TEXAS MARITAL PROPERTY RIGHTS

CASES AND MATERIALS

2009-2010

PAMELA E. GEORGE
PROFESSOR OF LAW
SOUTH TEXAS COLLEGE OF LAW

IMPRIMATUR PRESS

GRAIL & TUCKER LEGAL PUBLISHING, L.C.

525 WOODVIEW TOWER
1349 EMPIRE CENTRAL DR
DALLAS, TEXAS 75247
TELEPHONE: (800) 811-6725
FACSIMILE: (214) 879-9939
WWW.IMPRIMATURPRESS.COM

Printed in the United States of America

ISBN 978-1-60503-022-7

These materials are prepared for classroom use. It is not a substitute for specific legal research. The cases and laws are discussed generally and the author's comments should not be relied on for the basis of a legal opinion or course of action, without careful review of applicable authorities including those cases decided since the publication of this book.

Dedication

For My Mother and Brother
In Memory of my Father

Acknowledgment

This edition of Texas Marital Property Rights - Cases & Materials was necessitated by the many changes in the law that arose in the 2009 legislative session. I acknowledge and thank Dean James Alfini and Associate Dean Helen Jenkins of South Texas College of Law for their generous support of this project without which completion would have been most difficult. As the Fall 2009 semester begins, Dean Alfini will have stepped down as Dean and President of South Texas College of Law; it has been a joy to be a member of his faculty. As before, I extend special thanks to publishers Norm Grail and Jeff Tucker for their patience and confidence. In addition, I thank Christi Sprouse, Faculty Secretary, who has worked with me on this project and seamlessly facilitated this long distance endeavor.

Preface

This year, 2009, will mark my 28th year as a professor at South Texas College of Law. I have taught Texas marital property law for much of that time. This text has evolved over these many years. The text is intended to be used as a casebook for a 3-hour course in Texas Marital Property Rights. In assembling this text, the objective was to provide the student with an understanding of Texas marital property rights, beginning with its roots in Spanish/Mexican law, which still provides the rationale for many decisions and continuing through the most recent decisions. Law students and lawyers alike should be familiar with early as well as recent cases. The earliest cases often provided useful and analogous facts and theories, and can also provide guidance, if only by distinguishing current from past cases.

Although some of the cases have been edited, the goal was to present a practical view of marital property problems and how those problems interrelate with other marital property and procedural issues. Hopefully this compilation will avoid study within a vacuum, outside of any realistic context. Despite the fact that the Texas community property system is longstanding and well established, there remain numerous unresolved issues. The Notes, Comments & Questions presented throughout the book are designed to spur discussion of those unresolved areas, as well as provide an understanding of basic concepts. The NCQs are based upon questions I have posed to my classes for nearly three decades. In addition, an appendix of the most recent version of relevant statutes and constitutional provisions can be found at the back of the book. Some of the more recent or more difficult statutes have also been presented throughout the text together with commentary in hopes of aiding a deeper understanding.

It is my mission to keep this text fresh and ever evolving. In that regard I would welcome comments, recommendations, and suggestions, be they from students or teachers. Feel free to e-mail as follows: pgeorge@stcl.edu.

Pamela Elizabeth George
July 2009
Santa Fe, New Mexico

Table of Contents

Chapter 1
The Texas Marital Property System

Chapter 2
Characterization of Marital Property

Chapter 3
Claims for Economic Contribution and Reimbursement

Chapter 4
Management and Liability of Property During the Marriage

Chapter 5
Dissolution of the Marriage by Divorce

Chapter 6
Interspousal Torts

Chapter 7
Property Rights that Arise When There is No Formal Marriage

Chapter 8
Homestead

Appendix

Chapter 1

The Texas Marital Property System

A. Introduction

The study of marital property law focuses upon the effect that marriage has upon property ownership. From ownership springs the right to manage property during marriage. Along with ownership, the right to manage property may affect whether or not the property will be liable for debts or obligations incurred prior to or during a marriage. Likewise, the disposition of property on death or divorce is affected by its ownership.

In essence, a marital property system governs ownership, management, liability, and disposition of all property possessed during and upon dissolution of a marriage. Texas marital property is governed by community property principles derived from Spanish law. Texas is one of only nine community property states. Originally, there were eight community property states: Texas, Arizona, California, Idaho, Louisiana, Nevada, New Mexico and Washington. With its enactment of the Wisconsin Marital Property Act, which was effective January 1, 1986, Wisconsin became the ninth community property state.[1]

Although the basic discipline of community property is consistent from community property state to community property state, the narrower principles encompassed within each state can differ greatly from state to state. In addition, you will discover that in Texas, community property is constitutionally driven. For that and other reasons, the community property determinations of other states and the underlying rationale may not be transferable to Texas. Although the opinions of other state courts and certain federal cases will be peripherally mentioned, this text will focus on Texas law. The opinions of other jurisdictions are included only when there is an undecided issue or a concept that may be clarified in a manner consistent with or which might impact the Texas rationale.

1. An Overview of the Texas Constitution and Marital Property

As Justice Walker of the Texas Supreme Court has explained, in Texas "[a]ll marital property is . . . either separate or community." *Hilley v. Hilley*, 342 S.W.2d 565 (Tex. 1961). That is, Texas marital property is owned by a spouse separately or by the community; although ownership can be held by a combination of separate and community ownership interests.

The Texas Constitution specifically defines separate property. *See* TEX. CONST. art XVI, §15. Although the current Texas Constitution, adopted in 1876, has been amended numerous times, the basic separate property definition has remained constant. The amendments to art. XVI § 15 have removed gender based references and have broadened the means of acquiring separate property, but have not changed the original basic separate property definition which has existed for more than 150 years, predating the constitution of 1876.[2] Simply put, separate property is that owned or claimed before marriage or that acquired after by gift, devise, or descent. The evolution of TEX. CONST. art XVI, §15 will be set forth within this text. Likewise, very early cases which address the ownership of marital property are included within Chapter 1 of this text and less frequently throughout the remainder of the text. Because the basic definition of separate property has not changed since 1876, the early cases do not merely provide an historical perspective; rather, they provide viable precedent, of-

---

[1] Howard S. Erlanger & June M. Weisberger, *From Common Law to Community Property: Wisconsin's Marital Property Act Four Years Later*, 1990 WIS. L. REV. 769, 770, 790. (Wisconsin is the first and only state to base its marital property system on the Uniform Marital Property Act).

[2] *See* TEX. CONST. art. 7 §19 (1845). (First Texas state constitution contained like separate property language).

ten cited in current opinions. These early cases will be viewed in light of the constitution as it existed at the time the opinions were rendered.

The Texas Constitution does not specifically define community property. As we progress through the text, we will see that case law has provided some guidance as to how we recognize community property. It has been said that "[t]he principle which lies at the foundation of the whole system of community property is, that whatever is acquired by the joint efforts of the husband and wife, shall be their common property." *De Blane v. Hugh Lynch & Co.*, 23 Tex. 25, 29. (1859). This principle is also known as acquisition under the doctrine of onerous title. *Graham v. Franco*, 488 S.W.2d 390, 392 (1972). In contrast, community property has also been simply defined as that property which does not meet the constitutional definition of separate property, utilizing the doctrine of implied exclusion. *Arnold v. Leonard*, 273 S.W.2d 799, 802 (1925). Although these analytical doctrines can coexist, it will become evident that sometimes they are mutually exclusive.

The Texas Constitution is the touchstone for the characterization of marital property. The one thing that must never be forgotten is that the constitutional definition of separate property reigns supreme and cannot be impinged upon by either the legislature or husband and wife. *See Arnold v. Leonard*, 273 S.W.2d 799, 801 (1925); *Kellett v. Trice*, 95 Tex. 160, 66 S.W.2d 51 (1902). While holding that the constitutional definition of marital property cannot be changed by legislation or by contract, the courts have recognized that the constitutional definition encompasses more than literal interpretation would allow. The constitution does provide that laws may be passed to more clearly define the wife's rights in her separate property and that held as community property with her husband. So, while the constitution does not address the concepts of marital property management or of liability, the courts have also sustained the power of the Legislature to enact statutes dealing with management and liability of marital property. This first chapter will introduce this balancing of strict construction against the legislature's power to define.

2. An Overview of the Statutes and Marital Property

Even though the Texas Constitution provides only a definition of separate property, the legislature, within the Texas Family Code, has provided not only a separate property definition, but a community property definition as well. The definition of separate property is found in TEX. FAM. CODE § 3.001 which, except for subsection (3), tracks, the definition found in TEX. CONST. art. XVI § 15. Specifically, TEX. FAM. CODE § 3.001, titled "Separate Property," provides:

> A spouse's separate property consists of:
>
> (1) the property owned or claimed by the spouse before marriage;
>
> (2) the property acquired by the spouse during marriage by gift, devise or descent.
>
> (3) the recovery for personal injuries sustained by the spouse during marriage, except any recovery for loss of earning capacity during marriage.

The definition of community property is found in TEX. FAM. CODE § 3.002, which provides:

> Community property consists of the property, other than separate property, acquired by either spouse during marriage.

Of course, the legislature did not stop with mere definitions of separate and community property. Indeed, entire chapters of the Texas Family Code are dedicated to marital property matters, most notably: Chapter 1 - Marital Property Rights and Liabilities §§ 3.001-3.410; Chapter 4 - Premarital and Marital Property Agreements §§ 4.001-4.206; Chapter 5 - Homestead Rights §§ 5.001-5.108; Chapter 7 - Award of Marital Property §§ 7.001-7.008; Chapter 8 - Maintenance §§ 8.001-8.305. These chapters of the Texas Family Code, along with other chapters relevant to this course can be found in the Appendix at the end of this text.

3. The Community Property Presumption and Characterization

The goal in most marital property cases is to determine whether marital property is a spouse's separate property or community property. The term "characterization" or the phrase "to characterize" means to determine whether marital property was acquired at a time or in a manner which would deem it separate property of a spouse or whether it will simply be presumed community property. The task of characterization begins with the application of a primary principle known as the community property presumption. The community property presumption provides the first step in the analysis of every marital property case, whether during marriage or upon dissolution of a marriage by death or divorce. This presumption has served as the cornerstone for case analysis since the Texas Legislature adopted the Spanish model of community property laws in 1840.[3] The presumption, a product of the common law, is now codified at TEX. FAM. CODE § 3.003(a) which provides:

> Property possessed by either spouse during or on dissolution of marriage is presumed to be community property.

In applying this presumption, the operative word is "possessed." The presumption is not limited to property purchased or otherwise acquired during marriage. Thus, upon death or divorce all property possessed by the spouses is presumed to be community property.

This presumption can only be rebutted by clear and convincing proof that the property in question is separate property. TEX. FAM. CODE § 3.003 (b). If the property, by application of constitutional or statutory definitions or judicial precedent, is characterized as separate property, then the community property presumption has been rebutted.

Many practical reasons exist for characterizing marital property as either separate or community property. Upon dissolution of the marriage, different criteria control the disposition of separate property and of community property.

In a death case, the testate deceased spouse can devise only his separate property and one-half of the community property. Likewise, the separate property and the community property of the intestate deceased spouse will descend under different sections of the Probate Code and will be distributed in different manners.

In a divorce case, the trial court has broad discretion in the division of community property, but cannot divest title to separate property. In addition, during marriage, characterization is essential in identifying the spouse or spouses with power to manage marital property under TEX. FAM. CODE §§ 3.101, 3.102, and §§ 3.301-3.309. Characterization is also essential in determining, under section TEX. FAM. CODE § 3.202, the extent to which marital property is liable for obligations incurred either before or after marriage by a spouse to a third party, as well as the order in which property is subject to execution under section TEX. FAM. CODE § 3.203.

The cases that follow provide lesson in characterization, in rebutting the community property presumption, that are used today.

---

3 William O. Huie, *The Texas Constitutional Definition of the Wife's Separate Property*, 35 TEX. L REV. 1054 (1957).

Question

A potential client pulls up in front of your office driving a new (paper tags) red Corvette. Client enters your office and states, simply, that a divorce is desired and that when the marriage began Client had an estate of $500,000 which, in the single year the marriage has endured, has been reduced to $300,000. Client just wants out of the marriage and let's you know that in Client's opinion the divorce should be very simple because no community property was acquired. Client further explains that the estate was less at the end of marriage, which can be proved by looking at the reduction to $300,000, and that all should be awarded to Client. How would you respond to Client?

car is presump comm prop.

B. The Constitution of 1876

1. Article XVI § 15 as effective 1876-1947

The Texas Constitution of 1876, article XVI § 15, defines separate property as follows:

> All property, both real and personal of the wife, owned or claimed by her before marriage, and acquired afterward by gift, devise or descent, shall be her separate property; and laws shall be passed more clearly defining the rights of the wife, in relation as well to her separate property as that held in common with her husband. Laws shall also be passed providing for the registration of the wife's separate property.

The above constitutional provision begins the study of Texas marital property. This same definition of separate property appeared without change in the earlier Constitutions of 1845, 1861, and 1866. The provision was omitted from the Reconstruction Constitution of 1869 which merely provided that the rights of married women to their separate property should be protected by law. For a discussion of the early background and history of the provision, *see Arnold v. Leonard*, 273 S.W. 799, 800-801 (Tex. 1925); William O. Huie, *The Texas Constitutional Definition of the Wife's Separate Property*, 35 TEX. L. REV. 1056 (1957). Notably, the definition of separate property has been expanded but not significantly altered since that time. *See* TEX. CONST. art. XVI § 15 (1948); TEX. CONST. art. XVI § 15.

Questions

1. What appears to be the single most limiting aspect of the definition of separate property as set forth above?

2. Women were not in the Texas Legislature and, in fact, could not vote when the above definition was adopted. Why would a government run by men extend such property rights to women?

---

2. Statutes and Decisions, 1845-1947

The first case in this section *De Blane v. Hugh Lynch & Co.*, is nearly a century and a half old. The issue is the character of cotton grown during marriage on the separately owned lands of the wife. Character of these crops is in issue because creditors levied against the bales of cotton to satisfy a debt owed by husband. At the time, only the separate property of the wife would have been safe from creditors. As noted in the introduction, the definition of separate property has not substantively changed since 1845; likewise, the analysis and application of that definition has also remained unchanged for more than 150 years. This case provides precedent for the characterization of crops. As you read *De Blane*, think of current situations to which the case might be applied; realize that the precedent is more than 150 years old. Also note that this case was recently cited by the Austin Court of Appeals in *Winger v. Pianka*, 831 S.W.2d 853 (Tex. App.—Austin 1992, writ denied).

DeBlane is followed in *Stringfellow v. Sorrells*, which guides us in the characterization of livestock and their progeny and *Arnold v. Leonard* which addresses the characterization of rents and revenues. *Kellett v. Trice* introduces the strict interpretation of the Texas Constitution as it relates to marital property and the restrictions that such an interpretation places upon individuals; extension of the restrictions to the legislature is seen in *Arnold v. Leonard.* Once again, the analysis within these opinions is as viable today as when written. This section culminates with *North Texas Traction Co. v. Hill*, which focuses upon the characterization of personal injury recoveries; although the decision would probably stand today, the characterization of the recovery would be different as will be established in the next section by *Graham v. Franco.*

DE BLANE
v.
HUGH LYNCH & CO.
23 Tex. 25
(1859)

BELL, JUSTICE.

On the 27th day of October, 1847, Hugh Lynch & Co. obtained judgment in the district court for Liberty County, against Volizard DeBlane, for the sum of one hundred and twenty-three dollars and eighty cents, debt, and seventeen dollars and fifteen cents, costs.

On this judgment an execution was issued, and levied on ten bales of cotton. The cotton was claimed by the present appellant as her separate property. The appellant is the wife of Volizard DeBlane, the defendant in the execution. There was a trial of the right of property. The proof was, that the ten bales of cotton levied on was the crop, or a portion of the crop, of the year 1848, grown upon land which was the separate property of Madame DeBlane, and produced by the labor of slaves which were also the separate property of Madame DeBlane.

Under the instruction of the court, the Hon. C.W. Buckley presiding, the jury returned a verdict that the cotton was liable to the execution. There was judgment accordingly, and from that judgment Madame DeBlane has appealed.

The only question presented is, whether the cotton grown upon the land of the wife, by the labor of the slaves of the wife, remained her separate property, or became the common property of the husband and wife. If the cotton was common or community property, it was, of course, subject to the exception; if it remained the separate property of the wife, it was not subject to the execution.

We are of opinion that the cotton was community property, and subject to the execution.

So far as I am informed, the proposition that crops produced on the land of the wife, remain the separate property of the wife, is founded and supported upon what is supposed to be the true import of the term "increase of land," used in the act of 1848, better defining the marital rights of parties.

It will be observed that the act of January 20, 1840, did not use the expression "increase of land." That statute provided "that neither the lands nor slaves which the wife may own, or to which she may have any right, title, or claim, at the time of her marriage, nor the lands or slaves to which she may acquire, during the coverture, any right, title, or claim, by gift, devise, or descent, nor the increase of such slaves, in each case, nor the paraphernalia as defined at common law, which the wife may have at the time of the marriage, or which she may acquire during the coverture, as aforesaid, shall, by virtue of the marriage, become the property of the husband, but shall remain the separate property of the wife."

The statute of 1848 provides, that "all property, both real and personal, of the wife, owned or claimed by her before marriage, and that acquired afterwards by gift, devise or descent, as also the increase of all lands or slaves thus acquired, shall be the separate property of the wife."

In an etymological sense, it cannot be doubted, that the word "increase," as applied to land, or to the soil, means that which grows out of it, or that which is produced by the cultivation of it. The word is frequently employed in this sense in the English Bible. Instances of it will be found in the twenty-fifth chapter of the book of Leviticus. It is there said, "and for thy cattle, and for the beast that are in thy land, shall all the increase thereof be meat." Again, it is said; "behold, we shall not save nor gather in our increase." So, in the sixty-seventh Psalm, the expression occurs, "then shall the earth yield her increase." That the word was properly used as applying to the produce of the soil cannot be doubted, when it is remembered, that the translators of King James' Bible have perhaps never been surpassed in accurate scholarship. But to adopt this meaning of the word "increase", as used in our statute, and to interpret the statute accordingly, would, we think, lead to results wholly inconsistent with the recognized principles of law upon which the system of community property is based. It would also lead to results inequitable and unreasonable. If it be admitted, that the "increase of land" meant by our statute, is the product of the soil itself, then it would follow, that a crop grown on the land of her husband, by the labor of the slaves of the wife, would be the separate property of the husband, because it was the "increase" of his land. The husband has, by the statute, the control and management of the separate property of the wife; and if the husband owned land, as separate property, and the wife owned slaves, as separate property, the husband could always employ the wife's slaves in the cultivation of his own land, and thus add to his separate property by the use of her separate property.

The principle which lies at the foundation of the whole system of community property is, that whatever is acquired by the joint efforts of the husband and wife, shall be their common property. It would be an unnecessary consumption of time, to quote authorities for this proposition.

It is true, that in a particular case, satisfactory proof might be made, that the wife contributed nothing to the acquisitions; or, on the other hand, that the acquisitions of property were owing wholly to the wife's industry. But from the very nature of the marriage relation, the law cannot permit inquiries into such matters. The law, therefore, conclusively presumes that whatever is acquired, except by gift, devise or descent, or by the exchange of one kind of property for another kind, is acquired by their mutual industry. If a crop is made by the labor of the wife's slaves on the wife's land, it is community property, because the law presumes that the husband's skill or care contributed to its production; or, that he, in some other way, contributed to the common acquisitions.

It cannot be objected, that this rule will subject the *corpus* of the wife's estate to be diminished for her support, while the husband enjoyed the proceeds or fruits of her property. The law (HART. DIG. art. 2416) provides, that the wife may have so much of the proceeds of her separate property set apart for the support of herself, and for the nurture and education of her children, as the courts of the country may deem necessary, under the circumstances of any particular case. On the other hand, as was before said, a literal construction of the words of the statute, "the increase of land," would enable the husband to make acquisitions of separate property, by the use of the separate property of his wife. And in this way his children by another wife might become rich, while her children by another husband might remain comparatively poor. The judgment of the court below is affirmed.

Notes, Comments & Questions

1. *De Blane* contrasts with a California decision of the same period which, applying a constitutional provision identical to that of the Texas Constitution, held that dividends from separate property of the

wife were the wife's separate property. *George v. Ransom*, 15 Cal. 322 (Cal. 1860). Texas courts have adhered strictly to the doctrine that dividends, interest, rent, and other income derived from separate property of a spouse are community property. *See Estate of Wyly v. Commissioner*, 610 F.2d 1282 (5th Cir. 1980). *But see* art. XVI, § 15 of the Texas Constitution as amended, effective November 25, 1980, and § 3.005 of the Family Code, originally enacted as § 5.04 and originally effective September 1, 1981.

2. What does the court perceive to be the inequity of crops grown on separate property being characterized as separate property?

3. What does the court identify as the "principle which lies at the foundation of the whole system of community property?" This "principle" should be kept in mind as you continue to read cases. What is a descriptive name for the "principle"?

4. Keep Madame De Blane's situation in mind as you progress through the text. Consider whether the decision would have been different if the case had been decided at a later time.

STRINGFELLOW
v.
SORRELLS
18 S.W. 689
(Tex. 1891)

MARR, JUSTICE.

Before and at the time of her marriage to W.J. Sorrells in the year 1884 the appellee, Mrs. C.V. Sorrells, owned in her own right, together with other separate property, two mules. These animals were then colts, and worth $35 each; and a portion of their present value, as a result of their growth and avoirdupois as the years rolled on, is the subject of this controversy. The appellant, in the year 1888, held a just debt, merged into a valid judgment, for a small sum against the husband of the appellee, and in satisfaction of which he caused a writ of execution to be levied upon these mules of the wife during that year. At the time of the levy the animals were grown, and each of them worth in the market $75, instead of $35 as originally. The husband had managed and cared for the mules since the marriage, and the community estate furnished the provender for the animals during the intermediate time.

The appellee replevied the property, and duly made her claim thereto under the statute, "to try the rights of property." The case came up to the district court from a justice court, and the former court rendered a judgment in favor of the wife. The appellant insists that the enhanced value of the mules, which has resulted from the attention of the husband and the food furnished by the community since the marriage, and amounts to $80, is an *increase* of the separate estate of the wife, and consequently is community property, and liable to his execution. There is a modicum of plausibility in his contention, based upon the construction given by the Supreme Court to "the increase of the lands" of the wife, but these decisions were inspired by the necessity of protecting, not of destroying, her estate. *De Blane v. Lynch*, 23 Tex. 25; *Forbes v. Dunham*, 24 Tex. 611; *White v. Lynch*, 26 Tex. 195; *Cleveland v. Cole*, 65 Tex. 402; *Epperson v. Jones*, *id.* at 425; *Braden v. Gose*, 57 Tex. 37; *Carr v. Tucker*, 42 Tex. 336.

The Supreme Court has often decided what is not "the increase of the wife's lands," but, so far as we are aware, have not decided what *is*; and we are not required to do so now. The rule contended for would be most impracticable in application. The equitable criterion, if any were admissible in cases like the present, should be the expenses to the husband or the community, regarded as an investment of rearing the mules, not the increased value, which may be due to other causes, subject to be offset by the value of their use, if anything. This would add to "confusion worse confounded." As applied to livestock belonging to the wife, "the *increase*" of such property has been invariably (ever since the decision of the Supreme Court in *Howard v. York*, 20 Tex. 670) recognized in the reported cases to denote the progeny of the original stock or their descendants. This construction comports with the etymology of the term, and accords with the universal understanding. *De Blane v. Lynch, supra*. The record therefore develops no "increase" of these particular mules in the sense that would add to or constitute a part of the community estate. They are still the same animals which the wife owned at the time of her marriage, and, mule like, they have stubbornly refused "to bring forth after their kind."

The sex of these particular mules, nor their capacity for reproduction, if any, is not disclosed by the record, but the general rule, founded on common knowledge, with possibly some sporadic exceptions, must be recognized that mules do not "increase, multiply, and replenish the earth," according to the ordinary laws of procreation and the generic command. It would seem, therefore, that there can be no "increase" of the wife's separate estate, if composed solely of specific mules at the time of her marriage. In cases of other live stock, his interest, recognized by law, in the offsprings thereof, compensates the husband and the community, but the erratic mule standeth apart, "like patience on a monument, smiling at grief." It would tend to entirely destroy the corpus of the wife's estate, consisting of live personal property, to declare that an augmentation in weight or value should be deemed an "increase" of the property itself, so as to constitute a part of the community to that extent. Suppose it should decline under the ministrations of the husband, what, then, would compensate the wife? Fortunately she does not hold her separate property by so precarious a tenure as to depend upon the fluctuations of weight or the prices in the market. If she did, then the alert creditor would only need to abide his time in confidence of ultimately seizing, upon a ruthless execution, the flock, the drove, and feathered tribe of the wife. The law too closely guards "with flaming sword and cherubim" the sacred rights of the good housewife in her own "separate property" to admit of such grave consequences.

We need only to add that the use of the mules, and the products of their labor, may be supposed to compensate the community for the provender consumed, and the husband would scarcely demand any recompense for the felicity of teaching them how "to work in the traces."

We conclude that the judgment of the district court is a most righteous one, and ought to be affirmed.

STAYTON, CHIEF JUSTICE. Affirmed, as per opinion of Commission of Appeals.

Notes, Comments & Questions

1. The Texas Supreme Court in *Stringfellow v. Sorrells* declines to decide what is an "increase of the wife's lands." What do you think "an increase of the wife's lands" is?

2. Take note of the court's next to the last sentence in *Stringfellow v. Sorrells*. Think about what that sentence might foreshadow.

3. Under the Texas statutes, as interpreted by early decisions, the husband possessed sole management powers over all the marital property, including the separate property of the wife, except that the wife's joinder was required in deeds conveying real estate which was homestead or which was separate property of the wife. The husband's creditors could reach the husband's separate property, and the community property but not the wife's separate property.

4. The husband's control over the wife's separate property could easily be used to his advantage and to her ultimate disadvantage. The Texas Supreme Court expressed this concern in *De Blane*. Do you recall that argument? Another such situation arose in *Kellet v. Trice*. Keep *Kellet* in mind throughout the course, especially when the most recent amendment to TEX. CONST. art. XVI, § 15 is discussed. *See also* TEX. FAM. CODE §§ 4.201-.206.

KELLET
v.
TRICE
66 S.W. 51
(Tex. 1902)

[In *Kellet v. Trice*, husband and wife, shortly prior to divorce, joined in execution of a deed conveying separate property of the wife to a trustee "for the purpose of divesting the separate estate and title of us in and to the property (hereinafter described) in which each of us shall hereafter own . . . an equal undivided community interest. . . ."

On the following day the trustee conveyed the property to the husband as the community property of the husband and wife, through a deed containing the recital that it had been executed for the same purpose as the prior deed. In post-divorce litigation between the former husband and wife, the court held that the deeds were not effective to change the separate property of the wife to community property. The court said:]

. . . On the other hand, the policy of the law protects the wife's property from liability for her husband's debts, and she cannot make it subject to them by mere agreement not amounting to some kind of legal conveyance. *Magee v. White*, 23 Tex. 180. Her property is protected also against alienations by the husband, and she cannot, by power of attorney or other mere agreement, enable him to divest her title. *Cannon v. Boutwell*, 53 Tex. 626.

The power to convey does not, therefore, enable her to contract generally with reference to her separate property, but only to dispose, in whole or in part, of her title; and the only operation which her conveyances have is to pass such title or some interest in it. *Wadkins v. Watson, supra.*

The effect of her conveyances, as well as those of others, is governed by the law applicable to the existing facts under which they are made; and the case therefore resolves itself into the inquiry: Did the facts essential to make the property in question community property exist when the transaction took place; and, if not, could the husband and wife, by their mere volition, make it such in the manner attempted?

Property of husband and wife in this state gets its character as belonging separately to one of them or in common to both from the statutes defining their separate and community estates. Property which either of them owns before marriage and that which he or she acquires afterwards by gift, devise, or descent is his or her separate property. Property acquired by either after marriage otherwise than by gift, devise, or descent is their common property. By construction, property which is acquired after marriage in exchange for separate property, or which is purchased with separate funds, is held to belong to that estate which furnished the consideration. Separate property of either spouse may be conveyed to the other in such way as to become his or her separate property, and community property may be so conveyed by the husband to the wife as to make it hers separately. This is true, not because the parties chose to name the property separate, but because the facts transpire to bring it within the statutory definition; and the law, operating upon such facts, vests title in accordance with them. The act of the parties is such as the law defines as necessary to create the separate right. Therefore, the question whether particular property is separate or community must depend upon the existence or nonexistence of the facts, which, by the rules of law, give character to it, and not merely upon the stipulations of the parties that it shall belong to one class or the other. Thus, when one spouse passes to the other by gift his or her title to separate property, it could not become the community property of both, because the law declares that property so acquired shall be the separate property of the donee; and a gift by the husband to the wife of his interest in community property would become the separate property of the donee for the same reason. And so property acquired in the name of either spouse during marriage, otherwise than by gift, devise, or descent, or in exchange for separate property, would, by force of the statute, be community property. It is true that in the acquisition or afterwards, the husband may give to the wife all his interest in the property, and thus, by gift, make it hers; but at last this would be true only because the facts defined in the law exist and the separate right is derived through a gift, the husband having full power over the community estate.

If the deeds in question were without consideration, and passed title to the husband, under these rules of law they would vest in him a separate title to the land, because it is the wife's separate title that is attempted to be conveyed, and the conveyance would be a gift. Yet the deeds in effect declare that they shall not have this, but a different, operation. The one power the wife had was to convey her title, and, by her conveyance, invest her grantee with the right conveyed. The power she tried to exercise was, by the form of a conveyance, to make a contract changing the legal character of the property. As we have seen, the power of conveying does not include the power to do any such thing. It has been held in several cases that husband and wife cannot, by their mere agreements, alter the character given to property by the law acting upon the facts under which it is acquired. *Cox v. Miller*, 54 Tex. 27; *Green v. Ferguson*, 62 Tex. 529.

The admissions made in these cases that community property in existence, or as it comes into existence, may be made the separate property of the wife by gift from the husband, are thoroughly consistent with what we have said. The gift fulfills the requirements of the law under which the title of one is transferred to the other so as to become separate. Here the attempt of the wife is to make a gift without at the same time so conveying her title as to make the gift have its proper effect.

Recurring to the principles already stated, we see that, while a married woman, through the intervention of a trustee, may give or sell her property to her husband so as to make it his and, therefore, subject to his control and to his debts, and may also mortgage it to secure his debts, the power is withheld from her, while retaining, to empower him to alienate it, or to subject it to his debts. A more effectual method of defeating the last-named restrictions could not be devised than that employed in this case if it were upheld. All the mischiefs sought to be guarded against would at once flow from such a transaction, and this shows that the objections to it are not of a merely technical character. In our opinion, such transactions have no place in our laws regulating marital rights.

A statement of the effect of a real conveyance by the wife of her separate property, through the medium of a trustee, to her husband, such as has been upheld by this court, will serve to illustrate the difference between it and the transaction in question. By such a conveyance, the wife's title, or a part of it, to the whole or a part of the property would pass to and vest in the husband, and such interest as was conveyed would become his separate property. If only a part were conveyed, the remainder would continue to be her separate property, and would be protected from her husband's debts, as well as from alienation by him. Here the wife, while she pretends to divest her whole separate title, does not convey it to her husband, but declares that the instrument shall only operate to make the property belong to the community estate, the effect of which would be to vest in her husband an interest and in herself an interest of a different character from that which she owned and pretended to convey, and to put the whole forever beyond her control, and subject to that of the husband alone. This makes it apparent that this is not really a conveyance of her title such as she could make, but only an agreement by which a change in the character of such title is attempted, without the existence of the facts necessary, under the law, to effect the change.

The wife may hold the title to community property, legally acquired, as well as the husband. If, without consideration, she and her husband should execute such an instrument to a trustee upon the trust that he should reconvey the property to her, and should provide that it should thereby become community property, would it not be evident that the entire substance of such instruments would be the agreement to change the property from separate to community, and that in reality there would be no conveyance of her separate title? We instance a case in which there is no consideration because we do not wish to go beyond the facts of this case.

It is not necessary to hold that a married woman's separate property may not be so conveyed as to become, in law, community property. It may be that a purchase may be made of such property by the husband with community funds, so that the consideration will belong to the wife separately, and the property taking its place will belong to the community estate. If this is true, it is because the law, and not the mere agreement, would give such effect to the transaction. No such case is presented here.

The deeds are without valuable consideration. The recitals of money paid are evidently merely formal and nominal (*Lewis v. Simon*, 72 Tex. 475, 10 S.W. 554); and, besides, according to the recitals, equal sums were paid to each party, so that the wife received no more than she paid. The other recitals merely give the reasons and purposes actuating the parties and show no benefit to the wife, or detriment, disadvantage, or inconvenience to the husband whatever. The transaction, if the instrument should have effect, would operate wholly to the benefit of the husband without pecuniary consideration received by the wife.

We conclude that the transaction did not change from separate to community the property mentioned in the deeds, and this, with what we have said, answers the questions asked.

Notes, Comments & Questions

1. If spouses wanted to transform separate property into community, what were the available means in 1902?

2. Take a quick look at the Texas Family Code, *see* Appendix, and determine whether the means to transform separate property into community have been expanded.

3. If there has been an expansion of the means to transform separate property into community, when and how did such expansion occur?

---

3. Statutory Changes, 1911-1917

Between 1911 and 1921, several newly enacted statutes were intended to enlarge the rights and powers of married women with respect to marital property

Tex. Laws 1911, Ch. 52, at 92 empowered a married woman to obtain an order from the district court to remove her disabilities of coverture and to declare her feme sole for mercantile and trading purposes.

Tex. Laws 1913, Ch. 32 at 61 effected the following changes in articles 4621 and 4622 as they had existed previously:

(1) The wife acquired the power to manage her separate property, except that the joinder of the husband was required for the conveyance of real estate or the transfer of stocks and bonds.

(2) The wife acquired the power of control, management, and disposition of what was later termed the "special community property" consisting of the personal earnings of the wife, the rents from the wife's real estate, the interest on bonds and notes belonging to her and dividends on stocks owned by her.

(3) Exemption from liability for debts contracted by the husband was extended to the wife's special community property as well as to her separate property. The wife's separate property was held to be exempt from debts incurred by the husband's prior to the 1913 statute.

Tex. Laws 1915, Ch. 54, at 103 added a completely new section to the statute, which provided as follows:

> All property or moneys received as compensation for personal injuries sustained by the wife shall be her separate property, except such actual and necessary expenses as may have accumulated against the husband for hospital fees, medical bills and all other expenses incident to the collection of said compensation.

Finally, Tex. Laws 1917, Ch. 194, at 436 further amended article 4621 to define rents and revenues derived from separate property of either spouse as separate property of that spouse.

The case of *Kellet v. Trice* combined with these statutory changes set the stage for *Arnold v. Leonard.*

ARNOLD
v.
LEONARD
273 S.W. 799
(Tex. 1925)

GREENWOOD, JUSTICE.

The Court of Civil Appeals states the nature and facts of this case and the question which the Supreme Court is requested to determine as follows:

> The suit was brought by the appellee, Mrs. Adele E. Leonard, a married woman, joined pro forma by her husband, St. Clair Leonard, for an injunction to restrain the appellant, Gus I. Arnold, as administrator of the estate of Gus Schultz, deceased, from seizing or attempting to

subject certain rents and revenues from a number of pieces of real estate in the city of Galveston, all being the separate estate of the wife, Mrs. Adele E. Leonard, to the payment of a judgment owned and held by the appellant against St. Clair Leonard, the husband.

The facts alleged in the bill for injunction were agreed to be true by both parties to the suit, and showed, as recited, that all the real property involved is owned by Mrs. Adele E. Leonard, the wife, as her separate estate; that the judgment held and owned by the appellant in his capacity as administrator of the estate of Schultz was against the husband, St. Clair Leonard, and represented a community indebtedness; that in these circumstances the administrator was seeking, by threatening the issuance of writs of garnishment on the judgment against various renters and tenants of Mrs. Leonard's separate real estate, to subject the rents and revenues thereof to the payment of this judgment.

The appellant in the trial court answered the petition and prayer for an injunction with a special exception to the effect that it appeared from the allegations of the petition itself that the rent and revenues, the collection of which was so sought to be enjoined, constituted the community estate of Mrs. Adele E. Leonard and her husband, St. Clair Leonard, and by virtue of the Constitution of Texas, Article 16, § 15, the rents and revenues of the separate estate of the wife are community property and subject to the debts of the husband, and that Article 4621, Chapter 3, Title, 68, of the Revised Statutes of Texas of 1911, and the amendment thereof by the act of the regular session of the Thirty-Seventh Legislature, Chapter 130, Section 1, which undertakes to declare the rents and revenues of the wife's separate real property to be her separate estate, is contrary to the terms of the Constitution referred to, and is therefore void.

The trial court overruled the special exception of the appellant and granted the injunction prayed for by the appellees, restraining the appellant from in any manner undertaking to have the rents and revenues from the separate real property of the appellee, Mrs. Adele E. Leonard, applied to the liquidation of the judgment so held against her husband, holding that the rents and revenues of her separate estate constituted her separate property and were beyond the reach of a creditor of the community estate of the husband and wife.

It being obvious that the sole question involved in the case is as to the constitutionality of said Revised Statutes, Article 4621, because of the importance of the question and of some doubt entertained by different members of this court as to the correctness of the trial court's determination of it, we deem it advisable to certify for your decision the following question:

> Is the act of the Legislature above stated, which declares the rents and revenues of the wife's separate real property to be her separate estate, violative of Article 16, Section 15, of our State Constitution? In this connection we call attention to the case of *Rudasill v. Rudasill*, 219 S.W. 843.

* * *

Section 15 of Article XVI of the Constitution declares:

All property, both real and personal, of the wife, owned or claimed by her before marriage, and that acquired afterward by gift, devise, or descent, shall be her separate property; and laws shall be passed more clearly defining the rights of the wife, in relation as well to her separate property as that held in common with her husband. Laws shall also be passed providing for the registration of the wife's separate property.

This section is found, without a single word changed, in the Constitutions of 1845, 1861, and 1866. Section 19, Article VII, Constitutions of 1845, 1861, and 1866; Vol. IV, SAYLES' TEXAS STATUTES, pages 209, 246, 321.

Prior to the adoption of the Constitution of 1845, the wife's separate property had been so defined by the act approved January 20, 1840 as to include the lands and slaves owned or claimed by the wife at the time of her marriage and the land and slaves acquired by her during coverture by gift, devise, or descent, together with the increase of such slaves, and her paraphernalia.

It is undeniable that under the Act of 1840 all property other than that specifically defined as separate property of the wife was intended to belong to the separate estate of the husband or to become common property of the husband and wife. Such is the express provision of the Act. Section 19 of Article VII of the Constitution of 1845 was essentially an enlargement of the wife's separate estate. Under the act of 1840 all the wife's right to personal property passed to the husband, with the solitary exception of slaves and their increase. *Owen v. Tankersley*, 12 Tex. 407; Section 66, SPEER'S LAW OF MARITAL RIGHTS IN TEXAS; 30 C. J. 530, § 52c. By the constitutional provision *all* property, both real and personal, owned or claimed by the wife before marriage and that acquired by the wife afterwards by gift, devise, or descent became her separate property. We can conceive of no sound reason for concluding that the terms of the Constitution of 1845 were not meant to furnish the sole measure of the wife's separate estate, as had the Act of 1840, with its less liberal provision for the wife. Whatever the language of Section 19 of Article VII meant in the Constitution of 1845, that language has the same signification in Section 15 of Article XVI of the Constitution of 1876. *Muench v. Oppenheimer*, 86 Tex. 570, 26 S.W. 496; *Cox v. Robison*, 105 Tex. 430, 150 S.W. 1149.

The plain and obvious import of the language of the Constitution is to prescribe a test by which to determine when an acquest by the wife becomes a portion of the wife's separate estate. The test during coverture relates to the method by which the property is acquired. If the method be by gift, devise, or descent to the wife, then the Constitution makes the property belong to the wife's separate estate. If the method of acquiring during marriage be different, then the property falls without the class of separate estate of the wife, as fixed by the Constitution. We think the Supreme Court was doing no more than giving effect to the words of the Constitution when it said, through CHIEF JUSTICE WILLIE, "But of the property which a wife may acquire during marriage, none becomes her separate estate except such as is derived by gift, devise or descent." *Ezell v. Dodson*, 60 Tex. 332.

We have no doubt that the people in adopting the Constitution in 1845, as in 1876, understood that it was intended to put the matter of the classes of property constituting the wife's separate estate beyond legislative control. Thereby both the wife and the husband were given constitutional guaranty of the status of all property derived by means of or through the wife. Our duty is plain to give effect to the people's will. COOLEY'S CONSTITUTIONAL LIMITATIONS (7th Ed.) p. 89.

It is a rule of construction of constitutions that ordinarily, when the circumstances are specified under which any right is to be acquired, there is an implied prohibition against the legislative power to either add to or withdraw from the circumstances specified. *Koy v. Schneider*, 110 Tex. 378, 218 S.W. 479, 221 S.W. 880; *Dickson v. Strickland* (Tex. Sup.) 265 S.W. 1015; *Ex parte Vallandigham*, 1 Wall. 252, 17 L.Ed. 589; COOLEY'S CONSTITUTIONAL LIMITATIONS, p. 99; 6 R.C.L. § 43. Hence, when the Constitution says that as to property, not owned or claimed by the wife at marriage, it becomes her separate property when acquired in one of three specified modes, the Legislature is prohibited from saying that property acquired after marriage in some other mode may also become the wife's separate property.

The rule of implied exclusion is no more binding in construing statutes than in interpreting constitutions. In *Howard v. York*, 20 Tex. 672, in an opinion of Judge Roberts, it is said that for the Legislature to preserve to the wife's separate property increase of land and slaves "impliedly negatives the idea that the increase of any other property becomes separate property."

Had it been the purpose of the Constitution to empower the Legislature to add to the wife's separate property, it is hardly to be doubted that the power would have been conferred, when the framers of the Constitution were expressly authorizing the enactment of laws to more clearly define the rights of the wife in relation to both her separate property and community property.

It is said that expressions, such as that quoted from *Howard v. York, supra*, show that the Supreme Court has inferentially sanctioned the exercise by the Legislature, since 1848, of the power to add other property than that specified in the Constitution to the wife's separate estate. So, it is contended, we ought not to override the long-continued legislative interpretation of the constitutional provision.

It is true that the Act of March 12, 1848 provided that the wife's separate estate should include not only "all property, both real and personal, of the wife owned or claimed by her before marriage, and that acquired afterwards by gift, devise, or descent" but "also the increase of lands or slaves thus acquired." 3 GAMMEL'S LAWS OF TEXAS, p. 77; 2 BATTS' ANNOTATED CIVIL STATUTES OF TEXAS, p. 262. Since the abolition of slavery, the statutes have continued to declare that the increase of lands owned or claimed by the wife before marriage and of lands acquired by her during marriage by gift, devise, or descent shall belong to the wife's separate estate. Article 2851, R.S. of 1879; Article 4621, R.S. of 1911.

Save as to increase of lands or slaves, there never was any attempt at anything like statutory enlargement of the wife's separate property until the Legislature passed the Acts of 1917 and 1921, referred to in the certificate of the Court of Civil Appeals. These latter acts undertake to add to the wife's separate property not only all property mentioned in the Constitution and increase of the wife's separate lands, but "the rents and revenues derived therefrom."

The Supreme Court at an early date determined that the increase of slaves belonged not to the owner or owners of the parents but to the owner of the mother only, regardless of dates of birth of such increase before or after the enactment of the Act of 1840 or of 1848. The decision was based on a principle of the law of slavery in the United States which forbade the inhumanity of separating a young child from the child's mother. *Cartwright v. Cartwright*, 18 Tex. 628, 636. Application of the principle would have given the wife's separate estate the increase of that estate's female slaves, under the constitutional provision without aid from statute.

The court refused to hold that crops raised by labor of the wife's separate slaves on the wife's separate lands became increase of either lands or slaves or of both. *De Blane v. Lynch*, 23 Tex. 29. And, after slavery, crops grown on the wife's lands, with labor and money furnished wholly from her separate estate, were held to become community property. *Cleveland v. Cole*, 65 Tex. 405. Likewise, rents of the wife's separate lands have been consistently considered to belong to the community estate. *Rhine v. Blake*, 59 Tex. 243, 244; *Conner v. Hawkins*, 66 Tex. 639, 2 S.W. 520; *Hayden v. McMillan*, 4 Tex. Civ. App. 479, 23 S.W. 430: *Shepflin v. Small*, 4 Tex. Civ. App. 121, 23 S.W. 433. Nothing has ever been considered by this Court to come within the statutory phrase "increase of lands" unless it was such profit as may arise from the lands' own enhancement in value or such profit as may accrue from exchange of the lands for other more valuable property. *Rose v. Houston*, 11 Tex. 324, 62 Am. Dec. 478; *Evans v. Purinton*, 12 Tex. Civ. App. 158, 34 S.W. 350, with writ of error refused; *Cabell v. Menczer* 35 S.W. 207, 208. It is evident that everything relating to land that has been recognized by the Supreme Court as becoming separate property of the wife is embraced within the constitutional definition of her separate property, if we bear in mind that property remains separate through all mutations and changes. The Court, through CHIEF JUSTICE STAYTON, was merely applying this familiar principle in saying:

> Property purchased with money the separate property of husband or wife, or taken in exchange for the separate property of either, becomes the separate property of the person whose

> money purchases or whose property is given in exchange, in the absence of some agreement express or implied to the contrary, and if the thing purchased or taken in exchange increases in value this necessarily inures to the benefit of its owner. *Dixon v. Sanderson*, 72 Tex. 362, 10 S.W. 535, 536, 18 Am. St. Rep. 801.

With the Court declining to give effect to any attempt before 1917 at enlargement by statute of the wife's constitutional separate estate, we cannot feel bound to acquiesce in any supposed successful, long continued, and unchallenged assertion of such legislative power.

Moreover, the Legislature itself seems to have considered from 1879 to 1917 that it was not undertaking to add anything to the wife's constitutional separate estate by its provision for the preservation to the estate of the increase of her lands. For, it constantly declared, between those dates, that all property "acquired by either husband or wife during the marriage, except that which is acquired by gift, devise or descent, shall be deemed the common property of the husband and wife." Article 2852, R.S. of 1879, and Article 4621, R.S. of 1911.

Since rents and revenues derived from the wife's separate lands are entirely without the constitutional definition of the wife's separate property, and since the Legislature can neither enlarge nor diminish such property, it follows that the portions of the Acts of 1917 and 1921, which undertake to make rents and revenues from the wife's separate lands a part of her separate estate, are invalid.

* * *

By an Act approved March 21, 1913, it was provided that "neither the separate property of the wife, nor the rents from the wife's separate real estate, nor the interest on bonds and notes belonging to her, nor dividends on stocks owned by her, nor her personal earnings shall be subject to the payment of debts contracted by the husband;" and the act committed the classes of property enumerated as exempt from payment of the husband's debts to "the control, management, and disposition of the wife alone," provided the joinder of the husband was necessary in an incumbrance or conveyance of the wife's separate lands, and in a transfer of her stocks and bonds, unless she was authorized to act alone by an order of the District Court, and provided that the husband and wife must join in a conveyance of the homestead. The Acts of 1917 and 1921 retain each and all of the above provisions of the Act of 1913.

There can be no doubt that the Act of 1913 left the rents and revenues of the wife's separate lands assets of the community estate. *Red River Nat'l. Bank v. Ferguson*, 109 Tex. 290, 206 S.W. 923; *Whitney Hardware Co. v. McMahan*, 111 Tex. 245, 231 S.W. 694; *Scott v. Scott* 170 S.W. 273; *Tannehill v. Tannehill* 171 S.W. 1051. Nor can there be any doubt that the act of 1913 and the subsequent acts intended to exempt rents of the wife's separate lands from payment of a community debt contracted by the husband. The provision of the Acts of 1917 and 1921, declaring the exemption, is separate and distinct from the portions of the Acts undertaking to change the ownership of rents and revenues from the wife's separate lands. Hence such provision might be operative in each Act despite failure of the purpose to make the rents separate property of the wife. *Western Union Tel. Co. v. State*, 62 Tex. 633.

The Supreme Court of the United States upholds the validity of legislation conferring on the wife not only the right to manage but the right to dispose of community property, so long as the husband's interest attaches to the proceeds of such property.

Speaking through CHIEF JUSTICE WHITE, the Court states its conclusions as follows:

> The Legislature could as well have provided that the wife could convey, as the husband; and if it had power to say that either could dispose of the community interest of the other,

it could say that neither could do so. Changing the manner of conveyance did not alter the status of ownership. It could not make the interest of either spouse in community lands greater or less.

* * *

It is a misconception of that system to suppose that because power was vested in the husband to dispose of the community acquired during marriage, as if it were his own, therefore by law the community property belonged solely to the husband. The conferring on the husband the legal agency to administer and dispose of the property involved no negation of the community, since the common ownership would attach to the result of the sale of the property. *Warburton v. White*, 176 U.S. 484, 20 S. Ct. 404, 44 L. Ed. 555.

To the same effect is *Arnett v. Reade*, 220 U.S. 318 to 320, 31 S. Ct. 425, 55 L. Ed. 477, 36 L.R.A. (N.S.) 1040.

These conclusions harmonize with the conceptions underlying the Texas decisions that the wife's capacity to own and hold property is as complete as that of the husband; that each marital partner owns an estate in the community property equal to that of the other partner; and that statutes empowering the husband to manage the wife's separate lands and community assets make the husband essentially a trustee, accountable as such to the separate estate of the wife, or to the community. *Edrington v. Mayfield*, 5 Tex. 366 to 368; SPEER'S LAW OF MARITAL RIGHTS IN TEXAS, § 296; *Richardson v. Hutchins*, 68 Tex. 89, 3 S.W. 276; *Dority v. Dority*, 96 Tex. 224 to 226, 71 S.W. 950, 60 L.R.A. 941; *Waggoner Bank & Trust Co. v. Warren*, 111 Tex. 322, 234 S.W. 387.

We see no escape from the deduction that if the Legislature may rightfully place such portions of the community as it may deem best under the wife's separate control and make same subject to disposition by her alone, it may likewise exempt the same from payment of the husband's debts, without the exemption being open to successful constitutional attack by either the husband or his creditors.

* * *

The sum of our conclusions is: The Legislature, in defining the wife's rights in and to her separate property and property held in common with her husband, could lawfully deprive the husband of the power granted him for many years to manage and control the wife's separate property and portions of the community property which were derived from use of the wife's separate property or from her personal exertions, and could confide the management, control, and disposition thereof to the wife alone, and could exempt, not only her separate property, but said portions of the community from payment of the husband's debts. In making this grant of enlarged rights to the wife and working the corresponding diminution in rights to be exercised by the husband, the Legislature was lawfully defining the wife's rights in both her separate estate and common property, as expressly authorized by the Constitution. But the Legislature could not divest the husband of all interest in and to property which, under the Constitution, was guaranteed either to the community or to the husband's separate estate, and use the same to enlarge the wife's separate estate beyond its constitutional limits.

We, therefore, answer to the certified questions that so much of the Act of 1917 and of the Act of 1921 as undertook to declare the rents and revenues of the wife's separate realty to be her separate estate was violative of Section 15, of Article XVI, and of Section 35, of Article III of the Constitution, but that the provisions of said Acts, and of the prior Act of 1913, are valid, which render the rents and revenues of the wife's separate lands free from liability to forced sale for the payment of debts contracted by the husband.

Questions

1. What rule arises from *Arnold v. Leonard*?
2. In what way does this case comport with *Kellet v. Trice*?
3. What if Madame De Blane's case had been heard concurrently with *Arnold v. Leonard*?
4. Why is the limit on legislative power irrelevant to the outcome of *Arnold v. Leonard*?
5. What would be the only means to accomplish the change attempted by the Legislature, but disallowed by the Texas Supreme Court in *Arnold v. Leonard*?

NORTHERN TEXAS TRACTION CO.
v.
HILL

297 S.W. 778
(Tex. Civ. App.—El Paso 1927, writ ref'd)

PELPHREY, CHIEF JUSTICE.

Appellee, joined by her husband, T.A. Lambert, originally filed this suit in the Sixty-Eighth district court of Dallas county, Tex., against appellant. She thereafter, under the name of Mrs. Nettie Hill (joined by her husband, R.H. Hill), filed her second amended original petition.

She alleged in said amended petition that at the time of the original filing of the suit she was the wife of T.A. Lambert, but that since said filing she had been divorced from said Lambert and had married R.H. Hill, who was joined as plaintiff.

Appellee alleged that on or about October 24, 1923, appellant owned, operated, and controlled a system of interurban electric railway extending from the city of Dallas to the city of Fort Worth; that on said date while riding in an automobile driven by her then husband, T.A. Lambert, an interurban car, owned and operated by appellant, collided with said automobile, and as a result of such collision appellee suffered certain injuries.

Appellee more particularly alleged that appellant was guilty of negligence per se in that it had failed to keep the crossing in the condition required by the ordinances of the city of Dallas, and that the motorman failed and neglected to warn appellee as the ordinances required, and that the motorman failed to keep a proper lookout for vehicles approaching the crossing where the accident occurred.

Appellant answered by general demurrer, special exceptions to appellee's petition, general denial, and contributory negligence on the part of appellee and her then husband, T.A. Lambert. Appellee filed a supplemental petition containing special exceptions and a general denial. The case was tried before a jury, and resulted in a verdict in favor of appellee for $7,500. From a judgment on said verdict the Northern Texas Traction Company has appealed to this court.

Appellant bases its appeal on 34 separate propositions, all of which we deem it unnecessary to discuss.

Appellant specially excepted in its first amended original answer to appellee's petition because T.A. Lambert, who was the husband of the appellee at the time of the accident, was not made a party plaintiff. This exception was by the court overruled, and appellant assigns error thereto. We agree with appellant in its contention and hold that T.A. Lambert was a necessary party plaintiff, and that appellant's exception should have been sustained.

The right to sue for damages for a tort is a choice in action and property, within the legal sense of that term. *Ezell v. Dodson*, 60 Tex. 331; 2 BISHOP ON MARRIED WOMEN, art 271; SPEER ON LAW OF MARRIED WOMEN, art 193. The right to sue, being property in the legal sense of the term, was the community property of appellee and T.A. Lambert, unless by law it is made her separate property.

Article 4615, Revised Statutes of 1925, reads as follows:

> All property or moneys received as compensation for personal injuries sustained by the wife shall be her separate property, except such actual and necessary expenses as may have accumulated against the husband for hospital fees, medical bills, and all other expenses incident to the collection of said compensation.

It is contended by appellant that this statement is in contravention of article 16, § 15, of the Constitution, and in support of its contention cites a decision of our Supreme Court in the case of *Arnold v. Leonard*, 114 Tex. 535, 273 S.W. 799.

The constitutional provision is as follows:

> All property, both real and personal, of the wife, owned or claimed by her before marriage, and that acquired afterward by gift, devise or descent, shall be her separate property; and laws shall be passed more clearly defining the rights of the wife, in relation as well to her separate property as that held in common with her husband. Laws shall also be passed providing for the registration of the wife's separate property.

As said by the court in *Arnold v. Leonard, supra*:

> But the Legislature could not divest the husband of all interest in and to property which under the Constitution, was guaranteed either to the community or to the husband's separate estate and use the same to enlarge the wife's separate estate beyond its constitutional limits.
>
> It is a rule of construction of Constitutions that ordinarily when the circumstances are specified under which any right is to be acquired there is an implied prohibition against legislative power to either add to or withdraw from the circumstances specified. *Koy v. Schneider*, 110 Tex. 378, 218 S.W. 479, 221 S.W. 880; *Dickson v. Strickland*, 114 Tex. 176, 265 S.W. 1015; *Ex parte [Vallandigham] Vallandigham*, 1 Wall 252 [17 L. Ed. 589]; COOLEY'S CONSTITUTIONAL LIMITATIONS, p. 99; 6 R.C.L. § 43. Hence, when the Constitution says that as to property, not owned or claimed by the wife at marriage, it becomes her separate property when acquired in one of three specified modes, the Legislature is prohibited from saying that property acquired after marriage in some other mode may also become the wife's separate property."

The court held in the above-cited case the acts of the Legislature, which undertook to make the rents and revenues from the wife's separate bonds a part of her separate property, invalid.

We think the same reasoning applies in the present case, and hold article 4615, R.S. 1925, to be unconstitutional. Article 4619, Revised Statutes 1925, reads as follows:

> "All property acquired by either the husband or wife during marriage, except that which is the separate property of either, shall be deemed the common property of the husband and wife, and during coverture may be disposed of by the husband only.

By this article the cause of action, not being the separate property of either, became the community property of T.A. Lambert and appellee, vesting in each a half interest therein. *Fort Worth & R.G. Ry. Co. v. Robertson*, 55 Tex. Civ. App. 309, 121 S.W. 202; *Id.*, 103 Tex. 504, 121 S.W. 202, Ann. Cas. 1913A. 231, Judge Dunklin so held in construing a similar statute in a dissenting opinion in the above case, and the Supreme Court agreed with his opinion in 103 Tex. 504, 131 S.W. 400, Ann. Cas. 1913A, 231. Therefore T.A. Lambert, having a half interest in the right of action, was necessary party plaintiff. Appellant pleaded contributory negligence on the part of T.A. Lambert, and appellee in her supplemental petition specially excepted to said plea on the ground that the negligence of the husband is not imputable to the wife.

This exception was by the court sustained, and appellant assigns error to the court's action. If we are correct in our conclusion that the right of action was the community property of T.A. Lambert and appellee, then we must also conclude that the negligence of Lambert, if he was negligent, would be a defense to this action, for to hold otherwise would be to allow him to recover regardless of his own negligence. As was said by the Supreme Court in *Gulf C.& S. R. Ry. Co. v. James S. Greenlee et ux.*, 62 Tex. 344:

> Under the circumstances of this case it is quite clear that Mrs. Greenlee might well rely upon the prudence and caution of her husband in making the approach to, as well as crossing, the railroad. The correlative of the proposition is also true, that she would be bound by his negligence or want of due care.
>
> *See also Mo. Pacific Ry. Co. v. White*, 80 Tex. 202 15 S.W. 808.

* * *

In our opinion, it is unnecessary to discuss the other assignments.

The judgment of the trial court is reversed and the cause remanded.

Notes, Comments & Questions

1. *Northern Texas Traction* is not the end of the road on the characterization of personal injury damages. After reading *Graham v. Franco*, consider whether the holding in *Northern Texas Traction* would be sustained under that later analysis.

2. Was the doctrine of implied exclusion properly applied in *Northern Texas Traction*? Come back to this question after you read *Graham v. Franco*.

3. The following excerpts are from TEX. REV. CIV. STAT. 1925 and describe the roles and rights of husband and wife as regards ownership and management of marital property under the statutes which existed until January 1, 1968, when the Matrimonial Property Act of 1967 became effective. These excerpts are included only to provide you with a better understanding of the historical context in which the preceding case and some of the following cases arose.

Management and Liability

Art. 4613. [4621] [2967] [2851] Husband's separate property.

All property of the husband, both real and personal, owned or claimed by him before marriage, and that acquired afterward by gift, devise, or descent, as also the increase of all lands thus acquired, and the rents and revenues derived therefrom, shall be his separate property. The separate property of the husband shall not be subject to the debts contracted by the wife, either before or after marriage, except for necessaries furnished herself and children after her marriage with him, nor for torts of the wife. During marriage the husband shall have the sole management, control and disposition of his separate property, both real and personal. [Acts 1848, p. 77; G.L., Vol. 3, p. 77; Const., Art. 16, § 15; Acts 1913, p. 61; Acts 1917, p. 436; Acts 1921, p. 251.]

Art. 4614. [4621] [2967] [2851] Wife's separate property.

All property of the wife, both real and personal, owned or claimed by her before marriage, and that acquired afterward by gift, devise or descent, as also the increase of all lands thus acquired, and the rents and revenues derived therefrom, the interest on bonds and notes belonging to her and dividends on stocks owned by her, shall be the separate property of the wife. The wife shall have the sole management, control and disposition of her separate property, both real and personal; provided, however, the joinder of the husband in the manner now provided by law for conveyances of the separate real estate of the wife shall be necessary to the encumbrance or conveyance by the wife of her lands, and the joint signature of the husband and wife shall be necessary to a transfer of stocks and bonds belonging to her or of which she may be given control by this law. [*Id.*]

Art 4616. [4621] [2967] [2851] Wife's separate property protected.

Neither the separate property of the wife, nor the rents from the wife's separate real estate, nor the interest on bonds and notes belonging to her, nor dividends on stocks owned by her, nor her personal earnings, shall be subject to the payment of debts contracted by the husband nor of torts of the husband. [Acts 1848, p. 77; G.L., Vol. 3, p. 77; Const., Art. 16, § 15; Acts 1913, p. 61; Acts 1917, p. 436; Acts 1921, p. 251.]

Art. 4619. [4622] Community property.

All property acquired by either the husband or wife during marriage, except that which is the separate property of either, shall be deemed the common property of the husband and wife, and during coverture may be disposed of by the husband only. All the effects which the husband and wife possess at the time the marriage may be dissolved shall be regarded as common effects or gains, unless the contrary be satisfactorily proved. [Acts 1840, p. 3; G.L., Vol. 2, p. 177; Acts 1913, p. 61.]

Art. 4620. [4627] [2973] [2857] Community property liable for debts.

The community property of the husband and wife shall be liable for their debts contracted during marriage, except in such cases as are specially excepted by law. [Acts 1856, p. 51; G.L., Vol. 4, p. 469; P.D., 4646.]

Art. 4621. [4621] 2967] [2851] Community property not liable.

The community property of the husband and wife shall not be liable for debts or damages resulting from contracts of the wife except for necessaries furnished herself and children, unless the husband joins in the execution of the contract; provided, that her rights with reference to the community property on permanent abandonment by the husband shall not be affected by this provision. [Acts 1848, p. 77; Const., Art. 16, § 15; Acts 1913, p. 61; Acts 1917, p. 436; Acts 1921, p. 252.]

Art. 4623. [4624] [2970] [2854] Subject to debts of wife.

Neither the separate property of the husband nor the community property other than the personal earnings of the wife, and the income, rents and revenues from her separate property, shall be subject to the payment of debts contracted by the wife, except those contracted for necessaries furnished her or her children. The wife shall never be the joint maker of a note or a surety on any bond or obligation of another without the joinder of her husband with her in making such contract. [*Id.*; Acts 1848, p. 77; G.L. Vol. 3, p. 77.]

Litigation

Art. 1983. [1839] [1200] [1204] For wife's separate property.

The husband may sue either alone or jointly with his wife for the recovery of the separate property of the wife; and, in case he fails or neglects so to do, she may sue alone by authority of the court. [Acts 1840, p. 3; G.L. Vol. 2, p. 177; P.D. 4636.]

Art. 1984. [1840] [1201] [1205] Against husband and wife for necessaries.

The husband and wife shall be jointly sued for all debts contracted by the wife for necessaries furnished herself or children, and for expenses which may have been incurred by the wife for the benefit of her separate property. [Acts 1848, p. 77; G.L. Vol. 3, p. 78; P.D. 4643.]

Art. 1985. [1841] 1202] [1206] For wife's debts, etc.

The husband shall be joined in suits for separate debts and demands against the wife, but no personal judgment shall be rendered against the husband. [Acts 1846, p. 363; G.L. Vol. 2, p. 1669; P.D. 9]

Conveyance of Real Estate

Art. 1299. [1114] [635] [559] Conveyance of separate lands of wife.

The husband and wife shall join in the conveyance of real estate, the separate property of the wife; and no such conveyance shall take effect until the same shall have been acknowledged by her privily and apart from her husband before some officer authorized by law to take acknowledgments to deeds for the purpose of being recorded, and certified to in the mode pointed out in articles 6605 and 6608. [Acts 1897, p. 41; G.L. Vol. 10, p. 1095.]

Art. 1300. [1115] [636] [560] Conveyance of homestead.

The homestead of the family shall not be sold and conveyed by the owner, if a married man, without the consent of the wife. Such consent shall be evidenced by the wife joining in the conveyance, and signing her name thereto, and by her separate acknowledgment thereof taken and certified to before the proper officer, and in the mode pointed out in articles 6605 and 6608. [*Id.*]

Art. 6605. [6802] [4618] [4310] Acknowledgment of married woman.

No acknowledgment of a married woman to any conveyance or other instrument purporting to be executed by her shall be taken, unless she has had the same shown to her, and then and there fully explained by the officer taking the acknowledgment on an examination privily and apart from her husband; nor shall her husband certify to the same, unless she thereupon acknowledges to such officer that the same is her act and deed, that she has willingly signed the same, and that she wishes not to retract it. [Acts 1846, p. 156; P.D. 1003; G.L. Vol. 2, p. 1462.]

Art. 6606. [6803] [4619] [4311] Certificate of officer.

An officer taking the acknowledgment of a deed, or other instrument of writing, must place thereon his official certificate, signed by him and given under his seal of office, substantially in form as hereinafter prescribed.

Art. 6607. [6804] [4620] [4312] Form of certificate.

The form of an ordinary certificate of acknowledgment must be substantially as follows:

"The State of __________",
"County of ____________".

"Before me____________(here insert the name and character of the officer) on this day personally appeared ___________, known to me (or proved to me on the oath of__________) to be the person whose name is subscribed to the foregoing instrument and acknowledged to me that he executed the same for the purposes and consideration therein expressed."

(Seal) "Given under my hand and seal of office this_______day of ___________, A.D.______."

Art. 6608. [6805] [4621] [4313] Form by a married woman.

The certificate of acknowledgment of a married woman must be substantially in the following form:

"The State of ____________",
"County of ____________".

"Before me____________(here insert the name and character of the officer) on this day personally appeared ___________, wife of ______, known to me (or proved to me on the oath of__________) to be the person whose name is subscribed to the foregoing instrument, and having been examined by me privily and apart from her husband, and having the same fully explained to her, she, the said __________, acknowledged such instrument to be her act and deed, and declared that she had willingly signed the same for the purposes and consideration therein expressed, and that she did not with to retract it.

(Seal) "Given under my and seal of office this _______day of_______, A.D.______.

4. Special attention should be paid to Art. 6608 as set forth above. At a time when young people were attending Woodstock, women in Texas were finally (as of 1968) being liberated from the requirement of Articles 1299, 1300, 6605 and 6608, that they be taken separate and apart from their husbands to have explained to them and to privately sign acknowledgments, be they general or specifically for conveyance of their separate real estate or homestead.

5. The doctrine of implied exclusion, as explained in *Arnold v. Leonard*, continued to be utilized in response to attempts by private parties to change the character of property or acquire separate property by means not recognized in TEX. CONST. art. XVI § 15.

(a) In *Gorman v. Gause*, 56 S.W.2d 855 (Tex. Comm. App. 1933, judgment adopted) the court applied the doctrine of implied exclusion to a prenuptial agreement (or postnuptial, as the date executed was disputed). The agreement in *Gorman* declared that no property acquired during the marriage would be community. The court viewed this agreement as an attempt by the parties to fix the character of marital property by means different from that recognized in the state constitution, holding the agreement to be void and unenforceable. The court, depending upon *Arnold v. Leonard*, reasoned:

> [I]f the legislature is powerless to enact a law enlarging the wife's separate estate beyond its constitutional limits, it is clear that . . . such enlargement [cannot be] accomplished by mere agreement of the parties made in contemplation of marriage.

(b) In *Strickland v. Wester*, 112 S.W. 2d 1047 (Tex. 1938), the court held that a deed executed by a husband conveying property to his wife was effective as a gift. Prior to reaching this result, the court disposed of another contention of counsel, saying:

> According to the testimony of Mrs. Wester, she purchased this lot from her husband with money which she had earned as a school teacher. She had been teaching 27 years at the date of the trial, and many years ago she and her husband, who was also a teacher during his lifetime, entered into an agreement that her personal earnings should be her separate property. That agreement was not valid, for the community property law cannot be changed by contract.

c) In *King v. Bruce*, 201 S.W. 2d 803 (Tex. 1947), a husband and wife attempted to partition their community property into the separate property of each via an elaborate series of transactions. The court held the couple's attempt ineffective, as it was not recognized by the Texas Constitution as a means of acquiring separate property.

According to some authorities, *King v. Bruce* gave rise to TEX. CONST. art. XVI § 15 (1948) which finally enlarged the rights of spouses to partition and exchange their community property to create separate property.

6. Although the doctrine of implied exclusion and the analysis resting thereon are still used today, the impact is weakened as will be demonstrated in *Graham v. Franco*, 488 S.W.2d 390 (Tex. 1972).

7. What license have you seen, thus far, taken with the separate property parameters established by the Texas Constitution?

C. The Constitution as Amended in 1948

1. Article XVI § 15 as effective 1948-1980

TEX. CONST. art. XVI, § 15 (1948)

§ 15. Separate and Community Property of Husband and Wife

All property, both real and personal, of the wife, owned or claimed by her before marriage, and that acquired afterward by gift, devise or descent, shall be the separate property of the wife; and laws shall be passed more clearly defining the rights of the wife, in relation as well to her separate property as that held in common with her husband; provided that husband and wife, without prejudice to pre-existing creditors, may from time to time by written instrument as if the wife were a feme sole partition between themselves in severalty or into equal undivided interests all or any part of their existing community property, or exchange between themselves the community interest of one spouse in any property for the community interest of the other spouse in other community property, whereupon the portion or interest set aside to each spouse shall be and constitute a part of the separate property of such spouse.

This Amendment is self-operative, but laws may properly be passed prescribing requirements as to the form and manner of execution of such instruments, and providing for their recordation, and for such other reasonable requirements not inconsistent herewith as the Legislature may from time to time consider proper with relation to the subject of this Amendment. Should the Legislature pass an Act dealing with the subject of this Amendment and prescribing requirements as to the form and manner of the execution of such instruments and providing for their recordation and other reasonable requirements not inconsistent herewith and anticipatory hereto, such Act shall not be invalid by reason of its anticipatory character and shall take effect just as though this Constitutional Amendment was in effect when the Act was passed.

Notes, Comments & Questions

1. By what two means may spouses create separate property?

2. Explain the difference between those means.

3. How are creditors protected?

4. Although the right to partition or exchange community property has been expanded in the most recent versions of the Texas Constitution, the strictness with which the courts met initial efforts to partition and exchange cannot be ignored. As you read the following notes and cases, be mindful of the precise application of the Constitutional requirements by the Texas courts.

---

2. Statutes and Decisions, 1948-1967

In the classic case of *Hilley v. Hilley*, 342 S.W. 2d 565 (Tex. 1961), the court held that community property could not be used to create a joint tenancy with right of survivorship between the spouses. Such a transaction was not an interspousal gift, but was an attempt to transfer a survivorship right or interest in community property between the spouses for a valuable consideration. Because consideration paid by each spouse is derived from the community estate, the right or interest which each acquired would remain part of the community estate. Thus, the court held that the attempted transaction did not comport with the constitutional requisites and that the property remained community property. The court pointed out, however, that the spouses could make an effective survivorship agreement with reference to separate property owned by either or both. Six years later, after section 46 of the Probate Code had been amended, *Hilley* was followed in *Williams v. McKnight*, 402 S.W. 2d 505 (Tex. 1966).

As we will see, as of 1988, the Texas Constitution allows spouses to agree that all or part of their community property will become the separate property of the surviving spouse on the death of the other spouse. TEX. CONST. art. XVI, §15. Today, the two step process of partition and then establishment of a joint tenancy with right of survivorship is not needed. So, why include *Williams v. McKnight* and the notes and cases that follow? *Hilley v. Hilley*, *Williams v. McKnight*, and their progeny are the most important cases of the period following the 1948 amendment to the Texas Constitution. In 1948, spouses were given the right to create separate property by partition or exchange. This new right to create separate property was taken too far by the legislature and spouses who overstepped constitutional boundaries, bypassing partition or exchange, in an attempt to create separate property. The cases that follow are relevant not only for an understanding of the evolution of Texas marital property law, but also because they exemplify the strict interpretation of TEX. CONST. art. XVI, §15. These cases can be used to persuade a court that, historically, a liberal interpretation of TEX. CONST. art. XVI, §15 has been rejected and that a strict interpretation has, historically, been utilized and should continue to be so used.

WILLIAMS
v.
McKNIGHT
402 S.W.2d 505
(Tex. 1966)

POPE, JUSTICE.

Petitioner, D.D. Williams, as Independent Executor and Trustee under the will of James N. McKnight, Jr., deceased, filed this action against Mabel S. McKnight, the decedent's widow, to recover for the estate one-half of three savings accounts which she withdrew after the death of her husband. Petitioner contends that the funds belonged to the community estate of Mr. and Mrs. McKnight. Respondent, Mabel McKnight, contends that she and her husband complied with the 1961 amendment to Section 46 of the V.A.T.A. Probate Code by executing an agreement as to each account and that the agreements effected a partition of their community funds and the creation of joint accounts with rights of survivorship in her as the survivor. The trial court and the Court of Civil Appeals sustained that contention and held that the funds belonged to the widow as the survivor. 391 S.W.2d 813. We reverse the judgments of the courts below and render judgment that the funds were community funds, one-half of which belong to the estate of James N. McKnight.

The case is before us on an agreed statement of facts. James N. McKnight and his wife, Mabel S. McKnight, in 1962 made three separate deposits of $10,000 in savings accounts with three different institutions. All of the funds came from their community funds and nothing was thereafter added to or withdrawn from the accounts. On May 9, 1962, they deposited $10,000 with the City National Bank in Wichita Falls, Texas. On February 4, 1963, they deposited a like amount with the First-Wichita National Bank of Wichita Falls, Texas. They signed the signature cards at each of the banks. The agreements on the cards at those two banks were substantially the same. That of the First-Wichita National Bank was as follows:

> The joint depositors signing above agree, each with the other and with the above named bank, that all sums now or later deposited by either or both of such joint depositors in such account with all accumulations thereon, are and shall be owned by them jointly with the right of survivorship. The amounts in such savings account may be withdrawn by any one of such depositors or by the survivor or either of the survivors after the death of the other joint depositor or depositors. Each appoints the other his agent with power to deposit in said joint account moneys of the other and for that purpose to enforce any check, draft, note or instrument payable to the order of the other or all of such joint depositors, and each hereby ratifies and confirms any and all representations hereafter made by any of them with respect to the loss, theft or destruction of the passbook herewith issued to them. Payment to the survivor or either of these survivors shall be subject to the laws relating to inheritance and succession taxes and all rules and regulations made pursuant thereto. The rights of the bank hereunder this agreement shall not be changed or terminated by the said depositors or either of them except by written notice to the said bank which shall not affect transactions theretofore made.

On May 9, 1962, the McKnights made a similar deposit in Parker Savings and Loan Association, Wichita Falls, Texas. The signature card they signed at that institution also purported to create a joint tenancy with right of survivorship but it contained the additional agreement: "It is agreed by the signatory parties with each other and by the parties with you, that the funds placed in or added to the account by any one of the parties is and shall be conclusively intended to be a gift at that time of such funds to the other signatory party or parties to the extent of his or their pro rata interest in that account." Respondent does not, however, contend that she owns the account by reason of a gift. Her only contention with respect to this deposit is that Section 46 of the Probate Code authorized the creation out of community funds of a joint account with right of survivorship.

In *Hilley v. Hilley*, 161 Tex. 569, 342 S.W.2d 565 (1961), this Court held that to create a joint tenancy with right of survivorship out of community property, such property must be transmuted into separate property by partition prior to the agreement creating the joint tenancy with right of survivorship. Further, we held that the partition must be accomplished in accordance with the provisions of Article 4624a, VERNON'S ANN. TEX. CIV. ST.,[1] since Section 46 of the Probate Code did not inferen-

[1] Art. 4624a. Section 1. "A husband and wife, without prejudice to pre-existing creditors, may from time to time, by written instrument as if the wife were a feme sole, partition between themselves in severalty or into equal undivided interests all or any part of their existing community property, or exchange between themselves the community interest of one spouse in any property for the community interest of the other spouse in other community property. Such partition or exchange shall be effectuated by a written instrument subscribed and acknowledged by both spouses in the manner now required by law for the conveyance of realty; whereupon the property or interest in property set aside to each spouse by such instrument shall be and constitute a part of the separate property of such spouses."

"Such partition shall not be good or effectual against a purchaser in good faith, without notice thereof and for a valuable consideration, nor against any creditor unless filed for record with the County Clerk of the county or counties in which such property shall be situated."

"If such instrument purports to exchange property or to partition property between the husband and wife, otherwise than as equal undivided interest in the same property, or as equal shares or units of identical personal property, such

tially repeal or modify such statutes as Articles 4613, 4614, 4619, 4624a and 881a-23.[2] The thrust of our holding in *Hilley* was that the separate property of spouses, not community property, may be the subject of a joint tenancy between them, with right of survivorship. When the property is initially community, it must be rendered separate by statutory partition before survivorship rights arise from a joint tenancy agreement between husband and wife.

Shortly after our opinion in *Hilley*, the Fifty-Seventh Legislature in 1961, amended Section 46 of the Probate Code by adding one sentence. The section, as it existed before amendment is here stated and the sentence that the Fifty-Seventh Legislature added is italicized:

> Where two (2) or more persons hold an estate, real, personal, or mixed, jointly, and one (1) joint owner dies before severance, his interest in said joint estate shall not survive to the remaining joint owner or joint owners, but shall descend to, and be vested in, the heirs or legal representatives of such deceased joint owner in the same manner as if his interest had been severed and ascertained. Provided, however, that by an agreement in writing of joint owners of property, the interest of any joint owner who dies may be made to survive to the surviving joint owner or joint owners, but no such agreement shall be inferred from the mere fact that the property is held in joint ownership. *It is specifically provided that any husband and his wife may, by written agreement, create a joint estate out of their community property, with rights of survivorship.*

The amendment attempts to authorize spouses to create a joint estate with rights of survivorship out of their community property. In *Hilley*, we stated the reasons that this result could not constitutionally be accomplished, and those reasons are as valid after the amendment as they were before. Constitutional limitations are as binding upon the Legislature as they are upon the Judiciary.

Section 46 does not speak of partition. Moreover, it is a very old principle of law that the husband and wife cannot, by mere agreement, partition and transfer their community property to each other and effect a change of the class of the estate which the Constitution fixes upon the property. *Green v. Ferguson*, 62 Tex. 525, 529 (1884); *Cox v. Miller*, 54 Tex. 16 (1880); *Pevehouse v. Lubbock National Bank*, 79 S.W.2d 1107 (Tex. Civ. App. 1935, no writ). Neither Section 46 nor the agreements between Mr. and Mrs. McKnight mention a partition, but Mrs. McKnight urges that it was implicit in both the statute and the agreements. This contention is necessary in order to arrive at the separate property which alone may be the subject of an agreement for a joint tenancy with right of survivorship between husband and wife. This same contention was urged in *Hilley* and we rejected it as a fictional partition of community property into separate property. When the Constitution authorized a marital partition of property, it did not contemplate that fictions, presumptions, nor even legislative declarations of intention would undo constitutionally defined community properties. *Arnold v. Leonard*, 114 Tex. 535, 273 S.W. 799 (1925). Mr. and Mrs. McKnight could not make an effective agreement concerning their community funds until they first reduced those funds to their separate estates. Unless we indulge in the fictions denounced in *Hilley*, it is clear that they did not deal with their separate estates in the instant case.

instrument shall not be valid unless approved by the Court upon written application of the husband and wife, addressed to the District Court of the county in which they or either of them reside. Such petition must set out facts showing that the transaction is not to the disadvantage of the wife, and shall be filed and docketed as in other cases, and at any time thereafter the District Court may, in term time, take up and hear said petition and evidence in regard thereto, and enter an order accordingly either approving or disapproving the transaction."

[2] Article 881a-23 was later amended and provided that the parties could partition community funds by a written and acknowledged instrument. Acts 1957, 55th Leg., p. 1319, ch. 445. It was again amended after the date of the McKnight deposits and is now Section 6.09 of Article 852a. Acts 1963, 58th Leg., p. 269, ch. 113.

In so far as Section 46 authorizes spouses to create by agreement a joint estate with rights of survivorship *out of their community property*, it is violative of the Constitution. Statutory partition with the resulting separate property is the necessary prerequisite to a written agreement between husband and wife to create a joint estate with rights of survivorship.

An amicus curiae brief suggests, though it is not so contended by the parties, that at least with respect to the account with the Parker Savings and Loan Association, we should hold that there was a gift from the husband to the wife of his community interest, and that this was a gift of the present right to withdraw funds from the account as well as title to the entire account at his death if she survived him. As discussed in *Hilley*, there was consideration from each; and it was derived from the community estate. Consideration precludes the idea of a gift. *Kearse v. Kearse*, 276 S.W. 690 (Tex. Comm. App.1925). The right or interest of the spouses for that reason remained a part of the community estate.

The judgments of the courts below are reversed and judgment is here rendered that petitioner have and recover from respondent, Mabel McKnight, one-half of the three savings accounts in the sum of $15,000 together with interest from the time of her withdrawal of those funds from the respective depositories.

Notes, Comments & Questions

1. In *Davis v. East Texas Sav. & Loan Ass'n*, 354 S.W.2d 926 (Tex. 1962), the court held that the spouses could utilize separate property to create a valid joint tenancy with right of survivorship, with the spouses as joint tenants. In *Krueger v. Williams*, 359 S.W.2d 48 (Tex. 1962), the court held that a spouse, utilizing community property, could create a valid joint tenancy with right of survivorship with the spouse and a third party as joint tenants.

2. Much later, *Williams v. McKnight* was followed in *Maples v. Nimitz*, 615 S.W.2d 690 (Tex. 1981).

3. In 1967, the Texas Legislature enacted statutes dealing with marital property, achieving some of the goals which had been sought unsuccessfully in the legislation which preceded *Arnold v. Leonard*. The 1967 legislation is Tex. Laws 1967, ch. 309 at 735, sometimes referred to as the Matrimonial Property Act of 1967, effective January 1, 1968. The substantive provisions of this statute were reenacted and appear today in Chapters 3, 4 and 5 of the Texas Family Code.

4. Perhaps the most strict application of the constitutional partition requisites can be found more recently in *Jameson v. Bain*, 693 S.W.2d 676 (Tex. App.—San Antonio 1985, no writ). In this case, the partition/joint tenancy card was signed in the wrong order; that is, the spouses did not *first* partition the property, but rather, did so *after* creating a joint tenancy. The attempt was not successful, even under the 1980 amendments to the Constitution. Although today joint tenancies can be obtained by partitioning community funds, these strict precedents cannot be ignored when determining whether one has complied with constitutional requisites.

---

3. Statutes and Decisions, 1968-1980

This section begins with *Few v. Charter Oak Fire Ins. Co.*, where attorney for an injured wife took the bold step of suing for worker's compensation damages in wife's own name. What is of interest here is the balance between rules of procedure and statutes, as well as the basic rights of management and control that are finally being extended to women. At first glance, the next case of *Graham v. Franco* appears to be simply a case characterizing personal injury damages sought by wife. However, the more important aspect of the case is the court's determination of whether a statute that characterizes personal injury recoveries as separate property is constitutional, especially in light of earlier case law, including *Arnold v. Leonard.* The historical and constitutional underpinnings of the opinion cannot be ignored. This section culminates with *Williams v. Williams*, a premarital agreement opinion out of the Texas Supreme Court that reiterates the importance of complying with TEX. CONST. art. XVI, §15. This principle endures today even though TEX. CONST. art. XVI, §15 has been greatly expanded. Do not consider *Williams* to be simply a homestead case; rather it is a case in which only the homestead clause of the premarital agreement was upheld because the remainder was found to be unconstitutional. The analysis of the Texas Supreme Court provides a template for future cases.

FEW
v.
CHARTER OAK FIRE INS. CO.
463 S.W.2d 424
(Tex. 1971)

POPE, JUSTICE.

Mary Frances Few, joining her husband pro forma, sued Charter Oak Fire Insurance Company for total and permanent incapacity suffered in the course of her employment with Safeway Grocery in Mineola, Texas. The trial court awarded judgment for the plaintiffs, naming both Mary Frances and her husband in the judgment. The court of civil appeals, with a divided court, reversed the judgment for plaintiffs and remanded the cause for re-trial, holding that the husband was an indispensable party and that he was not joined as a real party.

* * *

Mary Frances Few and her husband, Milburn Few, had been married for many years prior to her accident on June 20, 1968, and they are still married. For this reason her workmen's compensation award was their community property. *Pickens v. Pickens*, 125 Tex. 410, 83 S.W.2d 951, 953 (1935). Community ownership may also be called a joint ownership. *Dillard v. Dillard*, 341 S.W.2d 668 (Tex. Civ. App.1961, writ ref. n.r.e.); *Hitchcock v. Cassel*, 275 S.W.2d 205 (Tex. Civ. App.1955, writ ref. n.r.e.). Rule 39, Texas Rules of Civil Procedure, as it was worded at the time of the trial,[2] provided that persons having a joint interest shall be made parties. It was this rule which prompted the court of civil appeals to hold that the wife's husband was an indispensable party. The court relied upon our recent opinion in *Petroleum Anchor Equipment Co., Inc. v. Tyra*, 406 S.W.2d 891, 892-893 (Tex. 1966), in which we applied Rule 39. In that case we held that persons who hold a joint interest shall or must be made parties and are indispensable parties.

---

[2] The rule was changed, effective January 1, 1971.

If only Rule 39 were involved in the case before us, our decision would be controlled by our earlier decision in *Petroleum Anchor*. However, we are now faced with two relevant statutes enacted by the legislature. Article V, Sec. 25, of the Texas Constitution, VERNON'S ANN. ST. vests in the Supreme Court the power to establish rules of procedure "not inconsistent with the law of the State." Legislative authority for this power is found in Article 1731a, Sec. 2. Rule 39 was established pursuant to this power. As the constitutional provision indicates, this is a limited power; and when a rule of the court conflicts with a legislative enactment, the rule must yield. *Missouri, K. & T.R. Co. v. Beasley*, 106 Tex. 160, 155 S.W. 183 (1913), *rehearing denied*, 106 Tex. 160, 160 S.W. 471.

Articles 4621 and 4626 are the statutes which control this case. Enacted by the 60th Legislature and effective January 1, 1968, they provided:

> Art. 4621.
>
> * * *
>
> During marriage each spouse shall have sole management, control and disposition of that community property which he or she would have owned if a single person, including (but not limited to) his or her personal earnings, the revenues from his or her separate property, the recoveries for personal injuries awarded to him or her, and the increase, mutations and revenues of all property subject to his or her sole management, control and disposition; the earnings of an unemancipated minor are subject to the management, control and disposition of the parents or parent having custody of the minor; if community property subject to the sole management, control and disposition of one spouse is mixed or combined with community property subject to the sole management, control and disposition of the other spouse, the mixed or combined community property is subject to the joint management, control and disposition of the spouses unless the spouses otherwise provide; any other community property is subject to the joint management, control, and disposition of the husband and wife.
>
> Art. 4626.
>
> * * *
>
> A spouse may sue and be sued without the joinder of the other spouse. When claims or liabilities are joint and several, the spouses may be joined under the rules relating to joinder of parties generally.

Articles 4621 and 4626 were designed to correct an anomalous situation concerning the rights of a Texas wife. Almost from the beginning of Texas history, the right of a wife to own property has been recognized, but it has taken more than a century to give the wife managerial powers over that which she owns.

The Constitution of 1836 recognized the community property system of Mexico and Spain and on January 20, 1840, the Fourth Congress of the Republic determined to follow that system in matters of marital property. 2 GAMMEL LAWS OF TEXAS 177-178 (1840). The system has proved to be much fairer in its recognition of the wife's rights of ownership than that afforded her by the common law. 1 DE FUNIAK, PRINCIPLES OF COMMUNITY PROPERTY, Sec. 3 (1943).

The common law had visited upon a wife an intolerable state of civil disability both in owning and managing property. As expressed by Vaughn, that system "suspended the wife's legal existence during the marriage, or at least consolidated it into that of the husband." Vaughn, *The Policy of Community Property and Inter-Spousal Transactions*, 19 Bay. L. Rev. 20, 48-49 (1967). At common law, the husband and wife were one, and the husband was that one. *Murphy v. Coffey*, 33 Tex. 508 (1870). The woman's legal existence, according to BLACKSTONE, was merged into that of her husband, "under whose wing, protection, and cover, she performs everything; and is therefore called in our law—French, a feme covert, and is said to be under the protection and influence of her husband, her baron, or lord, and her condition during her marriage is called her coverture.

* * *

If the wife be injured in her person or her property, she can bring no action for redress without her husband's concurrence, and in his name, as well as her own."

* * *

ERLICH'S BLACKSTONE, pp. 83, 84 (1959).

The Republic treated the wife's right to manage her property differently from her right to own that property. The same act of the Fourth Congress which recognized the community property system of ownership, took from the wife any powers to manage what she owned and gave the sole management of the wife's property to the husband. 2 GAMMEL, LAWS OF TEXAS 178 (1840). It has been the law of Texas for more than a century that, except in limited situations, only the husband could bring suit for community recoveries arising out of a wife's loss of earning capacity. *Roberts v. Magnolia Petroleum Co.*, 142 S.W.2d 315 (Tex. Civ. App. 1940, writ ref., (135 Tex. 289, 143 S.W.2d 79)); *Loper v. Western U. Teleg. Co.*, 70 Tex. 689, 8 S.W. 600 (1888); *Gallagher v. Bowie*, 66 Tex. 265, 17 S.W. 407 (1886); *Ezell v. Dodson*, 60 Tex. 331 (1883); *Murphy v. Coffey, supra*; *Firence Footwear Co. v. Campbell*, 406 S.W.2d 516, 411 S.W.2d 636 (Tex. Civ. App. 1967, writ ref. n.r.e.); *Urban v. Field*, 137 S.W.2d 137 (Tex. Civ. App. 1940, no writ).

Seventy years ago Judge Ocie Speer deplored the situation which recognized the wife's equality of ownership, yet denied that equality with respect to a wife's management of what she owned. He wrote:

> The foolish fiction that her existence is merged in that of her husband has given way to the more enlightened recognition of her identity as an individual, and her consequent capacity to own property, to make contracts, and to sue and be sued. Yet, as though fearing serious consequences of much moment, it has not altogether removed her fetters, but is slowly, yet surely, tending, through the course of legislative acts and judicial interpretations, toward the enlargement of her rights and powers, which will in time culminate in a proper recognition of all her civil rights. SPEER, THE LAW OF MARRIED WOMEN IN TEXAS, § 25 (1901).

Efforts to rectify the wife's inferior legal powers as the manager of her property have been infrequent; and over-broad corrective legislation changing the definition of community property has been stricken down on constitutional grounds. *See* Huie, § 11, *Commentary-Community Property Law*, 13 VERNON'S TEX. STATS., p. 39; *Northern Texas Traction Co. v. Hill*, 297 S.W. 778 (Tex. Civ. App.1927, writ ref.).

The disabilities of coverture remained as a remnant of the common law until 1967. During the intervening years, the wife in fact was still covert; her husband was still lord and baron. The 60th Legislature, in enacting Articles 4621 and 4626, avoided the constitutional difficulties arising from an attempt to modify legislatively the constitutional definition of community property. These statutes leave undisturbed the definition of community property, but more clearly define the managerial rights of each spouse. Article 4621 gave the injured spouse powers to manage that community which she would have owned if a single person, including recoveries for personal injuries. Article 4626 authorized the wife to sue without joining her husband, but it also provided that in the case of joint and several claims, the spouses "may be joined under the rules relating to joinder of parties generally."

Charter Oak argues that Rule 39(a) is the rule of joinder to which Article 4626 referred in its phrase "under the rules relating to the joinder of parties generally." However, the statute, unlike Rule 39(a) is permissive in terms. It is our opinion that the legislature, in using permissive terms, was recognizing that while the spouses' ownership interest in certain property may be joint, the managerial interest in the same property would be several. The legislature surely did not intend by the use of the phrase "may be joined" in Article 4626 to take away the sole managerial authority which it had just established in Article 4621. In terms of the facts presently before us, Mr. Few would be a proper party to the suit because of his ownership interest in the workmen's compensation benefit. However, he was not an indispensable party in view of his wife's sole managerial interest in the benefit. *See*, 23 S.W.L.J. 55 (1969); 22 S.w. L.J. 132 (1968). We hold that Mary Frances Few properly sued without joining her husband for the recovery of workmen's compensation benefits arising out of her own injury.

* * *

Notes, Comments & Questions

1. Why was the worker's compensation claim summarily characterized as community property?
2. Is there a general rule of legal analysis that emerges from this case?
3. Review TEX. FAM. CODE § 3.001(3).

GRAHAM
v.
FRANCO
488 S.W.2d 390
(Tex. 1972)

GREENHILL, CHIEF JUSTICE.

The writ of error was granted in this case to pass upon the constitutionality of a statute which provides: "The recovery awarded for personal injuries sustained by either spouse during marriage shall be the separate property of that spouse except for any recovery for loss of earning capacity during marriage." We hold that the statute, as construed, is constitutional. We also hold that the acts of negligence of the husband as found by the jury are not imputed to the wife so as to bar her recovery.

This action arises out of a rear end collision. The car in which the plaintiffs, Mr. and Mrs. Franco, were riding was struck from the rear at night by a truck owned by Bill Graham and driven by Roosevelt Tillis. The Francos testified that Mr. Franco was driving down the right side of the highway with lights burning. As to the rear lights, the testimony was that they had recently been checked and found to be in good order. The truck driver testified that the Franco car was stopped on the highway with its lights off.

The jury found that the truck driver was negligent in failing to keep a proper lookout. It also found that the acts of Mr. Franco in stopping his car on the highway and in having the car upon the highway without a rear light burning constituted negligence. Each of such acts was found to be a proximate cause. There were no allegations or findings that the wife, Mrs. Franco, was guilty of negligence in any respect.

The jury found that Mr. Franco's damages were "zero." It also found that Mrs. Franco's medical expenses were $2,212.92; but her damages, resulting from the occurrence in question, were likewise found to be "zero." The trial court entered judgment for the defendants.

As to Mr. Franco, the Court of Civil Appeals affirmed. His contributory negligence was held to have barred his recovery, and the question of his damages became immaterial. As to Mrs. Franco, that court reversed and remanded for a new trial. It found that the answer to the damages issue of "zero" was against the great weight and preponderance of the evidence. It recited, among other things, that she was in the hospital for 13 days, several of which were in intensive care.

The Character of Recovery for Personal Injury

The Court of Civil Appeals, in holding the statute constitutional, held that a wife would be entitled to recover, as her separate property, damages for injury to her body, including disfigurement, loss or impairment of the use of the body, and physical pain and suffering, both past and present. It excluded from her separate recovery loss of earnings, medical expenses, and "all other damages." These latter items were held to be recoverable by the community of the husband and wife.

In arriving at a proper solution of this problem, it is necessary to begin with law as it existed at the time of the adoption of our Texas constitutions and to ascertain the purpose of those portions of the constitutions which provide for the separate and community estates. Generally speaking, our civil procedure and our rules of necessary parties were adopted from the English; but the substantive rights of the spouses in separate and community property were taken from Spain and Mexico. In England, the spouses were one; and generally, the husband was dominant. He generally controlled the property of the wife and most litigation. He, at least, was generally a necessary party.

The problem in this litigation begins with the early Texas case of *Ezell v. Dodson*, 60 Tex. 331 (1883). The court had before it the right of a wife to sue alone for her personal injuries growing out of an assault. The defendant filed exceptions on the ground that the husband was a necessary party. The wife refused to amend, and the trial court dismissed her suit. This Court affirmed. We have examined the transcript in that case, and the only question was one of necessary parties. The character of the recovery, if any, whether separate or community, was not at issue. Nevertheless, by dictum, the court added that the assault and battery upon the wife gave rise to a chose in action; that the chose in action was property; and since it was acquired after marriage and not by way of gift, devise or descent, it would be community property. Thus the dictum was that an injury to the wife constitutes an asset or claim of the community estate.

The holding of *Ezell* was correct on the parties question as the law then existed. But we are of the opinion that its dictum was wrong for the reasons set out below and as ably discussed by Dean Leon Green in his analysis of the Texas Death Act in 26 Texas Law Review 461 at 466 et seq.

After *Ezell*, the question as to the character of the recovery for personal injuries, whether separate or community, was not examined in depth. The courts simply followed the dictum of *Ezell*.

The basic question is the interpretation of Section 15 of Article 16 of the Texas Constitution. With the key words underscored by us, it provides:

> All *property*, both real and personal, of the wife, *owned* or claimed by her before marriage, and that *acquired* afterward by gift, devise or descent, shall be the separate property of the wife; . . .

This Court in *Arnold v. Leonard*, 114 Tex. 535, 273 S.W. 799 (1925), held unconstitutional a statute which attempted to declare as separate property the rents and revenues from the wife's separate realty. The holding of that case is so limited; and in view of the history of our community property system and laws, it was a correct decision. The language of the opinion, however, is broad. The reasoning of the court in *Arnold v. Leonard*, and of cases following it, is one of implied exclusion; i.e., if property was acquired during marriage by any other means than gift, devise, or descent, it was and is necessarily community.

A much later case of this Court reverted to a test more akin to that prevailing under the Spanish and Mexican law, and several early opinions of this Court, dealing with community property. It applied an affirmative test; i.e., that property is community which is acquired by the work, efforts or labor of the spouses or their agents, as income from their property, or as a gift to the community. Such property, acquired by the joint efforts of the spouses, was regarded as acquired by "onerous title" and belonged to the community. *Norris v. Vaughan*, 152 Tex. 491, 260 S.W.2d 676 (1953); *De Blane v. Lynch*, 23 Tex. 25 (1859); *Smith v. Strahan*, 16 Tex. 314 (1856); *Epperson v. Jones*, 65 Tex. 425 (1886); DE FUNIAK, PRINCIPLES OF COMMUNITY PROPERTY (1971) § 62; MOYNIHAN, COMMUNITY PROPERTY, 2 AMERICAN LAW OF PROPERTY (1952) § 7.16. Under this reasoning, it is clear that the personal injuries to the wife are not "acquired" by the efforts of the spouses and would not belong to the community. Thus in *Norris v. Vaughan, supra*, JUSTICE SMITH wrote for this Court that:

> The principle which lies at the foundation of the whole system of community property is, that whatever is acquired by the joint efforts of the husband and wife, shall be their common property.

It is not necessary, however, to here make a decision on the correctness or applicability of *Norris v. Vaughan* and related cases and the concept of "onerous title."

The dictum of *Ezell* reasoned, as indicated, that if the wife were injured after marriage, this created a chose in action; that a chose in action [a cause of action for personal injuries] was property; that this property (chose in action) was acquired after marriage; and since it was not acquired by gift, devise or descent, it belonged to the community.

There is a large body of law, including cases by this Court, that a chose in action (a cause of action) for injuries to the *person* (as contrasted to injuries to *property*) was not regarded as *property* at the time of the adoption of our constitution. This Court stated the general rule in *G.H. & S.A. Ry. v. Freeman*, 57 Tex. 156 (1882):

> Mere personal torts die with the party and are not assignable. 'Such are actions of slander, libel, assault and battery, false imprisonment, *crim. con.*, seduction, etc. On the other hand, when the injury affects the estate rather than the person, when the action is brought for damage to the estate and not for injury to the person, personal feelings or character, the right of action could be bought and sold. Such right of action, upon the death, bankruptcy or insolvency of the party injured, passes to the executor or assignee as a part of his assets, because it affects his estate, and *not his personal rights*.' * * * In the American notes to the case of *Row v. Daudon*, . . . the rule stated above is treated as the general rule in America. 57 Tex. at 158.

The *Freeman* case was followed in *Stewart v. H. & T.C. Ry. Co.*, 62 Tex. 246 (1884).

At common law, a cause of action (chose in action) for damage to *property was* property and could be transferred and inherited. But a cause of action for *personal injuries* at common law was not inheritable or assignable. As is stated in MCKAY, LAW OF COMMUNITY PROPERTY § 182 (2nd ed. 1925), and relevant here as speaking as of the time our constitution was adopted:

By the clear weight of common law authority, a cause of action for personal injury is not property in any sense, nor for any purpose till it has been reduced to judgment; and the judgment, as property, takes its character as separate or common from the right violated in committing the wrong—the personal injury.

The *Ezell* opinion cites two authorities for the proposition that a chose in action for personal injuries is property: 2 BISHOP ON MARRIED WOMEN § 271, and C.*B. & Q. RR. Co. v. Dunn*, 52 Ill. 260 (1869). Bishop does not say that a chose in action for personal injuries is *property*. It says only that "the right to sue for a tort which one has suffered is a chose in action," and that after marriage the suit must be brought in the joint names of the husband and wife,—the *procedural* point before the *Ezell* court. Bishop continues, "But where the injury is in whole or in part to the wife, the right to sue for the injury to her is her postnuptial chose in action."

The other authority cited in *Ezell*, the *Dunn* opinion by the Illinois court, is one based on the construction of the intent of the Illinois Legislature in enacting a statute to change the common law. That opinion demonstrated that the Illinois Legislature intended that the cause of action for damages arising out of personal injuries should become *property*. Moreover, contrary to *Ezell*, the Illinois court said that it was *the wife's property*:

> Who is the natural owner of the right? Not the husband, because the injury did not accrue to him; it was wholly personal to the wife. It was her body that was bruised; it was she who suffered the agonizing mental and physical pain. 52 Ill. at 264.

Assuming that a chose in action arising out of a personal injury to a spouse is, or created, "property," the character of the "property" was personal to the one spouse injured at common law.

MCKAY, in his work on COMMUNITY PROPERTY cited above, says, at page 269, that in a personal injury, the right violated is to personal security; that no right is more intensely separate than this; and that the violator of this separate right gives rise to a separate cause of action. "This right belonged to the wife at common law, and so did the cause of action for its violation. There has never been any mistake about this in the common law authorities . . . ."

Similarly under Spanish law, an injury to the wife gave rise to rights in *her*, for her separate estate, not to the community. A recognized authority in this area, DE FUNIAK, writes in "PRINCIPLES OF COMMUNITY PROPERTY," Section 81, that:

> There is no question that this ["delictus" or "delict"] included the wife as a person wronged . . . with the right to be made whole so nearly as was possible . . . . Thus, the injury to the person of a wife was compensable to her to the extent that she was wronged or dishonored by such injury. . . .

That authority concludes that injuries to the wife were her separate right under the Spanish and Mexican law upon which our system of community property law was based.

Professor Joseph W. McKnight, whose views are similar to those of Dean Leon Green referred to above, concluded:

> The sort of recovery for personal loss referred to by Article 4615 was not construed as a property interest either under the common law as adopted in Texas in 1840 or under the Spanish law which prevailed prior to 1840 and thereafter with respect to marital property and other family matters. It is perhaps worthy of note that, even today, neither the federal Internal Revenue Code nor the federal Bankruptcy Act treats such losses as property interests. TRIAL LAWYERS FORUM 7 at 31 (1968).

It was also recognized at the time of the adoption of our various constitutions including that of 1876, that as to property which was exchanged for other property, and damages which were awarded to the separate property of a spouse, the recovery would be separate in character. *Love v. Robertson*, 7 Tex. 6 (1851); *Rose v. Houston*, 11 Tex. 324 (1854); *Chapman v. Allen*, 15 Tex. 278 (1855); *Cleveland v. Cole*, 65 Tex. 402 (1886); *San Antonio & A.P. Ry. Co. v. Flato*, 13 Tex. Civ. App. 214, 35 S.W. 859 (1896).

Under this line of authorities, able scholars have reasoned that the body of the wife brought into the marriage was peculiarly her own; and that if any "property" was involved in a personal injury to the wife, it was peculiarly hers. If her house, her separate property, were set afire and destroyed by a third person, the recovery should be her separate property. If an automobile were owned by the wife before marriage and was injured or destroyed, the recovery should go to repay the loss or damage to her separate property. So, the reasoning continues, if the arm of the wife is cut off, the recovery for the loss because of disfigurement and for the attendant pain and suffering should go to the wife. The reasoning is that the recovery is a replacement, in so far as practicable, and not the "acquisition" of an asset by the community estate. *See* Huie, *Definition of Wife's Separate Property*, 35 TEXAS LAW REVIEW 1054 at 1061 (1957); McKnight, *Personal Injury as Separate Property*, 3 TRIAL LAWYERS FORUM 7 (1968); McKnight, *Matrimonial Property*, 26 SOUTHWESTERN LAW JOURNAL 31 at 36 (1972); McSwain, *The New Marital Property Statutes*, 2 FAMILY LAW NEWSLETTER (STATE BAR OF TEXAS), number 3 (1968).

Other noted writers outside of Texas agree with Dean Green that the *Ezell* dictum and cases following it are incorrectly decided. Green, *The Texas Death Act*, 26 TEXAS LAW REVIEW 461 at 466 et seq.; MOYNIHAN, 2 AMERICAN LAW OF PROPERTY (1952) § 7.16; MCKAY, LAW OF COMMUNITY PROPERTY §§ 182, 184, and 378. In Section 398, MCKAY concludes,

> But neither at common law or by the law of community does he [the husband] hold the wife's right to personal security and should not be permitted to recover for the violation of this right. It does not belong to him nor to the community. The wife's physical pain and suffering are not his loss nor the loss of the community.

In the light of the foregoing, it is our conclusion that, in adopting the provisions of Section 15 of Article 16 of our constitution, the people did not intend to change the common law or the Spanish law under which Texas operated so as to make a cause of action for injuries to the wife an asset of the community. A personal injury, and the chose in action created, was not "property" at common law as then understood, and it was not property "acquired" by any community effort. If it was "property" under the common law, the Spanish law, or the Texas law, its character was separate, or personal, to the wife. In using the word "property," the framers of the constitution apparently had in mind property which could be given, bought and sold, and passed by will or by inheritance. A chose in action, or cause of action, arising out of injury to the wife was none of these. So, as stated, the dictum of *Ezell v. Dodson* was in error, and it still is. Granted our great reluctance to disapprove or overrule decisions in the field of property, or in the field of contracts upon which people deliberately rely, we consider it our particular duty to follow the constitution and to right the wrongs especially where the Legislature has felt strongly enough about it to take the action it has. This Court has, in the past, corrected the dictum of its previous decisions when the dictum was wrong. *Valmont Plantations v. State of Texas*, 163 Tex. 381, 355 S.W.2d 502 (1962). We have also overruled opinions where we regard them as erroneous. *Watkins v. Southcrest Baptist Church*, 399 S.W.2d 530 at 535 (Tex. 1966), and *Howle v. Camp Amon Carter*, 470 S.W.2d 629 at 630 (Tex. 1971). The dictum of *Ezell v. Dodson* is therefore overruled.

Most of the opinions of this Court dealing with injuries to the wife after *Ezell* were, like *Ezell*, concerned with procedural matters, mainly the question of who could or should, or should not, bring the suit. The merits of the question of the character of the recovery, whether separate or community, apparently were not re-examined. *Texas Central Ry. Co. v. Burnett*, 61 Tex. 638 (1884); *G.C. & S.F. Ry. v. Greenlee*, 62 Tex. 344 (1884); *Missouri Pacific Ry. Co. v. White*, 80 Tex. 202, 15 S.W. 808 (1891). These and other opinions are likewise overruled to the extent that they conflict with this opinion.

The Legislature in 1915 attempted to change the rule by a statute which was too broad. That statute was carried forward in the Revised Statutes of Texas of 1925 as Article 4615. It provided, in effect, that *all* recovery by the wife for personal injuries, except medical expenses, should be her separate property. This included loss of earnings which under common law and community property concepts at the time of the adoption of our constitution were community. The earnings of the spouses were funds acquired by the efforts of a spouse which have been considered part of the community of the spouses. That statute and the drafting of its successor are analyzed by Joseph W. McKnight in his article, *Personal Injury as Separate Property*, 3 TRIAL LAWYERS FORUM 7 (1968).

A court of civil appeals held that the above statute was unconstitutional. *Northern Texas Traction Co. v. Hill*, 297 S.W. 778 (Tex. Civ. App. 1927, writ refused). Because the statute classified all recovery, including personal earnings, to be separate, it was a correct decision as above indicated. But the court in the *Hill* case wrote too broadly and cited only the dictum of *Ezell v. Dodson* for its broad language. To the extent that the holding of the Northern Texas Traction Co. case conflicts with this opinion, it is overruled.

Our holding is that, independent of the statute involved, recovery for personal injuries to the body of the wife, including disfigurement and physical pain and suffering, past and future, is separate property of the wife. And, of course, a statute which provides that such recovery shall be the separate property of the wife is constitutional.

Recovery for Medical Expenses and Loss of Earning Capacity

Though there is room for a difference of opinion, our research indicates that the recovery for medical and related expenses is for the community. The reasoning has been that it is the burden of the community to pay these expenses. MOYNIHAN in 2 AMERICAN LAW OF COMMUNITY PROPERTY (1952) says at page 160:

> Although it would on principle seem the sounder view that damages recovered for pain, suffering and bodily disfigurement are the separate property of the injured spouse, it does not follow that all elements of damage for personal injury are properly classified as separate property. Damages for impairment of earning capacity and consequential damages in the nature of medical, hospital and nursing expenses are properly recoverable for the community.

DE FUNIAK writes in Section 82 of PRINCIPLES OF COMMUNITY PROPERTY, that while recovery for injuries to the spouse should be separate, the rule is different for other elements of recovery:

> But on the other hand, if injury deprives the marital community of the earnings or services of the spouse, that is an injury to the marital community; likewise there is loss to the community where the community funds are expended for hospital and medical expenses. . . .[1] If the wife is contributing earnings to the marital community, any injury interrupting or lowering those earnings is equally, as in the case of the husband, an injury to the community. . . .

[1] We do not have before us, and express no opinion upon a situation which might show that the medical expenses were paid from the separate funds of the injured spouse.

He also states that:

> The earning capacity, as such, would presumably be translated into earnings during the marriage, which would be community property.

To the extent that the marital partnership has incurred medical or other expenses and has lost wages, both spouses have been damaged by the injury to the spouse; and both spouses have a claim against the wrongdoer. The recovery, therefore, is community in character. This Court has held, however, that the wife could bring suit alone for medical services. *Few v. Charter Oak Fire Ins. Co.*, 463 S.W.2d 424 (1971).

Contributory Negligence of Husband

The Texas cases which have denied the wife a recovery for her personal injuries have for their basis the reasoning that, following *Ezell*, the recovery would be community property. Since the husband was negligent, he should not be permitted to recover for his own wrong; and since the husband shares in a recovery for the community property, there should be no recovery. Dean Page Keeton, in analyzing the holdings in the early cases, writes that, "it might be said that contributory negligence is a bar, not because it is unjust to hold the defendant but because it is unjust for the negligent plaintiff [the husband] to benefit from his own wrong." And "it is for this reason that the Texas courts . . . will not allow an injured spouse to recover for personal injuries, where the other spouse contributes to produce the injuries by negligent conduct." Keeton, *Imputed Contributory Negligence*, 13 TEXAS LAW REVIEW 161 at 177 and 179 (1935). This reasoning is spelled out in *Northern Texas Traction Co. v. Hill*, 297 S.W. 778 (Tex. Civ. App. 1927, writ refused) where the court pointed out that the husband had a "half interest" in the cause of action. Hence his contributory negligence would be a defense, "for to hold otherwise would be to allow him to recover regardless of his own negligence." 297 S.W. at 780.

In other situations, our decisions have not denied a wife to recover where the husband has been guilty of wrongdoing. Thus in *Nickerson v. Nickerson*, 65 Tex. 281 (1886), the husband and a third party had the wife wrongfully imprisoned. It was argued that she should not be permitted to recover from the third person because the recovery would be community, and hence the husband would profit from his own wrong. Before the case came to trial, there was a divorce. Contrary to the dictum of *Ezell* and in line with the other authorities cited above, this Court held:

> . . . like other choses in action (for injuries to the person) not reduced to possession during the coverture, the sum recovered would be her separate estate. 65 Tex. at 283.

In any event, the reason for the rule that the negligence of the husband should be imputed to the wife (that he would profit from his own wrong) falls where the recovery for her injuries is her separate property. We have held that such recovery is her separate property, and the recovery will not be to him or the community. Therefore, the contributory negligence of the husband does not bar the recovery by the wife. Cases which have followed the dictum of *Ezell* and have used the community property defense ("imputed negligence") are therefore wrong and should be overruled. Accordingly, the language in *Missouri Pacific Ry. Co. v. White*, 80 Tex. 202, 15 S.W. 808 (an adopted opinion by the Commission of Appeals, 1891), and the holding of *Dallas Railway & Terminal Company v. High*, 129 Tex. 219, 103 S.W.2d 735 (1937), and cases following them such as *Northern Texas Traction Co.* referred to above, are overruled in so far as they conflict with this opinion. In the case at bar, the only acts of contributory negligence pleaded, submitted, and found were those of Mr. Franco. Mrs. Franco is therefore not barred from those items for which she may recover, set out above.

Where, as in the case of medical expenses and lost earnings, the recovery would be community, the contributory negligence of the husband must be attributed to the marital community so far as affects any right of action on behalf of the marital community. DE FUNIAK, PRINCIPLES OF COMMUNITY PROPERTY (1971) § 83.

Other points are brought forward which include questions dealing with the admissibility of evidence dealing with contributory negligence, or not, of the husband in stopping his car upon the highway without proper lights burning. We have examined all the points, and we are in substantial agreement with their handling by the Court of Civil Appeals. They are overruled.

The opinion and judgment of the Court of Civil Appeals was that the part of the judgment of the trial court which denied a recovery to the husband was affirmed; but as to the wife, that court reversed the judgment of the trial court and remanded the cause for a new trial. The effect of the judgment of the Court of Civil Appeals was to sever the cause of action of the wife for such damages as she may be entitled to recover, but its judgment did not so provide. We order such a severance. Accordingly, the judgment of the Court of Civil Appeals is reformed to provide for a severance; and as reformed, it is affirmed.

Notes, Comments & Questions

1. Did *Graham v. Franco* change the law regarding characterization of personal injury damages?

2. Does *Graham v. Franco* skirt implied exclusion?

3. Note the discussion in *Graham v. Franco* of the respective doctrines of implied exclusion and of onerous title. How does the court limit the doctrine of implied exclusion? Consider these doctrines when reading the cases that follow such as *Eggemeyer v. Eggemeyer*, 554 S.W.2d 137 (Tex. 1977) and *Williams v. Williams*, 569 S.W.2d 867 (Tex. 1978), *Vallone v. Vallone*, 644 S.W.2d 455 (Tex. 1982), *infra*, and *Jensen v. Jensen*, 665 S.W.2d 107 (Tex. 1984), *infra;* all appear to be influenced by the doctrine of onerous title.

4. *Graham v. Franco* was followed in *Southwestern Bell Telephone Co. v. Thomas*, 554 S.W.2d 672 (Tex. 1977), where the trial court had rendered judgment for the plaintiffs, Mr. and Mrs. Thomas, for damages sustained when a car driven by Mr. Thomas in which Mrs. Thomas was a passenger had been struck from the rear by a truck owned by Southwestern Bell. The Court of Civil Appeals had affirmed, but the Supreme Court reversed and remanded the case as to personal injuries of Mr. Thomas and as to past and future medical expenses of Mr. and Mrs. Thomas, because of the failure of the trial court to submit the issue of contributory negligence, and said:

> Mrs. Thomas' recovery of damages for personal injuries is not barred by contributory negligence on Mr. Thomas's part. *Graham v. Franco*, 488 S.W.2d 390 (Tex. 1972). Her claim for personal injuries is severed, and the judgments below are in that regard affirmed.

5. In *Schwing v. Bluebonnet Express, Inc.*, 489 S.W.2d 279 (Tex. 1973), the court held that in a wrongful death action for the death of a wife, contributory negligence of the husband would be imputed to bar the husband's cause of action, but that it would not serve as a bar to the cause of action of the children. Although the accident occurred in 1964, prior to enactment of the Matrimonial Property Act of 1967 and prior to the decision in *Graham v. Franco*, the court pointed out that the decision in *Franco* did not turn on provisions of the statute but rested on constitutional grounds.

6. The case of *Graham v. Franco* opened the door for personal injury actions and recoveries to be considered marital property, giving rise to a need to characterize as separate or community property. Other characterization of personal injury cases will be considered within Chapter 2.

7. In *Graham v. Franco*, were medical expenses characterized?

8. Identify other damages which might be recovered in a personal injury case. How might those damages be characterized?

WILLIAMS
v.
WILLIAMS
569 S.W.2d 867
(Tex. 1978)

McGEE, JUSTICE.

The question presented by this cause is whether a premarital agreement to waive the constitutional and statutory rights of a surviving spouse to a homestead and other exempt property is valid. The trial court held such an agreement to be valid. The court of civil appeals reversed the judgment. 548 S.W.2d 492. We reverse the judgment of the court of civil appeals and affirm that of the trial court.

William Wesley Williams, Sr., and Mildred Disch Lawrence were married on September 9, 1973. Both parties had children by previous marriages and both brought substantial property into this marriage. Four days before their marriage, the parties executed a premarital agreement. The basic agreement containing the provisions relative to the waiver of the homestead right and right to have exempt property set aside to the survivor provided:

> "Whereas the parties desire that all property now owned or hereafter acquired by each of them shall, for testamentary disposition, be free from any claim of the other that may arise by reason of their contemplated marriage, "It is therefore agreed:
>
> "1. Property to be separately owned. After the solemnization of the marriage between the parties, each of them shall separately retain all rights in his or her own property, whether now owned or hereafter acquired, and each of them shall have the absolute and unrestricted right to dispose of such separate property, free from any claim that may be made by the other by reason of their marriage, and with the same effect as if no marriage had been consummated between them."

A supplemental agreement was simultaneously executed and incorporated into the basic agreement. It disclosed the properties that each spouse would bring into the marriage, set forth certain guidelines concerning living and other incidental expenses to be incurred during the marriage, and further provided:

> "5. All income from the separate estate of each party, including dividends, interest, rents and salaries, and any increases, sales proceeds, reinvestments or changes in said separate estate, shall remain under control of the party receiving the same and shall be deposited in such party's separate account. It is the intent of the parties that such income, except for the personal living expenses hereinabove set forth, shall remain the separate property of each party."

The marriage lasted but 141 days. Shortly after the parties were married, Mr. Williams became ill and died on January 29, 1974. He died testate and his sole devisees were his children, William Wesley Williams, Jr. and Geneva W. Canion, who are the petitioners in this cause. Approximately one year after the death of their father, and relying on the executed premarital agreement, they requested possession of the residence, the household furnishings therein, and a 1971 Chrysler automobile. It is undisputed that the property sought had been the separate property of the deceased and had been devised to the petitioners. Mildred Williams refused to abide by the premarital agreement, choosing instead to claim her rights as a surviving spouse. TEX. CONST. art. XVI, § 52; TEX. PROB. CODE ANN. §§ 271, 272, 284 (1956).

As a result of Mrs. Williams' refusal to vacate the property, the children filed this suit for declaratory judgment. The case was withdrawn from the jury and the trial court rendered judgment in favor of the children. The trial court held that the portion of the premarital agreement by which Mrs. Williams relinquished her constitutional and statutory rights to the homestead was valid and binding on her. The court then ruled that the agreement was void to the extent that it provided that income or other property acquired during marriage should be the separate property of the party who earned or whose property produced such income or acquisition. But the trial court held that the valid and void provisions of the agreement were severable and ordered that the children recover possession of the residence, all personal property belonging to their father at the time of his death, and the Chrysler automobile.

Article XVI, section 52 of the Texas Constitution provides that the homestead shall not be partitioned among the heirs of the deceased during the lifetime of the surviving husband or wife, or so long as the survivor may elect to use or occupy the same as a homestead.[1] This is sometimes referred to as the probate homestead. O. SPEER, TEXAS FAMILY LAW § 36:62, at 208 (5th ed. 1977). This homestead right of the survivor has been held to be one in the nature of a legal life estate or life estate created by operation of law. *See Sparks v. Robertson*, 203 S.W.2d 622 (Tex. Civ. App.—Austin 1947, writ ref'd); *White v. Blackman*, 168 S.W.2d 531 (Tex. Civ. App.—Texarkana 1942, writ ref'd w.o.m.); *Petrus v. Cage Bros.*, 128 S.W.2d 537 (Tex. Civ. App.—San Antonio 1939, writ ref'd); Comment, *The Widow's Exemption in Texas*, 25 BAYLOR L. REV. 346, 347 (1973). The Probate Code requires that the probate homestead and certain exempt personal property[2] be set aside to the surviving spouse. TEX. PROB. CODE ANN. §§ 271, 272, 283, 284 (1956). These rights are provided by law for the protection of the family and to secure a home for the surviving spouse. Therefore, we must decide whether these rights may be waived by a premarital agreement.

The statutory authorization for premarital agreements in Texas is section 5.41 of the Family Code.[3] This statute should be construed as broadly as possible in order to allow the parties as much flexibility to contract with respect to property or other rights incident to the marriage, provided the constitutional and statutory definitions of separate and community property or the requirements of public policy are not violated. *See generally* O. SPEER, TEXAS FAMILY LAW § 16:5, at 192 (5th ed. 1976); McKnight, *Commentary to the Texas Family Code*, Title 1, 5 TEX. TECH. L. REV. 281, 374-76 (1974).

---

[1] TEX. CONST. art. XVI, § 52 reads as follows:

"On the death of the husband or wife, or both, the homestead shall descend and vest in like manner as other real property of the deceased, and shall be governed by the same laws of descent and distribution, but it shall not be partitioned among the heirs of the deceased during the lifetime of the surviving husband or wife, or so long as the survivor may elect to use or occupy the same as a homestead, or so long as the guardian of the minor children of the deceased may be permitted, under the order of the proper court having the jurisdiction, to use and occupy the same."

[2] TEX. REV. CIV. STAT. ANN. art. 3836 (Supp. 1976-77).

[3] TEX. FAMILY CODE ANN. § 5.41 (1975) provides in pertinent part:

"(a) Before marriage, persons intending to marry may enter into a marital property agreement as they may desire.

"(b) The agreement must be in writing and subscribed by all the parties."

Mrs. Williams argues that the policy of the law favoring the security of the widow by preventing an improvident relinquishment of the homestead, or other similar rights, is paramount to the policy of the law favoring flexibility in premarital agreements. Decisions from Kansas and North Dakota support this view. . . . The weight of authority and the better rule, however, allows the premarital waiver of these rights. . . . (cites omitted)

Furthermore, the premarital agreement in question does not violate the public policy of this state. The parties to the agreement were mature individuals. There was no suggestion of fraud, overreaching, or a lack of understanding. Full disclosure was made of the nature and extent of the property interests involved. Both parties had substantial separate property which they desired to preserve for themselves. There were no interests of any minor children to protect. Viewing this agreement in light of these facts and circumstances, as well as the underlying purpose of the transaction, we are of the opinion that neither party would be adversely affected by the premarital agreement.

Mrs. Williams also contends that article XVI, section 52 of the Texas Constitution, in effect, prohibits the premarital agreement now before us. This contention, however, is based on an incorrect interpretation of section 52. While a "surviving" spouse is granted the right to occupy the homestead by section 52, such language is not to be construed as a constitutional prohibition to a waiver of that right by prospective spouses. Therefore, we hold that Mrs. Williams waived her rights to the probate homestead and exempt property by the premarital agreement in question.

The trial court correctly concluded that the agreement was void to the extent that income or other property acquired during marriage should be the separate property of the party who earned or whose property produced such income or acquisition. Such provisions were no more than a mere agreement between the parties to establish the character of the property prior to its acquisition during marriage in violation of both the Texas Constitution and the Family Code, TEX. CONST. art. XVI, § 15; TEX. FAMILY CODE ANN. § 5.01 (1975); see *Gorman v. Gause*, 56 S.W.2d 855 (Tex. Comm'n App.1933, jdmt. adopted); *Arnold v. Leonard*, 114 Tex. 535, 273 S.W. 799 (1925); *Hilley v. Hilley*, 161 Tex. 569, 342 S.W.2d 565 (1961). Mrs. Williams contends that the entire agreement is vitiated by these void provisions. On the assumption that the provisions in question constituted part of the consideration for the agreement, she asserts that when a contract is based upon several considerations, one or more of which is illegal, then the entire contract is void. *Edwards County v. Jennings*, 89 Tex. 618, 35 S.W. 1053 (1806); *Patrizi v. McAninch*, 153 Tex. 389, 269 S.W.2d 343 (1954). We disagree.

We are of the opinion that the agreement here is controlled instead by the rule that where the consideration for the agreement is valid, an agreement containing more than one promise is not necessarily rendered invalid by the illegality of one of the promises. In such a case, the invalid provisions may be severed and the valid portions of the agreement upheld provided the invalid provision does not constitute the main or essential purpose of the agreement. *See Wicks v. Comves*, 110 Tex. 532, 221 S.W. 938 (1920); *C.C. Slaughter Cattle Co. v. Potter County*, 235 S.W. 295 (Tex. Civ. App.—Amarillo 1921), *aff'd*, 254 S.W. 775 (Tex. Comm'n App.1923, jdmt. adopted); *cf. Smith v. Morton Independent School District*, 85 S.W.2d 853 (Tex. Civ. App.—Amarillo 1935, writ dism'd). *See also* 6A A. CORBIN, CONTRACTS § 1521 (1962); J. CALAMARI & J. PERILLO, CONTRACTS § 22-4 (2d ed. 1977); 17 AM. JUR. 2D, *Contracts* § 230 (1964). Mutual promises to marry, subsequently performed, provide valid consideration for the premarital agreement in question. The invalid provisions of the agreement are only a part of the many reciprocal promises in the agreement concerning the rights of the parties to the marriage. Moreover, they did not constitute the main or essential purpose of the agreement. Therefore, we hold that the trial court was correct in severing the invalid provisions from the premarital agreement and enforcing the valid provisions regarding Mrs. Williams' waiver of her rights as a surviving spouse to the homestead and other exempt property.

Accordingly, we reverse the judgment of the court of civil appeals and affirm that of the trial court.

CHADICK, JUSTICE, dissenting.

I respectfully dissent. I would affirm the judgment of the court of civil appeals.

On September 5, 1973, Mildred Disch Lawrence and William Wesley Williams, Sr. executed an antenuptial agreement. Four days later they were married. The antenuptial agreement was evidenced by two separately executed documents which the trial court correctly treated as a single contract. One agreement contained these provisions:

> Whereas the parties desire that all property now owned or hereafter acquired by each of them shall, for testamentary disposition, be free from any claim of the other that may arise by reason of their contemplated marriage, It is therefore agreed:
>
> 1. Property to be separately owned. After the solemnization of the marriage between the parties, each of them shall separately retain all rights in his or her own property, whether now owned or hereafter acquired, and each of them shall have the absolute and unrestricted right to dispose of such separate property, free from any claim that may be made by the other by reason of their marriage, and with the same effect as if no marriage had been consummated between them.

The supplemental agreement listed the properties that each spouse would bring into the marriage and then provided:

> 5. All income from the separate estate of each party, including dividends, interest, rents and salaries, and any increases, sales proceeds, reinvestments or changes in said separate estate, shall remain under control of the party receiving the same and shall be deposited in such party's separate account. It is the intent of the parties that such income, except for the personal living expenses hereinabove set forth, shall remain the separate property of each party.

The trial court withdrew the case from the jury and rendered judgment. It declared, as recited in the judgment, that the contract was void insofar as it provided "that income or other property acquired during marriage . . . should be the separate property of the party who earned or whose property produced such income or acquisition." That, of course, was a correct decision, since the contractual provision violated section 15 of article XVI[1] of the Texas Constitution, as well as section 5.01 of the Texas Family Code.[2] *Hilley v. Hilley*, 161 Tex. 569, 342 S.W.2d 565 (1961); *Gorman v. Gause*, 56

---

[1] § 15. Separate and Community Property of Husband and Wife

All property, both real and personal, of the wife, owned or claimed by her before marriage, and that acquired afterward by gift, devise or descent, shall be the separate property of the wife; and laws shall be passed more clearly defining the rights of the wife, in relation as well to her separate property as that held in common with her husband. . . .

[2] Section 5.01. Marital Property Characterized

(a) A spouse's separate property consists of:

(1) the property owned or claimed by the spouse before marriage;

(2) the property acquired by the spouse during marriage by gift, devise, or descent; and

(3) the recovery for personal injuries sustained by the spouse during marriage, except any recovery for loss of earning capacity during marriage.

(b) Community property consists of the property, other than separate property, acquired by either spouse during marriage.

S.W.2d 855 (Tex. Comm'n App.1933, jdmt. adopted); *Arnold v. Leonard*, 114 Tex. 535, 273 S.W. 799 (1925).

The trial court ruled, however, that the part of the agreement which relinquished the constitutional and statutory right to the homestead was valid. It then concluded that the void and valid parts of the single contract were severable and that Mrs. Williams had relinquished her rights to the homestead.

I.

* * *

II.

The protection of a widow from creditors following her husband's death finds its origins in the Spanish law. *Green v. Crow*, 17 Tex. 180, 184 (1856). The Third Congress of the Republic enacted the Exemption Act of 1839,[3] 2 H. GAMMEL, LAWS OF TEXAS 125 (1898); HARTLEY'S DIGEST OF THE LAWS OF TEXAS, art. 1270, at 405-06 (1850), and the Seventh Congress in 1843 amended the probate law by requiring the judge of the probate court to set apart the exempt real and personal property in the husband's estate "for the sole use and benefit of the widow and children of the deceased." 2 H. GAMMEL, LAWS OF TEXAS 834 (1898). When the Republic joined the United States, Texas became the first state to incorporate into its fundamental law a provision protecting the homestead rights of the family. W. NUNN, TEXAS HOMESTEAD AND OTHER EXEMPTIONS, § 3 (1931); Cole, *The Homestead Law in Texas*, 3 TEXAS L. REV. 217, 233 n. 74 (1925).

The first constitution of the State of Texas defined the homestead, freed it from forced sale, and then said "nor shall the owner, if a married man, be at liberty to alienate the same, unless by the consent of the wife, in such manner as the legislature may hereafter point out."[4] 2 H. GAMMEL, LAWS OF TEXAS 1294 (1898). The first legislature responded in 1846 by enacting section 26 of the 1846 Probate Act which set apart for the sole use and benefit of the widow and children, if there be either or any, of the deceased, all such property as by the Constitution and law of the State, has been or shall be declared not to be subject to forced sale. . . . 1846 Tex. Gen. Laws, An Act To Organize Probate Courts, § 26, at 317-18; 2 H. GAMMEL, LAWS OF TEXAS 1623-24 (1898).

That section also provided that when the estate contained none of the exempted "specific articles," the probate judge was empowered to conduct a sale of the deceased's property to procure them.

The Constitutions of 1861, 1866, and 1869 contained provisions which protected the homestead. W. NUNN, TEXAS HOMESTEAD AND OTHER EXEMPTIONS, § 4 (1931). Our present Constitution of 1876 enlarged the homestead exemption beyond those of the earlier constitutions and extended its benefits

---

[3] AN ACT Entitled an act to exempt certain property therein named from execution.

Sec. 1. Be it enacted by the Senate and House of Representatives of the Republic of Texas in Congress assembled, That from and after the passage of this act, there shall be reserved to every citizen or head of a family in this Republic, free and independent of the power of a writ of fire facias, or other execution issuing from any court of competent jurisdiction whatever, fifty acres of land or one town lot, including his or her homestead, and improvements not exceeding five hundred dollars in value, all house hold and kitchen furniture, (provided it does not exceed in value two hundred dollars, all implements of husbandry,) (provided they shall not exceed fifty dollars in value,) all tools, apparatus and books belonging to the trade or profession of any citizen, five milk cows, one yoke of work oxen or one horse, twenty hogs, and one year's provisions; and that all laws and parts of laws contravening or opposing the provisions of this act, be and the same are hereby repealed: Provided, The passage of this act shall not interfere with contracts between parties heretofore made. JOHN M. HANSFORD, Speaker of the House of Representatives. DAVID G. BURNET, President of the Senate. Approved, January 26, 1839. MIRABEAU B. LAMAR.

[4] TEX. CONST. art. VII, § 22 (1845).

to "unmarried adults, male and female." The constitutional protection of the right has, since 1876, been embodied in sections 50-52 of article XVI of the Constitution. The homestead right of the surviving spouse and children is found in section 52 in these words:

> On the death of the husband or wife, or both, the homestead shall descend and vest in like manner as other real property of the deceased, and shall be governed by the same laws of descent and distribution, but it shall not be partitioned among the heirs of the deceased during the lifetime of the surviving husband or wife, or so long as the survivor may elect to use or occupy the same as a homestead, or so long as the guardian of the minor children of the deceased may be permitted, under the order of the proper court having the jurisdiction, to use and occupy the same.

Strong and sound policies have supported and enforced the homestead right from the earliest times in Texas. As stated by CHIEF JUSTICE HEMPHILL, the object of the homestead law was

> to confer on the beneficiary a home as an asylum, a refuge which cannot be invaded nor its tranquility or serenity disturbed, and in which may be nurtured and cherished those feelings of individual independence which lie at the foundation and are essential to the permanency of our institutions. As a measure of sound policy, it cannot be too highly commended. . . . *Wood v. Wheeler*, 7 Tex. 13, 22 (1851).

JUSTICE LIPSCOMB in *Trawick v. Harris*, 8 Tex. 312, 314-15 (1852), stressed the soundness of the policy for the homestead protection.

> That the interest and protection of the wife entered largely into the consideration that induced the provision in our Constitution protecting the homestead there cannot be the smallest doubt; that she should have an asylum from which the creditor by the process of the law could not force her and her children, and rudely drive them from a home sanctified by so many sweet and endearing recollections, to become homeless and houseless wanderers, to be exposed not only to physical suffering but also to the more baneful and blighting influences so often and so successfully brought to bear on the unfortunate, when necessity and not the will consents to infamy. Protect the home of the wife, and the opportunity is in some measure afforded her by frugality and honest industry to support herself and children, and to prevent some of the worst calamities that the profligacy of the husband would bring on them. These were doubtless some of the considerations that influenced the framers of our Constitution in ingrafting the homestead protection as a cardinal law of the land.

The homestead laws are designed to protect the stability and welfare of the state. *Andrews v. Security Nat'l Bank*, 121 Tex. 409, 50 S.W.2d 253, 256 (1932); *Black v. Rockmore*, 50 Tex. 88, 96 (1878); 2 G. THOMPSON, REAL PROPERTY, § 970 (2d ed. 1939). By protecting citizens against being driven from their homes, there is some measure of protection against their becoming dependent on the state for housing. Moreover, the protection of the home is intended to encourage citizens to contribute as productive members of society. TEX. CONST. ANN. art. XVI, § 50, comment (Vernon 1955); W. NUNN, TEXAS HOMESTEAD AND OTHER EXEMPTIONS, § 2 (1931); 2 G. THOMPSON, REAL PROPERTY, § 1970 (2d ed. 1939). The Constitution's protection of the family has been expanded by a judicial history of liberal construction which effectuates the homestead law's beneficial purpose, "in accord with the humane principles and wise governmental policy upon which all homestead laws rest." *Woods v. Alvarado State Bank*, 118 Tex. 586, 19 S.W.2d 35, 38 (1929). The homestead law "is entitled to the most liberal construction for the accomplishment of its objects." *Trawick v. Harris*, 8 Tex. 312, 316 (1852). *See also Andrews v. Security Nat'l Bank*, 121 Tex. 409, 50 S.W.2d 253, 256 (1932); *Hall v. Fields*, 81 Tex. 553, 17 S.W. 82 (1891); *Blum v. Gaines*, 57 Tex. 119, 121 (1882); *Black v. Rockmore*, 50 Tex. 88, 96 (1878); *Allison v. Brookshire*, 38 Tex. 199, 201 (1873); *Reconstruction Finance Corp.*

v. Burgess, 155 S.W.2d 977, 980 (Tex. Civ. App.—Waco 1941, writ ref'd); *Panhandle Constr. Co. v. Head*, 134 S.W.2d 779, 781 (Tex. Civ. App.—Amarillo 1939, writ ref'd).

The answer to our problem, while found in the history and the purposes of the homestead, is apparent in the Constitution itself. Article XVI, section 52, of the Texas Constitution states that upon the death of the husband or wife, or both, the homestead descends and vests as other real property, but then adds a positive prohibition about partitioning under the circumstances of this case. These are the words of the Constitution, which control our decision:

> but it (the homestead) shall not be partitioned among the heirs of the deceased during the lifetime of the surviving husband or wife, or so long as the survivor may elect to use or occupy the same as a homestead, or so long as the guardian of the minor children of the deceased may be permitted, under the order of the proper court having the jurisdiction, to use and occupy the same.

It may be argued that, there being no children born of this marriage, effect should be given the antenuptial agreement. In fact, some jurisdictions make the distinction and permit an antenuptial agreement to forego homestead if there are no children. *See, e.g., Zachman v. Zachman*, 201 Ill. 380, 66 N.E. 256 (1903). Those cases do not arise under a direct constitutional prohibition as we have in Texas. The Texas Constitution directly addresses both the situation in which there are children and the situation in which there are none. It treats the two identically, and specifically prohibits a partition in each instance. To permit the relinquishment in this instance should logically compel the same result when the survivor has children at home. It is the clarity of the constitutional provision, no doubt, which explains why this problem has not previously been presented to a Texas court.

Some states have considered whether a premarital agreement may operate to defeat a homestead, and there is a conflict between their decisions. The agreements have been held void in Arkansas, Kansas, North Dakota and Vermont. . . .

Other jurisdictions, including Arizona, Illinois, Iowa, Minnesota, and Oregon, have given effect to the antenuptial agreements.

When the Texas Constitution addresses a problem, as it has in the case of survivor's right to a homestead, precedents from other jurisdictions become immaterial and unpersuasive. But of the jurisdictions considering the question of validity, apparently only the Kansas courts contended with a similar constitutional homestead provision. KAN. CONST. art. XV, § 9. It has been held in Kansas that the probate homestead rights provided by the Kansas Constitution, KAN. CONST. art. XV, § 9, and statute, KAN. PROB. CODE ANN. § 59-401, are for the protection of the family. Those rights cannot be varied or avoided by an antenuptial contract which provides that, should the wife survive the husband, she is to have no part in his estate. *In re Neis' Estate*, 170 Kan. 254, 225 P.2d 110, 117-18 (1950); *In re Garden's Estate*, 158 Kan. 554, 148 P.2d 745, 753-54 (1944); *Boulls v. Boulls*, 137 Kan. 880, 22 P.2d 465, 467 (1933). The policy considered by the Kansas courts in holding void any antenuptial agreements to waive the probate homestead is consistent with the approach that Texas has taken on the protection of homestead rights. The constitutional basis for voiding such agreements is stronger in Texas because the probate homestead provision, TEX. CONST. art. XVI, § 52, specifically defines the right.

III.

Despite the constitutional protection that Texas has historically given the probate homestead, the majority holds that the right may be waived by antenuptial agreement. Even if that is true, nowhere in the present antenuptial agreement is the homestead right expressly mentioned or specifically waived. The agreement contains only the general language that each spouse's separate property shall be "free from any claim" by the other spouse that may arise as a result of the marriage. It must be in this general language, if at all, that the majority finds waiver of the homestead right.

It has been held that "contracts of the wife in restraint of her right to the homestead, made either in contemplation of marriage or after marriage, should be closely scrutinized." *McCormick v. McNeel*, 53 Tex. 15, 20 (1880).[5] Because of the importance of the homestead right and the public policy that creates its agreements to abridge the right, if upheld, should be done so only if, after close examination, it is determined that the waiver is clear and explicit. "The right to a widow's . . . probate homestead cannot be waived by an ante-nuptial agreement not clear and explicit as to what rights were being waived." *Smith v. Tang*, 100 Ariz. 196, 412 P.2d 697, 704 (1966). The constitutionally protected home of a widow should not be taken away because of a generally worded antenuptial waiver. Moreover, contrary to the recitation in the majority opinion, there is nothing in this summary judgment record which shows that Mrs. Williams had full knowledge of the homestead right alleged to have been waived.

The antenuptial agreement in the present case fails to adequately identify the probate homestead or to clearly show that Mrs. Williams was waiving her right to it. Waiver should not be enforced against her.

I would affirm the judgment of the court of civil appeals.

STEAKLEY and POPE, JJ., join in this dissent.

Notes, Comments & Questions

1. After *Williams*, what appears to be the only provision which might be included in a premarital agreement?

2. What are the means by which spouses might change the character of property?

3. How about future spouses?

4. *Williams*, coupled with the desire of the general public, yielded an amendment to the Texas Constitution in 1980. Can you surmise what that amendment might be?

5. At the same time that the courts and the legislature were dealing with matters of marital property, the very atmosphere was changing with regard to the rights of women. The stage was set for some big changes, as evidenced by the passage of the Equal Rights Amendment.

The TEX. CONST. art. I, § 3a passed in 1972 provides as follows:

> Equality under the law shall not be denied or abridged because of sex, race, color, creed, or national origin. This amendment is self-operative.

Although the Equal Rights Amendment does not deal specifically with the definition of separate property, its influence can be observed in the 1980 amendment to the Constitution in which separate property is no longer defined solely in terms of the wife; rather, it is defined in relation to both spouses.

---

[5] In *McCormick* the widow elected to recover on a promissory note executed in consideration for an antenuptial deed relinquishing her homestead right and not to recover the homestead itself. The Court concluded that since the widow voluntarily elected to recover on the note at the trial, it would not interfere on her behalf to protect her homestead right.

The Equal Rights Amendment also influenced statutes. For example, TEX. FAM. CODE § 2.501 extended the duty to support to both spouses. *See also* TEX. FAM. CODE §§ 6.501, 6.502.

Case law has also embraced the Equal Rights Amendment beginning with dictum in *Felsenthal v. McMillan*, 493 S.W.2d 729 (Tex. 1973), indicates that if the question had been before the court in that case, the court would have recognized the existence of a cause of action by the wife for the tort of criminal conversation, corresponding to the husband's cause of action existing at common law. The tort of criminal conversation was abolished in Texas by legislation in 1975, when § 1.106 was added to the Family Code.

In *Vick v. Pioneer Oil Co.*, 569 S.W.2d 631 (Tex. Civ. App.—Amarillo 1978, no writ), the court held TEX. REV. CIV. STAT. ANN. art. 5172a § 4, providing overtime pay to women, to be unconstitutional under the Equal Rights Amendment. The court also found that the statute violated the Equal Employment Act, 42 U.S.C. § 2000e-2(a) because it favored one sex in employment practices.

Likewise, the Texas Equal Rights Amendment affected long held preferences that were based on gender in paternity and custody litigation. For example, In re *J.W.T.*, 872 S.W.2d 189 (Tex. 1994) established that a biological father has a constitutional right to establish paternity even though the mother and the presumed father—the husband—object. Also, the "tender years doctrine" which historically gave preference to a mother in custody litigation would be violative of the Equal Rights Amendment to the Texas Constitution. *See Dennis v. Smith*, 962 S.W.2d 67 (Tex. App.—Houston [1st Dist.] 1997, writ denied). *See also* the decisions recognizing the wife's derivative cause of action for loss of consortium, *Whittlesey v. Miller*, 572 S.W.2d 665 (Tex. 1978); *Reed Tool Co. v. Copelin*, 610 S.W.2d 736 (Tex. 1980); *Minyard Food Stores v. Newman*, 612 S.W.2d 198 (Tex. 1980).

In a related area of the law, the United States Supreme Court held in *Orr v. Orr*, 440 U.S. 268 (1979), that an Alabama statute which provided for the award of alimony to wives, but not to husbands, was unconstitutional. During that same year, the Texas Family Code was amended to authorize the award of temporary support during the pendency of divorce proceedings to husbands as well as wives.

It is clear that today's Supreme Court would hold unconstitutional, as a denial of equal protection, the Texas statutes as they existed prior to 1968, giving the husband sole management powers over the community property. *See Kirchberg v. Feenstra*, 450 U.S. 455 (1981). Presumably, the provisions of the present Family Code relating to management of community property would be held valid under the criteria applied in *Kirchberg*.

6. A review of the principles surrounding interspousal transfers is probably prudent at this point.

Either spouse may make a gift to the other spouse of his separate property or of his interest in community property. The property gifted becomes the separate property of the donee spouse. As to gifts of separate property, *see Bishop v. Bishop*, 359 S.W.2d 869 (Tex. 1962); *Dyer v. Dyer*, 616 S.W.2d 663 (Tex. Civ. App.—Corpus Christi 1981, writ dism'd). As to gifts of community property, *see Story v. Marshall*, 24 Tex. 306 (1859); *Parson v. United States*, 460 F.2d 228 (5th Cir. 1972); *Wyly v. Commissioner*, 610 F.2d 1282 (5th Cir.1980). *See also* TEX. CONST. art. XVI § 15 as it exists today.

Whether a gift has been made is a question of fact to be answered by the fact finder, be it judge or jury. The facts must support that a gift has been made. *See Bishop v. Bishop*, 359 S.W.2d 869 (Tex. 1963); *Daubert v. United States*, 533 F. Supp. 66 (U.S.D.C., W.D. Tex. 1981); *Akin v. Akin*, 649 S.W.2d 700 (Tex. App.—Fort Worth 1983, writ ref'd n.r.e.).

Moreover, while property purchased by the community estate from the separate estate of a spouse for a valuable consideration is community property, it is not possible for a gift to be made to the community estate, because of the constitutional definition. *Kellet v. Trice*, 66 S.W. 51 (Tex. 1902); *Tittle v. Tittle*, 220 S.W.2d 637 (Tex. 1949); *McLemore v. McLemore*, 641 S.W.2d 395 (Tex. App.—Tyler 1982, no writ).

7. The issue of gifts led probate attorneys to be concerned about the 1948 version of TEX. CONST. art. XVI, § 15. Under the 1948 amendment, if a spouse gifted to the other spouse an income producing asset, the income produced was characterized as community property by operation of Texas law. Accordingly, the gifting spouse retained an interest in that community income, even though the underlying asset was now the other spouse's separate property.

The Commissioner of Internal Revenue, citing 26 U.S.C. § 2036 (a)(1) and abandoning 30 years of practice based on the dicta found in *Commissioner v. Estate of Hinds*, 180 F.2d 930 (5th Cir. 1950), took the position that the donor spouse had retained an interest in the gifted property and that half of the gifted asset and half of the income should be reported in the donor spouse's estate tax return. The Commissioner's position was tested in *Estate of Wyly v. Commissioner*, 610 F.2d 1282 (5th Cir 1980). The Commissioner failed. The Fifth Circuit, Justice Garza writing for the majority, explained:

> . . . it is our conclusion that § 2036(a)(1) does not sweep the value of these transfers into the donor's gross estate. To summarize our review of federal and state law, we have held that the donor's community property interest in the income produced by these transferred properties is so limited, contingent, and expectant that it does not amount to a "right to the income," within the Act as defined by *United States v. Byrum, supra.* The interest is neither "significant," or "substantial" as the Supreme Court and this Court have called for in *United States v. Estate of Grace* and *In Re Estate of Lumpkin, supra*, and is therefore not subject to estate tax under this section. We have further held that the interest arises Only by operation of a mandatory definition contained in the Texas constitution which spouses may not circumvent, and that thus it is neither "retained" within the meaning of the Act, nor arisen "under" the transfers concerned.

8. The position that the Commissioner was taking in *Wyly* concerned probate attorneys who had planned numerous estates with the idea of eliminating assets from one spouse's estate by gifting them to the other. The probate bar did not wait for *Wyly* to be decided. Rather, they supported a constitutional amendment, approved by the voters, and which is now found in the 1980 amendment. Can you identify that portion of the amendment in the current TEX. CONST. art. XVI, §15?

D. The Constitution as Amended in 1980, 1987 and 1999

1. The Current Constitutional Provision

The current version of TEX. CONST. art. XVI, § 15 is set forth below. The numbers within brackets are not found in the official version and have been added so each of the clauses may be easily referenced.

> TEX. CONST. art. XVI, § 15. Separate and Community Property of Husband and Wife.
>
> [1] All property, both real and personal, of a spouse owned or claimed before marriage, and that acquired afterward by gift, devise or descent, shall be the separate property of that spouse; [2] and laws shall be passed more clearly defining the rights of the spouses, in relation to separate and community property, provided that persons about to marry and spouses, without the intention to defraud pre-existing creditors, may by written instrument from time to time partition between themselves all or part of their property, then existing or to be acquired, or exchange between themselves the community interest of one spouse or future spouse in any other community property then existing or to be acquired, whereupon the portion or interest set aside to each spouse shall be and constitute a part of the separate property and estate of such spouse or future spouse; [3] and the spouses may from time to time, by written instrument, agree between themselves that the income or property from all or part of the separate property then owned by one of them, or which thereafter might be acquired, shall be the separate property of that spouse; [4] and if one spouse makes a gift of property to the other that gift is presumed to include all the income or property which might arise from that gift of property; [5] and spouses may agree in writing that all or part of their community property becomes the property of the surviving spouse on the death of a spouse; [6] and spouses may agree in writing that all or part of the separate property owned by either or both of them shall be the spouses' community property.

Clauses 1-4, as amended Nov. 4, 1980, effective November 25, 1980. Clause 5 passed by voters on November 3, 1987, effective January 1, 1988. Clause 6 passed by voters of November 2, 1999, effective January 1, 2000.

Mastery of this constitutional provision, knowing how and when it is applied, is basic to understanding and successfully completing the study of Texas marital property law. For a deeper understanding of Texas Marital property law, this version of TEX. CONST. art. XVI, § 15 should be compared and contrasted to previous versions. The clauses are analyzed below.

Clause 1 - Separate Property Defined.

The first clause does nothing more than reiterate the definition of separate property that has been Texas law since before the Civil War. Today, however, the gender neutral term spouse, rather than wife, is used. As before, it is provided that all property owned or claimed before marriage or that acquired afterward by gift, devise or descent is the separate property of the owning or claiming spouse. Since 1866 the legislature has had the power to pass laws more clearly defining those rights - this would include rights of management and liability. *See Arnold v. Leonard*, 114 Tex. 535, 273 S.W. 799 (1925). The remaining clauses give to the spouses, and in some instances future spouses, the expanded power to change the character of property.

Clause 2 - Partition and Exchange Extended to Spouses & Future Spouses.

The second clause provides that spouses and future spouses may partition *or* exchange their property that is existing or that will be acquired in the future; the property partitioned or exchanged will become the separate property of the spouses. This second clause extends to future spouses and to property to be acquired in the future. Is this a change from the 1948 version that allowed partition or exchange of property? How so?

This clause allows for a partition and exchange to take place prior to the marriage. It is not enough that those about to marry, future spouses, merely agree that their property will be separate property, there must be an actual partition or exchange.

For example, if one spouse or future spouse has a separate property bank account that earns interest (community property) and the other has a separate property stock account that throws off dividends (community property), they may keep the rights in and to those accounts plus all interest or dividends separate *if* there is an exchange of such rights with the other spouse or future spouse. There is no requirement that the exchange be equal. However, if the future spouses had merely agreed (not exchanged) that all increases would be and remain the owning spouse's separate property, it is unlikely that such would withstand a constitutional challenge.

Spouses and future spouses may even exchange rights in and to their salaries so that their respective salaries become their separate property.

A partition is generally used when there is existing property or an identifiable account and the parties partition it into equal undivided interests or into specifically described portions.

This second clause of the constitution can only be utilized if there is no intent to defraud pre-existing creditors. If future spouses or spouses have pre-existing creditors and make an exchange or partition with the intent to defraud such creditors, the agreement will come into question and may be held ineffective. Is this a change from the 1948 version?

Clause 3 - Agreements are Limited to Spouses and Income Producing Property.

The third clause provides that *spouses* may from time to time, by written instrument, agree between themselves that the income from property from all or part of the separate property then owned or which thereafter might be acquired by one of them, shall be the separate property of the owning, spouse.

This clause allows the spouses to merely agree; this clause does not allow future spouses to simply agree. Only spouses can agree and they can only agree that *property or income arising from their separate property* might be and remain their separate property. For example, under this clause spouses can agree that rental income from a separate property rent house be and remain the owning spouse's separate property. Likewise, spouses can agree that dividends paid on separately owned stock will be and remain the owning spouse's separate property. Spouses cannot merely agree that their salary will be separate property, because such would not arise from separately owned property. Thus, if a spouse happens to be an attorney at a mega law firm, or a doctor employed by their own closely held corporation, the spouses cannot simply agree that their salary will be separate property. Why? Because salary is not income that arises from separate property.

In order to make separate property earned income separate, one must go back to the preceding clause 2 which requires a partition or an exchange. This is a very tricky and often overlooked limitation. Knowing what you know about the strict interpretation of the constitution, what would be the effect of a mere agreement that salary would be and remain a spouse's separate property?

To reiterate, future spouse's can only partition or exchange. This interpretation was accepted in *Fanning v. Fanning*, 828 S.W. 2d 135 (Tex. App.—Waco 1992), *aff'd. in part, rev'd. in part*, 846 S.W. 2d 225 (Tex. 1993). In *Fanning* the Waco court recognized that "the 1980 amendment did not authorize persons intending to marry to enter into agreements that the income from one spouse's separate property would thereafter be the owner's separate property. Therefore, we hold the trial court correctly concluded that paragraph 6.01 of the premarital agreement was unenforceable to the extent that the parties merely agreed that 'as soon as legally possible all income from their respective separate estates shall be the separate property of the spouse from whose estate such income is derived.' " *Id.* at 141.

Because the Texas Constitution remains the ultimate authority on the character of marital property a premarital agreement entered into cannot violate the constitutional definition of separate and community property and any attempt to change the character of property must be done in accordance with the Texas Constitution. That is, partitions or exchanges must be used by future spouses to change the character of any property (i.e., income from separate property, salary) from community to separate. Spouses must also use partition or exchange to change the community character of property, other than that community income that arises from a spouse's separate property which can be converted from community to separate by mere agreement. Some courts have been quite liberal in their interpretations of agreements, concluding that parties about to be married may agree to exchange their community property interests and thereby maintain as separate property future income from separate property and earnings acquired during the marriage. *See, e.g., Dokmanovic v. Schwarz*, 880 S.W.2d 272, 273-76 (Tex. App.—Houston [14th Dist.] 1994, no writ); *Winger v. Pianka*, 831 S.W.2d 853, 858 (Tex. App.—Austin 1992, writ denied); *see also Calmes v. United States*, 926 F.Supp 582, 586-88 (N.D. Tex.)(applying Texas law). Accordingly, it appears that exchanges have, to some extent, been inferred.

Clause 4 - Income Follows a Gift Between Spouses.

Clause 4 provides that if one spouse makes a gift of property to the other, that gift is presumed to include all the income or property which might arise from that gifted property. This clause is often referred to as the *Wyly* Amendment. *See* discussion *supra* at page 52, note 7.

This reference arises from *Estate of Wyly v. Commissioner*, 610 F.2d 1282 (5th Cir. 1980). *Wyly* arose when the Commissioner of Internal Revenue reversed a position held for more than twenty-five years and attempted to levy taxes on income-producing property conveyed from one spouse to the other. Although such conveyance was a gift, by operation of Texas law the gifting spouse retained an interest in the income arising from that property; accordingly, the Commissioner wanted to tax the gifting spouse.

In order to avoid this result, the Texas Constitution was amended and Clause 4 was enacted. However, it should be noted, that the Fifth Circuit ultimately held that the act does not automatically render some portion of value of property gifted by a Texas spouse to the other included in the giving spouse's gross estate. The problem was solved by clause 4 and by the Fifth Circuit; today, income from a gift between spouses follows the gift. This applies only to gifts between spouses, not gifts from third parties.

Clause 5 - Spouses Can Establish Rights of Survivorship in Community Property.

Clause 5 provides that spouses may agree in writing that all or part of their community property becomes the property of the surviving spouse on the death of a spouse. This clause was not effective until 1988, hopefully it did away with the many problems that arose when spouses attempted to establish a joint tenancy with a right of survivorship in property such as community bank accounts. It is assumed that this clause will eliminate the results of *Hilley v. Hilley*, 342 S.W.2d 565 (Tex. *Williams v. McKnight*, 402 S.W.2d 505 (Tex. 1966); *Jameson v. Bain*, 693 S.W.2d 676 (Tex. App. San Antonio 1985, no writ). Joint tenancies with rights of survivorship had been regularly "shot down" because the parties failed to first partition the property into separate property. Now spouses can agree that the community property will be the separate property of the surviving spouse.

Clause 6 - Only Spouses Can Convert Separate Property to Community.

Clause 6, effective January 1, 2000, provides that spouses may agree in writing that all or part of the separate property owned by either or both of them shall be the spouses' community property.

This clause, a long time in coming, was pushed more by the probate bar than the family law bar; it is recognized as an excellent estate planning tool. For example, a monied spouse by very specific agreement, could transform their separate property into the couple's community property. Upon doing so, half of the monied spouse's estate would be removed from the estate's value upon the death of the monied spouse.

Although this clause aids in estate planning, it can yield big problems for the family law attorney. Once separate property is transformed into community property, a divorce court has the absolute right to make a just and right division. The spouse that had previously owned the separate property could, theoretically, be divested of the entirety of what had at one time been separate property. If the property had remained separate, a trial court would not be able to divest the owning spouse of their separate property. *Eggemeyer v. Eggemeyer*, 554 S.W. 2d 137 (Tex. 1997). While this is an incredible estate planning tool, divorce lawyers should be concerned that a meek property-owning spouse could be left to the mercy of a manipulative and stronger spouse, thereby giving the more powerful spouse the right to acquire the less powerful spouse's separate estate.

---

2. Statutes Control Enforcement of Pre- and Post-Marital Agreements

The Uniform Premarital Agreement Act which governs premarital agreements is found at TEX. FAM. CODE §§ 4.001-.010. The most important thing to remember is that the Texas Constitution, though not referenced in the statute, does reign supreme when it comes to the enforcement of premarital agreements. Marital property agreements, also called post-marital agreements, are governed by TEX. FAM. CODE §§ 4.101-.106. The enforcement provisions governing of pre and post-marital agreements are identical.

A premarital and post marital property agreement is not enforceable if the party against whom enforcement is sought proves that:

* * *

(1) the party did not sign the agreement voluntarily; or
(2) the agreement was unconscionable when it was signed and, before signing the agreement, that party:

(A) was not provided a fair and reasonable disclosure of the property or financial obligations of the other party;

(B) did not voluntarily and expressly waive, in writing, any right to disclosure of the property or financial obligations of the other property beyond the disclosure provided; and

(C) did not have or reasonably could not have had adequate knowledge of the property or financial obligations of the other party.

* * *

These enforcement provisions found at TEX. FAM. CODE 4.006 and 4.105 do not encompass agreements which have as their purpose changing separate property into community property. However, all other marital property agreements are held to this standard.

One of the most important things to note is that the fair and reasonable disclosure regarding the property and liabilities of the parties must be given *before* the signing of the agreement. Accordingly, when any pre or post-marital agreement is drafted, a separate disclosure document should be drafted and a time of signing, which precedes the signing of the pre- or post-marital agreement, should be established. In addition, the statute specifies that unconscionability is to be decided by the court and the remedies and defenses provided in the statutes are exclusive. This exclusivity prohibits the use of common law defenses as was recognized, albeit prematurely, in *Daniel v. Daniel*, 779 S.W.2d 110 (Tex. App.—Houston [1st Dist.] 1989, no writ). Nonetheless, as we will see in *Sheshunoff v. Sheshunoff*, 172 S.W.3d 686, (Tex. App.—Austin 2005, pet. denied), common law defenses are probably subsumed in the determination of whether a party signed an agreement voluntarily.

---

3. Enforcement of Agreements to Convert Separate Property to Community Property.

As with pre and post-marital agreements, the agreements to convert separate property into community property must be in writing and signed by the spouses. The property to be converted must be specifically identified and it must specify that the properties are being converted to the spouses' community property. The mere transfer of the spouse's separate property to the name of the other spouse or to the name of both spouses is not sufficient to convert the property to community property. TEX. FAM. CODE § 4.203.

The enforcement provisions for the agreements to convert are set forth in TEX. FAM. CODE § 4.205. As with pre and post-marital agreements, an agreement is not enforceable if the spouse against whom enforcement is sought proves that the spouse did not execute the agreement voluntarily. It is also unenforceable if proven that they did not receive a fair and reasonable disclosure of the legal effect of converting the property to community property.

The code does provide that an agreement which contains a statutorily provided statement or substantially similar words prominently displayed in bold face type, capital letters, or underlined, is rebuttably presumed to provide a fair and reasonable disclosure of the legal effect of converting property to community. The statute provides the language which will yield the rebuttable presumption, as follows:

> "THIS INSTRUMENT CHANGES SEPARATE PROPERTY TO COMMUNITY PROPERTY. THIS MAY HAVE ADVERSE CONSEQUENCES DURING MARRIAGE AND ON TERMINATION OF THE MARRIAGE BY DEATH OR DIVORCE. FOR EXAMPLE:
>
> "EXPOSURE TO CREDITORS. IF YOU SIGN THIS AGREEMENT, ALL OR PART OF THE SEPARATE PROPERTY BEING CONVERTED TO COMMUNITY PROPERTY MAY BECOME SUBJECT TO THE LIABILITIES OF YOUR SPOUSE. IF YOU DO NOT SIGN THIS AGREEMENT, YOUR SEPARATE PROPERTY IS GENERALLY NOT SUBJECT TO THE LIABILITIES OF YOUR SPOUSE UNLESS YOU ARE PERSONALLY LIABLE UNDER ANOTHER RULE OF LAW.
>
> "LOSS OF MANAGEMENT RIGHTS. IF YOU SIGN THIS AGREEMENT, ALL OR PART OF THE SEPARATE PROPERTY BEING CONVERTED TO COMMUNITY

PROPERTY MAY BECOME SUBJECT TO EITHER THE JOINT MANAGEMENT, CONTROL, AND DISPOSITION OF YOU AND YOUR SPOUSE OR THE SOLE MANAGEMENT, CONTROL, AND DISPOSITION OF YOUR SPOUSE ALONE. IN THAT EVENT, YOU WILL LOSE YOUR MANAGEMENT RIGHTS OVER THE PROPERTY. IF YOU DO NOT SIGN THIS AGREEMENT, YOU WILL GENERALLY RETAIN THOSE RIGHTS.

"LOSS OF PROPERTY OWNERSHIP. IF YOU SIGN THIS AGREEMENT AND YOUR MARRIAGE IS SUBSEQUENTLY TERMINATED BY DEATH OF EITHER SPOUSE OR BY A DIVORCE, ALL OR PART OF THE SEPARATE PROPERTY BEING CONVERTED TO COMMUNITY MAY BECOME THE SOLE PROPERTY OF YOUR SPOUSE OR YOUR SPOUSE'S HEIRS. IF YOU DO NOT SIGN THIS AGREEMENT, YOU GENERALLY CANNOT BE DEPRIVED OF OWNERSHIP OF YOUR SEPARATE PROPERTY ON TERMINATION OF YOUR MARRIAGE, WHETHER BY DEATH OR DIVORCE."

TEX. FAM. CODE § 4.204(b).

This section of the Family Code also provides that if a proceeding regarding enforcement of an agreement which converts separate property to community property occurs after the death of the spouse against whom enforcement is sought, the proof required by subsection A, that being the rebuttable presumption to provide and fair and reasonable disclosure, may be established by an heir of the spouse or personal representative of the estate of that spouse.

---

4. Will Contracts

Since *Weidner v. Crowther*, 301 S.W.2d 621 (Tex. 1957), it has been generally accepted that interspousal will contracts do not constitute a change in the constitutional definition of separate property. In this regard, Section 59A of the Probate Code, titled Contracts Concerning Succession, must be considered.

§ 59A. Contracts Concerning Succession

(a) A contract to make a will or devise, or not to revoke a will or devise, if executed or entered into on or after September 1, 1979, can be established only by provisions of a will stating that a contract does exist and stating the material provisions of the contract.

(b) The execution of a joint will or reciprocal wills does not by itself suffice as evidence of the existence of a contract.

Likewise, the following probate code sections cannot be ignored.

§ 37. Passage of Title Upon Intestacy and Under a Will

When a person dies, leaving a lawful will, all of his estate devised or bequeathed by such will, and all powers of appointment granted in such will, shall vest immediately in the devisees or legatees of such estate and the donees of such powers; and all the estate of such person, not devised or bequeathed, shall vest immediately in his heirs at law; subject, however, to the payment of the debts of the testator or intestate, except such as is exempted by law, and subject to the payment of court-ordered child support payments that are delinquent on the date of the person's death; and whenever a person dies intestate, all of his estate shall vest immediately in his heirs at law, but with the exception aforesaid shall still be liable and subject in their hands to the payment of the debts of the intestate and the delinquent child support payments; but upon the issuance of letters testamentary or of administration upon any such estate, the executor or administrator shall have the right to possession of the estate as it existed at the death of the testator or intestate, with the exception aforesaid; and he shall recover possession of and hold such estate in trust to be disposed of in accordance with the law.

§ 38. Persons Who Take Upon Intestacy

(a) Intestate Leaving No Husband or Wife. Where any person, having title to any estate, real, personal or mixed, shall die intestate, leaving no husband or wife, it shall descend and pass in parcenary to his kindred, male and female, in the following course:

1. To his children and their descendants.

2. If there be no children nor their descendants, then to his father and mother, in equal portions. But if only the father or mother survive the intestate, then his estate shall be divided into two equal portions, one of which shall pass to such survivor, and the other half shall pass to the brothers and sisters of the deceased, and to their descendants; but if there be none such, then the whole estate shall be inherited by the surviving father or mother.

3. If there be neither father nor mother, then the whole of such estate shall pass to the brothers and sisters of the intestate, and to their descendants.

4. If there be none of the kindred aforesaid, then the inheritance shall be divided into two moieties, one of which shall go to the paternal and the other to the maternal kindred, in the following course: To the grandfather and grandmother in equal portions, but if only one of these be living, then the estate shall be divided into two equal parts, one of which shall go to such survivor, and the other shall go to the descendant or descendants of such deceased grandfather or grandmother. If there be no such descendants, then the whole estate shall be inherited by the surviving grandfather or grandmother. If there be no surviving grandfather or grandmother, then the whole of such estate shall go to their descendants, and so on without end, passing in like manner to the nearest lineal ancestors and their descendants.

(b) Intestate Leaving Husband or Wife. Where any person having title to any estate, real, personal or mixed, other than a community estate, shall die intestate as to such estate, and shall leave a surviving husband or wife, such estate of such intestate shall descend and pass as follows:

1. If the deceased have a child or children, or their descendants, the surviving husband or wife shall take one-third of the personal estate, and the balance of such personal estate shall go to the child or children of the deceased and their descendants. The surviving husband or wife shall also be entitled to an estate for life, in one-third of the land of the intestate, with remainder to the child or children of the intestate and their descendants.

2. If the deceased have no child or children, or their descendants, then the surviving husband or wife shall be entitled to all the personal estate, and to one-half of the lands of the intestate, without remainder to any person, and the other half shall pass and be inherited according to the rules of descent and distribution; provided, however, that if the deceased has neither surviving father nor mother nor surviving brothers or sisters, or their descendants, then the surviving husband or wife shall be entitled to the whole of the estate of such intestate.

§ 45. Community Estate

(a) On the intestate death of one of the spouses to a marriage, the community property estate of the deceased spouse passes to the surviving spouse if:

1. no child or other descendant of the deceased spouse survives the deceased spouse; or

2. all surviving children and descendants of the deceased spouse are also children or descendants of the surviving spouse.

(b) On the intestate death of one of the spouses to a marriage, if a child or other descendant of the deceased spouse survives the deceased spouse and the child or descendant is not a child or descendant of the surviving souse, one-half of the community estate is retained by the surviving spouse and the other one-half passes to the children or descendants of the deceased spouse. The descendants shall inherit only such portion of said property to which they would be entitled under Section 43 of this code. In every case, the community estate passes charged with the debts against it.

§ 46. Joint Tenancies

(a) If two or more persons hold an interest in property jointly, and one joint owner dies before severance, the interest of the decedent in the joint estate shall not survive to the remaining joint owner or owners but shall pass by will or intestacy from the decedent as if the decedent's interest had been severed. The joint owners may agree in writing, however, that the interest of any joint owner who dies shall survive to the surviving joint owner or owners, but no such agreement shall be inferred from the mere fact that the property is held in joint ownership.

(b) Subsection (a) does not apply to agreements between spouses regarding their community property. Agreements between spouses regarding rights of survivorship in community property are governed by Part 3 of Chapter XI of this code.[1]

If spouses are contemplating an agreement which includes survivorship rights in community property, TEX. PROB. CODE, Chapter XI, Part 3 titled "Community Property with Right of Survivorship" should be consulted.

---

5. Separation Agreements

"Separation Agreement" has many meanings. Texas does not recognize a "legal separation." Therefore, Texas courts cannot order a "legal separation." However, upon the filing of divorce, Texas courts may issue orders governing all aspects of the separation that *precede* the legal divorce. *See* TEX. FAM. CODE §§ 6.501-.506.

During the separation preceding the divorce, a couple may change ownership of their community property by a proper partition and exchange agreement. *See* TEX. FAM. CODE § 4.102. Particular enforcement provisions apply to the marital property agreement. *See* TEX. FAM. CODE § 4.105.

The requirements for changing the management and control of community property are much less strict than changing the ownership of community property. *See Le Blanc v. Waller*, 603 S.W.2d 265 (Tex. App. 1980). Therefore, a couple may desire to change the management and control of community property while separated.

A couple may also simply enter into an agreement in contemplation of divorce. Such an agreement must pass a trial court's "just and right" review. *See* TEX. FAM. CODE § 7.006.

---

[1] Texas Probate Code § 451 et seq.

Early Texas cases held that when spouses have separated, a deed partitioning the community property is effective. The leading case is *Rains v. Wheeler*, 76 Tex. 390 (Tex. 1890).

More recently, in *Amarillo National Bank v. Liston*, 464 S.W.2d 395 (Tex. Civ. App.—Amarillo 1970, writ ref'd n.r.e), the court held such an agreement to be invalid because the agreement did not comply with the constitutional and statutory requirements for the partition of community property.

---

6. Statutes and Decisions 1980 to Present

BRADLEY
v.
BRADLEY
725 S.W.2d 503
(Tex. App.—Corpus Christi 1987, no writ)

UTTER, JUSTICE.

This is an appeal from a decree of divorce in which the trial court held that "no community property other than personal effects has been accumulated by the parties." We reverse the judgment of the trial court and remand for a new trial.

The parties were married on July 31, 1982 and were divorced on July 9, 1986. On July 26, 1982, prior to their marriage, appellant and appellee entered into a prenuptial agreement. During the marriage, appellant was not gainfully employed outside the home, and appellee's income was derived from his medical practice.

In interpreting the prenuptial agreement, the trial court found that "the separate property of each of the parties as well as the revenues, increases, and income from such separate property, and from the respective personal efforts of each party belongs to that party." The trial court obviously considered appellee's income as being derived from appellee's personal efforts and concluded that such income was appellee's separate property.

By her second point of error, appellant contends that the trial court erred in determining that the prenuptial agreement operated to convert appellee's income from personal earnings into his separate property.

Paragraph 2, entitled "Stipulations of Parties," provides that "the general purpose and intent of the parties" is:

> (a) that VICTOR and MARGARET will each continue to own and to manage his or her separate property;
>
> (b) that all revenues, increases, and income from such separate property, and from their respective personal efforts will be subject to the sole management and control of the party whose separate property or personal efforts generated such revenues or income,
>
> (c) that the parties will do any and all things necessary in order to establish or preserve the separate character of all revenues, increases, and income from such separate property, and from their respective personal efforts, ...

Section (b) merely restates TEX. FAM. CODE ANN. § 5.22 (Vernon 1975). Section (c) sets out the parties' intent to preserve the "separate property character" of "their respective personal efforts." However, the "respective personal efforts" do not acquire separate property character until they have partitioned and exchanged their respective community property interests in the income from each other's personal efforts.

Paragraph 7 of the agreement, entitled "Annual Partition and/or Exchange of the Community Estate, Pursuant to Section 5.42 of the Texas Family Code," provides:

> that on or before the 15th day of April of each year during the existence of this marriage, VICTOR and MARGARET will fairly and reasonably partition (and/or exchange) in writing all of the community estate of the parties on hand that will have accumulated since January 1 of the preceding year whether it be in the form of cash, realty, or other assets.

Upon acquisition, appellee's earnings from his personal efforts became community property. They remain community property until partitioned and exchanged pursuant to TEX. CONST. art. XVI, § 15, and TEX. FAM. CODE ANN. § 5.42 (Vernon Supp.1987). The prenuptial agreement does not itself effect a partition and exchange of the parties' respective community interests in each other's personal earnings. It merely evinces an intent to do so in the future. Appellee testified and admitted that they have never done so.

Section 7 also provides that "[t]he failure of the parties to partition in writing the community estate, if any, . . . shall not constitute a waiver of the parties' obligations and rights hereunder." Appellee contends that this provision should be interpreted to mean "that any *failure* by them to conduct their annual partitions would *not* constitute a waiver of their rights to claim the separate character of their property." [emphasis appellee's] Appellee's interpretation of this provision is contrary to the express provisions of TEX. CONST. art. XVI, § 15, which requires a "written instrument" in order to partition and exchange community property interests.

We hold that the prenuptial agreement itself does not operate to partition and exchange the community property interests in each other's income from personal efforts. To the contrary, it merely contemplates a partition and exchange of community property interests in the future. Therefore, the trial court erred in its interpretation of the prenuptial agreement and in holding that appellee's income from his personal earnings was his separate property. Appellant's second point of error is sustained.

Appellant's third point of error, which contends that the trial court erred in determining that there was no community property of the estate, is also sustained.

The trial court has broad discretion in dividing the property in a divorce action and its division will not be disturbed absent an abuse of discretion. *Reid v. Reid*, 658 S.W.2d 863 (Tex. App.—Corpus Christi 1983, no writ). The trial court's mischaracterization of property will require a reversal only if we determine that the division of the property made was, because of the legal error upon which it was based, so unfair as to constitute an abuse of discretion. *Cook v. Cook*, 679 S.W.2d 581 (Tex. App.—San Antonio 1984, no writ). In other words, appellant must show that, due to the trial court's legal error, the division of the property was so disproportionate so as to be manifestly unfair. *Reid v. Reid*, 658 S.W.2d at 865. Furthermore, appellant must show that the trial court would have probably made a different division of the property if it had been properly characterized. *Id.*

In this case, the trial court made no division of the property of the marital estate because it determined that there was no community property to divide. The trial court decided that the marital estate consisted entirely of separate property and awarded it accordingly. Had the trial court properly characterized appellee's personal earnings, it would probably have made a different division of it. Therefore, the trial court's error in characterizing appellee's personal earnings resulted in a division which was so disproportionate as to be manifestly unfair.

Furthermore, "[w]hen determining what would constitute a fair division of the marital estate, the court may consider such factors as disparity of income or of earning capacity of the parties, their relative physical conditions and financial conditions, the size of their separate estates, business opportunities available to each spouse, and the nature of the property involved." *Cook v. Cook*, 679 S.W.2d at 585. Appellee's annual earnings are approximately $200,000.00, while appellant apparently was a housewife with no income. Appellee admitted that appellant has no profession or vocation. In view of appellee's significantly greater income and earning capacity, the award to appellee of 100% of the community property constitutes a clear abuse of discretion and is manifestly unjust.

That portion of the trial court's judgment which dissolves the marriage of the parties is left undisturbed. The portion of the judgment dividing the marital estate is REVERSED and REMANDED to the trial court for further proceedings consistent with this opinion.

Having addressed the controlling issues, we decline to discuss appellant's remaining points of error. TEX. R. APP. P. 90.

* * *

Questions

1. Why was section 7 of the above agreement ineffective?
2. How would you change the agreement to accomplish the goals of Dr. Bradley?

DEWEY
v.
DEWEY

745 S.W.2d 514
(Tex. App.—Corpus Christi 1988, writ denied)

UTTER, JUSTICE.

This appeal is from a judgment which granted a divorce to the parties and divided the parties' community estate. We affirm the judgment of the trial court.

The parties were married on March 18, 1984, after having executed a pre-marital agreement. Appellee filed suit for divorce on December 8, 1985, but later non-suited her petition and proceeded on appellant's cross-petition for divorce. On April 28, 1986, a decree of divorce and property division was approved and signed by the parties, their respective attorneys, and the court.

Appellee filed a motion for new trial on May 9, 1986, alleging she had been mentally incompetent when the above divorce decree was entered. After hearing the motion, the court set aside the April 28, 1986, divorce decree in its entirety, and granted a new trial. After a jury trial, the final judgment was signed granting a divorce to the parties and dividing the property therein.

Appellant contends in his first point of error that the trial court erred by granting a new trial on both the divorce and the property issues because appellee did not request that the divorce be set aside in her motion for new trial. Appellant complains that he was harmed by the court's setting aside the "divorce" because after the April 28, 1986, divorce decree was approved, he allegedly transferred certain funds from his separate property into his retirement account. Appellant asserts that the trial court viewed appellant's action as transforming separate property into community property because the community estate had been extended up until the December 19, 1986, judgment setting aside the divorce entered by the trial court.

In her motion for new trial, appellee requested that the "Final Decree of Divorce" should be set aside and a new trial granted. Appellee thereafter stated in her motion that she was requesting a new trial because she was of unsound mind at the time the decree was entered and was incapable of making rational divisions of their community assets. Nowhere did she limit her motion for new trial to the division of property.

Even if appellee had limited her request to the issue of property division, the court, in granting a new trial, would not have been restricted to the grounds set forth in the motion for new trial. *Napier v. Napier*, 555 S.W.2d 186, 188-89 (Tex. Civ. App.—El Paso 1977, no writ); *Brown v. American Finance Co.*, 432 S.W.2d, 564, 567 (Tex. Civ. App.—Dallas 1968, writ ref'd n.r.e.). Furthermore, the issue of divorce and the issue of property division are neither separable nor severable under Tex. R. Civ. P. 41, 174, and 320. *Vautrain v. Vautrain*, 646 S.W.2d 309, 315 (Tex. App.—Fort Worth 1983, writ dism'd); *Underhill v. Underhill*, 614 S.W.2d 178, 181 (Tex. Civ. App.—Houston [14th Dist.] 1981, writ ref'd n.r.e.). We hold there was no final judgment of divorce until December 19, 1986, when all issues and parties of the case were disposed of. Appellant's first point of error is overruled.

Appellant contends in his second point of error that the court erred in finding the parties had accumulated a community estate, because the pre-marital agreement precluded it. Appellant complains in his third point of error that the court erred in refusing to disregard the jury's answer to special issue number five because the answer was contrary to the great weight and preponderance of the evidence. Special issue number five asked the jury to determine whether the parties, in executing the pre-marital agreement, intended to make the income of each party the separate property of the party receiving the income. The jury answered that the parties did not.

In considering a "no evidence," "insufficient evidence," or "against the great weight and preponderance of the evidence" point of error, we will follow the well-established test set forth in *Pool v. Ford Motor Co.*, 715 S.W.2d 629 (Tex. 1986); *Dyson v. Olin Corp.*, 692 S.W.2d 456 (Tex. 1985); *Glover v. Texas General Indemnity Co.*, 619 S.W.2d 400 (Tex. 1981); *Garza v. Alviar*, 395 S.W.2d 821 (Tex. 1965); *Allied Finance Co. v. Garza*, 626 S.W.2d 120 (Tex. App.—Corpus Christi 1981, writ ref'd n.r.e.); and Calvert, *No Evidence and Insufficient Evidence Points of Error*, 38 Texas L. Rev. 361 (1960).

Neither party complains of the validity of the pre-marital agreement. The pre-marital agreement should be interpreted according to the true intentions of the parties as expressed in the instrument. *Coker v. Coker*, 650 S.W.2d 391, 393-94 (Tex. 1983); *Miller v. Miller*, 700 S.W.2d 941, 951 (Tex. App.—Dallas 1985, writ ref'd n.r.e.). No single provision taken alone will be given controlling effect; rather, every provision must be considered with reference to the whole instrument. *Coker*, 650 S.W.2d at 393-94.

The pre-marital agreement clearly states that all profits, dividends, interest, and proceeds that accumulate after marriage from each of the parties' separate property will remain that party's separate property. Appellant thereafter listed his professional corporation, George C. Dewey, M.D., P.A., as part of his separate property.

Appellant's professional corporation and appellant are legally distinct entities. *Cf. Sun Towers v. Heckler*, 725 F.2d 315, 331 (5th Cir. 1984), *cert. denied*, 469 U.S. 823, 83 L. Ed. 2d 45, 105 S.Ct. 100

(1984); *Massachusetts v. Davis*, 140 Tex. 398, 168 S.W.2d 216, 222 (1943). The corporate entity is the owner, and any contribution made by appellant to the professional corporation became corporate property which may not be characterized as either the separate or community property of the individual stockholders. *Cf. Marshall v. Marshall*, 735 S.W.2d 587, 594 (Tex. App.—Dallas 1987, writ ref'd n.r.e.) (applies rule to contributions made to spouse's partnership). Any rights or ownership interest appellant had in the professional corporation, however, could and did become appellant's separate property by virtue of the pre-marital agreement as did any profits, dividends, interest, or proceeds which accrued therefrom. *Williams v. Williams*, 720 S.W.2d 246, 249-50 (Tex. App.—Houston [14th Dist.] 1986, no writ).

The pre-marital agreement, however, did not mention appellant's salary received from the corporation during marriage; nor did it state that there would be no accumulation of a community estate. It merely asserted that the listed property and all profits, dividends, interest and proceeds resulting from that property should remain appellant's separate property. Since appellant's income was not expressly listed in the pre-marital agreement and it was apparently acquired during marriage, it was clearly community property. TEX. FAM. CODE ANN. §§ 5.01, 5.02 (Vernon 1975); *Maben v. Maben*, 574 S.W.2d 229, 232 (Tex. Civ. App.—Fort Worth 1978, no writ). Therefore, there is no ambiguity present on the face of the agreement and parol evidence shall not be considered. *Miller*, 700 S.W.2d at 951. We find the evidence presented was sufficient to support the jury's answer. Appellant's second and third points of error are overruled.

Appellant contends in his sixth point of error that the trial court impermissibly invaded his separate estate by awarding certain jewelry to appellee. Appellant argues that he received the jewelry as a "gift" from appellee and that it was part of his separate estate.

Three elements are necessary to establish the existence of a gift: 1) intent to make a gift; 2) delivery of the property; and 3) acceptance of the property. *Grimsley v. Grimsley*, 632 S.W.2d 174, 177 (Tex. App.—Corpus Christi 1982, no writ). Moreover, it was appellant's burden to show a gift had been made. *Diaz v. Cantu*, 586 S.W.2d 576, 580 (Tex. Civ. App.—Corpus Christi 1979, writ ref'd n.r.e.).

The record reveals that appellee "intended to return" the jewelry and that she delivered the jewelry to appellant and that appellant apparently accepted the jewelry. However, no evidence was presented that appellee intended to make a "gift" of the jewelry to appellant. On the contrary, the evidence indicates that appellant's mental condition had been deteriorating since March of 1986, and that she was depressed and didn't care about anything. In fact, the April 28, 1986 decree of divorce was later set aside by the court because appellee was not mentally competent to enter into a valid, binding contract at that time. Based on this evidence, the jury found that appellee did not make a gift of her jewelry to appellant. The evidence was sufficient to support the jury's answer. Appellant's sixth point of error is overruled.

Appellant contends in his seventh point of error that the trial court erred in characterizing the George C. Dewey, M.D., P.A. Defined Contribution Plan as community property because the plan was both owned by appellant's separate property professional association and established prior to the parties' marriage. Appellant complains in his ninth point of error that the trial court erred in refusing to disregard the jury's answers to special issues No. 7 and No. 9 because the evidence was insufficient as a matter of law or was against the great weight and preponderance of the evidence.

Special Issue No. 7:
Do you find from a preponderance of the evidence that monies deposited by George C. Dewey, M.D., P.A. into the George C. Dewey Defined Contribution Plan were profits and/or proceeds of the professional association?

The jury answered, "We do not."

Special Issue No. 9:
From a preponderance of the evidence, do you find that the George C. Dewey Defined Contribution Pension Plan is the separate property of George C. Dewey?
The jury answered, "We do not.

Retirement and pension plans are regarded as a mode of employee compensation earned during a given period of employment. *Cearley v. Cearley*, 544 S.W.2d 661, 662 (Tex. 1976); *Whorrall v. Whorrall*, 691 S.W.2d 32, 37-38 (Tex. App.—Austin 1985, writ dism'd). It is also well established that an employee spouse's accrued benefits in a retirement and pension plan which have been earned during marriage, but which have not vested and matured at the time of divorce, constitute a contingent interest in property and a community asset subject to division upon divorce. *Cearley*, 544 S.W.2d at 666; *May v. May*, 716 S.W.2d 705, 707 (Tex. App.—Corpus Christi 1986, no writ).

Appellant's contention that the Defined Contribution Plan belonged to appellant's separate property professional association is without merit. The record reveals that the professional association was appellant's employer and all rights to receipt of the plan's benefits were in appellant as an employee, not the professional association. Moreover, the pre-marital agreement merely states the Defined Benefit-Investment Fund Pension Plan is appellant's separate property, and does not mention appellant's Defined Contribution Plan. We find that the Defined Contribution Plan was not a continuation of the plan listed in the pre-marital agreement, but an entirely different plan. Therefore, the Defined Contribution Plan constituted community property subject to division on divorce.

Appellant relies on case law involving real property and stock acquisitions to support the proposition that since the Defined Contribution Plan was commenced prior to the parties' marriage, it was appellant's separate property. The inception of title doctrine simply does not apply in cases involving retirement or pension benefits, and appellant has cited no cases involving pension plans in support of his proposition. The Defined Contribution Plan was clearly a form of deferred "employee" compensation. In fact, only upon reaching the normal retirement age, separation from service from the professional association, or upon becoming 100 percent disabled, would he be allowed to withdraw from the plan. The only pertinent time period, therefore, concerns that in which the parties were married. Any benefits in the pension plan which accrued on appellant's behalf during the marriage was community property subject to division on divorce. TEX. CONST. art. XVI, § 15. Thus, the date the "professional association" originated the plan is irrelevant.

We conclude the trial court did not err in characterizing the Defined Contribution Plan as community property. We further conclude that the record, as a whole, reveals that there is sufficient evidence to support the jury's answers to special issues No. 7 and No. 9. Appellant's seventh and ninth points of error are overruled.

Appellant contends in his eighth point of error that the trial court erred in failing to reimburse appellant's separate estate for contributions made to the Defined Contribution Plan from appellant's separate property. Specifically, appellant argues that a portion of a $29,700 deposit to such plan made on April 29, 1986, came from an insurance policy which was owned by appellant's separate property professional association.

Since the professional association was appellant's employer, the source of the funds placed in the Defined Contribution Plan is immaterial. The professional association and appellant are legally distinct entities. If the professional association borrowed the money from an insurance policy to fund the pension plan, as argued in appellant's brief, then it is the professional association, and not appellant, who is liable for the debt. Appellant, in receiving the benefits, was simply being compensated for his work, which was clearly community property. Thus, appellant has not met his burden of pleading and proving that expenditures were made from his separate property for the benefit of the community and that they were reimbursable. *Cf. Vallone v. Vallone*, 644 S.W.2d 455, 459 (Tex. 1983); *Jensen v. Jensen*, 665 S.W.2d 107, 110 (Tex. 1984). Appellant's eighth point of error is overruled.

Appellant contends in his fourth and fifth points of error that the trial court erred in awarding appellee $20,000 in cash payable by appellant. Appellant complains that the award impermissibly invaded appellant's separate estate and thereby contravened the statutes and public policy of this state which prohibit alimony. Appellant's tenth point of error contends that the trial court abused its discretion in dividing the community estate because the division is so unequal as to be manifestly unjust.

In reviewing the actions of the trial court, there is a presumption that the trial court exercised its discretion properly. *Murff v. Murff*, 615 S.W.2d 696, 699 (Tex. 1981); *Bell v. Bell*, 513 S.W.2d 20, 22 (Tex. 1974). The trial court has wide discretion in dividing the parties' community estate and that division should be corrected on appeal only where a clear abuse of discretion has been shown. *Murff*, 615 S.W.2d at 698; *Mata v. Mata*, 710 S.W.2d 756, 760 (Tex. App.—Corpus Christi 1986, no writ).

The trial court may order appellant to pay appellee "cash" even though community property did not consist of any cash. *Weaks v. Weaks*, 471 S.W.2d 454, 455 (Tex. Civ. App.—Beaumont 1971, writ dism'd). Moreover, the mere fact that the community estate is not divided equally does not constitute an abuse of discretion as long as there is a reasonable basis for that division. *Mata*, 710 S.W.2d at 760; *Voronin v. Voronin*, 662 S.W.2d 102, 106-07 (Tex. App.—Austin 1983, writ dism'd). Factors to be considered include: 1) the relative earning capacity and business experience of the parties; 2) the educational background of the parties; 3) the size of separate estates; 4) the age, health and physical condition of the parties; 5) the fault in breaking up the marriage; 6) the benefits the innocent spouse would have received had this marriage continued; and 7) the probable need for future support. *Zamora v. Zamora*, 611 S.W.2d 660, 662 (Tex. Civ. App.—Corpus Christi 1980, no writ); *Erger v. Erger*, 590 S.W.2d 186, 188 (Tex. Civ. App.—Fort Worth 1979, writ dism'd); *Cooper v. Cooper*, 513 S.W.2d 229, 233-34 (Tex. Civ. App.—Houston [1st Dist.] 1974, no writ).

At the outset, we find that the $20,000 cash award to appellee was entirely referable to community assets available upon dissolution of the marriage. The accumulated value of the Defined Contribution Plan and the Bon Aire residence alone were in excess of the $20,000 cash award to appellee. The fact that there is still an indebtedness on some of these community assets is irrelevant. Their total equity value is still in excess of $20,000.00. We conclude, therefore, that the award neither impermissibly invaded appellant's separate estate, nor constituted alimony in contravention of statutes and public policy.

We further find the trial court did not abuse its discretion in dividing the community property. Appellant was a radiologist with an annual gross income in excess of $200,000. His separate property professional association generated approximately $336,000 per year and offered him numerous fringe benefits, most of which were granted at his own discretion because he was the association's only employee. Appellant's separate estate was extremely large and included among others, a separate property residence, bank accounts, pension plan benefits accrued prior to marriage, and an I.R.A. Appellee, on the other hand, was a charge nurse earning around $18,000 per year (although her most recent tax records reflected earnings of only $9,707) and was in poor health. In addition, the jury found appellant was at fault in breaking up the marriage by finding him guilty of such cruel treatment towards appellee, that further living together was insupportable. Appellant's fourth, fifth and tenth points of error are overruled.

The judgment of the trial court is AFFIRMED.

Question

Often times, even an enforceable premarital agreement does not accomplish the goal of the proponent. What would you have changed in the agreement to fulfill the doctor's goals?

DANIEL
v.
DANIEL

779 S.W.2d 110
(Tex. App.—Houston [1st Dist.] 1989, no writ)

EVANS, CHIEF JUSTICE.

This is an appeal from a divorce decree that confirmed the validity and enforceability of a postnuptial property agreement and, pursuant to said agreement, effected a division of the parties' marital estate.

The parties to this action, Mr. and Mrs. James Daniel, married in February 1981. After five years of marriage, they entered into a "Property Agreement," dated February 14, 1986, which is the principal subject of this dispute. In this Property Agreement, which covered properties owned, both separate and communal, each spouse agreed that: (1) all income, on and after the date of the Agreement, from a spouse's separate property (owned then or in the future) would become the separate property of that spouse; (2) all monies earned through a spouse's personal services and efforts would become the separate property of that spouse; (3) past and future trust distributions to Mrs. Daniel from any trust created by her prior to the marriage would become her separate property; and (4) trust distributions to Mr. Daniel, from any trust of which he was the beneficiary, would become his separate property. The Property Agreement also provided that each spouse transfer to the other spouse, as the other's separate property, such rights, claims, and property interests as were consistent with, and in furtherance of, the provisions of the Agreement.

Historically in Texas, a husband and wife could not, by "mere agreement," change their community property into separate property. *See Kellet v. Trice*, 95 Tex. 160, 170, 66 S.W. 51, 54 (1902); Cameron, Hoffman & Yutterberg, *Marital and Premarital Agreements*, 39 BAYLOR L.REV. 1095 (1987). In 1980, however, Texas voters approved an amendment to art. XVI, sec. 15 of the Texas Constitution, which allows a husband and wife, without prejudice to pre-existing creditors, to enter into written agreements for the partition or exchange of their community interests into separately owned properties. To implement this constitutional amendment, the 67th Legislature amended subchapter C of chapter 5 of the Texas Family Code, effective September 1, 1981.[1] Six years later, the 70th Legislature again amended subchapter C, designating it "Property Agreements," and dividing it into two parts.[2]

---

[1] Ch. 782, sec. 2, 1981 Tex.Gen.Laws 2964, 2964-65, amending sections 5.41 and 5.42, and adding sections 5.43, 5.44, 5.45, and 5.46.

[2] Ch. 678, sec. 1, 1987 Tex.Gen.Laws 2530, effective September 1, 1987. Part 1, entitled "Uniform Premarital Agreement Act," includes sections 5.41-5.50, and Part 2, entitled "Other Property Agreements," includes sections 5.51-5.56.

In this case, we are concerned only with Part 2, sections 5.52, 5.53, and 5.55, which pertain to post-nuptial agreements. These sections provide:

§ 5.52. Partition or Exchange of Community Property.

At any time, the spouses may partition or exchange between themselves any part of their community property, then existing or to be acquired, as they may desire. Property or a property interest transferred to a spouse by a partition or exchange agreement becomes his or her separate property.

§ 5.53. Agreements Between Spouses Concerning Income or Property Derived from Separate Property.

At any time, the spouses may agree that the income or property arising from the separate property then owned by one of them, or which may thereafter be acquired, shall be the separate property of the owner.

§ 5.55. Enforcement.

(a) A partition or exchange agreement is not enforceable if the party against whom enforcement is sought proves that:

(1) that party did not execute the agreement voluntarily; or

(2) the agreement was unconscionable when it was executed and, before execution of the agreement, that party:

(A) was not provided a fair and reasonable disclosure of the property or financial obligations of the other party;

(B) did not voluntarily and expressly waive, in writing, any right to disclosure of the property or financial obligations of the other party beyond the disclosure provided; and

(C) did not have, or reasonably could not have had, an adequate knowledge of the property or financial obligations of the other party.

(b) An issue of unconscionability of a partition or exchange agreement shall be decided by the court as a matter of law."

Tex. FAM. CODE ANN. secs. 5.52, 5.53, and 5.55 (Vernon Supp.1989).

Mrs. Daniel instituted this divorce action on September 23, 1987. By answer and counterclaim to her supplemental petition, Mr. Daniel asserted that the Property Agreement was unenforceable and should be set aside on theories of fraud, unconscionability, unjust enrichment, and breach of fiduciary duty.

The case was tried to a jury, and when both sides rested, the court directed a verdict in favor of Mrs. Daniel. In its judgment, the trial court concluded in part:

"Only three issues, under the pleadings and evidence, and the stipulation of counsel were in dispute as follows:

(1) the validity and effectiveness of the provisions of the Property Agreement between the parties dated February 14, 1986 concerning:

(a) the retroactive characterization of income;

(b) the transfer of Husband's interest in accumulated income earned prior to the date of the Agreement on Wife's separate property, particularly the Jean Warren Young Trust "A".

(2) the ownership and partition of an IRS refund check for calendar 1986, and the ownership of a claim for refund for calendar 1983; and

(3) the award of attorney's fees and expenses.

The Court was of the opinion that FC § 5.55 is to be utilized in determining the enforceability of the Property Agreement of the parties dated February 14, 1986. The Court finds that there are no pleadings nor any evidence suggesting that Respondent did not voluntarily execute said agreement as provided by FC § 5.55(a)(1). The Court further finds that said agreement is not unconscionable as a matter of law as provided by FC § 5.55(a)(2) and § 5.55(b).

The Court further finds that the common law defenses asserted by Respondent have been superseded by FC § 5.55 but, nevertheless, finds there is not sufficient evidence to warrant submission of special issues thereon to the jury. Accordingly, the Court finds that said agreement is valid and enforceable as a matter of law.

The Court further finds that it is undisputed that the federal income tax paid by the parties in 1983, 1984, 1985 and 1986 was paid (except for a small payment made by Respondent in the form of withholding) by a trust established by Petitioner in 1959 which, under the Property Agreement dated February 14, 1986, is her separate property."

In separate amended findings of fact and conclusions of law, the court found that Mr. Daniel voluntarily executed the Property Agreement, and that the evidence was insufficient to warrant submission of special issues on any common law defense. The court concluded, as a matter of law, that the agreement was not unconscionable and that it was valid and enforceable.

On this appeal, Mr. Daniel asserts 18 points of error, which are grouped to reflect common issues.

We first consider Mr. Daniel's points of error 1, 13, 14, and 15, in which he contends that the court erred in determining the enforceability of the Property Agreement under the current TEX. FAM. CODE ANN. sec. 5.55 (Vernon Supp.1989), rather than the 1981 version of that section.

In 1987, when the 70th Legislature amended chapter 5 of the Texas Family Code, it did not expressly provide that the amendatory provisions should be given retrospective application. In the absence of such a provision, the amendment would not usually be applied retrospectively to agreements executed before its effective date. *See Brooks v. Texas Employers Ins. Ass'n*, 358 S.W.2d 412, 413-14 (Tex. Civ. App.—Houston 1962, writ ref'd n.r.e.). However, the general rule does not control here, because the amendatory statute is both procedural and remedial in nature. *See Phil. H. Pierce Co. v. Watkins*, 114 Tex. 153, 158, 263 S.W. 905, 907 (1924). Section 5.55 establishes a statutory procedural scheme for challenging the enforceability of a post-nuptial property agreement executed pursuant to the statute. The amendatory provisions simply set forth the revised procedures to be followed by the courts in litigation occurring after the effective date of the amendment.[3] Thus, the trial court properly applied the provisions of section 5.55 to Mr. Daniel's action challenging the validity of the Property Agreement.

Mr. Daniel also argues, under these same points, that section 5.55 is inapplicable to the Property Agreement because it is not "a partition or exchange agreement," as that term is used in section 5.55.

We also disagree with this argument. There is no indication that the legislature intended, by using the general term "partition or exchange agreement" in section 5.55, to limit the enforcement provisions of that section to those agreements covered by section 5.52, entitled "Partition or Exchange of Community Property," and not those agreements covered by other sections of subchapter C, Part 2, as "Other Property Agreements." It seems evident that the legislature intended income arrangements between spouses, which are covered by section 5.53, entitled "Agreements Between Spouses Con-

[3] We further note that our supreme court has recently held a court of appeals is bound to apply the law as it existed at the time the divorce decree was signed. Sadler v. Sadler, 769 S.W.2d 886 (Tex. 1989). The decree in this case was signed on March 18, 1988, when the current section 5.55 was in effect.

cerning Income from Property Derived," to be enforced in the same manner as partition and exchange agreements covered by section 5.52.

In construing a statute, we must adopt an interpretation that will carry out the legislature's manifest purpose and intent. *Coastal States Gas Producing Co. v. Pate*, 158 Tex. 171, 176, 309 S.W.2d 828, 831 (1958). In ascertaining such intent, we must consider that the legislature intended a fair, reasonable, and sensible construction. *Clark v. Pearson & Co.*, 121 Tex. 34, 45, 39 S.W.2d 27, 32 (1931); *Calvert v. A-1 Bit & Tool Co.*, 256 S.W.2d 224, 231 (Tex. Civ. App.—Austin 1953, writ ref'd n.r.e.).

We perceive no rational basis for the legislature to have intended spouses' post-nuptial income arrangements, covered by section 5.53, to be enforced differently from partition and exchange of community property agreements, covered by section 5.52. Thus, we hold that the trial court properly applied the enforcement provisions of section 5.55 to all aspects of the Property Agreement, including those provisions relating to income derived from separate properties.

We accordingly overrule Mr. Daniel's points of error 1, 13, 14, and 15.

Secondly, we consider Mr. Daniel's contentions, under points of error 7 through 12, that assert the trial court erred in deciding, as a matter of law, that the evidence was legally insufficient to warrant the submission of issues to the jury on Mr. Daniel's asserted common law defenses. Although Mr. Daniel does not enumerate in his brief the common law defenses he sought to have submitted to the jury, his answer and counterclaim to Mrs. Daniel's supplemental petition suggest they are in the nature of actual and constructive fraud, breach of fiduciary duty to make full disclosure, and unjust enrichment.

Preliminarily, the legislature did not expressly provide that the enforcement provisions of section 5.55 constitute the exclusive remedy for challenging the enforceability of a property agreement executed pursuant to the Family Code. Therefore, we must look to the language of the statute to determine if the legislature intended that result.

As we view the statute, the legislature simply intended to recognize the validity of voluntary property agreements between a husband and wife, when such agreements were not unconscionable, and were based on a fair and reasonable disclosure of the parties' respective assets and financial obligations. Although the statute places the burden of proof on the party challenging the enforceability of a property agreement, it also alleviates the need for proof of all elements required in common law defenses.[4]

Because the amendatory statute is procedural and remedial in nature, we must adopt a construction that, in the absence of an express legislative provision to the contrary, will prevent forfeiture of a valuable right or remedy. *Stephenson v. Stephenson*, 22 S.W. 150, 151 (Tex. 1893); *Hope Oil Corp. v. Humble Oil & Refining Co.*, 43 S.W.2d 272, 273 (Tex. Civ. App.—San Antonio 1931, no writ).

We conclude that the legislature, by the enactment of the enforcement provisions of section 5.55, did not intend such provisions to replace all common law defenses, and that the statute simply provides an additional statutory remedy for persons challenging property agreements executed pursuant to the Family Code. *Compare Smith v. Baldwin*, 611 S.W.2d 611, 616-17 (Tex. 1980) (Texas Deceptive Trade Practices Act held not to displace common law remedies). We accordingly hold that the

[4] Under section 5.55, the challenging party simply has to prove: (a) that the agreement was involuntary; or (b) that it was unconscionable, and that he or she was not provided, and did not effectively waive, his or her right to a fair and reasonable disclosure about the other party's assets and liabilities. Thus, the contesting party does not have to prove knowledge or reliance, as would be necessary in a fraud common law defense.

trial court erred in deciding, as a matter of law, that section 5.55 superseded Mr. Daniel's common law defenses.

We now address Mr. Daniel's assertions that the trial court erred in instructing a verdict in Mrs. Daniel's favor, based on its determination that the evidence was legally insufficient to justify submission of common law defenses to the jury.

The issues raised by Mr. Daniel's assertions are: (1) does the record contain any evidence that Mrs. Daniel failed to make good faith disclosure of material facts within her knowledge; and (2) if there was such evidence, does the record conclusively establish that Mr. Daniel voluntarily and intelligently waived his right to such disclosure.[5]

Texas courts have closely scrutinized property agreements made by spouses during marriage. Because of the confidential relationship between a husband and a wife, courts have imposed the same duties of good faith and fair dealing on spouses as required of partners and other fiduciaries. *See Johnson v. Peckham*, 132 Tex. 148, 151-52, 120 S.W.2d 786, 787-88 (1938); *Miller v. Miller*, 700 S.W.2d 941, 945-47 (Tex. App.—Dallas 1985, writ ref'd n.r.e.); *Bohn v. Bohn*, 455 S.W.2d 401, 405 (Tex. Civ. App.—Houston [1st Dist.] 1970, writ dism'd w.o.j.).

Because Mr. Daniel appeals from a directed verdict, every inference that may properly be drawn from the evidence must be indulged in his favor, and if there is evidence of probative value requiring the jury's decision on either of these issues, the trial court's judgment must be reversed. *See White v. White*, 141 Tex. 328, 331, 172 S.W.2d 295, 296 (1943); *Estate of Grimes v. Dorchester Gas Producing Co.*, 707 S.W.2d 196, 201 (Tex. App.—Amarillo 1986, writ ref'd n.r.e.).

The thrust of Mr. Daniel's complaint is that Mrs. Daniel and her attorney failed to disclose the existence of over $1 million of community income, which had accumulated to Mrs. Daniel's separate property in a grantor trust designated in the Property Agreement as "Trust A." Mr. Daniel contends he was not given complete access to this information, and that Mrs. Daniel's failure to disclose the accumulation of her income amounted to constructive fraud.

Mr. Daniel is a licensed attorney and a certified public accountant. He graduated from the University of Texas in 1951 and, after serving two years in the army, worked as a state bank examiner. He returned to school for an accounting degree, and in 1960 or 1961, he earned a certified public accounting certificate. Mr. Daniel then worked for the national accounting firm of Ernst and Ernst, continuing his academic studies in the evenings at the University of Houston Law Center. He earned a law degree in 1967. Mr. Daniel then worked for Fish Engineering Company, marrying his first wife, the daughter of Ray Fish, the founder of that company. He was employed as vice-president and assistant to the president of Fish Engineering before he started his own venture capital firm, known as Daniel Enterprises, Inc. Mr. Daniel owns substantial assets as separate property, including a remainder interest under a testamentary trust established by his father's will.

Mrs. Daniel was the youngest daughter of the founder of Warren Petroleum Company in Oklahoma. In 1959, her parents gave her substantial sums of money, which she placed in a newly established trust created for her own benefit. This trust is referred to in the Property Agreement as "Trust A." At the time of trial, the trust residual was valued at about $12 million.

[5] Mr. Daniel does not contend that Mrs. Daniel made affirmative misrepresentations concerning her properties, and on oral submission, he stipulates there is no evidence showing an intent to defraud. He contends only that Mrs. Daniel failed to meet her fiduciary duty to fully disclose the extent of the income that had accumulated to her separate properties.

Both Mr. and Mrs. Daniel had prior marriages, and children by those marriages. In the fall of 1985, Mrs. Daniel, after preliminary discussion with Mr. Daniel, went to see Mr. Tom Eubanks of the law firm of Baker & Botts to discuss a post-nuptial agreement. Mr. Eubanks was a mutual friend of the Daniels and had served on a bank board with Mr. Daniel. After several months delay, due to the death of Mrs. Daniel's daughter, Mr. Eubanks prepared drafts of a proposed agreement, which culminated in the Property Agreement that is the subject of this suit. Mr. Eubanks testified that this was a "vigorously negotiated transaction," which the parties negotiated at "arms-length." Essentially, the Agreement provided that the income from Mrs. Daniel's separate property and efforts was to be her separate property, and income from Mr. Daniel's separate property and efforts was to be his separate property. The Agreement also provided that income from Mrs. Daniel's separate trust property, which had been community property when first earned, would become her separate property.

At the instance of Mr. Eubanks, Mr. Daniel had the proposed Property Agreement reviewed by Mr. Thomas Crowell of the law firm of Hutcheson & Grundy. Mr. Crowell testified that the Agreement had been negotiated in a friendly and amicable manner, and that Mr. Daniel had agreed to make the Agreement to preserve marital harmony with his wife. Mr. Crowell said that his assignment from Mr. Daniel was limited to a review of specific areas of the Agreement, and that he did not have a full picture of the parties' entire financial situation. He testified that he did not pass on the fairness of the contract because Mr. Daniel did not ask him to do so.

On the day the document was executed, Mr. Eubanks, at the written suggestion of Mr. Daniel, inserted in the final draft some additional language that referred for the first time to Mrs. Daniel's "Trust A," as well as to "any other trust created by wife prior to the marriage of the parties."

Mr. Daniel testified that he was acting as a husband, not as a professional, in dealing with the Property Agreement, and that he was trying to accommodate his wife's wishes in doing so. He said he was unaware that more than $1 million of community income had been accumulated and was being held in "Trust A."

Mr. Daniel contends that, because he negotiated with his wife "out of a sense of trust," her failure, and that of her attorney, to disclose vital information to him constituted a constructive fraud.

We disagree with Mr. Daniel's contention. We find no evidence of any act of bad faith on the part of Mrs. Daniel or her counsel. Instead, the evidence conclusively establishes, as a matter of law, that Mr. Daniel was given reasonable opportunity to ascertain the true facts, and that he knowingly chose not to follow that opportunity.

The record shows that Mr. and Mrs. Daniel filed joint income tax returns for the years 1981 to 1986. Mr. Chris Parsons of Deloitte, Haskins & Sells, the accounting firm that prepared these returns, testified that the returns showed line by line the various types of entities and the income generated by them. Among these income-generating entities was "Trust A." Mr. Daniel admitted that he had reviewed the tax returns and that he had not misunderstood their import. He knew, therefore, that "Trust A" generated substantial income for each of the years during his marriage to Mrs. Daniel.

At trial, and on this appeal, Mr. Daniel complains that, even though he knew that sizeable amounts of income were accruing to "Trust A," he did not know, and Mrs. Daniel never advised him, the trust income was being accumulated and was not being distributed. He testified that Mrs. Daniel sometimes complained to him that too much of the income was being distributed for charitable purposes, leaving him with the impression that there was very little left in the trust after such contributions.

At trial, Mr. Daniel was examined about his review of the income tax returns, and whether he could have determined the amount of charitable contributions being made from income accruing to "Trust A."

> Q. Now couldn't you have read the income tax returns that you signed and found out precisely how much money was donated to the family hospital and other family charities around Tulsa?
>
> A. Yes.

Based on this and other testimony of Mr. Daniel, the trial court could have determined, as a matter of law, that Mr. Daniel had information available to him from which he could readily have learned the amount of undistributed income in "Trust A," had he chosen to have that information.

Mr. Daniel also complains that he did not know, and had never been advised, about income accruing from certain tax-free bonds in Mrs. Daniel's custody account. He acknowledged, however, that he did know Mrs. Daniel had "a number of tax free bonds."

Mr. Daniel further admitted that he never asked his lawyer, Mr. Crowell, to inquire into the distribution of the income from "Trust A," or the extent of the income accruing to the tax-free bonds. He simply explained that his purpose in making the Property Agreement was to provide his wife "comfort" regarding her estate and her assets, and that he had not been interested in the size of her estate. He said he had not asked any questions about the extent of her properties *because of their mutual understanding that he would not inquire into her properties, and she would not inquire into his.*

Mr. Daniel also acknowledged that he had read and understood the following stipulations in the Property Agreement:

> Each of the Parties acknowledges that the other has fully acquainted him or her with the other's means and resources, that he or she has ascertained and weighed all of the facts, conditions, and circumstances likely to influence his or her judgment.
>
> Husband acknowledges that he realizes that the total of Wife's Income and said trust distribution is now substantially greater than the total of his Income and said trust distributions.
>
> Each of the Parties recognizes that this Agreement may be substantially more beneficial, overall and as to particulars, to one than the other and that each nevertheless wishes to enter into this Agreement.
>
> This Agreement sets forth the entire understanding of the Parties as to the subject matter of this Agreement; and neither Husband nor Wife has relied upon any representation of the other, except as those representations are especially set forth in this Agreement."

When one spouse knowingly elects not to inquire into matters that affect his or her interest, he or she may not later complain that he or she did not know the full circumstances of the transaction. . . .

Mr. Daniel is a licensed attorney, a certified public accountant, and an experienced businessman. He admitted he read and understood the terms of the Property Agreement, as well as the joint income tax returns he and his wife filed during the six years of their marriage. He knew of the sizeable amount of income accruing to "Trust A," and he knew that his wife owned a number of tax-free bonds. However, for his own, albeit laudable motives, i.e. his concern for the mental comfort of his wife, he voluntarily chose not to make any inquiry into those matters. He also instructed his attorney not to make any such inquiry for him. Moreover, when Mr. Daniel executed the written Property Agreement, he confirmed in writing his choice not to make any inquiry into the value and extent of his wife's property. Under these undisputed facts, the trial court did not err in concluding, as a matter of law, that Mr. Daniel presented no evidence justifying the submission of common law defenses to the jury.

Accordingly, while we sustain Mr. Daniel's point of error seven, we overrule his points of error 8 through 12, and in so doing, find point of error seven to have been harmless. *First Employees Ins. Co. v. Skinner*, 646 S.W.2d 170, 172 (Tex. 1983).

* * *

Finally, in points of error 16 and 17, Mr. Daniel contends that the trial court erred in finding that the Daniels' federal income tax for the years 1983 through 1986 had been paid principally from Mrs. Daniel's "Trust A," rather than from the income of such trust. As we interpret these points of error, Mr. Daniel contends there is no evidence, or factually insufficient evidence, to support the trial court's finding.

In cross-examination of Mr. Daniel, he was asked:

> "Q. Mr. Daniel, you heard Mr. Parsons testify earlier that all of the income taxes reported on your '84, 5 and 6 income tax returns were paid by Jean Daniel from Trust "A". You heard him say that?
>
> A. Yes.
>
> Q. You don't quarrel with that, do you?
>
> A. No.

Based on this testimony, the trial court did not err in determining as a matter of law, that the income tax for the years in question was paid out of Mrs. Daniel's trust fund.

We accordingly overrule these two points of error.

We affirm the judgment of the trial court.

COHEN, JUSTICE, concurring.

I agree with the result and most of the reasoning in the majority opinion, but, unlike the majority, I would hold that Family Code § 5.55 provides the exclusive means of attacking a post-marital property agreement. This section of the Family Code was enacted in order to make it easier to enforce marital property agreements. *Compare Sadler v. Sadler*, 769 S.W.2d 886 (Tex. 1989) (construing the purpose of Section 5.46). It accomplished this by shifting the burden of proof to the spouse attacking the property agreement. In so doing, the legislature did not enact a cumulative remedies provision as it did, for example, in the Deceptive Trade Practices Act. Section 5.55, relating to post-marital agreements, was amended in the same bill that amended the present sec. 5.46 of the Family Code, which was part of the Uniform Premarital Agreement Act. The language of sections 5.55 and 5.46 is nearly identical.

I doubt that the legislature would have enacted such statutes, if it simultaneously intended to retain all the non-uniform common-law defenses that made it so difficult to uphold marital property agreements. If common-law defenses are still available, the legislature has made it harder to uphold marital property agreements by retaining all the old traps, while adding two new ones in the form of sections 5.55 and 5.46.

One court has recently disregarded a jury finding that a property agreement was unfair. It upheld the challenged agreement because there was no evidence of the elements required by sec. 5.46. *Chiles v. Chiles*, 779 S.W.2d 127 (Tex. App.—Houston [14th Dist.] 1989). This is the same as holding that sec. 5.46 is the exclusive means of challenging a premarital agreement. I would follow *Chiles* and extend it to hold that sec. 5.55 is the exclusive means of challenging a post-marital agreement.

Notes, Comments & Questions

1. *Daniel v. Daniel* was instrumental in the adoption of TEX. FAM. CODE §§ 4.006(c) and 4.105(c).
2. What is the practical effect of the two sections referenced in the previous comment?

BECK
v.
BECK
814 S.W.2d 745
(Tex. 1991)

CORNYN, JUSTICE.

This is a suit to determine the enforceability of a premarital agreement, entered into in 1977, under section 5.41 of the Texas Family Code[1] and article XVI, section 15, of the Texas Constitution. The trial court granted summary judgment to Lillian Beck, holding that the premarital agreement at issue was enforceable under the 1948 amendment to article XVI, section 15, of the Texas Constitution.[2] The court of appeals affirmed the trial court's judgment. 792 S.W.2d 813. We affirm the judgment of the court of appeals, but for different reasons.

Audrian and Lillian Beck entered into a premarital agreement on October 27, 1977, pursuant to section 5.41(a) of the Texas Family Code,[3] which purported to authorize premarital agreements. Lillian's attorney drafted the agreement. Audrian's attorney reviewed the agreement, which Audrian and Lillian executed in his office. Paragraph four of the agreement provides:

"Notwithstanding that under the laws of the State of Texas the income from respective separate properties of Audrian and Lillian will be community property, they hereby agree that all the properties of every kind and nature, real and personal, held or standing in the name of only one of them shall be considered as a separate property of the one of them in whose name such property is held or stands, and that only properties, whether real or personal, held or standing in their joint names shall be considered as community property."

Audrian died on March 3, 1981. His will was admitted to probate on April 10, 1981. The probate court issued letters testamentary to Ronald Beck, Audrian's only child by a previous marriage, and appointed him independent executor of Audrian's estate.

---

[1] Act of May 14, 1969, 61st Leg., R.S., ch. 888, § 1, 1969 Tex.Gen.Laws 2707, 2729, amended by Act of June 15, 1973, 63rd Leg., R.S., ch. 577, § 31, 1973 Tex.Gen.Laws 1596, 1608 (current version at TEX.FAM.CODE ANN. §§ 5.42, .43, .56 (Vernon Supp.1991)).

[2] TEX. CONST. art. XVI, § 15 (1876, amended 1948).

[3] "Before marriage, persons intending to marry may enter into a marital property agreement as they may desire." Act of May 14, 1969, 61st Leg., R.S., ch. 888, 1969 Tex.Gen.Laws 2707, 2729, amended by Act of June 18, 1987, 70th Leg., R.S., ch. 678, 1987 Tex.Gen.Laws 2530, 2531-32 (current version at TEX.FAM.CODE ANN. §§ 5.42, .43, .56 (Vernon Supp.1991)).

Ronald, in both his individual capacity and in his capacity as independent executor of Audrian's estate, brought suit in the district court against Lillian on March 2, 1984. In his first amended petition, he requested, among other things, a declaratory judgment that the premarital agreement was unenforceable under the 1948 amendment to article XVI, section 15, of the Texas Constitution. The underlying dispute between Ronald and Lillian is whether Audrian's estate owns a one-half interest in the income generated by Lillian's separate property. The disputed property includes income from rental properties and bank accounts, as well as "income and earnings from [Lillian's] separate estate."

In the trial court, Ronald and Lillian both filed motions for partial summary judgment on the issue of the enforceability of the premarital agreement under the Texas Constitution. The trial court granted Lillian's motion for summary judgment. The court of appeals affirmed, holding that the agreement was enforceable under the 1948 amendment to article XVI, section 15, as an "exchange" of each spouse's community interest in future income from separate property. 792 S.W.2d at 816.

The 1948 amendment to article XVI, section 15, of the Texas Constitution provided:

> "All property, both real and personal, of the wife, owned or claimed by her before marriage, and that acquired afterward by gift, devise or descent, shall be the separate property of the wife; and laws shall be passed more clearly defining the rights of the wife, in relation as well to her separate property as that held in common with her husband; provided that husband and wife, without prejudice to pre-existing creditors, may from time to time by written instrument as if the wife were a feme sole partition between themselves in severalty or into equal undivided interests all or any part of their existing community property, or exchange between themselves the community interest of one spouse in any property for the community interest of the other spouse in other community property, whereupon the portion or interest set aside to each spouse shall be and constitute a part of the separate property of such spouse."

This court construed the 1948 amendment in *Williams v. Williams*, 569 S.W.2d 867 (Tex. 1978). We stated that any agreement attempting to recharacterize income or property acquired during marriage as separate property was "void" under article XVI, section 15, of the Texas Constitution. *Id.* at 870.

The court of appeals held that we construed only the "partition" language of the 1948 amendment in our decision in *Williams* and did not reach the issue of whether the agreement could be upheld as an "exchange" of each spouse's community interest. We disagree. In *Williams*, we simply stated that the premarital agreement violated the Texas Constitution and did not distinguish between a "partition" and an "exchange" of property. *Id.* Therefore, the court of appeals' holding, based on the distinction between a "partition" and an "exchange," was erroneous.

Having determined that the premarital agreement is unenforceable under the 1948 amendment, we must decide whether the retroactive application of the 1980 constitutional amendment to article XVI, section 15, of the Texas Constitution can uphold the premarital agreement. The 1980 amendment specifically provided in pertinent part:

> Spouses may from time to time, by written instrument, agree between themselves that the income or property from all or part of the separate property then owned by one of them, or which thereafter might be acquired, shall be the separate property of that spouse.

Tex. H.R.J. Res. 54, 66th Leg., R.S., 1979 Tex. Gen. Laws 3227, 3227.

Ronald contends that the premarital agreement at issue is not enforceable under Williams. Lillian argues that we can apply the 1980 amendment because it was the law in effect when the trial judge rendered judgment. *See Sadler v. Sadler*, 769 S.W.2d 886, 886 (Tex. 1989); *Chiles v. Chiles*, 779

S.W.2d 127, 129 (Tex. App.—Houston [14th Dist.] 1989, writ denied); *Daniel v. Daniel*, 779 S.W.2d 110, 113 n. 3 (Tex. App.—Houston [1st Dist.] 1989, no writ). We agree with Lillian that the agreement is enforceable, but for different reasons.

This court has previously held that the legislature has the power to cure statutes that are invalid under the Texas Constitution by proposing a constitutional amendment that is adopted by the citizens of Texas. *Hutchinson v. Patching*, 103 Tex. 497, 129 S.W. 603 (1910). By passing a constitutional amendment that specifically refers to the invalid statute, the legislature can expressly validate not only the statute, but all actions taken in reliance on the validity of that statute. *Id.* at 501-02, 129 S.W. at 605; *accord Ex parte Southern Ry. Co.*, 556 So.2d 1082, 1090 (Ala.1989); *Fullam v. Brock*, 271 N.C. 145, 155 S.E.2d 737, 741 (1967); *Red Rover Copper Co. v. Industrial Comm'n*, 58 Ariz. 203, 118 P.2d 1102, 1105 (1941); *People ex rel. McClelland v. Roberts*, 148 N.Y. 360, 42 N.E. 1082, 1085 (1896).

The legislature may also impliedly validate an invalid statute by passing a constitutional amendment to cure it. This power is termed the doctrine of implied validation. It permits a constitutional amendment to impliedly validate a statute that was originally beyond the legislature's power to enact if it does not impair the obligation of a contract or impair vested rights. Annotation, *Removal or Suspension of Constitutional Limitation As Affecting Statute Previously Enacted*, 171 A.L.R. 1070, 1072-73 (1947). Several courts in other jurisdictions have adopted the implied validation doctrine. *E.g.*, *Paluck v. Board of County Comm'rs*, 307 N.W.2d 852, 855 (N.D.1981); *Matthews v. Quinton*, 362 P.2d 932, 938-39 (Alaska 1961); *Golden v. People ex rel. Baker*, 101 Colo. 381, 74 P.2d 715, 716 (1937). No court in this state has adopted the doctrine, although one commentator has proposed it as a potential basis for retroactively applying our 1980 constitutional amendment to uphold premarital agreements entered into under section 5.41 of the Texas Family Code. McKnight, *The Constitutional Redefinition of Texas Matrimonial Property As It Affects Antenuptial and Interspousal Transactions*, 13 St. Mary's L.J. 449, 474-75 (1982) [hereinafter McKnight].

In deciding whether the 1980 amendment to article XVI, section 15, of the Texas Constitution impliedly validated section 5.41 of the Texas Family Code and all agreements entered into pursuant to this statute, we must first ascertain whether the legislature intended to apply the amendment retroactively. *See* McKnight at 475. To do so, we look to the language of the amendment, its legislative history, its purpose and the circumstances of its enactment. *Cf.* Tex. Gov't Code Ann. § 311.023 (Vernon 1988) (Statute Construction Aids).

The language of the statute itself is silent regarding any intended validation of section 5.41 or premarital agreements executed before 1980. However, the legislative history of the amendment, its purpose and the circumstances of its enactment persuade us that the legislature intended to cure section 5.41 and validate contracts entered into before the amendment became effective.

The legislative history of the 1980 amendment is enlightening. In a public hearing on House Joint Resolution 54,[4] held on February 28, 1979, before the House Committee on Constitutional Amendments, one witness testified:

> The idea here is just to make it a simple change to allow people to do what they wanted to do all along, and then find out under Texas law or what happens with the IRS later, that surprise, you can't do that. [Emphasis added.]

This testimony demonstrates that one purpose of the amendment was to uphold the intentions of spouses who entered into premarital agreements before 1980. Further, other testimony during the

[4] Tex.H.R.J.Res. 54, 66th Leg., R.S., 1979 Tex.Gen.Laws 3227, 3227.

public hearing and the floor debate in the Texas House of Representatives on April 10, 1979, indicates that the legislators sought to supersede the effect of this court's decision in *Williams* and the federal tax court's ruling in *Estate of Castleberry v. Commissioner of the Internal Revenue Service.*[5] Finally, the circumstances of the passage of the amendment less than two years after *Williams* and *Castleberry* indicate the legislature's intent to apply the constitutional amendment to agreements entered into before 1980. *See* Note, *The 1980 Texas Marital Property Amendment: An Analysis of Its Meaning and Effect*, 33 BAYLOR L. REV. 307, 317 n. 71 (1981).

The amicus curiae contends that retroactive application of the 1980 amendment in this case would impair a vested right. *See* TEX. CONST. art. I, § 16 ("No bill of attainder, ex post facto law, *retroactive law*, or any law impairing the obligation of contracts, shall be made."). The amicus argues that Audrian had a vested right in one-half of Lillian's income because it was characterized as community property by operation of law. *See Hopkins v. Bacon*, 282 U.S. 122, 51 S.Ct. 62, 75 L.Ed. 249 (1930). We disagree. We believe that retroactive application of the 1980 amendment to article XVI, section 15, of the Texas Constitution would not impair any vested rights in this case.

The existence of any vested rights depends on whether the contract was void or voidable when Ronald and Lillian executed it in 1977. Audrian did not have a vested right in one-half of Lillian's income by operation of law, because Lillian had a voidable interest in the contract that the 1980 constitutional amendment impliedly validated. The voidable nature of this interest arises from an exception to the general rule that contracts violating the law are void. 15 S. WILLISTON, A TREATISE ON THE LAW OF CONTRACTS § 1762, at 201-02 (1972) (quoting *Doherty v. Bartlett*, 81 F.2d 920, 926 (1st Cir.1936)) [hereinafter WILLISTON, LAW OF CONTRACTS]. This exception is set out in the RESTATEMENT (SECOND) OF CONTRACTS, which provides:

> In some instances, refusal to enforce a term may frustrate rather than further public policy. This is likely to be the case where legislation was enacted to protect a class of persons to which the promisee belongs in transactions of the kind involved. In such instances, there is no policy against the enforcement of the promise by one who belongs to that class.

RESTATEMENT (SECOND) OF CONTRACTS § 179 comment c (1981) (emphasis added)[6]; *see also* 6A A. CORBIN, CORBIN ON CONTRACTS § 1540, at 833-34 (1962); 14 WILLISTON, LAW OF CONTRACTS § 1630A, at 25.

When the Texas Legislature originally proposed the adoption of the Spanish model of community property laws, it failed to include a constitutional provision incorporating the Spanish rule that future spouses could contract to recharacterize their property as they desired. Cameron, Hoffman & Ytterberg, *Marital and Premarital Agreements*, 39 BAYLOR L. REV. 1095, 1099-1100 (1987) [hereinafter Cameron]; Note, *Antenuptial Agreements: Perspectives On the Texas Constitution and the Community Property System*, 56 TEXAS L. REV. 861, 862-63 (1978) [hereinafter Note]. Early court decisions interpreted our community property laws as establishing an inflexible system that forbade contracts attempting to recharacterize community property. *E.g., Gorman v. Gause*, 56 S.W.2d 855 (Tex. Comm'n App. 1933, judgm't adopted). These decisions were the legal manifestations of the now outmoded belief that women were not capable of managing their affairs and needed the law's protection. CAMERON at 1100; Note at 863.

---

[5] 68 T.C. 682 (1977), *rev'd*, 610 F.2d 1282 (5th Cir.1980). This case held that one-half of the income from a wife's separate property must be included in her husband's gross estate for federal estate tax purposes.

[6] We adopted section 601 of the RESTATEMENT OF CONTRACTS in Hughes v. Hess, 141 Tex. 511, 172 S.W.2d 301 (1943). This section became comment c to section 179 of the RESTATEMENT (SECOND) OF CONTRACTS.

Because Lillian is a member of the class intended to be protected by our earlier community property laws, the legislature and the citizens of Texas may, and did, validate premarital agreements such as this. The legislature and citizens could validate this premarital agreement because it was voidable when the parties entered into it. Because the contract was voidable, Audrian's community property rights in one-half of the income generated by Lillian's separate property never arose by operation of law.

We do not consider our statement in *Williams* that the agreement was "void" to be controlling here. The issue whether the premarital agreement was void or voidable was not before us in *Williams.* Nor was the question of implied validation, as the 1980 amendment had not yet been adopted. The only issue before this court was whether a premarital agreement waiving homestead rights and the exempt personal property set aside was constitutional. *Williams*, 569 S.W.2d at 868; *see also* McKnight at 450. This case, on the other hand, turns on the legal effect of the agreement when it was executed in 1977. Therefore, our prior classification of the agreement as "void," rather than "voidable," is not controlling under these facts. *See Wiener v. Zwieb*, 105 Tex. 262, 269, 141 S.W. 771, 774 (1911).

We hold that the 1980 amendment to article XVI, section 15, of the Texas Constitution demonstrates an intention on the part of the legislature and the people of Texas to not only authorize future premarital agreements, but to impliedly validate section 5.41 of the Texas Family Code and all premarital agreements entered into before 1980 pursuant to that statute. The legislature and the people of Texas have made the public policy determination that premarital agreements should be enforced. If we refuse to enforce Audrian's and Lillian's premarital agreement, we would thwart, rather than advance, our state's public policy enforcing these contracts. This, we decline to do.

Accordingly, we affirm the judgment of the court of appeals.

COOK, JUSTICE, concurring.

The instant contract, as did the contract in *Williams v. Williams*, 569 S.W.2d 867 (Tex. 1978), violated the law when it was written. Contracts violating the law are ordinarily void. 15 S. WILLISTON, A TREATISE ON THE LAW OF CONTRACTS § 1762, at 201-02 (1972). However, such contracts may be upheld when to do otherwise would actually frustrate public policy. RESTATEMENT (SECOND) OF CONTRACTS § 179 comment c (1981). If the contract entered into by Audrian and Lillian Beck were not enforced, the public policy that spouses may divide their property as Audrian and Lillian did would be thwarted.

I write separately to emphasize that retroactive validation based on subsequent law should be conservatively applied. This doctrine should be used only where the public policy is so clearly and broadly stated as to be unmistakable. The amendment of the state constitution to allow recharacterization of property is such an instance.

I concur in the judgment of this court.

Questions

1. What do you believe JUSTICE CORNYN was alluding to when he said, ". . . Lillian is a member of the class intended to be protected by our earlier community property laws, . . . ?"

2. Could this reasoning affect application of the *Beck* result across genders?

3. What effect does *Beck* have on other clauses of TEX. CONST. art. XVI, § 15?

FANNING
v.
FANNING

828 S.W.2d 135 (Tex. App.—Waco 1992),
aff'd in part, rev'd in part, 847 S.W.2d 225 (Tex. 1993)

CUMMINGS, JUSTICE.

Whitney Fanning appeals the final decree of divorce in which the trial court awarded the vast majority of the Fannings' assets and the custody of their three children to Nita Fanning. Because the court failed to enforce a premarital agreement and an enforceable partition agreement, we reverse that part of the judgment divesting Whitney Fanning of title to his separate property and dividing the community property contrary to the agreement of the parties. However, we affirm that part of the judgment awarding custody of the children to Nita Fanning and ordering Whitney Fanning to pay $3,000 per month for the support of the children.

THE PREMARITAL AGREEMENT

Whitney Fanning and Nita Kissel entered into a premarital agreement on August 15, 1980, pursuant to section 5.41(a) of the Texas Family Code,[1] which purported to authorize premarital agreements. Both parties were practicing attorneys when the premarital agreement was executed. They were married on September 27, 1980.

In point two, Whitney Fanning contends that the trial court erred in setting aside the premarital agreement because (1) the court erroneously concluded that the agreement was unconstitutional and void, (2) the court erroneously concluded that the agreement did not operate to partition or exchange the future income from separate property or the community interest in income from personal efforts. (3) Nita Fanning failed to satisfy the burden of proof required by section 5.46 of the Texas Family Code, and (4) the evidence was legally or factually insufficient to support the court's failure to enforce the premarital agreement.

Paragraph six of the agreement provides

> 6.01) During their marriage, all income and revenue (other than that which is part of the property itself) from the separate property of each party hereto is the community property of the parties if so defined by Texas law. However, the parties understand that the 66th Texas legislature approved H.J.R. 54, to be submitted to the voters on November 1980, by the terms of which spouses may, by agreement between themselves, provide that the income from separate property owned by either of them, or thereafter acquired, shall be the separate property of the spouse owning such separate property. If such amendment to Article XVI, Section 15, of the Texas Constitution is approved by the voters, the parties agree that as soon as legally possible all income from their respective estates shall be the separate property of the spouse from whose separate estate such income is derived.
>
> 6.02) The parties agree that each may, from time to time, designate certain banks as his or her agent to assist in carrying out this Agreement by administering accounts in the name of the respective party, by the name of the party adding "as separate property," or otherwise, to the end that all funds which are deposited to the separate accounts of the parties hereto and in-

---

[1] "Before marriage, persons intending to marry may enter into a marital property agreement as they may desire." Act of June 2, 1969, 61st Leg., R.S., ch. 888, § 1, 1969 Tex.Gen.Laws 2707, 2729, amended by Act of June 1, 1987, 70th Leg., R.S., ch. 678, § 1, 1987 Tex.Gen.Laws 2530, 2530-32 (current version at TEX.FAM.CODE ANN. §§ 5.41-.50 (Vernon Supp.1992)).

come therefrom will be identified as the separate property of the party in whose name such funds are held. As received, the respective parties shall deposit funds received that are the income or revenue from their respective separate property into one of their respective several or separate property accounts created in their respective and on deposit (if not before) such funds shall be the separate property of the spouse whose separate property produced such income or revenue, if so provided by this Agreement. The parties hereto hereby instruct any bank holding such funds on deposit as provided in this paragraph that such funds are the separate property of the party in whose name such deposit was made as provided in this paragraph.

VALIDITY OF THE PREMARITAL AGREEMENT

When this premarital agreement was executed in August 1980, it was void to the extent that it attempted to recharacterize income or other property acquired during the marriage as separate property. *See Williams v. Williams*, 569 S.W.2d 867, 870 (Tex. 1978).[2] Furthermore, income and revenue from separate property was community property because it was not acquired by "gift, devise or descent." *See* TEX. CONST. art. XVI, § 15. However, article XVI, section 15, of the Texas Constitution was amended in November 1980 to allow "persons about to marry and spouses" to partition or exchange community property "then existing or to be acquired" in the future. *Id.* The 1980 amendment also provided that "the spouses may from time to time, by written instrument, agree between themselves that the income or property from all or part of the separate property then owned by one of them, or which thereafter might be acquired, shall be the separate property of that spouse. . . ." TEX. CONST. art. XVI, § 15 (1980, amended 1987).[3]

The Texas Supreme Court held in *Beck* that the 1980 constitutional amendment impliedly validated section 5.41 of the Texas Family Code and all agreements entered into before November 4, 1980, pursuant to that statute. *Beck*, 814 S.W.2d at 749. In *Beck*, the parties agreed that "all the properties . . . held or standing in the name of only one of them shall be considered as a separate property of the one of them in whose name such property is held or stands." *Id.* at 746. Apparently, the supreme court found that the agreement was validated by the clause authorizing the "partition . . . or exchange . . . of community property . . . to be acquired." *See id.* at 747.

Because paragraph 6.02 of the Fannings' premarital agreement was substantially similar to the agreement upheld in *Beck*, that portion of the agreement was enforceable. Therefore, the court erred in setting aside paragraph 6.02 of the premarital agreement.

Unlike the agreement upheld in *Beck*, however, paragraph 6.01 of the Fannings' premarital agreement deals with income from separate property, regardless of whether it was deposited into an account designated as the separate property of one of the spouses. *See id.* at 746. Although the portion of the constitutional amendment validating the partition and exchange of property "then existing or to be acquired" applies to "persons about to marry and spouses," the portion of the amendment validating written agreements concerning income or property derived from separate property applies only to spouses. *See* TEX. CONST. art. XVI, § 15.[4]

---

[2] *But see* Beck v. Beck, 814 S.W.2d 745, 749 (Tex. 1991) (agreement entered under the 1948 amendment to article XVI, section 15, of the Texas Constitution was "voidable" rather than "void").

[3] Non-substantive changes were made to this clause by constitutional amendment in 1987. Article XVI, section 15, of the Texas Constitution now provides, "spouses also may from time to time, by written instrument, agree between themselves that the income or property from all or part of the separate property then owned or which thereafter might be acquired by only one of them, shall be the separate property of that spouse. . . ." TEX.CONST. art. XVI, § 15.

[4] This constitutional distinction between partition and exchange agreements and agreements concerning income from separate property was reflected by the 1981 and 1987 amendments to the Texas Family Code, enacted by the

Section 5.41 of the Texas Family Code, as it existed at the time the Fannings entered into the premarital agreement, appeared to allow persons intending to marry to enter into enforceable agreements concerning their property as they saw fit.[5] The scope of section 5.41 was addressed by the Texas Supreme Court in *Williams*:

> This statute should be construed as broadly as possible in order to allow the parties as much flexibility to contract with respect to property or other rights incident to the marriage, provided the constitutional and statutory definitions of separate and community property or the requirements of public policy are not violated. *Williams*, 569 S.W.2d at 870.

Because the Texas Constitution remains the ultimate authority on the character of marital property, a premarital agreement entered into pursuant to section 5.41 may not violate the constitutional definitions of separate and community property. *See Arnold v. Leonard*, 273 S.W. 799, 802 (Tex. 1925). We note that the Texas Supreme Court in *Beck* addressed only the retroactive application of the 1980 amendment, rather than the scope of premarital agreements authorized by that amendment. *See Beck*, 814 S.W.2d at 748.

The 1980 amendment did not authorize persons intending to marry to enter into agreements that the income from one spouse's separate property would thereafter be the owner's separate property.[6] Therefore, we hold that the trial court correctly concluded that paragraph 6.01 of the premarital agreement was unenforceable to the extent the parties merely agreed that "as soon as legally possible all income from their respective separate estates shall be the separate property of the spouse from whose estate such income is derived."

According to section 5.44 of the Texas Family Code, "A premarital agreement becomes effective on marriage." TEX. FAM. CODE ANN. § 5.44 (Vernon Supp.1992). As a result, some commentators have suggested that, by statutory definition, a premarital agreement is between spouses who are authorized to enter into agreements concerning income or property derived from separate property.[7] However, the constitutional distinction between partition and exchange agreements and agreements concerning income from separate property cannot be redefined by the legislature. *See Arnold*, 273 S.W. at 802. Therefore, section 5.44 provides no basis for validating paragraph 6.01 of the premarital agreement.

Arguably, a premarital agreement could partition or exchange income from separate property as property to be acquired in the future.[8] However, the language of paragraph 6.01 indicates that the parties were not contemplating a partition or exchange of property to be acquired during the marriage. Instead, paragraph 6.01 expressly refers to the portion of the 1980 amendment that authorized agreements concerning income or property derived from separate property. Because they were clearly at-

---

legislature to implement the 1980 amendment to article XVI, section 15, of the Texas Constitution. Although section 5.53 of the Texas Family Code authorizes agreements between spouses concerning income or property derived from separate property, the Texas Uniform Premarital Agreement Act does not expressly authorize such an agreement between "prospective spouses." *See* TEX.FAM.CODE ANN. §§ 5.41-.50, 5.53 (Vernon Supp.1992).

[5] *See* Cameron, Hoffman & Ytterberg, *Marital and Premarital Agreements*, 39 BAYLOR L. REV. 1095, 1101-02 (1987).

[6] *See* Featherston & Springer, *Marital Property Law in Texas: The Past, Present and Future*, 39 BAYLOR L. REV. 861, 884 (1987).

[7] *See* Mercing, *The Uniform Premarital Agreement Act: Survey of its Impact in Texas and Across the Nation*, 42 BAYLOR L. REV. 825, 844 (1990).

[8] Section 5.41 of the Texas Family Code, as amended in 1987, defines property as "an interest, present or future, legal or equitable, vested or contingent, in real or personal property, *including income and earnings*." TEX.FAM.CODE ANN. § 5.41(2) (Vernon Supp.1992) (emphasis added).

tempting to implement the portion of the 1980 amendment that applied only to spouses, we hold that paragraph 6.01 was not validated by the constitutional amendment authorizing the partition and exchange of property to be acquired in the future. Therefore, the income from separate property remained community property unless otherwise recharacterized by a valid provision of the premarital agreement or an enforceable partition agreement executed during the marriage. As in *Williams*, the invalid provision is severable from the valid portions of the agreement because the invalid provision does not constitute the agreement's main or essential purpose. *See Williams*, 569 S.W.2d at 871.

Paragraph two of the premarital agreement provided that the property described in Schedule A "is and shall remain the separate property of Future Husband," and that the property described in Schedule B "is and shall remain the separate property of Future Wife." The "incomes and revenues from Whitney E. Fanning practice of law" were designated as his separate property. Likewise, "all incomes derived from future Wife's law practice" were designated as her separate property. In *Huff v. Huff*, 554 S.W.2d 841, 842-44 (Tex. Civ. App.—Waco, 1977, writ dism'd), this court held that section 5.41 of the Texas Family Code authorized such an agreement. Furthermore, as a partition or exchange of property to be acquired in the future, this agreement was impliedly validated by the 1980 constitutional amendment. *See* TEX. CONST. art. XVI, § 15. Therefore, the court erred in finding that during the marriage all income earned by Whitney Fanning in the practice of law was community property. The court also erred in concluding that the provision of the premarital agreement providing for the exchange of future earnings from the practice of law was "unconstitutional and therefore void at the time of its execution." However, to the extent that either spouse earned income from personal efforts other than the practice of law, the court correctly concluded that the premarital agreement, "did not operate to partition and/or exchange the community property interests in the parties' income from personal efforts."

In point five, Whitney Fanning argues that the court erred in refusing to make an equal division of the community property. Paragraph ten of the premarital agreement provides:

> In the event the parties marriage is dissolved by divorce or annulment by any court, wherever located, each party is to retain his or her separate estate as his or her separate property following the dissolution. *All community property is to be divided equally between the parties according to its value.* To effectuate this provision, Future Husband and Future Wife relinquish and disclaim any right they may have to seek a division of their property other than in accordance with this paragraph, and agree to indemnify the other for the value of any property that may be awarded by a court in excess of the value that would result if division were in accordance with this paragraph." (Emphasis added).

In determining the validity of paragraph ten, we again construe the former section 5.41 of the Texas Family Code[9] "as broadly as possible in order to allow the parties as much flexibility to contract . . . , provided the constitutional and statutory definitions of separate and community property or the requirements of public policy are not violated." *See Williams*, 569 S.W.2d at 870. Article XVI, section 15, of the Texas Constitution provides that "the portion or interest set aside to each spouse shall be and constitute a part of the separate property and estate of such spouse or future spouse." TEX. CONST. art XVI, § 15. By definition, a partition or exchange of community property results in the recharacterization of community property. Because an agreement to equally divide the commu-

[9] Section 5.43(a)(3) of the Texas Family Code now authorizes parties to a premarital agreement to contract with respect to "the disposition of property on separation [or] marital dissolution. . . ." TEX.FAM.CODE ANN. § 5.43(a)(3) (Vernon Supp.1992). However, as in Beck, 814 S.W.2d at 746, we apply the law in effect at the time the agreement was executed. The retroactive application of sections 5.46 and 5.55 of the Texas Family Code is distinguishable because the enforcement provisions of the statute are procedural in nature. *See* TEX.FAM.CODE ANN. §§ 5.46, .55 (Vernon Supp.1992).

nity property involves the disposition of community property upon dissolution rather than the recharacterization of community property as separate property, the 1980 amendment to the constitution does not appear to authorize such an agreement. However, article XVI, section 15, also authorizes the legislature to more clearly define "the rights of the spouses, in relation to separate and community property. . . ." *Id.* This is exactly what the legislature was attempting to do in the former section 5.41 of the Texas Family Code, as well as in the Uniform Premarital Agreement Act, which replaced section 5.41 in 1987. Therefore, paragraph ten of the premarital agreement was constitutionally authorized by section 5.41.[10]

An agreement to equally divide community property also appears to encroach upon the trial court's statutory duty to "order a division of the estate of the parties in a manner that the court deems just and right, having due regard for the rights of each party. . . ." *See* TEX. FAM. CODE ANN. § 3.63(a) (Vernon Supp.1992). However, because section 5.41 had more clearly defined "the rights of the parties," the trial court, according to section 3.63(a), must give "due regard" to the terms of a premarital agreement authorized by the constitution. *See* TEX. CONST. art. XVI, § 15; TEX. FAM. CODE ANN. § 3.63(a) (Vernon Supp.1992). Therefore, the court erred to the extent that it failed to equally divide any community property of the parties.

ENFORCEABILITY OF THE PREMARITAL AGREEMENT

The court expressly found that "[O]n or about August 15, 1980, the parties executed an Agreement in Contemplation of Marriage." However, the court did not find that the agreement was executed involuntarily or that it was unconscionable. *See* TEX. FAM. CODE ANN. § 5.46 (Vernon Supp.1992). Because Whitney Fanning requested additional findings of fact related to the court's failure to enforce the premarital agreement, the judgment may not be supported upon appeal by a presumed finding that the agreement was unenforceable under section 5.46. *See* TEX. R. CIV. P. 299.

The premarital agreement, with the exception of paragraph 6.01, was both valid and enforceable. Because the trial court erred in setting the premarital agreement aside, points two and five are sustained.

THE PARTITION AGREEMENTS

Whitney and Nita Fanning executed partition agreements on August 14, 1981, and May 14, 1986, pursuant to section 5.42 of the Texas Family Code,[11] which purported to authorize the partition or exchange of community property. Each partition agreement recharacterized property listed on attached exhibits as the separate property of the designated spouse. In points one and three, Whitney Fanning contends that the court erred in setting aside the 1986 partition agreement and in refusing to enforce the 1981 partition agreement.

---

[10] Act of June 2, 1969, 61st Leg., R.S., ch. 888, § 1, Tex.Gen.Laws 2707, 2729, (amended 1987).

[11] When the 1981 partition was executed, section 5.42(a) of the Texas Family Code provided: "At any time, the spouses may partition between themselves, in severalty or in equal undivided interests, all or any part of their community property. They may exchange between themselves the interest of one spouse in any community property for the interest of the other spouse in other community property. A partition or exchange must be in writing and subscribed by both parties." Act of June 2, 1969, 61st Leg., R.S., ch. 888, § 1, 1969 Tex.Gen.Laws 2707, 2729, amended by Act of May 22, 1981, 67th Leg., R.S., ch. 782, § 2, 1981 Tex.Gen.Laws 2964, 2965. When the 1986 partition was executed, section 5.42 of the Texas Family Code provided: "At any time, the spouses may partition or exchange between themselves any part of their community property, then existing or to be acquired, as they may desire. Property or a property interest transferred to a spouse by a partition or exchange agreement becomes his or her separate property." Act of May 22, 1981, 67th Leg., R.S., ch. 782, § 2, 1981 Tex.Gen.Laws 2964, 2965, amended by Act of June 1, 1987, 70th Leg., R.S., ch. 678, § 1, 1987 Tex.Gen.Laws 2530, 2531-32 (current version at TEX.FAM.CODE ANN. § 5.52 (Vernon Supp.1992)).

VALIDITY OF THE PARTITION AGREEMENTS

The court concluded that neither partition agreement operated "to partition and/or exchange the community property interest in future income from the separate estates of the parties." In fact, neither partition agreement provides "that the income or property from all or part of the separate property then owned or which thereafter might be acquired by only one of them, shall be the separate property of that spouse." *See* TEX. CONST. art XVI, § 15.

However, both of the partition agreements provide that:

> There shall be from this day no community property interest in the above described real and personal property and we shall each hold the above described real and personal property as our sole and separate property in the manner indicated to the exclusion of the other spouse."

This provision extended the partition and exchange of the property listed on the attached exhibits to property "to be acquired" in the future, as authorized by the 1980 constitutional amendment. *See* TEX. CONST. art. XVI, § 15. Therefore, as in *Beck*, the future income from the separate-property assets listed on the attached exhibits remained the separate property of the designated spouse. *See Beck*, 814 S.W.2d at 746.

The court also concluded that neither partition agreement operated "to partition and/or exchange the community property interest in the parties' income from personal efforts." Although such an agreement was authorized by the 1980 constitutional amendment, as the partition or exchange of community property "to be acquired" in the future, neither partition agreement attempted to recharacterize the parties' income from personal efforts as separate property. *See* TEX. CONST. art XVI, § 15.

The 1986 partition agreement designated Whitney Fanning's law practice as his separate property. However, because the 1986 partition agreement did not expressly designate the income from his law practice as his separate property, the court correctly concluded that neither partition agreement operated to partition or exchange the community-property interest in the parties' income from personal efforts. *See Dewey v. Dewey*, 745 S.W.2d 514, 517 (Tex. App.—Corpus Christi 1988, writ denied). This is of little consequence, however, because the premarital agreement had previously effected a partition or exchange of the community-property interest in the primary source of the parties' income from personal efforts—"all incomes and revenues from [the] Whitney E. Fanning practice of law."

ENFORCEABILITY OF THE PARTITION AGREEMENTS

The court concluded as a matter of law that the 1986 partition agreement was unconscionable. The court also found that:

> Prior to the execution of the Partition Agreement dated May 12, 1986, Nita Kissel Fanning was not provided a fair and reasonable disclosure of the property or financial obligations of the other party; and Nita Kissel Fanning did not voluntarily and expressly waive, in writing, the right to disclosure of the property or financial obligations of the other party beyond the disclosure provided; and Nita Kissel Fanning did not have, or reasonably could not have had, an adequate knowledge of the property or financial obligations of the other party.

Whitney Fanning argues that the evidence was legally or factually insufficient to support the court's conclusion of law that the agreement was unconscionable or the court's findings of fact related to the disclosure of property or financial obligations. Concisely stated, Whitney Fanning contends that Nita Fanning failed to carry her burden of proof under section 5.55 of the Texas Family Code. Section 5.55 provides that:

> (a) A partition or exchange agreement is not enforceable if the party against whom enforcement is sought proves that:

(1) that party did not execute the agreement voluntarily; or

(2) the agreement was unconscionable when it was executed and, before execution of the agreement, that party:

(A) was not provided a fair and reasonable disclosure of the property or financial obligations of the other party;

(B) did not voluntarily and expressly waive, in writing, any right to disclosure of the property or financial obligations of the party beyond the disclosure provided; and

(C) did not have, or reasonably could not have had, an adequate knowledge of the property or financial obligations of the other party.

(b) An issue of unconscionability of a partition or exchange agreement shall be decided by the court as a matter of law."

TEX. FAM. CODE ANN. § 5.55 (Vernon Supp.1992).

In response, Nita Fanning argues that section 5.55 does not apply to the 1986 partition agreement. Prior to September 1, 1987, the enforcement of marital agreements was governed by section 5.45.[12] When the legislature amended the Texas Family Code in 1987, it did not expressly provide that the amendatory provisions should be given retrospective application. However, the general rule is that, in the absence of an express intention to the contrary, legislation dealing with a procedural matter applies to pending litigation to the extent that subsequent steps in the case are to be taken under the new rule. *Brooks v. Texas Employers Ins. Ass'n*, 358 S.W.2d 412, 414 (Tex. Civ. App.—Houston 1962, writ ref'd n.r.e.). Section 5.55 simply sets forth the revised procedural scheme for challenging the enforceability of a partition or exchange agreement. Therefore, Nita Fanning had the burden of proof under section 5.55 because the provisions of former section 5.45 no longer applied. *See Daniel v. Daniel*, 779 S.W.2d 110, 113 (Tex. App.—Houston [1st Dist.] 1989, no writ).

Although section 5.55(b) provides that the issue of unconscionability shall be decided by the court as a matter of law, the legislature and the courts have not defined "unconscionable" in the context of marital-property agreements. *See* TEX. FAM. CODE ANN. § 5.55(b) (Vernon Supp.1992). Instead, the issue of unconscionability must be addressed on a case-by-case basis, looking to the entire atmosphere in which the agreement was made. *See Pearce v. Pearce*, 824 S.W.2d 195, 199 (Tex. App.—El Paso, 1991, no writ). In *Chiles v. Chiles*, 779 S.W.2d 127, 129 (Tex. App.—Houston [14th Dist.] 1989, writ denied), the court held that a factual finding that an agreement was unfair to one spouse did not satisfy the burden of proof required by the statute.

In *Wade v. Austin*, 524 S.W.2d 79, 86 (Tex. Civ. App.—Texarkana 1975, no writ), the court addressed unconscionability of a contract under section 2.302 of the Texas Business and Commerce Code:

> In determining whether a contract is unconscionable or not, the court must look to the entire atmosphere in which the agreement was made, the alternatives, if any, which were available to the parties at the time of the making of the contract; the non-bargaining ability of one party; whether the contract is illegal or against public policy, and, whether the contact is oppressive or unreasonable. At the same time, a party who knowingly enters a lawful but improvident contract is not entitled to protection by the courts. . . . A contract is not unenforceable on the ground that it yields a return disproportionate to the expenditures in time and money, where there has been no mistake or unfairness and the party against whom it is sought to be enforced has received and enjoyed the benefits.

[12] Act of May 22, 1981, 67th Leg., R.S., ch. 782, § 2, 1981 Tex.Gen.Laws 2964, 2965, amended by Act of June 1, 1987, 70th Leg., R.S., ch. 678, § 1, 1987 Tex.Gen.Laws 2530, 2531-32 (current version at TEX.FAM.CODE ANN. § 5.55 (Vernon Supp.1992)).

As in *Wade*, we will focus upon the circumstances at the time the agreement was executed rather than the disproportionate effect of the agreement. *See id.* Mr. Fanning testified that severe marital problems developed in April and May 1986. On the night before the agreement was signed, Mrs. Fanning had played tennis as a substitute in a mixed-doubles tennis league. When she returned home, Mr. Fanning would not talk to her, and he was "pouting." She testified that, when she asked him what was wrong, he expressed his concern about going to prison in connection with a criminal investigation against the district attorney of McLennan County. According to Mrs. Fanning, her husband wanted to make sure that she did not take all the money he had accumulated and "run off with someone else" while he was in prison—a possibility that he envisioned because she had played tennis with another man that night.

Mrs. Fanning testified that Mr. Fanning assured her that he would never use the agreement against her; and that he threatened to divorce her and take the children if she did not sign the partition agreement. At that time, Mr. Fanning had won ten consecutive custody cases for fathers. Because Mrs. Fanning considered his threats to be valid, she believed that her only alternative was to sign the agreement. *See Matthews v. Matthews*, 725 S.W.2d 275, 279 (Tex. App.—Houston [1st Dist.] 1987, writ ref'd n.r.e.) (threatening to permanently deprive spouse of custody of the children constituted duress in the execution of a partition agreement).

That night, Mr. Fanning got out of bed and went to his law office to prepare the partition agreement. He called her the next day and told her to come to the office to sign the agreement. Although she remembered signing the partition agreement, she did not remember signing the accompanying deeds. She testified, however, that she would have signed whatever he put in front of her that day. A witness called by Mrs. Fanning testified that Mr. Fanning "just doesn't take no for an answer." According to the witness, when Mr. Fanning "wants to do something, he wants to do it and he wants to do it his way." Even the psychologist who testified on Mr. Fanning's behalf characterized him as manipulative and that, given his competitiveness, his manipulative tendencies, and his aggression, "he could get very angry and be retaliatory."

Considering the circumstances, the alternatives, and Nita Fanning's bargaining ability, we hold that the court did not err in concluding that the 1986 partition agreement was unconscionable when it was executed. Next, we must determine if the evidence is legally or factually sufficient to support the court's findings related to the disclosure of Mr. Fanning's property or financial obligations.

On direct examination, Mrs. Fanning testified that "At no time did [she] have a disclosure nor did [she] waive in writing any disclosure, which [she] since learned was a requirement." She believed that her husband wanted to keep her "ignorant of everything for [her] own protection" during the criminal investigation against the district attorney. She also testified that, because the district attorney's house had been searched, her husband was afraid that their house would be searched and that there was no safe place in Waco to keep anything.

Mrs. Fanning also testified that she did not have any knowledge of how much money was in an account, how much money her husband was making, or how much property he actually owned. Furthermore, Mr. Fanning's own psychologist described him as secretive. We find the evidence legally and factually sufficient to support the court's findings related to Mr. Fanning's failure to disclose his property or financial obligations. Therefore, we overrule point of error one.

The court expressly found that "On or about August 14, 1981, the parties executed a Partition Agreement." However, the court did not find that the 1981 partition agreement was executed involuntarily or that it was unconscionable. *See* TEX. FAM. CODE ANN. § 5.55 (Vernon Supp.1992). Because Whitney Fanning requested additional findings of fact related to the court's failure to enforce the 1981 partition agreement, the judgment may not be supported upon appeal by a presumed finding that the agreement was unenforceable under section 5.55. *See* TEX. R. CIV. P. 299.

The 1981 partition agreement was both valid and enforceable. Because the trial court erred in refusing to enforce the 1981 partition agreement, point three is sustained.

DIVESTITURE OF SEPARATE PROPERTY

In point four, Whitney Fanning contends that the trial court's failure to enforce the premarital agreement and the partition agreements resulted in the divestiture of his separate property. Because the court correctly concluded that the 1986 partition agreement was unenforceable, we will limit our discussion to any divestiture resulting from the court's failure to enforce the premarital agreement and the 1981 partition agreement. Although trial courts have a broad latitude in the division of the marital community property, that discretion does not extend to a taking of the fee title to the separate property of one spouse and its donation to the other spouse. *Eggemeyer v. Eggemeyer*, 554 S.W.2d 137, 142 (Tex. 1977). Separate property may, however, be set aside to assure compliance with an order for child support. *Id.*; TEX. FAM. CODE ANN. § 14.05(a) (Vernon Supp.1992).

In amended findings of fact, the court found that "All property not specifically listed as separate property in these Findings of Fact is community property of the parties." Although assets valued at approximately $50,000 were listed as Nita Fanning's separate property, nothing was listed as Whitney Fanning's separate property. In an amended conclusion of law, the trial court concluded that a divestiture of Whitney Fanning's interest in the assets awarded to Nita Fanning was "a just and fair division of the assets of the parties." The court awarded Nita Fanning at least a fifty-percent interest in a number of assets that appear to have been recharacterized as Whitney Fanning's separate property by the premarital agreement and the 1981 partition agreement. Some of the assets recharacterized by agreement as his separate property, such as "all retirement and pension accounts in his name," were expressly awarded to Nita Fanning by the trial court. However, it is unclear from the divorce decree whether certain other assets awarded to Nita Fanning are the same as or traceable to similar assets recharacterized by agreement as Whitney Fanning's separate property. Because the court's failure to enforce the premarital agreement and the 1981 partition agreement resulted in the divestiture of his separate property, we sustain point of error four with regard to the property recharacterized by those two agreements. On remand, the court must determine the character of the assets according to the valid and enforceable agreements of the parties. As in *Eggemeyer*, however, the trial court is also instructed to determine whether any further arrangements for the support of the children should be made pursuant to section 14.05 of the Texas Family Code. *See Eggemeyer*, 554 S.W.2d at 142; TEX. FAM. CODE ANN. § 14.05 (Vernon Supp.1992).

Because our disposition of points two through five requires a reversal and remand regarding the property division, we do not reach points six and seven, which are related to the court's just and right division of community property.

BREACH OF FIDUCIARY DUTY

In point eight, Whitney Fanning contends that the trial court erred in finding that he breached his fiduciary duty and that Nita Fanning suffered damage in the amount of $245,000. He argues that these findings were not supported by legally or factually sufficient evidence, or that they were based upon erroneously admitted hearsay evidence. The court filed the following findings of fact related to a breach of fiduciary duty:

> Whitney Ely Fanning breached his fiduciary duty to his wife by diverting community assets for the use and benefit of his paramour and her family and by disposing of community money without the consent of Nita Kissel Fanning and to her detriment.

Whitney Ely Fanning breached his fiduciary duty to his wife by disposing of and/or secreting significant community assets, to-wit: a certificate of deposit in the Cayman National Bank and Trust Company Limited, in the approximate amount of $295,000.

Nita Kissel Fanning has suffered damage in the amount of $245,000 as a result of the breach of Whitney Ely Fanning's fiduciary duty.

The courts have taken a dim view toward gifts by the husband to "strangers" of the marriage, "particularly of the female variety." *Spruill v. Spruill*, 624 S.W.2d 694, 697 (Tex. App.—El Paso 1981, writ dism'd). Constructive fraud is the breach of a legal or equitable duty, which the law declares fraudulent because it violates a fiduciary relationship. *Carnes v. Meador*, 533 S.W.2d 365, 370 (Tex. Civ. App.—Dallas 1975, writ ref'd n.r.e.). Such a trust relationship exists between a husband and wife with regard to the community property controlled by one spouse. *Id.* Thus, a presumption of constructive fraud arises when a spouse unfairly disposes of the other spouse's interest in community property. *Id.* The burden of proof is, therefore, upon the disposing spouse to prove the fairness of the disposition of the other spouse's one-half community ownership. *Id.*

Mr. Fanning testified that in April 1987 he wrote a check in the amount of $13,000 that "probably would have been for the down payment" on a house purchased by his paramour, Carol Villareal. Mrs. Fanning identified this as one of the checks missing from the documents produced by her husband prior to trial. Mr. Fanning also acknowledged that, in December 1987, he wrote a $3,000 check to Villareal for cosmetic surgery. He described the check as a bonus resulting from her employment with his law practice. However, Mrs. Fanning testified that, at about the same time, her husband told her they could not afford treatment recommended by her orthodontist and that Mr. Fanning refused to agree to pay for it. Mr. Fanning took Villareal to Mexico in 1987 and to Jamaica in 1989. He also testified that in 1988 he gave $6,000 to Villareal's mother for the purchase of an automobile. In *Mazique v. Mazique*, 742 S.W.2d 805, 807-08 (Tex. App.—Houston [1st Dist.] 1987, no writ), the court held that similar evidence was legally and factually sufficient to support the trial court's award of damages for constructive fraud.

Mr. Fanning also admitted that he contributed $40,000 to charitable organizations several months prior to trial. Property possessed by either spouse during marriage is presumed to be community property. TEX. FAM. CODE ANN. § 5.02 (Vernon Supp.1992). He testified that all gifts were made out of separate property, but he failed to rebut the community-property presumption by offering clear and convincing evidence tracing the property and its mutations back to his separate estate. *See Scott v. Scott*, 805 S.W.2d 835, 837 (Tex. App.—Waco 1991, writ denied). Although one spouse may make moderate gifts of community property for just causes, excessive or capricious gifts made with intent to defraud the other spouse may be set aside as a constructive fraud. *Hartman v. Crain*, 398 S.W.2d 387, 390 (Tex. Civ. App.—Houston 1966, no writ). One of Whitney Fanning's secretaries testified that Mr. Fanning mailed a significant sum of money to a number of charities during the summer of 1989. She also testified that Mr. Fanning's other secretary obtained a list of charities from the library and that each of the secretaries was responsible for addressing two hundred envelopes. We hold that the trial court rightfully could have considered the circumstances and timing of the charitable contributions in finding that such a disposition of community funds was unfair to the rights of Nita Fanning.

Mrs. Fanning testified that her husband made cash withdrawals from his personal account totaling $94,850 in 1987 and $50,050 in 1988 and the court admitted other evidence of significant cash withdrawals from his personal and office accounts. Although property possessed by either spouse during marriage is presumed to be community property, this presumption may be rebutted by clear and convincing evidence tracing the property and its mutations back to a spouse's separate estate. *Scott*, 805 S.W.2d at 837; TEX. FAM. CODE ANN. § 5.02 (Vernon Supp.1992). Because the court had previously concluded that the premarital agreement was unconstitutional and void, the court assumed that the funds in Whitney Fanning's personal and office accounts were community property. However, because the premarital agreement had recharacterized "accounts in the name of the respective party" as separate property, no fraud on the marital estate would have resulted from the disposition of funds from a bank account in his name.

Over Whitney Fanning's hearsay objection, the court admitted into evidence copies of two deposit slips reflecting a certificate of deposit in a Cayman Island bank. Mrs. Fanning testified that the funds in the Cayman Island account were from her husband's law practice. Again, the court erroneously concluded that these funds were community property. Because the premarital agreement effectively recharacterized the income from Whitney Fanning's law practice as his separate property, he owed no fiduciary duty to his wife with regard to the funds on deposit in the Cayman Island account. It is, therefore, unnecessary to address the hearsay complaint.

We hold that there is legally and factually sufficient evidence to support the court's finding that Whitney Fanning breached his fiduciary duty by "diverting community assets for the use and benefit of his paramour," and by "disposing of community assets without the consent" of Nita Fanning. However, there is no evidence to support a finding of a breach of fiduciary duty with regard to funds withdrawn from bank accounts in Whitney Fanning's name or the certificate of deposit in the Cayman Island bank. As a result, the court's award of damages is excessive. Therefore, we sustain point of error eight in part and remand for the trial court to determine the amount of community funds disposed of unfairly by Whitney Fanning.

* * *

Accordingly, the portion of the judgment granting the divorce, awarding custody, and ordering child-support payments is severed from the property division and affirmed. *See Scott*, 805 S.W.2d at 842. The portion of the judgment related to the division of property and the breach of fiduciary duty is reversed, and that portion of the cause is remanded for the trial court to enforce the premarital agreement and the 1981 partition agreement and to reconsider the amount of damages caused by the breach of fiduciary duty.

FANNING
v.
FANNING

847 S.W.2d 225
(Tex. 1993)

OPINION ON MOTION FOR REHEARING

PER CURIAM.

In this divorce case Nita Fanning challenges the validity of a prenuptial agreement, claiming that it is unconstitutional and also that it was executed under duress and is unconscionable. The trial court found the agreement unconstitutional but did not make findings for Nita on her other claims; the court also refused Whitney Fanning's request to find that the agreement was voluntarily entered into. The trial court granted the divorce, awarded custody of the couple's three children to Nita, ordered Whitney to pay child support, awarded Nita damages for Whitney's breach of fiduciary duty based in part on the unenforceability of the prenuptial agreement, and divided the marital estate. While the case was pending before the court of appeals, this Court issued its opinion in *Beck v. Beck*, 814 S.W.2d 745 (Tex. 1991), as a result of which the appeals court held that the premarital agreement is not unconstitutional and that it should be enforced. The court of appeals reversed the property division and award of damages for breach of fiduciary duty, and remanded the case for reconsideration of these issues and enforcement of the premarital agreement. In all other respects the divorce decree was affirmed. 828 S.W.2d 135.

We agree that the case must be remanded to the trial court, but we conclude that the issues to be reconsidered should not be so narrowly confined. The trial court should not, in the interest of justice, be required to enforce the premarital agreement but should have the opportunity to reconsider Nita's other challenges to its enforceability. Nita's failure to request, and the trial court's failure to make, findings regarding duress and unconscionability may well have been premised on the reasoning that those claims need not be addressed if the agreement was unconstitutional. We have broad discretion to remand a case in the interest of justice, TEX. R. APP. P. 180, and have often done so when "it appears from the record that the losing party might be able to recover under some other established legal theory that was not developed at the first trial." *Westgate, Ltd. v. State*, 843 S.W.2d 448, 455 (Tex. 1992) (citing authorities). It may be necessary for the trial court to redetermine the property division regardless of the enforceability of the premarital agreement, but it need not redetermine damages unless the agreement is found to be enforceable. If the damages Nita claims for breach of fiduciary duty are unliquidated and a retrial to determine those damages is necessary, Whitney's liability for alleged breaches must also be retried as long as that liability is contested. TEX. R. APP. P. 184(b).

Accordingly, a majority of the Court without hearing oral argument grants Nita Fanning's motion for rehearing, grants her application for writ of error, reverses that portion of the judgment of the court of appeals requiring the trial court to enforce the premarital agreement, and affirms the judgment in all other respects. The case is remanded to the trial court for further proceedings consistent with this opinion.

Notes, Comments & Questions

1. *Fanning v. Fanning* exemplifies the reality of marital property cases—such are seldom one dimensional.

2. The Waco Court of Appeals mentions that Mrs. Fanning believed that signing the agreement was her only alternative when faced with Mr. Fanning's threat to divorce her and obtain custody of the children. Following this observation, the court cites *Matthews v. Matthews*, 725 S.W.2d 275, 279 (Tex. App.—Houston [1st Dist.] 1986, writ ref'd n.r.e.). Take the time to look up and review *Matthews*. Were Mrs. Fanning and Mrs. Matthews so similarly situated that each should have been considered under duress at time of signing?

3. What do you think of the action taken by the Texas Supreme Court?

4. For more on the issue of unconscionability, *see Fazakerly v. Fazakerly*, 996 S.W.2d 260 (Tex. App.—Eastland 1999, pet. denied); *Marsh v. Marsh*, 949 S.W.2d 734 (Tex. App.—Houston [14th Dist.] 1997, no writ).

LARSON
v.
PRIGOFF

No. 05-99-01755-CV, 2003 WL 13352
(Tex. App.—Dallas Jan. 8. 2001, no pet. h.)
(not designated for publication)

Before Justices Morris, Whittington, and Fitzgerald.

OPINION

Fitzgerald, Justice.

In this appeal from a divorce proceeding, appellant Nancy Marie Larson brings a single point of error complaining the trial court erred in failing to find that a premarital agreement was unconscionable and unenforceable. We affirm.

Appellee Morris Prigoff, a podiatrist, and Larson, the office manager for Prigoff's medical clinic, were married on December 30, 1988. Immediately prior to their marriage, Prigoff and Larson entered into a premarital agreement. The agreement was designed to identify and maintain the separate property that each brought to the marriage and to provide that property acquired during the marriage would remain the separate property of the acquiring party. The agreement contemplates that there would be no community property; rather, all the property would be either the separate property of Larson or Prigoff. The agreement further provides for certain payments by Prigoff to Larson in the event of a divorce.

By at least 1997, the marriage became insupportable, and Larson sued for divorce. During the divorce proceedings, Larson challenged the provisions of the premarital agreement which recharacterized as separate property earnings received and income arising from separate property during the marriage. Larson contended that these provisions are unconstitutional under the Texas constitution. She also argued the premarital agreement is contrary to federal law to the extent the agreement denies benefits to Larson from certain of Prigoff's retirement accounts. Both sides filed motions for summary judgment seeking a ruling to determine whether the premarital agreement is enforceable. The trial court, however, determined that the issue should not be resolved by summary judgment and suggested that a "Request for Declaratory Relief pursuant [to] CPRC ch. 37 would be the proper vehicle to address the enforceability of the pre-nuptial agreement." Thereafter, a request for declaratory relief was presented to the court, and the issue was tried to the bench.[1]

The trial court found in favor of Prigoff. The court's ruling was later incorporated into a final decree of divorce. Additionally, Larson requested and received findings of fact and conclusions of law. Generally, the court found that the premarital agreement is not unconscionable, it is in "substantial

[1] Although the parties agree that such a request was presented to and determined by the court, neither the request, any response thereto, nor the reporter's record of the proceeding has been included in the appellate record. The parties also have not indicated who initiated the request for declaratory relief. In their briefs, the parties characterize the request as a "motion for declaratory judgment." It would appear that the appropriate manner of presenting a request for declaratory judgment to the court would have been for one of the parties to bring a declaratory judgment claim in an amended petition and have the matter set for trial. *See* Tex.Civ. Prac. & Rem. Code § 37.007 (Vernon 2000) ("If a proceeding under this chapter involves the determination of an issue of fact, the issue may be tried and determined in the same manner as issues of fact are tried and determined in other civil actions in the court in which the proceeding is pending."). Appellant, however, has not complained of any procedural irregularity in the manner by which the request for declaratory relief was presented to or determined by the trial court. Therefore, we do not consider the matter further.

compliance" with the laws and constitution of this state, its provisions are enforceable, and property should be awarded to both parties pursuant to the terms of the agreement.

Larson contends that the provisions of the premarital agreement providing that personal earnings received and income arising from separate property during the marriage are to be separate property are invalid pursuant to the Texas constitution. She reasons, therefore, that the agreement as a whole is unconscionable and unenforceable. We conclude appellant's complaints lack merit.

Texas law generally favors premarital agreements. *See Beck v. Beck*, 814 S.W.2d 745, 749 (Tex. 1991)(public policy dictates that premarital agreements should be enforced); *Grossman v. Grossman*, 799 S.W.2d 511, 513 (Tex. App.—Corpus Christi 1990, no writ) (premarital agreements are presumptively valid). The enforceability of premarital agreements is governed by the family code. In relevant part, the code provides:

> (a) A premarital agreement is not enforceable if the party against whom enforcement is requested proves that:
> (1) the party did not sign the agreement voluntarily; or
> (2) the agreement was unconscionable when it was signed and, before signing the agreement, that party:
> (A) was not provided a fair and reasonable disclosure of the property or financial obligations of the other party;
> (B) did not voluntarily and expressly waive, in writing, any right to disclosure of the property or financial obligations of the other party beyond the disclosure provided; and
> (C) did not have, or reasonably could not have had, adequate knowledge of the property or financial obligations of the other party.

TEX. FAM. CODE ANN. § 4.006 (Vernon 1998).

Preliminarily, we note Larson has failed to provide this Court with a complete record. Larson acknowledges in her brief that both the pleadings and reporter's record pertaining to the enforceability of the premarital agreement are not included in the appellate record. In a presubmission motion, Larson filed a motion for leave to supplement the record. We denied her motion without prejudice, noting leave was no longer required under the current appellate rules, Larson did not seek the assistance of this Court to compel preparation of the record, and Larson could supplement the record herself as she deemed necessary.

The record does not reflect that Larson made any attempt to supplement the record following the denial of her motion. The complaining party has the burden to bring forth a record to support its contention. *See Simon v. York Crane & Rigging Co.*, 739 S.W.2d 793, 795 (Tex. 1987); *American Paging of Texas, Inc. v. El Paso Paging, Inc.*, 9 S.W.3d 237, 240 (Tex. App.—El Paso 1999, pet. denied); *see also* TEX. R. APP. P. 34.6(b)(1), 35.3(b). Absent a record, we indulge every presumption in favor of the trial court's findings and presume that the evidence before the trial court was adequate to support its decision. *See Bryant v. United Shortline Inc. Assur. Services, N.A.*, 972 S.W.2d 26, 31 (Tex.1998); *Simon*, 739 S.W.2d at 795. Therefore, were Larson's argument on appeal based exclusively on section 4.006 of the family code, which requires factual determinations by the trial court, we would be constrained to hold that we must presume the missing record contains evidence supporting the judgment.

Larson, however, purports not to base her claim of unenforceability exclusively on section 4.006. Rather, she contends the premarital agreement is unconscionable and unenforceable under the family code because certain provisions of the agreement are unconstitutional. Nevertheless, Larson's attempt to recast her argument under section 4.006 in terms of a constitutional issue is equally unavailing. First, Larson confuses at least two separate issues: unconstitutionality of the agreement's provisions and unenforceability of the agreement. Even were we to agree that certain provisions of the agreement are unconstitutional, that would not necessarily render the entire premarital agreement unenforceable. *See Williams v. Williams*, 569 S.W.2d 867, 870-71 (Tex.1978); *Fanning v. Fanning*, 828 S.W.2d 135, 142 (Tex. App.—Waco 1992, writ granted), *rev'd on other grounds*, 847 S.W.2d 225 (Tex. 1993). Before the trial court could properly conclude the entire agreement is unenforceable, it would be incumbent upon Larson to demonstrate that the unconstitutional provisions are not severable but constitute the main or essential purpose of the agreement. *See Williams*, 569 S.W.2d at 871. Nothing in the record demonstrates Larson did so. Therefore, we cannot conclude the trial court erred in finding the agreement as a whole to be enforceable. *See Bryant*, 972 S.W.2d at 31; *Simon*, 739 S.W.2d at 795.

Further, evidence of unconscionability alone is insufficient to render a premarital agreement unenforceable under the family code. Section 4.006 of the family code provides that unconscionability is only a starting point in the analysis. Even if a premarital agreement is unconscionable, the party challenging the agreement must also demonstrate she has satisfied each of the three conditions set forth in 4.006(a)(2), regarding disclosure of the future spouse's financial condition. The record does not demonstrate Larson established she satisfied either sections 4.006(a)(2)(A) or 4.006(a)(2)(C), and the trial court specifically made findings against her regarding these two provisions. In the absence of a reporter's record, we must presume the record supports the trial court's determination. *See Bryant*, 972 S.W.2d at 31; *Simon*, 739 S.W .2d at 795.

Additionally, we cannot accept Larson's initial premise that the income and earnings provisions of the premarital agreement are unconstitutional. Other courts which have addressed this issue have concluded that parties about to be married may agree to exchange their community property interests and thereby maintain as separate property future income from separate property and earnings acquired during the marriage. *See, e.g., Dokmanovic v. Schwarz*, 880 S.W.2d 272, 273-76 (Tex. App.—Houston [14th Dist.] 1994, no writ); *Winger v. Pianka*, 831 S.W.2d 853, 858 (Tex. App.—Austin 1992, writ denied); *Fanning*, 828 S.W.2d at 142; *see also Calmes v. United States*, 926 F.Supp 582, 586-88 (N.D. Tex.)(applying Texas law). We agree. The exchange which occurred here does not violate the Texas constitution.

Finally, we also conclude Larson failed to demonstrate that the retirement accounts at issue are governed by federal law. Larson contends that the provisions of the premarital agreement as they relate to certain of Prigoff's retirement accounts are unenforceable pursuant to the Employee Retirement Income Security Act of 1974 (ERISA). *See* 29 U.S.C.A. §§ 1001-1461 (West 1999 & Supp.2000). Prigoff, however, contends that ERISA does not apply to his retirement accounts because he did not engage in interstate commerce. *See* 29 U.S.C. § 1003(a) (West 1999) (providing that ERISA is applicable to employee benefit plans established or maintained by an employer engaged in interstate commerce). The trial court found in favor of Prigoff. Because Larson has failed to provide us with a record of the applicable trial court proceedings, we must presume the record supports the trial court's conclusion and uphold the judgment of the trial court. *See Bryant*, 972 S.W.2d at 31; *Simon*, 739 S.W.2d at 795.

For the foregoing reasons, we overrule Larson's point of error and affirm the judgment of the trial court.

Note

Larson v. Prigoff is replete with procedural problems; nevertheless, the court's handling of the constitutional claim is interesting and provides insight into how such a claim should (or should not) be pleaded and proved.

ORSONO
v.
ORSONO

76 S.W.3d 509
(Tex. App.—Houston [14th Dist] 2002, no pet.)

BRISTER, CHIEF JUSTICE.

In this divorce action, appellant Gloria Hernandez DeAnda Osorno, former spouse of appellee Henry Osorno, contests (1) the enforcement of the couple's premarital agreement, (2) the denial of her motion for continuance, and (3) the division of the marital estate. We affirm in part and reverse and remand in part.

Gloria was forty years old when she met Henry in February 1992. In August, Gloria discovered she was pregnant. According to her, Henry wanted her to have an abortion, which she refused for religious reasons. In September, Henry agreed to marry her if she signed a premarital agreement. Both Henry and Gloria signed an Agreement in Contemplation of Marriage on October 9, 1992, and were married the following day.

Henry filed for divorce on December 22, 1998. Gloria contested the enforceability of the premarital agreement. A hearing was held before a master at which both Henry and Gloria testified. The master found the agreement enforceable.

Enforceability of the Premarital Agreement

As the party attacking a premarital agreement, Gloria had the burden to show (1) she did not sign the agreement voluntarily or (2) it was unconscionable and she did not receive proper disclosure of Henry's property. TEX. FAM.CODE ANN. § 4.006(a) (Vernon 1998). Gloria relies on the first ground, arguing she signed the premarital agreement involuntarily because she was forty, unmarried, and pregnant. The Family Code provides no definition of "voluntarily." In construing section 4.006(a), this Court has previously referred to commercial law governing enforcement of contracts for guidance. *See Marsh v. Marsh*, 949 S.W.2d 734, 739-40 (Tex.App.—Houston [14th Dist.] 1997, no writ) (looking to contract cases for definition of "unconscionable").

For duress to be a contract defense, it must consist of a threat to do something the threatening party has no legal right to do. *See Brown v. Aztec Rig Equip., Inc.*, 921 S.W.2d 835, 845 (Tex. App.—Houston [14th Dist.] 1996, writ denied). In this case, aside from his moral duties, Henry had no legal duty to marry Gloria. His threat to do something he had the legal right to do is insufficient to invalidate the premarital agreement. Gloria was faced with difficult choices, but we cannot find her decision to sign the agreement was involuntary. *See In re Marriage of Dawley*, 17 Cal.3d 342, 131 Cal.Rptr. 3, 551 P.2d 323, 331 (1976) (refusing to set aside premarital agreement signed under pressure of unplanned pregnancy). We overrule Gloria's first point of error.

* * *

Just and Right Division of the Marital Estate

In her second point, Gloria asserts there is no evidence to support the trial court's disproportionate division of the marital estate.[1] *See* TEX. FAM.CODE ANN. § 7.001. The trial court exercises wide discretion in this division, and we may reverse only in a case of clear abuse. *Murff v. Murff*, 615 S.W.2d 696, 700 (Tex. 1981).

---

[1] Although the master conducted the trial on the merits, the trial court signed the divorce decree.

In this case, there are no findings of fact or conclusions of law, and the divorce decree does not expressly list what property was found to be separate or community. Assuming all property in the "Division of Marital Estate" portion of the decree was community, *see Magill v. Magill*, 816 S.W.2d 530, 532-33 (Tex. App.—Houston [1st Dist.] 1991, writ denied) (finding property listed under designation "estate of the parties is divided as follows" was characterized as community property), the court awarded almost three-fourths of the estate to Henry (using his own property values). Although the court was not required to divide the marital estate equally, there must be a reasonable basis for the division. *Zieba v. Martin*, 928 S.W.2d 782, 790 (Tex. App.—Houston [14th Dist.] 1996, no writ). Here, there was none, as the evidence established Henry was in much better financial shape than Gloria.[2]

The inequity of this division shrinks or even disappears if several of the assets awarded to Henry were his separate property. Henry argues that accounts listed in the decree totaling almost $100,000 were designated his separate property in the parties' premarital agreement. But the only evidence as to the source of funds placed in those accounts was Henry's testimony; no deposit slips or bank records were offered tracing the money to support Henry's claim. Without tracing, Henry's testimony cannot overcome the community property presumption. *See Evans v. Evans*, 14 S.W.3d 343, 346 (Tex. App.—Houston [14th Dist.] 2000, no pet.); *Robles v. Robles*, 965 S.W.2d 605, 614 (Tex. App.—Houston [1st Dist.] 1998, pet. denied) (explaining that mere testimony without tracing is generally insufficient). Because the evidence is insufficient to support a separate-property finding, we sustain Gloria's second point of error.

We affirm the judgment finding the premarital agreement enforceable, but reverse the portion of the final decree of divorce dealing with the division of the marital estate and remand for a just and right division of the community estate. *See Evans*, 14 S.W.3d at 347 (holding mischaracterization that materially affected just and right division required remand).

Questions

1. It is clear that pregnancy will not be considered as duress causing one to sign a premarital agreement.

2. What other similar circumstances frequently encountered in "matters of the heart," will also fail to meet the duress standards?

---

[2] Testimony showed Henry earned a base salary of $7,355 per month in addition to an annual incentive bonus of up to $42,000, while Gloria owned an unprofitable retail clothing store she had funded by a $56,000 personal injury settlement. Although Gloria and Henry were named joint-managing conservators of their child, Gloria (who had stayed at home for nearly seven years raising their son) was to maintain his primary residence, with Henry to pay $1,200 per month in child support. While the evidence relating to the other applicable factors is conflicting, none lends support for a division in Henry's favor. *See Zieba*, 928 S.W.2d at 790-91. At the time of trial, Gloria was scheduled to have back surgery related to a 1994 car accident. Both parties used community assets to pay separate debts, and after the petition for divorce was filed, Henry replaced a $250,000 universal life insurance policy with a $400,000 term policy, spending the cash value. There was no testimony that Henry's educational background was more limited than Gloria's or that Gloria was at fault in the breakup of the marriage.

SHESHUNOFF
v.
SHESHUNOFF
172 S.W.3d 686
(Tex. App.—Austin 2005, pet. denied)

PEMBERTON, JUSTICE.

The principal issue in this case concerns the enforceability of a marital property agreement. *See* TEX. FAM.CODE ANN. § 4.105 (West 1998). Applying section 4.105 to the defensive theories that were timely raised in this case, we affirm the district court's judgment enforcing the agreement.

BACKGROUND

The Marital Property Agreement

Appellant Alexander Sheshunoff and Appellee Gabrielle Sheshunoff were married in 1971. Before their marriage, the couple entered into an agreement governing various rights and obligations relating to their marital property, and they devised a new one in 1990. Beginning in 2002, the couple, each with assistance of several attorneys, accountants, and other professional advisors, began negotiating an elaborate thirty-seven page Marital Property Agreement that addressed the couple's respective rights to their substantial marital assets. They eventually executed the Agreement in February 2003. In April 2003, Ms. Sheshunoff filed for divorce and sought the benefit of the agreed-upon property division.

The circumstances surrounding the formation of the Agreement are at the root of the present controversy. According to Mr. Sheshunoff, the Agreement shifted large amounts of the couple's marital assets to Ms. Sheshunoff and large amounts of marital liabilities to him for tax and estate planning purposes. Mr. Sheshunoff asserts that, throughout the negotiations, he had understood and intended that this arrangement was solely to achieve tax and estate planning benefits and that neither party had any intention to actually divorce. Mr. Sheshunoff claims that Ms. Sheshunoff and her lawyers misled him to believe that she shared this intent when, in fact, she was plotting to file for divorce (and avail herself of the highly favorable property division) once she persuaded him to sign the agreement. Ms. Sheshunoff denies these allegations.

* * *

DISCUSSION

Mr. Sheshunoff brings five issues on appeal. First, he contends that the district court erred in granting its partial summary judgment foreclosing his involuntariness defense; he does not complain of the court's ruling regarding unconscionability and lack of disclosure. In his second issue, Mr. Sheshunoff argues that the district court abused its discretion in striking his amended pleadings. In his third issue, Mr. Sheshunoff asserts that the district court erred in severing and referring his reformation claims to arbitration because Ms. Sheshunoff had waived her right to seek arbitration and had failed to exhaust her remedy of mediation as a precedent to arbitration. In his fourth issue, Mr. Sheshunoff complains that the district court erred in striking his jury demand, while in his fifth issue he contends that the district court erred in granting final summary judgment because he had raised genuine issues of material fact regarding his stricken pleadings and severed claims.[6]

---

[6] [Footnote omitted.]

Partial Summary Judgment

In his first issue, Mr. Sheshunoff challenges the district court's granting of partial summary judgment foreclosing his involuntary-execution defense to the Marital Property Agreement. Specifically, he argues that (1) he has raised a fact issue with regard to the common-law defenses of fraudulent inducement and duress; and (2) this evidence also raises a fact issue regarding involuntary execution under section 4.05 of the family code.

* * *

The involuntary execution defense

Our disposition of Mr. Sheshunoff's first issue requires us to evaluate Mr. Sheshunoff's summary-judgment evidence against the standard of "involuntary execution" in section 4.105 of the family code. The parties dispute the meaning of "involuntary execution" and the extent to which it can be proven by evidence of common-law defenses like fraud or duress. We accordingly first clarify the nature of this statutory defense before turning to Mr. Sheshunoff's summary-judgment evidence.

Overview of section 4.105

Section 4.105 of the family code provides:

> (a) A partition or exchange agreement is not enforceable if the party against whom enforcement is requested proves that:
>
> (1) the party did not sign the agreement voluntarily; or
>
> (2) the agreement was unconscionable when it was signed and, before execution of the agreement, that party:
>
> (A) was not provided a fair and reasonable disclosure of the property or financial obligations of the other party;
>
> (B) did not voluntarily and expressly waive, in writing, any right to disclosure of the property or financial obligations of the other party beyond the disclosure provided; and
>
> (C) did not have, or reasonably could not have had, adequate knowledge of the property or financial obligations of the other party.
>
> (b) An issue of unconscionability of a partition or exchange agreement shall be decided by the court as a matter of law.
>
> (c) The remedies and defenses in this section are the exclusive remedies or defenses, including common law remedies or defenses.

See TEX. FAM.CODE ANN. § 4.105(a). There is no dispute on appeal that the Marital Property Agreement is a "partition or exchange agreement" within the meaning of section 4.105.

Language parallel to that in section 4.105 appears in section 4.006 of the family code, which governs enforceability of premarital, or "antenuptial," agreements. *See* TEX. FAM.CODE ANN. § 4.006 (West 1998). Subsections (a) and (b) of each provision track the language of the Uniform Premarital Agreement Act. * * * These portions of the Uniform Act evolved from a debate between commissioners who desired certainty in the enforcement of marital property agreements and those who urged that such agreements should be routinely scrutinized for substantive fairness. * * * The former view dominated the debate: the Act provided that a premarital agreement that was voluntarily executed would be enforced, even if unconscionable, as long as the opposing party knew or should have known of the other party's assets, or waived such disclosure. *Id.* The commissioners considered that the voluntariness of a premarital agreement may turn, in part, upon whether the agreement was entered into knowingly, in the sense that the parties understood the terms or basic effect of the agreement. *Id.*

Before the Texas Legislature adopted our version of the Uniform Act, Texas law had required a party seeking to enforce a marital property agreement to prove, by clear and convincing evidence, that the other party had given informed consent and that the agreement had not been procured by fraud, duress, or overreaching. Act of June 18, 1987, 70th Leg., R.S., ch. 678, § 1, sec. 5.46, 1987 Tex. Gen. Laws 2530, 2530-31; *see Williams v. Williams*, 720 S.W.2d 246, 248 (Tex. App.—Houston [14th Dist.] 1986, no writ).[7] Dissatisfaction with this difficult burden of proof led to the legislature's adoption of the Uniform Act in 1987. * * * By shifting the burden of proof to the party opposing enforcement and by adopting the Uniform Act's concept that voluntarily executed marital property agreements should be enforced even if unconscionable (unless inadequate disclosure can be proven), the Texas Legislature manifested a strong policy preference that marital property agreements should be enforced whenever persons who are married or intend to marry voluntarily enter into them. *See Beck v. Beck*, 814 S.W.2d 745, 749 (Tex.1991) (public policy dictates that premarital agreements should be enforced), *cert. denied*, 503 U.S. 907, 112 S.Ct. 1266, 117 L.Ed.2d 494 (1992); *Grossman v. Grossman*, 799 S.W.2d 511, 513 (Tex. App.—Corpus Christi 1990, no writ) (premarital agreements are presumptively valid). Barring constitutional impediments, we must defer to these legislative policy pronouncements. *See Battaglia v. Alexander*, No. 02-0701, ___ S.W.3d ___, ___, 2005 WL 1252326, *17, 48 Tex. Sup. J. 720, 2005 Tex. LEXIS 419, at *62 (May 27, 2005).

As originally enacted, sections 4.006 and 4.105, like the Uniform Act, contained only subsections (a) and (b). *See* Act of June 1, 1987, 70th Leg., R.S., ch. 678, § 1, secs. 5.46, .55, 1987 Tex. Gen. Laws 2530, 2530-31. In 1993, however, the legislature departed from the Uniform Act and added subsection (c) to each. *See* Act of April 30, 1993, 73d Leg., R.S., ch. 136, §§ 1, 2, 1993 Tex. Gen. Laws 283, 283. This amendment apparently responded to *Daniel v. Daniel*, in which our sister court in Houston held that, absent explicit legislative provision to the contrary, the involuntary execution and unconscionability defenses should be construed to "simply provide[ ] an additional statutory remedy for persons challenging property agreements executed pursuant to the Family Code" and not "to replace all common law defenses." 779 S.W.2d 110, 114 (Tex. App.—Houston [1st Dist.] 1989, no writ). Thus, the *Daniel* court concluded that parties could assert *both* the statutory defenses under section 4.105 *and* common-law contractual defenses against the enforcement of partition and exchange agreements. *Id.* at 114. In subsection (c), the legislature supplied the explicit legislative intent found lacking by the Daniel court, providing that the "remedies and defenses in this section are the exclusive remedies or defenses, including common law remedies or defenses." * * *

Involuntary execution and common-law defenses

While maintaining that proof of fraud and duress is also evidence of involuntary execution, Mr. Sheshunoff asserts that involuntary execution "is a broader, less specific defense" than fraud and duress and that he accordingly does not necessarily have to prove each common-law element of either defense to prove involuntary execution. In contrast, Ms. Sheshunoff seems to construe subsection (c) of section 4.105 to foreclose the possibility that proof of a common-law defense like duress or fraud could also be proof of involuntary execution, though elsewhere she has appeared to concede that proof of duress might be proof of involuntary execution.

To ascertain the relationship between involuntary execution and fraud or duress, we first examine the meaning of "voluntarily" in section 4.105. Neither the family code nor the Uniform Act defines "voluntarily," nor does the legislative history of either provide much guidance regarding the intended meaning of the term. We can obtain some guidance from dictionary definitions.[8] The ordinary mean-

---

[7] [Footnote omitted.]

[8] [Footnote omitted.]

ing of "voluntarily," as reflected in dictionary definitions, entails (1) intentional action, as opposed to inadvertent or accidental action, (2) that is the product of the exercise of free will.[9]

The official comments accompanying the Uniform Act suggest that common-law concepts including duress, lack of capacity, fraud, and undue influence, along with the parties' relative bargaining power and knowledge regarding the meaning and effect of the agreement, could bear upon the ultimate determination of voluntariness. *See Marriage of Bonds*, 99 Cal.Rptr.2d 252, 5 P.3d at 824-25 (concluding that "the question is viewed as one involving such ordinary contract defenses as fraud, undue influence, or duress, along with some examination of the parties' knowledge of the rights being waived, or at least knowledge of the intent of the agreement"); *Marriage of Shirilla*, 319 Mont. 385, 89 P.3d 1, 3 (2004) ("The party seeking to avoid a premarital agreement may prevail by establishing that the agreement was involuntary, and that evidence of lack of capacity, duress, fraud, and undue influence, as demonstrated by a number of factors uniquely probative of coercion in the premarital context, would be relevant in establishing the involuntariness of the agreement."). Some courts, moreover, have equated voluntariness under the Uniform Act with "procedural fairness," which takes account of such factors as coercion, duress, undue influence, and the parties' relative bargaining power and sophistication. *See Marriage of Bonds*, 99 Cal.Rptr.2d 252, 5 P.3d at 826-27.

Texas courts have construed "voluntarily" under sections 4.105 and 4.006 in a generally consistent manner. In *Nesmith v. Berger*, for example, we assumed without deciding that the appellant's definition of "voluntarily," derived from common-law duress concepts, controlled our inquiry under section 4.006: "an action is taken by design, intentionally, purposefully, by choice, of one's own accord, or by the free exercise of will." 64 S.W.3d 110, 113-16 (Tex. App.—Austin 2001, pet. denied) (*citing Prigmore v. Hardware Mut. Ins. Co. of Minn.*, 225 S.W.2d 897, 899 (Tex. Civ. App.—Amarillo 1949, no writ)).[10] We applied this definition to an involuntary execution claim predicated on a husband's threat not to go on a planned honeymoon unless his wife first signed a premarital agreement. *Id.* at 111-15. Citing evidence of the parties' mutual desire to enter into such an agreement, the wife's motives for entering into the agreement, bargaining over terms, and both parties' subsequent compliance with the agreement, we overruled a great weight and preponderance challenge to the trial court ruling enforcing the agreement. *Id.* We concluded that "[i]n light of the bargaining that accompanied every step of the relationship between the parties before and during their marriage, we cannot say that [the husband's] proposed bargain to finalize the terms of the long-contemplated agreement before leaving on a honeymoon exerted such undue influence as to deprive [the wife] of her free will in signing the agreement." *Id.* at 115 (emphasis added); *see also Marsh v. Marsh*, 949 S.W.2d 734, 740-43 (Tex. App.—Houston [14th Dist.] 1997, no pet.) (in reviewing unconscionability defense,

---

[9] Webster's Third New International Dictionary defines "voluntarily" as "in a voluntary manner: of one's own free will: spontaneously," and "voluntary" as "proceeding from the will: produced in or by an act of choice," "performed, made or given of one's own free will," "done by design or intention: not accidental," and "acting of oneself: not constrained, impelled, or influenced by another." Webster's Third New International Dictionary 2564 (1986). Similarly, the American Heritage Dictionary defines "voluntary" as "[a]rising from one's own free will: acting on one's own initiative," "normally controlled by or subject to individual volition," "[c]apable of exercising will, volitional," and "[a]cting or performed without external persuasion or compulsion." American Heritage Dictionary 1436 (1973).

Some definitions, moreover, indicate that voluntariness implies knowledge of "essential facts." Black's Law Dictionary defines "voluntarily" as "[d]one by design or intention, intentional, proposed, intended or not accidental, intentionally and without coercion," and "voluntary" as "[u]nconstrained by interference; unimpelled by another's influence; spontaneous; acting of oneself. Done by design or intention. Proceeding from the free and unrestrained will of the person. Produced in or by an act of choice. Resulting from free choice. The word, especially in statutes, often implies knowledge of essential facts." Black's Law Dictionary 813 (7th ed.1999).

[10] [Footnote omitted.]

considering whether evidence of threats, fraud, overreaching, duress, or misrepresentations, as well as parties' relative sophistication, experience, and bargaining power).[11]

In *Nesmith*, we relied in part on the Fort Worth court's analysis in *Matelski v. Matelski*, 840 S.W.2d 124, 128-29 (Tex. App.—Fort Worth 1992, no writ). *Matelski*, like some other decisions from our sister courts, simply equates involuntary execution with common-law duress.[12] *See Osorno v. Osorno*, 76 S.W.3d 509, 510-11 (Tex. App.—Houston [14th Dist.] 2002, no pet.) (as matter of law, no duress in premarital agreement based on threat by party to commit act they have legal right to do).[13]

The ordinary meaning of "voluntary," the legislative history and application of the Uniform Act, and the manner in which Texas courts have construed the term compel us to agree with Mr. Sheshunoff—although the presence of such factors as fraud, duress, and undue influence may bear upon the inquiry, Mr. Sheshunoff does not have to prove each element of these common-law defenses to establish the ultimate issue of involuntary execution. *See Daniel*, 779 S.W.2d at 114 & n.4 (observing that involuntary execution "alleviates the need for proof of all elements required in common law defenses," such as knowledge or reliance elements of fraud). We implied as much in Nesmith, where we looked not to the elements of common-law defenses but directly to the controlling issue of whether the party resisting enforcement executed the agreement voluntarily. *See Nesmith*, 64 S.W.3d at 114-15. This approach is consistent with the text of section 4.105, which refers not to common-law concepts but solely to whether the party signed the agreement voluntarily. TEX. FAM.CODE ANN. § 4.105(a)(1); *see Office of the Attorney Gen. of Tex. v. Lee*, 92 S.W.3d 526, 528 (Tex. 2002).[14]

Ms. Sheshunoff contends that the legislature's addition of subsection (c) renders irrelevant the history and application of the involuntary execution defenses under the Uniform Act. We disagree. Subsection (c) was intended to clarify merely that, contrary to *Daniel*, parties cannot assert common-law defenses in addition to the defenses enumerated in section 4.105. It does not prohibit us from considering as potential evidence of involuntary execution proof of conduct that Mr. Sheshunoff asserts constitutes fraud or duress.

In sum, we conclude that section 4.105 sets out the exclusive remedies available to prevent enforcement of a postmarital agreement, and that, although common-law defenses may inform our analysis of "voluntariness," they will not necessarily control.

* * *

. . . Mr. Sheshunoff advances two theories of involuntary execution: (1) he was forced into signing the Agreement; and (2) he was misled into signing it in the belief that Ms. Sheshunoff would not actually seek a divorce and avail herself of her rights to the agreed-upon property division.

---

[11] [Footnote omitted.]

[12] The *Matelski* court described the elements of duress as follows:

> There can be no duress unless there is a threat to do some act which the party threatening has no legal right to do. Such threat must be of such character as to destroy the free agency of the party to whom it is directed. It must overcome his will and cause him to do that which he would not otherwise do, and that which he was not legally bound to do. The restraint caused by such threat must be imminent. It must be such that the person to whom it is directed has no present means of protection.

Matelski v. Matelski, 840 S.W.2d 124, 129 (Tex.App.-Fort Worth 1992, no writ) (*quoting Dale v. Simon*, 267 S.W. 467, 470 (Tex.Com.App.1924, judgm't adopted)).

[13] [Footnote omitted.]

[14] [Footnote omitted.]

To support his first involuntary execution theory, Mr. Sheshunoff presented an affidavit in which he claims that Ms. Sheshunoff threatened him that, unless he signed the Marital Property Agreement, "she would withdraw her loan guarantee" she had advanced his company, Alex Sheshunoff Management, L.P., "and have the Bank of America immediately call the line of credit," leading to dire consequences for the company. He attaches copies of the loan documents, which demonstrate that (1) Ms. Sheshunoff, along with Mr. Sheshunoff, was a guarantor on a $1 million loan agreement between Bank of America and Alex Sheshunoff Management Services, L.P.;[17] and (2) the promissory note provided that Bank of America "will have no obligation to advance funds" on the company's revolving line of credit if "any guarantor seeks, claims, or otherwise attempts to limit, modify, or revoke such guarantor's guarantees of this Note or any other loan with Lender." However, this evidence shows, at most, that Ms. Sheshunoff threatened to withdraw her loan guarantee and that her doing so would have entitled Bank of America to cut off the line of credit. Mr. Sheshunoff offers no proof, and only the conclusory statement in his affidavit, regarding the likelihood that Bank of America in fact would have exercised this contractual right, at Ms. Sheshunoff's behest or otherwise.[18] Absent such proof, the jury could not reasonably infer—and could only speculate—that Ms. Sheshunoff's alleged threat to withdraw the loan guarantee presented the sort of imminent threat that Texas law has considered capable of overwhelming free will and rendering Mr. Sheshunoff's execution of the Marital Property Agreement involuntary. *See Wright v. Sydow*, No. 14-03-00222-CV, 173 S.W.3d 534, 544, 2004 WL 3153293, *5, 2004 Tex.App. LEXIS 10541, at *15 (Tex. App.—Houston [14th Dist.] 2004, pet. denied); *King v. Bishop*, 879 S.W.2d 222, 223 (Tex. App.—Houston [14th Dist.] 1994, no writ); *Charping v. Light*, 578 S.W.2d 462, 464 (Tex. Civ. App.—Austin 1979, no writ) (quoting *Dale v. Simon*, 267 S.W. 467, 470 (Tex. Com. App.1924, judgm't adopted)). It is thus no evidence.[19]

As for Mr. Sheshunoff's second theory of involuntary execution, he does not dispute that he and his team of lawyers and advisors knew that the Agreement explicitly provided for the property division he now characterizes as "draconian" and that it would be effective if the parties divorced. Nor, significantly, does Mr. Sheshunoff claim that he was misled concerning the presence of these terms in the Agreement or that they were concealed from him.[20] Rather, Mr. Sheshunoff contends only that he was misled concerning Ms. Sheshunoff's subjective intent to avail herself of her rights under the Agreement. Although not singularly determinative, it is significant that our sister courts have held that this type of conduct, even if proven, would not constitute fraud under Texas law. *See In re GTE Mobilnet of S. Tex. Ltd. P'ship*, 123 S.W.3d 795, 799-800 (Tex. App.—Beaumont 2003, orig. proceeding) (alleged misrepresentations that company would not enforce contractual arbitration clause known to parties could not constitute fraudulent inducement as matter of law). Similarly, we would impermissibly deviate from the statutory language—and the legislature's manifest intent to facilitate enforcement of marital property agreements—by holding that a party who executes a marital property agreement with knowledge and understanding of its terms nonetheless did so "involuntarily" because he or she believed the other party would not enforce the agreement.

We accordingly conclude that Mr. Sheshunoff has failed to raise a fact issue regarding his involuntary execution defense. Our conclusion is not altered by Mr. Sheshunoff's assertions that Ms. Sheshunoff, as his spouse, owed him a fiduciary duty to be truthful during their negotiations. *See Buckner v. Buckner*, 815 S.W.2d 877, 880 (Tex. App.—Tyler 1991, no writ). Assuming without deciding that such a duty would apply under the circumstances of this case,[21] the Texas Legislature en-

[17] [Footnote omitted.]

[18] [Footnote omitted.]

[19] [Footnote omitted.]

[20] [Footnote omitted.]

[21] [Footnote omitted.]

acted section 4.105 with the understanding that married spouses owing fiduciary duties to one another would negotiate and execute marital property agreements. *See* TEX. GOV'T CODE ANN. § 311.023 (West 2005) (court to consider laws on same or similar subjects when construing statutes); *Argonaut Ins. Co. v. Baker*, 87 S.W.3d 526, 530-31 (Tex. 2002) (quoting *Acker v. Texas Water Comm'n*, 790 S.W.2d 299, 301 (Tex. 1990) ("A statute is presumed to have been enacted by the legislature with complete knowledge of the existing law and with reference to it.")). Notwithstanding these duties, the legislature manifested the strong policy preference that voluntarily made marital property agreements be enforced. We have concluded that Mr. Sheshunoff has not raised a fact issue regarding the sort of involuntary execution the legislature could have intended to bar enforcement of marital property agreements. That conclusion would control even in the face of the fiduciary duties Mr. Sheshunoff claims.

We accordingly hold that the district court did not err in granting Ms. Sheshunoff's motion for partial summary judgment. We overrule Mr. Sheshunoff's first issue.

* * *

Questions

1. Describe a situation in which the signing of a premarital agreement would be unconscionable.
2. Do you think the defense of involuntary signing is frequently used? Why? Why not?

Chapter 2

Characterization of Marital Property

A. An Overview of the Community Property Presumption and Its Rebuttal

The community property presumption is the primary principle that governs Texas marital property law. Today, this common law principle has been codified in the TEXAS FAMILY CODE which provides that all "[p]roperty possessed by either spouse during or on dissolution of marriage is presumed to be community property." TEX. FAM. CODE § 3.003(a).

The analysis of each case begins with the presumption that all property possessed during marriage or at the time a marriage is dissolved is community in character. The presumption applies to all property possessed, not just property acquired after marriage. The first case in this chapter, *Foster v. Christensen*, 67 S.W.2d 246 (Tex. Comm'n App. 1934, judgm't adopted), illustrates that a spouse (or party) who claims that all or some of the property possessed at or upon dissolution of marriage is separate, has the right to prove the separate character. That is, there is a right to rebut the community property presumption. In order to successfully rebut the community property presumption, a party must present clear and convincing evidence that the property is separate. TEX. FAM.CODE ANN. § 3.003.

Rebutting the community property presumption will be the focus of this chapter and will continue to be peripherally addressed throughout the rest of this text. If the community property presumption is successfully rebutted, the property in issue is then characterized as the separate property of one or both spouses.

This overview provides an introduction to some of the basic principles of characterization. At first glance, these principles may seem confusing, if not contradictory. Rest assured that after reading the cases within this chapter, the principles will become clear and, hopefully, any confusion will disappear.

The Fourteenth Court of Appeals has recently explained the community property presumption and its rebuttal, thus:

> The nature of property as separate or community is determined by the time and circumstances of its acquisition. *See Leighton v. Leighton*, 921 S.W.2d 365, 367 (Tex. App.—Houston [1st Dist.] 1996, no writ) (citing *Carter v. Carter*, 736 S.W.2d 775, 780 (Tex. App.—Houston [14th Dist.] 1987, no writ)). All property possessed by either spouse during or on the dissolution of marriage is presumed to be community property. *See* TEX. FAM.CODE ANN. § 3.003 (Vernon 1998). This presumption applies to dissolution by death as well as divorce. *See Smith v. Lanier*, 998 S.W.2d 324, 331-32 (Tex. App.—Austin 1999, pet. denied) (citing *George v. Reynolds*, 53 S.W.2d 490, 494 (Tex. Civ. App.—Eastland 1932, writ dism'd)). To overcome the presumption, a party must present clear and convincing evidence that the property is separate. *See* TEX. FAM.CODE ANN. § 3.003 (Vernon 1998). This evidence must generally trace and clearly identify the property as separate. *See Bahr v. Kohr*, 980 S.W.2d 723, 728 (Tex. App.—San Antonio 1998, no pet.) (citing *McKinley v. McKinley*, 496 S.W.2d 540, 543 (Tex. 1973)). A party may not overcome the presumption merely by showing that separate property was used to pay all or some of the installments on a note for property acquired during marriage; the payments create a right to reimbursement for the spouse, but not a separate property interest. *See Broussard v. Tian*, 295 S.W.2d 405, 406, 156 Tex. 371 (1956).

Evans v. Evans, 14 S.W.3d 343 (Tex. App.—Houston [14th Dist. 2000, no pet.).

The first sentence of the above excerpt, "[t]he nature of property as separate or community is determined by the time and circumstances of its acquisition," is not mere boilerplate, but one of the controlling tenets in the characterization of marital property. The simplest example of this principle is referred to as "inception of title," which can be used as a means to rebut the community property presumption. If a party can prove that the property was owned or claimed before marriage, then title incepted before marriage and it is deemed separate property. For the most part, if property is acquired after marriage, then it is community property; however, as will be discussed below, certain circumstances can result in the acquisition of separate property during marriage. If property is acquired by the community and then paid for, in whole or in part by the separate property of a spouse, it is still community property; characterization is set at acquisition, not by source of payment. By the same token, if property is owned or claimed before marriage, but paid for in whole or in part by community funds after marriage, it is still separate property; again, characterization is set at time of acquisition, not source of payment. Of course either of these examples might lead to claims for reimbursement or economic contribution (economic contribution is only applicable to case filed before September 1, 2009, but such claims do not affect the character of the property.

When property is owned or claimed before marriage (when title incepts before marriage) such property is the separate property of one or both spouses. The converse, however, is not true. Property acquired after marriage is not always community; if acquired by gift, devise or descent it is separate property. Likewise, separate property can be acquired after marriage if the funds or credit used to acquire property during marriage is separate. The operative word here is acquire, which is very different from simply paying off a community obligation with separate funds.

In order to establish that property acquired during marriage is separate property one may use the tool of tracing. As mentioned in *Evans v. Evans*, tracing is another means of establishing separate property. Separate funds or property can be traced into a purchase or acquisition during marriage to the end that the property acquired after marriage is separate property. *Carter v. Carter*, 736 S.W.2d 775 (Tex. App.—Houston [14th Dist.] 1987, no writ). Property acquired after marriage which at acquisition was partially paid for by separate funds and the remainder by the community can yield a tenancy in common between a spouse's separate estate and the community. *See Gleich v. Bongio*, 99 S.W.2d 881 (Tex. 1937). This is very different from a community acquisition that is later paid for by a spouse's separate property, which only yields a reimbursement or economic contribution claim in favor of the separate estate, not separate ownership.

Likewise, separate monies can be traced through bank accounts into which separate and community funds have been deposited. *Snider v. Snider*, 613 S.W.2d 8 (Tex. Civ. App.—Dallas 1981, no writ). The Texas Courts have recognized the application of several different means of tracing such funds, including: (1) dollar for dollar, *Latham v. Allison*, 560 S.W.2d 481 (Tex. Civ. App.—Fort Worth 1978, writ ref'd n.r.e.); (2) one dollar has the same value as another, or community out first, *Sibley v. Sibley*, 286 S.W.2d 657 (Tex. Civ. App.—Dallas 1935, writ dism'd); (3) community depletion of possible community funds, *Coggin v. Coggin*, 204 S.W.2d 47, 52 (Tex. Civ. App.—Amarillo 1947, no writ); and, (4) the intent, clearing house or conduit method. *McKinley v. McKinley*, 496 S.W.2d 540, 543 (Tex. 1973).

Although not referenced in *Evans*, a presumption of separate character can arise by virtue of a conveyance through which title is acquired. During marriage, a gift to a spouse from any source is the donee spouse's separate property. A conveyance between spouses or to another who is the natural object of one's bounty can give rise to a presumption of gift. This gift presumption can usually be rebutted by parol evidence that the property is community. *See* RESTATEMENT (THIRD) OF TRUSTS § 9, *Purchase-Money Resulting Trusts* (ALI 2003). However, if such a conveyance is evidenced by a significant recital in the deed or other instrument of conveyance, there arises an even stronger presumption. When there is a significant recital, the separate character recitation cannot be rebutted by parol evidence unless there exists equitable grounds for reformation such as fraud or mistake.

It cannot be overlooked that, ordinarily and historically, income and property arising from gifted property is community property. If a gift is made to a spouse by one that is not the spouse of the donee, the income is community property. For example, if wife's father makes a gift of stock to wife that produces dividends, the dividends are community property, but of course the underlying stock, as a gift, is separate. However, if the donor and the donee are spouses, there is an exception to this rule. TEX. CONST. art XVI § 15, provides that "if one spouse makes a gift of property to the other that gift is presumed to include all the income or property which might arise from that gift of property." So, if husband gifts to wife dividend producing stock, both the stock and the dividends are the separate property of the wife.

The separate characterization of property through credit transactions is an ever evolving means of establishing the separate character of property. The credit section of this chapter begins with a note on the most liberal case of *McClintic v. Midland Grocery & Dry Goods, Co.*, 154 S.W. 1157 (Tex. 1913) and culminates with *Ray v. United States*, 385 F.Supp. 372 (S.D. Tex. 1974) *aff'd per curiam* 538 F.2d 1228 (5th Cir. 1976). These cases will illustrate how property acquired during marriage can be acquired on separate credit, thus resulting in separate property acquired during marriage. The requirements for such separate acquisitions have grown more stringent as time has passed, but such is still a viable means of acquiring separate property during a marriage.

Although there is a dispute between the Texas courts of appeal when it comes to the characterization of personal injury damage recoveries, at least one court, has rejected the community property presumption and determined that under statute personal injury recoveries are to be presumed separate property. *See Osborn v. Osborn*, 961 S.W.2d 408 (Tex. App.—Houston [1st Dist.] 1997, no writ); TEX. FAM. CODE ANN. § 3.001 (3). (Vernon 1998). The dispute on whether to use the community property presumption or the statutory definition of separate property that addresses personal injury recoveries will be examined in the final section of this chapter. This difference of opinion has been further complicated by the Texas Supreme Court in it application of inception of title when characterizing worker's compensation benefits. *See Lewis v. Lewis*, 944 S.W.2d 630 (Tex. 1997).

As mentioned above, the first case in this chapter, *Foster v. Christensen*, establishes the right to rebut the community property presumption.

FOSTER
v.
CHRISTENSEN

67 S.W.2d 246
(Tex. Comm'n App. 1934, judgmt adopted)

SMEDLEY, JUDGE.

On April 15, 1916, W. H. Foster and his wife, Loula, conveyed to George A. Newgent and his wife, Frances F. Newgent, who was the daughter of Mr. and Mrs. Foster, certain land containing

55.6 acres in Kleberg county, Tex.; the deed reciting a cash payment of $600, the execution by the grantees of a note in the sum of $580, to be paid in yearly installments amounting each to one-fourth of the annual crops raised on the land, and the assumption of eight promissory vendor's lien notes, each in the sum of $200 theretofore executed by W. H. Foster to Theodore F. Koch. A vendor's lien was expressly retained to secure all the unpaid purchase money. The deed contained no statement that the land was intended to be the separate property of either of the grantees.

A petition in bankruptcy was filed against George A. Newgent, and he was adjudged a bankrupt on November 1, 1922. In the schedules filed by him he listed among his debts the $580 note and also a balance of $800 and interest due on the eight $200 notes above described, and among his assets he listed the above-described land. The claim of the bankrupt that the land was exempt as homestead was contested by a creditor, and after a hearing before the referee an order was entered December 31, 1923, declaring that the land was not homestead, but was subject to the payment of the claims of the creditors. This order recited that the hearing was had after notice "to the creditors and other interested parties."

On application of the trustee, an order was entered November 17, 1924, directing the trustee to sell said tract of land free of all liens at public auction after publishing notice of the sale. This order does not recite that it was entered after a hearing or pursuant to any notice. On December 9, 1924, an order was entered by the referee reciting that the trustee had reported the sale of said land in accordance with the order of sale to defendant in error Pete Christensen for the sum of $608, approving the report, and directing the trustee to execute a deed to the purchaser conveying the land to him free of liens. On the next day the trustee executed the deed as directed.

On April 17, 1925, W. H. Foster and wife filed suit in the district court of Nueces County, Tex., against George A. Newgent, Frances F. Newgent, Pete Christensen, and A. L. Ray and wife. This suit was for recovery of the principal and interest due upon the $580 note and a renewal of same executed on March 24, 1924, and for foreclosure of the lien. . . . On June 9, 1925, Newgent and wife, as defendants in that suit, filed a waiver of service, and on that day judgment was rendered in favor of the plaintiffs reciting the default of the defendant Christensen and of the Rays and foreclosing the lien. At the sheriff's sale the land was bought by W.H. Foster and wife.

* * *

[Suit was then filed by Christiansen to set aside the default judgment.]

The trial court sustained demurrers to practically all of the answer except that part of the same alleging Mrs. Newgent's separate ownership of the land, the execution of the $580 note, the retention of the lien securing it, and its renewal. All evidence offered by plaintiffs in error for the purpose of proving Mrs. Newgent's separate ownership of the land, notice to defendant in error of such claim, and that plaintiffs in error were not notified of and did not appear in the proceedings in bankruptcy, was excluded, and judgment was rendered for defendant in error following an instructed verdict. The Court of Civil Appeals affirmed the judgment of the trial court, apparently, as shown by its opinion on motion for rehearing, upon the sole ground that the claims asserted by plaintiffs in error were in effect a collateral attack upon the orders of the court of bankruptcy which could not be entertained. 42 S.W. 2d 460.

A careful consideration of the nature of the wife's separate property and of the rule against collateral attack leads us to a different conclusion.

The land, of course, presumptively became the community property of Mr. and Mrs. Newgent when it was conveyed to them jointly with no recital of her separate ownership; but her ownership of the land as her separate property would have been established by proof of the allegations in the answer that the cash payment was made out of her separate funds and that it was agreed at the time by the parties to the deed that the land should be her separate property and that the balance of the purchase money should be paid out of her separate funds. The effect of such proof would not be altered by the fact that the husband joined in the promise to pay the balance of the purchase money. *See McClintic v. Midland Grocery & Dry Goods Co.*, 106 Tex. 32, 154 S. W. 1157; *Presidio Mining Co. v. Bullis*, 68 Tex. 581, 4 S. W. 860; *Carter v. Bolin* (Tex. Civ. App.) 30 S. W. 1084; SPEER'S LAW OF MARITAL RIGHTS (3d Ed.) §§ 428-429.

When the wife's separate funds are used to pay but part of the purchase price of land acquired by the husband and wife during marriage, she has, in the absence of a different intention, an interest or equity in the land in proportion to such payment by her. The wife's separate ownership of property, although standing in the name of her husband or appearing on record to be community property, may be proven as any other fact by any competent evidence, including parol evidence, surrounding circumstances, and declarations of the parties. See the authorities last above cited and *Cummins v. Cummins*, (Tex. Civ. App.) 224 S. W. 903; SPEER'S LAW OF MARITAL RIGHTS (3d Ed.) §§ 406, 428, 429, 437.

Her ownership of separate property is a separate and individual ownership, and not merely a claim or inchoate right. In *Read v. Allen*, 56 Tex. 182, 193, it is said: "With us, husband and wife, as regards their personal property, unless when otherwise provided by statute, are separate and distinct persons in law." That case holds that a wife not actually a party to a suit is not bound by the judgment rendered in the suit even though her husband is a party, for the reason that the presence of her husband as a party to the suit does not make the wife constructively a party.

Judgment of foreclosure and sale in a suit against the husband when the land is the separate property of the wife does not affect her title and does not estop her. *Williamson v. Conner*, 92 Tex. 581, 50 S. W. 697; *Wilson v. Johnson*, 94 Tex. 272, 60 S. W. 242, 243. In the opinion in the case last cited, Judge Gaines said: "A judgment against him in a suit to recover property belonging to her in her own right, to which she is not a party, does not bind her."

Even though the title to the land was taken in the name of her husband, if it in fact is the wife's separate property, her title cannot be affected by any disposition made of it by her husband's will. *Mitchell v. Mitchell*, 80 Tex. 101, 15 S. W. 705. Judge Speer, speaking of the nature of the wife's separate property, says: "Her estate is separate in the sense that it belongs to her rather than to her husband, the community or any other person." SPEER'S LAW OF MARITAL RIGHTS (3d Ed.) § 399.

A writ of error was refused in the case of *Citizens' State Bank v. Jeffries* (Tex. Civ. App.) 2 S.W.2d 317, in which the court held that a wife is not a party to proceedings in bankruptcy against her husband, and that his wrongful designation in such proceedings of property as homestead, other than the true homestead, will not estop her from claiming the true homestead.

Since the wife's ownership of separate property is a separate, distinct, and independent ownership, Mrs. Newgent was not bound by the proceedings in bankruptcy (if in fact the land or an interest in it was her separate property) unless she was a party to such proceedings; and if she was not a party to them, the rule against collateral attack has no application to her.

* * *

Since the wife's separate property or interest is equitable in its nature when the title appears of record to be in the community, she may lose her title through its acquisition from the husband by an innocent purchaser for value. *Patty v. Middleton*, 82 Tex. 586, 17 S. W. 909; SPEER'S LAW OF MARITAL RIGHTS (3d Ed.) §§ 439, 448, and cases cited.

From the foregoing authorities and the rules announced by them it necessarily follows, in our opinion, that Mrs. Newgent was not a party to the proceedings in bankruptcy merely because she was the wife of the bankrupt; that if she was not in fact a party to the proceedings under which the land was sold, the purchaser acquired only such title as her husband had, and not the title that she may have separately owned, provided of course the purchaser was not a purchaser for value without notice of her claim of title; and that proof by her of her ownership of the land, or an interest in it, as her separate property, she not being a party to such proceedings, would not violate the rule against collateral attack.

* * *

Defendant in error contends that the court of bankruptcy by its order with reference to the claim of homestead made by the bankrupt determined against Mrs. Newgent her claim of separate ownership, and that a recital of that order proved that she was a party to the proceeding in which it was entered. The order, however, does not undertake to determine whether the land was community or separate property. It merely rejects the bankrupt's claim that the land was exempt as his homestead, and adjudges that as against such claim the land is subject to the payment of the claims of creditors. The recital of notice in the order is that notice was issued and mailed "to the creditors and other interested parties." This is not a recital that Mrs. Newgent was notified of, or appeared at, the hearing. The order does not even recite that all interested parties were notified.

* * *

It follows that the trial court erred in sustaining exceptions to the pleadings and in excluding evidence offered with respect to Mrs. Newgent's claim of separate ownership, the payments made by her on the purchase price of the land, the want of service upon her, her nonappearance as a party in the proceedings in bankruptcy, and notice to defendant in error of her claim of ownership.

Facts might possibly have existed which would have estopped Mrs. Newgent from asserting her claim of separate ownership against defendant in error, but defendant in error did not plead or prove facts sufficient so to estop her. *See John v. Battle*, 58 Tex. 591; *In re Torchia* (C. C. A.) 188 F. 207; *In re Jacobson* (C. C. A.) 4 F.2d 211; SPEER'S LAW OF MARITAL RIGHTS (3d Ed.) §§ 271-275, 277.

* * *

Evidence offered by Mrs. Newgent of payments made by her to the bank out of her separate funds prior to the trustee's sale should have been admitted as tending to prove her claim of separate ownership of the land, or of an interest in it.

On another trial, under proper pleadings and in order to adjust equities, evidence should be admitted as to payments which may have been made in good faith by any of the parties upon any debt secured by a prior existing lien or for taxes, and by which payments the true owner of the land must necessarily have been benefited.

* * *

We recommend that the judgment of the Court of Civil Appeals and that of the trial court be reversed and the cause remanded for trial in accordance with this opinion.

* * *

CURETON, CHIEF JUSTICE.

The judgments of the District Court and Court of Civil Appeals are both reversed, and cause remanded, as recommended by the Commission of Appeals.

We approve the holdings of the Commission of Appeals on the questions discussed in its opinion.

Questions

1. By what proof could the separate character of the wife's property be established?

2. The court mentions that the property was conveyed to the couple jointly, "with no recital of her separate ownership." Can you describe the "recital" to which the court refers?

3. Is the character of the wife's property ever resolved?

MAPLES v. NIMITZ

615 S.W.2d 690
(Tex. 1981)

BARROW, JUSTICE.

Necil Nimitz, administratrix of the estate of Ruth Cochran Maples, filed this cause against Frank L. (Jack) Maples, Jr., independent executor of the estate of Frank L. Maples, Sr., seeking to recover property allegedly belonging to the estate of Ruth Maples. The trial court rendered judgment on the jury verdict that all realty and personalty in dispute was the community property of Frank and Ruth Maples and Ruth's estate was awarded judgment for one-half of such property. The court of civil appeals reformed the trial court judgment to delete recovery for funds on deposit at a named bank and, as reformed, affirmed the trial court judgment. 610 S.W.2d 794. Only Jack Maples complains of the judgment of the court of civil appeals. We affirm.

Ruth Cochran and Frank Maples were married in 1951 and lived together until Ruth's death in 1977. Frank died a year later. The couple operated Maples Trailer Park in Orange during their marriage. There were no children born of this marriage. Ruth had three children by a prior marriage, including Necil Nimitz; and Jack was Frank Maples' son by a prior marriage. Ownership of two items of property are in controversy on this appeal: (1) thirteen and one-half acres of land; and (2) a savings account with the First Savings Association of Orange, Texas in the name of "Mr. or Mrs. Frank Maples."

A ten acre tract on which the couple operated Maples Trailer Park was conveyed to Frank in 1921. In 1948 Frank acquired an eight acre tract of undeveloped land across the street from the ten acre tract. However, all but three and one-half acres of the latter tract was sold before Ruth's death. It is undisputed that both tracts were his separate property at the time of their acquisition. For purposes of this appeal, both tracts are considered as one piece of property. Jack testified that in 1955 Frank conveyed the land to him. In 1972, during the marriage of Frank and Ruth, the property was conveyed to Frank by Jack and it remained in Frank's possession until the death of Ruth. Under these facts, there is a presumption that the property was community property of Frank and Ruth at her death. Section 5.02 of the Family Code provides that "(P)roperty possessed by either spouse during or on dissolution of marriage is presumed to be community property." *See: Cockerham v. Cockerham*, 527 S.W.2d 162 (Tex. 1975); *McKinley v. McKinley*, 496 S.W.2d 540 (Tex. 1973); *Tarver v. Tarver*, 394 S.W.2d 780 (Tex. 1965).

Jack recognizes the validity of this presumption but urges that it is inapplicable in this cause for two reasons: (1) the 1955 deed was not introduced into evidence and Jack's oral testimony that there was a conveyance is ineffective to convey legal title from Frank Maples to Jack; and (2) assuming that title was in him prior to the 1972 conveyance, Jack urges that he merely held it in trust for his father and that by the 1972 deed, he merely reconveyed Frank's separate property.

It must be recognized at the outset that this was not a trespass to try title case and Mrs. Nimitz was not required to establish a formal chain of title. Jack's unchallenged admission against interest that the tract was conveyed to him in 1955 was sufficient to establish this fact. This admission is corroborated by the fact that the inventory of Frank Maples' safety deposit box which was made subsequent to his death included a 1955 deed from Frank to Jack.

A more difficult question is raised by Jack's contention that he was merely holding the property in trust for his father from 1955 until 1972. Jack testified that his father conveyed the land to him in 1955 because his father had sustained a heart attack and because of threats of some unexplained nature by the Nimitz family. It is established that the property was exclusively in Jack's name for seventeen years. During that period six deeds of trust on this property were executed by Jack as security for loans. Jack testified that these loans were made to his father for improvements to the trailer park, although Jack conceded that all loans were made in Jack's name. Although the 1972 deed recites consideration, Jack testified that none was actually paid by his father. Jack urges that his return of the property to his father in 1972 was in the nature of a gift. Since Jack was an interested party and his uncorroborated testimony that Frank paid no consideration for the 1972 deed could not be disputed by Mrs. Nimitz, this testimony was not conclusive. *Praetorian Mutual Life Insurance Co. v. Sherman*, 455 S.W.2d 201 (Tex. 1970). We conclude there is more than a scintilla of evidence that the property belonged to Jack before it was conveyed to Frank in 1972 for a valuable consideration.

The jury found in response to Issue No. 1 "that the land conveyed in a deed to Frank L. Maples, Sr. from Frank L. (Jack) Maples, Jr. on the 19th day of April 1972 is the community property of Frank and Ruth Cochran Maples." Jack objected to the submission of Issue No. 1 because it calls for a legal conclusion. In connection with this objection, Jack requested issues which would have inquired if the land was conveyed to Frank by Jack as a gift. These requested issues were refused by the trial court. The trial court instructed the jury in connection with Issue No. 1 that all property acquired during marriage by gift is separate property. "Community property" was also defined by the trial court. Jack did not object to these explanatory instructions given with Issue No. 1.

Rule 277, Texas Rules of Civil Procedure, as amended effective September 1, 1973, authorizes the trial court in its discretion to submit issues broadly. This amended rule expressly provides that in submitting the case, "the court shall submit such explanatory instructions and definitions as shall be proper to enable the jury to render a verdict and in such instances the charge shall not be subject to the objection that it is a general charge." Here the broad issue when properly considered with the court's instructions required the jury to resolve the disputed fact issue as to whether Jack was holding the property in trust for his father from 1955 until 1972. The court did not err in submitting the issue broadly along with appropriate instructions. *Brown v. American Transfer & Storage Co.*, 601 S.W.2d 931 (Tex. 1980); *Republic Ins. Co. v. Bolton*, 564 S.W.2d 440 (Tex. Civ. App.—Dallas 1978, writ ref'd n.r.e.).

We conclude that the courts below properly held that under the verdict of the jury the real estate conveyed to Frank during his marriage to Ruth was community property. Her estate was correctly awarded an undivided one-half interest in this property.

* * *

The judgment of the court of civil appeals is affirmed.

WALLACE, J., notes his dissent.

Notes, Comments & Questions

1. *Maples v. Nimitz* focuses on the acquisition of property, or perhaps more accurately, the re-acquisition of property. The re-acquisition was during marriage and, thus, the community property presumption prevailed.

2. Why did Jack's "trust" theory fail?

3. A portion of *Maples v. Nimitz* was deleted from this casebook. That deleted portion addressed the character of bank accounts that the parties had attempted to hold as joint tenants with right of survivorship. This attempt was unsuccessful even in light of a probate code section that appeared to sanction the attempt. The court, citing *Williams v. McKnight*, 402 S.W.2d 505 (Tex. 1966) and other cases, held that without adherence to the two-step procedure, a joint tenancy with right of survivorship could not be created, i.e. there must be a partition before a joint tenancy can be established. Would such be the outcome today?

B. The Doctrine of Inception of Title

For more than 150 years, the Texas Constitution in its various incarnations has recognized that property owned or claimed by a spouse before marriage is the separate property of that spouse. It is not the simple passing of title that controls character, but rather it is the date on which the ownership or claim arises that controls; if the ownership of or claim to property arises before marriage, then the property is separate. *Welder v. Lambert*, 44 S.W. 281 (Tex. 1898), is the seminal inception of title case, making clear that transfer of paper title does not necessarily control inception of title and thus, does not control characterization.

Welder v. Lambert concerns land obtained under Mexican contracts to colonize issued in 1834 by the states of Coahuila and Texas. As you read *Welder v. Lambert* pay special attention to the court's determination of when a claim, capable of affecting character, arises. Although we are no longer concerned with contracts to colonize, as you read *Welder v. Lambert*, consider the circumstances in which it might be applied today.

WELDER
v.
LAMBERT
44 S.W. 281
(1898)

GAINES, CHIEF JUSTICE.

In this case certain questions have been certified by the court of civil appeals for the First supreme judicial district for our decision. The statement and questions are as follows:

The appellants, Dolores Welder and others, brought the suit against the appellees, Pat Lambert and others, in form for the partition of a part of 4½ leagues of land situated in Refugio county, on the west side of the San Antonio river, granted to the impresarios, James Power and James Hewitson, as premium lands, for the introduction of colonists, under a contract with the state of Coahuila and Texas. There had been a partition of the interests of Power and Hewitson, and the 4 1/2 leagues above mentioned were set apart to Power. The contract for colonization was made June 11, 1828. The grant of the 4½ leagues was made October 12, 1834, and the other premium lands were granted in December, 1834. Power was twice married. In July, 1832, he married Dolores de la Portilla. By this marriage there were two children, the appellant Dolores Welder and a son, James Power, who was the father of the other appellants. The appellants are the only heirs of Dolores, the first wife. She died in 1836. Afterwards James Power married Tomasa de la Portilla, a sister of the first wife, who bore him five children. James Power died in 1852, and Tomasa, his second wife, died in 1893. The appellees represent the entire interest of the five children by the second marriage. Appellants contend that the land was the community property of James Power and his first wife, Dolores, and that they are entitled to one-half thereof in the right of their mother, and to two-sevenths of the remaining one-half in their right as heirs of James Power, while appellees contend that the land was the separate property of James Power, and that the appellants are only entitled to two-sevenths of the whole.

The contract of Power and Hewitson with the State of Coahuila and Texas was for a colony within the littoral leagues, and received the approbation of the Supreme Government. Article 1 refers to the approbation of the supreme government, and states that the government admits the project, so far as conformable to the law of April 24, 1824. It defines the limits of the colony, which was afterwards, on March 13, 1829, augmented, and the colony was established in the augmentation limits. The remaining articles of the contract are as follows:

> Art. 2d. In view of the described territory, the impresarios remain obligated to introduce and settle, on their own account, two hundred, instead of four hundred, families, which they offered; it being an express condition that one-half of this contract shall be Mexican families, and the rest alien families, from Ireland.
>
> Art. 3rd. All possessions, with corresponding titles, found within the territory described in Art. 1st, shall be respected by the colonists of this contract; the impresarios being charged with compliance with this obligation.
>
> Art. 4th. Whenever any land may be required, as useful and advantageous, owing to its locality and circumstances, for the construction of some fortress, wharf, or store, for the defense of the port, or establishment of public administration, the impresarios shall have no right to prevent the occupation of any land or interesting point that it may be advantageous to take for any of the indicated objects, or any other not herein expressed.
>
> Art. 5th. In conformity to the law of March 24, 1825, the impresarios remain obligated to introduce and settle the two hundred families mentioned in Art. 2d within the term of six years, counted from this day, on penalty of forfeiting the rights and donations granted them by the same law.
>
> Art. 6th. The families, besides being Catholic, as the law requires, must be of good character; establishing these qualifications with certificates by the authorities of the country whence they came.
>
> Art. 7th. It is an obligation of the impresarios not to introduce nor permit within their colony criminals, vagrants, or men of bad conduct. They shall cause all persons in such circumstances to leave their territory, and in case of resistance the armed force must be resorted to.
>
> Art. 8th. To this end, whenever there shall be a sufficient number of men the National Civic Militia shall be organized, in full compliance with the law.
>
> Art. 9th. Whenever they shall have introduced at least one hundred families, they shall notify the Government, in order that it may send a Commissioner to give to the colonists possession of their lands, and to establish towns in conformity to the law and to the instructions which he shall receive.
>
> Art. 10th. After the particular application of lands to colonists, and of premiums to the impresarios, shall have been made, the Government alone shall have the power to dispose of the lands remaining vacant.
>
> Art. 11th. Official communications with the government or authorities in the state, and all public instruments and deeds, must be written in the Castillian language.
>
> Art. 12th. In all other cases not expressed in the articles of the present contract, the impresarios shall subject themselves to the general constitution and laws, and to the particular constitution and laws of the state.
>
> And his Excellency the Governor, and the attorney, in the name of the impresarios, having agreed to every one of the articles of the present covenant, obligated themselves

reciprocally to punctual compliance herewith before me, the Secretary of State, and signed hereto for perpetuation. And, the original proceedings remaining archived, a testimonio of the whole proceedings was ordered to be delivered in duplicates to the party interested for his protection, Leona Vicario, June 11th, 1828. - Jose Maria Viesca - Victor Blanco - Juan Antonio Padillo, Secretary. This is a copy. Santiago del Valle, Sec.

Dolores de la Portilla had no separate means when she married Power and did not receive anything from any source after her marriage. The evidence shows that colonists were introduced both before and after the marriage; but it is uncertain how many were introduced before and how many were introduced after. If the respective interests in the land are to be established by proof as to what proportion of the consideration for the grant was of the separate estate of Power and what of the community estate of himself and his wife Dolores, the party having the burden of proof will be at great disadvantage on account of the uncertainty of the evidence.

* * *

Upon the foregoing statement, the opinion of the supreme court is requested upon the following questions:

1. Did the fact that the grant to the land in controversy was made after the marriage of James Power and Dolores de la Portilla create the presumption that the land was the community property of the said James Power and his said wife Dolores?

2. Upon an issue of fact as to how much of the consideration for the grant was of the separate estate of Power and how much was of the community estate of himself and his wife, on which party should the burden of proof rest?

3. What efforts or expenditures of Power should be estimated in determining the extent of the separate and community interests in the land? Should his expenditures and labors in obtaining the contract be taken into the estimation?

4. What was the character of the title inherited by the appellants from their mother? Was it legal or equitable?

* * *

Preliminary to answering the questions certified, we deem it expedient to determine what the respective interests of Power and his first wife were in the lands at the time the final title was extended. The Spanish law being at that time in force, the result of the inquiry must depend upon the principles of that system of jurisprudence. There are decisions of this court which bear upon the question but there are none that we have found, in which the precise point has been considered. The Spanish authors, having no precedents to guide them, are necessarily confined to the enunciation of general principles, which fall short of declaring the law as to the specific question before us.

We are of the opinion that the concession made to Power and Hewitson under the law of Coahuila and Texas of March 24, 1825, by which, in consideration of their stipulating to introduce into the State a certain number of families, they were given the right to a premium in lands to be selected and granted to them upon their compliance with the agreement, has all the elements of a contract; and it seems to us that it is a matter of no moment whether the right so acquired was alienable or not. It was a fixed contract right, which entitled them to acquire the lands by a compliance with its conditions, and, as we think, was property, under the Spanish law. Escriche, in his Dictionary, treats of the respective rights of the husband and wife in the property held by them under the words "Bienes Gananciales," and he there says: "Among 'las bienes gananciales' are not considered: (1) Those which the consorts had at the time of contracting the marriage. . . ." ESCRICHE DIC. LEG. p. 367. In defining the meaning of the word "bienes," he uses this language: "Under the word 'bienes' are included, also, 'las acciones,' of whatever kind they may be. 'Acque bonis adnumeratur quod est in actionibus, petitionibus, persecutionibus.' " *Id.* p. 362. The first class of "acciones" defined by the author cited are shares in a partnership or incorporated company. *Id.* p. 48. Then, again, under a separate head, he defines the word "accion" as follows:

> The right to demand anything, and the method of judicial procedure which we have for the recovery of that which is ours, or which another owes us. * * * "La accion," meant in the first sense that is, such as a right which belongs to us to demand anything,—may be considered movable or immovable [that is—personal or real] by reason of its object, although it may be neither the one nor the other in its nature.

Id. p. 49. The result is that all choses in action owned by either of the consorts before marriage, remain the separate property of such consort.

If contracts be property, and if all property held by either the husband or wife at the time of the marriage be the separate property of the consort who held it, it follows that the right of acquisition secured to Power by the contract of himself and Hewitson with the State of Coahuila and Texas remained his separate property upon his marriage, and did not fall into the community.

But this comes short of settling the point under consideration. The inquiry still remains, is the status of the property to be determined by the acquisition of the final title or by the origin of the title? Upon this point we have found no direct expression in the authorities upon the Spanish law. But in Louisiana, where the community system prevails, the question has been set at rest by repeated decisions of the Supreme Court of that State. * * *

* * *

Our own decisions are in harmony with the principles announced in the cases referred to, although as we have said—the precise point seems not to have been determined. In *Mills v. Brown*, 69 Tex. 244, 6 S.W. 612, a widow, the head of a family, was entitled to acquire a homestead by settling upon the public domain, causing a survey to be made of the land, and by a continued residence thereon with an improvement of the same. While still a widow, she made application for the land, and paid the surveying fees. Thereafter, she married, and moved with her husband upon the property. The conditions of the law were complied with, and, she having died, a patent issued to her heirs. The question came up in a suit between the heirs and a purchaser holding under the husband. It was held that the land was community, and not separate property, and that the heirs were entitled to recover only one-half and the surveying fees paid by her mother. The court, speaking through Chief Justice Willie, say:

> To ascertain, therefore, the status of the property in controversy, we must find out by whom the first actual settlement upon it was made, of what the family consisted who first occupied the land, and in whose behalf an application could thereafter be made for a homestead pre-emption. The evidence upon that point is clear and undisputed. The settlement was made by Yarborough and his wife, formerly Mary Roberts, and her children by a former marriage. This initial and absolutely essential step was the joint enterprise of husband and wife. The occupation was continued by them jointly so long as the wife lived, and by the husband till the title matured. Considered in reference to this state of facts alone, there cannot be a shadow of a doubt that the husband had the same interest in the land as that held by the wife or her heirs, and that it was community estate. We are of opinion that the facts that Yarborough's wife had, before marriage, filed a pre-emption claim to the land and paid the surveying fees out of her own money, do not affect the right

> of her husband to a community interest in the homestead pre-emption. The law, as we have seen, does not contemplate that a survey shall be made on an application therefore filed until the pre-emptors have actually settled upon the land. Such acts must necessarily inure to the benefit of the family who make the first settlement, and no steps taken previous to that time by any member thereof for the benefit of any portion of the family and the exclusion of the remainder, can defeat the object of the law, which is to give to actual settlers a home upon land previously occupied by them.

In *Manchaca v. Field*, 62 Tex. 135, the husband obtained a concession for the purchase of 11 leagues of land, to be selected by him under the twenty-fourth section of the Colonization law of March 24, 1825. He obtained the final title to 10 leagues under the concession granted to him, but before the extension of that title the wife died. The grant was held to be community property. In that case the court say:

> It is urged by the defendants that, although the concession had issued in the lifetime of Mrs. Sanches, no step had been taken to appropriate any land under it; that, before the grant could be made effectual by the issuance of the final title, it was necessary to obtain the consent of the impresario to locate the concession within his colony; that the particular land must have been selected, and surveyed and classified by an authorized surveyor, and the survey and classification approved by the commissioner, and that the fees of the impresario and other colonial officials, and the amount due the government for the land according to its classification, must have been paid or secured; and that the mere concession, which was nothing more than a license to purchase so many leagues of the public domain, to be subsequently selected, and at a price and on terms to be subsequently determined, ought not to be treated as property in being at the death of Mrs. Sanches, so as to entitle her heirs to claim a community interest in the land afterwards granted under it. There is much force in the argument, and it finds an apparent sanction in *Webb v. Webb*, 15 Tex. 274; *Walters v. Jewett*, 28 Tex. 192, and perhaps other decisions of this court, but the later decisions and the weight of authority seem to favor the proposition of appellants, that the concession, having a money value, and being the subject of sale, was property, in which Mrs. Sanches had a community interest, which descended to her heirs at her death, and which attached to the grant subsequently extended in the name of her husband. *Porter v. Chronister*, 58 Tex. 54; *Wilkinson v. Wilkinson*, 20 Tex. 244; *Yates v. Houston*, 3 Tex. 433.

See also, *Hodge v. Donald*, 55 Tex. 344. All these cases turned upon the determination of the question whether or not the party taking the initial step in the acquisition of the property was at the time married or single.

Nor do we regard either the ruling in *Webb v. Webb*, 15 Tex. 275, or that in *Walters v. Jewett*, 28 Tex. 192, as being in conflict with these views. In the former, Judge Lipscomb, speaking for the court, says:

> The question presented by this statement of facts is, was the property in controversy held by the husband and wife, at the time of her death, as community property? If it was, there is no question but that her heirs are entitled to the one-half, after the payment of the community debts. The statement of facts shows conclusively that the title to the land was not obtained until after the dissolution of the matrimonial relations by the death of the wife. Does it show that anything had been done before this dissolution, giving a right in law to demand the title that subsequently issued to the husband, on which an equity could be raised in favor of the heirs of the wife, and attach to the land? The record of the statement of facts shows that the land had been selected before the death of the wife, but does not

> show in what way it had been selected,—whether by application to the commissioner, or in any other way. It does not show that the requisite qualifications of the applicant had been decided upon by the commissioner, or that anything had been done that was essential to the validity of the grant, prior to the death of the wife. We have no evidence that the necessary qualification of the colonist had been adjudicated upon by the commissioner before the date of the title; and at that time the husband was qualified, as a head of a family, to have received the same quantity of land, as his children were in the country with him.

This extract, as we think, makes it manifest that if it had been shown that the land had been lawfully selected and the qualifications of the husband adjudicated before the death of the wife, the result would have been different. The ruling that the immigration of the husband with the wife did not, of itself, entitle the latter to a half interest in the land granted by reason of that immigration, may be in conflict with other decisions upon that point; but, in so far as the decision bears upon the question under consideration, it seems to us to be in accord with our cases previously cited.

In *Walters v. Jewett*, *supra*, we do not understand the court to hold that the heirs of the wife were not originally entitled in equity to an interest in the land by reason of their mother's community right. There, during the life of the wife, the husband sold one-half of his right to acquire land from the Republic by reason of his immigration as the head of a family. After her death he sold the other half. Both sales were made before the certificate issued. The certificate was issued to Jewett, his assignee, and the patent issued in the name of Jewett. The court held that the heirs of the wife had a mere equitable claim upon the land, and that it could not be recovered in an action of trespass to try title.

In most of the cases cited, where the initial step in procuring title was taken, the purpose was to acquire a specific tract of land. In that respect the case before us is different. Power and Hewitson were not entitled, upon compliance with the conditions of their contract, to any specific tract or tracts. They were entitled only to so many leagues of land which were to be selected. In this respect it does not differ from the case of *Manchaca v. Field*, before cited. In that case, however, the concession was obtained while Sanches was a married man, and the lands were held to be of the community although the final title was not extended until after the death of the wife. If he had been single at the date of the concession and had married before the issuing of the title, the lands would doubtless have been held his separate property and the case would have been precisely in point.

In this cause the title originated in the contract of Power and Hewitson with the State of Coahuila and Texas. That contract, in the language of the Louisiana court, was the 'cause' of the title. Power was single when it was entered into, and the right to earn the lands acquired by it was his separate property. The title relates to its origin, and must take the impress of its character from it.

The rule of the Spanish law as to improvements made with community funds upon the separate property of the husband or wife is thus stated by SCHMIDT: "Money expended in improving property belonging to one of the spouses belongs to the community, but gives the other no claims to the property itself." SCHMIDT, SPANISH LAW, art. 48. It was so ruled by the Supreme Court of Louisiana in cases in which the rights of the parties depended upon the laws of Spain. *Hughey v. Barrow*, 4 La. Ann. 248; *Frique v. Hopkins*, 4 Mart. N.S. 212. These were cases in which the lands of one of the spouses were improved from community funds. We find no rule laid down in the Spanish laws which applies to a case precisely like this. But, as we understand that law, improvements, such as buildings and the like, made upon the land of one of the consorts by the community must, upon partition, be credited to the community estate, and are made a charge upon the property. 2 FEBRERO REFORMADO, arts. 2403, 2404, p. 95. The question here must therefore be determined by analogy to that principle. In *Mills v. Brown*, before cited, the expense of acquiring the land, which was held to be community property, was borne in part by the separate money of the wife. It was ruled that the heirs of the wife were entitled to one-half of the land, as community, and to a reimbursement of one-half of the expense so paid as a charge upon the husband's half of the property itself. They were not entitled to recover the other half of such expense, because they received one-half of the land, and in that had one-half of the benefit of the expense. This decision would, we think, be absolutely controlling but for the fact that it is a ruling upon our own statutes, and not upon the Spanish law. But we think that the principle was deduced from the latter law. In the case of *Moseman's Succession* [*Succession of Moseman*, 38 La.Ann. 219], before cited, the doctrine was distinctly announced and applied. It follows, as we think, that upon partition of the property in controversy, the land was chargeable in favor of the community with whatever the community may have contributed in labor and funds to its acquisition.

Having disposed of the preliminary points which, as we think, are necessarily involved in the questions propounded by the Court of Civil Appeals, we proceed to answer as follows:

1. Although both under our statute and under the Spanish law, the presumption of community property arises from the naked fact that it was acquired during the marriage, yet when, as in this case, upon the exhibition of the whole title it appears that its origin preceded the marriage and that it was the separate property of one of the spouses, we are of the opinion that the presumption no longer prevails.

2. The lands in controversy appearing to be of the separate estate of Power, we are of opinion that in order for the heirs of the first wife to establish a charge upon them for a reimbursement of community funds expended in their acquisition, the burden was upon them to prove that the funds had been so expended. 2 FEBRERO REFORMADO, art. 2414, p. 98.

3. We do not deem it necessary to decide the third question. The lands being the separate property of Power, and the heirs of the wife as such having no title in the property itself, the questions are: Were community funds invested in acquiring them? And if so, how much?

4. The fourth question we consider abstract. We think this sufficiently appears from what we have already said.

* * *

This opinion will be certified to the Court of Civil Appeals of the First Supreme Judicial District as an answer to the questions propounded.

Questions

1. When does title incept under a claim of homestead?

2. When does title incept under a claim of adverse possession?

3. Why the different treatment?

4. The court in the *Welder v. Lambert* opinion touches upon the concepts of reimbursement and pro rata characterization. Explain each concept within the *Welder v. Lambert* context.

5. With land grants and contracts to colonize no longer being available, can you think of a present day application of the case of *Welder v. Lambert*? See the next case, *Carter v. Carter*, for a hint.

CARTER
v.
CARTER
736 S.W.2d 775
(Tex. App.—Houston [14th Dist.] 1987, no writ)

SEARS, JUSTICE.

Nancy Marie Carter (appellant) appeals from a division of property in a divorce decree. At issue is the characterization of certain stocks and bonds and a house in Montgomery County, Texas, which were awarded to Donald H. Carter, Jr. (appellee) as his separate property. At appellant's request, the trial court filed Findings of Fact and Conclusions of Law. Appellant did not file any objections to these findings nor did she request any additional findings. In eight points of error appellant alleges the trial court abused its discretion in characterizing the stocks and the house as separate property or in failing to impose a constructive trust on the house. We affirm.

* * *

Points of error three through eight concern the characterization of the parties' home. Once again, we begin our inquiry with the presumption that property possessed by either spouse during or on dissolution of marriage is community property. A spouse claiming separate ownership must overcome this presumption by clear and convincing evidence.

Appellee testified that on October 29, 1974, he signed an earnest money contract on the Montgomery County house and secured it with a $1,000 check written on his separate account. This was prior to the December 7, 1974, marriage. The closing took place on January 15, 1975, and both parties signed the note and deed of trust. Appellee further testified that the down payment at closing was also paid out of his separate account.

The trial court found the following:

> 13. The earnest money contract providing for the purchase of Lot 91 of Hiwon, Section 1, Panorama Village, a subdivision in Montgomery County, Texas with DONALD H. CARTER, JR., individually, as purchaser, was signed prior to the date of his marriage to NANCY MARIE CARTER and the $1,000 of earnest money was paid prior to his marriage to NANCY MARIE CARTER.

The court then found that the lot was appellee's separate property and awarded appellant reimbursement of $30,000 for her share of funds expended by the community estate for improvement of the lot.

Ownership of real property is governed by the rule that "the character of title to property as separate or community depends upon the existence or nonexistence of the marriage at the time of the incipiency of the right in virtue of which the title is finally extended, and that the title, when extended, relates back to that time." *Creamer v. Briscoe*, 101 Tex. 490, 109 S.W. 911, 912 (1908). Appellee acquired a right to title to the property when he entered into the earnest money contract. *Wierzchula v. Wierzchula*, 623 S.W.2d 730, 732 (Tex. Civ. App.—Houston [1st Dist.] 1981, no writ). As the date of execution of the earnest money contract was prior to the marriage, appellee's right to title preceded the marriage and the separate character of the property was thereby established.

In point of error four appellant claims that there was insufficient "clear and convincing" evidence that appellee had acquired the right to title in the property prior to the marriage. Appellant bases her argument on the fact that the earnest money contract was not admitted into evidence and on the lack of evidence in the record to indicate when the contract was *accepted* by the seller. The unchallenged trial court finding was that the contract was signed prior to the marriage. The date of acceptance by the seller is not relevant.

Although the earnest money contract was not in evidence, appellee put into evidence, without objection, a check for $1,000, dated October 19, 1974 (the alleged date the contract was signed) made out to Eagle Title Company. The check appears to have been cashed on November 7, 1974, one month prior to the marriage. This evidence was corroborated by appellant, who testified that she thought the earnest money contract was signed in October and that she was not a party to its execution. Point of error four is overruled.

In point of error seven appellant argues that the deed is the best evidence of title to real property. She contends that the earnest money contract merged into the deed; therefore, the right to acquire the property ripened after the marriage. Appellant cites *Duke v. Duke*, for this proposition. 605 S.W.2d 408, 410 (Tex. Civ. App.—El Paso 1980, writ dism'd w.o.j.). However, though the earnest money contract in *Duke* had been entered into prior to marriage, it provided that the property would be conveyed to "James H. Duke and wife, Barbara J. Duke." This is but an illustration of the rule that in the absence of fraud, accident or mistake, all prior agreements entered into between the parties are considered merged in the deed. *Commercial Bank, Unincorporated, of Mason, Texas v. Satterwhite*, 413 S.W.2d 905, 909 (Tex. 1967). In this case, there is no evidence that both spouses were named in the earnest money contract. Therefore, *Duke* is not applicable and point of error seven is overruled.

Appellant's points of error three, five and six concern several presumptions that she argues affect the separate property characterization of Lot 91. In point of error three appellant asserts that the trial court abused its discretion in characterizing the property as appellee's separate property because where a deed to real property is made to both spouses, a presumption is raised that the spouses agreed the property would be community.

The cases cited by appellant in support of this presumption both involve properties acquired after marriage.[1] The separate or community nature of property is determined by the time and circumstances of its acquisition. *Ray v. United States*, 385 F.Supp. 372, 377 (S.D.Tex. 1974), *aff'd*, 538 F.2d 1228 (5th Cir. 1976); *Lindsay v. Clayman*, 151 Tex. 593, 254 S.W.2d 777, 780 (1952). The trial court characterized Lot 91 as appellee's separate property because the parties were not married at the time the property was acquired and because appellee alone signed the earnest money contract and paid the earnest money. Where there is no evidence of gift, the fact that the deed is in both names does not change the character of the property.

Appellant applies this same reasoning to point of error six regarding insufficient evidence to rebut the presumption that Lot 91 is community because it was purchased with community credit. Appellant contends that as a result of the note being signed after the marriage, there arises a presumption that the property is community because a debt acquired by either spouse during marriage is presumptively a community debt.

In support of her argument appellant cites *Wierzchula*, 623 S.W.2d at 732, which in turn cited *Gleich v. Bongio*, 128 Tex. 606, 99 S.W.2d 881 (1937). *Gleich* involved property purchased during marriage partly with separate funds of the husband and partly on the credit of the community. The *Gleich* court stated, "Money borrowed on a community obligation is community property. Similarly, property acquired on the credit of the community is community property." 99 S.W.2d at 883. *Wierzchula* did concern a situation very similar to the one before us in that an earnest

[1] Belkin v. Ray, 142 Tex. 71, 176 S.W.2d 162 (1943); Gonzalez v. Guajardo de Gonzalez, 541 S.W.2d 865 (Tex. Civ. App.—Waco 1976, no writ).

money contract was signed in the husband's name prior to marriage with the earnest money paid from his separate funds. However, once an earnest money contract is signed and the separate property character attaches, it is immaterial that a community debt may exist or that part of the unpaid purchase price is thereafter paid from community funds. The community estate is only entitled to reimbursement from the separate estate for community funds expended on the separate property. Appellant received such reimbursement. Points of error three and six are thus overruled.

In point of error five appellant argues that there was insufficient evidence to rebut the presumption that because the deed was in both parties' names appellee made a gift or advancement of one-half interest in the property to her. When a spouse uses separate property consideration to pay for land acquired during the marriage, and takes title to the land in the name of both husband and wife, it is presumed that the spouse intended the interest placed in the other to be a gift. *Cockerham*, 527 S.W.2d at 168. However, this presumption is rebuttable, and parol evidence is admissible to show that a gift was not intended. *Peterson v. Peterson*, 595 S.W.2d 889, 892 (Tex. Civ. App.—Austin 1980, writ dism'd w.o.j.).

Appellee testified that he did not intend to make a gift of one-half interest in Lot 91 to appellant. He testified that he did not request that both names be placed on the note and deed of trust. He merely accepted and signed the papers prepared by the savings and loan company. The parties had recently moved to Texas from Michigan and were unfamiliar with Texas community property laws. In addition, appellant offered no evidence that a gift was intended. In finding that Lot 91 was appellee's separate property, the trial court impliedly found that appellee made no gift to appellant. We find no evidence of gift and any such presumption is rebutted by the evidence. Therefore, point of error five is overruled.

* * *

Notes, Comments & Questions

1. When did Mr. Carter acquire the right to the home?

2. The deed for the home named both Mr. and Mrs. Carter. Is the naming of husband and wife prima facie proof of community property?

3. Does the character of the consideration affect the community property presumption?

4. What claim may Mrs. Carter make regarding the home?

5. Later in the course, we will be discussing resurrected claims for reimbursement and claims under the "almost defunct" economic contribution statutes. At this time, please review TEX. FAM. CODE §§ 3.401-3.410 and § 7.007. Keep these statutes in mind when reimbursement is addressed in upcoming chapters.

BROWN
v.
FOSTER LUMBER CO.

178 S.W. 787

(Tex. Civ. App.—Galveston, 1915, writ ref'd)

PLEASANTS, CHIEF JUSTICE.

This is an action of trespass to try title brought by appellee against R.P. Brown and the Michigan Diamond Oil & Refining company to recover the D.M. Bullock 601½ acre survey in San Jacinto county. After the trial began plaintiff took a nonsuit as to the Oil & Refining Company.

The defendant R.P. Brown disclaimed title to all the land, except a tract of 160 acres described in his answer, as to which he pleaded not guilty. He also pleaded limitation of 10 years; that the land was the separate property of his wife; and that it was, and had been since 1875, the homestead of himself and wife.

Mary E. Brown, the wife of defendant, filed petition in intervention, in which she claimed the 100 acres of land as her separate property, alleging that it was conveyed to her by James Smith in 1875 for her sole and separate use, and that she paid for said land with property and money belonging to her separate estate. She also pleaded limitation of 10 years, and that the property had been her homestead since 1875.

The trial in the court below without a jury resulted in a judgment for plaintiff against appellants, R.P. Brown and Mary E. Brown, for the entire tract of 601½ acres.

The record discloses the following facts: The D.M. Bullock survey was patented to M.O. Dimon, assignee, on April 3, 1852. Dimon conveyed it to Gabriel Freidberger on February 7, 1866. In 1873 or 1874 James Smith settled upon the Bullock survey, and in 1875 he sold the 160 acres now claimed by appellants, and upon which he then lived, to Mrs. Brown, for a consideration of $150. This consideration was paid by Mrs. Brown out of her separate estate. After she bought from Smith, she and her husband took possession of the 160 acres and lived thereon continuously for 12 or 13 years, cultivating and using a portion thereof and claiming the whole 160 acres. They afterwards bought a tract of 56 acres upon the Patterson survey adjoining the 160 acres claimed by them on the Bullock and built them a house on said 56 acres. Their dwelling house was near the line of the 160 acres, and the fencing on the two tracts was connected, and both tracts have been used for homestead purposes up to the present time. On May 12, 1899, Gabriel Freidberger brought suit in the district court of San Jacinto county against R.P. Brown and others, to recover the title and possession of the Bullock survey. Mrs. Brown was not a party to this suit, had no knowledge of the fact that the suit was pending, and knew nothing of the judgment that was rendered therein. On October 18, 1900, the following judgment was rendered in said suit:

> On this the 18th day of October, 1900, the above case came to be heard, and the defendant R.P. Brown having agreed to take nothing and to surrender all right and claim that he had or might have at the time of filing of this suit, and the defendant McWilliams having wholly failed to make answer to this petition herein filed in this case, thereupon judgment was asked for and taken in the above styled and numbered cause against the said McWilliams, and Mrs. E.J. McDaniels, one of the defendants in said cause, made and entered into an agreement with the plaintiff G. Freidberger that she take 80 acres of said land which her improvements now stand on, the same to be taken as near as possible out of the northeast corner of the hereinafter described lands, and the said Freidberger is to have and recover the timber on said 80 acres of land, and that the title of said lands be divested out

of each and all of the defendants, except the said E.J. McDaniels who is to have the above 80 acres, and the title to this balance of said land be invested in the said Freidberger, and the title to the said above 80 acres to be divested out of said Freidberger (except the timber on said 80 acres) and invested in the said McDaniels, which said land is described as follows: [Here follows description of the Bullock survey.] It is therefore ordered, adjudged, and decreed by the court that the plaintiff G. Freidberger do have and recover of the defendants, James McWilliams, R.P. Brown, and Mrs. E.J. McDaniels, the lands sued for in plaintiff's petition, except the 80 acres heretofore mentioned and excepted, and the said E.J. McDaniels is to recover the same 80 acres.

On February 7, 1902, Gabriel Freidberger conveyed to the Foster Lumber Company a portion of the Bullock survey, described as follows:

> All the unsold tract or parcel of land situated in San Jacinto county, Tex., being 601½ acres of land patented to M.O. Dimon, assignee of D. M. Bullock, April 3, 1852. No. 337, certificate 178, and described by metes and bounds as follows: [Here follows field notes of Bullock survey]—save and except 80 acres of said land decreed by the district court of said San Jacinto county in the case of *G. Freidberger v. R.P. Brown*, et al., No. 858, of date October 18, 1900, to belong to Mrs. E.J. McDaniels, to be taken by her out of said land where her improvements stand, and the same to be taken, as near as possible, out of the northeast corner thereof.

Under appropriate assignments of error, the appellants assail the judgment of the trial court upon three grounds: First. It is contended that the undisputed evidence shows the 160 acres of land in controversy was the separate property of Mrs. Brown, and she, not being a party to the suit of Freidberger against her husband, R.P. Brown, and others, in which an agreed judgment was rendered in favor of plaintiff for all of the Bullock survey, is not bound by said judgment. Second. If the property was not owned by Mrs. Brown in her separate right, it was the homestead of herself and husband, and she, not having been a party to the suit above mentioned, is not bound by the judgment therein rendered. Third. That the deed from Freidberger to appellee conveys only the unsold portion of the Bullock survey, less the 80 acre tract described in said deed: and there being no evidence showing what portion of the survey had been sold by Freidberger before his conveyance to appellee, or showing that none of said survey had been sold by him prior to said conveyance, said deed does not show title in appellee to the 160 acres of said survey involved in this suit.

We agree with the trial judge in the conclusion that neither of the first two contentions of appellants can be sustained. It is true that the undisputed evidence shows that the deed from James Smith to Mrs. Brown conveyed the land to her in the separate right, and that the consideration for such conveyance was paid by Mrs. Brown out of funds belonging to her separate estate, but the undisputed evidence further shows that Smith had no title to the land, and Mrs. Brown therefore acquired none by said deed. The only title acquired by her was a limitation title which ripened under the adverse claim and possession of herself and husband, and it is clear that property so acquired is community. Until the 10 years adverse claim and possession had expired, the title to the 160 acres remained in Freidberger, and, when this possession ripened into title, it vested in the community, notwithstanding the fact that when such adverse possession began and during all of the 10 years of such possession, Mrs. Brown claimed the land as her separate property under her deed from Smith.

It is now well settled that notwithstanding the fact that the property was the homestead, the wife was not a necessary party to the suit brought by Freidberger for its recovery. Her claim of homestead would have been no defense to said suit, and for that reason it was unnecessary to make her a party to the suit, and she is bound by the judgment rendered against her husband. Such judgment is not void, and cannot be collaterally attacked. *Childress v. Robinson* (Civ. App.) 161 S.W. 78; *Jergens v. Schiele*, 61 Tex. 255; *City of San Antonio v. Berry*, 92 Tex. 327, 48 S.W. 496; *Collins v. Ferguson*, 22 Tex. Civ. App. 552, 56 S.W. 225; *Brown v. Humphrey*, 43 Tex. Civ. App. 23, 95 S.W. 23; *Breath v. Flowers*, 43 Tex. Civ. App. 516, 95 S.W. 26; *Central Coal & Coke Co. v. Henry* (Civ. App.) 47 S.W. 281; SPEER ON LAW OF MARRIED WOMEN, § 295.

If the agreement of R.P. Brown was made in fraud of the homestead rights of his wife, or if the judgment was by mistake or fraud not entered in accordance with the true agreement made by R.P. Brown, it could only be set aside in a timely direct proceeding brought for that purpose.

We think the third contention of appellants above stated is sound and must be sustained. As we construe the deed from Freidberger to appellee, before set out, it conveys only the unsold portion of the Bullock survey, less the 80 acres mentioned in said deed. If this construction of the deed is correct, it follows that said deed does not show title in appellee to the 160 acres of said survey in controversy, in the absence of evidence showing what portion of the survey had been previously sold by the grantor, or that none of said survey had been sold prior to the conveyance to appellee. The deed is not void for insufficiency of description, but upon its face it does not identify with certainty the 160 acres involved in this suit as a part of the land thereby conveyed. This identification can be made by extrinsic evidence; but, in the absence of such evidence, it cannot be held that title to said 160 acres passed by said deed. *Smith v. Clay*, 57 S.W. 74.

For the reason indicated, judgment of the court below is reversed, and the cause remanded.

Reversed and remanded.

Appellants' Motion for Rehearing Denied.

In a very able motion for rehearing filed by counsel for appellant it is earnestly insisted that we erred in holding in our former opinion herein that the title acquired by possession under the 10 year statute by appellant R.P. Brown and wife was community property and not the separate property of Mrs. Brown. In support of this contention, appellant cites the case of *Alford Bros. v. Williams*, 41 Tex. Civ. App. 436, 91 S.W. 636, decided by this court and in which the opinion was written by the writer of this opinion. That opinion is in direct conflict with our present holding, but we regard it as also in conflict with the rule now recognized by the courts of this state. That case did not reach the Supreme Court, but the case of *Ry. Co. v. Speights*, 59 S.W. 572, cited in the opinion as authority for our holding, did reach that court, and our decision upon the question here involved was not affirmed; the court stating in its opinion that it was unnecessary to decide the question. In subsequent cases from this and other Courts of Civil Appeals a contrary rule to that announced by us in the *Alford* case has been followed, and the writer has reached the conclusion that the rule announced in the *Alford* case is not the correct rule. The deed to Mrs. Brown from one who held no title vested in her no right in the land as against the owners of the title, and, up to the very time that the 10 years possession by herself and husband was completed, she had no title to the land and no right of any kind in the land as against the owners of the title. How, then, can it be said that the deed to her was the inception of the title afterwards acquired by herself and husband by their 10 years occupancy and claim to the land? As the title to the land was acquired during the existence of the marriage relation and did not have its inception in any right acquired by Mrs. Brown before her marriage, we think it should be held to be community property. *Bishop v. Lusk*, 8 Tex. Civ. App. 30, 27 S.W. 306; *Cook v. Houston Oil Co.*, 154 S.W. 281. As pointed out in the *Cook* case, the holding in the case of *Bishop v. Lusk* is apparently approved by our Supreme Court in the case of *Creamer v. Briscoe*, 101 Tex. 494, 109 S.W. 911, 7 L.R.A. (N.S.) 154, 130 Am. St. Rep. 869.

We adhere to the conclusions expressed in our main opinion upon all of the questions presented by the motion for rehearing, and it follows that the motion is overruled.

Questions

1. Why didn't Mrs. Brown's title relate back to her purchase from Mr. Smith?
2. Why didn't it matter that the purchase was made with Mrs. Brown's separate funds?
3. When and by what means did the right to the property possibly incept?

Because of the many different relationships and property transfers described in *Strong v. Garrett*, you may want to draw a flowchart as you read.

STRONG v. GARRETT

224 S.W.2d 471
(1949)

HICKMAN, CHIEF JUSTICE.

This is an action in trespass to try title to 62½ acres of land in the Juan Y'Barbo Grant, in Rusk County. The plaintiffs in the trial court were Jesse Joseph Strong and his sister Alma B. Strong. The defendants were Leuvinia Lewis and husband, Cleveland Lewis, Charlie Garrett and wife, Evie Garrett, and Mrs. Georgia Bateman, and Claud and John Bateman. Charlie Garrett was awarded title to the land on his cross action in the trial court, and that judgment was affirmed by the Court of Civil Appeals. 218 S.W.2d 873. The Strongs and the Lewises are the petitioners before this Court.

The common source of title is Mrs. M.B. James. A predecessor in title to Mrs. James divided the Juan Y'Barbo Grant into six tracts of 62½ acres each. These tracts had identical metes and bounds description, except for the point of origin. They were numbered 1 through 6. Before title passed to Mrs. James her predecessor had conveyed away all of the tracts except Tract No. 3. In December, 1902, Mrs. James, who owned only Tract No. 3, conveyed to Anderson Strong 62½ acres out of the Y'Barbo Grant, but the metes and bounds description covered Tract No. 2. In that deed a vendor's lien was retained to secure a purchase money note. Shortly thereafter Anderson Strong moved upon Tract No. 3. In all subsequent dealings with this land, including proceedings in a lawsuit later to be mentioned, and also including some of the pleadings in the instant case, the land has carried the metes and bounds description of Tract No. 2. Prior to this suit the land had never been described in any of the instruments by the tract number, but always by the metes and bounds description covering Tract No. 2.

After receiving the deed from Mrs. James describing Tract No. 2, Anderson Strong, as early as 1905, and probably earlier, began living upon Tract No. 3, cultivating it and otherwise exercising full control over it, appropriating same as a homestead until his death in 1916. On December 27,

1906, he married Fannie Daniels, and the plaintiffs Jesse Joseph Strong and Alma B. Strong were born to that marriage. In January, 1911, Anderson and Fannie Strong were divorced, and in the divorce decree Anderson was awarded title to "62 acres of land, the same being the land bought by the plaintiff (Anderson Strong) from Mrs. M.B. James, and known as the Anderson Strong place and being the place where he now lives N. E. of Henderson, in Rusk County, Texas." The land was not otherwise described in the judgment. After the divorce decree, Fannie and her children remained in Rusk County until 1920, when they moved to Chicago, Illinois, where they still reside.

In 1912 Anderson Strong married Ida Young, who at that time had a daughter named Leuvinia. Leuvinia and her present husband, Cleveland Lewis, are parties to this suit. On March 25, 1916, Anderson Strong died intestate, leaving as his survivors his wife, Ida Young Strong, and his two children by his first marriage, the plaintiffs herein. The probate court ordered the homestead place of Anderson Strong, which was not described by metes and bounds, but which was sufficiently described to make certain that it was the land upon which he lived and which is the subject matter of this suit, set aside to the widow Ida Young Strong, subject to a vendor's lien against the property. As a matter of fact, the vendor's lien note by its terms was a lien against Tract No. 2, and not the land in suit.

On December 23, 1917, Ida Young Strong married respondent Charlie Garrett, and together they resided upon a farm owned by Garrett, near the land in suit, until Ida's death, intestate, in 1936. The following year, 1937, Charlie Garrett married his present wife, Evie. A short time before Ida Young Strong married Charlie Garrett she conveyed to him, by warranty deed, a tract of land described by metes and bounds as in the other instruments. That deed and the description therein contained will be considered more particularly later on in this opinion

As stated above, title to all the land in suit has been awarded to Charlie Garrett. In order to test the correctness of that award it becomes necessary to determine what character of title, if any, Anderson Strong acquired, and then trace that title to the date this action was filed. The Batemans, who were made defendants in the trial court, are the heirs of Mrs. James, Anderson Strong's vendor. They filed disclaimers in the case, and no further notice need be taken of them, since unquestionably the title has passed from Mrs. James and her heirs. None of the parties have record title to Tract No. 3, the land in suit. The deed from Mrs. James to Anderson Strong described by metes and bounds Tract No. 2. The deed is free of ambiguity, and there is no basis for the application of any rule of construction by which it could be held that the deed conveyed Tract No. 3. Standing unreformed, the deed did not convey title to Tract No. 3. *Davis v. George*, 104 Tex. 106, 134 S.W. 326. But it does not follow that Anderson Strong acquired no title at all. The undisputed facts establish that he acquired title by limitation. The deed from Mrs. James to him was executed prior to his marriage. He took possession of the land as early as 1905, while single, and continued to occupy it until his death in 1916. While he had no record title to the land which he occupied and used during that period, he did have an equitable right upon which he could successfully have maintained a suit to reform the deed. That right existed during the remainder of his lifetime. Anderson Strong having gone into possession of the land intended to be conveyed, and having exercised acts of ownership thereto, and his title not having been questioned by Mrs. James or those in privity with her, the statute of limitation of four years would not have been a bar to a suit by him for reformation. *Howard v. Young*, Tex. Civ. App., 210 S.W.2d 241, error refused, N.R.E.; *Payne v. Ross*, 10 Tex. Civ. App. 419, 30 S.W. 670. But it is a bar to his children, the plaintiffs herein, who have not been in possession of the land or exercised acts of ownership thereto; and the courts below did not err in failing to reform the deed for their benefit, in view of Charlie Garrett's plea of limitation of four years. Article 5529, R.C.S.

The period of limitation was completed during his marriage to his second wife, Ida Young Strong. This question then must be decided: Was this title "acquired" during his marriage to Ida Young Strong, and therefore community property under Article 4619, R.C.S., Vernon's Ann. Civ. St. art. 4619, or was it "claimed" by Anderson Strong before his marriage, and therefore his separate property under Article 4613, R.C.S., Vernon's Ann. Civ. St. art. 4613? Had Anderson Strong entered upon this land as a naked trespasser, without any property right therein, he would have had no basis for a claim of title until the full period of limitation had run. Property thus acquired by pure limitation, where the period began before marriage and ended during the marriage relation, is community property. *Brown v. Foster Lumber Co.*, Tex. Civ. App., 178 S.W. 787, writ refused; *O'Meara v. Williams*, Tex. Civ. App., 137 S.W.2d 66, error dismissed, correct judgment. This rule is recognized in *Hutto v. Cook*, 139 Tex. 571, 164 S.W.2d 513. But Anderson Strong was not a trespasser. He had a property right with respect to this land, and although he had no record title thereto, and his title was ripened by limitation, still when that period of limitation expired his title took character from his original claim, and the property became his separate estate. *Sauvage v. Wauhop*, Tex. Civ. App., 143 S.W. 259, writ dismissed; 23 TEX. JUR., *Husband and Wife*, § 109. *See also Creamer v. Briscoe*, 101 Tex. 490, 109 S.W. 911, 17 L.R.A., N.S., 154, 130 Am. St. Rep. 869, *and Simpson v. Oats*, 102 Tex. 186, 114 S.W. 105. Our conclusion is that according to the record before us Anderson Strong owned this property as his separate estate at the time of his death.

The plaintiffs were Anderson Strong's only children, and upon his death they inherited the land, subject to the homestead right of his widow, Ida Young Strong, and subject also to her life estate in one-third of the land. Article 2571, R.C.S.

Charlie Garrett was the vendee under a general warranty deed executed by Ida Young Strong after the death of Anderson Strong. After that deed was executed, Charlie Garrett took possession of the land, and shortly thereafter married Ida Young Strong, who had executed the deed to him. The deed from Ida Young Strong to Charlie Garrett contained the same erroneous description by metes and bounds as the deed from Mrs. James to Anderson Strong, but it went further and stated that the land was that tract which had been set apart to her by the Probate Court of Rusk County, and the tract which her former husband, Anderson Strong, had purchased from Mrs. James. The order of the probate court set aside to Ida Young Strong "the tract of land used as homestead," subject to the vendor's lien note against same. The tract in suit was the homestead of Anderson Strong.

It is the general rule that a particular description in a deed will prevail over a general description. *Cullers v. Platt*, 81 Tex. 258, 16 S.W. 1003; *Klein v. Humble Oil & Refining Co.*, 126 Tex. 450, 86 S.W.2d 1077. But the situation here may be distinguished from that in the cases in which this general rule has been applied. In this case the general description does not enlarge the particular, but is wholly repugnant to it, in that it describes an entirely different tract of land. It is clear that the grantor intended to convey the land set aside to her by the probate court, and not the land set forth in the metes and bounds description, to which she had no title whatever. In order to give the deed the effect intended by the parties the general description must prevail over the specific description. The general rule will not be applied when the grantor's true intention to convey the land covered by the general description clearly and unmistakably appears from the language of the entire instrument. *Arambula v. Sullivan*, 80 Tex. 615, 16 S.W. 436; *Sun Oil Co. v. Burns*, 125 Tex. 549, 84 S.W.2d 442. Construing this deed from its four corners, we think it unmistakably appears that the intention of Ida Young Strong was to convey to Charlie Garrett Tract No. 3, the home place, and we therefore hold that the general description prevails and Charlie Garrett went into possession of this land, not as a trespasser, but under a deed with covenants of general warranty.

While Ida Young Strong purported to convey to Charlie Garrett the fee title to the land, the only interest she owned in the land was a life estate in one-third thereof, and that was all the interest which passed to him by the deed. He therefore entered as the owner of an estate in one-third of the land, which estate has since terminated by the death of Ida Young Strong Garrett. Therefore whatever title Charlie Garrett acquired to this land was a limitation title. Since he claimed under a deed from the life tenant, Ida Young Strong Garrett, limitation could not begin to run against plaintiffs as to the one-third remainder interest protected by the life estate until her death in 1936. That period was not completed prior to the institution of this suit, and we hold that the trial court erred in decreeing that the plaintiffs take nothing. According to the record before us it should have awarded to them the title to one-third of this land, at least.

There is another error for which the case must be reversed. The evidence fails to show that Charlie Garrett matured title by limitation to the interest of plaintiff Jesse Joseph Strong after he attained his majority.

Still another error requiring reversal consists of the fact that Charlie Garrett has recovered this land from Leuvinia Lewis and husband, the parties in actual possession thereof under a claim of ownership, although he has not sued them for it. In his first amended original answer and cross action he sued the plaintiffs and the Lewises. That petition described Tract No. 2. In his second amended original answer and cross action, upon which he went to trial, he described the land correctly, but the Lewises were not named therein. That pleading, by its own recital, was "in lieu of all other answers filed herein by said defendants." That portion of the judgment is therefore, without foundation in the pleadings (Rule 301), and the record does not show that the issue was tried by consent of the parties under Rule 67.

In deciding the question of res judicata, raised by the Lewises because of a former suit with Garrett, the Court of Civil Appeals held that a petition in trespass to try title, which described Tract No. 2, could not be given the effect of adjudicating the title to Tract No. 3. That same situation exists here. If it should be held that Charlie Garrett's pleadings in this case put in issue the title to Tract No. 3, as between him and the Lewises, then it would follow that the pleadings in a former suit put the title to that tract in issue, and the judgment in that suit that he take nothing vested title in Leuvinia Lewis. But the Court of Civil Appeals correctly held that the judgment in that case was not res judicata as to Tract No.3.

In view of another trial, it is our duty to discuss other questions raised by the parties, which will most certainly arise again.

In order to be able to prescribe against the Strongs under the statutes of limitation to their two-thirds possessory interest, it was not necessary that Charlie Garrett bring home to them actual notice of his adverse holding. His entry under a duly recorded deed purporting to convey the entire fee, plus his long-continued, open and exclusive possession through tenants, was sufficient to warrant the inference of notice to the Strongs, his co-tenants out of possession. *Phillipson v. Flynn*, 83 Tex. 580, 19 S.W. 136; *Jones v. Siler*, 129 Tex. 18, 100 S.W.2d 352; *Republic Production Co. v. Lee*, 132 Tex. 254, 121 S.W.2d 973.

This question then arises: Did this two-thirds interest, if acquired by Charlie Garrett by limitation, become his separate property or the community property of either his first or his second marriage? It will be kept in mind that his first wife, Ida Young Strong Garrett, died in 1936, and that Leuvinia Lewis was her only child and is claiming under her.

We held above that Anderson Strong entered upon this land prior to his marriage with an equitable right in the entire tract, and that therefore the entire tract became his separate estate when full title matured by limitation. The situation with regard to Charlie Garrett is different. He entered under a deed, but it gave him no "claim" to the entire tract, for his vendor owned only a life estate in one-third thereof. As to the other two-thirds interest, Garrett must be treated as a naked trespasser, and the title thereto was "acquired" by him, if at all, after marriage. The property was therefore the community of Charlie Garrett and either his first or second wife, depending upon when the period of limitation was completed. There is no definite finding below as to when the limitation title was acquired. If it was acquired after his second marriage, Leuvinia Lewis would have no claim thereto; but if it was acquired during his first marriage, then Leuvinia Lewis, as the only child of Garrett's first wife, would have inherited a one-half interest therein, but for the application of the doctrine next discussed.

Prior to her marriage to Charlie Garrett, Ida Young Strong executed and delivered to him a warranty deed, purporting to convey the fee to the entire tract. If, therefore, she later acquired a community interest in the land through the adverse possession of her husband, no reason is perceived why that title would not pass to him under the doctrine of after-acquired title.

Charlie Garrett claims title to the land on the ground that he discharged a vendor's lien note against it. In her deed to Anderson Strong, Mrs. James retained a vendor's lien to secure a note given as a part of the purchase price. That lien was upon Tract No. 2, and not upon the land in suit. Garrett paid off that note to the holders after it had been renewed by Anderson Strong and later by his widow, Ida Young Strong. We agree with the holding of the Court of Civil Appeals that the payment of that note would not vest title to this property in Garrett. It may have created in him an equitable lien, but could not vest title to the land in him.

The Strongs did not plead minority in answer to the limitation plea of Charlie Garrett. However, they made proof of their ages, which disclosed that during much of the period of time covered by the transactions narrated in this opinion they were minors. No objection was made to the introduction of this evidence, and no question of the sufficiency of the pleadings to raise the issue was presented to the trial court. The pleadings should therefore be treated as if the issue of minority had been raised. TEX. R. CIV. P. Rule No. 67. That question should be eliminated before another trial.

Charlie Garrett pleaded the statute of limitation of five years (Art. 5509), but his proof did not meet the requirements of that Article.

It will be understood that we do not intend by this opinion to foreclose any fact issue in the case. Our conclusions of fact have been based upon the record before us on this appeal, which may be different upon another trial, when more fully developed.

The judgments of both courts below are reversed, and the case is remanded to the district court.

HARVEY, J., not sitting.

Questions

1. Why were Anderson Strong and Charlie Garrett's claims treated so differently?

2. Charlie Garrett's claim of adverse possession against the property in which Ida had a one-third life estate interest did not begin to run until Ida's death. Why?

McCURDY
v.
McCURDY
372 S.W.2d 381
(Tex. Civ. App.—Waco 1963, writ ref'd)

WILSON, JUSTICE.

The problem we are required to solve is whether proceeds of life insurance policies issued to the insured husband before marriage naming his estate as beneficiary (a) belong to the separate estate of the husband after his death, only in proportion to the amount of premiums paid by him before marriage; or (b) belong entirely to his separate estate, with right of reimbursement to the community based on the amount of premiums paid from community funds during marriage. Appellant urges the first solution; appellee the second, adopted by the trial court, and by us.

The facts are stipulated. Insured and his wife were married August 3, 1960, and their marriage continued until his death, March 16, 1962. Both policies of life insurance were issued to the insured husband before marriage, naming his estate beneficiary. One policy was issued May 22, 1956; the other, February 13, 1959. The 1959 policy was "converted" February 12, 1962, as authorized by the original policy. The nature of the conversion is not shown. Of the total premiums on the two policies, $1094.66 was paid by the husband before marriage; $657.60 was paid during coverture from community funds. The executor named in the husband's will listed the proceeds as a part of the husband's separate estate. The widow's action against the executor sought determination of the status of the proceeds. The trial court concluded the proceeds constituted a part of the husband's separate estate and decreed that the community estate of husband and wife should be reimbursed on the basis of the payments made out of community funds for premiums. The policies are not in evidence. No issue of fraud is suggested by the parties. There is no other evidence. The pleadings allege insured's will made specific bequests of $3000 each to his widow and their two children, of $5000 to his parents, with the rest of his estate to be held in trust for the use of his parents, his brother and his widow, who is appellant here.

The problem is directly presented for the first time in this State under these facts. In all other cases we have examined which reached the question, and where the beneficiary was insured's estate, the policies were issued during marriage. Our decision is restricted to the stated facts.

In *Brown v. Lee*, Tex., 371 S.W.2d 694, 7 S.Ct. J., 10, the Supreme Court said that by amendment of the definition of "property" in Art. 23(1), Vernon's Ann. Tex. Stats., to include "life insurance policies, and the effects thereof," the Legislature has aligned "Texas with other community property states in adhering to the theory that the right to receive insurance proceeds payable at a future but uncertain date is 'property.' Such property is said to be in the nature of a chose in action which matures at the death of the insured." In that case, however, the policy was also issued during coverture.

In approaching solution to this problem we must look somewhat beyond the immediate consequences of decision in this case. A dominant factor in our conclusion is an effort, within the broad principles of dissonant precedent, to fit life insurance proceeds under the present facts to the pattern of Texas community property law as applied to other types of property. The Legislature has apparently sought to do by amending Art. 23, Sec. 1.

That pattern, as to realty, title to which is acquired before marriage, and a portion of the consideration for which is thereafter paid from community, fixes the character of title at the time of its inception or acquisition. It "depends upon the existence or nonexistence of the marriage at the time of the incipiency of the right in virtue of which the title is finally extended." *Creamer v. Briscoe*, 101 Tex. 490, 109 S.W. 911, 912, 17 L.R.A.,N.S., 154, 130 Am. St. Rep. 869. In such a case as this, realty is held to be the husband's separate property. *Colden v. Alexander*, 141 Tex. 134, 171 S.W.2d 328, 334.

The Supreme Court of Louisiana had settled the present problem in 1886 in *In re Moseman's Estate*, 38 La. Ann. 219, by holding that where a life insurance policy was acquired before marriage, payable to the insured husband's estate, under community property law the right to proceeds remained the insured's separate estate, as vested before marriage, notwithstanding part of the premiums were paid thereafter from the community. Twelve years later CHIEF JUSTICE GAINES utilized that very holding to establish the analogy to realty similarly acquired, *Welder v. Lambert*, 91 Tex. 510, 44 S.W. 281, 284; and to sustain the holding that a fixed contract right acquired before marriage was property the 'character [of which] takes its impress from the date of the contract. The Texas pattern is not generally different as to personalty. *Schmidt v. Huppman*, 73 Tex. 112, 11 S.W. 175. *See Hilley v. Hilley*, 161 Tex. 569, 342 S.W.2d 565, 568.

The grappling by Texas courts with the community property aspects of life insurance has been admirably analyzed by William O Huie, *5th Ann. Taxation Conf., II Texas Institutes*, 104, 109 (1957), 17 TEX. L. REV. 121, 146; 18 TEX. L. REV. 121, 147 (1940); by Judge Wisdom, *Commissioner of Int. Rev. v. Chase Manhattan Bank*, 5 Cir., 259 F.2d 231, *cert. den.*, 359 U.S. 913, 79 S.Ct. 589, 3 L.Ed.2d 575; and by George E. Ray, 26 TEX. BAR JOURNAL 835. It is not necessary to repeat the analysis.

Why do we not adopt the California solution formula of proportionate premium payments suggested by the respected author of the first cited treatises? California has done what we think should here be done; it has made its solution as to life insurance proceeds consonant with its other community property law. In *Modern Woodmen of America v. Gray*, 113 Cal.App. 729, 1931, 299 P. 754, where it first considered the problem, the California court stated it would apply the apportionment method so as to follow the California rule as to realty that the inception of title doctrine does not apply (citing *Vieux v. Vieux*, 80 Cal. App. 222, 251 P. 640, where the latter principle was reflected). In *Forbes v. Forbes*, 118 Cal. App. 324, 257 P.2d 721, 722, the same court confirms its reason: "Contrary to the rule adopted in most community property states, under which the community has only the right of reimbursement for payments made with community funds", it is stated, "California gives to the community a protanto community property interest in such property in the ratio" which the separate and community payments bear to each other in the case of other types of property; and "[t]he same rule has repeatedly been applied in the case of life insurance policies procured by the husband before marriage." Apparently Washington also has followed its general tracing rule, *see Jacobs v. Hoitt*, 119 Wash. 283, 205 P. 414; *In re Coffey's Estate*, 195 Wash. 379, 81 P.2d 283, 286.

We think our decision harmonizes with what is said to be elsewhere the general rule: "If either spouse before marriage procures a policy of life insurance on his own or another's life, in his favor or in favor of his estate, the policy and its proceeds are his separate property. His rights to the proceeds date from the policy." MCKAY, COMMUNITY PROPERTY (2d ed.) Sec. 479, p. 316. It is consistent with the holdings of the Supreme Court of New Mexico, *In re Miller's Estate*, 44 N.M. 214, 100 P.2d 908, 910 syl. 2; and of Louisiana, *In re Moseman's Estate*, 38 La. Ann. 219.

Two reasons for applying the tracing principle to give proportionate ownership of proceeds are suggested, II TEXAS INSTITUTES, *supra*, 111: (a) simplicity; (b) just results. These are good reasons, and we have carefully considered others. It does not appear that the inception of title rule is less simple: each method requires computation of the amount of premiums paid out of community funds. Many incidental problems resulting from attempted application of the proportionate ownership rule are avoided. If simplicity be a virtue, we think the inception of title rule is simpler. It facilitates application of general principles of community property law. The inception of title rule is not less equitable in results. While in this case the proceeds which would be proportionately attributable to the community under the tracing theory happened to exceed the community premium payments, in another case the gross premiums so paid out might well exceed the total proceeds. To permit the nature of the property to be determined by the monetary result is not necessarily equitable; and apparent inequity may result under either method, depending on the facts in each case.[1]

In II TEXAS INSTITUTES, above, the query is presented: "How are orthodox principles to be applied when there is a change of marital status?" We believe the inception of title test applied to other forms of property, though arbitrary, is more conducive to uniformity and a degree of certainty under the present facts; and that (although there is much to be said for the proportionate method) this is the best method by which orthodox principles may be here applied.

In our opinion the proceeds of the policies constitute the separate estate of the deceased insured, and the community estate is entitled to reimbursement on the basis of premiums paid with community funds.

Affirmed.

Notes, Comments & Questions

1. Explain the differences in the California and Texas approaches to characterization?
2. How can both these of approaches be right?
3. Do not forget TEX. FAM. CODE § 3.401 et seq.

---

[1] [Footnote omitted.]

PARSON
v.
UNITED STATES

460 F.2d 228
(5th Cir. 1972)

INGRAHAM, CIRCUIT JUDGE:

This is an appeal by the United States from a judgment by the district court sustaining a claim for refund of estate taxes paid by the estate of Dr. George W. Parson. *Parson v. United States*, 308 F. Supp. 1159 (E.D. Tex., 1970).

The case was submitted on a stipulation of facts which indicated that decedent Parson and his wife were married on April 24, 1926, and resided in Texarkana, Arkansas until January 1945, at which time they moved to Texarkana, Texas. They remained there as residents of Texas until decedent's accidental death on December 17, 1961.

I.

The first issue in this case revolves around an application made by decedent, while living in Texas, for a Lumbermen's Mutual Casualty Company insurance policy. On February 20, 1958, decedent signed an application and was issued a certificate providing for payment of $50,000 upon his accidental death. The first and all subsequent premiums were paid with community funds.

Decedent, on February 20, 1958, executed the following instrument in his application for this accident policy:

"COMPLETE ONLY ONE OF THESE SECTIONS

I. THIRD PARTY OWNERSHIP

If you wish a third party, who has an insurable interest in your life, to own this certificate, complete the following statement:

THIRD PARTY OWNERSHIP—It is agreed by the person to be insured that all right and title to the insurance applied for shall vest in and every incident of ownership thereof may be exercised and enjoyed irrevocably without the consent of any other person by:

Name of Owner (PLEASE PRINT)

/s/ Mrs. Beatrice Smither Parson

(Show Given Name-Example, Mary Jones-NOT Mrs. Edward F. Jones)

whose insurable interest is Wife (Example, Wife, Son, Daughter, etc.)

II. "REGULAR" BENEFICIARY PROGRAM

If you wish to retain ownership of this certificate state name of person(s) to whom benefits are to be paid in case of Accidental Death.

NAME OF BENEFICIARY (PLEASE PRINT) RELATIONSHIP

____________	____________
____________	____________

(Show Given Name-Example, Mary Jones-NOT Mrs. Edward F. Jones)

Signature of Applicant /s/ Geo. W. Parson"

Upon Dr. Parson's death the full proceeds were paid to appellee Beatrice Smither Parson as third party policy owner. The estate tax return excluded these proceeds from decedent's gross estate, but the Internal Revenue Service included one-half in the gross estate under § 2042(2) of the Internal Revenue Code.[1]

The district court held that the instrument executed by Dr. Parson was sufficient to divest himself of the "incidents of ownership" and to transfer his community interest in the policy to his wife, thus the proceeds were not includable in his gross estate.

The question before us is whether the instrument executed by Dr. Parson operated as an effective assignment or gift of his community interest in the policy.

Under § 2042(2), life insurance proceeds payable to a beneficiary (other than the executor) are includable in the gross estate if the decedent at his death possessed any of the "incidents of ownership" exercisable either alone or in conjunction with any other person. § 20.2042-1 of the Treasury Regulations defines these incidents as follows:

> (2) For purposes of this paragraph, the term 'incidents of ownership' is not limited in its meaning to ownership of the policy in the technical legal sense. Generally speaking, the term has reference to the right of the insured or his estate to the economic benefits of the policy. Thus, it includes the power to change the beneficiary, to surrender or cancel the policy, to assign the policy, to revoke an assignment, to pledge the policy for a loan or to obtain from the insurer a loan against the surrender value of the policy, etc.

In addition to this determination of decedent's possession of economic benefits, the Commissioner is required to consider whether ownership can be attributed under applicable state law. *See Catalano v. United States*, 429 F.2d 1058 (5th Cir., 1969); *Freedman v. United States*, 382 F.2d 742 (5th Cir., 1967). The government urges that under Texas law there is a presumption that property purchased with community funds is community property even though title is taken in the name of one spouse only, citing *Magee v. Young*, 145 Tex. 485, 198 S.W.2d 883 (1946); *Brick & Tile, Inc. v. Parker*, 143 Tex. 383, 186 S.W.2d 66 (1945), and *Freedman v. United States, supra*. The government's contention is that a Texas spouse does not make a gift of his community interest when community funds are used to buy life insurance, record title to which, though taken in the wife's name, is not limited to the use and benefit of her separate estate.

The government bases its argument primarily on *Freedman v. United States, supra*. There the decedent wife applied for a $50,000 life policy and the husband was named primary beneficiary. Under the terms of the policy all values, rights and privileges would belong to the person who entered his signature as "owner" in the blank space provided.[2] The husband signed the application in this space. All premiums were paid with community funds and on the wife's death the husband

---

[1] 26 U.S.C. § 2042 provides in pertinent part as follows:

The value of the gross estate shall include the value of all property:

(1) Receivable by the executor—To the extent of the amount receivable by the executor as insurance under policies on the life of the decedent.

(2) Receivable by other beneficiaries. To the extent of the amount receivable by all other beneficiaries as insurance under policies on the life of the decedent with respect to which the decedent possessed at his death any of the incidents of ownership, exercisable either alone or in conjunction with any other person.

[2] The clause read as follows:

Control. The ownership including all benefits, values, rights and privileges shall belong to the Owner named below, otherwise to the Proposed Insured.

attempted to exclude all the proceeds, which were paid to him as beneficiary, from her estate. The court, however, held that even though the husband signed the policy as owner, "the decedent did not perform an affirmative act which would clearly reflect an intention to make a gift of her community share." 382 F.2d at 747. The court concluded, therefore, that:

> In the absence of a clause expressly purporting to transfer Mrs. Freedman's community interest to her husband's separate estate, it must be assumed that she merely agreed for the policy to be owned by Mr. Freedman as the community's agent. 382 F.2d at 747.

Unlike the situation in *Freedman*, here Dr. Parson was forced to make a conscious decision between irrevocably assigning all rights, title and every incident of ownership to Mrs. Parson, or expressly retaining ownership and naming a beneficiary. He chose the former and Mrs. Parson received the proceeds as third party owner. Under the government's theory of the case, the proceeds would be includable in the gross estate under § 2042 either with or without the instrument Dr. Parson executed; in other words, he performed a useless act.

We do not view the decision in *Freedman* or Texas law as requiring this restrictive result. The court in *Freedman* recognized that the presumption of community property upon which the government relies is a rebuttable one. Thus, the court below was authorized to view the evidence and determine Dr. Parson's intention in executing the assignment of his interest. In a footnote to the *Freedman* opinion the court clarified its opinion as follows:

> An instrument of assignment or deed of gift would have satisfied the evidentiary requirements for a gift. *See Lamade v. Brownell*, M.D.Pa., 1965, 245 F.Supp. 691 where the district court held that the insured, by means of an absolute assignment, had succeeded in divesting himself of all incidents of ownership. If Mrs. Freedman had executed such an instrument, the primary question for the Court would have been whether a wife can make a gift of community property under Texas law. 382 F.2d at 747, n.10.

Dr. Parson's act in the instant case was as much an assignment or deed of gift as in the *Lamade* case;[3] all right, title, and incidents of ownership were irrevocably vested in the wife. Dr. Parson performed a positive affirmative act which the district court found clearly reflected an intention to make a gift of his community share. It makes no difference, contrary to the government's contention, that Dr. Parson achieved this at the time the policy was applied for. In *Prichard v. United States*, 397 F.2d 60, 64 (5th Cir., 1968), this court stated that "[a] husband may unconditionally make his wife the owner and beneficiary of an insurance policy on his life *when it is issued*, or later if he desires, so as to bar inclusion of it in his estate." *See Mercantile Trust Co. Nat'l. Ass'n. v. United States*, 312 F.Supp. 108, 111 (E.D., Mo., 1970). Nor does it matter that Mrs. Parson was the one who placed her name in the space designating the person to whom the policy was assigned, or that the instrument did not contain the words "for the use and benefit of her separate estate." A court must look to the realities of the situation and give effect to substance over form. *Prichard v. United States, supra.*

---

3 In *Lamade* the assignment provided:

> For Value Received I hereby assign Policy No. 11651016-A *And any other policy subsequently issued in lieu thereof* and pursuant to any right to convert granted therein, issued by the Metropolitan Life Insurance Company of New York on the Life of HOWARD J. LAMADE with all the proceeds thereof and all sums of money, interest, benefit and advantages whatsoever accrued and to accrue thereunder unto MURIEL B. LAMADE, address: 270 Grampian Boulevard, Williamsport, Pa., My wife, and to her executors, administrators, successors or assigns. (Emphasis in original)

Here, the district court did not err in its holding that Dr. Parson's intent was clear and that he had performed the "affirmative act" which irrevocably transferred every incident of ownership to Mrs. Parson and effectuated a gift of his community interest to her. We thus affirm the district court's opinion with regard to this Lumbermen's Mutual Casualty Company accident policy.

II.

A second controversy in this case involves the estate tax treatment to be accorded to fourteen life insurance policies, two of which were purchased by Dr. Parson prior to his marriage, but all of which were purchased by him prior to his establishing residence in Texas in 1945—hence, all fourteen policies were acquired while decedent was domiciled in a common law jurisdiction.

Prior to January 1945, all premiums on these policies were paid from Dr. Parson's separate property. All premiums paid thereafter were from the community funds of Dr. and Mrs. Parson. Dr. Parson possessed all the incidents of ownership on these policies at his death and the proceeds totaling $54,024.50 were paid to Mrs. Parson as beneficiary.

One-half of the proceeds was included in the gross estate in the estate tax return filed. The Commissioner of Internal Revenue included the full amount in the gross estate, less a deduction of $19,998.57 for the amount of premiums paid with community funds, but increased by $9,999.29, representing one-half of the premiums paid with community funds, on the ground that decedent beneficially owned that amount of proceeds under Texas law.[4]

The district court, however, held that the proper tax treatment was that the proceeds be includable in decedent's gross estate only in the proportion that premiums paid from decedent's separate property, plus one-half of the premiums paid from community property, bore to the total amount of all premiums paid.[5]

The government on this appeal urges that the district court erred as a matter of law in its application of the so-called "tracing principle" to the proceeds of the fourteen policies. Bound as we are under *Erie*, we agree and reverse the district court's holding with respect to these policies.

Under Texas law, property acquired by a husband and wife in another state prior to their moving to Texas will retain the character of ownership it had in the state from which it was removed. *McClain v. Holder*, 279 S.W.2d 105, 107 (Tex. Civ. App.—Galveston 1955, writ ref'd n.r.e). *See Wrightsman v. Commissioner of Internal Revenue*, 111 F.2d 227 (5th Cir., 1940); *Orr v. Pope*, 400 S.W.2d 614 (Tex. Civ. App.—Amarillo 1966, no writ hist.). Property which was characterized as separate at the time acquired remains separate, although subsequently paid for with community funds, subject to the community's right of reimbursement. *Hode v. Ellis*, 268 S.W.2d 275, 283 (Tex. Civ. App.—Ft. Worth 1954), *aff'd in part, rev'd in part*, 154 Tex. 341, 277 S.W.2d 900 (1955).

The determining question is whether under the circumstances of the instant case a Texas court would apply the so called "inception of title" approach as opposed to the tracing principle or proportionate ownership approach taken by the district court. In our opinion we have received an *Erie* gale in the form of *McCurdy v. McCurdy*, 372 S.W.2d 381 (Tex. Civ. App.—Waco, 1963, writ ref'd).[6] There, two insurance policies were issued to the husband on his life before marriage,

[4] Under the Commissioner's deficiency notice, Dr. Parson's gross estate would thus include $44,025.21 of the insurance proceeds on these fourteen policies.

[5] Under this holding the gross estate of Dr. Parson would include $37,734.58 of the proceeds.

[6] Under Rule 483 of the Supreme Court of Texas a writ of error is refused when the judgment of the Court of Civil Appeals is a correct one and the principles of law declared are correctly determined.

naming his estate beneficiary. Part of the premiums was paid from the husband's separate funds before marriage, and part was paid during coverture from community funds. The specific and *only* issue before the court was to resolve whether the *proceeds* of the policies belonged to the separate estate of the husband at his death only in proportion to the amount of premiums paid before marriage, or whether they belonged entirely to his separate estate with right of reimbursement to the community for premiums paid with community funds. The court chose the latter solution, the so-called inception of title rule. Having pointed out that California and Washington follow a proportionate premium formula, the court explained:

> We think our decision harmonizes with what is said to be elsewhere the general rule: "If either spouse before marriage procures a policy of life insurance on his own or another's life, in his favor or in favor of his estate, the policy and its proceeds are his separate property. His rights to the proceeds date from the policy." MCKAY, COMMUNITY PROPERTY (2d ed.) Sec. 479, p. 316. It is consistent with the holdings of the Supreme Court of New Mexico, *In re Miller's Estate*, 44 N.M. 214, 100 P.2d 908, 910 syl. 2; and of Louisiana, *In re Moseman's Estate*, 38 La. Ann. 219.
>
> Two reasons for applying the tracing principle to give proportionate ownership of proceeds are suggested, II TEXAS INSTITUTES, *supra*, 111: (a) simplicity; (b) just results. These are good reasons, and we have carefully considered others. It does not appear that the inception of title rule is less simple: each method requires computation of the amount of premiums paid out of community funds. Many incidental problems resulting from attempted application of the proportionate ownership rule are avoided. If simplicity be a virtue, we think the inception of title rule is simpler. It facilitates application of general principles of community property law. 372 S.W.2d at 383-384.

The court below relied on a district court opinion in *Stapf v. United States*, 189 F.Supp. 830 (N.D. Tex., 1960), *rev'd on other grounds*, 375 U.S. 118, 84 S.Ct. 248, 11 L.Ed.2d 195 (1963), in which the tracing principle was utilized. That case, however, was decided before the *McCurdy* opinion, which is the most recent pronouncement of Texas law. The court below attempted to distinguish *McCurdy* because estate tax principles were not there in issue. Nevertheless, the *McCurdy* court determined the ownership of the life insurance proceeds and the estate tax applies to property beneficially owned by the decedent.

The district court also attempted to distinguish *McCurdy* on the grounds that in the instant case all but two of Dr. Parson's policies were taken out after his marriage. The key factor, however, is that the policies were separate property because at the time of acquisition Dr. Parson was domiciled in a common law state.

We are not unmindful of the possible inequities which might arise from the slavish application of the "inception of title" rule of life insurance and other areas. Nevertheless, under *Erie* we cannot skirt the clear import of state decisional law solely because the result is harsh. *See Van Pendley v. Fidelity & Casualty Co. of New York*, 459 F.2d 259 (5th Cir. 1972) [at 262, 263].

The Commissioner's assessment of estate tax consequences for the fourteen life policies was correct and the judgment of the district court with respect to those policies is reversed and remanded.

Affirmed in part, reversed and remanded in part.

Notes, Comments & Questions

1. *Parson* is divided into two distinct issues, both dealing with life insurance. With regard to the first discussed policy, how is it possible for property purchased during marriage with community funds to be a spouse's separate property?

2. How is *Parson* distinguished from *Freedman*?

3. The second issue in *Parson* focuses on fourteen policies all purchased prior to the couple establishing residence in Texas. Two of those policies were purchased before Dr. Parson was married. Why are all of these policies treated in the same manner, utilizing the inception of title rule?

4. If the Parson's marriage had been dissolved by divorce rather than death, would the policies have been characterized differently? Hint, check your family code.

C. Tracing

Tracing is probably the most prevalent means of establishing the separate character of marital property. Tracing requires more than the statements of an interested party that separate funds were used to purchase the questioned property. Indeed, the testimony of an interested witness, when not corroborated, does not conclusively establish a fact even when uncontradicted. *Robles v. Robles*, 965 S.W.2d 605 (Tex. Civ.—Houston [1st Dist.] 1998, pet. denied). If the testimony of a party is uncorroborated, it is not conclusive. *Parmeter v. Parmeter*, 348 S.W.2d 51, 54 (Tex. Civ. App.—Dallas 1961, no writ); *see also Johnson v. Johnson*, 804 S.W.2d 296, 300 (Tex. App.—Houston [1st Dist.] 1991, no writ). Thus, it is probable that the clear and convincing burden of proof will not be met SOLELY by the testimony of an interested witness. TEX. FAM. CODE. ANN. § 3.003 (b).

When utilizing tracing, one must establish the time and/or means of acquiring the property in question. Often times this will require tracing the acquisition of the property in issue back through several bank accounts or to several other pieces of property. Documentary evidence though not specifically required, is usually the key to proving a separate property claim. The truly onerous nature of the tracing burden is evidenced by the cases that follow. Forensic accountants are often used to prove separate property claims via tracing. Notebooks are assembled to organize the many documents necessary to prove that property is separate. It is not unusual to present dozens of documents in support of one separate property claim. It is a burden that cannot be taken lightly and cannot be met by preparation on the eve of trial. Indeed, if one waits and does not provide documentary evidence in response to proper discovery requests, it is probable that one will not be allowed to prove the separate character of the subject property.

HARDEE
v.
VINCENT
147 S.W.2d 1072
(1941)

SLATTON, COMMISSIONER.

This is a suit brought in the district court for injunction and for damages by Edna Vincent, joined by her husband U. A. (Doc) Vincent, against the sheriff of Hutchison County, and Tootle-Campbell Dry Goods Company. One of the purposes of the suit was to restrain the levy of an execution issued out of the county court of Hutchison County, Texas, on a judgment rendered on November 3, 1937, in favor of Tootle-Campbell Dry Goods Company against U. A. (Doc) Vincent for the sum of $385.95. The property upon which the levy was about to be made consisted of a stock of merchandise and fixtures situated in a store building at Stinnett, Texas, alleged to belong to the separate estate of Mrs. Vincent. A motion to dissolve the temporary restraining order was filed and after hearing evidence the trial court granted a perpetual injunction in accordance with the prayer of Mrs. Vincent. The sheriff and the dry goods company appealed to the Court of Civil Appeals. The Amarillo Court of Civil Appeals affirmed the decree of the trial court. 127 S.W.2d 333. This Court granted a writ of error. Two contentions are presented to this Court, viz.: (1) that the pleadings of Mrs. Vincent are insufficient to show that the property involved belonged to her separate estate; (2) that the evidence failed to show that the property in question was paid for with the funds belonging to Mrs. Vincent's separate estate. We shall only consider the second contention. The evidence shows that U. A. (Doc) Vincent on the 16th day of December, 1935, transferred and conveyed to his wife, Mrs. Edna Vincent, lot No. 2, block 54, in the town of Stinnett, Texas, and all of the stock of merchandise and trade fixtures contained in said store. * * *

* * *

* * * Vincent further testified that payments on the meat fixtures had been made from funds arising from the meat department. Payment of the gasoline tanks have been made from money from the filling station business and likewise from the other department. Separate accounts were kept but all cash sales and money received from collections were placed in the cash register and deposited in the bank in a general fund. He further testified that the judgment in favor of the dry goods company against him was for merchandise purchased for his wife's business.

The evidence quoted is all the proof in the record. It is without dispute. It is settled in this state that "all property acquired by either the husband or the wife during marriage, by onerous title, is community estate, the burden of proving that any portion thus acquired is the separate estate of the wife rests upon the party asserting that fact." *Epperson v. Jones*, 65 Tex. 425.

The proof shows that dry goods and fixtures were purchased on a credit and paid for with funds out of the business; that groceries were bought and paid for with cash out of the business. Whether the cash paid for the merchandise and fixtures came out of the capital investment or profits of the business does not appear.

The testimony of Vincent, to wit: that "he did not claim any interest in the business" and that "it belonged to his wife" cannot be given the legal effect of rebutting the presumption of community property for the reason that profits derived from the wife's separate estate during marriage belong to the community estate of the husband and wife. *Epperson* case, *supra*.

It was incumbent upon Mrs. Vincent to show that the money used in the purchase of additional stocks of merchandise and fixtures came out of her separate estate. She attempted to do this by showing that the business belonged to her separate estate at the time of the conveyances to her on December 16, 1935. The case was tried on March 14, 1938, some two years and three months after the conveyances from Vincent. During such time, the stocks of merchandise and fixtures were bought and sold, thus presenting the all important issue as to whether the money used in the purchases of such additional stocks of merchandise and fixtures was profits from the business or capital investment.

Absent proof that the money so used came out of the capital investment, which is the state of the record, the presumption of the law, that property acquired by either husband or wife during marriage belongs to the community estate of the husband and wife, controls in the present case. It follows from what has been said that the stock of merchandise and fixtures acquired after December 16, 1935, belong to the community estate of Vincent and wife and is liable for the debts of the husband. *Smith et al. v. Bailey*, 66 Tex. 553, 1 S.W. 627; *Middlebrook et al. v. Zapp et al.*, 73 Tex. 29, 10 S.W. 732; *Epperson* case, *supra*.

The decree of the district court granting the injunction which was affirmed by the Court of Civil Appeals will be here reversed, the injunction dissolved and the cause remanded to the district court.

Opinion adopted by the Supreme Court February 12, 1941.

Notes, Comments & Questions

1. A sole proprietorship operating as a retail business leads to big problems when characterizing inventory. If a business was owned by a spouse before marriage, the pre-marital inventory has probably been sold or cannot be identified. Accordingly, a spouse will probably not be able to establish that inventory as separate property but will be relegated to an equitable remedy—reimbursement.

2. In *Schecter v. Schecter*, 579 S.W.2d 502 (Tex. Civ. App.—Dallas 1978, no writ), the Dallas Court of Appeals seems to open up an inventory to characterization as separate property. In that case the court said, in part:

> We next address the appellant's contention that the appellee failed to prove that the inventory of the "Vogue" was her separate property since she did not properly trace the inventory from the beginning to the end of the marriage. Thus, he argues that the property is community and that the court erred in failing to divide it. Appellant cites *Jones v. Epperson*, 69 Tex. 586, 7 S.W. 488 (1889); *Middlebrook v. Zapp*, 73 Tex. 29, 10 S.W. 732 (1889), and *Hardee v. Vincent*, 136 Tex. 99, 147 S.W.2d 1072, 1074 (1941) in support of his contention. These cases are all distinguishable. All three cases involved creditors levying on property that was claimed to be separate property as opposed to community. The courts refused to allow the mere allegation that such property was separate without more, to act as a defense to creditor's claims. In cases such as the one at bar where the division of the property is at issue, we hold that the rule set out in *Schmidt v. Huppmann*, 73 Tex. 112, 11 S.W. 175 (1889) controls. In *Schmidt*, the plaintiff ran a mercantile business. At the death of his wife, he filed an inventory and appraisement deducting the value of the inventory at the beginning of the marriage from the value at the end of the marriage. The heirs contested this and the Supreme Court held that the value of the inventory at the date of the marriage was the separate property of the husband. The court pointed out the following:
>
>> While the specific articles that made up the original stock had been sold, and their places supplied by others from time to time as the exigencies of the business required, the property was in fact the same, a stock of merchandise, and we think that there was not such a change in the property as would divest it of its separate character, to the extent of the goods owned by appellant at the time of the marriage. *Id.* at 116, 11 S.W. at 176.
>
> The rule in *Schmidt* was followed in *Blumer v. Kallison*, 297 S.W.2d 898 (Tex. Civ. App.—San Antonio 1956, writ ref'd n.r.e.) in an opinion by Justice Norvell. We hold that appellee sufficiently traced the inventory of the "Vogue" and thus, overrule this point.

3. Before accepting that inventory can be established as separate property, it should be noted, that the extract from *Schmidt v. Huppmann*, 11 S.W. 175 (Tex. 1889), quoted above in the excerpt from *Schecter*, is not complete. The full quotation is as follows:

> While the specific articles that made up the original stock had been sold and their places supplied by others from time to time as the exigencies of the business required, the property was in fact the same, a stock of merchandise, and we think there was not such change in the property as would divest it of its separate character to the extent of the goods owned by appellant at the time of the marriage.

Where it satisfactorily appears, as in this case, that one spouse brought into the partnership separate funds invested in a particular business, which business was carried on and the profits arising therefrom used in creating and building up the community estate, and the separate funds are employed in the same business at the dissolution of the partnership, upon settlement with the community estate *we think the spouse furnishing such separate funds is entitled to be reimbursed therefor*. *Lewis v. Lewis*, 18 Cal. 654; *Werner v. Kelly*, 9 La. Ann. 60; *Coons v. Stringer*, 14 La. Ann. 726. (Emphasis added).

Moreover, *Schmidt v. Huppmann* is a reimbursement case—not a tracing case. The court determined that the husband was entitled to be reimbursed for the value of his original inventory—not that husband had traced the separate original inventory *in specie*.

4. After reading the full quote of *Schmidt v. Huppmann*, what do you think of the *Schecter* decision?

NORRIS
v.
VAUGHAN
260 S.W.2d 676
(1953)

SMITH, JUSTICE.

The respondent, Hal H. Vaughan and Beaulah Hunsaker were married on August 16, 1941, and they lived together as husband and wife until the death of Mrs. Vaughan on May 17, 1947. The petitioner, Mrs. Norris, is the daughter of Mrs. Vaughan by a former marriage. Mrs. Vaughan died intestate, and Mrs. Norris is her sole and only heir. Petitioner admits in her pleadings that respondent was the owner of certain properties in his own separate right, but contends that this property was natural gas producing and that the income, as the result of gas production, after the date of the marriage of her mother to Mr. Vaughan, was and is community property. It was further alleged by petitioner that all of the property involved was in the possession of the respondent, and that a full and complete accounting, which she requested be made by respondent, would disclose that she owned an interest in property acquired between the dates of August 16, 1941 and May 17, 1947.

Prior to his marriage to petitioner's mother, the respondent owned as his separate estate:

(a) A 7/8ths determinable fee, as lessee, in seven producing gas wells, known as the "Pakan Wells";
(b) A 1/4th interest in the Shamrock Gas Co., a partnership;
(c) A 1/4th interest in the Vaughan Well Co., a partnership;
(d) A 1/2 interest in the partnership of Pendleton & Vaughan.

During the period of coverture the partnership of Pendleton & Vaughan drilled ten gas wells, seven of which were producers. These wells are known as the McDowell and Taylor wells. The Vaughan Well Co. drilled two producing gas wells, known as the Hill and Cantrell wells.

The respondent went to trial on his second amended original answer wherein he alleged that certain property was his separate property, and that certain other property was community property. A full discussion of the contention of the parties and the facts relating thereto will be given later in this opinion in disposing of the points presented to this Court for determination.

On March 21, 1950, the trial court, on its own motion, appointed an auditor, who prepared and filed a complete audit and inventory of all transactions enumerated in the order of the court, and the cause proceeded to trial on December 11, 1951. A jury was empaneled, but on the 13th day of December, 1951, by agreement of the parties, the jury was discharged, and the Court, after hearing the evidence, entered its judgment on March 10, 1952, awarding to the petitioner a community interest in the wells known as the McDowell and Taylor wells, and a house situated on Lots 11, 12 and 13, Block 50, of the Woodley Southside Addition to the town of Shamrock, Wheeler County, Texas. All other property involved was declared to be the separate property of the respondent and judgment was entered accordingly in his favor.

All parties excepted to the judgment and an appeal was duly perfected to the Court of Civil Appeals for the Seventh Supreme Judicial District of Texas, which court reversed and rendered the portion of the trial court's judgment which awarded to petitioner an interest in the McDowell and Taylor wells, and affirmed the judgment of the trial court as to the separate property. It also reversed and rendered judgment for petitioner for the title and possession of an undivided one-half interest in and to Lots 11, 12 and 13, Block 50, of the Woodley Southside Addition to the town of Shamrock. All parties agree that petitioner is entitled to this community interest.

Petitioner's second point attacks the judgment of the Court of Civil Appeals wherein it held that profits from gas wells owned by respondent prior to the marriage was not community property. Their first point urges that the dry gas rights and lease interests acquired by respondent during his marriage to petitioner's mother, as well as the wells drilled thereon, were community property, and that it was error for the Court of Civil Appeals to hold otherwise.

We will first consider the petitioner's contention that profit from the sale of natural gas produced from the respondent's separate gas wells is community property. Respondent owns, as lessee, seven wells producing natural gas in the "Pakan" area. These wells were acquired in 1937 and a "life of production" sales contract for all the gas produced by these wells was made with Lone Star Gas Co. in 1939. After the wells were connected to the Lone Star pipeline there was little or no effort required in their management or operation. It is well established in Texas that the lessee in the usual oil and gas lease obtains a determinable fee in the oil and gas in place, and thus an interest in realty. *Stephens County v. Mid-Kansas Oil & Gas Co.*, 113 Tex. 160, 254 S.W. 290, 29 A.L.R. 566; *Hager v. Stakes, Tax Collector*, 116 Tex. 453, 294 S.W. 835; *Stephens v. Stephens*, Tex. Civ. App., 292 S.W. 290. The lessee's determinable fee interest will last only so long as oil or gas is produced, and it is a matter of judicial knowledge that oil and gas producing territory will become exhausted in time. *U. S. v. Ludey*, 274 U.S. 295, 47 S.Ct. 608, 71 L.Ed. 1054, 1055. Therefore, production of this natural gas will in time exhaust the gas reserves which comprise the separate estate. Production and sale of the natural gas in this instance is equivalent to a piecemeal sale of the separate corpus, and funds acquired through a sale of the separate corpus, if traced, will remain separate property. *Love v. Robertson*, 7 Tex. 6; *Rose v. Houston*, 11 Tex. 324; *Gleich v. Bongio*, 128 Tex. 606, 99 S.W.2d 881. When royalty is paid for oil or gas produced from the separate property of the lessor, the courts of this state have held that such royalty is payment for the extraction or waste of the separate estate and therefore remains separate property. *Lessing v. Russek*, Tex. Civ. App., 234 S.W.2d 891; *Texas Co. v. Parks*, Tex. Civ. App., 247 S.W.2d 179; *Bantuelle v. Bantuelle*, Tex. Civ. App., 195 S.W.2d 686. The theory advanced in these cases being that royalty is payment for the extraction or sale of the minerals that comprise the separate estate.

As said in the case of *Kellett v. Trice*, 95 Tex. 160, 66 S.W. 51, 53, "Property of the husband and wife in this state gets its character as belonging separately to one of them or in common to both from the statutes defining their separate and community estates." *See* Articles 4613 and 4619, Vernon's Annotated Civil Statutes.

Petitioner relies on Article 4619, *supra*: "Sec. 1. All property acquired by either the husband or wife during marriage, except that which is the separate property of either, shall be deemed the common property of the husband and wife; and all the effects which the husband and wife possess at the time the marriage may be dissolved shall be regarded as common effects or gains, unless the contrary be satisfactorily proved. * * *"

The petitioner admits that while the gas was in place it was separate property and an interest in land, but she advances the argument that when it was produced the profit on the sale was community income. It is petitioner's theory that if the gas had been sold in place it would have unquestionably remained the separate property of respondent and could not be considered in any sense as property acquired during the marriage, but that the production and selling of the gas changes the status of the property from separate to community, and that the proceeds should be classed as property acquired during marriage, and having assumed this to be true, she advances the further theory that the property thus classified is presumed to be community property, in the absence of a showing to the contrary.

The first question for us to determine so far as the "Pakan" wells are concerned is this: Does oil and gas in place when it has been produced from separate property remain separate property and a part of the corpus, or should it be classed as community income? The second question which naturally follows is this: Does this record show any community effort on the part of either the husband or wife in connection with the production from the "Pakan" wells?

The holding in the case of *Stephens v. Stephens, supra*, is to the effect that so long as separate property can be definitely traced and identified it remains separate property regardless of the fact that the separate property may undergo "mutations and changes." We are in accord with this view. The opinion quotes with approval the Supreme Court of Wyoming in the case of *State v. Snyder*, 29 Wyo. 163, 212 P. 758, 762. In that case the Court said in part:

> Oil and gas, while in situ, are part of the realty; part of the corpus of the land. When a portion of it is taken away, the proceeds necessarily arise out of the corpus, and it is humanly impossible to change that simple, plain, physical fact. The character of the proceeds can, obviously, at least as between the beneficiaries, in no possible manner be changed by the nature of the documentary authority pursuant to which the oil and gas is taken out of the ground. Documents do not possess the power of an alchemist; neither do they wield a magician's wand. Whether the oil be taken out of the ground pursuant to a license, lease, sale, or any other grant, or without any authority whatever, could not in the slightest degree affect the physical fact that it comes from the corpus of the land. If taken and disposed of at all, the effect is clearly a permanent disposition of that much of the corpus, the principal of the land, and, irrespective of the authority pursuant to which that is done, the proceeds must go to the beneficiaries according to the rights existing between them.

The principle announced in the *Stephens* case, *supra*, applies with equal force to the present case. In that case, the party claiming the property involved to be separate property was the lessor in an oil and gas lease which provided that the lessee should pay to the lessor an equal 1/8th part of the oil produced and saved from the leased premises. In the present case, respondent was the lessee in the oil and gas leases covering the "Pakan" area. In the *Stephens* case the court held that the acts on the part of lessor in executing the lease and receiving the proceeds for his part of the oil produced did not convert his separate estate into community property. It further held that "no skill, labor, or supervision of either of the spouses, and no community property was expended in the sale or production."

This brings us to a consideration of petitioner's contentions in regard to the "Pakan" wells that, even if the gas produced is to be considered respondent's separate property by virtue of being a sale of the separate estate, community labor, talent and funds were expended on its production and sale, thus impressing community character upon the gas. This is a well recognized theory, and the cases cited by petitioner as supporting this proposition deal with problems such as the making of bricks from clay extracted from separate land, *Craxton v. Ryan*, 3 Willson, Civ. Cas. Ct. App. § 367, and finished lumber sawed from separate timber, *White v. Hugh Lynch & Co.*, 26 Tex. 195. In these cases it is obvious that a great deal of community effort was required to transmute the separate property into a new and more valuable state. In the instant case petitioner seeks to prove the expenditure of community effort and funds by evidence that some $9,146 was spent in repair and upkeep of these "Pakan" wells. Revenue from these wells was kept in Vaughan's separate bank account and the expense items were drawn from this account or deducted from gas runs prior to payment. The trial court, in its judgment, found as a fact "that there was no co-mingling of funds received by Hal H. Vaughan during this marriage period as all of the funds, both separate and that all of the funds, both separate and community, were readily traceable from the audit of his books." There was no showing that community funds were used in these maintenance operations. Respondent's uncontroverted testimony is that he made only one trip to the "Pakan" area during the period of his marriage, and that the wells required no management. He entered into the contract with the Lone Star Gas Co., and thereafter had nothing to do with the leases, except to collect for his part of the gas produced. It is petitioner's burden to prove an expenditure of community effort so as to impress community character upon the separate asset. We therefore hold that since there was not such an expenditure of community funds or effort as to impress community character on the gas produced from the "Pakan" wells and the $80,661 received as profit, the gas produced and the proceeds therefrom remain separate property.

The next asset to be considered is the respondent's one-fourth interest in the Shamrock Gas Co. This partnership maintained distribution facilities and retailed natural gas to residences in and around Shamrock, Texas. This Company buys its natural gas from the Vaughan Well Co. and owns no gas producing property of its own. Respondent acquired his interest in this partnership prior to his marriage and his interest therein would be his separate property. During the period of coverture the respondent drew some $28,100 in salary and profits from the Shamrock Gas Co. Such sums were community funds as income and salary from a business enterprise, but respondent's interest in the partnership retains its separate nature. *Hardee v. Vincent*, 136 Tex. 99, 147 S.W.2d 1072.

Respondent also owned a one-fourth interest in a partnership known as the Vaughan Well Co. This partnership's sole business is the acquisition of gas wells by drilling under lease agreements and selling gas production to the Shamrock Gas Co. Prior to the marriage this partnership owned three producing gas wells, known as the O'Gorman No. 1 and No. 2 and the Sims well. As in the case of gas produced from the "Pakan" wells, the exhaustion of the gas reserves owned by the partnership prior to marriage is an invasion of the assets comprising respondent's separate estate. As to the matter of community labor or talent utilized in the production of the natural gas produced by these wells, Art. 4613, V.A.C.S. gives the husband the sole right to manage, control, and dispose of his separate property. Reasonable control and management is necessary to preserve the separate estate and put it to productive use. In the instant case the production and maintenance operations on these gas wells are necessary to their use and preservation and are in the nature of reasonable control and management of the separate estate. Thus, community character would not be impressed upon these wells by means of respondent's activities in relation to production and maintenance. The same reasoning is applicable to the maintenance operations on the "Pakan" wells. We therefore hold that respondent's interest in the Sims and O'Gorman wells remains separate property.

We will next consider the question of ownership of two other wells, known as the Hill and Cantrell wells. These wells were drilled by the Vaughan Well Co. and the right to drill the wells was secured under and by virtue of certain oil and gas leases executed after the date of marriage of respondent. The Hill lease was executed July 31, 1945 by Guy Hill and wife, Estelle Hill, as lessors to A. N. and B. F. Holmes, as lessees.

The Cantrell lease was executed April 23, 1946 by C.G. Cantrell and wife, Ovilla Cantrell, as lessors to B.F. Holmes, as lessee. The lessees in these two leases later assigned to respondent a one-fourth interest in these leases in recognition of the one-fourth interest which he owned in the Vaughan Well Co., a partnership. The leases were taken in the name of A.N. and B.F. Holmes for the benefit of the four partners, A.N. Holmes, B.F. Holmes, W.S. Pendleton and Hal H. Vaughan. The principles of law which we believe control our disposition of the controversy with reference to these two wells will be applicable in deciding the petitioner's contention that the community obtained an interest in the gas wells drilled by Pendleton & Vaughan during the period of coverture. Pendleton & Vaughan drilled ten gas wells, known as the McDowell and Taylor wells, under "farmout" agreements with Magnolia Oil Company. By the terms of these agreements Magnolia would assign certain of its lease interests to Pendleton & Vaughan upon the completion of a well on the lease area. Negotiation and acquisition of the 'farmout' agreements were made after the respondent's marriage, and were at least partially due to his talent and labor. In SPEER ON LAW OF MARITAL RIGHTS IN TEXAS, p. 461, Sec. 379, it is said: "* * * The community rights may attach to any beneficial estate . . . whether perfected or merely inchoate. . . ." The community acquired the right to drill the Hill and Cantrell wells under the oil and gas leases heretofore mentioned, and negotiations and acquisition of the "farmout" agreements (the McDowell and Taylor wells) were entered into with Magnolia Oil Company after the respondent's marriage. The Hill and Cantrell oil leases recite a cash consideration of $5, and $10, respectively, and delay rental payments of $160 and $83.55, respectively, and the assignments of these leases executed on December 20, 1948 and December 13, 1948, respectively, each recite a consideration of "One Dollar and other good and valuable considerations." These assignments were executed after the death of Mrs. Vaughan, but it is clear that respondent actually owned the interest assigned on the dates the two leases were executed. In acquiring the leases in the name of one member of the partnership, the effort, talent and skill put forth by that member is just as though the respondent, Hal H. Vaughan, had exercised such activities.

The community's acquired rights were fixed and determined at the time the oil leases were executed and the "farmout" agreements were entered into. The community rights thus acquired cannot be nullified merely because the respondent elected to use separate funds in drilling the Hill and Cantrell wells under the oil and gas leases, and in carrying out his agreement with reference to the McDowell and Taylor wells.

In the case of *De Blane v. Hugh Lynch & Co.*, 23 Tex. 25, the court said: "The principle which lies at the foundation of the whole system of community property is, that whatever is acquired by the joint efforts of the husband and wife, shall be their common property. . . ."

The court, after announcing this principle of law, continued by saying: "If a crop is made by the labor of the wife's slaves on the wife's land, it is community property, because the law presumes that the husband's skill or care contributed to its production; or, that he, in some other way, contributed to the common acquisitions."

Any property or rights acquired by one of the spouses after marriage by toil, talent, industry or other productive faculty is community property. *Logan v. Logan*, Tex. Civ. App., 112 S.W.2d 515. Therefore, the right to drill the McDowell and Taylor wells and the Hill and Cantrell wells was a community asset and the dry gas rights obtained by the drilling of the wells are community in nature. The separate estate would be entitled to reimbursement by the community estate for funds expended in behalf of the community. *Dakan v. Dakan*, 125 Tex. 305, 83 S.W.2d 620; *Snodgrass v. Robertson*, Tex. Civ. App., 167 S.W.2d 534. The respondent contends that all funds expended in drilling the McDowell and Taylor wells by the partnership of Pendleton & Vaughan were separate funds, and that no community funds were so used. Respondent is only entitled to reimbursement for all sums spent out of his separate estate in drilling the wells, and all operating expenses spent in the production and management of the wells after drilling commenced.

Since we have held that the community's acquired rights were fixed and determined at the time the "farmout" agreements were entered into, it naturally follows that petitioner is entitled to an interest in the McDowell and Taylor wells. The trial court decreed that the community estate owned an undivided 169/512 interest in the dry gas rights acquired by Pendleton & Vaughan under the "farmout" agreements with Magnolia Oil Company. Title vested as of the date of the acquisition of the right to drill the gas wells, and the fact that respondent might have expended separate funds in the drilling, operating and management of these wells would not affect the title thus acquired. The proceeds from the sale of gas from these wells would be community property and not separate property. We hold that the community estate acquired a 169/512 interest in the McDowell and Taylor wells, subject to reimbursement to the separate estate of its share of the cost of drilling these wells, and payment of its proportionate share of the partnership operating and management expense from the date of drilling McDowell Well No. 1.

As was held in *Dakan v. Dakan, supra* (125 Tex. 305, 83 S.W.2d 627), "the final determination of the rights of the respective parties is to be determined upon equitable principles as to the amount of reimbursement." All sums which may be shown by the respondent to have been spent by him out of his separate estate when definitely determined will be in the nature of a charge against the community estate. Likewise, if it should be determined by the trial court that any community funds were expended in connection with the drilling and operation and management of these wells, the community is entitled to credit for such sums so expended. "The judgment must give to all the parties all the relief to which they may be entitled." *Dakan v. Dakan, supra*. For the purpose of ascertaining the exact sum expended by respondent out of his separate estate and the sum expended out of the community estate, it is necessary to remand these issues to the trial court.

Respondent also alleges that the Hill and Cantrell wells were drilled by Vaughan Well Co. by the use and expenditure of the separate funds of respondent and his associates, and that the community acquired no interest in these wells. Since community effort, skill and labor were exerted in the acquisition of the right to drill the wells, the community acquired a 1/8th interest in the oil and gas leases covering the Hill and Cantrell wells, subject to reimbursement to the separate estate of its share of the cost of drilling these wells, and payment of its proportionate share of the partnership expense in production and management. The record discloses the gas sales from the wells separately from May 17, 1947 to 1951, but for the years 1945 and 1946 the record combines the receipts from the five gas wells, which includes the Sims and O'Gorman wells. To determine the amount to which respondent may be entitled as reimbursement, and the total gas production and sales from these wells, it is necessary that this phase of the case be remanded to the trial court. In determining these matters the trial court will be governed by the rules of law hereinabove announced with reference to the McDowell and Taylor wells.

The final problem to be considered is the $10,971 reimbursement awarded by the trial court for separate funds expended for community living expenses. It is fundamental that the husband is obligated to furnish support for the community living and if no community funds are available he should utilize his separate funds. *Callahan v. Patterson*, 4 Tex. 61; *Coggin v. Coggin*, Tex. Civ. App., 204 S.W.2d 47. It is his duty to provide for the community and in this instance he chose to expend a portion of his separate estate so that the community standard of living could be as it was. Separate funds spent for community living in such a manner should be deemed a gift to the community for its well-being and use. Allowing a right of reimbursement at a later date would be inconsistent with the fundamental concept that a man should provide for his home and community.

From what has been said, that part of the judgment of the Court of Civil Appeals with reference to the Hill and Cantrell wells is reversed and judgment here rendered that petitioner recover an undivided 1/8 interest in and to the Hill and Cantrell wells, and that the case be remanded to the trial court for further consideration in accordance with this opinion.

The judgment of the Court of Civil Appeals in so far as it reverses the judgment of the trial court awarding the petitioner a community interest in the McDowell and Taylor wells drilled by Pendleton & Vaughan is reversed and judgment here rendered awarding to the community estate an undivided 169/512ths interest in the McDowell and Taylor wells.

The judgments of the trial court and Court of Civil Appeals holding that the community estate is indebted to respondent, Hal H. Vaughan, in the sum of $10,971.85 are reversed and judgment rendered that as to this item the respondent shall take nothing. In all other respects the judgment of the Court of Civil Appeals is affirmed.

Notes, Comments & Questions

1. How are oil royalties received from separate property characterized? How about bonuses? How about delay rentals?

2. Do you think that enough community effort can be expended "so as to impress community character upon a separate asset?"

3. The Court recognizes that a party has a right to expend reasonable control and maintenance over separate property as is "necessary to preserve the separate estate and put it to productive use." How much time and effort would be reasonable? Think about these questions when you read *Vallone v. Vallone*, 644 S.W.2d 455 (Tex. 1982). (Note the use of *Norris v. Vaughan* in JUSTICE SONDOCK's dissent in *Vallone*).

4. The Court in *Norris v. Vaughan* denied reimbursement for living expenses. Do you see a possible "loophole" in this holding?

5. *Norris v. Vaughan* is the seminal case on the tracing and characterization of income from separately owned oil properties. At the same time, the case is now wrong regarding the treatment of partnership property; it takes the "aggregate approach" to partnership rather than the "entity approach" now required after passage of the Uniform Partnership Act. Nevertheless, *Norris v. Vaughan* is an important case, as much for what is now perceived as incorrect holdings as it is for its correct holdings.

6. Cases explaining the proper treatment of partnership property upon divorce, utilizing the entity theory of partnership, will be found in Chapter 5. Dissolution of the Marriage by Divorce. Included will be *Marshall v. Marshall*, 735 S.W.2d 587 (Tex. App.—Dallas 1987, writ ref'd n.r.e.) and an excerpt from the recent and well written opinion, *Lifshutz v. Lifshutz*, WL 1080244 (Tex. App.—San Antonio April 26, 2006, no pet. hist).

7 One of the available tracing aids is known as the "community out first rule." This aid was first used in *Sibley v. Sibley*, 286 S.W.2d 657 (Tex. Civ. App.—Dallas 1955, writ dism'd). In *Sibley* the court explained the rule thus:

> The presumption is that where funds are commingled so as to prevent their proper identity as separate or community funds, they must be held to be community funds. However, there are exceptions to the rule or presumption. In divorce proceedings our courts have found no difficulty in following separate funds through bank accounts. *Farrow v. Farrow*, Tex. Civ. App., 238 S.W.2d 255; *Coggin v. Coggin*, Tex. Civ. App., 204 S.W.2d 47. Equity impresses a resulting trust on such funds in favor of the wife and where a trustee draws checks on a fund in which trust funds are mingled with those of the trustee, the trustee is presumed to have checked out his own money first, and is therefore an exception to the general rule. *U.S. Fidelity & Guaranty Co. v. First National Bank*, Tex. Civ. App., 81 S.W.2d 213; *Continental National Bank v. Weems*, 69 Tex. 489, S.W.2d 802, at page 805.

8. *Sibley v. Sibley* is considered to be the case that established the "community out first rule." What concept is this rule based upon?

9. *Sibley v. Sibley*, also made it clear that it was not enough to look at the beginning balance of an account and compare it to an ending balance to determine the character of funds in the account. The funds must be traced through the account. In *Tarver v. Tarver*, 394 S.W.2d 780 (Tex. 1965), husband's children from a previous marriage (CPM's) tried to convince the court that since the estate of their deceased mother and their father was nearly equal to the estate their father now shared with their step-mother some forty years later, that half of the estate of the second marriage must belong to the estate of their deceased mother and, consequently, the children should share in it as they had never received anything from their mother who had died intestate. The Texas Supreme Court rejected the children's argument upholding the trial court's finding that the children "had failed to trace any fund, assets or income of the first community estate into the properties acquired during the second marriage and on hand at the time the marriage was dissolved." 394 S.W.2d at 785.

10. The "community out first rule" is not always used when tracing funds through a bank account. For that reason, calling it a "rule" is somewhat of a misnomer. Many practitioners prefer to call it a tracing aid since it is not a hard and fast rule.

11. An alternative method of tracing has become known as the "intent," "clearinghouse," or "conduit" method. When using this method,, the "clear intention" behind the specific and exact dollar amount deposited into and withdrawn from the bank account is considered when determining whether the source of payment is separate or community funds.

12. As you read the next case, *McKinley v. McKinley*, note that is credited with laying the groundwork for the clearing house method. Can you figure out why? Hint, what is the character of the $53.81 that remains in the after the $10,400 was put into Certificate No. 101046?

McKINLEY
v.
McKINLEY

496 S.W.2d 540
(Tex. 1973)

DENTON, JUSTICE.

This is an action brought by Flora McKinley for an injunction, and by amended petition, to obtain a declaratory judgment that two savings certificates were the community property of Flora McKinley and her deceased husband, Royal McKinley. The trial court held that the savings certificates were community property, and rendered judgment in favor of Flora McKinley for $13,200, half of the total value of the certificates. The court of civil appeals affirmed after allowing an offset for funds admittedly withdrawn by Flora McKinley. 483 S.W.2d 310. Holding that a portion of the savings certificates are separate property, we reverse.

Flora and Royal McKinley were married on January 15, 1965. Prior to the marriage Royal opened two savings accounts which were the source of funds used to purchase the certificates which are the subject of this suit. Immediately prior to the marriage one account was in the amount of $9,570.27 in the Dallas Federal Savings and Loan, and the other account consisted of $9,535.63 in the First Federal Savings & Loan. Between January 15, 1965, and Royal's death on October 15, 1970, numerous deposits and withdrawals were made in both accounts, and on January 2, 1968, withdrawals from both accounts were used to purchase the savings certificates which are the property in contention in this appeal.

On November 4, 1970, Keith McKinley, as executor, filed an inventory and appraisement which listed the two savings certificates as the separate personal property of Royal. The inventory and appraisement were subsequently approved by an order of the probate court. On November 6, 1970, respondent initiated this suit in the district court against Keith McKinley individually, and as independent executor of the estate of Royal McKinley, deceased. The original petition prayed for an order restraining Keith McKinley from disposing of the assets of the estate. By her first amended original petition she further prayed for a declaratory judgment under Article 2524-1, Vernon's Ann. Tex. St., to declare the two savings certificates community property.

The trial court made findings of fact, that, *inter alia*, the sources of the money to purchase said savings certificates were the joint checking account and/or joint savings accounts; that no evidence of probative value was offered as to the nature of any of the transactions in regard to the two joint savings accounts; and that the deceased commingled all funds held by him in joint savings and checking accounts. The court then concluded that the said certificates heretofore mentioned in the total sum of $26,400 were the community property of the parties to the marriage and not the separate property of Royal C. McKinley.

The court of civil appeals held that the separate funds of Royal McKinley lost their identity because of the many transactions which commingled the funds in the name of both of them and the certificates became community property.

* * *

There are two savings certificates involved here: One in the amount of $10,400, and the other in the amount of $16,000. The $10,400 certificate was purchased from the First Federal Savings & Loan Association with funds which were in a savings account in that same institution. Similarly, the $16,000 certificate was purchased from the Dallas Federal Savings & Loan Association with funds which came primarily from monies in a savings account with Dallas Federal Savings &

Loan. For ease of discussion the certificates will be discussed separately and will be referred to by the name of the respective savings and loan association, or by the value of the certificate.

In late 1964, Royal McKinley had $9,500 on deposit in a First Federal Savings & Loan savings account. It is uncontroverted that this $9,500 was Royal's separate property. By December 31, 1965, the interest earned by this account was $472.03, and on January 5, 1966, $472.03 was withdrawn. The $9,500 originally deposited remained in the account and continued to earn interest until, on December 31, 1967, the account balance was $10,453.81. From January 5, 1966, to December 31, 1967, no withdrawals were made from this account, and all deposits are shown and the account statement to have been "dividends." On January 2, 1968, $10,400 was withdrawn from the savings account and, on the same date, was used to purchase First Federal Savings & Loan savings certificate No. 101046 in the amount of $10,400. The First Federal certificate remained on account and untouched until Royal's death on October 15, 1970.

In *Tarver v. Tarver*, 394 S.W.2d 780 (Tex. 1965), this Court reiterated the basic presumption that all property possessed by a husband and wife when their marriage is dissolved is their community property. At the time *Tarver* was decided the presumption was created by Article 4619, Sec. 1, Vernon's Texas Civil Statutes, and the presumption remains by the clear language of Section 5.02 of the Family Code, V.T.C.A.: "Property possessed by either spouse during or on dissolution of marriage is presumed to be community property." It is the general rule that to discharge the burden imposed by the statute a spouse, or one claiming through a spouse, must trace and clearly identify property claimed as separate property, *Tarver v. Tarver*, *supra*; *Wilson v. Wilson*, 145 Tex. 607, 201 S.W.2d 226 (1947); *Chapman v. Allen*, 15 Tex. 278, 283 (1885). It is further well settled that when the evidence shows that separate and community property have been so commingled as to defy resegregation and identification, the burden is not discharged and the statutory presumption prevails. *Tarver v. Tarver*, *supra*; *Hodge v. Ellis*, 154 Tex. 341, 277 S.W.2d 900 (1955).

In applying these principles to the $10,400 savings certificate, it seems clear that the $9,500 originally on deposit with the First Federal Savings & Loan was traced in its entirety into savings certificate No. 101046, and that $9,500 of that certificate was clearly identified as separate property. We therefore hold that $9,500 of savings certificate No. 101046 in the face amount of $10,400 is separate property.

With respect to the $16,000 savings certificate purchased from the Dallas Federal Savings & Loan Association, the tracing problem is a bit more difficult. It might be helpful to mention at the outset that the $16,000 certificate came into existence with the consolidation of three smaller certificates in the amounts of $10,000, $4,000 and $2,000. The sources of the funds used to purchase the $4,000 and the $2,000 certificates are known. The $4,000 came from a savings account opened in 1969 by Flora and Royal McKinley as joint tenants with right of survivorship; and the $2,000 came from a joint checking account. There can be no dispute that these monies were community funds. Our concern then is with the $10,000 which ultimately found its way into the $16,000 certificate.

In November 1964, savings account No. 61152, was opened by Royal McKinley with the Dallas Federal Savings & Loan Association, and on December 31, 1964, this account had a balance of $6,570.27. It is undisputed that this sum was Royal's separate property. Between January 15, 1965, the date of Royal and Flora's marriage, and January 2, 1968, the date the $10,000 in question was withdrawn to purchase savings certificate No. 106146, numerous deposits and withdrawals were made. Of $7,740.34 deposited during this period, $1,140.34 came from dividends earned by the account. The source of the remaining $6,600 deposited in this account is not known. Two withdrawals were made during this period: The first on January 5, 1966 was in an amount equal to the total of the dividends earned to that date ($437.99), and the second, on March 30, 1966, in the amount of $4,985.91. The January 2, 1968 withdrawal of $10,000, used to purchase the certificate, left a balance of $1,886.71 in the account.

With respect to the $16,000 savings certificate, petitioner made no attempt to trace any of the separate funds in the Dallas Federal Savings account, or to identify any amount claimed to be the separate property of Royal McKinley. The only evidence with regard to these monies is the account sheet from Dallas Federal Savings & Loan and it is wholly inconclusive as to the nature of funds deposited or withdrawn. To come to any conclusion about the property status of the $16,000 certificate would require surmise and speculation. The burden to overcome the statutory presumption was on Keith McKinley, and we cannot say that he has sustained that burden. We therefore hold that the Dallas Federal Savings & Loan certificate is community property.

The judgments below are reversed; the cause is remanded to the trial court for entry of judgment in accordance with this opinion.

Notes, Comments & Questions

1. In light of *Sibley v. Sibley* and *McKinley v. McKinley*, consider this. Grandmother gives Wife $30,000 on her birthday. This $30,000 is clearly the separate property of Wife. Grandmother specifically gives Wife the money as a birthday present to use for the purchase of a car. Wife deposits the $30,000 into the community's joint checking account that already has a balance of $4,000 in community funds. Wife immediately purchases her vehicle for $30,000.

   a. Is the first $4,000 expended on the car community or separate property?

   b. What if Wife only used $28,000 to purchase her car, what is the character of the remaining funds?

   c. What is the character of the car if Wife spent $32,000 on the purchase?

   d. What tracing aid would you use in representing Wife?

2. In *Latham v. Allison*, 560 S.W.2d 481 (Tex. Civ. App.—Fort Worth 1978, writ ref'd n.r.e.), the court calls *McKinley* "the most liberal tracing case that we have seen." Why?

LATHAM
v.
ALLISON

560 S.W.2d 481
(Tex. Civ. App.—Fort Worth 1977, writ ref'd n.r.e.)

SPURLOCK, JUSTICE.

This appeal arises out of a suit for an accounting and partition of property between two estates. Finding that the certificates of deposit and bank balances in dispute were the community property of O.M. Allison, Sr., and Nonnie Lula Allison, the trial court ordered that H.A. Latham as administrator of the estate of Nonnie Lula Allison recover from O.M. Allison, Jr., as executor of the estate of O.M. Allison, Sr., the sum of $28,470.59 plus interest at the judgment rate until paid. The personal representative of each estate has perfected an appeal to this court.

We reverse and render judgment for appellant, H. A. Latham, administrator of the estate of Nonnie Lula Allison, for $35,378.62 plus interest at 9% Per annum from December 6, 1976, until paid.

O.M. Allison, Sr., and Nonnie Lula Allison were married on April 12, 1953. There were no children born of this marriage. O.M. Allison, Sr. died in March 1970; Nonnie Lula Allison died in October, 1970.

* * *

Prior to her marriage, Nonnie Lula Allison owned as her separate property 144 shares of common stock of the Franklin Life Insurance Company. In varying amounts, this stock was sold during the period of 1959 to 1966. During their marriage, Mr. and Mrs. Allison, Sr. maintained a joint checking account at the First National Bank of Nocona, Texas. Appellant contends that the proceeds of the sale of this stock were deposited into this joint bank account. Further, he contends that the proceeds were then invested in savings certificates at several savings and loan associations, but were later deposited in other certificates at other financial institutions. As he is aware, appellant is confronted with a tracing problem.

In *Tarver v. Tarver*, 394 S.W.2d 780 (Tex. 1965), our Supreme Court reaffirmed the basic presumption that all property possessed by a husband and wife upon dissolution of their marriage is community property. TEX. FAMILY CODE ANN. § 5.02 (1975) perpetuates this same rule. *Tarver* provides that to discharge the burden imposed by the statute, a spouse (or one claiming through a spouse) must trace and clearly identify the property claimed as separate property; however, when the evidence shows that separate and community property have been so commingled so as to defy segregation and identification, the burden is not discharged and the statutory presumption prevails.

At the outset, we note that the burden of tracing is a difficult, but not impossible burden to sustain. Like other legal doctrines, it has evolved in Texas case law. To understand this development of the tracing concept in the Texas case law, *see Rose v. Houston*, 11 Tex. 324 (1854); *Hardee v. Vincent*, 136 Tex. 99, 147 S.W.2d 1072 (1941); *Lindemood v. Evans*, 166 S.W.2d 774 (Tex. Civ. App.—San Antonio 1942, writ ref'd); *Waheed v. Waheed*, 423 S.W.2d 159 (Tex. Civ.

App.—Eastland 1967, no writ); *West v. Austin National Bank*, 427 S.W.2d 906 (Tex. Civ. App.—San Antonio 1968, writ ref'd n.r.e.); *In Re Marriage of Greer*, 483 S.W.2d 490 (Tex. Civ. App.—Amarillo 1972, no writ); *Tarver, supra.*

We are aware of the Supreme Court's opinion in *McKinley v. McKinley*, 496 S.W.2d 540 (Tex. 1973). While it is the most liberal tracing case that we have seen, it still requires that the property be clearly traced and identified as separate property. In that case, Mr. Royal McKinley had $9500 on deposit in a First Federal Savings & Loan savings account. Because of accrued interest, the account balance had grown to $10,453.81. On January 2, 1968, $10,400 was withdrawn from the savings account and on that same day, it was used to purchase a $10,400 savings certificate in the same financial institution. Thereafter, the certificate remained untouched until Mr. McKinley's death. Accordingly, our Supreme Court ruled that $9500 could be traced into the $10,400 certificate as constituting the separate property of Mr. McKinley. There was no doubt in that case that the $9500 separate property was actually deposited into the $10,400 certificate, since it was only a transfer on the books of the same financial institution.

We will compare the facts of the case at bar to the *McKinley* case to determine whether appellant has sustained his burden of tracing to overcome the statutory community property presumption.

As illustrative of appellant's tracing of separate property, we shall examine his attempt to trace $5500. The following statements, in summary form, are taken from appellant's brief:

> (1) 72 shares are sold with transfer date of August 25, 1959. Proceeds of this sale were $6027.50.
>
> (2) Of the above proceeds, $5500 was deposited in Oak Cliff Savings & Loan Association on August 24, 1959. The above $5500 remained on deposit there until December 30, 1969 (along with $9500 additional funds) when the whole of the account in the sum of $15,000 was withdrawn.
>
> (3) On the above $15,000, the sum of $14,000 was deposited in a First National Bank of Nocona certificate of deposit where it remained through March 23, 1970, the date of death of O. M. Allison, Sr.
>
> Conclusion: $5500 of the $21,000 certificate of deposit drawn upon First National Bank of Nocona is a portion of the proceeds from the original sale of 72 shares of stock.

Unfortunately, only a few of these statements are supported by the evidence. For example, when the stock was sold for $6027.50, there is no evidence to indicate that the proceeds of that sale constituted the source of the $5500 that went into the Oak Cliff Savings & Loan Association. At best, such a contention is only conjecture. At the time of closing the Oak Cliff account, $15,000 was withdrawn, but again, there is no evidence that this withdrawal was the source of the $14,000 that was deposited into the First National Bank of Nocona.

When tracing separate property, it is not enough to show that separate funds could have been the source of a subsequent deposit of funds. Such conjecture does not constitute sufficient evidence to sustain appellant's burden of tracing to overcome the community property presumption of the TEX. FAMILY CODE ANN. § 5.02 (1975).

We have reviewed the other situations whereby appellant has attempted to trace separate property; however, there is a total absence of evidence to show that the various accounts were actually funded with the proceeds from the sale of the separate stock. Since appellant has not sustained his burden of tracing, the statutory community property presumption prevails. Appellant's first three points of error are overruled.

* * *

Costs of this appeal are taxed against appellee.

Question

A very clear rule emerges from *Latham v. Allison* regarding the level of proof to establish separate property through tracing. Can you find the rule?

GIBSON v. GIBSON

614 S.W.2d 487
(Tex. Civ. App.—Tyler 1981, no writ)

McKay, Justice.

This is an appeal from a divorce decree in which the trial court found certain property to be the separate property of one of the spouses.

Prior to his marriage to appellant Rena Gibson on June 12, 1976, appellee C.E. Gibson purchased a piece of property in Missouri. That property was sold after the marriage for $8,000, with $5,500 paid at closing and $2,500 to be paid later. Appellee deposited the $5,500 into his personal account in Missouri, but later transferred that amount to the couple's joint checking account in Richardson, Texas (joint account). At the time of this transfer, the joint account contained an indeterminate amount of separate funds belonging to appellant, (though there was testimony that such sum was negligible), as well as the proceeds from several social security checks received by each party during the marriage.

Three or four months after the Missouri property was sold, the Gibsons purchased a house and lot in Mesquite, Texas, for $9,900. Title was placed in the names of both parties. A note was executed by both parties to finance part of the cost, with appellee's separately owned truck and appellant's small insurance policy used as collateral. Appellee borrowed $990 from one of his daughters as a down payment, and the remainder of the purchase price ($5,500) came from the joint account.

It is appellee's contention that the $5,500 cash payment was part of the proceeds from the sale of his Missouri property. He also testified that the balance of the amount due him for the sale of his property ($2,500) was applied, when received, on the note for the house and lot in Mesquite. Additionally, appellee's daughter Rita had borrowed money from him prior to his marriage to appellant, and appellee claims that the $1,700 repaid on that loan was used to pay on the note. Appellant testified that six monthly payments made on the note, at $135 each, came from funds in the joint account apart from the sum claimed by appellee to be his separate property. The Mesquite realty was sold on July 29, 1977, for $17,500, and the proceeds of the sale were placed in the joint account.

Approximately one month later, the couple purchased a house and lot at Cedar Creek for $6,500, using cash from the joint account. At the same time, they bought a $5,300 Dodge Aspen Station Wagon. To cover $1,400 of the purchase price, appellee traded in his truck which he owned when married. The remainder of the sum was paid in cash, again coming from the joint account. The titles to the real property and the car were in the names of both parties.

Certain improvements were made on the Cedar Creek property, including the addition of a small room and the purchase of a metal building, carpet, furniture and a septic tank. The cost of these items totaled $2,300 and was paid out of the joint account. Appellee contends that his separate funds, i. e., the proceeds from the sale of the Mesquite property, were used to finance the improvements, as well as to purchase the Cedar Creek property and the station wagon.

The trial court found that the Cedar Creek property and the car were the separate property of appellee. Appellant brings one point of error in which she attacks the trial court's characterization of the property on the grounds that (1) there was insufficient evidence to overcome the community presumption as to property possessed by the parties upon dissolution of the marriage; (2) appellee failed to show that he never intended to make a gift of the property in question to appellant when title was placed in the names of both parties; and (3) the Mesquite property was purchased with commingled funds, and an installment note executed on the credit of the community.

A deed from a third party which is in the names of both husband and wife raises a community presumption which is rebuttable and "operates only in the absence of satisfactory proof to the contrary." *Sparks v. Humble Oil & Refining Co.*, 129 S.W.2d 468, 469 (Tex. Civ. App.—Texarkana 1939, writ ref'd); *Von Hutchins v. Pope*, 351 S.W.2d 642, 645 (Tex. Civ. App.—Houston 1961, writ ref'd n.r.e.). No presumption of gift to either spouse arises in such a situation, and therefore appellee was not prejudiced by failing to rebut it. Furthermore, no allegations of gift were made at trial and no evidence presented on that point, thereby precluding appellant from raising the argument on appeal.

The heart of appellant's attack on the trial court's judgment is that the separate and community property of Mr. and Mrs. Gibson became so commingled as to defy appellee's attempt to trace his separate funds into the Cedar Creek property and the station wagon. The Texas Family Code dictates that "(p)roperty possessed by either spouse during or on dissolution of marriage is presumed to be community property." TEX. FAM. CODE ANN. Art. 5.02 (Vernon 1975). To overcome this presumption, the party asserting separate ownership must clearly trace the original separate property into the particular assets on hand during the marriage, *Cockerham v. Cockerham*, 527 S.W.2d 162, 167 (Tex. 1973), but when the evidence shows that separate and community property have been so commingled as to defy resegregation and identification, the burden is not discharged and the statutory presumption that the entire mass is community controls its disposition. *McKinley v. McKinley*, 496 S.W.2d 540, 543 (Tex. 1973); *Tarver v. Tarver*, 394 S.W.2d 780, 783 (Tex. 1965). A spouse must prove separate ownership to the court by "clear and convincing" evidence or by "clear and satisfactory" evidence. *Newland v. Newland*, 529 S.W.2d 105, 107 (Tex. Civ. App.—Ft. Worth 1975, writ dism'd).[1] When tracing separate property, it is not enough

[1] The court in *Newland* seems to hold that a judgment need be supported only be a preponderance of the evidence, with the "clear and convincing" standard serving only as an "admonition to the judge to exercise great

to show that separate funds could have been the source of a subsequent deposit of funds. *Latham v. Allison*, 560 S.W.2d 481, 486 (Tex. Civ. App.—Ft. Worth 1978, writ ref'd n. r. e.).

Courts dealing with the tracing of separate property commingled with community funds have required varying degrees of particularity in identifying separate property. *See* 6 ST. MARY'S L. J. 234 (1974). Many Texas cases have been strict in demanding a "dollar for dollar" accounting of separate funds used to purchase an asset, the ownership of which is in dispute. *E.g., Schmeltz v. Gary*, 49 Tex. 49 (1878); *Latham v. Allison, supra*; *West v. Austin National Bank*, 427 S.W.2d 906 (Tex. Civ. App.—San Antonio 1968, writ ref'd n. r. e.); *Stanley v. Stanley*, 294 S.W.2d 132 (Tex. Civ. App.—Amarillo 1956, writ ref'd n. r. e., *cert. den'd* 354 U.S. 910, 77 S.Ct. 1296, 1 L.Ed.2d 1428).

Certain other courts have been more lenient in their treatment of the tracing problem. The philosophy prompting these decisions was expressed in *Farrow v. Farrow*, 238 S.W.2d 255, 257 (Tex. Civ. App.—Austin 1951, no writ): "One dollar has the same value as another and under the law there can be no commingling by the mixing of dollars when the number owned by the claimant is known." In *Sibley v. Sibley*, 286 S.W.2d 657 (Tex. Civ. App.—Dallas 1935, writ dism'd), the court allowed appellee to trace her separate property through a series of transactions, including the deposit of the proceeds from a sale of her separate realty into a joint account containing a substantial amount of community funds and separate funds belonging to the other spouse. According to *Sibley*, community funds will be presumed to have been drawn out before separate funds from a joint bank account.

In still other cases, spouses have been permitted to distinguish their separate funds commingled in a bank account with community money by proving that community withdrawals, *e.g.* for living expenses, equaled or exceeded community deposits. For example, in *Coggin v. Coggin*, 204 S.W.2d 47, 52 (Tex. Civ. App.—Amarillo 1947, no writ), evidence was presented to show that income from the wife's property totaled approximately $1,000 per year, while family living expenses were $200-$500 monthly. The court found that such community funds could not have been used to pay for the property in question since they had already been depleted in paying for the living expenses. *See DePuy v. DePuy*, 483 S.W.2d 883, 888 (Tex. Civ. App.—Corpus Christi 1972, no writ).

Even if this court were to employ the most lenient of the tracing rules set out above, we would have to hold that appellee failed to produce sufficient evidence to trace his separate property. No explicit "dollar for dollar" accounting of appellee's separate funds was made as it passed through the joint account. While the record tends to indicate that the Gibsons' monthly income, standing alone, was inadequate to purchase the disputed property, it is possible that some community funds may have been used, in addition to separate funds, to buy the car and the Cedar Creek realty. Appellee made no attempt to prove the precise amount of community funds in the joint account at the time separate funds were deposited. Neither was evidence presented by appellee to quantify community deposits and withdrawals at the time the purchases in question were made.[2] Appellee testified that all community funds were depleted during the month to pay for living expenses; however, appellee admitted to having no personal knowledge of how much was actually spent since appellant paid the monthly bills. No testimony was elicited from appellant as to monthly community expenditures.

---

caution in weighing the evidence." *Newland v. Newland, supra* at 108. *See* O. SPEER, TEXAS FAMILY LAW § 15.26 (5th ed. 1976).

[2] Appellee might have introduced bank records to prove these sums as in Lindsey v. Lindsey, 564 S.W.2d 143 (Tex. Civ. App.—Austin 1978, no writ).

For these reasons we hold that appellee has not presented sufficient evidence to prove his sole ownership of the station wagon and Cedar Creek property. We therefore reverse the judgment and remand the cause to the trial court.

Questions

1. The proof presented in *Gibson v. Gibson* is not atypical. Yet, it was not enough to carry the burden of proving separate property. How could you have improved upon the presentation of husband's case?

2. What three modes of tracing does the court identify in *Gibson*?

3. Which of the three modes would have best served Mr. Gibson?

SNIDER
v.
SNIDER

613 S.W.2d 8
(Tex. Civ. App.—Dallas 1981, no writ)

CARVER, JUSTICE.

* * *

The executors also urge that the trial court erred in holding that the deceased husband's savings account in the Mercantile Bank (which pre-existed the marriage) was found by the trial court to belong to the community estate because of subsequent deposits and withdrawals by the community. On the date of the marriage, the balance in the account was $27,642.45. Upon dissolution of the community by the husband's death, the balance was $35,809.80. The account grew by interest from time to time, as well as by new deposits, and was reduced by withdrawals from time to time. The witness Wofford testified that an additional deposit of $10,000.00 of separate funds of the husband was made after the marriage and that the remaining deposits, as well as withdrawals, were made by the community. The passbook for this account was introduced into evidence and supports the separate character and balance of the account on the date of marriage. Between the marriage on October 3, 1972, and October 20, 1972, no interest was earned and no deposits were made, but withdrawals reduced the balance to $19,642.45. Between October 20, 1972, and April 23, 1973, there were entries of earned interest, deposits of unknown character, and withdrawals, but the balance was never below $19,642.45. On April 23, 1973, a separate property deposit of $10,000.00 was made and the identifiable separate property interest in the account became $19,642.45 plus $10,000.00 or $29,642.45. Subsequent interest earned, deposits, and withdrawals to the date of the husband's death never reduced the account balance to or below $29,642.45. We hold that this record traces and identifies the husband's separate interest in the Mercantile savings account to the extent of $29,642.45 with the remainder of the account being deemed community for want of tracing or identity. *See McKinley v. McKinley*, 496 S.W.2d 540 (Tex. 1973); *Schmidt v. Huppmann*, 73 Tex. 112, 11 S.W. 175 (1889); *Peterson v. Peterson*, 595 S.W.2d 889 (Tex. Civ. App.—Austin 1980, no writ); *Harris v. Ventura*, 582 S.W.2d 853 (Tex. Civ. App.—Beaumont 1979, no writ); *Sibley v. Sibley*, 286 S.W.2d 657 (Tex. Civ. App.—Dallas 1955, writ dism'd).

* * *

Notes, Comments & Questions

1. Make a flow chart of the funds that move in and out of the *Snider* account. This method is the best way to understand tracing.

2. In tracing funds through a bank account, would you use the date the check was written or the date the check cleared? Why?

3. The following case, *Bakken*, addresses the character of increases in mutual funds, a common issue.

BAKKEN
v.
BAKKEN
503 S.W.2d 315
(Tex. Civ. App.—Dallas 1973, no writ)

BATEMAN, JUSTICE.

The appellee sought and obtained a decree of divorce from appellant, custody of their four minor children and an attorney's fee. We affirm.

* * *

Appellant also complains, in his fifth point of error, of that portion of the decree which set aside to appellee as her separate property 1,023 shares of Affiliated Fund stock and 384 shares of National Securities Series stock. It is undisputed that appellee's original shares in these two mutual funds were gifts from her father and thus her separate property. Appellant contends, however, that the shares in these Funds received by appellee during marriage were bought with earnings from the original shares and thus were community property, citing *Scofield v. Weiss*, 131 F.2d 631 (5th Cir. 1942).

Appellee testified without dispute that the quarterly cash dividends she received from these two mutual funds were used for the support of herself and her children, but that all her capital gain dividends were left with the mutual funds for the purchase of the additional shares in question.

Mutual funds assets usually consist of the stocks, bonds and other securities of a number of other corporations. Their income is generally of two kinds: (1) cash dividends received from the corporations whose stock they own, and (2) the profit or gain realized from the sale of such stocks. When these cash dividends are passed on to married owners of mutual fund shares who hold them as separate property, there is no question that these dividends become community property of the spouses. The question before us is whether the distributed capital gains retain their nature as separate property or become community property when passed on to married owners of the mutual fund shares.

We hold that since appellee's original shares in the two mutual funds were admittedly her separate property the profit or gain realized from the sale of capital assets of the mutual funds is also her separate property. If she had owned a farm of 100 acres, which had a value of $100 per acre or a total of $10,000 at the time of acquisition, and had sold 25 of these acres at $1,000 per acre, the entire $25,000, even though in excess of the original value of the entire farm, would clearly have been her separate property. *Estrada v. Reed*, 98 S.W.2d 1042, 1044 (Tex. Civ. App.—Amarillo 1936, writ ref'd); *Evans v. Purinton*, 34 S.W. 350 (Tex. Civ. App.—Fort Worth 1896, writ ref'd); *Cabell v. Menczer*, 35 S.W. 206 (Tex. Civ. App.—Dallas 1896, no writ). And any land, stocks, bonds or other property, in which she might invest the $25,000, would also have been her separate property, assuming its separate character was traceable. *Tarver v. Tarver*, 378 S.W.2d 381, 387 (Tex. Civ. App.—Texarkana 1964), *aff'd* 394 S.W.2d 780 (Tex. 1965); *Boyd v. Orr*, 170 S.W.2d 829, 833 (Tex. Civ. App.—Texarkana 1943, writ ref'd w.o.m.). We know of no reason why a different rule should apply to the sale of her interest in stocks owned by the corporate mutual fund of which she was a shareholder. Our holding is consistent with the rule that increases in the value of separate property arising from fortuitous causes such as market fluctuations or natural growth remain separate property. *Dillingham v. Dillingham*, 434 S.W.2d 459, 461 (Tex. Civ. App.—Fort Worth 1968, writ dism'd).

* * *

As reformed, the judgment is affirmed.

CARTER

v.

CARTER

736 S.W.2d 775

(Tex. App.—Houston [14th Dist.] 1987, no writ)

SEARS, JUSTICE

* * *

In her first two points of error appellant argues that the trial court abused its discretion by characterizing seventeen blocks of stock as separate property. She alleges there was insufficient evidence to show the stock was purchased with separate funds and that appellee failed to trace the original separate property into those stocks by clear and convincing evidence.

Property possessed by either spouse during or on dissolution of marriage is presumed to be community property. TEX. FAM. CODE ANN. § 5.02 (Vernon 1975). To overcome that presumption, a spouse asserting separate ownership must clearly trace the original separate property into the particular assets on hand during the marriage. *Cockerham v. Cockerham*, 527 S.W.2d 162, 167 (Tex. 1975).

The parties were married on December 7, 1974. Appellee testified that in April 1970 his father made a gift to him of 159 shares of Milk Proteins, Inc. (MPI) stock. MPI appears to have been a small, family-owned company that also employed appellee. In 1976, Stauffer Chemical Company bought MPI, employed appellee and converted his 159 shares of MPI stock into 4,645 shares of Stauffer stock. Appellee testified that in 1979 Stauffer had a two-for-one stock split, which doubled his shares to 9,290.

In January and April of 1981, appellee sold 1,156 and 1,000 shares of Stauffer stock, and, in 1982, he sold an additional 1,000 shares. The proceeds from those three sales went into community assets to pay community debts and living expenses. Appellee also traded in Stauffer stock apart from the converted shares, acquiring 166 shares as a Christmas gift from his father in 1981 and participating in six short sales in 1982 and 1983. The 166 shares were sold on June 13, 1984, and one-half of the proceeds went to appellant.

After he retired from Stauffer, appellee went to work for a securities firm. When he obtained his broker's license, appellee opened a margin account at the firm in his name only. He bought and sold stock on credit through that account, using his remaining Stauffer stock (some 6,134 shares) as collateral for the debt created within the account. On February 22, 1985, appellee sold 500 Stauffer shares to reduce the debt in his margin account. Shortly thereafter, he tendered 900 shares and then an additional 4,700 shares to Chesebrough-Pond's Inc. He accounted for all except thirty-four of the original 9,290 shares. Appellee used most of the $156,800 he received for the tender to pay off the debt within his separate margin account, to buy additional stock listed on his inventory (which he kept in his separate account) and to buy a van.

The trial court made the following findings of fact and conclusions of law pertaining to the stock:

FINDINGS OF FACT

12. The following assets were acquired by DONALD H. CARTER, JR. prior to his marriage to NANCY MARIE CARTER:

* * *

(i) 159 shares of the common stock of Milk Proteins Inc.

* * *

14. Following the marriage of DONALD H. CARTER, JR. and NANCY MARIE CARTER, the 159 shares of Milk Proteins Inc. stock was exchanged for 4,645 shares of Stauffer Chemical Company stock.

15. The following assets were acquired subsequent to the date of marriage of DONALD H. CARTER, JR. and NANCY MARIE CARTER, with funds acquired by DONALD H. CARTER, JR. as a result of the sale of shares of Stauffer Chemical Company stock which Stauffer stock was acquired in exchange for 159 shares of Milk Proteins Inc. stock:

[listed are shares in sixteen companies, $20,000 of Harris County Tax Free Bonds and a 1985 Chevrolet van].

CONCLUSIONS OF LAW

7. The 159 shares of Milk Proteins Inc. stock was the separate property of DONALD H. CARTER, JR.

* * *

---

9. The following assets are the separate property of DONALD H. CARTER, JR.: [listed are shares in sixteen companies, $20,000 of Harris County Tax Free Bonds and a 1985 Chevrolet van].

Appellee testified at length about the 159 shares of MPI stock and its subsequent metamorphosis. A 1974 income tax return was offered into evidence to show that dividends on the stock were reported for that year. Appellee testified that MPI dividends generally were declared at the end of the year and then dated the following year. This testimony lends credence to his claim of ownership of the stock in 1973 (and thus prior to the December 7, 1974, marriage). The parties' tax returns for the years 1975 through 1983 were also placed in evidence to reflect the trading that occurred in the Stauffer stock. Finally, on both the 1976 and 1977 tax returns, the notation (H) appears beside the Stauffer Chemical Company dividends reported on Schedule B. Schedule B instructs one to write (H), (W) or (J) to denote stock held separately by the husband or wife, or stock held jointly.

Appellant offered no evidence to refute appellee's testimony concerning the acquisition of the MPI stock. She merely concluded the shares "could have been acquired during the marriage." She argues, however, that appellee did not meet his tracing burden with clear and convincing evidence and that the uncorroborated testimony of an interested witness is not conclusive.

In Texas there are but two standards by which evidence is reviewed: factual sufficiency and legal sufficiency. The requirement of clear and convincing evidence is merely another method of stating that a cause of action must be supported by factually sufficient evidence. *Meadows v. Green*, 524 S.W.2d 509, 510 (Tex. 1975). *See also Sanders v. Harder*, 148 Tex. 593, 227 S.W.2d 206, 209 (1950); *Newland v. Newland*, 529 S.W.2d 105, 108 (Tex. Civ. App.—Fort Worth 1975, writ dism'd w.o.j.). We hold that the evidence was factually sufficient to support the trial court's characterization of the stock as separate property. We find further that most of appellee's testimony is corroborated. We must recognize that in a case of this nature there is rarely a third person to corroborate material agreements between spouses or actions by one spouse without the participation of the other. In these instances we must rely upon the fact finder to make findings based upon his belief or disbelief of the testimony before him. *Newland*, 529 S.W.2d at 108. Points of error one and two are overruled.

* * *

D. Presumptions Arising From Conveyance Through Which Title is Acquired

1. Resulting Trusts

When record title is conveyed to one or both spouses during marriage, the conveyance places legal title in the spouse or spouses named as the grantee and equitable title is presumed to be in the community. However, other rules take over when it is proved that consideration has been paid from a spouse's separate property. These other rules are found in the recently revised Restatement of Trusts which is set forth below.

Restatement (Third) of Trusts
2003

Part 1. Nature, Characteristics, And Types Of Trusts
Chapter 2. Resulting Trusts

§ 9. Purchase-Money Resulting Trusts

(1) Except as stated in Subsection (2), where a transfer of property is made to one person and the purchase price is paid by another, a resulting trust arises in favor of the person by whom the purchase price is paid unless

(a) the latter manifests an intention that no resulting trust should arise, or

(b) the transfer is made to accomplish an unlawful purpose, in which case a resulting trust does not arise if the policy against unjust enrichment of the transferee is outweighed by the policy against giving relief to a person who has entered into an illegal transaction.

(2) Where a transfer of property is made to one person and the purchase price is paid by another and the transferee is a spouse, descendant, or other natural object of the bounty of the person by whom the purchase price is paid, a resulting trust does not arise unless the latter manifests an intention that the transferee should not have the beneficial interest in the property.

In order to more easily understand § 9. Purchase-Money Resulting Trusts, the following examples are provided.

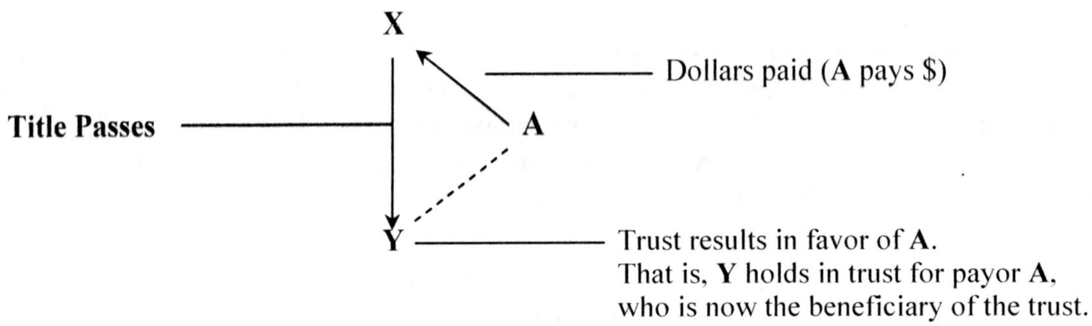

An illustration aid in understanding the "gift" presumption found in subsection (2) of § 9. Purchase-Money Resulting Trusts, is as follows:

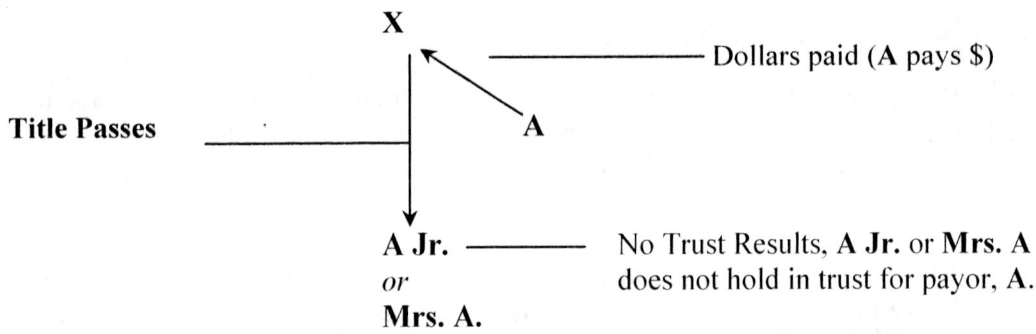

In applying the above rules, the consideration must be paid by the beneficiary or a legally binding commitment made for payment of the consideration by him prior to or at the time that the title passes. *Wright v. Wright*, 134 Tex. 82, 132 S.W.2d 847 (1939). With the exception to be noted later, parol evidence is admissible to rebut the presumption of the resulting trust.

Questions

1. Take a look at the illustration that follows the § 9(1) presumption. Answer the following questions:

a. Total purchase price is $1,000. A pays $500 and signs a note for $500 at the time title passes, but Y pays off the $500 note. What percentage represents A's interest? How about Y's interest?

b. Total purchase price is $1,000. A pays $500 and Y pays $500 at the time title passes. What is Y's interest? What is A's interest?

2. Take a look at the illustration that follows § 9(2). Answer the following questions:

a. A, father to A Jr., pays total purchase price of $1,000 and title passes to son, A Jr., at time of payment. What is A's interest?

b. What if father in scenario 1 provides his son with a letter before title passes asking son to simply hold the property which will be passed to him?

BYBEE
v.
BYBEE

644 S.W.2d 218
(Tex. App.—Fort Worth 1982, no writ)

HUGHES, JR., JUSTICE.

Rosalie Bybee sued Michael Wayne Bybee for divorce and property division. Following judgment, an appeal was taken by the husband limited to portions of the decree concerning the division of the property and debts of the parties. The principal question presented is whether the trial court erred in treating a one-half interest in 25 acres of land as property which was "jointly purchased" by the parties prior to their marriage. We agree that the trial court erred in awarding to the wife a one-fourth undivided interest in the realty. The judgment is reversed and remanded to the trial court for further proceedings not inconsistent with this opinion.

Husband and wife were married on March 10, 1979. Prior to their marriage, on September 9, 1978, Michael Bybee purchased a twenty-five acre tract of land located in Denton County. The purchase price for the land was $28,000.00.* The cash down payment was $2000.00, paid as follows: $1,000.00 was paid by Leon Bybee, grandfather of Michael, $800.00 was paid by Michael Bybee, and $200.00 of his future wife's funds were used for the down payment. The balance of the purchase price, $26,000.00, was represented by a promissory note, executed only by Michael Bybee, payable to the vendor.

It is uncontradicted that the deed to the property was taken in Michael Bybee's name only, and that he alone signed the promissory note and thereby became obligated to pay the balance thereof. Of course, based on these two facts alone, the inception of title rule dictates that the property could in no way be characterized as anything except the separate property of the husband. TEX. CONST. art. XVI, sec. 15 (1948); TEX. FAM. CODE ANN. sec. 5.01(a)(1) (1975).

On June 23, 1981, the husband gave a deed to his grandfather which conveyed to him a one-half undivided interest in the subject tract. Both parties agree that an undivided one-half interest in the land belongs to Leon Bybee.

---

* This footnote has been added by the author and does not appear in the original opinion. As will be evident later in the case, the purchase price for the land was $28,800—not $28,000. This correction was necessary for an understanding of the fractions referenced later in the case.

Concerning the remaining one-half undivided interest in and to the twenty-five acres, which is the only aspect of the trial court's property division which has been raised as error, the court filed findings of fact and conclusions of law, finding as fact the following:

> Shortly before the parties' marriage, the parties became the joint purchasers and owners of an undivided one-half (1/2) interest in a 25 acre tract of land located in Denton County, Texas, along with Leon Bybee, who was the joint purchaser of the remaining undivided one-half (1/2 interest in said 25 acre tract of land, whereby the said Leon Bybee . . . is the joint purchaser and owner of an undivided one-half (1/2) interest in said tract of land, the said ROSALIE BYBEE is the joint purchaser and owner of an undivided one-fourth (1/4) interest in said tract of land, and the said MICHAEL WAYNE BYBEE is the joint purchaser and owner of an undivided one-fourth (1/4) interest in said tract of land.
>
> And the Court finds that the Respondent MICHAEL WAYNE BYBEE did not have the said LEON BYBEE's name placed as a joint purchaser on the original Deed to the said 25 acre tract of land and did not have the said ROSALIE BYBEE's name, formerly ROSALIE GILBERT's name placed on the original Deed to said tract of land; and only after the parties separated and the parties divorce suit was filed, did the said MICHAEL WAYNE BYBEE execute a Deed to the said LEON BYBEE for an undivided one-half (1/2) interest in said tract of land, and the Court finds that the Respondent, MICHAEL WAYNE BYBEE admitted that the said LEON BYBEE was the joint purchaser and owner of an undivided one-half (1/2) interest in said 25 acre tract of land and that he and the said ROSALIE BYBEE were the joint purchasers and owners of the remaining undivided one-half interest in said tract of land.
>
> From this, the trial court concluded as follows:
>
> That ROSALIE BYBEE is the joint purchaser and owner of an undivided one-fourth (1/4) interest in and to a 25 acre tract of land located in Denton County, Texas as set out and described in Petitioner's Exhibit II and that MICHAEL WAYNE BYBEE is a joint purchaser and owner of an undivided one-fourth (1/4) interest in and to said tract of land, and that LEON BYBEE is the joint purchaser and owner of an undivided one-half (1/2) interest in said tract of land.

This court must review the case according to TEX. R. CIV. P. 299, which provides that "(w)here findings of fact and conclusions of law are filed by the trial court they shall form the basis of the judgment embraced therein. . . ." Here, the trial court found the parties to be "joint purchasers". The wife's name having not been found on the deed to the acreage, the only theory which could support the trial court's judgment is one based upon the law of trusts, specifically the theory of a resulting trust in favor of the wife. No such specific findings or conclusions have been filed by the trial court. Rule 299 further provides that "(t)he judgment may not be supported upon appeal by a presumption of finding upon any ground of recovery or defense, no element of which has been found by the trial court . . . ;" under this standard, even if a finding of "joint purchase" were to be held to be a finding of an element under the theory of resulting trust, the judgment of the trial court cannot be upheld.

In *Wright v. Wright*, 134 Tex. 82, 132 S.W.2d 847 (1939), the elements of a resulting trust were set out as follows:

> It is familiar law that a trust must result, if at all, at the very time a deed is taken and the legal title vested in the grantee. No oral agreement before or after the deed is taken, and no payments made after the title is vested, will create a resulting trust, unless the payments

are made in pursuance of an enforceable agreement upon the part of the beneficiary existing at the time the deed is executed. The trust must arise out of the transaction itself. The fundamental idea is that the beneficial title follows the consideration, and unless the one claiming the trust has paid the consideration, or become bound for same, at the very time of the making of the deed, no trust is created. *Id.*, 132 S.W.2d at 849.

It is undisputed that the parties utilized community funds to make payments on the land; this could not create a resulting trust under a "relation back" theory. There is no evidence of an enforceable agreement upon the part of the wife concerning payments made after the title was vested. The most that can be said is that the wife paid $200.00 towards the down payment on the land. Thereafter, the parties paid for the property with community funds, which simply gave rise to a claim by the wife for reimbursement for such funds expended to enhance the value of Michael Bybee's separate undivided interest in the property, less those expended to enhance the value of her own separate interest, if any.

Where a portion only of purchase money is contributed by a person who is not named in a deed, that person's ownership share is represented by the proportion that the contribution bears to the total price. *Wright v. Wright, supra*; *Wimberly v. Kneeland*, 293 S.W.2d 526 (Tex. Civ. App.—Galveston 1956, writ ref'd n.r.e.). In this case, where the future wife's contribution was $200.00 out of a total purchase price of $28,800.00, the smallest share that she would be entitled to would be a 1/144th undivided interest.

The parties could have orally agreed that they would be entitled to an agreed proportion of interest in and to the property; here, the wife was unable to testify to facts which would support the trial court's conclusion that she was a joint, equal owner with her husband of an undivided one-half of the subject tract. The husband claimed he paid $800.00 towards the $2000.00 down payment; the wife claimed he paid between $600.00 and $1000.00 towards the same. There was no agreed proportion of interest in the realty and hence no evidence upon which equal one-fourth interests could be awarded. *Newton v. Gardner*, 225 S.W.2d 598 (Tex. Civ. App.—Eastland 1949, writ ref'd n.r.e.); *Lanier v. Looney*, 2 S.W.2d 347 (Tex. Civ. App.—Dallas 1928, writ ref'd).

The equitable or beneficial title to land follows the consideration which was paid for the same. In order to establish beneficial title in her which was greater than the aforementioned 1/144th minimum share, it was incumbent upon the wife to present evidence that she became bound to her (future) husband to pay the balance of the purchase price, *Vicars v. Quinn*, 154 S.W.2d 947 (Tex. Civ. App.—El Paso 1941, no writ), or that she became bound to the vendor of the land to pay the balance of the purchase money, in her claimed proportionate share, before or at the time the land was conveyed to the future husband. *Faglie v. Williams*, 569 S.W.2d 557 (Tex. Civ. App.—Austin 1978, writ ref'd n.r.e.).

Finally, regarding the finding of the trial court which referred to Michael Bybee's admission at trial that he and his wife were co-owners of the remaining one-half interest in the land, the record reflects that after the parties were married (and after the deed to the property had been taken in his name), he told his wife that "she owned the part of my half, half of my half was hers." This single statement at trial, during the course of which Michael Bybee claimed he merely borrowed $200.00 from his future wife for the down payment on the acreage, was in the nature of an oral agreement or assurance made to his wife after the deed was taken. This could not be made the basis for declaring a resulting trust in favor of Rosalie Bybee because the same must arise at the time when title is taken. *Wright v. Wright, supra*; *Bunnell v. Bunnell*, 217 S.W.2d 78, 81 (Tex. Civ. App.—Waco 1949, no writ).

From the evidence adduced at trial and from our review of the findings and conclusions filed by the court, we hold there to be no evidence to support the trial court's judgment that awarded Rosalie Bybee a one-fourth undivided interest in and to the 25 acres of land. Further, the evidence and the findings and conclusions of the trial court were insufficient to establish a resulting trust in favor of Rosalie Bybee, at least to the extent of her adjudged interest in the land. By these holdings, we may not substitute our opinion for that of the trial court by rendering judgment for Michael Bybee because it is evident that our holdings have otherwise disturbed the overall division of the parties' property incident to their divorce. Remand of the entire cause (except the portion severing the marital bonds of the parties), with trial not inconsistent with this opinion, is hereby ordered.

Notes, Comments & Questions

1. If a deal had not been struck with the grandfather in *Bybee*, what would have been his interest?

2. Why wasn't a gift presumed to have been made by Mrs. Bybee to Mr. Bybee as to her $200 investment? That is, why wasn't her payment governed by § 9?

3. Conveyance to a Spouse or Spouses Containing No Significant Recital.

Before one can identify a conveyance with *no* significant recital, one must understand and be able to identify a significant recital. A recital in a deed is considered to be a significant recital if it states that the consideration is paid from the separate funds of a spouse, or if it states that the property is conveyed to a spouse as his or her separate property. *Brick & Tile, Inc. v. Parker*, 186 S.W.2d 66 (Tex. 1945); *Magee v. Young*, 198 S.W.2d 883 (Tex. 1946); *Henry S. Miller Co. v. Evans*, 452 S.W.2d 426 (Tex. 1970). A recital also can be significant if it states a conveyance is made out of love and affection or as a gift.

a. Third Party Grantor.

When the deed is from a third party as grantor to either spouse or to both of the spouses as grantee and the conveyance does not contain a significant recital, the normal community property presumption can be rebutted by parol evidence that the consideration was paid from the separate funds of one of the spouses, so that a resulting trust arises in favor of the separate estate of that spouse.

Wife as grantee: *Higgins v. Johnson*, 20 Tex. 389 (Tex. 1857); *Patterson v. Metzing*, 424 S.W.2d 255 (Tex. Civ. App.—Corpus Christi 1967, no writ); *Hampshire v. Hampshire*, 485 S.W.2d 314 (Tex. Civ. App.—Fort Worth 1972, no writ).

Husband as grantee: *Matador Land and Cattle Co. v. Cooper*, 87 S.W. 235 (Tex. Civ. App. 1905, no writ); *Alexander v. Alexander*, 373 S.W.2d 800 (Tex. Civ. App.—Corpus Christi 1963, no writ).

Both spouses named as grantees: *Sparks v. Humble Oil & Refining Co.*, 129 S.W.2d 468 (Tex. Civ. App.—Texarkana 1939, writ ref'd); *Von Hutchins v. Pope*, 351 S.W.2d 642 (Tex. Civ. App.—Houston [1st Dist.] 1961, writ ref'd n.r.e.).

b. Spouse as Grantor—Presumption of Gift

When the deed is from the husband to the wife as grantee and contains no significant recital, the normal community property presumption is replaced by the presumption that the husband is making a gift to the wife in the absence of parol evidence to rebut the presumption of gift. *Story v. Marshall*, 24 Tex. 305 (1859); *Dalton v. Pruett*, 483 S.W.2d 926 (Tex. Civ. App.—Texarkana 1972, no writ); *Babb v. McGee*, 507 S.W.2d 821 (Tex. Civ. App.—Dallas 1974, writ ref'd n.r.e.).

Since the wife did not have the power to convey lands without the joinder of her husband prior to 1968, there appear to bc no cases involving conveyances from the wife as grantor to the husband as grantee. Presumably, however, the outcome would be the same with regard to a deed from wife to husband executed after January 1, 1968.

SMITH
v.
STRAHAN
16 Tex. 314
(1856)

Suit by Watkins L. Smith, commenced September 12, 1853, against William H. Strahan, for the partition of certain four hundred acres of land among the heirs of Delilah Strahan, the deceased wife of said William. The other heirs, being three children of said Delilah and William, were made defendants. The plaintiff had married a fourth child, since deceased, leaving a child since deceased. The three other children, made defendants, two of them being minors and appearing by guardian, joined in the plaintiff's prayer for the partition. The father, William H. Strahan, alleged that the land, although the deed was taken in the name of his wife, Delilah, was paid for out of his separate property . . . .

* * *

In answer to issues submitted, there was a special verdict as follows: * * * The land in controversy was paid for by the separate property of W.H. Strahan. The deed from Patrick and Polly Reels to Delilah Strahan was not a gift or dedication to said Delilah from said W.H. Strahan. * * *

* * *

On this verdict the court rendered judgment for William H. Strahan, the father, confirming the title to said land in him. Motion for a new trial overruled. The plaintiff below and the children joined in the prosecution of this writ of error.

* * *

The plaintiff in error requested the court to charge the jury, that if they believe from the evidence that the land in controversy was purchased with the separate property of the defendant, W.H. Strahan, and that he had the deed taken in the name of his wife, Delilah Strahan, the presumption of the law is, that the land was donated to the said Delilah by her said husband, and it devolved on the said defendant, W.H. Strahan, to rebut that presumption by proof that she held the land from the date of the purchase thereof, for the benefit of, and in trust for, the said W.H. Strahan; which instruction the court refused to give, leaving (in the language of the bill of exceptions) the question of gift to the jury as a mere question of fact, and reserving the question of law to be applied by the court; and the court, after the finding, decided that property purchased with the separate property of the husband became and was his separate property, although he had the deed taken to his wife, as decided in *Houston v. Curl*, 8 Tex. 242. To which ruling the plaintiff and defendants excepted, etc.

* * *

HEMPHILL, CHIEF JUSTICE.

It is a general rule, that the trust of a legal estate, whether taken in the names of the purchaser and others jointly, or in the names of others without that of the purchaser, whether in one name or several, whether jointly or successively, results to the one who advances the purchase money; and this is in strict analogy to the rule of the common law, that where a feoffment was made without consideration, the use resulted to the feoffor. (2 STORY, EQ. sec. 1201; 2 Cox 92; 1 LEADING CASES IN EQUITY, p. 188.)

But there are exceptions to this rule as well established as the rule itself. For example, a purchase by a parent, in the name of a child, is deemed prima facie an advancement for the child, so as to rebut the presumption of a trust resulting for the parent. (2 STORY, sec. 1202, and the authorities above cited.) The moral obligation of the parent to provide for his children is said to be the foundation of this exception; and it is but a reasonable presumption that a purchase by a parent in the name of a child is for the benefit of the latter, in discharge of this obligation, and also as a token of his natural love and affection.

And a like presumption exists, also, in the case of a purchase by a husband in the name of the wife; and it is said that the presumption is stronger in case of a wife than of a child, for, at law, she cannot be the trustee of her husband. (2 STORY, sec. 1204; 2 Vernon, pp. 67, 683; 10 Ves. 360; HILL ON TRUSTEES, p. 135; DART ON VENDORS, 437; 19 Wendell 414; 3 Cushing, 194; 11 Paige 619; *Drummer v. Pitcher*, 2 Mylne & Keene, Eng. Chan. 7.)

The presumption of trust, when the purchase is taken in the name of a stranger, as it is raised, so it may be rebutted by parol evidence; and the presumption of an advancement, when taken in the name of a wife or child, may also be rebutted by evidence showing that the purchase was intended for the benefit of the husband or parent who advanced the purchase money.

* * *

The rational foundation for the presumption in favor of the wife is, that the purchase is intended as a provision for her; and this presumption will hold as well under our system as in others where the rights of the wife are not so much favored. It may, and would, under the operation of our laws, be generally more easily rebutted than it would be where the wife has no interest in community property, and a very restricted right to separate estate. The necessity for a provision would not so often exist in this state as in others where, by operation of law, the great proportion of the wife's property is absorbed by the husband. But the necessity might and would often exist in fact. The property of the wife might not be large, or in proportion to her condition and situation in life; and in fact, though eminent advantages are afforded the wife by our laws, yet her condition is not so much changed as to repel the presumption of benefit from a purchase made by a husband in her name out of his own separate funds.

The legal effect and operation of the deed is to vest the property in the wife. This effect would be rebutted in case a stranger were the nominee in the purchase. But the wife is not as a stranger to the husband. She has distinct rights and a separate estate, but he is bound for her support and maintenance, not only by law, but from the impulses of affection; and a conveyance to her, when the purchase money is advanced by himself, is not to be presumed *prima facie*, an arrangement for his convenience, but as importing to the wife a substantial benefit, and vesting in her the whole interest, as well legal as beneficial.

This is but a presumption, and may be rebutted by evidence; but the wife and her privies are entitled to the benefit of this presumption; and the court erred in refusing to instruct the jury that such was the inference of the law.

* * *

The judgment is ordered to be reversed, and the cause remanded for a new trial.

Notes, Comments & Questions

1. Perhaps one of the most interesting aspects *Smith v. Strahan* is that it was reversed on the basis of the jury charge. Today, 150 years later, a review of appellate cases reveals that errors in the jury charge still provide a prevalent basis for reversal.

2. In considering the RESTATEMENT (THIRD) OF TRUSTS, what portion of § 9 would you assign to the jury charge in *Smith v. Strahan* as given? What portion would you assign to the charge that should have been given?

3. We know that the community property presumption must be rebutted by clear and convincing evidence. The next case establishes the burden of proof which must be met to refute a gift presumption.

BOGART
v.
SOMER

762 S.W.2d 577
(Tex. 1988)

PER CURIAM.

At issue here is the standard of proof required to negate a presumption of gift in a constructive trust case. The trial court ruled that the proof required was by a preponderance of the evidence. The court of appeals reversed and remanded the cause to the trial court for a new trial. 749 S.W.2d 202. We denied the application for writ of error.

Allen and Gertrude Bogart purchased certain real property and placed record title in the name of their son-in-law, Joseph Somer. In April 1979, Gertrude Bogart died. Her estate beneficiaries were Phyllis (Bogart) Somer, Theodore Bogart and Lynn Bogart, her children, and Irene Warsaw, her sister. In February 1980, Allen Bogart died leaving his children, Phyllis (Bogart) Somer, Theodore Bogart, and Lynn Bogart as beneficiaries. After Gertrude and Allen Bogart's death, Theodore Bogart, Lynn Bogart and Irene Warsaw sought title to the realty held in Joseph Somer's name.

The trial court submitted an issue on lack of donative intent to the jury. The issue as submitted required a preponderance of the evidence to disprove intent. Based on the jury response that Allen and Gertrude Bogart lacked such intent, judgment was rendered that the beneficiaries of the Bogart estate owned the property and that Joseph Somer held it in constructive trust for them.

Somer appealed to the court of appeals which held that a presumption of gift exists when a father and mother-in-law place property in their son-in-law's name, and the party seeking to disprove the presumption must prove lack of donative intent by clear and convincing evidence. The court reversed the judgment of the trial court and remanded the cause for a new trial. 749 S.W.2d 202.

We approve the holding of the court of appeals that the burden of proof in refuting the presumption of gift is by clear and convincing evidence. The motion for rehearing on denial of the application for writ of error is overruled.

JOHNSON
v.
JOHNSON

584 S.W.2d 307
(Tex. Civ. App.—Texarkana 1979, no writ)

RAY, JUSTICE.

This is a divorce case. Stanley Joseph Johnson, appellee, and Adele Louise Johnson, appellant, both petitioned the court for a divorce and a division of the estate of the parties. A jury was waived and the case was tried to the court. The divorce was granted and the court entered a decree dissolving the marriage and dividing the estate of appellant and appellee. The residence of the parties was declared to be the separate property of the husband and it is from that portion of the judgment that the wife has perfected her appeal. No findings of fact or conclusions of law were filed by the trial court.

Appellant-wife submits two points of error for our consideration and asserts that the trial court erred in failing to find that she owned an undivided one-half interest in the residence as her separate property. The trial court found that the residence was the separate property of the husband. The law of this State relative to appellate review, in the absence of the filing of findings of fact and conclusions of law, is that the appellate court will not substitute its opinion for that of the trial court respecting the credibility of the witnesses and the weight to be given the evidence, but the appellate court will presume that the trial court found all facts in favor of its judgment and the appellate court will be bound by such findings if supported by sufficient evidence of probative force in the record. The judgment of the trial court will be affirmed.

The pertinent facts in this case are that appellee-husband proposed marriage in May of 1973; that he came from Florida to Longview in search of a dwelling; that on July 7, 1973, he signed a contract to purchase a house in which he alone was named as the purchaser; that the parties were married on August 14, 1973; that on August 24, 1973, a deed was executed naming both husband and wife as grantees; that the husband paid the entire purchase price out of his separate funds; and, that suit for divorce was filed on May 16, 1978.

Appellant contends that a presumption of gift of an undivided one-half interest in the house and land arose when the husband paid for the property out of his separate funds but had her named along with himself as the grantees in the deed. Ordinarily, property acquired during marriage is characterized as community property. TEX. FAMILY CODE ANN. § 5.01. There was a presumption that the property here involved was community, but that presumption was overcome when the parties stipulated that the house and land were paid for out of separate funds of the husband and that the contract to purchase the property was entered into prior to the marriage. However, because the deed named husband and wife as grantees, a second presumption arose, a presumption that the husband intended to give his wife an undivided one-half interest in the residence. *Hampshire v. Hampshire*, 485 S.W.2d 314 (Tex. Civ. App.—Fort Worth 1972, no writ); *Carriere v. Bodungen*, 500 S.W.2d 692 (Tex. Civ. App.—Corpus Christi 1973, no writ); 27 Sw. L.J. 27, 33 (1973).

The question before the trial court was whether or not the evidence adduced at the trial was sufficient to overcome the presumption of a gift to the wife of an undivided one-half interest in the property. The question before this Court is whether there was sufficient evidence of probative value presented to the trial court on which it could resolve the fact question of gift vel non. The favorable facts supporting the trial court's judgment are that:

> The inventory and appraisement filed by the wife pursuant to the order of the court shows that the wife did not claim an undivided one-half interest in the property as her separate property, but on the contrary, showed that she claimed no interest in real estate as her separate property; that the only interest claimed in the property in question was a community interest; that the wife testified in substance that the husband had never told her that he was making a gift to her of any interest in the property; that the wife assumed it was community property; that the husband had entered into a contract to purchase the property in which he alone was named as purchaser; that the husband paid for the property solely out of his separate funds; that he was unfamiliar with Texas community property laws; that he did not instruct anyone to insert the name of his wife in the deed; that he did not see the deed or examine it before it was recorded; that the inventory filed by the husband listed the residence as his separate property; that the husband's testimony was that he never talked to his wife about giving her the property and she never talked to him about his having given her any interest in the property; that he purchased the property for himself; and, there was nothing else in writing other than the deed to indicate a gift. We have concluded that the totality of the evidence in this case together with the inferences to be drawn therefrom sustain the trial court's judgment. The evidence was sufficient to overcome the presumption of a gift, thus leaving a fact issue to be determined by the trial court, the trier of the facts in this case. The issue of whether or not there was a gift was highly disputed. We cannot say that the trial court was without sufficient evidence to conclude that the husband did not intend to make a gift to the wife of an undivided one-half interest in the real property. The trial court was in a better position to determine the credibility of the witnesses and the weight to be given their testimony and we see no reason to substitute our judgment for that of the trial court.

While we have concluded that the evidence supports the trial court's judgment, there is yet another reason why this case should be affirmed. Appellant-wife received and accepted from appellee-husband the sum of $5,847.00 which represents a reimbursement to Mrs. Johnson for sums expended on the house out of her one-half of the community funds and some improvements from her separate funds. The court ordered the reimbursement when it declared the house to be the separate property of Mr. Johnson. By accepting payment of the $5,847.00, together with household furniture and other community assets, she has prejudiced the rights of Mr. Johnson, the non-appealing party. The general rule, with some narrow exceptions, is that a litigant cannot treat a judgment as both right and wrong, and if he voluntarily accepts the benefits of a judgment he cannot afterwards prosecute an appeal therefrom. *Carle v. Carle*, 149 Tex. 469, 234 S.W.2d 1002, 1004 (1950); *Swearingen v. Swearingen*, 487 S.W.2d 784 (Tex. Civ. App.—San Antonio 1972, writ dism'd). We further conclude that it can be inferred from the record that appellant-wife voluntarily accepted the benefits accorded her under the judgment and that she is therefore estopped to appeal.

The judgment of the trial court is affirmed.

PETERSON
v.
PETERSON
595 S.W.2d 889
(Tex. Civ. App.—Austin 1980, writ dism'd w.o.j.)

PHILLIPS, CHIEF JUSTICE.

Appellant Viola Peterson brought suit against Richard Martin Peterson, appellee, seeking a divorce and a division of the property of the parties. In particular, Mrs. Peterson claimed a community interest in the home purchased shortly after the wedding, relying first on the presumption that property acquired during the marriage is community, and alternatively, on the presumption that Mr. Peterson, by having Mrs. Peterson named as co-grantee in the deed, intended to make a gift to her of one-half of the property so conveyed. The trial court held that the property in question was the separate property of Mr. Peterson.

We affirm.

Inasmuch as appellant's points of error pertain to the legal and factual sufficiency of the evidence, we must review the evidence in its entirety.

Mr. and Mrs. Peterson, both of whom were in their fifties, were married on January 2, 1970. Approximately three months prior to the marriage they began shopping for a new home, and in November, 1969, a Standard Sales Contract was entered between Mr. Peterson and Crider-Layman Construction Company of Austin for the purchase of a house. At that time Mr. Peterson deposited a check for $2,000 with the builder, payable to Gracy Title Company, as earnest money. The sale closed on January 30, 1970, approximately one month after the parties were married. The deed named Richard M. Peterson and wife, Viola Peterson, as co-grantees. At the closing Mr. Peterson wrote a check payable to Gracy Title for $32,973.64, the balance of the purchase price.

At the trial Mr. Peterson testified that he paid the balance of the purchase price from his personal account, and that the check was drawn against a deposit in excess of $35,000 representing the proceeds from the sale of property which he had inherited from his mother. Further, Mrs. Peterson testified that she did not pay any of the purchase price from her separate funds.

On January 30, 1970, Mr. Peterson was notified that the sale would close that day. He testified that he phoned his wife to advise her of the closing, but that it was not necessary that she attend. It was at that point, according to Mr. Peterson, that he learned that his wife would not move into the house with him unless her name appeared on the deed. Mrs. Peterson testified to essentially the same facts, but she added that she told her husband that she would not move into the house unless she had a half-interest in the house.

Mr. Peterson testified that "I was real shocked. I didn't know what to do. I had just been married. I really didn't want to stir up any trouble at that early (stage) of a marriage . . . so I called . . . and asked . . . if we could get her name added to the deed right away. . . ." Mrs. Peterson's name was subsequently added to the deed and the sale was consummated. Mr. Peterson testified that he did not intend to make a gift to his wife of any interest in the house, but that he added her name to make her happy and to assure her that "she had a place to live the rest of her life," and "then at her death, it would be passed on to my children."

The trial court without aid of a jury found that the parties had acquired no community interest in the property. In the judgment the court stated:

> The Court finds that the entire purchase money for the property described in the deed to RICHARD M. PETERSON and VIOLA PETERSON dated January 30, 1970 . . . has been traced by clear and convincing evidence to the separate funds of RICHARD M. PETERSON. The presumption that property possessed by either spouse on the dissolution of a marriage is community property has been satisfactorily overcome by tracing with clear and convincing evidence the entire purchase money of the property herein described to the separate estate of the husband.
>
> The presumption of a gift created by the taking of title to real property in the name of husband and wife was rebutted by clear and convincing evidence establishing no intent to make a gift to the wife of any interest in the above described real estate."

Appellant, in her first point of error, contends that the trial court erred in finding that the parties' home was appellee's separate property because there was no evidence to overcome the community property presumption. Alternatively, appellant contends by her second and third points that such finding is against the great weight and preponderance of the evidence, and that the evidence is factually insufficient to support the court's finding. By her fourth point of error appellant complains that there was no evidence to support the court's finding that appellee had overcome the presumption that he had made a gift of one-half of the parties' home by naming appellant as co-grantee. Appellant also complains alternatively that such finding is against the great weight and preponderance of the evidence, and that the evidence is factually insufficient to support the court's finding.

We first note that the parties tried this case on the theory that property possessed by either spouse on the dissolution of a marriage is community property, and that appellee attempted to overcome the presumption by tracing the purchase price of the house to his separate funds. Although appellee entered into the contract for the purchase of the property prior to his marriage, he did not rely on the well-established rule that "existence or non-existence of the marriage at the time of incipiency of the right by which title finally vests determines whether the property is community or separate." *Creamer v. Briscoe*, 101 Tex. 490, 109 S.W. 911 (1908); *Williamson v. Williamson*, 457 S.W.2d 311 (Tex. Civ. App.—Austin 1970, no writ). Although we are of the opinion that this rule would be applicable since appellee's "right" to the property originated before the marriage, this theory has not been presented and is not before this Court.

* * *

In *Tarver v. Tarver*, 394 S.W.2d 780 (Tex. 1965), the Supreme Court of Texas restated the basic presumption that all property possessed by a husband and wife upon dissolution of their marriage is community property. TEX. FAMILY CODE ANN. § 5.02 (1975). *Tarver* provides that to discharge the burden imposed by the statute, a spouse must trace and clearly identify the property claimed as separate property.

Our courts have varied between a strict and lenient application of the tracing rules. In *McKinley v. McKinley*, 496 S.W.2d 540 (Tex. 1973), the Supreme Court applied the principles of tracing to a savings account. In that case Mr. McKinley had on deposit $9,500 of his separate funds in a savings account, earning interest, until the account balance was $10,453.81. Mr. McKinley thereafter withdrew $10,400 to purchase a savings certificate. The Supreme Court held that the $9,500 was clearly identified as separate property. This case has been described as the "most liberal tracing case that we have seen." *Latham v. Allison*, 560 S.W.2d 481 (Tex. Civ. App.—Fort Worth 1977, writ ref'd n.r.e.).

In the case at bar Mr. Peterson testified that he sold inherited property and deposited funds in excess of $35,000 into his personal bank account. He subsequently paid the balance of the purchase price from that same account. Appellant argues that no evidence was introduced to establish the beginning balance of that account on the date of marriage or to establish what deposits or withdrawals were made between the date of the marriage and the date of closing.

In reviewing appellant's "no evidence" point, after examining only that evidence in favor of the trial court's finding, we find probative evidence to support the trial court's finding that the community property presumption was overcome by tracing the entire purchase price to appellee's separate funds. In viewing the evidence in its entirety, we also find sufficient evidence to support the trial court's finding, and that the finding is not against the great weight and preponderance of the evidence. Mr. and Mrs. Peterson were married less than one month when Mr. Peterson made the payment from his personal account. Although Mrs. Peterson testified that she desired an interest in the house, under cross-examination she admitted that her only financial interest would be in maintaining the home landscaping, furniture, etc.

Relying upon *McKinley v. McKinley*, *supra*, we hold that appellee has traced the $32,973.64 to his separate property.

With respect to the deed wherein title to the property was taken in both names, we are faced with this presumption: when a husband uses separate property consideration to pay for land acquired during the marriage and takes title to the land in the name of the husband and wife, it is presumed he intended the interest placed in the wife to be a gift. *Cockerham v. Cockerham*, 527 S.W.2d 162 (Tex. 1975); *Hampshire v. Hampshire*, 485 S.W.2d 314 (Tex. Civ. App.—Corpus Christi 1973, no writ). The presumption is rebuttable, and parol evidence is admissible to show that a gift was not intended. *Galvan v. Galvan*, 534 S.W.2d 398 (Tex. Civ. App.—Austin 1976, writ dism'd).

In the instant case Mr. Peterson testified that he added his wife's name to the deed merely to consummate the sale. He said that he wanted to avoid any trouble at the early stage of his marriage, and wanted to accommodate his wife. He testified that he did not intend to give his wife a one-half interest in the home.

Mrs. Peterson, on the other hand, testified that she would not move into the house unless her name was on the deed. She also testified that she wanted a half-interest in the home, but offered no testimony that her husband meant to make a gift to her. She merely testified as to her own intentions. A review of events of the day of closing, January 30, 1970, evidences that Mr. Peterson had omitted his wife's name from the deed, and then only added her name at her insistence after she refused to go through with the purchase.

The trial court found that Mr. Peterson had overcome the presumption that he intended to make a gift of one-half interest in the house. Considering appellant's "no evidence" point, and reviewing only that evidence which supports the trial court's finding, we find some evidence to uphold the finding. Upon review of the record in its entirety, we further find sufficient evidence to uphold the finding, and that the finding is not against the great weight and preponderance of the evidence. Appellant's final three points of error are overruled.

The judgment of the trial court is affirmed.

Affirmed. (SMITH, J., not sitting).

PACE
v.
PACE

160 S.W.3d 706
(Tex. Civ. App.—Dallas 2005, pet. denied)

LANG-MIERS, JUSTICE.

Paul Max Pace appeals the division of property in this divorce case. Pace challenges the trial court's characterization of certain property as his wife's[1] separate property and argues this characterization prevented a just and right division of the couple's property. In eight issues, Pace argues (1) there is no evidence to support the trial court's findings of fact that the couple's Harvest Hill home and the assets in the Linda Ruth Thomas Management Trust (Management Trust) are Thomas's separate property, (2) the trial court erred by granting partial summary judgment in favor of Thomas and holding that the A.G. Edwards investment account (172 account) is Thomas's separate property because Thomas failed to rebut the community property presumption, and (3) the trial court abused its discretion in dividing the community estate because the mischaracterization of the Harvest Hill house and the 172 account as Thomas's separate property prevented a just and right division of the property. We affirm.

I. FACTUAL AND PROCEDURAL BACKGROUND

Thomas and Pace were married on March 8, 1997. Both had been married before and both had adult children from their previous marriages, but they had no children together. After four and one-half years of marriage, the parties separated and Thomas filed for divorce. Pace filed a counterpetition for divorce asserting his separate property and equitable interest claims as well as a claim for reimbursement against Thomas's separate property estate.

A. Thomas's Inheritance

Thomas inherited her parents' estates, consisting mostly of bonds and other securities, when they died in the mid-1990s. She invested this inheritance in the 172 account prior to her marriage to Pace. At the time of her marriage to Pace, the inheritance was valued at $2.7 million.

* * *

---

[1] The trial court's final decree of divorce changed Linda Ruth Thomas Pace's name to Linda Ruth Thomas. For clarity, we refer to her as Thomas.

C. Creation of the 204 Account and the Management Trust

Twenty-three days after they were married and after Pace refused to sign the prenuptial agreement, Thomas instructed A.G. Edwards to "sweep" all dividends, interest, and income from the 172 account and place the income in a new account (204 account) so that no community property would accrue in the 172 account.

About three years later, Thomas instructed her attorney to set up the Management Trust with Thomas as the donor, trustee, and sole beneficiary to segregate Thomas's separate property and to protect her from possible third party liability. The 172 account was transferred into the Management Trust and A.G. Edwards continued to "sweep" all dividends, interest, and income from that account into the 204 account.

D. The Harvest Hill House

When they were first married, Thomas and Pace lived in Thomas's house which she owned and lived in before their marriage. Two months after they were married, the Harvest Hill house was purchased. Thomas wrote a check for $1,000 as earnest money for the Harvest Hill house and a check for $200 for an inspection. Both checks were drawn on an account bearing only Thomas's name. Prior to closing, Thomas wired $194,102.53 from the 172 account to the title company in full payment of the Harvest Hill house. No credit or notes were obtained to purchase the house, and Pace did not contribute any money toward the purchase of the house.

A few days before closing, Pace told Thomas that he wanted to be on the deed to the Harvest Hill house because he did not want to feel like a tenant in the house. Thomas agreed to put his name on the deed, and Thomas and Pace both signed the settlement statement and the warranty deed. The settlement statement identified the purchasers as Pace and Thomas. The warranty deed identified the grantees as Pace and Thomas. Thomas and Pace resided in the Harvest Hill house until they separated. During that time, Thomas paid the ad valorem taxes, the fire and extended coverage insurance, and the upkeep of the Harvest Hill house from the 204 account.

* * *

E. Divorce Proceedings

Before trial, Thomas filed a motion for partial summary judgment seeking judgment as a matter of law denying Pace's community property characterization claims against her individually and as trustee of the Management Trust, that she did not commingle community property funds with her separate property assets contained in the Management Trust, and that all purchases of securities during the marriage were made with her separate property funds. Thomas supported her motion with her own affidavit and that of Shelley Turner, an employee of A.G. Edwards who handles the 172 account. Pace responded to the motion and attached four monthly statements for 1997 for the 172 account and three monthly statements for 1997 for the 204 account, along with the affidavit of Barbara Dossett, a bookkeeper and owner of The Taxpayer's Service who had inspected the account statements.

The trial court granted partial summary judgment in favor of Thomas sustaining Thomas's request to deny Pace's community property characterization and commingling claims against the 172 account, but not the other assets contained in the Management Trust. The remaining issues were tried to the court. The trial court granted the divorce and in the decree reaffirmed the prior partial summary judgment. The trial court also issued findings of fact and conclusions of law.

II. THE TRIAL COURT'S FINDINGS ARE SUPPORTED BY THE EVIDENCE

In his first through fourth issues on appeal, Pace argues there is no evidence to support the trial court's findings of fact characterizing the Harvest Hill house and the assets in the Management Trust, including the 172 account, as Thomas's separate property. We disagree.

* * *

B. Law of Separate and Community Property

In Texas, all marital property is either separate or community. *Hilley v. Hilley*, 161 Tex. 569, 573, 342 S.W.2d 565, 567 (Tex. 1961). Property possessed by either spouse during or upon the dissolution of their marriage is presumed to be community property. TEX. FAM. CODE ANN. § 3.003(a) (Vernon 1998). Property owned or claimed by a spouse before marriage remains that spouse's separate property during and after the marriage. TEX. CONST. XVI, § 15; TEX. FAM. CODE ANN. § 3.001 (Vernon 1998). Property purchased during the marriage with separate funds is separate property. *Hilley*, 161 Tex. at 573-74, 342 S.W.2d at 567. Clear and convincing evidence is necessary to establish that property is separate property. TEX. FAM. CODE ANN. § 3.003(b). A trial court may not divest a party of his separate property by a divorce decree. *In re Marriage of Murray*, 15 S.W.3d 202, 205 (Tex. App.—Texarkana 2000, no pet.) (citing *Eggemeyer v. Eggemeyer*, 554 S.W.2d 137, 142 (Tex. 1977)).

Property is characterized as separate or community at the time of the inception of title. The inception of title doctrine fixes the character of certain property interests when a party first acquires a right or claim to the property; title need not be vested at such time. *See, e.g., Henry S. Miller Co. v. Evans*, 452 S.W.2d 426, 430 (Tex. 1970); *Strong v. Garrett*, 148 Tex. 265, 224 S.W.2d 471 (1949); *Stavinoha v. Stavinoha*, 126 S.W.3d 604, 613 (Tex. App.—Houston [14th Dist.] 2004, no pet.).

C. The Harvest Hill House

In his first issue on appeal, Pace argues there is no evidence to support the trial court's finding of fact that "[a]fter the marriage, [Thomas] purchased the following property with separate monies: [the Harvest Hill house], value undisputed."

1. Applicable Law

A spouse who purchases real property during the marriage with her separate property, but takes title to the property in the names of both spouses is presumed to have made a gift to the other spouse of one-half interest in the property. *Cockerham v. Cockerham*, 527 S.W.2d 162, 167-68 (Tex. 1975); *Whorrall v. Whorrall*, 691 S.W.2d 32, 35 (Tex. App.—Austin 1985, writ dism'd). This presumption may be rebutted by clear and convincing evidence that there was no intent to make a gift. *Cockerham*, 527 S.W.2d at 168; *Whorrall*, 691 S.W.2d at 35.

2. Analysis

At trial, Pace claimed that Thomas made a gift to him of a one-half interest in the Harvest Hill house which Thomas claimed as her separate property and asked the court to award him that one-half interest. On appeal, Pace contends that the Harvest Hill house is presumed to be community property and that there is no evidence the Harvest Hill house is Thomas's separate property because there is no evidence the earnest money check was drawn on Thomas's separate property account. Although Pace did not raise this issue in the trial court, a complaint regarding the legal insufficiency of the evidence in a nonjury case may be made for the first time on appeal. TEX. R. APP. P. 33.1(d); *Yarbrough v. Yarbrough*, 151 S.W.3d 687, 689-90 (Tex. App.—Waco 2004, no pet. h.); *Nelson v. Najm*, 127 S.W.3d 170, 176 (Tex. App.—Houston [1st Dist.] 2003, pet. denied).

Thomas testified at trial that the earnest money check was paid from her separate funds and Pace offered no evidence to the contrary. Evidence in the trial court included an excerpt of Pace's deposition in which he admitted the Harvest Hill house was purchased completely with Thomas's separate property. This is some evidence that the earnest money check was drawn on Thomas's separate property account. Because the evidence is uncontroverted, it is also clear and convincing evidence that the funds used to purchase the Harvest Hill house were traced to Thomas's separate assets. *See Celso v. Celso*, 864 S.W.2d 652, 655 (Tex. App.—Tyler 1993, no writ) (where evidence is uncontroverted that husband's separate property assets were used to purchase house then evidence is clear and convincing that husband traced purchase of house to his separate property assets); *see also Holloway v. Holloway*, 671 S.W.2d 51, 55 (Tex. App.—Dallas 1983, writ dism'd) (party's uncontroverted testimony alone is sufficient to establish separate property nature of asset).[2]

We conclude the evidence was sufficient to support the trial court's finding that the Harvest Hill house was Thomas's separate property. Pace's first issue is overruled.

* * *

III. NO ISSUE OF FACT TO PRECLUDE PARTIAL SUMMARY JUDGMENT

In his fifth and sixth issues on appeal, Pace argues the trial court erred in granting and reaffirming Thomas' motion for partial summary judgment denying Pace's claim that the 172 account is community property because she failed to rebut the community property presumption. Pace contends that Thomas failed to conduct any tracing of the assets. Thomas responds that the trial court did not err because the affidavit of Dossett attached to Pace's response to her motion for partial summary judgment is not competent summary judgment evidence and, even if it were, it does not raise a genuine issue of material fact.

* * *

C. Analysis

Pace does not dispute that Thomas inherited the assets in the 172 account or that Thomas owned the 172 account prior to their marriage. Pace also does not claim that deposits were made into the 172 account from their community property incomes. Pace's argument is that the interest income from the 172 account was not swept properly into the 204 account and, as a result, was commingled with the underlying securities in the 172 account causing the entire 172 account to lose its identity as separate property. Pace argues Thomas failed to show the property was not commingled. We disagree.

Thomas testified that she set up the 204 account to hold the income generated by the 172 account to prevent commingling of the separate and community assets and that the income was transferred monthly. A spouse is competent to testify concerning the characterization of property without producing independent documentation such as bank records. *See Vannerson v. Vannerson*, 857 S.W.2d 659, 668 (Tex. App.—Houston [1st Dist.] 1993, writ denied). The testimony of a spouse seeking to overcome the community property presumption need not be corroborated to meet the clear and convincing standard. *Holloway*, 671 S.W.2d at 56; *Newland v. Newland*, 529 S.W.2d 105, 107-08 (Tex. Civ. App.—Fort Worth 1975, no writ); *but see Boyd v. Boyd*, 131 S.W.3d 605, 614-17 (Tex. App.—Fort Worth 2004, no pet. h.). However, a party's unsupported

[2] In fact, although not evidence, Pace's attorney even admitted during trial that the Harvest Hill house was purchased solely with Thomas's separate property.

and contradicted testimony may not meet the clear and convincing standard. *See Johnson v. Johnson*, 804 S.W.2d 296, 300-01 (Tex. App.—Houston [1st Dist] 1991, no writ).

In this case, Thomas's testimony is not unsupported or contradicted. Pace did not dispute that Thomas owned the 172 account as her separate property. And Turner corroborated Thomas's testimony that the community property income was never commingled with Thomas's separate property in the 172 account. The instructions to A.G. Edwards to sweep the income into a separate account also corroborated Thomas's and Turner's affidavits that the income from the 172 account was not commingled with the 172 account assets. Thomas's evidence adequately dispelled the community property presumption by showing the property was not commingled. *See Hanau*, 730 S.W.2d at 667; *Welder v. Welder*, 794 S.W.2d 420, 425 (Tex. App.—Corpus Christi 1990, no writ).

Additionally, Pace's evidence failed to raise a fact issue that the community property income had been commingled with the 172 account.[3] Dossett's affidavit does not controvert Thomas's summary judgment evidence that income on the 172 account was maintained as a credit and swept into the community 204 account. Instead, she states only that some interest earned on funds held in an interest-bearing account within the 172 account was not swept into the 204 account and that these funds were used to purchase new securities. But she does not identify the amount she contends should have been swept or the amount not swept, does not state that she has personal knowledge the interest was not swept, does not identify where the 172 or 204 account summaries support her theory, and does not explain the basis for her conclusion. In fact, her affidavit purports to explain, "[b]y way of example," but the explanation that follows does not refer to interest. Even with the supporting summaries, Dossett's statement that the interest from the interest-bearing account was not swept is a conclusion with no factual basis and is insufficient to raise a fact question.[4] *See Brown v. Brown*, 145 S.W.3d 745, 751-52 (Tex. App.—Dallas 2004, pet. denied); *Rizkallah v. Conner*, 952 S.W.2d 580, 587-88 (Tex. App.—Houston [1st Dist.] 1997, no pet.). As a result, there is no summary judgment evidence that the interest was not swept.

Dossett also stated that stock was sold for a profit in July and four days later those proceeds were invested in the 172 account. But proceeds from the sale of separate property are the separate property of the spouse whose property was sold. *Scott v. Scott*, 805 S.W.2d 835, 838 (Tex. App.—Waco 1991, no writ). Also, an increase or decrease in the value of separate property is an inherent part of the property itself and cannot be separated from it. *Dawson-Austin v. Austin*, 920 S.W.2d 776, 788 (Tex. App.—Dallas 1996), *rev'd on other grounds*, 968 S.W.2d 319 (Tex. 1998) (holding that an increase in the value of separate property stock remains separate property); *Smith v. Smith*, 22 S.W.3d 140, 150 (Tex. App.—Houston [14th Dist.] 2000, no pet.) (same). We conclude Pace failed to raise a fact issue concerning the separate property characterization of the 172 account.

We overrule Pace's fifth and sixth issues.

---

[3] Thomas argues the trial court should have granted her motion to strike Dossett's affidavit because Pace failed to disclose Dossett as a witness in discovery and because the affidavit is not competent summary judgment evidence. The trial court did not rule on the motion and, in fact, considered Dossett's affidavit in reaching its decision. Because we affirm the trial court's judgment, we need not reach the merits of this issue.

[4] If the correct amount was swept, mixing of dollars alone does not result in commingling. *See Trawick v. Trawick*, 671 S.W.2d 105, 110- 11 (Tex.App.-El Paso 1984, no writ) (one dollar has the same value as another dollar and no commingling by the mixing of dollars where the amount owned by each is known); *Farrow v. Farrow*, 238 S.W.2d 255, 257 (Tex.Civ.App.-Austin 1951, no writ) (same).

V. CONCLUSION

We conclude the evidence is sufficient to sustain the trial court's findings of fact that the Harvest Hill house and the assets in the Management Trust are Thomas's separate property. * * * We affirm the trial court's judgment.

Notes, Comments & Questions

1. The *Johnson* and *Peterson* cases make very good use of parol evidence to establish husband's separate property and to rebut any presumption of gift. Make sure that you understand why parol evidence can be used—there were no significant recitals.

2. Does the level of proof in *Pace* seem to equal that in *Johnson* or *Peterson*?

3. If you had represented the wives in *Johnson* and *Peterson* or husband in *Pace*, would you have presented their cases in a different manner?

4. Do you think the proof in *Johnson* and *Peterson* met the *Bogart v. Somer* level?

WHORRALL
v.
WHORRALL

691 S.W.2d 32
(Tex. App.—Austin 1985, writ dism'd w.o.j.)

SHANNON, CHIEF JUSTICE.

Appellant Richard E. Whorrall filed suit in the district court of Williamson County seeking a divorce from appellee Ilene Crafton Whorrall. By his suit, Richard also sought a division of the parties' community property. The union, being a "September marriage," produced no off-spring.

After a bench trial, the district court rendered judgment granting the divorce and dividing the community property between the parties. Upon appellant's request, the district court filed findings of fact and conclusions of law.

Richard claims that the district court erred (1) in awarding to Ilene all right, title, and interest in the parties' house located in Round Rock and . . . .

I.

THE HOUSE

The parties married on February 11, 1977. At that time, Richard was fifty-six and had been married before. Ilene was forty-four and had been married twice previously. About two weeks after their marriage, the couple purchased a house and lot located in Round Rock for $55,450.00. The purchase was financed as follows: the couple signed a note for $35,000.00 secured by a deed of trust; Richard contributed $500.00 of his separate funds as earnest money and Ilene paid $21,250.67 of her separate funds at closing for the down payment and closing costs.

In its findings and conclusions, the district court characterized the parties interest in the house as follows:

(1) Richard owned, as his separate property, a .9% interest in the house representing a value of $938.17. This separate interest was acquired by virtue of Richard's initial contribution of $500.00 from his separate property.

(2) Ilene owned, as her separate property, a 37.6% interest in the house valued at $39,973.70. This determination resulted from the district court's finding that Ilene contributed $21,250.67 of her separate funds toward the purchase of the house.

(3) The community estate owned a 61.6% undivided interest in the house valued at $32,387.40 (after subtracting the balance of the purchase money note).

In the judgment the district court vested the complete title in the house in Ilene. Accordingly, the district court awarded Ilene all of the community interest in the house as well as Richard's .9% separate interest.

By his point of error four, Richard asserts that the district court's finding that Ilene's separate estate owned a 37.6% undivided interest is supported by insufficient evidence. In reviewing factual sufficiency points of error, the reviewing court considers all of the evidence to determine whether the findings are so against the great weight and preponderance of the evidence as to be manifestly unjust. *In re King's Estate*, 150 Tex. 662, 244 S.W.2d 660 (1951).

It is trite learning that the weight and probative force of evidence is entirely for the fact finder. Likewise, the fact finder is the exclusive judge of the credibility of the witnesses and the weight to be attached to their testimony. The fact finder may believe the testimony of one witness and reject the testimony of other witnesses. Similarly, the fact finder may accept part of the testimony of one witness and disregard the remainder. The finder of fact may resolve conflicts and inconsistencies in the testimony of any one witness as well as the testimony of different witnesses. I RAY, LAW OF EVIDENCE § 3 (3rd ed. 1980).

The district court found that Ilene contributed $21,250.67 from her separate funds toward the purchase of the house. In addition, the parties stipulated that title to the house was taken in their joint names. Richard suggests that these undisputed facts give rise to three community property law presumptions which Ilene did not rebut by sufficient evidence. Accordingly, Richard argues that the district court should have concluded that the house was entirely the property of the community estate. This Court does not agree.

Richard urges first the presumption that property acquired during marriage is presumed to be a part of the community estate. TEX. FAM. CODE ANN. § 5.02 (1975). This presumption may be overcome by "clear and convincing" or "clear and satisfactory" proof, by identifying and tracing the property claimed as separate to a separate source of funds or credit used in its purchase. *McKinley v. McKinley*, 496 S.W.2d 540 (Tex. 1973); *Bilek v. Tupa*, 549 S.W.2d 217 (Tex. Civ. App. 1977, writ ref'd n.r.e.). Ilene testified that her $21,250.67 down payment was obtained from the sale of her duplex, the sale being made before her marriage to Richard. The couple purchased the house in Round Rock about two weeks after they were married. Upon examination, Richard conceded that this payment came from funds Ilene possessed before marriage. Accordingly, there was sufficient evidence of a clear and satisfactory nature to overcome this presumption.

Richard then points to the presumption that one spouse intends to make a gift to the other of one-half of his separate contribution made to purchase real estate during marriage when title to such real estate is taken in the name of both spouses. *Cockerham v. Cockerham*, 527 S.W.2d 162,

168 (Tex. 1975). This presumption, nevertheless, may be rebutted by evidence clearly establishing that there was no intention to make a gift. *Cockerham v. Cockerham, supra.*

Ilene testified that she had been through two previous marriages in which her husbands had been financially irresponsible and had taken financial advantage of her. She testified specifically that she did not intend to make a gift of one-half of the $21,250.67 as she "couldn't afford to do that." She explained further that she and Richard wanted to purchase a house and she put in the large down payment as a condition that he make all the remaining mortgage payments. Ilene also stated that her advancing the down payment was necessary because Richard "was broke" and told her that due to his recent divorce, "I don't have any money."

The outlined evidence overcame the presumption of gift, thereby leaving a fact issue to be determined by the district court. The great weight of the evidence supports the district court's determination of no intention by Ilene to make a gift to Richard of one-half of the $21,250.67 down payment.

Finally, Richard advances the argument that when real property is acquired during marriage and title to that property is taken in the name of both spouses, a presumption arises that the spouses agreed that the real estate would be owned by the community estate. *Gonzalez v. Guajardo de Gonzalez*, 541 S.W.2d 865 (Tex. Civ. App. 1976, no writ); *Robbins v. Robbins*, 519 S.W.2d 507 (Tex. Civ. App. 1975, no writ).

The evidence is conflicting as to the parties' agreement respecting the ownership of the house. Ilene testified that she and Richard discussed, before its purchase, the financing of the new house. She told Richard that she would be willing to make the large down payment "if that will constitute payment in full for my one-half interest in the house." She further related to Richard, "Then, if you make the mortgage payments and pay off the mortgage, we will own the house 50/50." Ilene further testified that the couple made an agreement that Richard would not become immediate half owner of the property upon purchase but "would own a full half interest in the house at the time that he paid off the mortgage."

Richard testified that the couple discussed purchasing a house before marriage and "We had an agreement that we would own the home equally, regardless of who paid what." He further testified:

> And we had quite a lot of conversation about it and the net of that conversation was that we were in love and it didn't make any difference who made the down payment. I said to her, 'I don't think I could live in a home with a wife if I wasn't the co-owner.' And she agreed and the agreement was that we would own the home equally.

Ascertaining the agreement of the parties is especially difficult in view of their lack of knowledge of community property law and their use of such terms as "jointly." It seems that Ilene thought that her down payment vested her with one-half interest in the house as her separate property and that her husband would acquire a separate one-half interest upon completing the balance of the payments. Her use of the term "jointly" could mean possibly that she intended that each party's separate estate own one-half of the house in a tenancy-in-common. Despite the legal inaccuracy (for the mortgage payments were made with community funds even though husband made them all), the tenor of Ilene's version of the agreement was that her down payment entitled her to own a portion of the residence as her separate property.

Richard argues that from the outset, the couple agreed to own the property "jointly," which he contends was an agreement to own the residence as community property. He further insists that the alleged condition of his making all the payments, if believed, "should be treated as a condition subsequent to the parties' agreement that they would own the property equally."

Richard invites this Court to measure his credibility against that of his former spouse and seeks to draw our attention to her acts which may reflect a lack of candor and fairness. The fact finder, not this Court, is the judge of the credibility of the witnesses and the weight to be accorded their testimony. *Harrell v. Sunylan Co.*, 128 Tex. 460, 97 S.W.2d 686 (1936). From all of the evidence, the fact finder could have concluded that the parties did not agree that the house would be a part of the community estate. On the other hand, the court could reasonably have concluded to the contrary. In such a situation, it is basic to our system of jurisprudence that the reviewing court may not substitute its view of the facts for that of the fact finder. *Benoit v. Wilson*, 150 Tex. 273, 239 S.W.2d 792 (1951). Richard's point of error is overruled.

By his fifth point, Richard asserts that the district court erred in awarding his .9% undivided separate interest in the house because the court had no power to award the separate property of one spouse to the other. Richard relies, of course, upon *Eggemeyer v. Eggemeyer*, 554 S.W.2d 137 (Tex. 1977). The Supreme Court in that opinion held that the trial court may not divest one spouse's fee interest in realty and award it to the other spouse. Even counsel for Ilene concedes that the district court erred in divesting Richard of that interest.

Ilene argues in support of the judgment that the error in divesting Richard of merely a .9% interest is harmless error. Furthermore, she argues that to require her to maintain a tenancy in common with a .9% interest is economically unrealistic and impracticable.

Although Ilene's position has practical appeal, *Eggemeyer* holds that a trial court has no authority to divest a fee interest of separate realty in order to award such to the other spouse, or, put another way, such action lies entirely outside the trial court's discretion. *See McLemore v. McLemore*, 641 S.W.2d 395 (Tex. App. 1982, no writ). Furthermore, this Court cannot conclude that the divestiture was harmless error pursuant to TEX. R. CIV. P. 434 when it plainly caused the rendition of an improper judgment. Point of error five is sustained.

* * *

Because the district court erroneously divested Richard of his .9% separate interest in the house, the judgment of the district court is modified to provide that Richard is a co-tenant in the house to the extent of his separate .9% interest. In all other respects the judgment is affirmed.

Questions

1. Why would husband in *Whorrall* have fought so strongly for a 0.9% interest?
2. Why did husband's 0.9% interest result in reversal?
3. How could the trial court on remand deal with a home in which each spouse has a separate property interest?

---

2. Conveyance Containing a Significant Recital

A significant recital can state: (1) that consideration is paid from a spouse's separate property; (2) that the property is conveyed to a spouse as his/her separate property; or, (3) that a conveyance is made to a spouse out of love and affection or as a gift.

MESSER
v.
JOHNSON
422 S.W.2d 908
(Tex. 1968)

WALKER, JUSTICE.

Real estate was conveyed to a married woman. Her husband joined in the deed as one of the grantors, and the instrument declared that the land was conveyed to the grantee as her separate estate and to her sole and separate use. The question to be decided is whether parol evidence may be received to show a resulting trust in favor of the community estate. We reaffirm the rule that it may not.

John E. Johnson and Pearl Johnson were married in 1930. The land in question was conveyed to the latter by H.T. Smith on June 9, 1943. John E. Johnson, who previously owned no interest in the property, is named in the deed as one of the grantors. He and H.T. Smith duly executed and acknowledged the instrument on the same day, and it was promptly filed for record. The deed recites a consideration of $12,480.00 paid in cash and expressly conveys the property to Pearl Johnson as "her sole and separate estate, and to her sole and separate use." This recital appears in the granting clause, the habendum clause and the warranty clause, but the deed does not state that the consideration was paid by the grantee out of her separate property.

Pearl Johnson died testate in 1961. Under the terms of her will, John E. Johnson was named independent executor without bond, was bequeathed all of her personal property, and was given a life estate in all of her real estate with remainder to Myrtle Messer et al, who are defendants in the present suit. Johnson was also given the power "to sell or mortgage any such portion of my real estate . . . that may be necessary for his comfortable support."

Johnson inventoried the land in the probate proceedings as community property. About three years later he instituted the present suit to establish a resulting trust in favor of the community and to obtain a construction of Pearl Johnson's will. After the suit was filed but before it was tried, he conveyed the land without warranty to his present wife, Esther Johnson, who was then substituted as plaintiff.

According to the evidence introduced at the trial, Johnson arranged for the purchase of the land and paid the $12,480.00 consideration out of community funds. He did not intend to give the property to Pearl but had it deeded to her because he was afraid of his son by a former marriage. He placed the title in her name as a matter of convenience to avoid any trouble with the son and to insure that neither the son nor anyone claiming through him could inherit the property in the event of Johnson's death. It also appears that the land was managed, used and held just as though it were community property.

Defendants objected to all testimony of this nature on the ground that it violated the parol evidence rule. Their objections were overruled and the case was submitted to the jury, which found: (1) that at the time of the conveyance, John E. and Pearl Johnson intended that the land would be their community property; and (2) that the title was conveyed to Pearl in trust for the use and benefit of herself and John. Judgment was rendered on the verdict decreeing that plaintiff owns an undivided one-half interest in the land in fee simple and an estate measured by the life of John in the other undivided one-half interest. The Court of Civil Appeals affirmed. 415 S.W.2d 276.

We assume without deciding that the issues submitted to the jury are raised by the extrinsic evidence introduced. Plaintiff says that the action of the trial court in admitting such evidence and basing its judgment thereon is supported by cases such as *McCutchen v. Purinton*, 84 Tex. 603, 19 S.W. 710. There, as here, the deed was from a third party to the wife. The instrument recited that the consideration was paid out of her separate estate and purported to convey the land to her as her separate property. Unlike the present case, however, the husband did not join in the deed and there is nothing to suggest that he participated in the transaction. It was held that the recitals in the deed, when uncontradicted and unexplained, overcame the presumption that the land was community property. The opinion further states that:

> If such recitals are untrue, and the payment of the consideration was in fact made with community funds, the evidence thereof would be admissible in a proper case to establish a resulting trust in favor of the community estate, as in other cases where the title is conveyed to one party, and the purchase money is paid by another.

The rule is otherwise where the deed to the wife is from the husband or the latter participates in the transaction to such an extent that he may fairly be regarded as a party to the instrument. In *Kahn v. Kahn*, 94 Tex. 114, 58 S.W. 825, the property had originally been conveyed to the wife, and the consideration was paid in part with funds belonging to the community estate, in part with the husband's separate funds and in part out of the wife's separate estate. Upon the representation that such a step was necessary to obtain a loan, the wife joined her husband in deeding the land to a third party, who then conveyed it to the husband. No loan was obtained, and the wife demanded that the property be reconveyed to her. The husband executed and delivered to her a deed which recited a consideration of $500.00 paid by the grantee "out of her separate funds, and for her separate use and benefit." The husband later attempted to recover an interest in the land by proving that his deed to the wife was made to keep peace in the family and that he did not intend to convey his interest to the grantee as her separate property. It was held that "without proof of fraud or mistake in the insertion of the recitals in the deed, parol evidence was not admissible to show that the maker of it did not intend to convey the property to his wife as her separate property, and this for the reason that the deed on its face clearly expressed such intent."

In *McKivett v. McKivett*, 123 Tex. 298, 70 S.W.2d 694, community realty was conveyed by a husband to his wife as her separate property. After the husband's death, his heirs sued to recover an interest in the property on the theory that his conveyance was executed pursuant to a prior agreement between the husband and wife that she would hold the title in trust for the community estate. The deed recited a contractual consideration, but the effect of this recital is not discussed in the opinion. In holding that extrinsic evidence was not admissible to show that the parties intended for the grantee to hold the property in trust, the Court said:

> The evidence offered in this case is of such character as to render the deed ineffective. It would prove that the beneficial title did not rest in the wife for her separate use, as the deed declared, but that it remained in the community. Such evidence would contradict the very statements in the deeds which the court held in *Kahn v. Kahn* to belong to that class of particular and contractual recitals which the parties may not deny. The deeds in express

terms declare the particular purpose or use for which the property is conveyed; that is, that it shall belong separately to the wife. Parol evidence should not be admitted to prove that it was conveyed for a different purpose or use.

It has also been held that an express or resulting trust in favor of the community may not be established by extrinsic evidence where property is conveyed by a third party to the wife as her separate estate and the husband participates in the transaction to such an extent that he should be regarded as a party to the instrument. *Lindsay v. Clayman*, 151 Tex. 593, 254 S.W.2d 777; *Loeb v. Wilhite*, Tex. Civ. App., 224 S.W.2d 343 (writ ref. n.r.e.). The opinions in *Lindsay* and *Loeb* emphasize the recitals of contractual consideration in the deed or contract of purchase there involved. As pointed out in *Jackson v. Hernandez*, 155 Tex. 249, 285 S.W.2d 184, however, the real basis for the application of the parol evidence rule in such cases is the stipulation in the deed that the land was conveyed to the grantee as her separate property, because the same constitutes a declaration that the grantee is to take the property for her own benefit.

It is clear then that extrinsic evidence was improperly admitted in the present case unless the line of decisions represented by *Kahn*, *McKivett*, *Lindsay* and *Loeb* is to be overruled. We are urged by an amicus curiae brief to relax the parol evidence rule here because there are situations in which the spouses will find it desirable to create an appearance of separate ownership while intending that the wife shall hold title in trust for the community estate. If the alleged oral agreement is one that might normally be made by the parties under the circumstances, it is argued, evidence thereof should be admitted and the trier of fact allowed to determine whether the recital of separate ownership was intended to be colorable only. In the event it was so intended, the argument continues, the oral agreement is necessarily "collateral" to the deed, because the parties could not have meant for the latter to express their entire agreement concerning ownership. *See* Fritz, *Marital Property—Effects of Recitals and Credit Purchases*, 41 TEX. L. REV. 1, 33; MCCORMICK ON EVIDENCE § 216.

The argument is appealing, because there are undoubtedly cases in which the parol evidence rule operates to defeat the true intention of the parties. On the other hand it is entirely proper to deny legal effect to prior or contemporaneous understandings when the parties intend for the written memorial to be the sole expression of their final agreement. The question often arises then as to whether only part of the transaction has been embodied in the writing and another part left in some other form. According to Professor Wigmore this depends wholly upon the intention of the parties, which must be determined from their conduct and language and the surrounding circumstances. In deciding upon such intent, however, "the chief and most satisfactory index for the judge is found in the circumstance whether or not the particular element of the alleged extrinsic negotiation is dealt with at all in the writing." IX WIGMORE ON EVIDENCE, 3rd ed. 1940, § 2430.

In this instance the deed declares in several places that the property was conveyed to the grantee as her separate property and to her sole and separate use. The ordinary and accepted meaning of these terms is that the grantee should take and hold the land for her own benefit. It also appears that John E. Johnson went out of his way to sign the deed when there was no reason for his doing so except to evidence an intention to make a gift to his wife. It is our opinion that in these circumstances the husband should not be heard to say that he did not intend to make his wife the beneficial owner of the land as the deed declared. We adhere, therefore, to the general rule that where an inter vivos written transfer of property stipulates that the transferee is to take the property for his own benefit, extrinsic evidence is not admissible, in the absence of equitable grounds for reformation or rescission, to show that he was intended to hold the property in trust. *See* RESTATEMENT, SECOND, TRUSTS § 38; IX WIGMORE ON EVIDENCE, 3rd ed. 1940, § 2437; I BOGERT ON TRUSTS, 2d ed. 1965, § 51. There is no allegation or evidence here of fraud, duress or mistake, and we hold that Pearl Johnson was the legal and equitable owner of the land as her separate property at the time of her death.

* * *

The will of Pearl Johnson empowered John E. Johnson to sell or mortgage any portion of her real estate that might be necessary for his comfortable support. This did not authorize him to defeat the interests of the remaindermen by making a gift of the land. *Nye v. Bradford*, 144 Tex. 618, 193 S.W.2d 165, 169 A.L.R. 1. It is undisputed that his conveyance to Esther Johnson, plaintiff, was made as a gift and did not constitute a sale or mortgage. The deed thus conveyed only the life estate of John E. Johnson in the land.

* * *

The judgments of the courts below are accordingly reversed and the cause is remanded to the district court with instructions to determine the status of the above mentioned oil and gas leases and overriding royalty interests and then render judgment not inconsistent with this opinion.

Notes, Comments & Questions

1. How might John Johnson have realized the benefit of the property in question?

2. When a significant recital exists, parol evidence to vary the deed is admissible in only the most specific circumstances. What are those circumstances?

3. When offered by a party to the transaction or by one in privity with a party to the transaction, parole evidence is not admissible to rebut a significant recital in the absence of allegations entitling the party to equitable relief. *See. e.g., McKivett v. McKivett*, 70 S.W.2d 694 (Tex. Comm'n App. 1034, opinion adopted); *Lindsay v. Clayman*, 254 S.W.2d 777 (Tex. 1952); *Messer v. Johnson*, 422 S.W.2d 908; *Henry s. Miller Co. v. Evans*, 452 S.W.2d 426 (Tex. 1970).

4. The non-grantee spouse is a party to the transaction if:

   a. he is the grantor, *McKivett v. McKivett, supra*; *Messer v. Johnson, supra*;

   b. he signs the executory contract of sale without joining in the deed, *Lindsay v. Clayman, supra*;

   c. he signs the promissory note and deed of trust executed as part of the transaction, *Hodge v. Ellis*, 277 S.W.2d 900 (Tex. 1955); or,

   d. he is merely present when the deed recitals are drafted, *Long v. Knox*, 291 S.W.2d 292 (Tex. 1956).

5. When the non-grantee spouse is *not* a party to the transaction, he may offer parol evidence to contradict the recital, and such evidence is admissible. *Smith v. Buss*, 144 S.W. 2d 529 (Tex. 1940); *Jackson v. Hernandez*, 285 S.W.2d 184 (Tex. 1955).

6. As you read the next case, think about it in the context of *Johnson, Peterson* and *Pace*, on the one hand, and *Messer v. Johnson* on the other.

RAYMOND
v.
RAYMOND
190 S.W.3d 77
(Tex. App.—Houston [1st Dist.] 2005, no pet.)

LAURA CARTER HIGLEY, JUSTICE.

Brenda Raymond filed for divorce from her husband Frank Raymond Jr., and the trial court granted the divorce. Subsequently, Brenda filed a motion for new trial, arguing errors in the division of property. The trial court denied the motion, and Brenda appealed.

In four points of error, Brenda argues that the trial court erred in (1) characterizing one piece of real property entirely as Frank's separate property; (2) overruling certain points of error in the motion for a new trial because the motion was not verified; and (3) not requiring reimbursement to the community estate for funds spent on Frank's separate real property. In a cross-point, Frank argues that Brenda is estopped from appealing the judgment.

We affirm in part and reverse and remand in part.

Background

Brenda Raymond, appellant, and Frank Raymond Jr., appellee, were married on June 20, 1987. Prior to this, Frank had bought two pieces of real property, one in Lake Jackson, Texas, and the other in Clute, Texas. After the marriage, Frank and Brenda had a house built on the Lake Jackson property. Also during the marriage, they refinanced the Clute property and subsequently paid off the balance of the loan. Later, on Brenda's urging, Frank executed a deed to Brenda conveying an undivided one-half interest in the Lake Jackson property. After the petition for divorce was filed, the court granted the divorce and awarded both the Lake Jackson and Clute properties to Frank as his separate property. The court did not award any funds to the community estate for money spent on the two properties.

* * *

Characterization of Real Property

In her first and second points of error, Brenda argues that the trial court erred in finding and ruling that the Lake Jackson property was entirely Frank's separate property.

A. Standard of Review

We review the trial court's characterization of property under an abuse of discretion standard. *Robles v. Robles*, 965 S.W.2d 605, 613 (Tex. App.—Houston [1st Dist.] 1998, pet. denied). The issue of whether property is separate or community property is determined by the facts that, according to rules of law, give character to the property. *McElwee v. McElwee*, 911 S.W.2d 182, 188 (Tex. App.—Houston [1st Dist.] 1995, writ denied). To determine whether there is legally sufficient evidence to support a finding, an appeals court considers only the evidence and inferences that support the finding and disregards all evidence and inferences that support the contrary. *Sherman v. First Nat'l Bank*, 760 S.W.2d 240, 242 (Tex. 1988); *Robles*, 965 S.W.2d at 615. If there is any evidence to support the finding, the appeals court must uphold the finding. *Sherman*, 760 S.W.2d at 242.

To determine whether the evidence was factually sufficient to support a finding, an appeals court considers and weighs all evidence that was before the trial court. *Cain v. Bain*, 709 S.W.2d 175, 176 (Tex. 1986). An appeals court sets a finding aside only if it is so against the great weight and preponderance of the evidence as to be manifestly unjust. *Id.* Similarly, a trial court's conclusions drawn from the facts may be reviewed to determine their correctness. *Herbage v. Snoddy*, 864 S.W.2d 695, 698 (Tex. App.—Houston [1st Dist.] 1993, writ denied).

B. Analysis

Prior to their marriage, Frank purchased property in Lake Jackson, Texas. Property purchased prior to marriage is that spouse's separate property. TEX. FAM.CODE ANN. § 3.001(1) (Vernon 1998). During the marriage, however, Frank executed a deed conveying an undivided one-half interest in the property to Brenda. It is the effect of this conveyance on the character of the property that we now review.

Both parties cite to cases holding that evidence of a gift of separate property from one spouse to another can be rebutted by evidence that a gift was not intended.[1] *See, e.g., In re Marriage of Morris*, 12 S.W.3d 877, 883 (Tex. App.—Texarkana 2000, no pet.); *Johnson v. Johnson*, 584 S.W.2d 307, 308-09 (Tex. Civ. App.—Texarkana 1979, no writ). The parties, however, cite to a line of cases that do not apply here. *Johnson* and the other cases in this line deal with situations where one spouse purchases real estate with his or her separate property, but both spouses' names appear as grantees on the deed *from that sale. Id.* at 308. In those cases, a rebuttable presumption is raised that the spouse intended to give the other spouse an undivided one-half interest in the property as a gift. *Id.* at 308-09.

Those are not the facts of the present case. Here, it is undisputed that Frank owned the property before the marriage, and he was the only grantee named on that deed. Therefore, it was his separate property from the inception. After Frank and Brenda married, Frank executed a separate deed to Brenda conveying an undivided one-half interest in the Lake Jackson property. Frank was the only grantor, and Brenda was the only grantee.

This case instead falls in line with *Massey* where we held that parol evidence is not admissible to vary the terms of an unambiguous document. *Massey v. Massey*, 807 S.W.2d 391, 405 (Tex. App.—Houston [1st Dist.] 1991, writ denied). It is for the court to construe an unambiguous document as a matter of law. *Coker v. Coker*, 650 S.W.2d 391, 393 (Tex. 1983); *Massey*, 807 S.W.2d at 405. A spouse who is a party to a deed transaction may not introduce parol or extrinsic evidence to contradict the express recitals in the deed without first tendering evidence of fraud, accident, or mistake. *Henry S. Miller Co. v. Evans*, 452 S.W.2d 426, 431-32 (Tex. 1970); *Massey*, 807 S.W.2d at 405. Evidence of the parties' intent can be introduced only if there is a latent or patent ambiguity. *Nat'l Union Fire Ins. Co. v. CBI Indus., Inc.*, 907 S.W.2d 517, 520 (Tex. 1995).

Frank never presented evidence at trial of fraud, accident, or mistake; nor did he establish any ambiguity in his deed to Brenda. Absent such evidence, the trial court erred in considering parol evidence of intent. *Dalton v. Pruett*, 483 S.W.2d 926, 929 (Tex. Civ. App.—Texarkana 1972, no writ). The deed was unambiguous on its face, and, as a matter of law, it effectively transferred an undivided one-half interest in the Lake Jackson property to Brenda.

---

[1] Both parties assume that the deed, reciting a consideration of $10.00 "and other valuable consideration," evidenced proof of a gift. We recognize that there is conflicting case law on whether this is evidence of a gift or of valuable consideration. *Compare* Saldana v. Saldana, 791 S.W.2d 316, 320 (Tex. App.—Corpus Christi 1990, no writ) (holding consideration of $1.00 is sufficient to evidence a sale), *with* Hall v. Barrett, 126 S.W.2d 1045, 1047 (Tex. Civ. App.—Forth Worth 1939, no writ) (holding that recited consideration of $10.00 is "usual and customary formal recitation used in deeds of gift"). Our holding on appellant's points of error, however, is the same regardless of whether the conveyance was a sale or gift. Therefore, we will assume, without holding, that the conveyance was a gift.

When there has been a conveyance of property by one spouse to another and a delivery of the deed, the presumption exists that it was the intention of the grantor spouse to make the property the separate property of the grantee spouse and in the absence of fraud, accident, or mistake, such conveyance cannot be disturbed. *Brothers v. Brothers*, No. 14-96-00364-CV, 1997 WL 7012, at *1 (Tex. App.—Houston [14th Dist.] Jan. 9, 1997, no writ) (not designated for publication) (*quoting Dyer v. Dyer*, 616 S.W.2d 663, 665 (Tex. Civ. App.-Corpus Christi 1981, writ dism'd)). Thus, we hold that an undivided one-half interest in the Lake Jackson property became Brenda's separate property.

Brenda's first and second points of error are sustained.

Questions

1. The court never informs us if the property was conveyed to wife as her sole and separate property, only that husband conveyed an undivided one-half interest of his separate property to wife. Do you think that is enough to deny the right to present parole evidence.

2. How does the court reconcile this with the cited case of *Johnson v. Johnson*?

3. Do the cases cited by the court for support involve deeds or other documents containing significant recitals?

4. Does the opinion give rise to a new rule of evidence regarding interspousal transfers?

E. Credit Transactions

Absent a premarital agreement, how can one acquire separate property during marriage if one does not receive it by gift, devise, or descent, or does not have the separate funds or property to purchase it? The answer is as simple if not priceless, CREDIT, separate credit.

How does one obtain separate credit during a marriage, especially in light of the community property presumption? The Texas Supreme Court tackled this question in 1913 in *McClintic v. Midland Grocery & Dry Goods, Co.*, 154 S.W.2d 1157 (Tex. 1913). In *McClintic*, Wife's brother gave her the down payment for certain real property and promised to provide her with funds each month to pay the mortgage. The property was taken in the name of the Husband and Wife and Husband and Wife signed the loan papers. Husband was sued by a creditor and the creditor attempted to levy against the land. Wife defended asserting that the land was her separate property and not subject to Husband's creditors. Based upon testimony of Husband, Wife, and Wife's brother, it was established that the down payment and subsequent payments given by brother to Wife were a gift to Wife and thus her separate property. *McClintic* is the first case in a long line of cases dealing with separate credit. It is unlikely, however, that given the *McClintic* proof today that the outcome would be the same. That is because one essential party did not testify—the mortgage holder, the lender. If Wife had defaulted, who would the creditor have gone against to collect?

Although spouses today can acquire property on their separate credit to the end that the property so acquired will be deemed separate, the proof needed to establish use of separate credit is beyond that presented in *McClintic*. Accordingly, *McClintic* is of little precedential value as regards the evidentiary burden.

The first case in this section, *Gleich v. Bongio*, concerns property purchased during marriage, the down payment being made from Husband's (and his brother's) separate property and the balance secured by community credit. Such is not an unusual means acquisition during marriage; property acquired in this way gives rise to a tenancy in common between the separate estate of husband and the community. The separate property down payment does not control the character of the credit; the credit is presumed to be community property.

The next case, *Broussard v. Tian*, involves a failed attempt by Husband to show that a bank did extend to him separate credit and, consequently, proving separate property.

The final case in this section, *Ray v. United States*, provides a roadmap for obtaining separate credit.

GLEICH
v.
BONGIO

99 S.W.2d 881 (Tex. 1937)

HICKMAN, COMMISSIONER.

This is a suit by plaintiff in error, Bertha Bongio Gleich, joined pro forma by her husband, August Gleich, Jr., against defendants in error, Felix Bongio, Sam Bongio, and the latter's wife, Margaret, to recover an undivided interest in certain lots situated in the city of Houston and for partition and an accounting. Felix Bongio was formerly the husband of plaintiff in error. No statement of facts accompanies the record, but the transcript contains a stipulation with regard to certain facts and the following findings of fact made by the trial court:

The Court finds that the following are the material facts proved in this case:

I.

That Felix F. Bongio and Bertha Bongio had been man and wife for approximately nine (9) years when divorced on or about the 5th day of May, 1930.

II.

That during the coverture of plaintiff, Felix F. Bongio and Sam Bongio purchased Lots one (1) Two (2) Three (3) Twelve (12) Thirteen (13) and Fourteen (14) in Block one (1) of the Brady Addition to the City of Houston, at a price of Twelve Thousand Dollars ($12,000.00) paying therefor the sum of Five Thousand Dollars ($5,000.00) Two Thousand Dollars ($2,000.00) of which was shown as paying the full purchase price of Lot Number Three (3) and Three Thousand Dollars ($3,000.00) been applied on the remaining five (5) lots, leaving Seven Thousand Dollars ($7,000.00), deferred payments thereon, secured by a vendor's lien on said five (5) lots.

That the cash payment of Five Thousand Dollars ($5,000.00), was made out of the separate estates of Felix Bongio and Sam Bongio, and that this same constituted their respective entire separate estates.

That subsequently lots Twelve (12) Thirteen (13) and Fourteen (14) were sold for a cash price of Eleven Thousand Five Hundred Dollars ($11,500.00), out of which the Seven Thousand Dollars ($7,000.00) vendor's lien was retired.

III.

That on October 26, 1929, Felix Bongio and Sam Bongio, joined by their wives, executed a deed of trust on the remaining lots to D. Guarino, to secure a note for Thirty-five Hundred Dollars ($3,500.00) for the purpose of constructing improvements on the said lots.

IV.

That there was no agreement at any time between Felix Bongio and Bertha Bongio that the said property in the Brady Addition, so purchased, was intended to be or become the separate property of Felix F. Bongio.

V.

> That the parties agreed between themselves as to the division of their personal community property at the time of their separation and in regard to their real property with the exception of the said six (6) lots in question in the Brady Addition, and part of this agreement consisted in the premises of Felix Bongio to pay the plaintiff the sum of Two Hundred Fifty Dollars ($250.00), for her interest in a separate lot, Fifty Dollars ($50.00) of which has been paid, leaving Two Hundred Dollars ($200.00) still due."

In the trial court it was decreed that plaintiff in error recover a 7/48 interest in and to lots 1, 2, and 3, subject to the indebtedness existing against same, together with the sum of $200, balance due under the settlement agreement. The decree adjudged "that a partition is here made," but no commissioners were appointed to make partition in kind, nor was any provision made for the sale of the lots and division of the proceeds. The decree contained a further provision "that in all other matters in controversy that plaintiff take nothing from defendants and that defendants recover nothing from plaintiffs by reason of their cross action." These provisions leave some uncertainty as to what disposition was made of the prayer for partition, but since the case is to be remanded to the trial court, we deem it unnecessary to construe the judgment with reference to the question of partition. The Court of Civil Appeals reversed the judgment of the trial court and rendered judgment that plaintiff in error take nothing by her suit to recover an interest in the lots. 71 S.W.2d 291. In our opinion neither judgment is correct.

It is obvious, we think, that plaintiff in error has no interest in lot No. 3. By the findings of fact that lot was purchased by Felix and Sam Bongio for $2,000, all of which consideration was paid in cash with their separate funds. No community funds or obligations formed a part of the consideration. That portion of the trial court's judgment awarding plaintiff in error an interest in that lot is erroneous. Since plaintiff in error practically concedes error in this particular, no further discussion thereof seems appropriate.

The status of lots 1 and 2 is different. These lots, together with lots 12, 13, and 14, were purchased by Felix and Sam Bongio for $10,000. The cash payment of $3,000 made on the purchase price was from their separate funds, but the deferred payment of $7,000 was evidenced by notes secured by a vendor's lien on all five lots. Later, Lots 12, 13, and 14 were sold for $11,500, and it was out of that fund that the deferred payment of $7,000 was made. The question thus presented is: What is the status of property, with reference to its being separate or community, when purchased during marriage partly with separate funds of the husband and partly on the credit of the community? The question presented cannot be distinguished from one in which a part of the purchase price is paid with the separate funds of the husband and the remainder with money borrowed on the credit of the community. 23 Tex. Jur., p. 127, *et seq.* § 104. Money borrowed on a community obligation is community property. Similarly, property acquired on the credit of the community is community property. Had no cash consideration been paid for these lots and the entire consideration been a community obligation, it would probably not be contended that the property is not wholly community. It would follow, it seems to us, as a matter of course, that, since a community obligation constituted a part of the purchase price, the community estate acquired a part interest in the lots. It seems to be the rule in some jurisdictions that property purchased partly with community funds and partly with separate funds of one of the spouses falls into the community, but in Texas, it has long been established that such an acquisition has the effect of creating a kind of tenancy in common between the separate and community estates, each owning an interest in the proportion that it supplies the consideration. The rule is well stated in 31 C.J., p. 40, § 1132, in this language:

> Generally purchases made partly with separate and partly with community funds will be community property to the extent and in the proportion that the consideration is furnished by the community, the spouse supplying the separate funds having a separate interest therein to the amount of his or her investment, the tenure of the whole property in such cases being by way of a sort of tenancy in common between the separate and community estates, ...

A long list of Texas cases are cited in support of the text and it is unquestionably a correct general statement of the established rule in this jurisdiction.

We quote from the opinion of JUSTICE WILLIAMS written while he was a member of the Court of Civil Appeals in the case of *Goddard v. Reagan*, 8 Tex. Civ. App. 272, 28 S.W. 352, as follows:

> * * * It also appeared that of $1,000, which was the consideration paid for the 200-acre tract, $700 was the money of the wife. The other $300 was borrowed from one Roach, for which the joint note of Reagan and wife was given, and the money so obtained was paid for the land. Some four or five weeks after the land had been thus paid for and acquired, the note given to Roach was paid out of funds of the wife, which had been received from Tennessee. It is claimed that from these facts it appears that the whole of the consideration for the 200 acres was paid with the wife's separate means. But this contention is contrary to the decisions of the Supreme Court. The money borrowed from Roach was community funds; the note given to him was a community debt, and when paid out of the wife's money became, perhaps, a claim in her favor against the common estate, or against her husband. The title to the land had, however, been acquired, and its status was fixed at the time of its acquisition. As $300 of the price paid for it was common funds, and $700 the separate funds of the wife, the equitable title in a three-tenths interest vested in the community estate, and seven-tenths in the wife. *Heidenheimer v. McKeen*, 63 Tex. 229; *Parker v. Coop*, 60 Tex. 111, 117. The court below held the whole of the 200 acres to have been the separate property of the wife, and for this the judgment must be reversed.

The case seems to have been tried on the theory that the rule above announced does not preclude or contradict a holding that the intention of the husband and wife at the time the property is acquired determines its status with reference to its separate or community character. The trial judge found as a fact that there was no agreement between the husband and wife that the property was intended to be or to become the separate property of the husband, and upon the basis of that fact finding concluded that it was, in part, community. Does the intention of the husband and wife at the time property is purchased upon a community obligation determine whether it is to become community property or the separate property of one of the spouses? It would appear that probably there is not complete harmony in the decisions on that question. Recent opinions of this Court, however, have pointed out the true nature of agreements having that effect.

In *Brokow v. Collet* (Tex. Com. App.) 1 S.W.(2d) 1090, 1091 it was held:

> * * * It does not lie in the power of the husband and wife by contract between themselves, made in advance, to set aside the Constitution of this state, as applied to the wife's separate property rights. * * *

In *Foster v. Christensen* (Tex. Com. App.) 67 S.W.2d 246, 249, Judge Smedley clearly expressed the true rule in this language:

> The land, of course, presumptively became the community property of Mr. and Mrs. Newgent when it was conveyed to them jointly with no recital of her separate ownership; but her ownership of the land as her separate property would have been established by proof of the allegations in the answer that the cash payment was made out of her separate funds and that it was agreed at the time by the parties to the deed that the land should be her separate property and that the balance of the purchase money should be paid out of her separate funds. * * * (Italics ours).

In the case of *Solether v. Trinity Fire Insurance Co.*, 124 Tex. 363, 78 S.W.2d 180, Judge (now Justice) Critz quoted with approval from Judge Smedley's opinion and reannounced the holding made therein: "The mere intention of the husband and wife cannot convert property purchased with an obligation binding upon the community into the separate estate of either spouse. To accomplish that purpose the vendor must have agreed with the vendee to look only to his or her separate estate for the satisfaction of the deferred payments."

The interest of plaintiff in error in lots 1 and 2 should be arrived at in this manner: Those lots, together with lots 12, 13, and 14, were purchased for a consideration of $10,000. Of this consideration ½ of $7,000, or $3,500, was furnished by the community of Felix and Bertha Bongio. The interest of that estate in the property was, therefore, 3500/10,000ths. The wife's interest is ½ of that fraction, or 3500/20,000ths, or 7/40th. Since lots 12, 13, and 14 have been sold, her interest is now 7/40th of lots 1 and 2.

The findings of fact disclose that Felix and Sam Bongio, joined by their wives, have executed a deed of trust lien to secure a note for $3,500, for the purpose of constructing improvements on the lots. The question is not sufficiently developed or briefed here for us to declare the respective rights growing out of this transaction, but, in view of another trial, we make this observation: One-half of this borrowed money became the community property of Felix Bongio and his then wife, now plaintiff in error. In so far as that fund may have been used, if it was used, to erect improvements on lot 3, the separate property of the husband, the community estate is entitled to an accounting, if such improvements enhanced the value of the property. The improvement of separate property with community funds does not change the status of the property, but may create equities in favor of the community. *Dakan v. Dakan*, 125 Tex. 305, 83 S.W.2d 620, may be consulted as a guide on this question upon another trial.

The judgment of the Court of Civil Appeals and trial court are both reversed and the cause remanded.

Opinion adopted by the Supreme Court January 6, 1937.

BROUSSARD
v.
TIAN
295 S.W.2d 405 (1956)

GARWOOD, JUSTICE.

This suit is one by the petitioner-plaintiff, Mrs. Broussard, for her half of an alleged 10/13 community interest in 520.5 acres of land in Limestone County, which latter was purchased by her former husband, the defendant-respondent, Tian, during their marriage, from the Federal Land Bank, the total consideration of $2,080 being $480 cash, which was paid out of the separate property of Tian, and $1,600 evidenced by a vendor's lien executed by him. Joined as codefendants were certain grantees or successors in title to Tian, but the rights of these additional parties (including Francis M. and Inez James, who admittedly may be now considered as without interest in the property) are not alleged to be any better than those of the respondent-defendant, Tian. The judgment of the trial court, affirmed by the Court of Civil Appeals, 290 S.W.2d 372, was against the petitioner-plaintiff. Our holding is to the contrary.

There is no written purchase contract in evidence. The deed, which ran to Tian, and the vendor's lien note and deed of trust, which he alone executed, contained no recitals purporting to deal with the community or separate status of the purchase or source of the consideration. However, not only the aforementioned $480 cash payment, but also several substantial payments of principal and interest on the note, were made out of the separate property of Tian, the balance due on the note being paid by his codefendant-grantees, and the community estate having thus paid out no money at all on the purchase.

On the other hand, as appears to be conceded-and necessarily so-by the respondents-defendant, the vendor's lien note being executed during the marriage by the husband, who is the community manager, and there being nothing in the note or related instruments to the contrary, the note is by presumption and in legal effect a community obligation, unless somehow lawfully shown to be otherwise. In the absence of any such showing, the result would necessarily be that, to the extent of the face of the note, the community furnished the original consideration for the purchase and thereby acquired a pro tanto ownership in the property, to wit, a 1600/2080 or 10/13 interest, of which the wife's half would be 5/13. The fact that the actual payment of all or some of the installments of the note were later made out of separate funds of the husband would not affect the community ownership, but would merely give rise to a debt or charge in favor of his estate against the community enforceable by appropriate proceedings. *Gleich v. Bongio*, 128 Tex. 606, 99 S.W.2d 881, in our view amply supports the foregoing statements. *See also Solether v. Trinity Fire Ins. Co.*, 124 Tex. 363, 78 S.W.2d 180.

It is also necessarily conceded that, assuming the above-mentioned showing as to the non-community character of the note could be made by parol, as, under the facts here, it would have to be if made at all, the respondents-defendant had the burden of making it. In this connection they introduced, over the objection of the petitioner-plaintiff, testimony of Tian which, when taken with other circumstances in evidence, they contend to be proof of an agreement between the grantor, Federal Land Bank, and Tian, sufficient under the above cited decisions, to make the note a separate property obligation of Tian and the property therefore entirely his separate estate. The single jury issue in the case was submitted under this theory, in response to which the jury found that there was such an agreement that the note "would be paid out of the separate property of M. J. Tian." If that finding is invalid, the judgment of the courts below against the petitioner-plaintiff cannot be sustained.

The petitioner-plaintiff asserts, in addition to other contentions, that the finding is wholly unsupported by the above-mentioned proof tendered by the respondents-defendant, even if parol evidence of such an agreement were admissible. We agree with this contention, and accordingly forego ruling on the other points raised by the petitioner-plaintiff, including the question of parol evidence.

The relevant portion of Tian's above-mentioned testimony is set out in the footnote.[1] It does tend to establish that the representatives of the grantor were interested in knowing whether Tian had means of one kind or another so as to render it probable that the note would be paid, and that Tian assured them he had certain means, which were of his separate estate, and intended to use these means to make payment. The respondents-defendant themselves, in their answer to the application, describe this testimony as follows:

> . . . and during this discussion, Johnson asked Tian, 'how he expected to make the deferred payments on this lans?' Tian told him that he had just received some bonus money from an oil lease and that he had some royalty under land that was being developed by the Gulf Oil Company, and that he could pay it out of this lease money, or out of the Gulf royalty. He then stated that this property was his separate property.

They then go on to say that this testimony plus the agreed facts that the sale was duly closed and the cash and sundry installment payments on the note were made by Tian out of his separate property lease money tends to show an "understanding that it (the note) would be paid out of his separate funds as he had stated."

Possibly the proof does amount to an 'understanding' in the sense that both parties considered the existence of the oil properties in question as a factor favorable to due discharge of the note. But it does not reflect a contract that it was to be paid out of these properties in particular, still less out of the separate property of Tian generally. The tenor of the discussion was simply that of an enquiry by the bank into the general prospects of the note being ultimately paid and an answer to that enquiry. The account of the conversation includes no statement from the bank representatives that they would make or recommend the sale on the strength of Tian's statement about his oil property or that the sale was to be conditioned on such property being retained by him or devoted to payment of the note, which was, of course, already secured by the vendor's lien. Still less is there anything to suggest that the bank, which initiated the discussion, had any interest in whether the source of payment of the note should be separate or community.

The events subsequent to the conversation do not modify or amplify the words favorably to Tian's contention. Considering that the grantor was an institution specializing in land loans and related transactions, the actual consummation of the sale without any written reference to the oil properties or to the separate or community character generally of the purchase suggests that there was not a special contract in this behalf rather than that there was. The fact that the cash consid-

---

[1] Q. What, if anything, did you tell them with regard to how you were going to make those payments, Mr. Tian? A. Mr. Dodson, I stood there, and I guess about 4 or 5 hours talking to him and he asked me emphatically how could I pay it. I said I owned surface soil, I have got royalty in a chain of title under a Gulf lease. I said I have got a lease that I have just made with Stanolind, and I said I can pay it out of the royalty . . . . He (Johnson) told me that he would have to go to the Board of Directors to get permission to all of their agreements. I told him I would pay it out of this lease I had and out of royalty I had from the Gulf.

Q. Did you or not tell him that that was your separate property? A. Absolutely my separate, I bought this Gulf out of some money I got from . . . .

Q. Outside of this 520 acres of land did you buy any real estate during the time that you and your wife were married? A. About four or five pieces.

eration and part of the note were later paid out of money accruing from the oil properties might well have been due to reasons other than an obligation so to pay them.

The fact that at the time of the purchase the spouses had been living apart for a considerable period does suggest a motive for Tian to avoid a community obligation; but the possibility or even probability of a general purpose to do business as a single man does not, under the circumstances, afford any proof of a contract between him and the bank to this effect. There is no proof that he discussed his domestic situation with the bank representatives. Actually, his reply to the question of whether he told the bank that his oil properties were separate is equivocal, although we assume it to mean that he did so state.

The judgments below are accordingly erroneous and must be reversed, and the petitioner, Mrs. Broussard, is entitled to recover against the respondents Tian and Burney her 5/13 interest in the property in question. Since the respondents have no alternative pleas for recovery of sums actually paid on the purchase money note, and no reason for remanding the case thus or otherwise appears, judgment must be here rendered for the petitioner for her interest aforesaid. It is so ordered.

Questions

1. Both *Gleich v. Bongio* and *Broussard v. Tian* were actions filed by former wives seeking their share of certain community property from former husbands. By what authority can they file such cases against their ex-husbands? Hint, check the Family Code.

2. What are the requisites for and limitations on filing such a suit?

3. What was Mr. Tian's marital status when he acquired the property in question?

4. The jury found that there was an agreement that the note on the property would be paid out of Mr. Tian's separate property. Why wasn't this finding sustained?

5. If you were drafting the note for Mr. Tian, what clause would you have included?

RAY
v.
UNITED STATES
385 F. Supp. 372 (S.D. Tex. 1974), *aff'd*
538 F.2d 1228 (5th Cir. 1976)

CARL O. BUE, JR., DISTRICT JUDGE.

In this action for refund of estate taxes paid by the Estate of Robert H. Ray, the defendant has counterclaimed, alleging that the estate was erroneously permitted to redeem certain Treasury Bonds at face value in payment of the estate taxes. The action is brought by Jack C. Pollard, Collette Lake Ray and Taylor Ray, the duly qualified and acting Independent Executors of the estate, and was heard by the Court without a jury. Jurisdiction vests in this Court by virtue of 28 U.S.C. § 1346(a)(1).

The facts relevant to this controversy indicate that on September 26, 1967, the decedent was found to be terminally ill, a victim of multiple myeloma or bone cancer. On the advice of decedent's attorney and with the consent of decedent's wife, Pollard, decedent's business partner, borrowed, as agent for decedent, $1,000,000 from the First City National Bank and signed a promissory note for that amount on December 26, 1967. The note, which was due in six months and bore interest at the rate of 6½ percent, contained the following language:

> Bank acknowledges that the proceeds of the loan evidenced by this note are and shall be the separate property of Robert H. Ray and hereby agrees that this indebtedness shall be paid out of his separate funds and that only his separate property (including the Government bonds purchased with proceeds of this loan) shall be liable for the payment of this indebtedness.
>
> Payment of this note is secured by a security agreement dated 12-26-67 covering $1,270,000.00 U.S. Treas, 3-1/2% Bds due 2-15-90.

Using the proceeds of this loan, Pollard purchased on the same date $1,270,000 par value 3½ percent United States Treasury Bonds due February 15, 1990, and signed a security agreement pledging the Treasury Bonds as security for the loan. This agreement contained the following stipulation:

> The term 'Liabilities' shall mean the indebtedness evidenced by note of even date herewith in the principal amount of $1,000,000.00 executed by Jack C. Pollard as Agent and Attorney in Fact for Robert H. Ray, payable to the order of Bank on or before six months.
>
> Notwithstanding anything herein to the contrary, Bank agrees that the Liabilities shall be paid out of the separate funds of Robert H. Ray and that only his separate property (including the Collateral) shall be liable for payment of the Liabilities.

At the time of the loan and subsequent purchase of the bonds, the decedent owned only a negligible amount of separate property, the vast majority of his assets consisting of community property. Decedent died on January 5, 1968, a resident of the State of Texas.

Plaintiffs timely filed Form 706, United States Estate Tax Return, on behalf of the estate with the District Director of Internal Revenue. The return reported the United States Treasury Bonds as the separate property of decedent and the note executed for the loan to purchase the bonds as a separate debt of the decedent. Accordingly, a marital deduction based upon the bonds being the decedent's separate property was claimed. By virtue of 26 U.S.C. § 6312(a) (since repealed, with respect to bonds issued after March 3, 1971, by Pub.L. No. 92-5 § 4(a), 85 Stat. 5),[1] a substantial portion of these bonds were then accepted by the Internal Revenue Service at their face value in payment of the estate taxes due as shown on the estate's tax return.

Subsequently, the Commissioner determined the bonds to be community rather than separate property and included only one-half of the bonds in the estate, thereby reducing the separate debt by one-half and disallowing the marital deduction. Additional taxes were assessed against the estate as the result of this determination. These were paid in part by the redemption of the remaining Treasury Bonds, which were redeemed by the Service at their face value.

Plaintiffs timely filed a claim for refund premised principally upon the Commissioner's characterization of the bonds as community property. Upon the disallowance of this claim, plaintiffs subsequently instituted this action. The complaint, supplemental complaint and counterclaim thus present for determination several issues:

> (1) whether the bonds purchased on December 26, 1967, constitute the separate property of the decedent;
>
> (2) whether the characterization of the bonds by the estate as separate property lacks economic substance and must be therefore disregarded;
>
> (3) whether the estate is entitled to a marital deduction;
>
> (4) whether the estate is entitled to deduct certain administrative expenses in full or whether these may be attributed in part to the community and deducted only in part.

The Government's counterclaim is premised upon the fact that the Internal Revenue Service redeemed at their face value in payment of the estate tax the totality of the bonds purchased on December 26, 1967. By virtue of the Commissioner's determination that only 50 percent of these bonds were includable in the decedent's estate, the Government argues that the other one-half of these bonds were erroneously redeemed at face value and should be reissued to the decedent's spouse. Additional payment would then be due to replace the reissued bonds.

THE U.S. TREASURY BONDS AS THE SEPARATE OR COMMUNITY PROPERTY OF THE DECEDENT

The separate property of a spouse is characterized in Texas by Article 5.01 of the Texas Family Code, V.T.C.A., as:

> (1) the property owned or claimed by the spouse before marriage;
>
> (2) the property acquired by the spouse during marriage by gift, devise or descent; and
>
> (3) the recovery for personal injuries sustained by the spouse during marriage, except any recovery for loss of earning capacity during marriage.

Community property is thus defined as all "property, other than separate property, acquired by either spouse during marriage." Under Texas law, the separate or community nature of property has been determined by courts at the time of acquisition under the inception of title rule. *See, e.g.*, *Lindsay v. Clayman*, 151 Tex. 593, 254 S.W.2d 777, 780 (1952). In transactions not involving

---

[1] That statute read, in pertinent part:

> It shall be lawful for the Secretary or his delegate to receive, at par with an adjustment for accrued interest, Treasury bills, notes and certificates of indebtedness issued by the United States in payment of any internal revenue taxes. . . .

credit or the indicia of a gift, courts have applied a tracing principle and characterized the subject property as separate or community or a combination thereof depending upon the nature of the funds or property actually used at the time of purchase to acquire it. *See, e.g., Freedman v. United States*, 382 F.2d 742 (5th Cir. 1967); *Duncan v. United States*, 247 F.2d 845 (5th Cir. 1957); *Gleich v. Bongio*, 128 Tex. 606, 99 S.W.2d 881, 883 (1937); *Baize v. Baize*, 460 S.W.2d 255 (Tex. Civ. App.—Eastland 1970, no writ). However, Texas courts have not uniformly traced the source of funds used in acquiring property during a marriage. Where the deed or purchase agreement contains a recitation that the property acquired is the separate property of one spouse and the other spouse has acquiesced in the transaction, the nature of the funds actually used to acquire the property has been viewed as irrelevant; the property is considered to be a gift. *See, e.g., Paudler v. Paudler*, 210 F.2d 765 (5th Cir. 1954); *Messer v. Johnson*, 422 S.W.2d 908 (Tex. 1968); *Lindsay v. Clayman, supra; McKivett v. McKivett*, 123 Tex. 298, 70 S.W.2d 694 (Tex. 1934). Likewise, Texas courts have recognized that when one spouse acquires property on credit with the creditor agreeing to look solely to the separate property of that spouse for compensation in the event of default, the spouse serving as the source of credit is considered the owner.[2] *See Broussard v. Tian*, 156 Tex. 371, 295 S.W.2d 405 (1956); *Gleich v. Bongio, supra*; *Dorfman v. Dorfman*, 457 S.W.2d 91, 95 (Tex. Civ. App.—Waco 1970, no writ); *Harrington v. Harrington*, 451 S.W.2d 797, 799 (Tex. Civ. App.—Houston [1st Dist.] 1967, writ dism'd); *Dillard v. Dillard*, 341 S.W.2d 668, 671 (Tex. Civ. App.—Ft. Worth 1960, writ ref. n.r.e.); *Carter v. Grabeel*, 341 S.W.2d 458, 460 (Tex. Civ. App.—Amarillo 1960, no writ); *Goodloe v. Williams*, 302 S.W.2d 235, 237 (Tex. Civ. App.—Texarkana 1957, writ ref.). *See generally* Huie, W., *Commentary—Community Property Law*, 13 Vernon's Annotated Revised Civil Statutes § 6 (1960).

Thus, by virtue of the inception of title rule in instances where property is purchased on credit, Texas courts have indicated that it is irrelevant if community funds were actually used to repay the separate debt.[3] *See Broussard v. Tian, supra; Lindsay v. Clayman, supra; Smith v. Buss*, 135 Tex. 566, 144 S.W. 529 (1940); *Orr v. Pope*, 400 S.W.2d 614 (Tex. Civ. App.—Amarillo 1960, writ. ref'd n.r.e.). Although the other spouse or the community may be entitled to reimbursement for the funds expended in repayment of the separate debt, title to the property still vests in the purchasing spouse. *See Broussard v. Tian, supra*; *Beeler v. Beeler*, 363 S.W.2d 305 (Tex. Civ. App.—Beaumont 1962, writ dism'd). Furthermore, courts have indicated that it is irrelevant under Texas law if the community or separate estate incurring the obligation has sufficient funds to repay its debt. *See Gleich v. Bongio, supra.*

Under a strict application of the above principles, the bonds in this instance should be treated as separate property. Decisions of the Texas courts have emphasized that the agreement between the creditor and the borrower is the primary indication of whether a debt is separate or community. It is evident from the loan agreement that the First City National Bank intended to look only to the decedent's separate estate for repayment. Thus, by virtue of this agreement the borrowed funds became the decedent's separate property, and the property purchased with these funds, the Treasury Bonds, is property acquired by separate property.

---

[2] It appears that the prior rule followed by Texas courts did not permit a married woman to obtain separate property by virtue of a credit transaction. *See* Farmers' State Bank v. Farmer, 157 S.W. 283 (Tex. Civ. App.—Amarillo 1913); Harrison v. Mansur-Tibbetts Implement Co., 16 Tex. Civ. App. 630, 41 S.W. 842 (1897); Schuster v. Bauman Jewelry Co., 79 Tex. 179, 15 S.W. 259 (Tex.1890). The Court does not find that this rule of law continues to be viable at the present time.

[3] In the absence of an explicit agreement between the debtor and the creditor to look only to the separate estate of one spouse for satisfaction of the indebtedness, property purchased on credit has been considered separate if it can be shown that the creditor expected payment from one spouse and that payment was actually made out of the separate estate. *See* Edsall v. Edsall, 240 S.W.2d 424 (Tex. Civ. App.—Eastland 1951, no writ).

The Government has advanced several arguments to defeat application of this principle. First, the Government argues that the application of this rule of law is contrary to the Texas Constitution[4] as well as to the decision of the Texas Supreme Court in *Hilley v. Hilley*, 161 Tex. 569, 342 S.W.2d 565 (1961).

> All marital property is thus either separate or community. If acquired before marriage by any method, or after marriage by gift, devise or descent, it is separate; otherwise it is community. There are only two exceptions. Property purchased with separate funds is separate and community property partitioned in the manner provided in Articles 4624a and 881a-23, becomes separate property. . . . While the husband may make a direct gift of his separate property or the community estate to his wife, the spouses cannot by a mere agreement change the character and nature of the rights and interest in property owned or acquired by them from that prescribed by law.

Id. at 567-568. Because this property was acquired after marriage, did not pass by devise or descent and was not acquired with separate funds, the Government argues that treating it as separate property is contrary to the definition of separate property as set forth by Texas law. Furthermore, the Government buttresses its argument by alleging that an agreement between the spouse and the vendor is irrelevant in determining the community or separate nature of property, absent a valid partition.

The Court does not find that treating these Treasury Bonds as separate property is inconsistent with either the decision in *Hilley* or the Texas Constitution. Neither authority considers the manner in which a court must determine the ownership of property acquired by virtue of a credit transaction. In credit cases, application of the tracing principle becomes much more complex. Indeed, title to the property could not be established until after the debt was paid if the tracing principle were strictly utilized. Such an approach is contrary to any application of the inception of title rule. Accordingly, the rule of *Gleich v. Bongio* supports application of this latter principle by requiring that property purchased on credit be determined at the time of acquisition by looking to the type of property that will be subjected to forfeiture in the event of a default.

Second, the Government claims that property purchased on credit should receive its community or separate characterization by virtue of the source of the funds from which the purchasing spouse expects to repay the loan. In applying such a rule in this case, the Government argues that the bonds must be considered community property, since the decedent had no separate property with which to repay the loan. In making this argument, the Government relies upon the case of *Edsall v. Edsall*, 240 S.W.2d 424 (Tex. Civ. App.—Eastland 1951, no writ), in which property purchased on credit was held to be separate because it was clearly evident that the purchaser intended to repay the short-term loan with separate property. However, the Court does not find that *Edsall* controls the result in this case. In *Edsall*, there was no agreement between the vendor and the purchaser to look only to the separate property of the purchaser for repayment of the purchase money debt. The legal principle recognized in *Gleich* actually was not before the court in *Edsall*.

---

[4] All property, both real and personal, of the wife, owned or claimed by her before marriage, and that acquired afterward by gift, devise or descent, shall be the separate property of the wife; and laws shall be passed more clearly defining the rights of the wife, in relation as well to her separate property as that held in common with her husband; provided that husband and wife, without prejudice to pre-existing creditors, may from time to time by written instrument as if the wife were a feme sole partition between themselves in severalty or into equal undivided interests all or any part of their existing community property, or exchange between themselves the community interest of one spouse in any property for the community interest of the other spouse in other community property, whereupon the portion or interest set aside to each spouse shall be and constitute a part of the separate property of such spouse. TEX.CONST. art. XVI, § 15, Vernon's Ann.St.

In the present suit there is a very explicit recitation in the promissory note executed by Pollard as well as in the agreement executed by the bank that it would look only to the separate property of the decedent including the Government bonds purchased with the proceeds of the loan for payment of the indebtedness. In view of the distinguishable factual circumstances, the Court cannot view *Edsall* as limiting the application of *Gleich* to the present case. In addition, the source of the repayment of the debt incurred has no materiality insofar as the separate or community character of the Government bonds is concerned, since any possible repayment of the indebtedness by the non-purchasing spouse from separate or community property would be equalized under the law by the right to reimbursement. *E.g.*, *Broussard v. Tian*, *supra*.

Third, the Government argues that it was necessary for the decedent to have made an initial down payment from his separate property before he could purchase property on his separate credit. Indeed, this crucial controversy between the parties arises because, contrary to the varying circumstances existing in the reported cases, the entire transaction in this instance was effected with borrowed funds, there being no initial down payment of separate property in any amount to establish the debt as separate in character under the inception in title rule. The Government's argument finds support in cases such as *Schuster v. Bauman Jewelry Co.*, 79 Tex. 179, 15 S.W. 259 (Tex. 1890), in which the court declared that "the wife's equity in such cases arises from the actual investment of her separate property." *Id.* at 260. Because the wife had not made a down payment with separate funds on property purchased partially on her separate credit and partially on the credit of the community, the court in that case held the property to be entirely community. This Court does not find this rationale to be supported by the more modern case law or the underlying concept of the separate credit principle. Where property is purchased partially with cash and partially with credit, courts have determined ownership proportionately by tracing the source of the cash payment and the source of the credit at the time of purchase. *See Gleich v. Bongio*, *supra*. However, when the separate cash down payment is absent and the entire transaction turns on the extension of credit, it would be economically unrealistic to apply any rule other than that applicable to the credit portion of transactions involving cash down payments. The Court can determine no valid reason for permitting a portion of property to be purchased on the separate credit of one spouse while not permitting that same spouse to obtain the entire property on his separate credit. In such instance the rule should be the same—property will take on the character of the consideration used to purchase it, whether that consideration be cash or credit.

Although the principle of permitting a spouse to independently acquire separate property through the use of separate credit has been vigorously challenged as lacking a strong conceptual basis in Texas property law, *see* Fritz, *Marital Property—Effects of Recitals and Credit Purchase*, 41 TEX. L. REV. 1 (1962), the principle appears to be well recognized and one which this Court would be reluctant to set aside in the absence of a more definitive expression from the Supreme Court of Texas. It seems that the rule set forth in *Gleich v. Bongio* is a judicial response to the practical problems inherent in determining the character of property purchased on credit. Unlike cash transactions, it does not appear nearly as feasible to "trace" the source of funds actually used to repay the loan in a credit transaction. Reliance upon such an approach in the present case would entail a delay in determining the separate or community character of property financed entirely through a loan which would normally be repaid over a considerable period of time. Similarly, strict application of the "tracing principle" to property purchased on credit would serve to circumvent the inception of title rule, since title actually would not be established until after the debt incurred in acquiring the property had been repaid.

It is conceded by both parties that the legal issues involved in this case raise unique questions as to the interpretation of Texas community property law. No resolution by this Court can reconcile existing conceptual inconsistencies found in the cases.[5] By applying the rule set forth in *Gleich*, the result is that all parties are cognizant at the time that property is acquired of whether it will be separate or community property. Although this same degree of certainty could be achieved by merely presuming that any property purchased on credit during the existence of a marriage is community, it appears to be more equitable to permit one spouse to encumber his own separate estate for the benefit of that estate so long as it does not jeopardize the community property of the other spouse. In that connection it is only too apparent from the record that what was community property before the Government bonds were purchased continued to be community property after such purchase. On the basis of the evidence presented and a consideration of the applicable Texas law, the Court can only conclude that the bonds purchased by the decedent on December 27, 1967, constituted his separate estate and should be treated accordingly for tax purposes.

* * *

Counsel for plaintiff will submit within thirty (30) days an appropriate judgment in accordance with the foregoing Memorandum and Opinion.

RAY
v.
UNITED STATES
538 F.2d 1228
(5th Cir. 1976)

PER CURIAM.

Shortly before his death, Robert H. Ray authorized Jack C. Pollard, acting as Ray's agent, to borrow $1,000,000 from the First City National Bank for the purpose of purchasing $1,270,000 par value United States Treasury Bonds. These bonds, known colloquially as "flower bonds," contained a provision making them redeemable at par prior to maturity to pay federal estate taxes, provided they were owned by the decedent at death and were included in his gross estate.[1] On December 26, 1967, Pollard signed a promissory note for $1,000,000 in which the bank acknowledged that the proceeds of the loan were the separate property of Robert H. Ray, that the indebtedness would be paid out of his separate funds, and that only his separate property, including the bonds, would secure the loan. Ray died ten days later.

---

[5] Actually Professor Fritz strongly urges abandonment of the inception of title rule when he states:

> It seems much more consistent with the general pattern of Texas marital property law to discountenance the inception-of-title rule altogether or to confine it to transactions initiated before marriage, and to recognize that the tracing of separate funds establishes separate ownership in a credit purchase, as it does in a cash purchase.

Recognizing the sharp cleavage in conceptual thinking over the thrust of *Gleich v. Bongio*, it is not for this Court to ignore its application in a case which on the relevant facts is uniquely within its gambit.

[1] The blooms are off the bonds. Once a hardy perennial, flower bonds are now virtually extinct. The applicable statute 26 U.S.C. § 6312(a), has been repealed with respect to bonds issued after May 3, 1971, by Pub.L. No. 92-5 § 4(a), 85 Stat. 5. *See* Ray v. United States, 385 F.Supp. 372, 376 (S.D.Tex.1974).

The plaintiffs, as executors of the decedent's estate, filed an Estate Tax Return with the District Director of Internal Revenue. The return reported the Treasury Bonds as the separate property of the decedent. It also reported the note as a separate debt of the decedent. The plaintiffs claimed a marital deduction based upon the decedent's separate ownership of the bonds. Pursuant to existing law, the Internal Revenue Service accepted a substantial portion of the bonds at their face value in payment of the estate taxes due.

The Commissioner subsequently determined that the bonds were community rather than separate property and included only one-half of the bonds in the estate. This had the effect of reducing the separate debt by one-half and disallowing the marital deduction. The plaintiffs paid the resulting additional tax assessment in part by redeeming the remaining bonds at face value. The plaintiffs filed a claim for refund, challenging the Commissioner's characterization of the bonds as community property. Based upon the Commissioner's determination that only half of these bonds were includable in the decedent's estate, the Government counterclaimed, arguing that one-half of the bonds were erroneously redeemed at face value. The District Court for the Southern District of Texas, Judge Carl O. Bue, Jr., upheld the plaintiffs' challenge. The Government has brought this appeal.

The Government argues on appeal that the District Court erred in holding that the Treasury Bonds were decedent's separate property rather than community property.[2] The crux of its argument is that the decedent, who had virtually no other separate property, could not have been expected to discharge his indebtedness to the bank out of other than community property. The Government asserts that therefore the Treasury Bonds purchased with the loaned funds must also be community property, notwithstanding the decedent's agreement with the bank that the latter would look only to the decedent's separate property for repayment. The Government contends that community funds were in fact used to repay the decedent's indebtedness to the bank.

In an excellent opinion in the court below, Judge Bue rejected the Government's argument. *See Ray v. United States*, 385 F.Supp. 372 (S.D.Tex. 1974). He observed that under Texas law the critical element in determining the status of property purchased on credit is the agreement of the creditor and the purchasing spouse that the proceeds of the loan are to be the debtor's separate property and that the creditor will look solely to the purchasing spouse's separate property for satisfaction of the indebtedness. *See Gleich v. Bongio*, 128 Tex. 606, 99 S.W.2d 881, 884 (1937). We adopt Judge Bue's opinion as the opinion of this Court.

The tax savings plan effectuated by a loan secured by the separate property of the spouse in the terminal days of the decedent's mortality was ingenious if not entirely ingenuous. Nevertheless, as the perceptive opinion of the trial court cogently demonstrates, the transaction was secure from the tax gatherer's scythe.

The judgment below is AFFIRMED.

---

[2] The Government does not challenge the decedent's purchase of the bonds as an invalid tax avoidance scheme. Its argument is simply that the bonds were community property under Texas law. Consequently, it argues, only one-half of the bonds were includable in the decedent's gross estate and thereby redeemable in payment of federal estate taxes. The availability of the marital deduction also turns on whether the bonds are characterized as separate or community property.

Questions

1. Finally, in *Ray*, we are given some guidance as to how to establish separate property with separate credit. What provisions in the agreements appear to support this outcome?

2. *Ray* also presents some very creative lawyering and brilliant estate planning. Simply put, a profit of $270,000 was realized in 10 days. Use of these bonds, known as flower bonds, in this way eventually led to their demise.

3. Reference to a "*Ray* Debt" often means that a creditor has agreed to look only to the separate estate of a spouse for repayment. This agreement means the community, any community, will not be liable for the debt. Understand the difference between a separate debt and a sole community debt.

4. Did Mr. Ray have a separate estate from which his debt could have been paid?

5. Where in the Constitution is separate property based upon separate credit found?

F. Personal Injury Recoveries—Which Presumption or Rule Controls?

The case of *Graham v. Franco*, 488 S.W.2d 390 (Tex. 1972) found in the first chapter is the seminal case on the characterization of personal injury recoveries. It is in the first chapter because it concerned the constitutionality of characterizing any part of such a recovery as separate property. The court clearly established that recoveries for personal injuries were separate property and, indeed, always had been. Loss of earning capacity, earnings during marriage, was established as community as were medical expenses incurred by the marital partnership.

Graham v. Franco is not, however, the last word on the characterization of personal injury recoveries. Although recovery for injury to the person is well accepted as the separate property of the injured spouse, a dispute has arisen between the courts of appeal. The issue is whether the community property presumption applies, leaving it up to the injured spouse to prove by clear and convincing evidence that the recovery or a portion thereof is separate; or, whether TEX. FAM. CODE ANN. § 3.001(3) provides a presumption that the injury recovery is separate property which must be rebutted by the party seeking community characterization.

The court in *Kyles v. Kyles*, 832 S.W.2d 194 (Tex. App.—Beaumont 1992, no writ) applied the community property presumption. Conversely, the court in *Osborn v. Osborn*, 961 S.W.2d 408 (Tex. App.—Houston [1st Dist.] 1997, no writ) rejected the community property presumption and determined that under statute personal injury recoveries are to be presumed separate property. This difference of opinion has been further complicated by the Texas Supreme Court in it application of inception of title when characterizing worker's compensation benefits. *See Lewis v. Lewis*, 944 S.W.2d 630 (Tex. 1997). Finally, personal injury recoveries also encompass damages which have not yet been characterized by the Texas Courts, such as punitive damages. These unresolved issues are the focus of this section.

KYLES
v.
KYLES
832 S.W.2d 194
(Tex. App.—Beaumont 1992, no writ)

WALKER, CHIEF JUSTICE.

This is a divorce case filed by Deloris White Kyles, appellant, against Charles H. Kyles, appellee. There were no children born to or adopted by the parties during marriage. The trial court dissolved the marriage and awarded various properties to the respective parties. The trial court also filed lengthy Findings of Fact and Conclusions of Law. The primary thrust of appellant's appeal has to do with the trial court's characterization of certain real and personal property, and the division of same.

* * *

In point of error number two, appellant contends that the trial court erred in characterizing the proceeds from a personal injury settlement received by appellee as his separate property. Appellant contends that the proceeds are presumed to be community property and that there is no evidence, or in the alternative, insufficient evidence, to rebut such presumption.

On or about June 26, 1984, while married to appellant, appellee was injured in a car accident. Appellee, husband, filed a lawsuit contending that he suffered various damages from the accident including lost wages and lost earning capacity. Husband eventually settled that lawsuit for $190,000.00.

During the divorce trial, the trial court admitted into evidence Petitioner's Exhibit 3, which is titled, "RELEASE." Petitioner's Exhibit 3 bears no signature on the spaces provided for the signatures of Charles Kyles and Deloris Kyles. Appellant tells us that appellee settled the lawsuit for $190,000.00 and executed a release and refers to Petitioner's Exhibit 3 which as stated, bears no signatures. Appellee, in his brief, makes only a one-sentence address to the missing signatures upon the "RELEASE" and states, "Appellant's reliance on the 'Release' is subject to substantial question since the 'Release' is not executed. The record does not contain any executed copy of a 'Release'." The trial court, in its findings of fact and conclusions of law, makes no reference to Petitioner's Exhibit 3. On page two of this five page Exhibit marked "Petitioner's Exhibit 3," we find the following language:

> It is understood and agreed that this is a FULL AND COMPLETE RELEASE, and includes all sums of any kind or character, including by way of illustration, but not by way of limitation: actual damages sustained by claimant; exemplary damages; medical, hospital, drug, or nursing bills; prosthetic devices; property damages; loss of wages or of profits; . . . .

The trial court found as a fact that the net settlement resulting from this Release was the amount of $122,330.19 and that at the time of trial, appellee had in his possession the sum of $69,000.00 of that settlement amount. The trial court also found that no part of such settlement funds were paid to appellee as a recovery for the loss of earning capacity, medical expenses or property damage during marriage.

All property possessed during marriage or on dissolution of marriage is presumed to be community property and the party claiming that such property is separate, must prove so by clear and convincing evidence. TEX. FAM. CODE ANN. § 5.02 (Vernon's Supp.1991). Thus, appellee has the burden of proving that the original settlement was his separate property in order to prove that the $69,000.00 remaining is indeed and in fact, his separate property.

At trial, counsel for appellant, Deloris Kyles, offered into evidence Petitioner's Exhibits 1 through 5, same being admitted by the trial court without objection from opposing counsel. Regarding Petitioner's Exhibit 3, we observe the following questions and answers:

> Q. Number 3 is the Release. Do you recall that? That's an instrument that you had to sign, Mr. Kyles. I think it is the one about which you and Deloris gave up all your rights and claims to that suit. Do you recall signing that, if you can identify that as an instrument that you signed to settle that lawsuit.
>
> A. I signed one to release the trucking company.
>
> Q. All right. Is that it, a copy of it?
>
> A. I don't know. I signed a release if that's what you are asking me.
>
> Q. All right.

We are hard put from the record to find clear and convincing evidence proffered by appellee to rebut the presumption that the settlement proceeds were community property. Without evidence to the contrary, it must be presumed that at least some of the settlement proceeds were attributable to lost wages or lost earning capacity which are community property. The only evidence we can find from the record, which comes close to addressing the issue, comes from appellee's testimony that it was his understanding that the entire settlement was for personal injuries and nothing else. However, in earlier testimony, appellee testified as follows:

Q. How much of that settlement was due to your lost wages in income?

A. I don't know.

Q. Some of it was, was it not?

A. It would have to be. It wasn't spelled out how much.

* * *

Q. You couldn't say one way or the other? You couldn't deny it, part of it was for lost wages?

A. I still don't know.

Since appellee did not prove what amount, if any, of the settlement proceeds were separate or community property, it must be conclusively presumed that the entire proceeds are community property. When a spouse receives a settlement from a lawsuit during marriage, some of which may be separate property and some of which may be community property, it is the spouse's burden to demonstrate what portion of the settlement is his separate property. *Moreno v. Alejandro*, 775 S.W.2d 735, 738 (Tex. App.—San Antonio 1989, writ denied). This Court has previously held that a spouse that receives a settlement arising out of a personal injury has a burden to show what portion of the recovery is his separate property. When some of the settlement may be for lost wages or lost earning capacity, the spouse who receives the settlement has the burden to show that none of the funds constitute payment for lost wages or lost earning capacity during marriage. In the absence of such evidence, the entire settlement proceeds are properly characterized as community property. *York v. York*, 579 S.W.2d 24, 25-26 (Tex. Civ. App.—Beaumont 1979, no writ), *see also*, *Patt v. Patt*, 689 S.W.2d 505, 509-510 (Tex. App.—Houston [1st Dist.] 1985, no writ).

In sustaining appellant's point of error number two, we hold that the trial court erred in its findings and conclusions that the settlement proceeds from the injury suffered by appellee constituted his separate property. The record offers no clear and convincing evidence what portion of the settlement, if any, is for personal injuries or what part is for lost wages or lost earning capacity. The most favorable evidence produced by appellee was the self-serving statement that it was his "understanding" that all the proceeds were for personal injuries. Such evidence standing alone does not overcome the presumption of community property. Appellant's point of error number two is sustained.

* * *

This case is hereby reversed and remanded to the trial court for further proceedings on the division of the parties' estate in view of and in conformity with our holding on those matters before this Court.

Notes, Comments & Questions

1. When settling a personal injury case, very little thought is given to the allocation of damages. Accordingly, a personal injury recovery is very seldom broken down into the elements of damage.

2. Whose duty is it to break down a personal injury settlement into the elements of damage—the personal injury attorney's or the divorce attorney's?

3. What kind of proof would you present if you represented the recipient of a personal injury recovery in a divorce?

4. The next case, *Osborn v. Osborn*, provides a very different take on the characterization of a personal injury recovery in that it does not apply the community property presumption.

OSBORN v. OSBORN

961 S.W.2d 408
(Tex. App.—Houston [1st Dist.] 1997, no writ)

O'CONNOR, JUSTICE.

Lon McVey Osborn appeals from a post-answer default judgment rendered against him in favor of Sara Osborn. We affirm in part and reverse and remand in part.

Facts

After 13 years of marriage, Sara Osborn sued Lon McVey Osborn for divorce.[1] Lon answered through his attorney, Elton L. Brownshadel. On March 27, 1995, the trial court issued a scheduling order setting the case for trial on October 9, 1995. The scheduling order contains Brownshadel's name and address. On October 2, 1995, the trial court signed an order permitting Brownshadel to withdraw as Lon's attorney of record.

On October 16, 1995, the trial court issued a second scheduling order setting the case for trial on January 8, 1996. The words "presently pro se" were handwritten beside the area designated for Lon's attorney's name. Beside the area designated for Lon's attorney's address were the handwritten words, "as in file."

On January 8, 1996, the case was called for trial, and Sara's attorney announced ready. Lon did not appear. Concerned about his absence, the trial court reset the case to January 11, 1996, and instructed Sara's attorney to send Lon a letter via messenger notifying him of the change. Sara's attorney arranged for a messenger service to deliver such a letter to Lon on January 8th. According to the messenger service's delivery sheet, nobody answered, so the messenger service taped the letter to Lon's front door.

---

[1] For convenience, we will refer to the parties by their first names.

On January 11, 1996, the case was called for trial. Sara's attorney announced ready, and again, Lon did not appear. The trial court waited approximately 15 minutes before proceeding with the bench trial. The final decree of divorce was signed January 17, 1996.

Lon obtained counsel and filed an unverified motion for new trial alleging he did not appear at the final hearing because (1) his attorney had medical problems; (2) he was involved with a personal injury lawsuit against Dr. Howard Cotler; and (3) he did not have actual notice of the final hearing. Lon also claimed (1) the second scheduling order was illegible; (2) the entry on the messenger service's sheet did not affirmatively state he was given notice; (3) he had a meritorious defense, namely that Sara is not entitled to 30% of any recovery in his personal injury lawsuit against Dr. Cotler; and, finally, (4) the granting of a new trial would not injure Sara.

The district court held a hearing on the motion for new trial, heard evidence in support of the motion, and overruled it.[2] After the hearing, Lon asked the trial court to make findings of fact and conclusions of law regarding the evidence heard at the motion for new trial hearing. On appeal, Lon challenges some of those findings.

***

Division of Recovery from Lawsuit

In point of error five, Lon argues that the evidence is legally and factually insufficient to rebut the statutory characterization of the potential recovery of Lon's personal injury lawsuit as his separate property. During trial, Sara testified Lon was injured in 1992, and the two of them filed a personal injury action.[4] At the time of the divorce, the personal injury lawsuit had not yet been tried and had not settled. The trial court found the claim arising from the personal injury lawsuit was community property.

The trial court did not file findings of fact and conclusions of law after the divorce trial; the only findings the court filed were those filed after the motion for new trial hearing. Under this point of error, Lon complains about the sufficiency of the evidence to support the finding made by the trial court that characterized his personal injury lawsuit as community property.[5] The only issue under this point is a legal issue—whether the trial court erred in characterizing all the damages in Lon's personal injury suit as community property. If the trial court mischaracterized Lon's separate property as community property, the error is one of law and is of constitutional dimensions. *Eggemeyer v. Eggemeyer*, 554 S.W.2d 137, 140 (Tex. 1977). We review the evidence from the divorce trial to see if there was any evidence that somehow transformed Lon's personal injury recovery into community property.

---

[2] There were actually two hearings on the motion for new trial. The first hearing was before a master and, because Lon appealed the master's finding, a second one was before the district court. We have no record from the first hearing.

[4] The case is styled *Lon Osborn and wife, Sara Osborn v. Dr. Howard Cotler, M.D., et al.* Sara filed the lawsuit for loss of consortium.

[5] The trial court made a finding and conclusions on the issue of the personal injury lawsuit. In finding of fact 12(j), the trial court characterized the personal injury lawsuit as community property. In conclusion of law 10, the trial court stated that no evidence was presented to establish that Lon had any separate property. In conclusion of law 11, the court held that all property other than that listed as separate property, was community property. An appellate court is not bound by the trial court's conclusions of law. Connelly v. Paul, 731 S.W.2d 657, 661 (Tex. App.—Houston [1st Dist.] 1987, no writ.). An appellate court is free to draw its own conclusions about the law. Austin Hardwoods, Inc. v. Vanden Berghe, 917 S.W.2d 320, 322 (Tex. App.—El Paso 1995, no writ).

The only evidence at the divorce trial regarding the personal injury lawsuit was from Sara. She testified that Lon had been injured during the marriage and a lawsuit was filed in both of their names. Although Sara did not introduce the petition from the personal injury suit, from her testimony it is clear the lawsuit requested the following types of damages: for Lon's personal injury, for Lon's lost wages, for Sara's claim for loss of consortium, and for medical costs and other expenses. Sara testified that the personal injury lawsuit had not been settled.

In a divorce proceeding, the trial court must order a division of the estate of the parties in a manner it deems just and right. TEX. FAM. CODE § 3.63 (1993). In making that division, the trial court has great discretion in dividing property to attain a fair and just result. *Leighton v. Leighton*, 921 S.W.2d 365, 368 (Tex. App.—Houston [1st Dist.] 1996, no writ). Only community property is subject to the trial court's "just and right" division. *Cameron v. Cameron*, 641 S.W.2d 210, 220 (Tex. 1982). In making its division, the trial court may not divest one party of his separate property. *Id.*

As a general rule, property possessed by either spouse during or on dissolution of marriage is presumed to be community property, and clear and convincing evidence is required to establish that such property is separate property. TEX. FAM. CODE § 5.02 (1993). To overcome the presumption of community property, the spouse claiming certain property as separate property must trace and clearly identify the property claimed to be separate. *Cockerham v. Cockerham*, 527 S.W.2d 162, 167 (Tex. 1975); *McElwee v. McElwee*, 911 S.W.2d 182, 189 (Tex. App.—Houston [1st Dist.] 1995, writ denied).

There is no presumption that a potential recovery for a personal injuries to the body of a spouse is community property. A recovery for personal injuries to the body of a spouse is separate property of that spouse. *Graham v. Franco*, 488 S.W.2d 390, 396 (Tex. 1972). Section 5.01 of the Family Code provides that the recovery for personal injuries sustained by a spouse during marriage (except any recovery for loss of earning capacity during marriage) is separate property. TEX. FAM. CODE § 5.01(a)(3). The damages that are the separate property of the injured spouse include those for disfigurement and for physical pain and suffering in the past and in the future. *Graham*, 488 S.W.2d at 396.

To the extent the marital partnership was injured, the community estate is entitled to recover damages. *Id.* The damages that belong to the community estate include lost wages of the injured spouse, damages for medical expenses, and other expenses associated with the injury to the community estate. *Id.*; *Huls v. Huls*, 616 S.W.2d 312, 315-16 (Tex. Civ. App.—Houston [1st Dist.] 1981, no writ). To the extent the other spouse was injured by loss of consortium, those damages are the separate property of the other spouse. *Whittlesey v. Miller*, 572 S.W.2d 665, 669 (Tex. 1978); *see also Reed Tool Co. v. Copelin*, 610 S.W.2d 736, 740 (Tex. 1981).

The trial court may not characterize separate property as community property. *Leighton*, 921 S.W.2d at 368; *Eggemeyer*, 554 S.W.2d at 140. When a court mischaracterizes separate property as community property, the error requires reversal because a spouse is divested of separate property. *Eggemeyer*, 554 S.W.2d at 140; *Leighton*, 921 S.W.2d at 368; *McElwee*, 911 S.W.2d at 189. If the mischaracterized property has value that would have affected the trial court's just and right division, then the mischaracterization is harmful and requires the appellate court to remand the entire community estate to the trial court for a just and right division of the properly characterized community property. *McElwee*, 911 S.W.2d at 189.

Sara argues that Lon had the burden at the trial to show how much of the recovery would be separate property and how much would be community property.[6] We disagree. The issue is decided by the trial court as a matter of law and has nothing to do with a presumption or a burden of proof. Because section 5.01 states that a spouse's recovery for a personal injuries to the spouse's body is separate property, Lon was not required to prove that. TEX. FAM. CODE § 5.01(a)(3).

Sara seems to complain that Lon did not inform her about the dollar value of damages he claimed for each type of injury. Lon's opinion regarding the amount of damages he claimed would not resolve the issue of what part of the recovery would be separate property and what part community property. Any estimate by Lon separating the dollar amount or percentage of recovery for injury to his body from the injury to the community and injury to Sara (for her loss of consortium) would be entirely speculative. Once the case is tried, the jury's answers will determine the amounts to be awarded for each type of injury. If the case is settled, Sara, as one of the plaintiffs, can participate in the allocation of damages to the different claims for damages.

We find the trial court erred in characterizing the recovery for Lon's personal injury lawsuit as community property. We sustain point of error five.[7]

On remand, the trial court is required to properly characterize the damages sought by the personal injury lawsuit. The damages for Lon's personal injury are his separate property; the damages for Sara's claim for loss of consortium are her separate property; the damages for Lon's lost wages, medical costs, and other expenses are community property. Because we cannot determine if the mischaracterization affected the trial court's just and right division, we remand the entire community estate for a just and right division based on properly characterized property.

We reverse that portion of the judgment dividing the property and remand this cause to the trial court for a new division of property. We affirm the remaining portions of the judgment.

Questions

1. Articulate the difference in the *Kyles* and *Osborne* approaches to the characterization of personal injury recoveries and the application of the community property presumption.

2. How does the First Court of Appeals foresee personal injury recoveries being characterized upon trial of the cause? What if the case is settled?

---

[6] In support of her argument, Sara cites cases in which a spouse received a lump sum award after settlement or trial for a personal injury suffered during the marriage. In those cases, the spouse was required to carry the burden to prove what part of the award was separate property. *See* Moreno v. Alejandro, 775 S.W.2d 735, 738 (Tex. App.—San Antonio 1989, writ denied). However, in this case there has been no lump sum award either by settlement or trial.

[7] Because of our disposition of point of error five, we need not reach point of error six, in which Lon argues the trial court abused its discretion in awarding Sara 30% of Lon's recovery.

LEWIS
v.
LEWIS

944 S.W.2d 630
(Tex. 1997)

PER CURIAM.

Is a workers' compensation settlement paid during marriage community property if the claimant's disability occurred prior to the marriage? The lower courts answered this question yes. 923 S.W.2d 837. We disagree.

Thomas Lewis suffered a work-related injury resulting in immediate permanent disability for which he claimed compensation. Seven months later he married Eva, and about ten months into the marriage he settled his compensation claim. The net proceeds, some $30,000, were deposited in Eva's account. About half of it was used to buy 15.25 acres of land deeded to both Thomas and Eva, and the balance was spent on living expenses. Several years later Eva filed for divorce. Thomas contended that the land was his separate property because it was purchased with the settlement funds. Eva contended that it was community property because Thomas received the funds while they were married. The trial court agreed with Eva and partitioned the property equally between them, giving Thomas the northern half and Eva the southern half. The court of appeals affirmed. 923 S.W.2d at 839.

A spouse's separate property includes "the recovery for personal injuries sustained by the spouse during marriage, except any recovery for loss of earning capacity during marriage." TEX. FAM. CODE § 5.01(a)(3). The character of compensation benefits paid during marriage is determined not by when the injury occurred, but by when the loss of earning capacity occurred. Thomas' loss did not occur during marriage. Thomas was determined to be permanently disabled from the date of his injury, some seven months before he married Eva. No further loss of earning capacity from his injury occurred during marriage. The payment he received during marriage was for a permanent loss he suffered before marriage.

Eva argues that because Thomas' disability was permanent and thus continued through marriage, part of his benefits should compensate the community for the loss it has suffered. By this theory, however, Eva would be entitled to part of Thomas' compensation benefits even if they had been paid before marriage. The argument is simply not credible. Thomas' loss was fully incurred before the community even existed, and while it continued, Eva does not contend that it worsened. In these circumstances the entire compensation benefits were Thomas' separate property.

Our conclusion is consistent with two other cases dealing with related situations. In *Charter Oak Fire Insurance Company v. Few*, 456 S.W.2d 156, 160 (Tex. Civ. App.—Tyler 1970), *rev'd on other grounds*, 463 S.W.2d 424 (Tex. 1971), the court of appeals held that a husband had a community interest in his wife's compensation benefits when her injury and disability occurred during marriage. In *General Insurance Company of America v. Casper*, 426 S.W.2d 606, 608 (Tex. Civ. App.—Tyler 1968, writ ref'd n.r.e.), the court held that a husband did not have a community interest in his wife's compensation benefits when her injury occurred during marriage but her disability did not begin until after divorce. In both those cases, as here, the issue is when the loss of earning capacity occurred. When it occurs outside marriage, compensation is separate property.

Because the land was purchased with Thomas' separate property and was thus itself separate property, the district court had no authority to partition half of it to Eva. We therefore conclude, without hearing argument, that the judgment of the court of appeals must be reversed. TEX. R. APP. P. 170. Inasmuch as the district court's error may have affected its determination of a just and right division of the community, we remand the case to that court for reconsideration of that determination. *See Jacobs v. Jacobs*, 687 S.W.2d 731 (Tex. 1985).

Notes, Comments & Questions

1. In *Lewis v. Lewis*, the Texas Supreme Court applies the inception of title rule to a worker's compensation settlement. If Lewis had lost his earning capacity during marriage and divorced a year after that loss, would the entire compensation be community property, based on inception?

2. Can you conceive of a more equitable way to deal with the hypothetical presented in question 1?

3. Is there any available authority to support your proposed solution?

Chapter 3

Claims for Reimbursement & Economic Contribution

A. Introduction

The concept of reimbursement has been touched upon in the first two chapters of this text, primarily by fleeting references within the cases. The purpose of a reimbursement claim is to provide a spouse a remedy when one marital estate (community, husband's separate, or wife's separate) has been utilized to either contribute to or improve another marital estate (community, husband's separate, or wife's separate). Reimbursement is used to satisfy a claim between marital estates.

Historically, a claim for reimbursement was viewed as a totally equitable remedy to be utilized at the trial court's discretion. However, many people (some legislators and their constituents) perceived that grave wrongs had resulted from this discretionary use of the reimbursement remedy; that is, reimbursement did not fully compensate the community for funds advanced to a spouse's separate estate or, conversely, the receiving estate did not fully compensate either husband's or wife's separate estate for funds advanced to either the community or the other spouse's separate estate.

Based on this perception, beginning in 1999 and ending in 2007, the Texas Legislature attempted to improve on common law reimbursement by adding the remedy of economic contribution and by limiting reimbursement as the bench and bar had come to know it. Justice Ann McClure of the El Paso Court of Appeals, Eighth Judicial District of Texas, has observed that "[f]amily law practitioners have dealt with reimbursement for decades, although the magic word did not appear in the Texas Family Code until the legislature created a statutory right of economic contribution in 2001." *Garcia v. Garcia*, 170 S.W. 3d 644, 649 (Tex. App.—El Paso 2005, no pet.). In the 2009 legislative session, the attempted legislative improvement to common law reimbursement, known as economic contribution has, to some extent, been abandoned in favor of common law reimbursement—with some statutory strictures. It is "to some extent" abandoned because economic contribution will still apply to those suits for dissolution of a marriage that were on file prior to September 1, 2009 or in which a spouse died prior to September 1, 2009.

Specifically, Section 13 of Acts 2009, 81st Leg., R.S., Senate Bill 866, provides:

> (a) In regard to a claim under Subchapter E, Chapter 3, Family Code, [formerly, Claims for Economic Contribution and Reimbursement, now Claims for Reimbursement] that arises from a suit for dissolution of a marriage, the changes in law made by this Act to that subchapter apply only to a claim made in a suit filed on or after the effective date of this Act. [September 1, 2009] A claim made in a suit filed before the effective date of this Act is governed by the law in effect on the date the suit was filed, and the former law is continued in effect for that purpose.
>
> (b) In regard to a claim under Subchapter E, Chapter 3, Family Code, [formerly, Claims for Economic Contribution and Reimbursement, now Claims for Reimbursement] that arises from the death of a spouse, the changes in law made by this Act to that subchapter apply only to a claim arising from a death that occurs on or after the effective date of this Act. [September 1, 2009] A claim arising from a death that occurs before the effective date of this Act is governed by the law in effect on the date the suit was filed, and the former law is continued in effect for that purpose.

Accordingly, practitioners, for a few years to come, will still have to be familiar with economic contribution as it existed prior to September 1, 2009. For this reason, one must understand the law as it existed prior to September 1, 2009. The partial statutory limits upon and later resurrection of common law reimbursement is explained below.

B. The Law, 1999-2001

The first attempt to rectify the perceived inequity of common law reimbursement was via the 1999 legislative amendments to the Texas Family Code which included the addition of Chapter 3, Subchapter E. Equitable Interest of Community Estate in Enhanced Value of Separate Property, §§ 3.401-3.406. These 1999 amendments were the most controversial marital property statutes that your author can remember in her 30 plus years of experience in this area of the law. Bench and bar were so concerned about the application of the "equitable interest" statutes that cases were settled in record numbers, perhaps, not a bad thing. The statutes engendered so much controversy that almost immediately after their enactment, work began to replace the 1999 statutes by the next—the 2001—legislative session.

C. The Law, 2001-9/1/2009

In 2001, the Texas Legislature repealed the "equitable interest" statutes and enacted Subchapter E. Claims for Economic Contribution & Reimbursement §§ 3.401 - 3.410 and § 7.007, Disposition of Claim for Economic Contribution or Claim for Reimbursement. These statutes were also met with skepticism. As Justice McClure observed, "Generally speaking these amendments were not well received by family law practitioners and both bench and bar have struggled with their application." *Garcia v. Garcia*, 170 S.W. 3d 644, 649 (Tex. App.—El Paso 2005, no pet.). Economic contribution law as it existed prior to September 1, 2009 is set forth below.

D. A Statutory Overview of the Former Economic Contribution Laws

Texas Family Code § 3.402 (as it existed prior to September 1, 2009) identified six possible claims for economic contribution, as the dollar amount of:

(1) the reduction of the principal amount of a debt secured by a lien on property owned before marriage, to the extent such debt existed at the time of marriage;

(2) the reduction of the principal amount of debt secured by a lien on property received by a spouse by gift, devise, or descent during a marriage, to the extent the debt existed at the time the property was received;

(3) the reduction of the principal amount of that part of a debt, including a home equity loan:

(A) incurred during a marriage;

(B) secured by a lien on the property; and

(C) incurred for the acquisition of, or for capital improvements, to the property;

(4) the reduction of the principal amount of that part of a debt:

(A) incurred during marriage;

(B) secured by a lien on property for owned by a spouse;

(C) for which the creditor agreed to look for repayment solely to the separate marital estate of the spouse on whose property such lien attached; and

(D) incurred for the acquisition of, or for capital improvements to, such property;

(5) the refinancing of the principal amount described by Subdivisions 1-4, to the extent the refinancing reduces that principal amount in a manner described by the appropriate subdivision; and

(6) capital improvements to property other than by incurring debt.

TEX. FAM. CODE § 3.402(a)(1)-(6) (now amended).

Prior to the passage of the foregoing economic contribution statute, the only remedy available for such claims was equitable reimbursement. The foregoing statute precluded one from using reimbursement for any of the claims enumerated above. Today, that has changed and reimbursement is the only remedy for dissolution cases filed or for deaths that occur after September 1, 2009. However, as regards the former law, there are a few other matters of which one should be aware.

Under the former law, the remedy of economic contribution did not include the dollar amount of (1) expenditures for ordinary maintenance and repair or for taxes paid on property, interest, or insurance; or,(2) the contribution by a spouse of time, toil, talent, or effort during the marriage. Although a spouse currently and previously has been able to make a claim for reimbursement for the contribution of a spouse of time, toil, talent, or effort during the marriage, traditionally reimbursement has not been recognized for expenditures for ordinary maintenance and repair or for taxes paid on property, interest, or insurance. The actual formula for a claim of economic contribution was set forth in Texas Family Code § 3.403, and is now repealed. This calculation will be reviewed in class; indeed, a work sheet for such calculation is still included in this Chapter of the text. Nonetheless, remember, this calculation will only be used in dissolution cases filed prior to September 1, 2009 or in when a spouse died before that same date.

E. An Overview of the Current Reimbursement Laws

Today, the six claims enumerated above in § 3.402 as it existed prior to September 1, 2009, as well as claims based upon (1) payment by one marital estate of the unsecured liabilities of another marital estate; (2) inadequate compensation for time, toil, talent, and effort of a spouse by a business entity under the control and direction of that spouse; and, (3) the reduction by the community estate of an unsecured debt incurred by the separate estate of one of the spouses, may all now be satisfied by use of a reimbursement claim. TEX. FAM. CODE § 3.402. In addition, it is specifically provided that trial courts shall resolve claims for reimbursement by using equitable principles, including that claims for reimbursement may be offset against one another. TEX. FAM. CODE § 3.402(b).

In contrast to the now defunct claims for economic contribution, reimbursement does allow for use and enjoyment of property during the marriage to be offset against the reimbursement claim, except that a spouse may not claim an offset for use and enjoyment of a primary or secondary separate residence for claims made by the community. TEX. FAM. CODE § 3.402(c). In addition, the party seeking an offset has the burden of proof. TEX. FAM. CODE § 3.402(e).

In addition, reimbursement for funds expended by a marital estate for improvements is measured by enhanced value to the benefited estate. TEX. FAM. CODE § 3.402(d). This is consistent with the case of *Anderson v. Gilliland*, 684 S.W.2d 673 (Tex. 1985), which can be found in the textual material of this chapter.

As with economic contribution, reimbursement does not create an ownership interest, only a claim against the benefited estate that matures upon dissolution of the marriage or upon the death of a spouse is available. TEX. FAM. CODE § 3.404.

Finally, whether a marriage is dissolved by dissolution proceeding or by death, a court may impose and equitable lien on the property of the benefited marital estate. TEX. FAM. CODE § 3.406. The imposition of a lien has been viewed as a narrow remedy, as evidenced in *Sheshtawy v. Sheshtawy*, 150 S.W.2d 772 (Tex. App.—San Antonio 2004, pet denied), thus:

> When dividing marital property on divorce, trial courts may impose equitable liens on one spouse's separate real property to secure the other spouse's claim for economic contribution or right of reimbursement for community improvements to that property. TEX. FAM. CODE ANN. § 3.407 (Vernon Supp.2004); *Heggen v. Pemelton*, 836 S.W.2d 145, 146 (Tex. 1992). Trial courts, however, may not impress such liens simply to ensure a just and right division. *Heggen*, 836 S.W.2d at 146.
>
> Here, Adel and Amal borrowed $135,000 and secured the loan with a lien on Adel's separate property, which was their home. The divorce decree ordered Adel to assume this community debt. In addition, the decree ordered Adel to secure, execute, acknowledge, and surrender a deed of trust on the home in favor of Amal in order to secure his assumption of the community debt. The trial court did not find that Amal had a claim for economic contribution or a claim of a right of reimbursement for community improvements to Adel's separate property. Thus, the trial court erred by imposing an equitable lien on Adel's separate property for reasons other than to secure Amal's claim for economic contribution or Amal's right of reimbursement. *See Heggen*, 836 S.W.2d at 146. We sustain Adel's fourth issue.

Sheshtawy, 150 S.W.2d at 779.

See also, *Langston v. Langston* 82 S.W.3d 686 (Tex. App.—Eastland 2002, no pet. h.) wherein it was established that while a court could impose an equitable lien on a spouse's separate property to secure a claim—be it for economic contribution or reimbursement—it could not simply award the contributing spouse the subject property. A lien will secure the claim and then if the claim is not satisfied, the lien will be subject to foreclosure, as would any other judgment lien. To allow a court to directly foreclose on title to a spouse's separate property and to vest title in the other spouse would be a divestiture of separate property. A two step process is needed—impose the lien and then foreclose.

There have been no changes to TEX. FAM. CODE § 3.409 which precludes reimbursement in five very specific circumstances, establishing that a court may not recognize a marital estate's claim for reimbursement for:

(1) the payment of child support, alimony, or spousal maintenance;

(2) the living expenses of a spouse or child of a spouse;

(3) contributions of property of nominal value;

(4) the payment of a liability of a nominal amount; or

(5) a student loan owed by a spouse.

TEX. FAM. CODE § 3.409.

Under the current and former statutes, a trial court is precluded from recognizing reimbursement for the payment of child support, alimony or spousal maintenance or for living expenses of a spouse or child of a spouse. TEX. FAM. CODE § 3.409(1), (2). This statute resolves what had been somewhat of a conflict in the courts of appeals.

In *Pelzig v. Berkebile*, 931 S.W.2d 398 (Tex. App.—Corpus Christi 1996, no writ), wife sought reimbursement for child support, college expenses, and alimony payments made to husband's child of a previous marriage and husband's former spouse. The court, reasoning that the wife was not deceived by the obligations and did not seek to have husband pay for same out of his separate estate, determined wife should not be reimbursed.

However, that same court did allow a wife to be reimbursed for community funds used by husband to pay for living expenses of a child born to another woman during the marriage of husband and wife. *Butler v. Butler*, 975 S.W.2d 765 (Tex. App.—Corpus Christi 1998, no writ). The child was born out of wedlock to husband and another woman while he was married to wife. In *Butler*, the reimbursement to the community was deemed justified by the appellate court. Under the current statute, the payment of child support cannot be reimbursed. TEX. FAM. CODE § 3.409(1). Query, can it be argued that this prohibition extends only to court-ordered child support? In *Butler*, the payments were not court ordered, but were voluntary.

Another case on the subject, *Farish v. Farish*, 982 S.W.2d 623 (Tex. App.—Houston [1st Dist.] 1998, no writ), held that court ordered child support payments are not subject to a claim for reimbursement from the community estate. This case recognizes the obligation of parents to support their children and further implies that if reimbursement was allowed, obligor parents could, ultimately, be paying such support twice—once during marriage and once upon dissolution by way of reimbursement.

F. Trial Court's Discretion in Dealing with Reimbursement Claims

Texas Family Code § 7.007 addresses a trial court's disposition of a claim for reimbursement, providing: In a decree of divorce or annulment, the court shall determine the rights of both spouses in a claim for reimbursement as provided by Subchapter E, Chapter 3, and the shall apply equitable principles to:

(1) determine whether to recognize the claim after taking into account all the relative circumstances of the spouses; and

(2) order a division of the claim for reimbursement, if appropriate, in a manner that the court considers just and right, having due regard for the rights of each party and any children of the marriage.

TEX. FAM. CODE § 7.007(b).

G. Reimbursement for Time, Toil, Talent, and Effort

The current Texas Family Code recognizes that a claim for reimbursement exists when there has been inadequate compensation for the time, toil, talent, and effort of a spouse by a business entity under the control and direction of that spouse. TEX. FAM. CODE § 3.402(a)(2). Accordingly, the cases which have addressed the measure of reimbursement for time, toil, talent, and effort of a spouse used to increase the value of a spouse's separate property business are the law. The codification or reimbursement has not affected the precedential value of the time, toil, talent, and effort reimbursement cases.

VALLONE
v.
VALLONE

644 S.W.2d 455
(Tex. 1982)

RAY, JUSTICE.

This is an appeal from a division of property in a divorce action. At issue is whether the trial court abused its discretion by not specifically considering the community's interest, if any, in the increase in value of the separate property portion of stock in a closely-held corporation in which all of the corporation's stock was issued in the husband's name. The stock was originally received in exchange for both community and separate assets. The court of civil appeals held that the trial court, "in making a division of the estate, did not take into consideration the large increment to [the husband's] separate property by reason of community labor and as a result the division of the estate was manifestly unfair to [the wife]." 618 S.W.2d 820, 824. We reverse the judgment of the court of civil appeals and affirm the judgment of the trial court.

The holding of the court of civil appeals in this case conflicts with the holding in *Hale v. Hale*, 557 S.W.2d 614 (Tex. Civ. App.—Texarkana 1977, no writ). In *Hale*, the court held that a contribution of community labor should not be taken into account in determining the amount of reimbursement that may be owing to the community by the benefited separate estate. Under TEX. REV. CIV. STAT. ANN. art. 1728 § 2, we have jurisdiction to review this case.

Tony and Leslie Vallone were married in 1966. During the first years of their marriage, Tony worked in a restaurant owned and operated by his father as a sole proprietorship. In January 1969, the assets of the restaurant were transferred to Tony from his father as a gift. Tony operated the restaurant as a sole proprietorship until its incorporation in August 1969. The initial capitalization consisted of $19,663 in assets. Included in the initial capital was the used restaurant equipment given to Tony by his father, valued at $9,365 (or slightly over 47% of the initial capital).

During the period beginning with the incorporation of the restaurant until the couple divorced, the business prospered. The restaurant business constituted the major asset of both the community estate and the husband's separate estate. Tony received approximately $200,000 per year as salary and bonus from the corporation. Many of the couple's personal transactions were handled through the corporation.

The trial court granted the divorce, awarded custody of the minor children to Tony, and filed findings of fact and conclusions of law in support of the division of property. The court found the business to be worth $1,000,000. Finding that 47% of its initial capitalization was traceable to Tony's separate estate, the trial court set aside a proportionate share of the corporate stock as Tony's separate property. The trial court then awarded Leslie 70% of the remaining stock as her share of the community interest in the corporation, subject to redemption provisions. The decree ordered Tony's Restaurant, Inc., to purchase Leslie's share of the stock for a cash payment of $77,000 and a $300,000 note personally guaranteed by Tony and secured by all of the stock in Tony's. The court of civil appeals calculated that Leslie received 51.4% of the net estate. Tony was ordered to assume all tax liabilities.

Leslie appealed the division of property. The court of civil appeals determined that the transfer of restaurant equipment from father to son was a gift, not a sale, and that the corporation was not operated as Tony's *alter ego*. But while further affirming the trial court's finding that 47% of the corporate stock was Tony's separate property, the court of civil appeals sustained Leslie's point of error that the trial court's division of the property was so manifestly unfair as to amount to an abuse of discretion, determining "that the court, in making a division of the estate, did not take into consideration the large increment to appellee's separate property by reason of community labor. . . ." 618 S.W.2d at 824.

The case comes to us in the following posture: Did the trial court abuse its discretion by ignoring community rights and equities which might have existed in the corporation?

At trial, Leslie asserted that the increase in the value of the corporation's stock should be considered as part of the community, alleging that the corporation existed as Tony's *alter ego*. She further requested reimbursement if, to quote from her pleadings, "(1) money or property of one of the petitioner's estates (separate or community); (2) has been used or expended to benefit the receiving estate (separate or community); (3) for which Petitioner's contributing estate received no quid pro quo; (4) thereby unjustly enriching the receiving estate."

Consideration of whether a corporation is an *alter ego* for purposes of determining whether assets held in the corporation's name should be treated as community property is an issue of fact from which the status of the property is determined. *Cockerham v. Cockerham*, 527 S.W.2d 162 (Tex. 1975); *Goetz v. Goetz*, 567 S.W.2d 892 (Tex. Civ. App.—Dallas 1978, no writ). The trial court and the court of civil appeals found that the restaurant corporation was not Tony's *alter ego*. No error of law has been correctly preserved on this point. Leslie's second cross-point states that the courts below erred in finding that the corporation was not the *alter ego* of Tony. For argument, Leslie adopts and incorporates by reference her point in her appellant's brief. The point was preserved in the court of civil appeals specifically as a "greater weight and preponderance of the evidence" point. A careful reading of the argument shows that the sum and substance of that point is directed towards a "greater weight and preponderance of the evidence" analysis. Authorities are cited to provide the framework in which the facts are to be construed. The court of civil appeals' opinion uses substantially the same *alter ego* test stated in Leslie's briefs. More importantly, Leslie's briefs in this Court do not assert that the court of civil appeals applied the wrong test or applied the correct test incorrectly. This leaves a factual determination which this Court does not have jurisdiction to decide. Similarly, Leslie challenged the characterization of the marital property in two points in her court of civil appeals brief. The first was a greater weight and preponderance of the evidence point and the second an insufficiency of the evidence point. The argument under the insufficiency point is clearly a *factual insufficiency* argument. We do not have jurisdiction to pass upon either of these points and are therefore bound by the finding of the courts below that the corporation was not the *alter ego* of Tony. In this respect, no constructive fraud was perpetrated upon the community.

Characterization of property as separate, however, does not necessarily preclude the right to reimbursement. Questions concerning the right to reimbursement do not concern which estate owns legal or equitable title in certain property. Rather, such questions entail

> the consideration of what is to be done with community property that by its very nature forms such a part of the separate estate of one spouse as not to be separable therefrom. The difficulty is not so much in deciding what is and what is not community property, but in deciding when and to what extent the separate estates should reimburse the community, and vice versa.

O. SPEER, TEXAS FAMILY LAW § 22.38 (5th ed. 1976).

When separate property is combined with community time, talent and labor, and both the community and the separate estate make claim upon the increment, the courts are confronted with conflicting principles of marital property law. It is fundamental that any property or rights acquired by one of the spouses after marriage by toil, talent, industry or other productive faculty belongs to the community estate. Nevertheless, the law contemplates that a spouse may expend a reasonable amount of talent or labor in the management and preservation of his or her separate estate without impressing a community character upon that estate. *Norris v. Vaughan*, 152 Tex. 491, 260 S.W.2d 676 (1953); *Hardee v. Vincent*, 136 Tex. 99, 147 S.W.2d 1072 (1941).

The rule of reimbursement is purely an equitable one. *Colden v. Alexander*, 141 Tex. 134. 171 S.W.2d 328 (1943). It obtains when the community estate in some way improves the separate estate of one of the spouses (or vice versa). The right of reimbursement is not an interest in property or an enforceable debt, per se, but an equitable right which arises upon dissolution of the marriage through death, divorce or annulment. *Burton v. Bell*, 380 S.W.2d 561 (Tex. 1964); *Dakan v. Dakan*, 125 Tex. 305, 83 S.W.2d 620 (1935).

A right of reimbursement arises when the funds or assets of one estate are used to benefit and enhance another estate without itself receiving some benefit. *Dakan v. Dakan, supra*. We hold it also arises when community time, talent and labor are utilized to benefit and enhance a spouse's separate estate, beyond whatever care, attention, and expenditure are necessary for the proper maintenance and preservation of the separate estate, without the community receiving adequate compensation.[1] To the extent that *Hale v. Hale, supra*, held that the expenditure of community

[1] Other community property states have formulated rules which permit the community to seek reimbursement for uncompensated community labors. Washington follows the rule that where a salary is paid to the spouse by a closely held corporation of which he owns all or substantially all of the stock, it is presumed that the community

time, talent and labor may under no circumstances give rise to an equitable right of reimbursement in the community's favor, it is hereby disapproved.

The party claiming the right of reimbursement has the burden of pleading and proving that the expenditures and improvements were made and that they are reimbursable. *Lindsay v. Clayman, supra*; *Wachendorfer v. Wachendorfer*, 615 S.W.2d 852 (Tex. Civ. App.—Houston [1st] 1981, no writ); *West v. Austin National Bank*, 427 S.W.2d 906 (Tex. Civ. App.—San Antonio 1968, writ ref'd n.r.e.). By her first cause of action, Leslie prayed for equitable reimbursement *if* community *funds or property* were used to benefit the separate estate of Tony to which end no compensation was had or received, thereby resulting in an unjust enrichment. As to this particular theory of recovery, the trial court found: "(3) The profits from . . . Tony's Restaurant, Inc., have been used, in large measure, for the benefit of the community estate and to build the community estate." Leslie objected to this finding of fact. Her several objections to the findings of fact and conclusions of law, together with those she urged the court to adopt, are in no way referable to the theory of reimbursement due to *time*, *talent* and *labor* expended by Tony on behalf of his separate estate to the detriment of the community estate. The only other causes of action pleaded by Leslie referable to reimbursement are those of constructive fraud arising out of Tony's alleged operation of the corporation as his *alter ego*.

Reimbursement is not available as a matter of law, but lies within the discretion of the court. In the absence of pleadings either specifically for or referable to reimbursement premised on uncompensated time, talent or labor, such recovery is waived and the failure of the trial court to consider the matter does not constitute error. *Burton v. Bell*, 380 S.W.2d 561, 567 (Tex. 1964); *Wachendorfer v. Wachendorfer, supra; Gaston v. Gaston*, 608 S.W.2d 332, 335 (Tex. Civ. App.—Tyler 1980, no writ); *Pruske v. Pruske*, 601 S.W.2d 746, 749 (Tex. Civ. App.—Austin 1980, writ dism'd).

Section 3.63 of the Texas Family Code affords the trial court wide latitude and discretion in dividing the community estate of the parties upon dissolution of their marriage. *Eggemeyer v. Eggemeyer*, 554 S.W.2d 137 (Tex. 1977); *McKnight v. McKnight*, 543 S.W.2d 863 (Tex. 1976). In reviewing the actions of the trial court, the appellate court will presume that the trial court exercised its discretion properly. *Murff v. Murff*, 615 S.W.2d 696 (Tex. 1981). The trial court's discretion will not be disturbed on appeal unless a clear abuse has been shown. *Cockerham v. Cockerham, supra*; *Bell v. Bell*, 513 S.W.2d 20 (Tex. 1974).

---

has been compensated for the services that spouse may have rendered. The enhanced value retains a separate character. *See* Hamlin v. Merlino, 44 Wash.2d 851, 272 P.2d 125, 129 (1954). In Arizona, the salary paid to the spouse must be fair and adequate, otherwise the entire increment in value will be deemed community property. *See* Nace v. Nace, 104 Ariz. 20, 448 P.2d 76 (1968). California applies either of two rules which provide for (1) allocation of a reasonable rate of return on the separate property to the separate estate and apportioning the remainder to the community, or (2) awarding the reasonable value of the spouse's services to the community. *See* Beam v. Bank of America, 6 Cal.3d 12, 98 Cal.Rptr. 137, 490 P.2d 257 (1971). Nevada courts likewise apply both California tests. *See* Johnson v. Johnson, 89 Nev. 244, 510 P.2d 625 (1973). As a rule, New Mexico reimburses or allocates to the community the reasonable value of the spouse's labors. *See* Katson v. Katson, 43 N.M. 214, 89 P.2d 524 (1939). Idaho courts are in accord. They consider a number of factors to determine if the salary paid the spouse is a fair compensation for labor expended, including the nature and size of the incorporated business, number of employees, and extent of the spouse's involvement and the growth pattern of the business. If the spouse has not taken an adequate compensation from the corporation, the courts will award the community the difference between the compensation received and what the corporation would have had to pay an employee to perform the same services. *See* Speer v. Quinlan, 96 Idaho 119, 525 P.2d 314 (1974).

We have carefully considered the entire record of this case to determine whether the trial court abused its discretion in dividing the community estate of the parties and have found no such abuse. *Humphrey v. Humphrey*, 593 S.W.2d 824 (Tex. Civ. App.—Houston [14th] 1980, writ dism'd). We therefore reverse the judgment of the court of civil appeals and affirm the judgment of the trial court.

SONDOCK, J., dissents in an opinion in which POPE, C.J., and MCGEE, J., join.

BARROW, J., dissents.

SONDOCK, JUSTICE dissenting.

I respectfully dissent. I believe that the majority has done the Bar a disservice by deciding this case on the basis of abuse of discretion. In applying this principle, the majority has confused discretion in *division* of property with discretion in *classifying* property. I recognize that a trial court has broad discretion in ordering a division of the property of the parties and that the division does not have to be on a 50/50 basis. A trial court, however, has no discretion in classifying property. I respectfully submit that it is impossible to decide whether there has been an abuse of discretion in division of the estate of the parties until this Court determines that a proper classification of the marital property has been made by the trial court.

The question presented by this case is: If during marriage, corporate stock owned by one spouse as separate property increases in value due to the time, talent, and toil of one or both spouses, does that increased value belong to the community estate or is it the separate property of the spouse who owns the stock? The increase is community property.

The majority recognizes as "fundamental" the proposition that "any property or rights acquired by one of the spouses after marriage by toil, talent, industry or other productive faculty belongs to the community estate." However, contrary to the mandate of *Norris v. Vaughan*, 152 Tex. 491, 260 S.W.2d 676 (1953), the majority indicates that the increase in the value of the stock in Tony's Restaurant, Inc., which the lower courts attributed to the time, talent, and toil of the spouses, is the separate property of the husband. The majority refuses to address this issue directly. They obviously have concluded, however, that the increase is the husband's separate property because they hold that the trial court did not abuse its discretion in dividing the property of the parties.

The majority further states that "when separate property is combined with community time, talent, and labor, and both the community and the separate estate make claim upon the increment, the courts are confronted with conflicting principles of marital property law." What the majority considers to be conflicting principles are the provisions in *Norris v. Vaughan*, *supra*, that: (1) classify all property acquired by time, talent, and toil, and (2) permit a spouse to expend a reasonable amount of time in the preservation of a separate estate. I submit that these are not conflicting principles of law. The provision that a spouse may preserve his separate property is simply a limitation on the general rule that requires spouses to direct their energy toward building the community estate rather than benefiting their individual interests. It defies logic to state that this Court in *Norris v. Vaughan*, *supra*, intended the definition of reasonable time to be interpreted to allow a spouse to spend 47% of his time building his separate estate. During marriage, the law will not permit a spouse to devote 100% of his time, talent, and toil on his own behalf in the operation of a sole proprietorship or a partnership and then claim 47% of the benefits as separate property. This conduct does not become acceptable in the eyes of the law merely because the same spouse does the same act through a corporate vehicle of his own creation.

* * *

The position of the majority ignores the basic principles underlying the community property system. Although the specific question presented by this case has never been answered by this Court, the underlying principle has been addressed many times. The only difference here is that the property involved—earnings/profits of the business—has been cloaked in corporate form.

During the marriage, Tony's Restaurant was started as a sole proprietorship. Later, the business was incorporated. Unidentified used restaurant equipment, which had a depreciated value of $9,365 in 1969, was transferred to the corporation as a part of the initial capitalization of $19,663. The trial court found that this used equipment was a gift to the husband from his father.[1] All of the stock was registered in the name of the husband and issued in one certificate, which does not bear the "sole and separate property" legend. At the time of divorce, the trial court upheld the husband's claim that 47% of the stock at its *present value* of $470,000 belonged to him as his sole and separate property.

Assuming that the evidence is sufficient to support the finding that 47% of the stock belonged to the husband as his sole and separate property,[2] the trial court erred in classifying the *increase in value* of that stock from $9,365 to $470,000 as the husband's separate property. Even though a business is created during the marriage from separate funds, the earnings of the business that result from a spouse's devotion of 100% of his or her time, talent, and toil belong to the community estate.

The issue of classifying the increase in the value of separate property as community property has been addressed by the Texas courts in various contexts.[3] The increase from a spouse's operation of a business always has been considered community property, even when the business itself was owned by one spouse prior to the marriage and thus was the separate property of that spouse.[4] *Epperson v. Jones*, 65 Tex. 425 (1886). In *Epperson*, this Court held that profits from the operation of a business are "community property, and cannot, therefore, be said to increase . . . [spouse's] separate estate to the extent of a single dollar." *Id.* at 428. *See Moss v. Gibbs*, 370 S.W.2d 452 (Tex. 1963); *Hardee v. Vincent*, 136 Tex. 99, 147 S.W.2d 1072 (Tex.

[1] The record does not support the majority's statement that the "assets of the restaurant were transferred to Tony."

[2] 618 S.W.2d at 822. The court of civil appeals refers to the evidence as being "scant." This is a classification that this opinion should not be construed as approving.

[3] *See* Arnold v. Leonard, 114 Tex. 535, 273 S.W. 799 (1925) (rents and revenues from separate property); Dixon v. Sanderson, 72 Tex. 359, 10 S.W. 535 (1888) (profits); Craxton, Wood & Co. v. Ryan, 3 Tex.Civ.Cas. 439 (1888) (bricks produced from a spouse's separate property); Braden v. Gose, 57 Tex. 37 (1882) (interest received on money in a separate bank account); White v. Lynch & Co., 26 Tex. 195 (1862) (timber produced from trees grown on separate real property); De Blane v. Lynch, 23 Tex. 25 (1859) (crops grown on separate realty).

[4] The increase in the instant case is distinguishable from an "inherent" increase in the value of separate property. The court of civil appeals noted: "The increase in the value of the stock . . . was directly attributable to the labors of one or both of the community partners. . . . All of the increase is attributable to the labor and skill of one (and probably both) of the spouses. This is clearly distinguishable . . . [from a situation where] separate property . . . increased in value because of reasons other than the time and effort of one or both of the spouses." 618 S.W.2d at 823-2

1941); *Smith v. Bailey*, 66 Tex. 553, 1 S.W. 627 (1886); *Cleveland v. Cole*, 65 Tex. 402 (1885); *Green v. Ferguson*, 62 Tex. 525 (1884).

* * *

Texas courts have considered this principle [whatever is acquired by joint efforts of the spouses in community property] so essential to the community property system that even fringe benefits arising from a spouse's labor, such as profit sharing, pension and retirement plans, including those that are noncontributing or are not vested or reduced to possession at the time of divorce, are considered community property. *Cearley v. Cearley*, 544 S.W.2d 661 (Tex. 1976); *Busby v. Busby*, 457 S.W.2d 551 (Tex. 1970); *Herring v. Blakeley*, 385 S.W.2d 843 (Tex. 1965); *Mora v. Mora*, 429 S.W.2d 660 (Tex. Civ. App.—San Antonio 1968, writ dism'd); *Kirkham v. Kirkham*, 335 S.W.2d 393 (Tex. Civ. App.—San Antonio 1960, no writ).

* * *

The majority justifies its holding that the trial court did not abuse its discretion in dividing the property by relying on the court of civil appeals' statement that the trial court awarded the wife 51.4% of the community estate. This overlooks the fact that the court of civil appeals remanded this case to permit the trial court to correct its error in excluding the increase in the value of the separate stock from the property to be divided. The majority does not recognize that if the trial court had properly classified the increase in the value of the stock, then the community property awarded to the wife would only represent approximately 30% of the parties' estate.

I cannot agree that awarding the wife 30% of the community property comports with the "just and right" requirement of section 3.63 of the Texas Family Code in a case in which the divorce was granted on a no-fault basis and the parties agreed on child custody. Two other material factors that the trial court should have considered in making its division were the respective earning capacities and business opportunities of the parties. In this case, the husband has an earning capacity of more than twenty times that of the wife and the difference in the business opportunities available to the respective parties is incalculable. More important, however, is the fact that included in the property awarded to the husband is the "goose that lays the golden egg"—Tony's restaurant itself. Additionally, under the trial court's classification, the husband has a separate estate of over $470,000 while the wife has none except gifts of personal effects.

When a trial court misclassifies over $450,000, or almost half of what the court of civil appeals noted was the largest community asset, it is impossible to conclude that the court did not commit reversible error. In effect, the trial judge eliminated over $450,000 from consideration as community property. * * *

* * *

A spouse who incorporates a family business with capital claimed as his or her separate property cannot change the community character of profits later earned and retained. By electing to elevate form over substance, the majority has created an option of election for a spouse, who by a simple ex parte paper transaction will be able to transform community earnings into separate property. Clearly, such an unauthorized mode of reclassifying property is contrary to the laws of this State.

Texas courts have prohibited spouses from changing community property into separate property by contract, *King v. Bruce*, 145 Tex. 647, 201 S.W.2d 803 (1947), or agreement, *Strickland v. Wester*, 131 Tex. 23, 112 S.W.2d 1047 (1938); *Gorman v. Gause*, 56 S.W.2d 855 (Tex. Comm'n

App. 1933, judgm't adopted); *Cox v. Miller*, 54 Tex. 16 (1880), or disclaimer, *Hardee v. Vincent*, *supra*. Until the 1948 amendment to article XV, section 16 of the Texas Constitution, spouses could not even partition community property. To the extent that the parties today can effectuate a change in the character of property from community to separate, such can be done only by strict compliance with the law. *Maples v. Nimitz*, 615 S.W.2d 690 (Tex. 1981); *Hilley v. Hilley*, 161 Tex. 569, 342 S.W.2d 565 (1961). Allowing a spouse to make the type of election the majority opinion creates will have ramifications of considerable magnitude given the widespread use of the corporate entity in the modern business world.

Basic principles and policies of community property support the proposition that the earnings of a spouse-owned business to which one or both spouses devote time, talent, and toil should be subject to division on divorce. * * *

* * *

Furthermore, I submit that this Court, in enunciating a rule requiring specific pleadings in family law matters, has effectively overruled what I believe has been the generally accepted rule for pleading in this area. The attitude toward pleading in divorce cases always has been liberal. Tests of sufficiency of pleadings in divorce cases have differed from that of cases in other areas. "The general rule as to the sufficiency of pleadings and quantum of proof applicable to civil cases generally does not apply to divorce cases in this state." [Citations omitted.] Further, in a divorce suit, the trial court may construe the pleadings of the parties with regard to property division more liberally than in other civil cases. [Citations omitted.]

There is a reason for the difference. For example, there is no true default judgment in a divorce suit. Even though the defendant fails to answer, full and satisfactory evidence must still be presented to warrant the granting of a divorce. General pleadings are encouraged and allegations of evidentiary facts are to be stricken from the pleadings. TEX. FAM. CODE ANN. § 3.52 (1975). A defendant (respondent) "need not answer on oath, and the petition shall not be taken as confessed for want of an answer." TEX. FAM. CODE ANN. § 3.53 (1975). The majority's holding will create confusion with the provisions of § 3.52 and § 3.53 of the Family Code and make it extremely difficult, if not impossible, for trial judges to continue to follow the mandate of § 3.63 of the Family Code.

Second, I cannot agree with the formalistic proposition that the wife's arguments do not adequately preserve the legal question of disregarding a wholly-owned corporation to divide community profits. This Court has always had a strong policy against elevating form over substance when construing points of error. * * *

* * *

The legal arguments in the instant case have been properly preserved and well presented. In fact, one of the wife's cross-points in this Court presents the argument, part of which is the synthesis of my dissenting opinion:

> CROSS-POINT I: The trial court and the Court of Appeals both erred in their finding that 47% of the stock in Tony's Restaurant, Inc., as well as the total value thereof, is the separate property of TONY VALLONE.

It is inconceivable that the majority could possibly construe this Cross-Point as presenting only "factual insufficiency" questions.

* * *

I would affirm the judgment of the court of civil appeals and reverse and remand the cause to the trial court for a division of the community estate in accordance with the principles of law set out in this opinion.

POPE, C.J., and MCGEE, J., join in this dissent.

BARROW, JUSTICE dissenting.

I respectfully dissent. I agree with the dissenting opinion of JUSTICE SONDOCK, but write to point out my specific disagreement with the majority opinion.

* * *

The issue upon which this Court is divided is whether the trial court abused its discretion in its division of the Vallones' community estate. A trial court is required to consider all community property owned by the spouses at the time of divorce when it divides the community estate pursuant to § 3.63 of the Family Code. *See Cameron v. Cameron*, 641 S.W.2d 210 (Tex. 1982). The division does not have to be equal and the court has broad discretion in its division of the community property. *Bell v. Bell*, 513 S.W.2d 20 (Tex. 1974). Here, however, the trial court erroneously found 47% of the current value of the couple's principal asset, i.e., Tony's Restaurant, was separate property and thus not subject to division or the exercise of its discretion. Considering the overall property division between the parties, I cannot agree that this erroneous characterization of such a significant part of the community estate was harmless error.

Furthermore, I do not agree that this error was not properly raised by the wife. A fair reading of this record clearly demonstrates that the basic area of dispute in the trial court, court of appeals and before us was the determination and valuation of the community interest in Tony's Restaurant. All courts were apprised of her complaint that the substantial increase in the valuation of Tony's Restaurant during the marriage was directly related to community effort.

I would reverse and remand the cause to the trial court for a division of the community estate after consideration of all community assets.

Notes, Comments & Questions

1. JUSTICE SONDOCK in her dissent states that the majority has confused discretion in division of property with discretion in classifying property. What does she mean?

2. What if Tony Vallone had not incorporated his restaurant?

3. How would the business have been characterized if operated as a sole proprietorship?

4. What monetary benefit did the incorporation effect?

5. Upon rendering *Vallone*, lawyers throughout the state perceived that the Supreme Court had settled the issue of reimbursement for time, toil, talent, and effort. This perception was momentarily tainted when following the *Vallone* opinion, the Supreme Court finally had a chance to substantively consider a case which presented the issue of reimbursement for time, toil, talent, and effort. This was the case of *Jensen v. Jensen*. The *Jensen* opinion appearing in this casebook was

preceded by two opinions which were withdrawn. Nevertheless, one should be cognizant of what the court held in those opinions, which this author refers to as *Jensen* I and *Jensen* II.

6. The following is an in depth analysis of the entire body of writing by the Supreme Court of Texas concerning *Jensen* reimbursement.

7. *Jensen* Reimbursement.

a. *Jensen I.*

Jensen v. Jensen, 26 Tex. Sup. Ct. J. 480 (July 6, 1983) (opinion withdrawn), deals with the increase in value of a separate property corporation as do all subsequent *Jensen* opinions.

The court in *Jensen I* was faced with deciding whether characterization or reimbursement principles should be applied to the enhanced or increased value of a separate property closely held corporate asset. However, in *Jensen I*, the solution as presented could hardly be considered definitive and did not explicitly resort to either characterization or reimbursement. The court held:

> An increase in the shares of stock, though separate property in origin, should belong to the community. We are not to be misunderstood as characterizing the stock as community property. Mr. Jensen's stock is and remains his separate property. However, *the enhanced value of the stock, which results from the time, toil, and effort of the spouse belongs to the community estate*. We intentionally avoid the use of the term "characterization." Moreover, in *Vallone*, while we talked of "reimbursement" we did so only as a method of compensating the community. (Emphasis added).

Jensen I says the increased value "belongs" to the community if it results from time, toil and efforts of the spouses. But the majority did not define exactly what "belongs" meant; the majority neither named or explained what they had created.

In addition to the lack of a name, the opinion presented other difficulties especially with respect to presumptions and burdens of proof. If the increased value is tantamount to a right of reimbursement, then the burden of proof is upon the spouse claiming the right of reimbursement to establish that the community has not been adequately compensated. However, if the increased value presents a question of characterization, the burden is on the spouse owning the separate property corporation to prove by clear and convincing evidence that it is separate property by showing that something other than the mere efforts of the spouse caused the increase and other similar facts.

JUSTICE WALLACE's dissent in *Jensen I* recognized the problems inherent in the circumstances of the *Jensen* case and set forth a solution based on reimbursement.

b. *Jensen II.*

Jensen v. Jensen, 27 Tex. Sup. Ct. J. 68 (November 9, 1983) (opinion withdrawn), was issued upon rehearing. The *Jensen II* opinion established that the court had not abandoned the inception of title rule as *Jensen I* seemed to indicate and characterized the stock of the closely held corporation involved in *Jensen* as separate property. However, the court recognized the community was entitled to some benefit by reason of the time, toil and effort expended by the husband which resulted in the increase in the value of the stock if he had not been adequately compensated.

The opinion changed from one of characterization (under the guise of the term "belongs") to one of reimbursement. There was a dispute, however, in the formula for reimbursement.

The majority, written by JUSTICE WALLACE, understandably relied upon the reasoning that JUSTICE WALLACE set forth in his dissenting opinion in *Jensen I*. The court held that the case now requires:

> . . . adoption of the rule that the community will be reimbursed for the value of the time and effort expended by either or both spouses to enhance the separate estate of either less the remuneration received for that time and effort in the forms of salary, bonus, dividends and other fringe benefits, those items being community property when received. *The enhanced value of the separate stock is one of the factors to be considered by the fact finder in determining the value of the community time and effort expended.* (Emphasis added).

Thus, the court found that the stock remained the separate property of the husband which had been acquired prior to marriage and was subject only to reimbursement claims of Mrs. Jensen if they could be proven. However, the court in *Jensen II* found that Mrs. Jensen had failed to meet her burden with regard to sustaining any reimbursement in light of the fact that the trial court found that Mr. Jensen had been adequately and reasonably compensated for the time and effort he expended in enhancing the value of the separate property stock. This holding resulted in reversal of the Court of Appeals opinion and an affirmance of the trial court's judgment. The Court adopted the reimbursement rule with regard to the increase in value of stock in a closely held corporation and in doing so noted that the adoption of such rule will obviate the need for the trial court to undertake the onerous and impossible burden that would be placed on it under the community ownership theory of attempting to determine just what factors actually contributed to the increase in the value of the stock and in what proportion.

c. *Jensen III.*

Jensen v. Jensen, 665 S.W.2d 107 (Tex. 1984) (as found below), was rendered on February 27, 1984, resulting in a withdrawal of the November 9, 1983, *Jensen II* opinion. The *Jensen III* opinion was also written by JUSTICE WALLACE. At first blush, the *Jensen III* opinion appears to be in keeping with the *Jensen II* opinion except for the fact that *Jensen III* remands the case to the trial court for the purpose of determining the amount of reimbursement, if any, due to the community as the result of the time, toil and talent expended by Mr. Jensen toward enhancement of the stock in the closely held corporation.

In addition to the obvious distinguishing factor of remand, there are more subtle deletions and additions which can be gleaned from the opinion only under the closest scrutiny.

But for the remand portion of the opinion, *Jensen III* is identical to the opinion in *Jensen II* until one reaches the ninth paragraph, which begins, "A consideration of the writings. . . ."

That paragraph ends by deleting a sentence found in *Jensen II*:

> [the] enhanced value of the separate stock is one of the factors to be considered by the fact finder in determining the value of the community time and effort expended. *Jensen II* at 69, 70.

Following this deletion, the opinion continues as it did in *Jensen II* until the court discusses the findings of the trial court, most especially the expert testimony regarding the reasonable value of the time, toil, and effort, and determines that remand is proper. With this background, on to *Jensen III*.

JENSEN
v.
JENSEN

665 S.W.2d 107
(Tex. 1984)

WALLACE, JUSTICE.

This court's opinion and judgment of November 9, 1983, are withdrawn and the following opinion is substituted therefor.

Petitioner, Robert Lee Jensen, and Respondent, Burlene Parks Jensen, were divorced on May 21, 1980. The decree of divorce provided that 48,455 shares of stock in RLJ Printing Co., Inc., acquired by Mr. Jensen four months prior to marriage, together with any increase in value in such stock which occurred during marriage, were the separate property of Mr. Jensen, and denied Mrs. Jensen any interest in the stock or its increased value. The court of appeals reversed and remanded, holding that the community should be compensated for an enhancement in value of the stock because such appreciated value had been due primarily to the time, toil and effort of Mr. Jensen. 629 S.W.2d 222. We remand to the trial court for determination of the amount, if any, of reimbursement to the community.

On March 21, 1975, Mr. Jensen formed the RLJ Printing Company, Inc. (RLJ) and for $1.56 per share acquired 48,455 of the 100,000 shares outstanding. On May 16, 1975, RLJ acquired Newspaper Enterprises, Inc., in what the trial court found to be a "unique business opportunity." The Jensens were married on July 21, 1975, separated on June 3, 1979, and divorced on May 21, 1980. At all pertinent times, Mr. Jensen was the key man in the operation of RLJ, which was a holding company whose sole assets consisted of all of the stock of Newspaper Enterprises, Inc. Mr. Jensen's compensation from RLJ, consisting of salary, bonuses and dividends, was $64,065.97 in 1976, $95,426.00 in 1977, $106,143.00 in 1978 and $115,000.00 in 1979.

The record does not reflect that any evaluation of the RLJ stock was made as of the date of the marriage. At trial, the per share value of the stock was $13.48 according to Mr. Jensen's expert and $25.77 according to Mrs. Jensen's expert.

The findings of fact and conclusions of law made by the trial court are as follows:

FINDINGS OF FACT

1. The RLJ Printing Company, Inc. was created by Respondent before the marriage of the parties.

2. RLJ Printing Company, Inc. acquired the stock of Newspaper Enterprises, Inc., 64 days before the marriage of the parties in a unique business opportunity.

3. RLJ Printing Company, Inc. is not an alter ego of the Respondent.

4. RLJ Printing Company, Inc. was not created in fraud of the rights of the community estate.

5. The salary paid Respondent has been adequate and reasonable.

6. The dividends paid Respondent have been adequate and reasonable.

7. The bonuses paid Respondent have been adequate and reasonable.

8. Respondent was the key man in the operation of RLJ Printing Company, Inc.

9. The successful operations of RLJ Printing Company, Inc. were primarily due to the time, toil and effort of Respondent.

CONCLUSIONS OF LAW

1. The community was not the equitable owner of any shares of RLJ Printing Company, Inc.

2. The community was not entitled to receive the value of the appreciation in shares of RLJ Printing Company, Inc. that was due to the successful operations of the company.

3. The community was not entitled to receive the value of the appreciation in shares of RLJ Printing Company, Inc., that was due to the time, toil and effort of Respondent.

The point of first impression squarely before us is how to treat, upon divorce, corporate stock owned by a spouse before marriage but which has increased in value during marriage due, at least in part, to the time and effort of either or both spouses.

The community property states have adopted variations of either "reimbursement" or "community ownership" theories. Common to both theories is the general concept that the community should receive whatever remuneration is paid to a spouse for his or her time and effort because the time and effort of each spouse belongs to the community. Though sharing a common conceptual basis, the two theories diverge when it comes to the valuation of the community's claim against separately owned stock that has appreciated by virtue of a spouse's time and effort. The "reimbursement" theory provides that the stock, as it appreciates, remains the separate property of the owner spouse. Under this theory, the community is entitled to reimbursement for the reasonable value of the time and effort of both or either of the spouses which contributed to the increase in value of the stock. The "community ownership" theory, on the other hand, holds that any increase in the value of the stock as a result of the time and effort of the owner spouse becomes community property.

A consideration of the writings of various scholars in this field, the treatment of the issue by our sister community property states, and the constitutional, statutory and case law of Texas leads to the conclusion that the reimbursement theory more nearly affords justice to both the community and separate estates. This theory requires adoption of the rule that the community will be reimbursed for the value of time and effort expended by either or both spouses to enhance the separate estate of either, other than that reasonably necessary to manage and preserve the separate estate, less the remuneration received for that time and effort in the form of salary, bonus, dividends and other fringe benefits, those items being community property when received.

This rule is a reasonable means of assuring that the community will be fully reimbursed for the value of community assets, i.e., time and effort expended, while at the same time providing that the property interest of the separate estate is also protected and preserved. As a practical matter, this rule will obviate the need for the trial court to undertake the onerous and quite often impossible burden that would be placed on it under the community ownership theory of attempting to determine just what factors actually contributed to the increase in value of the stock and in what proportion. The reimbursement theory of compensation is also consistent with the laws of Texas as found in the Texas Constitution, statutes and Supreme Court opinions set out below.

The Texas Constitution, Art. XVI, § 15, provides that property owned by a spouse before marriage remains the separate property of that spouse during marriage. In *Welder v. Lambert*, 91 Tex.

510, 44 S.W. 281 (1898), this Court decided that all property held by either a husband or a wife before marriage remains the separate property of such spouse and the status of the property is to be determined by the origin of the title to the property, and not by the acquisition of the final title. *Ibid.* This Court has consistently adhered to the rule expressed in *Welder*. *Dakan v. Dakan*, 125 Tex. 305, 83 S.W.2d 620, 624 (1935); *Creamer v. Briscoe*, 101 Tex. 490, 109 S.W. 911 (1908); *Peterson v. Peterson*, 595 S.W.2d 889 (Tex. Civ. App.—Austin 1980, writ ref'd n.r.e.); *Henry v. Reinle*, 245 S.W.2d 743, 744 (Tex. Civ. App.—Waco 1952, writ ref'd n.r.e.). The shares of RLJ stock thus remain the separate property of Mr. Jensen, subject only to the right of reimbursement, if any, proven by Mrs. Jensen.

The trial court found that Mr. Jensen was adequately and reasonably compensated for his time and effort expended in enhancing the value of the RLJ shares. This finding, if sustained, precludes Mrs. Jensen's right to reimbursement because that compensation was community property.

The only evidence offered at trial to establish the reasonableness of Mr. Jensen's compensation was the testimony of Mr. T. Wesley Hickman. Mr. Hickman was an expert in the field of corporate evaluation. It was his opinion that Mr. Jensen was reasonably compensated, but he based that opinion "primarily upon Mr. Jensen's percentage of the stock ownership." He further stated that without the stock ownership he seriously doubted that Mr. Jensen would have stayed with RLJ. His opinion as to reasonable compensation was primarily based upon Mr. Jensen's stock ownership and not upon the salary, bonuses and dividends received by the community due to the time, toil and effort of Mr. Jensen. Therefore the trial court's finding that Mr. Jensen's compensation was reasonable is without adequate support. Without that finding of fact there is no basis for the trial court's finding that "the community was not entitled to receive the value of the appreciation in shares of RLJ Printing Company, Inc. that was due to the time, toil and effort of respondent."

Upon retrial of this case the burden of proving a charge upon the shares of RLJ owned by Mr. Jensen will be upon the claimant, Mrs. Jensen. *Welder, supra*; *Burton v. Bell*, 380 S.W.2d 561 (Tex. 1964). The right to reimbursement is only for the value of the time, toil and effort expended to enhance the separate estate other than that reasonably necessary to manage and preserve the separate estate, for which the community did not receive adequate compensation. *Vallone v. Vallone*, 644 S.W.2d 455, 459 (Tex. 1982). However, if the right to reimbursement is proved, a lien shall not attach to Mr. Jensen's separate property shares. Rather, a money judgment may be awarded. *Burton v. Bell, supra.*

It has long been the rule of this court to remand to the trial court rather than to render judgment when the ends of justice will be better served thereby. Such remanding has often been ordered to supply additional testimony or to amend pleadings. *Karl & Kelly Company v. McLerran*, 646 S.W.2d 174 (Tex. 1983).

Therefore, pursuant to TEX. R. CIV. P. 505, we remand this cause to the trial court for the limited purpose of determining the amount of reimbursement, if any, due to the community as a result of the time, toil and talent expended by Mr. Jensen toward enhancement of the stock of RLJ. From the value of the time, toil and talent expended is to be subtracted the compensation paid to Mr. Jensen for such time, toil and talent in the form of salary, bonuses, dividends and other fringe benefits. Any remainder is the reimbursement due the community. This reimbursement, if any, shall be distributed by the trial court in addition to the property division heretofore made to the parties.

Concurring opinion by ROBERTSON, J.

ROBERTSON, JUSTICE concurring

I concur in the result reached by the majority. This Court in *Vallone v. Vallone*, 644 S.W.2d 455 (Tex. 1968), did not remand that cause to the trial court on the basis of Mrs. Vallone's failure to plead the affirmative relief of reimbursement. 644 S.W.2d at 458. Although Mrs. Jensen, like Mrs. Vallone, did not plead reimbursement this Court has remanded the cause of action in the interest of justice. The majority's opinion offers no explanation for the different disposition.

Until *Vallone*, Texas courts had traditionally followed a general rule of construing divorce pleadings liberally. *Cohen v. Cohen,* 194 S.W.2d 273, 275 (Tex. Civ. App.—Austin 1946, no writ). The majority opinion in *Vallone* appeared to mark the beginning of a shift to a policy requiring specific pleadings in family law matters. 644 S.W.2d at 466. However, the rise of the requirement of specific pleadings was short lived. The majority opinion, handed down thirteen months later, announces a return to a broad construction of divorce pleadings. Although a member of the majority in *Vallone*, I am of the opinion that this Court's return to a more liberal policy for construing divorce pleadings will provide trial judges with the freedom needed to reach just decisions in complex and sensitive family law actions.

Notes, Comments & Questions

1. Set out the formula for reimbursement for time, toil, talent, and effort.

2. How does one go about proving the factor of reasonable compensation?

3. What was wrong with the proof in *Jensen* regarding reasonable compensation?

4. Consider JUSTICE ROBERTSON's concurring opinion. As a litigator in a family law case, would you rely upon the more liberal policy of construing divorce pleadings as mentioned in the *Jensen* concurring opinion?

5. If the separate property corporation does not appreciate and the owning spouse worked day and night for little or no compensation, would there be a reimbursement claim?

6. As you read the next case, think about the presentation of proof for a reimbursement claim based upon time, toil, talent, and effort.

TRAWICK
v.
TRAWICK

671 S.W.2d 105
(Tex. App.—El Paso 1984, no writ)

STEPHEN F. PRESLAR, CHIEF JUSTICE.

This is an appeal from a judgment non obstante veredicto and from a directed verdict granted to the defendants below. Appellant sought a declaratory judgment awarding her an interest in the increased value of stock in a closely held corporation which was the separate property of her deceased husband, Stewart Trawick. She also asserted a community claim to other assets which defendant-executrix inventoried as separate property of the deceased. The court directed a verdict in favor of the separate estate with regard to the latter property. The issue of interest in the stock was submitted to the jury, which returned findings that the deceased had been undercompensated for his efforts in increasing the value of the stock and that the fifty-five percent of the increase in value was attributable to his efforts. Appellees' motion for judgment non obstante veredicto was granted and Appellant was deprived of any interest in the stock's value. We affirm in part and reverse and remand in part.

Sabine Machinery Company was founded by the deceased in 1968. It began operating as a corporation on January 1, 1976. Appellant and deceased married on November 12, 1976, and remained married until his death on October 26, 1980. At the time of his death, Stewart Trawick owned 750,000 shares of stock (three-fourths of all issued stock) in the corporation. Throughout the period in question, he was the president and chief operations officer of the business. He devoted his full business life to the corporation, was its actual day-to-day leader and was primarily responsible for its profit and growth. The parties stipulated that during the marriage the value of the corporation increased by $505,901.30.

Expert testimony from a certified public accountant indicated that just over one-half of the increase in value was solely attributable to Stewart Trawick's efforts. Consistent with the expert testimony and other direct evidence of his efforts, the jury found that fifty-five percent of the increase was the result of his work. When Stewart died, his will left none of the stock to the Appellant. . . .

In Ground of Error No. One, Appellant contends that the court erred in depriving her of an interest in the increased value of the corporate stock by granting judgment non obstante veredicto. The case was tried in January, 1982, prior to the three Supreme Court opinions in *Jensen v. Jensen*, 26 Tex. Sup. Ct. J. 480 (July 9, 1983), 27 Tex. Sup. Ct. J. 68 (November 9, 1983); 665 S.W.2d 107 (1984). At the time the case was tried, it was clear that one spouse could impose some form of community interest on the increased value of the other spouse's separate property where the increase was due to a manipulation of what would have been a reasonable flow of community income derived from the separate property. It was unclear what characterization should be attached to that interest and hence, the proper allocation of burden of pleading and proof was still in doubt. *See*: *Jensen I and Vallone v. Vallone*, 644 S.W.2d 455 (Tex. 1982). Appellant's pleadings were sufficient to encompass the community ownership theory as well as the reimbursement theory subsequently adopted in *Jensen II* and *Jensen III*. Under the community ownership theory, the ultimate burden of proof would have rested primarily on the advocate of the separate estate.

Under the present theory of recovery, the burden of establishing the various mathematical factors for reimbursement rests with the surviving spouse.

We do find that the *Jensen* opinions should be applied to the issues in this case. The fact that *Jensen* dealt with a distribution following divorce, as opposed to death, enhances the application of that case's theory of recovery here because some considerations which arise in the divorce context are not present and do not contribute further uncertainties to the values which are to be credited or debited to either estate (e.g. relative earning capacity).

While the reanalysis by the Supreme Court has helped to solidify the theory of recovery in this type of situation, we are still without a simple mathematical formula for resolution of this or any other such case. The facts of this case clearly pinpoint the factors which remain in shadow. *Jensen III* states:

> [T]he community will be reimbursed for the value of time and effort expended by either or both spouses to enhance the separate estate of either, other than that reasonably necessary to manage and preserve the separate estate, less the remuneration received for that time and effort in the form of salary, bonus, dividends and other fringe benefits, those items being community property when received.

In such a situation, we are confronted with two primary factors—1) increase in the value of separate property attributable to community effort and 2) undercompensation of the community for that effort. Appellant's pre-*Jensen* pleadings, proof, special issues and jury findings supported both elements. Because that is the case and because of the state of legal uncertainty at the time of trial, the degree to which those elements were satisfied leads us to reverse and remand in the interest of justice under TEX. R. CIV. P. Rule 434, as opposed to following the course taken in *Duncan v. Cessna Aircraft Co.*, 665 S.W.2d 414 (1984).

The remaining difficulty arises from the fact that the undercompensation elements consist of two sub-factors—1) what the reasonable value of the effort was and 2) what actual remuneration was received. A simple formulation of the reimbursement could be shown as:

  Attributable increase in value
- Actual remuneration

= Reimbursement

This would be neither realistic nor equitable. Such a formula would automatically equate the sum total of the increased value with the "value of time and effort expended by the community." Under *Jensen III* the enhanced value of the stock is one of the factors to be considered by the fact finder in determining the value of the community time and effort. Consequently, the appropriate computation is to determine the discrepancy between the reasonable value of the effort expended and the actual compensation received and then look to the enhanced value of the separate estate to satisfy that discrepancy. This approach was followed in *Faulkner v. Faulkner*, 582 S.W.2d 639 (Tex. Civ. App.—Dallas 1979, no writ). It is consistent with *Jensen III* and we find it most equitable in terms of the interests of the community and the separate estate of the deceased.

The pleadings and evidence addressed all factors comprising the more detailed formula. The stipulated enhancement in value was $505,901.30. The deceased owned seventy-five percent of the stock. The jury found, consistent with the lay and expert testimony, that fifty-five percent of the enhanced value was attributable to Stewart Trawick's work. Consequently, $208,684.29 was available to satisfy any claim by the community for undercompensation.

In given cases, the total enhanced value may equal or exceed the demonstrated right to reimbursement. We are not yet confronted with a question of right to reimbursement exceeding the enhanced value of a specific separate property asset and will not attempt to suggest the outcome of such a conflict.

Here, Stewart Trawick received a salary of $2,000.00 per month. The marital state existed during forty-eight months, resulting in $96,000.00 in salary. The corporation paid $17,000.00 in life insurance premiums, proceeds from which went to Appellant. Club membership dues for Appellant and the deceased amounted to $5,432.66. The deceased had the use of a new automobile, with no specific value appearing in the record. Appellant received $5,000.00 in company death benefits.

For purposes of retrial guidance, contrary to Appellees' position, several items should not be included in the actual compensation figure. These include the $96,000.00 in rental income which Stewart Trawick received by renting his separate real property to the corporation during three years of the period in question. That income was community property not by virtue of his labor and efforts on behalf of the corporation, but as income from a distinct, non-labor separate asset. While it may present an estate question, it is not part of the problem before us. The salary, vehicle and expense account provided Appellant for her labor should also be excluded from the calculation. Absent a showing that her employment was an absolute sham, this compensation is attributable to her toil and effort and not that of her deceased husband. In addition, the deceased's $8,000.00 expense account should not be included absent proof that his draws upon the account exceeded actual expenditures in his day-to-day conduct of company affairs. Absent such a showing this amounts to reimbursement of his out-of-pocket expenses and not compensation for his labor.

From the present record, the amount of actual remuneration which flowed to the community estate, through various forms of compensation, totaled $126,432.66 plus the value of an automobile during the forty-eight month period from November, 1976, through October, 1980.

The final factor to be determined in order to compute the degree of undercompensation, and hence reimbursement due, is the reasonable value of Trawick's labor and effort during that forty-eight month period. Some evidence was offered on this issue. No specific jury finding was sought or obtained. We see no justification for Appellees' theory that the judgment be affirmed on the basis of assumed findings of fact on this issue. As previously stated, we believe that this is a situation ripe for remand under Rule 434. Even in *Duncan*, *supra*, the Supreme Court stated that remand is appropriate where the party seeking such did present evidence that might allow relief under the proper theory on retrial. In *Duncan*, the defendant's offer of such proof was rejected by the court and no bill of exception was presented. This is not the case here.

The evidence and jury finding reflect that over $208,000.00 in increased value during a four-year period was solely attributable to the efforts of this one individual. This is clearly favorable to the Appellant. Appellees, on the other hand, offered evidence that Stewart Trawick's salary and fringe benefits were in appropriate proportion to those of the other corporate officers and employees. On its face, this evidence favors the Appellees, but perhaps it merely demonstrates an across-the-board undercompensation for labor and "excessive" retainage of value in the corporate entity. Finally, we note that expert witness James Daffron, C.P.A., testified that he had performed accounting and tax evaluations on other businesses in the Dallas area engaged in the same type of work, with similar sales levels, profit levels and corporate structure. He offered his opinion that officers in positions equivalent to that of Stewart Trawick, during the same time period, were receiving compensation from $60,000.00 to $100,000.00 per year, in addition to fringe benefits. His testimony was highly favorable to Appellant. The compensation range which he presented would support findings of remuneration deficit ranging from $144,000.00 to $304,000.00. Some portion of that range, of course, exceeds the well-established enhanced value of Stewart's estate. As previously stated, we are not yet confronted with a claim, jury finding or award exceeding the attributable enhanced value of the specific separate asset, and that is an issue unresolved by *Jensen III*. That opinion stated that the injured spouse does not gain a lien upon the specific asset of the deceased but rather a money judgment charged against the deceased's estate. Arguments can be made both for and against the use of the enhanced value figure as a ceiling of recovery. Upon retrial, both parties should proceed in a manner mindful of that issue. Point of Error No. One is sustained.

* * *

Point of Error No. Two relates to $69,965.00 in cash classified as the decedent's separate property. The party with the burden of tracing is aided by the rule that one dollar has the same value as another. Under the law, there can be no commingling by the mixing of dollars where the number owned by each claimant is known. *In the Matter of the Marriage of Tandy*, 532 S.W.2d 714, 717 (Tex. Civ. App.—Amarillo 1976, no writ); *Farrow v. Farrow*, 238 S.W.2d 255 (Tex. Civ. App.—Austin 1951, no writ). Here, the evidence shows that approximately nine months before the marriage, $21,765.00 was held in a safe deposit box belonging to Stewart Trawick. The day after Stewart died, the cash box held $76,465.00. Stewart's accountant testified that $21,765.00 was present in the same denominations as he counted prior to the marriage. J.W. Mitchell, Jr., testified he knew of a loan made by Sabine Machinery Company, prior to the establishment of the community estate, to a Mr. Beasley. Mitchell testified that he knew the repayments were charged against debt repayments that Stewart received from Sabine Machinery. Mitchell testified that he told Stewart to put the repayments in the safe deposit box. Cash envelopes totaling $19,700.00 were found when the box was opened after Stewart's death. Another $3,000.00 was shown to be debt repayment from Sabine to Stewart. The $500.00 came from accounts receivable that Stewart kept as his separate property when he incorporated the business. That $500.00 was paid the same day the note payment check was cashed. The dates on envelopes containing the last $25,000.00 corresponded to dates on which checks issued by Sabine Machinery to Stewart had been cashed. The payments were for a loan Stewart had made prior to marriage. The cash was clearly traced and the trial court properly ordered a directed verdict. Point of Error No. Two is overruled.

* * *

That portion of the trial court's judgment directing a verdict in favor of the Appellees with regard to the assets which are the subject of Points of Error Nos. Two through Five is affirmed. The judgment non obstante veredicto in favor of the Appellees with regard to reimbursement of the community estate for undercompensation from the Sabine Machinery Corporation is reversed and the cause remanded for retrial of that issue.

Questions

1. By what means did counsel diminish husband's contribution to the increase in value of the Sabine Machinery Co.?

2. What was the strategy in diminishing husband's contribution?

3. How was reasonable remuneration established?

4. Which payments to husband could be used as part of the actual remuneration? Why?

5. Which payments to husband could not be used as part of the actual remuneration? Why not?

6. Does the court establish a ceiling for reimbursement?

7. Should there be a ceiling for reimbursement?

H. Beginning Balance Reimbursement

Assuming that the claims for reimbursement listed in TEX. FAM. CODE § 3.408 are not exclusive, it thus appears that beginning balance reimbursement is not precluded by the current economic contribution/reimbursement statutes.

Oftentimes, a spouse will enter into a marriage with a substantial separate estate which will provide the base for the later economic success of the community. If that monied spouse cannot specifically trace those funds, reimbursement may offer some relief. The case of *Schmidt v. Huppman*, 11 S.W.2d 175 (1889) was mentioned in Chapter 2, page 141, as a note case in the discussion regarding the characterization of business inventories. As that discussion concluded, more often than not, a reimbursement claim will offer relief where a separate property inventory cannot be traced. In *Schmidt v. Huppman*, husband was able to recover the value of his separate property inventory upon which the community built a business, even though the inventory could not be traced in specie. This theory of beginning balance reimbursement has been applied beyond business inventories, as the next case evidences.

HORLOCK
v.
HORLOCK

533 S.W.2d 52
(Tex. Civ. App.—Houston [14th Dist.] 1975, writ dism'd w.o.j.)

COULSON, JUSTICE.

This is an appeal from a final decree of divorce. The principal issue is whether the court's property division is just and right.

Dorothy Gray Horlock, appellant, thirty-five years of age, and Roy M. Horlock, appellee, forty-one years of age, were married on November 22, 1966. Dorothy Gray Horlock had not been previously married. Roy M. Horlock was married to Margaret Boudreaux Horlock until her death on August 1, 1965. She bequeathed her entire estate to Roy M. Horlock. Three daughters were born to Margaret Boudreaux Horlock and Roy M. Horlock. One child, a son, was born to Dorothy Gray Horlock and Roy M. Horlock.

The parties separated on or about July 1, 1973. A final decree granting the appellant a divorce was entered on January 6, 1975. Custody of the son was granted to appellant. Appellee was ordered to pay child support of $750 per month, to pay for his son's medical hospitalization, to pay his son's medical and dental expenses in excess of $100 per year, to pay all of his son's orthodontic expenses, and to pay his son's private school tuition. Appellee was granted visitation rights with his son at specified times.

The divorce decree ordered a division of the Horlocks' estate and established responsibility for the discharge of debts and liabilities. The appellant's attorney was awarded a judgment against appellee of $15,000 for legal services rendered on appellant's behalf. All costs were adjudged against the appellee. Dorothy Horlock has brought this appeal.

Appellant's points of error concern four major issues. First, the appellant contends that certain gifts made during their marriage by Roy M. Horlock to his three daughters constituted fraud on the appellant's community estate. Second, the appellant challenges the trial court's determination that the separate estate of the appellee was entitled to reimbursement from the community estate for the proceeds from the sale of property owned by appellee prior to the date of the marriage (these proceeds having become totally commingled with the community estate of the parties). Third, the appellant contends that the trial court abused its discretion in the division of the parties' property because the division was not fair and equitable. Fourth, the appellant contends that the trial court erroneously determined that certain shares of capital stock in Collegiate Services Corporation were a part of the community property of the parties; her argument being that the stock was his separate property.

THE GIFTS TO THE CHILDREN

During the marriage, the appellee made gifts to his mother, who was blind and confined to a nursing home. He also made gifts to his three daughters and to his son. On appeal, the appellant has challenged only the gifts to the three daughters as being a fraud on her rights. The gifts ranged in value from $3,000 to $6,000 per year plus an amount equal to the lifetime federal gift tax exclusion for both the appellee and the appellant. The total value of the gifts to the three daughters was $131,517.

Appellant's contention that community property was used in making the gifts is not challenged by appellee. He did not tell the appellant that he was making the gifts to his three daughters, and admitted that the appellant would have strenuously protested had she known of the gifts. In 1972, appellee filed a gift tax return on which the appellant's name appeared. A third party signed the appellant's name to the return at the request of the appellee, who acted without the knowledge and consent of the appellant. The appellee and his accountant testified that the resulting income tax advantage generated by the gifts to his children was the motivation for the gifts. The appellee testified that in making the gifts he intended no deprivation of the appellant's rights. The trial court found that the appellee had not perpetrated an actual or constructive fraud upon the appellant by making the gifts to his three daughters.

To sustain a cause of action for actual fraud, the appellant has the burden of showing that the gifts were made with the primary purpose of depriving her from having the use and enjoyment of the assets comprising the gifts. Actual fraud involves dishonesty of purpose or intent to deceive. *Land v. Marshall*, 426 S.W.2d 841, 846 (Tex. Sup. 1968); *Archer v. Griffith*, 390 S.W.2d 735, 740 (Tex. Sup. 1964). Here, the appellant has failed to sustain her burden of showing an actual fraud. The evidence in support of appellant's position is conflicting. The appellee admitted that he made the gifts knowing that the appellant would not approve of them, however, there is ample evidence that the appellee's intention in making the gifts was to benefit both the community estate and the parties' individual estates upon the death of each or both of them.

The trial court found that at the time of the marriage, appellee owned property having a net value of approximately $1,000,000. Most, if not all of the community estate, would be classified as the special community of the husband under Texas Family Code Annotated, § 5.22. There may be a fraud on a spouse's community interest where the special community property of the other spouse is involved. However, the fact that it is a spouse's special community is important in considering the rights of disposition which accrue to that spouse given the special nature of that community property. It is not necessary that one spouse approve or agree with the dispositions made by the other spouse of that other spouse's special community property. *Murphy v. Metropolitan Life Insurance Company*, 498 S.W.2d 278 (Tex. Civ. App.—Houston (14th Dist.) 1973, writ ref'd n.r.e.). The single fact that the appellee intentionally prevented the appellant from finding out about the gifts which he made to his daughters does not constitute actual fraud.

In the instance of constructive fraud, a gift of one spouse's share of the community property will be set aside where the gift is unfair to that spouse. It was the appellee's burden to prove that the gifts were fair. *Murphy v. Metropolitan Life Ins. Co., supra*; *Givens v. Girard Life Insurance Company of America*, 480 S.W.2d 421 (Tex. Civ. App.—Dallas 1972, writ ref'd n.r.e.).

In considering the wife's claim of a constructive fraud against her share of the community property the courts have considered three primary factors. Those factors are the size of the gift in relation to the total size of the community estate, the adequacy of the estate remaining to support the wife in spite of the gift, and the relationship of the donor to the donee. *Givens v. Girard Life Insurance Company of America, supra*; *Hartman v. Crain*, 398 S.W.2d 387 (Tex. Civ. App.—Houston 1966, no writ).

Significant to the disposition of the issue of constructive fraud in this case are the findings of fact filed by the trial court. Among other things, the trial court found that Roy M. Horlock had three daughters by his prior marriage. At the time of the parties' separation the girls' ages were fourteen, seventeen and eighteen. The daughters inherited nothing from their deceased mother, whose will named Roy M. Horlock as her sole beneficiary of her substantial estate. The trial court further found that during their marriage, Dorothy Gray Horlock and Roy M. Horlock quarreled over Dorothy Gray Horlock's demands that Roy M. Horlock's daughters not share with her in his properties. She also demanded an interest in the properties owned by Roy M. Horlock prior to the marriage.

Roy M. Horlock's daughters are the natural objects of his bounty. The total value of the gifts to the daughters was $131,517. The trial court found as a fact that the appellee at the time of the marriage owned properties having a net value of approximately $1,000,000, and that at the time of the dissolution of the marriage appellant and appellee owned properties having a net value of approximately $3,000,000 to $4,000,000. It is evident that throughout the marriage the value of the estate was in excess of $1,000,000. Assuming the lower value of $1,000,000, the appellee's gifts to his three daughters constituted no more than 13.1517% of the total estate. The remaining minimum figure of approximately $870,000 in community funds would be sufficient to provide for the needs of the wife. The foregoing facts and considerations coupled with the tax advantages sought by the appellee removes the gifts by the appellee to his daughters from the pale of a constructive fraud upon the wife's portion of the community estate.

The appellant's first four points of error are overruled.

THE RIGHT OF THE HUSBAND'S SEPARATE ESTATE TO REIMBURSEMENT FROM THE COMMUNITY ESTATE

Appellant's points of error eight through eleven challenge the trial court's conclusions of law that the appellee is entitled to reimbursement for the use of his separate funds to enhance, improve, and increase the value of the community estate. The trial court concluded as a matter of law that regardless of appellee's equitable right of reimbursement, the property division made in the judgment is fair and equitable.

As a part of the findings of fact, the trial court found that at the time of the marriage the appellee owned properties having a net value of approximately $1,000,000. Subsequent to the marriage the appellee sold separate property real estate for approximately $700,000. The appellee also received payments in excess of $200,000 under certain contracts which had been entered into prior to the marriage and which the appellee had already performed. The total value of the separate property sold and collected subsequent to the marriage was $921,000. The appellee, in his role as manager of his separate estate and the parties' community estate, placed the proceeds of these sales into an investment account at the First City National Bank of Houston. The account existed prior to marriage and had been in use by the appellee, who was engaged in the real estate business. He had become established as a successful businessman in various phases of the building and apartment businesses, including construction, ownership and management.

The appellee commingled the proceeds of the sale of his separate property with the community property of the parties. The appellee admitted at trial and admits in his brief that the proceeds of the sale of his separate property have become completely commingled with the community estate. Appellee made no attempt at trial to trace the use of the proceeds of the sale of his separate property into any other transactions. The trial court determined in its conclusions of law that the appellee was entitled to reimbursement by reason of using his separate funds to enhance, improve and increase the value of the community estate. The trial court did not determine the amount of such reimbursement; however, the court did find as a fact that during the marriage specific properties owned by the appellee prior to the marriage were sold for a total sum in excess of $900,000, which was placed in the investment account at First City National Bank of Houston and thereafter used for the enhancement of the community estate.

The appellant requested additional findings of fact to compel the trial judge to specifically determine the amount of reimbursement to which the appellee's separate estate was entitled. However, the trial judge refused to reply to that request.

It is the appellant's position that the appellee is not entitled to reimbursement to his separate estate. The appellant further contends that, although the appellee may have utilized the proceeds of the sale of his separate property for the benefit of the community estate, the appellee allowed his separate property to become completely commingled with the community estate to a point at which segregation of the two estates is impossible. Appellant argues that the application of the doctrine of reimbursement is precluded by Texas Family Code Annotated § 5.02, which states:

"Property possessed by either spouse during or on dissolution of marriage is presumed to be community property."

The appellant contends that neither of the two recognized methods of escaping the effect of the presumption of community property, tracing or reimbursement, is applicable in this case. Here, tracing is impossible. Appellant contends that the appellee is also unable to rely upon reimbursement because the appellee cannot show that the specific use to which the proceeds of the sales of his separate property were put benefited the community. Appellant argues that the appellee cannot rely on the gross assumption that the $921,000 was used to benefit the community, in the absence of some direct evidence of how those funds were spent. It is the appellant's position that at the dissolution of a marriage, a spouse must trace and clearly identify separate property in order to discharge the burden of satisfactorily proving that such property is not community property. She relies on *Tarver v. Tarver*, 394 S.W.2d 780 (Tex. Sup. 1965); *Moor v. Moor*, 24 Tex. Civ. App. 150, 255 S.W. 231 (San Antonio 1900, no writ); and *Ervin v. Ervin*, 60 Tex. Civ. App. 537, 128 S.W. 1139 (1910, writ dism'd).

The cases cited by the appellant are not directly in point. In *Tarver* the parties challenging the trial court's determination that certain properties were community in nature proceeded under the theory of constructive trust and sought to be awarded a one-half interest in the properties themselves. The issue of reimbursement was not raised. The challenging parties were required to trace those funds held prior to the marriage into specific assets held at the dissolution of marriage in order to discharge their burden.

Moor is most frequently cited for the proposition that reimbursement will not be allowed when the husband commingles his separate estate with the community estate. *Moor* is discussed at length in a commentary by Professor Huie. Huie, *Commentary on the Community Property Laws of Texas*, 13 TEX. REV. CIV. STAT. ANN. 25 (1960). *See also Comment*, 36 TEXAS LAW REVIEW 196 (1955); 6 ST. MARY'S LAW JOURNAL 234 (1974). In *Moor* the husband first sought to trace the assets from his separate estate to that which he had commingled with the community estate. His claim for reimbursement was apparently an alternative claim. In that context, the husband attempted to pass the entire loss of a business venture onto the community estate rather than accepting a proportionate share of the loss on his separate estate. It should be observed that the remedy of reimbursement is equitable in nature. Considering the situation presented in *Moor*, the court equitably refused to sustain the husband's contentions.

Ervin is an example of a large number of cases wherein the husband failed to raise the claim of reimbursement. The arguments of appellant on the issue of reimbursement are not persuasive. It should be kept in mind that in seeking reimbursement the appellee does not ask to share in the actual assets which have been determined to be community property. Rather, the appellee seeks to recover an amount substantially equal to the amount of capital which he brought into the marriage as separate property and which he utilized for the benefit of the community estate.

Since the latter 1940's, courts in Texas have acted favorable toward allowing reimbursement and in allowing the tracing of separate funds. For example, in *Hartman v. Hartman*, 253 S.W.2d 480 (Tex. Civ. App. 1952, no writ), the husband was awarded reimbursement of $30,000 as compensation for the investment of his separate estate in the community business. The husband had entered into the marriage owning separate property valued at $37,794. He was engaged in the construction business and operated out of a single investment banking account. The evidence in *Hartman* showed that during the course of the marriage more than $200,000 passed through the bank account. The facts did not lend themselves to tracing, but the trial court did award reimbursement. *See also Schmidt v. Huppmann*, 73 Tex. 112, 11 S.W. 175 (1889); *Farrow v. Farrow*, 238 S.W.2d 255 (Tex. Civ. App.—Austin 1951, no writ). For examples of a more liberal treatment of the tracing doctrine, *see Blumer v. Kallison*, 297 S.W.2d 898 (Tex. Civ. App.—San Antonio 1956, writ ref'd n.r.e.); *Barrington v. Barrington*, 290 S.W.2d 297 (Tex. Civ. App.—Texarkana 1956, no writ). Another development in this area is exemplified by the case of *Sibley v. Sibley*, 286 S.W.2d 657 (Tex. Civ. App.—Dallas 1955, writ dism'd). *Sibley* stands for the proposition that where a bank account contains both community and separate monies, it is presumed that community monies are drawn out first.

Under these cases, the trial court was justified in awarding the husband a separate estate reimbursement. The husband's separate estate served as a strong foundation upon which the community's wealth was built. Throughout the marriage the husband utilized that foundation to provide for the appellant and to establish the $3,000,000 to $4,000,000 estate. Equity is well served by reimbursing him for that initial investment. In this case there is no question of fraud against the wife's estate, against the community, or against any third party creditor. One of these factors could shift the equities involved and preclude the appellee's recovery of reimbursement.

As a part of the appellant's argument on the question of reimbursement, complaint is made of the trial court's failure to make additional findings of fact and conclusions of law relative to the appellee's claim for reimbursement. The trial judge's reticence to make such findings served only to cloud the issue in the case on appeal. In view of the position which we take on the issue of reimbursement, the trial court's decision not to make additional findings of fact was harmless error. The trial court did not make specific findings as to each asset claimed as a source of reimbursement. Because no such findings were requested by the appellant, it is unnecessary for us to discuss the status of each of the assets claimed by the appellee as separate property.

THE DIVISION OF THE COMMUNITY ESTATE

Appellant's points of error 12 and 13 urge that the trial court's division of the community estate was so unfair and inequitable as to constitute an abuse of discretion.

The property division ordered by the court awarded to the appellant assets with a net value of $1,295,306. The appellee was awarded assets with a net value of $2,682,023. However, the record demonstrates that the husband by virtue of his investments in Collegiate Services Corporation, was under a contingent liability of roughly $2,000,000. Further, the court's property division allocated one-half of the Collegiate Service Corporation stock to the appellant but did not obligate the appellant to service the debt incident to the stock. The court found that the Collegiate Service Corporation stock did not have a market value, but that it had future potential. The effect of the judgment was to award the appellant the right to receive the benefits of any increase in value of the Collegiate Service Corporation stock without any obligation to service the debt coupled with such ownership.

The community estate's debt structure was examined in great detail during the trial of the case. Most of the community's assets served as security for outstanding debts. Some of the debts were free of personal liability. By the terms of the judgment the appellee was made responsible for the majority of the debt. Many debts were evidenced by promissory notes bearing short term maturity dates. In order for the appellee to successfully refinance the short term obligation and to service the long term indebtedness, it was necessary for him to have greater liquidity than the appellant. When considering the debt status of the community estate, it is clear that the unequal division of the community estate was necessary in the interest of preserving the community assets.

Such a consideration does not constitute an abuse of discretion. *Carle v. Carle*, 149 Tex. 469, 234 S.W.2d 1002 (1951); *Waggener v. Waggener*, 460 S.W.2d 251 (Tex. Civ. App.—Dallas 1970, no writ); *Dorfman v. Dorfman*, 457 S.W.2d 417 (Tex. Civ. App.—Texarkana 1970, no writ). The appellant's points 12 and 13 are overruled.

Appellant's points 14 and 15 involve the value of a washateria business awarded to the appellant which the appellee claimed to be community property but which the trial court determined to be the appellee's separate property. The appellant valued the washateria business at $100,000, five times its net income. The appellee valued the washateria at approximately $5,000. On appeal, the parties have reversed their positions. The appellee would prefer that the assets be valued at the higher level to decrease the difference between the appellee's and the appellant's share of the community estate. The appellant for the same reason seeks a value to be placed upon the washateria business at the lower figure of $5,000. It is admitted by the appellant that points 14 and 15 are of little importance in this appeal. We find points of error 14 and 15 are immaterial; they are overruled.

COLLEGIATE SERVICES CORPORATION STOCK

Prior to the marriage, the appellee owned 800 shares of Student Housing, Inc., a corporation engaged in providing off-campus housing for students at various colleges and universities. On February 6, 1969, Student Housing, Inc. merged with two other corporations to form Collegiate Services Corporation. As a result of that merger the appellee became the owner of 14,152 shares of Collegiate Services Corporation stock. A year after the merger, the parties acquired an additional 40 shares of stock in CSC.

At the time of the merger, the owners of Student Housing, Inc. contributed its assets and $200,000 in order to participate equally in the merger. The $200,000 was paid to Student Housing, Inc. to discharge certain obligations. This payment stabilized the debt structure of Student Housing, Inc. at the time of the merger. The CSC stock was issued to Mr. Horlock in exchange for his stock in Student Housing, Inc.

During the trial and on appeal the appellant attempted to demonstrate that the appellee's shares of CSC stock, presumed to be community property of the parties, were in fact the separate property of the appellee. The appellant further attempted to show that if the CSC stock was the appellee's separate property the community estate was entitled to a reimbursement of $100,000 for funds spent to maintain the appellee's interest in CSC. The trial court found that the appellee contributed separate and community funds of approximately $60,000 to maintain this investment prior to the merger of CSC and Student Housing, Inc. After the merger, the appellee made additional contributions of approximately $40,000 toward preserving the CSC investment. The court's division of the community property awarded one-half of the CSC stock to the appellant and one-half of the CSC stock to the appellee. However, it was ordered that only the appellee would be liable for the outstanding obligations accruing with the ownership of the CSC stock. In the event CSC calls upon its shareholders for additional contributions, the appellant may pass the cash call and thereby forfeit her stock in CSC to the appellee, or, the appellant may pay the cash call outright or upon terms specified in the judgment and retain her stock position in CSC.

The trial court made no specific findings as to the separate or community nature of the shares of CSC stock. However, the trial court in its conclusions of law enumerated those properties found to be the separate property of the appellee and did not include the CSC stock. From that conclusion of law it may be inferred that the trial court determined that the CSC stock was the community property of the parties. The appellant's position is that the CSC stock was the separate property of the appellee. Therefore, the appellant argues that the appellee owed the community estate a reimbursement of $100,000 for community funds spent to benefit the appellee's separate property, the CSC stock

The question presented is whether the appellant sustained her burden of overcoming the presumption that the CSC stock was the community property of the parties. There is no question that the original block of 14,152 shares of CSC stock was acquired by Mr. Horlock as a result of the merger of Student Housing, Inc. with the two other corporations. The shares of stock held by the appellee in Student Housing, Inc. were his separate property because he owned them prior to this marriage. Mutations and changes in the character of property do not affect the property's nature as separate or community, where it can be definitely traced and identified by clear and satisfactory proof. SPEER, MARITAL RIGHTS IN TEXAS § 389 (4th Edition) (1961).

The evidence clearly establishes that the 14,152 shares of CSC stock acquired as a result of the merger were a part of the appellee's separate property. The additional 40 shares of CSC stock acquired by the parties on May 31, 1970 was presumed to be community property rather than separate property of the appellee.

In the additional findings of fact, the trial court determined that separate and community funds in the approximate amount of $100,000 had been spent on the maintenance of the CSC investment. However, the trial court refused to make a determination of the amount of reimbursement due to the community estate by virtue of its contribution to the maintenance of the CSC investment. Because we find that, as a matter of law, the original 14,152 shares of CSC stock were the separate property of the appellee, the community estate is entitled to reimbursement from the separate estate of the appellee for that portion of the community estate expended on the maintenance of the CSC investment. It is the appellant's burden to establish the right of equitable reimbursement of the community estate from the separate estate of the appellee. The appellant is aided in meeting her burden by the presumption that assets purchased and money spent during marriage are community rather than separate property. *Hartman v. Hartman*, 253 S.W.2d 480 (Tex. Civ. App.—Austin 1952, no writ). The trial court's failure to determine that the 14,152 shares of CSC stock were a part of the separate estate of the appellee is error. Based upon the presumptions favoring the position of the appellant, the community estate is entitled to a reimbursement from the separate estate of the appellee in the sum of $100,000 expended during the period of the marriage. The $100,000 to be reimbursed to the community estate shall be divided $50,000 to the appellant and $50,000 to the appellee. Appellant's points of error number 5, 6 and 7 are sustained.

Texas Family Code § 3.63 provides that in a decree of divorce the court shall order a division of the parties' estate in a manner that the court deems just and right, having due regard for the rights of each party and any children of the marriage. The division of the property need not be equal if the circumstances will justify awarding more than one-half to one spouse. The court's power extends to separate as well as community property. A variety of factors may justify an unequal division. Here, the court could consider the fact that the husband owned assets with a net worth of over $1,000,000 at the time of the marriage and that the assets were utilized in developing the community estate.

The right of reimbursement is an equitable right. It may be considered by the trial court in the division of the properties of the parties. The generous provisions made for the support of the parties' son is an additional equitable consideration which may be considered in the division of the parties' properties. The debt structure of the assets of the parties and the necessity of the renegotiation of numerous short term debts by the husband, as well as the extensive contingent liability imposed upon the husband, are equities to be considered by the trial court in dividing the parties' properties. In exercising its equitable powers, the court may consider the fact that the parties' estate primarily consists of equitable interests in real property, much of which is unimproved, and the fact that the prevailing economic conditions constitute a threat to the community estate as an entirety. Upon reviewing the record in this case, we conclude that the court's property division is just and right.

The judgment of the trial court is modified to require the appellee to reimburse $100,000 to the community estate for advances used to maintain the CSC investment. Such reimbursement shall be paid $50,000 to the appellant and $50,000 to the appellee. In all other respects the judgment of the trial court is affirmed.

Notes, Comments & Questions

1. Once separate property is dissipated, can that exact property come back into the marital estate?

2. Identify the ways in which a court may deal with a reimbursement claim upon divorce.

3. Although not reimbursement issues, this case also delves into other issues that often arise in marital property cases—those of actual and constructive fraud.

   a. What are the requirements for a claim of actual fraud?

   b. What are the requirements for a case of constructive fraud?

4. Does the trial court's holding on actual fraud surprise you in any way?

5. It is often said that one must be careful for what one wishes as your wish may be granted. Does this adage apply in this case? (Hint—think washateria!)

I. Reimbursement for Improvements

In *Anderson v. Gilliland*, 684 S.W.2d 673 (Tex. 1985), the Texas Supreme Court settled a long standing dispute as to the proper measure of reimbursement for improvements made with the funds of one marital estate for the benefit of another marital estate. Prior to *Anderson v. Gilliland*, the views of the courts of appeal on the measure of improvement reimbursement varied. Three measures of reimbursement existed: (1) enhancement of value to the receiving estate or the cost of improvements, whichever is less; or, (2) enhancement alone, regardless of cost; or, (3) cost, regardless of enhancement. The Texas Supreme Court, in *Anderson*, held that "a claim for reimbursement for funds expended by an estate for improvements to another estate is to be measured by enhancement in value to the benefited estate. This rule is more likely to insure equitable treatment of both the contributing and benefited estates in most situations."

ANDERSON
v.
GILLILAND
684 S.W. 2d 673
(Tex. 1988)

WALLACE, JUSTICE.

This will probate suit presents the sole issue of what constitutes the measure of reimbursement.

Terri L. Anderson is the surviving daughter and devisee under the will of Lawrence Gilliland, deceased. Cleo Gilliland is the widow of Lawrence Gilliland and executrix of his estate.

At the date of the Gilliland's marriage, Mrs. Gilliland owned certain real property. During the marriage the community expended $20,237.89 to build a home on the property. At the time of Mr. Gilliland's death, this home had enhanced the separate property of Mrs. Gilliland by the sum of $54,000.00.

At trial Mrs. Anderson sought to have Mrs. Gilliland include one-half of the reimbursement due the community in the inventory of the estate of Lawrence Gilliland, because of the improvements the community made to the separate estate of Mrs. Gilliland. The trial court held that the proper measure of reimbursement was the enhanced value of Mrs. Gilliland's separate property. It ordered Mrs. Gilliland to include in the inventory an amount equal to one-half of the enhancement resulting from the improvements.

The trial court also found that approximately one-third of the expenditures for the home was from Mrs. Gilliland's separate funds. The court of appeals found that Mrs. Gilliland had not properly traced any separate funds into the home. 677 S.W.2d 105,appealing after remand624 S.W.2d 243. Mrs. Gilliland did not appeal that finding.

The court of appeals further held that the proper measure of reimbursement to an estate which has expended funds to erect improvements on another estate is the enhancement of value to the receiving estate or the cost of the improvements, whichever is less. The court of appeals rendered judgment finding the amount of reimbursement due the community was one-half of the $20,237.89 expended, less one-half of the outstanding mortgage of $10,154.00. The community monies expended in building the home were proceeds from the mortgage. We affirm the judgment of the court of appeals in part and reverse and render in part.

The various courts of appeals of Texas are not in agreement on the issue presented here. The Dallas Court of Appeals in this case acknowledged that its decision was contrary to that of the Fort Worth Court of Appeals in *Cook v. Cook*, 665 S.W.2d 161, (Tex. App.—Fort Worth 1983, writ ref'd n.r.e.). *Cook* follows *Harris v. Royal*, 446 S.W.2d 351 (Tex. Civ. App.—Waco 1969, writ ref'd n.r.e.). Both *Cook* and *Royal* held that enhancement alone, regardless of cost, is a proper measure of reimbursement in cases such as this.

Another view held by several courts is that the proper measure of reimbursement is enhancement or cost, whichever is less. *Hale v. Hale*, 557 S.W.2d 614, 615 (Tex. Civ. App.—Texarkana 1977, no writ); *Trevino v. Trevino*, 555 S.W.2d 792 (Tex. Civ. App.—Corpus Christi 1977, no writ); *Girard v. Girard*, 521 S.W.2d 714 (Tex. Civ. App.—Houston [1st Dist.] 1975, no writ).

A third measure of reimbursement set forth by another court is cost, regardless of enhancement. *In Re Higley*, 575 S.W.2d 432, 434 (Tex. Civ. App.—Amarillo 1978, no writ).

The confusion among the courts of appeals is due in great part to imprecise language by this court commencing with the decision of *Dakan v. Dakan*, 125 Tex. 305, 83 S.W.2d 620 (1935). In consecutive paragraphs *Dakan* held:

> * * * Hence results the rule that the community estate must be reimbursed for *the cost of the buildings* erected by joint labors or funds upon the separate property of one of the spouses. . . . *Furrh v. Winston*, 66 Tex. 521, 524, 1 S.W. 527, 529 (1886) (emphasis added),

and

> . . . in case of reimbursement for improvements, the amount of recovery is limited to the amount of enhancement of the property at the time of partition by virtue of the improvements placed thereon. *Clift v. Clift*, *supra*, [72 Tex. 144, 149, 10 S.W. 338 (1888).]

This court has stated in several cases that the proper measure of reimbursement is the enhanced value of the benefited estate resulting from the improvements. However, most of those statements have been dicta.

* * *

The right of an estate to reimbursement from another estate is an equitable right and should be determined by equitable principles. *Dakan*, 83 S.W.2d at 627, *supra*. Therefore, it is incumbent upon the courts to insure that a benefited estate is not required to pay more in reimbursement than the amount in which it was benefited by the other estate. Likewise, it is necessary to ascertain that the benefited estate pays no less than it has been benefited.

The "cost only" rule, if followed, would provide an easy-to-apply measure since it would not require proof of enhancement. However, such a rule would, in many instances, permit the owner of the benefited estate to be enriched at the expense of the contributing estate. This is true because the estate which contributes the capital necessary to construct the improvements would not share in the increase in value resulting from the investment. The "enhancement or cost, whichever is less" rule, however, would permit the benefited estate the maximum recovery at the expense of the contributing estate in all situations. This does not comport with equity.

We hold that a claim for reimbursement for funds expended by an estate for improvements to another estate is to be measured by the enhancement in value to the benefited estate. This rule is more likely to insure equitable treatment of both the contributing and benefited estates in most situations.

The judgment of the court of appeals is affirmed insofar as it holds that Mrs. Gilliland did not properly trace any separate funds to the improvements to her separate property. The judgment is reversed insofar as it holds that reimbursement is measured by the cost or enhancement, whichever is less. We render judgment for Terri L. Anderson and require Cleo Gilliland to include the sum of $21,923.00, representing one-half of the $54,000.00 enhancement to her separate property, less one-half of the outstanding mortgage on the property, in the inventory of the estate of Lawrence Gilliland.

J. Purchase Money Reimbursement—Equitable Offsets

In *Penick v. Penick*, the Texas Supreme Court held that the trial court was correct in considering off setting benefits in determining the measure of reimbursement for community funds used to pay a prenuptial purchase money debt. In *Penick*, the offsetting benefit was the tax deduction taken by the community for the depreciation in Husband's separate property.

Today, if there is a claim for reimbursement, "[b]enefits for the use and enjoyment of the property may be offset against a claim for reimbursement for expenditures to benefit a marital estate, except that the separate estate of a spouse may not claim an offset for use and enjoyment of a primary or secondary residence owned wholly or partly by the separate estate against contributions made by the community estate to the separate estate." TEX. FAM. CODE § 3.402(c).

However, if one wanted to take a more creative approach, one might ask the question, what is meant by "use and enjoyment?" Is a tax deduction "use and enjoyment?" Learned authorities in the field of Texas marital property law have contemplated this question.[1] The informal consensus appears to be that taking advantage of a tax break is not use and enjoyment of property. What do you think?

PENICK
v.
PENICK
783 S.W.2d 194
(Tex. 1988)

ROBERTSON, JUSTICE.

This divorce case concerns the proper measure for reimbursement when community funds are used to pay a prenuptial, purchase money debt. The specific issue is whether tax benefits derived by the community estate from a spouse's separate property may be considered and offset against the sum advanced by the community estate to reduce the principal of the debt on the separate property. In reversing the judgment of the trial court, the court of appeals held that the proper measure for reimbursement in this situation was to return to the community estate the actual amount expended on the principal of the separate property debt without consideration of offsetting benefits. 750 S.W.2d 247. We hold that the trial court properly considered offsetting benefits in determining the measure of reimbursement here and, accordingly, we reverse the judgment of the court of appeals and affirm the judgment of the trial court.

Robert and Maria Penick were married on March 13, 1975. At the time of the marriage Robert owned several residential rental properties. During the marriage Robert maintained and managed these properties. The community estate also purchased a few rental properties, but 90% of the community estate's income was derived from Robert's separate rental property.

---

[1] Cheryl Wilson, Jim Farris, Robert J. Piro, & Pamela George, *Is It a Tort If He Sonoras Too Loud? Creative and Innovative Marital Causes of Action*, New Frontiers in Marital Property, Scottsdale Arizona, (State Bar of Texas, October 2005).

Prior to trial, Robert and Maria entered into a written stipulation concerning Robert's separate real property. As a part of this stipulation, the parties agreed that the community estate had paid $104,500 to reduce the principal indebtedness on Robert's separate real property. Supported by the parties' joint tax returns, Robert testified at trial that the tax benefits to the community estate from the depreciation of his separate property exceeded the $104,500 expended by the community to reduce his separate property debt.

In determining the community property subject to division, the trial court concluded that no reimbursement was due the community because the community estate had on balance received a benefit, a reduction in its tax liability, by taking the depreciation of Robert's separate property. Maria appealed, arguing that the law of reimbursement did not permit Robert to offset any amount against those dollars paid by the community estate to reduce the principal of Robert's separate property debt. The court of appeals agreed that the community should be reimbursed for every dollar contributed to the principal of Robert's separate property debt, and so it remanded the cause to the trial court for a proper division of the community property, giving due regard to the $104,500 reimbursement owed the community estate.

The issue in this case is whether the trial court erred in considering the tax benefits received by the community estate through the depreciation of Robert's separate property as an offset against the amount paid by the community on the principal of Robert's prenuptial debt. The rules generally applicable to reimbursement claims for prenuptial debts and particularly the proper role for offsetting benefits are unsettled. *See generally*, Oldham, *Texas Reimbursement Law*, in STATE BAR OF TEXAS, ADVANCED FAMILY LAW COURSE (1988); Koons & Holmes, *Characterization and Reimbursement*, in STATE BAR OF TEXAS, ADVANCED FAMILY LAW COURSE (1987); Cook & Dudley, *Characterization, Tracing and Reimbursement*, in STATE BAR OF TEXAS, MARRIAGE DISSOLUTION (1987); Weekley, *Reimbursement Between Separate and Community Estates—The Current Texas View*, 39 BAYLOR L. REV. 945 (1987); Heard, Orsinger, & Strieber, *Characterization of Property and Reimbursement*, in STATE BAR OF TEXAS, ADVANCED FAMILY LAW COURSE (1986); Smith & Smith, *Reimbursement in Divorce Cases*, in STATE BAR OF TEXAS, MARRIAGE DISSOLUTION (1984); Smith, *Reimbursement*, in STATE BAR OF TEXAS, ADVANCED FAMILY LAW COURSE (1982). The confusion is, in part, attributable to this court's writings in *Dakan v. Dakan*, 125 Tex. 305, 83 S.W.2d 620 (1935), and *Colden v. Alexander*, 141 Tex. 134, 171 S.W.2d 328 (1943).

Dakan did not expressly consider the role of offsetting benefits in evaluating a claim for reimbursement. It simply provided that reimbursement for a purchase money advance should be at cost to the contributing estate. *Dakan*, 83 S.W.2d at 628. Eight years later in *Colden v. Alexander*, this court indicated that consideration of offsetting benefits was proper when measuring a reimbursement claim. Neither opinion is a paragon of clarity as the following oft-cited passage from *Colden* demonstrates:

> Of course, where the husband purchases land on credit before marriage, and pays the purchase money debt after marriage out of community funds, equity requires that the community estate be reimbursed. Under our law, the income during marriage from the estate of either the husband or the wife is community. The rule of reimbursement, as above announced, is purely an equitable one. Such being the case, we think it would follow that interest paid during coverture out of community funds on the prenuptial debts of either the husband or the wife on land, and taxes, would not even create an equitable claim for reim-

> bursement, unless it is shown that the expenditures by the community are greater than the benefits received.

Colden, 171 S.W.2d at 334 (citations omitted).

Dakan and *Colden* have spawned a dizzying array of alternative or conflicting principles and presumptions for evaluating a claim for reimbursement. From the cases interpreting *Dakan* and/or *Colden*, we have gleaned the following rules applicable to purchase money reimbursement claims. As a threshold requirement, it is typically held that the contributing estate need not show enhancement or the benefit of its contribution as a condition of reimbursement. *See, e.g., Nelson v. Nelson*, 713 S.W.2d 146 (Tex. App.—Texarkana 1986, no writ); *Fyffe v. Fyffe*, 670 S.W.2d 360 (Tex. App.—Texarkana 1984, writ dism'd w.o.j.). Instead, the payment by one marital estate of the debt of another creates a prima facie right of reimbursement.

From this general rule, some courts have carved an exception regarding interest, taxes and insurance. These courts indulge in a presumption that reimbursement is not due absent proof that the amount paid for these expenses was greater than the benefit received by the contributing estate. *See, e.g., Cook v. Cook*, 665 S.W.2d 161 (Tex. App.—Fort Worth 1983, writ ref'd n.r.e.); *Hawkins v. Hawkins*, 612 S.W.2d 683 (Tex. Civ. App.—El Paso 1981, no writ). This exception to the general rule is traceable to *Colden v. Alexander* and in application requires the party seeking reimbursement to show that the amount paid for taxes, interest and insurance exceeded the benefits received by the contributing estate.

Some courts, however, have rejected any concept of offsetting benefits, requiring instead that the contributing estate be fully reimbursed for all funds paid on the purchase money debt of another estate. *See, e.g., Hilton v. Hilton*, 678 S.W.2d 645 (Tex. App.—Houston [14th Dist.] 1984, no writ); *Brooks v. Brooks*, 612 S.W.2d 233 (Tex. Civ. App.—Waco 1981, no writ); *Pruske v. Pruske*, 601 S.W.2d 746 (Tex. Civ. App.—Austin 1980, writ dism'd w.o.j.). Still others have made the exception the rule, drawing no distinction between how the community funds were used and permitting reimbursement only upon a showing that expenditures exceeded benefits. *See, e.g., Allen v. Allen*, 704 S.W.2d 600 (Tex. App.—Fort Worth 1986, no writ); *Snider v. Snider*, 613 S.W.2d 8 (Tex. Civ. App.—Dallas 1981, no writ); *Klein v. Klein*, 370 S.W.2d 769 (Tex. Civ. App.—Eastland 1963, no writ).

The present writing of the court of appeals preserves many of the distinctions drawn in previous reimbursement cases. The court distinguishes the present case from those in which community funds were used to pay interest or taxes, thereby giving tacit approval to those cases which have found it appropriate to consider offsetting benefits when the community has paid certain separate property expenses other than the principal of the separate property debt. The court of appeals also distinguishes this case from those in which the community was alleged to have provided for improvements on separate property or to have provided time, talent and labor to benefit separate property. This disclaimer refers to the last two writings by this court on the subject of reimbursement, *Anderson v. Gilliland*, 684 S.W.2d 673 (Tex. 1985), and *Jensen v. Jensen*, 665 S.W.2d 107 (Tex. 1984).

Of these two cases *Anderson* is more closely analogous to our present case. It concerned the community's reimbursement claim for funds expended for capital improvements on a spouse's separate property. There, as here, we were faced with conflicting or inconsistent principles for evaluating the community's claim for reimbursement. Three distinct rules had evolved. In resolving this conflict we emphasized the equitable nature of the claim and selected what we considered the fairest measure, holding "that a claim for reimbursement for funds expended by an estate for improvements to another estate is to be measured by the enhancement in value to the benefited estate." *Anderson*, 684 S.W.2d at 675.

Noting that the correct measure for reimbursement under the present circumstances was unclear, the court of appeals held that the best rule was to reimburse the community for every dollar advanced on the principal of Robert's prenuptial, purchase money debt. The court of appeals further rejected consideration of any offsetting benefits under these circumstances. The court wrote that community funds used to pay the purchase price or to discharge encumbrances against separate property, as distinguished from the community's payment of taxes or interest on separate property should be reimbursed "without the necessity of proof that the expenditures exceeded benefits received by the community." 750 S.W.2d at 250.

This "dollar for dollar" reimbursement rule is inconsistent with the equitable approach we advocated in *Anderson*. The court of appeals, however, distinguishes *Anderson* because it concerned reimbursement for a capital improvement to separate property rather than reimbursement for a prenuptial, purchase money debt. A distinct and different set of rules have evolved for evaluating a reimbursement claim for capital improvements as opposed to one for purchase money.

Why we should have two distinct sets of rules for two very similar claims for reimbursement is another matter which is not entirely clear. One commentator has observed that there is no logical reason for calculating reimbursement differently in capital improvement cases and in purchase money cases and attributes the development of different rules to historical accident. Weekley, *Reimbursement Between Separate and Community Estates—The Current Texas View*, 39 BAYLOR L. REV. 945, 974 (1987). We are likewise at a loss to make a meaningful distinction between these two types of reimbursement. We view the advancement of funds by one marital estate to another under either transaction, payment of a purchase money debt or as a capital improvement, as essentially identical and therefore subject to the same kind of measurement.

Having disregarded the traditional dichotomy between reimbursement claims for purchase money debts and capital improvements, we turn again to the holding of the court of appeals. According to the court of appeals, the correct measure for reimbursement here is to return to the community the actual amount advanced to reduce the principal indebtedness on the separate property without regard to the benefits received in return by the community estate. Because the trial court considered the tax benefits realized by the community estate from the depreciation of Robert's separate property and offset this benefit against those community funds expended on the separate property, the court of appeals concluded that the trial court had abused its discretion. We disagree.

The outright rejection of offsetting benefits is inconsistent with the equitable nature of a claim for reimbursement. Most recently in *Jensen v. Jensen*, we embraced the concept of offsetting benefits. In *Anderson v. Gilliland*, we did not consider or mention offsetting benefits, but did emphasize that reimbursement is an equitable claim. As such, "a court of equity is bound to look at all the facts and circumstances and determine what is fair, just, and equitable." 27 AM. JUR. 2D, *Equity* § 102 at 624 (1966). The rule applied here by the court of appeals does not serve equity because it forecloses consideration of some of the facts and circumstances material to the reimbursement claim.

Admittedly it is difficult to announce a single formula which will balance the equities between each marital estate in every situation and for every kind of property and contribution. A useful analogy between an action for quantum meruit and a claim for reimbursement has been suggested:

> The equitable doctrine of quantum meruit is based upon the principle that one receiving benefits which are unjust for him to retain ought to make restitution or pay the value of the benefit to the party contributing the benefit. *Baldwin v. Smith*, 586 S.W.2d 624, 632 (Tex. Civ. App.—Tyler 1979), *rev'd on other grounds*, 611 S.W.2d 611 (Tex. 1980). Applied to claims for reimbursement, the doctrine might have three elements: (1) an estate has contributed to another estate, (2) the contributing estate has not received a quid pro quo, and (3) the benefited estate has thereby been unjustly enriched. Thus, achievement of equity between marital estates, a goal the Texas Supreme Court aspires to attain in *Anderson v. Gilliland*, would seem to necessitate a consideration of offset.

Koons and Holmes, *Characterization and Reimbursement*, in STATE BAR OF TEXAS, ADVANCED FAMILY LAW COURSE 48-9 (1987).

In the final analysis, great latitude must be given to the trial court in applying equitable principles to value a claim for reimbursement. As we said in *Dakan*, an equitable claim for reimbursement is not merely a balancing of the ledgers between the marital estates. *Dakan*, 83 S.W.2d at 627. The discretion to be exercised in evaluating a claim for reimbursement is equally as broad as that discretion subsequently exercised by the trial court in making a "just and right" division of the community property. TEX. FAM. CODE ANN. § 3.63 (Vernon Supp. 1988). In the present case the trial court did not abuse its discretion by considering the tax benefits returned to the contributing community estate and the effect the depreciation deduction had on the value of Robert's separate property.

The judgment of the court of appeals is reversed and the judgment of the trial court is affirmed.

COOK, J., concurs.

COOK, JUSTICE, concurring.

I concur with the majority opinion to the extent that tax benefits derived by the community estate from a spouse's separate property may be considered and offset against the sum advanced by the community estate to reduce the principal of the debt on the separate property.

However, I am concerned with certain language in the majority opinion and with the fact that it fails to set forth guidelines in handling reimbursement claims. This area of the law is fraught with confusion and remains unsettled in spite of the majority opinion. Therefore, I will set forth my understanding of the rules regarding reimbursement claims in an opinion on motion for rehearing.

Notes, Comments & Questions

1. TEX. FAM. CODE § 3.402(c) specifically provides that ". . . [b]enefits for the use and enjoyment of property may be offset against a claim for reimbursement for expenditures to benefit a marital estate. . . ." What is the "use and enjoyment" that the legislature probably had in mind?

2. In *Penick*, the court considered tax benefits received by the contributing community estate through the depreciation of Husband's separate property as an offset against the amount paid by the community on the principal of Husband's prenuptial debt. Decidedly, this is an unusual offset. Can you think of other offsets?

K. Availability of Reimbursement for Retained Earnings and Reimbursement for Use of Community Credit

Thomas v. Thomas exemplifies unique use of reimbursement theory. Based upon the assumption that the claims for reimbursement listed in TEX. FAM. CODE § 3.408(b) are not exclusive, the opinion which addresses reimbursement for retained Subchapter S earnings and use of community credit is still viable. The three separate opinions of the panel clearly indicate the difficulties in deciding the case. In addition to the reimbursement theory, the characterization of Subchapter S earnings is important to Texas marital property law.

THOMAS
v.
THOMAS

738 S.W.2d 342
(Tex. App.—Houston [1st Dist.] 1987, writ denied)

COHEN, JUSTICE.

In this appeal from a judgment dividing the marital estate, we must decide whether the retained earnings of a Subchapter S corporation are marital property subject to division on divorce. We hold that they are not.

The parties were married on November 17, 1968. Appellee filed for divorce in November 1983. Appellant was employed throughout the marriage as an executive with Proctor and Gamble.

Alexandria Coca-Cola Bottling Company Ltd. (hereafter the corporation) was founded in 1906 by appellant's grandfather. All stock in the corporation is owned by descendants of the founding family. Appellant has been Chairman of the Board since 1973. Between 1976 and 1982, appellant acquired approximately 16% of the stock in the corporation by gift and inheritance. It is undisputed that this stock is his separate property.

The corporation was a "Subchapter S" corporation at all relevant times, 26 U.S.C. § 1361 et seq. (1982 & Supp. 1984), and its income was treated as personal income of the shareholders for federal income tax purposes. Accordingly, the community estate paid federal income taxes on appellant's proportionate share of total corporate earnings, whether retained by the corporation or distributed to the shareholders, and the corporation neither owed nor paid federal corporate income tax on its income.

Between 1976 and 1984, the community received dividends of just over $500,000. The record does not disclose whether the community's federal income tax liabilities arising from the corporation's income exceeded whatever tax benefits may have arisen from ownership of the corporate stock.

It is undisputed that the corporation did not distribute all of its earnings to the shareholders. In special issue number three, the jury found that $146,000 of retained corporate income earned during the marriage was attributable to appellant's shares of stock.

The trial court's judgment provided:

> [Appellant] shall pay over to [appellee] forthwith (but no later than five (5) calendar days from his receipt thereof) one-half of any sums paid to him by the Coca Cola Bottling Company of Alexandria for his share of the earnings of that company until the sum of Seventy-Three Thousand and No/100 Dollars ($73,000.00) is paid over to [appellee]. [Appellant] is hereby appointed trustee for [appellee] under this provision until all sums due [appellee] have been paid to her and shall be accountable to [appellee] and the Court as trustee. [Appellant] shall notify the company of this award to [appellee] and shall take no action which is inconsistent with this Order. [Appellant] shall furnish [appellee] with a full disclosure and accounting of all sums received by him from the company until this portion of the judgment has been satisfied.

Appellant's third point of error contends that the trial court erred in awarding appellee $73,000 because those funds will be appellant's separate property, if and when he ever receives them.

The parties agree that the $73,000 award was based on special issue three and that it was based upon the trial court's implied characterization of the retained corporate earnings as community property. Therefore, we must decide whether the corporation's retained earnings are community property.

It is well established that unless the corporation is a spouse's alter ego, *Vallone v. Vallone*, 644 S.W.2d 455 (Tex. 1982), a court upon divorce may award only shares of stock, and not corporate assets. *McKnight v. McKnight*, 543 S.W.2d 863 (Tex. 1976). Moreover, a court may not divest a spouse of separate property corporate stock and award it to the other spouse. *Cameron v. Cameron*, 641 S.W.2d 210 (Tex. 1982). Appellee admits that in an ordinary corporation, retained earnings are a corporate asset. They are not marital property, separate or community. Appellee contends, however, that retained earnings of a Subchapter S corporation should be treated as community property because the community has paid federal income tax on them. This, she argues, justifies the recognition of a community interest in the retained earnings. We disagree.

Subchapter S status does not determine who owns the corporation's earnings. It merely provides an alternate method to tax the corporation's income. A Subchapter S corporation may distribute its income, but, like any other corporation, it is not required to do so. Corporate distributions, regardless of form, are controlled by state law. *See Commissioner v. Cohen*, 121 F.2d 348 (5th Cir. 1941); TEX. BUS. CORP. ACT. ANN. arts. 2.38, 2.39, 2.40 (Vernon 1980). The shareholder in a Subchapter S corporation has no greater rights over corporate property than a shareholder in any other corporation.

In *Suburban Utility Corp. v. Public Utility Commission*, 652 S.W.2d 358 (Tex. 1983), a rate case, the court held that a Subchapter S utility could deduct from its income federal taxes paid by its shareholders. Thus in a rate making proceeding governed by state law, the corporation was entitled to the expense deduction, even though the shareholders had paid the taxes. The court recognized that the earnings were owned by the corporation, not by the shareholders. It wrote: "Under Subchapter S . . . , a corporation may elect a tax status which protects the earnings and profits *of the corporation* from conventional corporate tax rates." (Emphasis added.) 652 S.W.2d at 363. The court thus recognized that the tax treatment of a Subchapter S corporation under federal law would not control the characterization of taxation expense under state law.

Other courts have recognized that Subchapter S status does not affect state tax liability. Thus, states may require Subchapter S corporations to pay state corporate income tax. *Commonwealth v. N.I. Inc.*, 31 Pa. Commw. 235, 375 A.2d 898 (1977), *aff'd*, 482 Pa. 261, 393 A.2d 653 (1978); *Brown v. Dept. of Revenue*, 558 S.W.2d 635 (Ky. Ct. App. 1977).

Courts in community property states have unanimously held that corporate earnings remained corporate property until distributed and, therefore, were not divisible on divorce. *Hoffmann v. Hoffmann*, 676 S.W.2d 817, 827 (Mo. 1984); *Simplot v. Simplot*, 96 Idaho 239, 526 P.2d 844 (1974); *Speer v. Speer*, 25 Cal. Rptr. 729, 209 Cal. App. 2d 233 (Cal. Ct. App.1962); *Gapsch v. Gapsch*, 76 Idaho 44, 277 P.2d 278 (1954).

We conclude that, while the corporation retained some earnings as "previously taxed income" of the shareholders, the earnings remained the corporation's exclusive property and never belonged to the appellant or the marital estate.

Appellee next contends that a Subchapter S corporation should be treated as a partnership because it is taxed like a partnership. Again, we disagree.

Federal law recognizes that Subchapter S does not convert a corporation to a partnership. *United States v. Richardson*, 469 F.2d 349 (10th Cir. 1972); *United States v. Silverman*, 359 F.Supp. 1113 (N.D. Ill. 1973); *Neal v. United States*, 313 F.Supp. 393 (C.D. Cal. 1970); *Wilhelm v. United States*, 257 F.Supp. 16 (D.C. Wyo. 1966); *R.S. Smero, Inc. v. Levine*, 51 A.D.2d 273, 381 N.Y.S.2d 337 (1976); *Motheral v. Motheral*, 514 S.W.2d 475, 477 (Tex. Civ. App.—Corpus Christi 1974, writ ref'd n.r.e.), relied on by the appellee, is not to the contrary.

We observe that the marital community benefits from the Subchapter S election. When corporate income is taxed as personal income, the corporation avoids tax liability, and the community avoids having dividends taxed twice, first as corporate income, and then, upon receipt, as personal income. *See* 26 U.S.C. sec. 1371, et seq. (1982 & Supp. 1984); *Shores Realty Co. v. United States*, 468 F.2d 572 (5th Cir. 1972); *Brown v. Dept. of Revenue*, 558 S.W.2d 635 (Ky. App. 1977). By avoiding corporate taxation, the corporation has more money to distribute as dividends. If the corporation has tax credits or losses, these reduce the community's taxable income. All the while, the corporate veil shields the shareholder from personal liability. Congress intended for shareholders in Subchapter S corporations to enjoy these substantial benefits

Upholding the trial court's order in this case could lead to undesirable and unpredictable results. It would tend to engraft upon our community property system the manifest complexities of federal tax law. If, by paying taxes, the community acquired an interest in a Subchapter S corporation's retained earnings, it presumably would also acquire an interest in property purchased with the reinvestment of those earnings. The bright line dividing the corporate estate from the marital estate would be dimmed. Such a result would not bode well for the future of this highly desirable corporate form.

We hold that previously taxed and retained earnings of a Subchapter S corporation are corporate assets, and are neither the community nor the separate property of the shareholder. Accordingly, the order that appellant pay $73,000 to appellee, when and if received as dividends from the corporation, improperly awards property that is not presently owned by the community and that will be appellant's separate property, if and when it is received. The third point of error is sustained.

In view of our disposition of the third point of error, it is not necessary for us to discuss the first, second, fourth, and fifth points of error.

In points of error six through twelve, appellant contends that the trial court erred in submitting special issues four and five, in which the jury found that the community should be reimbursed $150,000 because the community estate was used to enhance the value of appellant's corporate stock. Appellant also asserts that the evidence was factually and legally insufficient to support the jury's answers.

Based on the jury's findings, appellant became obligated to reimburse the community estate for $150,000. However, the judgment awarded the community's entire right of reimbursement to appellant. Thus, even if this obligation was erroneously imposed, appellant is not harmed, as long as the judgment eliminates the obligation by awarding it to him. Moreover, appellant does not contend that he was deprived of any other community property by virtue of his receipt of this specific community asset

We therefore hold that any error was harmless, unless awarding the right solely to appellant resulted in the overall property division being "so manifestly unjust that it constituted clear abuse of the trial court's discretion." *See Zisblatt v. Zisblatt*, 693 S.W.2d 944, 956 (Tex. App.—Fort Worth 1985, writ dism'd); *King v. King*, 661 S.W.2d 252 (Tex. App.—Houston [1st Dist.] 1983, no writ). Appellant makes no such contention. Accordingly, points of error six through twelve are overruled.

Insofar as it divides the community estate of the parties, the judgment is reversed, and the cause is remanded to the trial court for a re-division of the community estate.

DUNN, J., concurring and dissenting.

SAM BASS, J., dissenting and concurring.

DUNN, JUSTICE, concurring and dissenting.

I concur with the majority in the disposition of the Subchapter S issue, but I dissent from the holding with respect to the reimbursement issues.

The appellee asserts two separate claims for reimbursement, one for the appellant's time, toil, and talent used to enhance the value of his separate estate, and another for the use of community credit to enhance the value of the appellant's separate estate. With respect to the reimbursement claim for the appellant's time, toil, and talent, the "right to reimbursement is only for the value of the time, toil and effort expended to enhance the separate estate other than that reasonably necessary to manage and preserve the separate estate, for which the community did not receive adequate compensation." *Jensen v. Jensen*, 665 S.W.2d 107, 110 (Tex. 1984) (*Vallone v. Vallone*, 644 S.W.2d 455, 459 (Tex. 1982)). The appellee had the burden of introducing sufficient evidence to establish each of the elements of her reimbursement claim. *Id.* The appellee failed to introduce any evidence of the amount of time that was reasonably necessary for the appellant to spend managing and preserving his separate estate. Further, there is no evidence in the record concerning the value of the time, toil, and talent expended by the appellant beyond what was reasonably necessary to preserve his separate estate. The appellee has, therefore, failed to meet her burden of establishing the community's right to reimbursement for the appellant's time, toil, and talent expended on his separate property

With respect to the reimbursement claim based on the use of community credit to enhance the appellant's separate property, the appellee has again failed to satisfy her burden of going forward with evidence of each element of this claim. Initially, I note that this is not a case of community credit being used to construct an improvement on separate property.

On May 29, 1979, the Coca-Cola Bottling Co. borrowed $2,000,000, at a maximum interest rate of the prime rate + 1.35%, from the Guaranty Bank and Trust Co. of Alexandria, Louisiana. This loan was to be used to purchase land and construct improvements at the Coca-Cola bottling facility. The improvements were completed sometime in August 1980. On September 1, 1981, the Guaranty Bank and Trust Co. entered into an agreement, effective October 14, 1981, with the Industrial Development Board of the Parish of Rapides, Inc. for the issuance of industrial revenue bonds in the amount of $2,200,000 for the purpose of refinancing the May 29, 1979 loan to the Coca-Cola Bottling Co. Also on September 1, 1981, both the Coca-Cola Bottling Co. and the appellant and the appellee entered into agreements with Guaranty Bank and Trust Co. guaranteeing the payment of the principal and interest on the bonds. The purpose of this refinancing agreement was to reduce Coca-Cola Bottling Co.'s interest costs on its loan. The maximum interest rate payable on the bonds was 70% of the prime rate, with a total savings to the corporation of approximately $638,000.

Neither the parties' research nor ours has revealed a Texas case deciding the question of whether the community has a right to reimbursement for the use of its credit to secure a loan to refinance the husband's separate property debts. However, I am not willing to state, at this time, that this new reimbursement theory is without merit. I would analogize this situation to cases where separate debts are discharged with community funds. *See Villarreal v. Villarreal*, 618 S.W.2d 99 (Tex. Civ. App.—Corpus Christi 1981, no writ); *Hawkins v. Hawkins*, 612 S.W.2d 683 (Tex. Civ. App.—El Paso 1981, no writ). However, there is an important difference between the case before us and cases involving the discharge of a separate debt with community funds. When a debt is discharged, the cost to the community is obvious, but when a separate property debt is refinanced with the community acting as a guarantor, the cost to the community is not so readily ascertainable. In the latter situation, expert testimony would be required on the percentage risk undertaken by the community, and a dollar value would have to be assigned to that risk.

In the case before us, there is no testimony concerning the cost to the community resulting from the use of their credit to guarantee the refinancing of the separate property debt. Further, there is evidence in the record that even though the guarantee was for $2,200,000, and the net community assets were approximately $660,000, the appellant was nevertheless able to negotiate a loan from the River Oaks Bank & Trust Co. subsequent to the guarantee. The appellee has, therefore, failed to meet her burden of establishing the community's right to reimbursement for the use of the community credit.

Because I find that the community's claim for reimbursement was not supported by sufficient evidence, the question is whether this error "was reasonably calculated to cause and probably did cause rendition of an improper judgment in the case." TEX. R. APP. P. 81(b)(1). In a decree of divorce the court shall order a division of the estate of the parties in a manner that the court deems just and right. TEX. FAM. CODE ANN. sec. 3.63(a) (Vernon Supp. 1987).

My review of the record indicates that the trial judge's "just and right" division of the property constituted an approximately equal division of the community assets. However, this division was based on the jury's erroneous finding that the community had a $150,000 claim for reimbursement. Because of this reimbursement error, the community estate has now been reduced causing a disproportionate disposition of the property not in accordance with what the trial court determined was a "just and right" division of the property. I would remand this case to the trial judge for a new division of the community estate that does not include the $150,000 reimbursement claim. *Jacobs v. Jacobs*, 687 S.W.2d 731, 732 (Tex. 1985).

SAM BASS, JUSTICE, dissenting and concurring.

I concur with the majority concerning the reimbursement issues, and dissent as to whether "previously taxed income" of a Subchapter S corporation is community property, and thus, divisible upon divorce.

The community received dividends paid to appellant on his separately owned stock in the Alexandria Coca Cola Bottling Company Ltd. ("Corporation"). Appellant owns 16% of the stock, which he obtained by gift and inheritance from his parents.

The amounts of dividends were as follows:

1976 - $ 8,250.00;
1977 - $ 28,530.00;
1978 - $ 35,700.00;
1979 - $ 41,250.00;
1980 - $ 28,500.00;
1981 - $ 27,300.00;
1982 - $ 68,105.54;
1983 - $137,812.20;
1984 - $153,162.90;
1985 - $ 58,710.00.

These dividends were deposited in the joint account of Mr. and Mrs. Thomas and were used for living expenses and acquisition of community assets.

The corporation is a Subchapter S corporation, and by express stipulation and agreement of all of the shareholders of the corporation, its earnings are taxed to the shareholders individually. The jury found that $146,000 was the amount of earnings, which is called "previously taxed income," to the appellant that provided the basis of a $73,000 award to the appellee.

It is fundamental that the division of property upon divorce is largely within the discretion of the trial court. *McKnight v. McKnight*, 543 S.W.2d 863, 866 (Tex. 1976). The TEX. FAM. CODE ANN. § 3.63(a) (Vernon Supp. 1985), provides that:

> (a) In a decree of divorce or annulment the court shall order a division of the estate of the parties in a manner that the court deems just and right, having due regard for the rights of each party and any children of the marriage.

In applying this section of the Texas Family Code, courts have consistently held that:

> Section 3.63 of the Texas Family Code affords the trial court wide latitude and discretion in dividing the community estate of the parties upon dissolution of their marriage. In reviewing the actions of the trial court, the appellate court will presume that the trial court exercised its discretion properly. The trial court's discretion will not be disturbed on appeal unless a clear abuse has been shown.

Zisblatt v. Zisblatt, 693 S.W.2d 944, 956 (Tex. App.—Fort Worth 1985, writ dism'd).

Appellant argues that issue three, which relates to what, if any, is the "previously taxed income" of the corporation that can be attributed to the shares owned by appellant, should have included a request for reimbursement to the community or alternatively another theory of recovery. Additionally, appellant complains that issue three is not supported by any evidence and/or insufficient evidence for the jury finding supporting an award to the appellee of $73,000 of the "previously taxed income" when and if distributed by the corporation. Further, appellant alleges that the previously taxed and undistributed income held by the corporation was an award of corporate property or alimony and not community property subject to division upon divorce.

The evidence reveals that the entire income of the corporation for each year was immediately attributed on a proportional basis to the shareholders at the shareholders' expressed request. Each shareholder was required to pay income tax on the income attributed to them. The corporation, however, frequently failed to actually distribute all of the income attributed to the shareholders, and that income was retained in the corporation as "previously taxed income" distributable to the shareholders. Thus, the corporation accumulated "previously taxed income" of the shareholders as follows:

Prev. Taxed Income	Year	Appellant's Ownership	Amount Attributed To Appellant
160,000	1979	7½ %	12,000
30,000	1980	7½ %	2,250
250,000	1981	7½ %	18,750
240,000	1982	7½ %	18,000
280,000	1983	16 %	44,800

TOTAL			95,800

In 1984, the corporation accumulated $20,000 in "previously taxed income," and in the first five months of 1985, the corporation accumulated an additional $25,000 attributable to the appellant's interest in the corporation. The total of $153,800 agrees with the jury finding of $146,000. The trial court awarded the appellee one-half of that amount, when and if distributed, upon the basis that such was income previously distributable as "previously taxed income."

The law is well established that a property division upon divorce is solely within the discretion of the trial court. *McKnight*, 543 S.W.2d at 866. The jury has no power to divide the property, its answers are only advisory regarding the disposition of property; *Cockerham v. Cockerham*, 527 S.W.2d 162, 173 (Tex. 1975); *Roach v. Roach*, 672 S.W.2d 524, 529 (Tex. App.—Amarillo 1984, no writ). The jury can merely find specific facts to be used by the trial court in the exercise of its discretion. *Id.* Therefore, there was no need for a jury finding on whether some portion of the previously taxed undistributed income should be paid to appellee. This matter was solely in the discretion of the trial court.

Appellant also asserts that the undistributed "previously taxed income" of the corporation is not divisible upon divorce and therefore, the award to appellee constitutes alimony or the division of corporate property.

If a corporation is designated as a Subchapter S corporation, means that the corporation's undistributed taxable income is taxed to the shareholders, much like income of a partnership is taxed to individual partners. *Motheral v. Motheral*, 514 S.W.2d 475, 477 (Tex. Civ. App.—Corpus Christi 1974, writ ref'd n.r.e.). The undistributed income of separate property partnerships is treated as community property. *Grost v. Grost*, 561 S.W.2d 223, 229 (Tex. Civ. App.—Tyler 1977, writ dism'd). Texas courts consistently hold that portion of the partnership interest that consists of profits accumulated during marriage, whether or not distributed, is community property. *Norris v. Vaughan*, 152 Tex. 491, 260 S.W.2d 676, 681 (1953).

Accordingly, the trial court had complete discretion in the division of the undistributed but "previously taxed income" of the corporation upon divorce.

Appellant also alleges that there is no evidence, or insufficient evidence, to support the jury's finding of $146,000 on issue three.

The evidence in the record is that there was "previously taxed income" retained by the corporation that the community had not received, but that was properly due to the community. Further, appellee's expert witness testified that the undistributed "previously taxed income" since May 12, 1983, was $235,000.

Thus, the jury finding that the community owned $146,000 of the undistributed "previously taxed income" by the corporation is sufficiently supported by the evidence.

I respectfully dissent from the majority opinion on the subject of "previously taxed income," and I would affirm the judgment of the trial court on that issue.

Notes, Comments & Questions

1. In *Thomas* husband was awarded the $150,000 reimbursement. Why would he appeal?

2. Why would some commentators refer to this reimbursement as "phantom" reimbursement?

3. Why wasn't there a claim for reimbursement based upon time, toil, talent, and effort?

4. What claim for reimbursement regarding the Subchapter S might have provided the wife some relief?

5. Donn Fullenweider, wife's attorney in *Thomas*, was creative in formulating wife's claims and is an example of thoughtful and zealous lawyering. His success with the "use of community credit" basis for reimbursement proves that one should occasionally venture beyond tried and true claims. No venture, no gain!

6. For another creative use of reimbursement, *see Hilton v. Hilton*, 678 S.W.2d 645 (Tex. App.—Houston [14th Dist.] 1984, no writ) where husband was awarded community stock to reimburse him for separate property stock which he sold to retire a community debt. The stock used for reimbursement was the exact type of separate property stock that he had sold—Hilton Hotel Corpo-

ration stock. Why do you think he chose to sell separate property stock rather than to sell the existing community stock to retire the debt?

L. Economic Contribution Calculator

As mentioned throughout the introduction to this Chapter, the former statutory concept of Economic Contribution will not be applied unless a suit to dissolve a marriage is pending prior to September 1, 2009 or a spouse has died prior to September 1, 2009.

For this reason, application of the economic contribution remedy will be limited. However, should such a situation occur - in your practice or on the bar exam - on the following page you will find a Claim for Economic Contribution Calculator which was devised by Reginald Hirsch and Warren Cole, both premier family law attorneys.

CLAIM FOR ECONOMIC CONTRIBUTION CALCULATOR PER § 3.401 et seq.
(Assumes all criterion per statute exists (i.e. "secured by a lien on property," etc.)

A. EQUITY IN BENEFITED PROPERTY ON DATE OF DIVORCE/DISPOSITION		$ AMOUNT	TOTALS
1	FMV of the property on date of divorce/disposition:		
2	Principal amount of debt on date of divorce/disposition:	0.00	
3	**Total Equity – date of div./disp. (calculates automatically)**		0.00 **A**

B. ECONOMIC CONTRIBUTION BY CONTRIBUTING ESTATE (Debt Reduction)		$ AMOUNT	TOTALS
1	Principal amount of debt on Date of Marriage/Date of receipt as SP:		
2	Principal amount of debt on Date of Divorce/Disposition (same as A):	0.00	
3	**Total Amt. of Contribution by CE (calculates automatically)**		0.00 **B**

C. ECONOMIC CONTRIBUTION BY CONTRIBUTING ESTATE (Debt Refinancing)		$ AMOUNT	TOTALS
1	Principal amount of former debt on date of refinancing:		
2	Principal amount of former debt after refinancing (usually zero):	0.00	
3	**Total Amt. – Debt Ref. by CE (calculates automatically)**		0.00 **C**

D. ECONOMIC CONTRIBUTION-CAP. IMPROVEMENTS (Other Than Incurring Debt)		$ AMOUNT	TOTALS
1	Dollar Amount Contributed:		
	Total Val. Cap. Improvements (calculates automatically)		0.00 **D**

E. EQUITY IN PROPERTY–DATE OF MARRIAGE/1ST ECONOMIC CONTRIBUTION		$ AMOUNT	TOTALS
1	FMV on date of marriage or of first economic contribution:		
2	Principal amount of debt at date of marriage/1st economic contribution:	0.00	
3	**Total Equity – Date of Marr./1st Econ. Cont. (calculates automatically)**		0.00 **E**

F. ECONOMIC CONTRIBUTION BY BENEFITED ESTATE (During Marriage)		$ AMOUNT	TOTALS
1	Dollar Amount Contributed:		
	Total Econ. Contrib. by BE (calculates automatically)		0.00 **F**

$$ Amt. of the Claim [A x (B + C + D)/(B + C + D + E + F)] (calculates automatically):	
Percentage of Claim to Contributing Estate from Benefited Estate	

Chapter 4

Management and Liability of Property During Marriage

A. Introduction

Money problems can be one of the biggest concerns in a marriage. As debts mount, spouses want to know what property will be liable for the claims of creditors. Knowing the rules of marital property liability, especially in advance of problems that may arise, can aid in the protection of the marital estate and perhaps even save a marriage.

The liability of marital property is irretrievably linked to the management of marital property; accordingly, the concepts of management and liability cannot be effectively considered separately. The management and liability of marital property in Texas is statutorily driven. For this reason, the statutes will be set forth in the following overviews and they may be found in the Appendix.

B. Management, An Overview

The power to manage marital property includes the power to transfer title to a third person for consideration or by gift or by devise. It also includes the power to litigate and the power to incur obligations, either contractual or tortious, which would subject marital property to liability.

TEX. FAM. CODE § 3.101 provides that "[e]ach spouse has the sole management, control, and disposition of that spouse's separate property." This makes sense because a spouse should be and is able to do whatever they want with their separate property. This right to manage, control and dispose of separate property exists during the marriage and at death. A spouse in Texas is not required to devise any of their separate estate to their surviving spouse.

In contrast, a spouse's management and control over community property is balanced against the other spouse's rights to and interest in the community property. Specifically, TEX. FAM. CODE § 3.102 governs the management of community property and provides:

> (a) During marriage, each spouse has the sole management, control, and disposition of the community property that the spouse would have owned if single, including:
>
> (1) personal earnings;
>
> (2) revenue from separate property;
>
> (3) recoveries for personal injuries; and
>
> (4) the increase and mutations of, and the revenue from, all property subject to the spouse's sole management, control, and disposition.
>
> (b) If community property subject to the sole management, control, and disposition of one spouse is mixed or combined with community property subject to the sole management, control, and disposition of the other spouse, then the mixed or combined community property is subject to the joint management, control, and disposition of the spouses, unless the spouses provide otherwise by power of attorney in writing or other agreement.
>
> (c) Except as provided by Subsection (a), community property is subject to the joint management, control, and disposition of the spouses unless the spouses provide otherwise by power of attorney in writing or other agreement.

TEX. FAM. CODE § 3.102

Management and control of marital property is also clarified in relation to third parties so that third parties will be protected in their dealings with spouses. Assuming there is not a fraudulent transfer, a spouse should be able to sell a community asset in their name without the joinder of the other spouse; the third party purchaser should be able to depend upon the propriety of that sale. Specifically, TEX. FAM. CODE § 3.104 protects third parties, thus:

> (a) During marriage, property is presumed to be subject to the sole management, control, and disposition of a spouse if it is held in that spouse's name, as shown by muniment, contract, deposit of funds, or other evidence of ownership, or if it is in that spouse's possession and is not subject to such evidence of ownership.
>
> (b) A third person dealing with a spouse is entitled to rely, as against the other spouse or anyone claiming from that spouse, on that spouse's authority to deal with the property if:
>
> (1) the property is presumed to be subject to the sole management, control, and disposition of the spouse; and

(2) the person dealing with the spouse:

(A) is not a party to a fraud on the other spouse or another person; and

(B) does not have actual or constructive notice of the spouse's lack of authority.

TEX. FAM. CODE § 3.104.

Management is also addressed in TEX. FAM. CODE § 4.204 which governs the management of property converted from separate to community, providing that property converted to community property is subject to:

(1) the sole management, control, and disposition of the spouse in whose name the property is held;

(2) the sole management, control, and disposition of the spouse who transferred the property if the property is not subject to evidence of ownership;

(3) the joint management, control, and disposition of the spouses if the property is held in the name of both spouses; or

(4) the joint management, control, and disposition of the spouses if the property is not subject to evidence of ownership and was owned by both spouses before the property was converted to community property.

In addition, TEX. FAM. CODE § 3.103 provides that the earnings of the minor are subject to the joint management, control, and disposition of the parents of the minor, unless otherwise provided by agreement of the parents or by judicial order.

Notice that the foregoing management portions of the Texas Family Code do not simply characterize property as separate and community, but established further classification of community property into the sole management community property of either spouse or joint management community property. Thus the five management categories of marital property that are recognized are:

(1) Husband's separate property—sole management;
(2) Husband's sole management community property;
(3) Joint management community property;
(4) Wife's sole management community property;
(5) Wife's separate property—sole management.

The determination of whether marital property will be liable for a debt depends upon into which of the above categories the questioned property falls.

C. Liability, An Overview

Liability in the marital property realm is simply the determination of which of the five categories of marital property can be reached by a third party for satisfaction of an obligation incurred by one or both spouses. Just as marital property is categorized, so are the debts of the spouses.

The rules of marital property liability are set forth in TEX. FAM. CODE § 3.202, thus:

> (a) A spouse's separate property is not subject to liabilities of the other spouse unless both spouses are liable by other rules of law.
>
> (b) Unless both spouses are personally liable as provided by this subchapter, the community property subject to a spouse's sole management, control, and disposition is not subject to:
>
> (1) any liabilities that the other spouse incurred before marriage; or
>
> (2) any nontortious liabilities that the other spouse incurs during marriage.
>
> (c) The community property subject to a spouse's sole or joint management, control, and disposition is subject to the liabilities incurred by the spouse before or during marriage.
>
> (d) All community property is subject to tortious liability of either spouse incurred during marriage.

TEX. FAM. CODE § 3.202

In order to apply the foregoing statute, one must determine the category of marital property (husband's separate property or sole management community property, joint management community property, or wife's separate property or sole management community property) sought to satisfy the liability. In addition, one must also categorize the liability; that is, it must be determined,

(1) whether the liability is the sole liability of one spouse or the joint liability of both spouses;

(2) if a sole liability is involved, whether the liability is a separate property debt as described in *Ray v. United States*, 385 F.Supp. 372 (S.D. Tex. 1974), *aff'd per curiam*, 538 F.2d 1228 (5th Cir. 1976), *supra* at page 201; or

(3) if a sole liability is involved, whether it is a pre-marital liability; or

(4) if it is a post-marital liability, whether it is a nontortious liability; or

(5) if it is a post-marital liability, whether it is a tortious liability; or

(6) whether other rules of law are applicable.

The Texas Family Code also makes clear that the marital relationship in and of itself does not establish the liability of a spouse; indeed, it is only in the most limited of circumstances that the marital relationship, alone, can give rise to liability. Specifically, TEX. FAM. CODE § 3.201, provides:

> (a) A person is personally liable for the acts of the person's spouse only if:
>
> (1) the spouse acts as an agent for the person; or
>
> (2) the spouse incurs a debt for necessaries as provided by Subchapter F, Chapter 2.

(b) Except as provided by this subchapter, community property is not subject to a liability that arises from an act of a spouse.

(c) A spouse does not act as an agent for the other spouse solely because of the marriage relationship.

TEX. FAM. CODE § 3.201.

The following chart depicts marital property liability. To structure your analysis when determining which property is liable, characterize the debt and then determine the management of the property in question. Reference to this chart will greatly enhance your understanding of marital property liability.

Diagram of Marital Property Liability

	Husband's Separate Property	Husband's Sole Management. Community Property	Joint Management. Community Property	Wife's Sole Management. Community Property	Wife's Separate Property
Husband's Separate Property Debt*	■				
Husband's Pre-Marital Liabilities	■	■	■		
Husband's Non-Tortious Liabilities During Marriage	■	■	■		
Husband's Tortious Liabilities During Marriage	■	■	■	■	
Wife's Tortious Liabilities During Marriage		■	■	■	■
Wife's Non-Tortious Liabilities During Marriage			■	■	■
Wife's Pre-Marital Liabilities			■	■	■
Wife's Separate Property Debt*					■
Joint Liabilities Of Spouses	■	■	■	■	■

* The phrase "separate property debt" makes reference to a debt for which only separate property of the debtor spouse may be liable, as was exemplified in the case of *Ray v. United States*, 385 F. Supp. 372 (S.D.Tex. 1974), *aff'd per curiam*, 538 F.2d 1228 (5th Cir. 1976).

D. General Concepts

COCKERHAM
v.
COCKERHAM
527 S.W.2d 162
(Tex. 1975)

SAM D. JOHNSON, JUSTICE.

This is a divorce case in which the wife's trustee in bankruptcy has intervened. The trial court granted the divorce and made the property division to be discussed hereinafter. The court of civil appeals affirmed with one justice dissenting. 514 S.W.2d 150. We affirm the judgment of the court of civil appeals in part and reverse and render in part.

Petitioner Dorothy Cockerham brought this suit for divorce against her husband, respondent E.A. Cockerham. E.A. Cockerham filed a cross action for divorce alleging his wife had drained the community assets for the benefit of an individual named DeRay Houston. Petitioner Theodore Mack, trustee in bankruptcy of Dorothy Cockerham, intervened seeking to require the payment of indebtedness due the bankruptcy creditors out of the community property prior to its division between husband and wife. At trial the husband sought to prove, among other things, that the wife had made substantial gifts of community property to DeRay Houston in fraud of the husband's rights in the community. The jury rejected this argument in its answer to special issue number three:

> SPECIAL ISSUE NO. 3
>
> Do you find from a preponderance of the evidence that Dorothy Cockerham has made gifts of property to DeRay Houston?
>
> Answer "Yes" or "No."
>
> ANSWER: No.

Pursuant to the jury verdict, the trial court on September 11, 1972 entered a judgment granting the parties a divorce, awarding custody of the children to the husband, giving the wife visitation and restraining the wife from taking the children away from the husband's home. The judgment further recites, "The Court further finds that due to the intervention of the Trustee in Bankruptcy, the property rights of the parties herein are not determined at this time, but this Court retains jurisdiction of the property rights of such parties until finally determined at a future date."

About a year later, in September 1973, the cause was again called for trial for the purpose of determining the property rights of the parties. The property at issue in that trial, which is relevant to this appeal, included (1) a 198-acre tract claimed to be the homestead of the husband and wife, (2) a 320-acre tract on which the husband operated a dairy, and (3) a dairy business consisting of cattle, farm equipment and machinery, a milk base and milking equipment. Several claims were asserted against these properties. First, community debts totaling $47,985, which includes the sum of $36,200 due on indebtedness secured by a lien on the 198-acre tract, were alleged. Second, the trustee in bankruptcy asserted a claim for $68,933.99 to pay the wife's bankruptcy creditors and the bankruptcy expenses. These debts arose out of the operation of a dress shop by the wife during the last two years of the marriage. Finally, the husband alleged the wife had made fraudulent gifts of community assets in the amount of $19,317.14 to DeRay Houston.

Trial on the property rights of the parties was to the court which made findings of fact and conclusions of law.[1] The judgment of the trial court set aside the 198-acre homestead tract, along with household goods and furnishings, to the husband. The 320-acre tract was adjudicated to be one-half the separate property of the husband and one-half community property. The court required the $47,985 "community debts," which included the $36,200 due on the debt secured by a lien on the 198-acre tract, to be paid out of the community interest in the 320-acre tract of land and the other community property, consisting of the dairy business. After the community debts were paid the community property was to be divided equally between the parties. However, the husband was also awarded $9,658.57 (one-half of the $19,317.14 of community property which the trial court found to be fraudulently given by the wife to DeRay Houston) out of the wife's share of what remained of that equally divided property after payment of the community debts. The $68,933.99 due the trustee was to be satisfied out of the wife's share after the payment of all community debts and after further reducing her interest by the above-mentioned amount of $9,658.57.

Both Dorothy Cockerham and the trustee appealed from the judgment adjudicating the property rights to the court of civil appeals. That court affirmed the trial court's judgment, making, among others, the following determinations:

> 1. An undivided one-half of the 320-acre tract was E.A. Cockerham's separate property by reason of his prior ownership before marriage; the other undivided one-half of the 320-acre tract was the community property of E.A. and Dorothy Cockerham. Thus, there was a tenancy in common with respect to the 320-acre tract between the separate estate of E.A. Cockerham and the community estate.

---

[1] The findings of fact are substantially as follows: (1) The court held the 198-acre tract was the homestead of the parties and had an existing debt of $36,200 against it. The parties in addition owed $11,785 of other community debts for a total community indebtedness of $47,985. (2) As to the 320-acre tract, the findings recite ". . . that one-half thereof is community property and one-half the separate property of the said E.A. Cockerham by reason of his ownership to an undivided one-half interest thereof prior to his marriage with Dorothy Cockerham" and that the partition suit "was but a means of convenience provided by law to complete the purchase of the whole and secure a loan thereon." (3) The court made a finding which is contrary to the jury's answer to special issue number three, as above quoted. The court's finding was that Dorothy Cockerham made gifts of community assets to DeRay Houston in at least the sum of $19,317.14 in fraud of the community. The court further found that "this sum should be charged to the proportionate share owned by the said Dorothy Cockerham but subject to the community debts above set out." (4) The court found the dairy business, along with one-half of the 320 acres of land, to be community property and held the parties would take same subject to the community debt. (5) As to priority, the court found "that the property rights of the said Dorothy Cockerham set out herein are subject first to the judgment of this Court, and then subject to the rights of the Intervenor Trustee in Bankruptcy." Included in the conclusions of law were the following: (1) "The act of Dorothy Cockerham, over the protest of E.A. Cockerham, in using community funds in her store adventure; and having a joint bank account with a third party male; and in transferring inventory from her store to the supposed store of the third party male without accounting for same, was a fraud upon the rights of E.A. Cockerham, and for which she is entitled to have charged against her interest." (2) The estate is subject to the community debts ($47,985) and that Dorothy's share of the community property is chargeable with gifts made in fraud of the community. (3) One-half of the 320 acres is the separate property of E.A. Cockerham and one-half is the community property of E.A. Cockerham and Dorothy Cockerham. (4) As a final conclusion, the court stated, "The share or portion of Dorothy Cockerham is subject to the divisions of this Court, and the rights of the Intervenor Trustee inn the order as set out."

2. The dairy business operated by the husband on the 320-acre tract was under the sole management and control of the husband, E.A. Cockerham, "... and therefore under Section 5.61,[2] community property consisting of an undivided one-half of the 320 acres, the milking equipment, cattle, milk base, and farm equipment, was not subject to the 'non-tortious liabilities' of the wife, Dorothy Cockerham, same being the claims of the bankruptcy creditors of Dorothy Cockerham. ..."

3. The trial court had the power to disregard the jury's finding that the wife did not make gifts to DeRay Houston because the jury findings regarding the division of property were advisory only. There was evidence to support the trial court's finding that the property was fraudulently conveyed by the wife; the trial court acted within its discretion in charging the wife's share with the amounts given.

4. The trial court acted within its discretion in requiring the indebtedness secured by a lien on the 198-acre homestead tract to be paid out of the community property prior to the wife's bankruptcy creditors.

5. The division of community property was not so disproportionately favorable to the husband as to be an abuse of discretion.

Both Dorothy Cockerham and the trustee have filed applications for writ of error. Their contentions will be discussed separately.

APPLICATION OF THE TRUSTEE

The trustee brings fifteen points of error to this court. Basically he asserts error on the part of the court of civil appeals in not subjecting the whole 320-acre tract and all of the community property to the claims of the bankruptcy creditors, and in relegating those creditors to an inferior position with regard to priority. His initial contention is that the entire 320-acre tract was community property. Alternatively he argues that even if an undivided one-half interest in the 320-acre tract is the husband's separate property, the husband made a gift of one-half of his separate property interest to his wife. The trustee further argues that even if some part of the property is the separate property of the husband, it is nevertheless liable for the debts incurred in the operation of the dress shop.

THE 320-ACRE TRACT AS COMMUNITY OR SEPARATE PROPERTY.

When the Cockerhams were married on May 16, 1949, the husband, E.A. Cockerham, owned an undivided one-half interest in the 320-acre tract and his brother, Herman Cockerham, owned the other undivided one-half. The brothers conducted a farming and cattle raising operation on this property. A number of years later, in 1955, Herman Cockerham wanted to sell his undivided one-half interest in the 320 acres and his brother, E.A. Cockerham, wanted to buy him out. However, E.A. Cockerham had to get a loan on the property in order to pay his brother for his half. In order to accomplish these things, the two brothers went to a lawyer who filed a partition suit on behalf of E.A. and wife against Herman and wife and secured the court appointment of receiver. The receiver thereupon sold the 320-acre tract to E.A. and Dorothy Cockerham at private sale under the orders of the district court. The receiver's deed indicates a total consideration of $22,700, of which $11,400 cash was recited to have been paid by E.A. and Dorothy Cockerham and $11,300 cash furnished by John Hancock Mutual Life Insurance Company, who reserved a ven-

---

[2] Texas Family Code.

dor's lien on the land. It was undisputed, however, that E.A. and Dorothy Cockerham actually made no cash payment at all. It is also undisputed that the amount recited to have been paid in cash by E.A. Cockerham in this transaction ($11,400) was approximately the value of his undivided one-half interest in the property. The receiver's deed was a conveyance to E.A. and Dorothy Cockerham, in both names as grantees. All Dorothy seemed to know about this transaction was that her husband was buying his brother out of the 320-acre tract. The trial court held that these facts were sufficient to establish that an undivided one-half of the 320-acre tract was separate property of E.A. Cockerham "by reason of his ownership to an undivided one-half interest thereof prior to his marriage." The court of civil appeals affirmed, holding that there was a tenancy in common between the separate property of E.A. Cockerham and the community property. The trustee attacks this holding, asserting that the evidence is insufficient to support the conclusion of the court of civil appeals that E.A. Cockerham adequately traced his prior separate property ownership in the 320-acre tract.

Property possessed by either spouse during or on dissolution of marriage is presumed to be community property. Section 5.02[3]. In order to overcome this presumption, the party asserting separate ownership must clearly trace the original separate property into the particular assets on hand during the marriage. *E.g.*, *McKinley v. McKinley*, 496 S.W.2d 540, 543 (Tex. 1973); *Tarver v. Tarver*, 394 S.W.2d 780 (Tex. 1965). *See* Comment, *The Commingling of Separate and Community Funds: The Requirement of Tracing in Texas*, 6 ST. MARY'S L.J. 234 (1974).

In the instant case it was undisputed that the husband owned an undivided one-half interest in identifiable real property prior to marriage. The partition suit and sale was, as found by the trial court, only "a means of convenience provided by law to complete the purchase of the whole and secure a loan thereon." In addition, the cash consideration ($11,400) recited to have been paid by E.A. Cockerham in this transaction was the approximate value of his prior undivided interest in the property. No cash, however, actually changed hands. These facts are sufficient to justify the trial court in finding that E.A. Cockerham put up the interest he owned prior to marriage as partial consideration for the purchase. Since the interest he owned prior to marriage was an undivided one-half of the 320-acre tract, such undivided one-half interest remained his separate property.

The trustee alternatively contends that if the husband had a separate property interest in the 320 acres the record shows he made a gift of an undivided one-half of such separate property interest to his wife. In support of this position the trustee points out that title to the whole 320 acres was taken in the name of E.A. Cockerham and wife, Dorothy Cockerham, and asserts that it is well established that when a husband uses separate property consideration to pay for land acquired during the marriage and takes title to the land in the name of husband and wife, it is presumed he intended the interest placed in his wife to be a gift. *Smith v. Strahan*, 16 Tex. 314 (1856); *Tucker v. Carr*, 39 Tex. 98 (1873); *Tate v. Tate*, 299 S.W. 310 (Tex. Civ. App.—Eastland 1927, no writ); *Carriere v. Bodungen*, 500 S.W.2d 692 (Tex. Civ. App.—Corpus Christi 1973, no writ); *Hampshire v. Hampshire*, 485 S.W.2d 314 (Tex. Civ. App.—Fort Worth 1972, no writ); 1 MCCORMICK & RAY, TEXAS LAW OF EVIDENCE § 92 (2d ed. 1956). *See* POMEROY'S EQUITY JURISPRUDENCE § 1039 at 2354. This presumption, however, can be rebutted by evidence clearly establishing there was no intention to make a gift. *Smith v. Strahan*, *supra*; *Dean v. Dean*, 214 S.W. 505 (Tex. Civ. App.—1919, no writ); *Hampshire v. Hampshire*, *supra*; *Patterson v. Metzing*, 424 S.W.2d 255 (Tex. Civ. App.—Corpus Christi 1967, no writ); 1 MCCORMICK & RAY, *supra*.

---

[3] All references herein are to the Texas Family Code, hereinafter cited by section only.

In the instant case Dorothy Cockerham testified she never paid any attention to the purchase of the 320 acres; in fact, she claimed she never even saw the deed to the property until the preparation for the instant litigation. Her attitude toward the 320-acre tract has, until the instant suit, been largely one of complete disinterest—the 320 acres and the dairy business on it were her husband's business about which she paid little, if any, attention. She offered no testimony in support of the presumption that her husband meant to make a gift to her of part of his interest in the 320-acre tract. There is nothing in her testimony which would indicate any understanding that a gift had been made to her. The husband's testimony also tends to negate any idea that he intended a gift to his wife. The structure of the transaction whereby he bought his brother's interest in the 320-acre tract was of no concern to him; he left the transaction entirely to his lawyer. All he knew was that one day he went to the courthouse and then, "I just owned 160 acres worth of land." At trial he took the position that the whole 320 acres had always been *his land*. Moreover, the husband's brother, Herman, from whom he bought the property corroborated the testimony that the purchase was structured as it was solely to enable the husband to buy the property. Based upon this evidence the trial court entered two findings of fact which relate to whether the husband intended a gift to the wife. First, the court found the method used to purchase the 320 acres was but a "means of convenience" to complete the purchase. Second, the court entered a finding that "one-half (of the 320-acre tract) is community property and one-half the separate property of E.A. Cockerham." By entering these findings the court impliedly found that the presumption the husband intended a gift to the wife was sufficiently rebutted and that, in fact, there was no such intention. This finding must be upheld if it finds any support in the evidence. *Langlotz v. Citizens Fidelity Insurance Company*, 505 S.W.2d 249 (Tex. 1974); *Butler v. Hanson*, 455 S.W.2d 942 (Tex. 1970). Considering the record before us, we are unable to say there is no evidence to uphold the implied finding of the trial court that E.A. Cockerham did not intend to make a gift to his wife.

Since E.A. Cockerham adequately traced his prior separate interest in an undivided one-half of the 320-acre tract and sufficiently rebutted the presumption which arises from the fact that title was taken in the name of himself and his wife, a tenancy in common exists in the 320-acre tract between the undivided one-half separate property interest of E.A. Cockerham and the undivided one-half community property interest. *Gleich v. Bongio*, 128 Tex. 606, 99 S.W.2d 881 (1937).

THE TRUSTEE'S CLAIM AGAINST THE COMMUNITY PROPERTY.

As noted above, the community owned an undivided one-half interest in the 320-acre tract as tenant in common. In addition, the dairy business, which was purchased during marriage with community funds, is indisputedly community property.

The trustee claims the community interest in the 320-acre tract and the community property dairy business is subject to the dress shop obligations, relying on Section 5.61, which is entitled "Rules of Marital Property Liability" and which provides:

> (a) A spouse's separate property is not subject to liabilities of the other spouse unless both spouses are liable by other rules of law.
>
> (b) Unless both spouses are liable by other rules of law, the community property subject to a spouse's sole management, control, and disposition is not subject to:
>
> (1) any liabilities that the other spouse incurred before marriage; or
>
> (2) any nontortious liabilities that the other spouse incurs during marriage.

(c) The community property subject to a spouse's sole or joint management, control, and disposition is subject to the liabilities incurred by him or her before or during marriage.

(d) All the community property is subject to tortious liability of either spouse incurred during marriage.

The trustee argues, first, that the community property was subject to *joint* management, control and disposition and is thus liable for the debts incurred by Dorothy Cockerham in the operation of the dress shop under Section 5.61(c). Alternatively, the trustee contends that even if the dairy business was under the *sole* management of the husband within Section 5.61(b) the debts incurred in the operation of the dress shop are joint liabilities of the husband and wife and thus the dairy business is not insulated from liability by Section 5.61(b)(2), which protects sole management property only from non-tortious liabilities incurred by the other spouse. Thus the trustee argues the dairy business would be subject to these joint liabilities under Section 5.61(c), which provides that property subject to the sole management of a spouse is subject to liabilities incurred by that spouse.[4]

THE COMMUNITY PROPERTY AS JOINT OR SOLE MANAGEMENT PROPERTY.

Resolution of the issue of whether community property is joint or sole management property depends upon the construction and interpretation of Section 5.22, which pertains to the management of community property. At the time this case was tried that section read as follows:

(a) During marriage, each spouse has the sole management, control, and disposition of the community property that he or she would have owned if single, including but not limited to:

(1) personal earnings;

(2) revenue from separate property;

(3) recoveries for personal injuries; and

(4) the increase and mutations of, and the revenue from, all property subject to his or her sole management, control, and disposition.

(b) If community property subject to the sole management, control, and disposition of one spouse is mixed or combined with community property subject to the sole management, control, and disposition of the other spouse, then the mixed or combined community property is subject to the joint management, control, and disposition of the spouses, unless the spouses provide otherwise by power of attorney or other agreement in writing.

(c) Except as provided in Subsection (a) of this section, the community property is subject to the joint management, control, and disposition of the husband and wife, unless the spouses provide otherwise by power of attorney or other agreement in writing.[5]

The court of civil appeals pointed out that the dairy business on the 320-acre tract was operated solely by E.A. Cockerham; that it was near but not contiguous to the homestead tract; that it was in possession and control of the husband; that the wife took no part in its operation. Thus, reasoned the court of civil appeals, the community property dairy business along with the undi-

---

[4] The reference to liabilities 'incurred by him or her' in Section 5.61(c) is interpreted to mean liabilities incurred by the spouse referred to in that section.

[5] Effective January 1, 1974 Subsection (c) was changed to allow spouses to eliminate the requirement that an agreement to alter managerial powers be in writing.

vided one-half community property interest in the 320 acres upon which the business was located was under the sole management of E.A. Cockerham within the meaning of Section 5.22(a). The trustee disputes this holding, contending the dairy business does not fit into any of the specifically enumerated classifications of sole management property listed in Section 5.22(a). Since Section 5.22(c) provides that all property except property included in Subsection (a) is joint management property, the trustee reasons the dairy business and the community tract are thus subject to the joint management of the husband and wife.

With regard to the 320-acre tract, the record reveals E.A. Cockerham and his wife in effect borrowed the cash necessary to purchase the community interest by giving a note secured by a deed of trust on the property in return. Title to the property was taken in the name of both husband and wife; both husband and wife were obligated on the note. Under virtually identical circumstances these facts were considered sufficient to establish that the community interest was subject to the joint management of the husband and wife in *Cooper v. Texas Gulf Industries, Inc.*, 513 S.W.2d 200 (Tex. 1974). We therefore hold that the community interest in the undivided one-half of the 320-acre tract was subject to the joint management of E.A. Cockerham and his wife. Section 5.22(c).

The situation with respect to the dairy business is somewhat more complicated. As has been noted, the dairy is located on the 320-acre tract, which is one-half separate property of the husband and one-half community property. The dairy was acquired during the marriage when the husband converted his cattle operation into a dairy business. Over the years the proceeds from the business were invested in additional machinery and equipment causing the business to increase in size and worth. It is asserted the proceeds from the dairy business are "personal earnings" of the husband within Section 5.22(a)(1); that these earnings alone have caused the dairy business to grow and thus the business is the "increase and mutation" of the husband's personal earnings and is under the sole management of the husband. Section 5.22(a)(4). We do not agree. The income from the dairy business was produced not only by the labor of the husband but also by the use of capital improvements which were community property and by the use of the land on which the business was located. Personal earnings, on the other hand, are earnings solely by physical or mental labor, unaided by capital, except insofar as may be necessary to supply the means of such labor as, for example, the ax of a woodcutter or the pen and paper of a writer. *First Nat. Bank v. Davis*, 5 S.W.2d 753 (Tex. Com. App. 1928, holding approved); 1 SPEER'S MARITAL RIGHTS IN TEXAS § 421 at 625 (4th ed. 1961). We conclude the income produced by the dairy business was not "personal earnings" of the husband within Section 5.22(a)(1). The husband has not shown that this is property which he "would have owned if single." Section 5.22(a). The use of community assets was an integral part of the dairy business. We therefore hold the dairy business was thus under the joint management, control and disposition of the husband and wife under Section 5.22(c).

Since both the community interest in the 320-acre tract and the community dairy business were under the joint management of both E.A. Cockerham and his wife, they will be liable for the dress shop debts whether those debts are considered obligations of only the husband, of only the wife or joint obligations of both the husband and wife. Section 5.61(c).

THE TRUSTEE'S CLAIM AGAINST THE HUSBAND'S SEPARATE PROPERTY.

The trustee also seeks to hold the husband's separate property interest in an undivided one-half of the 320-acre tract liable for the dress shop debts. He argues that Section 5.61(a) does not insulate the husband's separate property from liability for the dress shop debts. He contends, first, that the dress shop debts are joint liabilities for which both spouses are liable. Alternatively, he claims that even if the dress shop debts are liabilities of the "other spouse" (wife) within Section 5.61, the husband is nevertheless also liable under "other rules of law" within the meaning of that statute. We sustain the trustee's first contention and thus find it unnecessary to consider his alternative argument.

The Character of the Dress Shop Debts.

In 1969 Dorothy Cockerham opened a dress shop in Hurst, Texas. The evidence is conflicting as to E.A. Cockerham's attitude toward this enterprise—she claimed he urged her to open the shop; he claimed he opposed the move but realized that not allowing her to open the shop would cause a divorce. Notwithstanding his alleged opposition, however, the wife did, in fact, open the shop using approximately $4,000 which was advanced to her by the husband.

Dorothy had financial difficulties from the beginning and in 1970 she moved the shop to Burleson, Texas in an attempt to improve sales. The business continued to flounder, however, and eventually resulted in bankruptcy. The debts asserted by the trustee represent, primarily, credit purchases of inventory for the store.

E.A. Cockerham never took part in the conduct or operation of the dress shop and all purchases for the shop were made by Dorothy. The husband claims this fact alone establishes that the debts incurred were solely those of his wife. The fact of physical operation of a business, however, is not wholly determinative of the character, as sole or joint, of the debts incurred in its operation. This is especially true since both husband and wife now have full capacity to contract. Section 4.03.

To determine whether a debt is only that of the contracting party or if it is instead that of both the husband and wife, it is necessary to examine the totality of the circumstances in which the debt arose. Of particular importance in the instant case is the consideration of implied assent to the debt by the noncontracting party, the husband.

The debts in the instant case arose, of course, during marriage. It is well established that debts contracted during marriage are presumed to be on the credit of the community and thus are joint community obligations, unless it is shown the creditor agreed to look solely to the separate estate of the contracting spouse for satisfaction. *Broussard v. Tian*, 156 Tex. 371, 295 S.W.2d 405 (1956); *Gleich v. Bongio, supra*. There is no evidence the parties who extended Dorothy Cockerham credit agreed to look solely to her separate estate for satisfaction, and thus, there are no facts to rebut the presumption these debts are community liabilities. Though this would establish the community character of the debts, the fact that the debts are community liabilities would not, without more, necessarily lead to the conclusion they were joint liabilities. Characterization of the debts as community liabilities is only one aspect of the circumstances to be considered in determining whether the debts are joint.

In the instant case the record is replete with factors which point to the conclusion that the dress shop debts were joint liabilities of both the husband and the wife. For example, it was the husband who advanced the wife the necessary capital to pay for the initial inventory of the store. In addition, it was the wife's practice, acquiesced in by her husband, to write checks for personal and family expenses on his personal checking account by signing his name rather than hers; this was done because the parties did not have a joint account. Their bank knew of this practice and honored the checks written by the wife on her husband's account. After the wife opened the dress shop she continued to write checks on her husband's account and often paid for merchandise for the store in this manner. The husband never forbade her to do so nor did he stop payment on any of the checks. On one occasion, as the business began to encounter difficulties, he borrowed $5,000 to pay off some of the dress shop debts because, in his words, "... I have always paid my debts." It is clear that he recognized these as his obligations. Though the husband now claims he did not authorize the dress shop liabilities, his actions were consistent with an implied assent to their establishment. In addition, there is some evidence of an expressed assent in that there was at least one instance in which he himself signed a check in the sum of $1,400 which was used to pay operational expenses of the dress shop. Moreover, the joint income tax returns of Dorothy and her husband for the years Dorothy had the dress shop reveal they took depreciation deductions on the dress shop equipment and wrote off substantial losses because of the dress shop operation. Because of this the Cockerhams paid very little, and in some years no, federal income tax even though the husband had a substantial income from his dairy business.

In view of the record presented to this court, we hold the dress shop debts are joint liabilities of both the husband and the wife. Since they are not liabilities of the "other spouse," Section 5.61(a) does not insulate the husband's separate property from liability for these debts. A joint liability is an obligation of both parties; the husband's separate property is therefore subject to the dress shop debts. *See e.g.*, 4 CORBIN ON CONTRACTS § 928 (1951).

THE TRUSTEE'S CLAIM FOR EQUALITY IN PRIORITY.

The order of the trial court, which was affirmed by the court of civil appeals, provided that the community debts would be paid out of the community estate and that the balance of the community property would be divided equally between the husband and wife, except for the payment to the husband, out of the wife's share, of $9,658.57, representing his share of community property allegedly disposed of in fraud of his rights. The wife's bankruptcy debts were to be satisfied out of the wife's share of the community property after payment of the $9,658.57 to the husband. The trustee argues first that the courts below erred in allowing the community creditors to be satisfied out of the community property before the bankruptcy creditors. The trustee claims all of the unsecured creditors, including the bankruptcy creditors, had an equal right to be paid out of the community property. We have determined that the debts asserted by the bankruptcy creditors are joint liabilities of the husband and the wife; they therefore have an equal right to be paid out of the community property and also may be satisfied out of the separate property of the husband.

The second argument of the trustee is that the courts below erred in subordinating the rights of the bankruptcy creditors to the claim of the husband against the wife. Any distribution of community property between the husband and wife, contends the trustee, must be done in subordination to the rights of creditors. *See* 3 SPEER'S MARITAL RIGHTS IN TEXAS § 840 (4th ed. 1961). We agree that the courts below erred in allowing the claim of the husband to be paid before the claim of the trustee. We reach this conclusion, however, upon a determination that the award to the husband was improper.

As noted above, the trial court found that Dorothy Cockerham had fraudulently taken community property and made gifts to DeRay Houston. This finding was in disregard of the jury's refusal to find that Dorothy had made such fraudulent gifts. As recognized by the court of civil appeals, the testimony was sharply conflicting on this issue and there was certainly at least some evidence to support the jury's answer. The court of civil appeals, however, held that the trial court had the power to disregard the jury's answer because answers of the jury regarding disposition of property are advisory only. Though the trial court has wide discretion in dividing the property of the spouses as it feels just and in disregarding advisory answers of the jury, it may not ignore the jury's answers which extend to issues of fact from which the status of property is determined. *Stafford v. Stafford*, 41 Tex. 111 (1874); *Rice v. Rice*, 21 Tex. 58 (1858); *Baker v. Baker*, 104 S.W.2d 531 (Tex. Civ. App.—San Antonio 1936, no writ). This is particularly true when the disposition of the property to the husband or wife is based solely on its status. In the instant case the award of part of the wife's share of community property to the husband was based only on the findings of the trial court that the property was property which had been fraudulently disposed of by the wife. This was directly related to the status of the property. The action of the trial court in disregarding the jury's answer regarding the status of the property was error. There was no basis for the award to the husband.

APPLICATION OF THE WIFE

Dorothy Cockerham contends the trial court's division of the property was so disproportionate as to be manifestly unjust and amounted to an abuse of discretion. Her main complaint is that the trial court awarded the 198-acre homestead tract and all the household furniture to her husband. Other than this, all of the community property was divided equally, subject to the community debts.

It is well established that the trial court has wide discretion in the division of property on divorce and it will be disturbed only when an abuse of discretion is shown. Section 3.63; *Hailey v. Hailey*, 160 Tex. 372, 331 S.W.2d 299 (1960); *Hedtke v. Hedtke*, 112 Tex. 404, 248 S.W. 21 (1923). Considering the record before us, we are unable to say the trial court abused its discretion.

We hold that the husband did not make a gift of an undivided one-half interest in his separate property interest in the 320-acre tract to the wife; that the 320-acre tract is one-half the separate property of the husband and one-half the community property of the husband and the wife; that a tenancy in common exists on the 320-acre tract between the undivided one-half community property interest and the undivided one-half separate property interest of the husband; that the undivided one-half community property interest in the 320-acre tract was under the joint management of the husband and the wife and is subject to the dress shop debts; that the dairy business was community property under the joint management of the husband and the wife and is liable for the dress shop debts; that the dress shop debts are joint obligations rendering the husband's separate property interest in the 320 acres liable for these obligations; that the bankruptcy creditors and the community creditors have an equal right to be satisfied out of the community property; that the trial court erred in disregarding the jury's answer regarding the status of the property allegedly given by the wife to DeRay Houston and the courts below erred in ordering a reduction in the wife's share of the community property in the sum of $9,658.57; and that the trial court's division of the property was not so disproportionate as to amount to an abuse of discretion.

The judgment of the court of civil appeals is accordingly affirmed in part and reversed and rendered in part in accordance with this opinion. The case is further remanded to the trial court for determination, pursuant to Section 5.62, of the order in which the property of the parties shall be subject to execution.

Dissenting opinion by REAVLEY, J., in which GREENHILL, C.J. and WALKER, J., join.

REAVLEY, JUSTICE (dissenting).

I disagree with the Court's holding that E.A. Cockerham is personally liable for, and his separate property subject to, the debts incurred by Dorothy Cockerham in the operation of the dress shops.[1] It is a long step through fact and law from the decision of the trial court that E.A. Cockerham is not liable personally for those debts, incurred by Dorothy "in her store adventure" which used community funds "over the protest of E.A. Cockerham," to the decision by this Court that he is personally liable.

What are the factors so "replete" in this record which the majority find to require that we take this step? We are given the following: (1) The husband "advanced" the wife money. He paid for the initial inventory and borrowed money at one time to enable her to meet her difficulties. (2) She was allowed to write checks on "his personal checking account." He signed one of the checks himself to pay an operational expense. (3) The husband and wife filed joint income tax returns and deducted for the dress shop losses. Since "his dairy business" was enjoying a substantial income, the deductions reduced the amount of tax that would otherwise have been due. (4) The husband gave his implied assent to the dress shop liabilities.

It must first be understood that there is no pleading and no contention that any creditor relied upon appearances that the husband was operating or responsible for these dress shops. Estoppel is not in the case. The facts by anyone's version would not take us in that direction. E.A. Cockerham worked at his dairy farm near Itasca and did little else. During the two years while Dorothy Cockerham had a dress shop, first in Hurst and then in Burleson, he went there 'once or maybe twice.' He did absolutely nothing toward the operation of these dress shops, and he took no interest in them except for his concern about the cost when he became aware of the difficulties several months before the collapse.

Money for this venture did indeed come out of the Itasca bank account. Quite a bit of it. But these were community funds and a community bank account. Except for the interests in land stated above, all that they owned was community property. The Court holds here that this community was under the joint management and control of both spouses. During the 22 years of their marriage they had kept their money in this account and the wife had always signed checks on the account by writing his name—sometimes adding "by wife." The references in the opinion to what he "advanced the wife" are inappropriate to the present Family Code and to the emancipation of married women.

The Cockerhams filed joint income tax returns through 1971. All income and all deductions were reported without any distinction between the separate or community nature of each. This is what spouses do in joint returns, and I know of no prior suggestion that the ownership of property or personal liabilities are thereby changed.

I had supposed that the Texas Family Code as enacted and amended by the 61st, 62nd and 63rd Legislatures places a creditor who deals with one spouse in a position where, in the event of subsequent unpaid debts and liabilities, he might not be able to reach that community property which is not held solely in the name of the spouse with whom he deals. Section 5.24 protects the creditor to the extent that he can assume the spouse has sole management of property in that spouse's name. However, the other community property may well be under the sole management

[1] E.A. Cockerham's separate property, prior to divorce, consisted of the one half interest in the 320 acres discussed in the opinion, and also his remainder interest in 130 acres which is not discussed. The latter interest was given to him by his mother, who retained a life estate.

of the other spouse by the terms of § 5.22, which so specifies for property that the other spouse "would have owned if single" and which also gives effect to agreements between the spouses, whether or not the agreement is known to the creditor. If the other spouse has sole management, under § 5.61 that property is beyond the creditor's reach. If that state of the law was disturbing to creditors, they can now relax while spouses with separate estates do the worrying. The Court today seems to hold that a wife (or husband) who assents to the husband (or wife) spending community funds in a venture thereby subjects her (or his) total estate to any liability that the husband's (or wife's) venture may precipitate.

Except for the liability for necessaries which each spouse may owe for the support of the other spouse, the separate property of a spouse should be subjected to liability for debts of the other spouse only to the extent and under the same rules of law that would make a non-family party liable. §§ 5.61(a), 3.59.

If the separate property of E.A. Cockerham is liable for the dress shop debts, discussion of sections of the Family Code and of the matters of joint or sole management are not necessary. The present case raises so many questions of interest that the majority does discuss a few unnecessary matters, and I shall discuss one.

In deciding the respective ownership of the 320 acres, the majority begins with the "well established" rule "that when a husband uses separate property consideration to pay for land acquired during the marriage and takes title to the land in the name of husband and wife, it is presumed he intended the interest placed in his wife to be a gift." The reason back of the rule is that a husband or parent owes a moral obligation to a wife or child, and a deed in the name of the wife or child is presumed to have been made in discharge of that moral obligation and as a gift to the natural object of his love and affection. If, however, the wife uses her separate money to purchase property and takes a deed in the name of the husband, the contrary presumption follows: he holds legal title under resulting trust for her benefit. *Smith v. Strahan*, 16 Tex. 314 (1856). Such differences in treatment are now passe. Comment, 9 HOUSTON L. REV. 120 (1971). For instruments executed after the date of the delivery of this opinion, I would apply the presumption in favor of a gift to either spouse. However, I would not presume a gift in favor of a spouse who is receiving an interest in the property irrespective of gift. In the present case, Dorothy and E.A. Cockerham were purchasing an undivided half interest for their community. This explains the appearance of Dorothy's name as grantee. No presumption of gift by him to her of his separate property interest is justified. I must add that under the writing of the majority, the presumption has become a very weak one. The husband testifies that the interest is his, and the wife, though in court, says nothing about a gift; presumption rebutted.

GREENHILL, C.J. and WALKER, J., join in this dissent.

Notes, Comments & Questions

1. Could you write a well-reasoned opinion for *Cockerham* using only one page and reaching the same result as the Texas Supreme Court?

2. If tried today, would any provision of the current Texas Family Code aid Mr. Cockerham?

3. If you need help on question 2 read the next case.

PROVIDIAN NAT'L BANK v. EBARB

180 S.W.3d 898
(Tex. App.—Beaumont 2005, no pet.)

GAULTNEY, JUSTICE.

Providian National Bank sued George Ebarb and Kerri Ebarb in April 1999 to recover amounts allegedly owed on a credit card. A month after the suit was filed, the Ebarbs were divorced. The Bank nonsuited the defendants, but in 2001 filed suit against them on the same debt. Providian obtained a default judgment against Kerri Ebarb. She did not appeal.

* * *

In issue four the Bank challenges the legal sufficiency of the evidence to support the trial court's adverse finding on the Bank's claim.[1] Having the burden of proof at trial, the Bank must demonstrate on appeal that the evidence establishes, as a matter of law, all vital facts in support of its claim that George Ebarb is personally liable for the debt. *See Dow Chem. Co. v. Francis*, 46 S.W.3d 237, 241 (Tex. 2001) (citing *Sterner v. Marathon Oil Co.*, 767 S.W.2d 686, 690 (Tex. 1989)).

The Bank did not present evidence that George Ebarb signed any document making him personally liable on the account. His signature was not on the application for credit. Instead, the Bank relied on evidence that George was "listed secondary" by the Bank on the account, and both spouses' names were on the credit card and the monthly statement issued by the Bank. There is also evidence George Ebarb became aware of the debt and made some payments on it. The billing was sent to the address where George and Kerri resided while married. However, when Providian's representative was asked at trial if there was any documentation "saying George Ebarb ever requested any credit be extended" to him, the representative replied "No."

Providian argues George Ebarb's subsequent awareness of the debt and payment of some of the monthly bills establish his liability, although there is no contract or other evidence setting out the agreement and responsibilities of the parties, no evidence Kerri was acting as George's agent,

[1] Since the Bank requests a rendition, rather than a remand for a new trial, we interpret issue four as a legal sufficiency issue, though the standard of review the Bank suggests we use is for factual sufficiency review.

and no evidence George agreed to be responsible for the debt. The Bank argues the evidence nevertheless establishes George's ratification of the debt. Ratification requires: "(1) approval by act, word, or conduct; (2) with full knowledge of the facts of the earlier act; and (3) with the intention of giving validity to the earlier act." *Gibson v. Bostick Roofing & Sheet Metal*, 148 S.W.3d 482, 492 (Tex.App.-El Paso 2004, no pet.). Ratification may occur when a person retains the benefits of a transaction after acquiring full knowledge. *Miller v. Kennedy & Minshew, P.C.*, 142 S.W.3d 325 at 343 (Tex.App.-Fort Worth 2003, pet. denied). Largely a matter of intent, ratification may be inferred by a party's course of conduct and need not be shown by express word or deed. *Miller*, 142 S.W.3d at 342-43; *Eikon King Street Manager, L.L.C. v. LSF King Street Manager, L.L.C.*, 109 S.W.3d 762, 768 (Tex.App.-Dallas 2003, pet. denied).

As factfinder in this bench trial, the trial court was the sole judge of the credibility of the witnesses and the weight to be given their testimony. *See City of Keller*, 168 S.W.3d at 819. When asked whether he knew anything about the debt of almost $4,500, George testified, "No. I didn't know things were that bad, no." There is no evidence he personally benefitted from or used the credit card. He testified part of the "divorce problems" involved financial problems created by Kerri. George indicated that at the time he "was married" and "was trying to help things out at the house and pay bills and try to be responsible and help." The trial judge reasonably may have concluded George's subsequent awareness of the credit card account and payment of some of the monthly bills did not establish his approval, full knowledge, or intent to assume personal liability for the debt Kerri had incurred. The Bank asks this Court to reverse the trial court's finding and render judgment that George Ebarb is personally liable for the entire amount of the debt. Based on the sparse record before us, we cannot conclude the Bank established ratification or its entitlement to that judgment as a matter of law. Issue four is overruled.

In issue five, the Bank argues the trial court erred in applying Tex. Fam.Code Ann. § 3.201 (Vernon 1998). Section 3.201 governs a person's liability for the acts of his or her spouse and provides as follows:

> (a) A person is personally liable for the acts of the person's spouse only if:
>
> (1) the spouse acts as an agent for the person; or
>
> (2) the spouse incurs a debt for necessaries as provided by Subchapter F, Chapter 2.
>
> (b) Except as provided by this subchapter, community property is not subject to a liability that arises from an act of a spouse.
>
> (c) A spouse does not act as an agent for the other spouse solely because of the marriage relationship.

TEX. FAM. CODE ANN. § 3.201 (Vernon 1998)(footnote omitted). In applying section 3.201, the trial court concluded under the circumstances George was not liable for Kerri's acts in incurring the debt with the Bank. Asserting error in applying the statute, the Bank relies on *Cockerham v. Cockerham*, 527 S.W.2d 162, 171 (Tex. 1975), and argues there is a presumption that debts incurred during marriage are "community debts" unless the creditor agreed to look solely to the contracting spouse's separate estate for satisfaction of the debt. *See also Sprick v. Sprick*, 25 S.W.3d 7, 13 (Tex. App.—El Paso 1999, pet. denied); *Morris v. Morris*, 894 S.W.2d 859, 863 (Tex. App.—Fort Worth 1995, no writ). However, that argument does not answer the question of whether a spouse is personally liable under section 3.201 on a particular debt. Subsequent to the holding in *Cockerham*, the Legislature amended the Family Code by adding former TEX. FAM. CODE ANN. § 4.031, now TEX. FAM. CODE ANN. § 3.201 (Vernon 1998). *See also* TEX. FAM.

CODE ANN. § 3.202 (Vernon 1998) (rules of marital property liability); *Patel v. Kuciemba*, 82 S.W.3d 589, 595 (Tex. App.—Corpus Christi 2002, pet. denied); *Nelson v. Citizens Bank & Trust Co. of Baytown, Texas*, 881 S.W.2d 128, 130-31 (Tex. App.—Houston [1st Dist.] 1994, no writ). The trial court properly looked to the provisions of that statute to determine whether George Ebarb was liable for the debt incurred by Kerri.

The Bank argues, regardless of section 3.201, community property is reachable by creditors under section 3.202. *See* TEX. FAM. CODE ANN. § 3.202 (Vernon 1998). The two sections of the Family Code relate to two distinct liability concepts. Section 3.201 governs a spouse's personal liability for the acts of his or her spouse, and section 3.202 sets out rules of marital property liability. However, we disagree that section 3.202 controls the claim here regardless of section 3.201. This is a suit in which the Bank sought to hold George Ebarb personally liable on the debt. The Bank was not attempting to take community property to satisfy the judgment against Kerri. The trial court found the Bank failed to establish George Ebarb is personally liable for the debt, either through Kerri's acts or through his own acts. We see no error in the trial court's application of section 3.201 based on the pleadings and evidence presented in this case. Issue five is overruled.

We reverse and render judgment that George Ebarb take nothing on his claim against Providian National Bank. We affirm the trial court's judgment that Providian National Bank take nothing on its claim against George Ebarb.

AFFIRMED IN PART; REVERSED AND RENDERED IN PART.

E. Management Rights

JAMAIL
v.
THOMAS

481 S.W.2d 485
(Tex. Civ. App.—Houston [1st Dist.] 1972, writ ref'd n.r.e)

BELL, CHIEF JUSTICE.

Appellant, an attorney, filed suit against appellees, Aetna Life & Casualty Company, Norman Chersky, Ronald Easley and James Richard Thomas, to recover damages for tortious interference with a contract of employment. The court, based on a jury verdict, rendered a judgment that appellant take nothing. Easley and Chersky were claim adjusters for Aetna.

On September 15, 1968, an automobile driven by James Richard Thomas hit the automobile owned and driven by Tommy Cochran. There was a rear end collision. The Cochrans' automobile was also occupied by Mrs. Cochran and a small child of the Cochrans. The next day Mrs. Cochran, who was injured, was taken to a hospital where she remained about three weeks. At the time Mr. and Mrs. Cochran were separated and a divorce suit was pending. They later became reconciled and a divorce was never granted. On September 16, Mr. Cochran went to appellant's office and talked to Mr. Barnett, an associate of appellant. At that time Cochran employed appellant as an attorney. The power of attorney was signed by Tommy Cochran only. It purported to employ appellant to represent the Cochrans in "my (our) claim for damages against all responsible parties because of our injuries and damages. . . ." The contract was a contingent fee one and assigned to appellant a 40% interest in "my (our) cause of action" if suit was filed and recovery was finally had without an appeal.

Aetna, Mr. Thomas' insurer, on January 6, 1969, made a settlement with Mr. and Mrs. Cochran and took a release signed by both of them. The release recited a total payment of $6,675.27. Its clear language effected a release by Mr. and Mrs. Cochran of any claims they had by reason of the collision.

In February, 1969, appellant filed suit against Thomas on behalf of Mr. and Mrs. Cochran. That petition is not in the record. Sometime after appellant learned of the settlement and release the suit was dismissed.

Appellant then filed this suit to recover his damages allegedly resulting from tortious interference by the appellees with his contract of employment. He went to trial on his Third Amended Original Petition. In the petition he alleged that "Thomas was guilty of negligence which proximately caused the collision . . . and resulting in injuries and damages to Mr. and Mrs. Tommy Cochran. . . ." Then followed a specification of the acts of negligence.

In the paragraph alleging injuries appellant asserted that in the collision Mrs. Cochran received injuries to her neck which caused her disability to such an extent that she could not carry on her duties as a housewife and the injuries caused her physical pain and mental anguish. It was alleged that Mrs. Cochran was hospitalized and that Mr. and Mrs. Cochran incurred medical bills.

Appellant then alleges he "was employed to represent Mr. and Mrs. Cochran in their claim for damages arising out of the collision. . . ." Appellant then asserts he filed suit in their behalf for recovery "for their losses and physical pain, mental suffering, impairment of the duties of a housewife and medical bills. . . ."

In his prayer appellant asked to recover 40% of the amount which probably would have been awarded to Mr. and Mrs. Cochran, or, alternatively, asked for 40% of the amount actually paid to Mr. and Mrs. Cochran by Aetna. Exemplary damages of $5,000.00 were asked.

The evidence shows that Mrs. Cochran received a neck injury and was hospitalized about three weeks. She was off from her work longer than that. Mr. Cochran was not injured. His automobile was damaged but the cost of repairs is not shown. The amount of the doctors' and hospital bills is not shown.

It appears that immediately Mr. Chersky contacted Mrs. Cochran at the hospital. Aetna determined their insured was probably liable. Aetna ascertained the net weekly earnings of Mrs. Cochran from her employment were $60.00 and started paying $120.00 per week. Some of the drafts were payable to Mr. and Mrs. Cochran and some to "Claimant." About January 6, 1969, a settlement was agreed on by Mrs. Cochran. A final payment of $4,820.00 was made. The check with a release was sent to Mr. and Mrs. Cochran. The release was to be signed by both Mr. and Mrs. Cochran and the check was payable to both. When the release was not timely returned, Aetna stopped payment on the check. Mr. Easley then took a release to the Cochran home and obtained the signature of both parties and then paid them $4,820.00. The total payment directly to the Cochrans including weekly payments was $6,675.27.

We feel the evidence conclusively establishes that Aetna, through Chersky and Easley, had knowledge of appellant's employment by Mr. Cochran. They nevertheless continued their negotiations with Mrs. Cochran. They never negotiated with Mr. Cochran except to obtain signing of the release. While Mrs. Cochran did not sign the contract she knew of it. An issue was raised by the evidence as to whether she ratified it.

The jury, in response to special issues, made, in effect, the following answers:

1. Issue No. 1. Failed to find that Mrs. Cochran ratified the contract.

2. Special Issue No. 2. Failed to find that Aetna through its representatives knowingly interfered with performance of the contract by securing the signing of the release by Tommy Cochran.

3. Issue No. 3. Failed to find that Aetna through its representatives knowingly interfered with performance of the contract by securing of the signing of the release by Mrs. Cochran.

Issue 4 was conditioned on an affirmative answer to Issue No. 2, and inquired as to whether Aetna acted with conscious indifference to the rights of appellant. Issue No. 6 was the compensatory damage issue and was conditioned on an affirmative answer to Issue No. 2. Issue No. 8 was the exemplary damage issue and was conditioned on an affirmative answer to Issue No. 4. These issues were unanswered because of the manner in which they were conditioned. All of these issues relate to recovery based on the conduct of Aetna insofar as Aetna allegedly interfered with the contractual relation between appellant and Mr. Cochran.

The other issues relate to the contractual relation between appellant and Mrs. Cochran. Specific notice of them is unnecessary in the light of the jury's failure to find ratification.

We are of the view that the terms of the contract are broad enough to encompass all of the damages resulting to both Mr. and Mrs. Cochran. We are also of the view that the release was effective to release all claims for all damages.

Appellant by his first four points of error asserts it was conclusively established that there was tortious interference with performance by obtaining the release from Mr. and Mrs. Cochran, and the trial court erred in rendering judgment against appellant and in refusing to grant appellant's motion for judgment notwithstanding the verdict, his motion for instructed verdict and his motion for new trial.

A reference to the motion for instructed verdict and for judgment notwithstanding the verdict reveals that appellant's theory was that the contract was between Mr. and Mrs. Cochran and him in that Mr. Cochran had contracted for himself and Mrs. Cochran with authority of Mrs. Cochran. This was also the theory plead.

There is no evidence showing actual authority and the mere relationship of husband and wife does not give the husband authority to contract with regard to the wife's separate property or community property committed by law to her sole management, control and right of disposition. *Taylor v. Gilbert Gertner Enterprises*, 466 S.W.2d 337 (Tex. Civ. App.—Houston, [1st Dist.] 1971, writ ref., n.r.e.). The husband could not assign the wife's interest in her cause of action.

Appellees urge that all recovery by the wife for personal injury, except loss of earning capacity during the marriage, is her separate property under Article 4615, Vernon's Ann. Civ. St., which was in effect at the time the injuries were received. This article is now Section 5.01 of the Texas Family Code, V.T.C.A. Also, appellees cite *Smith v. Smith*, 473 S.W.2d 299 (Tex. Civ. App.—Texarkana 1971, writ ref., n.r.e.); *Kirkpatrick v. Hurst*, 472 S.W.2d 295 (Tex. Civ. App.—Texarkana 1971, writ granted on another point).

We need not determine whether Aetna's payments directly to Mr. and Mrs. Cochran were her separate property.

As we read the record the payments made directly to the Cochrans were for damages for injuries received by Mrs. Cochran, including lost earnings up to the time of the release and in the future, if any, and physical pain and mental anguish. The record is confusing as to whether payment of hospital and doctors' bills was made directly to the creditor or was included in the payment to the Cochrans. In our view it makes no difference in the light of our holding.

Article 4621, V.A.T.S., in effect at all material times (now Section 5.22 Texas Family Code), read as follows:

> During marriage each spouse shall have sole management, control and disposition of that Community property which he or she would have owned if a single person (emphasis ours unless otherwise stated), including (but not limited to) . . . the recoveries for personal injuries awarded to him on her. . . .

The effect of this statute is to define the rights of each spouse with regard to community property. It does not deal with what constitutes separate property. It suffices to say that Article 4615 makes a recovery for personal injuries by a spouse his or her separate property except for loss of earning capacity during the marriage.

In the landmark case of *Arnold v. Leonard*, 114 Tex. 535, 273 S.W. 799, our Supreme Court held that Article 16, Section 15, Texas Constitution, Vernon's Ann. St., permitted the legislature to pass laws more clearly defining the wife's rights with regard to her separate property as well as that held in common with her husband.

The Texas cases cited by appellee, that we have above noticed, all deal with recovery by the wife for physical injury to the body, physical pain and mental anguish and damages for such injuries were held to be her separate property. The case of *Franco et ux. v. Graham*, 470 S.W.2d 429 (Tex. Civ. App.—Corpus Christi, writ granted), held the same and the opinion contained a statement that medical expenses were not included as an element of recovery as separate property under the term "the recovery awarded for personal injuries."

We hold that by virtue of Article 4621, the wife has the sole right to manage, control and dispose of her cause of action to recover damages for personal injuries which would clearly include injury to the physical structure of the body, physical pain, mental anguish, loss of earnings and impaired earning capacity. We also hold that under the facts of this case Mrs. Cochran had sole management, control and right of disposition of recovery for hospital and medical bills.

Whether the term "the recovery for personal injuries" standing alone includes such consequential damages as hospital and medical bills, we need not decide. Article 4621 gave "sole management, control, and disposition of that community property which" the husband or wife "would have owned if single." All of the items of recovery above listed would belong to the injured wife, if she had been single. She would be liable for hospital and medical bills either because of her contract or because of necessaries furnished. She would, were she single, own any recovery for them.

Professor Joseph W. McKnight, writing in 22 SOUTHWESTERN LAW JOURNAL, at page 132, reaches the following conclusion:

> . . . article 4621 provides that *all types* of recoveries for personal injuries are subject to the management, control and disposition of the person injured. The provisions of article 4615, dealing with ownership of the recovery, should be clearly distinguished from the management provisions of article 4621. . . . Article 4621 . . . does give the injured spouse management, control, and disposition over all of a personal injury recovery whether such recovery is community or separate or both. Regardless of characterization of various aspects of personal injury recoveries as separate or community property, *the injured spouse has the sole power to settle a dispute as to liability because of his or her management powers. . . .*

In the case of *Weatherford v. Elizondo*, 52 F.R.D. 122, the Honorable Ben Connally, District Judge, held that by virtue of the management powers conferred by Section 5.22 Texas Family Code (old Article 4621) to the injured spouse over personal injury recoveries, an injured wife was an indispensable party to a suit brought by the husband.

Appellant objected to the form of the definition of ratification accompanying Special Issue No. 1. The complaint is that the use of the term "full knowledge" places an undue burden on him.

We are of the view that ratification of an agreement or act requires that a party alleged to have ratified it have full knowledge of all the facts. 2 TEX. JUR. 2D, *Agency*, Section 38.

It is urged that the court erred in not including "acquiescence" in the definition of ratification and in refusing to give appellant's requested definition. There was no error. Appellant's requested definition was not substantially correct. Further, acquiescence is merely evidence of ratification. *Austin v. Jones*, 148 Ala. 659, 41 So. 408; *Allen v. Corn Exchange Bank*, 87 App. Div.

335, 84 N.Y.S. 1001. The definition given read: "By the term ratified . . . is meant the approval by act, word, or conduct, with full knowledge of the facts, of the prior act, with the intention of giving validity to such prior act." This definition is correct.

Points not specifically discussed have, in the light of our above holdings, become immaterial.

Affirmed.

ON MOTION FOR REHEARING

The appellant urges the fact that the checks were payable to both Mr. and Mrs. Cochran created a presumption that each was entitled to receive one-half. We are unable to agree. The pleadings and proof were that all injuries were to Mrs. Cochran. Appellant sought damages for tortious interference with a contract with Mr. and Mrs. Cochran. She did not make or ratify said contract.

The burden of proof was on the appellant to establish that included in the payments made were damages over which Mr. Cochran had control and also the amount thereof. This he had failed to do.

Motion overruled.

COLEMAN, JUSTICE (concurring).

This court has correctly overruled appellant's motion for rehearing of its judgment affirming the judgment of the trial court. Appellant proved a tortious interference with his employment contract, but he failed to produce any evidence from which the trial court could determine the amount of damage resulting to him by reason thereof. He did not show the amount of money paid to his client in settlement of the claim. The fact that the checks issued in settlement of the claim by the insurance company were made payable to both Mr. and Mrs. Cochran is evidence of payment of a consideration to both parties, but, in view of the pleadings and evidence in this case, the issuance of the checks payable to two payees does not establish that each payee received, or was entitled to receive, fifty per cent of the proceeds of the checks. There is no other evidence pertinent to the issue of damage, as issue on which appellant had the burden of proof. The judgment of the trial court was properly affirmed for the reason that appellant failed to produce evidence to sustain an award of damages in any amount other than nominal.

Notes, Comments & Questions

1. Obviously, this case took place long before *Texaco, Inc. v. Pennzoil*, 729 S.W.2d 768 (Tex. App.—Houston [1st Dist] 1987, writ ref'd n.r.e), *dism'd by agr.*, 748 S.W.2d 631 (Tex. App.—Houston [1st Dist] 1988, no writ). Nonetheless, you can see where greatness resides and how persistence ultimately pays off.

2. As to the marital property issues, what was Mr. Jamail's theory?

3. Why didn't it make any difference that the settlement may have encompassed community property?

McDONALD
v.
ROEMER
505 S.W.2d 698
(Tex. Civ. App.—San Antonio 1974, no writ)

BARROW, CHIEF JUSTICE.

Appellants, J.R. McDonald and wife, Mary McDonald, have perfected their appeal from a judgment entered on a jury verdict, whereby appellee recovered judgment against appellants for the sum of $1,500 as damages for breach of an agricultural lease of 64 acres of land in Wilson County.

* * *

The third point complains of the action of the trial court in rendering a judgment against J.R. McDonald in that there is no basis for liability against him. The ownership of the leased land was not shown. However, the lease was executed solely by Mary McDonald, as landlord, and the consideration was paid solely to her. There is absolutely no evidence to show any basis for liability against J.R. McDonald. This defect was timely urged to the trial court by a motion for judgment non obstante veredicto, as well as by motion for new trial. The trial court, therefore, erred in entering judgment against J.R. McDonald.

The judgment of the trial court against J.R. McDonald is reversed, and it is here rendered that appellee take nothing against him. The judgment against Mary McDonald is affirmed. The costs of this appeal are taxed one half to appellee and one half to appellant, Mary McDonald.

Questions

1. In *McDonald v. Roemer*, the court explains that the ownership of the leased land was not shown.

2. What difference, if any, would it make if the land was wife's separate property?

3. What difference, if any, would it make if the land was wife's sole management community property?

4. What difference, if any, would it make if the land was the joint management property of the spouses?

MEDENCO, INC.
v.
MYKLEBUST
615 S.W.2d 187
(Tex. 1981)

CAMPBELL, JUSTICE.

This is a post-divorce action against the former husband and his employer for fraudulent concealment and conspiracy for failing to voluntarily disclose information about his employment benefits. The trial court granted the motion for summary judgment for Defendants, Medenco, Inc. and Continental Prosthetics, Inc., and rendered judgment that Plaintiff, Gloria June Myklebust, take nothing. The Court of Civil Appeals reversed the judgment and remanded the cause. 605 S.W.2d 397. We reverse the judgment of the Court of Civil Appeals and affirm the judgment of the trial court.

Mr. Myklebust was employed by Medenco and one of its subsidiaries, Continental Prosthetics. Pursuant to his employment agreement, he was granted options to acquire Medenco stock. In January 1978, Mr. Myklebust terminated his employment and was entitled to exercise stock options to purchase 2,063 shares of Medenco common stock. Except for the stock options, he apparently was not entitled to receive any other employment or retirement benefits.

On March 13, 1978, the Myklebusts were divorced. During and after the divorce proceedings, Ms. Myklebust requested information from Medenco concerning Mr. Myklebust's employment and retirement benefits including stock options. Medenco refused to voluntarily disclose the information stating it considered the information to be confidential. However, Medenco offered, in writing, to release the information if the request was accompanied by the consent or instructions of Mr. Myklebust, by an appropriate court order, or by a subpoena duces tecum.

On March 29, Ms. Myklebust brought this suit against her former husband and his former employer, Medenco and one of its subsidiaries, Continental Prosthetics. She alleged that Mr. Myklebust fraudulently concealed community assets from her both during and after the divorce proceedings; that he purposely and maliciously prevented her from obtaining information concerning his stock options and other employment benefits; and, that Medenco and Continental Prosthetics acted in concert with Mr. Myklebust to defraud her of her interest in the stock options and other benefits.

Medenco filed a motion for summary judgment which alleged that Ms. Myklebust failed to state a cause of action. It also alleged that her claims were moot because Mr. Myklebust had no additional benefits. The trial court granted the motion for summary judgment and rendered judgment that Ms. Myklebust take nothing against Medenco and Continental Prosthetics.[1]

The Court of Civil Appeals held that an employer has a duty to voluntarily disclose the existence and nature of an employee's benefits to the employee's spouse upon reasonable request and proper identification. We disagree.

---

[1] The cause of action against Medenco and Continental Prosthetics was severed from the cause of action against Mr. Myklebust and a final judgment was rendered in favor of Medenco and Continental Prosthetics. Mr. Myklebust is not a party to this appeal.

We are of the opinion that it is not sound policy to create a duty for every employer in Texas to voluntarily disclose to non-employee spouses community property assets accrued by an employee spouse because of the employment. During marriage the duty to disclose is between the spouses.

If a divorce action is filed, the non-employee spouse can obtain information about the employee's work benefits through discovery proceedings. *See* Sales, *Pre-Trial Discovery in Texas*, 31 SW. L.J. 1017 (1977). The employee spouse as a party to the divorce is subject to (1) Rule 167,[2] Discovery and Production of Documents and Things for Inspection, Copying or Photographing, (2) Rule 168, Interrogatories to Parties, (3) Rule 169, Admission of Facts and of Genuineness of Documents, and (4) Rules 186, 186a and 201, Written or Oral Depositions of Witnesses, Subpoena Duces Tecum. The employer who is not a party to the divorce is subject to (1) Rule 167, Discovery and Production of Documents and Things for Inspection, Copying or Photographing[3] and (2) Rules 186, 186a and 201, Written or Oral Depositions of Witnesses, Subpoena Duces Tecum. If the employee spouse or employer refuses to disclose the information, the sanctions of Rules 170 and 215a may be imposed. *See* Comment, *Imposition and Selection of Sanctions in Texas Pretrial Discovery Procedure*, 31 BAYLOR L. REV. 191 (1979); Sales, *supra*. Ms. Myklebust did not attempt to use any of these methods of discovery during the divorce proceedings.

After divorce, the non-employee spouse has several legal remedies against the employee spouse for failing to disclose the requested information. These remedies include a suit for fraudulent concealment of community assets and for partition of undivided community property. The employee spouse and the employer are subject to the applicable discovery procedures discussed above.

This suit was filed 16 days after the divorce was granted, but before it became final. *See* Rule 329b, TEX. R. CIV. PRO. Ms. Myklebust filed a Notice of Intent to depose various Medenco officers. The trial court granted a protective order to this Notice. She does not complain of that order. Almost one year later, on March 8, 1979, Ms. Myklebust served interrogatories on Medenco inquiring about Mr. Myklebust's employment benefits. These were answered on April 6. No complaint was made of these answers.

During marriage, community property employment benefits acquired through employment are subject to the sole management, control and disposition of the employee spouse. TEX. FAM. CODE ANN. § 5.22(a). The employer owes a duty to the employee spouse to make reasonable disclosure of the nature and extent of the benefits held by the employer. If a final divorce decree awards any portion of the employment benefits to the non-employee spouse as separate property, the employer would owe the same duty of disclosure to the non-employee owner as it would the employee owner. Before disclosing the information, the employer may require proper proof of ownership and identity. After receiving a reasonable request from the non-employee owner, the employer must reply within a reasonable time.

We hold that an employer does not have a duty to voluntarily disclose the existence and nature of an employee's benefits to the employee's spouse. The judgment of the Court of Civil Appeals is reversed and the judgment of the trial court is affirmed.

---

[2] All references to rules are to Vernon's Texas Rules Annotated.

[3] Effective January 1, 1981, Rule 167 applies to nonparties as well as parties. TEX.R.CIV.P. 167. *See* Pope & McConnico, *Practicing Law With the 1981 Texas Rules*, 32 BAYLOR L. REV. 457, 468-69 (1980).

Questions

1. This case clearly indicates that the Texas Supreme Court expects a divorce case to be tried as any other civil cause. By what means could the wife have obtained the information she sought?

2. Do you think that the current rules of discovery would impact a case such as this one? How so?

3. Where did the wife's best claim lie?

COOPER
v.
TEXAS GULF INDUSTRIES, INC.

513 S.W.2d 200
(Tex. 1974)

SAM D. JOHNSON, JUSTICE.

Petitioners Dr. Griffin Cooper and his wife, Dolores, appeal from summary judgment that they take nothing in a suit for cancellation and rescission of a sale of real estate to them by Texas Gulf Industries, Inc. (T.G.I.). Cooper and his wife sued T.G.I. on September 28, 1971 alleging fraud as ground for rescission and cancellation of the sale. T.G.I. moved for summary judgment asserting Dr. Cooper previously filed a suit on December 29, 1970, which suit was dismissed with prejudice on January 29, 1971, and that such dismissal with prejudice was res judicata of the instant action. The trial court granted T.G.I.'s motion for summary judgment that plaintiffs take nothing and the court of civil appeals affirmed. 495 S.W.2d 273. We reverse and remand.

In the prior suit filed December 29, 1970 Dr. Cooper was the sole plaintiff. He sought to terminate a management contract on the property at issue and alternatively sought to rescind the sale of the property. The trial court dismissed the first suit "with prejudice."

The Coopers argue that dismissal of the prior suit with prejudice is not res judicata of the instant suit because Dolores Cooper, being a grantee along with her husband in the deed to the real estate at issue, was a necessary party to a suit to cancel and rescind the sale. Accordingly, the Coopers assert, the trial court had no jurisdiction in the prior case and the judgment of dismissal with prejudice is invalid.

A decision on whether a wife is an indispensable party in an action which concerns her joint community property necessitates (1) a study of the Texas Family Code, Section 5.22 (1971),[1] to

[1] Section 5.22 recites:

§ 5.22. Community Property: General Rules

(a) During marriage, each spouse has the sole management, control, and disposition of the community property that he or she would have owned if single, including but not limited to:

(1) personal earnings;

(2) revenue from separate property;

determine the nature of the community property, (2) a reexamination of the rule that a husband can act for and represent his wife in an action concerning their joint community property under the doctrine of virtual representation, and (3) a discussion of the application of Rule 39, as amended, Texas Rules of Civil Procedure (1971), concerning the joinder of parties.

THE NATURE OF THE COMMUNITY PROPERTY

T.G.I. says in its brief that the property in question is community property and the record bears this out. Both Coopers were named in the deed to the property in question and both signed a deed of trust executed in favor of T.G.I. Insofar as can be ascertained, both Coopers were obligated also on the notes given as consideration. Part of the consideration was payment of $45,000 in cash; the record does not reveal the source of these funds. Under Section 5.02, Texas Family Code (Supp. 1971), property possessed by either spouse during marriage is presumed to be community property. In light of this presumption, and the absence of contrary evidence in the record, the court adopts T.G.I.'s statement that the property involved is community.

Under Section 5.22 community property falls into two categories with respect to management: *sole* management community property and *joint* management community property. On the basis of the record before us, the court must assume that the property is subject to joint management. Section 5.24 says, "(d)uring marriage, property is presumed to be subject to the sole management, control, and disposition of a spouse *if* it is held in his or her name. . . ." (Emphasis added.) All of the evidence, as noted above, indicates joint ownership of and joint liability for the property in question.

THE DOCTRINE OF VIRTUAL REPRESENTATION

One of the basic questions in this case is whether Dr. Cooper, in bringing the first suit without the joinder of his wife, acted as a representative of the community; whether he "virtually represented" his wife in that action. If the doctrine has vitality, the dismissal with prejudice of that first suit would be binding upon the wife, Mrs. Dolores Cooper, and res judicata as to the second and instant suit.

Under the doctrine of virtual representation, a suit naming only the husband as a party is nonetheless binding on the wife. ... The basis for virtual representation is the husband's power of sole management of the entire community.

Section 5.22 of the Family Code takes away the husband's sole right to manage all of the couple's community property. When joint management community property is involved, the husband and wife are now *joint* managers. The wife is her husband's equal with respect to management;

---

(3) recoveries for personal injures; and

(4) the increase and mutations of, and the revenue from, all property subject to his or her sole management, control, and disposition.

(b) If community property subject to the sole management, control, and disposition of one spouse is mixed or combined with community property subject to the sole management, control, and disposition of the other spouse, then the mixed or combined community property is subject to the joint management, control, and disposition of the spouses, unless the spouses provide otherwise by power of attorney or other agreement in writing.

(c) Except as provided in Subsection (a) of this section, the community property is subject to the joint management, control, and disposition of the husband and wife, unless the spouses provide otherwise by power of attorney or other agreement in writing.

she stands in the same position as any other joint owner of property. While another section[2] provides that a spouse may sue and be sued without the joinder of the other, *neither* spouse may virtually represent the other. The rights of the wife, like the rights of the husband and the rights of any other joint owner, may be affected only by a suit in which the wife is called to answer. If one of the spouses wishes the other to represent him or her, Section 5.22(c) of the Family Code permits that arrangement provided the consenting spouse authorizes that representation by a power of attorney or other agreement in writing. No such writing is in evidence here.

Dolores Cooper was not a party to the first suit; the doctrine of virtual representation was abolished by the new Family Code; there was no writing authorizing her husband to represent her. Accordingly, her interest in the Coopers' joint management community property is untouched by the judgment of dismissal with prejudice of the first suit.

* * *

. . . we determine that the named parties in the first suit, Dr. Cooper and T.G.I., were properly before the court for the resolution of the issues between them; that the judgment of dismissal with prejudice resolved those issues and is necessarily res judicata as to the claims of Dr. Cooper in the second and instant suit; that the judgment of dismissal is not res judicata, however, with respect to the rights and claims of Mrs. Dolores Cooper; and finally, that the judgment of dismissal is conclusive as to Dr. Cooper except to the extent that it might have to be disregarded in giving Mrs. Cooper all the relief to which she may show herself entitled.

The judgments of the courts below are reversed and the cause remanded to the trial court for further proceedings consistent with this opinion.

Concurring opinion by WALKER, J., in which GREENHILL, C. J., joins.

WALKER, JUSTICE (concurring).

I am in general agreement with the opinion and concur in the judgment of the Court. It should be pointed out, however, that there has been no showing that Mrs. Dolores Cooper participated in the prior litigation. *See* 46 AM. JUR. 2D, *Judgments* § 535; RESTATEMENT, *Judgments* § 84.

[2] § 4.04. Joinder in Civil Suits

(a) A spouse may sue and be sued without the joinder of the other spouse.

(b) When claims or liabilities are joint and several, the spouses may be joined under the rules relating to joinder of parties generally.

Questions

1. How is the characterization of the property in question established?
2. How is the management of the property in question established?
3. What is the "doctrine of virtual representation?"
4. How may virtual representation be accomplished?
5. Are there any limits upon the conclusive nature of the judgment against Dr. Cooper?

DR. DONALD R. KLEIN & ASSOCIATES, M.D., P.A.
v.
KLEIN

637 S.W.2d 507
(Tex. App.—Eastland 1982, no writ)

RALEIGH BROWN, JUSTICE.

This is a suit brought in the County Court at Law No. 4 of Dallas County by Donald R. Klein and Associates, M.D., P.A., against Annabelle Sholdar Klein to recover for medical services performed by Dr. Klein on Mrs. Klein. The services were rendered Mrs. Klein while she was the wife of Joseph H. Klein, who subsequently died. A probate proceeding is pending on his estate. The trial court dismissed without prejudice to the association's right to file in the Probate Court. Klein and Associates appeal. We reverse and remand.

Mrs. Klein urges that the suit is a matter "incident to an estate" as contemplated by probate jurisdiction and, therefore, the County Court at Law had no jurisdiction.

TEX. PROB. CODE ANN. § 5A(a) (Vernon 1980) provides:

> (a) In proceedings in the constitutional county courts and statutory county courts at law, the phrases 'appertaining to estates' and 'incident to an estate' in this Code include the probate of wills, the issuance of letters testamentary and of administration, the determination of heirship, and also include, but are not limited to, all claims by or against an estate, all actions for trial of title to land incident to an estate and for the enforcement of liens thereon incident to an estate, all actions for trial of the right of property incident to an estate, and actions to construe wills, and generally all matters relating to the settlement, partition, and distribution of estates of wards and deceased persons.

TEX. PROB. CODE ANN. § 5A(b) provides in part:

> In situations where the jurisdiction of a statutory probate court is concurrent with that of a district court, any cause of action appertaining to estates or incident to an estate shall be brought in a statutory probate court rather than in the district court.

Dallas County has a statutory probate court. TEX. REV. CIV. STAT. ANN. art. 1970-31a (Vernon 1964). It is undisputed that at the time the services were rendered, Mrs. Klein was married to the deceased, Joseph H. Klein, and that any debt arising from the rendition of such services is a community obligation. Therefore, Mrs. Klein contends that the matter is one "incident to an estate" and is properly a matter for the probate court.

Dr. Klein argues that since the pleadings before the court clearly established that the County Court at Law had jurisdiction to hear the matter it erred in granting the motion to dismiss on jurisdictional grounds. He contends that he chose to sue only Mrs. Klein and was under no jurisdictional obligation to include the Estate of Joseph Klein. There is no showing that Dr. Klein has filed a claim against the Estate of Joseph Klein to satisfy the alleged debt.

TEX. FAM. CODE ANN. § 4.04 (Vernon 1975) provides:

> (a) A spouse may sue and be sued without the joinder of the other spouse. (b) When claims or liabilities are joint and several, the spouses may be joined under the rules relating to joinder of parties generally.

See also Cooper v. Texas Gulf Industries, Inc., 513 S.W.2d 200 (Tex. 1974).

The court in *Dulak v. Dulak*, 513 S.W.2d 205 (Tex. 1974), considering the matter of granting complete relief in an action regarding a community interest, said:

> In *Cooper*, *supra*, we made the further ruling that the omission of one of the spouses as a party in an action concerning their joint community property no longer renders a judgment void. Since jurisdiction with respect to the non-joinder of parties is now de-emphasized by force of amended Rule 39, we conclude that failure to join Helen Dulak in the suit below was not a jurisdictional defect and the judgment, unless otherwise erroneous, is binding upon those who were parties to the suit.

Since either spouse may be sued without the joinder of the other, it should not be a jurisdictional defect to sue Mrs. Klein without the joinder of the Estate of Joseph Klein. In the instant case there is no showing of any effort to make such estate a party, without the joinder of the Estate, the action could not be one "incident to an estate." In so holding we need not pass upon the issue of Mrs. Klein's individual liability. We merely hold that the trial court erred in dismissing the cause of action for want of jurisdiction.

The judgment is reversed, and the cause is remanded.

Questions

1. The right to sue is a management right; conversely, so is the right to be sued.
2. Why would Dr. Klein have made the decision *not* to join the estate of Mrs. Klein's husband?

F. Fraudulent Conveyances

GIVENS
v.
GIRARD LIFE INS. CO. OF AMERICA

480 S.W.2d 421
(Tex. Civ. App.—Dallas 1972, writ ref'd n.r.e.)

GUITTARD, ASSOCIATE JUSTICE.

Girard Life Insurance Company filed this interpleader action to determine ownership of insurance proceeds on the life of Walter Morris, deceased. The petition names as defendants Weedoll Givens, the designated beneficiary, and Edna Morris, widow of the insured. The principal question is whether designation by the husband of an unrelated person as beneficiary of life insurance purchased with community funds is constructive fraud on the wife.

The case was tried on an agreed statement of facts, which includes the following information. Walter and Edna Morris were married in 1928, and had several children, some of whom survive, but when he died on June 22, 1970, he had not lived with Edna for more than ten years. He held a certificate of insurance under a group life insurance policy obtained from Girard Life by his employer, who paid all the premiums and made no deductions from his pay for that purpose. On June 27, 1967, Morris changed the beneficiary to Weedoll Givens, who was not related to him by blood or marriage and was described in the designation as a friend. She had been acquainted with him since 1963, and their friendship continued until his death.

The policy provided a death benefit of $4,000, which the insurance company paid into court. Other assets are described as follows:

> The only known asset of the community estate of Walter Morris and Edna P. Morris, other than personal items, is approximately one acre of land near Fayetteville, Texas (and insurance policies, if same are considered assets of the community estate).

No will was found. Community indebtedness consisted of $350 on a television and stereo purchased by Edna Morris, taxes due on the acre of land near Fayetteville, and unpaid funeral expenses of $215.

The trial court held that the insurance proceeds were community property and that the change of beneficiary from his wife Edna Morris to the unrelated friend "was an act of constructive fraud upon the rights of Edna P. Morris as to her half of the proceeds." Accordingly, the judgment awarded one-half of the proceeds to the widow and the other half to the beneficiary, who appeals, contending that the stipulated facts fail to show any ground to defeat the prima facie case established by her designation as beneficiary. We hold that the facts support the judgment.

We agree with appellant that the rights of the insured husband under this contract were subject to his statutory power of management and disposition. Life insurance is defined as property by Vernon's TEX. REV. CIV. STAT. ANN. art. 23, subd. 1 (1969), and earnings during marriage are community property under TEX. FAM. CODE, § 5.01 (1969), V.T.C.A. Since the premiums paid by his employer were part of the compensation for his services, this insurance is deemed to be purchased out of his earnings and therefore community property. *Herring v. Blakeley*, 385 S.W.2d 843 (Tex. Sup. 1965); *Lee v. Lee*, 112 Tex. 392, 247 S.W. 828 (1923). Like other community property purchased with earnings, it was within his sole management, control and disposition under the Family Code[1] and the certificate issued in his name was subject to his disposition under a specific provision of the Insurance Code.[2] However, designation of a life insurance beneficiary is equivalent to a gift in the absence of a consideration moving from the beneficiary to the insured. *Evans v. Opperman*, 76 Tex. 293, 13 S.W. 312 (1890). Consequently, our question here is a particular aspect of the general question of the power of the managing spouse to make gifts of community property without consent of the other spouse. Reconciliation of the managerial power of one spouse with the interest of the other spouse as equal owner is a problem inherent in the concept of management by one spouse of marital property owned in common. This concept has come down to us from the laws of Spain and Mexico, and is carried forward in the statutes above mentioned without substantial change, except that the managerial powers of the husband have been restricted and those of the wife have been extended with respect to classes of property not now before us.

Our review of the authorities reveals that the husband's power to make gifts of community property has always been limited, though the limits have never been clearly defined. Early Spanish authorities expressed various opinions.[3] Probably the prevailing Spanish view was stated by the commentator ESCRICHE, as follows:

> . . . the husband can, without the consent of the wife, make *inter vivos* conveyances [of their community property] and even moderate donations for just causes; but excessive or capricious gifts will be null, and alienations made with intent to defraud the wife, who will

---

[1] TEX. FAM. CODE § 5.22 (1969):

Community Property: General Rules

(a) During marriage, each spouse has the sole management, control, and disposition of the community property that he or she would have owned if single, including but not limited to:

(1) personal earnings;

(2) revenue from separate property;

(3) recoveries for personal injuries; and

(4) the increase and mutations of, and the revenue from, all property subject to his or her sole management, control, and disposition.

(b) If community property subject to the sole management, control, and disposition of one spouse is mixed or combined with community property subject to the sole management, control, and disposition of the other spouse, then the mixed or combined community property is subject to the joint management, control, and disposition of the spouses, unless the spouses provide otherwise by power of attorney or other agreement in writing.

(c) Except as provided in Subsection (a) of this section, the community property is subject to the joint management, control and disposition of the husband and wife, unless the spouses provide otherwise by power of attorney or other agreement in writing."

[2] TEX. INS. CODE ANN. art. 3.49-3 (Supp.1972), V.A.T.S.: "A spouse shall have management, control and disposition of any contract of life insurance or annuity heretofore or hereafter issued in his or her name or to the extent provided by the contract or any assignment thereof without the joinder or consent of the other spouse." Appellant does not rely on this statute. Therefore, we express no opinion as to whether this statutory language indicates legislative intent to narrow the protection which the courts have given the widow under the constructive fraud doctrine or to broaden the management powers with respect to insurance purchased with earnings beyond those which the insured has under the Family Code, § 5.22(a), *supra*.

[3] Huie, *Community Property Laws as Applied to Life Insurance*, 18 TEX.L.REV. 121 (1940); DE FUNIAK, PRINCIPLES OF COMMUNITY PROPERTY, 2D ED. § 121 (1971).

have action in all these cases against the properties of the husband and against the possessor of the things conveyed.[4]

In *Stramler v. Coe*, 15 Tex. 211 at 216 (1855), CHIEF JUSTICE HEMPHILL, citing ESCRICHE and other Spanish authorities, declares:

> The husband has the active control and administration of the ganancial property during the matrimony. No consent of the wife is necessary to a valid alienation of such property by the husband. But excessive or capricious donations and sales, made with the intent to defraud the wife, would be void; and she would be entitled to her action against the property of the husband and against third possessors.

Prof. Huie has pointed our [sic] that this is almost a literal translation of ESCRICHE's language, and therefore the court must have intended to adopt the rule as laid down by ESCRICHE, but that the court's statement is ambiguous as to whether a showing of fraudulent intent is required with respect to donations as well as sales, whereas ESCRICHE made it clear that excessive or capricious gifts would be void without regard to whether the husband intended to defraud the wife.[5] This distinction seems to have been overlooked in later cases in which Texas courts have said that the husband may use his managerial powers to give away community property so long as he does so without intent to defraud the wife.[6] However, the Supreme Court has never held that proof of actual intent to defraud is required to avoid an "excessive or capricious" gift. Several courts of civil appeals have treated intent to defraud the wife as a fact issue to be submitted to the jury.[7] This approach has been criticized on the ground that making the validity of the gift depend on the subjective intent of the deceased husband leaves the wife's protection against excessive gifts inadequate and uncertain, and that the husband would never know in advance whether his gift would stand or fall, because its validity would depend upon a jury's speculation upon an issue of fact incapable of being accurately determined.[8]

We are persuaded that the widow should not have the burden of establishing fraudulent intent in order to protect her interest in the community property from abuse of her husband's managerial powers. This view is sustained by Texas authority. In appropriate cases our courts have dispensed with proof of fraudulent intent on the theory of constructive fraud, a judicial convention employed to achieve a just result in cases where the wrong to the wife is so clear that intent is immaterial. Thus an "excessive or capricious donation" was held to be "presumptively fraudulent" in *Hartman v. Crain*, 398 S.W.2d 387 (Tex. Civ. App.—Houston 1966, no writ). Also in *Martin v. Moran*, 11 Tex. Civ. App. 509, 32 S.W. 904 (Fort Worth 1895, no writ), the insured's designation of his own estate as beneficiary was held to be a fraud on the wife because he had no

---

[4] Translation quoted in Huie, *supra* note 3, at 123, *citing* ESCRICHE, DICCIONARIO DE LEGISLACION ANOTADO (1840) 71.

[5] Huie, *supra* note 3, at 128.

[6] Krueger v. Williams, 163 Tex. 545, 359 S.W.2d 48 (1962); Volunteer State Life Ins. Co. v. Hardin, 145 Tex. 245, 197 S.W.2d 105 (1946); Moody v. Smoot, 78 Tex. 119, 14 S.W. 285 (1890); Rowlett v. Mitchell, 52 Tex.Civ.App. 589, 114 S.W. 845 (Texarkana 1908, no writ).

[7] Aaron v. Aaron, 173 S.W.2d 310 (Tex.Civ.App.—Texarkana 1943, writ ref'd w.o.m.); Moore v. California-Western States Life Ins. Co., 67 S.W.2d 932 (Tex.Civ.App.—Amarillo 1934, writ dism'd); Shaw v. Shaw, 28 S.W.2d 173 (Tex.Civ.App.—Waco 1930, writ dism'd); Krenz v. Strohmeir, 177 S.W. 178 (Tex.Civ.App.—Austin 1915, writ ref'd).

[8] Huie, *supra* note 3, at 130 et seq.

power to give her interest in the community property to himself. The constructive fraud concept has been applied in cases in which the beneficiary has been changed from the wife to a relative of the insured, and the community estate remaining was insolvent or its assets so meager that the value of the property left in the hands of the surviving spouse was less than the proceeds of the policy. *Davis v. Prudential Ins. Co. of America*, 331 F.2d 346 (5th Cir. 1964); *Kemp v. Metropolitan Life Ins. Co.*, 205 F.2d 857 (5th Cir. 1953); *National Maritime Union v. Augustine*, 458 S.W.2d 832 (Tex. Civ. App.—Beaumont 1970, no writ). On the other hand, if adequate provision is made for the surviving spouse a gift to a relative, through life insurance or otherwise, is not considered fraudulent. *Krueger v. Williams*, 163 Tex. 545, 359 S.W.2d 48 (1962); *Brown v. Brown*, 282 S.W.2d 90 (Tex. Civ. App.—Waco 1955, writ ref'd n.r.e.); *Jones v. Jones*, 146 S.W. 265 (Tex. Civ. App.—San Antonio 1912, no writ).

All the cases above cited involved donees and beneficiaries related to the decedent. In such cases, as learned commentators have noted, the courts have considered objective factors in determining whether the situation was one in which the decedent might properly have made a gift of community funds, such as the relationship of the parties, whether special circumstances tended to justify the gift, and whether the community funds used for such purpose were reasonably in proportion to the community assets remaining.[9] Prof. Huie suggests that where life insurance is used as a means for distributing property at death to nondependent relatives, the principles of testamentary disposition of community property should apply, so that the beneficiary designation should be upheld only when reimbursement can be had from the husband's part of the community estate, and that gifts to the wife should also be considered on the question of constructive fraud.[10]

Although we have found no direct precedent dealing with application of the constructive fraud concept to an unrelated donee or beneficiary, the reasons for protecting the widow's interest against appropriation of community funds for relatives of the husband, such as a mother, sister or child of an earlier marriage, have even greater force when the beneficiary is entirely unrelated.[11] Persons outside the family do not ordinarily receive substantial gifts from donors in the modest circumstances of the deceased husband here. Neither are unrelated friends normally named as beneficiaries in life insurance contracts, which are designed primarily for protection of dependents on death of the insured by payment of debts and expenses and compensation for loss of support. *Warthan v. Haynes*, 155 Tex. 413, 288 S.W.2d 481 (1956). In our view, a husband's use of jointly owned funds to provide life insurance benefits to someone outside the family is so extraordinary as to raise a strong inference of misappropriation of the wife's interest in the community property. Consequently, we hold that purchase of life insurance with community funds for benefit of an unrelated person is constructively fraudulent in the absence of special justifying circumstances.

Under this holding the widow establishes constructive fraud prima facie by proof that life insurance was purchased with community funds for the benefit of an unrelated person, and the bene-

---

9 Johanson, *Revocable Trusts and Community Property*, 47 TEX. L. REV. 537, 568 (1969); 1 OAKES, SPEER'S MARITAL RIGHTS IN TEXAS, 4TH ED. § 434 at 642 (1961); DE FUNIAK, PRINCIPLES OF COMMUNITY PROPERTY, § 123 at 305 (1971). This passage from DE FUNIAK, as it appears in an earlier edition, is quoted with approval in support of the decision in Kemp v. Metropolitan Life Ins. Co., 205 F.2d 857 (5th Cir. 1953).

10 *Supra* note 3, at 145 et seq.

11 Johanson, *supra* note 9, at 568, citing cases in which gifts to mistresses have been declared fraudulent as against the wife. *See* Roberson v. Roberson, 420 S.W.2d 495 (Tex.Civ.App.—Houston [14th Dist.] 1967, writ ref'd n.r.e.); Watson v. Harris, 61 Tex.Civ.App. 263, 130 S.W. 237 (Austin 1910, no writ).

ficiary then has the burden to justify such use of community funds. What special circumstances would justify designation of an unrelated beneficiary cannot properly be determined in this case. All we know from the agreed statement about the relationship of the beneficiary to the insured is that they had been acquainted since 1963 and their friendship continued until the insured's death. This relationship does not support a substantial benefit to the unrelated friend from funds owned in common by the husband and wife. Neither can the friend's recovery of the entire proceeds be justified as equivalent to testamentary disposition of the insured's half of the community. No compensating benefits were provided by will for the widow, and although the agreed statement mentions "insurance policies," it does not disclose the amount or beneficiary of any policy other than the certificate in question. In the absence of any proof of these matters, we hold that the trial court was correct in awarding to the widow half the insurance proceeds[12] on the ground that the change of beneficiary from her to appellant Givens was an act of constructive fraud.

* * *

Questions

1. Why were the insurance policy proceeds community property?

2. Why have courts eliminated the need to prove fraudulent intent in cases such as this one?

3. How does a widow establish a prima facie case of constructive fraud?

4. What special circumstances might have justified the naming of an unrelated person as beneficiary?

5. This case revolves around a $4,000 death benefit. How can such a small dollar amount be considered excessive and capricious? (How much does an appeal cost?)

---

[12] Apparently the interest of the surviving spouse is limited to half the proceeds on the theory that the insured may dispose of his interest without limitation, as he can by will. Aaron v. Aaron, 173 S.W.2d 310 (Tex. Civ. App.—Texarkana 1943, writ ref'd w.o.m.); Huie, *supra* note 3, at 137; Comment, *The Community Life Insurance Policy*, 18 BAYLOR L. REV. 627, at 631 (1966). A question may be raised concerning the decedent's half as well as if survivor [sic] would otherwise have the whole burden of community debts, but that question is not before us.

MURPHY
v.
METROPOLITAN LIFE INS. CO.

498 S.W.2d 278
(Tex. Civ. App.—Houston [14th Dist.] 1973, writ ref'd n.r.e.)

TUNKS, CHIEF JUSTICE.

Bobby Buchanan died intestate on October 27, 1970. He left surviving him his mother, Alma Buchanan Alexander Murphy, his wife, Lena Buchanan, and three sons. Those individual parties will sometimes be referred to by their first names.

At the time of his death Bobby was and had been for many years an employee of Shell Chemical Corporation. As such he had acquired certain employee benefits. One such benefit was called a provident fund and had a value of about $33,000. His estate was the named beneficiary of the provident fund at the date of his death. Another benefit was under what was called a survivor's benefit plan. That benefit had a value of about $24,000. Under this plan the employer had certain rights, hereinafter discussed, with reference to designation of the beneficiary. Bobby also was the insured in a company group life insurance policy in the amount of $12,500. At the time of Bobby's death his mother was the designated beneficiary under the group life policy. Other items of property remaining at Bobby's death were a home valued at $10,000, automobiles valued at $500 and household furniture of which no value was established by the evidence.

After Bobby's death both the mother and the surviving wife filed claims for the benefits under the life insurance policy. The insurer, Metropolitan Life Insurance Company, because of the conflict, declined to pay either claimant. The mother then filed suit against the surviving wife and the insurer to recover the benefits. The insurer took the position of a stakeholder and tendered the money representing the benefits into court to be paid in accordance with the judicial determination as to the conflicting claims. The surviving wife answered and by cross-action asserted her claim to the benefits. After a non-jury trial the trial court adjudged that the mother and surviving wife each receive one half of the benefits. The mother appealed.

The life insurance policy in question was property. *Brown v. Lee*, 371 S.W.2d 694 (Tex. Sup. 1963); TEX. REV. CIV. STAT. ANN. art. 23, subd. 1 (1957). In response to pretrial interrogatories Lena characterized this policy as community property and no contrary contention is made by either party. Bobby, as the named insured, had the right to designate the beneficiary of the policy. TEX. INS. CODE ANN. art. 3.49-3 (1968), V.A.T.S. Also, since it was an incident to his employment, it was a part of the community which was subject to his "sole management, control, and disposition." TEX. FAMILY CODE ANN. § 5.22 (1970), V.T.C.A. However, his statutory authority to designate the beneficiary and to dispose of this item of the community was subject to limitation. He could not exercise that authority if, and to the extent that, such exercise was in fraud of his wife or resulted in a constructive fraud against her interest in the community. Before enactment of the cited article of the Insurance Code, it had long and firmly been established in Texas that one spouse could not give away the benefits of an insurance policy acquired with community funds if such gift was in actual fraud or resulted in constructive fraud of the other. *See* Huie, *Community Property Laws as Applied to Life Insurance*, 18 TEX. L. REV. 121 (1940) *and* Quilliam, *Gratuitous Transfers of Community Property to Third Persons*, 2 TEX. TECH. L. REV. 23 (1970). There is nothing in the language of the cited article from the Insurance Code that indicates an intent to depart from the rule or that the giving away of such a community property will not, under any circumstances, be fraudulent. The article is consistent with section 5.22 of the Family Code. The language of TEX. FAMILY CODE ANN. sec. 5.24 clearly indicates that, within the scope of legislative intent, the disposition of community property by one spouse having control thereof may sometimes constitute a fraud upon the other spouse.

In this case the trial judge found as a fact "that the intent of Bobby Buchanan in changing the beneficiary of said policy was arbitrary, capricious and improvident and was done to deprive his wife of benefit and not as a part of any considered estate planning." He recited conclusions of law to the effect that the changing of the beneficiary both was actual fraud and resulted in constructive fraud upon the rights of Lena Buchanan. We must review the record to determine whether the trial judge's quoted fact finding is supported by the evidence and whether the legal conclusions drawn therefrom were proper. In such review we must consider all of the evidence in the light most favorable to the appellee and may not hold the trial court's finding erroneous if there is any probative evidence supporting it unless the finding is so against the preponderance as to be manifestly wrong. *Cortez v. Cortez*, 457 S.W.2d 131 (Tex. Civ. App.—San Antonio 1970, no writ).

Bobby and Lena Buchanan were married in 1949. The insurance policy in question was issued in 1951. Lena originally was designated beneficiary. In the latter part of 1968 the couple separated for a period of about two months because of marital trouble. It was during this separation that Bobby changed the designation of beneficiary in the insurance policy from his wife to his mother. At the same time he changed the designation of beneficiary in his employee provident fund from his wife to his estate. Bobby did not tell Lena of these changes of beneficiary after the separation ended. The changes remained effective until his death. A fellow employee testified that in the year 1969 when Bobby was asked if he had a will he said, "I got that all taken care of where my boys will get everything I got." Those facts would constitute some circumstantial evidence that Bobby was motivated by ill feeling toward his wife in changing the beneficiary of the insurance policy.

Mrs. Murphy, Bobby's mother, was a widow. She was 64 years old at the date of Bobby's death. She owned a home in another city. Her only income was from a $98 monthly social security check and an oil payment varying from $5 to $60 monthly. Bobby was her only child. Bobby's father had been dead about seven years. Those facts would constitute some circumstantial evidence that Bobby was motivated by his moral obligation to his mother in changing the designation of beneficiary to her.

The total value of the community, including the benefits from the insurance policy, was about $80,000. The evidence shows that after Bobby's death his wife received over $45,000 from the community without regard to the insurance benefits. She received one half of the provident fund ($16,500), one half interest in the home ($5,000), one half interest in the cars ($250), and *all* of the survivor's benefit ($24,000). The fact that she would get more than half of the community without receiving any of the proceeds of the insurance policy is due to the fact that she received all, instead of half, of the survivor's benefit.

The record is not at all clear as to the legal nature of the survivor's benefit program maintained by Bobby's employer. It was obviously an incident to his employment contract and, if property at all, it was community property. We assume that this payment was pursuant to some employer-employee plan that was set out in a written instrument the terms of which would show whether it created any proprietary interest in the community estate. There is no such written instrument in evidence. The only explanation of the nature of such benefit is the oral testimony of a representative of the employer. He testifies that it is a program under which the company pays to survivors of active employees who die before reaching age 55 a sum representing twice the employee's annual salary. Under the plan the company, and not the employee, selects the survivor or survivors who are to be beneficiaries. He testified that an order of priority exists with reference to the company's election of the beneficiary as follows: 1st the surviving spouse, 2nd surviving children, 3rd surviving parents and 4th the decedent's estate. The weight to be given the priorities of that list by the company is not shown by evidence. The witness, in fact, called the payment a "gratuity" by the company. That conclusion by the witness is of doubtful validity. Neither the shareholders of the company nor the Internal Revenue Service would look upon the program with favor if a payment under it were a gratuity. However, Lena, in response to pretrial interrogatories, said that she did not claim that the payment under this plan was not a part of the community estate.

The law review articles by Huie and Quilliam, cited above, discuss the history of the judicial treatment by Texas Courts of a husband's gift of part of the community estate to an outsider. Another such discussion appears in Johanson, *Revocable Trusts and Community Property: The Substantive Problems*, 47 TEX. L. REV. 537 (1969). The opinion in *Givens v. Girard Life Insurance Company of America*, 480 S.W.2d 421 (Tex. Civ. App.—Dallas 1972, writ ref'd n.r.e.) includes another discussion of the subject. From those authorities and the cases cited therein it may be said that a husband may properly make a gift of a part of the community controlled by him, but that the propriety of such a gift requires the absence of fraud. As to what constitutes such fraud as will invalidate the gift the authorities speak of actual fraud and constructive fraud. A trust relationship exists between the husband and wife as to that portion of the community controlled by the husband. *Brownson v. New*, 259 S.W.2d 277 (Tex. Civ. App.—San Antonio 1953, writ dism'd). For that reason any unfair gift of community property by a husband to one outside of the community would be a constructive fraud. In an attack on such gift the wife does not have the burden of proving that it was motivated by the husband's actual fraudulent intent. At the wife's suit such a gift will be set aside, as to the wife's community share of the property given, if it is unfair to the wife. The burden of proving fairness is on the husband or his donee. *See Archer v. Griffith*, 390 S.W.2d 735 (Tex.Sup.1964); *Givens v. Girard Life Insurance Company of America*, *supra*; *Daves v. Lawyers Surety Corporation*, 459 S.W.2d 655 (Tex. Civ. App.—Amarillo 1970, writ ref'd n.r.e.); *Davis v. Prudential Insurance Company of America*, 331 F.2d 346 (5th Cir. 1964).

In this case the husband's gift was to his mother. She was a natural object of his bounty. She was indigent. He had at least a moral obligation to contribute to her support. By some arrangement not fully explained in the record the surviving wife still got more than half of the community, even if the gift was held valid. Those facts argue for the validity of the gift. They would have supported a fact finding by the trial judge to the effect that the gift was fair.

The gift here was a rather large one in relation to the size of the community estate—almost one-sixth. The total amount of the community estate left for the surviving wife, while substantial, did not provide her with a high degree of financial security. She had only a small earning capacity. She had no separate property. She had three sons to raise and educate. Under the rules of review set forth above by which this Court is bound, those facts placed it within the fact finding discretion of the trial judge to find that the husband's gift of the wife's share of the community interest in the insurance policy was unfair to the wife. That finding sustained the trial court's judgment setting aside the gift as to the wife's interest.

* * *

The judgment of the trial court is affirmed.

Questions

1. Is *Murphy* an actual or constructive fraud case?
2. If the trial court had found in favor of the decedent's mother, would a reversal have ensued?

---

fraud on comm

SPRUILL
v.
SPRUILL

624 S.W.2d 694
(Tex. App.—El Paso 1981, writ dism'd)

WARD, JUSTICE.

The husband appeals the property division from a divorce suit. Trial was to a jury and based on the verdict rendered, the Court entered the divorce and property division. We affirm the judgment of the trial Court.

The parties were married in August, 1966, and had two children. In February, 1977, the wife, Diane Spruill, filed her suit for divorce against her husband and joined as a party Defendant the husband's primary corporation, the Larry Spruill Company, Inc. The husband owned forty-eight percent of the capital stock of this company before his marriage and after marriage acquired the balance of the shares of capital stock by purchasing them with community funds. The evidence reveals that the husband was a successful mobile home dealer, the dealership being owned by the corporation. In addition to selling mobile homes, the husband had a fifty percent stock ownership in four other corporations which manufactured or sold apparatus in connection with mobile homes which he designed. The husband, for a substantial number of years prior to the divorce trial, had operated solely out of the Larry Spruill Company, Inc., or out of another of his corporations for all of his ordinary living expenses. The home where the parties lived was owned by the corporation and all of the motor vehicles, furniture and other assets, normally associated with being acquired by the community estate, were in fact owned by a corporate entity. The husband even paid for the food and other necessities of life from a corporate account. According to the husband's testimony, about the time that the divorce suit was filed, his business, from being very successful, took a turn for the worse. Thus, in December, 1976, he filed a financial statement with an Odessa bank showing that he and his wife had a net worth of approximately $400,000.00.

On January 1, 1977, and again in 1978, the husband executed several promissory notes in the approximate amount of $285,000.00 to his business partner in New Orleans and pledged all of the stock in all of the various companies as security. Further, according to the husband's version, the promissory note indebtedness finally came to the total sum of $358,000.00 by June of 1978, and in July, 1979, the partner filed suit in New Orleans to foreclose on all of the corporate stocks that the husband and wife owned, and after he obtained judgment this completely wiped out the community estate. Finally, according to the husband, the community thus lost the house, the furniture, all of the mobile home inventory, all monies, the motor vehicles, and every other conceivable community asset. After the foreclosure by the partner, the husband was then hired by the partner to continue acting as president of Larry Spruill Company, Inc., at a salary of $1,000.00 a month and, according to the husband, the partner still remained his friend, although he had impoverished both the husband, the wife, and the children. During this time, the husband executed a second lien note and deed of trust to the First National Bank of Odessa covering the home in question. Also during these proceedings, the husband left his wife and children and moved in with his girl friend.

The judgment entered granted the wife the divorce, awarded custody of the children to the wife, awarded to her the sum of $7,000.00 in cash which was in the registry of the Court, awarded to her the cash surrender value of all life insurance policies as described in the evidence and, in addition, the sum of $30,000.00 cash to be paid by the husband together with legal interest thereon from the date of the divorce judgment.

The Court further found and determined that Larry Spruill Company, Inc. and Lawrence Wayne Spruill were one and the same; that the Defendant corporation became the alter ego of the husband; and that the notes executed by the husband in favor of his partner and the pledging of the corporate stock of the various corporations were all done by the husband to create a false community debt with the intent to defraud the wife of her community interest in the stock. Based on this, the husband's interest, if any, in the corporate stock of the Larry Spruill Company, Inc. and the four other subsidiary corporations was awarded to the wife; the wife and the minor children were awarded the sole use and occupancy of the home, together with all household goods, furniture, and furnishing and equipment located therein, insofar as any interest of the husband and the Larry Spruill Company, Inc. were concerned; and finally, all corporate records and all personal property, of whatever nature of the Larry Spruill Company, Inc. and other corporations, were awarded to her.

This brings us to a point where we can consider the status of this appeal. In the first place, the Defendant, the Larry Spruill Company, Inc., has not appealed the judgment of the trial Court. Though the husband's brief refers to the corporation as an Appellant, the corporation did not file an appeal bond. Thus, the judgment as to the corporation is final and this Court has acquired no jurisdiction over the judgment insofar as it relates to that Defendant. Rule 356, TEX. R. CIV. P.; *Governing Board v. Pannill*, 561 S.W.2d 517, (Tex. Civ. App.—Texarkana 1977, writ ref'd n.r.e.).

In the second place, Larry Spruill makes many complaints regarding various jury findings regarding property without showing that he has been harmed or prejudiced in any way. The testimony by the husband was that at the time of trial the husband owned nothing but the clothes on his back. The Court found that the husband owned nothing, and this finding has not been attacked. An appellant will not be favored with a reversal for error that does not prejudice him even though it might prejudice another party. APPELLATE PROCEDURE IN TEXAS, 2D ED. sec. 20.3. With these ground rules before us, we will examine the points.

By his last point, the husband complains that the Court erred in entering judgment for the Plaintiff in the absence of the joinder of necessary parties. Under his argument, he contends that the partner and the First National Bank of Odessa were indispensable parties since the jury determined that both had participated with the husband in defrauding the wife of her ownership in the stocks and the house and, therefore, the judgment awarding the stocks and the house to her was void. We note that the Defendant husband did not raise the omission of these parties by any plea in abatement or by exception but chose to remain silent until he pointed the omissions out in his motion for directed verdict. If the parties were necessary parties rather than indispensable ones, the plea in abatement was necessary, otherwise, a waiver has been created. 2 MCDONALD, TEXAS

CIVIL PRACTICE sec. 7.13 (rev. 1970); 1 MCDONALD, TEXAS CIVIL PRACTICE sec. 3.33 (rev. 1981). In this case, the trial court has determined that the wife be awarded the ownership of the stock certificates, the home and its contents, only insofar as the judgment may effect the interest of the husband and wife. Under these circumstances, we hold that the missing parties were not indispensable parties. At best, a waiver has been presented. *See*, 1 MCDONALD, TEXAS CIVIL PRACTICE secs. 3.28.1, 3.29 (rev. 1981); annot. 63 A.L.R.3D 363 (1975). The point under consideration is overruled.

We will discuss two points that relate to a matter where the husband does have a definite interest, since the trial Court judgment for divorce did in effect award a monetary judgment in favor of the wife against her husband for $30,000.00. Professor Reed Quilliam has pointed out that the Courts have taken a dim view toward gifts by the husband to "strangers" of the marriage, particularly of the female variety. *See*, *Gratuitous Transfers of Community Property To Third Persons*, 2 TEX. TECH. L. REV. 23, p. 40 (1970). It has further been pointed out that a trust relationship exists between husband and wife as to that community property controlled by each spouse and a presumption of constructive fraud arises when a spouse unfairly disposes of the other spouse's one-half interest in community property. Because of this, the burden of proof is upon the disposing spouse to prove the fairness of the disposition of the other spouse's one-half community ownership. *See*, *Carnes v. Meador*, 533 S.W.2d 365, at 370, (Tex. Civ. App.—Dallas 1975, writ ref'd n.r.e.).

In this connection, proof was made in our case by the wife that before the divorce the husband was spending large sums of money on his girl friend. Regarding this evidence, two special issues were submitted. Issue Number Eight inquired if the husband spent community funds on the girl friend with the knowledge or consent of the wife. To this, the jury answered, "Yes." Issue Number Nine inquired as to what sum of money represented by community funds was spent on the girl friend. To this, the jury answered, "30,000.00."

Point Number Eight is that there was no evidence or insufficient evidence regarding the finding by the jury that the husband spent $30,000.00 in community funds on the girl friend. Under this point, the husband's whole brief consists of one sentence, pointing out that on one page of the Statement of Facts the wife stated she did not know how much the husband had spent on other women. This briefing leaves something to be desired since the Statement of Facts consists of twelve-hundred pages of testimony and volumes of exhibits. Regardless, we have reviewed the record and under the appropriate rules regarding our consideration of "no evidence" and "insufficient evidence" contentions, the Eighth Point is overruled.

We assume that Special Issue Number Eight was submitted in an attempt by the husband to establish a defense to the wife's contention that she should be repaid for these fraudulent expenditures. Point of Error Ten complains of the entry of the judgment in favor of the wife for the recovery of her judgment against the husband since the jury found that the wife was aware of or consented to the expenditure of the community funds on the girl friend. The problem with this defense submitted by the husband is twofold. In the first place, the husband by the answer that he has secured to Issue Number Eight has not established that the community funds were spent on the girl friend with the consent of the wife so as to constitute a defense to any constructive fraud of the wife's rights. As far as the answer to the issue is concerned, it could have been answered because it was with the knowledge of the wife. This would be no defense to the constructive fraud. In the second place, the way the issues are framed, the answer to Special Issue Number Eight does not establish that the wife had knowledge of or consented to an expenditure of any amount of money other than "community funds." For all we know, it could have been $5.00, as there is no tying the answer to Special Issue Number Eight with the answer to Special Issue Number Nine. The defense urged by the husband based on the jury finding to Special Issue Number Eight fails. Point of Error Number Ten is overruled.

We have examined the balance of the husband's points and they present either no merit or present points where the husband cannot be harmed or prejudiced in any way. The balance of the points are overruled. While there may be defects in the judgment regarding the award made to the wife against the husband, we cannot grant relief where points regarding those defects have not been made.

The judgment of the trial Court is affirmed.

Questions

1. Why do you think the husband received so little of the property?
2. What effect did the finding of alter ego have?
3. The appellate court found that husband was not prejudiced by the judgment. How was this conclusion reached?
4. Husband tried to defend his expenditures on his girlfriend; why did the defense fail?

MORRISON
v.
MORRISON

713 S.W.2d 377
(Tex. App.—Dallas 1986, writ dism'd)

GUILLOT, JUSTICE.

David Morrison appeals the property division in a divorce judgment. Trial was to the court. On appeal, David raises ten points of error contending that: (1) the trial court abused its discretion by inequitably dividing the community estate in favor of Carolyn; (2) the trial court had no jurisdiction to file its amended findings of fact and conclusions of law; and (3) the evidence was legally and factually insufficient to support the trial court's amended findings. We disagree with each contention and, for the reasons stated below, affirm the judgment of the trial court.

The record shows that David and Carolyn were married for over thirty-five years when David filed for divorce. David alleged as grounds for divorce insupportability and cruelty. Carolyn filed a counterclaim seeking a divorce on the grounds of insupportability, cruel treatment, adultery, and desertion. The judgment of divorce was entered July 17, 1985. The community property distributed by the discretion of the court was: (1) the residence valued at $62,473.00; (2) Focus on Dallas, Inc., Carolyn's corporate business valued at $139,000.00; and (3) David's insurance business valued at $14,000.00. The court awarded Carolyn the house and her business and awarded David $29,000.00 and his business.

The trial court filed findings of fact and conclusions of law on September 3, 1985. The court found that the marriage was insupportable because of conflict of personalities. After David perfected his appeal, Carolyn requested additional findings which the court filed on January 16, 1986. The court additionally found that David was at fault in the breakup of the marriage because of his alcoholism, adultery, and diversion of community assets for the benefit of other women.

With respect to the diversion of community assets, the trial court found that David spent "substantial amounts of community funds" on other women while married to Carolyn. David admitted he had secretly put a girlfriend on the insurance coverage of Focus on Dallas Inc. He also admitted: (1) taking other women to Hawaii and staying in fancy accommodations; (2) taking trips all over the country with various women; (3) paying traveling expenses for various women; (4) "advancing" cash to various women; (5) paying attorney's fees for one or more women; and (6) buying gifts for other women during his marriage. He also admitted paying $2,689.45 for rent for another woman's apartment and paying or "advancing" another woman $7,385.00.

In points of error one through five, David contends that the trial court awarded Carolyn 83.5% of the community estate and that this division was manifestly unjust. We disagree.

Section 3.63 of the Texas Family Code gives the trial court broad discretion in the division of community assets and the division made by the trial court will not be disturbed on appeal unless a clear abuse of discretion is shown. *Murff v. Murff*, 615 S.W.2d 696, 698 (Tex. 1981). In exercising this discretion the court may consider many factors, including fault in breaking up the marriage. *Id.* at 698. It is presumed that the trial court exercised its discretion properly and every reasonable presumption is resolved in favor of the trial court's exercise of discretion. *Id. Gutierrez v. Gutierrez*, 643 S.W.2d 786, 787 (Tex. App.—San Antonio 1982, no writ). Furthermore, unequal divisions of community property have been upheld where the facts warrant the inequality. *See Jones v. Jones*, 699 S.W.2d 583, 586 (Tex. App.—Texarkana 1985, no writ); *Cluck v. Cluck*, 647 S.W.2d 338, 343 (Tex. App.—San Antonio 1982, writ dism'd) (the appellate court affirmed a division in which appellant contended that the appellee received eighty-six percent of the community property).

In the instant case, Carolyn was entitled to reimbursement to her half of the community property because of David's misuse of community funds. The right of reimbursement is an equitable right which may be considered by the trial court in determining the division of community property. *Horlock v. Horlock*, 533 S.W.2d 52, 60-61 (Tex Civ. App.—Houston [14th Dist.] 1975, writ dism'd). We presume, therefore, that when the court divided the community, it awarded Carolyn a substantial reimbursement for the assets David diverted from her half of the community. *See Robbins v. Robbins*, 519 S.W.2d 507, 510-11 (Tex. Civ. App.—Fort Worth 1975, no writ) (the appellate court presumed that the wife's entitlement to reimbursement of her separate estate was taken into calculation by the trial court when it divided the parties' community property); TEX. R. CIV. P. 299. Furthermore, the trial court found David at fault in the breakup of the marriage because of his adultery. We presume that the trial court also considered this factor when it divided the community. *Gutierrez*, 643 S.W.2d at 787. Based on the evidence of Carolyn's right to reimbursement and David's adultery, we hold that the trial court did not abuse its discretion in awarding a disproportionate amount to Carolyn. *See Murff*, 615 S.W.2d at 698.

In points of error nine and ten, David attacks the sufficiency of the evidence to support the trial court's finding of his wrongful diversion of community assets. Because a trust relationship exists between husband and wife as to that community property controlled by each spouse, the burden of proof to show fairness in disposing of community assets is upon the disposing spouse. *Spruill v. Spruill*, 624 S.W.2d 694, 697 (Tex. App.—El Paso 1981, writ dism'd). Thus, once evidence of the expenditures of community funds was admitted, it was incumbent on David to justify the expenditures.

At trial David admitted paying $2,689.45 for another woman's apartment rent. He claimed that the payment was an "advance" but admitted that nothing was written on the check to indicate the advance. He also admitted "advancing" another woman $7,385.00, but offered no evidence of reimbursement. He also admitted taking trips all over the country with other women and paying legal fees and traveling expenses for other women. The extravagant nature of these expenditures and David's failure to document the transactions gave the court broad discretion in evaluating David's testimony. *Id. Gunter v. Molk*, 663 S.W.2d 674, 675 (Tex. App.—Beaumont 1983, writ ref'd n.r.e.). In a bench trial, the judge has broad discretion to reach his own conclusion after considering all the evidence and can accept or reject any or all the testimony of any witness. *Gunter*, 663 S.W.2d at 675. Consequently, the trial court could disregard David's testimony that these expenditures were "advances" or business expenses.

Moreover, the court could arrive at its own estimation of the total amount wrongfully spent. *Id.* David stated that he did not have bank records except for the two years preceding the trial. The trial court could reasonably infer that other funds or assets were wrongfully diverted from the community estate which could not be discovered because of the lack of records. We conclude that the evidence of David's expenditures and his failure to document or keep bank records is sufficient to support the trial court's finding that David wrongfully spent a substantial amount of community funds on other women.

David also contends that the evidence is insufficient to support the trial court's finding of his adultery. We disagree. At trial, David admitted taking other women to motels for "sexual encounters" but denied committing adultery because he claimed he was incapable of sexual intercourse. Adultery, however, can be shown by circumstantial evidence. *Miller v. Miller*, 306 S.W.2d 175, 176 (Tex. Civ. App.—San Antonio 1957, no writ). Furthermore, in evaluating David's testimony, the trial court could disregard David's uncorroborated claim of impotency. *Gunter*, 663 S.W.2d at 675. Consequently, we hold that David's testimony of his "sexual encounters" with other women is sufficient evidence of adultery to support the trial court's finding.

We conclude that the trial court properly exercised its discretion in dividing the community estate and that the disparity in the division favoring Carolyn was due to David's diversion of community assets and his adultery. Because the trial court's division of property was warranted by David's wrongful diversion of community assets and adultery, we need not address David's point of error relating to the court's finding of his alcoholism. Consequently, we overrule points of error one through five and points of error nine and ten.

* * *

Finally, David contends that his constitutional due process rights were violated because the court filed its amended findings after the court's jurisdiction over the case had expired. David, however, fails to allege any specific constitutional harm. He only complains of the extra expense required to file his supplemental brief in response to the untimely action of the court. Because

David does not show us any specific harm which resulted in a denial of his right to adequately present his appeal, we conclude that his due process rights were not violated. We overrule David's eighth point of error.

Affirmed.

Questions

1. In *Morrison*, how did the trial court deal with the wife's right to reimbursement for misuse of community funds?

2. Why didn't the wife have to establish the exact amount of community funds her husband wrongfully diverted?

3. In *Spruill*, the court found that the husband had defrauded his wife. Perhaps, the same fraud finding could be applied to the *Morrison* case. However, if fraud on the community exists, should a money judgment be allowed? What about punitive damages?

4. Read the next case and answer question 3 again.

SCHLUETER
v.
SCHLUETER

975 S.W.2d 584
(Tex. 1998)

GONZALEZ, JUSTICE.

This divorce case answers the question of what remedies are available to a spouse alleging fraud on the community committed by the other spouse. The husband transferred various community assets to his father shortly before he filed for divorce. The wife counterclaimed for divorce and brought independent tort claims against her husband and father-in-law, seeking damages for fraud, breach of fiduciary duty, and conspiracy. Based on favorable jury findings, the trial court ordered a disproportionate division of the community estate favoring the wife, and rendered judgment for the wife against the husband and his father for actual and exemplary damages. Holding that a tort cause of action for fraud on the community exists independent of a divorce proceeding, the court of appeals affirmed. 929 S.W.2d 94. We granted writ to resolve a conflict among courts of appeals. Because a wronged spouse has an adequate remedy for fraud on the community through the "just and right" property division upon divorce, we hold that there is no independent tort cause of action between spouses for damages to the community estate. Accordingly, we reverse the judgment against the husband and remand for a new division of the marital estate. We affirm the remainder of the court of appeals' judgment.

I

Richard and Karen Schlueter married in 1969. In December 1992, Mr. Schlueter began investing in emus. He contributed $3250 of community funds toward two pairs of the birds, but eventually sold his interest to his father, Hudson Schlueter, for $1,000. The emu business was worth at least $10,000 when the sale occurred. Mrs. Schlueter did not know the details of the business and did not find out that her husband had sold his interest to her father-in-law until after Mr. Schlueter filed for divorce.

Shortly before he filed for divorce, Mr. Schlueter accepted a $30,360.41 check from his employer as an incentive for early retirement. Mr. Schlueter turned the check over to his father for deposit in his father's account. His father then wrote himself a check for $12,565, allegedly to reimburse past loans to Mr. Schlueter. About a week later, Mr. Schlueter filed for divorce.

Mrs. Schlueter counterclaimed for divorce and added independent tort claims against her husband and father-in-law for fraud, breach of fiduciary duty, and conspiracy. All of Mrs. Schlueter's claims against her husband and father-in-law involve their depriving the Schlueters' community estate of assets. Mrs. Schlueter makes no claim that she was deprived of her separate property.

The jury heard the fraud and conspiracy claims in a bifurcated trial. The jury found that Mr. Schlueter committed actual and constructive fraud in dealing with the community assets, that he and his father had fraudulently transferred assets between them, and that they had engaged in a civil conspiracy to injure Mrs. Schlueter. The jury found that $12,850 would compensate the community for Mr. Schlueter's and his father's actions. It found that $35,000 would compensate the community for damage caused by the conspiracy. Finally, the jury found that Mr. Schlueter should pay $50,000 and his father $15,000 in exemplary damages.

At a later date, the trial court heard the divorce action without a jury, divided the marital assets, and rendered judgment on the jury verdict against Mr. Schlueter and his father jointly and severally for $12,850. In its Findings of Fact, the trial court determined that the joint and several judgment was part of the community estate. The court also awarded Mrs. Schlueter $30,000 in exemplary damages against her husband and $15,000 in exemplary damages against her father-in-law, and awarded Mrs. Schlueter $18,500 from her husband for attorney's fees on appeal.

The court of appeals affirmed. The court held that a spouse may bring an independent tort claim against the other spouse for fraud for which exemplary damages may be awarded, even when the fraud resulted only in a depletion of community assets and not the wronged spouse's separate estate. 929 S.W.2d at 99-100. The court of appeals based its holding on this Court's abrogation of the doctrine of interspousal immunity in the *Bounds*, *Price*, and *Twyman* decisions, and concluded that a person may bring any cause of action against his or her spouse. 929 S.W.2d at 99-100 (construing *Twyman v. Twyman*, 855 S.W.2d 619, 624 (Tex. 1993); *Price v. Price*, 732 S.W.2d 316, 319 (Tex. 1987); and *Bounds v. Caudle*, 560 S.W.2d 925, 927 (Tex. 1977)). The court of appeals also affirmed the judgment against the father-in-law, holding that the trial court had not abused its discretion in admitting into evidence a copy of a divorce decree involving Mr. Schlueter's brother.

Relying on *Belz v. Belz*, 667 S.W.2d 240, 247 (Tex. App.—Dallas 1984, writ ref'd n.r.e.), and *In re Marriage of Moore*, 890 S.W.2d 821, 829 (Tex. App.—Amarillo 1994, no writ), Mr. Schlueter alleges that the court of appeals committed reversible error in recognizing a separate cause of action for fraud on the community. Mr. Schlueter and his father, in the father's only point of erpoint of error, also assert that the court of appeals erred in holding that the trial court did not abuse its discretion in admitting into evidence a copy of the decree from Mr. Schlueter's brother's divorce.

II

The court of appeals reads the *Twyman*, *Price*, and *Bounds* decisions too broadly; these decisions do not control this case. In *Bounds*, we dealt with whether the interspousal immunity doctrine prevented a deceased woman's children from suing their stepfather for their mother's wrongful death. *Bounds*, 560 S.W.2d at 925. The stepfather had allegedly shot and killed his wife. We concluded that interspousal immunity should be abolished for willful or intentional torts. *Id.* at 926-27. From a policy perspective, we stated that suits for willful and intentional torts such as the physical attack in that case would not disrupt domestic tranquility in "a home which has already been strained to the point where an intentional physical attack could take place." *Id.* at 927.

We re-examined the doctrine in *Price v. Price*, 732 S.W.2d 316 (Tex. 1987). A wife sued her husband for negligence in causing her injuries in a motorcycle accident. Again this Court considered and rejected the argument that "peace and harmony" in the home would be damaged by suits between spouses, commenting that "[i]t is difficult to fathom how denying a forum for the redress of any wrong could be said to encourage domestic tranquility." *Id.* at 318. We followed up on our holding in *Bounds* by stating, "We now abolish [the interspousal immunity doctrine] completely as to any cause of action. We do not limit our holding to suits involving vehicular accidents only." *Id.* at 319.

Finally, in *Twyman*, we expressly adopted the tort of intentional infliction of emotional distress, and a plurality held that such a claim could be brought in a divorce proceeding. *Twyman*, 855 S.W.2d at 622, 624-26. The plurality noted that under *Bounds* and *Price*, there was no legal impediment to bringing a tort claim in a divorce action "based on either negligence or an intentional act such as assault or battery." *Twyman*, 855 S.W.2d at 624. Of course, by its facts, *Twyman* expanded that statement by allowing an intentional tort claim for emotional distress, which does not necessarily involve the physical aspects of assault or battery.

The salient characteristic distinguishing *Bounds*, *Price*, and *Twyman* from the case before us is that all three involved personal injury tort claims. *Twyman*, 855 S.W.2d at 621 (intentional infliction of emotional distress); *Price*, 732 S.W.2d at 316 (negligence claim for personal injuries); *Bounds*, 560 S.W.2d at 926 (wrongful death). *Cf. Cleaver v. George Staton Co., Inc.*, 908 S.W.2d 468, 471 n.2 (Tex. App.—Tyler 1995, writ denied) (distinguishing *Twyman*, which involved outrageous spousal conduct, and noting that the trial court could sort out the husband's claims against wife for breach of fiduciary duty and fraud on community estate in the property division, not by a separate cause of action). In discussing the potential for double recovery in *Twyman*, the Court pointed out that recovery for personal injuries of a spouse, including pain and suffering, is the separate property of the injured spouse, and therefore does not add to the marital estate. *Twyman*, 855 S.W.2d at 625 n.20 (citing TEX. FAM. CODE § 5.01(a)(3) (Act of May 31, 1969, 61st Leg., R.S., ch. 888, 1969 Tex. Gen. Laws 2707, 2726, *repealed by* Act of April 3, 1997, 75th Leg., R.S., ch. 7, § 3, 1997 Tex. Gen. Laws 8, 43)) (current version at TEX. FAM. CODE ANN. § 3.001(3)).

Likewise, in response to the concern that interspousal suits would result in fraud and collusion between the participants, the *Price* court stated, "we are unable to distinguish interspousal suits from other actions for personal injury." *Price*, 732 S.W.2d at 318. Therefore, despite its broad language stating that the Court was abolishing the interspousal immunity doctrine "completely as to any cause of action," *id.* at 319, the action in *Price* was one for personal injury, for which any recovery would be separate property of the injured spouse.

Moreover, a factor in *Price* that weighed heavily toward abolishing interspousal immunity "as to any cause of action" was the need to remedy the problem of denying a litigant a forum for the redress of a wrong. *Id.* at 318-19. The Court summed up the holding by saying that the result in the case was "compelled by the fundamental proposition of public policy that the courts should afford [such] redress." *Id.* at 320. However, redress is available in the present case without the creation of a separate tort cause of action between spouses.

Mrs. Schlueter sued her husband for improperly depleting community assets. This state's community property system provides that upon divorce, the trial court must enter a division of a married couple's estate "in a manner that the court deems just and right," considering the rights of the parties and any children of the marriage. TEX. FAM. CODE ANN. § 7.001. Such a standard may at times lead to a disproportionate division of assets and liabilities of the parties, depending on the circumstances that courts may consider in refusing to divide the marital estate equally.

As this Court stated in *Cameron v. Cameron*, 641 S.W.2d 210, 223 (Tex. 1982), "Community property owes its existence to the legal fact of marriage, and when the parties to that compact determine their relationship should end, property acquired during marriage is and should be divided among them in a just and right manner." This is distinguishable from recovery of separate property through an independent tort, which we allowed in *Twyman*, because "separate property . . . owes its existence to wholly extramarital factors, things unrelated to the marriage. In relation to that property, the parties are, in essence, strangers; they are separate." *Cameron*, 641 S.W.2d at 223. With these differences in mind, we hold that the well-developed "just and right" standard should continue to be the sole method used to account for and divide community property upon divorce.

Of course, there are also aspects of this state's community property system that provide additional remedies against a spouse for improper conduct involving the community estate. Texas recognizes the concept of fraud on the community, which is a wrong by one spouse that the court may consider in its division of the estate of the parties and that may justify an unequal division of the property. *See Belz v. Belz*, 667 S.W.2d 240, 247 (Tex. App.—Dallas 1984, writ ref'd n.r.e.). As the court in *Belz* aptly described it:

> [A] claim of fraud on the community is a means to an end, either to recover specific property wrongfully conveyed, . . . or . . . to obtain a greater share of the community estate upon divorce, in order to compensate the wronged spouse for his or her lost interest in the community estate.

Id. at 246-47. Just as in the present case, *Belz* involved alleged intentional deprivation of the wife's share of community assets. Nevertheless, despite the intentional nature of the claim, because the fraud was perpetrated on the community, the court correctly distinguished it from cases involving personal injuries for which recovery belongs to the separate estate. *Id.* at 246.

Additionally, it is well settled that a trial court may award a money judgment to one spouse against the other in order to achieve an equitable division of the community estate. *See Murff v. Murff*, 615 S.W.2d 696, 699 (Tex. 1981) (allowing money judgment against husband in division of community property where he had substantial sums in savings before separation that had disappeared by the time of trial). Of course, the money judgment can only be used as a means for the wronged spouse to recoup the value of his or her share of the community estate lost through the wrongdoer spouse's actions. *See Mazique v. Mazique*, 742 S.W.2d 805, 808 (Tex. App.—Houston [1st Dist.] 1987, no writ). Because the amount of the judgment is directly referable to a specific value of lost community property, it will never exceed the total value of the community estate. Still, a sound policy in favor of the wronged spouse is advanced: he or she should not suffer just because when it is time to divide the community, the other spouse has depleted the estate such that there is not enough money or property left to effect a just and right division.

The case of *In re Marriage of Moore*, 890 S.W.2d 821 (Tex. App.—Amarillo 1994, no writ), illustrates this aspect of marital property law. Mr. Moore filed for divorce, and Mrs. Moore counterclaimed for divorce and sought actual and exemplary damages for breach of fiduciary duty to the community estate. *Id.* at 825. Among other things, she alleged that Mr. Moore had conveyed community property to third parties in breach of his fiduciary duty not to commit fraud on the community. *Id.* at 825-26. The trial court found that Mr. Moore had breached his fiduciary duty, and assessed damages against him separate from the division of the marital estate. *Id.* at 825. Absent a voluntary remittitur by Mrs. Moore of the damages for breach of fiduciary duty, the court of appeals held that it would remand to the trial court for a new property division. *Id.* at 843.

The court correctly said:

> [A] trial court may award a money judgment to one spouse, even as damages for the other spouse's fraud on the community. However, that type of personal judgment is merely a means for recouping the defrauded spouse's share of the community property lost as a result of the wrongdoing spouse's breach of the trust relationship. Such a recovery is not awarded as "separate damages" for an independent cause of action.

Id. at 828 (citations omitted). The court concluded that the only recourse available to Mrs. Moore for Mr. Moore's breach of fiduciary duty to the community estate was an action for fraud on the community. *Id.* at 827. The court of appeals correctly determined that no independent cause of action exists in Texas to recover separate damages when the wrongful act defrauded the community estate. *Id.* at 829.

Trial courts also have wide discretion and are allowed to take many factors into consideration in making a just and right division, *see Murff*, 615 S.W.2d at 698-99, including wasting of community assets. *See* Barbara Anne Kazen, *Division of Property at the Time of Divorce*, 49 BAYLOR L. REV. 417, 424-28 (1997) (discussing factors that may be considered by a trial court in effecting a just and right property division). This too allows injured spouses like Mrs. Schlueter to recover her appropriate share of not only that property existing in the community at the time of divorce, but also that which was improperly depleted from the community estate. Waste of community assets is similar to the allegations against the husband here: that without the wife's knowledge or consent, he wrongfully depleted the community of assets of which Mrs. Schlueter was entitled a share. Such behavior is properly considered when dividing a community estate.

Mrs. Schlueter argues that allowing a separate tort cause of action for actual fraud is necessary so that exemplary damages may be awarded for the intentional acts of the wrongdoer spouse. However, heightened culpability does not change the essential character of the wrong: a deprivation of community assets as opposed to a tort committed against a person or his or her separate property. As discussed, the "just and right" standard with accompanying consideration of a wrongdoer spouse's fraud on community assets provides wronged spouses such as Mrs. Schlueter with redress. Moreover, as we have previously held, "recovery of punitive damages requires a finding of an independent tort with accompanying actual damages." *Twin City Fire Ins. Co. v. Davis*, 904 S.W.2d 663, 665 (Tex. 1995); *Federal Express Corp. v. Dutschmann*, 846 S.W.2d 282, 284 (Tex. 1993); *cf. Amoco Prod. Co. v. Alexander*, 622 S.W.2d 563, 571 (Tex. 1981) (explaining in breach of contract action that even if breach is malicious, intentional, or capricious, punitive damages not recoverable without a tort). Because of our holding in the present case that there is no independent tort cause of action for wrongful disposition by a spouse of community assets, the wronged spouse may not recover punitive damages from the other spouse.

However, despite the inappropriateness of punitive damages, it is a logical extension of a standard that calls for a "just and right" division to allow the court to consider that a spouse not only deprived the community of assets to the detriment of the other spouse, but may have done so with dishonesty of purpose or intent to deceive. *See Land v. Marshall*, 426 S.W.2d 841, 846 n.3 (Tex. 1968). This is the culpability needed for actual fraud on the community, which is one of the allegations by Mrs. Schlueter against Mr. Schlueter. Therefore, while we hold that a separate and independent tort action for actual fraud and accompanying exemplary damages against one's spouse do not exist in the context of a deprivation of community assets, if the wronged spouse can prove the heightened culpability of actual fraud, the trial court may consider it in the property division.[1]

III

With regard to the causes of action against Mr. Schlueter's father, he has not argued that these separate and independent tort claims against him as a third-party defendant should also be abolished. Therefore, we do not reach that issue. We note that the trial court's $12,850 judgment of actual damages against Mrs. Schlueter's father-in-law was awarded to the community estate. That judgment represents an asset returned to the community estate, making it monetarily whole. Therefore, the trial court, in its just and right division, may not effect a disproportionate property division *solely* to make up for that formerly lost asset. However, as we have already discussed, the trial court may take into account Mr. Schlueter's conduct that resulted in a defrauding of the community estate.

IV

As previously noted, both Mr. Schlueter and Mr. Schlueter's father, in his only point of error, assert that the trial court committed reversible error in admitting evidence regarding prior acts by Mr. Schlueter's father involving his other son's divorce. We conclude that the court of appeals has correctly decided this issue. 929 S.W.2d at 97-99.

V

Finally, Mr. Schlueter complains that the trial court's award of $18,500 to Mrs. Schlueter for attorney's fees on appeal was erroneous because the trial court had previously instructed the jury that it could consider attorney's fees as part of its exemplary damages award against him. Therefore, he argues that a separate attorney's fees award amounts to a double recovery. Because we have reversed the exemplary damage award against him, there is no possibility of double recovery, and we need not consider this argument.

However, a party should not be penalized for taking a successful appeal. Because we have reversed the damages award against Mr. Schlueter, we also reverse the award for attorney's fees on appeal.

---

[1] For a thorough discussion of issues relevant to this case, *see* Bradley L. Adams, *The Doctrine of Fraud on the Community*, 49 BAYLOR L. REV. 445, 450-64 (1997).

For all the foregoing reasons, we reverse the court of appeals' judgment against Richard Schlueter for actual and exemplary damages, and attorney's fees on appeal, and remand this cause to the trial court for a new property division. We affirm the remainder of the court of appeals' judgment.

JUSTICE GONZALEZ delivered the opinion of the Court, in which JUSTICE ENOCH, JUSTICE OWEN, JUSTICE BAKER, JUSTICE ABBOTT, and JUSTICE HANKINSON joined.

JUSTICE HECHT filed a dissenting opinion, in which CHIEF JUSTICE PHILLIPS joined.

JUSTICE SPECTOR filed a dissenting opinion.

Notes, Comments & Questions

1. As is clear from the court's opinion, a fraud on the community property is distinguished from personal injury tort claims. What is the basis for these claims being distinguishable?

2. The court holds that the wronged spouse cannot recover punitive damages from the other spouse. Why not?

3. On what must the wronged spouse rely for redress of a fraud on the community property?

4. How did the court handle the actual and punitive damages awarded from the husband's father to the wife?

5. Chapter 6 focuses upon interspousal torts. Consider this case as you read that chapter.

6. Following the Texas Supreme Court opinion in *Schlueter v. Schlueter*, Texas family law attorney's searched for a way to obtain more for their wronged clients than a just and right division of the community estate. Even though a trial court is authorized to award a money judgment to a spouse in order to achieve an equitable division, a money judgment can only be used as a means to recoup what was lost through the wrong doing spouse's actions. Under *Schlueter* one is limited to actual damages, punitive damages are not allowed.

7. In *Chu v. Hong*, 185 S.W.3d 307 (Tex. App.—Fort Worth 2006), *rev'd*, 249 S.W.3d 441 (Tex. 2008), the Fort Worth Court of Appeals considered a situation in which a spouse sold community property when divorce was imminent, thereby defrauding the community estate. As we know from *Schleuter*, in such cases, a trial court can order the spouse to return the property or take the fraud into account in making a just-and-right division. However, in *Chu v. Hong*, the trial court did neither. After finding the husband sold community property to third parties without his wife's consent, the trial court ordered the buyers to return the property to the wife but allowed the husband to keep the money they paid for it, and added a judgment against the buyers *and their lawyer* for more than $1.75 million. This trial court action was affirmed by the Fort Worth Court of Appeals. The practical effect of the trial court's decision and the appellate court's affirmance was thus: because one spouse defrauded the other, both are better off and the community estate vastly increased. The Texas Supreme Court granted the Petition for Review and issued the opinion that follows.

CHU v. HONG

249 S.W.3d 441
(Tex. 2008)

BRISTER, JUSTICE.

A spouse who gives away community property to friends or relatives when divorce is imminent has defrauded the community estate. In such cases, a trial court can order the spouse to return the property or take the fraud into account in making a just-and-right division.

But in this case the trial court did neither. After finding a husband sold community property to third parties without his wife's consent, the trial court ordered the buyers to return the property to the wife but allowed the husband to keep the money they paid for it, and added a judgment against the buyers and their lawyer for more than $1.75 million. Thus, because one spouse defrauded the other, both are better off and the community estate vastly increased. We hold the courts below erred in allowing one spouse to recover damages without first recovering the community property from the spouse who took it.

I. Background

While visiting her relatives in Korea in 1996, Chong Hui Hong (Hong) met and then married Gyu Chul Kim (Gyu). She then returned to Texas, Gyu soon followed, and in 1997 they bought a donut shop in Mansfield, Texas. Marital problems arose the next year, and Hong filed criminal assault charges against Gyu and withdrew an application for his green card. At about the same time, they both signed a contract to sell the donut shop for $180,000 to another couple, Myong Nam Kim and Kyon S. Kim (the Kims).

When the contract's closing date came and went with no action, the Kims stopped payment on their $20,000 downpayment check. Hong and Gyu then sent a letter (drafted by Hong but signed only by Gyu as Seller) demanding payment of the $20,000 and threatening criminal charges. In response, the Kims retained attorney William Chu, who demanded performance of the sales contract within four days and threatened civil litigation.

A few days later, Gyu appeared alone at Chu's office and agreed to close the sale. In the bill of sale (which Chu drafted), Gyu represented he was the lawful owner in every respect of the shop and had full authority to sell it. The Kims paid him $180,000: $90,000 in cash and checks, $46,668.29 by promissory note, and the rest by assuming a note Gyu and Hong still owed on their purchase of the shop. The Kims subsequently paid off both notes.

Sometime after the closing, Gyu wired the money he received from the sale to his parents in Korea. He then filed for divorce from Hong. Hong responded with a counterclaim for defrauding the community of the proceeds from the shop sale, and added a suit against the Kims and their attorney Chu for conversion and conspiracy. When his criminal assault case came to trial, Gyu was convicted and deported from the United States.

The divorce and fraud cases were tried five years later. Chu represented both himself and the Kims; Gyu appeared only by attorney and his deposition. A jury answered all questions favorable to Hong. In its final judgment, the trial court granted a divorce, declared the shop sale void and ordered the Kims to turn the premises and equipment over to Hong, allowed Hong and Gyu to each keep the marital property currently in their possession, and assessed no damages against Gyu other than attorney's fees of $65,000. The trial court assessed the same attorney's fees jointly against the other defendants, along with $247,000 for lost profits and interest, and punitive damages against the Kims for $20,000 and against their attorney Chu for $1,500,000. The Kims filed for bankruptcy, so only Chu appealed. In a divided opinion, the court of appeals affirmed.[1]

II. The Conversion Claim

The only direct liability finding against Chu was that he converted Hong's property. Because Chu received nothing but a legal fee that was paid by his own clients, there is no evidence to support this finding.

Hong concedes Chu got nothing but a legal fee, and does not dispute it was paid by his clients the Kims, which of course is precisely what one would expect. None of that money could have come from Gyu or Hong; as they were *selling* the shop rather than *buying* it, the flow of money was the other way around. Even if Chu's fee was paid solely from profits later earned from the shop (though there was no evidence to that effect), money can be converted only if it is specifically identified and held in trust.[2] As Hong parted with no cash in any transaction here, there is simply no evidence that Chu converted anything that belonged to her. Thus, the conversion finding cannot support the judgment against Chu.

III. The Conspiracy Claim

Jurors found Chu and the other defendants were part of a conspiracy. Conspiracy is a derivative tort requiring an unlawful means or purpose, which may include an underlying tort.[3] Chu did not object when the conspiracy question was submitted without conditioning it on any other tort finding.[4] Thus, it can support the judgment if there was some evidence of a conspiracy to commit any of the three other torts in the charge: fraudulent transfer, conversion, or breach of fiduciary duty.

While the jury found Hong's husband Gyu committed each of these torts, no judgment was entered against him on that basis for a very straightforward reason: such torts do not exist. Ten years ago in *Schlueter v. Schlueter*, we reaffirmed that under the community-property law of Texas, there is no independent tort cause of action for wrongful disposition by a spouse of community assets.[5] That is due to the essential character of the wrong: a deprivation of community assets as opposed to a tort committed against a person or his or her separate property.[6]

---

[1] 185 S.W.3d 507.

[2] *See* Mauriceville Nat'l Bank v. Zernial, 892 S.W.2d 858, 860 (Tex.1995); Houston Nat'l Bank v. Biber, 613 S.W.2d 771, 774 (Tex.Civ.App.—Houston [14th Dist.] 1981, writ ref _d n.r.e.)("The general rule is that trover lies for the conversion of money only when there is an obligation resting on the defendant not to convert to his own use specific coin or notes.").

[3] *See* NME Hosps., Inc. v. Rennels, 994 S.W.2d 142, 148 (Tex.1999); Tilton v. Marshall, 925 S.W.2d 672, 681 (Tex.1996).

[4] *Cf.* State Bar of Tex.. Texas Pattern Jury Charges-Business, Consumer, Insurance & Employment PJC 109.1 (2006) (providing that conspiracy question should be "[c]onditioned on findings of a statutory violation or a tort (other than negligence) that proximately caused damages").

[5] 975 S.W.2d 584, 589 (Tex.1998).

[6] *Id.*

As we noted in *Schlueter*, personal injury claims are the separate property of each spouse, and thus can be asserted between spouses as independent torts.[7] But waste, fraudulent transfer, or other damage to community property are claims belonging to the community itself, so they must be included in the trial court's just-and-right division of community property upon divorce.[8] Allowing independent torts between spouses for community damage would thus require fault to be determined twice-once in the tort action, and again in the property division. To avoid that, the just-and-right division is the sole method for adjudicating such claims, and no independent cause of action exists in Texas . . . when the wrongful act defrauded the community estate.[9]

In this case, Hong proved her former husband sent the proceeds of community property to his parents. While the trial court could take this into account in making a just-and-right division, *Schlueter* makes quite clear it could not be pleaded as an independent cause of action, at least against Gyu.[10]

Hong notes correctly that in *Schlueter* we did not decide whether torts against the community estate could be alleged against a third-party.[11] As a general matter, they clearly can; if a third party steals community property, surely either spouse or both can seek recovery in tort for it.[12]

But the question presented here is a narrower one: whether a third party can be held liable in tort when community property *is taken by one of the spouses.* We answered that question in the negative in *Cohrs v. Scott.*[13] There, a divorcing wife settled all her property claims against her husband, and then sought damages against a third party for helping her husband transfer two cars to a mistress. This Court held that the fraud having been initiated and carried out mainly by the husband, [the wife] must look primarily to him and his property to right the wrong.[14]

For several reasons, we believe that remains the proper rule. If one spouse retains the fruits from defrauding the community estate, it is hard to see how the estate as a whole has been damaged, not to mention why someone else should pay for it. While Gyu and the funds are in Korea, there was no evidence Hong could not recover them from him there; indeed, there was no evidence she even tried. The judgment here did not order Gyu to return those funds; instead, Hong ended up with the shop and Gyu ended up with the funds the Kims paid for it. We do not think one spouse should be able to double the community estate by defrauding the other.

---

7 *Id.* at 587 ("[R]ecovery for personal injuries of a spouse, including pain and suffering, is the separate property of the injured spouse, and therefore does not add to the marital estate.")(citing Twyman v. Twyman, 855 S.W.2d 619, 625 n. 20 (Tex.1993)).

8 *Id.* at 588-89; TEX. FAM. CODE § 7.001.

9 *Schlueter*, 975 S.W.2d at 588-89.

10 *Id.* at 589.

11 *Id.* at 590.

12 *See, e.g.*, Douglas v. Delp, 987 S.W.2d 879, 882-83 (Tex.1999)(holding legal malpractice claim was community property, and thus became part of one spouse's bankruptcy estate); Graham v. Franco, 488 S.W.2d 390, 396 (Tex.1972)(holding claim for medical expenses incurred and lost wages was community property, "and both spouses have a claim against the wrongdoer.").

13 161 Tex. 111, 338 S.W.2d 127, 133 (1960).

14 *Id.*

Further, if a spouse cannot be liable for tort and punitive damages in a case like this,[15] it is unclear under what theory co-conspirators can. Hong argues that Gyu's fraud against the community estate was still an unlawful act, even though it could only be addressed in the just-and-right property division. But co-conspirators are each responsible for the damage the conspiracy caused;[16] if Gyu's liability is limited to returning the property or adjusting the community division, the liability of co-conspirators should be as well. Moreover, if one spouse can enlarge the community estate by suing the other's relatives, many acrimonious divorce cases will undoubtedly become more so. That may be necessary when relatives have community property in their hands; but when they do not, little is gained by adding third parties if the property can be restored through orders between the former spouses.

We are especially reticent to open the door to such claims here against an opposing party's attorney. As an attorney, Chu had a fiduciary duty to further the best interests of his clients, the buyers;[17] imposing a second duty to the sellers would inevitably conflict with the first.[18] An attorney who personally steals goods or tells lies on a client's behalf may be liable for conversion or fraud in some cases.[19] But there are no such allegations here; the only claim is that Chu should have refused to draw up the bill of sale (although his client asked him to) because he knew one spouse was selling the shop without the other spouse's consent—even though neither spouse was his client. We need not approve of Chu's ethics to hold that *Schlueter* requires Hong to seek restitution from her own husband before seeking it from someone else's lawyer.

We disagree with Hong that *Schlueter* must yield to the provisions of the Uniform Fraudulent Transfer Act.[20]

Schlueter itself involved an alleged fraudulent transfer, and made no exception for that statute. Moreover, the two are entirely consistent: the Act provides for equitable remedies to rescind the fraudulent transfer,[21] or a damage assessment limited to the amount of the property transferred;[22] *Schlueter* allows precisely the same remedies against a former spouse.[23]

Finally, even if a conspiracy action existed despite *Schlueter*, the evidence here would not support it. Chu could only be liable for conspiracy if he agreed to the *injury* to be accomplished;

---

[15] *Schlueter*, 975 S.W.2d at 589.

[16] *State v. Standard Oil Co.*, 130 Tex. 313, 107 S.W.2d 550, 559 (1937).

[17] *Hoover Slovacek LLP v. Walton*, 206 S.W.3d 557, 560-61 (Tex.2006).

[18] *Barcelo v. Elliott*, 923 S.W.2d 575, 577 (Tex.1996) ("At common law, an attorney owes a duty of care only to his or her client. . . . Without this 'privity barrier,' the rationale goes, clients would lose control over the attorney-client relationship. . . .").

[19] *See, e.g.*, Estate of Stonecipher v. Estate of Butts, 686 S.W.2d 101, 103 (Tex.1985); Poole v. Houston & T.C. Ry. Co., 58 Tex. 134, 137-38 (1882); *cf.* McCamish, Martin, Brown & Loeffler v. F.E. Appling Interests, 991 S.W.2d 787, 794 (Tex.1999) (noting fraud actions cannot be brought against an opposing attorney in litigation as reliance in those circumstances is unreasonable).

[20] *See* TEX. BUS. & COM. CODE §§ 24.001-.013.

[21] *Id.* § 24.008.

[22] *Id.* § 24.009(b), (c).

[23] 975 S.W.2d at 588 ("[I]t is well settled that a trial court may award a money judgment to one spouse against the other in order to achieve an equitable division of the community estate. Of course, the money judgment can only be used as a means for the wronged spouse to recoup the value of his or her share of the community estate lost through the wrongdoer spouse's actions." (citation omitted)).

agreeing to the *conduct* ultimately resulting in injury is not enough.[24] Viewing all the evidence in a light favorable to the verdict,[25] Chu knew that Gyu was selling his wife's interest without her knowledge or consent. But Gyu told the Kims the money from the sale would be used to pay off a loan from his parents, and the rest would be shared with Hong; Hong denied there was any such loan, but there was no evidence Chu or the Kims knew that at the time. Conspiracy may be proved by inferences from circumstantial evidence,[26] but inferring an agreement to the ultimate injury generally arises "from joint participation in the transactions *and from enjoyment of the fruits of the transactions*."[27] As there was no evidence Chu's fee depended on keeping the proceeds from Hong, there is no basis for inferring he intended for her to be cheated.

Because Hong has no tort claim against her former husband under Texas community-property law, she has no conspiracy claim against Chu for conspiring in such a tort.[28] The courts below erred in concluding otherwise.

IV. The Aiding-a-Fiduciary-Breach Claim

Finally, the jury found that Chu knowingly participated, aided, or assisted Gyu in breaching his fiduciary duty to his former wife. Assuming such a claim exists and is somehow different from a conspiracy to breach his fiduciary duty, it too is excluded by *Schlueter* for the reasons noted above.

* * *

Accordingly, we reverse the court of appeals' judgment and render judgment that Hong take nothing against William Chu.

---

[24] *Tri v. J.T.T.*, 162 S.W.3d 552, 556-57 (Tex.2005).

[25] City of Keller v. Wilson, 168 S.W.3d 802, 819 (Tex.2005) ("Courts reviewing all the evidence in a light favorable to the verdict thus assume that jurors credited testimony favorable to the verdict and disbelieved testimony contrary to it.").

[26] Jernigan v. Wainer, 12 Tex. 189, 193 (1854) ("When men enter into conspiracies, they are not likely to call in a witness. . . . In such cases the injured party must necessarily have recourse to circumstantial evidence. For it is only by the inferences and deductions which men properly and naturally draw from the acts of others in such cases, that their intentions can be ascertained.").

[27] Int'l Bankers Life Ins. Co. v. Holloway, 368 S.W.2d 567, 582 (Tex.1963) (emphasis added).

[28] *See* Am. Tobacco Co., Inc. v. Grinnell, 951 S.W.2d 420, 438 (Tex.1997) (holding dismissal of tort claims required dismissal of conspiracy claim).

G. Liability of Marital Property

The rules of marital property liability were introduced in the over view at the beginning of this chapter. The cases that follow will provide a more in depth view of marital property liability. Do not forget the chart found at the beginning of this chapter, page 277, to help in your analysis of these cases.

Having just said, "do not forget the chart," that is exactly what we must do, "forget the chart," when dealing with "other rules of law."

BRODAY
v.
UNITED STATES
455 F.2d 1097
(5th Cir. 1972)

RONEY, CIRCUIT JUDGE.

Frank Broday married his present wife, Billie Shipman Broday, on June 7, 1966. As of that date, Billie Shipman was liable for income taxes assessed against her and her former husband, Joe Shipman (now deceased), for the taxable year 1962. In an effort to collect this tax, the District Director of Internal Revenue levied upon a checking account which held funds received as dividend income from Mr. Broday's separate property. Mr. Broday paid his wife's income tax liability and then filed a claim for refund on the ground that there was a wrongful levy upon the bank account. Holding that under Texas community property law the wife possessed a property right in the dividend income from the separate property of her husband, which property right is subject to a federal tax lien for prenuptial income taxes of the wife, we must reverse the decision of the lower court which awarded a refund to Mr. Broday.

I.

* * *

II.

The basic issue involved in this appeal is whether, under Texas property law, the community property bank account of which the husband had sole right to management and control is subject to levy for a federal tax debt of the wife incurred prior to marriage. The government is entitled to a lien for the tax plus interest upon all of the wife's "property and rights to property."[2] The question of whether and to what extent the wife has property and rights to property is determined under the applicable state law. *Aquilino v. United States*, 363 U.S. 509, 512-513, 80 S.Ct. 1277

---

[2] Section 6321 of the Internal Revenue Code of 1954.

Lien for taxes.

If any person liable to pay any tax neglects or refuses to pay the same after demand, the amount (including any interest, additional amount, addition to tax, or assessable penalty, together with any costs that may accrue in addition thereto) shall be a lien in favor of the United States upon all property and rights to property, whether real or personal, belonging to such person.

(1960), 4 L.Ed.2d 1365; *Morgan v. Commissioner of Internal Revenue*, 309 U.S. 78, 82, 60 S.Ct. 424 (1940), 84 L.Ed. 585. However, once it has been determined under state law that the taxpayer owns property or rights to property, federal law is controlling for the purpose of determining whether a lien will attach to such property or rights to property. *United States v. Bess*, 357 U.S. 51, 56-57, 78 S.Ct. 1054 (1958), 2 L.Ed.2d 1135.

There is no question that the bank account upon which the government levied constituted community property of Mr. and Mrs. Broday under Texas law. This point is made clear by the decision of this Court in *Commissioner of Internal Revenue v. Chase Manhattan Bank*, 259 F.2d 231, 239 (5th Cir. 1958), *cert. den.*, 359 U.S. 913, 79 S.Ct. 589 (1959), 3 L.Ed.2d 575, in which we said:

> All property accumulated during marriage is community property, unless it is received by gift, devise, or inheritance. In Texas even income derived from separate property belongs to the community, including interest and dividends from separately owned securities.

See Warren v. Schawe, 163 S.W.2d 415 (Tex. Civ. App. 1942). As community property, Mrs. Broday had a present vested interest therein equal and equivalent to that of her husband. *Hopkins v. Bacon*, 282 U.S. 122, 126-127, 51 S.Ct. 62 (1930), 75 L.Ed. 249; *see Poe v. Seaborn*, 282 U.S. 101, 51 S.Ct. 58 (1930), 75 L.Ed. 239; *Bender v. Pfaff*, 282 U.S. 127, 51 S.Ct. 64 (1930), 75 L.Ed. 252.

The taxpayer contends that Article 4620 of Vernon's Texas Civil Statutes Annotated, as amended by Acts of 1967, 60th Legislature, p. 738, ch. 309, Section 1,[3] which by its terms would operate to exempt the particular community property here in issue from the antenuptial debts of Mrs. Broday, is effective to prevent attachment of a federal tax lien on her vested present interest in such property. Taxpayer concedes that mere state exemption statutes are ineffective against a statutory lien of the federal government for federal taxes. *United States v. Hoper*, 242 F.2d 468 (7th Cir. 1957). However, he argues that Article 4620 gives a property right in the husband which transcends the federal tax law.

When the district court granted the taxpayer summary judgment in this case, it did not have the advantage of the *United States v. Mitchell*, 403 U.S. 190, 91 S.Ct. 1763 (1971), 29 L.Ed.2d 406, in which the Supreme Court by unanimous decision reversed the decisions of this Court in *Mitchell v. Commissioner of Internal Revenue*, 430 F.2d 1 (5th Cir.1970) and *Angello v. Metropolitan Life Ins. Co.*, 430 F.2d 7 (5th Cir. 1970). This Supreme Court decision controls the instant case. Indeed, it is pointed out in the government's brief that the taxpayer's brief in support of his motion for summary judgment before the trial court relied upon this Court's decisions in *Mitchell*, *Angello* and *Ramos v. Commissioner of Internal Revenue*, 429 F.2d 487 (5th Cir. 1970) as presenting the identical issue as the case at bar, and argued that those decisions were controlling. The decision in *Ramos* was based upon the *Mitchell* and *Angello* cases, and therefore was effectively overruled by the Supreme Court in *Mitchell*. Although those cases involved Louisiana community

[3] The community property subject to sole or joint management, control and disposition of a spouse shall be subject to the liabilities of that spouse incurred before or during marriage. The community property subject to the sole management, control and disposition of a spouse shall not be subject to any liabilities of the other spouse incurred before marriage or nontortious liabilities incurred by the other spouse during marriage unless both spouses are liable by other rules of law. All the spouses' community property is subject to liability for all torts committed by either spouse during marriage." Effective Jan. 1, 1970, Article 4620 was repealed by Acts of 1969, 61 Leg., p. 2707, ch. 888, § 6. However, similar language now appears in the new Texas Family Code, ch. 5.

property law, while this case involves Texas law, it was properly conceded below by the taxpayer that the law of Texas is identical to the law of Louisiana as to whether the community fund is liable for the wife's separate debts incurred before marriage.

In *Mitchell*, the Supreme Court held that under the laws of Louisiana a married woman has a present vested interest in community property equal to that of her husband and therefore is personally liable for federal income taxes on her one-half share of the community income, notwithstanding her subsequent election under state law to renounce all of her rights in the community. The Court rejected the contention that the taxpayers involved should not be personally liable for community debts because under Louisiana law their husbands had complete control over the community property.

Since a married woman in Louisiana or Texas has a vested interest in, and is the owner of, a half share of the community income sufficient to require her to pay income taxes thereon, it follows a *fortiori* that she has "property" or "rights to property" to which a federal tax lien would attach under Section 6321 of the Code.

We think that the taxpayer must fail in his argument that Article 4620 of Vernon's Texas Civil Statutes should be characterized in a different manner than an exemption statute. The Ninth Circuit cases of *United States v. Overman*, 424 F.2d 1142 (9th Cir.1970) (relating to the law of the State of Washington) and *In re Ackerman*, 424 F.2d 1148 (9th Cir.1970) (relating to the law of Arizona), which held against the taxpayer in cases similar to this one, were specifically approved in the opinion of the Supreme Court in *Mitchell*. In *Overman* the taxpayer advanced the argument that the state statute in issue was not merely an exemption statute but instead was one which defined property rights and therefore was controlling. In rejecting this argument, the Court noted "all that section 6321 requires is that the interest be 'property' or 'rights to property.' It is of no statutory moment how extensive may be those rights under state law, or what restrictions exist on the enjoyment of those rights." 424 F.2d at 1145. It appears clear from the decision in *Mitchell* that the right of the United States to enforce its liens does not depend upon state laws which regulate the rights of creditors generally and does not depend upon whether the "exemption" label is attached to the particular statute in question.

The only cases cited by the taxpayer in his brief in support of his position are *Bice v. Campbell*, 231 F.Supp. 948 (N.D. Tex. 1964) and *Mulcahy v. United States*, 251 F.Supp. 783 (S.D. Tex. 1966). It is apparent that these decisions are now incorrect because they are fundamentally incompatible with the decisions in *Mitchell*, *Overman* and *Ackerman*, *supra*.

Reversed.

Notes, Comments & Questions

1. In cases such as *Broday v. United States*, the courts look to state law to determine the spouse's property and rights to property. Once that determination is made, federal law is controlling for the purpose of determining whether a lien will attach.

2. If the wife had owed a similar debt to Neiman-Marcus, what property would have been liable?

3. The United States Supreme Court case of *Mitchell*, cited by the *Broday* court, is the controlling precedent. Explain the Louisiana law upon which the wife was relying in *Mitchell*.

MORTENSON
v.
TRAMMELL

604 S.W.2d 269
(Tex. Civ. App.—Corpus Christi 1980, writ ref'd n.r.e.)

* * *

In their 24th point, appellants assign error to the failure of the court to declare the balance on a $3,500.00 note to be the community property of the Trammells, thereby entitling the estate to one-half of the balance. The money was originally borrowed by Jo Ellen Trammell from the Rio Grande Building & Loan Association on March 28, 1973. She assigned as collateral for the note a certificate of deposit which was previously adjudicated to be her separate property (CD # 9697).

On the same day, Mrs. Trammell loaned the money to her daughter and son-in-law, Vicki and Daniel Bowen. As collateral for this loan, she received a secondary vendor's lien and deed of trust on property in Corpus Christi owned by the Bowens. The loan agreement recited that payment was to be made to both Victor and Jo Ellen instead of just Jo Ellen, who had originally secured the loan.

There is a presumption that any loan made by a spouse during marriage is an obligation of the community. *Faulkner v. Faulkner*, 582 S.W.2d 639 (Tex. Civ. App.—Dallas 1979, no writ). This presumption, however, can be overcome by presenting clear and satisfactory evidence that the creditor agreed to look solely to the separate estate of the contracting spouse for satisfaction. *Cockerham v. Cockerham, supra*; *Broussard v. Tian*, 156 Tex. 371, 295 S.W.2d 405 (1956), *cert. denied*, 353 U.S. 941, 77 S.Ct. 811, 1 L.Ed.2d 758; *Gleich v. Bongio*, 128 Tex. 606, 99 S.W.2d 881 (1937); *Carter v. Grabeel*, 341 S.W.2d 458 (Tex. Civ. App.—Amarillo 1960, no writ).

The creditor in the case here, the Rio Grande Bank & Loan Association, obviously intended to seek satisfaction of the debt from Mrs. Trammell alone by requiring her certificate of deposit as collateral. If a default on the note occurred, the Bank would have looked to Mrs. Trammell for repayment of the debt. Additionally, there is no indication that this debt was purchased on community credit because Mrs. Trammell took out the loan in her name alone and gave her separate property as collateral.

Even though the second note by the Bowens was made payable to both Victor and Jo Ellen Trammell, clear and convincing evidence was presented to the jury which supported their finding that the note receivable was the separate property of Mrs. Trammell. The loan made by Mrs. Trammell to her children was from money acquired on the credit of her separate estate. *See Trevino v. Trevino*, 555 S.W.2d 792 (Tex. Civ. App.—Corpus Christi 1977, no writ). Appellants' point 24 is overruled.

Notes, Comments & Questions

1. The case of *Ray v. United States*, 385 F. Supp. 372 (S.D. Tex. 1974), *aff'd*, 538 F.2d 1228 (5th Cir.1976), previously presented in Chapter 2, Section E. Credit Transactions, page 201, is the definitive case on a separate liability. That is, only the spouse's separate property will be liable. How does this case compare to *Ray*?

2. What do you think about looking to collateral to determine the character of property?

3. If the collateral in this case had been more volatile, perhaps stock rather than a certificate of deposit, would the outcome have been the same?

POPE PHOTO RECORDS, INC.
v.
MALONE

539 S.W.2d 224
(Tex. Civ. App.—Amarillo 1976, no writ)

REYNOLDS, ASSOCIATE JUSTICE.

A creditor sought to recover the balance of a debt incurred by a deceased husband from the lump sum proceeds of his life insurance received by his surviving widow. The trial court denied recovery. The insurance proceeds became the widow's separate property not shown to be subject to the debt. Affirmed.

When James Pat Malone died on 20 November 1973, eight insurance policies, the beneficiaries of which he had the contractual right to change, were in force on his life. He had gratuitously named his wife, Roberta E. Malone, as the beneficiary of each policy. One of them was issued prior to their marriage and none of its premiums was paid with community funds. The remaining seven policies were issued during the marriage and Mrs. Malone was named the beneficiary at the time each was issued. Six of the seven policies were issued prior to 1 January 1970 and all premiums on them were paid monthly or annually with community funds. The remaining policy was issued on 1 May 1971 in the face amount of $25,000 as an incident to Malone's employment on that date as president of the First National Bank in Hereford, Texas. The bank paid the monthly premium after deducting $15 per month from Malone's salary to apply toward the premium. The proceeds from the eight policies were paid to Mrs. Malone in lump sums aggregating $83,458.27.

Mrs. Malone qualified as the independent executrix of Malone's estate. She filed an inventory and appraisement omitting the insurance proceeds and reflecting that the community debts and claims against the estate exceeded the assets.

During his lifetime on 27 March 1970, James Pat Malone executed, and thereafter made two payments on, his interest bearing promissory note in the principle [sic] sum of $9,000 payable on demand to the order of National Litho & Printing Company. The note was transferred and assigned to Pope Photo Records, Inc. Following Malone's death, the balance due on the note was reduced to a judgment against, and a claim was made on, his estate. One payment was made on the debt from the estate assets and, after the assets were exhausted without payment of the debt in full, Pope Photo Records, Inc., proceeded against Roberta E. Malone individually. The suit, from which this appeal stems, sought the recovery of $4,416.73 as the principal due on the debt, together with interest and reasonable attorney's fees.

There was a bench trial. In addition to the development of the foregoing facts, there was testimony by the president of National Litho & Printing Company and sole owner of the stock of Pope Photo Records, Inc., that he made a loan to Malone in order for Malone to pay a bank note placed for collection, and that he had never talked with Mrs. Malone about the existence of the debt. After Malone's death, he referred the note to this attorney to get in touch with Mrs. Malone, who testified that she did not know about the debt until after her husband's death. Mrs. Malone conceded that the community estate was insolvent at the date of her husband's death, but she did not know when it first became insolvent. There was and is no contention that the estate was insolvent on 27 March 1970, the date of the debt, or on 1 May 1971, the date of the latest insurance policy naming Mrs. Malone as the beneficiary. At the conclusion of the trial, the court, later making and filing findings of fact and conclusions of law, rendered a take-nothing judgment from which Pope Photo Records, Inc., has appealed.

Pope initially contends the trial court erred in legally concluding that the insurance proceeds received by Mrs. Malone are not subject to its debt. It should be observed that presently in Texas when a husband insures his life with community funds, the right to receive the future insurance proceeds is community property in the nature of a chose in action maturing at the death of the husband. Consequently, the matured proceeds are community in character, "except where the named beneficiary is in fact surviving, in which case a gift of the policy rights to such beneficiary is presumed to have been intended and completed by the death of the insured." *Brown v. Lee*, 371 S.W.2d 694, 696 (Tex. 1963). The corollary is that by naming the wife the beneficiary, the husband manifests the intent to make a gift to her. Huie, *Community Property Laws as Applied to Life Insurance*, 17 TEX. L.R. 121, 123-24 (1939). Long standing is the coexisting rule that the insurance proceeds she receives at her husband's death are her separate property not subject to the husband's debts unless the proceeds have been assigned as collateral security therefor. *San Jacinto Bldg., Inc. v. Brown*, 79 S.W.2d 164, 166 (Tex. Civ. App.—Beaumont 1935, writ ref'd).

From these principles Pope argues that because the gratuitous gift of the insurance proceeds to Mrs. Malone was not completed until Malone's death when the community estate was insufficient to pay the existing debts, the intended gift was voided by § 24.03 of the Texas Business and Commerce Code (1968). Because that statute, as material here, does void a gratuitous transfer of property as to an existing creditor unless at the time of the transfer the debtor has enough property in this state subject to execution to pay all of his existing debts, the argumentative inference is that the insurance proceeds retained their community character, making them liable for the debt.

After an in-depth consideration, the very same argument, made under circumstances strikingly similar to those we review and also in reliance on the "gift . . . is . . . completed by the death of the insured" language in *Brown v. Lee*, *supra*, was rejected in *Parker Square State Bank v. Huttash*, 484 S.W.2d 429 (Tex. Civ. App.—Fort Worth 1972, writ ref'd n.r.e.). The holding indispensable to the rejection was that the controlling date of the transfer meant in V.T.C.A., Bus. & C. § 24.03, was the date the beneficiary was designated. In context, the holding is not, as Pope asserts that it is, in direct conflict with the *Brown v. Lee*, *supra*, language that the gift is "completed by the death of the insured." At least, the Supreme Court, after reviewing the *Huttash* opinion quoting that lan-

language from *Brown v. Lee, supra,* in connection with its consideration of the application for writ of error, did not reverse *Huttash* as it was authorized to do by Rule 483, Texas Rules of Civil Procedure, if the holding were in conflict with the *Brown v. Lee, supra,* decision. *See, e.g.,* CALVERT, APPLICATION FOR WRIT OF ERROR, APPELLATE PROCEDURE IN TEXAS, § 22.9. Thus, applied here in the absence of any contention that the Malones' community estate was insolvent on or before the last date Mrs. Malone was designated a beneficiary, the *Huttash* holding negates the applicability of V.T.C.A., BUS. & C. § 24.03, to void the gift to Mrs. Malone.

Next, Pope seeks to neutralize the trial court's factual finding that Malone became insolvent on or about 1 November 1973, but presents no point of error that insolvency on an earlier date was established conclusively or as a matter of law. The neutralization is sought as a predicate for an attack on the court's legal conclusion that no portion of the insurance proceeds is subject to Pope's debt even though a portion of the premiums was paid when Malone was insolvent. The two-prong challenge is viable only if Texas law permits the claimed right of recovery from the proportional part of the proceeds generated by premiums paid from the community when it was insolvent. The challenge is unavailing because it has been settled, again under circumstances similar to those in the case at bar, that Texas law does not sanction such recovery absent fraud in the formation of the insurance contract which is not alleged here. *San Jacinto Bldg., Inc. v. Brown, supra,* at 166-67. The only Texas case which Pope cites for its proposition is *Red River Nat. Bank v. De Berry,* 47 Tex. Civ. App. 96, 105 S.W. 998 (1907, no writ), where that holding is clearly based on a specifically pleaded Arkansas statute exempting from the claims of the husband's creditors only the insurance purchased by premiums not exceeding a set amount annually. The opinion in *San Jacinto Bldg., Inc. v. Brown, supra,* in discussing *De Berry* and stating that it actually is authority for the conclusion reached in *San Jacinto Bldg., Inc. v. Brown, supra,* that Texas law does not allow the husband's creditors to recover from the widow's insurance proceeds attributable to premiums paid during insolvency, points out that there is no like statute in Texas limiting or regulating in any manner the amount one may expend on premiums or that would render such payments transfers of property in fraud of creditors. 79 S.W.2d at 166.

Finally, Pope assigns error to the denial of judgment on its theory that its debt is a jointly incurred community debt to which Mrs. Malone's separate property is subject. The § 5.61(a) provision of the Texas Family Code (1975) is that a spouse's separate property is not subject to liabilities of the other spouse unless both spouses are liable by other rules of law. To escape the efficacy of the proviso, Pope proposes the application of the rule of *Cockerham v. Cockerham,* 527 S.W.2d 162 (Tex. 1975).

In *Cockerham,* a divorce case, the court subjected the husband's separate property to the debts incurred by the wife in her operation of the business during the marriage when the court found that the husband had impliedly, and to some extent expressly, consented to the establishment of the debts as joint liabilities. There, among other circumstances, the husband advanced the wife the necessary capital for the business inventory, the wife wrote checks on the husband's bank account to pay for merchandise, at least on one occasion the husband wrote a check to pay the operational expenses, and the husband borrowed money to pay some of the business debts which he recognized as his obligations.

But the facts of *Cockerham* are readily distinguishable from the facts before us, and the Supreme Court made it clear in *Cockerham* that an examination of the totality of the circumstances giving rise to the debt is necessary to determine joint liability. Here, Malone incurred the debt at issue to pay his prior bank note. The use made of the money represented by the bank note is merely speculated. It is undisputed that Mrs. Malone did not know of the debt until after her husband's death more than three and one-half years later. The totality of these circumstances, without more, is insufficient to remove the insulation installed by V.T.C.A., Family Code § 5.61(a), to protect Mrs. Malone's separate property from the debt incurred by her husband.

Each facet of Pope's points of error has been considered whether specifically mentioned or not. None of the points presents reversible error.

The judgment is affirmed.

Notes, Comments & Questions

1. In this case, the creditor relies upon an "other rule of law," that being TEX. BUS. & COMM. CODE § 24.03. To have relied successfully upon this section, what did the creditor have to prove?

2. Having failed in its initial theory, the creditor moves on to the *Cockerham* offense. Explain the *Cockerham* offense.

STEWART TITLE CO.
v.
HUDDLESTON

598 S.W.2d 321 (Tex. Civ. App.—San Antonio), *writ ref'd n.r.e. per curiam*, 608 S.W.2d 611 (Tex. 1980)

CADENA, CHIEF JUSTICE.

Defendants, Stewart Title Company, Louise Munn Jehl, Mildred Munn Martin and Francis J. Jehl, administrator of the estate of William O. Davis, appeal from a summary judgment declaring that the interest of plaintiff, Catherine Evans Huddleston, is free from the claims of defendants under certain judgment liens based on judgments recovered by defendants against Edward Huddleston, plaintiff's former husband.

The debts on which the judgments were based were incurred during the time that plaintiff and Edward were married, and must be regarded as community debts. The land in question was a part of the community estate of plaintiff and her former husband.

As a result of a divorce suit filed by plaintiff, a decree was rendered by a district court of Aransas County on January 6, 1975, terminating the marriage between plaintiff and Edward Huddleston. Prior to the date of the divorce plaintiff and her former husband had entered into an agreement concerning, among other things, the division of the property. This agreement, which was approved by the court, was incorporated by reference as a part of the decree of divorce. Under this agreement, plaintiff was awarded certain items, including real estate and cash, and Edward Huddleston was awarded certain personal and real property. According to the decree and agreement, each party received an undivided one-half interest in the real property involved in this litigation.

After the Huddlestons were divorced, defendants filed suit against plaintiff's former husband and were awarded judgments against him based on community debts. Plaintiff was not a party to such suits, was not served with citation and entered no appearances. Plaintiff is not named in any of the judgments. Subsequently, the holders of the judgments abstracted the judgments, thus perfecting their judgment liens.

On September 9, 1977, plaintiff filed suit for judgment declaring that defendants' claims under the abstracted judgments were not valid as to the land in question. Defendants answered and included prayers for foreclosure of the judgment liens against both plaintiff and her former husband. In addition, the Davis estate sought judgment against plaintiff on the original debt owed to the Davis estate.

The trial court rendered summary judgment declaring that plaintiff was not bound by the judgments against her former husband, and that her interest in the land in question was not subject to defendants' claims under the abstracted judgments. Subsequently, the trial court entered an order severing plaintiff's cause of action against defendants from that portion of the case involving defendants' claims against plaintiff.

Defendants first assert that the trial court erred in granting plaintiff's motion for summary judgment, because defendants were pre-existing creditors without notice of the disposition of the community estate by the divorce decree and settlement agreement.

It is true that a divorce decree does not diminish or limit the rights of creditors to proceed against either or both spouses for payment of debts owed to the creditors prior to the divorce decree. TEX. FAM. CODE ANN. § 3.63 (Vernon 1975); *Walker v. Walker*, 527 S.W.2d 200, 203 (Tex. Civ. App.—Fort Worth 1975, no writ). It is also true that nonexempt property remains subject to the claims of community creditors, even after divorce. A spouse who receives property which would, absent a divorce, be subject to the claims of creditors remains personally liable, and the property so received remains subject to being taken to satisfy the claims of the community creditors. *Swinford v. Alliance Fin. Co. of Casa View*, 424 S.W.2d 298, 301 (Tex. Civ. App.—Dallas 1968, writ dism'd), *cert. den.*, 393 U.S. 923, 89 S.Ct. 253, 21 L.Ed.2d 259 (1968).

The above rules, while well established, are not applicable here. As already pointed out, at the time that defendants filed their suits against Edward Huddleston, he and plaintiff had been divorced and owned the property in question as tenants in common. Since a judgment cannot have the effect of imposing joint liability on one who has not been made a party to the suit, it is clear that defendants' judgments against Edward Huddleston imposed no liability on plaintiff. *Zodiac Corp. v. General Elec. Credit Corp.*, 566 S.W.2d 341, 346 (Tex. Civ. App.—Tyler 1978, no writ). The adoption of the Family Code abolished the doctrine of virtual representation, under which the husband was deemed to represent the wife in any suit involving the liability of the community estate. *Dulak v. Dulak*, 513 S.W.2d 205, 207 (Tex. 1974). Even if the doctrine of virtual representation was still applicable between husband and wife, the power of the husband to act as the representative of the wife would not survive the dissolution of the marriage by divorce. *Roemer v. Traylor*, 60 Tex. Civ. App. 437, 128 S.W. 685, 689 (Tex. Civ. App.—Galveston 1910, writ ref'd).

The property settlement agreement and the divorce decree were not recorded in the office of the county clerk until some two years after defendants had abstracted their judgments against Edward Huddleston. From this fact defendants argue that they were not charged with notice of either the agreement or the decree and that both were void as to them. This contention is based on the provisions of Article 6627, TEX. REV. CIV. STAT. ANN. (Vernon Supp. 1980), and Sections 5.03

and 5.42(d), TEX. FAM. CODE ANN. (Vernon 1975). We consider defendants' argument to be beside the point. It overlooks the fact that no judgment against Edward Huddleston could be binding on plaintiff. An abstracted judgment creates a lien only on the property of the judgment debtor and does not extend to land owned by those who are not parties to the judgment. Plaintiff's interest in the land in question arose independently of the divorce and property settlement agreement. Its existence resulted from our laws concerning the nature of property acquired during marriage, and her interest in the land could be subjected to the payment of debts only on the basis of a judgment against her in a suit to which she was a party. This would have been true even if the judgment against Edward Huddleston had been rendered before he and plaintiff were divorced. Plaintiff's interest in the land in question after the divorce differs in no way from what her interest in such land would have been if there had been no agreement, and if the judgment made no mention of the property. Had the divorce court made no disposition of the property in the decree of divorce, plaintiff and her former husband would have remained owners of the property as tenants in common. *Busby v. Busby*, 457 S.W.2d 551, 554 (Tex. 1970); *Garrison v. Texas Commerce Bank*, 560 S.W.2d 451, 456 (Tex. Civ. App.—Houston (1st Dist.) 1977, writ ref'd n. r. e.). Therefore, even if the statutes relied on by defendants require that we give no effect to the separation agreement and property provisions of the divorce decree, plaintiff's claim to the land in question as a tenant in common remains undisturbed.

* * *

We find no merit in the contention that the trial court erred in entering the order of severance.

The judgment of the trial court is affirmed.

STEWART TITLE CO.
v.
HUDDLESTON

608 S.W.2d 611
(Tex. 1980)

PER CURIAM.

Catherine Evans Huddleston brought this suit seeking a declaration that judgment liens obtained by petitioners Stewart Title Company and the Estate of William O. Davis against her former husband, Edward Scott Huddleston, in suits filed after their divorce were invalid and void as to her and her property since she was not made a party to the suits against her former husband. Petitioners counter-claimed and sought foreclosure of their judgment liens against community property received by Catherine Evans Huddleston by the partition of the community property in connection with the divorce. The trial court severed the counter claims and granted Catherine Evans Huddleston's motion for summary judgment which declared that the judgments recovered by petitioners were invalid and void as to her and as to any property owned by her after the date of the divorce whether acquired by her either prior to or subsequent to that date. The court of civil appeals affirmed. 598 S.W.2d 321.

The summary judgment record establishes that the debts which formed the basis for petitioners' suits arose during the marriage of Catherine Evans and Edward Scott Huddleston and were presumptively community debts. The record further establishes that she received incident to the divorce action an undivided one-half interest in 19.2 acres of land located in Bexar County in the partition of community property.

We interpret the judgments of the courts below as not foreclosing a judgment in the severed cause that any community property acquired by Catherine Evans Huddleston as a part of the partition of the community property would be subject to judgment liens properly secured against her as a result of preexisting community debts. *See* Texas Family Code, § 5.42(c), Texas Revised Civil Statutes Annotated.

The applications for writ of error are refused, no reversible error.

Notes, Comments & Questions

1. Within the previous case, the court makes the observation that ". . . a divorce decree does not diminish or limit the rights of creditors to proceed against either or both spouses for payment of debts owed to the creditors prior to the divorce decree." What is the practical effect of this observation? What effect should this observation have upon a lawyer's advice to clients?

2. Why did Stewart Title Co. fail in its argument that it was not charged with notice of either the divorce or the appurtenant agreement?

3. Can a judgment be had against Catherine Huddleston by Stewart Title Co.?

LeBLANC
v.
WALLER

603 S.W.2d 265
(Tex. Civ. App.—Houston [14th Dist.] 1980, no writ)

PAUL PRESSLER, JUSTICE.

This is an appeal from the judgment in a divorce action wherein appellee, as an alleged creditor of the community, intervened, seeking enforcement of debts incurred during the marriage of appellant and her former husband. Appellant's former husband is not a party to this appeal. We affirm in part and reverse and render in part.

Appellant and Mr. LeBlanc were separated on or about September 15, 1978. At that time, they orally agreed to a division of their modest estate. There was no written partition agreement as contemplated by TEX. FAM. CODE ANN. § 5.42 (Vernon 1975). The presumption is, therefore, that all of the assets were community property. TEX. FAM. CODE ANN. § 5.02 (Vernon 1975). Immediately following the separation, Mr. LeBlanc became an independent plumbing contractor and, pursuant to such business, incurred an indebtedness to appellee for materials to be used in his plumbing business. The record reflects that appellant never had any contact with appellee prior to the divorce proceedings, was not a party to the transactions between Mr. LeBlanc and appellee, in no way benefited from those transactions, and did not in fact become aware of the indebtedness until shortly before the hearing for the divorce. She further testified that she was living alone at the time the debts were incurred and was financially supporting herself.

* * *

The debt having been incurred prior to the termination of the marriage, it is presumed to be a community debt. *Cockerham v. Cockerham*, 527 S.W.2d 162 (Tex. 1975). However, appellant contends that TEX. FAM. CODE ANN. § 5.61 (Vernon 1975) insulates her from liability for this debt allegedly incurred by her former husband. Section 5.61 provides in part:

> (b) Unless both spouses are liable by other rules of law, the community property subject to a spouse's sole management, control, and disposition is not subject to:
>
> (2) any nontortious liabilities that the other spouse incurs during marriage.

Appellant claims that all of the community property which was in her possession from the time the debt arose until the date of the divorce judgment was subject to her sole management, control, and disposition and therefore not subject to any nontortious liability incurred by Mr. LeBlanc subsequent to the time she gained sole management, control, and disposition of the assets. Neither party contends that any other "rules of law" are applicable to this situation.

TEX. FAM. CODE ANN. § 5.22 (Vernon 1975), which sets forth the guidelines for determining what constitutes community property subject to the sole management, control, and disposition of one spouse provides:

> (a) During marriage, each spouse has the sole management, control, and disposition of the community property that he or she would have owned if single, including but not limited to:
>
> (1) personal earnings;
>
> (2) revenue from separate property;
>
> (3) recoveries for personal injuries; and
>
> (4) the increase and mutations of, and the revenue from, all property subject to his or her sole management, control, and disposition.
>
> * * *
>
> (c) Except as provided in Subsection (a) of this section, the community property is subject to the joint management, control, and disposition of the husband and wife, unless the spouses provide otherwise by power of attorney in writing or other agreement. (Emphasis added.)

This "agreement" referred to in subsection (c) is not a partition agreement of the community, but rather an agreement to transfer the power of management, control, and disposition over certain community property assets from one spouse to the other. Appellant contends that the oral agreement for division of their property falls within the "other agreement" provision of subsection (c) above. We agree. Prior to 1974, Section 5.22(c) read, ". . . unless the spouses provide otherwise by power of attorney or other agreement in writing." In 1973 that section was amended to read, ". . . unless the spouses provide otherwise by power of attorney in writing or other agreement." This amendment became effective on January 1, 1974. Applying the standard rules of statutory construction, it is apparent that the Texas Legislature chose to remove the requirement that such an agreement be in writing.

In the case of *Evans v. Muller*, 510 S.W.2d 651 (Tex. Civ. App.—Austin) *rev'd per curiam*, 516 S.W.2d 923 (Tex. 1974), the Court of Civil Appeals concluded that a Section 5.22(c) oral agreement had been entered into, that there was no evidence that said agreement was designed to delay, defraud or hinder creditors, and that the property subject to that agreement was, therefore, insulated from liability by Section 5.61(b)(2). The Texas Supreme Court, in reversing the Court of Civil Appeals, *supra*, did not criticize its reasoning or interpretation of Section 5.22(c), but reversed simply on the basis that the agreement and trial were prior in time to the date on which the amendment removing the requirement for a written agreement became effective. The agreement having been made subsequent to the amendment, we hold that the oral agreement in this cause meets the requirements of Section 5.22(c).

However, it must also be determined whether the liability in question was incurred by Mr. LeBlanc alone or, instead, was a joint liability. TEX. FAM. CODE ANN. § 5.61(b)(2). The Texas Supreme Court, in *Cockerham v. Cockerham*, *supra*, has stated the applicable rule as follows:

> To determine whether a debt is only that of the contracting party or if it is instead that of both the husband and wife, it is necessary to examine the totality of the circumstances in which the debt arose. Of particular importance in the instant case is the consideration of implied assent to the debt by the noncontracting party, the husband.

The Court pointed out that, in the absence of some evidence that the creditor agreed to look solely to the separate estate of the contracting spouse for satisfaction, the debt, incurred during marriage, is presumed a community liability. The Court emphasized, however, that "(c)haracterization of the debts as community liabilities is only one aspect of the circumstances to be considered in determining whether the debts are joint." The other factors which the Court considered in determining whether the debts were joint liabilities were 1) who advanced the capital necessary to pay for the initial and additional inventory, 2) statements by the parties as to their willingness to pay the debt, 3) who signed the checks to pay for operational expenses, and 4) the treatment of depreciation deductions and shop losses on the parties' joint income tax return.

In the case before us, the noncontracting spouse had no knowledge of the liability until shortly before the inception of this action, did not participate in the business, did not realize any gain from it, nor have the opportunity to do so. There is no evidence of assent, implied or expressed, on appellant's part to incurring this debt. While the evidence reflects that appellee never agreed to look solely to Mr. LeBlanc's separate estate for satisfaction of this debt, that circumstance alone will not support the conclusion that it is a joint liability. There are no other circumstances reflected in the record, and, therefore, no evidence to rebut the conclusion that the liability was incurred by Mr. LeBlanc alone. Consequently, neither the community property under appellant's sole management, control, and disposition, nor her separate property is subject to this liability according to the terms of Section 5.61(a) and (b)(2). As the record reflects that there are no assets in appellant's possession or under her control which do not fall into one of those categories, appellant is not liable for this debt.

Affirmed in part and reversed and rendered in part.

Notes, Comments & Questions

1. Why did not the *LeBlanc* agreement affecting their marital property have to be in writing?

2. Why do creditors always seem to fall back on the *Cockerham* joint liability argument?

3. As you read these cases, make sure you are aware of current cites for applicable family law statutes.

H. Protection of Third Parties

SANBURN
v.
SCHULER
86 Tex. 116, 23 S.W. 641
(1893)

STAYTON, CHIEF JUSTICE.

The land in controversy was conveyed to Barron F. Deal, while he was the husband of Tina Deal, by a deed reciting a consideration of $1,000 paid, but there was nothing to show that the land was paid for with his separate estate, though this was the case.

Barron F. Deal died without leaving any children, but one sister and his wife survived.

After his death, his widow, for a valuable consideration, conveyed the land to a person who conveyed it to defendant on like consideration, and neither of the persons had notice that the land was paid for by Barron F. Deal with his separate means.

This action was brought by the sister of Barron F. Deal, as his sole heir, to recover the land, but judgment was rendered against her by the trial court, and on appeal that judgment was affirmed by the Court of Civil Appeals. 22 S.W. Rep. 119.

On application for writ of error, applicant insists that the decision is contrary to the rulings made in many cases, and especially to the decisions in *Edwards v. Brown*, 68 Tex. 329, 4 S.W. Rep. 380, and 5 S.W. Rep. 87, and *Patty v. Middleton*, 82 Tex. 586, 17 S.W. Rep. 909.

Since the decision of the case of *Cooke v. Bremond*, 27 Tex. 457, it has been steadily held that a purchaser for valuable consideration from a husband, of property acquired during marriage, will be protected against the claim of the wife, although the deed through which the property was acquired in terms conveyed the property to the wife, though the property was paid for with the separate funds of the wife, or was intended as a gift to her, unless the purchaser, through recitals in the deed or otherwise, was put upon inquiry or had notice of facts giving to the wife the superior right.

No reason exists for giving effect to this rule as to transactions occurring during the marriage, and for denying it in transactions occurring after the death of husband or wife.

It must be kept in mind, when dealing with a question of this kind, that the purchaser is protected because he purchases from and pays a valuable consideration to the person who apparently has title, through such means for transmitting title as the law prescribes.

The effect of a deed made to husband or wife during marriage must necessarily be the same after the death of one as while both are alive; and if from that, in connection with the statutes under which it must be construed, property appears to belong to the common estate, then a bona fide purchaser from the survivor must be protected against the claims of persons entitled to take, by inheritance only, the separate estate of the deceased member.

This necessarily results from the fact that the bona fide purchaser is entitled to rely upon the deed construed under the law; and this, nothing to the contrary appearing, made the land in controversy, acquired by onerous title during the marriage, common estate.

Such appearing to be the character of the property, the purchaser was bound to inquire who inherited the share of the deceased husband; and upon inquiry he ascertained that the deceased left neither child nor children, and then knew that the wife, under the statute, was the heir.

The property appearing to be common property, an inquiry as to what persons would inherit the separate estate of the deceased husband was irrelevant.

If any fact had been known to the purchaser which would have shown the superior right of the husband to the land, then a purchaser from the wife could not be deemed an innocent purchaser on the ground that he did not know that the deceased husband left a sister, for every purchaser must ascertain who is entitled to take by inheritance any particular property belonging to the estate of a deceased person dying intestate.

If the property be community property, in fact or presumptively, the purchaser must ascertain who is the heir of the deceased as to such property; but, if it be really or apparently the separate estate of the deceased, then he must ascertain who takes that by inheritance.

In so far as the right of the bona fide purchaser to protection is concerned, the operation of the statute of descent and distribution on the apparent title was to pass that to Mrs. Deal, as fully as would a conveyance by one having the apparent superior right pass that apparent right even to a purchaser with notice of the superior right of some third person; so that she, as well as a person holding apparent title by deed, could make a conveyance to a bona fide purchaser that would be protected against an unknown but superior right to that held by the vendor.

The statutes of descent and distribution are as effective in their operation to pass apparent title as is a deed, and a purchaser is entitled to rely upon title evidenced in the one way as fully as when evidenced in the other.

There is nothing in the opinion of the Court of Civil Appeals in conflict with the rules announced in the cases cited in the opinion of that court, nor to the rules announced in the cases of *Edwards v. Brown*, 68 Tex. 329, 4 S.W. Rep. 380, and 5 S.W. Rep. 87, and *Patty v. Middleton*, 82 Tex. 586, 17 S.W. Rep. 909. The motion to reconsider will be overruled.

Question

What inquiries must be made by a purchaser presented with a title that appears to establish community property?

MORAN
v.
ADLER
570 S.W.2d 883
(Tex. 1978)

POPE, JUSTICE.

The plaintiffs assert their rights as equitably adopted children to their stepmother's one-half community interest in two tracts of real estate. The defendant, Lester Adler, asserts his ownership in the land as a bona fide purchaser without notice of plaintiffs' claim that they are the adopted children of the stepmother. The trial court rendered judgment on a jury verdict for the plaintiffs but the court of civil appeals has reversed the judgment of the trial court and remanded the cause to that court. The court of civil appeals held that the jury findings about equitable adoption were not supported by clear, unequivocal and convincing evidence. 549 S.W.2d 760. We granted the writ to examine that standard of proof. We also granted defendant Adler's application which asserts his rights as a bona fide purchaser of the land without notice of the children's adoptive status. We reverse the judgments of the courts below and render judgment that plaintiffs take nothing.

The plaintiffs in this cause are Victor Moran, Jr., Xochitl Moran Hernandez, Yolanda Moran Coulter and Rene Moran. They are the children of Victor Moran, Sr. and Ester Landeros Moran. The mother died in 1929 and the next year Victor Moran married Ramona Guevara Moran. It is undisputed that the lands in suit were the community property of Victor Moran and Ramona, his second wife. Ramona died intestate in 1959, and in 1973 Mr. Moran borrowed sixty thousand dollars from the Laredo National Bank. He gave a deed of trust covering the tract to secure the loan and when he became delinquent the bank foreclosed the deed of trust lien. Lester Adler purchased the property at the foreclosure sale for seventy-five thousand dollars. Adler now asserts his rights as a purchaser from the bank who, he says, was an innocent purchaser for value and without notice of the claim by the children of the first marriage that they were equitably adopted by their stepmother, Ramona. The opinion of the court of civil appeals contains a full and correct statement of the testimony upon which the jury made its findings that Ramona, the stepmother, equitably adopted the four children of the earlier marriage. The testimony need not be repeated.

* * *

Defendant Lester Adler asserted his title to the lands by claiming that the bank took the mortgage on the property for a valuable consideration without notice of the claim by the Moran children that Ramona had adopted them. If the bank took the lien in good faith for a valuable consideration without notice, then Adler, regardless of his knowledge or notice, took good title as purchaser under the bona fide mortgagee at the foreclosure sale. . . . [Citations omitted.] The jury made findings that the Laredo National Bank at the time it took a deed of trust on the property had notice that the plaintiffs claimed the land, that the bank had knowledge of facts sufficient to put it on inquiry, and that a diligent inquiry would have revealed the claim by the plaintiffs to an undivided one-half interest in the property. The defendant, Adler, says there is no evidence to support those findings.

The court of civil appeals, without reaching Adler's no-evidence point, held that children who are equitably adopted are legal heirs of the adopting parent. It then distinguished an earlier decision of this court which held that equitably adopted children, unlike natural children and statutorily adopted children, receive only an equitable title from a deceased adoptive parent. The court of civil appeals quotes *Fleming v. Ashcroft*, 142 Tex. 41, 175 S.W.2d 401 (1943), and construes it to hold that the innocent purchaser doctrine protects a purchaser by cutting off an equitable title, but that the doctrine does not cut off a legal title. That case was decided in 1943. The court of civil appeals said that the Probate Code changed the status of equitably adopted children so that they are now "heirs at law." It held that equitably adopted children now inherit the same quality of title as a natural child or a statutorily adopted child, and for that reason, the court of civil appeals concluded that *Fleming* and its protection of innocent purchasers against the claim of an equitably adopted child was changed by the Probate Code.

It is our opinion that *Fleming* was not grounded upon the supposed distinction between legal and equitable title that is owned by an equitably adopted child. The real basis for protection of an innocent purchaser is explained in *Fleming* by its quotation from *Edwards v. Brown*, 68 Tex. 329, 337, 4 S.W. 380 (1887): "The policy of our laws is to protect purchasers against secret titles, whether they be legal or equitable. . . ."

The *Fleming* opinion cites three cases by this court that state that the holder of the apparent title[1] will be protected over the holder of the secret title. In *Edwards v. Brown*, *supra*, at issue was the rights of heirs of a spouse when title had been taken in the name of the other spouse. The court gave this as its reason for protecting an innocent purchaser who did not have notice of a holder of the legal estate who had not recorded his deed:

> But it may be further remarked that it does not follow that, because one may have the legal title, another may not acquire a superior equity as a bona fide purchaser. The holder of the legal estate by an unrecorded deed cannot prevail over a purchaser from his grantor, who has paid value without notice of the unrecorded conveyance. If a vendee is to be required to inquire into his vendor's family history in order to ascertain whether the property was community or not, why should he not be held to inquire into his business history and thus be affected with notice of secret trusts on behalf of partners or other third parties? 68 Tex. at 332-33, 4 S.W. at 381.

Marshburn v. Stewart, 113 Tex. 507, 254 S.W. 942 (1923), was another case cited in *Fleming*. The reason expressed in *Marshburn* for protecting the innocent purchaser even against an outstanding legal title, was that apparent title should prevail over hidden titles:

> While in this case the apparent title and the real title are both legal titles, we do not think, in view of the legal presumption of the sufficiency of the apparent title and the burden of proof imposed by our law on the holder of the real title to prove its superiority, that it should be given greater weight in determining the burden of proof on the question of notice than is given to an outstanding equitable title when asserted against a legal title. The

[1] The holder of the "apparent title," as used in this opinion, is the "one apparently invested with title" when viewed from the recorded instruments, "rely(ing) on the record." Waggoner v. Dodson, 96 Tex. 415, 422, 73 S.W. 517, 518 (1903). *See* Hennessy v. Blair, 107 Tex. 39, 42, 173 S.W. 871, 873 (1915); Patty v. Middleton, 82 Tex. 586, 590-91, 17 S.W. 909, 911 (1891); 4 F. LANGE, TEXAS PRACTICE: LAND TITLES AND TITLE EXAMINATION § 335, at 29 (1961); 5 F. LANGE, TEXAS PRACTICE: LAND TITLES AND TITLE EXAMINATIONS § 813, at 244 (1961). In determining the apparent title, one may also rely on well established legal presumptions operating on the recorded facts and knowledge of whether a grantee is, in fact, deceased. Thus when the recorded instruments show the husband purchased the land during marriage, one who purchases from the surviving wife acquires the "apparent title" because of the presumption that property purchased during marriage is community property. Sanburn v. Schuler, 86 Tex. 116, 23 S.W. 641 (1893).

> law having invested Mrs. Aiken, as survivor of the community, with the apparent legal title in fee simple to this land, and such apparent title having passed to Marshburn for an adequate and valuable consideration, we think before defendants in error can defeat the same they must further show that at the time he purchased he had notice of their rights. or that he had notice of facts sufficient to put him upon inquiry, and that such inquiry, pursued with reasonable diligence, would have necessarily discovered the real facts upon which their claim to the land involved in this suit is predicated. 113 Tex. at 513, 254 S.W. at 944.

The protection of the apparent title is also discussed in *Patty v. Middleton*, 82 Tex. 586, 17 S.W. 909 (1891), cited in *Fleming*:

> There is no doubt that in many opinions this court has used expressions to the effect that the rights of heirs of a deceased member of the matrimonial union, where the land was conveyed during the marriage to the survivor, was a legal estate, and the title transmitted by descent a legal title; but this is not true as matter of law, and to so hold when words or terms are used with reference to the right of bona fide purchaser from the survivor to whom the lands were directly conveyed would overturn all the long-recognized rules applicable to the question, for the question then is not as to the real interest which the wife or her heirs had, but as to the apparent right in the survivor as evidenced by the deeds through which the property was acquired. 82 Tex. at 592, 17 S.W. at 912.

The correct basis for the innocent purchaser doctrine is that of "the apparent title or the legal title as appearing of record" to an interest in land. *Simonds v. Stanolind Oil & Gas Co.*, 134 Tex. 332, 114 S.W.2d 226, 234 (1938). *See Slaughter v. Qualls*, 139 Tex. 340, 162 S.W.2d 671, 675 (1942); *Gholson v. Peeks*, 224 S.W.2d 778, 782 (Tex. Civ. App.—Eastland 1949, writ ref'd); *Federal Life Ins. Co. v. Martin*, 157 S.W.2d 149, 152 (Tex. Civ. App.—Texarkana 1941, writ ref'd); *Burton v. Connecticut General Life Ins. Co.*, 72 S.W.2d 318, 322 (Tex. Civ. App.—Fort Worth 1934, writ ref'd).

The doctrine which protects an innocent purchaser frequently finds its application in cases in which the legal title prevails over the equitable title. That confrontation occurs so frequently that many opinions place their holdings upon a legal-equitable distinction. *See, e.g., Mitchell v. Schofield*, 106 Tex. 512, 171 S.W. 1121 (1915); *Daniel v. Mason*, 90 Tex. 240, 38 S.W. 161 (1896); *Foster v. Christensen*, 67 S.W.2d 246 (Tex. Comm'n App. 1934, judgmt. adopted); *Heidelberg v. Harvey*, 391 S.W.2d 828 (Tex. Civ. App.—El Paso 1965, writ ref'd n. r. e.); *Connor v. Lane*, 355 S.W.2d 223 (Tex. Civ. App.—Waco 1962, no writ); *Landry v. Williamson*, 335 S.W.2d 400 (Tex. Civ. App.—Houston 1960, writ ref'd n. r. e.); *Stahl v. Westerman*, 250 S.W.2d 325 (Tex. Civ. App.—San Antonio 1952, no writ); *Balcomb v. Vasquez*, 241 S.W.2d 650 (Tex. Civ. App.—El Paso 1951, writ ref'd n.r.e.); *Moye v. Goolsbee*, 124 S.W.2d 925 (Tex. Civ. App.—Beaumont 1939, writ ref'd); *Home Owners' Loan Corp. v. Netterville*, 110 S.W.2d 628, 630 (Tex. Civ. App.—Beaumont 1937), *rev'd on other grounds*, 134 Tex. 30, 132 S.W.2d 93 (1939); *Love v. R. S. Allday Supply Co.*, 106 S.W.2d 830, 832 (Tex. Civ. App.—Eastland 1937, writ dism'd).

It is our opinion that *Fleming v. Ashcroft*, *supra*, correctly holds that a purchaser from the apparent legal heir, in the absence of notice to the contrary, can rely upon the presumption that there are no equitably adopted children. The reason for that rule is that the claim of the equitably adopted child is not apparent. There are neither birth nor adoption records which a purchaser can consult to protect himself. The proof of an equitable adoption is extrinsic, may come from any source, and in that sense is hidden or secret. This is particularly so after the alleged adoptive parent, Ramona Moran in this case, has died. A purchaser from the heirs must discover the apparent heirs, whether they are the natural or statutorily adopted children, at his own peril. But a child who is adopted by estoppel affords no legal record. As this court has held before, an equitable adoption or adoption by estoppel does not afford all of the legal consequences of a statutory adoption. *Heien v. Crabtree*, 369 S.W.2d 28, 30 (Tex. 1963).

There remains for consideration Adler's contention that the Laredo National Bank, through whom he acquired his title, was an innocent purchaser as a matter of law. He urges that there is no evidence either of knowledge or of facts which were sufficient to put the bank upon inquiry. We agree.

Strong v. Strong, 128 Tex. 470, 98 S.W.2d 346 (1936), was a holding that, as a matter of law, the defendant was protected as an innocent purchaser of an oil and gas lease. Plaintiffs were the children of Manuel Strong and his first wife Nancy Strong. Manuel and Nancy Strong acquired some land as their community property, but it was taken in his name. After the death of his first wife, Manuel and his second wife executed an oil and gas lease. The children of the first marriage brought suit in trespass to try title to recover the undivided interest which they had inherited from their mother. This court in its holding as a matter of law that the plaintiffs had not overcome the defense of innocent purchaser wrote:

> A purchaser of land must search the records, for they are the primary source of information as to title and he is charged with knowledge of the existence and contents of the recorded instruments affecting the title. [Citations omitted.] He must also make inquiry as to the rights or title of the possessor, for possession is equivalent to registration, in that it gives constructive notice of the possessor's rights. . . .
>
> The value and effectiveness of the registration statutes are to an extent impaired by the rule that possession gives constructive notice of title, but the rule is justified, or at least supported, as suggested by Mr. Pomeroy, by the fact that ordinarily the truth as to title may be readily obtained from the person in possession. We find no good reason, however, for imposing upon the purchaser the additional burden of ascertaining at his peril what may be the common reputation in the community as to the ownership of land. Reputation does not ordinarily afford a ready or dependable source of information. It has the fallibility of hearsay. Rights or titles to land should not be dependent upon the existence or nonexistence, the truth or the untruth, of common reputation, notoriety, or rumor. 98 S.W.2d at 348.

There was evidence that Victor Moran, following the death of his second wife, acting alone, executed oil and gas leases covering the property which were recorded. He executed surface leases and conveyances to tracts of land out of a larger tract, including one conveyance of two acres to one of the plaintiffs. Victor Moran was named as the sole owner in a condemnation proceeding instituted by the City of Laredo in 1970. He had previously given mortgages on the land to borrow money. At the time the bank took its mortgage on the property, none of the plaintiffs were in possession of the land, and the plaintiffs did not assert their claim prior to this suit.

Plaintiffs relied upon two items which they say were sufficient to put the bank upon inquiry. Plaintiff Rene Moran, a police officer, testified that he told virtually every member of the Laredo Police Department that he, his brother and his sisters claimed an interest in the land. That kind of reputation and hearsay evidence was rejected in *Strong v. Strong, supra*. The other item upon which the plaintiffs rely is an affidavit that Victor Moran, Sr. recorded in the Webb County deed records in 1968. He swore that plaintiffs were the natural children of him and his first wife, that they were not Ramona's natural children and that Ramona did not adopt them. The fact that Moran denied Ramona's adoption in the affidavit, argue the plaintiffs, put the Laredo National Bank on notice to make further inquiry about the negative of the statement. In our opinion, even actual knowledge of a second marriage does not put one on inquiry about the adoption of children of the first marriage by the new spouse of the second marriage. There is no stronger reason that such facts put one on notice than existed in *Strong v. Strong*. It is our opinion that the evidence relied upon by the plaintiffs in support of the jury's findings about the Laredo National Bank's knowledge or notice of facts about the equitable adoption is no more than a scintilla of evidence. *Joske v. Irvine*, 91 Tex. 574, 44 S.W. 1059 (1898).

We reverse the judgments of the courts below and render judgment that plaintiffs take nothing.

BARROW, J., not sitting.

Questions

1. How does the Supreme Court of Texas view the claim of the Moran children?
2. Is the claim to equitable title, legal title, or secret title?
3. Upon what facts did the children depend to charge the purchaser with knowledge or, at least, put him on inquiry?
3. Why were the facts referred to in question 2 insufficient to charge purchaser with knowledge or put him on inquiry?

WILLIAMS
v.
PORTLAND STATE BANK
514 S.W.2d 124
(Tex. Civ. App.—Beaumont 1974, writ dism'd)

STEPHENSON, JUSTICE.

Rose Lee Chivers Williams (plaintiff) brought this action to remove a cloud upon the title to the land involved. Portland State Bank (Bank) filed a cross-action against plaintiff and Thurman Lee Williams (Williams), her former husband, to recover on a note and for foreclosure of its lien upon such land. Trial was before the court, and judgment was rendered that plaintiff take nothing and the Bank recover on its note and foreclosing its lien. Williams did not appeal.

The basic questions in the case involve construction of Sections 5 .22 and 5.24 of the V.T.C.A., Family Code, as amended (1971), and are of first impression. The material part of those sections reads as follows:

§ 5.22. Community Property: General Rules

(a) During marriage, each spouse has the sole management, control, and disposition of the community property that he or she would have owned if single, including but not limited to:

(1) personal earnings;

(2) revenue from separate property;

(3) recoveries for personal injuries; and

(4) the increase and mutations of, and the revenue from, all property subject to his or her sole management, control, and disposition.

(b) If community property subject to the sole management, control, and disposition of one spouse is mixed or combined with community property subject to the sole management, control, and disposition of the other spouse, then the mixed or combined community property is subject to the joint management, control, and disposition of the spouses, unless the spouses provide otherwise by power of attorney in writing or other agreement.

(c) Except as provided in Subsection (a) of this section, the community property is subject to the joint management, control, and disposition of the husband and wife, unless the spouses provide otherwise by power of attorney in writing or other agreement.

§ 5.24. Presumption

(a) During marriage, property is presumed to be subject to the sole management, control, and disposition of a spouse if it is held in his or her name, as shown by muniment, contract, deposit of funds, or other evidence of ownership, or if it is in his or her possession and is not subject to such evidence of ownership.

(b) A third person dealing with a spouse is entitled to rely (as against the other spouse or anyone claiming from that spouse) on that spouse's authority to deal with the property if:

(1) the property is presumed to be subject to the sole management, control, and disposition of the spouse; and

(2) the person dealing with the spouse:

(A) is not a party to a fraud upon the other spouse or another person; and

(B) does not have actual or constructive notice of the spouse's lack of authority.

The record before us shows the following transpired:

(1) Plaintiff and Williams were married January 22, 1954.

(2) 77.44 acres of land, involved in this suit, were acquired as community property by deed dated April 4, 1963, in which plaintiff and Williams were named as grantees.

(3) 100 acres of land, involved in this suit, were acquired as community property by deed dated December 30, 1963, in which Williams was the sole grantee.

(4) A note in the amount of $25,000 and a deed of trust covering both tracts of land, dated June 23, 1971, were prepared to be executed by both plaintiff and Williams.

(5) Plaintiff refused to execute either of the papers, and Williams gave this information to Jeff E. Bell, Jr., president of defendant Bank.

(6) A new note and deed of trust of the same date and terms were immediately prepared for Williams to execute alone; which he did, and the loan was concluded.

(7) Plaintiff filed suit for divorce from Williams June 30, 1971.

(8) The Bank's deed of trust was filed for record July 27, 1971.

(9) Such divorce was granted November 17, 1971, and plaintiff was awarded title to the land involved in this suit, in the divorce decree. The Bank was not a party to such divorce suit.

(10) Williams did not pay the first annual installment on the note given the Bank, and plaintiff received a letter from the Bank dated July 11, 1972, informing her that notices were being posted to sell this land.

(11) This suit was filed July 25, 1972.

The trial court made findings of fact and conclusions of law, including the following: The land involved was not the homestead of plaintiff and Williams. Such land was their community property. The Bank and Williams were not a party to any fraud as to plaintiff.

We consider first the points of error complaining about the action of the trial court in permitting foreclosure of the deed of trust lien as to the 77.44 acre tract which was held in names of both plaintiff and Williams. We conclude that this situation is controlled by Section 5.22(c) of the Family Code which provides, in essence, that community property is subject to the joint management, control and disposition of the husband and wife except under certain circumstances which do not exist here. We construe this section to mean that Williams had no legal authority to encumber plaintiff's interest in this tract of land in both of their names.

We consider next the points of error complaining about the action of the trial court permitting foreclosure of the deed of trust lien as to the 100 acre tract of land held in Williams' name alone. Section 5.24 of the Family Code provides in part in essence that it is presumed that property held in the name of one spouse alone, is subject to the sole management, control and disposition of such spouse, and a third person dealing with that spouse is entitled to rely upon that spouse's authority to deal with the property in the absence of fraud or notice of the spouse's lack of authority. From the factual situation before us in this case, we meet the question as to whether knowledge by the president of the Bank making this loan that plaintiff had refused to execute the first note and deed of trust was notice that Williams lacked the authority to encumber plaintiff's interest in this tract of land.

There is no evidence in this record that Williams had actual authority to encumber plaintiff's interest in this land. Both testified upon this trial, and it is clear that he did not have such authority. There is also no evidence in this record that the Bank had actual specific knowledge that Williams had no authority from plaintiff to encumber her interest in this tract of land. However, this section of the Family Code does not require 'knowledge' of lack of authority, but uses the term "notice." There is an excellent discussion in *Flack v. First Nat. Bank of Dalhart*, 148 Tex. 495, 226 S.W.2d 628 (1950), as to the different meanings of the words "knowledge" and "notice" and the fact that the two words are not synonymous. This statement is then made in that case at page 632, to-wit:

> Whatever puts a person on inquiry ordinarily amounts in law to notice, provided inquiry has become a duty and would lead to knowledge of the facts by the exercise of ordinary diligence and understanding. In other words, one who has knowledge of such facts as would cause a prudent man to make further inquiry, is chargeable with notice of the facts which, by use of ordinary intelligence, he would have ascertained.

See also, *Continental Insur. Co. v. Stewart & Stevenson Serv.*, 306 S.W.2d 415, 422 (Tex. Civ. App.—Houston, 1957, error ref. n.r.e.).

Applying the law of the *Flack* case, *supra*, to the case before us, we hold the actual knowledge by the Bank that plaintiff had refused to sign the first note and deed of trust was sufficient as a matter of law to put the Bank on "notice" to make further inquiry as to the extent to Williams' authority to encumber plaintiff's interest in this tract of land. The use of ordinary diligence by the Bank would have revealed to the Bank that Williams had no such authority, and the presumption that he had such authority would have been rebutted.

We must still determine whether or not the execution of the note and deed of trust created a valid lien upon Williams' interest in both tracts of land. We hold that it did, and the trial court properly ordered foreclosure of such lien as to Williams' interest. A study of the pertinent sections gives us no reason to believe such a lien would be either void or voidable as to his interest.

We proceed to enter the judgment which should have been rendered by the trial court. That portion of the judgment decreeing that the Bank have and recover from Williams the sum of $25,000 with interest as provided, and for its attorney's fee and foreclosure of the deed of trust liens as to the undivided one-half interest owned by Williams is affirmed. The remaining portion of the original judgment as to the order of sale shall remain as stated. It is further ordered that the Bank take nothing as to plaintiff, and the cloud upon her one-half undivided interest, in both tracts of lands, is removed. The cost of this appeal shall be paid one-half by plaintiff and one-half by the Bank.

Affirmed in part and reversed and rendered in part.

Questions

1. What is the difference between notice and knowledge?
2. How did notice in this case affect the ultimate judgment obtained by the bank?

Chapter 5

Dissolution of the Marriage by Divorce

A. Introduction

Texas marital property law affects a number of legal disciplines including, but not limited to: estate planning; administration of estates; debtor-creditor rights; tort law; tax law; and, family law. Of course, none of these disciplines is so driven by Texas marital property law as is family law, particularly the divorce action. Accordingly, this entire chapter is devoted to divorce and how a variety of issues as well as properties, are dealt with upon divorce.

This chapter will begin with an analysis of the just and right division and proceed to an identification of the property that can be divided upon divorce. How certain properties should be characterized and valued upon divorce will also be addressed, with special attention paid to goodwill, retirement benefits, and stock options. Likewise, alimony and statutory maintenance will be explained. Post divorce issues, such as the treatment of property omitted from a divorce decree and appellate review are also included in the chapter.

B. The Just and Right Division

> In a decree of divorce or annulment the court shall order a division of the estate of the parties in a manner that the court deems just and right, having due regard for the rights of each party and any children of the marriage.

TEX. FAM. CODE § 7.001

The foregoing statute, TEX. FAM. CODE § 7.001, has often been hailed as a basis for the trial court's perceived, unbridled discretion to divide property upon divorce. A trial court may even reject a property division presented in a settlement agreement if it deems that such is not a just and right division. TEX. FAM. CODE § 7.006 provides:

> (a) To promote amicable settlement of disputes in a suit for divorce or annulment, the spouses may enter into a written agreement concerning the division of the property and the liabilities of the spouses and maintenance of either spouse. The agreement may be revised or repudiated before rendition of the divorce or annulment unless the agreement is binding under another rule of law.
>
> (b) If the court finds that the terms of the written agreement in a divorce or annulment are just and right, those terms are binding on the court. If the court approves the agreement, the court may set forth the agreement in full or incorporate the agreement by reference in the final decree.
>
> (c) If the court finds that the terms of the written agreement in a divorce or annulment are not just and right, the court may request the spouses to submit a revised agreement or may set the case for a contested hearing.

Although a settlement agreement may be binding under other rules of law, including those governing stipulations or mediated settlement agreements,[1] TEX. FAM. CODE § 7.006 (c) gives the trial court the power to reject a property settlement agreement that it finds does not meet the just and right standard. Unlike many community property states, a 50/50 division is not mandated; an even division is not even presumed, as a matter of law, to be just and right. Of course, what is just and right, lies within the discretion of the trial judge hearing the case, which can certainly vary from court to court.

The limits on the trial court's discretion will be discussed later in the chapter. This section will explore the factors that can be considered by the trial court in the making of a just and right division of marital property upon divorce. Prior to 1981, there had been a disagreement between the courts of appeal as to what factors could be considered by a trial court in exercising its discretion in the division of martial property. In *Murff v. Murff*, the Texas Supreme Court provided a non-exclusive list of factors that can be considered by a trial court in the division of property upon divorce.

---

[1] *See* Pamela E. George & Kim Thibodeaux, *"When Handshakes Won't Do" Rule 11, Stipulations and MSAs*, presented to 32nd Annual Advanced Family Law Course (State Bar of Texas, August 2006) reprinted in the Appendix. This paper is an introduction to "other rules of law" which might require enforcement of an agreement even if repudiated.

MURFF
v.
MURFF
615 S.W.2d 696
(Tex. 1981)

SPEARS, JUSTICE.

In this divorce case, petitioner, Wanda Faye Murff, was granted a divorce by the trial court from respondent, John Samuel Murff, after a non-jury trial. John Murff was dissatisfied with the trial court's division of the community property and appealed to the court of civil appeals. That court reversed the judgment of the trial court and remanded the cause for a new trial, holding that the trial court abused its discretion in the division of the parties' estate. 601 S.W.2d 116.

We granted Mrs. Murff's Application for Writ of Error on all five asserted points of error. We have jurisdiction of the case because the holding of the court of civil appeals on the issue of whether fault may be considered in dividing the property, conflicts with *Duncan v. Duncan*, 374 S.W.2d 800 (Tex. Civ. App.—Eastland 1964, no writ) and on the issue of whether disparity in earning power or capacity may be considered in dividing the property, with *In re Marriage of McCurdy*, 489 S.W.2d 712 (Tex. Civ. App.—Amarillo 1973, writ dism'd). We reverse the judgment of the court of civil appeals and affirm the judgment of the trial court and hold the trial court did not abuse its discretion in dividing the parties' property.

Mrs. Murff sought the divorce on three grounds: "no-fault" insupportability, and alternatively, adultery and cruel treatment, both "fault" grounds. Although the Decree of Divorce did not specify upon which ground the divorce was granted to Mrs. Murff, the Findings of Fact filed by the court stated that she had proved grounds under all three alternative grounds. In its division of the community estate of the parties, the trial court awarded the wife property valued by the trial court at $78,901, plus attorney's fees of $8,500, and awarded the husband property valued at $73,600, plus $30,000 of husband's claimed separate property. The trial court further found that by alternatively valuing the wife's retirement and annuity at $47,090.55 instead of $8,000, the property awarded the wife would be $117,991.55, plus attorney's fees of $8,500. The court of civil appeals found that the trial court abused its discretion in six particulars: (1) in giving consideration to "fault" of a spouse to justify a disparate division of the community property; (2) in giving consideration to disparity of "income" between spouses instead of considering a disparity of "need" between spouses; (3) in failing to consider an award of attorney's fees to the wife against the husband as an element of the court's division; (4) in failing to declare the identity of separate property and fix any charge thereon in favor of the community; (5) in failing to evaluate correctly the pension plans; and (6) in failing to *divide* the spouses' property and in imposing an inequitable money judgment in lieu of division.

Mr. and Mrs. Murff had been married over 22 years at the time of the divorce hearing. They had a 21-year old daughter who attended college at the time. The wife was 46; the husband 47. Both spouses had worked full-time during their marriage. At the time of the divorce, the wife's annual gross salary was $14,750 or $1,229 per month; her net monthly take-home pay was $927 per month. The husband's annual gross salary was $26,715; his gross pay per month was approximately $2,200 from which deductions were made for taxes, insurance and retirement; however, taking into consideration the added "service incentive pay," the husband's gross pay per month was almost $3,000 per month. Both husband and wife were members of a pension plan with their employers.

Mrs. Murff's first point of error is that the court of civil appeals erred in holding that the trial court could not consider fault in the breakup of the marriage in arriving at a "just and right" division of the community estate. We sustain this point, having recently ruled on the same question in *Young v. Young*, 609 S.W.2d 758 (Tex. 1980). We there held that in a divorce granted on a fault basis, the trial court may consider the fault of one spouse in breaking up the marriage when making a property division. In the instant case, the divorce was based upon both no-fault and fault grounds, thus *Young* is applicable. As we said in *Young*, however, "this does not mean that fault *must* be considered, only that it *may* be considered."

In her second point of error, Mrs. Murff attacks the holding of the court of civil appeals that the trial court erred in considering a disparity in the income of the spouses. The court of civil appeals has held that only the cure of the "necessitous circumstances" or "probable future necessities" may be considered in arriving at a just and right division.

The Texas Family Code § 3.63 provides for the division of the parties' property upon divorce:

> In a decree of divorce or annulment the court shall order a division of the estate of the parties in a manner that the court deems just and right, having due regard for the rights of each party and any children of the marriage.

The trial court has wide discretion in dividing the estate of the parties and that division should be corrected on appeal only when an abuse of discretion has been shown. *Hedtke v. Hedtke*, 112 Tex. 404, 248 S.W. 21 (1923).

Numerous courts of civil appeals decisions have recognized that a trial court may consider the disparity of incomes or of earning capacities of the parties in dividing the estate of the parties.[1] The cases cited in the margin recognize that community property need not be equally divided. In exercising its discretion the trial court may consider many factors and it is presumed that the trial court exercised its discretion properly. *Bell v. Bell*, 513 S.W.2d 20, 22 (Tex. 1974). These cases further indicate that the trial court may consider such factors as the spouses' capacities and abilities, benefits which the party not at fault would have derived from continuation of the marriage, business opportunities, education, relative physical conditions, relative financial condition and obligations, disparity of ages, size of separate estates, and the nature of the property. We believe that the consideration of such factors by the trial court is proper in making a "just and right" division of the property. Likewise, the consideration of a disparity in earning capacities or of incomes is proper and need not be limited by "necessitous" circumstances. *Bokhoven, supra*; *Means, supra*; *Cooper, supra, Allen, supra.*

We next address Mrs. Murff's contention that the court of civil appeals erred in holding that the trial court's award of a money judgment for $7,500 to her was an abuse of discretion because it was not used as a "device to avoid fractionating items in the estate to be divided." We disagree with the court of civil appeals that the trial court abused its discretion. There was evidence that the wife had only $300 in funds on hand, but that the husband had substantial sums in savings before the separation that had disappeared by the time of trial. Some $1,400 of the money judgment represented unpaid court-ordered temporary alimony for the wife from the pendency of the divorce action prior to trial. We find no abuse of the trial court's discretion under these facts. *Garrett v. Garrett*, 534 S.W.2d 381 (Tex. Civ. App.—Houston [1st Dist.] 1976, no writ); *In re Marriage of Jackson*, 506 S.W.2d 261 (Tex. Civ. App.—Amarillo 1974, writ dism'd).

---

[1] [Footnote omitted.]

Mrs. Murff next complains of the holding of the court of civil appeals that the trial court should have considered the attorney's fees awarded her as a factor in achieving a just and right division of the property. In *Carle v. Carle*, 149 Tex. 469, 234 S.W.2d 1002, 1005 (1950), this court, in responding to a certified question, said:

> In practical effect, a decree that the husband pay all of the wife's attorney's fees may be to award him less of the community estate than that awarded to the wife, but that alone does not condemn it. The attorney's fee is but a factor to be considered by the court in making an equitable division of the estate, considering the conditions and needs of the parties and all of the surrounding circumstances.

We agree with the statement of the court of civil appeals in this case that it is not clear whether the award of attorney's fees to the wife was taken into consideration by the trial court; however, there is likewise no indication in the trial court's judgment, findings of fact or conclusions of law that it did not take them into consideration in making its division. The failure to list the attorney's fees as "property" in the list of property awarded to the wife is no indication that they were not considered in the division, only that it was not considered "property." In either event, in applying the *Carle* standard, we find no abuse of discretion in awarding to the wife her attorney's fees under the circumstances of this case.

* * *

Finally, we consider Mrs. Murff's contention that the trial court correctly evaluated the pension plans of the parties and did not abuse its discretion in awarding each the anticipated benefits of these respective plans. The wife had been with her employer for 9 years and 11 months at the time of trial; ten years was required to vest her retirement rights. Prior to July 1, 1972, she had contributed to the employer's annuity plan from which she would receive $15.21 per month upon retirement at age 65. Since that date, she has contributed to a new retirement fund which would pay her an additional $344 per month upon retirement at age 65. The employer's insurance company placed a value of $2,500.55 on the annuity and $44,410 on the retirement.

The husband, on the other hand, could retire at age 55 and draw $651.30 per month, or substantially more than that if he waited until age 65. He had $9,420 in contributions to the fund which he could withdraw if his employment terminated. An actuarial consultant testified that based on retirement at age 60, his retirement had a present value of $68,667, using the Group Annuity Mortality Table, and $62,933, using the U.S. (Census) Life Table. Assuming retirement at age 55, the values were $61,872 and $58,729.

In its findings of fact, the trial court placed a present value of $58,700 on the husband's retirement and $8,000 on the wife's retirement. Although the method of interpolation used by the trial court in determining the value of the wife's retirement is not shown, it is clear that the value of the husband's retirement far exceeded that of the wife's. The husband could retire at age 55 at a much greater amount than the wife could at age 65. The trial court was not bound by the valuation placed on her retirement by the insurance company but could evaluate the pension plans under the circumstances based upon the differences in benefits in the plans, the amounts of contributions paid in and by whom, the expectancy of receiving the benefits, and other relevant information. The conclusion of the court of civil appeals that the wife's retirement was valued at the *current* value of the benefits but the husband's retirement was valued at the *potential* value of the benefits is without support in the record. The trial court in its findings of fact even measured the division of the property using the higher value for the wife's retirement and found the division would award the wife far less than the 65% division of the total property she had requested. Using either the $8,000 figure or the sum of $2,580.55 and $44,510 as the value of the wife's retirement, we hold that the trial court did not abuse its discretion in its division.

The trial court in a divorce case has the opportunity to observe the parties on the witness stand, determine their credibility, evaluate their needs and potentials, both social and economic. As the trier of fact, the court is empowered to use its legal knowledge and its human understanding and experience. Although many divorce cases have similarities, no two of them are exactly alike. Mathematical precision in dividing property in a divorce is usually not possible. Wide latitude and discretion rests in these trial courts and that discretion should only be disturbed in the case of clear abuse.

Accordingly, the judgment of the court of civil appeals is reversed and the judgment of the trial court is affirmed.

Notes, Comments & Questions

1. The *Murff* case does not provide an exclusive—all inclusive—list of the factors that may be considered by a trial court in dividing community property. Identify the *Murff* factors and then, add to them if you can.

2. Can you think of additional factors that a trial court might consider in dividing community property upon divorce? List them.

3. Can you recall any cases that have been previously studied which identified additional factors for consideration in the division of property? Name those cases and identify the factors.

4. In the case of *Young v. Young*, 609 S.W.2d 758 (Tex. 1980), which was cited in *Murff*, the court found that fault in the break-up of a marriage could be considered in the division of property. The court also found that the needs of an adult disabled child—for whom child support could not be ordered—was a proper factor to consider.

C. Divestiture of Separate Property Not Just and Right

At first glance, the discretion of the trial court seems to be bound only by the ambiguous "just and right" standard. However, case law, and more recently statutes, have reigned in what was once perceived as a trial court's near absolute power to exercise its discretion in a property division. Although the perception of unbridled discretion remains, the reality is not without constraints.

Perhaps the longest standing and currently unquestioned constraint is the prohibition against divesting a spouse of their separate property upon divorce. With the decision in *Eggemeyer v. Eggemeyer*, 554 S.W.2d 137 (Tex. 1977) the Texas Supreme Court put to rest any controversy and made clear that in cases of divorce a court cannot divest a spouse of their separate real property. Although argument has been made that this limitation is only applicable to divestiture of separate real property, the Texas Supreme court in *dictum* appears to extend the prohibition of divestiture to separate personalty. *See Cameron v. Cameron*, 641 S.W.2d 210 (Tex. 1982). Thus, the court's exercise of discretion in matters of division of property can only be exercised in relation to community property; a court cannot divest a spouse of separate property.

EGGEMEYER
v.
EGGEMEYER
554 S.W.2d 137
(Tex. 1977)

POPE, JUSTICE.

The question presented by this appeal is whether a trial court may in a divorce decree divest one spouse of his separate realty and transfer title to the other spouse. The court of civil appeals in reversing the judgment of the trial court has ruled that section 3.63 of the Family Code does not authorize such a divestiture of one's title to separate property. 535 S.W.2d 425. We affirm that judgment. This court has jurisdiction because the holding of the court of civil appeals conflicts with the holding in *Wilkerson v. Wilkerson*, 515 S.W.2d 52 (Tex. Civ. App. 1974, no writ).

The trial court granted Virginia Eggemeyer a divorce from Homer Eggemeyer and named her managing conservator of their four minor children. The trial court also awarded Virginia all of the community interest in the small family farm. Homer owned as his separate property an undivided one-third interest in the farm by reason of a gift from his mother. The trial court divested him of that interest and transferred his title to Virginia. The farm was already subject to a 20,101.80 dollar debt owing the Federal Land Bank of Houston as well as a second lien in the amount of 5,200 dollars. In divesting title from Homer, the court created and imposed still another lien against the property in the sum of 10,000 dollars which was ordered payable to Homer by Virginia on July 16, 1982, the date when the youngest of the four children reaches age eighteen. The trial court ordered Homer to pay one hundred dollars per child per month until each reaches eighteen. The court of civil appeals in reversing the divestiture of title followed the well-reasoned decision of *Ramirez v. Ramirez*, 524 S.W.2d 767 (Tex. Civ. App. 1975, no writ), and several previous decisions by this court.

It has long been the law that upon divorce the rents, revenues, and income from a spouse's separate property may be set aside for the support of the minor children. In support of that principle, the court of civil appeals properly cited *Hedtke v. Hedtke*, 112 Tex. 404, 248 S.W. 21 (1923); *Rice v. Rice*, 21 Tex. 58 (1858); *Fitts v. Fitts*, 14 Tex. 443 (1855), and section 14.05(a) of the Texas Family Code. The trial court could have but did not set over the father's separate interest in the farm to the mother for the support of the children during their minority. The court of civil appeals did remand the cause to the trial court to consider such an arrangement. That arrangement would have satisfied the law's command that Homer Eggemeyer must support his minor children without divesting Homer of his title in his separate property.

Article 4639a, enacted in 1935, for the first time authorized divorce courts to inquire into the financial circumstances of the parties and to make orders for child support. Prior to this article's enactment, the Texas courts fashioned a method for enforcing the parents' legal duty to provide child support. The parents' property, whether community or separate, was subjected to a trust or some other form of interim management to insure the payment of child support. *Cunningham v. Cunningham*, 120 Tex. 491, 40 S.W.2d 46 (1931); *Fitts v. Fitts, supra*. When the duty of support to the minor was fulfilled, the property was freed from the trust. This method did not divest nor transfer to another person the owner's fee title.

Virginia Eggemeyer states that section 3.63 of the Family Code authorizes the divestiture of Homer's separate realty and its vesting in her because the trial court can make such an order when it is "just and right." The statute is, of course, wholly silent about that matter. The argument is that the earlier article 4638 specifically prohibited the divestiture of title[1] whereas the Family Code does not.[2] From this omission, she argues the legislature intended to change the law and to authorize a divestiture. This is not a correct result for several reasons.

The legislative commentary which accompanied the section when it was being considered by the legislature stated: "This is a codification of present law." McKnight, *Commentary on Sec. 3.63*, 5 TEX. TECH L. REV. 337 (1974). The legislature believed it was making no change but was carrying forward the law as it then existed.

Section 14.05(a) of the Family Code supplies additional evidence of the legislature's intent to keep the law unchanged and as it was under article 4638. In construing section 3.63, section 14.05(a) has apparently escaped the consideration of the parties. As appears from the section's second sentence, section 14.05(a) carried forward into the Family Code what was well established by judicial precedent:

> § 14.05. Support of Child
>
> (a) The court may order either or both parents to make periodic payments or a lump-sum payment, or both, for the support of the child until he is 18 years of age in the manner and to the persons specified by the court in the decree. *In addition, the court may order a parent obligated to support a child to set aside property to be administered for the support of the child in the manner and by the persons specified by the court in the decree.* (Emphasis added.)

---

[1] Article 4638. [4634] [2980] [2864] Division of property. The court pronouncing a decree of divorce shall also decree and order a division of the estate of the parties in such a way as the court shall deem just and right, having due regard to the rights of each party and their children, if any. Nothing herein shall be construed to compel either party to divest himself or herself of the title to real estate. [P.D. 3452.]

[2] Section 3.63: In a decree of divorce or annulment the court shall order a division of the estate of the parties in a manner that the court deems just and right, having due regard for the rights of each party and any children of the marriage.

The legislature expressly authorized the setting aside of property "to be administered," not divested, and "for the support of the child," but not for the support of a spouse. That was a codification of existing law. Section 3.63 does not expressly authorize the divestiture of separate realty, but section 14.05 does expressly authorize an interim administration of a spouse's property to assure the payment of child support. The reasonable conclusion is the legislature in enacting section 14.05 was codifying existing law.

Other evidence of legislative intent is derived from that part of section 3.63 which declares a divorce decree shall order "a division of the estate of the parties in a manner that the court deems just and right." The only "estate of the parties" is community property. Under former article 4638, we construed "the estate of the parties" to mean community property. *Reardon v. Reardon*, 359 S.W.2d 329 (Tex. 1962); *Hailey v. Hailey*, 160 Tex. 372, 331 S.W.2d 299 (1960); *Mansfield v. Mansfield*, 308 S.W.2d 80 (Tex. Civ. App. 1958, writ dism'd). The community estate may logically be the subject of "a division." The statute does not authorize a division of the "estates" of the parties. McKnight, *Commentary on Sec. 3.63*, 5 TEX. TECH L. REV. 338 (1974).

A constitutional problem also arises from the trial court's decree that the husband's separate property shall become the separate property of the divorced wife. The nature of property is fixed by the Texas Constitution, and not by what is "just and right." Culpability may, despite no-fault divorce, be a basis for the dissolution of a marriage, but it is no basis for a redefinition of property at variance with the Texas Constitution. Section 15, article XVI of the Texas Constitution declares that a wife's property, owned or claimed by her before marriage, and that acquired afterward by gift, devise or descent shall be the separate property of the wife.[3] By reason of legislation, the husband's property is classified the same way.[4] If one spouse's separate property may by a divorce decree be changed from the separate property of the one spouse into the separate property of the other, there is a type of separate property which is not embraced within the constitutional definition of the term. This question has never been confronted by this court, and as Professor McKnight has written: "Thus a constitutional issue that has never been raised needs resolution." McKnight, *Matrimonial Property*, 27 SW. L.J. 37, 38 (1973).

This court held in *Arnold v. Leonard*, 114 Tex. 535, 273 S.W. 799 (1925), and again in *Graham v. Franco*, 488 S.W.2d 390, 392 (Tex. 1972), that the constitutional definition of separate property was intended to be exclusive and that it may not be altered or enlarged by an act of the legislature. *See also*, *Gorman v. Gause*, 56 S.W.2d 855 (Tex. Com. App. 1933, holding approved); Huie, *The Texas Constitutional Definition of the Wife's Separate Property*, 35 TEX. L. REV. 1054, 1057-1058 (1957). This court has also held that the legislature cannot transform one type of constitutionally defined

---

[3] All property, both real and personal, of the wife, owned or claimed by her before marriage, and that acquired afterward by gift, devise or descent, shall be the separate property of the wife. . . .

[4] Section 5.01. Marital Property Characterized

(a) A spouse's separate property consists of:

(1) the property owned or claimed by the spouse before marriage;

(2) the property acquired by the spouse during marriage by gift, devise, or descent; and

(3) the recovery for personal injuries sustained by the spouse during marriage, except any recovery for loss of earning capacity during marriage.

(b) Community property consists of the property, other than separate property, acquired by either spouse during marriage.

property into another type of property. *Williams v. McKnight*, 402 S.W.2d 505 (Tex. 1966). We said in *Hilley v. Hilley*, 161 Tex. 569, 342 S.W.2d 565, 567-568 (1961):

> All marital property is thus either separate or community. If acquired before marriage by any method, or after marriage by gift, devise or descent, it is separate; otherwise, it is community. . . . Property purchased with separate funds is separate . . . and community property partitioned in the manner provided in Articles 4624a and 881a-23, becomes separate property.

There is another constitutional problem. The protection of one's right to own property is said to be one of the most important purposes of government. That right has been described as fundamental, natural, inherent, inalienable, not derived from the legislature and as preexisting even constitutions. *Pennsylvania Coal Co. v. Mahon*, 260 U.S. 393, 43 S.Ct. 158 (1922), 67 L.Ed. 322; 28 A.L.R. 1321 (1924); 16 AM. JUR. 2D, *Constitutional Law* § 362 (1964). Article I, section 19, of the Texas Constitution[5] explains that no citizen of this state shall be deprived of his property except by the due course of the law of the land. The due course that protects citizens requires not only procedural but also substantive due course. *See* Interpretive Commentary after section 19, art. I, TEX. CONST., p. 448, VERNON'S TEX. CONST. "One person's property may not be taken for the benefit of another private person without a justifying public purpose, even though compensation be paid." *Thompson v. Consolidated Gas Co.*, 300 U.S. 55, 80, 57 S.Ct. 364(1936), 376, 81 L.Ed. 510. This court quoted and relied upon that statement from *Thompson* in *Marrs v. Railroad Commission*, 142 Tex. 293, 177 S.W.2d 941, 949 (1944). There is no contention that the taking of Homer's separate property and its transfer to Virginia is justified by any benefit to the public welfare. The taking was not grounded upon the police power; consequently, the taking from Homer would not have been a constitutional act even if the legislature had expressly authorized the divestiture of one person's property and its vesting in another person.

The court of civil appeals, as stated above, held correctly that the trial court may set aside either spouse's separate real property, its income, rents, or revenues for the support of the minor children. CHIEF JUSTICE HEMPHILL, writing in *Rice v. Rice*, 21 Tex. 58, 71 (1858) said:

> The separate property may be divided in cases of necessity; or the whole, both separate and community, may be kept together as in this case, for the benefit of the children; but the decree must not divest either party of their title in the lands or slaves. It will be no breach of the statute to decree the use of property, for some period, to the use of the children, reserving the fee of the property in the husband to be enjoyed by him after the expiration of the trust estate for the children.

The basis for the holding was the duty of the parent to support his children whether from the community or the separate estate. The trial court judgment which was approved in *Rice* was that a receiver under bond would take charge of the property, collect the proceeds, and apply them to the support, education, and maintenance of two minor children. *Rice*, *supra*, 64.

Virginia Eggemeyer strongly relies upon *Hedtke v. Hedtke*, 112 Tex. 404, 248 S.W. 21 (1923), as supporting her contention that Homer Eggemeyer's separate property may be transferred to her. The husband and father in that divorce action owned one hundred acres as his separate property which was also the family homestead. It was the homestead interest not the land itself, that was granted the wife and two children of the marriage "during the balance of the natural life of the plaintiff (mother)." The

[5] No citizen of this State shall be deprived of life, liberty, property, privileges or immunities, or in any manner disfranchised, except by the due course of the law of the land. TEX. CONST. art. I, § 19.

lands were adjudged the property of the husband, and the decree was that "Possession of said land to revert to said defendant, J.G. Hedtke at the termination of said homestead rights as herein provided. . . ." In that case, the reason for the rule was also expressed; it was the husband's burden to support his family. The court was overbroad in its statement that the divorced husband owed family obligations to the divorced wife as distinguished from their children, but the court clearly recognized the limitations upon divesting title:

> For the purpose of doing equity, the court may award all the personal property to either spouse, and may subject the income, rents, or revenues of all real estate belonging to either or both of the spouses, to the support of either or both of them, or to the education and support of the children.

The case concerned homestead rights, that is, the use of the husband's separate property upon which homestead rights accrued during marriage. Homestead rights are different from the community or separate character of property. In *Hedtke*, homestead rights were properly subject to the decree as a part of the court's order for support of the children. We should not extend this precedent which upholds a right to a continued use of separate property as homestead to a right to divest title in separate property.

The dictum of *Hedtke v. Hedtke, supra*, that a divorce court may dispose of "any and all property of the parties, separate or community" in the exercise of a wide discretion which will be corrected only where there is an abuse of discretion is, in general, a sound rule. *See, Hailey v. Hailey*, 160 Tex. 372, 331 S.W.2d 299 (1960). It was not, however, essential to the decision. The trial court had decreed the homestead right during the life of the divorced wife, but provided further that "[p]ossession of said land to revert to said defendant J.G. Hedtke, at the termination of said homestead rights. . . ." Trial courts have a broad latitude in the division of the marital community property, but that discretion does not extend to a taking of the fee to the separate property of the one and its donation to the other. This is the construction which this court has previously given *Rice* and *Hedtke*. *See Cunningham v. Cunningham*, 120 Tex. 491, 40 S.W.2d 46 (1931).

The language and holdings of a number of courts of civil appeals are reviewed and distinguished in *Ramirez v. Ramirez*, 524 S.W.2d 767 (Tex. Civ. App. 1975, no writ). We agree with that decision. We disapprove the language of *Wilkerson v. Wilkerson*, 515 S.W.2d 52 (Tex. Civ. App. 1974, no writ), as well as the language and holdings of those decisions which have construed section 3.63 of the Family Code at variance with this opinion, *Baxla v. Baxla*, 522 S.W.2d 736 (Tex. Civ. App. 1975, no writ); *In re Marriage of Butler*, 543 S.W.2d 147 (Tex. Civ. App. 1976, writ dism'd); *Burns v. Burns*, 541 S.W.2d 280 (Tex. Civ. App. 1976, no writ); *Dietz v. Dietz*, 540 S.W.2d 418 (Tex. Civ. App. 1976, no writ); *Merrell v. Merrell*, 527 S.W.2d 250 (Tex. Civ. App. 1975, writ ref'd n.r.e.); *Harrison v. Harrison*, 495 S.W.2d 1 (Tex. Civ. App. 1973, no writ); *In re Marriage of McCurdy*, 489 S.W.2d 712 (Tex. Civ. App. 1973, writ dism'd); *Medearis v. Medearis*, 487 S.W.2d 198 (Tex. Civ. App. 1972, no writ). *See* McKnight, *Division of Texas Marital Property on Divorce*, 8 ST. MARY'S L.J. 413, 444-449 (1976).

The correct rule, as stated by the court of civil appeals in this case, is that a parent owes a duty to support his child and that duty can be enforced against the parent and his separate property. A receiver or trustee may be named to assure compliance with the order for child support. The fee to the separate property, however, may not be divested.

We affirm the judgment of the court of civil appeals reversing the trial court's divestiture of the husband's separate property and remanding the cause to the trial court to determine whether an interim arrangement for the support of the children should be made.

STEAKLEY, J., joined by GREENHILL, C. J., and REAVLEY and YARBROUGH, JJ., dissent.

STEAKLEY, JUSTICE, dissenting.

The dissenting opinion delivered May 18, 1977 is withdrawn, and the following is substituted therefor.

This case presents a narrow and easily articulable question: Does Section 3.63 of the Texas Family Code authorize the divestiture of title to a spouse's separate real property where such action is necessary to effect a "just and right" division of the marital property of divorcing spouses? In the instant case the Court of Civil Appeals held the trial court did not have such authority, citing *Ramirez v. Ramirez*, 524 S.W.2d 767 (Tex. Civ. App.—Corpus Christi 1975, no writ). *Eggemeyer v. Eggemeyer*, 535 S.W.2d 425 (Tex. Civ. App.—Austin 1976). A majority of this Court affirms that holding. I would reverse the judgment of the Court of Civil Appeals and affirm that of the trial court, the effect of which would be to divest Homer Eggemeyer of a one-third undivided interest in the family farm, an interest which was his separate property by virtue of a gift from his mother.

Section 3.63 of the Texas Family Code provides:

> In a decree of divorce or annulment the court shall order a division of the estate of the parties in a manner that the court deems just and right, having due regard for the rights of each party and any children of the marriage.

TEX. FAMILY CODE ANN. § 3.63 (1975). The predecessor statute repealed by the enactment of the Family Code was Article 4638. It provided:

> The court pronouncing a decree of divorce shall also decree and order a division of the estate of the parties in such a way as the court shall deem just and right, having due regard to the rights of each party and their children, if any. *Nothing herein shall be construed to compel either party to divest himself or herself of the title to real estate.* [Emphasis added.]

See Tex. Laws 1841, *An Act Concerning Divorce and Alimony* §§ 1-14, at 19-22, 2 H. GAMMEL, LAWS OF TEXAS 483-486 (1898). The italicized sentence in Article 4638, and in all its predecessor statutes, was not carried forward in Section 3.63. Notwithstanding, the majority here holds that Section 3.63 does not authorize the trial court to divest a divorcing spouse of his or her separate real property when ordering a division of the marital estates. *Accord, Ramirez v. Ramirez, supra. Contra, Wilkerson v. Wilkerson*, 515 S.W.2d 52 (Tex. Civ. App.—Tyler 1974, no writ). Established principles of statutory construction require the opposite result. Furthermore, such a result does not contravene either the United States or Texas Constitution.

I.

The majority construes the phrase "estate of the parties" to mean only the community property of the spouses. Such a construction, while perhaps grammatically sound, is contrary to well-established Texas law and practice. In *Hedtke v. Hedtke*, 112 Tex. 404, 248 S.W. 21 (1923), this Court iterated the parameters of a trial court's discretion in dividing the property of divorcing spouses. Construing the language of Article 4638, the Court wrote:

> The estate subject to division, under the statute, include(s) all property of the parties whether community property or separate property. The meaning of the statute is not different from what it would have been had the word "property" been substituted in its phraseology for the word "estate." . . .

Id. at 22. The construction adopted by the Court in *Hedtke* has been accepted and adhered to ever since. *See, e.g.*, *In re Marriage of Jackson*, 506 S.W.2d 261 (Tex. Civ. App.—Amarillo 1974, writ dism'd); *Dorfman v. Dorfman*, 457 S.W.2d 417 (Tex. Civ. App.—Texarkana 1970, no writ); *Earnest v. Earnest*, 223 S.W.2d 681 (Tex. Civ. App.—Amarillo 1949, no writ); Smith, *Family Law*, 26 Sw.L.J. 51, 55 & n.30 (1972). The phrase "estate of the parties" was carried forward into Section 3.63. In construing a statute we must assume the Legislature was aware of prior judicial interpretations, and reenactment of a statute or portion thereof without a change in its language indicates approval of such prior judicial interpretations. *Koy v. Schneider*, 110 Tex. 369, 221 S.W. 880 (1920); *Gabbert v. City of Brownwood*, 176 S.W.2d 344 (Tex. Civ. App.—Eastland 1943, writ ref'd); 2A SUTHERLAND, STATUTES AND STATUTORY CONSTRUCTION § 45.12 (4th ed. 1973). Thus, I would construe "estate of the parties," in accordance with established Texas law, to mean all property of the parties, whether real or personal, separate or community.

I respectfully suggest the majority's construction of "estate of the parties" finds no support in the cited authorities, *Reardon v. Reardon*, 163 Tex. 605, 359 S.W.2d 329 (1962); *Hailey v. Hailey*, 160 Tex. 372, 331 S.W.2d 299 (1960), and *Mansfield v. Mansfield*, 308 S.W.2d 80 (Tex. Civ. App.—El Paso 1958, writ dism'd). None of these cases contain language purporting to construe the disputed phrase. In *Reardon* the Court of Civil Appeals, uncertain of the effect of a prior decision of this Court, certified a question to the Court. The only issue was whether or not the proviso of Article 4638 proscribing the divestiture of title to real estate was applicable to community property. This Court reiterated its holding in *Hailey, supra*, and held that the prohibition against the divestiture of title did not apply to community real property. No other issue was before the Court, and no other language of the statute was involved. Specifically, the Court did not expressly or impliedly ascribe a meaning to the phrase "estate of the parties." In *Hailey, supra*, the spouses owned two lots as community property. The trial court granted the parties a divorce and awarded one lot to each spouse. The Court of Civil Appeals reversed the trial court on the ground that it was error to award one lot to each party. This Court reinstated the trial court judgment, holding that the divestiture of a spouse's interest in community real property was not prohibited by the proviso of Art. 4638. Again, the opinion of this Court contained no construction of the phrase "estate of the parties." *Mansfield v. Mansfield, supra*, did not reach this Court, but it, too, involved the question of whether a trial court's division of community real property ran afoul of the statutory prohibition against divestiture of title to real estate. The Court of Civil Appeals there held that such divestiture was not proscribed by the statute. It did not purport to construe "the estate of the parties." The majority also cites an article by Professor McKnight as supporting its construction of "estate of the parties." *See*, McKnight, *Commentary on Sec. 3.63*, 5 TEX. TECH. L. REV. 338 (1974). McKnight does suggest that the majority's construction is logically supportable, but he also *notes* that the majority construction "would . . . *depart from long usage* with respect to discretionary division of separate personalty." *Id.* [Emphasis added.]

Reardon, Hailey, and *Mansfield, supra*, are important to the resolution of this case for another reason, however. Those cases establish beyond question that the Art. 4638 prohibition against the divestiture of title to real estate applied only to separate realty. The reasoning of this Court in *Hailey*, reaffirmed in *Reardon*, was that a division of community realty does not involve a divestiture of title but instead effects a partition of real property between persons already possessing title thereto.

The pronouncements of this Court in *Hedtke* and *Hailey* established the parameters of Article 4638 within which a trial court could exercise its discretion in dividing the property of a divorcing husband and wife. In *Hedtke* this Court construed "estate of the parties" to mean all property of the parties, community and separate. In *Hailey* we held the prohibition against divestiture of title to real estate applied only to the separate real property of the spouses and did not prohibit the division of community realty upon divorce. At the time of the enactment of Section 3.63 the law was clear—a court dividing the marital properties was authorized to award community realty, community personalty, and separate personalty to either spouse upon a determination that such was "just and right."[1] It could not, however, award one spouse's separate realty to the other because the last sentence of Article 4638 prohibited it.

There is no difference in the constitutional classification of separate real and separate personal property. It is therefore unmistakably implicit in the decisions of this Court and the various courts of civil appeals that absent the statutory prohibition against the divestiture of title to real estate, an award of separate realty would also be within the authority of the trial court in ordering a division of the estate of the divorcing parties. It was precisely this prohibition that was removed by the Legislature in the enactment of Section 3.63. Ordinarily, the fact "that significant words are omitted from the reenactment or amendment of a statute imports a conclusive presumption that the Legislature intended to exclude the object theretofore accomplished by the abandoned words." *Gateley v. Humphrey*, 151 Tex. 588, 254 S.W.2d 98 (1952). Stated differently, there is a presumption that if a change occurs in legislative language, a change was intended in legislative result. 2A SUTHERLAND, STATUTES AND STATUTORY CONSTRUCTION § 45.12 (4th ed. 1973). Where the language of a statute is plain and clear, it must be given effect as written. *Railroad Commission of Texas v. Miller*, 434 S.W.2d 670 (Tex. 1968); *Simmons v. Arnim*, 110 Tex. 309, 220 S.W. 66 (1920). I would give effect to the language of Section 3.63 and hold that a trial court adjudicating a divorce has the authority to divide all the marital properties, whether real or personal, separate or community.

In construing the statute, the majority relies on a statement by Professor McKnight that the legislative commentary which accompanied the statute stated: "This is a codification of present law." *See*, McKnight, *Commentary on Sec. 3.63*, 5 TEX. TECH. L. REV. 337 (1974). From this fact the majority concludes the Legislature believed it was making no change in the law by enacting Section 3.63. Clearly the courts recognized the Legislature had in fact changed the law. *See, e.g., Wilkerson, supra*; *Baxla v. Baxla*, 522 S.W.2d 736 (Tex. Civ. App.—Dallas 1975, no writ). The action of the courts in divesting title to separate realty made known to the Legislature the effect of its action. Furthermore, commentators were quick to point out the omission. *See, e.g.*, Smith, *Family Law*, 26 SW.L.J. 51, 55 (1972). The Legislature has met in regular session four times since the effective date of Section 3.63, and it has considered legislation to restore the prohibition against the divestiture of title to separate realty.[2] Yet it has chosen not to restore the statutory prohibition.

---

[1] *See also* Fitts v. Fitts, 14 Tex. 443 (1855); Rice v. Rice, 21 Tex. 58 (1858); Simons v. Simons, 23 Tex. 344 (1859); Cooper v. Cooper, 513 S.W.2d 229 (Tex.Civ.App.—Houston [1st Dist.] 1974, no writ); Dorfman v. Dorfman, 457 S.W.2d 417 (Tex.Civ.App.—Texarkana 1970, no writ); Keene v. Keene, 445 S.W.2d 624 (Tex.Civ.App.—Dallas 1969, writ dism'd); Roye v. Roye, 404 S.W.2d 92 (Tex.Civ.App.—Tyler 1966, no writ); Allen v. Allen, 284 S.W.2d 774 (Tex.Civ.App.—Galveston 1955, writ dism'd); Rylee v. Rylee, 244 S.W.2d 717 (Tex.Civ.App.—El Paso 1951, no writ); Donias v. Quintero, 227 S.W.2d 252 (Tex.Civ.App.—El Paso 1949, no writ); Jones v. Jones, 211 S.W.2d 269 (Tex.Civ.App.—El Paso 1944, no writ); Puckett v. Puckett, 205 S.W.2d 124 (Tex.Civ.App.—Texarkana 1947, no writ); Tims v. Tims, 201 S.W.2d 865 (Tex.Civ.App.—Amarillo 1947, writ dism'd); Smith v. Smith, 187 S.W.2d 116 (Tex.Civ.App.—Fort Worth 1945, no writ); Lewis v. Lewis, 179 S.W.2d 594 (Tex.Civ.App.—Fort Worth 1944, no writ); Hamm v. Hamm, 159 S.W.2d 183 (Tex.Civ.App.—Fort Worth 1942, no writ).

[2] *See* 63rd Legislature, House Bill No. 102; 65th Legislature, House Bill No. 524.

Section 14.05(a) of the Family Code is said to provide additional evidence that the Legislature intended to keep the law unchanged. I respectfully submit that Section 14.05 does not provide support for the majority's result and, indeed, is irrelevant to the question now before this Court. Section 14.05, entitled "Support of Child," is concerned with what provision may be made for the support of children of the marriage. It provides that "the court may order a parent obligated to support a child to set aside property to be administered for the support of the child in the manner and by the persons specified by the court in the decree." TEX. FAMILY CODE ANN. § 14.05(a) (1970). The majority points out that Section 14.05 does not authorize the divestiture of title to property in order to provide support for a child, nor does it provide for the support of the wife. The question before us is unrelated to the statutory obligations of support. We are here concerned only with what authority a trial court may exercise in dividing the property of the spouses upon divorce. Questions having to do with methods of enforcing the support obligations of a parent are totally independent of and apart from questions concerning the authority of a trial court to divide the marital properties between divorcing spouses "in a manner that the court deems just and right."

II.

The majority opinion concludes that its construction of Section 3.63 is mandated by the United States and Texas Constitutions. The argument is two-pronged. First, according to the majority, the constitutional definition of separate property is exclusive and does not permit the "creation" of separate property via the judicial act of divesting the separate property of one spouse and awarding it to the other. Secondly, the majority concludes that the taking of one spouse's separate property and its transfer to the other would violate the due process mandate that one person's property may not be taken for the benefit of another private person without a justifying public purpose.

The original predecessor statute to Section 3.63 was enacted in 1841 and was not materially amended until the enactment in 1969 of Section 3.63 of the Texas Family Code. The pertinent portion of Article 16, Section 15 of the Texas Constitution has had a similarly long life and has not been amended in any relevant particular. That section now provides, in pertinent part:

> Sec. 15. All property, both real and personal, of the wife, owned or claimed by her before marriage, and that acquired afterward by gift, devise or descent, shall be the separate property of the wife; *and laws shall be passed more clearly defining the rights of the wife, in relation as well to her separate property as that held in common with her husband*; . . . (Italics added).

The property of the husband is similarly characterized by statute. *See* TEX. FAMILY CODE ANN. § 5.01 (1975). The original predecessor of Article 16, Section 15 of the present Constitution was Article 7, Section 19 of the Texas Constitution of 1845. It was then provided in identical language:

> Sec. 19. All property both real and personal of the wife, owned or claimed by her before marriage, and that acquired afterwards by gift, devise, or descent, shall be her separate property; and laws shall be passed more clearly defining the rights of the wife, in relation as well to her separate property, as that held in common with her husband. . . .

Thus, the Legislature, in passing the original statute of 1841 and in re-enacting the statute through the years, culminating in the enactment of Section 3.63 of the Family Code in 1969, has acted pursuant to the constitutional mandate to pass laws "more clearly defining the rights of the [marital partners], in relation as well to [their] separate property, as that held in common with [the other spouse]."

The authority granted a trial court by Section 3.63 does not authorize the creation of a type of separate property inconsistent with the constitutional definition of the term. *See* Article 16, Section 15, *supra*. As noted above, the majority asserts that where a trial court divests one spouse's title to separate property and awards it to the other spouse as his or her separate property, the property cannot constitutionally become the separate property of the second spouse because it is neither "owned or claimed . . . before marriage" nor "acquired afterwards by gift, devise, or descent." This argument fails for two reasons. First, the property division directed by Section 3.63 occurs after the divorce of the parties, and Article 16, Section 15, providing for the initial characterization of property, does not control this situation. Secondly, the constitutional definition of separate property is not exclusive. There are numerous recognized classifications of separate property that consist of property "not owned or claimed" before marriage or "acquired afterward by gift, devise or descent." This is true, for example, of mutations of separate property and of post-marriage increases in the value of separately held land and personalty. *See Stringfellow v. Sorrells*, 82 Tex. 277, 18 S.W. 689 (1891); *Love v. Robertson*, 7 Tex. 6 (1851); *Lessing v. Russek*, 234 S.W.2d 891 (Tex. Civ. App.—Austin 1950, writ ref'd n.r.e.); *Evans v. Purinton*, 12 Tex. Civ. App. 158, 34 S.W. 350 (Tex. Civ. App.—1896, writ ref'd). *See also* McKnight, *supra*, at 337. Similarly, personal injury awards are the separate property of the injured spouse under the statutory mandate that a spouse's separate property includes the "recovery for personal injuries sustained by the spouse during marriage, except any recovery for loss of earning capacity during marriage." TEX. FAMILY CODE ANN. § 5.01(a) (1975).

In support of its holding that the constitutional definition of separate property was intended to be exclusive and that it may not be altered or enlarged by an act of the Legislature, the majority cites *Arnold v. Leonard*, 114 Tex. 535, 273 S.W. 799 (1925), and *Graham v. Franco*, 488 S.W.2d 390 (Tex. 1972). In *Arnold* this Court found to be unconstitutional a statute which provided that income from a wife's separate property was the separate property of the wife. After a lengthy review of relevant authority, this Court concluded the statute there in question impermissibly attempted to expand the constitutional definition of the wife's separate property, a definition the court held to be exclusive. However, this Court's most recent consideration of the constitutional definition of separate property suggests a more flexible approach. In *Graham v. Franco, supra*, the Court considered the constitutionality of a statute providing that personal injury recoveries were the separate property of the injured spouse. Discussing *Arnold v. Leonard, supra*, this Court recognized that the rationale of *Arnold* was "one of implied exclusion, i.e., if property was acquired during marriage by any other means than gift, devise, or descent, it was and is necessarily community." *Graham v. Franco, supra* at 392. Continuing, the Court wrote:

> A much later case of this Court reverted to a test more akin to that prevailing under the Spanish and Mexican law, and several early opinions of this Court, dealing with community property. It applied an affirmative test; i.e., that property is community which is acquired by the work, efforts or labor of the spouses or their agents, as income from their property, or as a gift to the community. Such property, acquired by the joint efforts of the spouses, was regarded as acquired by "onerous title" and belonged to the community. *Norris v. Vaughan*, 152 Tex. 491, 260 S.W.2d 676 (1953); *DeBlane v. Lynch*, 23 Tex. 25 (1859); *Smith v. Strahan*, 16 Tex. 314 (1856); *Epperson v. Jones*, 65 Tex. 425 (1886); DE FUNIAK, PRINCIPLES OF COMMUNITY PROPERTY (1971) § 62; MOYNIHAN, COMMUNITY PROPERTY, 2 AMERICAN LAW OF PROPERTY (1952) § 7.16.

Under this reasoning, it is clear that the personal injuries to the wife are not "acquired" by the efforts of the spouses and would not belong to the community. Thus in *Norris v. Vaughan, supra*, Justice Smith wrote for this Court that:

> The principle which lies at the foundation of the whole system of community property is, that whatever is acquired by the joint efforts of the husband and wife, shall be their common property.

Id. at 392-393. Thus, rather than emphasizing the exclusivity of the constitutional definition of separate property, *Graham* supports a more flexible interpretation of the provision, one recognizing that such flexibility is necessary in order to solve problems that occasionally arise in the application of existing principles of marital property law. *See* Huie, *The Texas Constitutional Definition of the Wife's Separate Property*, 35 TEX. L. REV. 1054, 1061 (1957).

The second constitutional ground upon which the majority relies is the absence of due process of law, or, as the Texas Constitution refers to it, "due course of the law of the land." TEX. CONST. art. I, § 19. The majority holds that a trial court's divestiture of title to one spouse's separate property and subsequent investiture of title in the other spouse would violate substantive due course, i.e., would be a taking of private property unjustified by a resultant benefit to the public welfare. The majority relies on the opinion of this Court in *Marrs v. Railroad Commission*, 142 Tex. 293, 177 S.W.2d 941 (1944), as supporting its holding. In *Marrs* it was alleged that, by virtue of an order of the Railroad Commission setting an arbitrarily low allowable in one section of an oil field, the plaintiffs' land was being drained of oil and gas. This Court upheld the plaintiffs' claim that the Commission's order resulted in an unconstitutional taking of private property and the gift of it to another private person without a justifying public purpose. *See Thompson v. Consolidated Gas Co.*, 300 U.S. 55, 57 S.Ct. 364 (1936), 81 L.Ed. 510. The only "public purpose" possibly served by the Commission's order was the conservation of valuable natural resources, but the evidence in *Marrs* did not indicate the order in question was necessary to accomplish that purpose.

The case of a statutory scheme for the division of property upon divorce, a scheme which authorizes a court to award one spouse's separate property to the other where necessary to effect a "just and right" property division, presents uniquely different questions. The special relationship between the state and the institution of marriage has often been recognized. *See, e.g., Williams v. North Carolina*, 317 U.S. 287, 63 S.Ct. 207 (1942), 87 L.Ed. 279. The nature and effect of this special relationship have been described as follows:

> Marriage, as creating the most important relation in life, as having more to do with the morals and civilization of a people than any other institution, has always been subject to the control of the legislature. That body prescribes the age at which parties may contract to marry, the procedure or form essential to constitute marriage, the duties and obligations it creates, *its effects upon the property rights of both, present and prospective*, and the acts which may constitute grounds for its dissolution. [Emphasis added.]

Maynard v. Hill, 125 U.S. 190, 205, 8 S.Ct. 723 (1887), 726, 31 L.Ed. 654. *See also Loving v. Virginia*, 388 U.S. 1, 87 S.Ct. 1817 (1966), 18 L.Ed.2d 1010 ("a social relation subject to the State's police power"); *Haddock v. Haddock*, 201 U.S. 562, 26 S.Ct. 525 (1906), 50 L.Ed. 867; *Andrews v. Andrews*, 188 U.S. 14, 23 S.Ct. 237 (1902), 47 L.Ed. 366; *Baker's Executors v. Kilgore*, 145 U.S. 487, 12 S.Ct. 943 (1891), 36 L.Ed. 786; 1 SIMPKINS, TEXAS FAMILY LAW § 1:1 (1975); 55 C.J.S. MARRIAGE § 2 (1948).[3] The broad regulatory powers of the state over the institution of marriage clearly extend to the division of property upon divorce. Furthermore, it is within the power of the

[3] One writer notes that marriage is a civil institution in reference to which "public interests overshadow private—one which public policy holds specially in the hands of the law for the public good, and over which the law presides in a manner not known in other departments." 1 BISHOP ON MARRIAGE, DIVORCE AND SEPARATION § 5 (1891).

Legislature to provide, as it impliedly has, that upon divorce one spouse's separate property can be awarded to the other where necessary to effect a "just and right" property division. Because of the state's pervasive interest in and control over the marriage relation, partners entering a marriage do so subject to the present and future laws of Texas governing the relationship. Section 3.63 of the Texas Family Code is such a law, and the action of a trial court dividing the marital property, both separate and community, pursuant to the statutory mandate, would not deny either party due course of the law of the land.

There is a public purpose served by the statutory investiture of trial courts with the broad power to divide the divorcing spouses' separate and community real and personal property as they deem "just and right." That purpose is to insure that one spouse does not, through artful management of the marital property, accumulate a separate estate of substantial value at the expense of the separate estate of the other spouse or at the expense of the community and then, upon divorce, retain that separate estate and relegate the other spouse to his or her separate estate and to the potentially depleted community estate. By prohibiting the invasion of a spouse's separate property where necessary to effect a just and right property division, the majority sanctions and promotes the societal disharmony resulting from inequitable property settlements upon divorce. In my view the Legislature sought to avoid this potential injustice by granting the trial court broad discretion in dividing the property of the marriage. The holding of the majority narrowly circumscribes that discretion and, in my opinion, is neither mandated by the Constitution nor comports with the statutory provisions.

As noted above, the constitutional rule relied upon by the majority mandates that one person's property may not be taken for the benefit of another private person without a justifying public purpose, even though compensation be paid. *See Marrs v. Railroad Commission, supra.* If this rule applies in the instant case to prohibit the divestiture of one spouse's title to separate property in order to equitably divide the property of the marriage, I suggest that the enforcement of a personal injury judgment is similarly prohibited. Clearly such a judgment takes one private person's property for the benefit of another, and if there is no "justifying public purpose" in the instant case, there is none in the hypothetical personal injury case. It seems to me there is a "justifying public purpose" in both situations. In a personal injury case, the state has an interest in seeing the injured party compensated for his negligently inflicted injury. In the absence of such compensation, the injured party might be unable to recover financially or spiritually from the accident. Additionally, it is equitable to provide that the negligent party should make reparation to those injured by his negligence. In the case of property division upon divorce, the state has an interest in seeing the property of the marriage equitably divided so as to avoid the imposition of undue financial hardship upon one spouse. Equitable property divisions minimize the deleterious financial and emotional effects of divorce and, therefore, minimize interpersonal conflict. Furthermore, it is just to allow a trial court broad discretion in dividing the marital property in order that each spouse might participate, to the extent deserved, in the economic gains of the marriage.

III.

To reiterate, I would hold that Section 3.63 authorizes a trial court to divest title to one spouse's separate real property and to award that property to the other spouse as his or her separate property. The Constitution does not prohibit such statutory authorization, and the clear language of the statute demands such an interpretation. I recognize that as a general rule separate property, whether real or personal, should be restored to its owner and the community property of the marriage divided as seems just and right. *Fitts v. Fitts*, 14 Tex. 443 (1855); *Fuhrman v. Fuhrman*, 302 S.W.2d 205 (Tex. Civ. App.—El Paso 1957, writ dism'd). As this Court wrote in *McElreath v. McElreath*, 162 Tex. 190, 345 S.W.2d 722 (1961), each spouse primarily "must look to the community property for her

[his] share of the material gains incident to an ill-starred marriage." *Id.* at 724. Furthermore, the conceptual basis of community property is the notion that spouses should share as equal partners in the benefits and burdens of the marriage. When the marriage is terminated, the primary fund to be divided is that comprised of assets acquired by the spouses as a community. The invasion of the separate property of one spouse for the benefit of the other can be justified only in exceptional circumstances. This is illustrated by the action of the Court of Civil Appeals in *Cooper v. Cooper*, 513 S.W.2d 229 (Tex. Civ. App.—Houston [1st Dist.] 1974, no writ).

I would reverse the judgment of the Court of Civil Appeals and affirm that of the trial court.

GREENHILL, C. J., and REAVLEY and YARBROUGH, JJ., join in this dissent.

Notes, Comments & Questions

1. Subsequent to the *Eggemeyer* decision, whether the trial court possessed the power, upon proper findings, to divest a spouse of title to separate personalty as part of the division of marital property upon divorce was not clear. A number of decisions from the courts of civil appeals reasoned that the language in *Eggemeyer* did not encompass separate personal property and that the holding in *Eggemeyer* was limited to separate real estate, the only property before the court in that decision. Representative of such decisions are *Muns v. Muns*, 567 S.W.2d 563 (Tex. Civ. App.—Dallas 1978, no writ), *York v. York*, 579 S.W.2d 24 (Tex. Civ. App.—Beaumont 1979, no writ), *In re Marriage of Trujillo*, 580 S.W.2d 873 (Tex. Civ. App.—Texarkana 1979, no writ); and *Campbell v. Campbell*, 586 S.W.2d 162, 168 (Tex. Civ. App.—Fort Worth 1979), *writ of error granted, opinion withdrawn*, 613 S.W.2d 236 (Tex. 1980).

2. The Supreme Court granted a writ of error in the aforementioned *Campbell* case. In an opinion reported in 23 Tex. Sup. Ct. J. 391 (1980), the court applied the doctrine of *stare decisis* to hold that the *Eggemeyer* decision applied to separate personalty as well as to separate realty. However, while the case still was pending in the Supreme Court, the parties settled the case. In an order reported in 613 S.W.2d 236 (Tex. 1980), the Supreme Court withdrew its opinion in the case which had not been published in the Southwestern Reporter. This question also has been addressed in *Cameron v. Cameron*, 641 S.W.2d210 (Tex. 1982).

3. Throughout this course, the rule that a divorce court cannot divest a spouse of separate property has been reiterated. This rule has almost taken on a mantra like quality in marital property practice. Nonetheless, the arguments made by JUSTICE STEAKLEY in his dissent in *Cameron* are worthy of contemplation. Review and outline his primary points of argument. Keep in mind that *Cameron* was a 5/4 decision.

McLEMORE
v.
McLEMORE
641 S.W.2d 395
(Tex. App.—Tyler 1982, no writ)

MCKAY, JUSTICE.

This appeal is from a division of property in a divorce. Appellant, Vernon Earl McLemore, appeals the award to Nancy Carol McLemore, appellee, of all title to their house and lot in San Augustine. He contends that since the deed of gift was made to him and appellee jointly, he was thereby vested, as a matter of law, with an undivided one-half interest in said realty as his separate property. He further contends that the trial court was prohibited, as a matter of law, from divesting him of title to this alleged separate property realty, and that such action was an abuse of the court's discretionary power under § 3.63 of the Texas Family Code.

We reverse and remand in part and affirm in part.

Appellant and appellee were married in 1962. Appellee filed this divorce action in 1980, and appellant filed a cross-action for divorce. Two children were born of this marriage.

The home in which the parties resided during the last several years of their marriage was purchased in 1964 by appellant's parents, Ray and Opal McLemore, and the parties moved into this home shortly thereafter. Said property was conveyed by appellant's parents to both parties as grantees in 1974. Contrary to the usual practice, the deed was neither introduced into evidence as an exhibit, nor read into the record. However, the testimony from all parties to the deed is undisputed that it named both appellant and appellee as grantees. Although appellee disputed the testimony of appellant and his parents that the conveyance was a gift rather than a sale, the trial court, sitting without a jury, found that the conveyance was a gift to the community estate of appellant and appellee.

In its divorce decree, the trial court awarded the house and lot to appellee as her sole and separate property and divested appellant of all right, title, and interest in and to such property, after finding that such division was just and right, having due regard for the rights of each party and of the children. Appellant duly filed a motion for new trial contesting this award on the ground that the house was separate property, having come into the marriage by gift, and that an award to appellee which divested appellant of title to this property violated the provisions of the constitution of the State of Texas. This motion was overruled by the trial court.

Appellant next requested that the trial court make and file its findings of fact and conclusions of law. The court did so, and the findings of fact pertinent to this appeal were as follows: (10) that Ray McLemore and Opal McLemore purchased the home in which the parties live in San Augustine, Texas, in October of 1964, and that no consideration was ever paid by Vernon McLemore or Nancy McLemore for said home; (11) that Ray McLemore and Opal McLemore made a gift of the property in San Augustine, Texas, to Vernon McLemore and Nancy McLemore in January of 1974; (12) that Ray McLemore and Opal McLemore intended to make a gift of the home to Vernon McLemore and Nancy McLemore jointly as a part of their community property and not to Vernon McLemore only.

The conclusions of law pertinent to this appeal were: (6) Ray McLemore and Opal McLemore did not make a gift of the home and lot located in San Augustine County, Texas, to Vernon McLemore individually, but to the community of Vernon McLemore and Nancy McLemore; (7) Ray McLemore and Opal McLemore intended to make a gift of the house and lot in San Augustine, Texas, to the community of Vernon McLemore and Nancy McLemore as reflected by the deed of January 1974.

Appellant brings three points of error. In point two, he contends the trial court erred in finding and concluding that Ray and Opal McLemore made a gift of the house and lot to the community of Vernon and Nancy McLemore. We sustain this point.

The law in Texas has long been settled that an attempted gift by a third party to the community estate vests each marital partner with a one-half undivided interest in the subject matter of the gift as his or her separate property. In the case of *Bradley v. Love*, 60 Tex. 472 (Tex. 1883), the facts were almost identical to those of the case at bar. There the wife's father made a gift of realty to the husband and wife jointly. The court concluded that such a conveyance would result in each marital partner having an undivided half interest in the land as separate property. *Id.* at 477-8.

Two years later, the court was again presented with a gift of realty from the wife's parents to the husband and wife jointly in *Rogan v. Williams & Co.*, 63 Tex. 123 (Tex. 1885). Again, the court concluded that the legal result of the conveyance was to vest husband and wife with one-half undivided interests as tenants in common, and that such interests were the separate property of each spouse. *Id.* at 129.

This doctrine has been followed by Texas courts through the years (*see King v. Summerville*, 80 S.W. 1050 (Tex. Civ. App. 1904) *aff'd*, 98 Tex. 332, 83 S.W. 680 (Tex. 1904)), and was recently reaffirmed in *White v. White*, 590 S.W.2d 587 (Tex. Civ. App.—Houston [1st Dist.] 1979, no writ). In *White* the wife's aunt conveyed certain realty to husband and wife jointly by deed of gift. The court, *citing Rogan v. Williams, supra*, held that such a gift vested in each grantee an undivided half interest as his or her separate property. *Id.* at 588.

Appellant's contention finds additional support in § 5.01, TEX. FAM. CODE ANN. (Vernon 1975), which provides that property acquired by a spouse during marriage by gift, devise, or descent is a spouse's separate property. The trial court found that the house and lot in the case at bar were acquired by gift. Therefore, the house and lot were separate property as a matter of law. Appellant's second point of error must therefore be sustained.

In his first and third points of error, appellant contends that the trial court erred as a matter of law and abused its discretion in awarding appellee the house and lot in San Augustine since appellant, as a matter of law, was vested with an undivided one-half interest in said realty as his separate property. We sustain these points.

Since appellant was vested with a one-half undivided interest in said realty as his separate property, the action of the trial court in divesting appellant of this interest and awarding it to appellee cannot stand under *Eggemeyer v. Eggemeyer*, 554 S.W.2d 137 (Tex. 1977). It is well established that divorce courts in this state may exercise wide discretion in making a division of the parties' property, and such discretion should not be disturbed on appeal unless a clear abuse thereof is shown. *Bell v. Bell*, 513 S.W.2d 20, 22 (Tex. 1974); *Jensen v. Jensen*, 629 S.W.2d 222, 225 (Tex. App.—Tyler 1982, no writ); *Musick v. Musick*, 590 S.W.2d 582, 585 (Tex. Civ. App.—Tyler 1979, no writ). However, that discretion does not extend to taking the fee to the separate real property of one spouse and awarding it to the other. *Eggemeyer, supra* at 142; *White, supra* at 589.

In *Jensen, supra* at 225, this court stated that although an appellant correctly complains that the trial court mischaracterized community property as separate property, to obtain reversal appellant must go further and show the trial court would have made a different division if the property had been properly characterized, *citing Smith v. Smith*, 620 S.W.2d 619, 625 (Tex. Civ. App.—Dallas 1981, no writ). This court further said that any other rule would presume harm from a trial court's error of law, and would contravene Rule 434, TEX. R. CIV. P. We adhere to these cases as a correct statement of the law in any case of mischaracterization of property by the trial court *other than* a case where separate realty is mischaracterized as community, and then taken from one spouse and awarded to the other. This is because the supreme court has stated in *Eggemeyer, supra*, that where the trial court takes the fee to separate realty of one spouse and donates it to the other, it is prima facie an abuse of discretion; or, stated another way, such action lies entirely outside the trial court's discretion. We note also that even the application of the above test would require reversal in the instant case. Had the trial court correctly characterized the house and lot as separate property, it obviously would have made a different division of the property. It certainly would not have taken appellant's interest and awarded it to appellee in direct contravention of the rule in *Eggemeyer*, *supra*.

A court of civil appeals may not render a property division but must remand the case to the trial court for proper division. *McKnight v. McKnight*, 543 S.W.2d 863, 866-8 (Tex. 1976).

Accordingly, that part of the judgment dividing the property of the parties is reversed and remanded for further proceedings. We affirm the judgment in all other respects.

Notes, Comments & Questions

1. This case presents an issue that is not atypical—gifts to spouses. This problem can arise with wedding gifts, the first gifts received by a couple, and can continue throughout the marriage. Very often future bad feelings, not to mention attorneys' fees, can be saved by an up-front understanding of gift implications.

2. What do you think about the trial court's "gift to the community" conclusion of law?

3. This case exemplifies the automatic reversal that ensues upon mischaracterization followed by divestiture.

4. Currently, is there a means by which the home in *McLemore* could be converted to community property?

5. For a case holding that an error in characterizing community property as separate property is not in itself reversible error, unless it results in an inequality in the division of property that constitutes an abuse of the trial court's discretion, *see Mundy v. Mundy*, 653 S.W.2d 954 (Tex. Civ. App.—Dallas 1983).

D. Quasi-Community Property and the Just and Right Division

In rendering a just and right division, the only error that a trial court can make that will guarantee reversal upon appeal is the divestiture of separate property. However, there are other errors that can increase an Appellant's chances for reversing a divorce court's division of property. For example, if quasi-community property is not properly characterized, such may provide a basis for reversal. Quasi-community property is that property acquired during marriage but acquired outside the state of Texas that would be considered community property if it had been acquired in Texas. The longstanding common law relating to quasi-community property upon divorce has been codified. In codifying the treatment of quasi community property upon divorce, the legislature has recognized additional constraints upon a trial court's division, primarily with regard to how certain assets must be characterized and treated. Specifically, TEX. FAM CODE § 7.002, Division and Disposition of Certain Property Under Special Circumstances, in pertinent part[1] provides:

> (a) In addition to the division of the estate of the parties required by Section 7.001, in a decree of divorce or annulment the court shall order a division of the following real and personal property, wherever situated, in a manner that the court deems just and right, having due regard for the rights of each party and any children of the marriage:
>
> (1) property that was acquired by either spouse while domiciled in another state and that would have been community property if the spouse who acquired the property had been domiciled in this state at the time of the acquisition; or
>
> (2) property that was acquired by either spouse in exchange for real or personal property and that would have been community property if the spouse who acquired the property so exchanged had been domiciled in this state at the time of its acquisition.
>
> (b) In a decree of divorce or annulment, the court shall award to a spouse the following real and personal property, wherever situated, as the separate property of the spouse:
>
> (1) property that was acquired by the spouse while domiciled in another state and that would have been the spouse's separate property if the spouse had been domiciled in this state at the time of acquisition; or
>
> (2) property that was acquired by the spouse in exchange for real or personal property and that would have been the spouse's separate property if the spouse had been domiciled in this state at the time of acquisition.

Cameron v. Cameron, 641 S.W.2d 210 (Tex. 1982) was tried prior to the codification of the quasi-community statutes. Nevertheless, after a lengthy analysis of the *Eggemeyer* bar against divestiture and its application to separate personalty, the Texas Supreme Court's decision rests on the proper treatment of quasi-community property. *Cameron* is followed by *Estate of Hanau v. Hanau*, 730 S.W.2d 663 (Tex. 1987) which is not a divorce case. Nevertheless, the Texas Supreme Court's opinion in *Hanau* distinguishes the treatment of quasi-community property upon death from treatment upon divorce and thus seemed appropriate and necessarily included.

---

[1] TEX. FAM. CODE § 7.002(c) which is not quoted above, requires a trial court to confirm, in a decree of divorce or annulment, certain properties as separate property of a spouse if partitioned or exchanged by the spouses in a written agreement.

CAMERON
v.
CAMERON
641 S.W.2d 210
(Tex. 1982)

POPE, JUSTICE.

The questions presented concern the trial court's division of military retirement pay and United States Savings Bonds between divorcing spouses in Texas. The property was acquired in states that do not have a community property system. The trial court awarded the wife thirty-five percent of the gross military retirement funds received in the future by the divorced husband and fifty percent of the United States Savings Bonds. Considerable other property was divided about which there is no dispute. The court of civil appeals reversed the judgment in part and held that the retirement pay and savings bonds, acquired by the spouses in a common law property state, were the husband's separate property and, thus, not subject to division. 608 S.W.2d 748. We reverse the judgment of the court of civil appeals with respect to the military retirement pay; we reverse the judgment of the court of civil appeals and affirm the trial court's judgment dividing the savings bonds.

Paul Cameron joined the United States Air Force on June 22, 1954. While in the military, Paul married Sue Akers in Midland, Texas, on September 29, 1957, and the couple immediately moved to California. The Camerons remained in California, a community property state, for only three months. During the balance of Mr. Cameron's military service, the two lived in Arkansas, Indiana, Maryland, Nebraska, Ohio and Oklahoma, all of which observe the common law property system. The Camerons' move to Texas in August 1977 coincided with Paul's retirement from the Air Force. At the time the divorce suit was filed in 1978, both spouses lived in Texas.

I. THE MILITARY RETIREMENT PAY

In awarding a fraction of Paul Cameron's military retirement pay to his wife, the trial court followed a number of Texas decisions approving such a division upon divorce. *Taggart v. Taggart*, 552 S.W.2d 422 (Tex. 1977); *Cearley v. Cearley*, 544 S.W.2d 661 (Tex. 1976); *Busby v. Busby*, 457 S.W.2d 551 (Tex. 1970); *Herring v. Blakeley*, 385 S.W.2d 843 (Tex. 1965). While this cause was on appeal, the United States Supreme Court held that the supremacy clause of the United States Constitution, article VI, precludes a state court from dividing military nondisability retirement pay on divorce. *McCarty v. McCarty*, 453 U.S. 210, 101 S. Ct. 2728 (1981), 69 L.Ed.2d 589. In the wake of *McCarty*, we held that the supremacy clause effectively foreclosed the division of military retirement benefits under Texas community property laws. *Trahan v. Trahan*, 626 S.W.2d 485, 487 (Tex. 1981); *see also In re Marriage of Jacanin*, 124 Cal. App. 3d 67, 177 Cal. Rptr. 86, 87-88 (Ct. App. 1981); *Dedon v. Dedon*, 404 So.2d 904, 905 (La. 1981); *Hill v. Hill*, 291 Md. 615, 436 A.2d 67, 70 (1981).

Mrs. Cameron urged that we should remand the cause to afford the trial court an opportunity to increase her award from the community property as a means of offsetting her loss of thirty-five percent of the future retirement pay. The United States Supreme Court had also closed the door to that remedy. *McCarty*, 453 U.S. at 228-29 n. 22, 101 S. Ct. at 2739 n. 22; *see also Hisquierdo v. Hisquierdo*, 439 U.S. 572, 588, 99 S. Ct. 802 (1979), 811, 59 L. Ed. 2d 1.

On September 9, 1982, the President signed into law the Uniformed Services Former Spouses' Protection Act, Pub. L. No. 97-252, 96 Stat. 730 (1982). The purpose of the act was to reverse the effect of the *McCarty* decision. Under the act, a divorce court may divide military retirement pay between the spouses in accordance with the law of the jurisdiction of that court. The act limits such division of retirement pay to periods beginning after June 25, 1981. *Id.* § 1002(a) [to be codified at 10 U.S.C. § 1408(c)(1)].

Paul Cameron served in the military for more than nineteen years of his twenty-one and a half year marriage to Sue Cameron. Under the act, Sue Cameron is entitled to receive a portion of Paul Cameron's retirement pay. The divorce decree, dated March 29, 1979, awards Sue Cameron "thirty-five percent (35%) of the gross present and future Military Retirement presently being received." Sue Cameron is entitled to recover that thirty-five percent, but not for the period from March 29, 1979 to June 25, 1981. Therefore, we affirm that part of the trial court judgment awarding Sue Cameron thirty-five percent of the military retirement pay, but only for the period beginning after June 25, 1981.

II. THE U.S. SAVINGS BONDS

The court of civil appeals characterized the funds earned by Mr. Cameron in common law jurisdictions as his separate property and, through tracing principles, decided the bonds acquired with the common law funds belonged in his separate, Texas estate. As a part of Mr. Cameron's separate estate, the bonds, according to the court of civil appeals, could not be divested by the trial court. Sue Cameron seeks to uphold the trial court's disposition of the bonds by arguing that we should overrule our decision in *Eggemeyer v. Eggemeyer*, 554 S.W.2d 137 (Tex. 1977), or, alternatively, treat separate personalty differently than separate realty. Although we view the nature of the savings bonds acquired in common law jurisdictions in a different light than the court of civil appeals, we first address these arguments advanced by Mrs. Cameron.

A. *Eggemeyer Correctly States the Law*

Since the early days of the Republic of Texas, Texas has carefully drawn a line between the separate and community property of spouses in an attempt to preserve the distinctions between and the integrity of the two classes of property. Any judicial divestiture of separate property would essentially disregard the constitutionally mandated distinction. At times pertinent to this action, the Texas Constitution has provided:

> All property, both real and personal, of the wife, owned or claimed by her before marriage, and that acquired afterward by gift, devise or descent, shall be the separate property of the wife. . . .

TEX. CONST. art. XVI, § 15. In interpreting this provision, the court in *Arnold v. Leonard*, 114 Tex. 535, 273 S.W. 799 (1925), ruled that the constitution contained the exclusive definition of separate property and that the legislature could neither alter nor enlarge upon it. Section 3.63 of the Family Code authorizes a "just and right" division of the estate of the parties, but it does not provide authority for the transmutation of one spouse's separate property into the other spouse's separate property. Allowing a trial court to divest separate property from one spouse and award it to the other spouse as part of the latter's separate estate would impermissibly enlarge the exclusive constitutional definition of separate property. *See Eggemeyer, supra*, at 140.

In addition to this constitutional reason for disallowing the divestiture of separate property on divorce, the statutory construction of section 3.63, TEX. FAM. CODE ANN., does not imbue our courts with the authority to divest separate property. The Fourth Congress of the Republic of Texas approved in 1840 an "Act adopting the Common Law of England . . . and to regulate the Marrital [sic] Rights of Parties." 1840 Laws of the Republic of Texas, at 3-6, 2 H. GAMMEL, LAWS OF TEXAS 177-

180 (1898). In defining separate and community property,[1] the congress decreed that land or slaves acquired *before* marriage or afterward by gift, devise or descent constituted separate property. All other marital acquisitions fell into the common or community estate of the spouses. One year later, the Fifth Congress of the Republic of Texas approved an act "Concerning Divorce and Alimony." The statute authorized a divorce court to "order a division of the estate of the parties . . . as shall seem just and right," and added, "that nothing herein contained shall be construed to compel either party to divest him or herself of title to real estate or to slaves." 1841 Laws of the Republic of Texas, *An Act Concerning Divorce and Alimony § 4*, at 20, 2 H. GAMMEL, LAWS OF TEXAS 484 (1898) (emphasis added); *see* McKnight, *Commentary on Sec. 3.63*, 5 TEX. TECH. L. REV. 337-338 (1974). The divorce statute made clear it was "the estate of the parties,"—the common property—that the court had the power to divide. In contrast, the congress directed that real estate and slaves—separate property as defined one year earlier by the Fourth Congress—should remain inviolate on divorce. The Fifth Congress, thus, forbade the divestiture of a spouse's separate property, as then defined, by the courts on divorce. Consequently, division of property by a divorce court was limited to the community estate.

The phrase "estate of the parties" has been carried forward in Texas divorce laws and now appears in TEX. FAM. CODE ANN. § 3.63(a). This court in *Eggemeyer, supra*, at 139, affirmed the construction that the phrase referred only to community property.[2] Four years after *Eggemeyer*, the 67th Texas Legislature amended section 3.63, but left undisturbed this court's decision that "estate of the parties" refers only to community property. In addition, the scheme enacted by the legislature in section 3.63(b) of the Family Code builds upon the law that property acquired before marriage or afterward by gift, devise or descent cannot be divided by Texas courts.[3] To now hold that the "estate of the par-

---

[1] Sec. 3. Be it further enacted, That neither the lands nor slaves which the wife may own, or to which she may have any right, title or claim at the time of her marriage, nor the lands nor slaves to which she may acquire, during the coverture, any right, title or claim, by gift, devise or descent, nor the increase of such slaves in each case, nor the paraphernalia as defined at Common Law, which the wife may have at the time of the marriage, or which she may acquire during the coverture as aforesaid, shall, by virtue of the marriage, become the property of the husband, but shall remain the separate property of the wife; Provided, however, That during the continuance of the marriage, the husband shall have the sole management of such lands and slaves.

Sec. 4. Be it further enacted, That all property which the husband or wife may bring into the marriage *except land and slaves and the wife's paraphernalia and all the property acquired during the marriage, except such land or slaves, or their increase, as may be acquired by either party, by gift, devise or descent*, and except also the wife's paraphernalia, acquired as aforesaid, and during the time aforesaid, shall be the common property of the husband and wife, and during the coverture may be sold or otherwise disposed of by the husband only; it shall be first liable for all the debts contracted by the husband during the marriage, and for debts contracted by the wife for necessaries during the same time; and upon the dissolution of the marriage, by death, after the payment of all such debts, the remainder of such common property shall go to the survivor, if the deceased have no descendant or descendants; but if the deceased have a descendant or descendants, the survivor shall have one half of such common property, and the other half shall pass to the descendant or descendants of the deceased.

1840 Laws of the Republic of Texas, An Act to Adopt the Common Law of England—To Repeal Certain Mexican Laws, and to Regulate the Marrital [sic] Rights of Parties §§ 3, 4, at 4, 2 H. GAMMEL, LAWS OF TEXAS 178 (1898) (emphasis added).

[2] The Arizona Supreme Court in construing its divorce statute providing for a "division of the property of the parties as to the court shall seem just and right," also determined that the phrase "property of the parties" referred only to the community property. Collier v. Collier, 73 Ariz. 405, 242 P.2d 537, 541 (1952).

[3] Amended section 3.63 now provides:

Section 3.63 Division of Property

(a) In a decree of divorce or annulment the court shall order a division of the estate of the parties in a manner that the court deems just and right, having due regard for the rights of each party and any children of

ties" encompasses separate as well as community property would thwart the intent of this most recent pronouncement by the legislature.

Section 3.63(a), moreover, authorizes a "division" of the parties' estate, but provides no authority for a court to "divest" a divorcing spouse's separate property. Castleberry, *Constitutional Limitations on the Division of Property Upon Divorce*, 10 ST. MARY'S L.J. 37, 48-55 (1978). As early as in the 1841 divorce statute discussed above, the Texas Congress drew a distinction between allowing courts to "order a *division* of the estate of the parties" while at the same time forbidding them "to compel either party to *divest* him or herself of the title to real estate or slaves." 1841 Laws of the Republic of Texas, *An Act Concerning Divorce and Alimony § 4*, at 20, 2 H. GAMMEL, LAWS OF TEXAS 484 (1898) (emphasis added). The 1981 amendment to TEX. FAM. CODE ANN. § 3.63 continues the use of the term "division" when addressing the courts' power to order a disposition of marital property. In *Hailey v. Hailey*, 160 Tex. 372, 331 S.W.2d 299 (1960), this court recognized and explained the difference between a "division" of property and a "divestiture" of property. A division of the community is similar to a partition of property and "is not a divesting of title of either owner. . . ." *Id.* at 377, 331 S.W.2d at 303. The division, we said, does not effect a conveyance or transfer of title; the transaction only dissolves the tenancy in common. One year later in *McElreath v. McElreath*, 162 Tex. 190, 345 S.W.2d 722 (1961), we repeated our holding in *Hailey*:

---

the marriage.

(b) In a decree of divorce or annulment the court shall also order a division of the following real and personal property, wherever situated, in a manner that the court deems just and right, having due regard for the rights of each party and any children of the marriage;

(1) property that was acquired by either spouse while domiciled elsewhere and that would have been *community property* if the spouse who acquired the property had been domiciled in this state at the time of the acquisition; or

(2) property that was acquired by either spouse in exchange for real or personal property, and that would have been *community property* if the spouse who acquired the property so exchanged had been domiciled in this state at the time of its acquisition.

TEX.FAM.CODE.ANN. § 3.63 (emphasis added).

The Bill Analysis for H.B. 753 prepared for the House Committee on Judiciary stated:

Division of Property. Two separate systems of marital property regimes exist in the various states: common law and community property. Each regime provides for the welfare and estate of both spouses upon dissolution of marriage. The end result is similar while the nomenclature is different. In community property states, like Texas, each spouse has legal title in property accumulated during the marriage. In common law states, the same property may belong to one spouse, but the other spouse is found to have acquired an equitable interest that can be vested upon dissolution of the marriage.

* * *

Suggested solutions would be to allow Texas courts to find an equitable interest in separate property, or to allow the courts to consider as *community property* that property which would have been *community* had it been acquired by someone domiciled in Texas at the time of acquisition.

* * *

Section 1. Amends Family Code, Section 3.63, to allow Texas courts to divide all property before them in a marriage dissolution suit which according to Texas law would be considered *community property* if the acquiring spouse had been domiciled in Texas at the time of acquisition.

HOUSE COMM. ON THE JUDICIARY, 67th Legislature of Texas, BILL ANALYSIS TO H.B. 753, p. 1 (1981) (emphasis added).

> Under our laws, permanent alimony is not recognized, nor is a Texas court authorized to *divest* either spouse of his or *her title to separate property, Hailey v. Hailey*, Tex. Sup., 331 S.W.2d 299, but the wife, in the main, must look to the community property for her share of the material gains incident to an ill-starred marriage.

Id. at 193, 345 S.W.2d at 724 (emphasis added). Thus, the terminology utilized first by the Texas Congress and carried forward to the present day by the Texas Legislature reinforces our decision that separate property is not subject to divestiture by courts on divorce.

It is also suggested that separate property may be divested and granted to the non-owning spouse as an exercise of the police power. The Texas Legislature, however, has not seen fit to exercise this power in favor of divestiture of spouses' separate property on divorce. Presently, section 3.63(a) of the Family Code is silent on the courts' power to take one spouse's property and give it to the other on divorce. In comparison, the California statute concerning the disposition of property on divorce, CAL. CIV. CODE § 4800, like TEX .FAM. CODE ANN. § 3.63(a), neither expressly prohibits nor provides for divestiture of separate property on divorce. Yet the California courts have consistently refused to interpret the statute as authorizing its courts to divest spouses of their separate property. One California court has explained:

> The jurisdiction of the court with respect to property in a divorce action is found in section 137 et seq. of the Civil Code. As a general rule and subject to certain exceptions not material here, the power of the court is limited to a disposition of the community property and a court is without power to pass upon a dispute as to separate property or the disposition of the same.

Roy v. Roy, 29 Cal. App. 2d 596, 85 P.2d 223 (Dist. Ct. App. 1938); *accord*, *Machado v. Machado*, 58 Cal. 2d 501, 375 P.2d 55, 58 (1962); *Fox v. Fox*, 18 Cal. 2d 645, 117 P.2d 325, 326 (1941); *Simpson v. Simpson*, 80 Cal. 237, 22 P. 167, 168 (1889). As recently as 1981 when the Texas Legislature considered and substantially amended TEX. FAM. CODE ANN. § 3.63,[4] it failed to assert any intention to use the police power it might have as a means of divestiture. We do not see, therefore, that the state has authorized the use of any power it might have to take separate property on divorce.

Texas property law contains a rich tradition of respect for the constitutional, TEX. CONST. art. XVI, § 15, and statutory, TEX. FAM. CODE ANN. § 5.01, boundaries between community and separate property. Our state's courts have steadfastly guarded these estates from, and have been alert to rectify fraudulent encroachment by one estate upon the other. *Land v. Marshall*, 426 S.W.2d 841 (Tex. 1968); *Krueger v. Williams*, 163 Tex. 545, 359 S.W.2d 48 (1962); *Volunteer State Life Ins. Co. v. Hardin*, 145 Tex. 245, 197 S.W.2d 105 (1946). The integrity of each estate has been protected by developed principles of law and accounting by which funds or assets may be traced. *Tarver v. Tarver*, 394 S.W.2d 780 (Tex. 1965); *Rose v. Houston*, 11 Tex. 324 (1854); *Love v. Robertson*, 7 Tex. 6 (1851). The law of reimbursement between separate and community estates of spouses at divorce has been recognized since an early date. *Rice v. Rice*, 21 Tex. 58 (1858); *see also Lindsay v. Clayman*, 151 Tex. 593, 254 S.W.2d 777 (1952); *Dakan v. Dakan*, 125 Tex. 305, 83 S.W.2d 620 (1935); *Schmidt v. Huppmann*, 73 Tex. 112, 11 S.W. 175 (1889). A decision that would throw all separate and community property of the divorcing spouses into a hotchpotch so a trial judge could divide the mass without regard to when or how it was acquired would raze much of our developed community property law.

---

[4] *See* note 3, *supra*.

As we look beyond the boundaries of Texas, we find our holding in *Eggemeyer* that separate property may not be divested puts Texas in conformity with the law in six of the seven other community property states. In Arizona, "The court in pronouncing the decree of divorce had no authority to compel either party to divest himself or herself of the title to separate property." *Wiltbank v. Wiltbank*, 18 Ariz. 435, 162 P. 60, 61 (1917); *see also Collier v. Collier*, 73 Ariz. 405, 242 P.2d 537 (1952); *Armstrong v. Armstrong*, 71 Ariz. 275, 226 P.2d 168 (1951); *Schwartz v. Schwartz*, 52 Ariz. 105, 79 P.2d 501 (1938); *Brown v. Brown*, 38 Ariz. 459, 300 P. 1007 (1931); *Warren v. Warren*, 2 Ariz. App. 206, 407 P.2d 395 (1966).

In California, the court may not assign the separate property of one spouse to the other, nor require one to pay the other any amount in lieu of an assignment or divestiture. *Fox v. Fox*, 18 Cal. 2d 645, 117 P.2d 325 (1941). "The power of the court to dispose of the property of the parties to a divorce action is limited to their community property. It is the general rule that the court has no jurisdiction to assign separate property of one spouse to the other. . . ." *Mitchell v. Marklund*, 238 Cal. App. 2d 398, 47 Cal. Rptr. 756 (Ct. App. 1965); *accord Reid v. Reid*, 112 Cal. 274, 44 P. 564 (1896); *Davis v. Davis*, 222 Cal. App. 2d 691, 35 Cal. Rptr. 281 (Ct. App. 1963); *Thomasset v. Thomasset*, 122 Cal. App. 2d 116, 264 P.2d 626 (Dist. Ct. App. 1954); *Barba v. Barba*, 103 Cal. App. 2d 395, 229 P.2d 465 (Dist. Ct. App. 1951); *Robinson v. Robinson*, 65 Cal. App. 2d 118, 150 P.2d 7 (Dist. Ct. App. 1944). The California rule may be summed up: "As a general rule and subject to certain exceptions not material here, the power of the court is limited to a disposition of the community property and a court is without power to pass on a dispute as to separate property or the disposition of the same." *Roy v. Roy*, 29 Cal. App. 2d 596, 85 P.2d 223 (Dist. Ct. App. 1938); *see also Machado v. Machado*, 58 Cal. 2d 501, 375 P.2d 55 (1962); *McKannay v. McKannay*, 68 Cal. App. 701, 230 P. 214 (Dist. Ct. App. 1924). In California, even the community property must be divided in equal parts rather than, as in Texas, fairly and equitably. CAL. CIV. CODE §§ 4800, 4801.

The Idaho Supreme Court, interpreting that state's divorce laws, stated, "The court has the power to divide the community property between the parties, but has no power or authority to award the wife's separate property, or any of it, to the husband." *Radermacher v. Radermacher*, 61 Idaho 261, 100 P.2d 955 (1940); *see also Simplot v. Simplot*, 95 Idaho 239, 526 P.2d 844 (1974).

Nevada courts cannot divest separate property and award it to a spouse in fulfillment of the statutory power to make an equitable disposition of the marital property. *Stojanovich v. Stojanovich*, 86 Nev. 789, 476 P.2d 950 (1970); *Jacobs v. Jacobs*, 83 Nev. 73, 422 P.2d 1005 (1967); *Thorne v. Thorne*, 74 Nev. 211, 326 P.2d 729 (1958). The New Mexico law regarding divestment of title parallels that of Nevada. *Ridgway v. Ridgway*, 94 N.M. 345, 610 P.2d 749 (1980). Louisiana also maintains a distinction on divorce between a couple's community and separate estates. *See generally Curtis v. Curtis*, 403 So.2d 56 (La. 1981); *Lane v. Lane*, 375 So.2d 660 (La. Ct. App. 1978), *writ denied*, 381 So.2d 1222 (La. 1980); LA. CIV. CODE ANN. arts. 149, 155, 159, 2341, 2365, 2367, 2369, 2369.1. The Nevada, New Mexico, and Louisiana legislatures have imposed upon spouses a continuing legal duty to provide support for a divorced spouse through alimony. While prohibiting divestment for property settlements, those states expressly permit a transfer in discharge of the legislatively enunciated duty to provide support. *See* LA. CIV. CODE ANN. art. 160; NEV. REV. STAT. § 125.150(3); N.M. STAT. ANN. § 40-4-7.B(1).

The State of Washington is the only community property jurisdiction that holds contrary to *Eggemeyer* and the rule in all other community property states. Even so, Washington permits divestment only in exceptional circumstances. *Morris v. Morris*, 69 Wash. 2d 506, 419 P.2d 129 (1966); *Browning v. Browning*, 46 Wash. 2d 538, 283 P.2d 125 (1955).

The National Conference of Commissioners on Uniform State Laws in the Uniform Marriage and Divorce Act has accepted the principle that separate property in community property states should not be subjected to divestment by a trial court on divorce. The recommended draft for community property jurisdictions affirmatively states that "the court shall assign each spouse's separate property to that spouse."[5] The comment explains that the commissioners from community property states adhered to the distinction between community and separate property, and the draft provides only for the division of community property. UNIF. MARRIAGE & DIVORCE ACT § 307 COMMISSIONERS' COMMENT, 9A U.L.A. 144 (1973).

In a broader context, Professor Marsh in his treatise, MARITAL PROPERTY IN CONFLICT OF LAWS 182 (1952), writes that "in none of the United States at the present time does either spouse acquire a marital-property interest in the property of the other owned at the time of marriage, whether movable or immovable." *Accord*, K. GRAY, REALLOCATION OF PROPERTY ON DIVORCE 127, 132 (1977). Section 257 of the RESTATEMENT OF CONFLICT OF LAWS (SECOND) and its comment affirms the principle that a spouse gains no marital property interest in the pre-marital acquisitions of the other spouse by virtue of the marriage.[6]

---

[5] [Section 307. Disposition of Property.]

In a proceeding for dissolution of the marriage, legal separation, or disposition of property following a decree of dissolution of the marriage or legal dissolution by a court which lacked personal jurisdiction over the absent spouse or lacked jurisdiction to dispose of the property, the court shall assign each spouse's *separate* property to that spouse. It also shall divide *community* property, without regard to marital misconduct, in just proportions after considering all relevant factors including:

(1) contribution of each spouse to acquisition of the marital property, including contribution of a spouse as homemaker;

(2) value of the property set apart for each spouse;

(3) duration of the marriage; and

(4) economic circumstances of each spouse when the division of property is to become effective, including the desirability of awarding the family home or the right to live therein for a reasonable period to the spouse having custody of any children.

Unif. Marriage & Divorce Act § 307 *alternative* B 9A U.L.A. 144 (1973) (emphasis added.

[6] The RESTATEMENT (SECOND) provides:

TITLE D. MARITAL PROPERTY

Introductory Note: The term "marital property," as used in the RESTATEMENT of this Subject, means any interest which one spouse acquires, solely by reason of the marital relation, in the immovables and movables of the other spouse, apart from the expectancy of inheriting upon the death of the other.

§ 257. Effect of Marriage on Existing Interests in Movables

Whether as a result of the marriage one spouse acquires an interest in the movables then owned by the other spouse is determined by the local law of the state which, with respect to the particular issue, has the most significant relationship to the spouses and the movables under the principles stated in § 6. This state will usually be that where the other spouse was domiciled at the time of the marriage.

Comment:

a. The rule of this Section is of minor importance, since in no State of the United States does a spouse acquire any marital property interest, as defined in the Introductory Note to this Title, in the movables owned by the other spouse at the time of the marriage.

RESTATEMENT (SECOND) OF CONFLICT OF LAWS § 257 (1971).

The undercurrent of arguments to this court in support of the divestment of separate property is that Texas does not allow permanent alimony.[7] Section 3.59, TEX. FAM. CODE ANN., authorizes support of a spouse only until a final decree. *See Eichelberger v. Eichelberger*, 582 S.W.2d 395, 402 (Tex. 1979). The policy against permanent alimony is so strong that the Texas Legislature has stated that the duty of support will be honored under the laws of other states except that the rule "shall not include alimony for a former wife." TEX. FAM. CODE ANN. § 21.21; *see McElreath v. McElreath*, 162 Tex. 190, 228-229, 345 S.W.2d 722, 747 (1961).

One reason that Texas denies permanent alimony is that more than a century and a half ago, the state, along with Louisiana, took the lead to give wives equality with their husbands in the ownership of property they acquired during coverture. The common law recognized the wife's existence only through the husband, who upon marriage became the owner of the wife's property. *Castleberry, supra*, at 55. In addition, spouses share the gains of their marriage equally under our community property legacy from Spain. Common law jurisdictions are yielding to this equal system of marital property ownership. *See* K. GRAY, *supra*, at 63-67, 132-133.

It is urged that we, by indirection, should resolve the problem of the state's lack of alimony laws by allowing our courts to divest a spouse of separate property and award it to the other spouse. In so doing, it is argued that we would be insuring the state that a worthy spouse[8] would receive the financial support necessary to keep him or her from being a charge of society. As noted earlier, New Mexico currently allows its courts to transfer spouses' separate property on divorce, but the statute permitting such expressly notes that the transfer is considered alimony. N.M. STAT. ANN. § 40-4-7.B(1). Divestiture of separate property for reason of financial support is nothing less than alimony. Our legislature has not authorized Texas courts to grant permanent alimony, and we do not perceive that it is our function to legislate in its stead.

Whatever may be the reasons for the strong Texas legislative policy against permanent alimony, this court will respect it. To do otherwise requires this court to disregard the rules of statutory construction, the history of the law prohibiting divestment of separate property, the developed law of the other community property states; it would wipe out the legal distinctions between property, generate unnecessary constitutional problems about the classification and taking of property, create a new cycle of problems in construing amended article 3.63(b) of the Family Code, and would be contrary to the directions the law is taking in both common and community property law states as well as in the provisions of the Uniform Marriage and Divorce Act. The rules stated in this cause and in *Eggemeyer* harmonize these problems and keep the Texas community law consistent with the law of the other community property states. If there is a need for permanent alimony, it must come from the legislature where the policy arguments can be fully addressed by the whole public.

---

[7] Texas is the only state that forbids an award of alimony. In 1980, Pennsylvania reformed its law to permit alimony, but at the same time, the state's reform statute excluded "separate" property from the term "marital property." Separate property is defined as that which is acquired before marriage and that which is acquired during marriage by gift, bequest, devise or descent. Only marital property is divisible upon divorce. *See* Freed & Foster, *Divorce in the Fifty States: An Overview*, 14 FAM.L.Q. 230-31 (1981).

[8] The parental duty to support children is not here involved. That duty exists independent of the character of property a spouse owns and may be enforced and secured by setting aside property, separate or community, to assure the children's support. Eggemeyer v. Eggemeyer, 554 S.W.2d 137 (Tex. 1977); Cunningham v. Cunningham, 120 Tex. 491, 40 S.W.2d 46 (1931); Hedtke v. Hedtke, 112 Tex. 404, 248 S.W. 21 (1923); Gulley v. Gulley, 111 Tex. 233, 231 S.W. 97 (1921).

B. Separate Personal Property, Like Separate Real Property, May Not Be Divested

The court in *Eggemeyer* was unanimous in its decision, as stated by the dissent, that the "estate of the parties" includes both real and personal property. In 1969, article 4638, later to become section 3.63 of the Family Code, was amended to eliminate the statutory prohibition concerning divestment of realty. As previously written, there was a question whether article 4638 meant that separate personalty could be divested. The Texas Legislature by its 1969 amendment of section 3.63 removed this provision, and as now written, the statute avoids the charge that it violates the due course of law, TEX. CONST. art. I, § 19, equal protection, TEX. CONST. art. I, § 3, and the constitutional classifications of property, TEX. CONST. art. XVI, § 15. *See also Castleberry, supra*, at 40-46.

Sue Cameron argues that *Eggemeyer* stands only for the narrow rule that separate realty may not be divested; separate personalty, she argues, may be divested. Only realty was involved in *Eggemeyer*, but, on the issue concerning an unconstitutional classification between realty and personalty, the entire court agreed that realty and personalty must be treated alike.[9] To hold that the owner of separate realty may not be divested of his property, but that the owner of vendor's lien notes secured by the same realty or that the owner of stock in a corporation owning the realty could be divested would be an unreasonable classification of property. *Railroad Commission v. Miller*, 434 S.W.2d 670 (Tex. 1968); *see San Antonio Retail Grocers, Inc. v. Lafferty*, 156 Tex. 574, 297 S.W.2d 813 (1957); *Ground Water Conservation Dist. No. 2 v. Hawley*, 304 S.W.2d 764 (Tex. Civ. App.—Amarillo, writ ref'd n.r.e.), *per curiam*, 157 Tex. 643, 306 S.W.2d 352 (1957). Landholders cannot be so favored over holders of other kinds of property. *Reed v. Reed*, 404 U.S. 71, 75, 92 S. Ct. 251 (1971), 253, 30 L. Ed. 2d 225; *State v. Standard Oil Co.*, 130 Tex. 313, 107 S.W.2d 550, 557 (1937). The term "property" includes every species of property. *Gulf, C. & S.F. Ry. v. Fuller*, 63 Tex. 467, 469 (1885); *Renault, Inc. v. City of Houston*, 415 S.W.2d 948 (Tex. Civ. App.—Waco), *rev'd on other grounds*, 431 S.W.2d 322 (Tex. 1968); *see Castleberry, supra*, at 46.

Our construction of the statute corresponds with the law that prevails in community property states. Arizona holds that there may be no divestment of either separate realty, *Porter v. Porter*, 67 Ariz. 273, 195 P.2d 132 (1948), or of separate personalty, *Warren v. Warren*, 2 Ariz. App. 206, 407 P.2d 395 (Ct. App. 1966). California denies a divestment of separate realty, *Reid v. Reid*, 112 Cal. 274, 44 P. 564 (1896), and treats separate personalty in the same manner, *Donovan v. Donovan*, 223 Cal. App. 2d 691, 36 Cal. Rptr. 225 (Dist. Ct. App. 1963). Idaho held the same in *Simplot v. Simplot*, 96 Idaho 239, 526 P.2d 844 (1974). In Nevada, neither the separate realty, *Thorne v. Thorne*, 74 Nev. 211, 326 P.2d 729 (1958), nor the separate personalty, *Zahringer v. Zahringer*, 76 Nev. 21, 348 P.2d 161 (1960), may be divested in settling marital property rights. We can find no justifiable reason for treating separate personalty in a different manner than separate realty in divorce proceedings. As a result, we reject Sue Cameron's argument to allow the divestiture of separate personalty upon divorce.

C. "Separate" Property Under Common Law and Community Property Regimes

Mr. Cameron acquired most of the U.S. Savings Bonds here at issue during his marriage to Sue Cameron while the couple was domiciled in common law states. Reviewing the action of the trial court, which had awarded Mrs. Cameron one-half of the bonds, the court of civil appeals characterized the bonds earned by Mr. Cameron in the common law jurisdictions as his separate property and held that the trial court could not divest a spouse's separate personalty. 608 S.W.2d at 751. We recognize that property acquired in common law jurisdictions has historically been termed "separate"

[9] The dissent stated: "There is no difference in the constitutional classification of separate real and separate personal property." *Eggemeyer, supra*, at 144 (STEAKLEY, J., dissenting).

property, but we hold that the property spouses acquire during marriage, except by gift, devise or descent should be divided upon divorce in Texas in the same manner as community property, irrespective of the domicile of the spouses when they acquire the property.

Characterization of the common law marital estate as separate property comes from the common law concept that the wife possessed no legal identity apart from her husband in whom legal title to the couple's property vested. *See* Oldham, *Property Division in a Texas Divorce of a Migrant Spouse: Heads He Wins, Tails She Loses?*, 19 HOUS. L. REV. 1, 3-15 (1981); *see generally Dickson v. Strickland*, 114 Tex. 176, 201-02, 265 S.W. 1012, 1021-22 (1924). Beginning with the enactment of the various Married Women's Property Laws throughout the nation during the nineteenth and early twentieth centuries, common law jurisdictions began to modify statutorily their archaic treatment of wives' rights in marital property. *See* Glendon, *Matrimonial Property: A Comparative Study of Law and Social Change*, 49 TUL. L. REV. 21, 28-35 (1974). As a result of the statutes, courts in thirty-nine of the forty-two common law property states[10] now possess power to fashion upon divorce an equitable distribution of property acquired during marriage. *See* Freed & Foster, *Divorce in the Fifty States: An Overview*, 14 FAM. L.Q. 229, 249-52 (1981). A husband in a common law state may now have full paper title to property, but the non-acquiring wife holds valid and substantial rights to an equitable share of the "separate" marital property on divorce. *See* H. MARSH, JR., MARITAL PROPERTY IN CONFLICTS OF LAW 22-67 (1952).[11]

Common law jurisdictions have been compelled to recognize the justness of a community property system which recognizes the rights of both the husband and wife during the period of their acquisition of real and personal property. Common law marital property is not and should not be regarded by Texas courts as "separate" property in the context of our community property law on divorce. *See* TEX. CONST. art. XVI, § 15. Four of the eight community property states in recent years have addressed this difference in meanings of terms and have recognized the distinctions between the community and common law property concepts of "separate" property. Each court has looked behind the label when dividing marital property, that which was acquired during marriage.

In *Hughes v. Hughes*, 91 N.M. 339, 573 P.2d 1194 (1978), the New Mexico Supreme Court considered the disparate natures of separate property in common law and community property states. The court held that New Mexico courts should not treat separate property as recognized in common law jurisdictions the same as separate property under community property laws. *Id.* at 1201-02. The court further held the bare legal principle that a wife has no legal title in her husband's separate common law marital property could not be accepted in light of the benefits, incidents, and immunities recognized as attaching to marital property in a wife's favor by courts in common law property states. *Id.* at 1197-99.

The Idaho Supreme Court in *Berle v. Berle*, 97 Idaho 452, 546 P.2d 407 (1976), also viewed the separate property concept in the common law state of New Jersey as significantly different from the concept of separate property under Idaho's community property laws. The trial court in *Berle* had characterized the husband's common law marital property as separate property and had concluded that Idaho's prohibition against divesting separate property entitled the husband to all the common law

[10] Even in those three states—Mississippi, Virginia, and West Virginia—the wife has some of the "bundle of sticks." Any injustice that accrues to divorcing parties from one of those three states, is the problem of their own archaic and unfair laws.

[11] In the thirty years since Professor Marsh published his work, the distinctions between marital property that is called "separate" property in common law and community property states have become more pronounced. *See* K. GRAY, *supra*, at 63-67.

property. In reversing the judgment of the trial court, the Idaho Supreme Court maintained that Idaho's prohibition of divestiture was restricted to "separate" property within the context of the community property laws and did not prevent that state's courts from acknowledging the rights of spouses to an equitable division of common law separate property on divorce. *Id.* at 409.

In *Rau v. Rau*, 6 Ariz. App. 362, 432 P.2d 910 (1967), the court of appeals in Arizona confronted a judgment in which an Arizona trial court had equally divided personalty (savings bonds) and realty (a farm) that the Raus bought with funds they acquired during their marriage in Illinois, a common law state. The court determined that a spouse in Illinois holds an equitable interest upon divorce to a fair and just division of jointly earned marital property even though title to such property rests in the name of only one spouse. Comparing the definition of separate property under Arizona statutory law[12] with the nature of separate property as found in Illinois, the court maintained that Arizona's prohibition against divestiture of spouses' "separate" property would not preclude a division of the Illinois common law separate property. *See also Braddock v. Braddock*, 91 Nev. 735, 542 P.2d 1060 (1975). We agree with the New Mexico, Idaho, Arizona, and Nevada courts that substantively distinguish common law marital property from the separate property of community property jurisdictions.

The 67th Texas Legislature last year adopted this sensible approach when it authorized a division, on divorce, of common law property acquired during marriage in a manner like they would divide community property on divorce. This amendment to TEX. FAM. CODE ANN. § 3.63 provides as follows:

> (b) In a decree of divorce or annulment the courts shall also order a division of the following real and personal property, wherever situated, in a manner that the court deems just and right, having due regard for the rights of each party and any children of the marriage:
>
> (1) property that was acquired by either spouse while domiciled elsewhere and that would have been community property if the spouse who acquired the property had been domiciled in the state at the time of the acquisition; or
>
> (2) property that was acquired by either spouse in exchange for real or personal property, and that would have been community property if the spouse who acquired the property so exchanged had been domiciled in this state at the time of its acquisition.

The bill analysis accompanying the subsequently adopted statute correctly explained:

> Two separate systems of marital property regimes exist in the various states: common law and community property. Each regime provides for the welfare and estate of both spouses upon dissolution of marriage. The end result is similar while the nomenclature is different. In community property states, like Texas, each spouse has legal title in property accumulated during the marriage. In common law states, the same property may belong to one spouse, but

---

[12] The court in *Rau* cited Arizona's community property definition of separate property, and except for its treatment of the increases, rents, issues and profits from separate property, it is the same definition we have in Texas.

Compare ARIZ.REV.STAT.ANN. § 25-213:

> A. All property, real and personal, of the husband, owned or claimed by him before marriage, and that acquired afterward by gift, devise or descent, and also the increase, rents, issues and profits thereof, is his separate property;

With TEX. CONST. art. XVI, § 15:

> All property, both real and personal, of a spouse owned or claimed before marriage, and that acquired afterward by gift, devise or descent, shall be the separate property of that spouse. . . .

> the other spouse is found to have acquired an equitable interest that can be vested upon dissolution of the marriage.

HOUSE COMM. ON THE JUDICIARY, 67th Legislature of Texas, BILL ANALYSIS TO H.B. 753, p. 1 (1981). In enacting subsection (b) of TEX. FAM. CODE ANN. § 3.63, the legislature established a workable, uncomplicated framework for effecting just divisions of common law marital property on divorce in Texas. The amendment, however, applies only to suits for divorce or annulment in which a hearing has not been held before September 1, 1981. 1981 Tex. Gen. Laws, ch. 712, § 3, at 2656. The trial court rendered a judgment divorcing the Camerons in 1979. Rather than returning in this cause to the now discredited approach of assuming the equivalence of "separate" property under community property systems and common law "separate" property, and rather than embarking upon a cumbersome conflict of laws approach[13] which produces essentially the same result, we judicially adopt TEX. FAM. CODE ANN. § 3.63(b) as part of the substantive law of this state.

It has been suggested that section 3.63(b) may run afoul of this court's decision in *Eggemeyer*, because the statute may unconstitutionally authorize trial courts to interfere with the rights of a spouse holding legal title to common law marital property. *See* Oldham, *supra*, at 37-46; Stewart & Orsinger, *Fitting a Round Peg into a Square Hole: Section 3.63, Texas Family Code, and the Marriage that Crosses State Lines*, 13 ST. MARY'S L.J. 477, 486-91 (1982).

As stated above, divorce courts in all but three of the common law jurisdictions may effect an equitable distribution of the marital assets upon divorce. The New Mexico Supreme Court explained in Hughes:

> The wife, in many common law states. . . , has inchoate equitable rights to her husband's separate property where she has made contributions to preserving and bettering that property, whereas in a typical community property state she has no such rights since she has community property rights instead.

Hughes, supra, at 1199. A Texas court that makes a distribution on divorce of the common law marital estate equivalent to what would occur in the common law jurisdiction where the couple was domiciled when they acquired the property, does not impair the rights of spouses in the common law marital property. No divestment transpires because the acquiring spouse loses no more in a Texas divorce than he loses in a judgment rendered in an equitable distribution common law state. *Berle, supra*, at 411. Our judicial adoption of the quasi-community property amendment to TEX. FAM. CODE ANN. § 3.63 does not violate article I, section 19 of the Texas Constitution.

III. CONCLUSION

The framework for the Spanish community property system of marital property builds upon a distinction between spouses' community and separate estates. This distinction springs from a reality that property acquired during marriage other than by gift, devise or descent is the product of a unique, joint endeavor undertaken by spouses. That is the concept of matrimony. Community property owes its existence to the legal fact of marriage, and when the parties to that compact determine their relationship should end, property acquired during marriage is and should be divided among them in a just and right manner. By way of contrast separate property, in the community property setting, owes its existence to wholly extramarital factors, things unrelated to the marriage. In relation to that property, the parties are, in essence, strangers; they are separate. Any property that arises independently of

[13] Professor J. Thomas Oldham has thoughtfully developed this viable concept in Oldham, *Property Division in a Texas Divorce of a Migrant Spouse, Heads He Wins, Tails She Loses*, 19 HOUS.L.REV. 1 (1981).

marriage as a means of "equitably" balancing the spouses' positions on divorce cannot be justified. Such a view rejects the viability of the community property system and ignores the carefully hewn jurisprudence that attempts to preserve the integrity of the two estates. The vast majority of common law property states have demonstrated that they too recognize the special nature of property acquired through the corroborative efforts of spouses. In adopting TEX. FAM. CODE ANN. § 3.63(b) as the substantive law of the state, we continue the national trend endorsing the use of marital property as the means of settling the equities between divorcing spouses.

We reverse that part of the judgment of the court of civil appeals that denied Sue Cameron fifty percent of the savings bonds and affirm the judgment of the trial court ordering the equal division.

We reverse that part of the judgment of the court of civil appeals that reversed the trial court's judgment that Sue Cameron receive thirty-five percent of the military retirement pay, and we render judgment awarding Sue Cameron her share of the military retirement pay but only from June 25, 1981.

Costs are adjudged against the respondent.

MCGEE, JUSTICE, concurring.

I agree with the judgment of the Court. I also concur in that portion of the majority opinion which holds that marital property acquired in a common law state is subject to division by a Texas court upon the parties' divorce. I cannot, however, accept the majority's unnecessary discussion of *Eggemeyer v. Eggemeyer*, 554 S.W.2d 137 (Tex. 1977). Since the entire Court agrees that the savings bonds at issue in this case are not separate property, the majority's discussion of separate personalty is *obitur dictum*. As in *Eggemeyer*, a majority of this Court has reached conclusions grounded on statutory and constitutional considerations not essential to the disposition of the case. Because I do not believe *Eggemeyer* correctly states the law in all respects, I respectfully disagree with the majority's statement to the contrary.

In *Eggemeyer*, the issue before the Court was whether the trial court, in its divorce decree, could "divest one spouse of his separate *realty* and transfer title to the other spouse." 554 S.W.2d at 138 (emphasis added). Virginia Eggemeyer's principal contention was that section 3.63, unlike former article 4638, did not restrict the power of the trial court to divide the separate realty of one spouse and award the other spouse a fee interest therein. The Court rejected this contention, holding that the legislature had intended to recodify the law as it existed before the enactment of the Family Code.

The majority opinion in *Eggemeyer*, however, transcended the precise issue before the Court and advanced three additional grounds for its decision:

> (1) the phrase "estate of the parties," as employed in section 3.63 of the Family Code refers only to the community property of the parties and prohibits the division of separate property;
>
> (2) a division of the separate property of one spouse would create a form of separate property not provided for in article XVI, section 15 of the Texas Constitution;
>
> (3) a division of the separate property of one spouse is a taking of property not justified by any public benefit, and deprives that spouse of his property without due process in violation of article I, section 19 of the Texas Constitution.

In this case, the majority states that these supposed limitations on the power of the trial court are equally applicable to an attempted division of separate personalty. For the following reasons, I disagree.

A. *Eggemeyer* Is Not Stare Decisis on the Divisibility of Separate Personalty Under the Family Code.

The first statutory ground advanced in *Eggemeyer* was that the legislature intended to enact the Family Code as a codification of existing law. 554 S.W.2d at 139. Article 4638, the forerunner of section 3.63, expressly prohibited divestiture of realty by a trial court when making a fair and just division of property in divorce proceedings. For over a hundred years, however, Texas courts divided separate personalty when equity demanded such a division. *Hedtke v. Hedtke*, 112 Tex. 404, 409, 248 S.W. 21, 22-23 (1923); *Fitts v. Fitts*, 14 Tex. 443, 450, 453 (1855); *Trader v. Trader*, 531 S.W.2d 189, 190 (Tex. Civ. App.—San Antonio 1975, writ dism'd); *Tullis v. Tullis*, 456 S.W.2d 172, 173 (Tex. Civ. App.—El Paso 1970, writ dism'd); *Dillingham v. Dillingham*, 434 S.W.2d 459, 461 (Tex. Civ. App.—Fort Worth 1968, writ dism'd); *Grant v. Grant*, 351 S.W.2d 897, 898 (Tex. Civ. App.—Waco 1961, writ dism'd); *McCart v. McCart*, 275 S.W.2d 155, 157 (Tex. Civ. App.—Fort Worth 1955, no writ); *Grisham v. Grisham*, 255 S.W.2d 891, 893 (Tex. Civ. App.—Waco 1953, no writ); *Hamm v. Hamm*, 159 S.W.2d 183, 185-86 (Tex. Civ. App.—Fort Worth 1942, no writ); *Dale v. Dale*, 141 S.W.2d 718, 719 (Tex. Civ. App.—Beaumont 1940, no writ).

The statutory prohibition of divestiture of realty was not carried forward in section 3.63 of the Family Code. Despite the obvious omission of that prohibition, the Court determined the legislative intent behind section 3.63 was to codify the law as it existed at that time. *Eggemeyer*, 554 S.W.2d at 139. Thus, section 3.63 did not authorize divestiture of separate realty upon divorce. *Id.*

This holding alone would have been sufficient to sustain the Court's judgment in *Eggemeyer*. Nevertheless, the Court advanced a second statutory ground as a basis for its decision. Upon examining section 3.63, the Court held that the "estate of the parties" was limited to community property. In so doing, the Court redefined the statutory language in a manner wholly different from that which existed previously. Consequently, the Court's construction of section 3.63 was inconsistent with its simultaneous determination that the Family Code codified the existing law.

In *Hedtke v. Hedtke*, 112 Tex. 404, 248 S.W. 21 (1923), this Court construed the phrase "estate of the parties" as follows:

> The estate subject to division, under the statute, includes *all property of the parties whether community property or separate property*. The meaning of the statute is not different from what it would have been had the word 'property' been substituted in its phraseology for the word "estate."

Id. at 408, 248 S.W. at 22 (emphasis added). Notwithstanding continued judicial and legislative acceptance of this construction, the majority in *Eggemeyer* examined several relatively recent cases and determined "estate of the parties" referred only to community property. *See Reardon v. Reardon*, 163 Tex. 605, 359 S.W.2d 329 (Tex. 1962); *Hailey v. Hailey*, 160 Tex. 372, 331 S.W.2d 299 (1960); *Mansfield v. Mansfield*, 308 S.W.2d 80 (Tex. Civ. App.—El Paso 1957, writ dism'd). Upon closer examination, it is clear those cases dealt solely with the question of whether title to community real estate could be divested. None of these cases purported to construe "estate of the parties."[1]

---

[1] In *Reardon v. Reardon*, the Court held that the prohibition against divestiture of title to real estate in article 4638 did not include community real estate. 163 Tex. at 607, 359 S.W.2d at 330. The most that should be taken from this holding is that the "estate of the parties" *does* include community realty. I do not believe the holding excludes from the definition the separate property of the spouses. If "estate of the parties" was intended to apply only to community property, that portion of article 4638 prohibiting divestiture of title to realty would have been mere surplusage.

The courts of this State historically have interpreted "estate of the parties" to mean all property of the parties, whether community or separate. *E.g., Hedtke v. Hedtke*, 112 Tex. at 408, 248 S.W. at 22; *Fitts v. Fitts*, 14 Tex. at 450; *Trader v. Trader*, 531 S.W.2d 189, 190 (Tex. Civ. App.—San Antonio 1975, writ dism'd). Any doubt as to the correct construction of a statute must be considered removed by consistent interpretation by the appellate courts. *Marmon v. Mustang Aviation, Inc.*, 430 S.W.2d 182, 193 (Tex. 1968); *see also Cunningham v. Cunningham*, 120 Tex. 491, 40 S.W.2d 46 (1931). As JUSTICE NORVELL cautioned in *Marmon*, the doctrine of *stare decisis* is especially weighty in statutory construction:

> It is one thing for the judicial branch to amend a statute and quite another thing to modify a rule of common law. And, to overrule a court's uniform interpretation of a statute which has persisted over a long period of years as evidenced by numerous decisions, is very like amending a statute. That is why the rule of stare decisis is highly binding in this field.

430 S.W.2d at 193. Because the definition of "estate of the parties" was not essential to the holding in *Eggemeyer*, and because it represented a departure from established construction, I do not regard the *Eggemeyer* definition as a correct statement of the law.[2]

B. *Eggemeyer* Is An Incorrect Construction of the Texas Constitution.

The Court's judgment in *Eggemeyer*, as noted above, was fully supported by the holding that section 3.63 was merely a recodification of existing law. Thus, it is not surprising that the subsequent discussion of the constitutional limitations on the division of separate property in general has been treated as dicta, *Muns v. Muns*, 567 S.W.2d 563, 565 (Tex. Civ. App.—Dallas 1978, no writ), and has not been viewed as prohibiting an award of one spouse's separate personalty to the other. *York v. York*, 579 S.W.2d 24, 25 (Tex. Civ. App.—Beaumont 1979, no writ); *Eichelberger v. Eichelberger*, 557 S.W.2d 587, 589 (Tex. Civ. App.—Waco 1977), *rev'd on other grounds*, 582 S.W.2d 395 (Tex. 1979). The constitutional bases of *Eggemeyer* should not be regarded as authoritative since this Court will not decide a case on constitutional grounds if the case can otherwise be disposed of. *See, e.g., Wood v. Wood*, 159 Tex. 350, 359, 320 S.W.2d 807, 813 (1959); *San Antonio General Drivers, Helpers Local No. 657 v. Thornton*, 156 Tex. 641, 647, 299 S.W.2d 911, 915 (1957); *Waller v. State*, 68 S.W.2d 601, 603 (Tex. Civ. App.—Amarillo 1934, writ ref'd). In my opinion, there are no constitutional limitations on the power of the trial court to divest a spouse of his or her separate property.

Prior to its amendment in 1980, article XVI, section 15 of the constitution provided as follows:

> All property, both real and personal, of the wife, owned prior to marriage or claimed by her before marriage by gift, devise or descent, shall be the separate property of the wife; and laws shall be passed more clearly defining the rights of the wife, in relation as well to her separate property as that held in common with her husband. . . .

In *Hailey v. Hailey*, the Court noted with approval the language in Ex parte Scott, 133 Tex. 1, 123 S.W.2d 306 (1939), that title to realty could not be divested. The Court held that the division of community real property is proper and does not violate article 4638 because a partition deed merely dissolves a tenancy in common and does not convey title. 160 Tex. at 375-76, 331 S.W.2d at 302-03. Accordingly, when a trial court orders a partition of community property, title to that property is not divested. In *Mansfield v. Mansfield* the holding was the same. 308 S.W.2d at 83.

[2] The fact that the legislature has not amended section 3.63 since the Court's decision in *Eggemeyer* is not evidence of the legislature's intent to limit the "estate of the parties" to community property. In light of the constitutional dicta in *Eggemeyer*, the legislature reasonably could have believed that any attempt to include separate property in the estate of the parties would have been unconstitutional.

Citing Arnold v. Leonard, 114 Tex. 535, 273 S.W. 799 (1925), the majority in *Eggemeyer* stated that the constitutional definition of separate property was exclusive and could not be altered or enlarged by the legislature. Thus, even if section 3.63 could be construed as permitting a divestiture of one spouse's separate realty, the trial court was still powerless to make an award of one spouse's separate property to the other in its divorce decree.

What the Court overlooked in *Eggemeyer* is that the division of property upon divorce does not occur during the marriage, but at the moment of divorce; the division of property and the divorce decree are a single, integrated action. Application of those rules which characterize property before and during marriage is inappropriate. An analogous situation involves community property that is not divided upon divorce. We have consistently held such property is owned by the ex-spouses separately as tenants in common. *Busby v. Busby*, 457 S.W.2d 551, 554 (Tex.1970); *Taylor v. Catalon*, 140 Tex. 38, 41-42, 166 S.W.2d 102, 104, (1942); *Kirkwood v. Domnan*, 80 Tex. 645, 647-48, 16 S.W. 428, 429 (1891). In both instances, this "separate property" is not within the constitutional definition, but is created by the fact of divorce.

There are, moreover, at least two additional situations in which property that is neither "owned prior to marriage" nor acquired thereafter by "gift, devise or descent" is treated as separate property. The first is a mutation of separate property. The second, personal injury awards, is particularly instructive for the purposes of this case. In *Graham v. Franco*, 488 S.W.2d 390 (Tex. 1972), we unanimously held that such awards were the separate property of the injured spouse despite their exclusion from the constitutional definition. More importantly, we limited *Arnold v. Leonard* to its facts. Thus, the most that can be gleaned from *Arnold v. Leonard* is that the legislature is powerless to enact a law classifying the rents and revenues of the wife's separate realty as her separate property.

There is, however, a more basic flaw in the "implied exclusion" reasoning of *Arnold v. Leonard*. Logically extended, it denies the existence of the husband's separate property since the constitution, until the 1980 amendment of article XVI, section 15, provided only for the separate property of the *wife*. Under a strict reading of *Arnold v. Leonard*, all property owned by the husband before marriage and acquired thereafter during marriage is necessarily *community*.

The fact that property is community or separate is pertinent to its division upon divorce. The courts of appeals have evolved several equitable rules which, quite properly, limit the trial court's discretion to award the separate property of one spouse to the other spouse to extraordinary circumstances. *Muns v. Muns*, 567 S.W.2d 563, 567 (Tex. Civ. App.—Dallas 1978, no writ); *Cooper v. Cooper*, 513 S.W.2d 229, 233 (Tex. Civ. App.—Houston [1st Dist.] 1974, no writ); *Bryant v. Bryant*, 478 S.W.2d 602, 605 (Tex. Civ. App.—Waco 1972, no writ); *Dorfman v. Dorfman*, 457 S.W.2d 91, 95 (Tex. Civ. App.—Waco 1970, no writ); *Keene v. Keene*, 445 S.W.2d 624, 626 (Tex. Civ. App.—Dallas 1969, writ dism'd). Equity and the theory of community property argue for such rules. For over a century, Texas courts awarded separate personalty upon divorce. Prior to *Eggemeyer*, this was not considered a constitutional problem. It was the *statutory* provision, not the constitution which prohibited the award of separate *realty* upon divorce. Therefore, I would hold that article XVI, section 15 of the constitution does not prohibit a trial court from dividing the separate property of one spouse upon divorce.

The second constitutional basis for the Court's decision in *Eggemeyer* was the due process clause of the Texas Constitution. TEX. CONST. art. I, § 19. In *Eggemeyer*, the Court stated that the division of one spouse's separate property was not justified by any benefit to the public welfare. Because this "taking" of private property was not grounded upon the police power, the legislature could not constitutionally authorize a division of one spouse's separate property.

I disagree with this holding. As stated in the dissent in *Eggemeyer*, "the special relationship between the State and the institution of marriage has often been recognized." 554 S.W.2d at 147. The state's interest in the marital relationship provides a sufficient and justifiable public purpose for divestiture of one spouse's separate property. *Maynard v. Hill*, 125 U.S. 190, 205, 8 S. Ct. 723 (1897). 726, 31 L. Ed. 654.

By ordering periodic child support payments, Texas courts are empowered to divest a parent of his separate personalty. TEX. FAM. CODE ANN. § 14.05. Likewise, the state imposes a duty upon the spouses to support each other during the marriage. *Id.* § 4.02. Although a spouse must look first to the community for support, the other spouse may be required to employ his or her separate funds if community funds are insufficient. *Norris v. Vaughan*, 152 Tex. 491, 502-03, 260 S.W.2d 676, 683 (1953); *Callahan v. Patterson*, 4 Tex. 61, 66 (1849). In neither case is there a violation of due process. The valid state interest in the marital relationship justifies the burdens imposed upon a spouse's separate property. That same valid state interest allows the state to provide rules for the dissolution of the marriage and the division of both separate and community property upon dissolution.

Section 3.63 of the Family Code and previous Texas divorce statutes have required the division of marital property according to equitable principles. In many circumstances, equity may require an unequal division of community property. *Bell v. Bell*, 513 S.W.2d 20, 22 (Tex. 1974). Likewise, in extreme cases, equity may require the trial court to award a portion of one spouse's separate personalty to the other. I would hold that article I, section 19 of the Texas Constitution is no impediment to an award of one spouse's separate property to the other.

The majority opinion suggests that allowing a divestiture of separate personalty under section 3.63, in light of the holding in *Eggemeyer* that separate realty cannot be divested, is a violation of equal protection under the Fourteenth Amendment of the United States Constitution and article I, section 3 of the Texas Constitution. The argument is that a classification based on land ownership arbitrarily discriminates against those persons owning separate personalty rather than separate realty. I do not find this contention persuasive.

The equal protection clauses of both the federal and state constitutions protect individuals against arbitrary discrimination by the state. The state, however, may classify its citizens into reasonable classes, and treat these different classes of persons in different ways. *Reed v. Reed*, 404 U.S. 71, 75, 92 S. Ct. 251, 253 (1971), 30 L.Ed.2d 225; *Railroad Commission v. Miller*, 434 S.W.2d 670, 673 (Tex. 1968); *Bjorgo v. Bjorgo*, 402 S.W.2d 143, 148 (Tex. 1966).

The test under both the state and federal constitutions is whether the classification is reasonable and not arbitrary. *Reed v. Reed*, 404 U.S. at 76, 92 S. Ct. at 254 (1971); *Railroad Commission v. Miller*, 434 S.W.2d at 673; *San Antonio Retail Grocers v. Lafferty*, 156 Tex. 574, 577, 297 S.W.2d 813, 815 (1957). There must be some ground of difference which has a fair and substantial relationship to the purpose of the legislation, so that all persons similarly situated are similarly treated. *New Orleans v. Dukes*, 427 U.S. 297, 303-04, 96 S. Ct. 2513, 2516-17, 49 L. Ed. 2d 511 (1976); *Railroad Commission v. Miller*, 434 S.W.2d at 673.

There is a rational purpose for the different treatment accorded owners of real and personal property by the trial courts upon divorce. Realty, by definition, is unique. By contrast, personalty is often fungible and more easily replaced than realty. If a spouse's personalty is genuinely unique and irreplaceable, the trial court can consider this fact under section 3.63.

C. A Divestiture of Separate Property Is Not an Award of Alimony.

The majority opinion asserts that a divestiture of separate property "is nothing less than alimony." Thus, the majority concludes that a division of one spouse's separate property is not only prohibited by section 3.63 and the Texas Constitution, but is also contrary to public policy. I disagree.

A divestiture of separate property and an award of alimony are totally different. Unlike a divestiture of separate property, alimony is a personal obligation of one spouse to support the other which continues after a final decree of divorce. *Francis v. Francis*, 412 S.W.2d 29, 32-33 (Tex. 1967). By contrast, a divestiture of separate property, like a division of community property, is an isolated event which occurs at the moment of divorce. Alimony and an award of separate property are two distinct means of achieving a single end: the financial support of the ex-spouse. Because Texas does not permit alimony, our courts, with the implicit approval of the legislature, have permitted divestiture of one spouse's separate personalty to ensure that the other spouse does not become a destitute ward of the state.

The majority also stresses that its opinion conforms with the law of other community property jurisdictions. While it is true that no state other than Washington permits a divestiture of separate property, it is equally true that the courts of these states are empowered to award permanent alimony. This is a critical distinction which the majority relegates to a footnote.

D. Conclusion.

Neither *Eggemeyer* nor the majority opinion in this case should be viewed as anything but dicta regarding the power of the trial court to divide separate personalty upon divorce. In my opinion, section 3.63 of the Family Code allows the trial court to divest a spouse of his or her separate personalty. Furthermore, I do not believe the Texas Constitution prohibits such a division.

BARROW and SONDOCK, JJ., join in this concurring opinion.

GREENHILL, CHIEF JUSTICE, concurring.

I agree with the substance of the concurring opinion of Mr. JUSTICE MCGEE.

I also agree with the holding of the Court that marital property acquired in a common-law jurisdiction is not separate property within the framework of the Texas community property laws.

The majority opinion gives several grounds for its holdings with which I obviously do not agree. Since there are many reasons given, it is not necessary to reach constitutional grounds, particularly the "due process" argument. A wise rule of opinion writing and appellate judgments is that constitutional grounds are not decided unless it is absolutely necessary.

A redeeming feature of the majority opinion, as I understand it, is that it does not reach the "due process" point. If it even suggests such a holding, it is unnecessary to the opinion.

The Court's opinion does not disavow the dictum of the earlier opinion in *Eggemeyer*. Separate personal property was not before the Court in *Eggemeyer*; and any observation about "due process" was, in my opinion, clearly dictum. With this state of the law, we also have the undisturbed language of *Hedtke* that it was permissible to deal differently with separate realty and separate personalty.

It is my hope, therefore, that the Court's power to deal with separate property, particularly separate personal property, may be addressed by the Legislature. After all, the Legislature is the policy making body of this state. In this context, the Legislature will have an alternative to enacting alimony statutes which will surely result if the "due process" dictum of *Eggemeyer* should ultimately prevail. The Legislature can change the "estate of the parties" and other statutory provisions; but it cannot change the "due process [due course] of law" of the Texas Constitution,—without a constitutional amendment.

Notes, Comments & Questions

1. How many pages of the *Cameron* opinion are inconsequential to the holding?

2. Does the Texas Supreme Court actually hold that separate personal property cannot be divested or is it dictum?

3. The court looks to all other community property states and with one exception concludes that those states may not divest a spouse of separate property. Do those states enjoy a remedy in divorce that Texas does not?

4. Why didn't the court resolve the lack of a Texas alimony law by allowing a divestiture of separate property?

5. Alimony pending divorce has long been allowed in Texas. Why is such not a divestiture of separate property?

6. In 1995, the Texas Legislature authorized post-divorce alimony in very limited circumstances. Read TEX. FAM. CODE §§ 8.001; 8.051-.060. Would these sections have provided relief to Mrs. Cameron?

7. The Supreme Court references TEX. FAM. CODE § 3.63 (b) (currently § 7.002) as authority for characterizing the savings bonds as community property and allowing division of same. However, §3.63 (b) applied only to divorce actions in which a hearing had not been held before September 1, 1981. The Camerons were divorced in 1979 so how could the rule of § 3.63 (b) be applied?

8. Though not a divorce case, the next case demonstrates the different treatment that property—which would be quasi-community property upon divorce—receives upon death.

9. In addition to the quasi-community property issue, *Cameron* also addresses military retirement and the effect of the supremacy clause of the United States Constitution on the division of benefits and the congressional solution. Although retirement benefits are addressed at section G. of this chapter, it should now be noted that when one of the parties to divorce proceedings holds rights to retirement benefits which arise under statutes, whether federal, state, or local, the provisions of the relevant statute and any applicable case law must be considered to determine whether the benefits are divisible upon divorce.

The classic example is military retirement benefits, which for many years the Texas courts had considered to be divisible upon divorce. However, on June 25, 1981 in *McCarty v. McCarty*, 453 U.S. 210, 101 S. Ct. 2728 (1981), the Supreme Court, construing the Act of Congress creating such benefits, held that the benefits were not divisible upon divorce. The *McCarty* decision was the law of the land until September 9, 1982, when the President signed into law the Uniformed Services Former Spouses' Protection Act, Pub. L. No. 97-252, 96 Stat. 730 (1982). The purpose of the Act was to reverse the effect of the *McCarty* decision. The effect of this statute on a divorce case pending at the time of enactment of the statute is dealt with in *Cameron v. Cameron*, 641 S.W.2d 210 (Tex. 1982). It has been held that the *McCarty* decision had no retroactive effect upon the division of military benefits in divorce decisions which became final prior to the decision in *McCarty*, *Segrest v. Segrest*, 649 S.W.2d 610 (Tex. 1983). Finally, although the court in *Cameron v. Cameron* awarded the wife a share of the military retirement benefits only for the period beginning after June 25, 1981, a strong probability exists that later decisions will hold the Uniformed Services Former Spouses' Protection Act applicable to periods both before and after June 25, 1981.

Another illustration of the problem relating to statutory retirement benefits is *Hisquierdo v. Hisquierdo*, 439 U.S. 572, 59 L. Ed. 2d 1 (1979), holding benefits payable under the Railroad Retirement Act of 1974 not divisible, and stating that it would be error for the trial court to make an off-setting award. *Hisquierdo* was followed in *Eichelberger v. Eichelberger*, 582 S.W.2d 395 (Tex. 1979), but in 1981, Congress amended the applicable statute, U.S. Code title 45, section 231a, to permit division of Railroad Retirement Benefits upon divorce under certain conditions.

Other examples of decisions holding that statutory retirement benefits are not divisible upon divorce, *Perez v. Perez*, 587 S.W.2d 671 (Tex. 1979) (Military Readjustment Benefits); *Ex parte Johnson*, 591 S.W.2d 453 (Tex. 1979) (Veterans Administration Retirement Fund). Obviously, the statutes in these decisions as well as statutes providing for other retirement benefits should be checked for amendments and later case law should be investigated before a determination can be made as to whether the benefits are divisible in any specific case.

ESTATE OF HANAU
v.
HANAU

730 S.W.2d 663
(Tex. 1987)

ROBERTSON, JUSTICE.

This case involves the question of whether the rule announced in *Cameron v. Cameron*, 641 S.W.2d 210 (Tex. 1982) applies to probate as well as divorce matters.

Robert and Dorris Hanau were married in Illinois in 1974 and five years later moved to Texas. After moving here, Robert prepared a will leaving his separate property to his children by a prior marriage, and his community property to Dorris. Robert and Dorris each had substantial amounts of separate property before the marriage, and at all times kept such property under their own names. While married and in Illinois, Robert accumulated numerous shares of stock through the use of his separate property. Under Illinois common law, this would have remained his separate property. Robert died in Texas in 1982 and Dorris was granted letters testamentary on May 10, 1982. In February 1983, Dorris transferred large amounts of the estate's stock to the son, Steven, and the daughter, Leslie Ann. In May 1983, however, Steven brought an original petition seeking to have Dorris removed as executrix, claiming that she was intentionally mismanaging and embezzling from the estate. Dorris soon thereafter filed an inventory and appraisal listing all of the property owned by Robert, claiming that all stocks obtained by Robert during their marriage were community property, even though they were originally acquired in a common law state. Thus, Dorris sought the return of some of the stock she had already delivered to the children. The parties stipulated that the stocks acquired before marriage were Robert's separate property and that stocks acquired while married in Texas were community property. The only question presented to the trial court was the status of those stocks bought during the marriage in Illinois using Robert's separate property.

The trial court severed the question of proper distribution of the assets and granted a partial summary judgment to Dorris on the characterization issue. The trial judge ruled that all the amounts that accrued during the marriage would be considered as community property in Texas, despite their characterization as separate property outside the state. He concluded that "the Texas Supreme Court in *Cameron v. Cameron* could not have intended to limit its new characterization of common law marital property to divorce proceedings, but rather intended that said characterization to be applied to any situation where the issue arose, including probate proceedings."

The court of appeals affirmed in part and reversed in part. 721 S.W.2d 515. The court determined that *Cameron* was not applicable to probate situations, rather it should be limited only to divorce matters. Therefore, the court held that most of the stocks should have been classified as separate property, and rendered judgment that they go to the son and daughter. The court did, however, affirm as to one specific stock (TransWorld) where it held that a proper tracing could not be shown so as to classify it as separate property. Both parties appeal here; Dorris as to the former holding, Steven as to the latter. We affirm in part and reverse and render in part.

In her application, Dorris relies exclusively on § 3.63 of the Family Code and *Cameron v. Cameron*, 641 S.W.2d 210 (Tex. 1982). Dorris admits that *Cameron* dealt with divorce rather than probate, but argues that this court intended to make "a fundamental change in its characterization of common law marital property." She argues that a broad interpretation of the result in *Cameron* should be applied because no distinction can be made between dissolution of the marriage by death or divorce. We disagree.

The long-standing general rule is that property which is separate property in the state of the matrimonial domicile at the time of its acquisition will not be treated for probate purposes as though acquired in Texas. *Oliver v. Robertson*, 41 Tex. 422, 425 (1874); *McClain v. Holder*, 279 S.W.2d 105, 107 (Tex. Civ. App.—Galveston 1955, writ ref'd n.r.e.). In *Cameron*, we held, however, that separate property acquired in common law jurisdictions merits different treatment in the limited context of divorce or annulment. While there were solid reasons for creating the *Cameron* rule in those situations, the same rationales are not applicable to probate procedures.

In *Cameron*, this court used three bases for its holding. First, the court examined the laws of some of the other community property states, and agreed that a difference exists between common law marital property and the separate property of community property jurisdictions. This court cited to several cases, including *Rau v. Rau*, 6 Ariz. App. 362, 432 P.2d 910 (Ariz. Ct. App. 1967), in support of its holding. In examining *Rau*, however, it is clear that the court there refused to apply the rule to probate cases because "the statutory regulation of rights of succession has been regarded as something apart from the determination of property rights between living persons." *Id.* at 914. Furthermore, nothing in the other cases used for support in *Cameron* reveals an intent to extend the rule to probate cases in those jurisdictions. *See Hughes v. Hughes*, 91 N.M. 339, 573 P.2d 1194 (1978); *Berle v. Berle*, 97 Idaho 452, 546 P.2d 407 (1976). In fact, it appears that the only community property states which have extended the rule reach such a result based completely upon statutory authority. *See* CALIFORNIA PROB. CODE § 66 (West 1985); IDAHO CODE § 15-2-201 (1971). Thus, there is no case law or trend which supports change of the rule here.

The second basis used in *Cameron* was the Texas legislature's action in adopting § 3.63 of the Family Code. Section 3.63 provides that a trial judge shall make a "just and right" division of property, which may include: "Property that was acquired by either spouse while domiciled elsewhere and that would have been community property if the spouse who acquired the property had been domiciled in the state at the time of the acquisition." Therefore, this court merely judicially adopted § 3.63 into the substantive law of this State. Dorris suggests that we apply § 3.63 to the probate situation, but by its own terms the Family Code provision applies only "in a decree of divorce or annulment." In addition, there is no provision similar to § 3.63 in the Probate Code, nor in any other statute of this state, which would logically require us to follow her suggestion. Therefore, there is also a lack of statutory authority which mitigates against extending *Cameron.*

The final foundation in *Cameron* dealt with the necessity of giving the trial court the power to effect an equitable distribution of property. Without such power, unfair results could occur because one spouse's equitable share of the other spouse's separate property under common law might not be considered under our community property definition of separate property. The *Cameron* holding merely made such an interest in common law separate property one which is susceptible to a Texas trial court's equitable division. The key is that there is no similar right in a probate proceeding, nor is there any need for any. If there is a valid will, the will should usually be enforced regardless of the equity of the devises or bequests within. *Huffman v. Huffman*, 161 Tex. 267, 339 S.W.2d 885, 889 (1960) (while a court can relax rules of construction, it may not redraft a will). Similarly, if the property is to pass through intestacy, a specified statutory formula is invoked which operates without the need to make equitable determinations. *See* TEX. PROB. CODE ANN. § 38 (Vernon 1980).

In sum, to extend *Cameron* would make a shambles of 150 years of Texas probate law, thus, without a clear showing of supporting case law, statutory authority or a clear need for such broad power in the trial court, we refuse to do so. Because the court of appeals refused to enlarge *Cameron*, its judgment on this point is affirmed.

In turning to the only other issue in this case, we must address whether the court of appeals erred in holding that the 200 shares of TransWorld stock were not properly traced.

The stipulations of the parties provided the following:

(1) Both parties owned considerable amounts of property before entering the marriage.

(2) After the marriage, both Robert and Dorris continued to keep their respective stock, bond and mutual funds accounts in their own names.

(3) During all times pertinent to this lawsuit, all transactions in Robert's account were from his income, and all transactions in Dorris' account were from her income.

(4) That the following transactions took place in the stock brokerage account of Robert:

A) On the date of marriage, there were 200 shares of Texaco stock in the account.

B) That while married and living in Illinois, the Texaco stock was sold for $5,755.00 and on the same date 200 shares of City Investing stock were purchased for $5,634.00.

C) After moving to Texas, the City Investing stock was sold for $6,021.00 and on the same date 200 shares of TransWorld stock were bought for $6,170.00. The court of appeals held that the above stipulations did not constitute sufficient evidence to overcome the community property presumption.

The court held that it is not sufficient "to show that the separate funds *could have been* the source of a subsequent deposit of funds," *citing Latham v. Allison*, 560 S.W.2d 481, 485 (Tex. Civ. App.—Fort Worth 1978, writ ref'd n.r.e.) (emphasis in original).

In *Tarver v. Tarver*, 394 S.W.2d 780, 783 (Tex.1965), this court held that all property possessed at the time of dissolution of the marriage is presumed to be community property. To show otherwise, the spouse must trace and clearly identify the property claimed as separate property. While the burden is difficult, it is not an impossible one to bear. *Latham*, at 484. But if the evidence shows that the separate property and community property are commingled so as to defy segregation and identification, the burden is not discharged and the statutory presumption prevails. *Latham*, at 484.

The account here has not been commingled, as it was stipulated that the decedent had always kept the property in his own name and that his wife had no power over the account. It certainly does not appear that the property has so radically changed as to "defy resegregation and identification" as said by this court in *McKinley v. McKinley*, 496 S.W.2d 540, 543 (Tex. 1973). Further, the petitioner has shown the chain of events leading from the Texaco stock to the TransWorld purchase and shown that no other transactions occurred on the days in question, which would have planted the seeds of doubt upon the possible source of the funds used to buy the stocks. Because the court of appeals' holding that the TransWorld stock was not properly traced was erroneous, we reverse the judgment of the court of appeals and render judgment that the TransWorld stock be transferred to Steven Hanau. The judgment is in all other things affirmed.

SPEARS, J., concurring.

I concur in the result reached by the court. *Cameron v. Cameron*, 641 S.W.2d 210, 221-23 (Tex. 1982) was based in large part upon Section 3.63 of the Family Code which provided statutory authorization for the characterization of property acquired outside of Texas as quasi-community property. No such provision is present in the Probate Code; therefore, I concur.

The court's opinion creates two rules for the characterization of the same property. A husband and wife from a common law state could retire to Texas with the majority of their property characterized as the husband's separate marital property. If the wife brought divorce proceedings, the "separate" marital property would be characterized as quasi-community property under *Cameron* and Section 3.63 of the Family Code. The trial court would then be authorized to divide the marital property between the spouses in a manner that it deemed just and right. Under the majority's decision in this case, the same husband could execute a will devising all the "separate" marital property to a third party leaving the wife without any means of support after he dies.

Most jurisdictions have some method to protect the interest and insure the support of surviving spouses. This court's holding leaves surviving spouses without the protection afforded by either common law or community property statutory schemes in certain situations. Accordingly, I urge the Legislature to eliminate this illogical and potentially inequitable difference in the characterization of marital property by adopting a Probate Code section similar to Section 3.63 of the Family Code and the probate codes of other jurisdictions. *See* CALIFORNIA PROB. CODE § 66 (West 1985); IDAHO CODE § 15-2-201 (1971).

Notes, Comments & Questions

1. We have read that the character of property is established at inception. How then can the means of marriage dissolution affect the character of property?

2. Should the probate code be changed to encompass quasi-community property?

3. What could be the rationale for this different treatment?

4. Remember, if a marriage is dissolved by death, property is characterized at situs of acquisition.

E. Valuation for Division

In order to make a just and right division of the community estate, the trial court must be presented with the value of the assets of the estate. Evidence of value of the community estate can be as simple as a spouse testifying to the value of a particular asset or can entail a battle of the experts. It is not unusual for spouses to present widely varying valuations of contested assets—remember the washateria in *Horlock v. Horlock*, 533 S.W.2d 52 (Tex. Civ. App.—Houston [14th Dist.] 1975, writ dism'd). Once presented with the evidence, the trial court must determine the value and make its just and right division.

If a spouse appeals the division of property, values of the assets are necessary; how else could one establish that a property division is or is not just and right? As obvious as the need for values may seem, many trial courts, for a variety of reasons, did not make such findings. There was a split within the courts of appeals as to whether the failure to provide values was reversible error. In 2001, the legislature addressed this problem with the passage of TEX. FAM. CODE § 6.711, Findings of Fact & Conclusions of Law, which provides:

> (a) In a suit for dissolution of a marriage in which the court has rendered a judgment dividing the estate of the parties, on request by a party, the court shall state in writing its findings of fact and conclusions of law concerning:
>
> (1) the characterization of each party's assets, liabilities, claims, and offsets on which disputed evidence has been presented; and
>
> (2) the value or amount of the community estate's assets, liabilities, claims, and offsets on which disputed evidence has been presented.
>
> (b) A request for findings of fact and conclusions of law under this section must conform to the Texas Rules of Civil Procedure.

The requirement that findings be made by the trial court when disputed evidence regarding characterization or value has been presented makes the appeal of a property division much easier. Nonetheless, the trial court must be presented with ample evidence of characterization and value and the findings must be properly requested. *See* TEX. R. CIV. P. 296-299a.

Cases abound regarding proper valuation of assets upon divorce. However, the following case tackles the issue of valuing a law partnership and whether to include goodwill in that value, as well as numerous other issues which might arise in a hotly contested divorce.

FINN
v.
FINN
658 S.W.2d 735
(Tex. App.—Dallas 1983, writ n.r.e.)
(en banc)

VANCE, JUSTICE.

The questions presented in this appeal concern the trial court's division of property upon the divorce of Frank and Joellen Finn. The wife asserts fourteen points contending that various errors committed by the trial court resulted in an unfair and unjust property division. For the reasons stated below, we hold that the wife was improperly denied discovery of documents essential to prove the value of the community interest in the husband's law practice. We therefore reverse and remand the property division for a new trial.

The Finns were married for more than twenty years. During the entire time the couple was married the husband worked for a large Dallas law firm. The law practice is structured as a partnership in which the husband has been a senior partner for over ten years. Although the wife also has a law degree, she did not practice law during the marriage, but instead devoted her time to maintaining the home and raising their four children. The parties agreed on the value of most of the community property, but the value of the husband's law practice was hotly contested.

1. *Goodwill of Law Firm.*

The wife contends that the trial court erred by instructing the jury to exclude the goodwill of the law firm and its future earning capacity from the valuation of the community interest in the husband's law practice. Relying on the Fort Worth Court of Civil Appeals decision in *Geesbreght v. Geesbreght*, 570 S.W.2d 427 (Tex. Civ. App.—Fort Worth 1978, writ dism'd), the wife argues that the husband's law firm has goodwill which is separate and apart from the husband's professional ability. Therefore, the wife argues that the husband's professional partnership is analogous to the professional corporation addressed by the court in *Geesbreght* and the goodwill attached to the law firm is property subject to division upon divorce.

The husband, relying on the supreme court opinion in *Nail v. Nail*, 486 S.W.2d 761 (Tex. 1972) contends that the goodwill is not a vested property right which fixes a benefit in any sum at a future time. In support of his contention, the husband notes that the partnership agreement under which the law firm operates makes no provision for compensating a senior partner for the goodwill of the firm in the event of his death or withdrawal. The husband argues that the goodwill of the professional partnership is analogous to the individual professional practice addressed by the court in *Nail*, in that under the terms of the operating agreement any benefit conferred on the husband due to the goodwill of the firm is a mere expectancy contingent on his continued participation in the firm. Thus, he argues, the goodwill is not property in the community estate subject to division on divorce.

In *Nail* the supreme court noted that "goodwill has no existence as property in and of itself, as a separate and distinct entity, but only as an incident of a continuing business having locality or name." *Nail*, 486 S.W.2d at 763. The court went on to state that professional goodwill attaches to the person of the professional as a result of confidence in his skill and ability. In the case of a solo practitioner the court held that goodwill did not possess value or constitute an asset separate and apart from the professional's ability. *Nail*, 486 S.W.2d at 764. Accordingly, the court held that the goodwill of the professional's practice that may have accrued during the marriage was not property in the community estate. The *Nail* court was particularly concerned with the fact that should a solo practitioner die or cease to practice the goodwill would cease to exist without its value having been realized in any manner other than by enhancing the practitioner's earning capacity. *Nail*, 486 S.W.2d at 764. The *Nail* court specifically reserved the question of goodwill that exists apart from the person of an individual member in a professional partnership or corporation.

In *Geesbreght* the Fort Worth Court of Civil Appeals considered the question of whether goodwill was property subject to division upon divorce in the context of a professional corporation. Dr. Geesbreght and his partner incorporated their professional practice with each partner holding one-half of the corporate stock. The corporation did not do business under the names of the two stockholders and employed many professionals, in addition to the two stockholders, to provide services on behalf of the corporation under its many contracts. The court noted that the corporation had a reputation for providing services in its own name that was built in large part upon the abilities of the professional employees. To that extent, goodwill existed in the corporation separate and apart from the personal ability and reputation of Dr. Geesbreght. *Geesbreght*, 570 S.W.2d at 435. The court went on to hold that this corporate goodwill had a commercial value and to the extent that it enhanced the value of Dr. Geesbreght's stock in the corporation, the goodwill was property subject to division upon divorce. *Geesbreght* 570 S.W.2d at 436. The issue of whether the community estate was entitled to share in the goodwill of the corporation was not before the *Geesbreght* court. It was undisputed that Dr. Geesbreght's stock in his professional corporation was community property and to the extent that the goodwill enhanced the value of the stock, it was community property subject to division upon divorce.

Read together, *Nail* and *Geesbreght* indicate a two-pronged test to determine whether the goodwill attached to a professional practice is subject to division upon divorce. First, goodwill must be determined to exist independently of the personal ability of the professional spouse. Second, if such goodwill is found to exist, then it must be determined whether that goodwill has a commercial value in which the community estate is entitled to share.

Evidence in the present case indicates that the husband's law firm has goodwill independent of his professional ability. Like the professional corporation in *Geesbreght*, the firm does not conduct business under the names of the senior partners, but rather operates under the names of two founding partners no longer practicing with the firm. The record reflects that at the time of trial the law firm consisted of twenty senior partners, twenty-two junior partners and forty-three associates. The husband has been practicing law with the firm for over twenty-five years; however, the firm has been providing legal services to the public for more than ninety years. A large part of the firm's reputation for providing services was built upon the professional abilities of the husband's predecessors in the firm as well as the abilities of his present partners and professional employees. Under these circumstances we recognize that the firm has goodwill independent and apart from the professional ability of the husband.

The inquiry does not stop here, as the wife contends, but must continue to determine whether his goodwill has commercial value to which the community estate is entitled. Without question the goodwill of a long established firm has commercial value. The question which confronts us is whether the community estate is entitled to share in the value of the law firm's goodwill.

The community estate is not entitled to a greater interest than that to which the husband is entitled in the firm's goodwill. The extent of the husband's interest is governed by the partnership agreement.[1] Under the terms of the partnership agreement, should the husband die or withdraw, he is entitled only to 1) the amount contained in his capital account, 2) any earned income which had not been distributed, and 3) his interest in the firm's reserve account less ten percent of his proportionate share in the accounts receivable for clients' disbursement.[2] By a vote of three fourths of the senior partners, the husband may be required to withdraw, and in that event he is entitled to the same compensation for his interest as provided for voluntary withdrawal should he continue to practice law elsewhere. Additional compensation is provided should the husband voluntarily withdraw from the firm and cease to practice law. The agreement does not provide any compensation for accrued goodwill to a partner who ceases to practice law with the firm, nor does it provide any mechanism to realize the value of the firm's goodwill.

The lack of any legal right of the husband to realize the value of the firm's goodwill is a decisive factor. It distinguishes the present case from *Geesbreght* wherein the corporate structure provided a mechanism which enabled Dr. Geesbreght to realize the value of accrued goodwill by enhancing the value of his stock. In the present case the only mechanism through which the husband may possibly realize the value of the accrued goodwill is through continuing to practice law as a member of the firm, a circumstance depending not only on his own individual capacity, but also on the uncontrolled discretion of his partners. Thus his position is no better than that of the physician in *Nail,* in which the supreme court found the value of accrued goodwill in an individual professional practice to be realized only through enhanced future earning capacity. Such realization in the future is no more than an expectancy entirely dependent on the husband's continued participation in the firm, and, therefore, is not property in the community estate. *Nail*, 486 S.W.2d at 764. Consequently, we hold that the

[1] The wife urges us to follow a line of California cases which have held the accrued good will of a professional practice to be community property subject to division upon divorce. Slater v. Slater, 100 Cal. App. 3d 241, 160 Cal. Rptr. 686 (1980); Webb v. Webb, 94 Cal. App. 3d 335, 156 Cal. Rptr. 334 (1979); Foster v. Foster, 42 Cal. App. 3d 577, 117 Cal. Rptr. 49 (1974); Lopez v. Lopez, 38 Cal. App.3d 93, 113 Cal. Rptr. 58 (1974); Golden v. Golden, 270 Cal. App.2d 401, 75 Cal. Rptr. 735 (1969); Mueller v. Mueller, 144 Cal. App.2d 245, 301 P.2d 90 (1956). She places particular emphasis upon the *Slater* case which held the wife was not bound by the provisions of the partnership agreement as to the extent of the husband's interest should he withdraw from the partnership to determine the present value of the husband's continued participation in the partnership. Following the rationale of the California courts, the wife urges us to disregard the provisions of the partnership agreement and find accrued goodwill to be community property subject to division. This we decline to do.

The California community property statute mandates an equal division of the community property upon divorce. CAL.CIV.CODE § 4800(a) (Deering Supp.1983). This has been interpreted to mean a mathematically equal division in the ideal situation. In re Juick, 21 Cal. App.3d 421, 98 Cal. Rptr. 324, 329 (1971). The court in California is not at liberty to make an unequal division of the community property due to disparate earning capacity between the spouses, business opportunities, education, relative physical conditions, relative financial condition and obligations, disparity of ages and size of separate estates. Thus the California court must consider the factor of accrued goodwill under the guise of community property if it is to be considered at all. Such is not the case in Texas. The Texas court is at liberty to make an unequal division of the community property which, when all factors are considered, is a just and right division. TEX. FAM. CODE ANN. § 3.63 (Vernon Supp. 1982-1983); Murff v. Murff, 615 S.W.2d 696, 699 (Tex. 1981). Thus, in Texas we are not placed in the position of being compelled to consider the accrued goodwill of a professional partnership as community property or omit it from consideration entirely as are the California courts. Under Texas community property law, we find the accrued goodwill of a professional partnership to be more properly considered as a factor enhancing earning capacity of the professional spouse rather than as community property to be valued and divided for the reasons set forth in the text of this opinion.

[2] The agreement also contains extensive provisions regarding retirement benefits which we find unnecessary to detail here.

trial court properly instructed the jury not to consider the law firm's accrued goodwill or future earning capacity[3] when placing a value on the community interest in the husband's law practice.

By this holding we do not mean that the husband's earning capacity as a member of the firm has no relevance to the division of the community estate. Under section 3.63 of the Family Code disparity in earning capacity of the spouses is a factor which may be considered when making a just and right division of the community property. *Murff v. Murff*, 615 S.W.2d 696, 698 (Tex. 1981). Although goodwill cannot properly be considered in determining the value of the community's interest in the law firm, to the extent that the husband's earning capacity is enhanced by his continued participation in the law firm, the court may consider this factor when assessing any disparity in earning capacity of the spouses.

2. *Limitation of Discovery.*

The wife contends that the trial court improperly denied discovery of the law firm's balance sheets, profit and loss statements, and records reflecting salaries and disbursements to senior partners. The trial court granted discovery of the firm's partnership agreement and retirement plan and of the husband's Internal Revenue Service K-1 schedules, which provide annual summaries of his share of the firm's assets and earnings. These documents, the wife contends, were insufficient to allow her to adequately prepare a valuation of the community interest in the firm. Specifically she complains that without the requested documents she is unable to determine the value of the firm's accrued goodwill and its earning capacity, which have a direct relation to the value of the community interest in the firm and to the disparity between the earning capacity of the spouses.

The husband contends that the wife was able to adequately determine the value of the community interest in the firm without the financial records withheld from her. He points out that the wife presented the testimony of two expert witnesses who were able to place a value on the community interest in the firm without the absent records. In addition the husband presented evidence of the value of the community interest in the firm through the managing partner, Harold Kleinman, who testified from notes he had made while examining the absent records. The husband argues that the wife was not harmed because sufficient evidence was presented on which to value the community interest in the firm. We do not agree.

The wife served the husband with a subpoena duces tecum requesting the disputed documents. He refused to comply with the request and the wife filed a motion to compel production of those documents not produced. At a hearing on the motion one of the wife's two expert witnesses, Lane McDaniel, testified that he needed the firm's yearly financial statements for the last five years plus any interim financial statements for the current year, the partnership agreement, any existing buy-sell agreement, and the husband's Internal Revenue Service K-1 schedules for the last five years in order

[3] Goodwill has been defined as "the advantage or benefit which is acquired by an establishment beyond the mere value of the capital stock, funds, or property employed therein, in consequence of the general public patronage and encouragement which it receives from constant or habitual customers on account of its local position, or common celebrity, or reputation for skill, or influence, or punctuality, or from other accidental circumstances or necessities, or even from ancient partialities or prejudices." Estate of Masquelette v. Commissioner of Internal Revenue, 239 F.2d 322, 325 (5th Cir. 1956) (quoting STORY, PARTNERSHIPS § 99). To the extent that the law firm's future earning capacity is attributable to goodwill, the propriety of its consideration in the valuation of the community estate's interest in the law firm is disposed of by our holding in regard to goodwill. To the extent that the law firm's future earning capacity is attributable to factors other than goodwill, it is not property in the community estate based on the same rationale applied to accrued goodwill.

to calculate the value of the husband's interest in the firm.[4] McDaniel's testimony was sufficient to demonstrate a need for the requested materials. The judge ordered that the partnership agreement and the husband's K-1 schedules be produced and denied the motion as to the firm's financial statements.

At trial one of the wife's expert witnesses, Jim Sampson, testified that the value of the husband's interest in the firm under the provisions of the partnership agreement was $161,000.[5] Sampson indicated he had calculated these values based on the formula provided in the partnership agreement using the figures contained in the couple's tax returns for the last five years and the firm's balance sheets for 1976, 1977 and eight months of 1978. Sampson did not indicate that he had access to any other financial records of the firm.

At trial, the wife's other expert, Lane McDaniel, testified that the value of the husband's interest in the tangible assets of the firm was $122,000. McDaniel indicated that he obtained this figure from Kleinman's prior testimony.

The managing partner of the firm, Harold Kleinman, testified as to the amount to which the husband would be entitled should he either leave the firm and continue to practice law or be forced to withdraw from the firm by a vote of the partners. He stated that the total due the husband under either of these circumstances was $122,342.00.[6] Kleinman's figure is almost $40,000.00 less than Sampson's figure. Kleinman testified that the source of his figures was the firm's "regular accounting records," and particularly the firm's balance sheet as of December 31, 1980, a document to which the court denied the wife access. This testimony was admitted over the wife's timely objection pointing out to the court that she had been denied access to records which were the basis of Kleinman's testimony.

Under these circumstances we find the denial of discovery deprived the wife of access to material information needed to effectively cross-examine Kleinman and to allow her experts all the information they required to accurately calculate the value of the husband's interest in the firm. Had the documents been produced as requested, the wife would have had the information necessary to effectively challenge the accuracy of Kleinman's testimony. Further, the wife's experts were not required to rely on secondary data in determining and presenting to the court her estimate of the value of the community interest in the firm.

The denial of discovery was material not only because it denied the wife information needed to adequately present her case to the court, but also because it deprived the trial court of sufficient evidence on which to base a valuation of the community interest in the law firm. The jury found the value of the community interest in the firm to be zero. On the husband's motion, the court disre-

[4] Although McDaniel stated during direct examination that he would like to have the K-1 schedules for all of the partners in the firm, he conceded on cross-examination that only the husband's K-1 schedule was necessary and that he did not need the K-1 schedules for the other partners. McDaniel was never asked on cross-examination to retract his previously stated need for the firm's financial statements nor did he do so voluntarily.

[5] Sampson also testified that the average amount of the husband's income from the firm for the last five years was $172,000. The husband is entitled to this additional sum under the partnership agreement only should he withdraw from the partnership voluntarily and cease to practice law.

[6] Kleinman testified that the balance remaining in the husband's undistributed earnings account was $45,853.08 and that the balance in the husband's capital account was $69,937.36. He also testified that the 10% deduction to be subtracted from the husband's share of the firm's reserve account was $1,638.00. The deduction figure should be equal to 10% of the husband's percentage interest in the accounts receivable for clients' disbursements. This figure was to be subtracted from the husband's proportionate share of the firm's reserve account. There was no testimony as to the amounts contained in either the firm's reserve account or its accounts receivable for clients' disbursements.

garded the jury's finding and substituted the value testified to by Kleinman as the value of the community interest in the firm.[7] The wife contends that there is no evidence of probative value to support the court's finding. We agree.

The husband's Internal Revenue Service K-1 schedules from 1975 through 1979 were admitted into evidence. From these forms it is possible to calculate the amount in the husband's capital account and the amount of his undistributed income for the years encompassed by the forms. However, the K-1 schedules do not reflect the amount to which the husband would be entitled from the firm's reserve account, the third item specified in the partnership agreement. The trial of this action commenced on December 8, 1980, and lasted for eight weeks. The K-1 schedules contained no information as to the amounts contained in the husband's various accounts with the firm at the time of divorce, approximately one year after the time represented in the most recent K-1 schedule admitted at trial. Nor do the figures contained in the K-1 schedules comport with the figures testified to by Kleinman which were substituted for the jury's finding by the court.

Kleinman's testimony consisted of figures obtained from the firm's current records which were not produced at any time. Of the $122,343 which Kleinman gave as the value of the husband's interest before deducting an earnings distribution of $45,853.08, the major component was $69,937.36, which, according to Kleinman, represented the husband's interest in the capital account. This figure, Kleinman said, was not based on computation, but was taken from "a schedule as of December 31, 1980, which lists each partner of the firm and lists opposite his or her name their capital account." The wife objected to this evidence on the ground that it constituted a summary with respect to which no underlying details had been provided.

Counsel for the husband offered to bring the document to court and allow it to be examined in camera. The judge, however, asked the witness whether the document would be cumulative of his testimony, and the witness replied that it would. On further examination, Kleinman explained that the bulk of the husband's capital account represented what the husband had actually paid for the "hard assets," the furniture and fixtures of the firm, over the period of twelve or thirteen years that he had been a senior partner, and that the "capital account" was a cumulation of such items. The wife's counsel objected to this testimony as being a summary of information from the firm's books that had not previously been made available to him and that he did not want to and could not do an accounting of firm's books at that point in the trial.

From these proceedings it appears that the wife's objection was not to the husband's failure to bring into court the document containing the cumulative figure, but that testimony based on this document was not competent because the document itself represented a summary of other figures which had not been made available for her examination.

This objection was well taken. Even if the document of December 31, 1980, had been offered, it would not have been admissible over the objection made. It was not a record of the husband's contributions made at or near the time of each transaction as required by the business records statute, TEX. REV. CIV. STAT. ANN. art. 3737e (Vernon Supp. 1982-1983). Neither were the underlying records authenticated in the manner required by the statute.

---

[7] From the language contained in the judgment it is apparent that the court deducted the amount of undistributed earnings the court had ordered disbursed to the husband to pay federal income taxes from the figure testified to by Kleinman, thus finding the value of the community interest in the firm to be $76,489.

Kleinman's testimony, based on unproved and unproduced records, was not susceptible of an adequate cross-examination, and neither did the wife's attorneys have an opportunity to subject the firm's records to an audit of their own. Consequently, the evidence was inadmissible. *Dallas Railway & Terminal Co. v. Guthrie*, 146 Tex. 585, 210 S.W.2d 550, 552 (1948).

Counsel for the wife did not waive the objection by advising the court that he had no time to look at the records and that it would be impossible to go through them and do an accounting of the figures at that point in the trial. When records are voluminous, the party relying on them, merely by making them accessible at the time of trial, cannot shift the burden to the opposing party to examine them and determine any objection to admissibility of testimony based on them. *Sherwin-Williams Co. v. Perry Co.*, 424 S.W.2d 940, 946 (Tex. Civ. App.—Austin 1968, writ ref'd n.r.e.). Oral testimony based on entries contained in written records without producing the source of such information is hearsay. *Delhi Gas Pipeline Co. v. Heddin*, 508 S.W.2d 417, 420 (Tex. Civ. App.—Tyler 1974, no writ). The lack of production of the underlying records renders Kleinman's testimony double-hearsay since the records themselves are hearsay until properly admitted as business records under article 3737e, TEX. REV. CIV. STAT. ANN. (Vernon Supp. 1982-1983). *Day & Zimmermann, Inc. v. Strickland*, 483 S.W.2d 541, 546 (Tex. Civ. App.—Texarkana 1972, writ ref'd n.r.e.). These records, like those in *Sherwin-Williams*, are hearsay, and any testimony based on them is "hearsay spawned in hearsay." *Sherwin-Williams Co.*, 424 S.W.2d at 946. Consequently, Kleinman's testimony does not establish the trial court's valuation as a matter of law. *See Xonu Intercontinental Industries v. Stauffer Chemical Co.*, 587 S.W.2d 757, 760 (Tex. Civ. App.—Corpus Christi 1979, no writ).

This problem was not cured by the testimony of the wife's experts. McDaniel accepted Kleinman's figure of $122,000 as the value of the husband's interest in the tangible assets of the firm and indicated that the source of his information was Kleinman's testimony, which was hearsay. Testimony based on the hearsay statements of others is nothing more than hearsay upon hearsay. *See Day & Zimmermann, Inc.*, 483 S.W.2d at 546; *Muro v. Houston Fire and Casualty Insurance Co.*, 329 S.W.2d 326, 332 (Tex. Civ. App.—San Antonio 1959, writ ref'd n.r.e.). Further, McDaniel based his testimony of value on factors other than those specified in the partnership agreement. We do not know what McDaniel's testimony would have been if further information had been developed by discovery or by cross-examination of Kleinman based on the underlying records.

The only other evidence as to the value of the husband's interest in the firm under the partnership agreement was the testimony of Sampson, the wife's other expert. Sampson's figure was more than 30% greater than Kleinman's figure, the one ultimately used by the trial court to determine the value of the community interest in the firm. However, Sampson did not have access to the then current financial statements of the firm, but was forced instead to estimate the amounts in the various relevant firm accounts using secondary sources of information. Sampson testified on the basis of the information available to him, which did not include the current information available to Kleinman, that the value of the husband's interest according to the formula in the partnership agreement was $161,000. In the light of this testimony, the trial court could not properly hold as a matter of law that the value (before deducting the earnings distribution of $45,853.04) was $122,342.

The wife was entitled to inspect those financial records of the firm necessary to calculate the husband's interest in the firm under the formula contained in the partnership agreement. The fact that one of her experts was able to estimate that amount from secondary sources of information does not negate her right to the most accurate information available. We recognize the need to protect the confidentiality of the firm's records. However, this need not be an absolute bar to discovery because the court may order an *in camera* inspection of the documents to protect their privacy. *Maresca v. Marks*, 362 S.W.2d 299, 301 (Tex. 1962); *Crane v. Tunks*, 160 Tex. 182, 328 S.W.2d 434, 440 (1959).

We find that the denial of discovery was such a denial of the rights of the wife as was reasonably calculated to cause and probably did cause the rendition of an improper judgment. The husband's interest in the firm was a major asset of the community estate. Lack of this discovery left the trial court's valuation of this asset without proper support in the evidence. Since this interest is the largest item of the community estate, and its value was the principal contested issue at the trial with respect to the division of the property of the parties, we conclude that without a proper valuation the trial court could not properly exercise its discretion in making a "just and right" division within section 3.63 of the Texas Family Code. Under these circumstances we hold that the trial court's division of the community estate was an abuse of discretion. Consequently, that portion of the judgment dividing the community property must be remanded for a new trial. TEX. R. CIV. P. 434.

With respect to the wife's pre-trial motion for discovery, we are unable to determine precisely which records should have been produced. Much of the information requested was for the purpose of determining the goodwill of the firm, a matter we hold should not be considered in determining the husband's interest. Neither is the wife entitled to examine the records of all the partners, but only those bearing on the husband's interest. Relevant information from the firm's balance sheet for 1980 and possibly for several previous years should be furnished. The court will have to determine, perhaps after hearing evidence, what additional records, if any, should be furnished in order to determine the husband's earning capacity and the value of his interest in the firm as determined by the partnership agreement. If relevant figures based on an independent audit are available, further examination of the firm's records may not be necessary.

If remand is necessary, we have been urged by amicus curiae to remand only on the issue of the value of the community interest in the law firm and not to remand the entire property division. This we cannot do. Article 3.63 of in Texas Family Code requires that the property division be just and right. The husband's interest in the firm constitutes a large percentage of the community estate and any change in its valuation may distort the division and require a redistribution of the property. The trial court must have before it all of the property of the parties in order to make the just and right division mandated by Article 3.63. Therefore, the entire property division is remanded for a new trial.

3. *Issues on Retrial*

The wife has raised several contentions with respect to problems that may recur on retrial. These include the propriety of including $126,400 in the property awarded to the wife comprised of gold coins which were not shown to exist; the propriety of awarding four life insurance policies to the husband contrary to a stipulation that they were to be awarded to the wife as her separate property; the propriety of charging the wife fees for guardians ad litem appointed over her objection; and the propriety of denying the wife an award for her attorney's fees. We have considered these contentions in light of our order remanding the property division for a new trial.

a. *The Gold Coins*

With respect to the gold coins the wife contends that the property division was unjust because the trial court included the gold coins in the property awarded to her when there was no evidence that these coins were in the possession of either party at the time of trial. The wife admitted that she had removed the coins from the couple's safety deposit box and placed them in paper folders in their house. The wife asserts that the coins disappeared from the house while she was out of the state and accuses her husband of taking them while she was gone. The husband admits having searched the house while the wife was gone and having seen the paper folders, but insists that the folders were empty when he saw them. A special issue was submitted to the jury asking whether the husband or anyone acting in his behalf had removed the coins from the house. Based on the jury's negative response to this issue, the trial court credited the gold coins to the wife's share of the community property, impliedly finding that the coins or the proceeds from them were still in the wife's possession.[8]

On remand, the court should ask the jury to determine whether each of the parties has possession of the coins or has received the benefit of having had them. If neither spouse is found to have benefited from possession of the coins, then they cannot properly be included in the property awarded to either spouse.

b. *The Life Insurance*

The wife also contends that the trial court erred in awarding four life insurance policies covering the husband's life to him although the parties had agreed that the policies were to be awarded to her. The wife claims that the policies are her separate property and that in reliance on the written agreement she did not proceed at trial to present evidence as to the separate character of the property. The stipulation states that the wife "shall have as her separate property and estate" the insurance policies in question. The language used does not indicate that the present character of the property is "separate," but rather indicates an agreement by the parties that the policies are to be awarded to the wife as her separate property upon division of the community estate. We find this language to be more in the nature of a property settlement agreement and not a stipulation as to the character of the property. The trial court is not bound by the parties' written agreement which does not purport to settle the entire property division and is not incorporated in the judgment. *See Harding v. Harding*, 461 S.W.2d 235 (Tex. Civ. App.—San Antonio 1970, no writ). The court must follow the mandate of section 3.63 of the Family Code and make a just and right division of the property regardless of any agreement between the spouses. Before such an agreement can become binding on the court, the court must find that the agreement is fair, just and equitable and has been entered into without coercion or other undue influence. *See Morgan v. Morgan*, 622 S.W.2d 447, 450 (Tex. App.—Beaumont 1981, no writ). However, on retrial the wife should have an opportunity to establish that the policies are her separate property, and, therefore, not property subject to division in the community estate. *Cameron v. Cameron*, 641 S.W.2d 210, 219 (Tex. 1982).

c. *The Guardians Ad Litem*

The wife next contends that the trial court erred in appointing guardians ad litem for two of the couple's minor children at the husband's request, over her objection. She argues that the trial court abused its discretion in charging her with one-half of the guardians' fees because they had no ascertainable duties to perform, performed no discovery, and participated minimally in the trial. If the guardians were entitled to any fees for this minimal representation, the wife contends that the husband should have been charged with all of those fees because the guardians were appointed on his motion which the wife opposed. We do not agree.

---

[8] The judgment awarded the wife, among other items as follows:

B. Fifty (50) Mexican fifty Peso gold coins already in the possession and/or control of RESPONDENT JOELLEN FINN.

C. One Hundred Seventy-Five (175) Austrian 100 Coronas already in the possession and/or control of RESPONDENT JOELLEN FINN.

Under section 11.10(a) of the Texas Family Code the court may appoint a guardian ad litem to represent the interests of the child in a suit affecting the parent-child relationship. TEX. FAM. CODE ANN. § 11.10(a) (Vernon Supp. 1982-1983). Such an appointment will not be overturned unless an abuse of discretion is shown. *Swearingen v. Swearingen*, 578 S.W.2d 829, 831 (Tex. Civ. App.—Houston [1st Dist.] 1979, writ dism'd). Custody of the minor children was highly contested in the present case. Whether the guardians made any substantial contribution to the trial is a matter of hindsight which does not control the question of abuse of discretion. Trial of the custody issue took almost four weeks and accounts for fifteen volumes of the statement of facts. Under these circumstances, we find the trial court did not abuse its discretion in appointing the guardians ad litem.

The amount of compensation awarded to the guardians ad litem is also within the discretion of the court and will not be overturned unless a clear abuse of discretion is apparent from the records. *Poston v. Poston*, 572 S.W.2d 800, 802 (Tex. Civ. App.—Houston [1st Dist.] 1978, no writ). The record indicates that the guardians attended the four weeks of trial concerning the issue of custody as well as several pre-trial hearings. The court's award of fees to the guardians ad litem was supported by evidence in the record and was not an abuse of discretion.

The parents of the minor child whose interests are being protected by the appointed guardian ad litem are required to pay the guardian's fee unless they are indigent. TEX. FAM. CODE ANN. § 11.10(e) (Vernon Supp. 1982-1983). As the parents of the two minor children whose interests the court sought to protect by the appointment of guardians ad litem, both the husband and the wife were liable for their fees. The liabilities of the parties are one factor to be considered by the court when making a just and right division of the property under section 3.63 of the Texas Family Code. *Goren v. Goren*, 531 S.W.2d 897, 899 (Tex. Civ. App.—Houston [1st Dist.] 1975, writ dism'd); *see Horlock v. Horlock*, 533 S.W.2d 52, 58 (Tex. Civ. App.—Houston [14th Dist.] 1975, writ dism'd). This debt will be a factor to be considered by the court when dividing the property on remand.

d. *The Wife's Attorney's Fees*

The wife also complains of the court's failure to award her any attorney's fees. Two special issues were submitted to the jury regarding the reasonableness and necessity of the services of her attorney and the amount to be awarded for those services. The jury found the services rendered by the wife's attorney were not reasonable and necessary and, therefore, did not reach the question of the amount to be awarded. Based on the jury's answers to those special issues, the court did not award the wife any attorney's fees. The wife contends that the jury's answers to the two special issues on her attorney's fees were against the great weight and preponderance of the evidence and that the court erred in denying her attorney's fees.

The court is not required to award either spouse attorney's fees, but rather the attorneys' fees are one factor to be considered when making a just and right division of the property. *Carle v. Carle*, 149 Tex. 469, 234 S.W.2d 1002, 1005 (1950); *Austin v. Austin*, 619 S.W.2d 290, 292 (Tex. Civ. App.—Austin 1981, no writ); *Brooks v. Brooks*, 612 S.W.2d 233, 238 (Tex. Civ. App.—Waco 1981, no writ). On remand of the property division, the reasonable and necessary attorney's fees of both parties will be a factor considered by the court in making a just and right division of the property.

We note that over half of the statement of facts filed in this appeal concerns the issue of child custody, which the wife did not challenge. That portion of the statement of facts was used by the wife solely to challenge the need for the appointment of guardians ad litem for two of the minor children, an issue on which she did not prevail. We therefore tax one-half of the costs to the wife and one-half of the costs to the husband. TEX. R. CIV. P. 448.

The original opinion is withdrawn. The judgment is reversed with respect to the property division and affirmed in all other respects. The cause is remanded for a new trial limited solely to the issue of the property division.

GUITTARD, C.J., and ALLEN, SHUMPERT and SPARLING, JJ., join in this majority opinion.

GUILLOT, J., did not participate in this case.

STEWART, J., concurring.

I respectfully disagree with the majority's holding that the value of the law firm's goodwill is not to be considered in evaluating the community's partnership interest. The firm's goodwill is an asset of the partnership entity, and it does not belong to either the separate or community estate of the individual partners. Bromberg, *Source and Comment*, TEX. REV. CIV. STAT. ANN. art. 6132b, § 28-A (Vernon 1970). Thus, the *Nail* decision is inapplicable here. The goodwill of the law partnership is analogous to the corporate goodwill addressed by the court in *Geesbreght v. Geesbreght*, 570 S.W.2d 427, 435 (Tex. Civ. App.—Fort Worth 1978, writ dism'd). The firm's good will enhances the value of the community partnership interest.

The partnership agreement does not control the value of the individual partnership interests. The asset being divided is the husband's interest in the partnership as a going business, not his contractual death benefits or withdrawal rights. *Slater v. Slater*, 100 Cal. App. 3d 241, 160 Cal. Rptr. 686, 688-689 (1980). The formula in the partnership agreement may represent the present value of the husband's interest, but it should not preclude a consideration of other facts. *Slater*, 160 Cal. Rptr. at 689; *Stern v. Stern*, 66 N.J. 340, 331 A.2d 257 (1975). The value of the husband's interest should be based on the present value of the partnership entity as a going business, which would include consideration of partnership goodwill, if any. Goodwill is property and, although intangible, it is an integral part of a business, the same as its physical assets. *Taormina v. Culicchia*, 355 S.W.2d 569, 573 (Tex. Civ. App.—El Paso 1962, writ ref'd n.r.e.); *Ordway-Saunders Co. v. Little*, 568 S.W.2d 711, 717 (Tex. Civ. App.—Amarillo 1978, writ ref'd n.r.e.). Whether the law firm possessed goodwill, and, if so, its value are fact questions for the trier of facts. *Taormina*, 355 S.W.2d at 574.

The majority are concerned with future contingencies. All assets of the community estate are valued as of the time of dissolution of the marriage. There is no valid reason to exclude a professional partnership interest from this basic rule when the partner intends to continue as a member of the firm.

I otherwise concur.

AKIN, J., joins in this opinion.

AKIN, JUSTICE, concurring.

Although I agree that the judgment should be reversed, I agree also with JUSTICE STEWART that the goodwill of the husband's law partnership should be considered in arriving at the husband's interest in that partnership. Hence, I have joined in that opinion and concur in the result reached by the majority.

Apart from these grounds for reversal of the judgment, I would also reverse the judgment dividing between the parties the costs of two guardian ad litems, one for each of the parties' minor children. In this respect, in my view but one guardian ad litem was needed, if any, because the interests of the two children were not in conflict, but rather parallel. Indeed, throughout this long trial both guardian ad litems were present but did nothing except submit bills for trial time on an hourly basis. Thus, I fail to understand why two were necessary to protect the interests of these children. Consequently, I would hold that the appointment of a guardian ad litem for each child was an abuse of discretion. Since the husband moved the court to appoint each of these guardian ad litems, I would assess the costs of each against the husband.

In my view, courts are often too free with litigants' funds in appointing and in compensating unneeded guardian ad litems. Indeed, the guardian ad litem fees in this case were a significant sum with respect to the total community estate. Consequently, judges should appoint a guardian ad litem only where absolutely necessary to protect the children's' interests and then to exercise restraint on the guardian ad litems as to whether the time expended was necessary to protect the wards. In this case, the judge permitted both guardian ad litems to sit throughout the entire trial, even though neither participated and even though much of the testimony and trial time concerned matters other than the children's' interest. Nevertheless, each guardian ad litem was paid on an hourly basis as though each was actively engaged in a contested trial, which was not the case here.

Additionally, I fail to understand why the children's interests in this case were not represented under the doctrine of virtual representation by either their mother or by their father, each of whom was represented by competent counsel. *Oaklawn Preservation Society v. Board of Managers Dallas County Hospital Dist.*, 566 S.W.2d 315 (Tex. Civ. App.—Dallas 1978, writ ref'd n.r.e.). This doctrine is particularly applicable here since the record shows that each child's interests were fully represented by each parent's attorney. Accordingly, I would reverse also on this ground and assess all of the guardian ad litem fees to the husband who caused their appointment.

STEWART, J., joins in this opinion.

STEPHENS, J., dissenting.

* * *

THE MISSING GOLD COINS

Our record reveals that the wife first filed suit for divorce September 22, 1978. Before that time, and in contemplation of filing for divorce, she removed all of the gold coins from a jointly controlled safe deposit box at one bank in Dallas, to another, in her name alone, without the knowledge of the husband. Later when the husband learned of this transfer, she moved them to a third bank and again established a safe deposit box in her name alone.

The first divorce suit, to which the husband had filed no cross-action, was scheduled for trial on July 14, 1980, before a visiting judge. On that morning the wife dismissed her suit. On that same morning, she and her sister drove to the bank where she emptied her safe deposit box of all gold coins, consisting of 275 Austrian four ducats, 55 gold Krugerrands, 50 Mexican peso gold coins, and 175 Austrian one hundred coronas. While at the bank, her sister rented a safe deposit box in her name, making the wife a co-signatory on the box. The wife testified that her sister rented the box because she had a book which she wished to keep in it, and denied that she transferred any of the gold coins into her sister's box. The wife also took possession of five buckets of silver coins, each containing $1,000.00 face value, which had pledged as collateral on a loan at that bank, made for her personal benefit, without the knowledge of the husband.

The wife and her sister left the bank, drove to her home on Harvest Hill, took the coins into the house, and the sister left. The wife agrees that the market value of the gold coins in her exclusive possession could have been in excess of $500,000.00 during this interval of time.

After her sister left the Harvest Hill address on the morning of July 14, 1980, the wife hid the gold and silver coins in various places in the house. She testified that she did not spend the night or the next three nights at that house, although she did stay there some of the time during those days. On July 18, 1980, the wife left Dallas and was gone for one month. During this time her whereabouts were unknown to the husband. When she returned to Dallas, she accused her husband of removing the 175 gold Austrian Coronas and 50 Mexican pesos, but made no accusation as to the other coins. She testified that upon her discovery of the missing coins she notified neither the police nor any insurance company of their disappearance. In answer to special issue, the jury found that neither the husband nor anyone acting in his behalf removed these coins from the Harvest Hill address.

On October 7, 1980, long after the wife returned to Dallas, she negotiated a loan from a Dallas Bank in the amount of $120,000.00, securing it with the remaining gold and silver coins, valued by the bank at $190,475.00.

This evidence shows that the wife, on July 14, 1980, was in possession of the gold coins in question. The jury absolved her husband from later taking them. It is highly unlikely that burglars removed only these specific coins, leaving all the remaining ones, as well as other valuables in the house, during the wife's absence. Under these facts, the trial judge was clearly justified in charging the wife, the last party in possession, with the gold coins. *See Arrington v. Arrington*, 613 S.W.2d 565 (Tex. Civ. App.—Fort Worth 1981, no writ); *Baxla v. Baxla*, 522 S.W.2d 736 (Tex. Civ. App.—Dallas 1975, no writ); *Grothe v. Grothe*, 590 S.W.2d 238 (Tex. Civ. App.—Austin 1979, no writ).

In summary, I must challenge the wisdom of the majority's reversal and remand this case for a new trial as to the property division. First, the law is clear that unless error in the trial results in a manifestly unfair division of the property, the error is harmless. Second, the majority agree that no part of the good-will of Thompson & Knight is a divisible asset in this case, so good-will is not in issue. All of the other values having been stipulated by the parties, this leaves only the capital account of the husband in the firm of Thompson & Knight disputed. Perhaps a new trial as to property will produce a more precise proffer of evidence as to this computer print-out figure, yet the figure will unquestionably be the same. The result then will be not a more fair and just division of the parties' estate between the parties; instead, it will be a dissipation of the capital account, and perhaps more, to pay the additional lawyer fees, accounting fees, witness fees, and other expense of litigation, resulting, finally, in a lesser sum to be realized by the parties. This litigation has been long, tedious, expensive, and emotional for the parties and their children. It should be ended. The trial court's judgment should in all things be affirmed.

CARVER, STOREY, WHITHAM and ROWE, JJ., join in this dissenting opinion.

Notes, Comments & Questions

1. If, after reading *Finn v. Finn*, you are still unsure about the concept of goodwill, reading *Nail v. Nail*, 486 S.W.2d 761 (Tex. 1972) and *Geesbreght v. Geesbreght*, 570 S.W.2d 427 (Tex. Civ. App.—Fort Worth 1978, writ dism'd) may help. Understanding the facts and circumstances which give rise to the varying goodwill rules may clarify this concept.

2. In the *Finn* case, wife's experts and husband's experts were very close in their valuation of husband's interest in the law firm. Why then did the trial court's limitation on discovery yield reversible error?

3. Why was husband's trial offer of valuation data too little, too late?

4. In Justice Stephen's dissenting opinion, he opines that the decision is an impermissible application of the appellate standard of review. What does he mean?

5. In weighing the "gold coin" story, what do you think?

6. The Texas Supreme Court granted and then withdrew the writ in the case of *Guzman v. Guzman*, 827 S.W.2d 445 (Tex. App.—Corpus Christi 1992) *writ granted, then withdrawn*, 843 S.W.2d 486 (Tex. 1992). The issue in *Guzman* was whether professional goodwill that does not exist separate and apart from a professional's skills is property subject to a just and right division upon divorce. The court of appeals, compelled to follow the holding in *Nail v. Nail*, 486 S.W.2d 761 (Tex. 1972), held that such goodwill was not divisible; however, the court of appeals noted that wife's argument that such goodwill should be divided was not a frivolous argument. The Corpus Christi Court obviously had some misgivings about the *Nail* approach to goodwill. The case was taken to the Texas Supreme Court, where the writ was granted but withdrawn with the following statement:

> On procedural grounds, and without reference to the merits, we withdraw our order granting the application for writ of error as improvidently granted, and deny the application. *Guzman v. Guzman*, 843 S.W.2d 486 (Tex. 1992).

7. Can you speculate on the "procedural grounds?"

8. Does the Texas Supreme Court's action in *Guzman* give you any idea as to its view on goodwill?

9. If you were representing the non-working spouse in a divorce case and were facing a similar goodwill issue, how would you use *Guzman*?

10. In *Rathmell v. Morrison*, 732 S.W.2d 6 (Tex. App.—Houston [14th Dist.] 1987, no writ), a court for the first time specifically recognized that a "non-professional" may have goodwill. The court stated:

> Appellant [John] is not a lawyer or doctor, as were the professionals in *Nail*, *Geesbreght*, and *Finn*. Nevertheless, it is clear that appellant did develop professional goodwill as the term is used in *Nail*. . . . the key to the financial success of the Rathmell companies was John's personality, social contacts, and specialized knowledge of the problems and solutions peculiar to insuring businesses and associations. . . . The goodwill that arose because of these attributes in John attached as a result of confidence in his skill and ability and did not possess value or constitute an asset separate and apart from John's person or his individual ability to practice his profession, and would be extinguished if he died, or retired, or was disabled. 732 S.W.2d at 18.

11. In *Keith v. Keith*, 763 S.W.2d 950 (Tex. App.—Fort Worth 1989, no writ), the court examined the *Finn* use of the partnership agreement as a basis for valuation and disagreed, thus:

> Charles relies on the case of *Finn v. Finn*, 658 S.W.2d 735 (Tex.App.—Dallas 1983, writ ref'd n.r.e.) (en banc). In that case the court found the community estate would not be entitled to a greater interest in the goodwill of an ongoing law firm than that to which the husband was entitled under the terms of the partnership agreement in the event of his death or withdrawal. Since the husband's partnership agreement provided that he had no interest in the good will in the event of his death or withdrawal, the court held there was no community interest in the firm's good will at divorce. *Id.* at 742.

For the reasons stated in her opinion, we agree with the concurring opinion of Justice Annette Stewart in that case to the effect that the formula set forth in the partnership agreement with respect to death or withdrawal of the partner is not necessarily determinative of the value of a spouse's interest in the ongoing partnership as of the time of divorce. *Id.* at 749; *see In re Marriage of Slater*, 100 Cal. App. 3d 241, 160 Cal. Rptr. 686, 688-89 (1979). We overrule point of error number three.

In points of error numbers four and five, Charles asserts there is no evidence to support the trial court's findings that Glenda would not have signed the partnership agreement if she had thought it would defeat her community interest in the partnership and that the partnership agreement was not intended to apply to the evaluation of the business in case of divorce of either partner. Both of these points of error are dependent upon the presumption that a determination of the value of Charles' interest in the partnership business is necessarily limited by the terms of the partnership agreement. Since we have found the value is not so limited, we overrule points of error numbers four and five.

F. Partnership Distributions

A business entity can affect the character of marital property. Likewise the manner in which business entities make payment to partners or stock holders can also affect characterization as these next cases show.

MARSHALL
v.
MARSHALL
735 S.W.2d 587
(Tex. App.—Dallas 1987, writ ref'd n.r.e.)

STEWART, JUSTICE.

Arlene O. Marshall and J.W. "Woody" Marshall sued each other for divorce. In four points of error, Arlene contends that the trial court (1) abused its discretion in denying her claims for reimbursement for community funds used to pay Woody's separate debt and for gifts of community funds to Woody's daughter and grandson; (2) erred in ruling that the community estate is not liable for all unpaid debts of Leasing Telephone Concepts, Incorporated (LTC), including those incurred after June 25, 1984; (3) abused its discretion in dividing the household furnishings in kind; and (4) erred in awarding her only $5,500 for the value of the Mercedes automobile wrongfully taken from her possession by Woody.

In two cross-points, Woody asserts that the trial court erred in finding that he gave Arlene a usufructuary right in the Mercedes automobile which he wrongfully terminated and in ordering him to pay $12,500 of Arlene's attorney fees. In one cross-point, Marshall Pipe and Supply Company (the partnership) maintains that the trial court erred in denying its claim to ownership of the household furnishings used by the spouses during marriage. We affirm in part, reverse and render in part, and reverse and remand in part.

Approximately five months after being divorced from their first marriage, the parties remarried on March 18, 1983. On June 25, 1984, Woody filed for a divorce from their second marriage, and later the same day Arlene also filed for divorce. The suits were consolidated with Woody designated as petitioner and Arlene as cross-petitioner. The trial court entered the decree of divorce on December 31, 1985. The marriage involved no children. By agreement, on appeal, Arlene is designated as appellant and Woody as appellee. Neither party appeals the divorce itself. We develop the facts as they relate to the points.

I.

ARLENE'S REIMBURSEMENT CLAIMS

In her first point of error, Arlene argues that the trial court incorrectly characterized the disbursements by the partnership to Woody as his separate property and that, as a result, the trial court abused its discretion in denying her claim that Woody should be ordered to reimburse the community for (1) $125,375.50 of community funds used to pay Woody's 1982 taxes, a separate debt incurred before the marriage, and (2) $63,325.58 of community funds that Woody gave to his daughter during the marriage.

EXTENT OF COMMUNITY EARNINGS

To resolve Arlene's contentions, we must first determine the extent of the community earnings during the marriage. The partnership disbursed $542,315.72 to Woody during the marriage. The partnership records and Woody's tax returns reflect that some amounts were distributed as "salary" and other amounts were distributed as "distributions of profits." Woody argues that only $22,400 of the amount disbursed was salary and that the rest was a return of capital and, therefore, his separate property. Arlene argues that all the disbursements were either salary or distributions of profits and, therefore, community.

Arlene first argues that all partnership disbursements to Woody during marriage were community property because they were acquired during the marriage, TEX. FAM. CODE ANN. § 5.01(b) (Vernon 1975), and, therefore, are presumed to have been community property. *Id.* § 5.02. She further contends that whatever is earned from the labor and effort of either spouse is community property, *Givens v. Girard Life Insurance Co.*, 480 S.W.2d 421, 423 (Tex. Civ. App.—Dallas 1972, writ ref'd n.r.e.); thus, all the disbursements are community property because they are compensation for Woody's labor and effort on behalf of the partnership. Finally, she maintains that the partnership distributions are revenues and profits from Woody's separate property, thereby making them community property, *Arnold v. Leonard*, 114 Tex. 535, 273 S.W. 799 (1925); consequently, whether classified as "distributions of profits" or "salary," all disbursements are community.

Woody brings three responses to justify the separate property characterization of the trial court. First, he argues that he and Arlene entered into a prior separate property agreement providing that all income arising from separate property owned or acquired by either spouse would be the separate property of said spouse. Second, he argues that the distributions from the partnership were distributions of capital and were, therefore, his separate property. Third, he contends that all community property distributions to him and to Arlene during the marriage had been consumed by them.

SEPARATE PROPERTY AGREEMENT

We first consider whether the separate property agreement (the agreement) has any bearing on the present case. The parties were first married on April 26, 1982. On June 14, 1982, they executed a separate property agreement, which provides: "All income and/or property arising from the separate property now owned by [said spouse] or hereafter acquired by [said spouse], shall be the sole and separate property of [said spouse]." The October 15, 1982, judgment of divorce recited that the agreement was valid.

Approximately five months later the parties remarried, and it is from this marriage that the parties seek a divorce and a property division. Arlene's brief ignores the existence of the agreement; Woody's argues that the agreement is still in effect.

Woody relies primarily upon *Sorrels v. Sorrels*, 592 S.W.2d 692 (Tex. Civ. App.—Amarillo 1979, writ ref'd n.r.e.). In *Sorrels*, the property settlement incident to the parties' first divorce required Mr. Sorrels to pay alimony to Mrs. Sorrels after the divorce. It further provided that "should [Mrs. Sorrels] remarry, such remarriage shall have no effect upon obligations of [Mr. Sorrels] to make the aforesaid payments." Mr. and Mrs. Sorrels subsequently remarried and divorced for a second time, and Mr. Sorrels argued that the second marriage invalidated the payment obligations. The court disagreed. The agreement had whatever legal force the law of contracts would give it. *Id.* at 696.

Sorrels is distinguishable. In *Sorrels*, the agreement specifically stipulated that a subsequent remarriage would have no bearing on the alimony payments. In the present case, no express provision provides for the termination or continuation of the agreement.

When the duration of the contract is not expressly dictated by the agreement, courts will frequently presume that the parties intended that the agreement should continue for a reasonable time. *Beckner v. Barrett*, 81 S.W.2d 719 (Tex. Civ. App.—Dallas 1935, writ dism'd w.o.j.). When it appears, from the intrinsic nature of the agreement, that an agreement is necessarily limited as to duration by the happening of any one of several contingencies, this ascertainable contingency determines the duration. *See Brittian v. General Telephone Co.*, 533 S.W.2d 886 (Tex. Civ. App.—Fort Worth 1976, writ dism'd w.o.j.); *Kennedy v. McMullen*, 39 S.W.2d 168 (Tex. Civ. App.—Beaumont 1931, writ ref'd).

The agreement in this case was executed less than two months after the first marriage. The agreement recites:

> WHEREAS, JOSEPH WOODROW MARSHALL and ARLENE O'BRIEN MARSHALL were married on April 26, 1982, *and are now husband and wife*;
>
> WHEREAS, at the time of said marriage each owned separate property and each expects that each might *hereafter* acquire separate property; and
>
> WHEREAS, both desire the income and/or property arising from all of the respective separate property now owned or which *hereinafter* might be acquired by each shall be the respective separate property of each, it is therefore agreed between them as follows: * * *

(Emphasis added.) We conclude from these provisions that the parties were contracting in relation to the existing marriage only. It is unreasonable to assume that they anticipated a series of remarriages and divorces. The first divorce is the ascertainable contingency that determined the duration of the agreement; consequently, the agreement has no bearing on either the second marriage or the second divorce. The agreement does not justify the trial court's separate characterization of the partnership distributions.

DISTRIBUTIONS FROM CAPITAL

Woody's second response is that the distributions from the partnership, other than the salary in the partnership agreement, were from his capital account and were, therefore, his separate property. We develop Woody's argument and the reasons why we disagree with it below.

The partnership engaged in the business of exploring for, developing, and producing oil and gas. The partnership acquired all its oil and gas leases before the second marriage. The partnership agreement provides that it will pay Woody \$700 in salary per month. For the duration of the marriage, the amount comes to \$22,400. The partnership agreement also provides that all other distributions are from the distributee's share of the profits. The partnership disbursed \$542,315.72 to Woody during the marriage. Woody maintains that only \$22,400 was community property and that the rest was a return of capital.

The Texas Uniform Partnership Act (UPA) provides that unless the partners agree otherwise, no partner is entitled to remuneration for acting in the partnership business and that each partner is to share equally in the profits. TEX. REV. CIV. STAT. ANN. art. 6132b, § 18(1)(a) & (f) (Vernon 1970). Because the agreement is controlling, Woody concedes that the \$22,400 is community.

Woody next points to *Norris v. Vaughan*, 152 Tex. 491, 260 S.W.2d 676 (1953). In *Norris*, the husband owned a separate determinable fee interest in the "Pakan" wells and an interest in a separate partnership that was in the sole business of acquiring gas wells, drilling under lease agreements, and selling the gas. The Texas Supreme Court held that the proceeds from the production and sale of oil and gas from the "Pakan" wells and from the three leases acquired by the partnership before the husband's marriage were the husband's separate property.

The Supreme Court applied the aggregate theory of partnership and treated the individual partners as owners of the partnership property. Thus, the court characterized partnership property as separate or community, depending upon whether the partnership acquired its property rights before or after the marriage of the partner/husband. Because the husband had acquired his interest in the partnership before the marriage, that interest was his separate property. Likewise, because the partnership had owned its interest in three producing gas wells prior to the husband's marriage, the court held that the husband's interest in the three wells was his separate property and the gas produced from them was "an invasion of the assets comprising [husband's] separate estate." *Id.* 260 S.W.2d at 681. The court further held that the proceeds from the sale of oil and gas produced from separate property remains separate so long as the oil and gas can be definitely traced and identified. The court reasoned that, since oil and gas in place are part of the corpus of the land, when they are produced, they simply undergo a mutation. Similarly, when the oil and gas production is sold, the proceeds are derived from the piecemeal sale of a separate asset, the corpus of land, and remain separate property. *Id.* at 679-80.

Woody contends that the *Norris v. Vaughan* analysis is applicable in this case because it is undisputed that his partnership interest is his separate property, that the primary business of the partnership is production of oil and gas, that all the partnership leases were acquired prior to marriage, and that the proceeds from the sale of oil and gas are simply mutations of the oil and gas in place, and, therefore, all partnership proceeds from these sales distributed during the marriage remain his separate property.

Arlene has two responses. First, she argues that the adoption of the Uniform Partnership Act in 1961 has amended *Norris*. Second, she contends that because Woody's tax returns and the partnership's own records reflect that Woody received $334,891 in salary for the years 1983 and 1984, Woody cannot now gainsay them. Arlene emphasizes that whether the distributions are for salary or from partnership profits makes no difference, since both salary and profits from separate property become community property. *Trawick v. Trawick*, 671 S.W.2d 105, 109 (Tex. App.—El Paso 1984, no writ).

With the passage of the Uniform Partnership Act in 1961, Texas discarded the aggregate theory and adopted the entity theory of partnership. Under the UPA, partnership property is owned by the partnership itself and not by the individual partners. In the absence of fraud, such property is neither community nor separate property of the individual partners. A partner's partnership interest, the right to receive his share of the profits and surpluses from the business, is the only property right a partner has that is subject to a community or separate property characterization. TEX. REV. CIV. STAT. ANN. at 6132b §§ 8, 26, & 28-A; Note, *Community Rights and the Business Partnership*, 57 TEXAS L. REV. 1018, (1979); Bromberg, *Commentary on the Texas Uniform Partnership Act*, 7 TEX. REV. CIV. STAT. ANN. 300-01 & 321 (Vernon 1970). Further, if the partner receives his share of profits during marriage, those profits are community property, regardless of whether the partner's interest in the partnership is separate or community in nature. TEX. FAM. CODE ANN. § 5.01(b) (Vernon 1975); *Arnold v. Leonard*, 273 S.W. at 799; Note, 57 TEXAS L. REV. at 1032.

The Supreme Court recognized the changes in partnership law wrought by the adoption of the UPA in *McKnight v. McKnight*, 543 S.W.2d 863 (Tex. 1976). There the court determined that the only partnership-related property a trial court can award upon dissolution of a partner's marriage is the partnership interest. *Id.* at 867-68; *see Haney v. Fenley, Bate, Deaton & Porter*, 618 S.W.2d 541, 542 (Tex. 1981).

Initially, we note that according to the partnership records, Woody's distributions were a series of draws allocated to him, Arlene, and Debra (Woody's daughter), many of which were based on payments by the partnership to personal creditors on behalf of one of these three. The major "distribution" each year was the partnership's payment of Woody's individual income tax liability. It is true that a portion of the distributions was closed to Woody's capital account at the end of the year, but this was simply a bookkeeping entry after the fact.

The amount closed to the capital accounts of both partners, Woody and his ex-wife, Ruby, was based on the total of their draws for the year. In this manner the accountant determined their personal income and their income tax thereon; the accountant then had the partnership pay their personal income tax. These amounts are reflected on the partnership returns as "withdrawals and distributions" in the reconciliation of the partners' capital accounts. Woody's draws throughout each year at issue, and historically, always exceeded Ruby's. Consequently, Woody's excess draws were allocated to salary for Woody on the partnership books and reported as "guaranteed payments for partners" on the partnership tax returns. Woody reported all disbursements received from the partnership, either directly or indirectly, as ordinary income on the spouses' joint tax returns for 1983 and 1984.

Woody apparently relies on the rule that mutations of separate property remain separate if properly traced. *Norris*, 260 S.W.2d at 679. However, a withdrawal from a partnership capital account is not a return of capital in the sense that it may be characterized as a mutation of a partner's separate property contribution to the partnership and thereby remain separate. Such characterization is contrary to the UPA and implies that the partner retains an ownership interest in his capital contribution. He does not; the partnership entity becomes the owner, and the partner's contribution becomes partnership property which cannot be characterized as either separate or community property of the individual partners. TEX. REV. CIV. STAT. ANN. art. 6132b, §§ 8, 25, & 28-A(1) (Vernon 1970); Bromberg, 17 TEX. REV. CIV. STAT. ANN. at 300-01. Thus, there can be no mutation of a partner's separate contribution; that rule is inapplicable in determining the characterization of a partnership distribution from a partner's capital account.

Further, the *Norris v. Vaughan* characterization of proceeds from the production of oil and gas is inapplicable to a partnership receipt of such proceeds, for they are simply partnership property and are not subject to characterization as separate or community property. TEX. REV. CIV. STAT. ANN. art. 6132b, §§ 8, 25, & 28-A(1) (Vernon 1970); *McKnight v. McKnight*, 543 S.W.2d at 867; Bromberg, 17 TEX. REV. CIV. STAT. ANN. at 300-01. In this case, all monies disbursed by the partnership were made from current income. The partnership agreement provides that "any and all distributions . . . of any kind or character over and above the salary here provided . . . shall be charged against any such distributee's share of the profits of the business." Under these facts, we hold that all of the partnership distributions that Woody received were either salary under the partnership agreement or distributions of profits of the partnership.

Although the partnership utilized the bookkeeping device of allocating to salary Woody's withdrawals that were in excess of Ruby's, that device does not make such distributions "salary" contrary to the partnership agreement. The withdrawals nevertheless were distributions of partnership income or profits and, thus, community. We hold that all distributions by the partnership to Woody during the course of the second marriage were community property. Woody's second argument in support of the trial court's separate characterization of the partnership distributions is overruled.

CONSUMPTION OF COMMUNITY DISTRIBUTIONS DURING THE MARRIAGE

Finally, Woody argues that regardless of whether his partnership distributions during marriage were separate or community, the spouses consumed all income during the marriage. Therefore, argues Woody, any mischaracterization of these distributions was harmless error. Woody relies upon (1) the trial court's finding that "all income received by the community in exchange for community labor was consumed during the marriage," (2) Arlene's reliance on his testimony that he and she "might have some community property in a house on Bonnard Street. That would be all I know of," and (3) Woody's own analysis of the distributions, which results in a maximum total community income of $328,067.

We disagree with Woody; the evidence does not show that the spouses consumed all income during the marriage. First, the finding of the trial court addresses only the portion of the income attributable to community labor and fails to address other income received by the community. Second, Woody's testimony has no probative value on the issue because it is based on his lay conclusion concerning the characterization of the property at issue, which is a question of law reserved for the court to decide. Third, we held earlier that the partnership disbursed $542,315.72 to Woody, all of which was community income. Woody's analysis addresses only $328,067 of that amount, which still leaves $214,248.72 of community income unaccounted for. Consequently, we hold that the evidence does not show that the spouses consumed all income during the marriage and that the trial court's mischaracterization of the partnership distributions is not harmless error. Woody's argument that the spouses consumed all community income during the marriage is overruled.

WOODY'S 1982 TAX DEBTS

Having determined that all partnership distributions to Woody during the marriage were community property, we turn to Arlene's contention that the community should be reimbursed for the $125,375.50 that the partnership paid during the marriage for the balance due on Woody's 1982 taxes. It is undisputed that Woody's 1982 tax liability was his separate debt. This payment was charged to Woody's account by the partnership and became part of the total funds distributed to Woody during the marriage. Woody and Arlene reported this figure as part of their income on their joint 1983 tax return, and the community paid taxes on it. The trial court found that the source of the funds used by the partnership to pay Woody's 1982 taxes was the "proceeds of production which were earned prior to marriage." It further found, "[T]he payment [of the taxes] by the partnership gives rise to no claim to Arlene Marshall upon which relief can be granted." It is evident from these findings that the trial court denied Arlene's claim for reimbursement regarding these funds because the trial court concluded that the funds could be characterized as separate or community depending upon when the partnership earned them. This finding is based on the *Norris v. Vaughan* rationale. The partnership funds used to pay Woody's 1982 taxes were neither separate nor community until the partnership disbursed the money for the taxes. At that point, the money became revenue acquired during marriage from Woody's separate partnership interest; consequently, the funds were community property. TEX. FAM. CODE ANN. §§ 5.01(b) & 5.02 (Vernon 1975); *Arnold v. Leonard*, 273 S.W. at 802. Accordingly, we remand Arlene's claim for reimbursement for one half of the money paid for Woody's 1982 taxes to the trial court for its redetermination in light of our holding that these funds were community property.

GIFTS TO WOODY'S DAUGHTER

Arlene also maintains that the community is entitled to reimbursement for funds that Woody gave to his daughter, Debra, and her son, Dustin, during the marriage. She asserts that the evidence reveals that Woody, or the partnership on his behalf, gave Debra and Dustin community funds totaling \$103,235.44 during the marriage; that the community received benefits from exemptions and deductions on the parties' joint tax returns for 1983 and 1984 of \$38,909.86; and that the balance of \$63,325.58 was composed of gifts which were unfair and which constituted constructive fraud on the community.

Although the trial court made no specific finding regarding whether the gifts were made from separate or community funds, it found in relation to the gifts:

> A. No dishonesty of purpose or intent to deceive Arlene Marshall;
>
> B. That the transfers were not made with the primary purpose of depriving Arlene Marshall from having the use and enjoyment of the assets comprising the transfer; . . . .
>
> D. No breach of a fiduciary relationship which resulted in injury. Based upon the above findings of fact, the court also finds no fraud either actual or constructive.

From these findings, we conclude that the trial court assumed that the gifts were made from community funds in ruling on Arlene's claim for reimbursement based on these gifts. Therefore, we need not remand this claim, as we have the claim for reimbursement for the 1982 tax payment, because of a mischaracterization of funds used.

Arlene argues that the trial court erred in placing the burden on her to prove constructive fraud because the law presumes constructive fraud when a spouse makes gifts to a stranger to the marriage. She further relies on the trial court's statement, "[T]here's already evidence in this trial that Mrs. Marshall did not actively consent to the giving of those gifts to the daughter." Finally, she maintains that there is insufficient evidence to support a finding that the gifts were fair.

We agree that when there is constructive fraud, the burden is on the donor to prove that the gifts of his or her share of the community property are fair; otherwise the gift will be set aside. *Horlock v. Horlock*, 533 S.W.2d 52, 55 (Tex. Civ. App.—Houston [14th Dist.] 1975, writ ref'd n.r.e.). The courts consider three primary factors in determining whether the wife's claim of constructive fraud exists: the size of the gift in relation to the total size of the community estate, the adequacy of the estate remaining to support the wife in spite of the gift, and the relationship of the donor to the donee. *Id.*

We conclude that the evidence supports the trial court's finding of no constructive fraud. The community received \$542,315.72 during the marriage as Woody's special community property. The contested gifts of \$63,375.58 are only 11.7 percent of this amount. The remaining \$478,940.14 in community funds from the partnership was sufficient to support the wife. Finally, Woody made the gifts to his daughter and grandson, the natural objects of his bounty. We also agree with the trial court's finding that there was no intent to deceive Arlene. She knew about the gifts, and although she may not have actively consented to them, there is also no evidence that she objected to them. We overrule Arlene's complaint of the trial court's denial of her claim for reimbursement for gifts to Debra and Dustin.

* * *

II

LTC DEBTS

In point of error two, Arlene contends that the trial court incorrectly ruled that the community estate is not liable for all unpaid debts of the business Leasing Telephone Concepts, Incorporated (LTC), including those incurred after June 25, 1984. Arlene began LTC in May of 1984. The trial court signed an agreed temporary order on August 17, 1984, that provided, "Each party shall be responsible for the debts incurred by him or her on or after June 25, 1984." Arlene terminated LTC in December 1984, at which time LTC was indebted in the amount of $60,000. The trial court ruled that the $60,000 debt of LTC was Arlene's responsibility by virtue of the August 17, 1984, temporary order.

In its finding, the trial court found that the August 17 order provided, "[E]ach party will be *solely liable* for any debt incurred by them subsequent to June 25, 1984." (Emphasis added.) This finding is a misstatement of the terms of the order. The trial court also found that this provision "controlled" these subsequent debts. In the judgment, the court characterized the debts incurred by Arlene after June 25, 1984, including those debts associated with LTC, as her separate debts and obligations. Arlene contends that this mischaracterization of the LTC debt as her separate debt resulted in the trial court's abusing its discretion in dividing the community debts and that this part of this case should be reversed and remanded.

We agree with Arlene that a provision in an agreed temporary order indicating which debts a spouse will be responsible for during the pendency of the case neither binds the trial court in its division of property and debts after a trial on the merits nor transforms community debts into the separate debts of the spouse incurring them. It is undisputed that the LTC debt was incurred during marriage and that, but for the agreed temporary order, it should be characterized as a community debt. Because we conclude the temporary order in not controlling, we hold that the LTC debt is a community debt. We sustain Arlene's second point of error.

III.

HOUSEHOLD FURNISHINGS

In point of error three, Arlene contends that the trial court abused its discretion by dividing in kind the household furnishings located at the house on Bonnard Drive. Arlene argues that no evidence supports a division in kind, and, in any event, the division of the furnishings was neither just nor right, as required by section 3.63 of the Texas Family Code. The trial court's division of marital property will not be disturbed on appeal absent a showing of an abuse of discretion. *Murff v. Murff*, 615 S.W.2d 696, 698 (Tex. 1981). This court must indulge every reasonable presumption in favor of a proper exercise of discretion by the trial court in dividing property. *Van Dyke v. Van Dyke*, 624 S.W.2d 800 (Tex. Civ. App.—Houston [14th Dist.] 1981, no writ). Arlene has failed to show that the trial court abused its discretion in dividing the household furnishings. Her third point of error is overruled.

In the partnership's cross-point one, it argues that the trial court erred in finding that the evidence failed to rebut the presumption that the furnishings belonged to the community and erred in awarding Arlene the furnishings listed in part II of exhibit A to the decree of divorce. The partnership attacks the trial court's findings as erroneous in that the unrefuted evidence establishes that the furnishings belong to the partnership and, furthermore, as a matter of law one cannot make a gift of property to the community estate. For the reasons given below, we hold that the trial court erred in ruling that the evidence failed to rebut the community presumption.

Woody testified that the partnership purchased the furnishings before the marriage, that the partnership owned all the furnishings, and that he and Arlene moved the furnishings from two houses owned by the partnership into the house on Bonnard Drive. Arlene agreed that the partnership had owned the furnishings, but she explained that Woody told her that whatever furnishings they moved into the Bonnard Drive house would become part of their community estate and that she understood Woody to mean that the furnishings would become hers and his jointly. Woody never denied making these statements to Arlene. There is also evidence that the partnership continued to carry the furnishings as an asset on its books and records.

Two possible scenarios exist. First, the partnership merely lent the furnishings. Second, the partnership made a gift of the furnishings. However, if the partnership intended a gift to the community, as Arlene contends, a gift to the community does not result; rather, when a third party attempts to make a gift to the community estate, the gift vests in each marital spouse, both taking a one-half undivided interest in the subject matter of the gift as his or her separate property. *McLemore v. McLemore*, 641 S.W.2d 395, 397 (Tex. Civ. App.—Tyler 1982, no writ); *Ramsower v. Pieper*, 114 S.W.2d 1188 (Tex. Civ. App.—Austin 1938, no writ) (applied to gift of personal property). Consequently, under either scenario, the furnishings do not become community property. The evidence is sufficient to rebut the presumption that the furnishings were community property. We sustain the partnership's cross-point one in this regard.

However, the partnership contends that we should render judgment declaring that it owns the furnishings. We overrule this contention. Although we have determined that the furnishings do not belong to the community, the question remains whether the partnership lent or gave the furnishings to Arlene and Woody. As the evidence is conflicting, the trial court is the proper court to resolve this question of fact. We remand this issue to the trial court for its determination.

IV.

THE MERCEDES

In her fourth point, Arlene contends that there is no evidence to support the judgment of the trial court that only $5,500 represents the value of the Mercedes wrongfully taken by Woody from Arlene's possession. The partnership maintains that it owned the Mercedes prior to the parties' marriage and that Woody permitted Arlene merely to use the Mercedes. Woody denies giving Arlene the car. The trial court decided *sua sponte* that Woody gave Arlene a usufruct that was her sole and separate property and that Woody wrongfully terminated her usufruct. Woody brings a cross-point wherein he argues that the trial court erred in finding a usufruct. In the alternative, the partnership and Woody argue that if Arlene did have a usufructuary right that Woody wrongfully terminated, then the trial court correctly found that Woody should pay Arlene only $5,500 in damages for its wrongful termination.

No usufruct is involved in the present case. A usufruct is the right of using and enjoying and receiving the profits of property that belongs to another, and a usufructuary is a person who has the usufruct or right of enjoying anything in which he has no property interest. *In re Adjudication of the Water Rights of the Upper Guadalupe Segment of the Guadalupe River Basin*, 642 S.W.2d 438, 444 (Tex. 1982) (Texas Supreme Court relies upon *Sparks v. Spence*, 40 Tex. 693 (1874), and *Cartwright v. Cartwright*, 18 Tex. 626 (1857); *Sparks*, 40 Tex. at 700; *Kelly v. Lansford*, 572 S.W.2d 369, 372

(Tex. Civ. App.—Fort Worth 1978, writ ref'd n.r.e.) (court relies upon C.J.S.); 91 C.J.S. *Usufruct* 550 (1955) (C.J.S. relies upon *Sparks*, 40 Tex. at 700, and *Cartwright*, 18 Tex. at 628).

Three types of usufructs exist. First, there are the *natural* profits produced by the subject of the usufruct. For example, the profits produced spontaneously by the earth or animals, such as timber, herbs, fruit, wool, milk, and the young of cattle are natural. Second, there are *industrial* profits, which are profits produced by cultivation, such as crops of grain. Third, there are civil profits, which are rents, freights, and revenues from annuities and from other effects or rights. *Cartwright v. Cartwright*, 18 Tex. 626, 628 (1857) (Texas Supreme Court relies upon *Cartwright* for another proposition in *Kelly v. Marlin*, 714 S.W.2d 303, 308 (Tex. 1986). A usufruct is a right to profits or something tangible originating from other property. The right to drive the partnership Mercedes is not a tangible profit; therefore, Arlene's right to drive the partnership Mercedes is not a usufruct.

Arlene argues simply that the unclaimed depreciation of the Mercedes was $10,833.33, not $5,500. She does not argue that the trial court erred in ruling that she received only a usufruct to the Mercedes and not the Mercedes itself. Because we hold that there is no usufruct and because Arlene does not complain of the trial court's implied finding that the partnership did not give the Mercedes itself to her, we hold that the Mercedes belongs to the partnership and that, therefore, when Woody retook possession of it, he did not commit conversion. Accordingly, we reverse the trial court's judgment ordering Woody to pay Arlene $5,500 for the wrongful termination of her usufructuary right in the Mercedes, and we render judgment that Arlene take nothing on her Mercedes claim.

V.

AWARD OF ATTORNEY'S FEES

In Woody's final cross-point, he contends that the trial court erred in finding the agreed August 17, 1984, temporary orders were inapplicable to the attorney's fees of Arlene's attorney but were applicable to the attorney's fees of Woody's attorney. The trial court ordered Woody to pay $12,500 in attorney's fees to Arlene's attorneys. Woody contends that under the terms of the temporary order and as a matter of law Arlene's attorney's fees are her sole responsibility. The entry of a final judgment inconsistent in its terms with an earlier temporary order operates to set aside the temporary order. *Cf. Hill v. Robinson*, 592 S.W.2d 376 (Tex. Civ. App.—Tyler 1979, writ ref'd n.r.e.) (final judgment and interlocutory judgment). The trial court may award attorney's fees as part of the division of the community estate. *See Murff v. Murff*, 615 S.W.2d at 699. Woody's cross-point is overruled.

In his final cross-point, Woody also argues that there was no evidence that the $2,500 fee to Arlene's first attorney was reasonable and necessary and that there was no evidence that the $10,000 fee to Arlene's second attorney was reasonable and necessary. When deciding a "no evidence" question, appellate courts are to consider only the evidence and the inferences tending to support the finding and to disregard all evidence and inferences to the contrary. *Mitsubishi Aircraft International, Inc. v. Maurer*, 675 S.W.2d 286 (Tex. App.—Dallas 1984, no writ). Arlene's first attorney testified explicitly that the services she performed for Arlene were reasonable and necessary. Arlene's second attorney testified that his fees were reasonable and his services were necessary. Woody's final cross-point is overruled.

CONCLUSION

Regarding Arlene's first point of error, which complains of the denial of her reimbursement claims, we affirm the trial court's denial of Arlene's claim for reimbursement for gifts to Woody's daughter and grandson. We reverse the trial court's denial of Arlene's claim for reimbursement to the community for $125,375.50 used to pay Woody's 1982 income tax and remand this claim to the trial court for its reconsideration in the light of this opinion.

In point of error two, Arlene contends that the trial court improperly characterized the LTC debts, including those incurred after June 25, 1984, as her separate obligation. We reverse the trial court's determinations that the LTC debts were Arlene's separate debts.

Regarding the furnishings, the subject of Arlene's third point of error and the partnership's first cross-point, we reverse the trial court's treatment of the furnishings as community property. We remand the matter of the furnishings to the trial court for it to determine whether the partnership lent or gave the furnishings to Arlene and Woody.

Arlene's fourth point of error and Woody's first cross-point address the trial court's ruling that Woody wrongfully terminated Arlene's usufructuary right to the Mercedes. We reverse the trial court's judgment awarding Arlene $5,500 for the wrongful termination of her usufructuary right in the Mercedes, and we render judgment that Arlene take nothing on her Mercedes claim. We overrule Woody's second cross-point, which attacks the trial court's award of Arlene's attorney's fees.

Because the trial court mischaracterized Woody's partnership distributions as his separate property, the LTC debts as Arlene's separate liability, and the furnishings as community property, we reverse and remand the entire property and debt division, including the award of attorney's fees incident thereto, to the trial court for its redivision in light of this opinion. *McKnight v. McKnight*, 543 S.W.2d at 868.

Notes, Comments & Questions

1. *Marshall v. Marshall* is an excellent example of the complicated, if not convoluted, nature of many divorce cases. As in *Marshall*, seldom does an ample estate give rise to a singular issue. To the contrary, ample estates often beget numerous issues.

2. In his attempt to escape Arlene's reimbursement claims, Woody argued three theories. One theory was that the $542,315.72 distributed by his partnership was not community property, but was his separate and traceable investment in the partnership capital account. Why did this argument fail?

3. Make sure that you can identify and understand the shortcomings of Woody's three arguments.

4. In another argument, Woody attempts to rely on the case of *Sorrels, v. Sorrels*, 592 S.W.2d 692 (Tex. Civ. App.—Amarillo 1979, writ ref'd n.r.e.). Assuming you understand why *Sorrels* is not applicable, why is the *Sorrels* case itself ironic?

5. Why is *Norris v. Vaughan* of no help to Woody?

6. Identify the requisite elements to prove constructive fraud on the community.

7. Do temporary orders of the trial court serve to characterize property? Why or why not?

8. What is a usufruct?

LIFSHUTZ
v.
LIFSHUTZ
199 S.W. 3d 9
(Tex. App.—San Antonio 2006, pet. denied)

LOPEZ, JUSTICE

* * *

B. Distribution of Berlee Lumber Company Stock

In his second issue, James challenges the finding by the trial court "that 1/3 of the stock of Berlee Lumber Company was distributed by Liberty Partnership to JAMES G. LIFSHUTZ as a non liquidating community distribution and then recontributed by JAMES G. LIFSHUTZ to Liberty Financial during the reorganization and reimbursement was therefore due the community estate." In the final divorce decree, the trial court further found, "that the distribution of Berlee stock should be and is hereby characterized as community property and when contributed by JAMES G. LIFSHUTZ to his separate corporate entities, JAMES G. LIFSHUTZ' separate estate was enhanced between \$1,100,000.00-\$1,780,630.00."

The evidence presented on this issue is conflicting. In 1990, Liberty Properties Partnership appeared to have acquired the stock of Berlee Lumber Company from Barnard Lifshutz, James's father. Although there is conflicting evidence with regard to the recording of this transfer in the stock book, the remainder of the evidence appears to support a finding that the stock was transferred to Liberty Properties Partnership. In 1996, the Berlee stock was transferred from Liberty Properties Partnership to Liberty Financial Corporation. The trial court found that this transfer resulted in a distribution from the partnership to James, causing it to become a community property asset before it was then recontributed to Liberty Financial Corporation.

Kymberly called several experts in both legal and accounting or tax fields who testified that the transfer caused a distribution to James. James called several experts who testified to the contrary.

Janet E. Stigent-Burns, a certified public accountant, stated she reviewed the 1996 tax return, including the K1, financial statements, general ledgers, work paper entries, and various items in the minute book, corporate records, and partnership records. The 1996 partnership return showed a distribution to the partners consisting of the Berlee stock, a note receivable from Texas Home Improvement, and various cash distributions. Burns characterized the distribution as community property. Burns testified that the value of the distribution of Berlee stock was \$1,108,348.00. On cross-examination, Burns stated that she was unaware of another way the transaction could be documented for tax purposes if the transfer was direct from Liberty Properties Partnership to Liberty Financial Corporation. Burns stated that the direct transfer could not be accomplished without a deemed or constructive distribution to James and his brothers. Burns also testified that the financial statement and tax return for Liberty Financial Corporation documenting the contribution of the Berlee stock and James's individual tax return contained entries that were inconsistent with a direct transfer.

Norman Seeman, a certified public accountant, prepared the tax returns for James and the Entities. Although Seeman agreed that the tax returns showed the Berlee stock as being distributed, Seeman stated that the "amount wasn't distributed. This amount was transferred to another corporation." Seeman later insisted that the Berlee stock was not distributed, stating:

> Don't use the word "distributed." You keep coming back—it wasn't distributed. This was part of a recapitalization. It was transferred from one company to the other. You keep saying distributed, and it wasn't distributed.

Seeman testified that he did not intend the entries to reflect a distribution but a direct transfer of the Berlee stock from the partnership to the corporation.

Peter Wolverton, a tax attorney with a masters in taxation, reviewed the tax returns of Liberty Properties Partnership and Liberty Financial Corporation. Wolverton stated that the partnership reported the transaction as a distribution of Berlee stock to James and his brothers. Wolverton further testified that Liberty Financial treated the transaction as a contribution to capital by James and his brothers to Liberty Financial. Wolverton stated that if Berlee had transferred the stock to Liberty Financial directly and thereby became a shareholder, the transaction would have resulted in a $3,000,000 taxable gain. If the stock was transferred directly and Berlee did not become a shareholder as part of a tax reorganization, the Berlee stock would have a zero basis, and Liberty Financial would not be able to deduct any losses with regard to that asset. Wolverton stated that the fair market value of Berlee at the time of transfer was $3,400,000.00.

Stanley Blend, a tax attorney, testified that in planning the reorganization, the Berlee stock was to be transferred from the partnership to the corporation. Blend agreed that for federal income tax purposes, the transfer of the stock was shown as a distribution to the partners; however, Blend asserted that it could have been shown as a direct investment. Blend stated that the stock certificates reflected that the ownership was transferred from the partnership to the corporation under Texas substantive law.

William Bradley, a certified public accountant, testified that the tax returns contained one acceptable way in which the direct transfer of the stock could be reported; however, other methods could also have been used. Bradley agreed that the direct transfer would "possibly" require the Berlee stock to be reflected on Liberty Financial's books with a zero basis.

James relies on *Thomas v. Thomas*, 738 S.W.2d 342 (Tex. App.—Houston [1st Dist.] 1987, writ denied), to support his position. In *Thomas*, a spouse was claiming that retained earnings in a Subchapter S corporation should be considered marital property because the income of Subchapter S corporations is treated as the personal income of the shareholders for tax purposes. 738 S.W.2d at 343-44. The court noted that Subchapter S status does not determine who owns the corporation's earnings but merely provided an alternative method to tax the corporation's income. *Id.* at 344. "A Subchapter S corporation may distribute its income, but, like any other corporation, it is not required to do so. Corporate distributions, regardless of form, are controlled by state law." *Id.* The court agreed with the unanimous holding of the courts in community property states that "corporate earnings remained corporate property until distributed and, therefore, were not divisible on divorce." *Id.* at 344.

Thomas would be more on point if Liberty Properties Partnership had retained its interest in the Berlee stock. In that case, the Berlee stock would be a retained partnership asset and would not be a part of the community property estate. The distinction in this case is that the Berlee stock was undisputedly transferred, and the question is whether it resulted in a distribution to James.

Kymberly relies on *Marshall v. Marshall*, 735 S.W.2d 587 (Tex. App.—Dallas 1987, writ ref'd n.r.e.), to support her position. In *Marshall*, the husband owned a separate property interest in a partnership. The partnership engaged in oil and gas exploration and production. *Id.* at 594. The partnership acquired all of its oil and gas leases before the marriage. *Id.* The partnership disbursed $542,315.72 to the husband during the marriage. *Id.* The husband maintained that only the

$22,400.00 paid as salary was community property. *Id.* The court rejected the husband's argument and held that the distributions of partnership income or profits were community property. *Id.* at 595.

In view of *Marshall*, James argues that the distribution in this case was an asset distribution and not a profit distribution; therefore, James contends that *Marshall* is not controlling. In *Marshall*, the court noted:

> [A] withdrawal from a partnership capital account is not a return of capital in the sense that it may be characterized as a mutation of a partner's separate property contribution to the partnership and thereby remain separate. Such characterization is contrary to the UPA and implies that the partner retains an ownership interest in his capital contribution. He does not; the partnership entity becomes the owner, and the partner's contribution becomes partnership property which cannot be characterized as either separate or community property of the individual partners. Thus, there can be no mutation of a partner's separate contribution; that rule is inapplicable in determining the characterization of a partnership distribution from a partner's capital account.

735 S.W.2d at 594. Whether the distribution was of an asset or cash, the distribution was from the capital account to which *Marshall* states that the "mutation of a partner's separate contribution" does not apply. As one commentator has explained:

> As with trusts, a partnership can be an effective means of preserving the separate property character of assets contributed to the partnership and the undistributed income thereon. The partner's spouse does not have an interest in the assets of the partnership until the assets and profits are actually distributed to the partner either in the form of partnership income or return of capital. To the extent that income distributions are made from the partnership, the distributions will be characterized as community property. Further, to the extent that distributions from the partnership include a return of the partner's separate capital contribution, the distribution will be characterized as community income because the partnership entity becomes the owner of the capital contribution. Thus, no mutation of the partner's separate property contribution occurs. Essentially, the rule of mutation of separate property is inapplicable in characterizing a partnership distribution from a partner's capital account.

Lisa H. Jamieson, *Marital Property Issues in the Modern Estate Plan*, 49 BAYLOR L. REV. 391, 402 (1997) (citing *Marshall*).

Even if we accept that the manner in which a transaction is documented for tax purposes is not controlling, it still must be considered as some evidence. Furthermore, although traditionally the stock book of a corporation might be decisive with regard to the manner in which stock ownership was transferred, evidence was presented in this case that could cause the trial court to question the validity of the stock book to accurately reflect the conveyance of the corporate stock. There was evidence that when the stock book was reviewed in 1993, it did not reflect the conveyance of the Berlee stock to Liberty Properties Partnership in 1990 although a subsequent review of the stock book revealed certificates dated in 1990. The trial court could have found that in light of that evidence, the stock book was not credible evidence of the manner in which the Berlee stock was conveyed because the stock certificates could be created at any time and back dated. Accordingly, the evidence is sufficient to support the trial court's finding that a distribution occurred.

Texas has adhered to the entity theory of partnership since the Texas Uniform Partnership Act was enacted in 1961. *See Haney v. Fenley, Bate, Deaton & Porter*, 618 S.W.2d 541, 542 (Tex.1981); *Burnap v. Linnartz*, 914 S.W.2d 142, 150 (Tex. App.—San Antonio 1995, writ denied). Under the entity theory, all property brought into the partnership is partnership property and, as partnership property, does not retain either a community or separate property nature. *See Harris v. Harris*, 765 S.W.2d 798, 804 (Tex. App.—Houston [14th Dist.] 1989, writ denied). "This is an area in which the community property principles and the Texas version of the Uniform Partnership Act conflict." 38 ALOYSIUS A. LEOPOLD, TEXAS PRACTICE: MARITAL PROPERTY AND HOMESTEADS § 7.10 (1993). "[W]hen an individual partner contributes property into a partnership, the partner loses individual interest in the property and, since the partnership itself is the new owner, the property can no longer be classified as separate or community." *Id.* at § 4.10. Accordingly, since partnership property does not retain a separate character, distributions from the partnership are considered community property, regardless of whether the distribution is of income or of an asset.[4] *Marshall*, 735 S.W.2d at 594.

* * *

Notes, Comments & Questions

1. How a partnership, corporation, or other business entity deals with profits, recapitalization, dissolution, repayment of loans, or distributions can affect their characterization. Accordingly, one should seek counsel if attempting a distribution on the *Lifshutz* scale.

2. Likewise, tax treatment can weigh in on the ultimate question of characterization. One should be careful in making decisions for tax purposes without being fully aware of the possible effect on the character of marital property. Although tax treatment does not control the character of marital property, it can be used as evidence to support or destroy an assertion of the separate or community character of property.

---

[4] We recognize that a Louisiana appellate court has drawn a distinction between distributions of income and distributions of a capital asset. Guilott v. Guilott, 361 So.2d 1271, 1276-77 (La. Ct. App.1978, writ denied). In *Guilott*, however, the court did not analyze the effect of the entity theory of partnerships in concluding that a distribution of the capital assets of the partnership, as distinguished from fruits or earnings, was the wife's separate property. We further note that Wolverton testified that the accumulated profits in Liberty Properties exceeded the aggregate distributions, which included the Berlee stock distribution.

G. Retirement and Other Employee Benefits Including Stock Options

The family home and the spouses' retirement benefits often vie for the position as a couple's most valuable community asset. The home, however, has not yielded the controversy that surrounds the valuation of retirement benefits. Indeed, prior to 1976, non-vested retirement benefits were not even considered property subject to division on divorce.

The study of retirement benefits requires that one be familiar with defined benefit retirement plans and defined contribution retirement plans.

Defined benefit plans utilize one's years of service and salary or average salary and plugs the figures into a formula which yields a monthly, yearly, or lump sum payment. The formulas vary from company to company. Military retirement is a type of defined benefit plan.

A defined contribution plan is based upon actual contributions into a spouse's retirement account either by the employer or the spouse or a combination, thereof. These plans may also be invested in a variety of assets such as stocks, bonds, or even cash accounts. Usually a party is able to ascertain exactly how much is in their defined contribution plan at date of marriage. In contrast, it is trickier to determine how much a defined benefit plan is worth at date of marriage, but as you will see that fiction has and will be entertained. The beginning balance of a retirement plan is important because that is usually a spouse's separate property.

1. Statutes Relating to Retirement Benefits, Other Employee Benefits, and Stock Options

The 2009 legislative session yielded some changes in the statutes dealing with retirement benefits, other employee benefit plans, and stock options. Some of the changes include a repeal of statutes that were passed in the 2005 legislative session. One statute that did not change is TEX. FAM CODE § 7.003 which governs the disposition of retirement, employee benefit and other plans. This statute simply requires that the trial court, in a decree of divorce or annulment, *shall* determine the rights of both spouses in such benefits. Realize that this section governs all employee benefit plans, even stock options; it provides as follows:

> § 7.003. Disposition of Retirement and Employment Benefits and Other Plans
>
> In a decree of divorce or annulment, the court shall determine the rights of both spouses in a pension, retirement plan, annuity, individual retirement account, employee stock option plan, stock option, or other form of savings, bonus, profit-sharing, or other employer plan or financial plan of an employee or a participant, regardless of whether the person is self-employed, in the nature of compensation or savings.

Although the disposition statute, § 7.003, did not change, the statutes that, as of 2005, set forth the means to determine separate and community interests in retirement plans and other employee plans, including stock options, have, to some extent been repealed. To the extent that the statutes have been repealed, we now look to the common law that previously governed the determination of separate and community interests.

The statute which had and does govern the determination of marital property interests in employee benefits is TEX. FAM. CODE § 3.007, set forth below in its entirety. The statute is set forth so that one can see the changes that occurred in the 2009 legislative. As with reimbursement and economic contribution, it is important to understand how the law existed prior to the 2009 changes because the changes made to TEX. FAM. CODE § 3.007 apply to a suit for dissolution of a marriage pending before a trial court on or filed after the effective date of the Act, which is September 1, 2009. The changes also apply to the estate of a person who dies on or after the effective date, September 1, 2009. The statute provides as follows:

§ 3. 007. Property Interest in Certain Employee Benefits

~~(a) A spouse who is a participant in a defined benefit retirement plan has a separate property interest in the monthly accrued benefit the spouse had a right to receive on normal retirement age, as defined by the plan, as of the date of marriage, regardless of whether the benefit had vested.~~

~~(b) The community property interest in a defined benefit plan shall be determined as if the spouse began to participate in the plan on the date of marriage and ended that participation on the date of dissolution or termination of the marriage, regardless of whether the benefit had vested.~~

(c) The separate property interest of a spouse in a defined contribution retirement plan may be traced using the tracing and characterization principles that apply to a nonretirement asset.

(d) A spouse who is a participant in an employer-provided stock option plan or an employer-provided restricted stock plan has a separate property interest in the options or restricted stock granted to the spouse under the plan as follows:

(1) if the option or stock was granted to the spouse before marriage but required continued employment during marriage before the grant could be exercised or the restriction removed, the spouse's separate property interest is equal to the fraction of the option or restricted stock in which:

(A) the numerator is the sum of:

(i) the period from the date the option or stock was granted until the date of marriage; and

(ii) If the option or stock also required the continued employment following the date of dissolution of the marriage before the grant could be exercised or the restriction removed, the period from the date of dissolution of the marriage until the date the grant could be exercised or the restriction removed; and

(B) the denominator is the period from the date the option or stock was granted until the date the grant could be exercised or the restriction removed; and

(2) if the option or stock was granted to the spouse during the marriage but required continued employment following the date of dissolution of the ~~after~~ marriage before the grant could be exercised or the restriction removed, the spouse's separate property interest is equal to the fraction of the option or restricted stock in which:

(A) the numerator is the period from the date of dissolution or termination of the marriage until the date the grant could be exercised or the restriction removed; and

(B) the denominator is the period from the date the option or stock was granted until the date the grant could be exercised or the restriction removed.

(e) The computation described by Subsection (d) applies to each component of the benefit requiring varying periods of employment before the grant could be exercised or the restriction removed.

~~(f) The characterization of the marital property interest in an option or restricted stock described by Subsection (d) must be recalculated if, after the initial division of the option or~~

~~stock, the vesting occurs on a date earlier than the vesting date stated in the original grant of the option or stock. The recalculation required by this subsection must adjust for the shortened vesting period and applies to options and stock granted before and during the marriage.~~

As can be seen from the foregoing, the determination of a spouse's separate property interest in defined contribution retirement plans has remained as it was in 2005. Similarly, in 2009, a spouse's separate property interest in stock options has been clarified. However, when it comes to defined benefit retirement plans, the legislature struck the portion of the statute which defined community and separate interests, those being TEX. FAM. CODE § 3.007 (a) (b) (repealed).

The repeal of these statutes now requires that a determination of the community and separate interests in defined benefit retirement plans be based on the common law.

---

2. Retirement Benefits Cases

Case law regarding retirement benefits has evolved over the past 30+ years. It is the one area of divorce law that the Texas Supreme Court has, with some regularity, addressed. A synopsis of the most important retirement benefit cases and the text of the entire case *May v. May*, 716 S.W.2d 705 (Tex. App.—Corpus Christi 1986, no writ) is set forth below. The following synopsis will provide guidance for determining separate and community interests in defined benefit retirement plans. Even though lengthy, the entire *May* opinion is included because it provides a thorough analysis of the Texas Supreme Court cases that have shaped retirement law in the state of Texas. If on can understand the *May* opinion, one will understand the common law of Texas retirement benefits.

a. *Cearley v. Cearley*, 544 S.W.2d (Tex. 1976).

Military retirement benefits, a defined benefit plan, were at issue in *Cearley*. The trial court in *Cearley v. Cearley*, ordered that "if" and "when" the husband received his retirement benefits, wife should receive one-half of 18, (representing the years they had been married and he had been employed) over the number of years of active service until retirement. This decision of the trial court was reversed by the court of appeals, finding that a trial court was without authority to order division of a husband's prospective military retirement benefits because no vested interest had been acquired in the benefits at the time of the divorce judgment.

Upon review, the Texas Supreme Court held that military retirement pensions earned during the marriage were community property. The Texas Supreme Court flatly rejected the argument that retirement benefits were a mere expectancy because husband had not retired prior to divorce or because the rights were subject to forfeiture by death or dishonorable discharge prior to his retirement. The court held that the benefits were community property even though the benefits had not matured and were not at the time of divorce subject to possession and enjoyment. The Texas Supreme Court recognized that community rights may exist in interests that cannot be reduced to possession at the time of dissolution of the marriage, such as remainder or reversion rights. The Court further held that the trial court properly settled the matter in the divorce judgment by awarding "if, as and when" the retirement benefits reach maturity, thus taking into account the contingency. The trial court's award was affirmed.

---

b. *Taggart v. Taggart*, 552 S.W.2d 422 (Tex. 1977).

In *Taggart*, the retirement benefits were not divided upon divorce; but rather, were addressed in a post-divorce action that focused on the retirement benefits as omitted property. (Post divorce division of omitted property will be addressed later in this chapter at section J. Post-Judgment Actions.) Based upon the *Cearley* decision, the *Taggart* court held that wife owned as part of her community estate a share in the contingent right to military retirement benefits even though the right had not matured at the time of divorce.

However, the Texas Supreme Court held that the trial did not make the correct computation of wife's fractional interest. The trial court used 20 years as the denominator in computing Ann Taggart's half interest in the husband's retirement benefits. However, at the end of 20 years, the husband was not entitled to receive any retirement benefits because he had to serve an additional 10 years in fleet reserve. Thus, the denominator to determine the community interest should have been the 30 years that he had to serve. Thus, the correct computation of the community interest is:

$$\frac{246 \text{ (months married \& in service)}}{360 \text{ (months in service at date of retirement)}} \quad X \text{ (value of retirement pay)}$$

The 246 represents the months that Ann was married to George while he was serving in the military. The 360 represents George's entire military service. This fraction of the military retirement pay, 246/360ths, represents the community interest. Ann was awarded 1/2 of this community interest because at the time a spouse automatically received 1/2 of property that was not divided upon divorce. Today, the trial court makes a just and right division of the omitted property. *See* TEX. FAM. CODE §§ 9.201-.204.

The next case, *Berry v. Berry*, took the place of *Taggart* for purposes of valuing a defined benefit plan. However, even in light of *Berry*, *Taggart* was good law *if* the spouse had retired at date of divorce.

---

c. *Berry v. Berry*, 647 S.W.2d 945 (Tex. 1983).

Berry represents a big change in the valuation of defined benefit plans. The Texas Supreme Court in *Berry* approved a completely new formula in the valuation of a defined benefit plan that has not matured as of date of divorce. The pertinent facts in this case include the following:

Mr. and Mrs. Berry were married on November 11, 1939. On May 22, 1940, Mr. Berry was employed by Southwestern Bell Telephone Company. The couple was divorced on September 13, 1966. The decree of divorce did not mention the distribution of retirement benefits; thus, they were omitted. Mr. Berry continued working for Southwestern Bell until his retirement in June, 1978. After retirement, Mrs. Berry brought suit to collect her share of the retirement benefits.

The Southwestern Bell retirement benefit plan is a defined benefit plan. The formulas used in these plans vary from company to company, but Mr. Berry's retirement benefit was based upon the highest salary paid over a consecutive 60 month period which was multiplied by a factor obtained from total length of service. The district staff manager for employee benefits for Southwestern Bell testified that at date of trial, Mr. Berry was being paid benefits in the amount of $946.34 a month. He further testified that had Mr. Berry been eligible to retire on September 13, 1966, the date of divorce—the retirement benefits would have amounted to $221.21. Based upon this assumption, wife was entitled to receive $110.60 of each month's retirement benefit paid to Mr. Berry. At the time of the suit, Mrs. Berry would have been entitled to receive ½ of any omitted asset; today an omitted asset would be subject to a just and right division.

The formula used by the trial court was:

$$1/2 \text{ (W's share)} \times \frac{26 \text{ (years married \& employed)}}{26 \text{ (years employed at divorce)}} \times \$221.21 \text{ (value at divorce)} = \$110.60$$

The court of appeals reversed the trial court's judgment and instead, using *Taggart*, determined that wife should be awarded one-half of 26/38 x $946.34, the amount Mr. Berry received at retirement. Thus, the court of appeals determined that Mrs. Berry should receive $323.74.

$$1/2 \text{ (W's share)} \times \frac{26 \text{ (years married \& employed)}}{38 \text{ (years employed at retirement)}} \times \$946.34 \text{ (value at retirement)} = \$323.74$$

Upon review, the Texas Supreme Court affirmed the trial court's decision and determined that all monies which Mr. Berry earned after the divorce were his separate property and could not be divested by an award to Mrs. Berry. Because the monies earned after divorce were his separate property, the community fraction could not encompass the years of service after the divorce. Thus, the denominator and the value of the plan were frozen at date of divorce; a fiction was imposed to obtain the value of the retirement benefits at divorce date.

The *Berry* Court explained that they were not to be understood as overruling *Taggart v. Taggart* insofar as that, and other opinions, approve an apportionment formula for determining the extent of community interest in retirement benefits that are already being received. However, they note that when the value of such benefits is in issue, the benefits are to be apportioned to the spouses based upon the value of the community interest at the time of the divorce.

---

d. *May v. May*, 716 S.W.2d 705 (Tex. App.—Corpus Christi 1986, no writ). *May* presents a well-analyzed application of the *Berry* formula.

OPINION

NYE, CHIEF JUSTICE.

This is an appeal from a division of retirement benefits in a divorce action. In anticipation of their divorce, the parties entered into an agreement which disposed of many of the matters in controversy. The matters that were submitted to the trial court concerned the characterization and division of appellant's three retirement plans. This appeal concerns only the trial court's disposition of two of the plans.

Appellant's first two points of error and appellee's cross-point complain of the division of appellant's San Antonio Fire Department pension benefits. The third point of error concerns appellant's Air National Guard benefits.

The trial court divided appellant's accrued, non-vested, and unmatured civilian retirement benefits earned from the San Antonio Fire Department.[1] The trial court made the following findings of fact:

1. Parties were married on April 8, 1967.

12. Respondent began his employment with the City of San Antonio in June, 1969, and accumulated retirement credit continuously from that date through the date of trial.

13. Respondent [had] worked 15 years out of the 20 years which are required for the retirement to vest.

14. The number of months Respondent was married while accumulating credit towards City of San Antonio retirement, through trial, [equaled] 184 months.

15. That a certified actuary determining the present value of Respondent's Fireman Retirement was stipulated to and admitted into evidence without objection. If Respondent retired [at] the date of divorce his present monthly Accrued Pension Benefit would be $667.79.

16. The present value of Petitioner's community interest in Respondent's City of San Antonio Retirement plan is $25,000. Said amount reflects the value of Petitioner's interest in Respondent's Fire Department Retirement plan projected upon contingencies and anticipated future value based upon historical inflation trends.

The trial court awarded appellee (the non-employee spouse) the following portion of appellant's benefits:

1 -- 2	X	months married in plan (184) --------------- months in plan at retirement	X	amount of monthly benefit employee would be receiving on date of divorce whether eligible or not ($667.79)	X	100% + total percentage of cost of living increases granted by employer from 12-31-84 to retirement

[1] We use the term "accrued" benefits in the actuarial sense, meaning the specific dollar amount allotted to an employee at any given time under the pension plan. By "vested" benefits, we mean that the employee has an unconditional ownership interest in certain pension benefits. By "matured" benefits, we mean that the employee qualifies for immediate possession and enjoyment of the benefits. Comment, *An Interdisciplinary Analysis of the Division of Pension Benefits In Divorce and Post-Judgment Partition Actions: Cures for the Inequities in Berry v. Berry*, 37 BAYLOR L. REV. 106, 121-22 (1985).

An employee spouse's accrued benefits in a retirement plan which have been earned during marriage, but which have not vested and matured at the time of divorce, constitute a contingent interest in property and a community asset subject to division upon divorce. *Cearley v. Cearley*, 544 S.W.2d 661, 666 (Tex. 1976); *Miser v. Miser*, 475 S.W.2d 597, 600 (Tex. Civ. App.—Dallas 1971, writ dism'd). Although this is a well-settled point in Texas law, uncertainty still exists as to the proper method of dividing future interests in retirement benefits.

Upon divorce, the non-employee spouse is entitled to a certain percentage (in this case, the trial court awarded one-half) of the community interest in the pension benefits. Unless the marriage spans the entire term of employment under the plan through to retirement, so that all benefits were earned during the marriage and are community property, an apportionment must be made between those benefits earned during marriage and those earned while not married, which are separate property. Once the community's fractional interest has been determined, the value of the benefits is multiplied by that fraction which yields the specific amount of the non-employee spouse's interest in the benefits. This method of division is reflected in the following formula:

$$\frac{1}{2} \quad \text{X} \quad \frac{\text{no. months married under plan}}{\text{no. months employed under plan}} \quad \text{X} \quad \text{value} \quad = \quad \text{amount of non-employee spouse's share}$$

(Community Share)	(Community Interest)	(Value)	(Amount of Share)

See Division of Pension Benefits, 37 BAYLOR L.REV. at 136. This relatively straight-forward equation is still the source of much confusion. The uncertainty has arisen in part because the denominator of the community interest fraction and the valuation element have not been consistently defined in case law. The "number of months employed under the plan" has been calculated at both the time of divorce and the time of retirement. The valuation variable has also been calculated for both the date of divorce and the date of retirement. The dates at which these two variables should be calculated is the central question to be determined in this case.

The leading cases in this area are *Taggart v. Taggart*, 552 S.W.2d 422 (Tex. 1977), which spoke to the apportionment element of the equation, and *Berry v. Berry*, 647 S.W.2d 945 (Tex. 1983), which primarily considered the valuation element. Each of these elements has been considered by the Supreme Court in relative isolation from one another. However, these two elements operate jointly in any division of retirement benefits. The interplay between these two variables is reflected in the instant case where the trial court apparently used a mixed formula for division by calculating the apportionment denominator from the date of retirement (*Taggart*) and the valuation element from the date of divorce (*Berry*).

Both parties agree that the trial court erred in this regard. Appellant argues in his first point of error that the trial court abused its discretion, as a matter of law, by calculating the denominator in the apportionment fraction as of the date of retirement instead of the date of divorce, thereby divesting appellant of some of his separate property. By cross-point, appellee agrees that the trial court abused its discretion in calculating the apportionment fraction from the date of retirement instead of divorce. However, appellee contends that this miscalculation divests her of separate property by multiplying a continually reducing apportionment fraction by a value which already has been discounted back to the value of the benefits at the time of divorce. The trial court improperly calculated these two variables of the formula, and we find that this formula used by the trial court was incorrect. It worked to the detriment of the non-employee spouse.

Taggart v. Taggart involved the partition of military retirement benefits. The employee spouse began employment under the plan in 1943, married in 1947, completed twenty years of service and was eligible for retirement in 1964, divorced in 1968, and actually retired in 1974. The trial court had awarded the non-employee spouse "four-ninths *of all retirement pay*," which the employee spouse had and would receive after retirement. (Emphasis added). Four-ninths represents one-half of the fractional amount of time the parties had been married and accumulating benefits over the employee spouse's years of service as of 1964, the date he was eligible to retire (three and one-half years before divorce). The trial court then applied this fraction to the value of the benefits as of the date of retirement.

The Supreme Court ruled the trial court had incorrectly computed the apportionment formula. 552 S.W.2d at 424. The Court reasoned that it was the employee spouse's thirty years of service (360 months) which entitled him to the benefits he received at retirement. The Court held that the correct calculation was "one-half of 246/360 th's of the retirement pay." Although the Court makes no specific mention of the value of the benefits, we can infer that it used the trial court's valuation date, retirement. *See Heisterberg v. Standridge*, 656 S.W.2d 138, 147 n. 4 (Tex. App.—Austin 1983, no writ). The *Taggart* formula can be expressed as:

$$\frac{1}{2} \times \frac{\text{no. months married under plan}}{\text{no. months employed under plan as of the date of retirement}} \times \text{value of benefits as of the date retirement} = \text{non-employee spouse's share}$$

	Apportionment (d/r)	Value (d/r)	

Ten years after *Taggart*, the Supreme Court decided *Berry v. Berry*. That case involved the partition of civilian retirement benefits. The parties were married in 1939, before Mr. Berry became employed under the plan in 1940. The couple was divorced in 1966, while the benefits were still unmatured. Mr. Berry retired in 1978, after thirty-eight years of service, and began receiving retirement benefits.

The trial court awarded Mrs. Berry one-half of the benefits "as would have existed at the time of divorce." There was evidence that Mr. Berry actually received \$946.34 per month in retirement benefits, but that had he been eligible to retire at the time of his divorce his monthly benefits would have amounted to \$221.21. To reach the result it did, the trial court must have calculated the apportionment fraction as of the date of divorce. Thus, the equation would be:

1		no. years married under plan
--	X	-----------
2		no. years employed under plan as of date of divorce

1		26				
--	X	--	X	$221.21	=	$110.60/mo.
2		26				

The Court of Appeals reversed and applied the *Taggart* division formula. It ruled that, since Mr. Berry had been employed thirty-eight years under the plan, the community's interest was 26/38 or 34.21% "of all benefits received by Mr. Berry." The Court obviously valued the benefits as of date of retirement. Under the Court of Appeals' *Taggart* formula, Mrs. Berry would have been entitled to:

1		26				
--	X	--	X	$946.34	=	$323.74/mo.
2		38				

In its opinion, the Supreme Court, for the first time, recognized that other factors affect the division of retirement benefits. The Court noted that, under this retirement plan, the "total length of service under the plan is used as a multiplier in order to reach the amount of benefits payable." Additionally, it noted that "the highest salary paid an employee over a consecutive sixty-month period" was another factor used in computing benefits under this plan. Mr. Berry's highest paid sixty months were in his last five post-divorce years. He had received twelve to fourteen pay raises after his divorce, and had benefited from an improved retirement plan due to union negotiations. To value the benefits as of the date of retirement would allow Mrs. Berry to share in the increases in benefits due to Mr. Berry's post-divorce earnings and efforts.

The Court pointed out that it had already held that retirement benefits should be valued as of the date of divorce. *Herring v. Blakeley*, 385 S.W.2d 843, 848 (Tex. 1965). Then the Court quoted *In Re Marriage of Rister*, 512 S.W.2d 72, 74 (Tex. Civ. App.—Amarillo 1974, no writ), in which that court recognized that valuing benefits at the date of retirement would allow the non-employee spouse to receive benefits accruing to the employee spouse as a result of increased future earnings after the divorce.

This recognition points out a limitation of the *Taggart* formula. Valuing retirement benefits as of the date of retirement and then multiplying by half of the community's proportional share assumes that the community's interest in the benefits is equally earned during each month of employment, so that the non-employee spouse is entitled to a straight percentage of the whole benefit. *Heisterberg v. Standridge*, 656 S.W.2d at 145. Such was not the case in *Berry*, and is not the case in most, if not all, retirement plans.

The Supreme Court, in *Berry*, expressly declined to overrule *Taggart.* The Court cautioned that, while it "did apply a formula based on the number of months in which marriage coincided with employment, divided by the number of months Taggart was in the Navy," *Taggart* should not be read as ruling on the date at which benefits should be valued.[2]

In *Berry*, the Court held that when the value of benefits is in issue, the benefits are to be apportioned based on their value at the date of divorce. Although the Supreme Court did not overrule *Taggart*, neither did it follow *Taggart*, on the facts of the case, and apply an apportionment formula dated at retirement to the value of the benefits as of the date of divorce. The *Berry* Court affirmed the trial court and awarded Mrs. Berry \$110.60 of Mr. Berry's \$946.34 monthly retirement payments. Had the Court applied a *Taggart* fraction to the *Berry* value, as did the trial court in the case at bar, Mrs. Berry only would have been entitled to:

$$\frac{1}{2} \quad X \quad \frac{26}{38} \quad X \quad \$221.21 \quad = \quad \$\,75.67/\text{mo.}$$

We view the present body of law to mean that the *Taggart* formula is applicable in cases where apportionment is the only issue. We perceive such cases to be those where the parties are divorced after the employee spouse has retired or terminated employment under the plan. *See Anderson v. Anderson*, 707 S.W.2d 166 (Tex. App.—Corpus Christi, 1986, writ ref'd n.r.e.); *Harrell v. Harrell*, 700 S.W.2d 645 (Tex. App.—Corpus Christi 1986, no writ); *Workings v. Workings*, 700 S.W.2d 251 (Tex. App.—Dallas 1985, no writ); *Neese v. Neese*, 669 S.W.2d 388 (Tex. App.—Eastland 1984, writ ref'd n.r.e.). In these instances, the concern is to shield the accrued benefits attributable to the employee spouse's premarriage earnings, if any, from the non-employee spouse. This is the function of the apportionment fraction. There is no danger that the non-employee spouse might reap some benefit from the employee spouse's post-divorce earnings because there are none.[3]

In any case where divorce occurs prior to the employee spouse's retirement or termination of employment (i.e., where the amount of retirement benefits could still be increased by future earnings), valuation necessarily becomes an issue in the division, and *Berry*, by its own terms, controls. When the employee spouse continues to accrue additional benefits under the plan because of continued employment, there is a danger that the non-employee spouse's share might comprise some of the value of the accrued benefits earned after divorce. *Berry* prohibits such a result. It requires the benefits be valued as of the date of divorce, not retirement.

Because the case at bar is one in which divorce occurred before retirement, *Berry* dictates that the benefits be valued as of the date of divorce. We hold that equity and the rule against divestiture of separate personal property dictate that the denominator of the apportionment fraction must be calculated from the date of divorce also. The trial court in this case ordered a division of benefits accord-

---

[2] One commentator has suggested that, in not overruling *Taggart*, the Court merely intended to "renew prior supreme court approval of apportionment as the preferred 'method' of dividing pension benefits . . . [and] to reassure the continued viability of apportionment and the 'if, as, and when' method of distribution. . . ." *Division of Pension Benefits* 37 BAYLOR L. REV. at 144-45.

[3] If one assumes that retirement benefits are not equally earned in each year of employment under a plan, one could logically argue that, in instances where the employee spouse was employed and accruing benefits under a plan for a significant period of time before marriage, a straight *Taggart* formula division might divest the employee spouse of separate property even if retirement occurs before divorce, unless the value of the benefits attributable to premarriage earnings is factored out of the division formula.

ing to a formula which divides the benefits as valued at the date of divorce by an apportionment fraction calculated from the date of retirement. This mixture of the two formulas was error, because it divested the non-employee spouse of a portion of her separate property. *But see Dunn v. Dunn*, 703 S.W.2d 317 (Tex. App.—San Antonio 1985, writ ref'd n.r.e.); *Rankin v. Bateman*, 686 S.W.2d 707 (Tex. App.—San Antonio 1985, writ ref'd n.r.e.).

The *Taggart* apportionment fraction is a reducing fraction in that the non-employee spouse's share reduces as the employee spouse continues employment under the plan after divorce. In *Taggart*, the non-employee spouse's share was determined by comparing the time married to the entire period of employment under the plan; yet, that ratio was applied against the value of the plan benefits which accumulated over the same period. In *Berry*, the value of the benefits was frozen at the date of divorce, as was the non-employee's pro rata share. Accordingly, we hold that in cases such as this, where the *Berry* valuation is mandated, the denominator of the apportionment fraction must also be calculated as of the date of divorce.

In the instant case, the parties were married before appellant began employment under the plan. As of the date of divorce, appellant had worked 184 months under the plan while married; therefore, the apportionment fraction would be 184/184. Appellant argues that, under the *Berry* formula, appellee's share of his retirement benefits should be:

$$\frac{1}{2} \times \frac{184}{184} \times \$667.79 = \$333.89 \text{ (as, if, and when received)}$$

The value in this equation is based on Finding of Fact Number Fifteen in which the trial court found that, if appellant had retired at the date of divorce, the amount of his monthly benefit payment would be $667.79. At trial, the actuary testified as follows:

> MR. RESENDEZ: So typically what I am saying, Your Honor, is that if this person on a hypothetical basis continues to work and retires at 20 years and then is retired until death, he would receive $667.79 per month, which has a present value of $68,446.63. Her share would be equal to $251.76. This amount is roughly 37.7 percent of the $667.79.

In his second point of error, appellant complains of the fourth variable in the trial court's division formula which awarded appellee a portion of the total percentage of the cost of living increases granted by appellant's employer from the date of divorce to the date of retirement. Appellant argues the trial court abused its discretion in making this award, as it unlawfully divests him of separate property. We agree.

We find that this issue is again controlled by *Berry*. The Supreme Court stated, "we reject the concept of inflation as a factor for our consideration as it relates to the current value of retirement benefits." *Berry*, 647 S.W.2d at 947. Thus, *Berry* prohibits non-employee spouses from sharing in post-divorce increases in retirement benefits, as that would be a divestiture of separate property under *Cameron v. Cameron*, 641 S.W.2d 210 (Tex. 1982). *See also Heisterberg v. Standridge*, 656 S.W.2d at 146.

The case at bar is clearly distinguishable from *Neese v. Neese*, 669 S.W.2d 388, cited by appellee. In that case, the employee spouse was retired and receiving benefits when the parties divorced. The court in that case found that *Berry* was not controlling because all of the benefit increases were community property as there had been no post-divorce employment or accrual of benefits. Thus, both spouses were entitled to share in the increases and decreases in retirement benefits. This Court also reached the same holding based upon a similar fact situation in *Harrell v. Harrell*, 700 S.W.2d at 647-48.

The employee spouse in the instant case did not retire before divorce; therefore, *Berry* prohibits the non-employee spouse, appellee, from sharing in any post-divorce increases in the value of appellant's retirement benefits.[4] The trial court erred in awarding appellee any portion of appellant's post-divorce cost of living increases.

By his third point of error, appellant complains the trial court abused its discretion in mischaracterizing his separate property interest in his Air National Guard retirement benefits as community property, thereby divesting him of separate property.

The trial awarded appellant the Air National Guard retirement plan in its entirety. The trial court also modified the parties' property settlement agreement by ordering appellant to pay appellee $5,164.00 from community property funds set aside to him in the agreement. Appellant claims the court awarded him his retirement benefits provided that he pay appellee this lump sum in return for exclusive rights in the plan.

Appellant complains that the trial court should have divided these benefits according to the *Berry* formula, instead of awarding appellee a lump sum. We find nothing in the record to reflect the present value of the total benefits under the plan.

TEX. FAM. CODE ANN. § 3.63(a) (Vernon Supp. 1986) authorizes a trial court to divide the estate of the parties in a manner the trial court deems just and right. This trial court was well within its discretion to award appellant all of these benefits instead of dividing them. *See In re Marriage of Butler*, 543 S.W.2d 147, 150 (Tex. Civ. App.—Texarkana 1976, writ dism'd). It would also be in the trial court's discretion to order appellant to pay a lump sum to appellee in lieu of any interest she has in the benefits. The trial court has broad discretion in the division of property upon divorce, and this discretion will not be disturbed on appeal unless there is an abuse of discretion. *McKnight v. McKnight*, 543 S.W.2d 863, 866 (Tex. 1976). Appellant's third point of error is overruled.

The judgment of the trial court is affirmed insofar as it awards appellant all the benefits from his Air National Guard plan and awards appellee the sum of $5,164.00.

The portion of the judgment which awards appellee an interest in post-divorce cost-of-living increases in appellant's San Antonio Fire Department retirement benefits is reversed. We here render judgment that appellee take none of these increases.

The portion of the judgment which awards appellee an interest in appellant's San Antonio Fire Department retirement benefits is also reversed. We sever and remand to the trial court with instructions to divide the benefits according to the *Berry* formula, with the denominator of the apportionment calculated as of the date of divorce and then multiplied by the value of the benefits as of the same date, whatever amount the trial court determines that value to be. TEX. R. CIV. P. 434.

AFFIRMED in part; REVERSED and RENDERED in part; and REVERSED and REMANDED in part.

---

[4] We are mindful that this rigid prohibition may deprive the non-employee spouse of increases he/she may fairly be entitled to, *see Division of Pension Benefits*, 37 BAYLOR L. REV. at 152-64; however, *Berry* governs in this regard.

e. *Humble v. Humble*, 805 S.W.2d 558 (Tex. App.—Beaumont 1991, *writ denied*).

In *Humble*, the court was dealing with a defined benefit plan. Mrs. Humble was married to Mr. Humble during his highest wage earning years, and yet, under the *Berry* formula, these high earning years were considered of no more value than the years at the first of his employment. By using the *Berry* formula, Mrs. Humble received only 13.5% of the benefits, when, in the last ten years during marriage, Mr. Humble's pay and benefits had increased fourfold.

Mrs. Humble proposed that she should receive 1/2 of the amount that the retirement benefits had increased during the marriage. In her attempt to convince the court that such was fair, Mrs. Humble showed that if Husband had been married during the entirety of his employment - the first 30 years to Wife 1, the final 10 years to her, Wife 2—that using *Berry* to value both wive's interests would leave a significant part of the retirement benefits unaccounted for—a windfall to Husband. The Beaumont Court of Appeals opined:

> Appellant attempts to support her point of error number three by way of hypothetical analysis. Appellant asks this Court to assume that Mr. Humble married on the date of his employment and divorced one day prior to his marriage to our "Mrs. Humble". Appellant then determines the value of the community interest in the pension plan of the first marriage by freezing the value of the benefits at the time of the divorce as mandated by *Berry.* Using the apportionment method, the value of the community interest of the second marriage in the retirement benefit is calculated. Appellant adds the value of first marriage interest to the second marriage interest to demonstrate a gap.
>
> Appellant then concludes that it is the application of the apportionment formula that causes the gap. Even though we applaud appellant's creativity, we nevertheless, disagree. It is apparent that under appellant's hypothetical, a gap is indeed produced by applying *Berry* to the first marriage. *Berry* freezes those benefits as of the time of the divorce. *Berry*, in effect, fails to recognize the contribution that years of service during the first marriage makes to the final divorce/retirement benefit in the second marriage. It is *Berry's* effect on this first marriage, by freezing those benefits, that creates the gap in appellant's hypothetical situation.
>
> It is always interesting to hypothetically dismantle any opinion which is precisely what good lawyers should do and we agree that hypothetically under *Berry* an inequity could be created. However, in dealing with the real life situation before us, Mrs. Humble, appellant in our case, occupied the same position of the second wife in the hypothetical situation.
>
> We are of the opinion that the trial court in our case applied well established Texas law and also reached the correct result both mathematically and equitably. Appellant's point of error number three is overruled.

Humble v. Humble, 805 S.W.2d at 562.

The new statutes have done little to resolve this inequity. It appears that under the new rules, rather than the spouse with the benefits reaping the windfall, it may go to the community. Under the new statute it appears that any windfall will now be subject to a just and right division.

A better understanding of the *Humble* problem is illustrated by the following hypothetical.

> H married W1 in May 1958. At the time of divorce H was working for Hexxon. H's employment began the day he was married to W1. H has always been a frugal man and he has a

special aversion to lawyer's and their offices. H decided to "do his own divorce" from W1. H drafts the divorce papers but fails to mention retirement benefits from Hexxon in the division of property. The retirement plan is a defined benefit plan. At the time of divorce, May 1978, he had been married to W1 and employed 240 months, he was making $50,000 per year and his retirement plan had a lump sum worth of $200,000.

Immediately after his divorce, from W1, (the very next day), he married W2 in May 1978. In May 1998, he has filed for divorce from W2 and retired. At the date of retirement he was making $200,000 per year and his retirement plan—the same plan he had at the time of employment with Hexxon, has a lump sum worth of two million dollars ($2,000,000). H has been employed for a total of 480 months, 240 of which were when he was married to W2. W1 has intervened in the divorce proceedings between W2 and H. W1 is seeking her share of the retirement benefits. Of course, W2 wants her share, as well.

Using the *Berry* formula figure the interest of W1 and W2. Is there a windfall? Who benefits?

---

f. *Pelzig v. Berkebile*, 931 S.W.2d 398 (Tex. App.—Corpus Christi 1996, no writ).

Pelzig v. Berkebile involves a defined contribution retirement plan. Husband in this case contributed to two retirement accounts. The accounts were funded by contributions from Husband and supplemented by a corresponding contribution from his employer. Thus, unlike *Berry*, these were not *defined benefit* plans; rather, these were *defined contribution* plans. At date of marriage husband's accounts held $31,912.27. What is in issue is the value of the benefits at date of divorce, and the formula to be used in dividing the benefits into separate and community property.

Being a defined contribution plan, husband's benefits were not controlled by his length of service, but by the amount of money he put into the plan. The court found that simply subtracting the pre-marriage sum from the sum available at divorce would yield community property. Thus, the court found that only $31,912.00 represents separate property; any additional contributions and interest, be it on separate or community contributions, were deemed to be community. This is a very harsh case when considering a party's retirement plan; that is, one's separate property cannot increase at all in a defined contribution plan. In contrast, if husband had placed this money in a simple stock account, increases in value of that stock would have remained his separate property.

Today, the Husband in *Pelzig* would be allowed to use tracing and characterization principles to establish his separate property interest. For example, if the account at time of marriage held $30,000 in stock, that stock and any increase to those original shares would be and remain his separate property. Of course, husband would have to trace and prove his separate interest by clear and convincing evidence.

---

3. Stock Options

Unlike retirement benefits, the characterization and valuation of stock options have not been addressed by the Texas Supreme Court, although several courts of appeal have issued opinions on the subject. Before the Texas Supreme Court had the opportunity to address the stock option issue, the legislature addressed it in 2005 and refined it in 2009. Accordingly, stock options are now governed by TEX. FAM. CODE §§ 3.007 (d) and (e).

---

4. Other Statutes Dealing with Employee Benefits

In addition to the above discussed portions of the Texas Family Code which are relevant to a spouse's employment benefits, there are others, the full text of which can be found in the Appendix. Read the following statutes: TEX. FAM. CODE § 7.004. Disposition of Rights in Insurance; TEX. FAM. CODE, Chapter 9. Post-Decree Proceedings, Subchapter B. Post Decree Qualified Domestic Relations Order; TEX. FAM. CODE §§ 9.301. Pre-Decree Designation of Ex-Spouse as Beneficiary of Life Insurance; 9.302. Pre-Decree Designation of Ex-Spouse as Beneficiary in Retirement Benefits and Other Financial Plans.

Finally, in matter of Insurance and ERISA, the following case should be read. *Manning v. Hayes*, 212 F.3d 866 (5th Cir. 2000), *certiorari denied* 121 S.Ct. 1401, 532 U.S. 941, 149 L.Ed.2d 345.

---

5. Texas Retirement and ERISA

KENNEDY
v.
PLAN ADMINISTRATOR FOR DuPONT SAVINGS &INVESTMENT PLAN
129 S.Ct. 865 (2009)

SOUTER, JUSTICE.

The Employee Retirement Income Security Act of 1974 (ERISA), 88 Stat. 829, 29 U.S.C. § 1001 *et seq*., generally obligates administrators to manage ERISA plans "in accordance with the documents and instruments governing" them.§ 1104(a)(1)(D). At a more specific level, the Act requires covered pension benefit plans to "provide that benefits . . . under the plan may not be assigned or alienated," § 1056(d)(1), but this bar does not apply to qualified domestic relations orders (QDROs), § 1056(d)(3). The question here is whether the terms of the limitation on assignment or alienation invalidated the act of a divorced spouse, the designated beneficiary under her ex-husband's ERISA pension plan, who purported to waive her entitlement by a federal common law waiver embodied in a divorce decree that was not a QDRO. We hold that such a waiver is not rendered invalid by the text of the antialienation provision, but that the plan administrator properly disregarded the waiver owing to its conflict with the designation made by the former husband in accordance with plan documents.

I

The decedent, William Kennedy, worked for E.I. DuPont de Nemours & Company and was a participant in its savings and investment plan (SIP), with power both to "designate any beneficiary or beneficiaries . . . to receive all or part" of the funds upon his death, and to "replace or revoke such designation." App. 48. The plan requires "[a]ll authorizations, designations and requests concerning the Plan [to] be made by employees in the manner prescribed by the [plan administrator]," *id.*, at 52, and provides forms for designating or changing a beneficiary, *id.*, at 34, 56-57. If at the time the participant dies "no surviving spouse exists and no beneficiary designation is in effect, distribution shall be made to, or in accordance with the directions of, the executor or administrator of the decedent's estate." *Id.*, at 48.

The SIP is an ERISA " 'employee pension benefit plan,' " 497 F.3d 426, 427 (C.A.5 2007); 29 U.S.C. § 1002(2), and the parties do not dispute that the plan satisfies ERISA's antialienation provision, § 1056(d)(1), which requires it to "provide that benefits provided under the plan may not be assigned or alienated."[1] The plan does, however, permit a beneficiary to submit a "qualified disclaimer" of benefits as defined under the Tax Code, *see* 26 U.S.C. § 2518, which has the effect of switching the beneficiary to an "alternate . . . determined according to a valid beneficiary designation made by the deceased." Supp. Record 86-87 (Exh. 15).

In 1971, William married Liv Kennedy, and, in 1974, he signed a form designating her to take benefits under the SIP, but naming no contingent beneficiary to take if she disclaimed her interest. 497 F.3d, at 427. William and Liv divorced in 1994, subject to a decree that Liv "is . . . divested of all right, title, interest, and claim in and to . . . [a]ny and all sums . . . the proceeds [from], and any other rights related to any . . . retirement plan, pension plan, or like benefit program existing by reason of [William's] past or present or future employment." App. to Pet. for Cert. 64-65. William did not, however, execute any documents removing Liv as the SIP beneficiary, 497 F.3d, at 428, even though he did execute a new beneficiary-designation form naming his daughter, Kari Kennedy, as the beneficiary under DuPont's Pension and Retirement Plan, also governed by ERISA.

On William's death in 2001, petitioner Kari Kennedy was named executrix and asked DuPont to distribute the SIP funds to William's Estate. *Ibid.* DuPont, instead, relied on William's designation form and paid the balance of some $400,000 to Liv. *Ibid.* The Estate then sued respondents DuPont and the SIP plan administrator (together, DuPont), claiming that the divorce decree amounted to a waiver of the SIP benefits on Liv's part, and that DuPont had violated ERISA by paying the benefits to William's designee.[2]

---

[1] The plan states that "[e]xcept as provided by Section 401(a)(13) of the [Internal Revenue] Code, no assignment of the rights or interests of account holders under this Plan will be permitted or recognized, nor shall such rights or interests be subject to attachment or other legal processes for debts." App. 50-51. Title 26 U.S.C. § 401(a)(13)(A), in language substantially tracking the text of § 1056(d)(1), provides that "[a] trust shall not constitute a qualified trust under this section unless the plan of which such trust is a part provides that benefits provided under the plan may not be assigned or alienated."

[2] The Estate now says that William's beneficiary-designation form for the Pension and Retirement Plan applied to the SIP as well, but the form on its face applies only to DuPont's "Pension and Retirement Plan." App. 62. In the District Court, in fact, the Estate stipulated that William "never executed any forms or documents to remove or replace Liv Kennedy as his sole beneficiary under either the SIP or [a plan that merged into the SIP]." *Id.*, at 28. In any event, the Estate did not raise this argument in the Court of Appeals, and we will not address it in the first instance. *See* Taylor v. Freeland & Kronz, 503 U.S. 638, 645-646, 112 S.Ct. 1644, 118 L.Ed.2d 280 (1992).

So far as it matters here, the District Court entered summary judgment for the Estate, to which it ordered DuPont to pay the value of the SIP benefits. The court relied on Fifth Circuit precedent establishing that a beneficiary can waive his rights to the proceeds of an ERISA plan " 'provided that the waiver is explicit, voluntary, and made in good faith.' " App. to Pet. for Cert. 38 (quoting *Manning v. Hayes*, 212 F.3d 866, 874 (C.A.5 2000)).

The Fifth Circuit nonetheless reversed, distinguishing prior decisions enforcing federal common law waivers of ERISA benefits because they involved life-insurance policies, which are considered " 'welfare plan[s]' " under ERISA and consequently free of the antialienation provision. 497 F.3d, at 429. The Court of Appeals held that Liv's waiver constituted an assignment or alienation of her interest in the SIP benefits to the Estate, and so could not be honored. *Id.*, at 430. The court relied heavily on the ERISA provision for bypassing the antialienation provision when a marriage breaks up: under 29 U.S.C. § 1056(d)(3),[3] a court order that satisfies certain statutory requirements is known as a qualified domestic relations order, which is exempt from the bar on assignment or alienation. Because the Kennedys' divorce decree was not a QDRO, the Fifth Circuit reasoned that it could not give effect to Liv's waiver incorporated in it, given that "ERISA provides a specific mechanism-the QDRO-for addressing the elimination of a spouse's interest in plan benefits, but that mechanism is *not* invoked." 497 F.3d, at 431.

We granted certiorari to resolve a split among the Courts of Appeals and State Supreme Courts over a divorced spouse's ability to waive pension plan benefits through a divorce decree not amounting to a QDRO.[4] 552 U.S. ___, 128 S.Ct. 1225, 170 L.Ed.2d 57 (2008). We subsequently realized that this case implicates the further split over whether a beneficiary's federal common law waiver of plan benefits is effective where that waiver is inconsistent with plan documents,[5] and after oral argument we invited supplemental briefing on that latter issue, upon which the disposition of this case ultimately turns. We now affirm, albeit on reasoning different from the Fifth Circuit's rationale.

II

A

By its terms, the antialienation provision, § 1056(d)(1), requires a plan to provide expressly that benefits be neither "assigned" nor "alienated," the operative verbs having histories of legal meaning: to "assign" is "[t]o transfer; as to assign property, or some interest therein," BLACK'S LAW DICTIONARY 152 (4th rev. ed.1968), and to "alienate" is "[t]o convey; to transfer the title to property," *id.*, at 96. We think it fair to say that Liv did not assign or alienate anything to William or to the Estate later standing in his shoes.

---

[3] Section 1056(d)(3)(A) provides that the antialienation provision _shall apply to the creation, assignment, or recognition of a right to any benefit payable with respect to a participant pursuant to a domestic relations order, except that paragraph (1) shall not apply if the order is determined to be a qualified domestic relations order._

[4] *Compare* Altobelli v. IBM Corp., 77 F.3d 78 (C.A.4 1996) (federal common law waiver in divorce decree does not conflict with antialienation provision); Fox Valley & Vicinity Constr. Workers Pension Fund v. Brown, 897 F.2d 275 (C.A.7 1990) (en banc) (same); Keen v. Weaver, 121 S.W.3d 721 (Tex.2003) (same), *with* McGowan v. NJR Serv. Corp., 423 F.3d 241 (C.A.3 2005) (federal common law waiver in divorce decree barred by antialienation provision).

[5] Compare *Altobelli, supra* (federal common law waiver controls); Mohamed v. Kerr, 53 F.3d 911 (C.A.8 1995) (same); Brandon v. Travelers Ins. Co., 18 F.3d 1321 (C.A.5 1994) (same); *Fox Valley*, 897 F.2d 275 (same); Strong v. Omaha Constr. Industry Pension Plan, 270 Neb. 1, 701 N.W.2d 320 (2005) (same); *Keen, supra* (same), with Metropolitan Life Ins. Co. v. Marsh, 119 F.3d 415 (C.A.6 1997) (plan documents control); Krishna v. Colgate Palmolive Co., 7 F.3d 11 (C.A.2 1993) (same).

The Fifth Circuit saw the waiver as an assignment or alienation to the Estate, thinking that Liv's waiver transferred the SIP benefits to whoever would be next in line; without a designated contingent beneficiary, the Estate would take them. The court found support in the applicable Treasury Department regulation that defines "assignment" and "alienation" to include

> "[a]ny direct or indirect arrangement (whether revocable or irrevocable) whereby a party acquires from a participant or beneficiary a right or interest enforceable against the plan in, or to, all or any part of a plan benefit payment which is, or may become, payable to the participant or beneficiary." 26 CFR § 1.401(a)-13(c)(1)(ii) (2008).

See Boggs v. Boggs, 520 U.S. 833, 851-852, 117 S.Ct. 1754, 138 L.Ed.2d 45 (1997) (relying upon the regulation to interpret the meaning of "assignment" and "alienation" in § 1056(d)(1)). The Circuit treated Liv's waiver as an " 'indirect arrangement' " whereby the Estate gained an " 'interest enforceable against the plan.' " 497 F.3d, at 430.

Casting the alienation net this far, though, raises questions that leave one in doubt. Although it is possible to speak of the waiver as an "arrangement" having the indirect effect of a transfer to the next possible beneficiary, it would be odd usage to speak of an estate as the transferee of its own decedent's property, just as it would be to speak of the decedent in his lifetime as his own transferee. And treating the estate or even the ultimate estate beneficiary as the assignee or transferee would be strange under the terms of the regulation: it would be hard to say the estate or future beneficiary "acquires" a right or interest when at the time of the waiver there was no estate and the beneficiary of a future estate might be anyone's guess. If there were a contingent beneficiary (or the participant made a subsequent designation) the estate would get no interest; as for an estate beneficiary, the identity could ultimately turn on the law of intestacy applied to facts as yet unknown, or on the contents of the participant's subsequent will, or simply on the participant's future exercise of (or failure to invoke) the power to designate a new beneficiary directly under the terms of the plan. Thus, if such a waiver created an "arrangement" assigning or transferring anything under the statute, the assignor would be blindfolded, operating, at best, on the fringe of what "assignment" or "alienation" normally suggests.

The questionability of this broad reading is confirmed by exceptions to it that are apparent right off the bat. Take the case of a surviving spouse's interest in pension benefits, for example. Depending on the circumstances, a surviving spouse has a right to a survivor's annuity or to a lump-sum payment on the death of the participant, unless the spouse has waived the right and the participant has eliminated the survivor annuity benefit or designated a different beneficiary. *See Boggs, supra*, at 843, 117 S.Ct. 1754; 29 U.S.C. §§ 1055(a), (b)(1)(C), (c)(2). This waiver by a spouse is plainly not barred by the antialienation provision. Likewise, DuPont concedes that a qualified disclaimer under the Tax Code, which allows a party to refuse an interest in property and thereby eliminate federal tax, would not violate the antialienation provision. *See* Brief for Respondents 21-23; 26 U.S.C. § 2518. In each example, though, we fail to see how these waivers would be permissible under the Fifth Circuit's reading of the statute and regulation.

Our doubts, and the exceptions that call the Fifth Circuit's reading into question, point us toward authority we have drawn on before, the law of trusts that "serves as ERISA's backdrop." *Beck v. Pace Int'l Union*, 551 U.S. 96, 101, 127 S.Ct. 2310, 168 L.Ed.2d 1 (2007). We explained before that § 1056(d)(1) is much like a spendthrift trust provision barring assignment or alienation of a benefit, *see Boggs, supra*, at 852, 117 S.Ct. 1754, and the cognate trust law is highly suggestive here. Although the beneficiary of a spendthrift trust traditionally lacked the means to transfer his beneficial interest to anyone else, he did have the power to disclaim prior to accepting it, so long as the disclaimer made no attempt to direct the interest to a beneficiary in his stead. *See* 2 RESTATEMENT (THIRD) OF TRUSTS § 58(1), Comment *c*, p. 359 (2001) ("A designated beneficiary of a spendthrift trust is not required to accept or retain an interest prescribed by the terms of the trust. . . . On the other hand, a purported disclaimer by which the beneficiary attempts to direct who is to receive the interest is a precluded transfer"); E. GRISWOLD, SPENDTHRIFT TRUSTS § 524, p. 603 (2d ed. 1947) ("The American cases, though not entirely clear, generally take the view that the interest under a spendthrift trust may be disclaimed"); *Roseberry v. Moncure*, 245 Va. 436, 439, 429 S.E.2d 4, 6 (1993) (" 'If a trust is created without notice to the beneficiary or the beneficiary has not accepted the beneficial interest under the trust, he can disclaim' " (quoting 1 A. SCOTT & W. FRATCHER, LAW OF TRUSTS § 36.1, p. 389 (4th ed.1987) (hereinafter FRATCHER))).

We do not mean that the whole law of spendthrift trusts and disclaimers turns up in § 1056(d)(1), but the general principle that a designated spendthrift can disclaim his trust interest magnifies the improbability that a statute written with an eye on the old law would effectively force a beneficiary to take an interest willy-nilly. Common sense and common law both say that "[t]he law certainly is not so absurd as to force a man to take an estate against his will." *Townson v. Tickell*, 3 Barn. & Ald. 31, 36, 106 Eng. Rep. 575, 576-577 (K.B.1819).[6]

The Treasury is certainly comfortable with the state of the old law, for the way it reads its own regulation "no party 'acquires from' a beneficiary a 'right or interest enforceable against the plan' pursuant to a beneficiary's waiver of rights where the beneficiary does not attempt to direct her interest in pension benefits to another person." Brief for United States as *Amicus Curiae* 18. And, being neither "plainly erroneous [n]or inconsistent with the regulation," the Treasury Department's interpretation of its regulation is controlling. *Auer v. Robbins*, 519 U.S. 452, 461, 117 S.Ct. 905, 137 L.Ed.2d 79 (1997).[7]

---

[6] DuPont argues that Liv's waiver would have been an invalid disclaimer at common law because it was given for consideration in the divorce settlement. But the authorities DuPont cites fail to support the proposition that a beneficiary's otherwise valid disclaimer was invalid at common law because she received consideration. *See* Roseberry v. Moncure, 245 Va., at 439, 429 S.E.2d, at 6; Smith v. Bank of Del., 43 Del.Ch. 124, 126-127, 219 A.2d 576, 577 (1966); Preminger v. Union Bank & Trust Co., 54 Mich.App. 361, 368-369, 220 N.W.2d 795, 798-799 (1974); 4 FRATCHER § 337.1 (4th ed.1989); 1 RESTATEMENT (SECOND) OF TRUSTS § 36, Comment *c* (1957). It is true that the receipt of consideration prevents a beneficiary from making a qualified disclaimer for gift tax purposes, *see* 26 CFR § 25.2518-2 (2008), and there is common law authority for the proposition that a renunciation by a devisee is ineffective against existing creditors if "it is shown that those who would take such property on renunciation had agreed to pay to the devisee something of value in consideration of such renunciation." 6 W. BOWE & D. PARKER, PAGE ON LAW OF WILLS § 49.5, p. 48 (2005); *see also* Schoonover v. Osborne, 193 Iowa 474, 478-479, 187 N.W. 20, 22 (1922). But at common law the receipt of consideration did not necessarily render a disclaimer invalid. *See* Commerce Trust Co. v. Fast, 396 S.W.2d 683, 686-687 (Mo.1965); Central Nat. Bank v. Eells, 5 Ohio Misc. 187, 189-192, 215 N.E.2d 77, 80-81 (Ohio Prob.Ct.1965); *In re* Wimperis, [1914] 1 Ch. 502, 508-510; *see also In re* Estate of Baird, 131 Wash.2d 514, 519, n. 5, 933 P.2d 1031, 1034, n. 5 (1997). In any event, our point is not that Liv's waiver was a valid disclaimer at common law: only that reading the terms of 29 U.S.C. § 1056(d)(1) to bar all non-QDRO waivers is unsound in light of background common law principles.

[7] It is true that the Government's position regarding the applicability of the antialienation provision to a waiver has fluctuated. The Labor Department previously took the position that "application of such a federal common-law waiver rule to pension plans would conflict with ERISA's anti-alienation provision." Brief for Secretary of Labor as *Amicus Curiae* 16 in Keen v. Weaver, No. 01-0447 (Tex.2003). And it likewise asserted that "waiver of pension benefits is generally impermissible under [§ 1056(d)(1)]." Brief for Secretary of Labor as *Amicus Curiae* 5 in *In re Estate of Egelhoff*, No. 67626-7 (Wash.2001). The Labor Department has reconsidered that view and has now taken the Treasury's position. Brief for United States as *Amicus Curiae* 20, n. 6. But "the change in interpretation alone presents no separate ground for disregarding the [Treasury's and the Labor] Department's present interpretation."

The Fifth Circuit found "significant support" for its contrary holding in the QDRO subsections, reasoning that "[i]n the marital-dissolution context, the QDRO provisions supply the *sole* exception to the anti-alienation provision," 497 F.3d, at 430, a point that echoes in DuPont's argument here. But the negative implication of the QDRO language is not that simple. If a QDRO provided a way for a former spouse like Liv merely to waive benefits, this would be powerful evidence that the antialienation provision was meant to deny any effect to a waiver within a divorce decree but not a QDRO, else there would have been no need for the QDRO exception. But this is not so, and DuPont's argument rests on a false premise. In fact, a beneficiary seeking only to relinquish her right to benefits cannot do this by a QDRO, for a QDRO by definition requires that it be the "creat[ion] or recogni[tion of] the existence of an alternate payee's right to, or assign[ment] to an alternate payee [of] the right to, receive all or a portion of the benefits payable with respect to a participant under a plan." 29 U.S.C. § 1056(d)(3)(B)(i)(I). There is no QDRO for a simple waiver; there must be some succeeding designation of an alternate payee.[8] Not being a mechanism for simply renouncing a claim to benefits, then, the QDRO provisions shed no light on whether a beneficiary may waive by a non-QDRO.

In sum, Liv did not attempt to direct her interest in the SIP benefits to the Estate or any other potential beneficiary, and accordingly we think that the better view is that her waiver did not constitute an assignment or alienation rendered void under the terms of § 1056(d)(1).

B

DuPont has three other reasons for saying that Liv's waiver was barred by ERISA. They are unavailing.

First, it argues that even if the waiver is not an assignment or alienation barred under the terms of § 1056(d)(1), § 1056(d)(3)(A) still prohibits it, in providing that § 1056(d)(1) "shall apply to the creation, assignment, or recognition of a right to any benefit payable with respect to a participant pursuant to a domestic relations order [that is not a QDRO]." At the very least, DuPont reasons, Liv's waiver included a "recognition" of William's rights with respect to the SIP benefits. But DuPont overlooks the point that when subsection (d)(3)(A) provides that the bar to assignments or alienations extends to non-QDRO domestic relations orders, it does nothing to expand the scope of prohibited assignment and alienation under subsection (d)(1). Whether Liv's action is seen as a waiver or as a domestic relations order that incorporated a waiver, subsection (d)(1) does not cover it and § 1056(d)(3)(A) does not independently bar it.

Second, DuPont relies upon § 1056(d)(3)(H)(iii)(II), providing that if a domestic relations order is not a QDRO, "the plan administrator shall pay the segregated amounts (including any interest thereon) to the person or persons who would have been entitled to such amounts if there had been no order." According to DuPont, because the divorce decree was not a QDRO this provision calls for paying benefits as if there had been no order. But DuPont has wrenched this language out of its setting, reading clause (iii) of subparagraph (H) as if there were no clause (i):

Long Island Care at Home, Ltd. v. Coke, 551 U.S. 158, 171, 127 S.Ct. 2339, 168 L.Ed.2d 54 (2007). Nor does the fact that the interpretation is stated in a legal brief make it unworthy of deference, as "[t]here is simply no reason to suspect that the interpretation does not reflect the agency's fair and considered judgment on the matter in question." *Auer*, 519 U.S., at 462, 117 S.Ct. 905.

[8] Even if one understands Liv's waiver to have resulted somehow in her interest reverting to William, he does not qualify as an "alternate payee," which is defined by statute as "any spouse, former spouse, child, or other dependent of a participant who is recognized by a domestic relations order as having a right to receive all, or a portion of, the benefits payable under a plan with respect to such participant." 29 U.S.C. § 1056(d)(3)(K).

> "During any period in which the issue of whether a domestic relations order is a qualified domestic relations order is being determined . . . the plan administrator shall separately account for the amounts (hereinafter in this subparagraph referred to as the "segregated amounts') which would have been payable to the alternate payee during such period if the order had been determined to be a qualified domestic relations order." § 1056(d)(3)(H)(i).

Thus it is clear that subparagraph (H) speaks of a domestic relations order that distributes certain benefits (the "segregated amounts") to an alternate payee, when the question for the plan administrator is whether the order is effective as a QDRO. That is the circumstance in which, for want of a QDRO, clause (iii) tells the plan administrator not to pay the alternate, but to distribute the segregated amounts as if there had been no order. Clause (iii) does not, as DuPont suggests, state a general rule that a non-QDRO domestic relations order is a nullity in any proceeding that would affect the determination of a beneficiary. And of course clause (iii) says nothing here at all; the divorce decree names no alternate payee, and there are consequently no "segregated amounts."

Third, DuPont claims that a plan cannot recognize a waiver of benefits in a non-QDRO divorce decree because ERISA preempts "any and all State laws insofar as they may now or hereafter relate to any employee benefit plan," with "State law" being defined to include "decisions" or "other State action having the effect of law."[9] §§ 1144(a), (c)(1). DuPont says that Liv's waiver, expressed in a state-court decision and related to an employee benefit plan, is thus preempted. But recognizing a waiver in a divorce decree would not be giving effect to state law; the argument is that the waiver should be treated as a creature of federal common law, in which case its setting in a state divorce decree would be only happenstance. A court would merely be applying federal law to a document that might also have independent significance under state law. *See, e.g., Melton v. Melton*, 324 F.3d 941, 945-946 (C.A.7 2003); *Clift v. Clift*, 210 F.3d 268, 271-272 (C.A.5 2000); *Lyman Lumber Co. v. Hill*, 877 F.2d 692, 693-694 (C.A.8 1989).

III

The waiver's escape from inevitable nullity under the express terms of the antialienation clause does not, however, control the decision of this case, and the question remains whether the plan administrator was required to honor Liv's waiver with the consequence of distributing the SIP balance to the Estate.[10] We hold that it was not, and that the plan administrator did its statutory ERISA duty by paying the benefits to Liv in conformity with the plan documents.

---

[9] This preemption provision does not apply to QDROs. *See* § 1144(b)(7).

[10] Despite our following answer to the question here, our conclusion that § 1056(d)(1) does not make a nullity of a waiver leaves open any questions about a waiver's effect in circumstances in which it is consistent with plan documents. Nor do we express any view as to whether the Estate could have brought an action in state or federal court against Liv to obtain the benefits after they were distributed. *Compare* Boggs v. Boggs, 520 U.S. 833, 853, 117 S.Ct. 1754, 138 L.Ed.2d 45 (1997) ("If state law is not preempted, the diversion of retirement benefits will occur regardless of whether the interest in the pension plan is enforced against the plan or the recipient of the pension benefit"), *with* Sweebe v. Sweebe, 474 Mich. 151, 156-159, 712 N.W.2d 708, 712-713 (2006) (distinguishing *Boggs* and holding that "while a plan administrator must pay benefits to the named beneficiary as required by ERISA," after the benefits are distributed _the consensual terms of a prior contractual agreement may prevent the named beneficiary from retaining those proceeds"); Pardee v. Pardee, 2005 OK CIV APP. 27, __ 20, 27, 112 P.3d 308, 313-314, 315-316 (2004) (distinguishing *Boggs* and holding that ERISA did not preempt enforcement of allocation of ERISA benefits in state-court divorce decree as "the pension plan funds were no longer entitled to ERISA protection once the plan funds were distributed").

ERISA requires "[e]very employee benefit plan [to] be established and maintained pursuant to a written instrument," 29 U.S.C. § 1102(a)(1), "specify[ing] the basis on which payments are made to and from the plan," § 1102(b)(4). The plan administrator is obliged to act _in accordance with the documents and instruments governing the plan insofar as such documents and instruments are consistent with the provisions of [Title I] and [Title IV] of [ERISA]," § 1104(a)(1)(D), and the Act provides no exemption from this duty when it comes time to pay benefits. On the contrary, § 1132(a)(1)(B) (which the Estate happens to invoke against DuPont here) reinforces the directive, with its provision that a participant or beneficiary may bring a cause of action "to recover benefits due to him under the terms of his plan, to enforce his rights under the terms of the plan, or to clarify his rights to future benefits under the terms of the plan."

The Estate's claim therefore stands or falls by "the terms of the plan," § 1132(a)(1)(B), a straightforward rule of hewing to the directives of the plan documents that lets employers " 'establish a uniform administrative scheme, [with] a set of standard procedures to guide processing of claims and disbursement of benefits.' "[11] *Egelhoff v. Egelhoff*, 532 U.S. 141, 148, 121 S.Ct. 1322, 149 L.Ed.2d 264 (2001) (quoting *Fort Halifax Packing Co. v. Coyne*, 482 U.S. 1, 9, 107 S.Ct. 2211, 96 L.Ed.2d 1 (1987)); *see also Curtiss-Wright Corp. v. Schoonejongen*, 514 U.S. 73, 83, 115 S.Ct. 1223, 131 L.Ed.2d 94 (1995) (ERISA's statutory scheme "is built around reliance on the face of written plan documents"). The point is that by giving a plan participant a clear set of instructions for making his own instructions clear, ERISA forecloses any justification for enquiries into nice expressions of intent, in favor of the virtues of adhering to an uncomplicated rule: "simple administration, avoid[ing] double liability, and ensur[ing] that beneficiaries get what's coming quickly, without the folderol essential under less-certain rules." *Fox Valley & Vicinity Const. Workers Pension Fund v. Brown*, 897 F.2d 275, 283 (C.A.7 1990) (Easterbrook, J., dissenting).

And the cost of less certain rules would be too plain. Plan administrators would be forced "to examine a multitude of external documents that might purport to affect the dispensation of benefits." *Altobelli v. IBM Corp.*, 77 F.3d 78, 82-83 (C.A.4 1996) (Wilkinson, C. J., dissenting), and be drawn into litigation like this over the meaning and enforceability of purported waivers. The Estate's suggestion that a plan administrator could resolve these sorts of disputes through interpleader actions merely restates the problem with the Estate's position: it would destroy a plan administrator's ability to look at the plan documents and records conforming to them to get clear distribution instructions, without going into court.

---

[11] We express no view regarding the ability of a participant or beneficiary to bring a cause of action under 29 U.S.C. § 1132(a)(1)(B) where the terms of the plan fail to conform to the requirements of ERISA and the party seeks to recover under the terms of the statute.

The Estate of course is right that this guarantee of simplicity is not absolute. The very enforceability of QDROs means that sometimes a plan administrator must look for the beneficiaries outside plan documents notwithstanding § 1104(a)(1)(D); § 1056(d)(3)(J) provides that a "person who is an alternate payee under a [QDRO] shall be considered for purposes of any provision of [ERISA] a beneficiary under the plan." But this in effect means that a plan administrator who enforces a QDRO must be said to enforce plan documents, not ignore them. In any case, a QDRO enquiry is relatively discrete, given the specific and objective criteria for a domestic relations order that qualifies as a QDRO,[12] *see* §§ 1056(d)(3)(C), (D), requirements that amount to a statutory checklist working to "spare [an administrator] from litigation-fomenting ambiguities," *Metropolitan Life Ins. Co. v. Wheaton*, 42 F.3d 1080, 1084 (C.A.7 1994). This is a far cry from asking a plan administrator to figure out whether a claimed federal common law waiver was knowing and voluntary, whether its language addressed the particular benefits at issue, and so forth, on into factually complex and subjective determinations. *See, e.g., Altobelli, supra*, at 83 (Wilkinson, C. J., dissenting) ("[W]aiver provisions are often sweeping in their terms, leaving their precise effect on plan benefits unclear"); *Mohamed v. Kerr*, 53 F.3d 911, 915 (C.A.8 1995) (making "fact-driven determination" that marriage termination agreement constituted a valid waiver under federal common law).

These are good and sufficient reasons for holding the line, just as we have done in cases of state laws that might blur the bright-line requirement to follow plan documents in distributing benefits. Two recent preemption cases are instructive here. *Boggs v. Boggs*, 520 U.S. 833, 117 S.Ct. 1754, 138 L.Ed.2d 45, held that ERISA preempted a state law permitting the testamentary transfer of a nonparticipant spouse's community property interest in undistributed pension plan benefits. We rejected the entreaty to create "through case law . . . a new class of persons for whom plan assets are to be held and administered," explaining that "[t]he statute is not amenable to this sweeping extratextual extension." *Id.*, at 850, 117 S.Ct. 1754. And in *Egelhoff* we held that ERISA preempted a state law providing that the designation of a spouse as the beneficiary of a nonprobate asset is revoked automatically upon divorce. 532 U.S., at 143, 121 S.Ct. 1322. We said the law was at fault for standing in the way of making payments "simply by identifying the beneficiary specified by the plan documents," *id.*, at 148, 121 S.Ct. 1322, and thus for purporting to "undermine the congressional goal of 'minimiz[ing] the administrative and financial burden[s]' on plan administrators," *id.*, at 149-150, 121 S.Ct. 1322 (quoting *Ingersoll-Rand Co. v. McClendon*, 498 U.S. 133, 142, 111 S.Ct. 478, 112 L.Ed.2d 474 (1990)); *see Egelhoff, supra*, at 147, n. 1, 121 S.Ct. 1322 (identifying "the conflict between the plan documents (which require making payments to the named beneficiary) and the statute (which requires making payments to someone else)").

What goes for inconsistent state law goes for a federal common law of waiver that might obscure a plan administrator's duty to act "in accordance with the documents and instruments." *See Mertens v. Hewitt Associates*, 508 U.S. 248, 259, 113 S.Ct. 2063, 124 L.Ed.2d 161 (1993) ("The authority of courts to develop a 'federal common law' under ERISA . . . is not the authority to revise the text of

[12] To qualify as a QDRO, a divorce decree must "clearly specif[y]" the name and last known mailing address of the participant and the name and mailing address of each alternate payee covered by the order; the amount or percentage of the participant's benefits to be paid by the plan to each such alternate payee or the manner in which such amount or percentage is to be determined; the number of payments or period to which the order applies; and each plan to which such order applies. § 1056(d)(3)(C). A domestic relations order cannot qualify as a QDRO if it requires a plan to provide any type or form of benefit, or any option, not otherwise provided under the plan; requires the plan to provide increased benefits; or requires the payment of benefits to an alternate payee that are required to be paid to another alternate payee under another order previously determined to be a QDRO. § 1056(d)(3)(D). A plan is required to establish written procedures for determining whether a domestic relations order is a QDRO. § 1056(d)(3)(G)(ii).

the statute"). And this case does as well as any other in pointing out the wisdom of protecting the plan documents rule. Under the terms of the SIP Liv was William's designated beneficiary. The plan provided an easy way for William to change the designation, but for whatever reason he did not. The plan provided a way to disclaim an interest in the SIP account, but Liv did not purport to follow it.[13] The plan administrator therefore did exactly what § 1104(a)(1)(D) required: "the documents control, and those name [the ex-wife]." *McMillan v. Parrott*, 913 F.2d 310, 312 (C.A.6 1990).

It is no answer, as the Estate argues, that William's beneficiary-designation form should not control because it is not one of the "documents and instruments governing the plan" under § 1104(a)(1)(D) and was not treated as a plan document by the plan administrator. That is beside the point. It is uncontested that the SIP and the summary plan description are "documents and instruments governing the plan." *See Curtiss-Wright Corp.*, 514 U.S., at 84, 115 S.Ct. 1223 (explaining that 29 U.S.C. §§ 1024(b)(2) and (b)(4) require a plan administrator to make available the "governing plan documents"). Those documents provide that the plan administrator will pay benefits to a participant's designated beneficiary, with designations and changes to be made in a particular way. William's designation of Liv as his beneficiary was made in the way required; Liv's waiver was not.[14]

IV

Although Liv's waiver was not rendered a nullity by the terms of § 1056, the plan administrator properly distributed the SIP benefits to Liv in accordance with the plan documents. The judgment of the Court of Appeals is affirmed on the latter ground.

It is so ordered.

Questions

1. What section of the Texas Family Code might come into question after this case?
2. How so?
3. What advice will you give a divorcing client after reading this case?

---

[13] The Estate does not contend that Liv's waiver was a valid disclaimer under the terms of the plan. We do not address a situation in which the plan documents provide no means for a beneficiary to renounce an interest in benefits.

[14] The Estate also contends that requiring a plan administrator to distribute benefits in conformity with plan documents will allow a beneficiary who murders a participant to obtain benefits under the terms of the plan. The "slayer" case is not before us, and we do not address it. *See* Egelhoff v. Egelhoff, 532 U.S. 141, 152, 121 S.Ct. 1322, 149 L.Ed.2d 264 (2001) (declining to decide whether ERISA preempts state statutes forbidding a murdering heir from receiving property as a result of the killing).

H. Alimony or Maintenance

Only recently have the Texas courts been able to order that a spouse make post-divorce maintenance payments. Although temporary alimony has long been allowed, post divorce alimony has not. The denial of post divorce alimony was based on the argument that payment of alimony after the end of the marriage was a divestiture of separate property - money earned after divorce.

Although the spouses could agree that alimony would be a part of their settlement agreement, the agreement to pay alimony could only be enforced as a contract. Such an agreement could not be enforced under the court's contempt powers. *See Francis v. Francis*, 412 S.W.2d 29 (Tex. 1967). More recently, the Austin Court of Appeals in *Cardwell v. Sicola Cardwell*, 978 S.W.2d 722 (Tex. App.—Austin 1998, writ denied) recognized that spousal support agreements are governed by the law of contracts and determined that support payments should continue after obligor husband's death.

As a preface to the next case, read Texas Family Code, Chapter 8, Maintenance. Note that the word "alimony" is not present in the Texas Family Code. What do you think is the significance of the legislature's decision not to use the word alimony?

In re MARRIAGE OF HALE

975 S.W.2d 694
(Tex. App.—Texarkana 1998, no writ)

CORNELIUS, CHIEF JUSTICE.

Steve Hale appeals from a divorce decree that directs him to pay his ex-wife, Tara Hale, post-divorce spousal maintenance for three years at a rate of $300.00 per month. Mr. Hale contends that the evidence is legally and factually insufficient to support the court's award of spousal maintenance and that the trial court abused its discretion by making such an award.

The parties were married on January 11, 1985. They have two minor children. The court found that the parties should be appointed joint managing conservators, with each parent establishing the primary residence of one child. Mrs. Hale was fifteen years of age when she married, and she did not return to school. During the marriage she got several jobs, but was unable to keep the jobs because Mr. Hale insisted that she quit work. Mrs. Hale testified that her husband was a controlling personality to the point of obsession.

The court found that Mr. Hale earned over $36,000.00 as a logger during the year preceding the divorce. The court found that Mrs. Hale earned $867.00 per month. The court ordered Mr. Hale to pay $175.00 per month as child support. The decree ordered Mrs. Hale to provide and pay for health insurance, and directed Mr. Hale to pay her seventy-five percent of the monthly health insurance premium. Mrs. Hale was awarded a 1985 pickup truck with the attendant debt, a horse with its underlying $4,500.00 debt, together with some furniture and household goods. Mr. Hale received his 1995 truck with its debt and other furniture and household goods. He continues to live in the house that they built on his father's property while they were married.

The evidence shows that Mrs. Hale is now attending night school seeking to obtain a G.E.D., and that she has been employed with a local company during most of the one-year separation from her husband.

The court found that Mr. Hale had engaged in violence toward his wife, that the marriage existed for over ten years, and that Mrs. Hale lacked sufficient property, "including property distributed to her under this decree, to provide for her minimum reasonable needs and that she clearly lacks earning ability in the labor market adequate to provide support for her minimum reasonable needs."

The court also found that Mrs. Hale has little education or employment skills, that the parties made excessive expenditures of $22,000.00 when they built a home on property owned by Mr. Hale's father, and that Mrs. Hale would receive no benefit from that expenditure.

The spousal maintenance statutes provide in part:

§ 8.002. Eligibility for Maintenance

In a suit for dissolution of a marriage or in a proceeding for maintenance in a court with personal jurisdiction over both former spouses following the dissolution of their marriage by a court that lacked personal jurisdiction over an absent spouse, the court may order maintenance for either spouse only if:

(1) the spouse from whom maintenance is requested was convicted of or received deferred adjudication for a criminal offense that also constitutes an act of family violence under Chapter 71 and the offense occurred:

(A) within two years before the date on which a suit for dissolution of the marriage is filed; or

(B) while the suit is pending; or

(2) the duration of the marriage was 10 years or longer, the spouse seeking maintenance lacks sufficient property, including property distributed to the spouse under this code, to provide for the spouse's minimum reasonable needs, as limited by Section 8.005, and the spouse seeking maintenance:

(A) is unable to support himself or herself through appropriate employment because of an incapacitating physical or mental disability;

(B) is the custodian of a child who requires substantial care and personal supervision because a physical or mental disability makes it necessary, taking into consideration the needs of the child, that the spouse not be employed outside the home; or

(C) clearly lacks earning ability in the labor market adequate to provide support for the spouse's minimum reasonable needs, as limited by Section 8.005.

§ 8.003. Factors in Determining Maintenance

A court that determines that a spouse is eligible to receive maintenance under this chapter shall determine the nature, amount, duration, and manner of periodic payments by considering all relevant factors, including:

(1) the financial resources of the spouse seeking maintenance, including the community and separate property and liabilities apportioned to that spouse in the dissolution proceeding, and that spouse's ability to meet the spouse's needs independently;

(2) the education and employment skills of the spouses, the time necessary to acquire sufficient education or training to enable the spouse seeking maintenance to find appropriate

employment, the availability of that education or training, and the feasibility of that education or training;

(3) the duration of the marriage;

(4) the age, employment history, earning ability, and physical and emotional condition of the spouse seeking maintenance;

(5) the ability of the spouse from whom maintenance is requested to meet that spouse's personal needs and to provide periodic child support payments, if applicable, while meeting the personal needs of the spouse seeking maintenance;

(6) acts by either spouse resulting in excessive or abnormal expenditures or destruction, concealment, or fraudulent disposition of community property, joint tenancy, or other property held in common;

(7) the comparative financial resources of the spouses, including medical, retirement, insurance, or other benefits, and the separate property of each spouse;

(8) the contribution by one spouse to the education, training, or increased earning power of the other spouse;

(9) the property brought to the marriage by either spouse;

(10) the contribution of a spouse as homemaker;

(11) marital misconduct of the spouse seeking maintenance; and

(12) the efforts of the spouse seeking maintenance to pursue available employment counseling as provided by Chapter 304, Labor Code.

§ 8.004. Presumption

(a) Except as provided by Subsection (b), it is presumed that maintenance is not warranted unless the spouse seeking maintenance has exercised diligence in:

(1) seeking suitable employment; or

(2) developing the necessary skills to become self-supporting during a period of separation and during the time the suit for dissolution of the marriage is pending.

(b) This section does not apply to a spouse who is not able to satisfy the presumption in Subsection (a) because of an incapacitating physical or mental disability.

TEX. FAM. CODE ANN. §§ 8.002, 8.003, 8.004 (Vernon Pamph. 1998).

We first consider what standard of review we should use for this kind of appeal. The statute does not specify the proper standard of review. An order for spousal maintenance is similar to an award of child support, where the standard of review is abuse of discretion, so we will use that standard here.[1] In making an abuse of discretion review in a child support context, we have held that factual and legal insufficiency of the evidence are part of the abuse of discretion review and are not independent grounds for reversal. *In re Marriage of Driver*, 895 S.W.2d 875, 877 (Tex. App.—Texarkana 1995, no writ). A review of the sufficiency of the evidence is subsumed into the review for abuse of discretion.

A trial court's award of child support will not be reversed unless an abuse of discretion is shown. *Gillespie v. Gillespie*, 644 S.W.2d 449, 451 (Tex. 1982); *In re Hidalgo*, 938 S.W.2d 492, 498 (Tex. App.—Texarkana 1996, no writ). Thus, we will reverse only if the court abused its discretion by act-

[1] This type of review was also applied in DuBois v. DuBois, 956 S.W.2d 607, 612 (Tex. App.—Tyler 1997, no writ).

ing without reference to any guiding rules or principles or by acting arbitrarily or unreasonably. *Worford v. Stamper*, 801 S.W.2d 108, 109 (Tex. 1990). There is no abuse of discretion if some evidence supports the decision. *Dennis v. Smith*, 962 S.W.2d 67, 68 (Tex. App.—Houston [1st Dist.] 1997, writ denied); *Holley v. Holley*, 864 S.W.2d 703, 706 (Tex. App.—Houston [1st Dist.] 1993, writ denied).

We view the evidence in the light most favorable to the trial court's actions and indulge every legal presumption in favor of the judgment. If there is some probative and substantive evidence to support the judgment, the trial court did not abuse its discretion. *DuBois v. DuBois*, 956 S.W.2d 607, 610 (Tex. App.—Tyler 1997, no writ).[2]

There is evidence that Mrs. Hale was only fifteen when she married, that she did not graduate from high school, and that her husband hindered her efforts to complete her education or find employment outside the home. There is evidence that a substantial part of the family's estate went into building a house on Mr. Hale's father's property, in which they had no ownership interest. There is evidence that Mrs. Hale had sought and obtained employment, that she was making a set amount of money each month, and that the money she earned was insufficient to meet her needs. She had no rental/mortgage payment because she was living in a house that belonged to her mother, but even then she was unable to earn sufficient money to meet her minimum reasonable needs. Her mother testified that she was providing money to help Mrs. Hale meet her expenses. Mrs. Hale's Exhibit 4 set out her expenses as follows:

Groceries & Household Supplies	220	
Utilities	120	
Auto Payment	143	
Gas	120	
Auto Insurance	35	
School Lunches	20	
Credit Union	63	
Credit Cards	130	
	$851	[Leaving $24.00 per month for all other expenses]

The schedule of expenses, however, is just a generalized list and does not include other essential needs that everyone has, such as her portion of health premiums, uncovered medical expenses, drugs and medicines, clothing, and the like.

Viewing all these circumstances, and especially considering Mrs. Hale's uncertain and very limited earning capacity, we cannot conclude that the trial court abused its discretion in awarding spousal maintenance.

---

[2] Findings of fact in a case tried to the court have the same force and dignity as a jury's verdict. Anderson v. City of Seven Points, 806 S.W.2d 791, 794 (Tex. 1991). In reviewing a no evidence point of error, we consider only the evidence and inferences that, when viewed in their most favorable light, tend to support the finding and disregard all evidence and inferences to the contrary. Davis v. City of San Antonio, 752 S.W.2d 518, 522 (Tex. 1988). In reviewing the factual sufficiency of the evidence, we examine all of the evidence. Plas-Tex, Inc. v. U.S. Steel Corp., 772 S.W.2d 442, 445 (Tex. 1989). The finding will be set aside only if the evidence, standing alone, is too weak to support the finding or the finding is so against the great weight and preponderance of the evidence that it is clearly wrong and manifestly unjust. Cain v. Bain, 709 S.W.2d 175, 176 (Tex. 1986); In re King's Estate, 150 Tex. 662, 244 S.W.2d 660, 661 (1951); In re Pecht, 874 S.W.2d 797, 800 (Tex. App.—Texarkana 1994, no writ).

Mr. Hale contends that the spousal maintenance statute presumes that if a person f employment, an order for maintenance is improper. Although the statute does not contain guage, he suggests that because the statute was linked to a welfare bill, the simple fact that Mrs. Ha is employed precludes an award of spousal maintenance. We have not been provided with any authority to support this position, and it is not supported by the express language of the statute. In the absence of some clear indication that the Legislature intended that result, we will not make such a presumption.

Mr. Hale also contends that, as a matter of law, a person who earns a net wage of $865.00 per month has sufficient income to provide for her reasonable minimum needs. He points out that Mrs. Hale will be receiving child support, so her income will be raised from that source, and he suggests that the credit card bills are not appropriate for consideration. He also argues that the federal minimum wage statute sets as a matter of law the wage necessary to meet minimum reasonable needs. We disagree.

The term "minimum reasonable needs" is not defined by statute, and there appear to be no cases defining the term. Deciding what the minimum reasonable need is for a particular individual or family is a fact-specific determination that ordinarily should be made by the trial court. Mr. Hale argues that a credit card bill is not a "need," but credit cards are realities of modern life and are often used to provide family "needs" or to preserve property when savings or current income are insufficient to do so.

We cannot accept the proposition that the federal minimum wage statute, as a matter of law, dictates what amount will provide the "minimum reasonable needs" of an individual or family. Indeed, it is common knowledge that the minimum wage, standing alone, is usually inadequate to support a family. We are unwilling to hold that the minimum wage is adequate in every case.

In a separate argument, Mr. Hale states that the maintenance award is improper because the Family Code prohibits maintenance if the recipient cohabits with another person in a permanent place of abode on a continuing conjugal basis, and that Mrs. Hale now lives with a man to whom she is not married. TEX. FAM. CODE ANN. § 8.007 (Vernon Pamph. 1998). Hale has not, however, directed us to any evidence that this allegation is true.[3] In the absence of any evidence to support this assertion, we cannot find that the trial court erroneously applied the law.

Although he has no point of error on this issue, Mr. Hale also argues very briefly that the maintenance statute is unconstitutional because it constitutes a taking without due course of law, citing *Eggemeyer v. Eggemeyer*, 554 S.W.2d 137, 140 (Tex. 1977). Mr. Hale did not raise the constitutional argument in the trial court, so he has waived that issue on appeal.

The judgment of the trial court is affirmed.

---

[3] Further, in her brief Mrs. Hale explicitly denies that this is correct.

I. Appellate Review of the Property Division

Justice Ann McClure, Eighth Court of Appeals at El Paso, is board certified in Texas Family Law and a former President of the Family Law Section of the State Bar of Texas. In the case of *Tate v. Tate*, 55 S.W.3d 1 (Tex. App.—El Paso 2000, no pet.) Justice McClure has succinctly explained the presentation of an appeal of a property division upon divorce:

Variations on a Mischaracterization Theme

> Three fact scenarios establish the appropriate structure of an appellant's characterization contention. First, suppose Wife claims Blackacre is her separate property and Husband claims the asset is community property. Second, suppose the trial court characterizes it as community property and awards it to Wife. On appeal, Wife must establish error; she must challenge that the characterization is against the great weight and preponderance of the evidence [a factual sufficiency complaint] or that separate property status was established as a matter of law [a legal sufficiency complaint]. She must also establish that the characterization error was harmful—because of the mischaracterization, the overall division of property constitutes an abuse of discretion. *In re Marriage of Morris*, 12 S.W.3d 877, 884 (Tex. App.—Texarkana 2000, no pet. h.) (mere mischaracterization of separate property as community property does not require reversal; it is appellant's burden to prove that any disparity in the division was caused by the mischaracterization of property and that it was of such substantial proportions that it constituted an abuse of the trial court's discretion); *Magill v. Magill*, 816 S.W.2d 530, 533 (Tex. App.—Houston [1st Dist.] 1991, writ denied) (accord).
>
> Now suppose that given the same fact pattern, the trial court characterizes Blackacre as Wife's separate property and awards it to her. This time, Husband appeals. He must first establish error by challenging the legal or factual sufficiency of the evidence to support the separate property characterization. He must also conduct a harm analysis—because of the mischaracterization, the overall division of property constitutes an abuse of discretion. *Vandiver v. Vandiver*, 4 S.W.3d 300, 302 (Tex. App.—Corpus Christi 1999, pet. filed) (mischaracterization of community property as separate property is not reversible unless the mischaracterization had more than a *de minimus* effect on the just and right division).
>
> It is only in the third scenario that reversible error exists as a matter of law. In this example, Wife claims Blackacre is separate property and Husband claims it is community property. The trial court characterizes it as community property and awards it to *Husband*. If Wife can establish that Blackacre is her separate property, it is unnecessary to show harm because divestiture of separate property is reversible error. *Eggemeyer v. Eggemeyer*, 554 S.W.2d 137, 140 (Tex. 1977); *In re Marriage of Morris*, 12 S.W.3d at 881. In this singular instance, there is no need to demonstrate that the overall property division constitutes an abuse of discretion.

Tate v. Tate, 55 S.W.3d at 6,7.

In light of Justice McClure's succinct explanation, only two cases are presented in this section. *McKnight v. McKnight*, 543 S.W.2d 863 (Tex. 1976) clearly establishes that the division of property is solely within the province of the trial judge. *McElwee v. McElwee*, 911 S.W.2d 182 (Tex. App.—Houston 1995, writ denied) explains that when a mischaracterization yields more than a *de minimis* effect on the division of property, the abuse of discretion standard is met. *McElwee v. McElwee*, 911 S.W.2d 182 (Tex. App.—Houston [1st Dist.] 1995, writ denied).

McKNIGHT
v.
McKNIGHT
543 S.W.2d 863
(Tex. 1976)

MCGEE, JUSTICE.

This case concerns the division of property in a divorce action. Robert E. McKnight, the husband, appealed from the division of property made by the trial court alleging abuse of discretion and asserting that an improper division was made of partnership property. The court of civil appeals reversed the trial court and rendered another property division. 535 S.W.2d 658. We reverse the court of civil appeals regarding its disposition of the property and remand the case to the trial court; we affirm that part of the court of civil appeals' judgment which maintains the trial court's decree of divorce and award of child custody.

* * *

Petitioner and respondent were married in 1952. During this marriage the couple had seven children, four of whom were minors at the time of this suit. Disharmony arose in the marriage and the parties separated on May 24, 1972. The wife filed suit for divorce on May 21, 1973. Incident to the divorce were the issues of child custody and the division of property.

The district court entered its decree of divorce on October 15, 1974, awarding custody of three minor children to the husband and custody of the youngest child to the wife. Two of the remaining children, who were not minors, chose to live with the husband. The third child was married and not living with the family.

The trial court divided the property in its divorce decree without expressing the value of the property awarded. The wife was given all the distributions and disbursements from her father's estate which included shares of stock in 16 different companies, all the cash or deposits in three financial institutions held in her name or the husband's name, 3,500 shares of stock of First International Bancshares, 50 shares of stock of the Fort Davis State Bank, the cash surrender value of all the life insurance policies owned by or in the name of either the husband or wife, all the household goods and furnishings of the family home, a 1972 Buick station wagon and one share of stock in the membership of the Odessa Country Club. The wife was also awarded one-fourth of all the cattle and animal stock owned by the McKnight Ranch Company, a partnership in which the husband was part owner, and one-half of the monies in the McKnight Ranch account. The cattle were to be selected by the wife and delivered in kind. The husband was awarded 206 shares of First International Bancshares, 12 shares of stock in the Fort Davis State Bank, ownership of life insurance held in his name, subject to the cash surrender value awarded the wife, the family home, and any interest owned by the husband in 12 drill sites located in Odessa, Texas. The husband was awarded one-fourth of all McKnight Ranch Company cattle, subject to the distribution and award to the wife, one-half interest in the McKnight Ranch Company and its equipment, subject to any outstanding indebtedness of the company. The husband was given his interest in 23,040 acres of ranch land in Crane County, Texas, and any real estate interest held in his name in the Jeff, McCutcheon and Grierson Ranches located in Jeff Davis County, Texas. The husband was required to assume any tax liability incurred during the marriage with any tax refund being split between husband and wife. The husband was also ordered to pay attorney's fees in the sum of $9,750, all court costs, and child support payments of $600 a month for the child in the wife's custody.

The court of civil appeals held that the trial court "abused its discretion in regards to the rights of the children of the marriage." The court stated that this abuse resulted because "the children are the obligation of the husband, yet he is stripped of all cash, a portion of his livestock, left a business to operate but no funds to operate it with, and ordered to pay debts. The day-to-day expense of five children requires cash or a readily available source of cash. . . ." 535 S.W.2d at 660.

The rationale for the court of civil appeals' holding is the lack of immediate cash assets to operate the ranch and provide for the children. The court remedied this situation by first relieving some of the husband's tax liability. The court reversed that part of the judgment ordering the husband to pay any taxes incurred during the marriage and stated that "(j)udgment is here rendered that the parties share equally, 50-50, any income tax liability incurred during the marriage. . . ." 535 S.W.2d at 661. The court of civil appeals next reversed the portion of the judgment awarding the wife all the deposits in the financial institutions named by the trial court. The court of civil appeals stated that "judgment is here rendered" that all deposits in the name of the wife would remain hers but that any deposits excepting the McKnight Ranch account, held in the name of the husband or jointly in the name of the husband and wife, would be shared equally. The court also reversed the trial court's award of the cash surrender value of various life insurance policies stating that "judgment is here rendered that the ownership and cash surrender value of any policies of life insurance standing in the name of Robert E. McKnight or owned by him are awarded to him." The court reversed the wife's award of any specific McKnight Ranch Company property holding that such an award was in violation of the Texas Uniform Partnership Act, Texas Revised Civil Statutes Annotated article 6132b, and rendered judgment that the husband recover one-half interest in the partnership of McKnight Ranch Company.

We believe the court of civil appeals erred in rendering specific awards of property rather than remanding the case to the trial court after it determined that there was an abuse of discretion. It is well settled that the trial court has broad discretion in determining the disposition of property in divorce actions and this discretion will not be disturbed unless an abuse of discretion is shown. *Cockerham v. Cockerham*, 527 S.W.2d 162 (Tex. 1975); *Bell v. Bell*, 513 S.W.2d 20 (Tex. 1974); TEX. FAMILY CODE ANN. § 3.63 (1975). The role of the court of civil appeals in reviewing cases where property is divided in a divorce action is to determine only if there is an abuse of discretion. *Hooper v. Hooper*, 403 S.W.2d 215 (Tex. Civ. App.—Amarillo 1966, writ dism'd w.o.j.); *Wilson v. Wilson*, 225 S.W.2d 236 (Tex. Civ. App.—Fort Worth 1949, no writ). When the court of civil appeals rendered specific awards of property, it was in effect substituting its determination of "just and right" for the trial court's determination. TEX. FAMILY CODE ANN. § 3.63 (1975). The court of civil appeals in so rendering was infringing upon the trial court's discretion provided in section 3.63 of the Family Code. This case directly conflicts with the rule announced in *Hooper v. Hooper* and *Wilson v. Wilson*. In *Hooper* the court of civil appeals determined that the trial court had abused its discretion and remanded the case with this language: "We are not to be understood to hold that the property should be divided equally or any other definite proportion. That is not the prerogative of this court. We are simply charged with the authority to determine whether the division of the property made by the judgment should be upheld." 403 S.W.2d at 217. In *Wilson* the court of civil appeals held there had been an abuse of discretion in disposing of certain property. The court did not hold that the property should be divided equally or in any named proportion but stated that "(o)ur only authority is to determine whether the disposition of property made by the judgment should be upheld." Courts of civil appeals in reviewing property divisions on divorce do not have the authority to render judgments dividing the property of the spouses.

The husband contends that authority for the action of the court of civil appeals can be found in Texas Rules of Civil Procedure 434 which states: "When the judgment or decree of the court below shall be reversed, the court shall proceed to render such judgment or decree as the court below should have rendered, except when it is necessary that some matter of fact be ascertained or the damage to be assessed or the matter to be decreed is uncertain, in either of which cases the cause shall be remanded for a new trial." The "matter to be decreed" in this case is a "just and right" division of the property in compliance with the Family Code. The court of civil appeals could not render a property division under the authority of Rule 434 because the matter to be decreed was dependent on the discretion of the trial court.

The husband also contends that the court of civil appeals derives authority for its action from *Fuhrman v. Fuhrman*, 302 S.W.2d 205 (Tex. Civ. App.—El Paso 1957, writ dism'd w.o.j.). There the court of civil appeals reviewed a divorce case where the trial court awarded each spouse their own separate property and the community property was divided equally between them. The court held that the trial court had incorrectly determined that 6613.9 shares of stock was community property and because no findings were made which justified a different method of division from that which was made, the court of civil appeals remanded the case with instructions to set aside the stock as separate, not community, property. The case did not deal with the court of civil appeals rendering an award because of an abuse of discretion and we do not find that it lends authority to the court of civil appeals in the present case. The respondent has failed to cite any case where a court of civil appeals sought to remedy an abuse of discretion by rendering an award of property rather than remanding the case to the trial court. Other cases relied on by the husband are cases where the court of civil appeals has ordered a new trial subject to remittitur of property pursuant to the court's holding regarding an equitable division. *Cooper v. Cooper*, 513 S.W.2d 229 (Tex. Civ. App.—Houston (1st Dist.) 1974, no writ); *Dietz v. Dietz*, 540 S.W.2d 418 (Tex. Civ. App.—El Paso 1976, no writ). These cases are distinguishable from the present case because the courts of civil appeals in *Cooper* and *Dietz* would remand the case for a new trial or would affirm a judgment for the division of property if a party would remit certain property to the other spouse. In these situations the option lay with one of the parties to either retry the case or remit some property, but in the present case the property is divested without the party having an option. Mr. McKnight also cites cases in which the courts of civil appeals rendered a judgment either granting or denying a divorce decree due to an error of the trial court regarding a ground relied on for the divorce. None of those cases mentions property division and the judgment of the court of civil appeals only grants or denies a divorce. These cases are not authority for the court of civil appeals in this case.

The trial court also awarded the wife specific properties of the McKnight Ranch Company. The company was run as a partnership with Mr. McKnight owning a 50 percent interest, his father owning a 30 percent interest and his sister owning the remaining 20 percent. The court of civil appeals held that under the Texas Uniform Partnership Act, Texas Revised Civil Statutes Annotated article 6132b, the rights of a divorcing spouse can only attach to the husband's interest in the partnership and not specific partnership property. The court of civil appeals was correct in its holding that the trial court erred in awarding specific partnership property. The Texas Uniform Partnership Act provides:

§ 28-A. Extent of Community Property Rights of a Partner's Spouse.

(1) A partner's rights in specific partnership property are not community property.

(2) A partner's interest in the partnership may be community property.

(3) A partner's right to participate in the management is not community property.

§ 28-B. Effect of Death or Divorce on Interest in the Partnership.

(1)(A) On the divorce of a partner, the partner's spouse shall, to the extent of such spouse's interest in the partnership, be regarded for purposes of this Act as an assignee and purchaser of such interest from such partner.

The trial court detailed a division of the partnership cattle between the husband and wife and awarded the wife one-half of the partnership bank account. The court of civil appeals held the award violated the Act and rendered that the husband recover one-half interest in the partnership with the wife getting no interest in the partnership. While we think the court of civil appeals was correct in its application of the Act, the court should have remanded this issue with the other issues of property division rather than making an award to the husband. It would have been proper for the trial court in its discretion to have given the wife an interest in the partnership. The court of civil appeals by rendering that the husband take a one-half interest in the partnership was infringing on the discretion of the trial court.

The judgment of the court of civil appeals is reversed and the cause is remanded to the trial court for division of the property. In all other respects the judgment of the court of civil appeals is affirmed.

Notes, Comments & Questions

1. The Section of the Texas Uniform Partnership Act quoted above no longer exists in that form. Rather, the relevant statute is TEX. REV. CIV. STAT. art 6132b-5.05. Nonetheless, the holding of the *McKnight* case remains good law, actual partnership assets cannot be taken from the partnership and divided between the divorcing spouses because the assets belong to the business entity. This of course presupposes that the business entity is not disregarded or in some way pierced by the court.

2. What is the role of the court of appeals in reviewing cases where property is divided in a divorce action?

3. The next case, *McElwee v. McElwee*, 911 S.W.2d 182 (Tex. App.—Houston [1st Dist.] 1995, writ denied), provides a somewhat easier route in obtaining a reversal based upon mischaracterization.

McELWEE
v.
McELWEE

911 S.W.2d 182
(Tex. App.—Houston [1st Dist.] 1995, writ denied)

HUTSON-DUNN, JUSTICE.

Appellant, Edward M. McElwee, the respondent in the trial court below, appealed from a judgment of divorce and a property division. The three issues before this Court are: (1) whether the trial court erred in denying appellant's motion to recuse Judge Bill Elliott; (2) whether Judge Elliott was disqualified to hear the matter; and (3) whether the trial court committed reversible error in mischaracterizing community property as separate property of the appellee, Mary Louise McElwee. Because appellant has waived the issue of recusal and because appellant did not show Judge Elliott was disqualified, we affirm the trial court's denial of the motion to recuse and overrule appellant's point of error regarding disqualification. Because the trial court's mischaracterization of community property materially affected the property division, we sustain appellant's second point of error. Finally, having found merit in appellant's arguments, we overrule appellee's cross- point.

Summary of Facts

Edward M. McElwee (Edward) and Mary Louise McElwee (Mary) were married on October 8, 1949. At the time of their marriage, Edward worked as a United States Air Force jet fighter pilot and Mary attended college.

In 1982, Mary filed for divorce and employed Vern Thrower as her attorney. However, wishing to preserve the marriage, Mary reconciled with Edward, and the divorce action was dismissed. Mary filed for divorce, once again, in August 1991. Finding that Edward was guilty of cruel treatment toward Mary, the trial court rendered a judgment of divorce. Without including five properties which the court characterized as Mary's separate property, the court awarded approximately 60.8% of the community property to Mary and 39.2% to Edward.

The Parties' Pleadings

Edward raises two points of error. . . .

In his second point of error, Edward argues the trial court erred by mischaracterizing community property as Mary's separate property. He argues this error requires reversal because it deprived him of his interest in a substantial portion of the community estate. In reply points two through four, Mary asserts that Edward waived error with respect to mischaracterization because he did not object to the trial court's characterization of the property and because he did not brief his points of error in an abuse of discretion standard. In reply points five through seven, Mary asserts that the trial court's error, if any, does not require reversal because, despite any mischaracterization, the trial court's division was not an abuse of discretion. Mary also raises a cross-point asserting that she should be awarded damages because Edward took this appeal without sufficient cause and for delay pursuant to Texas Rule of Appellate Procedure 84.

Analysis

* * *

In point of error two, Edward argues the trial court erred by mischaracterizing certain community properties as Mary's separate property. Edward argues the evidence was legally insufficient, or in the alternative factually insufficient, to rebut the presumption that the property was community property. The five properties in question are: (1) a USAA Gold Fund Mutual Fund Account held in Mary's name and valued at approximately $7,553.54; (2) a Savings of America account listed in Mary's name and valued at approximately $4,489.73; (3) a Savings of America account in the name of Mary or Beulah Hoffpauir and valued at approximately $2,796.96; (4) a Savings of America account listed in Mary's name and valued at approximately $8,971.37; and (5) an America United Life annuity with a monthly payout of $154.00.

Edward asserts the court has erred on three grounds. First, he argues Mary did not rebut the community property presumption because she failed to trace and clearly identify any property she claimed to be separate. Second, he claims that all five accounts were created with money from Mary's disability payments, which are community property as a matter of law. Finally, he claims that, even if some of the money in the accounts was separate property, any interest accruing on separate property is community property as a matter of law. Moreover, he asserts that the error was harmful because separate property cannot be considered in making a just and right division of the marital estate.

Mary argues that Edward waived any error in the characterization of the property because he neither objected to the court's characterization of the property at rendition nor raised the error in his motion for new trial. In the alternative, she argues that any error was harmless because the division of property was not an abuse of discretion, but was just and right.

As a preliminary matter, Edward did not waive his point of error regarding mischaracterization. Generally, to preserve error for appellate review, a party must present a timely request, objection, or motion to the trial court, stating the grounds for the ruling desired. TEX. R. APP. P. 52(a). However, a party complaining of factual or legal insufficiency points on appeal from a nonjury trial is not required to comply with rule 52(a). TEX. R. APP. P. 52(d). Edward raised his second point of error based on both legal and factual sufficiency of the evidence to support the trial court's characterization and division of property. Therefore, we will address the merits of his argument.

Article XVI, section 15 of the Texas Constitution provides that all of a wife's property, owned or claimed by her before marriage or acquired after marriage by gift, devise, or descent shall be her separate property. TEX. CONST. art. XVI, § 15. The Family Code extended this definition to a husband's property.[2] This constitutional definition of separate property is exclusive and may not be enlarged by

---

[2] Section 5.01 of the Family Code provides:

§ 5.01. Marital Property Characterized

(a) A spouse's separate property consists of:

(1) the property owned or claimed by the spouse before marriage;

(2) the property acquired by the spouse during marriage by gift, devise, or descent; and

(3) the recovery for personal injuries sustained by the spouse during marriage, except any recovery for loss of earning capacity during marriage.

(b) Community property consists of the property, other than separate property, acquired by either spouse during marriage.

legislative action. *Eggemeyer v. Eggemeyer*, 554 S.W.2d 137, 140 (Tex. 1977). A court may not decree that the separate property of one spouse shall become the separate property of the other spouse because the nature of separate property is determined by the Constitution, rather than by what is "just and right." *Eggemeyer*, 554 S.W.2d at 140.

The Family Code codifies the constitutional presumption that all property possessed by a husband and wife at the time of the dissolution of their marriage is community property. TEX. FAM. CODE ANN. § 5.02 (Vernon Supp. 1995). The party asserting that property is separate property bears the burden of rebutting the community property presumption by clear and convincing evidence. TEX. FAM. CODE ANN. § 5.02 (Vernon 1993); *Wilson v. Wilson*, 145 Tex. 607, 201 S.W.2d 226, 227 (1947). To rebut the presumption, a spouse must generally trace and clearly identify property claimed as separate property. *McKinley v. McKinley*, 496 S.W.2d 540, 543 (Tex. 1973); *Tarver v. Tarver*, 394 S.W.2d 780, 783 (Tex. 1965). If the evidence shows that "separate and community property have been so commingled as to defy resegregation and identification, the burden is not discharged and the statutory presumption prevails." *McKinley*, 496 S.W.2d at 543.

The issue of whether property is separate or community property is determined by the facts which, according to rules of law, give character to the property. *Hilley v. Hilley*, 161 Tex. 569, 342 S.W.2d 565, 568 (1961). Mere testimony that property was purchased with separate property funds, without any tracing of the funds, is generally insufficient to rebut the presumption. *See Schmeltz v. Garey*, 49 Tex. 49, 60-61 (Tex. 1878).

Applying the above tenets, we must consider the evidence related to the nature of the property in question. Mary testified that the accounts at issue were created with her disability income, which was derived from benefits provided by her employer, and with proceeds from the sale of timber off of her separate property. Her disability income was derived from benefits provided by her employer. Between 1987 and November 1993, Mary received $1500 each month, contingent only upon an annual medical examination. Mary testified that the three Savings of America accounts were created with money from her disability pay. The American United Life Annuity was also a disability benefit provided by Mary's employer. However, the evidence is conflicting regarding the source of the USAA Gold Fund mutual fund. While Mary's inventory and testimony on direct examination reflect that the account was created with the proceeds from the sale of timber off of her separate property, she testified on cross-examination that the USAA Gold Fund account and the three Savings of America accounts were created with her disability pay. Nevertheless, the question giving rise to her cross-examination testimony was somewhat confusing. For purposes of this opinion, we presume that Mary clearly claims the USAA Gold Fund mutual fund was created with the proceeds from the sale of timber taken from her separate property.

Matured private retirement, annuity and pension benefits earned by a spouse during marriage are part of the community estate. *See Allard v. Frech*, 754 S.W.2d 111, 114 (Tex. 1988), *cert. denied*, 488 U.S. 1006, 109 S.Ct. 788, 102 L. Ed. 2d 779 (1989); *Taggart v. Taggart*, 552 S.W.2d 422, 423 (Tex. 1977); *Cearley v. Cearley*, 544 S.W.2d 661, 662 (Tex. 1976). Disability plans which are part of an employee benefit package are also community property. *Ex parte Burson*, 615 S.W.2d 192, 194 n. 2 (Tex. 1981); *Marshall v. Marshall*, 511 S.W.2d 72, 74 (Tex. Civ. App.—Houston [1st Dist.] 1974, no writ). Hence, Mary's disability income was community property.[3]

Tex. Fam. Code Ann. § 5.01 (Vernon 1993).

[3] Section 5.01 of the Family Code provides that recoveries for personal injuries sustained during the marriage are separate property unless the recovery is for loss of earning capacity. TEX. FAM. CODE ANN. § 5.01(a)(3) (Vernon 1993). This Court has already held that disability retirement benefits are not recoveries for personal injuries, but are

In addition, the proceeds from the sale of timber off of Mary's separate property were also community property. Rents and revenues from separate property are community property. *See Moss v. Gibbs*, 370 S.W.2d 452, 454 (Tex. 1963). Like crops, timber grown on separate property is community property. *White v. Lynch*, 23 Tex. 195, 196 (1862) (ruling that lumber was community property, despite the fact that it was sawed at a separate property mill by separate property labor); *see also Connor v. Hawkins*, 66 Tex. 639, 2 S.W. 520, 521 (1886); *De Blane v. Lynch*, 23 Tex. 25, 27 (1859).

Therefore, both the proceeds from the timber and the disability benefits were community property. Consequently, the USAA Gold Fund mutual fund and the three Savings of America accounts were community property because they were created with community property. The American United Life Annuity was community property because it was a disability benefit which matured during the marriage. The trial court erred in ruling that these five accounts were Mary's separate property.

Trial courts have broad discretion in making a "just and right"[4] division of the community estate, and this discretion is not disturbed on appeal unless a clear abuse of discretion is shown. *Murff v. Murff*, 615 S.W.2d 696, 698 (Tex. 1981). When a court mischaracterizes *separate* property as *community* property, the error requires reversal because the subsequent division divests a spouse of his or her separate property. *Eggemeyer*, 554 S.W.2d at 140.

The issue of whether a court commits reversible error by mischaracterizing *community* property as *separate* property has not been directly decided by our Supreme Court. However, the high court has held that "once reversible error affecting the 'just and right' division of the community estate is found, the court of appeals must remand the entire community estate for a new division." *Jacobs v. Jacobs*, 687 S.W.2d 731, 733 (Tex. 1985). Only the trial court may make a just and right division of community property. TEX. FAM. CODE ANN. § 3.63 (Vernon 1993). The appellate court's role is to determine only if the trial court abused its discretion in making the division. *See Jacobs*, 687 S.W.2d at 732-33; *McKnight v. McKnight*, 543 S.W.2d 863, 866-68 (Tex. 1976). If the trial court mischaracterizes community property as separate property, then the property does not get divided as part of the community estate. If the mischaracterized property has value that would have affected the trial court's just and right division, then the mischaracterization is harmful and requires the appellate court to remand the entire community estate to the trial court for a just and right division of the properly characterized community property. If, on the other hand, the mischaracterized property had only a *de minimis* effect on the trial court's just and right division, then the trial court's error is not an abuse of discretion.[5]

We recognize that some appellate decisions have held that a trial court's error in mischaracterizing community property as separate property does not require reversal unless the appellate court finds that the trial court would have made a different division if the property had been properly characterized. *See King v. King*, 661 S.W.2d 252, 254 (Tex. App.—Houston [1st Dist.] 1983, no writ); *see also Bradley v. Bradley*, 725 S.W.2d 503, 505 (Tex. App.—Corpus Christi 1987, no writ); *Cook v. Cook*,

---

earned property rights. *Marshall*, 511 S.W.2d at 74. Mary's disability income is also part of the "bundle of benefits" provided by her employer. *Id.*

[4] The Family Code authorizes a trial court to make a "just and right" division of the parties' estate, having due regard for the rights of the parties. TEX. FAM. CODE ANN. § 3.63 (Vernon 1993).

[5] The doctrine of *de minimis non curat lex* controls the disposition when a mischaracterization creates no significant effect on the trial court's property division. Under this doctrine, the "law does not care for, or take notice of, very small or trifling matters." BLACK'S LAW DICTIONARY 431 (6th ed. 1990); *see, e.g.*, Phillips v. Parrish, 814 S.W.2d 501, 506 (Tex. App.—Houston [1st Dist.] 1991, writ denied).

679 S.W.2d 581, 585 (Tex. App.—San Antonio 1984, no writ); *McLemore v. McLemore*, 641 S.W.2d 395, 398 (Tex. App.—Tyler 1982, no writ); *Smith v. Smith*, 620 S.W.2d 619, 623 (Tex. Civ. App.—Dallas 1981, no writ). In general, the cases hold that reversal is required only if the appellant shows that, due to the trial court's legal error, the resulting division constituted an abuse of discretion. *King*, 661 S.W.2d at 254; *Bradley*, 725 S.W.2d at 505. Although this Court has not revisited this rule since *Jacobs*, other courts have continued to apply the rule without analyzing it in light of *Jacobs*. *See Iglinsky v. Iglinsky*, 735 S.W.2d 536, 539 (Tex. App.—Tyler 1987, no writ); *Bradley*, 725 S.W.2d at 505. We disagree with these courts.

The facts of this case illustrate why this Court cannot presume that the trial court would have made the same division despite the mischaracterization. At rendition, the trial court judge stated that he had made an approximately 61%/39% division[6] in Mary's favor. Because the division did not consider the approximately $45,000 in mischaracterized property, the court actually made an approximately 64%/36% division in Mary's favor.[7] We do not suggest that, under the facts of this case, the trial court judge did not have the power to make a more or less disproportionate division. However, under *Jacobs* and *McKnight*, only the trial court has the power to make a just and right division of the community estate. *Jacobs*, 687 S.W.2d at 733; *McKnight*, 543 S.W.2d at 865 (stating "a court of civil appeals has no authority to render its own property division"). To hold that this Court may not remand the case unless we determine that the distribution actually made by the trial court, considering the mischaracterization, is not an abuse of discretion effectively permits this Court to award a completely new division of the community estate—a 64%/36% division, rather than a 61%/39% division. Yet, this Court does not have the power to render a new division. Therefore, in light of Jacobs, we rule that when a mischaracterization has more than a mere *de minimis* effect upon the trial court's division, the appellate court must remand the community estate to the trial court for a just and right division based upon the correct characterization of the property.

In this case the trial court's error affected the court's property division. Hence, we reverse and remand the cause for a just and right division of the community estate. In addition, because the value

---

[6] Mary has argued that we should ignore this statement because it was a mere finding of fact recited in the judgment which conflicts with findings of fact which were later filed by the trial court. Under rule 299a, if findings of fact are recited in a judgment and are in conflict with the findings of fact made pursuant to rules 297 and 298, the latter findings are controlling for appellate purposes. TEX.R.CIV.P. 299a. However, the allegedly conflicting findings Mary cites are conclusions of law, properly filed under the heading "CONCLUSIONS OF LAW." Rule 299a simply does not apply.

[7] The trial court found the community estate to be valued at $534,300. We assume the court meant $534,700 because the court awarded Edward assets amounting to $209,900, and awarded Mary assets amounting to $324,800 ($209,900 + $324,800 = $534,700). Therefore, the trial court found that it awarded 39.2% of the community estate to Edward and 60.8% to Mary.

The trial court did not assess a value for the annuity because Edward did not offer a value at trial. Edward has asked this Court to take judicial notice of his calculated value of the annuity. We decline to do so. However, assuming without deciding the annuity was valued at $21,602.20, as he suggests, the total value of the mischaracterized properties amounts to $45,413.80 ($7,553.54 + $4489.73 + $2796.96 + $8971.37 + $21602.20 = $45,413.80). Adding the value of the mischaracterized assets to the total value of the community estate found by the trial court, the correct value of the community estate is $580,113.80 ($534,700 + 45,413.80 = $580,113.80).

Therefore, Mary received community property valued at $370,213.80 ($324,800 + $45,413.80 = $370,213.80). Edward received community property valued at $209,900. Thus, the court awarded approximately 64% of the community estate to Mary ($370,213.80 / $580,113.80 = .64). The court awarded Edward 36% of the community assets ($209,900/$580,113.80 = .36).

of the America United Life annuity has not yet been determined, the trial court must assess the value, if any, of the annuity before disposing of the property.

We sustain appellant's second point of error.

Finally, Mary raises a cross-point asserting that she should be awarded damages because Edward took this appeal without sufficient cause and for delay pursuant to TEX. R. APP. P. 84. We find his appeal was not frivolous; therefore, Mary's request for damages under appellate rule 84 is denied.

We overrule appellee's cross-point.

We affirm the portion of the trial court's judgment that denies appellant's motion to recuse. In addition, we affirm the portion of the trial court's judgment that pertains to the divorce. We reverse the portion of the judgment pertaining to the property division and remand that part of the judgment to the trial court with instructions that the trial court make a just and right division consistent with this opinion.

Notes, Comments & Questions

1. The *McElwee* case was remanded because appellate courts do not have the authority to render judgments dividing property and the 3 percent difference effected by the mischaracterization, if affirmed, was deemed to be the rendition of a judgment different than that made by the trial court. That is, an appellate court cannot substitute its judgment for a trial court's division of property. *Compare McElwee* to *Grossnickle v. Grossnickle*, 935 S.W.2d 830 (Tex. App.—Texarkana 1996, writ denied), in which the court held a 3 percent error in division of the estate was not reversible.

2. To take advantage of the *McElwee* holding, findings of fact can help. Why? What findings would you request?

3. The *McElwee* case was remanded to the trial court for a just and right division consistent with the opinion. Upon remand, the wife was awarded an even greater share of the community property. Husband appealed again; the court of appeals affirmed. *McElwee v. McElwee*, Cause No. 01-97-00460-CV (Tex. App.—Houston [1st Dist.] June 3, 1999, pet. denied).

J. Other Post-Judgment Actions

1. Motions in Aid and Clarification of Judgment

The signing of a decree of divorce does not necessarily mean the end of the divorce controversy. Often times, all of the documents necessary to transfer property are not signed simultaneously with the divorce. A spouse can end up in a position of not being able to obtain the property he or she was awarded because the decree is not specific enough to be enforced. The late, and well respected Judge Sam Emison of the 257th Judicial District Court, Harris County, Texas presided over *McKinley v. McKinley*. Judge Emison fashioned the aid and clarification remedy and is owed a debt of gratitude. Judge Emison's remedy has now been codified. *See* TEX. FAM. CODE §§ 9.001-.014, concentrating on §§ 9.007-.009. When reading the statutes and the case of *Shanks v. Treadway*, pay special attention to the limitations placed upon clarifications to a decree.

Ex parte McKINLEY
578 S.W.2d 437
(Tex. Civ. App.—Houston [1st Dist.] 1979, no writ)

EVANS, JUSTICE.

In this original proceeding for a writ of habeas corpus, Patricia Ann McKinley complains of an order of contempt issued by the 257th Family District Court.

The relator's application recites that under the terms of the divorce decree in question the respondent was ordered to execute a general warranty deed conveying to the relator his undivided interest in their community owned home and relator was directed to execute a promissory note payable to respondent in the principal amount of $14,000.00, bearing interest at the rate of 9% per annum, and providing that principal and interest would be payable six months after the emancipation of the parties' two children. Under the terms of the decree the relator was also ordered to execute a deed of trust securing the payment of the note. The relator did not execute the note and deed of trust as contemplated by the divorce decree, and the respondent then brought the contempt proceedings in question.

On June 13, 1978, the trial court entered an order in the contempt proceedings, denying the respondent's motion for contempt, but ordering the relator to execute and deliver to the respondent, or to his attorney, on or before 9:00 o'clock a.m. on July 24, 1978, a real estate lien note and deed of trust in the form of those attached to the order as exhibits. Subsequently on October 5, 1978, the trial court found the relator in contempt by reason of her failure to execute and deliver the note and deed of trust as required by the aforementioned order and directed that she be confined in the Harris County Jail from day to day until the note and deed of trust were executed and delivered into court.

The relator contends that the contempt order is void because the property in question was her separate property and she argues, in effect, that the divorce decree was, therefore, invalid insofar as it sought to impose a lien on her property. She also contends that the order of June 13, 1978, did not sufficiently apprise her of her obligations under that order; that the motion for contempt did not sufficiently detail the alleged acts of disobedience under such order; and that the contempt order did not sufficiently explain the manner in which she might purge herself of the contempt. She further contends that the pleading and evidence did not establish the fact of her contempt and that the Court was without authority to enter the order upon which the contempt was based, having lost jurisdiction of the cause before the order was entered.

This proceeding constitutes a collateral attack on the trial court's contempt order, and this court may not grant a writ of habeas corpus relieving the relator from the imposition of that order unless the order is void on its face or is so completely without evidentiary support as to render it void. *Ex parte Butler*, 523 S.W.2d 309 (Tex. Civ. App.—Houston (1st Dist.) 1975, no writ). If the record shows merely that the order was erroneously entered, as distinguished from being completely void, this court is without authority to grant relator's application. *Ex parte Rhodes*, 163 Tex. 31, 352 S.W.2d 249 (1961).

The divorce court was empowered to award the community homestead to the relator and to require the respondent to execute a general warranty deed conveying to the relator his interest in the community property. It was also authorized to require that the relator compensate the respondent for his community interest in the property and to provide that this be accomplished by means of a deferred payment. Thus, it was proper for the divorce decree to provide that the relator would be required to execute a note evidencing the deferred payment and a deed of trust securing payment of the note. The divorce decree sufficiently sets forth the material terms of the note and deed of trust to be executed, and the decree is not void for uncertainty merely because it fails to specify a date certain when the relator would be required to execute the note and deed of trust. The subsequent order entered by the trial court in aid of its decree set forth with particularity the form of the note and deed of trust to be executed by the relator and the date and time when the documents were to be executed and delivered. The trial court was authorized to issue this order in aid and clarification of its prior decree and for the purpose of effectuating the terms of the decree. *Schwartz v. Jefferson*, 520 S.W.2d 881 (Tex. 1975); *Bush v. Bush*, 265 S.W.2d 676 (Tex. Civ. App.—El Paso 1954, no writ). The order is not void.

The order of commitment recites that after hearing the testimony and the evidence the court found that the relator had wilfully disobeyed its order by failing to execute and deliver to the respondent, or his attorney, on or before the specified date, a note and a deed of trust in the form of those attached to its prior order, and it ordered the relator confined in the Harris County Jail from day to day until the note and deed of trust had been executed and delivered to the court. The contempt motion sufficiently details the relator's alleged acts of disobedience and the commitment order sufficiently indicates the manner in which the relator may purge herself of the contempt.

The relator is remanded to the Sheriff of Harris County, Texas for confinement in accordance with the trial court's order of commitment.

SUPPLEMENTAL OPINION

The trial court has certified to this court that relator has purged herself of contempt by the execution and delivery of the documents specified in the trial court's order. This court's former opinion and judgment dated February 1, 1979; are, therefore, vacated and relator is ordered discharged from custody.

SHANKS v. TREADWAY

110 S.W.3d 444
(Tex. 2003)

O'NEILL, JUSTICE.

The issue in this case is the proper interpretation of a 1981 divorce decree that divided, among other assets, retirement benefits stemming from one spouse's employment both during and after the marriage. The trial court held that the divorce decree awarded the non-employee spouse a specific percentage of the retirement benefits valued at the date of divorce. The court of appeals reversed, concluding that the decree unambiguously awarded the non-employee spouse a percentage of the total amount of the benefits on the date of retirement. 110 S.W.3d 1, 6. We hold that the court of appeals correctly interpreted the decree. Accordingly, we affirm the court of appeals' judgment.

I. Background

Kenda Carolyn Treadway and George Payton Shanks married in 1962. George started working for American Airlines in 1966 and began participating in American's retirement program the following year. The program included both a defined benefit plan and a defined contribution plan.[1] George continued to work for American until his retirement in 1998.

George and Kenda divorced in 1981. In the divorce decree, the district court awarded Kenda a twenty-five percent interest in George's retirement benefits, and neither party appealed the judgment. The relevant portions of the decree provide:

The Court finds that [George] has earned certain employee benefits under a pension plan arising out of past employment as an employee of American Airlines.

[Kenda] is awarded a "pro-rata interest" (as hereinafter defined) of any and all sums received or paid to [George] from such pension plan and such sum or sums shall be payable to [Kenda] if, as and when paid by American Airlines or the trustee of such plan to [George] as pension or retirement employee benefits existing because of [George's] employment.

IT IS DECREED that [Kenda's] "pro-rata interest" shall be defined as that sum of money equal to 25% of the total sum or sums paid or to be paid to [George] from such pension or retirement plan.

* * *

IT IS FURTHER DECREED that all remaining right, title and interest in and to such American Airlines pension and/or retirement plan shall be and is hereby set aside to [George].

On March 9, 1998, approximately two months before his scheduled retirement date, George filed a Motion to Sign Qualified Domestic Relations Order ("QDRO"). *See* TEX. FAM. CODE § 9.102. In his motion, George proposed that the court calculate the value of both the defined benefit and defined

---

[1] Generally, an employee participating in a defined benefit plan will receive a future benefit based on a specified formula that often takes into account earnings, length of service, or both. Brown, Comment, *An Interdisciplinary Analysis of the Division of Pension Benefits in Divorce and Post-Judgment Partition Actions: Cures for the Inequities in Berry v. Berry*, 37 BAYLOR L. REV. 107, 115-16 (1985). A defined contribution plan, on the other hand, is funded by contributions of a specified amount that are invested or placed in a trust fund, and the employee is entitled upon retirement to those contributions plus the earnings thereon. *Id.* at 113.

contribution plans as of the date of divorce in awarding Kenda her twenty-five percent interest. In response, Kenda asserted that *res judicata* barred the attempted collateral attack. She requested that the district court sign her proposed QDRO, awarding her twenty-five percent of the total amount of the benefits to be paid to George.

The district court signed two QDROs—George's QDRO dividing the defined benefit plan valued at the date of divorce *and* Kenda's QDRO dividing both plans valued as of the date that George actually received payment. In light of the inconsistent orders, George moved for reconsideration. The court granted George's motion, vacated Kenda's QDRO, and entered another QDRO valuing the defined contribution plan at the date of divorce. Kenda appealed.

The court of appeals reversed the judgment, concluding that the trial court's QDROs impermissibly altered the substantive division of property made in the original divorce decree. 110 S.W.3d at 3. The court held that the divorce decree unambiguously awarded Kenda "a twenty-five percent interest of the '*total* sum or sums paid or to be paid' from [George's] pension plans and [did] not limit her award to a percentage of the benefits accrued in the plans prior to the divorce." *Id.* at 6. The court therefore remanded the case to the district court to enter a revised QDRO awarding Kenda a twenty-five percent interest in the entire amount to be paid to George as retirement benefits. We agree with the appellate court's interpretation of the decree and therefore affirm the court of appeals' judgment.

II. Dividing Retirement Benefits

We begin with an overview of the law that was in effect in this area at the time the decree was entered to demonstrate the complexities involved in dividing retirement benefits upon divorce. Our decisions focused first on the recognition of pension interests as community property rights and then on the separate issues of apportionment and valuation of benefits. In *Cearley v. Cearley*, we considered whether future pension benefits constitute community property rights subject to equitable division upon divorce. 544 S.W.2d 661, 663-64 (Tex.1976). We approved of the proposition that even "non-vested[2] pension rights are ... a contingent interest in property," and "to the extent that such rights derive from employment during coverture, they comprise a community asset subject to division in a dissolution proceeding." *Id.* (quoting *Brown v. Brown*, 15 Cal.3d 838, 126 Cal.Rptr. 633, 544 P.2d 561, 562 (1976)). We also discussed the difficulty of computing the present value of such a contingent interest and approved the method of making the award of the non-employee spouse's community interest "effective if, as, and when the benefits are received by the [employee] spouse." *Id.* at 666.

The 1983 case *Berry v. Berry*, 647 S.W.2d 945 (Tex.1983), currently governs the division of retirement benefits. However, when the decree in question was entered in 1981, *Cearley* and *Taggart v. Taggart*, 552 S.W.2d 422 (Tex. 1977), provided trial courts the formula to use in determining the community interest in retirement benefits and the non-employee spouse's share of that interest. The Court used a fraction to apportion the community interest: the number of months married under the plan divided by the total number of months employed under the plan at the time of retirement. *Taggart*, 552 S.W.2d at 424. That fraction was multiplied by the non-employee spouse's "just and right" share in the community interest as determined by the trial court (often fifty percent) and then

---

[2] Pension plan benefits become vested when the employee has an unconditional ownership interest in them; that is, the employee has the right to receive the accrued benefits upon retirement whether or not he is working for the same employer. Brown, 37 BAYLOR L. REV. at 119. In contrast, pension benefits are "matured" when the employee is entitled to "immediate collection and enjoyment." *Id.*

multiplied by the value of the benefits received by the employee spouse at retirement. *Id.*[3] When the trial court entered George and Kenda's divorce decree, it should have employed the *Taggart* formula to divide the retirement benefits, though of course the court would not have been able to insert numbers for the denominator of the community interest fraction or the value of the benefits, which could not be determined until retirement.

III. Interpreting the Divorce Decree

Notwithstanding the state of the law at the time the divorce decree was entered, this case does not involve a direct appeal, and we must interpret the decree to determine not what the trial court should have done but, if possible, what the court actually did. When interpreting a divorce decree, courts apply the general rules regarding construction of judgments. *Wilde v. Murchie*, 949 S.W.2d 331, 332 (Tex. 1997) (per curiam) (citing *Constance v. Constance*, 544 S.W.2d 659, 660 (Tex. 1976)). Judgments should be construed as a whole to harmonize and give effect to the entire decree. *Constance*, 544 S.W.2d at 660. "[I]f the decree, when read as a whole, is unambiguous as to the property's disposition, the court must effectuate the order in light of the literal language used." *Wilde*, 949 S.W.2d at 332; *see also Baxter v. Ruddle*, 794 S.W.2d 761, 763 (Tex.1990). If the decree is ambiguous, the court should review the record along with the decree to aid in interpreting the judgment. *Wilde*, 949 S.W.2d at 332. In addition, if a judgment is ambiguous--that is, subject to more than one reasonable interpretation--courts should adopt the construction that correctly applies the law. *MacGregor v. Rich*, 941 S.W.2d 74, 75 (Tex.1997) (per curiam). As with other written instruments, whether a divorce decree is ambiguous is a question of law. *Coker v. Coker*, 650 S.W.2d 391, 394 (Tex.1983).

The decree in question identifies George's pension plan as "arising out of past employment," but then states that Kenda is entitled to "a 'pro rata interest' . . . of any and all sums received or paid to [George] from such pension plan. . . ." The decree also defines "pro rata interest" as "25% of the total sum or sums paid or to be paid to [George] from such pension or retirement plan." The decree does not set out a specific *Taggart*-like formula to be used in calculating Kenda's interest.

The court of appeals concluded, and we agree, that the decree is unambiguous, and Kenda should receive twenty-five percent of George's total retirement benefits. The phrase "arising out of *past* employment as an employee of American Airlines" (emphasis added) does not render the decree ambiguous, as George argues; rather, it merely serves to identify more specifically the property that is being divided (i.e., George's retirement plan).[4] As noted by the court of appeals, the trial court

[3] The *Berry* decision altered this formula. 647 S.W.2d at 947. Although the Court in *Berry* expressly declined to overrule *Taggart* with regard to the apportionment fraction, it nevertheless effected a change in the fraction's denominator to the number of months employed under the plan at the time of divorce. *Id.*; *see also Grier v. Grier*, 731 S.W.2d 931, 932 (Tex.1987). *Berry* altered the valuation portion of the formula as well, requiring the value of the benefits to be calculated at the date of divorce to avoid invading the employee spouse's separate property. 647 S.W.2d at 947. It should be noted that serious concerns have been raised regarding the *Berry* formula's failure to account for post-divorce increases in the value of retirement benefits attributable to community property contributions to the plan. Brown, 37 BAYLOR L. REV. at 152-62. In addition, the problems associated with valuing benefits differ depending on the type of plan being divided. *Id.* at 112-17, 152-62 (discussing the differences between defined benefit plans and defined contribution plans). However, the facts of the case currently before the Court do not provide us the opportunity to address those concerns in this opinion.

[4] Although George's retirement benefits include both a defined benefit plan and a defined contribution plan, the decree referred to them as a single plan. Because this is not a direct appeal, it is unnecessary to address at length the myriad differences between the two types of plans. Nevertheless, trial courts should take into serious consideration the kind of plan at issue when dividing and valuing retirement benefits. *See supra* note 3; Brown, 37 BAYLOR L.REV. at 134-36, 156-62.

awarded Kenda an interest of all sums received under such *plan*, not an interest of presently accrued benefits under such plan. 110 S.W.3d at 6. And the plan that was in existence at the time of the divorce and referred to in the decree is the same plan in effect now that George has retired. The fact that the plan's value may have increased since the divorce does not affect the decree's plain language, which simply cannot reasonably be construed to award Kenda an interest only in the plan benefits that had accrued on the date of divorce. Whether intentional or not, the court that entered the decree failed to limit the community interest pursuant to the *Taggart* apportionment fraction and instead clearly gave Kenda a twenty-five percent interest in the *total* amount (whatever that might be) to be paid to George under the plan.

Viewing the division of the plan benefits in light of the decree as a whole, the fact that the court awarded Kenda only a twenty-five percent interest in the plan also supports our interpretation. Trial judges must carefully review all community assets in making a "just and right" division of those assets, and the retirement benefits were one of the assets considered in this case. *See Busby v. Busby*, 457 S.W.2d 551, 555 (Tex.1970). Given the complexities involved in dividing this type of asset, perhaps the trial court intended to achieve an overall just and right division by awarding Kenda a lesser interest in the total value of the plan at retirement rather than a greater interest in a smaller portion of the benefits. We simply cannot know with certainty because the decree was never appealed. In any event, our responsibility is to construe the decree as written.

It is true, as George points out, that Texas law prohibits courts from divesting spouses of their separate property. *Eggemeyer v. Eggemeyer*, 554 S.W.2d 137, 139-40 (Tex.1977). But George therefore urges us to interpret the decree to award Kenda an interest in only the community portion of the plan to avoid attributing to the trial court an intent to divide separate property, which it lacked authority to do. That argument is flawed in two respects. First, it overlooks the fact that applying *Taggart*, which was the controlling law at the time the decree was entered and required benefits to be valued at the time of their disbursement, would probably divest George of a portion of his separate property anyway. In fact, the reason the Court altered the requisite formula in *Berry* was to avoid invading a spouse's separate property. *See supra* note 3; *Berry*, 647 S.W.2d at 947.[5] This tension demonstrates the difficulty inherent in dividing pension plans that involve both separate and community property and indicates that interpreting such a division is not as simple as presuming a lack of intent to divide separate property.[6]

Such an analysis is also problematic because the fact that the district court erroneously applied the law when it entered the divorce decree does not alter the decree's plain language. In *Baxter*, which was decided after *Berry*, the divorce decree in question awarded the non-employee spouse "37 1/2% of [the employee spouse's] gross benefits, if, as and when he received them. The decree also provided that [the non-employee spouse] was to receive 37 1/2% of the total benefits that [the employee spouse] received each month." 794 S.W.2d at 763 (emphasis removed). We held that "[t]his language unambiguously provided that [the non-employee spouse] was to receive 37 1/2% of the total retirement benefits received by [the employee spouse] each month, including any post-divorce in-

---

[5] We reiterate that even after *Berry* was decided, concerns about invading separate property remained. Brown, 37 BAYLOR L. REV. at 152-62.

[6] We recognize the importance of safeguarding individual property rights, but significantly, it was not until 1977 in *Eggemeyer* that this Court expressly and unequivocally held that a court cannot divest a spouse of his or her separate property upon divorce. *Eggemeyer*, 554 S.W.2d at 142.

creases." *Id.*[7] We therefore enforced the decree as written even though it conflicted with *Berry. Id.* Similarly, we must enforce the decree as written in this case even though it conflicts with *Taggart.*

Kenda argues that the district court cannot change the substantive division of property made in the original decree. We agree. While the court may enter a "clarifying order" to enforce compliance with an insufficiently specific decree, TEX. FAM. CODE § 9.008(b), a court "may not amend, modify, alter, or change the division of property made or approved in the decree of divorce." *Id.* § 9.007(a). The original decree in this case is unambiguous, and the trial court had no authority to enter an order altering or modifying the original disposition of property. *Id.*; *Pierce v. Pierce*, 850 S.W.2d 675, 679 (Tex. App.—El Paso 1993, writ denied); *see also McGehee v. Epley*, 661 S.W.2d 924, 925-26 (Tex.1983) (stating that clarification orders cannot be used to effect a substantive change in a divorce decree after the trial court's judgment becomes final). George's remedy for a substantive error of law by the trial court was by direct appeal, and he cannot now collaterally attack the judgment. *Mapco, Inc. v. Forrest*, 795 S.W.2d 700, 703 (Tex.1990); *Baxter*, 794 S.W.2d at 762; *Stinson v. Stinson*, 668 S.W.2d 840, 841 (Tex. App.—San Antonio 1984, writ ref'd n.r.e.). The district court was therefore without authority to enter a QDRO altering the terms of the decree by limiting Kenda to a twenty-five percent interest in the benefits that had accrued under the plan at the time of the divorce.

IV. Conclusion

The divorce decree is unambiguous and awarded Kenda Treadway twenty-five percent of George Shanks's total retirement benefits. The court of appeals was correct in reversing the district court's judgment, and we therefore affirm the judgment of the court of appeals.

---

[7] We note, however, that we disagree with the court of appeals' conclusion in this case that the phrase "if, as, and when received" is "a term of art evidencing an intent to value a pension plan at the time of receipt rather than at the time of divorce." 110 S.W.3d at 6. In *Cearley*, when we recognized contingent pension benefits as community property rights subject to division upon divorce, we acknowledged that "it may be necessary in many instances for the judgment to make the apportionment to the nonretiring spouse effective if, as, and when the benefits are received by the [employee] spouse." 544 S.W.2d at 666. The term thus reflects the contingent nature of the community's interest in the retirement benefits and not necessarily the value of that interest.

2. Omitted Property

Throughout the course, we have read cases in which former spouses have returned to court to obtain their share of community property not divided upon divorce. *See e.g. Gleich v. Bongio*, 99 S.W.2d 881 (Tex. 1937); *Broussard v. Tian*, 295 S.W.2d 405 (Tex. 1956). These are known as omitted property cases and are now governed by TEX. FAM. CODE §§ 9.201-.204. The biggest change with the codification of the right to divide omitted property is that the trial court may now make a just and right division of that property, rather than having to award a 50% interest as a tenant in common. *See* TEX. FAM. CODE §§ 9.203 and 9.204.

MILLER
v.
MILLER
700 S.W.2d 941
(Tex. App.—Dallas 1985, writ ref'd n.r.e.)

GUITTARD, CHIEF JUSTICE.

Our prior opinion of August 30, 1985, is withdrawn and this opinion substituted.

Judy Miller sued her former husband, Howard Miller, to rescind a shareholders' agreement regarding corporate stock acquired by Howard before their divorce and allegedly not disposed of by the parties' divorce decree. After a jury trial resulting in some findings favorable to Judy and others favorable to Howard, the trial court denied rescission and granted Howard specific performance of a purchase option provided in the shareholders' agreement. Judy contends that the trial court erred in refusing to rescind the agreement because of Howard's nondisclosure of material facts and his failure to establish that the agreement was fair to her. We agree and, consequently, reverse the judgment of the trial court in part, render judgment for Judy in part, and affirm the judgment of the trial court in part.

FACTUAL BACKGROUND

On July 15, 1978, Judy and Howard separated. Howard was employed as an engineer. Sometime in 1978, Howard and three other engineers began discussions regarding the formation of a company to design and produce a novel electronic telephone switching system to be known as the "IBX." Such a company, InteCom, Inc., was eventually formed in January 1979. At that time Howard acquired a twenty-five percent ownership interest in InteCom, represented by 250 shares of stock. Later, additional shares were issued to the founders, ultimately bringing the total shares held in Howard's name to 710,355 shares. Exxon Enterprises, Inc. was enlisted to provide financial backing. Exxon agreed to invest $1,500,000 in InteCom in exchange for 1,500,000 shares of stock. Exxon's investment was based almost exclusively on the abilities of the four founding stockholders. For that reason, Exxon demanded that the founders remain in control of InteCom and keep an interest in InteCom. Exxon's demand was embodied in the shareholders' agreement in question.

The agreement provided that a founder could not sell his shares in InteCom without offering them first to the other founders and then to Exxon. The other founders were to have thirty days in which to exercise their options to purchase the shares of the selling founder. Exxon then had thirty days in which to exercise its option to purchase those shares not sold to the other founders. A formula set out in the agreement determined the purchase price of shares sold by a founder to another founder or to Exxon. If the option was not exercised by any of the other founders or Exxon, the shares could be offered to third parties, but only at the same price the shares were offered to the other founders or Exxon. If they were not purchased by a third party within a certain period of time, they had to be reoffered to the other founders and then to Exxon at a new price determined by the formula.

The agreement also required each founder to cause his wife to sign the agreement "for the purpose of agreeing to be bound by the terms of this Agreement." The agreement provided that, in the event of a divorce, the wife had to first offer to sell her shares in InteCom, if any, to her husband at a price also to be determined by a formula set forth in the agreement. If the husband did not purchase the wife's shares within thirty days, then the remaining founders had the right to purchase the wife's shares for a period of thirty days, and then, if the remaining founders did not purchase the wife's shares, Exxon had the right to purchase the wife's shares, again for a period of thirty days. Shares not purchased by the husband, the other founders, or Exxon could then be sold to any third party for a period of ninety days at the same price and on the same conditions and terms initially offered to the founders and Exxon. At the end of the ninety-day period, the wife had to offer her shares again to her husband, then to the other founders, and then to Exxon at a new price determined by formula. Howard contends that the agreement gave him the right to acquire Judy's community interest in the shares for $2,500.

On April 10, 1979, Howard filed a petition for divorce. On the next day, April 11, 1979, before the parties divorced but after they separated, Howard approached Judy with the agreement. It is undisputed that Howard did not explain the agreement to Judy and that he failed to disclose to her certain information regarding the agreement. Howard testified that he gave the agreement to Judy to take home and asked her to return it to him by the next morning. Judy testified that when Howard handed her the agreement, she read it, signed it, and never asked Howard or anyone else any questions about it. She testified that she considered the agreement binding on her. Later Judy also read and signed another agreement concerning InteCom, a "Stock Purchase Agreement," dated July 1, 1980, which she testified she also considered binding on her.

Later, on August 23, 1980, Howard and Judy were divorced. At the time of the divorce, Howard's 250 shares of stock had grown to 710,355 through stock splits, stock dividends, and stock issues. Although there is some dispute about whether Howard and Judy discussed the agreement between its signing and the divorce, there is no dispute that Judy did not complain about the agreement until some two years after the divorce when she learned from an electronics magazine that InteCom was worth more than she had previously believed it to be worth. Then, on October 20, 1982, Judy filed this suit against Howard. After Judy's suit was filed, Howard attempted to exercise his option to purchase Judy's shares in InteCom.

In Judy's trial pleadings, she sought rescission of the shareholders' agreement and partition of the 710,355 shares of InteCom owned by Howard at the time of the divorce and alternatively actual and exemplary damages. These requests for relief were based on the theories of actual fraud and constructive fraud by breach of a confidential or fiduciary duty. Howard denied that Judy had any interest in the stock and alternatively counterclaimed for specific performance of the purchase option in the agreement and for attorney's fees.

JURY FINDINGS

The jury found that Howard made the following representations to Judy:

(1) that the agreement was an agreement between Exxon and the founders that placed certain restrictions on the stock; and

(2) that the agreement was an agreement to get the company started.

The jury found that these representations were false and material, but that Howard did not make them with the intention that Judy rely on them in deciding whether to sign the agreement. Because of these negative answers, other issues related to the fraud claim were not reached. The jury also found that Howard failed to disclose the following to Judy:

(1) that on or about April 11, 1979, InteCom, Inc. issued to Exxon Enterprises, Inc. 1,500,000 shares of stock in InteCom at a price of $1.00 per share in return for a capital contribution to InteCom, Inc. of $1,500,000;

(2) that upon divorce the agreement of April 11, 1979, required Judy to sell to Howard and others any and all interest which she had in InteCom, Inc.;

(3) that shares of the InteCom stock held in Howard's name at that time had a fair cash market value; and

(4) that InteCom was in the process of developing the "IBX" system, which if successfully developed would be in great demand.

The jury found that these undisclosed facts were material, but that Howard had not failed to disclose them with the intention of inducing Judy to sign the agreement. Because of these negative answers, the jury did not reach other issues inquiring whether Judy would not have signed the agreement if Howard had disclosed any of these matters and whether Howard's failure to disclose any of them was a proximate cause of any loss or damage to Judy.

With respect to Judy's claim of breach of fiduciary duty, the jury found (1) that a confidential relationship existed between Judy and Howard at the time that Howard presented the agreement to Judy, (2) that Howard acted in good faith at the time he presented the agreement to Judy, and (3) that the restrictions imposed by the agreement on Judy's rights of ownership or transfer of her stock interest were reasonably related to the corporate interest of InteCom as of April 11, 1979. However, the jury answered "we do not" to the issue inquiring whether, under the facts and circumstances of the case, the agreement is fair to Judy.

TRIAL COURT'S JUDGMENT

The trial court ruled as a matter of law that the 710,375 shares of InteCom stock had not been divided in the divorce decree and that Judy and Howard held the stock as tenants in common. Both Howard and Judy moved for judgment, and Howard additionally moved the trial court to disregard certain jury findings, including the finding of a confidential relationship between him and Judy and the finding that the agreement was not fair to Judy. The trial court ordered the stock evenly divided between Howard and Judy. However, the trial court also granted Howard's motion to disregard certain jury findings, declared the shareholders' agreement to be valid and in full force and effect, and ordered Judy to sell all her shares to Howard at the price set according to the formula in the agreement as of September 22, 1980, thirty days after the divorce decree.

In this court, Judy presents various points of error challenging the trial court's refusal to rescind the agreement. We find these points dispositive of this appeal; thus, we do not decide Judy's other points. Howard presents several cross-points, which we consider and overrule.

BREACH OF FIDUCIARY DUTY

Judy does not complain of the jury's adverse findings on the issues of actual fraud. Nor does she attack the negative findings on the issues inquiring whether Howard failed to disclose material facts with the intent to induce her to sign the stockholders' agreement. She contends, however, that she is entitled to rescission of the agreement because of the jury's finding that a confidential relationship existed between her and Howard when Howard presented the agreement to her and the jury's finding that the agreement was not fair to her. She insists that the finding of a confidential relationship established a fiduciary duty on the part of Howard, that this fiduciary duty casts on him the burden to show that the agreement was fair to her, and that his failure to discharge this burden of showing that the agreement was fair provides the grounds for rescission.

We conclude that Judy's contention is correct. Most of the facts are not in dispute. The record shows that as a founder, officer, and director of InteCom, Howard had an insider's knowledge of the affairs and prospects of the corporation. In particular, he knew that on the very day he presented the agreement to Judy for her signature, InteCom had made an agreement with Exxon to sell 1,500,000 shares of stock to Exxon for one dollar per share. Although Judy had heard that Exxon was expected to provide financial backing for the enterprise and saw Exxon's name in the agreement itself, she was not aware that Exxon had agreed to purchase shares at this price. Howard also knew the technical details of the telephone switching system being developed, the potential demand for it, and the prospect that Exxon might initiate a public offering of the shares. None of this information was known to Judy.

During their marriage Howard had handled all their business affairs. Although the parties had separated and a divorce suit was pending, they had no disagreement concerning financial matters at the time the agreement was signed. They visited an attorney together and employed him to file a "friendly" divorce suit, but they did not ask his assistance in dividing their property. Howard was still paying Judy's living expenses, including the rent on an apartment to which Judy had moved. The nature of their relationship is indicated by the manner in which they divided their property. They made their own division agreement, which Howard wrote down and presented to the attorney as a basis for an agreed divorce decree. Judy testified that she still trusted Howard in these matters. This evidence supports the jury's finding of a confidential relationship between the parties.

Recognition of a fiduciary duty in this case is based not only on the personal relationship between Howard and Judy but also on Howard's position as a founder, officer, and director of InteCom. Authorities are divided on the question of whether an officer and director of a corporation has a general fiduciary duty to disclose to a stockholder his knowledge of information affecting the value of the stock before purchasing it from the stockholder. Some courts have followed the so-called "majority rule" that a director or officer does not stand in a fiduciary relation to a stockholder in respect to his stock and, therefore, has the same right as any other stockholder to trade freely in the corporation's stock. *Seitz v. Frey*, 152 Minn. 170, 188 N.W. 266, 268 (1922); *Schuur v. Berry*, 285 Mich. 654, 281 N.W. 393 (1938); 3A W. FLETCHER, CYCLOPEDIA OF THE LAW OF PRIVATE CORPORATIONS, § 1168.1, at 283 (rev. perm. ed. 1975) [hereinafter cited as FLETCHER]. Other courts have held that officers and directors have a fiduciary duty to individual stockholders, as well as to the corporation itself and, thus, cannot properly purchase stock from a stockholder without giving him the benefit of any official knowledge they have of information that may increase the value of the stock. *Dawson v. National Life*

Insurance Co. of United States, 176 Iowa 362, 157 N.W. 929 (1916); *Jacobson v. Yaschik*, 249 S.C. 577, 155 S.E.2d 601 (1967); 3A FLETCHER § 1168.2, at 288-89. Still other courts, while recognizing the "majority rule" as a general principle, have applied a "special facts" exception imposing on the officer or director a limited fiduciary duty to disclose any knowledge of special matters relating to the corporate business—e.g., merger, assured sale, etc.—that may affect the value of the stock. *Strong v. Repide*, 213 U.S. 419, 29 S. Ct. 521, 53 L. Ed. 853 (1909); *Hobart v. Hobart Estate Co.*, 26 Cal. 2d 412, 159 P.2d 958 (1945); 3A FLETCHER § 1171, at 293-94. No Texas decision on the point has been found.

We conclude that the facts of this case, as stated above, are sufficient to bring it within the "special facts" exception to the so-called "majority rule," and, therefore, we need not consider whether the more general duty required by the "minority rule" should be imposed. Applying the "special facts" doctrine to the present case, we conclude that before Howard could contract with Judy concerning the InteCom stock, he had the duty to disclose to her the facts that Exxon was purchasing 1,500,000 shares at one dollar per share and that if IBX was developed, it would be in great demand. Because of the confidential relationship between the parties, as found by the jury, together with the special information known to Howard as a founding officer and director of InteCom, particularly the contemporaneous purchase by Exxon of 1,500,000 shares at one dollar per share, we hold that Howard had a fiduciary duty to deal fairly with Judy in acquiring from her any rights in the InteCom stock.

Since this duty has been established, we must determine where the burden of proof lies concerning the fairness or unfairness of the shareholders' agreement as between Judy and Howard and whether that burden has been discharged. The leading Texas case on this question is *Johnson v. Peckham*, 132 Tex. 148, 120 S.W.2d 786, 787-88 (1938), which concerned a partner's duty to disclose to a co-partner, whose interest he was purchasing, facts affecting the value of the partnership property. The Supreme Court held that because of the fiduciary relationship, the purchasing partner had the "absolute duty" to disclose to the selling partner material facts within his knowledge and that such a sale would be sustained "only when it is made in good faith, for a fair consideration and as full and complete disclosure of all important information as to value." Accordingly, the court held that the selling partner did not have the burden to establish reliance on the purchasing partner to make such disclosure and that the trial court had properly refused a requested issue inquiring whether the purchaser relied on the seller to make such disclosure. Following this decision, Texas courts have applied a presumption of unfairness to transactions between a fiduciary and a party to whom he owes a duty of disclosure, thus casting on the fiduciary the burden to establish fairness. *Texas Bank & Trust Co. v. Moore*, 595 S.W.2d 502, 509 (Tex. 1980); *Archer v. Griffith*, 390 S.W.2d 735, 740 (Tex. 1964); *Ginther v. Taub*, 570 S.W. 516, 525 (Tex. Civ. App.—Waco 1978, writ ref'd n.r.e.). Accordingly, we conclude that Howard had the burden of proving the fairness of the shareholders' agreement to Judy.

In determining whether Howard has met this burden of proving the fairness of the agreement, we note that what constitutes the required fairness has been variously stated, depending on the facts in the particular case. Although the supreme court said proof of "good faith" is necessary to sustain the transaction in *Johnson*, 120 S.W.2d at 787, the *Johnson* opinion itself recognizes that good faith does not in itself establish fairness. *Id.* at 788; *accord Archer*, 390 S.W.2d at 740; *Cartwright v. Minton*, 318 S.W.2d 449, 452-53 (Tex. Civ. App.—Eastland 1958, writ ref'd n.r.e.) (*quoting Murphy v. Cartwright*, 202 F.2d 71, 73 (5th Cir. 1953)). The fiduciary must also show that the transaction was "fair, honest, and equitable." *Archer*, 390 S.W.2d at 740. In *Stephens County Museum, Inc. v. Swenson*, 517 S.W.2d 257, 261 (Tex. 1974), the ultimate issues were held to be whether the fiduciary "had made reasonable use of the confidence placed in him and whether the transactions were ultimately fair and equitable." Although breach of such a fiduciary duty is referred to in the above authorities as "constructive fraud," it is to be distinguished from other types of "constructive fraud" in which the entire burden rests on the party asserting it. *See, e.g., Clem v. Fulgham*, 14 S.W.2d 812, 813 (Tex. Comm'n App. 1929, judgmt adopted) (suit to rescind deed for innocent misrepresentation); *Capitol Rod & Gun Club v. Lower Colorado River Authority*, 622 S.W.2d 887, 893 (Tex. App.—Austin 1981, writ ref'd n.r.e.) (reformation of deed for "legal fraud").

This issue of fairness has been held to be one proper for jury determination. *Stephens County Museum*, 517 S.W.2d at 261; *Archer*, 390 S.W.2d at 742; *Carnes v. Meador*, 533 S.W.2d 365, 371-72 (Tex. Civ. App.—Dallas 1975, writ ref'd n.r.e.).

The special issue submitted to the jury on this question was:

> DO YOU FIND FROM A PREPONDERANCE OF THE EVIDENCE that the Shareholders' Agreement of April 11, 1979, under all the facts and circumstances of this case, is fair to Judy Miller?
>
> The jury answered "We do not."[2] Howard argues that this answer should be disregarded because the evidence establishes as a matter of law that the agreement was fair to Judy. Judy maintains, on that the other hand, that the jury finding on this issue is supported by the evidence and entitles her to judgment.

In establishing the fairness of a transaction between a fiduciary and his beneficiary, some of the most important factors are whether the fiduciary made a full disclosure, whether the consideration (if any) is adequate, and whether the beneficiary had the benefit of independent advice. G. BOGERT, HANDBOOK OF THE LAW OF TRUSTS AND TRUSTEES § 544, at 446 (rev. 2d ed. 1978) [hereinafter cited as BOGERT]. In the present case, it is undisputed that Howard did not make a full disclosure and that Judy had no independent advice. The consideration question is complex in view of Exxon's participation. Another crucial inquiry bearing on the issue of fairness is whether the fiduciary has benefited or profited at the expense of the beneficiary. *International Bankers Life Insurance Co. v. Holloway*, 368 S.W.2d 567, 576 (Tex. 1963); *Cole v. McCanlies*, 620 S.W.2d 713, 715 (Tex. Civ. App.—Dallas 1981, writ ref'd n.r.e.). The transaction is unfair if the fiduciary significantly benefits from it at the expense of the beneficiary as viewed in the light of circumstances existing at the time of the transaction. *Archer*, 390 S.W.2d at 740.

Applying this principle to the facts of the case, we hold that the evidence is sufficient to support the jury's negative answer to the fairness issue. Although Howard testified that the agreement was prepared by Exxon, which insisted on its execution as a condition of its investment in InteCom, and that the provisions in question were designed solely to encourage the founders to continue their involvement with and contributions to InteCom, we conclude that the evidence justifies the inference that Howard gained a benefit at Judy's expense because her rights under the agreement were not equal to his. In the event of a divorce, which the parties were then contemplating, Judy did not have the same opportunity that Howard had to continue his connection with InteCom and profit by whatever appreciation might have been anticipated in the value of the shares. Howard had an option to purchase her shares, but Judy had no corresponding option or offsetting benefit. Although Howard testified that the agreement was required by Exxon, his testimony, coming from an interested party, does not conclusively establish that Exxon would not have considered a modification of the agreement in

[2] There is no complaint in this Court that the issue inquired whether the agreement *is* fair to Judy, rather than whether it *was* fair at the time it was made.

this respect. The record contains no details of the negotiations with Exxon. No witness from Exxon testified that the provision concerning options on divorce of the founders was required by Exxon or was indispensable to its participation. We hold that Howard failed to establish as a matter of law that the agreement was fair because he failed to prove that he did not gain any benefit from it at Judy's expense.

Howard argues that after Judy failed to get favorable findings on several series of issues submitting independent grounds of recovery, individual answers from several of these series cannot be put together to support a recovery on a different ground. He insists that no recovery can be allowed on this constructive fraud theory—i.e., the breach of fiduciary duty theory—because the jury answered "we do not" to the inquiry of whether Howard failed to disclose certain information with intent to induce Judy to sign the agreement and, due to this negative answer, did not reach the issues inquiring whether Judy would have signed the agreement if Howard had disclosed this information and whether Howard's failure to disclose any of them was a proximate cause of any loss or damage to Judy. We disagree.

Although these issues may have been necessary to a recovery of damages, an alternative claim in Judy's petition, we conclude that they are not necessary to rescission in view of other jury findings. Furthermore, these issues are immaterial to our holding that Howard had a fiduciary duty casting on him the burden to show that the transaction was fair and also to our holding that Howard failed to discharge this burden. The jury findings that Howard did not act in bad faith, that his failure to disclose was not done with intent to induce Judy to sign the agreement, and that the restrictions imposed on Judy's stock ownership were reasonably related to the corporate interests of InteCom are also evidentiary and not controlling.

Howard contends further that as a matter of law he has negated the materiality of the facts that the jury found he failed to disclose and that he has also negated any causal relation between these nondisclosures and any damage to Judy because Judy admitted on cross-examination that she would have signed the agreement even if all these facts had been disclosed. Again, we cannot agree.

Under the charge as submitted by the court, materiality of the nondisclosed facts did not depend on Judy's state of mind. The court defined "material fact" as a "fact which a reasonable person, under the same or similar circumstances, would attach importance to in determining his course of conduct or action." If the facts known to Howard were "material" in this sense, he had a fiduciary duty to disclose them, and his breach of this duty cannot be excused on the ground that Judy has failed to establish her reliance on Howard's duty to disclose them. *Johnson*, 120 S.W.2d at 787-88. In view of Howard's burden under *Johnson, Moore*, and the other authorities cited to prove the fairness of the agreement, we conclude that he also had the burden to prove that knowledge of these facts would not have deterred Judy from signing the agreement, if, indeed, he can be excused from his breach of fiduciary duty on this ground.

With respect to Howard's contention that he has established as a matter of law the lack of a causal relation between his nondisclosure and Judy's signing of the agreement, our review of the evidence discloses that Judy's testimony is not altogether clear on this point. Judy testified that she went to Howard's house at his request, examined the agreement briefly, and signed it because he asked her to sign it. She knew nothing about community property and was not aware that she had any interest in the InteCom stock. She said Howard asked her to sign the agreement because he needed it to get the company started, but that he did not explain it to her. She did not know about the options for purchase of her stock. She said that she would not have signed the agreement without further investigation if she had known that it could have required her to sell her half interest in Howard's shares for

$2,500 (two cents per share) and she had thought it was worth one dollar per share—the price at which Exxon was buying InteCom stock. The rule that a party is presumed to know what he signs is not applied strictly in a confidential relationship. *Oar v. Davis*, 135 S.W. 710, 712-13 (Tex. Civ. App.—Dallas 1911), *aff'd*, 105 Tex. 479, 151 S.W. 794 (1912).

As we have previously stated, Judy admitted on cross-examination that she had read the shareholders' agreement, but not page by page, and that she would have signed it regardless of the value of the stock. She also admitted that the status of the "IBX" would have made no difference to her. If she had known that the agreement contained an option in favor of Howard, she might have had some questions and would have had an attorney look it over, but she could not say that she would not have signed the agreement. On further cross- examination, Judy testified that even if Howard had told her everything there was to know about InteCom's relations with Exxon, she probably would have signed the agreement anyway, that she "had no way of saying" that she would not have signed it.

The attempt to discover what course of action a party would have taken under hypothetical circumstances different from those under which a contract was actually signed involves an element of speculation in the nature of an opinion rather than a fact. Thus, we regard Judy's testimony, taken as a whole, as equivocal. She thinks that if she had had more information, she might have asked some questions and would have sought legal counsel, but she has no idea what advice she would have received or what she would have done if she had received legal advice. Lack of independent advice is itself a factor relevant to fairness. BOGERT, § 544, at 446. At the time she signed, InteCom's prospects and the value of its stock, of which she knew nothing, did not concern her. Her husband, whom she still trusted in these matters, asked her to sign it because he needed it to get the company started. She was in this frame of mind, according to her testimony, when she signed the agreement.

We conclude that this testimony cannot be taken as a judicial admission that Howard's breach of his fiduciary duty had no effect on her signing. Testimony of a party that merely contradicts some other portion of the party's testimony does not have conclusive effect; to be a judicial admission, it must be deliberate, clear, and unequivocal. *Tex-Wis Co. v. Johnson*, 534 S.W.2d 895, 901 (Tex. 1976); *United States Fidelity & Guaranty Co. v. Carr*, 242 S.W.2d 224, 229 (Tex. Civ. App.—San Antonio 1951, writ ref'd). Thus, we cannot hold that Judy has judicially admitted that disclosure of the facts that Howard admittedly failed to disclose, and which the jury found would have been considered important by a reasonable person, would have had no bearing on her decision to sign the shareholders' agreement.

In the light of all the evidence, we hold that the evidence is sufficient to support the jury's finding of a confidential relationship and the negative finding on the fairness issue. We hold further that Howard failed to discharge his burden to show that the shareholders' agreement was fair and, consequently, that the trial court erred in denying Judy rescission of the agreement.

* * *

EFFECT OF DIVORCE DECREE

We now consider Howard's cross-points complaining of other rulings of the trial court. First, Howard contends that Judy's interest in the stock was allotted to him by the divorce decree. We cannot agree.

Both parties approved the decree, which purports to divide their property in accordance with a written agreement between them. The decree expressly lists and disposes of other corporate stock but does not mention the InteCom stock. In the present suit, the parties stipulated that out of 710,355 shares of the InteCom stock, one certificate for 625,000 shares was actually in Howard's possession at his residence at the time of the divorce and that the remaining 85,355 shares, represented by three certificates and pledged to various lenders, were in Howard's constructive possession. Howard contends that the InteCom stock was disposed of in that portion of the decree that allots the following to him as his separate property:

> *All personal property* in possession of Petitioner at this time at the residence located at 3204 Lynbrook Drive, Plano, Collin County, Texas, including without limitation Petitioner's jewelry, clothing, furniture, fixtures, items of personalty and other such personal effects in his possession. [Emphasis added.]

Howard argues that the stock certificate is "personal property" and that, therefore, the shares in his possession, actual or constructive, were included in the quoted provision of the divorce decree. Judy contends that the decree does not dispose of intangible property rights such as shares of stock, relying on *Dessommes v. Dessommes*, 505 S.W.2d 673, 677 (Tex. Civ. App.—Dallas 1973, writ ref'd n.r.e.), in which we held that a decree similar to the one in the present case did not include retirement benefits. She also insists that Howard is bound by his testimony at trial that he did not consider the InteCom stock included in the divorce decree.

An agreed judgment must be interpreted as if it were a contract between the parties, and the interpretation of the judgment is governed by the laws relating to contracts. *Hutchings v. Bates*, 406 S.W.2d 419, 420 (Tex. 1966); *Ex parte Jones*, 163 Tex. 513, 358 S.W.2d 370, 375 (1962). In construing a written contract, the primary concern of the court is to ascertain the true intentions of the parties as expressed in the instrument. *Ideal Lease Service, Inc. v. Amoco Production Co.*, 662 S.W.2d 951, 952 (Tex. 1983); *Coker v. Coker*, 650 S.W.2d 391, 393 (Tex. 1983). If the intention expressed on the face of the contract is doubtful, resort may be had to parol evidence of the situation and the surroundings of the parties to resolve the doubt. Similarly, resolution of an ambiguity in an agreed judgment turns upon the intentions of the parties as disclosed by the provisions of the judgment and the surrounding circumstances, which may be clarified through the admission of extrinsic evidence. *Johnson v. Johnson*, 572 S.W.2d 364, 366 (Tex. Civ. App.—Amarillo 1978, no writ). Since the divorce decree does not expressly dispose of the InteCom stock, but does expressly dispose of other corporate stock, and since both Judy and Howard testified that they did not intend that the decree should include the InteCom stock, we hold that the trial court correctly ruled that the divorce decree did not dispose of it and that Judy and Howard held it as tenants in common after the divorce.

EXCLUSION OF ORAL AGREEMENT

Howard asserted in the trial court that he and Judy orally agreed, after their separation but before their divorce, that property "acquired by each would be the separate property of the acquiring spouse." The trial court excluded Howard's testimony regarding the oral agreement and refused to submit any special issues regarding it. Howard now maintains that the trial court's rulings were erroneous because the agreement was made after separation and in contemplation of divorce. He cites cases beginning with *Rains v. Wheeler*, 76 Tex. 390, 13 S.W. 324, 326 (1890), holding that spouses may make a valid partition of their community property after a permanent separation. He notes that two of those cases, *Loston v. Loston*, 424 S.W.2d 316, 317 (Tex. Civ. App.—Houston [14th Dist.] 1968, writ dism'd); and *Callicoatte v. Callicoatte*, 417 S.W.2d 618, 621 (Tex. Civ. App.—Waco 1967, writ ref'd n.r.e.), concerned oral agreements made after the 1948 amendment to article XVI, section 15, of the Texas Constitution, and also after enactment of Tex. Laws 1949, p. 450, ch. 242, now embodied in section 5.44 of the Texas Family Code (Vernon Supp. 1985). The 1948 amendment permits spouses to make written partition of their community property. Section 5.44 of the Family Code requires partition of community property to be "in writing and subscribed by all parties." Accordingly, he argues that the constitutional amendment and the statute requiring written agreements of partition of community property generally do not affect agreements made after permanent separation. We do not agree.

We do not regard *Loston* or *Callicoatte* as authoritative on this question because neither of those opinions indicates that the constitutional or statutory requirement of a written agreement were called to the attention of the court. We follow instead *Recio v. Recio*, 666 S.W.2d 645, 649 (Tex. App.—Corpus Christi 1984, no writ), which expressly holds that an oral agreement partitioning community property at the time of a divorce is unenforceable because not in writing and subscribed by both parties, as required by section 5.44 and its predecessor. In our view, the *Recio* decision is sound because section 5.44 contains no exception for partitions made after separation, and we see no reason why a writing should be required when the spouses are living together but not when they have separated. Consequently, we hold that the trial court did not err in excluding Howard's testimony concerning the alleged oral agreement.

* * *

SUMMARY

In summary, we find no merit in any of Howard's cross-points. We hold that the divorce decree did not dispose of the InteCom stock and that Howard and Judy held the InteCom stock as tenants in common, that Howard owed a fiduciary duty to Judy based on their confidential relationship and his position as officer and director of InteCom, and that the evidence does not establish as a matter of law that the agreement was fair to Judy. The jury's findings establish a fiduciary duty and a breach of that duty, and its failure to find that the agreement was fair to Judy entitled Judy to rescission of the agreement as between her and Howard. The nonjoinder of the other signatories to the agreement does not preclude rescission of the agreement as between Howard and Judy.

Thus, we affirm that portion of the trial court's judgment declaring that Judy and Howard hold the InteCom stock as tenants in common and equally partitioning the stock between them. In all other respects, we reverse the judgment of the trial court and render judgment for Judy rescinding the shareholders' agreement of April 11, 1979, as between Judy Miller and Howard Miller only. The rights and liabilities of the other signatories to that agreement are not affected by this judgment.

Our opinion of August 30, 1985, is withdrawn and this opinion is substituted. Appellee's motion for rehearing is overruled.

Notes, Comments & Questions

1. By what two positions did Howard owe a fiduciary duty to Judy?

2. It has been said that marriage gives rise to a confidential relationship, a fiduciary relationship. Do you think that any fiduciary duty arising from marriage continues through divorce? *See Bass v. Bass*, 790 S.W.2d 113 (Tex. App.—Fort Worth 1990, no writ), holding that a fiduciary relationship "does not continue when a husband and wife hire numerous independent professional counsel to represent them respectively in a contested divorce proceeding." *Id.* at 119.

Chapter 6

Interspousal Torts

A. Introduction

The interspousal tort immunity doctrine was abrogated as to willful or intentional torts by the Texas Supreme Court in the case of *Bounds v. Caudle*, 560 S.W.2d 925 (Tex. 1977). Prior to this time, spouses could not sue one another in tort. As explained by the Texas Supreme Court in *Bounds v. Caudle*:

> . . . the doctrine of interspousal tort immunity had its origin in the common law and is based on the legal fiction that the husband and wife became one person in law. Under this concept, married women lost their capacity to sue or be sued without the joinder of the husband. The wife's personal and property rights as well as her legal existence were considered suspended during the marriage. . . . This concept necessarily made it impossible for one spouse to maintain an action against the other. *Id.* at 926.

This was the law in Texas and throughout a majority of the states. However in 1977, the Texas Supreme Court held in *Bounds v. Caudle* there was no sound basis for barring a suit for intentional tort between spouses. *Id.* at 927. The court abolished the interspousal tort immunity doctrine for willful and intentional torts that occurred between spouses on or after March 1, 1971.

The March 1, 1971 date is significant because that is the date Dr. Bounds shot and killed his wife. Thus, the court deemed proper a subsequent wrongful death action brought by Mrs. Bounds' heirs and allowed recovery.

Despite the abrogation in *Bounds v. Caudle*, the doctrine of interspousal tort immunity remained intact and applicable for a decade to cases that were not based on willful and intentional acts. That is, spouses could not sue one another for negligent torts. *See Bruno v. Bruno* 589 S.W.2d 179 (Tex. Civ. App.—Waco 1979, writ ref'd n.r.e.). The doctrine was not completely abrogated until the summer of 1987. *Price v. Price*, 732 S.W.2d 316 (Tex. 1987).

The following cases track the evolution of the complete abrogation of the interspousal tort immunity doctrine. This action of the Texas Supreme Court should open numerous creative avenues of recovery in family law matters and should result in some unusual cases.

B. Cases

MOGFORD
v.
MOGFORD

616 S.W.2d 936
(Tex.Civ.App.—San Antonio 1981, writ ref'd n.r.e.)

ESQUIVEL, JUSTICE.

This is an appeal of a divorce case in which a cause of action for personal injuries was joined in the trial court. No appeal is taken from that part of the judgment granting the divorce. To our knowledge, it is a case of first impression in this state.

Appellee, Dorothy Mogford, the wife of appellant, Lorenzo Mogford, for thirty-one years, sued for divorce in the district court. At the time of the divorce there were no minor children of the marriage. By her Second Amended Original Petition, appellee joined a cause of action for personal injuries arising out of willful and intentional torts committed upon her person by appellant during the marriage. In her petition, appellee sought \$100,000.00 actual damages and \$100,000.00 in punitive damages. The trial of the cause was to a jury. The jury awarded appellee \$20,000 in damages for injuries and mental anguish caused by appellant's abuse of her. No punitive damages were awarded. The decree of divorce entered by the trial court on August 31, 1979, stated the grounds for the divorce. In answers to special issues presented to the jury, it was found that appellant was guilty of cruel treatment of appellee; that during the marriage appellant had committed adultery; that appellant had willfully and intentionally struck and abused appellee during the marriage, and that appellee was injured as a result of the willful and intentional acts of appellant. The trial judge also made a division of the community property and entered a corrective judgment nunc pro tunc, so that temporary orders issued during the pendency of the divorce would continue in effect until the appeal was exhausted.

Appellant cites eight points of error on appeal. Because of the nature and importance of this case we will examine each point of error individually. This case delves into the unclear realm of interspousal tort immunity on which there is a dearth of cases that we can consider to guide us. As far as we have been able to determine there are no cases specifically on point with this particular case in this state.

Appellant's first point of error is as follows:

> IT WAS FUNDAMENTAL ERROR FOR THE TRIAL COURT TO RENDER JUDGMENT AGAINST APPELLANT FOR CLAIMED INJURIES RESULTING FROM ALLEGED TORTIOUS CONDUCT OF APPELLANT DURING THEIR MARRIAGE AND BEFORE ANY SEPARATION. UNDER THE STATUTORY LAW OF 'INTERSPOUSAL IMMUNITY' APPELLEE NEITHER HAS NOR HAD ANY CAUSE OF ACTION FOR THE INJURY CLAIMED, IF ANY INJURIES THERE WERE.

This point of error is the one relied on and briefed most exhaustively by both parties. Appellant's attorney argues forcefully that, "under the Constitution and laws of the State of Texas neither the wife nor the husband has any cause of action based upon the tortious conduct (willful or otherwise) of either against the other." Appellant's contention is that the common law doctrine of interspousal tort immunity is still applicable in Texas despite the recent erosion of this concept in the statutes, case law, and learned treatises. Appellant states that the common law was originally adopted by statute and that it remains in force today by statute. Appellant quotes from Vernon's Annotated Texas Statutes Article 1: "The common law of England so far as it is not inconsistent with the Constitution and the laws of this State, shall together with such Constitution and laws be the rule of decision and shall continue in force until altered or repealed by the Legislature."

Appellant urges that under this reasoning, the doctrine of interspousal tort immunity was transformed into statutory law because this common law concept of ancient England has been adopted by the Legislature of this State.

Appellant's argument fails in this case. The common law disability that prohibits one spouse from bringing a suit for grievances against the other has for some time been in retreat in this state. Equity, equality and justice have long cried out for a remedy to an aggrieved spouse for such heinous and despicable behavior inflicted by one spouse upon the other.

A passage in the landmark decision of *Bounds v. Caudle*, 560 S.W.2d 925, 926 (Tex. 1977), states quite succinctly the foundation on which the common law doctrine rested:

> The doctrine of interspousal tort immunity had its origin in the common law and is based on the legal fiction that the husband and wife became one person in law. Under this concept married women lost their capacity to sue or to be sued without the joinder of the husband. The wife's personal and property rights as well as her legal existence were considered suspended during the marriage. The husband acquired all of his wife's choses in action and could assert them in his own name and he became liable for the torts of his wife. This concept necessarily made it impossible for one spouse to maintain an action against the other. It is quite evident that the concept of the unity of the husband and wife as one person has been abandoned so far as the laws of this state are concerned. A woman is no longer viewed as an appendage of her husband. She is an individual with rights and duties of her own and not merely a subservient chattel of the male.

The Texas Family Code now provides that a wife's recovery for personal injuries other than for loss of earning capacity is part of her separate estate. TEX. FAM. CODE ANN. § 5.01(a)(3) (Vernon 1979). The Family Code permits a spouse to sue and be sued without the joinder of the other spouse. TEX. FAM. CODE ANN. § 4.04 (Vernon 1979). Under section 5.21 of the Family Code, the wife has sole management, control and disposition of her separate estate. TEX. FAM. CODE ANN. § 5.21 (Vernon 1979). It is not difficult to see that these statutory changes make the common law rationale for the doctrine obsolete under recent laws enacted by the Legislature. The fictional unity of the marriage relationship has also been dramatically altered by the emergence of women's rights over the past eighty years. The Supreme Court of Texas in *Bounds v. Caudle*, wisely ruled that there is no sound basis in barring a suit for an intentional tort, and accordingly abolished the rule of interspousal tort immunity to the extent that it served as a bar to all claims for willful and intentional torts arising out of a wrongful death action.

There is no doubt in our minds that the unity and harmony of the family is of paramount importance to our society, but so is the physical and mental well-being of the individuals that comprise the family. A family in which willful or intentional torts have caused injury and mental anguish to occur is not likely to be more disrupted by allowing a spouse to redress a grievance in the courts of equity. The usual occurrence is that when such physical attacks occur, the marriage is already in deep trouble. It is most difficult to perceive how allowing a suit for injury could disrupt the marriage even more. As a matter of public policy, we feel that the disallowance of such actions could do more to destroy a family than to allow them. This is because the allowance of such suits provides a means to redress a wrong committed upon a family member who is otherwise virtually powerless to stop such abuses. Perhaps, it is not unlikely that the allowance of such actions would serve as a deterrent or restraint upon a violent family member who is disposed to batter his or her spouse and children. It is our opinion that the theoretical basis for the disallowance of such suits which is pinned upon public policy must give way to a more urgent policy need, that being the redress of a wrong committed upon the person of an individual. Indeed, several other states have gone so far as to allow suits between spouses to take place with regard to intentional torts, and in some cases even negligent torts. *Johnson v. Johnson*, 201 Ala. 41, 77 So. 335 (1917); *Cramer v. Cramer*, 379 P.2d 95 (Alaska 1963); *Leach v. Leach*, 227 Ark. 599, 300 S.W.2d 15 (1957); *Klein v. Klein*, 58 Cal.2d 692, 26 Cal. Rptr. 102, 376 P.2d 70 (1962); *Self v. Self*, 58 Cal.2d 683, 26 Cal. Rptr. 97, 376 P.2d 65 (1962); *Foster v. Foster*, 264 N.C. 694, 142 S.E.2d 638 (1965).

Justice Greenhill in the recent case of *Robertson et al. v. The Estate of Byron M. McKnight*, 609 S.W.2d 534 (Tex. 1980), stated, "While Texas does not permit spouses to recover from each other for negligently inflicted injuries, a rule which does permit such a suit does not violate good morals or natural justice." Indeed, we believe that justice is served by stating what is already obvious; the legislature by its actions has mortally wounded the doctrine of interspousal tort immunity and we will not take heroic steps to insure its survival. We are not unheeding to policy arguments that would serve to controvert our position, but the dignity of the individual demands that at the same time we must heavily weigh many compelling factors in favor of allowing the trial court's judgment to stand. We have done this with great care and reflection. Accordingly, appellant's Point of Error No. 1 is overruled.

Appellant's Second Point of Error is as follows:

> THE TRIAL COURT WAS GUILTY OF FUNDAMENTAL ERROR IN RENDERING JUDGMENT FOR THE APPELLEE'S CLAIMED PERSONAL INJURIES IN THIS CAUSE, BECAUSE THE INSTANT CAUSE IS ONE FOR DIVORCE AND THE DISTRICT COURT IS WITHOUT POWER, AUTHORITY OR JURISDICTION TO CONSIDER A TORT CLAIM IN A DIVORCE ACTION.

This case was initiated on August 3, 1977, with the filing of appellee's original petition. This petition requested that the court grant a divorce and divide the marital property, together with a prayer for the issuance of temporary orders. On October 30, 1978, following the Supreme Court's decision in *Bounds v. Caudle*, appellee filed her second amended original petition which in addition to matters previously pled, contained a claim for damages resulting from the willful and intentional torts of appellant.

The district court unquestionably had jurisdiction to consider the divorce case. The amount in controversy also gave the court jurisdiction to consider the personal injury case. TEX. CONST. Art. V, § 8, Tex. Rev. Civ. Stat. Ann. art. 1906, §§ 2, 6 (Vernon 1964). A plaintiff in his or her petition may join as independent claims any or as many claims either legal or equitable or both as he may have against the opposing party. TEX. R. CIV. P. 51(a); 1 TEX. JUR. 3D *Actions* § 52 (1979). Further, a party may state as many separate claims as he or she has regardless of consistency and whether they are based on legal or equitable grounds or both. TEX. R. CIV. P. 48; 1 TEX. JUR. 3D *Actions* § 52, (1979). The courts favor the avoidance of a multiplicity of suits. The courts favor resolution in one suit of all matters existing between the parties and arising out of the same transaction. *Parkhill Produce Company v. Pecos Valley Southern Railway Company*, 348 S.W.2d 208 (Tex. Civ. App.—San Antonio 1961, writ ref'd n.r.e.). Appellant's remedy if he did not want both causes of action to be considered at the same trial, was to file a motion for severance. Any claim against a party may be severed and proceeded with separately. TEX. R. CIV. P. 41; 1 TEX. JUR. 3D *Actions* § 77 (1979). This refers to a claim that is a severable part of a controversy that involves more than one cause of action. *Rose v. Baker*, 143 Tex. 202, 183 S.W.2d 438 (1944). It is obvious from the record before us that the divorce action and the claim for personal injuries were set out in separate counts. Appellant's failure to request a severance of the two causes of action waived his right to have this matter reviewed on appeal. *Lewis v. Texas Employers' Insurance Association*, 151 Tex. 95, 246 S.W.2d 599 (1952). In light of this, appellant's point of error no. 2 is overruled.

* * *

Notes, Comments & Questions

1. Which spouse, victim or tort-feasor, would be most likely to desire the joining of a tort with a divorce action? Why?

2. Which spouse would be most likely to fight a joinder? Why?

3. What problems can you envision if a joinder is allowed?

4. Rather than endure a tort trial, why not just claim cruelty and ask for a disproportionate division of the community estate?

5. *Mogford v. Mogford* does not present the last word on the joinder of tort claims with divorce actions. Later in this chapter the case of *Twyman v. Twyman*, 855 S.W.2d 619 (Tex. 1993) and the note case *Brinkman v. Brinkman*, 966 S.W.2d 780 (Tex. App.—San Antonio 1998, no writ) will provide further insight into this issue.

PRICE
v.
PRICE

732 S.W.2d 316
(Tex. 1987)

KILGARLIN, JUSTICE.

This case presents us with the opportunity to re-examine the validity of the doctrine of interspousal immunity. The case originated as a civil action of negligence for personal injuries brought by Kimberly Parmenter Price against her husband, Duane Price. Duane Price's motion for summary judgment was granted. The court of appeals affirmed that judgment. 718 S.W.2d 65. We reverse the judgment of the court of appeals and remand this cause to the trial court.

In July of 1983, Kimberly Parmenter, at the time a feme sole, was injured when a motorcycle on which she was riding collided with a truck. The motorcycle was driven by Duane Price. Six months after the accident, Duane and Kimberly were married. After marriage, Kimberly brought this action seeking recovery from her husband, Duane, and from the driver of the truck, claiming that the negligence of these drivers had caused her injuries. The driver of the truck and his employer settled. The trial court, in granting summary judgment for Duane, relied on the doctrine that one spouse could not sue another for negligent conduct.

The doctrine of interspousal immunity is a part of the common law, having been judicially created. Its origins are shrouded in antiquity, but the basis of the doctrine is "*that a husband and wife are one person*." *Firebrass v. Pennant*, 2 Wils. 255, 256 (C.P. 1764) (emphasis in original).

A woman's disability during coverture was an essential ingredient in fostering the doctrine. As was stated in *Thompson v. Thompson*, 218 U.S. 611, 614-15, 31 S.Ct. 111, 54 L.Ed. 1180 (1910):

> At common law the husband and wife were regarded as one,—the legal existence of the wife during coverture being merged in that of the husband; and, generally speaking, the wife was incapable of making contracts, of acquiring property or disposing of the same without her husband's consent. They could not enter into contracts with each other, nor were they liable for torts committed by one against the other" (emphasis added).

An earlier thesis on American law expanded the concept of superiority of the husband over the wife even to the extent of restraining her liberty or disciplining her. 2 KENT'S COM. 174 (8th ed. 1854). While in this, the last quarter of the twentieth century, such views seem preposterous, recognition that those views were prevalent in the law makes easily understandable why suits by wives against husbands were not permitted.

However, the husband/wife unity argument as grounds for the doctrine was severely impeded by the adoption of what were known as Married Women Acts. These legislative acts occurred principally in the latter half of the nineteenth century and early twentieth century. *See, e.g.*, 1877 CONN. PUB. ACTS c. 114; GA. CODE ANN. § 7142 (1913); 1949 KAN. SESS. LAWS 23-20 (1868); MASS. GEN. L. ch. 209 §§ 1-13 (1845); MO. REV. STAT. §§ 1735 & 8304 (1909); MONT. CODE ANN. §§ 1439-1441 (1887); 1893 PA. LAWS 345 § 3; *and* 1913 Tex. Gen. Laws ch. 32, p. 61. These acts, while varying from state to state, generally gave wives the rights to own, acquire and dispose of property; to contract; and, to sue in respect to their property and contracts. Most importantly, many of the statutes specifically abolished the doctrine of the oneness of husband and wife.

With the demise of the legal fiction of the merger of husband and wife into a single entity, the doctrine of interspousal immunity found support in considerations of marital harmony, as well as the potential for collusive lawsuits. RESTATEMENT (SECOND) OF TORTS § 895F, *comment d* (1979).

American jurisdictions, in upholding the doctrine, early on espoused the premise that a civil suit by one spouse against another would destroy the harmony of the home. One court, in a fire and brimstone opinion upholding the prohibition against suits between spouses, foresaw all manner of evil should the immunity doctrine be terminated. In *Ritter v. Ritter*, 31 Pa. 396 (1858), that court, while observing that a favorite maxim at common law was that marriage makes a man and woman one person at law, also said:

> Nothing could so complete that severance [of the marriage relationship] and degradation, as to throw open litigation to the parties. The maddest advocate for woman's rights, and for the abolition on earth of all divine institutions, could wish for no more decisive blow from the courts than this. The flames which litigation would kindle on the domestic hearth would consume in an instant the conjugal bond, and bring on a new era indeed—an era of universal discord, of unchastity, of bastardy, of dissoluteness, of violence, cruelty, and murders."

The second argument for barring interspousal suits, the possibility of collusive lawsuits, is entirely inconsistent with the subjugation of wife to husband and preservation of happy homes theses. Nevertheless, such inconsistency did not seem to trouble the courts. The possibility of collusion was alluded to in *Abbott v. Abbott*, 67 Me. 304 (1877), where it was suggested that a widow could raid her deceased husband's estate by claiming all sorts of wrongs by him during his lifetime. The fraud theory expanded into vogue with the advent of insurance to cover vehicular accidents. In *Newton v. Weber*, 119 Misc. Rep. 240, 196 N.Y.S. 113, 114 (1922), the court said of allowing a tort action by a wife against her husband, "[t]he maintenance of an action of this character, unless the sole purpose be a raid upon an insurance company, would not add to conjugal happiness and unison."

Without ascribing any reasons for doing so, Texas adopted the doctrine of interspousal immunity one hundred years ago in *Nickerson* and *Matson v. Nickerson*, 65 Tex. 281 (1886), *citing* as authority only COOLEY ON TORTS, *Peters v. Peters*, 42 Iowa 182 (1875), *and Langendyke v. Langendyke*, 44 Barb. 366 (N.Y.1863). *Nickerson* barred all civil actions for tort between husband and wife.

Neither *Cooley* nor either case relied upon offered logic for the doctrine. Those authorities merely stated that the law forbade suits by one spouse against the other for personal injuries.

The doctrine remained firmly established as Texas law until *Bounds v. Caudle*, 560 S.W.2d 925 (Tex. 1977). *Bounds* abrogated the rule as to intentional torts. In *Bounds*, this court concluded that suits for willful or intentional torts would not disrupt domestic tranquility since "the peace and harmony of a home" which had "been strained to the point where an intentional physical attack could take place" could not be further impaired by allowing a suit to recover damages. *Id.* at 927.

Is there today any policy justification for retaining this feudal concept of the rights of parties to a marriage? Apparently, our colleagues on the Court of Criminal Appeals have decided "no" in respect to the marital discord argument. With their September 1, 1986 promulgation of TEX. R. CRIM. EV. 504, that court abolished the long-standing rule that one spouse could prevent the other from voluntarily giving testimony in a criminal prosecution. "The Fourth Court of Appeals also questioned the justification of the policy when it observed:

> [W]hile the new legislation [the Married Women Acts] forced recognition of the rights of a married woman to recover from her husband if he broke the leg of her mule, the courts continued to clothe him with immunity if he tortiously broke his wife's leg."
>
> * * *
>
> It has never been satisfactorily explained how permitting the wife to recover for her husband's conduct which tortiously injures her property would not disrupt domestic harmony, while allowing her to recover for bodily injury would. *Sneed v. Sneed*, 705 S.W.2d 392, 394 (Tex. App.—San Antonio 1986, writ ref'd n.r.e.).
>
> It was likewise that court, in upholding the summary judgment in this case, that said:
>
> Although neither courts nor commentators have satisfactorily explained how denying relief to the injured spouse will promote harmony, we are constrained to follow the unambiguous, if indefensible, precedent set by *Nickerson* and *Bounds*.

718 S.W.2d at 66.

Dean William Prosser, a preeminent commentator on tort law, certainly agreed that the doctrine is indefensible. He has stated:

> Stress has been laid upon the danger of fictitious and fraudulent claims, on the very dubious assumption that a wife's love for her husband is such that she is more likely to bring a false suit against him than a genuine one; and likewise the possibility of trivial actions for minor annoyances, which might well be taken care of by finding consent to all ordinary fictions of wedlock—or at least assumption of risk! The chief reason relied upon by all these courts, however, is that personal tort actions between husband and wife would disrupt and destroy the peace and harmony of the home, which is against the policy of the law. This is on the bald theory that after a husband has beaten his wife, there is a state of peace and harmony left to be disturbed; and that if she is sufficiently injured or angry to sue him for it, she will be soothed and deterred from reprisals by denying her the legal remedy—and this even though she has left him or divorced him for that very ground, and although the same courts refuse to find any disruption of domestic tranquility if she sues him for a tort to her property, or brings a criminal prosecution against him. If this reasoning appeals to the reader, let him by all means adopt it.

PROSSER, LAW OF TORTS, § 122 at 863 (4th ed. 1971). While it is true that part of this quote involves intentional rather than negligent torts, the arguments in favor of interspousal immunity are generally equally applicable, and lacking, as to both. It is difficult to fathom how denying a forum for the redress of any wrong could be said to encourage domestic tranquility. It is equally difficult to see how suits based in tort would destroy domestic tranquility, while property and contract actions do not.

As to the potential for fraud and collusion, we are unable to distinguish interspousal suits from other actions for personal injury. In *Whitworth v. Bynum*, 699 S.W.2d 194, 197 (Tex. 1985), this court "refuse[d] to indulge in the assumption that close relatives will prevaricate so as to promote a spurious lawsuit." Our system of justice is capable of ascertaining the existence of fraud and collusion. The Supreme Court of West Virginia, abolishing the rule in *Coffindaffer v. Coffindaffer*, 161 W.Va. 557, 244 S.E.2d 338, 343 (1978), stated:

> Anyone who has confronted insurance defense counsel in personal injury cases knows that it is a rare occasion when the false or collusive claim escapes their searching examination. We do an injustice not only to the intelligence of jurors, but to the efficacy of the adversary system, when we express undue concern over the quantum of collusive or meritless lawsuits. There is, to be sure, a difference between the ability to file a suit and to achieve a successful result. It is upon the anvil of litigation that the merit of a case is finally determined. Forged in the heat of trial, few but the meritorious survive.

In regards to both the domestic tranquility and fraud arguments, Prosser and Dean Page Keeton have said "almost no legal writer has had any use for these arguments, and under repeated criticisms and reiterated attacks on them in the courts, judicial perception of these arguments has slowly shifted." W. PROSSER & P. KEETON, LAW OF TORTS § 122 at 902 (5th ed. 1984).

Other jurisdictions have preceded us in either completely or partially abolishing the doctrine of interspousal immunity. . . .

The doctrine of interspousal immunity has previously been abrogated as to some causes of action in this jurisdiction. We now abolish that doctrine completely as to any cause of action. We do not limit our holding to suits involving vehicular accidents only, as has been done by some jurisdictions and as has been urged upon us in this case. To do so would be to negate meritorious claims such as was presented in *Stafford v. Stafford*, 726 S.W.2d 14 (Tex. 1987). In that case a husband had transmitted a venereal disease to his wife, resulting in an infection that ultimately caused Mrs. Stafford the loss of her ovaries and fallopian tubes, ending for all time her ability to bear children. While we ruled for her, the issue of interspousal immunity had not been preserved for our review. To leave in place a bar to suits like that of Mrs. Stafford or other suits involving non-vehicular torts would amount to a repudiation of the constitutional guarantee of equal protection of the laws. TEX. CONST. ANN. art. I, § 3. This we will not do.

Our result today is compelled by the fundamental proposition of public policy that the courts should afford redress for a wrong, and the failure of the rationale supporting the doctrine to withstand scrutiny. We therefore reverse the judgment of the court of appeals upholding the trial court's summary judgment, and remand this cause to the trial court for further proceedings.

MAUZY, J., concurs with an opinion.

MAUZY, JUSTICE, concurring.

Although I concur whole-heartedly in the opinion of the court, I am compelled to voice my outrage at the recent action of our State Board of Insurance. With its opinion today, the court has rid Texas common-law of an archaic doctrine. Yet, the State Board of Insurance has now incorporated this same senseless doctrine into contract law. It recently prescribed a standard auto policy endorsement that expressly excludes liability coverage for intrafamily suits. 12 Tex. Reg. 1126 (1987) (Form 575 adopted as part of amendments to *Rules and Rates Governing the Insuring of Automobiles and Standard Endorsements*). The Board's action cannot have any rational justification; and it does not in any way serve the interests of the people of Texas.

Notes, Comments & Questions

1. In *Price*, the Texas Supreme Court takes a very rational and well reasoned approach to dismantling the longstanding rationale for denying a wife the right to sue her husband in a negligence based tort. Do you agree?

2. In the *Price* case, how broad was the Texas Supreme Court's abrogation of the interspousal tort immunity doctrine? Find the language.

3. For what reason, other than the problem with proving intent, would a spouse desire to bring a negligence based tort, rather than an intentional tort against the other spouse.

4. Earlier in this course, we studied the recent Texas Supreme Court opinion of *Schlueter v. Schlueter*, 975 S.W.2d 584 (Tex. 1998). Review that opinion when considering the discussion of *Price v. Price* as set forth in the nest case, *Twyman v. Twyman.*

5. *Twyman*, the following opinion, is very lengthy. Not only is there a majority opinion, but there was also the following opinions rendered:

   a. GONZALEZ—concurred in part and filed opinion
   b. PHILLIPS—concurred in part, dissented in part, filed opinion
   c. HECHT—concurred in part, dissented in part, filed opinion; joined by ENOCH
   d. SPECTOR—dissented and filed opinion; joined by DOGGETT

6. Although only the majority opinion is presented in this text, a review of the entire *Twyman* opinion will provides a thorough understanding of the court's position on the question of emotional distress.

TWYMAN
v.
TWYMAN
855 S.W.2d 619
(Tex. 1993)

CORNYN, JUSTICE.

In this case we decide whether a claim for infliction of emotional distress can be brought in a divorce proceeding. Because the judgment of the court of appeals is based on negligent infliction of emotional distress, and cannot be affirmed on that or any other basis, we reverse the judgment of that court and remand this cause for a new trial in the interest of justice. TEX. R. APP .P. 180. We deem a new trial appropriate because of our recent decision that no cause of action for negligent infliction of emotional distress exists in Texas. Today, however, we expressly adopt the tort of intentional infliction of emotional distress, and hold that such a claim can be brought in a divorce proceeding.

I.

Sheila and William Twyman married in 1969. Sheila filed for divorce in 1985. She later amended her divorce petition to add a general claim for emotional harm without specifying whether the claim was based on negligent or intentional infliction of emotional distress. In her amended petition, Sheila alleged that William "intentionally and cruelly" attempted to engage her in "deviate sexual acts."[1] Following a bench trial, the court rendered judgment dissolving the marriage, dividing the marital estate, awarding conservatorship of the children to Sheila, ordering William to pay child support, and awarding Sheila $15,000 plus interest for her claim for emotional distress. William appealed that portion of the judgment based on emotional distress, contending that interspousal tort immunity precluded Sheila's recovery for negligent infliction of emotional distress. The court of appeals affirmed the judgment, holding that Sheila could recover for William's negligent infliction of emotional distress. 790 S.W.2d 819.

While this case has been pending, we have refused to adopt the tort of negligent infliction of emotional distress. *See Boyles v. Kerr*, 855 S.W.2d 593 (Tex. 1993). Thus the judgment of the court of appeals cannot be affirmed. We consider, therefore, whether the court of appeals' judgment may be affirmed on alternative grounds. Because Sheila's pleadings alleging a general claim for emotional harm are broad enough to encompass a claim for intentional infliction of emotional distress, we consider whether the trial court's judgment may be sustained on that legal theory.

[1] At trial, Sheila testified that William pursued sadomasochistic bondage activities with her, even though he knew that she feared such activities because she had been raped at knife-point before their marriage. The trial court found that William "attempted to emotionally coerce [Sheila] in 'bondage' on an ongoing basis. . . ." and "engaged in a continuing course of conduct of attempting to coerce her to join in his practices of 'bondage' by continually asserting that their marriage could be saved only by [Sheila] participating with him in his practices of 'bondage.' "

While this court has never expressly recognized the tort of intentional infliction of emotional distress, we found no reversible error in the court of appeals' opinion in *Tidelands Automobile Club v. Walters*, which did so. 699 S.W.2d 939 (Tex. App.—Beaumont 1985, writ ref'd n.r.e.). There, the court of appeals adopted the elements of the tort as expressed in the RESTATEMENT (SECOND) OF TORTS § 46 (1965). The RESTATEMENT elements of intentional infliction of emotional distress are: 1) the defendant acted intentionally or recklessly, 2) the conduct was extreme and outrageous, 3) the actions of the defendant caused the plaintiff emotional distress, and 4) the emotional distress suffered by the plaintiff was severe. *Id.* According to the RESTATEMENT, liability for outrageous conduct should be found "only where the conduct has been so outrageous in character, and so extreme in degree, as to go beyond all possible bounds of decency, and to be regarded as atrocious, and utterly intolerable in a civilized community." *Id.* cmt. d. Of the forty-six states that have recognized this tort, forty-three have adopted this *Restatement* formulation.[2] The other three states, although not adopting the *Restatement* definition, require the equivalent of "outrageous" conduct.[3] Today we become the forty-seventh state to adopt the tort of intentional infliction of emotional distress as set out in § 46(1) of the RESTATEMENT (SECOND) OF TORTS.

We do not, however, adopt this tort only because of its broad acceptance in jurisdictions throughout the United States. As distinguished from the tort of negligent infliction of emotional distress, we believe the rigorous legal standards of the RESTATEMENT formulation of intentional infliction of emotional distress help to assure a meaningful delineation between inadvertence and intentionally or recklessly outrageous misconduct. The requirements of intent, extreme and outrageous conduct, and severe emotional distress before liability can be established will, we think, strike a proper balance between diverse interests in a free society. That balance, at minimum, must allow freedom of individual action while providing reasonable opportunity for redress for victims of conduct that is determined to be utterly intolerable in a civilized community.

This holding represents a middle ground between the polar positions adopted by various members of the court.[4] JUSTICE HECHT, joined by JUSTICE ENOCH, in arguing against our express adoption of the tort of intentional infliction of emotional distress, maintains that judges and juries are guided by insufficient standards, that liability may be imposed arbitrarily, that reported cases either supporting or refusing to support an award of damages disclose no uniform patterns, and that the sensitivities of aggrieved people are entirely too subjective and unpredictable. We disagree, and believe that such objections could just as easily be made to well-established causes of action in Texas. For example, one might also contend that the legal standards for ordinary negligence

[2] [Footnote omitted.]

[3] *See* Hall v. The May Dep't Stores Co., 292 Or. 131, 637 P.2d 126, 129 (1981) (requiring "some extraordinary transgression of the bounds of socially tolerable conduct"); Chedester v. Stecker, 64 Haw. 464, 643 P.2d 532, 535 (1982) (requiring the conduct to be "unreasonable," which the court equated with "outrageous" as defined in RESTATEMENT § 46); Sears Roebuck & Co. v. Devers, 405 So.2d 898, 901 (Miss. 1981) (finding liability may exist "where there is something about the defendant's conduct which evokes outrage or revulsion").

[4] Five members of the court—CHIEF JUSTICE PHILLIPS and JUSTICES GONZALEZ, HIGHTOWER, DOGGETT, SPECTOR and myself—agree that the judgment of the court of appeals must be reversed: JUSTICES GONZALEZ, HIGHTOWER, and I form a plurality of the court who recognize the tort of intentional infliction of emotional distress in the marital context and who remand this case for a new trial in the interests of justice; CHIEF JUSTICE PHILLIPS would recognize the tort, but not apply it to married couples and would reverse and render; JUSTICES HECHT and ENOCH would not recognize the tort under any circumstances and would reverse and render. JUSTICES DOGGETT and SPECTOR would recognize the tort in the marital context but would affirm the judgment of the court of appeals.

gence are vague, and that juries must necessarily rely on their own notions of fault. Because jurors' ideas about what is "ordinary" and "reasonable" may vary, the same arguments about lack of uniformity, unpredictability, and personal sensitivities could be made. Yet just as we trust juries to decide questions of negligence, proximate cause, and damages, when guided by appropriate legal standards we think them equally capable of resolving factual disputes giving rise to the tort of intentional infliction of emotional distress.

JUSTICE SPECTOR, joined by JUSTICE DOGGETT, on the other hand, agrees with us that this tort should be adopted, but uses this case as another opportunity to question the wisdom of our decision in *Boyles*, in which we refused to adopt the tort of negligent infliction of emotional distress. They join some amici curiae[5] in implying that the court has disregarded the tort's unique role in addressing women's psychic injuries. One need only identify those who have brought claims for negligent infliction of emotional distress, however, to dispel the suggestion that women will be disproportionately affected. Of the thirty-four Texas appellate cases in which a claim for negligent infliction of emotional distress was alleged,[6] thirteen were brought by women,[7] twelve were brought by men,[8] seven by husbands and wives jointly,[9] one by an executrix on behalf of an es-

---

[5] *E.g.*, Women and the Law Section of the State Bar of Texas.

[6] We note these cases not for their precedential value, but as examples of cases in which a claimant brought an action for negligent infliction of emotional distress.

[7] Boyles v. Kerr, 855 S.W.2d 593 (Tex. 1993); Smith v. Chasewood Bank, No. B14-92-00302-CV, 1993 WL 81584 (Tex. App.—Houston [14th Dist.], March 25, 1993, n.w.h.) (not designated for publication) (brought individually and on behalf of husband's estate); Schauer v. Koperwhats, 856 S.W.2d 437 (Tex. App.—Houston [1st Dist.], 1993, n.w.h.); Hennigan v. I.P. Petroleum Co., 848 S.W.2d 276 (Tex. App.—Beaumont, 1993, n.w.h.); Jones v. Legal Copy, Inc., 846 S.W.2d 922 (Tex. App.—Houston [1st Dist.] 1993, no writ); Gibson v. Matrix Resources, Inc. of Texas, 05-91-01502-CV, 1993 WL 42881 (Tex. App.—Dallas, Feb. 17, 1993) (not designated for publication); Weirich v. Weirich, 833 S.W.2d 942 (Tex. 1992); Natividad v. Alexsis, Inc., 833 S.W.2d 545 (Tex. App.—El Paso 1992, writ granted); McAlister v. Medina Elec. Co-op., Inc., 830 S.W.2d 659 (Tex. App.—San Antonio, 1992, writ denied); Massey v. Massey, 807 S.W.2d 391 (Tex. App.—Houston [1st Dist.] 1991, writ pending); Blair v. Blair, 01-89-01035-CV, 1991 WL 9266 (Tex. App.—Houston [1st Dist.] 1991, writ denied) (not designated for publication); Twyman v. Twyman, 790 S.W.2d 819 (Tex. App.—Austin 1990, writ granted); Chiles v. Chiles, 779 S.W.2d 127 (Tex. App.—Houston [14th Dist.] 1989, writ denied).

[8] Izen v. Royall, 01-92-1216-CV, 1993 WL 66813 (Tex. App.—Houston [1st Dist.], March 11, 1993, n.w.h.); Garcia v. San Antonio Hous. Auth., 859 S.W.2d 78 (Tex. App.—San Antonio, 1993, n.w.h.); Krupka v. U.S. Videotel and Encode Intern., No. B14-92-00398-CV, 1993 WL 46571 (Tex. App.—Houston [14th Dist.], Feb. 25, 1993, n.w.h.) (not designated for publication); Birdo v. Williams, _____ S.W.2d _____, No. 01-91-00294-CV, 1992 WL 347121 (Tex. App.—Houston [1st Dist.], Nov. 25, 1992, n.w.h.); Daniels v. Pecan Valley Ranch, Inc., 831 S.W.2d 372 (Tex. App.—San Antonio 1992, writ denied); C.T.W. v. B.C.G., 809 S.W.2d 788, 796 (Tex. App.—Beaumont 1991, no writ) (brought on behalf of two male children); Johnson v. Rollen, 818 S.W.2d 180 (Tex. App.—Houston [1st Dist.] 1991, no writ); Gumm v. Owen, 815 S.W.2d 259 (Tex. App.—El Paso 1991, no writ); Wavell v. Caller Times Pub. Co., 809 S.W.2d 633 (Tex. App.—Corpus Christi 1991, writ denied); McNamara v. Freedom Newspapers, Inc., 802 S.W.2d 901 (Tex. App.—Corpus Christi 1991, writ denied); Southwestern Bell Tel. Co. v. Wilson, 768 S.W.2d 755 (Tex. App.—Corpus Christi 1988, writ denied); Hinojosa v. South Texas Drilling & Exploration, Inc., 727 S.W.2d 320 (Tex. App.—San Antonio 1987, no writ).

[9] Channel 4, KGBT v. Briggs, 759 S.W.2d 939 (Tex. 1988); St. Elizabeth Hosp. v. Garrard, 730 S.W.2d 649 (Tex. 1987), overruled by Boyles v. Kerr, 855 S.W.2d 593; Resolution Trust Corp. v. Cook, 840 S.W.2d 42 (Tex. App.—Amarillo 1992, writ denied) (awarding damages for negligent infliction of emotional distress to both spouses); Campos v. Ysleta General Hosp., Inc., 836 S.W.2d 791 (Tex. App.—San Antonio 1992, writ denied); Valenzuela v. Aquino, 800 S.W.2d 301 (Tex. App.—Corpus Christi 1990, writ granted); State Nat. Bank v. Academia, Inc., 802 S.W.2d 282 (Tex. App.—Corpus Christi 1990, writ denied); Hewitt v. Chadwick, 760 S.W.2d 333 (Tex. App.—Texarkana 1988, no writ).

tate,[10] and one by a corporation.[11] These cases demonstrate that the tort has been alleged by litigants in a wide variety of circumstances. There is simply no factual or legal basis for the suggestion that by choosing not to recognize this particular tort, the court demonstrates insensitivity to female claimants.

JUSTICE SPECTOR also argues that because of our refusal to recognize the tort of negligent infliction of emotional distress some wrongs will go uncompensated because of the difficulty in proving the actor's intent when the actor intends nothing more than to satisfy his own desires. *Infra*, 855 S.W.2d at 644. But in Sheila Twyman's case, and in countless other cases involving both men and women, we believe that our adoption of the RESTATEMENT formulation of the tort of intentional infliction of emotional distress provides a reasonable opportunity for redress for outrageous conduct.

Of course, rarely will a defendant admit knowing of a substantial certainty that emotional harm would befall the victim. Juries, however, are free to discredit the defendant's protestations that no harm was intended and to draw necessary inferences to establish intent. *See McGalliard v. Kuhlmann*, 722 S.W.2d 694, 697 (Tex. 1986); *Fichtner v. Richardson*, 708 S.W.2d 479, 483 (Tex. App.—Dallas 1986, writ ref'd n.r.e.) ("The jury may believe all, part, or none of the testimony in arriving at the finding it concludes is the most reasonable"); *see also Walters v. American States Ins. Co.*, 654 S.W.2d 423, 426 (Tex. 1983) (holding that jury is free to make a reasonable inferential leap based on evidence). Ironically, for JUSTICE SPECTOR to argue in favor of applying a negligence standard to this case is to argue that as a matter of law the emotional harm William caused was foreseeable but not substantially certain to occur.[12] We disagree with that characterization and believe that on retrial the factfinder should be permitted to consider whether William knew with substantial certainty that his actions would probably cause Sheila emotional harm.

Moreover, Section 46 of the RESTATEMENT definition of the tort expressly includes situations in which the actor recklessly inflicts emotional distress. An actor is reckless when he "knows or has reason to know . . . of facts which create a high degree of risk of . . . harm to another, and deliberately proceeds to act, or fails to act, in conscious disregard of, or indifference to that risk." RESTATEMENT (SECOND) § 500, cmt. a. Again, on retrial, the jury may consider whether William acted recklessly toward Sheila.

II.

We now consider whether the cause of action for intentional infliction of emotional distress may be brought in a divorce proceeding.[13] In *Bounds v. Caudle*, this court unanimously abolished

[10] Godinet v. Thomas, 824 S.W.2d 632 (Tex. App.—Houston [14th Dist.] 1991, writ denied) (brought on behalf of a woman).

[11] Brazosport Bank of Tex. v. Oak Park Townhouses, 837 S.W.2d 652 (Tex. App.—Houston [14th Dist.] 1992) *rev'd and remanded*, 851 S.W.2d 189 (Tex. 1993).

[12] One amicus asserts that such a "twisted" classification of this conduct is due to the struggle to bring a claim within insurance coverage. *See Amicus Brief of United States Automobile Association*, p. 5.

[13] CHIEF JUSTICE PHILLIPS, and JUSTICES HECHT and ENOCH rue the court's decision to permit the tort of intentional infliction of emotional distress to be brought in divorce proceedings. But it appears that much of what they disapprove of is related to the consequences of recognizing any tort action between divorcing spouses. Their criticisms would seem to be better directed at the court's earlier decisions to abrogate the doctrine of interspousal tort immunity in Bounds v. Caudle, 560 S.W.2d 925 (Tex. 1977), and Price v. Price, 732 S.W.2d 316 (Tex. 1987).

the doctrine of interspousal immunity for intentional torts. 560 S.W.2d 925 (Tex. 1977). Ten years later, we abrogated interspousal immunity "completely as to any cause of action,"[14] including negligence actions for personal injuries. *Price v. Price*, 732 S.W.2d 316, 319 (Tex. 1987). Under the rules established in *Caudle* and *Price*, there appears to be no legal impediment to bringing a tort claim in a divorce action based on either negligence or an intentional act such as assault or battery.[15]

The more difficult issue is when the tort claim must be brought and how the tort award should be considered when making a "just and right" division of the marital estate. *See* TEX. FAM. CODE § 3.63(b). Of the states that have answered this question, several have held that the tort case and the divorce case must be litigated separately. *See e.g. Walther v. Walther*, 709 P.2d 387, 388 (Utah 1985); *Windauer v. O'Connor*, 107 Ariz. 267, 485 P.2d 1157 (1971); *Simmons v. Simmons*, 773 P.2d 602, 605 (Colo. Ct. App.1988). Other states require joinder of the two actions. *See, e.g. Tevis v. Tevis*, 79 N.J. 422, 400 A.2d 1189, 1196 (1979); *Weil v. Lammon*, 503 So.2d 830, 832 (Ala. 1987).

We believe that the best approach lies between these two extremes. As in other civil actions, joinder of the tort cause of action should be permitted,[16] but subject to the principles of res judicata.[17] *See Barr v. The Resolution Trust Corp.*, 837 S.W.2d 627, 631 (Tex. 1992) (reaffirming the transactional approach to res judicata analysis). *See also* TEX. R. CIV. P. 51; *Henriksen v. Cameron*, 622 A.2d 1135 (Me. 1993). Of course, how such claims are ultimately tried is within the sound discretion of the trial court. *See* TEX. R. CIV. P. 174. But joinder of tort claims with the divorce, when feasible, is encouraged. Resolving both the tort and divorce actions in the same proceeding avoids two trials based at least in part on the same facts, and settles in one suit "all matters existing between the parties."[18] *Mogford*, 616 S.W.2d at 940 (*citing Parkhill Produce Co. v. Pecos Valley S. Ry.*, 348 S.W.2d 208, 209 (Tex. Civ. App.—San Antonio 1961) writ ref'd n.r.e. *per curiam*, 163 Tex. 88, 352 S.W.2d 723 (1961)).

---

[14] CHIEF JUSTICE PHILLIPS' statement that "all conduct actionable between strangers is [not] automatically actionable between spouses" cannot be reconciled with this language. *See* 855 S.W.2d at 627 (PHILLIPS, C.J., dissenting).

[15] We necessarily disapprove of the contrary holding in Chiles v. Chiles, 779 S.W.2d 127 (Tex.App.—Houston [14th Dist.] 1989, writ denied) (declining to recognize intentional infliction of emotional distress as a separate cause of action in a divorce suit).

[16] A [divorce action] plaintiff . . . may join as independent claims any or as many claims either legal or equitable or both as he may have against the opposing party. . . . Further . . . [either] party may state as many separate claims as he or she has regardless of consistency and whether they are based on legal or equitable grounds or both. *Mogford v. Mogford*, 616 S.W.2d 936, 940 (Tex. Civ. App.—San Antonio 1981, writ ref'd n.r.e.).

[17] We anticipate that most tort cases between spouses will be joined with the divorce proceeding, however, situations may exist in which the facts supporting the tort action will be different from those supporting a petition for divorce.

[18] By holding that these actions may be brought in a single lawsuit we are not authorizing the use of contingent fee arrangements in family law matters. *See* TEX. DISCIPLINARY R. PROF. CONDUCT 1.04 & cmt. 9 (1989), reprinted in TEX. GOV'T CODE ANN., tit. 2, subtit. G app. (Vernon Supp. 1993) (STATE BAR RULES art. 10, § 9). Rather, attorneys should enter two separate fee arrangements, one for the divorce and the other for the tort claim. *See* Andrew Schepard, *Divorce, Interspousal Torts, and Res Judicata*, 24 FAM. L. Q. 127, 151-52 (1990).

When a tort action is tried with the divorce, however, it is imperative that the court avoid awarding a double recovery.[19] When dividing the marital estate, the court may take into account several factors, including the fault of the parties if pleaded. *See Murff v. Murff*, 615 S.W.2d 696, 699 (Tex. 1981). The trial court may also consider "such factors as the spouses' capacities and abilities, benefits which the party not at fault would have derived from continuation of the marriage, business opportunities, education, relative physical conditions, relative financial condition and obligations, disparity of ages, size of separate estates, and the nature to the property." *Id. See also Young v. Young*, 609 S.W.2d 758, 761 (Tex. 1980); *Bell v. Bell*, 513 S.W.2d 20, 22 (Tex. 1974). However, a spouse should not be allowed to recover tort damages and a disproportionate division of the community estate based on the same conduct. Therefore, when a factfinder awards tort damages to a divorcing spouse, the court may not consider the same tortious acts when dividing the marital estate. Contrary to CHIEF JUSTICE PHILLIPS' contention, an award for tortious conduct does not replace an analysis of the remaining factors to be considered when the trial court divides the marital estate. 855 S.W.2d at 626 (PHILLIPS, C.J., dissenting). The court may still award a disproportionate division of property for reasons other than the tortious conduct. To avoid the potential problem of double recovery, the factfinder should consider the damages awarded in the tort action when dividing the parties' property. If a jury is used to render an advisory division of the parties' estate, the judge should limit, by appropriate instruction, the jury's consideration of the alleged tortious acts and later consider the award of damages in determining a just and right division of the marital estate.[20]

Sheila Twyman cannot recover based on the findings of fact made by the trial court in this case.[21] It is likely, however, that this case proceeded on a theory of negligent infliction of emotional distress in reliance on this court's holding in *St. Elizabeth Hospital v. Garrard*, 730 S.W.2d 649 (Tex. 1987), which we recently overruled. *See Boyles v. Kerr*, 855 S.W.2d 593 (Tex. 1992). As we noted in *Boyles*, this court has broad discretion to remand for a new trial in the interest of justice when it appears that a case proceeded under the wrong legal theory, and when it appears that the facts when developed on retrial may support recovery on an alternative theory. *Id.* at 603. *See also American Title Ins. Co. v. Byrd*, 384 S.W.2d 683 (Tex. 1964); *Dahlberg v. Holden*, 150 Tex. 179, 238 S.W.2d 699 (1951). When, as here, a party presents her case in reliance on prece-

---

[19] For a discussion of the possibility of double recovery in this type of case, *see* Shepard, *supra* at 146-47.

[20] In Texas, recovery for personal injuries of a spouse, including pain and suffering, is the separate property of that spouse. TEX. FAM. CODE § 5.01(a)(3); Graham v. Franco, 488 S.W.2d 390, 396 (Tex. 1972). Therefore, an award to one spouse from the other does not add to the marital estate, and raises no possibility that the tort award becomes "self-offsetting." *See* Barbara H. Young, *Interspousal Torts and Divorce: Problems, Policies, Procedures*, 27 J. FAM. L. 489, 511 (1989).

[21] The RESTATEMENT calls for the court to first determine whether the conduct may be reasonably regarded as so extreme and outrageous as to allow recovery and whether severe emotional distress can be found. RESTATEMENT (SECOND) OF TORTS § 46 (1965) cmt. h; *see also* Horton v. Montgomery Ward & Co., 827 S.W.2d 361, 369 (Tex. App.—San Antonio 1992, writ denied); Tidelands Auto. Club v. Walters, 699 S.W.2d 939, 945 (Tex. App.—Beaumont 1985, writ ref'd n.r.e.). The trial court made no findings of outrageous behavior or severe emotional distress, and the judgment was based specifically and exclusively on negligent infliction of emotional distress. The divorce decree recites: After considering the pleadings, the evidence, and the arguments of the attorneys, the Court finds the facts and law support judgment for Petition [sic] in her tort for negligent infliction of emotional distress upon Petitioner.

Additionally, the trial court made a disproportionate property division based on William's cruel treatment and adultery. It appears that such an award may allow Sheila a double recovery based on the same conduct. A new trial conducted in accordance with the principles announced in this decision should rectify this problem.

dent that has been recently overruled, remand is appropriate. *See Scott v. Liebman*, 404 S.W.2d 288, 294 (Tex. 1966). Therefore, in the interest of justice, we reverse the judgment of the court of appeals and remand this cause to the trial court for a new trial.

Concurring opinion by JUSTICE GONZALEZ.

Concurring and Dissenting opinion by CHIEF JUSTICE PHILLIPS.

Concurring and Dissenting opinion by JUSTICE HECHT joined by JUSTICE ENOCH.

Dissenting opinion by JUSTICE SPECTOR joined by JUSTICE DOGGETT.

(JUSTICE GAMMAGE not sitting)

Notes, Comments & Questions

1. In the *Twyman* opinion, the Texas Supreme Court warns against the potential problem of double recovery, stating, "[i]f a jury is used to render an advisory division of the parties' estate, the judge should limit, by appropriate instruction, the jury's consideration of the alleged tortious acts and later consider the award of damages in determining a just and right division of the marital estate." What kind of jury instruction do you envision?

2. How could findings of fact guard against an allegation of double recovery?

3. The case of *Brinkman v. Brinkman*, 966 S.W.2d 780 (Tex. App.—San Antonio 1998, no cert.) establishes the strength of the double recovery principle, thus:

> . . . we do not believe that the present case presents a situation in which "the facts supporting [the] tort action [are] different from those supporting [the] petition for divorce" as anticipated by the *Twyman* court. *See Twyman*, 855 S.W.2d at 625 n. 17. In fact, because the tort at issue here was made a part of the divorce proceedings, this appears to be the type of case in which the *Twyman* court encouraged joinder. *Id.* at 625; *see Mogford v. Mogford*, 616 S.W.2d 936, 940-41 (Tex. App.—San Antonio 1981, writ ref'd n.r.e.) (stating that, in a case involving the joinder of a divorce and a personal injury claim, "the courts favor the avoidance of a multiplicity of suits . . . the courts favor resolution in one suit of all matters existing between parties and arising out of the same transaction"). If Ms. Brinkman's personal injury claim was not fully litigated in the divorce action, it certainly could have been with the use of diligence, as is required by the principles of res judicata. *See Barr*, 837 S.W.2d at 631 (holding "a subsequent suit will be barred if it arises out of the same subject matter of a previous suit and which through the exercise of diligence, could have been litigated in a prior suit.").
>
> When Ms. Brinkman chose to allege cruel treatment as grounds for divorce in order to receive a disproportionate share of community property, she was bound to assert all of her claims for cruel treatment arising out of the marriage. To hold otherwise would enable a spouse to use one instance of abuse as grounds for receiving a large amount of temporary spousal support or a greater share of community property, and then another instance of abuse to obtain actual and punitive damages from the former spouse. In cases in which the marriage involved long-term abuse, the number of lawsuits between the spouses could

> multiply exponentially. The prevention of such a situation is one purpose of res judicata. . . .
>
> Because Ms. Brinkman knew about her personal injury claim against Mr. Brinkman and used it to her advantage in the divorce proceeding, the claim should have been joined with the divorce action. If such joinder would have caused undue complication of the divorce proceeding, the proper remedy would have been severance, not the filing of a second suit after the first had been resolved. *See Mogford*, 616 S.W.2d at 941 (holding that appellant's remedy, if he did not want both divorce and personal injury claim considered at the same trial, was to file a motion for severance). Requiring joinder under these facts is consistent with the purposes of res judicata. Accordingly, the trial court did not err in finding that Ms. Brinkman's personal injury claim is barred by res judicata.
>
> The judgment of the trial court is affirmed.

4. After reading the excerpt of the *Brinkman* case, would you rely on the permissive nature of joinder to put off the filing of a tort by one spouse against the other spouse?

5. In addition to joinder, the issue of limitations has also been the subject of much controversy among family law experts since the abolition of interspousal immunity. Although this issue has not been specifically addressed in Texas, the case of *Armstrong v. Armstrong*, 750 S.W.2d 45 (Tex. App.—Fort Worth 1988, writ denied) supports the application of the two year statute of limitations to causes in tort which arise between spouses. The marital relationship was not utilized to toll the limitations period.

Chapter 7

Property Rights That Arise When There is No Formal Marriage

A. Introduction

One need not be ceremonially married in order to have property rights arise from a romantic relationship. The relationships which give rise to certain property rights include the following: (1) meretricious relationships; (2) putative spouses; and (3) common law marriages.

It is important to understand the technical definitions of each of these three informal relationships so that one can recognize the existence of such a relationship. It is also important to understand that the facts and circumstances which give rise to these relationships are not necessarily transferable between states. That is, facts which might give rise to a common law marriage in Texas would give rise to no more than a meretricious relationship in California because California is one of the 36 states that do not recognize common law marriage. Accordingly, one must be cautious in the use of these terms.

A meretricious relationship is cohabitation by persons who both know they are not married to one another. In discussing, researching, and analyzing meretricious relationships, it must be remembered that many states refer to what Texas would recognize as a common law marriage or, as a putative spouse, as meretricious because no legitimate status is accorded such relationships in those particular states.

A putative spouse is one who in good faith believes that he/she is married, but in reality cannot be married because of the existence of an unknown impediment, such as an undissolved prior marriage. One or both spouses may be innocent of the existence of the impediment. The property rights of a putative spouse, as to property acquired during the putative relationship, are the same as a lawful spouse but end when the innocent spouse learns of the putative status. Although spouses have been known to be punitive, a putative spouse is not necessarily punitive. Invariably the term "punitive spouse" appears on exams.

Common law marriage is now governed by statute, a statute that has been frequently amended of late. *See* TEX. FAM. CODE § 2.401. In Texas, parties to a common law marriage are afforded the same status as those who have been ceremonially married. The evolution of the common law marriage statutes are presented in this chapter at Section D. Common Law Marriages.

B. Meretricious Relationships

The concept of property rights arising from meretricious relationships is not a new one, although it has never been widely accepted. This was especially true in bible belt states that did not want to see a woman profit from her sins. For example, in the case of *Rehak v. Mathis*, 238 S.E. 81 (Ga. 1977), a female cohabitant filed an action in equity against defendant seeking her portion of purchase money interest in a house which parties had allegedly purchased together, as well as an amount for services rendered to defendant over the 18-year period during which they cohabited. The lower court granted the male partner's motion for summary judgment. The Georgia Supreme Court affirmed the summary judgment, holding that cohabitation would constitute immoral consideration precluding the female cohabitant from recovery. In his dissent, Justice Hill opined,

> . . . courts normally do not deny judicial relief to sinners. If that were the rule, the caseload in all courts would be drastically reduced. Courts normally do not deny judicial relief where both plaintiff and defendant have been immoral. If that were the rule, the divorce rate would be reduced.

Ever progressive, Texas did not hold to such narrow views. However, the recognition of such property rights was not heralded until the California case of *Marvin v. Marvin*, 557 P.2d 106 (1976). In *Marvin v. Marvin*, 557 P.2d 106 (Cal. 1976), the female plaintiff claimed that she and the defendant, actor Lee Marvin, had lived together under an agreement which required her to give up her career as an entertainer and singer in order to devote her full time to defendant as a companion, homemaker, housekeeper and cook. In return the defendant agreed to provide for all of her financial support and needs for the rest of her life. Claiming breach of the agreement, plaintiff sought to impress a constructive trust upon one-half of the property acquired by defendant during the course of the relationship. The trial court granted judgment for the defendant on the pleadings. The Supreme Court of California reversed and remanded, holding that plaintiff's petition stated a cause of action. The court summarized its decision as follows:

> We conclude that the judicial barriers that may stand in the way of a policy based upon the fulfillment of the reasonable expectations of the parties to a nonmarital relationship should be removed. As we have explained, the courts now hold that express agreements will be enforced unless they rest on an unlawful meretricious consideration. We add that in the absence of an express agreement, the courts may look to a variety of other remedies in order to protect the parties' lawful expectations.
>
> The courts may inquire into the conduct of the parties to determine whether that conduct demonstrates an implied contract or implied agreement of partnership or joint venture (*see Estate of Thornton* (1972) 81 Wash.2d 72, 499 P.2d 864), or some other tacit understanding between the parties. The courts may, when appropriate, employ principles of constructive trust (*see Omer v. Omer* (1974) 11 Wash. App. 386, 523 P.2d 957) or resulting trust (*see Hyman v. Hyman* (Tex. Civ. App. 1954) 275 S.W.2d 149). Finally, a nonmarital partner may recover in quantum meruit for the reasonable value of household services rendered less the reasonable value of support received if he can show that he rendered services with expectation of monetary reward. (*See Hill v. Estate of Westbrook, supra*, 39 Cal.2d 458, 462, 247 P.2d 19.)
>
> Since we have determined that plaintiff's complaint states a cause of action for breach of an express contract, and, as we have explained can be amended to state a cause of action independent of allegations of express contract, we must conclude that the trial court erred in granting defendant a judgment on the pleadings.

The Supreme Court of California specifically recognized no less than seven means of recovery for one involved in a meretricious relationship. In addition, the court included a footnote which would allow seemingly unlimited remedies. Specifically, footnote 25 provided:

> Our opinion does not preclude the evolution of additional equitable remedies to protect the expectations of the parties to a nonmarital relationship in cases in which the existing remedies prove inadequate; the suitability of such remedies may be determined in later cases in light of the factual setting in which they arise.

Following the 1976 opinion of the California Supreme Court, the case was remanded to the trial court. The trial court ordered the defendant, Lee Marvin, to pay to plaintiff, Michelle Marvin, the sum of $104,000, to be used by her primarily for economic rehabilitation; thus, rehabilitative alimony or palimony was born.

On appeal, the court held that the trial court had not based the award on any of the remedies specifically recognized by the California Supreme Court. Although argument was made that the trial court had merely applied equitable remedies as recognized in footnote 25, the court of appeals nonetheless held that:

> A court of equity admittedly has broad powers, but it may not create totally new substantive rights under the guise of doing equity. . . . [I]t is clear that no basis whatsoever, either in equity or in law, exists for the challenged rehabilitative award. It therefore must be deleted.

Marvin v. Marvin, 176 Cal. Rptr 555, 559, 122 Cal. App. 3d 871, 876 (1981); *see also* Annot., *Property Rights Arising From Relationship of Couple Cohabiting Without Marriage*, 3 A.L.R. 4th 13 (1981).

HAYWORTH
v.
WILLIAMS
116 S.W. 43
(Tex. 1909)

BROWN, JUSTICE.

Certified question from the Court of Civil Appeals of the Second district, as follows:

> The above-styled cause is now pending before us on a motion for rehearing. The opinion rendered by us on the original hearing will accompany this certificate, and is made a part of it. The members of this court are agreed upon the ground of reversal upon which the cause was originally reversed, but are not agreed as to the legal sufficiency of the evidence to support appellee Margreth's plea of limitation against the deceased Thomas Jefferson, or even to authorize the submission of such issue should the evidence be the same on another trial.

* * *

The Court of Civil Appeals has submitted three questions, which, for convenience, we formulate as follows:

First Question: Did the evidence in the record raise the issue of 10-year limitation in favor of Margreth Williams against Thomas Jefferson?

Briefly, the evidence bearing upon this question is as follows: In 1859 Thomas Jefferson, being then a married man and living in the state of Pennsylvania, entered into a marriage, in form, with Margreth Williams, who, at the time, knew that Jefferson was a married man, he having a living wife. Subsequently, Jefferson and Margreth Williams removed from Pennsylvania to the city of New Orleans, La., where they remained until 1880, when Jefferson, with Margreth and their children, removed to Cooke county, Tex., and he bought the land in controversy in this suit. The land was deeded to Jefferson for a recited cash consideration, paid at the time. In a short time after the purchase, Jefferson, with Margreth and their illegitimate children, moved upon the land, where he remained with them but a few months and then returned to New Orleans. Margreth Williams with her children remained upon the land, cultivating the same and improving it by building fences, etc., during which time she claimed the land as her own and claimed to be the wife of Thomas Jefferson. She says that she claimed the land because she was the wife of Thomas Jefferson; Margreth Williams and her children resided upon the land until this suit was brought on the 9th day of September, 1905. Thomas Jefferson returned to the place at intervals; sometimes would be gone for a number of years at a time. On the occasions of his visits he would remain with them but a very short time, when New Orleans. Thomas Jefferson brought a suit against Margreth Williams for divorce, claiming that she was his wife, but subsequently dismissed that suit. He instituted this suit for the purpose of recovering the land, and during the pendency of it he died. Appellant was appointed temporary administrator and made a party to the suit. In order for the statute of limitation of 10 years to be effective in favor of Margreth Williams, it was necessary that she should have claimed the title to the land adversely to Thomas Jefferson, in whom the title was. Her claim to the land as his wife through the deed by which title was conveyed to him was not such adverse possession as would confer a right upon her. We therefore answer that the evidence was not sufficient to raise the issue of limitation in favor of Margreth Williams.

* * *

Third Question: Is Margreth Williams, notwithstanding the invalidity of her marriage, under the facts of this case, entitled to an interest in the property because she contributed to its acquisition?

The records show that in 1880 the land in suit was conveyed by deed regularly executed to Thomas Jefferson for a recited cash consideration, acknowledged to have been paid by him at the time. Margreth Williams' right in this property is a question of fact to be submitted to the jury under proper instructions. If Margreth Williams can show that the money with which the land was purchased was acquired in whole or in part by her labor in connection with Thomas Jefferson before the time when the land was purchased, then she would be entitled to a share in the land in the proportion that her labor contributed in producing the purchase money. Nothing which she did contributing to the improvement of the property or otherwise in connection with Thomas Jefferson after the deed was made and the land paid for can affect the title. Her right must have existed in the fund which purchased the land, and no trust in favor of Margreth Williams will arise out of the dealings between her and Jefferson after the title had vested in him. *Allen v. Allen* (Tex.) 107 S. W. 528; *Kinlow v. Kinlow*, 72 Tex. 639, 10 S. W. 729.

It is not necessary that Margreth Williams should prove that she produced by her labor a part of the very money that was used in purchasing the land. If she and Thomas Jefferson were working together to a common purpose, and the proceeds of labor performed by them became the joint property of the two, then she would occupy the position that a man would have occupied in relation to Thomas Jefferson under the same circumstances; each would own the property acquired in proportion to the value of his labor contributed to the acquisition of it. In the statement of the evidence in this case by the court as it is submitted to us, there is no mention made of the financial condition of Thomas Jefferson or of Margreth Williams at the time that they united their fortunes unlawfully, nor his financial condition at the time he came to Texas. The source from which the money was derived for the purchase of the land is not made to appear. The legal title was vested in Thomas Jefferson by the deed, and, in order to participate in that, Margreth Williams must show a state of facts which made Thomas Jefferson a trustee for her benefit, and must prove such facts as will enable the jury to say whether or not she contributed anything to the purchase of the land, and, if so, the proportion of her contribution.

Notes, Comments & Questions

1. *Hayworth v. Williams* is an outstanding example of the progressive view that the courts in Texas historically have taken in cases regarding women and property rights.

2. What theories did the court in *Hayworth* advance as a means of relief for Margreth Williams?

3. In 1982, a Texas court followed *Hayworth* in resolving the claim of two parties who had been involved in an alleged lesbian relationship. *See Small v. Harper*, 638 S.W.2d 24 (Tex. App.—Houston [1st Dist.] 1982, writ ref'd n.r.e.).

HARRINGTON
v.
HARRINGTON

742 S.W.2d 722
(Tex. App.—Houston [1st Dist.] 1987, no writ)

DUGGAN, JUSTICE.

In this appeal from a divorce judgment, the appellant attacks the court-ordered division of certain real property that he claims as his separate property. The divorce decree recites:

> The Court further finds that the property situated at 2639 Talbot, Houston, Harris County, Texas, was purchased for the mutual benefit, use and ownership of both parties and accordingly, it is ORDERED that BRIAN K. HARRINGTON and M. GAY FOWLER HARRINGTON be awarded and each party is hereby awarded as tenants in common an undivided one-half interest in said property. . . ."

In two points of error, the appellant contends that the court abused its discretion in concluding that the parties owned the Talbot property as tenants in common, because (1) that finding unconstitutionally divested him of his separate property, resulting in an unjust division, and (2) there was no evidence to support a finding of oral partnership/joint venture, and the evidence establishes that the appellant owned the property as separate property for two years before the marriage.

The appellant asserts that he acquired the property two years before the marriage, that no common law marriage existed at that time, and that the credit application and title to the property were solely in his name. He argues that there is no evidence to support a finding by the trial judge that this was community property, and he has rebutted any presumption that the property was community property. Thus, he argues, the trial court unconstitutionally divested him of his separate property when it awarded a one-half interest of the Talbot property to the appellee as community property. He quotes the language of the trial judge at the end of the hearing, "Thee [sic] Court finds the Talbot Street property to be part of the community, and the parties will own it as tenants-in-common." The docket sheet shows a similar entry.

The appellee does not dispute the appellant's discussion of authorities that define the difference between separate and community property. But she asserts that these principles do not apply to this case, because the trial court did not, as the appellant contends, erroneously designate the Talbot property as community property and divide it as such. Rather, the court found that the property was purchased by the parties as tenants in common, pursuant to an oral partnership. Thus, the court merely recognized that the parties owned the property as partners before their marriage, and upon divorce, the court correctly granted the appellant his undivided one-half interest as his separate property.

At the appellant's request, the trial court made findings of fact and conclusions of law. The court found, inter alia, that the parties began to live together in December 1971; that they were ceremonially married on December 18, 1977; and that they stopped living together as husband and wife on May 30, 1985. The court found that they lived in leased residences in their joint names from 1972 until the purchase of the Talbot Street residence; that in the spring of 1975, the parties agreed to look for a home to purchase in West University Place; that they looked for prospective homes together for a period of approximately three months; that both parties agreed on the choice of the home to purchase, i.e., the Talbot Street property; and that both parties attended the closing of the sale of the Talbot Street house. The court further found that at the time of purchase, the appellee had a bachelor's degree in journalism; that the appellant had a master of business degree in finance and had taken courses in business law; and that at that time of the purchase, the appellee was terminating her employment to attend law school full time.

The court further found that at the time of the purchase of the home, the parties agreed that title to the property would be taken in the appellant's name, at appellant's suggestion, for credit purposes and convenience only, but intended the residence to be owned, used, and enjoyed jointly. The parties expended labor and money in improvements to the home and planned to use the appellee's separate property funds to remodel the home. Finally, the court found that the reason for the marriage was to have children and that the appellee became pregnant immediately after the parties married.

The trial court concluded that the parties entered into an oral partnership/joint venture to own and occupy the home located on Talbot Street jointly; that they took title to the home in appellant's name for convenience and credit purposes only; and that the parties owned the home as tenants in common.

When a judgment is rendered in writing and then signed, it becomes the official judgment of the court. *See Wood v. Griffin & Brand*, 671 S.W.2d 125, 130 (Tex. App.—Corpus Christi 1984, no writ). Recitals in a judgment or signed order of the court control over a conflicting docket entry. *See Hamilton v. Empire Gas & Fuel Co.*, 134 Tex. 377, 110 S.W.2d 561, 566 (1937); *Verret v. Verret*, 570 S.W.2d 138 (Tex. Civ. App.—Houston [1st Dist.] 1978, no writ); *Tejas Trail Property Owners Ass'n v. Holt*, 516 S.W.2d 441, 446 (Tex. Civ. App.—Fort Worth 1974, no writ).

The judgment of the court and its findings of fact and conclusions of law do not characterize the Talbot Street property as community property. We thus disagree with the appellant's basic premise in point of error one that the court erroneously divided that property as community property, and improperly divested him of his separate property. Because of this holding, the appellant's argument and authorities are inapplicable to the present case, and we overrule point of error one.

In point of error two, the appellant contends that the court erred in concluding that the parties owned the Talbot Street home as tenants in common, because there is no evidence to support a finding of oral partnership/joint venture. The appellant contends that the record establishes as a matter of law that he owned the home as his separate property for three years before the marriage.

A partnership is generally defined as an association among two or more persons to carry on as co-owners a business for profit. *See, e.g.*, TEX. REV. CIV. STAT. ANN. art. 6132b, sec. 6 (Vernon 1970). A joint venture is similar, but is generally limited to a single transaction. *C.C. Roddy, Inc. v. Carlisle*, 391 S.W.2d 765 (Tex. Civ. App.—Fort Worth 1965, writ ref'd n.r.e.). In determining whether a partnership exists between spouses or cohabitants in the purchase or ownership of property, the parties' intent is an important factor. *Negrini v. Plus Two Advertising, Inc.*, 695 S.W.2d 624, 631 (Tex. App.—Houston [1st Dist.] 1985, no writ); *see also Cluck v. Sheets*, 141 Tex. 219, 171 S.W.2d 860 (1943); *Small v. Harper*, 638 S.W.2d 24 (Tex. App.—Houston [1st Dist.] 1982, writ ref'd n.r.e.).

In reviewing a "no evidence" point of error, we consider only the evidence and inferences that tend to support the finding, and we disregard all evidence and inferences to the contrary. *King v. Bauer*, 688 S.W.2d 845, 846 (Tex. 1985); *Garza v. Alviar*, 395 S.W.2d 821, 823 (Tex. 1965). If there is any evidence of probative force to support the finding, the point must be overruled and the finding upheld. *In re King's Estate*, 150 Tex. 662, 244 S.W.2d 660 (1951).

The appellee pled that an oral partnership existed in the parties' purchase and ownership of the property, entitling her to an undivided one-half interest in the property. After making the findings of fact described above, the trial judge also reached that conclusion and entered judgment for the appellee on this question. After reviewing the record, we find that there is some evidence of probative force to support the court's findings and conclusion.

There was testimony that the parties lived together for about three years in residences leased in both their names; that they eventually decided that they wanted to live in a house together and went house-hunting together; and that they found the house that they liked after about three months. The appellee testified that she had no legal background at the time the Talbot house was purchased, and that she did not then understand the nature of separate versus community property. She testified that the appellant told her that because she was earning so little money at the time, he would apply for the loan himself and put his name on it. She agreed and had no concern that he would ever assert that the property was his alone. She testified that they always referred to the property as "our home," and that the appellant never claimed the property was his alone before the separation. They both contributed to improving the house, including painting, wall papering, remodeling, and repairs. At no time did the appellant ever indicate to her that he intended her to have no ownership interest in the house. The appellee also testified that she spent much of her separate property income on the house and on living expenses for the children, and that although she and her husband had separate bank accounts, she did not carefully segregate out her separate property income until after the separation.

Viewing only the evidence that tends to support the verdict and drawing the inferences favorable to the verdict, we find that there is some evidence to support the trial court's findings and conclusion that the parties intended to purchase and own the Talbot Street property as partners. We thus find no abuse of discretion in the trial court's judgment that that property is owned by the parties as tenants in common, with each having an undivided one-half interest as separate property.

The judgment of the trial court is affirmed.

Notes, Comments & Questions

1. The *Harrington* case presents the most typical factual situation which gives rise to a claim of property rights during a meretricious relationship; specifically, persons living together, acquiring property, and then marrying.

2. How might one avert the type of controversy that arises in *Harrington*?

C. Putative Spouse

The facts of *Davis v. Davis* are most succinctly set forth by the lower appellate court. The following excerpt is from *Davis v. Davis*, 507 S.W.2d 841 (Tex. Civ. App.—Houston [14th Dist.] 1974), and serves as an introduction to the opinion of the Texas Supreme Court.

> Charles Mason Davis originally married in 1951, and Beverly Nell Davis Lange and Lawrence Riley Davis are the children of this marriage. This first marriage was terminated by divorce in 1965. In 1966 Charles Davis married a second time. This marriage terminated in divorce in 1967, and he married Mary in the same year. Charles Delary Davis was born in 1967. After entering the third marriage, the deceased worked on off-shore oil rigs in South America, and he went to Australia in 1967 to do similar work for the Reading & Bates Offshore Drilling Company. In 1968 he was transferred to Singapore. On October 2, 1968, the deceased engaged in a Buddhist wedding ceremony with Nancy and signed a Chinese marriage contract. They lived together as husband and wife in Singapore. Sometime after this marriage ceremony, a copy of Mary's divorce petition arrived at the couple's apartment in Singapore (the divorce was never prosecuted to completion). Charles Mason Davis drowned as a result of a ship collision in the Sea of Java on December 24, 1970. Approximately one month later, Nancy Melissa Davis was born to Nancy, and Bessie Nell Davis was born to Mary.
>
> The deceased (who dies intestate) left a $50,000 life insurance policy with his estate named as beneficiary, as well as $1,399.88 in wages and a boat and motor. Nancy was appointed administratrix in Chambers County and (two weeks later) Mary was appointed administratrix in Liberty County.

Davis v. Davis, 507 S.W.2d at 842.

DAVIS
v.
DAVIS
521 S.W.2d 603
(Tex. 1975)

REAVLEY, JUSTICE.

Charles Davis was killed by shipwreck in the Sea of Java on December 24, 1970, at the age of 36 years. The Probate Court of Chambers County, where the administration of his estate is pending, is in possession of the small amount of his personal property, together with wages due from his employer, Reading & Bates Offshore Drilling Company, and the proceeds of a group accidental death insurance policy which was purchased by that employer and issued a few days prior to the death of Charles. The insurer has paid $51,031.38 into the registry of the Chambers County Court. This litigation will determine the heirship of Charles Davis and the manner of division of this property.

Charles married Mary Nell in Liberty County in 1966, and in 1967 he departed for Australia without her on an assignment with Reading & Bates. After a year or so in Australia he was in Iran briefly, and then in August of 1968 he was assigned to Singapore. On October 2, 1968, a Buddhist wedding

wedding ceremony was performed to unite Charles and Nancy, and they lived together as man and wife in Singapore from that time until his death. Approximately one month after his death, both Mary Nell and Nancy gave birth to daughters.

This controversy ensues over the status and rights of Mary Nell and Nancy, and of the daughter of each. The County Probate Court held that Nancy was the lawful widow of Charles and that both of these daughters were entitled to inherit as children of Charles. The District Court, after an appeal and de novo trial without a jury, decided that Mary Nell was the widow, that Nancy was the putative wife, but that the daughter born to Mary Nell after the death of Charles was not his child and was not entitled to inherit any portion of his estate. The Court of Civil Appeals agreed that Mary Nell was the lawful widow and that her daughter was not the child of Charles, but it held that Nancy was not the putative wife at the time of the death of Charles. 507 S.W.2d 841. The only difference between the District Court and the Court of Civil Appeals in the division of the property was in the allotment to Nancy. What did not go to Nancy, under either judgment, went one-half to Mary Nell and the remaining one-half in equal parts to the children of Charles. The District Court awarded Nancy one-half of the wages due and the insurance proceeds; the Court of Civil Appeals judgment gave her nothing. Both Courts ruled that Mary Nell's daughter was not the child of Charles, and both ruled that Nancy's daughter inherited as a child of Charles. Even though the Court of Civil Appeals held that Nancy's putative status was terminated prior to the death of Charles, that holding would not prevent the daughter from being a legitimate child of their marriage. V.A.T.S. Probate Code, § 42.

Nancy is here contending that she is the lawful widow or, at least, that she was the putative wife. Mary Nell's daughter contends that she is the legitimate child of Charles.

We hold, first, that Nancy was not the lawful widow of Charles. While it is initially presumed that Charles and Mary Nell were divorced prior to the wedding ceremony between Charles and Nancy (*Texas Employers' Insurance Ass'n v. Elder*, 155 Tex. 27, 282 S.W.2d 371, 1955; VERNON'S TEX. FAMILY CODE ANN. § 2.01, 1973), the evidence presented by Mary Nell was legally adequate to rebut that presumption. It is shown that the records in Chambers and Liberty Counties reflect no divorce between them, that the records of the State of Queensland, Australia, show no divorce during the period from September 1, 1967 to December 31, 1970, and that the records in Singapore show no divorce between them during that same period. It is not necessary in order to rebut the presumption that Mary Nell prove the nonexistence of divorce in every jurisdiction where proceedings could have been possible; it is only necessary to rule out those proceedings where Charles might reasonably have been expected to have pursued them. *Caruso v. Lucius*, 448 S.W.2d 711 (Tex. Civ. App. 1969, writ ref'd n.r.e.). The trial court was entitled to find that there had been no divorce between Charles and Mary Nell and that Mary Nell was therefore his lawful widow.

We next hold that Nancy was the putative wife of Charles. A written contract of marriage (the Chinese document and the English translation), signed by Charles and Nancy, together with her father and another witness, certifying the marriage as being solemnized on October 2, 1968, was placed in evidence. Nancy and two other witnesses testified to the full formality of the ceremony, which was held in the home of her parents with all of her family participating and with twenty persons in attendance. For more than two years thereafter, and until the date of his death, Charles and Nancy lived together as man and wife. Nancy testified that Charles told her of his previous marriage but also assured her that he was divorced and free to marry her. The evidence clearly warrants the finding that Nancy entered this relationship in good faith. The attorney for Mary Nell, however, having proved that official Singapore records show no registration of this marriage prior to the death of Charles, contends that the marriage was entirely void and of no legal effect under Singapore law. He placed in evidence photographic copies of a portion of the pages of what appears to be an official publication of the law of the Republic of Singapore. There was no pleading as to the law of Singapore, nor do these pages establish the total effect of that law as it pertains to Nancy and Charles. Even if there had been an adequate pleading and if we assume that these copies faithfully reflect some of the pages of an official publication, on this record the Texas courts cannot determine that the total law of Singapore would brand the relationship of Nancy and Charles as meretricious. *See generally*: Thomas, *Proof of Foreign Law in Texas*, 25 Sw.L.J. 554 (1971).

The Court of Civil Appeals has held that even though Nancy may have become the putative wife of Charles at the outset and continued in that relationship for two years thereafter, at a time prior to his death she was put on notice that he was not divorced from Mary Nell—where—upon her putative standing terminated. The evidence on this point turns on the following testimony by Nancy:

> Q: Now, during—well—subsequent to April 2, 1968 and before December 23, 1970, you learned, did you not, that Mary Nell Davis was trying to get a divorce from Charles Davis?
>
> A: I didn't learn nothing of that.
>
> Q: Well, you remember you (sic) asking that question on your deposition?
>
> A: You asking me whether I received—
>
> Q: No ma'am, I didn't ask you if you received it. I asked you if you learned that Mary Nell Davis was trying to get a divorce from Charles?
>
> A: I learned it.
>
> Q: Yes. A: I know it.

The interrogation on the occasion of Nancy's deposition, which was introduced at the trial by the lawyer for Nancy to show a waiver of the dead man's statute, does not throw much light on this matter except for her statements that she knew that Charles was asked to sign a paper which came in the mail at a time when she was pregnant with the child born after the death of Charles. This testimony does not establish conclusively her lack of good faith. In the first place, it is not clear when Nancy understood that Mary Nell was 'trying to get a divorce.' She appreciated the facts as of the time of the trial, but it is not clear that she did so prior to the death of Charles. And even if she knew that these were divorce papers, it does not necessarily follow that Nancy had any reason to believe that Charles had been dishonest with her and had not obtained a prior divorce from Mary Nell. Before we charge Nancy with bad faith or impose upon her a duty to investigate matters, we must take into account that she was in Singapore and not in Texas, that she knew nothing of Texas law, and that she was a 20 year old Chinese woman who had always lived in Singapore and was then expecting a child by a husband who had given her no reason to believe that he had another wife. The trial court was entitled to find in her favor; we hold that the record does not conclusively establish her lack of good faith.

As a putative wife Nancy is entitled to the same right in the property acquired during her marital relationship with Charles as if she were a lawful wife. *Lee v. Lee*, 112 Tex. 392, 247 S.W. 828 (1923); SPEER'S MARITAL RIGHTS IN TEXAS § 56 (4th ed. 1961). In her case it will be half of the wages owed by the employer at the date of his death as well as half of the proceeds from the insurance policy which was furnished by the employer as an incident of the employment.

This brings us to the question of the legitimacy of Mary Nell's daughter who was born a month after the death of Charles. We agree with the Court of Civil Appeals that impossibility of access between Charles and Mary Nell, during the time when this child might have been conceived, has not been proved unless we consider the testimony to that effect by Mary Nell herself. Whether her testimony may be considered depends on whether we apply the Rule of Lord Mansfield, so-called because it was Lord Mansfield in *Goodright v. Moss*, 98 Eng. Rep. 1257 who said in 1777 that husband and wife 'shall not be permitted to say after marriage that they had no connection and therefore that the offspring is spurious.' This rule has been applied to exclude testimony to facts that would bastardize one's own child as of the time of birth. *Esparza v. Esparza*, 382 S.W.2d 162 (Tex. Civ. App. 1964, no writ). It has even been used to exclude testimony on the ground that the effect would not be in accord with the innocence of married persons. *Burtis v. Weiser*, 195 S.W.2d 841 (Tex. Civ. App.1946, writ ref'd); *Contra*, *Gravley v. Gravley*, 353 S.W.2d 333 (Tex. Civ. App. 1962, writ dism'd).

Until the Court of Civil Appeals opinion in the present case, Texas courts have accepted Lord Mansfield's Rule as the law of this state. *Adams v. Adams*, 456 S.W.2d 222 (Tex. Civ. App. 1970, no writ); *Barnett v. Barnett*, 451 S.W.2d 939 (Tex. Civ. App. 1970, writ dism'd); *Longoria v. Longoria*, 324 S.W.2d 244 (Tex. Civ. App. 1959), *writ dism'd per curiam*, 160 Tex. 134, 327 S.W.2d 453 (1959); *Carnes v. Kay*, 210 S.W.2d 882 (Tex. Civ. App. 1948, no writ); *Gonzalez v. Gonzalez*, 177 S.W.2d 328 (Tex. Civ. App. 1943, no writ); *Moore v. Moore*, 299 S.W. 653 (Tex. Civ. App. 1927, no writ); *Pinkard v. Pinkard*, 252 S.W. 265 (Tex. Civ. App.1923, no writ). All the while there has been widespread denunciation of the Rule. WIGMORE ON EVIDENCE § 2063 (2nd ed. 1923); 1 MCCORMICK & RAY, TEXAS LAW OF EVIDENCE § 90 (2nd ed. 1956); *Note*, 6 TEX.TECH.L.REV. 231 (1974).

Rules that exclude evidence bearing directly on the truth to be determined ought not to survive without very good cause. The testimony of a spouse on the matter of non-access by the other spouse is, subject to the usual tests of credibility, clearly the best evidence of that fact. The present case is one where all of the testimony establishes beyond any reasonable doubt that Mary Nell's daughter is not the child of Charles. Then why should the courts refuse to accept the truth? And is there not a valid objection to allowing the child of another father to inherit part of this estate? Some courts have said that the Rule is required for the protection of the child. This may or may not be its consequence. It may be harmful to the interest of the child. *E.g.*, *Esparza v. Esparza*, 382 S.W.2d 162 (Tex. Civ. App. 1964, no writ); *U.S.F. & G. Co. v. Henderson*, 53 S.W.2d 811 (Tex. Civ. App. 1932, no writ).

The contention is made that this is a rule which cannot be changed by judicial decision, because it was adopted in 1840 by statute as part of the common law. Art. 1, Vernon's Ann. Civ. St. This argument is often made and sometimes accepted (*e.g.*, *Gonzalez v. Gonzalez*, 177 S.W.2d 328, Tex. Civ. App. 1943, no writ), but it misunderstands what the common law was and is. The common law of England was conformable to 'the law of Nature, the law of God, to common sense, to legal reason, justice, and humanity.' BROOM, COMMENTARIES ON THE COMMON LAW, p. 21, (4th ed. 1869). *Calvin's Case*, 7 Co. 1a, 77, Eng.Rept. 377, 391 et seq. (K.B.1608); *Forbes v. Cochrane*, 107 Eng. Rep. 450, 455, 458 et seq. (K.B.1824). Lord Mansfield proclaimed the basis of this very rule to be 'decency, morality and policy.' The system and tradition that we call the 'common law' is not a body of law which evolved within historic England or a bygone age to stand immutable ever afterward. It is the guide and governance of this Court today—in the absence of a mandate of the Constitution or statute. Learned Hand said that our common law is 'a combination of custom and its successive adaptations. The judges receive it and profess to treat it as authoritative, while they gently mould it the better to fit changed ideas.' THE SPIRIT OF LIBERTY p. 52 (1952). 'This flexibility and capacity for growth and adaptation is the peculiar boast and excellence of the common law.' *Hurtado v. California*, 110 U.S. 516, 530, 4 S.Ct. 111, 118, 28 L.Ed. 232 (1884). '(A)s life is always in flux, so the common law, which is merely life's explanation as the lawyer and the judge, law's spokesmen, are always making it, must also be.' Hutcheson, *The Common Law of the Constitution*, 15 TEX. L. REV. 317, 319 (1937).

This Court has not regarded the legislative adoption of the common law as installing all of the prior rules of English courts with statutory authority. It held that we would look to the declaration of the courts of the several states to determine the body of common law in 1840, and that this should be effectuated only so far as not inconsistent with the conditions and circumstances of the people of this state. *Grigsby v. Reib*, 105 Tex. 597, 153 S.W. 1124 (1913); *Diversion Lake Club v. Heath*, 126 Tex. 129, 86 S.W.2d 441 (1935). This Court has often rejected earlier rules of common law, including those in force in 1840. *E.g., Roberts v. Short*, 1 Tex. 373 (1846); *Mud Creek Irr., Agr. & Mfg. Co. v. Vivian*, 74 Tex. 170, 11 S.W. 1078 (1889); *Dickson v. Strickland*, 114 Tex. 176, 265 S.W. 1012 (1924); *Billings v. Atkinson*, 489 S.W.2d 858 (Tex. 1973).

It does not follow that this Court, or any court, is entitled to apply or not apply the rules of law according to preference in the individual case. Those who depend upon the law require continuity and predictability. If the administration of justice is to be effective in the trial courts, the rules must not be constantly shuffled. The appellate court must always start with the rule of precedent and either apply it faithfully or modify the rule if it is not consistent with the prevailing customs and precepts of the legal profession and of the community, giving particular attention to that portion of the community most concerned and affected by the rule.

If *Lord Mansfield's Rule* were one that had been counted upon in the planning of property rights, it should be left to the Legislature to change. That is no obstacle in this case. *The Rule* has never prevented proof of non-access of spouses for a determination of illegitimacy of a child born or conceived during wedlock. The exclusion has only applied to testimony by the spouses themselves. Proof of illegitimacy has been made more difficult, but there is no rule of law that prevents the fact from being shown if other evidence is available. Regarding blindfolds on triers of fact with disfavor, and finding no justification for perpetuating this decree by Lord Mansfield, we hold that testimony of non-access between man and woman is admissible from any witness knowledgeable of the fact.

The judgment of the Court of Civil Appeals is reversed; the judgment of the District Court is affirmed.

Questions

1. Which spouse, the legal spouse or the putative spouse, appears to receive the greater share of Charles' estate? Why?
2. Has *Lord Mansfield's Rule* recently been abrogated?
3. If so, what was the catalyst?

D. Common Law Marriage

As noted in the introduction, common law marriage is now governed by the Texas Family Code. The genesis of the common law marriage statute, since its inception in 1970, is set forth below.

§ 1.91. Proof of Informal Marriage. [Effective 1970 through Sept. 1, 1989.]

(a) In any judicial, administrative or other proceeding, the marriage of a man and woman may be proved by evidence that:

(1) A declaration of their marriage had been executed under section 1.92 of this code; or

(2) they agreed to be married, and after the agreement they lived together in this state as husband and wife and there represented to others that they were married.

(b) In the proceeding in which a marriage is to be proved under Section (a)(2) of this section, the agreement of the parties may be inferred if it is proved that they lived together as husband and wife and represented to others that they were married.

§ 1.91. Proof of Informal Marriage. [Effective Sept. 1, 1989 through Aug. 31, 1997.]

(a) In any judicial, administrative or other proceeding, the marriage of a man and woman may be proved by evidence that:

(1) A declaration of their marriage had been executed under section 1.92 of this code; or

(2) they agreed to be married, and after the agreement they lived together in this state as husband and wife and there represented to others that they were married.

(b) A proceeding in which a marriage is to be proved under this section must be commenced not later than one year after the date on which the relationship ended or not later that one year after September 1, 1989, whichever is later.

§ 2.401. Proof on Informal Marriage. [Effective Sept. 1, 1997 through Aug. 31, 2005.]

(a) In any judicial, administrative or other proceeding, the marriage of a man and woman may be proved by evidence that:

(1) A declaration of their marriage had been executed under section 1.92 of this code; or

(2) they agreed to be married, and after the agreement they lived together in this state as husband and wife and there represented to others that they were married.

(b) If a proceeding in which a marriage is to be proved as provided by subsection (a)(2) is not commenced before the second anniversary of the date on which the parties separated and ceased living together, it is rebuttably presumed that the parties did not enter into an agreement to be married.

§ 2.401. Proof on Informal Marriage.[1] [Effective Sept. 1, 2005 through present.]

(a) In a judicial, administrative, or other proceeding, the marriage of a man and woman may be proved by evidence that:

(1) a declaration of their marriage has been signed as provided by this subchapter; or

---

[1] Subsection (d) was added by the Legislature in 2005 in an attempt to stop polygamous relationships in Texas.

(2) the man and woman agreed to be married and after the agreement they lived together in this state as husband and wife and there represented to others that they were married.

(b) If a proceeding in which a marriage is to be proved as provided by Subsection (a)(2) is not commenced before the second anniversary of the date on which the parties separated and ceased living together, it is rebuttably presumed that the parties did not enter into an agreement to be married.

(c) A person under 18 years of age may not:

(1) be a party to an informal marriage; or

(2) execute a declaration of informal marriage under Section 2.402.

(d) A person may not be a party to an informal marriage or execute a declaration of an informal marriage if the person is presently married to a person who is not the other party to the informal marriage or declaration of an informal marriage, as applicable.

It was the case of *Claveria v. Claveria* that gave rise to the 1989 amendment. What is of utmost interest about the *Claveria* case is that a common law marriage is proved in the face of denials by both parties to the common law marriage. As you read the case, consider the how and why of such a result.

CLAVERIA
v.
CLAVERIA
615 S.W.2d 164
(Tex. 1981)

POPE, JUSTICE.

The question presented is whether there is some evidence, more than a scintilla, of a common-law marriage. This case arose as a probate matter in which Patricio Claveria contested the will of Otha Faye McQuaid Claveria. The probate court dismissed the contest after sustaining a plea to abate which stated that Patricio was not an interested person as defined by the Probate Code.[1] The trial court concluded that Patricio had no interest in the estate property because his ceremonial marriage to Otha Faye was void by reason of a prior undissolved common-law marriage. The court of civil appeals reversed the judgment, holding that there was no evidence of the prior common-law marriage. 597 S.W.2d 434. We hold that there was evidence of the marriage and remand the cause to the court of civil appeals to determine the factual insufficiency points.

Otha Faye died testate on March 4, 1978, leaving all of her property to her two children by a former marriage. Patricio and Otha Faye were ceremonially married in November, 1974, and he claims a community and homestead interest in the property acquired since that time. His only claim in the trial court and on appeal is that he is an interested party by reason of his marriage to Otha Faye. He has not asserted that he has an interest as a putative spouse nor because of any other right of ownership in the

---

[1] § 3. Definitions and Use of Terms When used in this Code, unless otherwise apparent from the context:

(r) "Interested persons" or "persons interested" means heirs, devisees, spouses, creditors, or any others having a property right in, or claim against, the estate being administered; and anyone interested in the welfare of a minor or incompetent ward.

property. The inference should not be drawn from this opinion, that a marriage is always essential to proof of an interest in an estate. The points that were presented in the court of civil appeals relate only to the validity of the marriage between Patricio and Otha Faye.

After Patricio's and Otha Faye's ceremonial marriage, they lived together as husband and wife until Otha Faye died on March 4, 1978. We must begin, therefore, with the presumption that their marriage was valid. TEX. FAM. CODE ANN. § 2.01.[2] The presumption that the most recent marriage is a valid one continues until one proves the impediment of a prior marriage and its continuing validity. *Texas Employers' Ins. Ass'n v. Elder*, 155 Tex. 27, 282 S.W.2d 371 (1955); *Nixon v. Wichita Land & Cattle Co.*, 84 Tex. 408, 19 S.W. 560 (1892); *Carroll v. Carroll*, 20 Tex. 731 (1858); *Lockhart v. White*, 18 Tex. 102 (1856); *Yates v. Houston*, 3 Tex. 433 (1848). *See also* Allen, *Presumption of the Validity of a Second Marriage*, 20 BAYLOR L. REV. 206 (1968); Annot., *Presumption as to Validity of Second Marriage*, 14 A.L.R.2d 7 (1950); 52 AM. JUR. 2D *Marriage* §§ 140-167 (1970).

After some evidence of a prior and continuing marriage has been introduced, the weight of such evidence must be determined by the finder of fact. *Davis v. Davis*, 521 S.W.2d 603 (Tex. 1975); *Woods v. Hardware Mut. Casualty Co.*, 141 S.W.2d 972 (Tex. Civ. App.—Austin 1940, writ ref'd). *See* O. SPEER, TEXAS FAMILY LAW §§ 1:46, 5:90 (5th ed. 1975); 38 TEX. JUR. 2D *Marriage* §§ 44-46 (1962); Note, *Evidence—Sufficiency of Evidence to Rebut Presumption of Validity of Second Marriage*, 1 BAYLOR L. REV. 203 (1948); Note, *Workman's Compensation Presumption of Validity of Second Marriage to Allow Beneficiary to Recover*, 6 BAYLOR L. REV. 242 (1954); *Allen, supra*, at 215-17; Note, *Marriage Evidence*, 33 TEXAS L. REV. 1097 (1955).

A valid common-law marriage consists of three elements: (1) an agreement presently to be husband and wife; (2) living together as husband and wife; and (3) holding each other out to the public as such. *Collora v. Navarro*, 574 S.W.2d 65 (Tex. 1978); *Humphreys v. Humphreys*, 364 S.W.2d 177 (Tex. 1963). This law has been codified in the Family Code.[3]

---

[2] Section 2.01. State Policy

In order to promote the public health and welfare and to provide the necessary records, this code prescribes detailed and specific rules to be followed in establishing the marriage relationship. However, in order to provide stability for those entering into the marriage relationship in good faith and to provide legitimacy and security for the children of the relationship, it is the policy of this state to preserve and uphold each marriage against claims of invalidity unless strong reasons exist for holding it void or voidable. Therefore, every marriage entered into in this state is considered valid unless it is expressly made void by this chapter or unless it is expressly made voidable by this chapter and is annulled as provided by this chapter. When two or more marriages of a person to different spouses are alleged, the most recent marriage is presumed to be valid as against each marriage that precedes it until one who asserts the validity of a prior marriage proves its validity.

[3] § 1.91. Proof of Certain Informal Marriages

(a) In any judicial, administrative, or other proceeding, the marriage of a man and woman may be proved by evidence that:

(1) a declaration of their marriage has been executed under Section 1.92 of this code; or

(2) they agreed to be married, and after the agreement they lived together in this state as husband and wife and there represented to others that they were married.

(b) In any proceeding in which a marriage is to be proved under Subsection (a) (2) of this section, the agreement of the parties to marry may be inferred if it is proved that they lived together as husband and wife and represented to others that they were married.

Marriage, whether ceremonial or common-law, is proved by the same character of evidence necessary to establish any other fact. *Stafford v. Stafford*, 41 Tex. 111 (1874); O. SPEER, TEXAS FAMILY LAW § 5:89 (5th ed. 1975). Thus, proof of common-law marriage may be shown by the conduct of the parties, or by such circumstances as their addressing each other as husband and wife, acknowledging their children as legitimate, joining in conveyances as spouses, and occupying the same dwelling place. *Bonds v. Foster*, 36 Tex. 68 (1871); O. SPEER, *supra* § 5:89; 38 TEX. JUR. 2D *Marriage* § 42 (1962).

In reviewing the record on the "no evidence" point, this court must consider only the evidence and reasonable inferences from the evidence, which, viewed in their most favorable light, supports the trial court's judgment, and must disregard all the evidence and inferences to the contrary. *Bounds v. Caudle*, 560 S.W.2d 925 (Tex. 1977); *In re King's Estate*, 150 Tex. 662, 244 S.W.2d 660 (1952); Calvert, *"No Evidence" and "Insufficient Evidence" Points of Error*, 38 TEXAS L. REV. 361 (1960).

When two persons not living together occasionally refer to each other as a spouse, these isolated references have been held, in some instances as a matter of law, not to have established a common-law marriage. *See Ex parte Threet*, 160 Tex. 482, 333 S.W.2d 361 (1960); *Drummond v. Benson*, 133 S.W.2d 154 (Tex. Civ. App.—San Antonio 1939, writ ref'd). Further, the act of one of the parties to an alleged common-law marriage in celebrating a ceremonial marriage with another person without having first obtained a divorce, tends to discredit the first relationship and to show that it was not valid. *Higgins v. Higgins*, 246 S.W.2d 271 (Tex. Civ. App.—Austin 1952, no writ); *Nye v. State*, 77 Tex. Cr. R. 389, 179 S.W. 100 (1915). Still, the circumstances of each case must be determined based upon its own facts. *Collora v. Navarro, supra* at 70; O. SPEER, *supra* at § 2:3; Annot., *Judicial Declaration of Validity or Existence of Common-Law Marriage*, 92 A.L.R.2d 1102 (1963).

The record discloses several items of direct evidence which establish the fact of a prior undissolved common-law marriage between Patricio Claveria and Carolina Mendoza Claveria. Both Patricio and Carolina testified at the trial; and while they both denied they had ever been married, they both also produced evidence of their common-law marriage. Some of their denials appear from the record to express the belief that the questions concerned a ceremonial marriage. In any event, there was evidence about the elements of a common-law marriage.

Patricio and Carolina both testified that they had lived together in 1967 in San Antonio for some two and a half months. A deposition that Patricio gave in a worker's compensation case in 1972, two years before his ceremonial marriage to Otha Faye, is also in the record. In that earlier court proceeding, he testified that he was married, and that his wife's name was Carolina. He testified that his wife was not employed, that she was a housewife. When asked if she had been a housewife for several years, he answered "About 16 years married." The evidence was not retracted nor otherwise explained.

Patricio and Carolina lived together in a house and lot in San Antonio that they purchased through the Veterans Administration. The grantees in the deed were Patricio Claveria and wife, Carolina Claveria. They executed a deed of trust to secure the payment of the purchase price in the amount of five thousand three hundred and fifty dollars, and they did so as husband and wife. The acknowledgment to the deed of trust was taken as husband and wife and there was a recital, in the quaint custom of the times, that Carolina was examined "privily and apart from her husband" when the document was explained to her. Carolina admitted that she had signed the document and had done so as a wife. This is direct evidence of the common-law marriage. *Red Eagle v. Cannon*, 201 Okl. 511, 208 P.2d 557 (1949).

Carolina testified that she had lived all her life in San Antonio. Patricio testified that he had lived only in San Antonio and Dallas. Certificates from the district clerks of Bexar and Dallas Counties show that there has been no divorce or annulment decree from either of those counties which involved Patricio or Carolina. *Caruso v. Lucius*, 448 S.W.2d 711 (Tex. Civ. App.—Austin 1970, writ ref'd n.r.e.); *Woods v. Hardware Mut. Casualty Co., supra* ; TEX. REV. CIV. STAT. ANN. art. 3731a § 5.

We have in this case direct evidence by Patricio that he and Carolina were husband and wife and that they lived together as such. We have the recorded deed in which both Patricio and Carolina represented to the Veterans Administration that they were married. We have the notarial acknowledgment by both of them that they were husband and wife. We have Patricio's and Carolina's solemn acknowledgment which was filed in the public records. There is, therefore, some evidence that the two lived together and held themselves out to the public as husband and wife. From the nature of that proof, their agreement to be married may also be inferred. TEX. FAM. CODE ANN. § 1.91(b).

The law recognizes a common-law marriage, but a common-law divorce is unknown to Texas law. The marriage arises out of the state of facts; but once the common-law status exists, it, like any other marriage, may be terminated only by death or a court decree. Once the marriage exists, the spouses' subsequent denials of the marriage, if disbelieved, do not undo the marriage. *De Beque v. Ligon*, 292 S.W. 157 (Tex. Comm'n App. 1927, holding approved).

Patricio also urges that the common-law marriage between him and Carolina was impossible, because Carolina was already married in 1967 when the common-law marriage arose, having ceremonial married Luis Ochoa in 1945, some twenty-two years earlier. Carolina so testified, but the trial court, in this instance, determined that there was no existing impediment at the time of Carolina's and Patricio's common-law marriage. An alleged spouse's testimony is not conclusive. *Oldham v. McIver*, 49 Tex. 556 (1878); O. SPEER, *supra* at § 1:35. The trial court could also rely upon the unrebutted presumption of the validity of the 1967 common-law marriage of Patricio and Carolina, TEX. FAM. CODE ANN. § 2.01. *Texas Employers' Ins. Ass'n v. Elder, supra*. Carolina testified in this case that she and Luis Ochoa lived together two months, separated, and that she had not seen him since 1945. The long absence of Luis Ochoa for twenty-two years before the 1967 common-law marriage, without any proof that he was still alive at that time, gave rise to the presumption of his death. TEX. REV. CIV. STAT. ANN. art. 5541*; Zurich Gen. Accident & Liability Ins. Co. v. Hill*, 251 S.W.2d 948 (Tex. Civ. App.—Texarkana 1952, writ ref'd n.r.e.); *see also* O. SPEER, *supra* at § 1:45; 1 R. RAY TEXAS LAW OF EVIDENCE § 83 (TEXAS PRACTICE 3D ED. 1980).

The court of civil appeals was in error in its holding that there was no evidence of an undissolved common-law marriage between Patricio and Carolina and in rendering judgment that no such marriage arose. We reverse the judgment of the court of civil appeals and remand the cause to that court to pass upon the factual insufficiency and the great weight of the evidence points that were presented to that court but not decided.

Notes, Comments & Questions

1. How did Otha Faye's children raise, prove, and succeed on the issue of common law marriage when both Patricio Claveria and Carolina Mendoza denied the existence of any such marriage?

2. The court made the statement, "common law divorce is unknown to Texas law." What is the practical effect of this statement?

3. Why did not Patricio's assertions, that Carolina's previous ceremonial marriage to Luis Ochoa was not dissolved by divorce, affect his marriage to Carolina?

4. Although common law marriage claims are unusual, they are not non-existent. The case of *Winfield v. Renfro*, 821 S.W.2d 640 (Tex. App.—Houston [1st Dist.] 1991, writ denied) provides insight into the type of evidence that might be presented in support of a common law marriage claim. Although the jury in *Winfield* did find a common law marriage, the case was reversed due to a defective jury charge. Specifically, the jury was questioned if the parties had represented to others that they were married—not that they ***there*** [in Texas] had represented to others that they were married. In light of the evidence that the couple had held out in other locales, the charge as given was deemed harmful and required reversal.

5. The following case is based upon the common law marriage statute that was effective between 1989 and 1995. Nonetheless, the holding of the Texas Supreme Court regarding evidentiary matters is applicable to the statute as it exists today.

RUSSELL
v.
RUSSELL
865 S.W.2d 929
(Tex. 1993)

HIGHTOWER, JUSTICE.

In these consolidated cases, we consider the effect of a 1989 amendment to section 1.91 of the Texas Family Code, entitled "Proof of Certain Informal Marriages," concerning evidence of an agreement to be "informally" married. In each case, the trial court found that an informal marriage existed. The courts of appeal, however, reached conflicting results. In *Russell v. Russell*, the Ninth Court of Appeals affirmed the existence of an informal marriage although it reversed and remanded the case to the trial court to determine when the informal marriage began. 838 S.W.2d 909. In *Weaber v. Lorensen*, the Fifth Court of Appeals held that there was no evidence that the parties agreed to be married, reversed the trial court's judgment and rendered judgment that a valid marriage did not exist. 840 S.W.2d 644. We hold that under section 1.91 of the Family Code, as amended in 1989, an agreement to be married may be established by direct or circumstantial evidence. For the reasons explained herein, we reverse the judgments in *Russell v. Russell* and *Weaber v. Lorensen* and remand those causes to the Ninth and Fifth Courts of Appeal for further proceedings consistent with this opinion.

In *Russell v. Russell*, James and Margaret Russell were ceremonially married in Texas in 1981. In the period before the ceremonial marriage—1964 to 1981—the parties cohabited intermittently and had five children, all supported and acknowledged by James. Margaret alleged that she and James were married on or about April 17, 1964. The trial court, sitting without a jury, found that there was a common law marriage which began March 22, 1972. The court of appeals, interpreting the 1989 amendment to section 1.91(b) of the Texas Family Code, affirmed the existence of an informal marriage although it reversed and remanded the case to the trial court to determine when the informal marriage began. Concerning the 1989 amendment, the court of appeals stated "that regardless of the amendment of sec. 1.91(b), an agreement to be married may be inferred from direct or circumstantial evidence which preponderates that the parties lived together in the State of Texas and did, in Texas, represent to others that they were married." 838 S.W.2d at 913.

In *Lorensen v. Weaber*, Vivian Weaber and Ronald Lorensen began cohabitating on or about February 6, 1982. Lorensen is a pipefitter and his job required frequent moves. In January 1991, the couple separated and Weaber filed suit for divorce in February 1991. The trial court sitting without a jury found that the parties were married, without formalities, on February 16, 1982. The court of appeals held that there was no evidence that the parties agreed to be married, reversed the trial court's judgment and rendered judgment that a valid marriage did not exist.

I.

Weaber and *Russell* argue that under the 1989 amendment to section 1.91 of the Texas Family Code, an agreement to be "informally" married may be established by direct or circumstantial evidence. We agree.

Common law marriages have been recognized in Texas since 1847. *Tarpley v. Poage's Adm'r*, 2 Tex. 139, 149 (1847). From this beginning, Texas has rejected the necessity of ritual formalities to establish the marriage relationship. However, Texas' recognition of common law marriages has been described as "grudging." Kathryn S. Vaughn, *Comment, The Recent Changes to the Texas Informal Marriage Statute: Limitation or Abolition of Common-Law Marriage?*, 28 HOUS. L. REV. 1131, 1150 (1991) (hereinafter Recent Changes). *See Texas Employers' Insurance Ass'n v. Elder*, 274 S.W.2d 144, 147 (Tex. Civ. App.—Fort Worth 1954), *aff'd. on other grounds*, 155 Tex 27, 282 S.W.2d 371 (1955) ("[t]he law does not favor, but merely tolerates . . . common-law marriages. . . .").

Despite strong pressure to do so, in 1970 the Texas legislature refused to abolish common law marriages when it enacted Title 1 of the Family Code. *Recent Changes*, 28 HOUS. L. REV. at 1150; Woodrow M. Bonesio, *Comment, Marriage and Divorce Under the Texas Family Code*, 8 HOUS. L. REV. 100, 107 (1970). As enacted, section 1.91 stated:

> (a) In any judicial, administrative, or other proceeding, the marriage of a man and woman may be proved by evidence that:
>
> (1) a declaration of their marriage has been executed under Section 1.92 of this code;
>
> or
>
> (2) they agreed to be married, and after the agreement they lived together in this state as husband and wife and there represented to others that they were married.
>
> (b) In any proceeding in which a marriage is to be proved under Subsection (a)(2) of this section, the agreement of the parties to marry may be inferred if it is proved that they lived together as husband and wife and represented to others that they were married.

In sections 1.91(a)(1) and 1.92-95, the legislature added a provision allowing a couple to file a declaration of informal marriage with the county clerk. Although such a declaration constitutes prima facie proof of the parties informal marriage, the parties need not make the declaration to have a valid common law marriage.

In 1989, some members of the legislature attempted to abolish common law marriage. *See* Tex. H.B. 588, 71st Leg., R.S. (1989); *Recent Changes*, 28 HOUS. L. REV. at 1151. The effort failed, but the legislature amended section 1.91(b) to make proof of common law marriages more difficult in Texas. *See* Act of June 14, 1989, 71st Leg., R.S., ch. 369, s 9, 1989 Tex. Gen. Laws 1458, 1459 (codified at TEX. FAM. CODE ANN. § 1.91(b)). Section 1.91 now states:

> (a) In any judicial, administrative, or other proceeding, the marriage of a man and woman may be proved by evidence that:
>
> (1) a declaration of their marriage has been executed under Section 1.92 of this code;
>
> or
>
> (2) they agreed to be married, and after the agreement they lived together in this state as husband and wife and there represented to others that they were married.
>
> (b) *A proceeding in which a marriage is to be proved under this section must be commenced not later than one year after the date on which the relationship ended or not later than one year after September 1, 1989, whichever is later.*

(Emphasis added). Prior to the 1989 amendment, section 1.91 permitted courts to infer or imply the couple's marriage agreement from evidence which established cohabitation and public representation. *See Estate of Claveria v. Claveria*, 615 S.W.2d 164, 166 (Tex. 1981); *Howard v. Howard*, 459 S.W.2d 901, 903-04 (Tex. Civ. App.—Houston [1st Dist.] 1970, no writ).

II.

For suits filed on or after September 1, 1989, the existence of a common law marriage in Texas requires proof of each of the three elements of an informal marriage set forth in section 1.91(a)(2) no later than one year after the relationship ended. The elements are (1) an agreement to be married, (2) after the agreement, the couple lived together in this state as husband and wife, and (3) the couple represented to others that they were married. The 1989 amendment defines the burden of proof for informal marriages and eliminates the ability of courts to simply infer an agreement to marry from evidence that they lived together as husband and wife and represented to others that they were married. One commentator described the effect of the 1989 amendment as follows:

> Rather than abolishing the doctrine of informal marriage as had been proposed on numerous occasions in the past, the legislature tightened the rules for reliance on the doctrine by repealing the provision that allowed a court to infer an agreement to be married from proof of cohabitation and holding-out. This amendment, therefore, raises the question of how the elements of agreement may hereafter be proved.
>
> In the future one of two basic fact patterns will develop depending on whether both parties are living. If both parties to the alleged informal marriage are alive, one of them will commonly deny the agreement. When the other party to the alleged informal union offers direct evidence of an express agreement to be presently married, the trier of fact will be required to weigh the testimony in the context of other evidence of the relationship. If one of the parties is dead, the survivor will be required to meet the limitation imposed by Evidence Rule 601(b) by providing corroboration of an alleged transaction with the decedent. Under most circum-

> stances the proponent of the marriage will have an easier case in the latter instance unless there is convincing evidence that the decedent denied the existence of the agreement. If evidence of an express agreement to marry is not offered, the fact-finder will have to treat the facts of cohabitation and holding-out as circumstantial evidence of the agreement in order to find a tacit agreement to be married. This process is, however, virtually identical to the prior process of inference. But by repealing the provision authorizing the fact-finder to infer an agreement from proof of two elements of an informal marriage, the legislature has not excluded a finding of a tacit agreement to be married. In making such a finding, however, it seems that the evidence of holding-out must be more convincing than before the 1989 agreement.
>
> In a society in which non-marital cohabitation for extended periods of time is far more common than it once was, the fact-finder will have to weigh the evidence of a tacit agreement more carefully than in the past. As the statute now stands, an occasional uncontradicted reference to a cohabitant as "my wife" or "my husband" or "mine" will not prove a tacit agreement to be married without corroboration. Such a reference by the contestant of the union will, of course, be stronger evidence of an agreement than such a statement by the proponent. The non-social context of the contestant's reference to the proponent as his "wife" or her "husband" will also receive closer scrutiny. If the statement is made in a self-serving context, the fact-finder may be expected to disbelieve the truth of the statement. A forthright assertion of marriage with the consequence of liability (as when an alleged spouse seeks admission of the other to a hospital) may, on the other hand be far more probative of a tacit agreement to be married.

Joseph W. McKnight, *Family Law: Husband and Wife*, 44 SW. L.J. 1, 2-3 (1990) (footnotes omitted). *But see Recent Changes*, 28 HOUS. L. REV. at 1151 (The 1989 amendment "effectively abolished common-law marriage in Texas.").

"Any ultimate fact may be proved by circumstantial evidence." *State v. $11,014.00*, 820 S.W.2d 783, 785 (Tex. 1991); *Farley v. M M Cattle Co.*, 529 S.W.2d 751, 755 (Tex. 1975). "A fact is established by circumstantial evidence when the fact may be fairly and reasonable inferred from other facts proved in the case." *Dallas County Flood Control v. Cross*, 815 S.W.2d 271, 279-80 (Tex. App.—Dallas 1991, writ denied); *Walter Baxter Seed Co. v. Rivera*, 677 S.W.2d 241, 244 (Tex. App.—Corpus Christi 1984, writ ref'd n.r.e.). Proof of an agreement to be married may be made by circumstantial evidence or conduct of the parties. "[I]n order to establish a common law marriage as a matter of law, it is not necessary to establish each element by direct proof, as each element may be established by circumstantial, as well as direct, evidence." *Tompkins v. State*, 774 S.W.2d 195, 208-09 (Tex. Crim. App. 1987), *cert. granted*, 486 U.S. 1053 (1988), *judgmt aff'd*, 490 U.S.754 (1989). "Marriage, whether ceremonial or common-law, although the character of the evidence might be different, is proved as any other fact might be proved." *Tompkins*, 774 S.W.2d at 209. *See Estate of Claveria v. Claveria*, 615 S.W.2d at 166. Proof of cohabitation and representations to others that the couple are married may constitute circumstantial evidence of an agreement to be married. However, the circumstances of each case must be determined based upon its own facts.[1] We conclude that section 1.91, as amended in 1989, does not require direct evidence of an agreement to be married in order

[1] One of the dissent's primary complaints appears to be that this court has failed to provide a "bright line" test concerning the evidence which does and does not constitute circumstantial evidence of an agreement to be married. However, as in most evidentiary matters subject to legal and factual sufficiency review, each case must be evaluated based upon its own facts and no "bright line" test may be applied.

to establish a common law marriage, but that the agreement may be proved by circumstantial evidence.[2]

III.

Although an agreement to be married may be proved by circumstantial evidence, it is subject to legal and factual sufficiency review on appeal to the court of appeals and legal sufficiency review on appeal to this court. *See, e.g., Estate of Claveria v. Claveria*, 615 S.W.2d at 165-67; *Winfield v. Renfro*, 821 S.W.2d 640, 645-46 (Tex. App.—Houston [1st Dist.] 1991, writ denied). However, there must be legally and/or factually sufficient evidence concerning each element of a common law marriage. A finding that there is legally and/or factually sufficient evidence of cohabitation and public representation will not necessarily constitute legally and/or factually sufficient evidence of an agreement to be married. There must also be legally and/or factually sufficient evidence of an agreement to be married which may include direct and/or circumstantial evidence.

In *Russell v. Russell*, the court of appeals considered whether there was legally or factually sufficient evidence to support the trial court's finding that a common law marriage existed.[3] The court held "that the evidence which we have recited clearly shows cohabitation and holding out, and is, standing alone, sufficient for our overruling . . . [James Russell's] no evidence point." 838 S.W.2d at 915-16. The court further held that the "evidence of holding out to be husband and wife, brought about at the insistence of . . . [James Russell], was evidence of sufficient weight for the trial court to 'infer' an agreement to be married." 838 S.W.2d at 917.[4] Assuming that legally or factually sufficient evidence of cohabitation and public representation existed, the court erroneously failed to consider whether there was legally or factually sufficient evidence of an agreement to be married and erroneously inferred an agreement to be married.

In *Lorensen v. Weaber*, the court of appeals considered whether there was legally sufficient evidence to support the trial court's finding that a common law marriage existed between the parties. The court of appeals held that there was no evidence that the parties agreed to be married, stating that "[w]hile it is unclear how specific the evidence of an agreement to be married must be after the statutory provision allowing inference of an agreement was repealed, it is clear that such evidence does not exist in this case." 840 S.W.2d at 647. However, it is unclear whether the court considered any circumstantial evidence when it determined that there was legally insufficient evidence of an agreement to be married.[5]

In *Russell v. Russell*, the court erroneously failed to consider whether there was legally or factually sufficient evidence of an agreement to be married and erroneously inferred an agreement to be

[2] The dissent erroneously argues at great length that this court is ignoring the 1989 amendment to section 1.91 and is interpreting the amendment as having no effect on the proof required by section 1.91. Before the 1989 amendment, the existence of an agreement to be married was effectively presumed upon proof of cohabitation and public representation. However, after the 1989 amendment, the existence of an agreement to be married must be proved either by direct or circumstantial evidence. In addition, the dissent is attempting to further amend section 1.91 to add the requirement that an agreement to be married must be proved by direct evidence and may not be proved by circumstantial evidence.

[3] Contrary to the dissent's assertion, this court has not misread the court of appeals' opinion in *Russell v. Russell*.

[4] The court did not consider evidence of cohabitation because "the evidence clearly supports far more than a mere passive cohabital relationship between . . . [James and Margaret Russell]. The evidence shows that . . . [they] lived together for long periods of time." 838 S.W.2d at 916.

[5] We express no opinion concerning the legal sufficiency of the evidence in either cause.

married. Before this court, Russell asserts that the court of appeals misconstrued the effect of the 1989 amendment to section 1.91 and erred in finding that there was legally and factually sufficient evidence to support the trial court's finding that a common law marriage existed. In *Weaber v. Lorensen*, it is unclear whether the court considered any circumstantial evidence when it determined that there was legally insufficient evidence of an agreement to be married. Before this court, Weaber asserts only that the court of appeals misconstrued the effect of the 1989 amendment to section 1.91. Since Russell will probably involve factual sufficiency questions and Weaber did not assert a legal sufficiency challenge in this court, the entire causes are remanded to their respective courts of appeal.[6]

Accordingly, we reverse the judgments in *Russell v. Russell* and *Weaber v. Lorensen* and remand those causes to the Ninth and Fifth Courts of Appeal for further proceedings consistent with this opinion.

PHILLIPS, C.J., and DOGGETT, CORNYN, GAMMAGE, ENOCH and SPECTOR, JJ., join in the opinion and the judgment.

GONZALEZ, J. joined by HECHT, J., dissents.

GONZALEZ, J., dissenting.

In 1989 the legislature repealed the Family Code provision which provided that an agreement to enter into a common-law marriage could be inferred if one of the parties proved that they lived together as husband and wife and represented to others that they were married. Today, the Court ignores this amendment and in effect holds that a fact finder can look to cohabitation and holding-out as circumstantial evidence of an agreement to be married. This approach is identical to the process of inferences that the legislature repealed. Under our constitution, the legislature is authorized to make this change and we should not disregard it. To do so violates the separation of powers doctrine. I would affirm the judgment of the court of appeals in *Lorensen v. Weaber*[1] and reverse and render in *Russell v. Russell*.[2]

---

[6] The dissent also erroneously implies that Flores v. Flores, 847 S.W.2d 648 (Tex.App.—Waco 1993, writ denied) is inconsistent with the court's opinion. *Flores* recognized "that the plain meaning of the statute [section 1.91], as it now exists, allows proof of an agreement to be married by direct evidence, by a combination of direct and circumstantial evidence, or by wholly circumstantial evidence." *Id.* at 652. The court then proceeded to review the record to determine whether there was legally sufficient evidence of an agreement to be married. The court concluded that the evidence was legally insufficient to support an agreement to be married. *Id.*

[1] 840 S.W.2d 644. Vivian Weaber and Ronald Lorensen began a relationship in 1982. They lived together in Illinois, Iowa, New Mexico, and California before moving to Texas in 1990. During their relationship, they rented property under the names of Vivian and Ronald Lorensen, and used the name Lorensen for certain utility bills. Mr. Lorensen filed as a "single" person on his tax returns, but claimed Ms. Weaber as his dependent, designating her as a "friend" on each return. There were no children born to them. The trial court held that a common-law marriage existed, but the court of appeals reversed and rendered on the basis that there was no evidence of an agreement to be married.

[2] 838 S.W.2d 909. Believing that death was imminent, James and Margaret Russell were ceremonially married in Texas in 1981. Prior to this ceremony, from 1964 to 1981, not only did Mr. Russell father five children with Mrs. Russell, but during this same period, he fathered and supported other children by other women. The underlying issue in this case is whether the parties entered into a common-law marriage before the ceremonial marriage so that Mrs. Russell can share the assets that Mr. Russell acquired before 1981. The trial court found a common-law marriage and the court of appeals agreed, but it reversed and remanded because the evidence was factually insufficient to support the finding of the date of inception of the marriage.

I. The Amendment

The 1989 amendment to section 1.91 of the Texas Family Code requires direct evidence of an agreement to be married in order to establish an informal marriage. Prior to the amendment, subsection (b) of section 1.91 allowed courts to infer the existence of an agreement to be married as long as the elements of cohabitation and holding-out were proved. Subsection (b) was repealed by the 1989 amendment and replaced with a statute of limitations.[3]

As acknowledged by the Court, by amending the statute, the legislature intended that each of the elements listed in subsection (a)(2), an agreement to be married, cohabitation, and holding-out, must be proved. It is no longer permissible simply to infer the existence of an agreement to be married from proof of cohabitation and holding-out. While I agree that each element must now be proved, I do not agree with the Court that an agreement to be married can be proved by circumstantial evidence.

The court of appeals in Russell held that the requisite agreement could be "inferred from direct or circumstantial evidence which preponderates that the parties lived together in the State of Texas and did, in Texas, represent to others that they were married." *Russell* at 913. According to the *Russell* court, circumstantial evidence of an agreement to be married would include having lived together, having held oneself out as being married, and any evidence which would go, directly or indirectly, to prove cohabitation or holding oneself out as married. *Id.* The *Russell* court held that allowing the agreement to be proved by circumstantial evidence would be necessary, since an express agreement would be rare and difficult to prove. *Id.* Today, the Court supports this result, citing the proposition that "[a]ny ultimate fact may be proved by circumstantial evidence." *State v. $11,014.00*, 820 S.W.2d 783, 785 (Tex. 1991).

---

[3] Prior to the 1989 amendment, section 1.91 of the Texas Family Code, entitled "Proof of Certain Informal Marriages" read:

> (a) In any judicial, administrative, or other proceeding, the marriage of a man and woman may be proved by evidence that:
>
> * * *
>
> (2) they agreed to be married, and after the agreement they lived together in this state as husband and wife and they represented to others that they were married.
>
> (b) In any proceeding in which a marriage is to be proved under Subsection (a)(2) of this section, the agreement of the parties to marry may be inferred if it is proved that they lived together as husband and wife and represented to others that they were married.
>
> Act of May 14, 1969, 61st Leg., R.S., ch. 888, § 1.91, 1969 Tex. Gen. Laws 2707, 2717, *amended* by Act of June 14, 1989, 71st Leg., R.S., ch. 369, § 9, 1989 Tex. Gen. Laws 1458, 1459. (emphasis added).

The section was amended in 1989 to read:

> (a) In any judicial, administrative, or other proceeding, the marriage of a man and a woman may be proved by evidence that:
>
> * * *
>
> (2) they agreed to be married, and after the agreement they lived together in this state as husband and wife and they represented to others that they were married.
>
> (b) A proceeding in which a marriage is to be proved under this section must be commenced not later than one year after the date on which the relationship ended or not later than one year after September 1, 1989, whichever is later.

TEX.FAM.CODEANN. § 1.91 (Vernon 1993).

Both the *Russell* court of appeals and this Court ignore the intent of the legislature in amending the statute. Under their interpretation of the statute, the amendment did nothing more than add a statute of limitations; it did not affect the proof necessary to show the existence of an agreement to be married. Under this interpretation, the legislature accomplished nothing by repealing the old subsection (b). This interpretation violates a fundamental tenet that the legislature is never presumed to do a useless act. *Hunter v. Fort Worth Capital Corp.*, 620 S.W.2d 547, 551 (Tex. 1981); *Cameron v. Terrell & Garrett, Inc.*, 618 S.W.2d 535, 540 (Tex. 1981) (holding that every word or phrase excluded from a statute is presumed to be excluded for a purpose).

In my opinion, the only conceivable reason to omit the language regarding permissible inferences in the new version of the statute is that the legislature sought to inform Texans that these inferences are no longer permissible—that an agreement to be married must be proved by direct evidence. The state of the law prior to the 1989 amendment allowed the existence of an agreement to be married to be proved by proving cohabitation and holding-out. By deleting the provision which permitted this inference to be made, the legislature indicated a clear intent not to allow such inferences in the future. *See Allen Sales and Servicecenter, Inc. v. Ryan*, 525 S.W.2d 863, 866 (Tex. 1975) (holding that statutes should be construed consistent with existing law unless a contrary intent is clear); *Transportation Ins. Co. v. Maksyn*, 580 S.W.2d 334, 338 (Tex. 1979) (holding that deletion of a provision indicates a legislative intent to reject the proposition stated in the deleted language).

II. The Effect

The legislature retained the requirement of an agreement to be married in order to prove an informal marriage. However, Section 1.91 no longer permits the existence of an agreement to be inferred upon proof of the other required elements, cohabitation and holding oneself out as married. It follows that an agreement to be married cannot be proved circumstantially using the evidence that proves cohabitation and holding-out, because this requires making an inference that the legislature no longer permits. To suggest, as the Court does today, that the legislature meant that proof of cohabitation and holding-out no longer gives rise to an inference of an agreement to be married, but now is circumstantial evidence of that agreement, flies in the face of reason. In both cases, the evidence used to prove cohabitation and holding-out gives rise to the inference of the existence of an agreement. Are we to believe that the legislature wants Texas courts to continue as before, and simply call it something different?

In my opinion, an agreement to be married must be proved directly in order to find an informal marriage under Texas Family Code Section 1.91. This direct proof can be written or oral. When one party claims that an agreement existed and the other denies it, the issue becomes one of credibility for the fact finder to resolve. This approach probably will make it more difficult to prove an informal marriage, but I believe that is what the legislature intended when it amended the statute. If, as in *Weaber*, no party is willing to state, under oath, that there was an explicit agreement to be married, an agreement should not be inferred. This rule will prevent "accidental" marriages, in which cohabitation and holding-out were used, under the old act, to bind a party who never intended to enter into a marriage, formal or informal. The intent to enter into a marriage must be affirmatively shown, which is, I believe, what the legislature intended.

* * *

Notes, Comments & Questions

1. The Texas Supreme Court's holding in *Russell*, that circumstantial evidence may be used to establish a common law marriage, is still good law equally applicable to the current statute.

2. Judge Paul Brown, of the Federal District Court for the Eastern District of Texas, addressed the constitutionality of the 1989 common law marriage statute in the case of *White v. State Farm Mutual Insurance Co.*, 907 F.Supp. 1012 (E. Dist. Tex. 1995). Finding the statute unconstitutional, Judge Brown reasoned thus:

* * *

A. Existence of a Common Law Marriage

> Texas has long recognized that persons who desire to live as husband and wife need not necessarily formalize their desires by engaging in a ceremonial wedding. *See, e.g.*, *Grigsby v. Reib*, 105 Tex. 597, 153 S.W. 1124 (1913). Section 1.91(a)(2) of the Texas Family Code is the codification of the common law's requirements for an informal or "common law" marriage. In order to prove a common law marriage in Texas, a party must satisfy three elements: (1) that the couple agreed to be married; (2) after their agreement, the couple lived together in Texas as husband and wife; and (3) the couple represented to others that they were married. TEX. FAM. CODE § 1.91(a)(2). The existence of a common law marriage is a question of fact, with the burden of proof being on the party seeking to establish the marriage. *Weaver v. State*, 855 S.W.2d 116 (Tex. App.—Houston [14th Dist.] 1993, no pet.).
>
> State Farm argues that White has not shown that a marriage relationship existed between she and McLaughlin under "any method recognized by the laws of the State of Texas." State Farm further contends that even if a common law marriage existed between White and McLaughlin, that it terminated at least three years prior to the accident in November 1993. White responds by showing that the investigation by State Farm either establishes or, at the very least, causes a fact issue to arise regarding her common law marriage. Moreover, White maintains, and correctly so, that State Farm's argument regarding termination of the alleged common law marriage is erroneous under Texas law.
>
> The Court finds that State Farm has failed to carry its burden regarding the nonexistence of White's common law marriage. Moreover, contrary to State Farm's position, once a common law relationship exists, it is treated with the same dignity as a ceremonial marriage and may only terminate by death, divorce, or annulment. *Claveria v. Claveria*, 615 S.W.2d 164, 165, 167 (Tex. 1981). There is no "common law divorce" in Texas and the mere passage of time and ceasing of cohabitation will not serve to terminate a common law marriage once it is in existence. *See id.*; *Home Indemnity Company v. Edwards*, 488 S.W.2d 561, 563 (Tex. Civ. App.—Ft. Worth 1972, writ ref'd n.r.e.). Accordingly, the Court is of the opinion that fact issues remain as to the existence of a common law marriage between White and McLaughlin and that State Farm's motion should be denied on this issue.

B. Limitations under TEX. FAM. CODE *§ 1.91(b)*

> State Farm next argues that even if a common law marriage existed between White and McLaughlin, White is barred from asserting its existence by the one year statute of limitations

contained in TEX. FAM. CODE § 1.91(b).[2] White contends that she complied with the statute by bringing this action within one year of McLaughlin's death. Alternatively, White maintains that section 1.91(b) violates the Due Process and Equal Protection clauses of the United States and Texas Constitutions, as well as the Open Courts provision of the Texas Constitution.

1. "Proceedings" under section 1.91(b)

Section 1.91(b) of the Texas Family Code provides as follows:

> A proceeding in which a marriage is to be proved under this section must be commenced not later than one year after the date on which the relationship ended or not later than one year after September 1, 1989, whichever is later.

In deciding the issue before it, the Court must first determine if the instant proceeding qualifies as a "proceeding in which a marriage is to be proved." From reviewing the case law, it is apparent that Texas' courts do not limit the applicability of section 1.91(b) to only domestic relations cases. Proceedings under section 1.91(b) have run the gamut from probate to criminal cases. *Villages of Greenbriar v. Torres*, 874 S.W.2d 259, 265 (Tex. App.—Houston [1st Dist.] 1994, writ denied) (stating that limitations of section 1.91(b) in probate proceeding is a bar to proof of heirship); *Riley v. State*, 849 S.W.2d 901, 902-03 (Tex. App.—Austin 1993, pet. ref'd) (holding that section 1.91(b) limitation barred the state from proving a previous common law marriage by the defendant for purposes of invalidating a subsequent marriage and a claim of spousal privilege). Thus, the Court concludes that this case qualifies as a "proceeding" under section 1.91(b).

2. Commencing of the Limitations Period

The Court now focuses on White's argument that she has complied with section 1.91(b) by commencing this suit within a year of McLaughlin's death. White contends that because a common law marriage may end only by divorce, death, or annulment, that the statute of limitations does not begin to run until one of those events occurs. Texas courts have squarely addressed the issue of when the statute begins to run and have answered the question adverse to White's contention.

White's argument turns on the issue of when the common law relationship ends. The Court notes that the Legislature chose to craft the statute using the ending of the "relationship" and not the marriage as the beginning of the running of limitations. Texas courts have consistently interpreted the ending of the relationship to be the date on which cohabitation ceases. *Georgiades v. Di Ferrante*, 871 S.W.2d 878, 881 (Tex. App.—Houston [14th Dist.] 1994, writ denied); *Riley*, 849 S.W.2d at 902. Had White and McLaughlin been cohabitating at the time of his death, then the statute would have run from November 1993. However, the evidence clearly shows, and White has admitted, that they ceased cohabitation during 1989,

---

[2] The Court is aware that section 1.91(b) of the Texas Family Code has recently been amended. The version under consideration in this case was enacted in 1989. The 1995 amendment deletes the absolute bar contained in the 1989 version. TEX.FAM.CODE § 1.91(b) (Vernon Supp. 1996). However, because the Legislature specifically provided that the 1995 amendment not be applied retroactively, unless otherwise noted, any reference to section 1.91(b) is a reference to the 1989 version. TEX.FAM.CODE § 1.91(b) historical and statutory notes (Vernon Supp. 1996) [Act of May 29, 1995, 74th Leg., R.S., ch. 891, § 1, 1995].

some four years prior to the filing of this action. Therefore, the Court finds the statute began running in 1989, and this suit was filed after the statute had run.

3. Constitutional Challenges

White maintains that section 1.91(b) violates the Equal Protection and Due Process clauses of the United States and Texas Constitutions and the Open Courts provision of the Texas Constitution. Because the Court is of the opinion that section 1.91(b) is unconstitutional as a violation of the equal protection clause, the Court chooses not to address White's other arguments.

White presents two very distinct classes to the Court: ceremoniously married persons and informally or common law married persons. White contends section 1.91(b) is unconstitutional because it carves out special treatment for ceremoniously married couples.

Under Equal Protection analysis of a government's classification, a court must apply differing standards of review depending upon the right or classification involved. If a classification causes a disadvantage to a "suspect class" or threatens a "fundamental right," then the standard of strict scrutiny is applied. *Plyler v. Doe*, 457 U.S. 202, 217, 102 S.Ct. 2382, 2394-95, 72 L.Ed.2d 786 (1982). If a classification, however, does not involve a suspect class or fundamental right, then the standard of rationality is applied. *Vance v. Bradley*, 440 U.S. 93, 95-97, 99 S.Ct. 939, 942-43, 59 L.Ed.2d 171 (1979).

White does not argue that 1.91(b) disadvantages a suspect class. Moreover, the Court is unable to find the protection of a marital estate or community property rights impinges upon a "fundamental right." *See Dannelley v. Almond*, 827 S.W.2d 582, 585 (Tex. App.—Houston [14th Dist.] 1992, no writ). Accordingly, the Court must decide whether the one year prove-up period contained in section 1.91(b) is reasonably related to a legitimate governmental interest.

In 1989, certain members of the Texas Legislature made a significant effort to abolish common law marriages in Texas. *Russell v. Russell*, 865 S.W.2d 929, 931 (Tex. 1993). The effort failed and section 1.91(b) was the resulting compromise. *Id.* Texas' interest in requiring "timely" proof of informal marriages is to facilitate divorce and probate proceedings by limiting the staleness of evidence presented at those proceedings. *See Dannelley*, 827 S.W.2d at 586. The Court has concluded that the goal of 1.91(b) was to prevent Texas courts from having to rely on stale evidence in proceedings to adjudicate property interests. Section 1.91(b)'s purpose is not solely to have formal proof of informal marriages. The Court finds that a state's efforts at limiting the use of stale evidence in court proceedings is a legitimate governmental interest.

The Court must now determine whether the one-year limitation is rationally related to the accomplishment of the state's interest. In answering this question, the Court chooses to rely on the Supreme Court's decision in *Mills*. In *Mills*, the Court examined the constitutionality of a similar one-year limitation in Texas on proving up the legitimacy of a child. *Mills v. Habluetzel*, 456 U.S. 91, 102 S.Ct. 1549, 71 L.Ed.2d 770 (1982). The Court held that the statute was unconstitutional as a violation of equal protection. *Id.* at 102-03, 102 S.Ct. at 1556. In reaching its decision, the Court found that given the importance of the rights involved and the social, as well as legal, impediments to a legitimacy determination, the one- year time period was too short. *Id.* at 98-03, 102 S.Ct. at 1554-56.

In applying the rationale of *Mills* to White's case, this Court finds that section 1.91(b) is unconstitutional. First, the Court is concerned by the severity of the bar section 1.91(b) presents. By way of example, assume a couple has been common law married for a lengthy time period and has filed no formal declaration of marriage. During their marriage, the couple has acquired a house, automobiles, investments, financial accounts, and retirement benefits. The couple has also had two children during their period of marriage. Should this couple cease cohabitating and neither file for a divorce or a declaratory judgment seeking to prove the existence of the marriage within one year, under section 1.91(b), all community property rights are extinguished. Moreover, the legitimacy of the children of the marriage is also now placed at issue, because section 1.91(b) puts the couple in a position as if they were never married. *Dannelley*, 827 S.W.2d at 585.

Assuming the same scenario as detailed above for a ceremoniously married couple and the result is the opposite. A formally married couple can separate and cease cohabitating for any number of years, even until death, and Texas law protects the ceremoniously married couple's community property interests, as well as protecting the legitimacy of any children of the marriage. Texas law does this despite the fact that proof of the origin of property and any contributions made by each spouse's separate estate may grow incredibly stale.

Moreover, like the Court in *Mills*, this Court is concerned by the impediments that exist to filing a proceeding under section 1.91(b) in the one-year time period. As discussed above, the statute begins running when cohabitation ceases. If a common law couple ceases cohabitation, but is attempting to reconcile, the statute may run without there ever being any intent that the marriage cease.

The Court finds that section 1.91(b) is not rationally related to Texas' interest in aiding in the conduct of divorce and probate proceedings. The Court recognizes that the Legislature has the power to limit proof of common law marriages, however, the one-year limitation is too short a time period. Moreover, the same concerns of staleness exist in sorting out the property in a formal marriage, yet the law does not require those spouses to take action or forfeit these very significant marital rights and interests. The state's interest is not rationally furthered by the one-year limitation. Therefore, section 1.91(b) is unconstitutional as a violation of the Equal Protection clause of the United States Constitution. State Farm's motion for summary judgment on the basis of section 1.91(b) should be denied.

* * *

3. A portion of the prior code section which governed common law marriages, as discussed in *White v. State Farm Mutual Automobile Insurance Company*, provided as follows:

   Section 1.91(b) of the Texas Family Code provides as follows:

   > A proceeding in which a marriage is to be proved under this section must be commenced not later than one year after the date on which the relationship ended or not later than one year after September 1, 1989, whichever is later.

   When does a relationship end?

4. Is the current code section any more explicit?

5. Having read the excerpt from *White v. State Farm Mutual Automobile Insurance Company*, do you think that the current common law marriage statute is constitutional?

6. What is the rationale behind the continued recognition of common law marriages?

7. In 1998, the Texas Supreme Court, in a consolidation of two cases, *Shepard v. Ledford*, 962 S.W.2d 28 (Tex. 1998), was considered the statute of limitations imposed by the 1989 version of the Texas common law marriage statute. The limitations being that "[a] proceeding in which a marriage is to be proved under this section must be commenced not later than one year after the date on which the relationship ended or not later than one year after September 1, 1989, whichever is later."

The Texas Supreme Court held as follows:

* * *

IV. Conclusion

A. Shepard v. Ledford

> While we affirm the court of appeals' judgement in this case, we disapprove of the court of appeals' determination that Family Code section 1.91(b) conflicts with MLIIA section 10.01 Section 1.91(b) is a time limit [1 year] for bringing a proceeding to prove the requisite elements of a common-law marriage. However, because the parties stipulated to the Landlords' common-law marriage, Mrs. Ledford had standing to bring a wrongful death claim without meeting section 1.91(b)'s requirements. Furthermore, Mrs. Ledford, as Mr. Ledford's sole heir, also has standing to assert his survival action.

* * *

B. Transamerican v. Fuentes

> Mrs. Fuentes had no standing to file a wrongful death claim because she did not file a proceeding to prove the existence of a common-law marriage within [1 year] section 1.91(b)'s time limit. Therefore, she is barred from maintaining her wrongful death claim against Transamerican. [limitations 2 years] Accordingly, we reverse the court of appeals' judgment and render judgment that Mrs. Fuentes take nothing.

Shepard v. Ledford, 962 S.W.2d at 35.

8. Does the current statute do away with any such limitations problems; i.e. when the common law marriage statute of limitation is shorter than the tort statute of limitation?

Chapter 8

Homestead

A. The Texas Constitution

The starting point for the study of Texas homestead law is Article XVI of the Texas Constitution. Three sections of Article XVI deal with homestead. Section 50 establishes exemptions of the homestead from liability for most debts and also establishes restrictions upon homestead conveyance. Section 51 defines homestead in terms of acreage; in the past such was defined in terms of acreage or value. Section 52 creates the so-called survivorship or probate homestead.

---

1. TEX. CONST. art. XVI, § 50

§ 50. Homestead; Protection from Forced Sale; Mortgages, Trusts Deeds and Liens.

(a) The homestead of a family, or of a single adult person, shall be, and is hereby protected from forced sale, for the payment of all debts except for:

(1) the purchase money thereof, or a part of such purchase money;

(2) the taxes due thereon;

(3) an owelty of partition imposed against the entirety of the property by a court order or by a written agreement of the parties to the partition, including a debt of one spouse in favor of the other spouse resulting from a division or an award of a family homestead in a divorce proceeding;

(4) the refinance of a lien against a homestead, including a federal tax lien resulting from the tax debt of both spouses, if the homestead is a family homestead, or from the tax debt of the owner;

(5) work and material used in constructing new improvements thereon, if contracted for in writing, or work and material used to repair or renovate existing improvements thereon if:

(A) the work and material are contracted for in writing, with the consent of both spouses, in the case of a family homestead, given in the same manner as is required in making a sale and conveyance of the homestead;

(B) the contract for the work and material is not executed by the owner or the owner's spouse before the fifth day after the owner makes written application for any extension of credit for the work and material, unless the work and material are necessary to complete immediate repairs to conditions on the homestead property that materially affect the health or safety of the owner or person residing in the homestead and the owner of the homestead acknowledges such in writing;

(C) the contract for the work and material expressly provides that the owner may rescind the contract without penalty or charge within three days after the execution of the contract by all parties, unless the work and material are necessary to complete immediate repairs to conditions on the homestead property that materially affect the health or safety of the owner or person residing in the homestead and the owner of the homestead acknowledges such in writing; and

(D) the contract for the work and material is executed by the owner and the owner's spouse only at the office of a third-party lender making an extension of credit for the work and material, an attorney at law, or a title company;

(6) an extension of credit that:

(A) is secured by a voluntary lien on the homestead created under a written agreement with the consent of each owner and each owner's spouse;

(B) is of a principal amount that when added to the aggregate total of the outstanding principal balances of all other indebtedness secured by valid encumbrances of record against the homestead does not exceed 80 percent of the fair market value of the homestead on the date the extension of credit is made;

(C) is without recourse for personal liability against each owner and the spouse of each owner, unless the owner or spouse obtained the extension of credit by actual fraud;

(D) is secured by a lien that may be foreclosed upon only by a court order;

(E) does not require the owner or the owner's spouse to pay, in addition to any interest, fees to any person that are necessary to originate, evaluate, maintain, record, insure, or service the extension of credit that exceed, in the aggregate, three percent of the original principal amount of the extension of credit;

(F) is not a form of open-end account that may be debited from time to time or under which credit may be extended from time to time unless the open-end account is a home equity line of credit;

(G) is payable in advance without penalty or other charge;

(H) is not secured by any additional real or personal property other than the homestead;

(I) is not secured by homestead property that on the date of closing is designated for agricultural use as provided by statutes governing property tax, unless such homestead property is used primarily for the production of milk;

(J) may not be accelerated because of a decrease in the market value of the homestead or because of the owner's default under other indebtedness not secured by a prior valid encumbrance against the homestead;

(K) is the only debt secured by the homestead at the time the extension of credit is made unless the other debt was made for a purpose described by Subsections (a)(1)-(a)(5) or Subsection (a)(8) of this section;

(L) is scheduled to be repaid:

(i) in substantially equal successive periodic installments, not more often than every 14 days and not less often than monthly, beginning no later than two months from the date the extension of credit is made, each of which equals or exceeds the amount of accrued interest as of the date of the scheduled installment; or

(ii) if the extension of credit is a home equity line of credit, in periodic payments described under Subsection (t)(8) of this section;

(M) is closed not before:

(i) the 12th day after the later of the date that the owner of the homestead submits a loan application to the lender for the extension of credit or the date that the lender provides the owner a copy of the notice prescribed by Subsection (g) of this section;

(ii) one business day after the date that the owner of the homestead receives a copy of the loan application if not previously provided and a final itemized disclosure of the actual fees, points, interest, costs, and charges that will be charged at closing. If a bona fide emergency or another good cause exists and the lender obtains the written consent of the owner, the lender may provide the documentation to the owner or the lender may modify previously provided documentation on the date of closing; and

(iii) the first anniversary of the closing date of any other extension of credit described by Subsection (a)(6) of this section secured by the same homestead property, except a refinance described by Paragraph (Q)(x)(f) of this subdivision, unless the owner on oath requests an earlier closing due to a state of emergency that:

(a) has been declared by the president of the United States or the governor as provided by law; and

(b) applies to the area where the homestead is located;

(N) is closed only at the office of the lender, an attorney at law, or a title company;

(O) permits a lender to contract for and receive any fixed or variable rate of interest authorized under statute;

(P) is made by one of the following that has not been found by a federal regulatory agency to have engaged in the practice of refusing to make loans because the applicants for the loans reside or the property proposed to secure the loans is located in a certain area:

(i) a bank, savings and loan association, savings bank, or credit union doing business under the laws of this state or the United States;

(ii) a federally chartered lending instrumentality or a person approved as a mortgagee by the United States government to make federally insured loans;

(iii) a person licensed to make regulated loans, as provided by statute of this state;

(iv) a person who sold the homestead property to the current owner and who provided all or part of the financing for the purchase;

(v) a person who is related to the homestead property owner within the second degree of affinity or consanguinity; or

(vi) a person regulated by this state as a mortgage broker; and

(Q) is made on the condition that:

(i) the owner of the homestead is not required to apply the proceeds of the extension of credit to repay another debt except debt secured by the homestead or debt to another lender;

(ii) the owner of the homestead not assign wages as security for the extension of credit;

(iii) the owner of the homestead not sign any instrument in which blanks relating to substantive terms of agreement are left to be filled in;

(iv) the owner of the homestead not sign a confession of judgment or power of attorney to the lender or to a third person to confess judgment or to appear for the owner in a judicial proceeding;

(v) at the time the extension of credit is made, the owner of the homestead shall receive a copy of the final loan application and all executed documents signed by the owner at closing related to the extension of credit;

(vi) the security instruments securing the extension of credit contain a disclosure that the extension of credit is the type of credit defined by Section 50(a)(6), Article XVI, Texas Constitution;

(vii) within a reasonable time after termination and full payment of the extension of credit, the lender cancel and return the promissory note to the owner of the homestead and give the owner, in recordable form, a release of the lien securing the extension of credit or a copy of an endorsement and assignment of the lien to a lender that is refinancing the extension of credit;

(viii) the owner of the homestead and any spouse of the owner may, within three days after the extension of credit is made, rescind the extension of credit without penalty or charge;

(ix) the owner of the homestead and the lender sign a written acknowledgment as to the fair market value of the homestead property on the date the extension of credit is made;

(x) except as provided by Subparagraph (xi) of this paragraph, the lender or any holder of the note for the extension of credit shall forfeit all principal and interest of the extension of credit if the lender or holder fails to comply with the lender's or holder's obligations under the extension of credit and fails to correct the failure to comply not later than the 60th day after the date the lender or holder is notified by the borrower of the lender's failure to comply by:

(a) paying to the owner an amount equal to any overcharge paid by the owner under or related to the extension of credit if the owner has paid an amount that exceeds an amount stated in the applicable Paragraph (E), (G), or (O) of this subdivision;

(b) sending the owner a written acknowledgement that the lien is valid only in the amount that the extension of credit does not exceed the percentage described by Paragraph (B) of this subdivision, if applicable, or is not secured by property described under Paragraph (H) or (I) of this subdivision, if applicable;

(c) sending the owner a written notice modifying any other amount, percentage, term, or other provision prohibited by this section to a permitted amount, percentage, term, or other provision and adjusting the account of the borrower to ensure that the borrower is not required to pay more than an amount permitted by this section and is not subject to any other term or provision prohibited by this section;

(d) delivering the required documents to the borrower if the lender fails to comply with Subparagraph (v) of this paragraph or obtaining the appropriate signatures if the lender fails to comply with Subparagraph (ix) of this paragraph;

(e) sending the owner a written acknowledgement, if the failure to comply is prohibited by Paragraph (K) of this subdivision, that the accrual of interest and all of the owner's obligations under the extension of credit are abated while any prior lien prohibited under Paragraph (K) remains secured by the homestead; or

(f) if the failure to comply cannot be cured under Subparagraphs (x)(a)-(e) of this paragraph, curing the failure to comply by a refund or credit to the owner of $1,000 and offering the owner the right to refinance the extension of credit with the lender or holder for the remaining term of the loan at no cost to the owner on the same terms, including interest, as the original extension of credit with any modifications necessary to comply with this section or on terms on which the owner and the lender or holder otherwise agree that comply with this section; and

(xi) the lender or any holder of the note for the extension of credit shall forfeit all principal and interest of the extension of credit if the extension of credit is made by a person other than a person described under Paragraph (P) of this subdivision or if the lien was not created under a written agreement with the consent of each owner and each owner's spouse, unless each owner and each owner's spouse who did not initially consent subsequently consents;

(7) a reverse mortgage; or

(8) the conversion and refinance of a personal property lien secured by a manufactured home to a lien on real property, including the refinance of the purchase price of the manufactured home, the cost of installing the manufactured home on the real property, and the refinance of the purchase price of the real property.

(b) An owner or claimant of the property claimed as homestead may not sell or abandon the homestead without the consent of each owner and the spouse of each owner, given in such manner as may be prescribed by law.

(c) No mortgage, trust deed, or other lien on the homestead shall ever be valid unless it secures a debt described by this section, whether such mortgage, trust deed, or other lien, shall have been created by the owner alone, or together with his or her spouse, in case the owner is married. All pretended sales of the homestead involving any condition of defeasance shall be void.

(d) A purchaser or lender for value without actual knowledge may conclusively rely on an affidavit that designates other property as the homestead of the affiant and that states that the property to be conveyed or encumbered is not the homestead of the affiant.

(e) A refinance of debt secured by a homestead and described by any subsection under Subsections (a)(1)-(a)(5) that includes the advance of additional funds may not be secured by a valid lien against the homestead unless:

(1) the refinance of the debt is an extension of credit described by Subsection (a)(6) of this section; or

(2) the advance of all the additional funds is for reasonable costs necessary to refinance such debt or for a purpose described by Subsection (a)(2), (a)(3), or (a)(5) of this section.

(f) A refinance of debt secured by the homestead, any portion of which is an extension of credit described by Subsection (a)(6) of this section, may not be secured by a valid lien against the homestead unless the refinance of the debt is an extension of credit described by Subsection (a)(6) or (a)(7) of this section.

(g) An extension of credit described by Subsection (a)(6) of this section may be secured by a valid lien against homestead property if the extension of credit is not closed before the 12th day after the lender provides the owner with the following written notice on a separate instrument:

"NOTICE CONCERNING EXTENSIONS OF CREDIT DEFINED BY SECTION 50(a)(6), ARTICLE XVI, TEXAS CONSTITUTION:

"SECTION 50(a)(6), ARTICLE XVI, OF THE TEXAS CONSTITUTION ALLOWS CERTAIN LOANS TO BE SECURED AGAINST THE EQUITY IN YOUR HOME. SUCH LOANS ARE COMMONLY KNOWN AS EQUITY LOANS. IF YOU DO NOT REPAY THE LOAN OR IF YOU FAIL TO MEET THE TERMS OF THE LOAN, THE LENDER MAY FORECLOSE AND SELL YOUR HOME. THE CONSTITUTION PROVIDES THAT:

"(A) THE LOAN MUST BE VOLUNTARILY CREATED WITH THE CONSENT OF EACH OWNER OF YOUR HOME AND EACH OWNER'S SPOUSE;

"(B) THE PRINCIPAL LOAN AMOUNT AT THE TIME THE LOAN IS MADE MUST NOT EXCEED AN AMOUNT THAT, WHEN ADDED TO THE PRINCIPAL BALANCES OF ALL OTHER LIENS AGAINST YOUR HOME, IS MORE THAN 80 PERCENT OF THE FAIR MARKET VALUE OF YOUR HOME;

"(C) THE LOAN MUST BE WITHOUT RECOURSE FOR PERSONAL LIABILITY AGAINST YOU AND YOUR SPOUSE UNLESS YOU OR YOUR SPOUSE OBTAINED THIS EXTENSION OF CREDIT BY ACTUAL FRAUD;

"(D) THE LIEN SECURING THE LOAN MAY BE FORECLOSED UPON ONLY WITH A COURT ORDER;

"(E) FEES AND CHARGES TO MAKE THE LOAN MAY NOT EXCEED 3 PERCENT OF THE LOAN AMOUNT;

"(F) THE LOAN MAY NOT BE AN OPEN-END ACCOUNT THAT MAY BE DEBITED FROM TIME TO TIME OR UNDER WHICH CREDIT MAY BE EXTENDED FROM TIME TO TIME UNLESS IT IS A HOME EQUITY LINE OF CREDIT;

"(G) YOU MAY PREPAY THE LOAN WITHOUT PENALTY OR CHARGE;

"(H) NO ADDITIONAL COLLATERAL MAY BE SECURITY FOR THE LOAN;

"(I) THE LOAN MAY NOT BE SECURED BY HOMESTEAD PROPERTY THAT IS DESIGNATED FOR AGRICULTURAL USE AS OF THE DATE OF CLOSING, UNLESS THE AGRICULTURAL HOMESTEAD PROPERTY IS USED PRIMARILY FOR THE PRODUCTION OF MILK;

"(J) YOU ARE NOT REQUIRED TO REPAY THE LOAN EARLIER THAN AGREED SOLELY BECAUSE THE FAIR MARKET VALUE OF YOUR HOME DECREASES OR BECAUSE YOU DEFAULT ON ANOTHER LOAN THAT IS NOT SECURED BY YOUR HOME;

"(K) ONLY ONE LOAN DESCRIBED BY SECTION 50(a)(6), ARTICLE XVI, OF THE TEXAS CONSTITUTION MAY BE SECURED WITH YOUR HOME AT ANY GIVEN TIME;

"(L) THE LOAN MUST BE SCHEDULED TO BE REPAID IN PAYMENTS THAT EQUAL OR EXCEED THE AMOUNT OF ACCRUED INTEREST FOR EACH PAYMENT PERIOD;

"(M) THE LOAN MAY NOT CLOSE BEFORE 12 DAYS AFTER YOU SUBMIT A LOAN APPLICATION TO THE LENDER OR BEFORE 12 DAYS AFTER YOU RECEIVE THIS NOTICE, WHICHEVER DATE IS LATER; AND MAY NOT WITHOUT YOUR CONSENT CLOSE BEFORE ONE BUSINESS DAY AFTER THE DATE ON WHICH YOU RECEIVE A COPY OF YOUR LOAN APPLICATION IF NOT PREVIOUSLY PROVIDED AND A FINAL ITEMIZED DISCLOSURE OF THE ACTUAL FEES, POINTS, INTEREST, COSTS, AND CHARGES THAT WILL BE CHARGED AT CLOSING; AND IF YOUR HOME WAS SECURITY FOR THE SAME TYPE OF LOAN WITHIN THE PAST YEAR, A NEW LOAN SECURED BY THE SAME PROPERTY MAY NOT CLOSE BEFORE ONE YEAR HAS PASSED FROM THE CLOSING DATE OF THE OTHER LOAN, UNLESS ON OATH YOU REQUEST AN EARLIER CLOSING DUE TO A DECLARED STATE OF EMERGENCY;

"(N) THE LOAN MAY CLOSE ONLY AT THE OFFICE OF THE LENDER, TITLE COMPANY, OR AN ATTORNEY AT LAW;

"(O) THE LENDER MAY CHARGE ANY FIXED OR VARIABLE RATE OF INTEREST AUTHORIZED BY STATUTE;

"(P) ONLY A LAWFULLY AUTHORIZED LENDER MAY MAKE LOANS DESCRIBED BY SECTION 50(a)(6), ARTICLE XVI, OF THE TEXAS CONSTITUTION;

"(Q) LOANS DESCRIBED BY SECTION 50(a)(6), ARTICLE XVI, OF THE TEXAS CONSTITUTION MUST:

"(1) NOT REQUIRE YOU TO APPLY THE PROCEEDS TO ANOTHER

DEBT EXCEPT A DEBT THAT IS SECURED BY YOUR HOME OR OWED TO ANOTHER LENDER;

"(2) NOT REQUIRE THAT YOU ASSIGN WAGES AS SECURITY;

"(3) NOT REQUIRE THAT YOU EXECUTE INSTRUMENTS WHICH HAVE BLANKS FOR SUBSTANTIVE TERMS OF AGREEMENT LEFT TO BE FILLED IN;

"(4) NOT REQUIRE THAT YOU SIGN A CONFESSION OF JUDGMENT OR POWER OF ATTORNEY TO ANOTHER PERSON TO CONFESS JUDGMENT OR APPEAR IN A LEGAL PROCEEDING ON YOUR BEHALF;

"(5) PROVIDE THAT YOU RECEIVE A COPY OF YOUR FINAL LOAN APPLICATION AND ALL EXECUTED DOCUMENTS YOU SIGN AT CLOSING;

"(6) PROVIDE THAT THE SECURITY INSTRUMENTS CONTAIN A DISCLOSURE THAT THIS LOAN IS A LOAN DEFINED BY SECTION 50(a)(6), ARTICLE XVI, OF THE TEXAS CONSTITUTION;

"(7) PROVIDE THAT WHEN THE LOAN IS PAID IN FULL, THE LENDER WILL SIGN AND GIVE YOU A RELEASE OF LIEN OR AN ASSIGNMENT OF THE LIEN, WHICHEVER IS APPROPRIATE;

"(8) PROVIDE THAT YOU MAY, WITHIN 3 DAYS AFTER CLOSING, RESCIND THE LOAN WITHOUT PENALTY OR CHARGE;

"(9) PROVIDE THAT YOU AND THE LENDER ACKNOWLEDGE THE FAIR MARKET VALUE OF YOUR HOME ON THE DATE THE LOAN CLOSES; AND

"(10) PROVIDE THAT THE LENDER WILL FORFEIT ALL PRINCIPAL AND INTEREST IF THE LENDER FAILS TO COMPLY WITH THE LENDER'S OBLIGATIONS UNLESS THE LENDER CURES THE FAILURE TO COMPLY AS PROVIDED BY SECTION 50(a)(6)(Q)(x), ARTICLE XVI, OF THE TEXAS CONSTITUTION; AND

"(R) IF THE LOAN IS A HOME EQUITY LINE OF CREDIT:

"(1) YOU MAY REQUEST ADVANCES, REPAY MONEY, AND REBORROW MONEY UNDER THE LINE OF CREDIT;

"(2) EACH ADVANCE UNDER THE LINE OF CREDIT MUST BE IN AN AMOUNT OF AT LEAST $4,000;

"(3) YOU MAY NOT USE A CREDIT CARD, DEBIT CARD, OR SIMILAR DEVICE, OR PREPRINTED CHECK THAT YOU DID NOT SOLICIT, TO OBTAIN ADVANCES UNDER THE LINE OF CREDIT;

"(4) ANY FEES THE LENDER CHARGES MAY BE CHARGED AND COLLECTED ONLY AT THE TIME THE LINE OF CREDIT IS ESTABLISHED AND THE LENDER MAY NOT CHARGE A FEE IN CONNECTION WITH ANY ADVANCE;

"(5) THE MAXIMUM PRINCIPAL AMOUNT THAT MAY BE EXTENDED, WHEN ADDED TO ALL OTHER DEBTS SECURED BY YOUR HOME, MAY NOT EXCEED 80 PERCENT OF THE FAIR MARKET VALUE OF YOUR HOME ON THE DATE THE LINE OF CREDIT IS ESTABLISHED;

"(6) IF THE PRINCIPAL BALANCE UNDER THE LINE OF CREDIT AT ANY TIME EXCEEDS 50 PERCENT OF THE FAIR MARKET VALUE OF YOUR HOME, AS DETERMINED ON THE DATE THE LINE OF CREDIT IS ESTABLISHED, YOU MAY NOT CONTINUE TO REQUEST ADVANCES

UNDER THE LINE OF CREDIT UNTIL THE BALANCE IS LESS THAN 50 PERCENT OF THE FAIR MARKET VALUE; AND

"(7) THE LENDER MAY NOT UNILATERALLY AMEND THE TERMS OF THE LINE OF CREDIT.

"THIS NOTICE IS ONLY A SUMMARY OF YOUR RIGHTS UNDER THE TEXAS CONSTITUTION. YOUR RIGHTS ARE GOVERNED BY SECTION 50, ARTICLE XVI, OF THE TEXAS CONSTITUTION, AND NOT BY THIS NOTICE."

If the discussions with the borrower are conducted primarily in a language other than English, the lender shall, before closing, provide an additional copy of the notice translated into the written language in which the discussions were conducted.

(h) A lender or assignee for value may conclusively rely on the written acknowledgment as to the fair market value of the homestead property made in accordance with Subsection (a)(6)(Q)(ix) of this section if:

(1) the value acknowledged to is the value estimate in an appraisal or evaluation prepared in accordance with a state or federal requirement applicable to an extension of credit under Subsection (a)(6); and

(2) the lender or assignee does not have actual knowledge at the time of the payment of value or advance of funds by the lender or assignee that the fair market value stated in the written acknowledgment was incorrect.

(i) This subsection shall not affect or impair any right of the borrower to recover damages from the lender or assignee under applicable law for wrongful foreclosure. A purchaser for value without actual knowledge may conclusively presume that a lien securing an extension of credit described by Subsection (a)(6) of this section was a valid lien securing the extension of credit with homestead property if:

(1) the security instruments securing the extension of credit contain a disclosure that the extension of credit secured by the lien was the type of credit defined by Section 50(a)(6), Article XVI, Texas Constitution;

(2) the purchaser acquires the title to the property pursuant to or after the foreclosure of the voluntary lien; and

(3) the purchaser is not the lender or assignee under the extension of credit.

(j) Subsection (a)(6) and Subsections (e)-(i) of this section are not severable, and none of those provisions would have been enacted without the others. If any of those provisions are held to be preempted by the laws of the United States, all of those provisions are invalid. This subsection shall not apply to any lien or extension of credit made after January 1, 1998, and before the date any provision under Subsection (a)(6) or Subsections (e)-(i) is held to be preempted.

(k) "Reverse mortgage" means an extension of credit:

(1) that is secured by a voluntary lien on homestead property created by a written agreement with the consent of each owner and each owner's spouse;

(2) that is made to a person who is or whose spouse is 62 years or older;

(3) that is made without recourse for personal liability against each owner and the spouse of each owner;

(4) under which advances are provided to a borrower based on the equity in a borrower's homestead;

(5) that does not permit the lender to reduce the amount or number of advances because of an adjustment in the interest rate if periodic advances are to be made;

(6) that requires no payment of principal or interest until:

(A) all borrowers have died;

(B) the homestead property securing the loan is sold or otherwise transferred;

(C) all borrowers cease occupying the homestead property for a period of longer than 12 consecutive months without prior written approval from the lender; or

(D) the borrower:

(i) defaults on an obligation specified in the loan documents to repair and maintain, pay taxes and assessments on, or insure the homestead property;

(ii) commits actual fraud in connection with the loan; or

(iii) fails to maintain the priority of the lender's lien on the homestead property, after the lender gives notice to the borrower, by promptly discharging any lien that has priority or may obtain priority over the lender's lien within 10 days after the date the borrower receives the notice, unless the borrower:

(a) agrees in writing to the payment of the obligation secured by the lien in a manner acceptable to the lender;

(b) contests in good faith the lien by, or defends against enforcement of the lien in, legal proceedings so as to prevent the enforcement of the lien or forfeiture of any part of the homestead property; or

(c) secures from the holder of the lien an agreement satisfactory to the lender subordinating the lien to all amounts secured by the lender's lien on the homestead property;

(7) that provides that if the lender fails to make loan advances as required in the loan documents and if the lender fails to cure the default as required in the loan documents after notice from the borrower, the lender forfeits all principal and interest of the reverse mortgage, provided, however, that this subdivision does not apply when a governmental agency or instrumentality takes an assignment of the loan in order to cure the default;

(8) that is not made unless the owner of the homestead attests in writing that the owner received counseling regarding the advisability and availability of reverse mortgages and other financial alternatives;

(9) that requires the lender, at the time the loan is made, to disclose to the borrower by written notice the specific provisions contained in Subdivision (6) of this subsection under which the borrower is required to repay the loan;

(10) that does not permit the lender to commence foreclosure until the lender gives notice to the borrower, in the manner provided for a notice by mail related to the foreclosure of liens under Subsection (a)(6) of this section, that a ground for foreclosure exists and gives the borrower at least 30 days, or at least 20 days in the event of a default under Subdivision (6)(D)(iii) of this subsection, to:

(A) remedy the condition creating the ground for foreclosure;

(B) pay the debt secured by the homestead property from proceeds of the sale of the homestead property by the borrower or from any other sources; or

(C) convey the homestead property to the lender by a deed in lieu of foreclosure; and

(11) that is secured by a lien that may be foreclosed upon only by a court order, if the foreclosure is for a ground other than a ground stated by Subdivision (6)(A) or (B) of this subsection.

(l) Advances made under a reverse mortgage and interest on those advances have priority over a lien filed for record in the real property records in the county where the homestead property is located after the reverse mortgage is filed for record in the real property records of that county.

(m) A reverse mortgage may provide for an interest rate that is fixed or adjustable and may also provide for interest that is contingent on appreciation in the fair market value of the homestead property. Although payment of principal or interest shall not be required under a reverse mortgage until the entire loan becomes due and payable, interest may accrue and be compounded during the term of the loan as provided by the reverse mortgage loan agreement.

(n) A reverse mortgage that is secured by a valid lien against homestead property may be made or acquired without regard to the following provisions of any other law of this state:

(1) a limitation on the purpose and use of future advances or other mortgage proceeds;

(2) a limitation on future advances to a term of years or a limitation on the term of open-end account advances;

(3) a limitation on the term during which future advances take priority over intervening advances;

(4) a requirement that a maximum loan amount be stated in the reverse mortgage loan documents;

(5) a prohibition on balloon payments;

(6) a prohibition on compound interest and interest on interest;

(7) a prohibition on contracting for, charging, or receiving any rate of interest authorized by any law of this state authorizing a lender to contract for a rate of interest; and

(8) a requirement that a percentage of the reverse mortgage proceeds be advanced before the assignment of the reverse mortgage.

(o) For the purposes of determining eligibility under any statute relating to payments, allowances, benefits, or services provided on a means-tested basis by this state, including supplemental security income, low-income energy assistance, property tax relief, medical assistance, and general assistance:

(1) reverse mortgage loan advances made to a borrower are considered proceeds from a loan and not income; and

(2) undisbursed funds under a reverse mortgage loan are considered equity in a borrower's home and not proceeds from a loan.

(p) The advances made on a reverse mortgage loan under which more than one advance is made must be made according to the terms established by the loan documents by one or more of the following methods:

(1) an initial advance at any time and future advances at regular intervals;

(2) an initial advance at any time and future advances at regular intervals in which the amounts advanced may be reduced, for one or more advances, at the request of the borrower;

(3) an initial advance at any time and future advances at times and in amounts requested by the borrower until the credit limit established by the loan documents is reached;

(4) an initial advance at any time, future advances at times and in amounts requested by the borrower until the credit limit established by the loan documents is reached, and subsequent advances at times and in amounts requested by the borrower according to the terms established by the loan documents to the extent that the outstanding balance is repaid; or

(5) at any time by the lender, on behalf of the borrower, if the borrower fails to timely pay any of the following that the borrower is obligated to pay under the loan documents to the extent necessary to protect the lender's interest in or the value of the homestead property:

(A) taxes;

(B) insurance;

(C) costs of repairs or maintenance performed by a person or company that is not an employee of the lender or a person or company that directly or indirectly controls, is controlled by, or is under common control with the lender;

(D) assessments levied against the homestead property; and

(E) any lien that has, or may obtain, priority over the lender's lien as it is established in the loan documents.

(q) To the extent that any statutes of this state, including without limitation, Section 41.001 of the Texas Property Code, purport to limit encumbrances that may properly be fixed on homestead property in a manner that does not permit encumbrances for extensions of credit described in Subsection (a)(6) or (a)(7) of this section, the same shall be superseded to the extent that such encumbrances shall be permitted to be fixed upon homestead property in the manner provided for by this amendment.

(r) The supreme court shall promulgate rules of civil procedure for expedited foreclosure proceedings related to the foreclosure of liens under Subsection (a)(6) of this section and to foreclosure of a reverse mortgage lien that requires a court order.

(s) The Finance Commission of Texas shall appoint a director to conduct research on the availability, quality, and prices of financial services and research the practices of business entities in the state that provide financial services under this section. The director shall collect information and produce reports on lending activity of those making loans under this section. The director shall report his or her findings to the legislature not later than December 1 of each year.

(t) A home equity line of credit is a form of an open-end account that may be debited from time to time, under which credit may be extended from time to time and under which:

(1) the owner requests advances, repays money, and reborrows money;

(2) any single debit or advance is not less than $4,000;

(3) the owner does not use a credit card, debit card, or similar device, or preprinted check unsolicited by the borrower, to obtain an advance;

(4) any fees described by Subsection (a)(6)(E) of this section are charged and collected only at the time the extension of credit is established and no fee is charged or collected in connection with any debit or advance;

(5) the maximum principal amount that may be extended under the account, when added to the aggregate total of the outstanding principal balances of all indebtedness secured by the homestead on the date the extension of credit is established, does not exceed an amount described under Subsection (a)(6)(B) of this section;

(6) no additional debits or advances are made if the total principal amount outstanding exceeds an amount equal to 50 percent of the fair market value of the homestead as determined on the date the account is established;

(7) the lender or holder may not unilaterally amend the extension of credit; and

(8) repayment is to be made in regular periodic installments, not more often than every 14 days and not less often than monthly, beginning not later than two months from the date the extension of credit is established, and:

(A) during the period during which the owner may request advances, each installment equals or exceeds the amount of accrued interest; and

(B) after the period during which the owner may request advances, installments are substantially equal.

(Amended Nov. 6, 1973, and Nov. 7, 1995; Subsecs. (a)-(d) amended and (e)-(s) added Nov. 4, 1997; Subsecs. (k), (p), and (r) amended Nov. 2, 1999; Subsec. (a) amended Nov. 6, 2001; Subsecs. (a), (f), and (g) amended and (t) and (u) added Sept. 13, 2003; Subsec. (p) amended and (v) added Nov. 8, 2005; Subsecs. (a), (g), and (t) amended Nov. 6, 2007.)

---

2. Tex. Const. art. XVI, § 51

§ 51. Amount of Homestead; Uses.

The homestead, not in a town or city, shall consist of not more than two hundred acres of land, which may be in one or more parcels, with the improvements thereon; the homestead in a city, town or village, shall consist of lot or contiguous lots amounting to not more than 10 acres of land, together with any improvements on the land; provided, that the homestead in a city, town or village shall be used for the purposes of a home, or as both an urban home and a place to exercise a calling or business, of the homestead claimant, whether a single adult person, or the head of a family; provided also, that any temporary renting of the homestead shall not change the character of the same, when no other homestead has been acquired; provided further that a release or refinance of an existing lien against a homestead as to a part of the homestead does not create an additional burden on the part of the homestead property that is unreleased or subject to the refinance, and a new lien is not invalid only for that reason.

(Amended Nov. 3, 1970, Nov. 6, 1973, Nov. 8, 1983, and Nov. 2, 1999.)

NOTE: The joint resolution amending Sec. 51 in 1983 included a section that did not purport to amend the constitution and that provided the following:

"This amendment applies to all homesteads in this state, including homesteads acquired before the adoption of this amendment."

---

3. Tex. Const. art. XVI, § 52

§ 52. Descent and Distribution of Homestead; Restrictions on Partition

On the death of the husband or wife, or both, the homestead shall descend and vest in like manner as other real property of the deceased, and shall be governed by the same laws of descent and distribution, but it shall not be partitioned among the heirs of the deceased during the lifetime of the surviving husband or wife, or so long as the survivor may elect to use or occupy the same as a homestead, or so long as the guardian of the minor children of the deceased may be permitted, under the order of the proper court having the jurisdiction, to use and occupy the same.

B. Statutes

The Texas Property Code addresses homestead, as follows:

Property Code
Title 5. Exempt Property and Liens
Subtitle A. Property Exempt from Creditor's Claims
CHAPTER 41. INTERESTS IN LAND
SUBCHAPTER A. EXEMPTIONS IN LAND DEFINED

§ 41.001. Interest in Land Exempt from Seizure.

(a) A homestead and one or more lots used for a place of burial of the dead are exempt from seizure for the claims of creditors except for encumbrances properly fixed on homestead property.

(b) Encumbrances may be properly fixed on homestead property for:

(1) purchase money;

(2) taxes on the property;

(3) work and material used in constructing improvements on the property if contracted for in writing as provided by Sections 53.254(a), (b), and (c);

(4) an owelty of partition imposed against the entirety of the property by a court order or by a written agreement of the parties to the partition, including a debt of one spouse in favor of the other spouse resulting from a division or an award of a family homestead in a divorce proceeding;

(5) the refinance of a lien against a homestead, including a federal tax lien resulting from the tax debt of both spouses, if the homestead is a family homestead, or from the tax debt of the owner;

(6) an extension of credit that meets the requirements of Section 50(a)(6), Article XVI, Texas Constitution; or

(7) a reverse mortgage that meets the requirements of Sections 50(k)-(p), Article XVI, Texas Constitution.

(c) The homestead claimant's proceeds of a sale of a homestead are not subject to seizure for a creditor's claim for six months after the date of sale.

Amended by Acts 1985, 69th Leg., ch. 840, § 1, eff. June 15, 1985; Acts 1993, 73rd Leg., ch. 48, § 2, eff. Sept. 1, 1993; Acts 1995, 74th Leg., ch. 121, § 1.01, eff. May 17, 1995; Acts 1995, 74th Leg., ch. 121, § 2.01; Acts 1997, 75th Leg., ch. 526, § 1, eff. Sept. 1, 1997; Acts 2001, 77th Leg., ch. 516, § 1, eff. Sept. 1, 2001.

§ 41.002. Definition of Homestead.

(a) If used for the purposes of an urban home or as both an urban home and a place to exercise a calling or business, the homestead of a family or a single, adult person, not otherwise entitled to a homestead, shall consist of not more than 10 acres of land which may be in one or more contiguous lots, together with any improvements thereon.

(b) If used for the purposes of a rural home, the homestead shall consist of:

(1) for a family, not more than 200 acres, which may be in one or more parcels, with the improvements thereon; or

(2) for a single, adult person, not otherwise entitled to a homestead, not more than 100 acres, which may be in one or more parcels, with the improvements thereon.

(c) A homestead is considered to be urban if, at the time the designation is made, the property is:

(1) located within the limits of a municipality or its extraterritorial jurisdiction or a platted subdivision; and

(2) served by police protection, paid or volunteer fire protection, and at least three of the following services provided by a municipality or under contract to a municipality:

(A) electric;

(B) natural gas;

(C) sewer;

(D) storm sewer; and

(E) water.

(d) The definition of a homestead as provided in this section applies to all homesteads in this state whenever created.

Amended by Acts 1985, 69th Leg., ch. 840, § 1, eff. June 15, 1985; Acts 1989, 71st Leg., ch. 391, § 2, eff. Aug. 28, 1989; Acts 1999, 76th Leg., ch. 1510, § 1, eff. Jan. 1, 2000; Acts 1999, 76th Leg., ch. 1510, § 2, eff. Sept. 1, 1999.

§ 41.0021. Homestead in Qualifying Trust.

(a) In this section, "qualifying trust" means an express trust:

(1) in which the instrument or court order creating the express trust provides that a settlor or beneficiary of the trust has the right to:

(A) revoke the trust without the consent of another person;

(B) exercise an inter vivos general power of appointment over the property that qualifies for the homestead exemption; or

(C) use and occupy the residential property as the settlor's or beneficiary's principal residence at no cost to the settlor or beneficiary, other than payment of taxes and other costs and expenses specified in the instrument or court order:

(i) for the life of the settlor or beneficiary;

(ii) for the shorter of the life of the settlor or beneficiary or a term of years specified in the instrument or court order; or

(iii) until the date the trust is revoked or terminated by an instrument or court order recorded in the real property records of the county in which the property is located and that describes the property with sufficient certainty to identify the property; and

(2) the trustee of which acquires the property in an instrument of title or under a court order that:

(A) describes the property with sufficient certainty to identify the property and the interest acquired; and

(B) is recorded in the real property records of the county in which the property is located.

(b) Property that a settlor or beneficiary occupies and uses in a manner described by this subchapter and in which the settlor or beneficiary owns a beneficial interest through a qualifying trust is considered the homestead of the settlor or beneficiary under Section 50, Article

XVI, Texas Constitution, and Section 41.001.

(c) A married person who transfers property to the trustee of a qualifying trust must comply with the requirements relating to the joinder of the person's spouse as provided by Chapter 5, Family Code.

(d) A trustee may sell, convey, or encumber property transferred as described by Subsection (c) without the joinder of either spouse unless expressly prohibited by the instrument or court order creating the trust.

(e) This section does not affect the rights of a surviving spouse or surviving children under Section 52, Article XVI, Texas Constitution, or Part 3, Chapter VIII, Texas Probate Code.

Added by Acts 2009, 81st Leg., R.S., ch. 984, § 1, eff. Sept. 1, 2009.

Section 2 of Acts 2009, 81st Leg., R.S., ch. 984, provides:

This Act applies only to a transfer that is effective on or after the effective date of this Act. A transfer that is effective before the effective date of this Act is governed by the law as it existed immediately before the effective date of this Act, and that law is continued in effect for that purpose.

§ 41.003. Temporary Renting of a Homestead.

Temporary renting of a homestead does not change its homestead character if the homestead claimant has not acquired another homestead.

Amended by Acts 1985, 69th Leg., ch. 840, § 1, eff. June 15, 1985.

§ 41.004. Abandonment of a Homestead.

If a homestead claimant is married, a homestead cannot be abandoned without the consent of the claimant's spouse.

Added by Acts 1985, 69th Leg., ch. 840, § 1, eff. June 15, 1985.

§ 41.005. Voluntary Designation of Homestead.

(a) If a rural homestead of a family is part of one or more parcels containing a total of more than 200 acres, the head of the family and, if married, that person's spouse may voluntarily designate not more than 200 acres of the property as the homestead. If a rural homestead of a single adult person, not otherwise entitled to a homestead, is part of one or more parcels containing a total of more than 100 acres, the person may voluntarily designate not more than 100 acres of the property as the homestead.

(b) If an urban homestead of a family, or an urban homestead of a single adult person not otherwise entitled to a homestead, is part of one or more contiguous lots containing a total of more than 10 acres, the head of the family and, if married, that person's spouse or the single adult person, as applicable, may voluntarily designate not more than 10 acres of the property as the homestead.

(c) Except as provided by Subsection (e) or Subchapter B, to designate property as a homestead, a person or persons, as applicable, must make the designation in an instrument that is signed and acknowledged or proved in the manner required for the recording of other instruments. The person or persons must file the designation with the county clerk of the county in which all or part of the property is located. The clerk shall record the designation in the county deed records. The designation must contain:

(1) a description sufficient to identify the property designated;

(2) a statement by the person or persons who executed the instrument that the property is designated as the homestead of the person's family or as the homestead of a single

adult person not otherwise entitled to a homestead;

(3) the name of the current record title holder of the property; and

(4) for a rural homestead, the number of acres designated and, if there is more than one survey, the number of acres in each.

(d) A person or persons, as applicable, may change the boundaries of a homestead designated under Subsection (c) by executing and recording an instrument in the manner required for a voluntary designation under that subsection. A change under this subsection does not impair rights acquired by a party before the change.

(e) Except as otherwise provided by this subsection, property on which a person receives an exemption from taxation under Section 11.43, Tax Code, is considered to have been designated as the person's homestead for purposes of this subchapter if the property is listed as the person's residence homestead on the most recent appraisal roll for the appraisal district established for the county in which the property is located. If a person designates property as a homestead under Subsection (c) or Subchapter B and a different property is considered to have been designated as the person's homestead under this subsection, the designation under Subsection (c) or Subchapter B, as applicable, prevails for purposes of this chapter.

(f) If a person or persons, as applicable, have not made a voluntary designation of a homestead under this section as of the time a writ of execution is issued against the person, any designation of the person's or persons' homestead must be made in accordance with Subchapter B.

(g) An instrument that made a voluntary designation of a homestead in accordance with prior law and that is on file with the county clerk on September 1, 1987, is considered a voluntary designation of a homestead under this section.

Added by Acts 1987, 70th Leg., ch. 727, § 1, eff. Aug. 31, 1987. Amended by Acts 1993, 73rd Leg., ch. 48, § 3, eff. Sept. 1, 1993; Acts 1993, 73rd Leg., ch. 297, § 1, eff. Aug. 1, 1993; Acts 1997, 75th Leg., ch. 846, § 1, eff. Sept. 1, 1997; Acts 1999, 76th Leg., ch. 1510, § 3, eff. Jan. 1, 2000.

§ 41.0051. Disclaimer and Disclosure Required.

(a) A person may not deliver a written advertisement offering, for a fee, to designate property as a homestead as provided by Section 41.005 unless there is a disclaimer on the advertisement that is conspicuous and printed in 14-point boldface type or 14-point uppercase typewritten letters that makes the following statement or a substantially similar statement:

THIS DOCUMENT IS AN ADVERTISEMENT OF SERVICES. IT IS NOT AN OFFICIAL DOCUMENT OF THE STATE OF TEXAS.

(b) A person who solicits solely by mail or by telephone a homeowner to pay a fee for the service of applying for a property tax refund from a tax appraisal district or other governmental body on behalf of the homeowner shall, before accepting money from the homeowner or signing a contract with the homeowner for the person's services, disclose to the homeowner the name of the tax appraisal district or other governmental body that owes the homeowner a refund.

(c) A person's failure to provide a disclaimer on an advertisement as required by Subsection (a) or to provide the disclosure required by Subsection (b) is considered a false, misleading, or deceptive act or practice for purposes of Section 17.46(a), Business & Commerce Code, and is subject to action by the consumer protection division of the attorney general's office as provided by Section 17.46(a), Business & Commerce Code.

Added by Acts 2001, 77th Leg., ch. 341, § 1, eff. Sept. 1, 2001. Amended by Acts 2003, 78th Leg., ch.

1191, § 1, 2, eff. Sept. 1, 2003.

§ 41.006. Certain Sales of Homestead.

(a) Except as provided by Subsection (c), any sale or purported sale in whole or in part of a homestead at a fixed purchase price that is less than the appraised fair market value of the property at the time of the sale or purported sale, and in connection with which the buyer of the property executes a lease of the property to the seller at lease payments that exceed the fair rental value of the property, is considered to be a loan with all payments made from the seller to the buyer in excess of the sales price considered to be interest subject to Title 4, Finance Code.

(b) The taking of any deed in connection with a transaction described by this section is a deceptive trade practice under Subchapter E, Chapter 17, Business & Commerce Code, and the deed is void and no lien attaches to the homestead property as a result of the purported sale.

(c) This section does not apply to the sale of a family homestead to a parent, stepparent, grandparent, child, stepchild, brother, half brother, sister, half sister, or grandchild of an adult member of the family.

Added by Acts 1987, 70th Leg., ch. 1130, § 1, eff. Sept. 1, 1987. Amended by Acts 1999, 76th Leg., ch. 62, § 7.84, eff. Sept. 1, 1999.

§ 41.007. Home Improvement Contract.

(a) A contract described by Section 41.001(b)(3) must contain the following warning conspicuously printed, stamped, or typed in a size equal to at least 10-point bold type or computer equivalent, next to the owner's signature line on the contract:

> "IMPORTANT NOTICE: You and your contractor are responsible for meeting the terms and conditions of this contract. If you sign this contract and you fail to meet the terms and conditions of this contract, you may lose your legal ownership rights in your home. KNOW YOUR RIGHTS AND DUTIES UNDER THE LAW."

(b) A violation of Subsection (a) of this section is a false, misleading, or deceptive act or practice within the meaning of Section 17.46, Business & Commerce Code, and is actionable in a public or private suit brought under the provisions of the Deceptive Trade Practices-Consumer Protection Act (Subchapter E, Chapter 17, Business & Commerce Code).

Added by Acts 1987, 70th Leg., ch. 116, § 1, eff. Sept. 1, 1987. Renumbered from § 41.005 by Acts 1989, 71st Leg., ch. 2, § 16.01(30), eff. Aug. 28, 1989. Amended by Acts 1993, 73rd Leg., ch. 48, § 4, eff. Sept. 1, 1993.

§ 41.008. Conflict with Federal Law.

To the extent of any conflict between this subchapter and any federal law that imposes an upper limit on the amount, including the monetary amount or acreage amount, of homestead property a person may exempt from seizure, this subchapter prevails to the extent allowed under federal law.

Added by Acts 1999, 76th Leg., ch. 1510, § 4.

SUBCHAPTER B. DESIGNATION OF A HOMESTEAD IN AID OF ENFORCEMENT OF A JUDGMENT DEBT

§ 41.021. Notice to Designate.

If an execution is issued against a holder of an interest in land of which a homestead may be a part and the judgment debtor has not made a voluntary designation of a homestead under Section 41.005, the judgment creditor may give the judgment debtor notice to designate the homestead as defined in Section 41.002. The notice shall state that if the judgment debtor fails to designate the homestead within the time allowed by Section 41.022, the court will appoint a commissioner to make the designation at the expense of the judgment debtor.

Amended by Acts 1985, 69th Leg., ch. 840, § 1, eff. June 15, 1985; Acts 1987, 70th Leg., ch. 727, § 2, eff. Aug. 31, 1987.

§ 41.022. Designation by Homestead Claimant.

At any time before 10 a.m. on the Monday next after the expiration of 20 days after the date of service of the notice to designate, the judgment debtor may designate the homestead as defined in Section 41.002 by filing a written designation, signed by the judgment debtor, with the justice or clerk of the court from which the writ of execution was issued, together with a plat of the area designated.

Amended by Acts 1985, 69th Leg., ch. 840, § 1, eff. June 15, 1985.

§ 41.023. Designation by Commissioner.

(a) If a judgment debtor who has not made a voluntary designation of a homestead under Section 41.005 does not designate a homestead as provided in Section 41.022, on motion of the judgment creditor, filed within 90 days after the issuance of the writ of execution, the court from which the writ of execution issued shall appoint a commissioner to designate the judgment debtor's homestead. The court may appoint a surveyor and others as may be necessary to assist the commissioner. The commissioner shall file his designation of the judgment debtor's homestead in a written report, together with a plat of the area designated, with the justice or clerk of the court not more than 60 days after the order of appointment is signed or within such time as the court may allow.

(b) Within 10 days after the commissioner's report is filed, the judgment debtor or the judgment creditor may request a hearing on the issue of whether the report should be confirmed, rejected, or modified as may be deemed appropriate in the particular circumstances of the case. The commissioner's report may be contradicted by evidence from either party, when exceptions to it or any item thereof have been filed before the hearing, but not otherwise. After the hearing, or if there is no hearing requested, the court shall designate the homestead as deemed appropriate and order sale of the excess.

(c) The commissioner, a surveyor, and others appointed to assist the commissioner are entitled to such fees and expenses as are deemed reasonable by the court. The court shall tax these fees and expenses against the judgment debtor as part of the costs of execution.

Amended by Acts 1985, 69th Leg., ch. 840, § 1, eff. June 15, 1985; Acts 1987, 70th Leg., ch. 727, § 3, eff. Aug. 31, 1987.

§ 41.024. Sale of Excess.

An officer holding an execution sale of property of a judgment debtor whose homestead has been designated under this chapter may sell the excess of the judgment debtor's interest in land not included in the homestead.

Amended by Acts 1985, 69th Leg., ch. 840, § 1, eff. June 15, 1985; Acts 1987, 70th Leg., ch. 727, § 4, eff. Aug. 31, 1987.

CHAPTER 53. MECHANIC'S, CONTRACTOR'S, OR MATERIALMAN'S LIEN
SUBCHAPTER K. RESIDENTIAL CONSTRUCTION PROJECTS

§ 53.254. Homestead.

(a) To fix a lien on a homestead, the person who is to furnish material or perform labor and the owner must execute a written contract setting forth the terms of the agreement.

(b) The contract must be executed before the material is furnished or the labor is performed.

(c) If the owner is married, the contract must be signed by both spouses.

(d) If the contract is made by an original contractor, the contract inures to the benefit of all persons who labor or furnish material for the original contractor.

(e) The contract must be filed with the county clerk of the county in which the homestead is located. The county clerk shall record the contract in records kept for that purpose.

(f) An affidavit for lien filed under this subchapter that relates to a homestead must contain the following notice conspicuously printed, stamped, or typed in a size equal to at least 10-point boldface or the computer equivalent, at the top of the page:

"NOTICE: THIS IS NOT A LIEN. THIS IS ONLY AN AFFIDAVIT CLAIMING A LIEN."

(g) For the lien on a homestead to be valid, the notice required to be given to the owner under Section 53.252 must include or have attached the following statement:

"If a subcontractor or supplier who furnishes materials or performs labor for construction of improvements on your property is not paid, your property may be subject to a lien for the unpaid amount if:

(1) after receiving notice of the unpaid claim from the claimant, you fail to withhold payment to your contractor that is sufficient to cover the unpaid claim until the dispute is resolved; or

(2) during construction and for 30 days after completion of construction, you fail to retain 10 percent of the contract price or 10 percent of the value of the work performed by your contractor.

"If you have complied with the law regarding the 10 percent retainage and you have withheld payment to the contractor sufficient to cover any written notice of claim and have paid that amount, if any, to the claimant, any lien claim filed on your property by a subcontractor or supplier, other than a person who contracted directly with you, will not be a valid lien on your property. In addition, except for the required 10 percent retainage, you are not liable to a subcontractor or supplier for any amount paid to your contractor before you received written notice of the claim."

Added by Acts 1997, 75th Leg., ch. 526, § 23, eff. Sept. 1, 1997.

C. Cases

1. Possessory Interest in Land

Oftentimes a homestead claim can be based upon an interest that does not meet the laymen's traditional perception of homestead. The following case is an excellent example.

CAPITAL AGGREGATES, INC.
v.
WALKER
448 S.W.2d 830
(Tex. Civ. App.—Austin 1969, writ ref'd n.r.e.)

HUGHES, JUSTICE.

Appellant, Capitol Aggregates, Inc., obtained a money judgment against appellee, Clyde Walker, in the court below, Cause No. 167,482, for the sum of $10,077.27, plus interest and costs, and the judgment being unpaid, appellant caused an execution to issue by the clerk of the court which, pursuant to such judgment, was placed in the hands of T.O. Lang, Sheriff of Travis County. Sheriff Lang levied this execution, or at least attempted to levy it upon a 'mobile trailer home' occupied by Mr. Walker and his family as a home. This suit was brought by Clyde Walker and wife Hazel Walker, against Sheriff Lang and Capitol Aggregates, Inc., to permanently enjoin the levy of execution against the 'mobile trailer home,' the Walkers contending it was their homestead and exempt from execution under the Constitution and laws of this State. Trial to the court, without a jury, resulted in a judgment permanently enjoining the parties sued from levying or attempting to levy the execution on and from selling or attempting to sell the 'mobile trailer home' of appellees. Only Capitol Aggregates, Inc., has appealed.

The trial court made and filed findings of fact and conclusions of law, those pertinent here being:

> 2. Plaintiffs, Hazel Walker and Clyde Walker, sold their home on Fortview Road in Austin, Texas, sometime in the year 1968, took, the proceeds therefrom and made a so-called 'down payment' on the purchase price of and did purchase and become the owners of what was frequently shorthandly referred to in the testimony as a 'trailer home.'
>
> 3. The 'trailer home' is an enclosed structure containing three bedrooms, one and one-half baths, a living room and a kitchen, and containing such other facilities sufficient to meet the domestic and physical needs of human beings who might abode therein.
>
> 4. As originally purchased by the plaintiffs, such structure had affixed to the underside thereof axles to which wheels were attached. By virtue of such attachment, said structure was then 'mobile' and 'movable' in the sense that, by the application of sufficient force, such as that generated by the power of an ordinary automobile, such structure could be moved from one place to another comparatively more easily than it could be dragged or if the invention of the wheel and axle were not among the devices of our modern technology.

5. At the time of such purchase of such structure, the plaintiffs then owned a leasehold estate in a lot of land situated in what was characterized in the testimony as a 'trailer park' located at 1600-G Barton Springs Road in the City of Austin, Texas. Immediately after such purchase of such structure by the plaintiffs, they caused such structure to be moved to said lot in which they then owned such leasehold estate. There the plaintiffs caused said wheels to be removed from such structure and such structure to be set upon what was referred to in the testimony as 'cement blocks' on said lot. Such structure's gas, water and sewage facilities were connected to the gas, water and sewage systems located under the surface of and being a part of the aforesaid lot of land. The structure's electrical system was connected to the electrical service furnished as a part of said leasehold estate. By such setting on such blocks, the underside of said structure was held up from the actual surface of the soil of the earth a distance of approximately two feet. Although the plaintiffs did not themselves 'fasten' such structure to such blocks or soil, either by hairpin or steel cable embedded in concrete, I take judicial notice of the law of gravity and frictional adhesion and find that such structure was thereupon affixed by the plaintiffs to the lot of land in which they then held the aforesaid leasehold estate and that such structure was then, in all reasonable and practical sense of the terms, immovable and without mobility except by external application thereto of some great force such as that of a severe hurricane or powerful bulldozer.

6. I find that such affixation to said land by the plaintiffs was with the intention to enhance the usability of said leasehold estate in said land as the plaintiffs' home so long as the plaintiffs held said estate in said land.

7. I find that, except for some periods of time during which the plaintiff, Clyde Walker, was temporarily separated from Hazel Walker, the plaintiffs in fact have continuously from the time said structure was affixed as aforesaid to and including the date of trial, resided and abode in such structure upon said land and have used, occupied and enjoyed said land and said structure thereon as a home for themselves and their family.

Conclusions of Law:

The plaintiffs' ownership interest in the aforesaid structure is an interest in a homestead within the meaning of Article 16, Sections 50 and 51, Constitution of the State of Texas, and Articles 3832 and 3833 of the Revised Civil Statutes of Texas, and therefore exempt from forced sale under execution.

Appellant's first point is that there was no evidence to support the finding of the trial court that the house trailer (mobile home) was affixed to the land.[1]

We do not believe we are required to recite all of the testimony bearing on and sustaining the finding of the court challenged here for the reason that, except perhaps as to the intent of appellees, appellant does not deny the factual findings of the court, but rather questions their legal effect.

Mr. Walker, who had been in the concrete business for many years, testified that the method used in placing his trailer on concrete blocks was the same as used by house movers who move and relocate entire houses. In some areas where hurricanes are common, mobile homes are bolted to the concrete blocks.

[1] The substance of this point is also included in Point III B.

On cross examination, Mr. Walker testified:

Q Mr. Walker, had you been around trailer parks much before you moved into this one?

A Not a great lot, no, sir. Just saw them and visited in one or two or three.

Q Do you know whether or not it might be a common practice to take wheels off and sell them and buy some more when you need them and then maybe sell those when you want to put the trailer down again and so forth?

A Well, I wouldn't know about that. That wasn't the reason we took ours off.

Q Well, you took yours off so that you could sell them, and you did, in fact, get some money for them, didn't you?

A We got a hundred dollars for them because we never intended to move the trailer. We didn't need them. We didn't want them.'

Mr. L. Paul Meadows, Sr., who operated the trailer park where appellees' mobile home was located, testified:

Q In the operation of your business there, do you have some people who come and park their mobile homes for a long period of time and some who come for very short periods of time?

A Well, frankly, I have one that's been there almost ten years and then some six and seven years, and on like that. Just comers and goers, I don't have, but the man next door has overnight parking. Small homes. Most of mine are comers and stayers.'

* * *

To us, it seems, under this record, that the mobile trailer of appellees is as physically attached to the land as frame houses built on concrete blocks or cedar posts.

Regarding the intention of appellees in the matter, we take the following rules laid down in *O'Neal v. Quilter*, 111 Tex. 345, 234 S.W. 528, 529 (1921), as our guide:

> The controlling question in the case is, was it Quilter's intention, at the time he built the house on O'Neil's premises, that it should be a permanent accession to the freehold? This intention is to be ascertained from the facts and circumstances attendant upon the placing of the house there.
>
> The principles governing the question are well expressed in *Hutchins v. Masterson*, 46 Texas (551) 554, 26 Am. Rep. 286, wherein the court says:
>
> > The weight of the modern authorities establishes the doctrine that the true criterion for determining whether a chattel has become an immovable fixture consists in the united application of the following tests:
> >
> > 1. Has there been a real or constructive annexation of the article in question to the realty?
> >
> > 2. Was there a fitness or adaption of such article to the uses or purposes of the realty with which it is connected?
> >
> > 3. Whether or not it was the intention of the party making the annexation that the chattel should become a permanent accession to the freehold; this intention being inferable from the nature of the article, the relation and situation of the parties interested, the policy of the law in respect thereto, the mode of annexation, and purpose or use for which the annexation is made.

> And of these three tests pre-eminence is to be given to the question of intention to make the article a permanent accession to the freehold, while the others are chiefly of value as evidence of this intention.' *See Moody v. Aiken*, 50 Texas (65) 74; *Willis & Bro. Morris*, 66 Texas 628, 1 S.W. 799, 59 Am. Rep. 634; *Jones v. Bull*, 85 Texas 136, 19 S.W. 1031.

> Quilter was a tenant at will. O'Neal had the authority and right to terminate his occupancy of the premises at any time. That fact, in the absence of an agreement to the contrary, is persuasive that the placing of the house thereon by Quilter was for his temporary use and benefit.
>
> Looking to the intention of Quilter in building the box house on O'Neal's land, it is not to be presumed that it was his purpose to enhance the value of the freehold, his tenancy being indefinite and uncertain, and the building being of a nature which could be removed without injury to the land. The legal presumption is just to the contrary, that it was not his intention to enhance the value of the freehold, but to place the house there for his own use and benefit, and that it should retain its character as personalty. *Cullers & Henry v. James*, 66 Texas 494, 1 S.W. 314.
>
> In discussing this same principle, CHIEF JUSTICE GAINES, in the case of *Wright v. MacDonnell*, 88 Texas (140) 150, 30 S.W. (907) 911, uses the following language:
>
> > Whether it is or is not the intention of the parties in any particular case to make them the property of the landlord is the very point to be determined. An intention on part of the tenant to surrender a valuable right ought not to be lightly implied, though such intention might be made manifest by the circumstances of the particular case.

The question of intention here, it being our opinion that there was legally sufficient evidence to support finding of fact 6, supra, was for the trier of the facts.

Appellant relies upon *Gann v. Montgomery*, 210 S.W.2d 255, Tex. Civ. App., Fort Worth, writ ref. n.r.e. (1948). In that case a house trailer in which the Ganns and their two children had lived for more than two years, they having no other home, was moved to Mexia where it was parked on property rented by Mr. Gann's parents, and with their permission to leave it there while Mr. Gann sought work. While the trailer was so located, Mr. Gann borrowed money, giving a chattel mortgage on the trailer as security. On default of the debt, suit was brought and judgment of debt and foreclosure was obtained. The Ganns brought suit to enjoin execution of the judgment of foreclosure, at which time the trailer had been moved to Fort Worth Army Airfield in which, presumably, the Ganns had no private estate. The trial court denied relief and his judgment was affirmed.

We have no difficulty in distinguishing this case. Not only are the facts there not comparable with the facts here but the finding of the trier of the facts there was adverse to the claim of homestead, whereas it is favorable here.

See Clark v. Vitz, 190 S.W.2d 736, Tex. Civ. App., Dallas, writ ref. (1945), where the Court held that a trailer set on blocks and used for family purposes became a part of the homestead property on which it was located, the trailer and homestead being commonly owned, and was exempt from execution. Here, too, the findings of the trier of facts was favorable to the homestead claimant, and his judgment was affirmed.

Appellant also relies upon the definition of 'house trailer' found in Art. 1436-1, VERNON'S TEX. PENAL CODE as indicating legislative intent that a 'house trailer' should always be a chattel. Sec. 2a of such Article provides:

> Sec. 2a. The term 'House Trailer' means a vehicle without automotive power designed for human habitation and for carrying persons and property upon its own structure and for being drawn by a motor vehicle.

We cannot agree that this definition of a 'house trailer' has any bearing on the question of homestead. All homesteads, excluding the land, consist of an aggregation of chattels. It is their attachment to realty which gives them homestead character. *See* Vol. 28, *Homesteads*, TEX. JUR. 2D, Sec. 10, p. 380.

While not of evidentiary value here, we quote from the August 20, 1969 issue of Investor's Reader as illustrative of the modern concept of mobile homes:

> On the other hand, mobile homes have not been very mobile for a good many years now. In fact, the chairman-president feels the term is a misnomer. 'Most mobile homes are so big it takes a truck to move them. Some 85% of the owners live in them on a permanent basis and 60% of the homes stay right at their original site.' The one key element of mobility is they are fully manufactured and equipped at a factory, then towed to their intended location, usually a trailer park.

We overrule Point I and complementary Point III B.

Point II is that there is no evidence to support finding that appellees held a leasehold estate in the Trailer Park, and Point III A is that a homestead depends upon an estate in land greater than appellees had in the land on which the house trailer was located. These points are closely related and will be discussed and determined together.

Appellees placed their trailer house in Trailer Park under a verbal month to month rental agreement with the operator of the Park, the landlord, Mr. L. Paul Meadows, Sr. When this case was heard on petition for a temporary injunction, Mr. Meadows testified that he had given appellees notice that their tenancy would terminate the next day. However, Mr. Meadows and appellees entered into an agreement that appellees would be permitted to remain in the space occupied by them pending termination of this litigation conditioned upon their prompt payment of rent, other charges and abiding by the rules of the park.

It is our opinion that a month to month tenancy is a sufficient interest in realty to sustain a homestead claim. Appellant *cites*, *Hampton v. Gilliland*, 23 Tex. Civ. App. 87, 56 S.W. 572, Tex. Civ. App., Galveston, no writ (1900); *Ellis v. Bingham*, 150 S.W. 602, Tex. Civ. App., Texarkana, no writ (1912) *and Greene v. White*, 137 Tex . 361, 153 S.W.2d 575, 136 A.L.R. 626 (1941) as indicating a contrary conclusion.

The facts in *Hampton* are complicated, but as we understand them the homestead claimant had no right to occupy the residence on the farm in question except as tenant of his mother who owned a life estate therein. Such right of occupancy and possession did not accrue during the lifetime of the claimant, he having only a remainderman's estate therein, and no homestead right passed to his widow on his death. It is well settled that a remainderman cannot have a homestead interest in the property so long as the prior estate is undetermined. *Homesteads*, Vol. 28, TEX. JUR. 2D, Sec. 54, p. 437. This case is not helpful here. Appellees owned the trailer and had the right of immediate occupancy and possession of it.

Ellis involved an execution on ungathered crops. The Court held the execution should not be enjoined for the reason that the claimant's possession of the premises was incidental to his work in making the crop and would not support a homestead claim.

Greene, too, has complicated facts. We are referred to a statement by the Court that a man and wife living on land and claiming it by adverse possession but, prior to perfecting limitation title 'could have no homestead right or interest in land to which they had no title.' In such case the claimant would not have the right of possession or title and there would be nothing to which a claim of homestead could attach.

There are many authorities holding that a possessory interest in a lot or lots is sufficient to support a claim of homestead, the other requisites being present. *See Homesteads*, Vol. 28, TEX. JUR. 2D, Sec. 58, p. 443.

We believe the best statement of the law in this respect and under facts closely analogous to those present here is found in *First National Bank of Kaufman v. Dismukes*, 241 S.W. 199, Tex. Civ. App., Texarkana, no writ (1922), from which we quote:

> The only question presented on the appeal is that of whether or not a homestead will attach to a business house or 'warehouse' that is constructed on leased premises. In point of fact the warehouse' was used by the husband, as the head of a family, as a place to exercise his business, at the time and since the deed of trust was made and filed. As the homestead right or privilege is of constitutional creation, its nature, character and extent depend upon the law creating and defining it. "The homestead in a city, town or village," as defined by the Constitution of this state—'
>
>> shall consist of . . . a lot or lots not to exceed in value five thousand dollars at the time of their designation as the homestead, without reference to the value of any improvements thereon; provided, that the same shall be used for the purposes of a home, or as a place to exercise the calling or business of the head of a family; provided, also, the temporary renting of the homestead shall not change the character of the same when no other homestead has been acquired. CONST. art. 16, § 51; article 3786, Complete Stat. of 1920.
>
> Ownership of the fee in the "lot or lots" is not, by any terms of the law, essential to the existence of the homestead. The only limitation of the law is as to value and the use of the property. While the law is in terms of 'lot or lots' of land, yet the object was to secure to the family a place of family residence and a place for the head of the family to actually exercise his calling or business to support the family. A "house" is necessarily embraced in the word "homestead." *Franklin v. Coffee*, 18 Tex. 413, 70 Am. Dec . 292; *Cullers v. James*, 66 Tex. 494, 1 S.W. 314. As stated in this latter case:
>
>> If the head of a family owns a house and no interest or estate in the land on which it stands, the house is a chattel. If he occupies it with his family, it is their home. He may be compelled to move it from one lot to another as fast as legal process can oust him, still, though ambulatory, unsatisfactory, and in all its appointments mean; though it advertises the thriftless poverty of its proprietors, and is a caricature of the princely possibility of the exemption laws, it is the home of a family, and is embraced in the spirit and purpose, if not the letter, of the Constitution. The same principles under our present Constitution must be applied to the place of business of the head of the family.

(3) Hence, giving effect to the plain intent of the Homestead Act, any possessory interest in a lot or lots, the fee simple title not being required to support it, coupled with the requisite occupancy by the husband and his family, is sufficient to support a homestead claim. Consequently, if any possessory interest in the lot or lots less than the fee-simple title is sufficient to entitle a claimant to the benefits of the provisions of the Homestead Act, it follows logically that the homestead right and privilege attaches to a tenement or building, coupled with the requisite occupancy, erected upon leased or rented premises. *Cullers v. James, supra*; *Low v. Tandy*, 70 Tex. 745, 8 S.W. 620; *Phillips v. Warner* (Tex. Sup.) 16 S.W . 423; *(Anheuser-Busch) Brewing Ass'n v. Smith* (Tex. Civ. App.) 26 S.W . 94; *Ellis v. Bingham* (Tex. Civ. App.) 150 S.W. 602.

(4) It does not appear, it is true, in the record the kind of lease, or duration of the same, that appellee has in the land. An exclusive, uninterrupted possession of the premises does appear. That is sufficient as against a judgment creditor. Where a head of a family is in the exclusive possession, as here, of a lot of land actually occupied by him as a business homestead, it does not concern the judgment creditor whether such claimant possesses a lease for a long term of years or of less duration.'

This case has been cited many times with approval. We follow it and hold that the possessory interest held by appellees in the lot to which their trailer house was affixed is sufficient to support a claim of homestead in the trailer house of appellees, all other requisites of a homestead being present. We overrule the points under discussion.

Finding no error, the judgment of the trial court is affirmed.

Notes, Comments & Questions

1. It is the opinion of the *Capital Aggregates* Court that "a month to month tenancy is a sufficient interest in realty to sustain a homestead claim." Explain the rationale back of this holding.

2. In *Rose v. Carney's Lumber Co.*, 565 S.W.2d 571 (Tex. Civ. App.—Tyler 1978, no writ), the court held that equitable title to land, acquired under a contract of purchase, is sufficient as a basis for a claim of homestead.

---

2. Family or Single Adult Homestead

Before adoption of the 1973 amendments to Sections 50 and 51 of the Texas Constitution, and the amendment of Article 3833, effective January 1, 1974, the only possible homestead was the family homestead. Thereafter, it became possible for the homestead to consist either of a family homestead or a single adult homestead.

Despite the recent recognition of single adult homestead, it is still necessary to consider the requirements for the existence of a family and the consequences of termination of family status. Under current law, a single adult may only claim a 100-acre rural homestead, whereas a family may claim 200 acres. Thus, it might behoove an unmarried rural homestead claimant to nonetheless establish family status, per the next case.

RENALDO
v.
BANK OF SAN ANTONIO
630 S.W.2d 638
(Tex. 1982)

McGEE, JUSTICE.

This is a suit for declaratory judgment to determine the validity of a deed of trust. The primary question presented in this cause is whether a divorced husband who is under a legal obligation to support his child could and did establish a homestead prior to the 1974 amendments to the Texas homestead laws.[1] The trial court, sitting without a jury, rendered judgment declaring the deed of trust void as against the asserted homestead exemption. The court of civil appeals reversed the trial court's judgment and rendered judgment denying the homestead exemption and declaring the deed of trust valid. 626 S.W.2d 318. We reverse the judgment of the court of civil appeals and affirm the judgment of the trial court.

Jeremy and Patti Renaldo were married in 1968. The couple established a home at 110 Brittany in San Antonio, Texas, where they lived until their separation on or about August 22, 1972. On March 28, 1972, Jeremy and Patti entered into an agreement in contemplation of divorce whereby Patti would receive as her separate property the residence at 110 Brittany and Jeremy would receive as his separate property a house at 602 Santa Monica in San Antonio, Texas. The following day Jeremy purchased the 602 Santa Monica property from third parties.

A decree of divorce was rendered on December 5, 1972. The first child of the marriage was born December 19, 1972, two weeks after the divorce. The divorce decree incorporated the March 28 property settlement agreement and further provided that Patti would have custody of the child, that Jeremy would make periodic child support payments, and that he would have certain visitation rights.

Jeremy moved onto the 602 Santa Monica property around the time of divorce and has continued to live there without interruption. Jeremy's son lived with his mother most of the time but was a fre-

[1] Effective January 1, 1974, TEX. REV. CIV. STAT. ANN. art. 3833 was amended to provide a homestead exemption to "a single, adult person, not a constituent of a family."

quent visitor at his father's house. While the divorce decree provided for visitation of only 2 ½ hours per week, there was testimony at trial that the child often spent the night with Jeremy, and that the child had his own room at Jeremy's house.

On September 24, 1973, Jeremy executed a deed of trust covering the 602 Santa Monica residence to the Bank of San Antonio. The deed of trust was requested by the Bank to secure a pre-existing commercial debt. None of the money received from the Bank was used to purchase, pay taxes on, or improve the property in question. Jeremy brought this suit to declare the deed of trust invalid, asserting that the 602 Santa Monica property was his homestead.

In order to sustain his homestead claim, Jeremy had the burden to prove he had established a family homestead in the Santa Monica property prior to the execution of the deed of trust. This necessarily involves evidence that he was part of a family unit at the time the property acquired its asserted homestead character. The court of civil appeals reversed the trial court's judgment on the basis that Jeremy failed to establish a homestead at 602 Santa Monica prior to his divorce. Apparently, that court was of the opinion that any homestead rights of a divorced person must have existed prior to the divorce. We disagree.

The cases clearly establish that a family unit entitled to a homestead may consist of a divorced person and a dependent child. *E.g., Woods v. Alvarado State Bank*, 118 Tex. 586, 19 S.W.2d 35 (1929); *Speer & Goodnight v. Sykes*, 102 Tex. 451, 119 S.W. 86 (1909); *Hall v. Fields*, 81 Tex. 553, 17 S.W. 82 (1891); *Zapp v. Strohmeyer*, 75 Tex. 638, 13 S.W. 9 (1890). This is true even though custody of the child may have been awarded to the other spouse, so long as the obligation for support continues and a genuine parent-child relationship exists. In *Schulz v. L. E. Whitham & Co.*, 119 Tex. 211, 27 S.W.2d 1093, 1095 (1930), we summarized the law in this area as follows:

> (A)lthough the husband and wife may be divorced, and although the children may have been awarded to her, and may not live with him, yet so long as they are minors, to whom he owes a duty of support, he is entitled to a homestead as the head of a family.

The Bank contends that this rule applies only if the divorced person is continuing to claim a homestead which was established prior to divorce, but that a separate homestead may not be dedicated after divorce.

While a number of the cited cases hold that a homestead continues through divorce where one spouse remains on the property, a single parent's homestead rights are not limited to that situation. In *Woods v. Alvarado State Bank*, 118 Tex. 586, 19 S.W.2d 35 (1929), this Court upheld a 200-acre homestead exemption in a 228-acre tract belonging to J.D. Woods, even though he had acquired some of the land after his divorce. The trial court had sustained the homestead claim only as to the original 104 acres he had owned and occupied as a homestead prior to his divorce. On appeal, we held Woods was entitled to the full 200-acre exemption because he was the head of a family consisting of himself and a minor son at the time he acquired the additional acreage. *Cf. Lane v. Phillips*, 69 Tex. 240, 6 S.W. 610 (1887) (single father of illegitimate children was entitled to claim a homestead exemption).

The fact that Jeremy's ex-wife, Patti, continued to reside at the couple's original homestead after divorce does not affect Jeremy's right to establish a separate homestead elsewhere. A divorced parent's right to a family homestead derives from the relationship to his or her children. As we stated in *Zapp v. Strohmeyer*, 75 Tex. 638, 13 S.W. 9, 10 (1890), "(t)he head of the family, or the two heads of families, that there may be after divorce, are entitled to hold their homesteads against forced sale. . . ."

Jeremy proved that he was the head of a family and he was therefore entitled to establish a homestead. He introduced evidence that, prior to the execution of the deed of trust, he had occupied 602 Santa Monica with the intent of making it his home where his son could regularly visit. We affirm the trial court's judgment sustaining the homestead and declaring the Bank's deed of trust void.

The judgment of the court of civil appeals is reversed and the judgment of the trial court is affirmed.

NOTES, COMMENTS & QUESTIONS

1. Many decisions deal with the question of what comprises a "family" for purposes of the homestead claim. It is well-settled that it is not necessary for the family to include both husband and wife.

2. In the leading case, *Woods v. Alvarado State Bank*, 19 S.W.2d 35, Tex. 1929, it was held that, following divorce, the former husband and two minor children, who, though awarded to the mother, continued to live with the father, constituted a family for homestead purposes.

3. In *Central Life Ass. Soc. v. Gray*, 32 S.W.2d 259 (Tex. Civ. App.—Waco 1939, writ ref'd), the court pointed out that the relationship is one of status, that there must be a legal or moral obligation on the head of the family to support the other member or members, and that there must be a corresponding dependence upon the part of such member or members for such support. Examples given in *Central Life* included brother and sister, when there is a moral obligation on the part of the brother to support and care for the sister and when the necessity or such care and support exists; a widow who had voluntarily assumed the care of children of a stepdaughter; and a single woman who had assumed responsibility for rearing nephews and nieces.

4. In *Tanton v. State Nat'l Bank of El Paso*, 79 S.W.2d 833 (Tex. 1935), it was held that a family consisting solely of a husband and wife is terminated upon divorce, so that the spouse retaining title to the land formerly comprising the family homestead is no longer entitled to homestead protection. That is, if after the divorce the party claiming the homestead was not head of a family—did not have custody of children—the homestead claim was not valid. However, the Texas Supreme Court in *Eggemeyer v. Eggemeyer*, 623 S.W.2d 462 (Tex. 1981) made the following observation:

> However, with the 1973 amendment to Article 16, Section 50, providing for a single adult homestead, this rule necessarily become obsolete. It seems to be well-settled that once a homestead has been shown to exist, . . . there is a presumption that the homestead continues in absence of evidence to the contrary.

Id. at 465

5. Although a single person can claim a 100 acre rural homestead, it is interesting to note that a surviving spouse is not considered single for homestead purposes. For example, in the case of *Riley v. Riley*, 972 S.W.2d 149 at 153 (Tex. App.—Texarkana 1998, no writ), the court determined that the widow's homestead should be 200 acres. The court reasoned thus:

> Appellants also argue that the probate court erred in allowing conveyance of the separate real property because Bobbie Riley has a homestead right in only 100 acres of the separate real property of her deceased husband's estate and, therefore, did not have homestead rights in the separate property oil and gas production of the estate.

By statute, a single person living alone is entitled to 100 acres as a rural homestead.[10] Appellants argue that Bobbie Riley is only entitled to homestead rights in 100 acres, and because she lives in a home on the property in question, the homestead would logically be located where the home is located, the 160-acre Home Place tract. The River Place, which produces oil and gas royalties, would be excluded from Bobbie Riley's homestead, they argue. Further, Appellants contend they are entitled to one half of the approximately $36,000 in oil and gas royalties received by Bobbie Riley since Elbert Riley's death, pursuant to Section 38 of the Probate Code,[11] which sets out the rules of descent and distribution in cases of intestacy.

Section 41.002(b)(2) of the Property Code deals with exemption from creditors and states that, for a single, adult person, for the purposes of a rural home, the homestead shall consist of not more than 100 acres, which may be in one or more parcels, with the improvements thereon, if that person is not otherwise entitled to a homestead.[12] Bobbie Riley is "otherwise entitled to a homestead" under Sections 282 and 283 of the Probate Code[13] and Article XVI, Section 52 of the Texas Constitution, which gives a deceased spouse's survivor and minor children the right to occupy the homestead for life.

The Texas Constitution sets out the definition and acreage limitations of homesteads as 200 acres.[14] Section 271 of the Probate Code provides that in administering an estate, the court shall "set apart for the use and benefit of the surviving spouse and minor children and unmarried children remaining with the family of the deceased, all such property of the estate as is exempt from execution or forced sale by the constitution and laws of the state."[15] Section 272 provides that "the homestead shall be delivered to the surviving spouse, if there be one, and if there be no surviving spouse, to the guardian of the minor children and unmarried children, if any, living with the family."[16]

During their marriage, the Rileys were entitled to claim a rural homestead of 200 acres on Elbert Riley's separate property land.[17] A surviving spouse has the same homestead rights in the property as both spouses had prior to the death of one spouse.[18] The status of the homestead is immediately ascertainable upon the death of the decedent.[19] Bobbie Riley is rightfully entitled to 200 acres as her homestead under the Texas Constitution.

6. Two distinct lines of cases deal with the situation in which the husband is awarded title to real estate upon divorce, and the wife is awarded a money judgment against the husband. In one line of cases, where the divorce judgment does not fix a lien against the real estate, and the husband desig-

---

[10] TEX. PROP. CODE ANN. § 41.002(b)(2) (Vernon Supp.1998).

[11] TEX. PROB. CODE ANN. § 38 (Vernon 1980).

[12] TEX. PROP. CODE ANN. § 41.002(b)(2) (Vernon Supp.1998).

[13] TEX. PROB. CODE ANN. §§ 282, 283 (Vernon 1980).

[14] TEX. CONST. art XVI, §§ 50-52.

[15] TEX. PROB. CODE ANN. § 271(a) (Vernon Supp.1998) (emphasis added).

[16] TEX. PROB. CODE ANN. § 272 (Vernon 1980).

[17] TEX. CONST. art. XVI, § 51.

[18] TEX. CONST. art. XVI, § 52; TEX. PROB. CODE ANN. §§ 282, 283 (Vernon 1980); Hunter v. Clark, 687 S.W.2d 811, 814 (Tex. App.—San Antonio 1985, no writ).

[19] National Union Fire Ins. Co. of Pittsburgh v. Olson, 920 S.W.2d 458, 462 (Tex. App.—Austin 1996, no writ).

nates the real estate as his homestead before an abstract of judgment is filed, the homestead exemption prevails over the judgment lien. *See, e.g., Wierzchula v. Wierzchula*, 623 S.W.2d 730 (Tex. Civ. App.—Houston [1st Dist.] 1981, no writ); *Ealy v. Ealy*, 616 S.W.2d 420 (Tex. Civ. App.—Texarkana 1981); *Spence v. Spence*, 455 S.W.2d 365 (Tex. Civ. App.—Houston [14th Dist.] 1970, writ ref'd n.r.e.). In the second line of cases, in which the divorce judgment creates a lien against the real estate, the lien prevails over the asserted homestead exemption. *See, e.g., Lettieri v. Lettieri*, 654 S.W.2d 554 (Tex. Civ. App.—Fort Worth 1983); *Day v. Day*, 610 S.W.2d 195 (Tex. Civ. App.—Tyler 1980, writ ref'd n.r.e.). However, when no express lien is reserved, an equitable vendor's lien may arise if the obligation arises out of a settlement agreement. *McGoodwin v. McGoodwin*, 671 S.W.2d 880 (Tex. 1984).

McGOODWIN
v.
McGOODWIN

671 S.W.2d 880
(Tex. 1984)

BARROW, JUSTICE.

Our opinion and judgment delivered on March 4, 1984 are withdrawn, and the following is substituted.

This is a suit to enforce a lien. Patsy McGoodwin sued her former husband, James L. McGoodwin, and his son, James R. McGoodwin, seeking to force the sale of a certain tract of land. After a bench trial, the trial court decreed that the property be sold to satisfy Patsy's claim. The court of appeals affirmed. 656 S.W.2d 202 (1983). We modify those judgments, and as modified we affirm.

James and Patsy acquired the twenty-two acres of land now in question during their marriage. They moved onto the property, and James has lived there ever since. James and Patsy were divorced, and by its divorce decree the court approved a property settlement agreement reached by the parties and divided their property according to that agreement. The agreement awarded James the twenty-two acres of land as his separate property. In return, James agreed to pay Patsy "$22,500 as consideration for the conveyance of [Patsy's] 1/2 interest" in the land. Patsy agreed to convey her interest upon payment of the consideration by James. James has not paid this consideration, but asserts full ownership. After the divorce, James conveyed a remainder interest in the land to his son as a gift and reserved a life estate to himself.

Patsy brought this suit to subject the land to forced sale to satisfy her claim for the unpaid consideration. Patsy claims that a vendor's lien in her favor is implied by the property settlement agreement between her and James. The trial court agreed and ordered the vendor's lien foreclosed and the property sold. In addition, the court held the deed from James to his son void. This latter holding is not attacked before this court. James insists, however, that no vendor's lien arose from the property settlement agreement. Since the land in question is his homestead, James contends, it is exempt from forced sale to satisfy his debt to her.

The issue to be decided is a narrow one. Does a divorce decree that approves a property settlement agreement by which the husband agrees to pay a sum of money as consideration for the wife's interest in a particular piece of real estate imply a vendor's lien in favor of the wife? The significance of this issue is clear. A vendor's lien is a lien for purchase money. If Patsy holds such a lien, she is entitled to enforce it through foreclosure notwithstanding James's homestead claim. TEX. CONST. art. XVI, § 50.

* * *

Correct resolution of the question presented requires first an understanding of the effect given a marital property settlement agreement by Texas law. Such an agreement, though incorporated into a final divorce decree, is treated as a contract, and its legal force and its meaning are governed by the law of contracts, not by the law of judgments. *Francis v. Francis*, 412 S.W.2d 29, 33 (Tex. 1967); *Ex parte Jones*, 163 Tex. 513, 358 S.W.2d 370, 375 (1962); *Martinez v. Guajardo*, 464 S.W.2d 944, 946-47 (Tex. Civ. App.—San Antonio 1971, no writ). The property settlement provision now considered is one that directs the payment of money as consideration for the conveyance of an interest in real estate. Its construction, therefore, is dictated by the law regarding contracts for the sale of land.

Established Texas law holds that when no express lien is reserved in a deed and the purchase money is not paid, a lien nevertheless arises by implication in favor of the vendor to secure payment of the purchase money. That vendor's lien may be enforced in a suit brought for that purpose. *White, Smith & Baldwin v. Downs*, 40 Tex. 225, 226, 231-32 (1874); *Briscoe v. Bronaugh*, 1 Tex. 326, 329-30 (1846); *Delley v. Unknown Stockholders of the Brotherly and Sisterly Club of Christ, Inc.*, 509 S.W.2d 709, 714 (Tex. Civ. App.—Tyler 1974, writ ref'd n.r.e.). In the seminal Texas case on this point, this court explained:

> "There is," it has been said, "a natural equity that the land should stand charged with so much of the purchase money as was not paid, and that without any special agreement for that purpose." Vern. 267; 4 Kent, 152. It is founded upon an implied trust between the vendor and purchaser. The latter is regarded as the trustee of his vendor, receiving the contract or conveyance, to hold it for the use of the vendor until the purchase money is paid. . . . This equitable mortgage exists in every case of sale where the money is not paid, unless it be otherwise agreed by the parties either expressly or by acts showing that the lien was not intended to be retained. . . . Prima facie the lien exists and it lies on the purchaser to show that the vendor agreed to waive it. *Briscoe*, 1 Tex. at 330 (emphasis original). This same concept was stated more succinctly in *Downs*: "[The vendor's] lien arose by implication, as a natural equity creating a constructive trust in the vendee, that he should not keep the estate of another without paying for it." 40 Tex. at 231.

We must now apply these settled principles to the facts of the instant case. During her marriage to James, Patsy owned an undivided one-half interest in the twenty-two acre tract of land. In the property settlement agreement, Patsy contracted to sell her interest to James in exchange for $22,500. That agreement was incorporated into the property division order of the final divorce decree.[1] Because the purchase money was not paid at the time of the divorce decree, a vendor's lien arose in Patsy's favor

[1] The court has been cited to the following cases as authority for the proposition that Patsy is not entitled to any lien because none was expressly provided in the settlement agreement: Ealy v. Ealy, 616 S.W.2d 420 (Tex. Civ. App.—Texarkana 1981, writ dism'd); Spence v. Spence, 455 S.W.2d 365 (Tex. Civ. App.—Houston [14th Dist.] 1970, writ ref'd n.r.e.); Goldberg v. Goldberg, 425 S.W.2d 830 (Tex. Civ. App.—Fort Worth 1968, no writ); Goldberg v. Goldberg, 392 S.W.2d 168 (Tex. Civ. App.—Fort Worth 1965, no writ). These cases are all distinguished from the present case by the fact that each involved court-ordered, not agreed, property divisions in which the trial court elected not to charge the land with a lien.

against the undivided one-half interest she had sold. This purchase money lien is superior to James's claim of homestead.

The $22,500 purchase money remained unpaid, and Patsy brought this suit to enforce her vendor's lien. Patsy is entitled to foreclosure of her vendor's lien, and the courts below so held. Her lien, however, is against only the interest she sold—an undivided one-half interest—and it is only that interest that can be sold to satisfy her claim. Accordingly, we modify the judgments of the courts below to decree foreclosure on and sale of an undivided one-half interest in the twenty-two acre tract.

As modified, we affirm the judgments of the courts below.

Notes, Comments & Questions

1. Although Patsy McGoodwin eventually won her case, how could the entire problem have been dealt with in an easier way?

2. James McGoodwin did not attack the trial court's finding that the deed to his son was void. Would it have made a difference if the conveyance was not void?

3. Do not forget that liens can also be placed upon separate property homesteads to secure claims for economic contribution. *See* TEX. FAM. CODE § 3.401.

---

3. Rural Homestead

What are the requirements to claim a rural homestead? Can there be a rural business homestead? How is a rural area determined? All these questions are answered by the cases below.

EXALL ET AL.
v.
SECURITY MORTGAGE & TRUST CO.
39 S.W. 959
(Tex. Civ. App. 1897, writ ref'd)

JAMES, C.J.

The land in controversy is a tract of 219 acres, near, but outside of, the city of Dallas, acquired by Henry Exall in November, 1889, which he immediately converted into a stock farm, and upon which he conducted the business of breeding, training, and boarding horses, and he has made use of the property in this manner ever since. He was and is the head of a family, and at the time he acquired this land, and ever since, has resided in the city of Dallas. During this time he and his family boarded in Dallas, as they had previously done, having no residence homestead in the city; and it is admitted that at the time the mortgage was given appellee on said farm Exall had formed no intention of residing thereon. In March, 1891, Exall, joined by his wife, mortgaged the farm to appellee by deeds of trust, and at sale thereunder appellee became the purchaser thereof, and the latter has brought this action in trespass to try title. The defenses are all founded upon the theory that the farm was exempt as homestead. From our view of the law governing the right of the parties the above facts are all that are necessary to be stated.

It was held by the district judge that the constitution does not exempt a place of business in the country unless the head of the family resides on some part of the land claimed as homestead, or intends to reside thereon; and that, if he lives in a city, with no intention of moving upon the property claimed as homestead, he cannot have exempt 200 acres of land which he uses only as a stock farm, for business purposes. The only position that can be taken, and the one that is taken by appellants, is that the land was entitled to exemption as a place of business in the country, and depends on the proper construction of section 51, art. 16 of the constitution. It is claimed that the first proviso that appears in the section, vis: "Provided that the same shall be used for the purpose of a home or as a place to exercise the calling or business of the head of the family," was intended to refer to the rural as well as the urban homestead, and that, Exall having no residence homestead or business homestead (as contended by appellants on the facts) in the city, he could live in the city, without any intention of living on the country tract, and have this, to the extend of 200 acres, as a business homestead. This view is opposed to all the supreme court has said in cases in which the intention of the convention in adopting said section is discussed. That court has, in language that is unmistakable, stated, and to our mind demonstrated, that the section was meant to apply alone to the urban homestead. *Miller v. Menke*, 56 Tex. 539; *Swearingen v. Bassett*, 63 Tex. 267. Nor do we find anything in any of the decisions which tends to hold a different view. The homestead in the country, it is provided, shall consist of not more than 200 acres, in one or more parcels, with the improvements thereon. Under the rule as it was before the constitution of 1876, as well as now, the condition to such a homestead was that the head of the family should use it, or some part of it, as a home, or at least have an intention to do so. There was no necessity for enlarging this exemption for business purposes. If any part of the land, or any parcel thereof, was made to fulfill the condition of residence, the whole was exempt as homestead, irrespective of what use was made, if any, of the remainder; consequently the mention of a use for business purposes in connection with this exemption would have been meaningless and superfluous. In the opinion on rehearing in *Miller v. Menke*, JUDGE STAYTON says:

> The exemption for rural homestead gives not only the home or residence of the family, but not exceeding two hundred acres of land, in one or more parcels: enough to enable the head of the family thereon to exercise his calling or business, agricultural or other, and thereby provide a support for his family.
>
> While the use to which the property is applied operates as a designation of the homestead in either case, yet the use of the rural homestead other wise than as the home of the family is not necessary to preserve such a homestead to the full extent of the area provided by the constitution; while in reference to the urban homestead the use of the home of the family as a residence will not be sufficient to protect and keep alive the exemption of a place for the head of the family to exercise his calling or business which is detached and separate from the home.
>
> The letter and spirit of the constitution harmonizes the urban exemption with that, before its adoption, given only to the rural, and exempts to each a place not only for the shelter of the family, but also a place where the head may exercise his calling or business.

The interpretation of said sections as indicated by these expressions is consistent with reason and correct rules of construction, and the result which it leads to is that the proviso in question was intended to have reference only to a town or city homestead, and that there is no such thing as a homestead exemption outside a town or city in a tract not used or intended to be used as a home, and which is applied only to business uses. We concur with the ruling of the district court on this question. It renders unnecessary all other questions in the case, except the fourteenth assignment of error, which is, the court erred in rendering judgment against J.M. Dickson on his disclaimer. The judgment was properly rendered against Dickson for the land, and in his favor for costs. *Johnson v. Schumacher*, 72 Tex. 334, 12 S.W. 207. Affirmed.

RILEY
v.
RILEY
972 S.W.2d 149
(Tex. App.—Texarkana 1998, no writ)

GRANT, JUSTICE.

* * *

We next address whether homestead acreage can be comprised of different parcels. If used for the purposes of a rural home, the homestead may be in one or more parcels.[20] To establish a homestead claim in rural property, the claimant must reside on part of the property and use the property for purposes of a home, although the claimant need not reside on all the parcels so long as the other tracts are used for the support of the family.[21] Bobbie Riley is entitled to 200 acres and to designate which 200 acres she wants to claim as her homestead as long as it is part of the property used by the family for homestead. She claims a homestead in 140 acres of the Home Place and 59.7 acres of the River Place, including the production of oil and gas.

The question, then, is whether a claimant may select only a portion of that land on which her home is located so that she may also select a portion of land elsewhere to make up her 200 acres of homestead. Specific to this case, may Bobbie Riley designate as her homestead a 140-acre portion of the 160 acres which is the site of her residence so that she can also designate 59.7 mineral- rich acres elsewhere?

A homestead claimant may exclude part of a tract actually occupied to obtain more acreage in another tract.[22] However, such claimant must show that the second tract satisfies the requirement that the land is used for support of the family.[23] Bobbie Riley testified that both parcels of property were farmed and ranched during the marriage for their support and that both parcels are presently used for running livestock. Testimony that cattle is grazed on the property shows use of the property in a manner which establishes homestead rights.[24] Bobbie Riley also testified that the River Place has been oil- and gas-producing property since her marriage to Elbert Riley. The evidence supports the conclusion that the Rileys used the properties in such a manner as to establish homestead rights in the properties.

Bobbie Riley may properly designate as her homestead a 140-acre portion of the 160-acre Home Place, which is the site of her residence, and also designate 59.7 acres of the River Place.

* * *

---

[20] TEX. PROP. CODE ANN. § 41.002(b)(1) (Vernon Supp.1998).

[21] NCNB Texas Nat'l Bank v. Carpenter, 849 S.W.2d 875, 879 (Tex. App.—Fort Worth 1993, no writ).

[22] Affleck v. Wangemann, 93 Tex. 351, 55 S.W. 312, 313 (1900); Mayfield Co. v. Pepper, 76 S.W.2d 216, 217 (Tex. Civ. App.—Texarkana 1934), *rev'd on other grounds*, 129 Tex. 307, 103 S.W.2d 737 (1937).

[23] Carpenter, 849 S.W.2d at 879.

[24] Fajkus v. First Nat'l Bank of Giddings, 735 S.W.2d 882, 884 (Tex. App.—Austin 1987, writ denied).

LEE
v.
NORTH TEXAS PRODUCTION CREDIT ASSOC.
570 F.2d 1301
(5th Cir. 1978)

Before GOLDBERG, AINSWORTH, and HILL, CIRCUIT JUDGES.

PER CURIAM:

This appeal concerns the entitlement of bankrupts to a rural homestead exemption for two parcels of property in the vicinity of Oak Grove, Texas. Fortuitously, there is Fifth Circuit precedent for the fact that Oak Grove was a village in 1934. *Buttram v. Harris*, 73 F.2d 679 (5th Cir. 1934). In the case at bar, the district court, reversing the decision of the bankruptcy judge,[1] held that "the facts and circumstances which gave life to the village in (1934) do not presently exist and are not binding upon the Court in deciding this case." Recognizing the effects of changing times, we agree and affirm on the basis of the district court's memorandum opinion, reproduced below as an Appendix.

AFFIRMED.

MEMORANDUM OPINION

This matter is before this Court on appeal, wherein Billy James Lee and wife, Dorothy Kirk Lee, Bankrupts, have filed objections to the decision of the Bankruptcy Court rendered on January 26, 1977. The Bankrupts contend that they are entitled to a rural homestead exemption, and as a consequence, two tracts of land, one tract, consisting of one and one-eighth acre of land and upon which the Bankrupt's house is situated, and the other, containing 193.99 acres and separated three to four miles from the first, are exempt property. However, the Bankruptcy Court, in its decision, held that Oak Grove is a village, the Bankrupt's smaller tract and residence is located therein, and as a result thereof, they are entitled to an urban homestead exemption which does not include their 193.99 acre tract. This Court is of the opinion, for the reasons stated hereafter, that such ruling was erroneous in that Oak Grove is not presently a village.

The record discloses that Oak Grove is located at the intersection of Highway 82 and Farm to Market road 1326. Likewise, within a radius of two-tenths of a mile from the intersection, there are eleven houses, a convenience store where groceries and gas may be purchased, and an abandoned church. Six-tenths of a mile north of the intersection, there are two sawmills, and two additional houses, including that of the Bankrupts. Disregarding the distance of the two houses and sawmills and any argument therein concerning the limits or boundaries of Oak Grove, it is a village, if at all, on the strength of the houses, store, sawmills and abandoned building. It is the opinion of this Court that such is insufficient to constitute a village.

---

[1] Appellants contend that the district court can overturn the decision of the bankruptcy judge only when that decision is clearly erroneous. Here there is no dispute as to the underlying facts; the district court disagreed with the bankruptcy judge only as to the legal effect to be accorded to those facts. In such circumstances, the scope of review is much broader than is the case with respect to contested basic facts or questions of credibility. Shaw v. United States Rubber Company, 361 F.2d 679 (5th Cir. 1966); *see also* 9 WRIGHT & MILLER, FEDERAL PRACTICE AND PROCEDURE: CIVIL §§ 2588, 2589. Here the district court acted within the appropriate scope of review.

While there is no doubt that Oak Grove was a village in 1934, *Buttram v. Harris*, 73 F.2d 679 (5th Cir. 1934),[1] it is the conclusion of this Court that the facts and circumstances which gave life to the village in that year do not presently exist and are not binding upon the Court in deciding this case. Moreover, to stamp the lable (sic) of village upon this crossroad collection of buildings, would do violence to the meaning and intent of the word as used within Section 51 of Article 16 of the Texas Constitution. In the case of *In re Buie*, N.D.Tex., 287 F. 896, Judge Atwell aptly described a similar circumstance by stating:

> The record shows in this case that the entire county of Kaufman is heavily populated or settled; but to hold that a community, such as the record discloses in this case, is a "town," within the meaning of the constitutional provision under consideration, would eventually mean that there can be no rural homestead in Texas, because the people of the country are as gregarious as the people of the city, and they naturally place their residences and accompanying outbuildings at such corners or places on their farms as will touch the public roads and be nearer their neighbors.

Notes, Comments & Questions

1. *In M.H. Lauchheimer & Sons v. Saunders*, 76 S.W. 750 (Tex. 1903), the court held that whether a homestead is considered urban or rural depends upon conditions existing at the time the adverse right is first asserted.

2. Can you think of an area within your vicinity which may give rise to an urban versus rural controversy?

3. In *Cocke v. Conquest* 35 S.W.2d 673 (Tex. 1931), four separate tracts within an eight-mile radius, aggregating 188 acres, were held to comprise a rural homestead, when the claimant resided on one tract and used all four tracts for farming and ranching, *see also Rancho Oil Co. v. Powell*, 175 S.W.2D 960 (Tex. 1943).

---

[1] *Buttram v. Harris*, was rendered on November 26, 1934, and at that time, Oak Grove consisted of a flag station of the Texas and Pacific Railroad, two stores, a school and two teachers and seventy-five pupils, two filling stations, a gristmill, a bus line stop, post office, and a blacksmith shop. Likewise, there were twelve or fourteen houses averaging from three to six dwellers.

4. Urban Homestead

An urban homestead can present some interesting concerns because it encompasses business as well as residence.

FORD
v.
AETNA INS. CO.
424 S.W.2d 612
(Tex. 1968)

GREENHILL, JUSTICE.

In a previous suit, Aetna Insurance Company recovered a judgment for approximately $138,000 against H.M. Ford and others. 394 S.W.2d 693 (Tex. Civ. App.1965, write ref'd n.r.e.). In an effort to satisfy that judgment, Aetna got out execution against the properties of Ford. . . . Ford . . . had two non-contiguous lots in the same block in Sinton, both of which he claimed to use in his plumbing business, and both of which he claimed as business homestead.

Ford and his wife brought this action against Aetna and the Constable of Precinct 1, San Patricio County, to enjoin the sale under writ of execution of the . . . lots claimed as business homestead. The trial court granted Ford a temporary injunction. The Court of Civil Appeals sitting at Eastland . . . held . . . that because the two city lots were not contiguous, only one lot could be exempt as business homestead. In reversing the judgment of the trial court on temporary injunction, it held that Ford could elect which of the lots he would claim as business homestead. 417 S.W.2d 448.

. . . Ford contends that business lots need not be contiguous, and that there was evidence to sustain the action of the trial court in enjoining the sale of both lots. The questions before us are whether the fact that the two town lots are not contiguous prevents their constituting 'a place' for a business homestead; and assuming that two non-contiguous lots may constitute 'a place' for a business homestead, whether there was an abuse of discretion by the trial court in granting the temporary injunction to stay the sale.

As stated, the two lots claimed by the Fords as their business homestead are not adjacent or contiguous. The lots, both in Block 35 in Sinton, are separated by an alley. They are also separated laterally a distance of 25 feet. As illustrated by the diagram below, not drawn to scale, they are so closely situated to one another as to be capable of use in a single business.

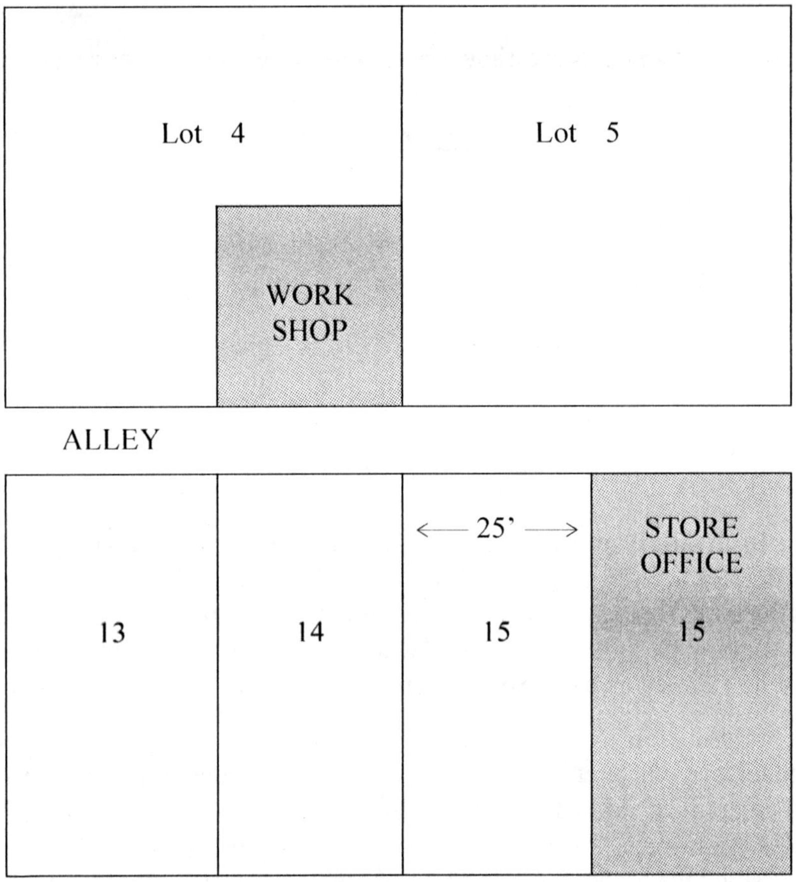

Mr. Ford testified that both lots were necessary and convenient for use in the exercise of his plumbing business, and that both were actually used in such business. His office, warehouse and sales area were located on lot 16, while the building on lot 4 contained his workshop and a storage area. While it is disputed, there is evidence in the record to support the Fords' contention that both lots were collectively used and necessary to the operation of his plumbing business.

Art. 16, Sec. 51, Texas Constitution, Vernon's Ann. St., defines the business homestead as follows:

> The homestead in a city . . . shall consist of lot, or lots . . . used . . . as a place to exercise the calling or business of the head of the family. . . .

In *McDonald v. Campbell*, 57 Tex. 614 (1882), this Court was first called upon to determine the extent of the business homestead exemption where the claimant claimed two non-contiguous lots. The plaintiff had execution levied on a house and lot owned by a druggist, who contended the house constituted part of his business homestead. The defendant's drug store was not contiguous to the house in question, which was used as a store room where patent medicines and other items used in the drug store were kept. In holding that the house was not exempt from execution as part of the business homestead, the Court said:

> We are of the opinion that the facts do not show that the use made of the house as a mere wareroom in which to store away articles of merchandise connected with the business in which the defendant was engaged as a druggist, was, in a legal and proper sense, the use of

that house and lot in the exercise of the defendant's calling or business. Whilst the law means to allow the head of a family, exempt from execution, one or more lots where he may exercise his vocation and conduct his business, its scope is not intended to extend so far as to protect from execution a lot or lots in excess of the lot or lots on which the vocation or the business of the head of the family is followed, even though such extra lots might be actually used in a way which was incidentally useful or profitable to the business which was being followed. Such supernumerary lots must be deemed merely auxiliary to the business office, station, store, shop or other like place of business; they are superfluous to the necessities of a trade homestead, which, according to the spirit of the constitution, demands no more than a sufficiency of lots whereupon to exercise the calling or business of the head of the family. Under the evidence in this case, we conceive that the drug store and lot was the defendant's place of business, and that the house in controversy was merely a place where the defendant stored certain goods in connection with his business as a druggist. We cannot believe that a proper construction of the constitution will so far expand its liberal provisions as to make them include lots indefinite in number, at the pleasure of the beneficiary,—limited only by their value not to exceed $5,000, when designated, without regard to their improvements,—and exacting no other requirement for exemption than their appropriation to collateral service and use in the business which the owner may be conducting on some other lot elsewhere in the town or city. 57 Tex. at 617.

The Court reached a similar result in *Rock Island Plow Co. v. Alten*, 102 Tex. 366, 116 S.W. 1144 (1909). In that case, the judgment debtor owned four lots which he claimed as business homestead. He operated a hardware and implement store on the front two lots, which were separated from his other two lots by a single lot owned by a third party; thus the front two lots were not contiguous to the back two lots. He used these latter two lots to store and expose for sale second-hand implements and vehicles which he had taken in trade, and to assemble vehicles and implements before placing them in his warehouse. The water closet used by his customers and himself was also located on the back lot. This Court held that the back two lots were not protected by the business homestead exemption, saying:

> . . . that portion which is devoted to the business must constitute a place, that is, one place, at which the business is transacted. It may consist of more than one lot if so used as to make them a place for transacting that business. . . .'
>
> The language applied to the lots to be used for the purposes of a home and the lots dedicated to the transaction of the business of the head of the family presents a sharp contrast in the character of the two exemptions. For the residence, or family homestead, it is not required that all of the lots should be used as "the domestic or hearthstone home," only that they be used "for the purposes of the home. . . . In contrast to that language, it is provided that for the business exemption the lots must constitute a place to exercise the calling or business of the head of a family which forbids the construction that such lots might be used "for the purposes" or in aid of the business of the family." 116 S.W. at 1144.

It is apparent from the quoted language of the above cases that the non-contiguity of the lots involved was not the controlling factor in determining that such non-contiguous lots were not part of the business homestead. Instead, the Court determined that the business homestead exemption was limited only to those lots actually used in the exercise of the business; and therefore lots merely used 'in connection with' the business or 'in aid of' the business actually conducted on another lot were not protected by the business homestead exemption.

Some writers and legal scholars have concluded from these two cases that the business homestead exemption cannot, under any circumstances, extend to two or more non-contiguous lots. *See, e.g.* NUNN, TEXAS HOMESTEAD AND OTHER EXEMPTIONS 137 (1931); Comment, 8 S.W.L.J. 90, 92 (1954): Note, 16 TEXAS L. REV. 108 (1938). Dean McSwain also reached this conclusion from the *Rock Island Plow* case but stated that it constituted an unduly restrictive holding. McSwain, *The Texas Business Homestead*, 15 BAYLOR L. REV. 39, 42 (1963). Several courts of civil appeals have reached the same conclusion in dicta, although the mere fact of non-contiguity never seems to have been the controlling consideration. *See, e.g. Campbell v. First National Bank in Lubbock*, 88 S.W.2d 1084 (Tex. Civ. App.1935, writ ref'd); *Harrington v. Mayo*, 61 Tex. Civ. App. 610, 130 S.W. 650 (1910, no writ); *Parrish v. Frey*, 18 Tex. Civ. App. 271, 44 S.W. 322 (1898, writ ref'd).

The holding that mere non-contiguity of lots will defeat the business homestead exemption is not compelled by either the literal language of the constitution or the *Campbell* and *Rock Island* cases. The constitutional definition of "lots used as a place . . . of business" is not expressly limited to contiguous lots. Since two adjacent lots with two buildings could clearly be exempted as business homestead, *Rock Island Plow Co. v. Alten, supra*, there is no logical reason why two non-contiguous lots collectively used as a place for the exercise of a single business cannot similarly be exempt.

We are further persuaded to this conclusion by the use of the wording 'lot or lots' in the constitution. "Lots" for homestead purposes are tracts of land designated by use, and the word is not limited to the boundaries of platted lots of a city or subdivision. *Hargadine v. Whitfield*, 71 Tex. 482, 9 S.W. 475 (1888). Thus a tract of platted contiguous lots would be "a lot" for homestead purposes, and the constitutional exemption of "lots" would be meaningless if contiguity were required.

We hold, therefore, that the business homestead exemption may extend to two non-contiguous lots when such lots are used as a place for the operation of the business of the head of a family, and both are essential to and necessary for such business, not merely being used in aid of the business.

In a hearing on an application for a temporary injunction, the only question before the trial court is the right of the applicant to a preservation of the status quo of the subject matter of the suit pending a final trial of the case on its merits. *Transport Company of Texas v. Robertson Transports, Inc.*, 152 Tex. 551, 261 S.W.2d 549 (1953). Since we have held that the fact that the lots are not contiguous does not, standing alone, prevent their being "a place" of business for homestead purposes, and since the Fords adduced evidence at the hearing for temporary injunction to support their contention that both lots were actually and necessarily used as a place for the operation of the plumbing business, no abuse of discretion by the trial court was shown.

The judgment of the Court of Civil Appeals reversing in part the judgment of the trial court and remanding the cause for further proceedings in accordance with its opinion is reversed, and the judgment of the trial court is affirmed.

GRIFFEN, J. dissenting.

VISTRON CORP.
v.
WINSTEAD

521 S.W.2d 754
(Tex. Civ. App.—Eastland 1975, no writ)

WALTER, JUSTICE.

Vistron Corporation and Don Mooney, Sheriff, have appealed from a permanent injunction order. The statement of the case and the statement of the facts have been correctly stated by the appellant and they are as follows:

> Vistron Corporation, appellant herein, obtained judgment against R.E. Winstead, appellee herein on the 10th of January, 1974 for the sum of $4,694.44 on an open account. Such judgment was abstracted and a Writ of Execution was issued out of the District Court of the 50th Judicial District and delivered to the Sheriff of Baylor County, Texas, and at such time as R.E. Winstead, appellee, was notified of such Writ of Execution, he caused to be filed a petition for injunction and the Judge of the 50th Judicial District Court of Baylor County, Texas, granted a temporary restraining order, and after hearing, entered a judgment making such temporary order a permanent injunction. And such order restrained Vistron Corporation and Don Mooney, Sheriff of Baylor County, from executing against the described real estate.
>
> The appellants' point of error is as follows:
>
> The District Court erred in rendering judgment preventing the execution against the described real estate for the reason that such judgment in effect grants to the Appellee, R.E. Winstead, both an urban homestead situated in the City of Seymour, Texas, and a rural homestead situated in Baylor County, Texas.

R.E. Winstead resides with his wife and children in a home that he owns within the city limits of the incorporated city of Seymour, Texas. Mr. Winstead operates his fertilizer business on a 2.5 acre tract of land approximately two-tenths of a mile from the city limits of Seymour on the Wichita Falls highway. The record reveals that businesses are located on each side of the highway from the center of the city past Winstead's place of business. Winstead testified there were businesses close to and beyond his business on the highway. He named the Triangle Hotel, Venues Motel and MacDermott Equipment Company.

In *Purdy v. Grove*, 35 S.W.2d 1078 (Tex. Civ. App.—Eastland 1931, writ ref.), the court said:

> * * * The urban homestead provided by the Constitution of Texas contemplates a lot or lots used for the purposes specified in such Constitution located in one urban community, whether governed by one or more municipal bodies, and not a lot or lots situated in widely separated urban communities. That statement is a significant one, and indicates that municipal boundary lines in such cases, like the corporate existence of a city, town, or village, are unimportant considerations in determining the location of or the right to claim the urban homestead, or a part thereof. Evidently, as used in this provision of the Constitution (section 51, art. 16), "a city, town, or village' means 'an aggregation of inhabitants and a collection of occupied dwellings and other buildings." *State ex rel. Wilke v. Stein et al.* (Tex. Com. App.) 26 § .W.(2d) 182, 184. There would appear to be no legal obstacle to a family residence homestead being located in Dallas and a business homestead in connection therewith in Highland

Park; the two adjoining municipalities being separated merely by a corporate line. The test would be, Are the parts of the one homestead located in one urban community?

We also cite in support and confirmation of the conclusions relating to the business homestead, NUNN ON EXEMPTIONS, p. 125, an excellent text recently published. In discussing limitations, (a) to (h), under which property may be impressed with the homestead character, the author states:

* * *

(b) That there can be but one residence homestead.

(c) That he can have but one business homestead, and such place of business is limited to one place.

(d) That the business homestead or place of business, together with the urban residence homestead, must be located in the same city, town or village, in that the two together constitute but one homestead.

* * *

It follows that the four propositions under consideration are overruled.

In *Woods v. Alvarado State Bank*, 118 Tex. 586, 19 S.W.2d 35 (1929), the Supreme Court said:

The rule that homestead laws are to be liberally construed to effectuate their beneficent purpose is one of general acceptation.

In *Connelly v. Johnson*, 259 S.W. 634 (Tex. Civ. App.—San Antonio 1924, no writ), the court said:

Liberal construction must be given to effectuate the purpose and intent of the framers of the Constitution, to protect the homestead right of the families.

We hold that Winstead's 2.5 acre tract of land described in the judgment is his homestead, and is not subject to forced sale. *Lewis v. Morrison Supply Company*, 231 F.2d 632 (1956).

We have examined appellants' point of error and find no merit in it. It is overruled.

The judgment is affirmed.

McKEE
v.
SMITH

965 S.W.2d 52
(Tex. App.—Fort Worth 1998, writ denied)

DAUPHINOT, JUSTICE.

Appellant Robert McKee attempted to force the sale of a piece of real property owned by Appellee Wanda Smith to satisfy a judgment against her. Wanda leases the property to Don A. Smith, Ph.D., Inc., a corporation wholly owned by Wanda's husband Don. The corporation is the family's only means of support and the property its only place of business.

Appellees claimed that the property was protected by the business homestead exemption. The trial court agreed and enjoined the forced sale. In his sole point, McKee contends that real estate leased to a corporation is not protected by the business homestead exemption.

The Texas Constitution has since 1876 exempted from forced sale debtors' real property used as their family's primary place of business.[1] The property code also provides for this business homestead exemption.[2] It is well-settled that real property titled to a corporation which is wholly owned by a family member is not protected by a business homestead exemption.[3] However, Texas state court case law is silent as to whether the business homestead exemption applies to real property titled to a family member but leased to a corporation wholly owned by a family member. The Fifth Circuit Court of Appeals, applying Texas law, found that the exemption would apply.[4]

The business homestead exemption was designed to protect property titled to a family member at which family "members may pursue such business or avocation as may be necessary for the support and comfort of the family."[5] The Texas Supreme Court directs us to construe the business homestead exemption liberally toward these ends.[6] Consequently, we follow the Fifth Circuit in finding that the business homestead exemption applies to real property titled to a family member but leased to a corporation wholly owned by a family member. We overrule McKee's sole point and affirm the trial court's judgment.

Questions

1. Texas Constitution art. XVI § 51 provides that an urban homestead may be used "as both an urban home *and* a place to exercise a calling or business of the homestead claimant, . . ." (emphasis added). How would you distinguish lots used "to exercise a calling or business" from lots used in aid of a business? Provide examples.

2. What various incorporated areas exist in your locale?

---

[1] *See* Waggener v. Haskell, 89 Tex. 435, 35 S.W. 1, 1-2 (1896) (citing TEX. CONST. art. XVI, § 51).

[2] TEX. PROP. CODE ANN. §§ 41.001-.002 (Vernon Supp.1998).

[3] *See* Nash v. Conatser, 410 S.W.2d 512, 521-22 (Tex. Civ. App.—Dallas 1966, no writ); Nowlin v. Wm. Cameron & Co., 54 S.W.2d 1035, 1035-36 (Tex. Civ. App.—Fort Worth 1932, writ ref'd).

[4] *See* In re John Taylor Co., 935 F.2d 75, 76-77 (5th Cir.1991).

[5] C.D. Shamburger Lumber Co. v. Delavan, 106 S.W.2d 351, 355 (Tex. Civ. App.—Amarillo 1937, writ ref'd) (quoting Pryor v. Stone, 19 Tex. 371, 373 (1857)).

6 *See* Cocke v. Conquest, 120 Tex. 43, 35 S.W.2d 673, 678 (1931); Woods v. Alvarado State Bank, 118 Tex. 586, 19 S.W.2d 35, 35 (1929).

5. Establishing the Homestead Claim

Very often a person will not reside upon property which has been designated as homestead in response to a creditor's claim. Is physical presence always necessary? Is it the defining factor?

CHESWICK
v.
FREEMAN
287 S.W.2d 171
(Tex. 1956)

HICKMAN, CHIEF JUSTICE.

Petitioner, Louise Freeman, obtained a judgment for money against respondent, Fred Freeman, her former husband, in Harris County in May, 1951, an interest in which judgment she assigned to petitioner Cheswick. The judgment was abstracted in Limestone County the following month, and thereafter an execution issued out of the Harris County court was caused to be levied on fifty acres of land in Limestone County as the property of respondent and notice to sell the property on October 2, 1951, was posted by the sheriff of that county. Respondent filed this suit to enjoin the sale and was awarded first a temporary restraining order, followed by a temporary injunction, which, upon final trial upon the merits, was made permanent. The trial court's judgment was affirmed by the Court of Civil Appeals. 282 S.W.2d 315.

The sole question for decision is whether the 50-acre tract of land was the homestead of respondent and, as such, exempt from sale under the execution. It is the contention of respondent that the property became his homestead following the death of his father in 1941, or in the alternative, that it became his homestead following the death of his mother in 1949. The facts bearing on the first contention may be briefly stated as follows: Respondent's father and mother owned a 67-acre tract of land in Limestone County, of which the 50-acre tract in controversy is a part, together with a nonadjacent 60-acre tract. This land was their homestead. The father died intestate in 1941. Following his death, respondent and his wife, with the consent of his mother, lived with her on the 67-acre tract until 1945, when they moved to Waco. In 1949 respondent's mother died intestate, after which he and his brother, her sole heirs, partitioned their parents' estate, respondent receiving as his portion the 50-acre tract here involved and the brother receiving the balance of the 67-acre tract together with the 60-acre tract. Respondent's use and occupancy of the land from 1941 to 1945 were of such nature as would have impressed his interest with the homestead character had the mother not been living at that time.

Under the provisions of Section 52, Article XVI, of our State Constitution, Vernon's Ann. St., upon the death of respondent's father this property became the homestead of his mother for her lifetime or so long as she might elect to use or occupy the same as her homestead. She continued to use and occupy the property as her homestead until her death, and no question of abandonment or waiver of her homestead right therein is presented. It is the rule that so long as respondent's mother continued to occupy this property as her homestead her possessory right therein was exclusive and precluded a similar right in her children. This property could not be impressed with two homestead rights at the same time, one in favor of the mother and the other in favor of her son. *Massillon Engine & Thresher Co. v. Barrow*, Tex. Com. App., 231 S.W. 368; *Rettig v. Houston West End Realty Co.*,

Tex. Com. App., 254 S.W. 765; *Johnson v. Prosper State Bank*, Tex. Civ. App., 125 S.W.2d 707, *affirmed by memorandum opinion* 134 Tex. 677, 138 S.W.2d 1117; *Cook v. Young*, Tex. Civ. App., 269 S.W.2d 457, no writ history. NUNN ON EXEMPTIONS, p. 120, correctly states the rule as established by the above authorities in this language:

> * * * The right to the use and occupancy as a homestead in the surviving parent is exclusive and precludes a similar right in the heirs of the deceased so long as such right is exercised by such survivor. And this is true although the heir may be upon the property with the consent of her surviving parent, for such holding cannot attach to the title taken by the heir, in that, the homestead rights of the survivor run to the entire homestead tract and exclude all others.

Respondent relies upon *Thompson & Sons Lumber Co. v. Clifton*, 132 Tex. 366, 124 S.W.2d 106, as an authority supporting his contention that he acquired a homestead right in this land during the lifetime of his mother. In our view that case affords no support for his position. The question of the right of a child to impress a homestead character upon land which is the homestead of one of his parents was not before the court for decision in that case. The opinion discloses that the parents of the homestead claimant had their home in the city of Mexia, but owned in community 600 acres of land outside of the city. A son resided on a portion of the 600 acres after the death of his mother but before the death of his father, who continued to live in his home in Mexia. Had the parents established a homestead right in the rural property, same would have been limited to 200 acres and claimant might have established a homestead in the excess, but there was no showing that they ever established such right.

This brings us to a consideration of the question of whether the respondent established a homestead right on this property after the death of his mother in 1949. The relevant facts are as follows: In 1945 respondent and his wife moved to Waco. After the death of his mother in 1949 respondent and his brother partitioned the land of their parents, respondent receiving in that partition the 50-acre tract here involved. Petitioners' judgment was abstracted in June, 1951, and execution issued in August of that year. After his mother's death, respondent and his wife continued to live in Waco until January, 1952, when they moved to the land here involved and lived there until March 1, 1954. Respondent testified that he intended at all times to make this tract of land the homestead of himself and family and that he had no property except this little tract of land. He further testified that he paid his poll tax in Limestone County in 1948, 1950, and 1952. His intention to make this property his homestead was not evidenced by any overt acts. He placed no improvements upon the land before returning to live on it in 1952; neither was he prevented from occupying same by unavoidable circumstances. The record would support no conclusion other than that respondent had in mind the intention to make this property his home at some future date, followed by occupancy thereof after the levy of the execution. Before the execution was levied no overt acts evidenced that intention. In our view these facts will not support the holding that this property became the homestead of respondent prior to the levy of the execution. In order to impress upon property a homestead character in the absence of actual occupancy, the head of the family must have intended to reside thereon with his family as a home and that intention must be evidenced by overt acts of preparation. Something must be done which impresses the land with the incidents of a home. Many of the earlier authorities establishing that doctrine are cited in *Lasseter v. Blackwell*, Tex. Com. App., 227 S.W. 944; and many of the later cases are cited in *Gilmore v. Dennison*, 131 Tex. 398, 115 S.W.2d 902.

In support of his claim that this property was impressed by the homestead character by him after the death of his mother in 1949, and before the levy of the execution in 1951, respondent places much reliance upon *Vaughan v. Sterling Nat. Bank & Trust Co. of New York*, Tex. Civ. App., 124 S.W.2d

440, error refused. In that case the homestead claimants were Mr. and Mrs. Traylor and the property upon which they claimed homestead rights was acquired by Mrs. Traylor under the will of her deceased father. It was found that the Traylors formed an intention to move upon the property upon the death of Mrs. Traylor's father, but were prevented from carrying out their intention by the illness of Mr. Traylor. About six months after her father's death the Traylors moved their piano and other furniture to the premises. That case might stand for the proposition that, when it is found that a bona fide intention existed to move upon the property as a home, but the move was delayed on account of the physical inability of the claimant to make same, no overt acts of intention are necessary to impress the property with the homestead character. That condition does not exist in the instant case.

Respondent also relies upon *Stevenson v. Wilson*, Tex. Civ. App., 130 S.W.2d 317, error refused, and *Stevenson v. Wilson*, Tex. Civ. App., 206 S.W.2d 613, no writ history. We think it unnecessary to make any further statement concerning those cases than that in that litigation there was testimony of overt acts of preparation performed by the homestead claimant evidencing an intention to occupy the property as a home.

It is our view that the trial court erred in granting the injunction, and that the Court of Civil Appeals erred in affirming the case. Accordingly, the judgments of both courts are reversed and the injunction dissolved.

CLARK
v.
SALINAS

628 S.W.2d 51
(Tex. 1982)

PER CURIAM.

John W. Clark sought to foreclose a judgment lien against a lot owned by Salinas. The subject matter of the judgment, out of which the lien arose, bore no relationship to the lot in question.

Salinas claimed the lot as a homestead. He sought and obtained a temporary injunction to enjoin a foreclosure sale. The trial court granted the temporary injunction. The court of appeals affirmed. 626 S.W.2d 118. The writ of error is refused, no reversible error, because the trial court did not abuse its discretion in granting the temporary injunction to preserve the status quo. *Navarro Auto Park Inc. v. City of San Antonio*, 580 S.W.2d 339 (Tex. 1979); *Davis v. Huey*, 571 S.W.2d 859 (Tex. 1978); *Anderson v. Tall Timbers Corporation*, 162 Tex. 450, 347 S.W.2d 592 (1961).

As set out more fully in the opinion of the court of appeals, Salinas had purchased the lot and intended to build a house on it as his homestead. He owned no other property. He had plans drawn up and purchased supplies from which to build the house, but he stored them on his mother's lot rather than on his lot. He had intended to build the house himself but was prevented from doing so because of an injury.

We are cited to *Cheswick v. Freeman*, 155 Tex. 372, 287 S.W.2d 171 (1956), *Gilmore v. Dennison*, 131 Tex. 398, 115 S.W.2d 902 (1938), and other cases. The court of appeals went beyond the upholding of the temporary injunction and held as a matter of law that the land had acquired the status of a homestead. It distinguished Cheswick and Gilmore.

We agree with the court of appeals that there was not an abuse of discretion in granting the temporary injunction to preserve the status quo. We, therefore, do not reach the merits of the case.

Questions

1. Why didn't Mr. Freeman's homestead right attach between 1941 and 1945?

2. Why didn't Mr. Freeman's homestead right attach in 1949, or any time between 1949 and prior to judgment abstracted against him?

3. How did the actions of Mr. Salinas differ from those of Mr. Freeman?

---

6. Abandonment

The cornerstone of a homestead claim often will be the use made of the claimed property. Use also can defeat a homestead claim.

ATWOOD
v.
GUARANTY CONST. CO.
63 S.W.2d 685
(Tex. 1933)

LEDDY, JUDGE.

Plaintiffs in error are husband and wife. In 1924 they acquired a lot 72 feet in width and 152.8 feet in length, extending through an entire city block in the city of Lubbock. They occupied as a home the residence situated on the east end of this lot, facing on Avenue O. They erected a garage near the north property line about 82 feet west of Avenue O. The west 70 feet of this lot, which fronted on Avenue P, had been separated from the remainder of the lot by a wire fence which seems later to have been torn down. The west end of the lot was unimproved and was used as a chicken yard and garden in connection with plaintiffs in error's homestead.

In 1929 plaintiffs in error decided to improve the west end of their home place by building two residences, with a double garage. These residences were to face on Avenue P. It was contemplated that the houses would be used for rental purposes; the income therefrom, after the payment of the cost of their construction, was to be used for the support of the plaintiffs in error.

In order to obtain funds with which to erect these rent houses, plaintiffs in error executed a promissory note for the contract price of the proposed improvements and secured the same by a duly executed mechanic's lien which described the entire lot.

This suit was brought by defendant in error, the owner of the note given by plaintiffs in error, to recover the balance due thereon and to foreclose the mechanic's lien on the property described in the mechanic's lien contract.

Plaintiffs in error admitted the debt and the existence of a mechanic's lien to secure the same. They urged no objection to a foreclosure of the lien against the west part of the lot upon which the improvements had been constructed. They sought, however, a cancellation of the lien in so far as it affected the east 80 feet of the lot upon which was situated the residence which they used and occupied as a homestead. The ground upon which they sought cancellation was that no valid lien could be created upon their homestead for the erection of improvements not made thereon.

The trial court sustained the defense urged by plaintiffs in error. It rendered judgment for defendant in error for the balance due on the note with a foreclosure of the mechanic's lien on the west 72 feet of said lot and canceled the mechanic's lien on the east 80 feet of said lot.

Defendant in error duly perfected an appeal to the Court of Civil Appeals. That court reversed the portion of the trial court's judgment foreclosing the mechanic's lien on the west part of said lot and rendered judgment in favor of defendant in error for a foreclosure of its mechanic's lien on the entire lot.

We conclude the trial court rendered a proper judgment and that the Court of Civil Appeals erred in not affirming the same.

The undisputed facts disclose that prior to the execution of the mechanic's lien contract for the erection of the two rent houses, the entire lot upon which plaintiffs in error's residence was situated constituted their homestead. They occupied the residence thereon as a place of abode for the family, while the west end of said lot was used in connection with their home as a chicken yard and for garden purposes.

The following plat* fairly presents the situation as it existed after the erection of the rent houses on the west end of the lot:

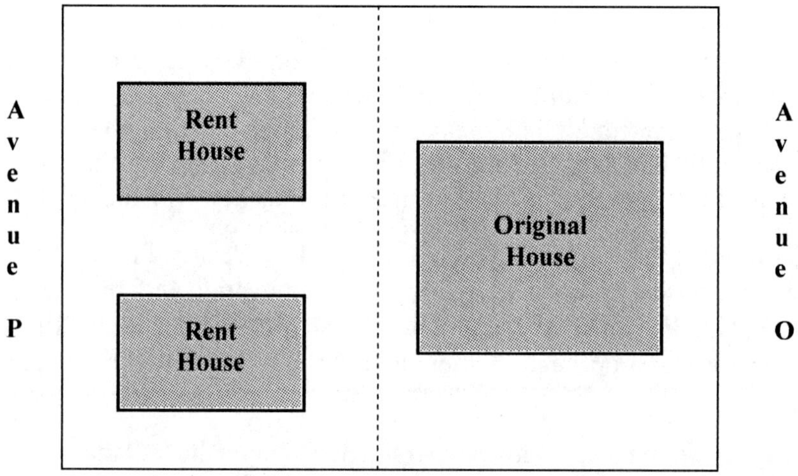

A valid lien can be created upon the homestead for any improvements made upon the tract dedicated to that purpose. The only limitation upon the power to create such liens is that the improvements must be of such a nature that they may reasonably and fairly be used in connection with the proper use and enjoyment of the property as a homestead. If the home owner permanently appropriates a portion of the home tract for a use inconsistent with that of the homestead, such act upon his part constitutes an abandonment of that portion of the tract for homestead purposes. *Strang v. Pray*, 89 Tex. 527, 35 S. W. 1054; *Wynne v. Hudson*, 66 Tex. 1, 17 S. W. 110; *Lipscomb v. Adamson Lumber Co.* (Tex. Civ. App.) 217 S. W. 228.

When plaintiff in error entered into a contract to build the two residences for rental purposes, his action operated to segregate from his home tract such part thereof as was reasonably necessary for the proper use and enjoyment of said rent property. The permanent appropriation of this portion of the home tract for purposes inconsistent with its use as a homestead operated as an abandonment of it for homestead purposes.

Under the Constitution and statutes of this state, a valid mechanic's lien can be fixed upon the homestead only for improvements made thereon. It necessarily follows that a lien cannot be fixed on the homestead for improvements made on property which constitutes no part of the family homestead.

* This is editor's simplified version of plat, not the court's exhibit.

While it is not necessary in order that a valid mechanic's lien may be created on the homestead that the improvements be made upon the residence which is used for the purpose of a home, nevertheless it is essential that before such lien can be fixed the improvements made thereon must be of such a nature as not to be inconsistent with the homestead use.

Defendant in error contends that the case of *Macomber et ux. v. Home Building & Loan Co.* (Tex. Civ. App.) 291 S. W. 294, in which a writ of error was refused by the Supreme Court, is decisive of its contention in this case. There is nothing in the opinion in the case relied on contrary to the holding made by us in this case. In that case it was shown that appellants owned lots 1 and 2 in block 42 in the city of Beaumont. They segregated a portion of their home tract, 60 by 100 feet in dimension, upon which to erect a dwelling to be used solely for rental purposes. In pursuance of this purpose they executed a mechanic's lien upon that portion of the lot upon which the dwelling was to be erected to secure the payment of a note given to cover the cost of erecting the dwelling. After the house was completed appellants used it for rental purposes. They then built a fence around it so as to cut off all of the 100 by 60 feet described in the mechanic's lien contract with the exception of 46 feet by 74 feet which was the amount of land actually covered by the rent house. Under these circumstances the court very properly held that the appellee was entitled to a foreclosure on the land described in the mechanic's lien contract. The effect of this holding was that appellants had segregated from their home tract 60 by 100 feet to be used in connection with the occupancy of the dwelling to be erected. Hence the lien created thereon was valid and they could not by subsequent action reduce the amount of land which they had solemnly agreed might be dedicated for use in connection with the rent house.

In the instant case plaintiffs in error have not abandoned the use of the east end of their lot for homestead purposes. Nor have they consented that it might be used in connection with the use of the rent houses. They have, however, conclusively evinced an intention to abandon the west 72 feet of the lot because it has been permanently appropriated by them to a use inconsistent with homestead purposes.

It is insisted that effect must be given to the testimony of Mrs. Atwood upon the trial that all of the lot was then their homestead as it had previously been. This was but a legal conclusion upon her part and is entitled to no weight when shown not to be justified by the facts upon which it was based.

Where a building to be used for rental purposes is erected upon a portion of a homestead tract, the mechanic's lien given for securing the cost of such improvements will attach to the land upon which the improvements are situated and which are essential to its proper use and enjoyment or such as may be shown was intended to be used in connection with such property. *Strang v. Pray, supra.* 1 JONES ON MTGS. § 142.

The surrounding facts and circumstances evince with reasonable clearness a purpose upon the part of plaintiffs in error to designate the west 72 feet as the amount of land which they deemed essential for use in connection with the occupancy of the rent houses. The dividing line between the home place and the rent houses is fairly shown to be the line upon which the rears of the garages on both lots are situated. It seems that at one time a fence was constructed on this line and that the rear of the garage on the home place was placed on approximately this line. We believe from all the surrounding circumstances that the trial court was justified in concluding that plaintiffs in error intended all of the land west of the rear of their garage to be used in connection with the rent houses.

We recommend that the judgment of the Court of Civil Appeals be reversed and the judgment of the trial court affirmed.

CURETON, CHIEF JUSTICE.

Judgment of the Court of Civil Appeals reversed, and judgment of the district court affirmed.

Notes, Comments & Questions

1. What if the plaintiffs in *Atwood v. Guaranty Construction Co.* had installed a swimming pool rather than built two rent houses?

2. Did the finding of abandonment work to the plaintiff's advantage?

3. What if there had been no such finding of abandonment?

4. Abandonment can occur by following another party's instructions. For example, in the case of *Power v. Chapman*, 994 S.W.2d 331 (Tex. App.—Texarkana 1999, no writ), the court opined, thus:

> In the third point of error, Power contends that the trial court erred in granting the motion for summary judgment because the prenuptial agreement prevented him from asserting his claim to homestead and other rights. It is unclear from the reading of the motion for summary judgment that this claim was contained in the motion and provided a basis for the relief granted.
>
> Nevertheless, Power argues that he did not waive his right to homestead property and that he moved from the home he had shared with the decedent only at Chapman's insistence when Power remarried. Power contends that *Hunter v. Clark* controls. 687 S.W.2d 811 (Tex. App.—San Antonio 1985, no writ). In *Hunter*, the court of appeals found a prenuptial agreement to be inadequate to waive homestead rights. The court failed to find an intent in the agreement that the property enumerated remain "free from any claim," including homestead rights, of either of the respective parties. *Hunter*, 687 S.W.2d at 816.
>
> The language in the prenuptial agreement involved here also fails to explicitly state that the property is to be free from any claim of the other spouse. However, Power moved out of the house in March 1992 when he remarried. Before marrying, Power asked Chapman if he could remain in the house, and Chapman stated that he could not have another woman in the house. Power did not protest Chapman's wishes and did not bring any claims regarding the deprivation of homestead rights until June 1994. Based on the circumstances, the trial court could have found that Power abandoned his homestead rights when he voluntarily moved out of the home following his remarriage. The third point of error is overruled.

---

7. Improvements

As a preface to this section, go back to section B. Statutes of this chapter and read TEX. PROP. CODE § 53.254

KEPLEY
v.
ZACHRY
116 S.W.2d 699
(Tex. 1938)

GERMAN, COMMISSIONER.

On April 15, 1927, James K. Kepley and wife, Nora Kepley, entered into a contract with H.B. Zachry for the construction of a dwelling house on certain lots of land situated in Laredo, Tex., constituting their homestead. Zachry was to furnish all labor and materials and was to construct and deliver the dwelling as a turnkey job for the lump sum of $15,500. The contract provided for a mechanics', materialmen's, laborers', and contractors' lien upon the homestead property to secure payment of the contract price. While this contract was signed by the parties on the date mentioned, it was not acknowledged as required by law until June 21, 1927. After the signing of the contract, Zachry proceeded with construction of the dwelling and prior to June 21, 1927, had expended in labor and materials about $8,000 thereon. After the acknowledgment of the contract, Zachry continued with the work and substantially completed the dwelling according to contract. The jury found that after June 21, 1927, Zachry expended for labor and materials in completing the dwelling the sum of $7,500.

This suit was instituted by defendant in error Zachry to recover a balance due upon the contract price for the dwelling, and to foreclose a lien against the homestead property for the amount of labor and materials furnished after June 21, 1927. He will be referred to as plaintiff. Kepley and wife will be referred to as defendants. The trial court awarded judgment in favor of plaintiff for $10,208.79, with interest, and allowed foreclosure of lien against the homestead for the sum of $5,660.97, with interest from June 16, 1934. This is the only part of the judgment that is brought into question. The Court of Civil Appeals affirmed the judgment of the district court allowing foreclosure of lien against the homestead. 90 S.W.2d 571. Upon that question writ of error was granted.

It is not claimed that plaintiff had any lien prior to the acknowledgment of the contract on June 21, 1927. It is contended, however, that he did acquire a lien for the value of materials and labor furnished after that date, and the Court of Civil Appeals so held.

Article 16, § 50, of our Constitution is as follows:

> The homestead of a family shall be, and is hereby protected from forced sale, for the payment of all debts except for the purchase money thereof, or a part of such purchase money, the taxes due thereon, or for work and material used in constructing improvements thereon, and in this last case only when the work and material are contracted for in writing, with the consent of the wife given in the same manner as is required in making a sale and conveyance of the homestead; nor shall the owner, if a married man, sell the homestead without the consent of the wife, given in such manner as may be prescribed by law. No mortgage, trust deed, or

> other lien on the homestead shall ever be valid, except for the purchase money therefor, or improvements made thereon, as hereinbefore provided, whether such mortgage, or trust deed, or other lien, shall have been created by the husband alone, or together with his wife; and all pretended sales of the homestead involving any condition of defeasance shall be void.

The applicable statute is article 5460 of the Revised Statutes of 1925 and is as follows:

> When material is furnished, labor performed, or improvements as defined in this title are made, or when erections or repairs are made upon homesteads, if the owner thereof is a married man, then to fix and secure the lien upon the same it shall be necessary for the person or persons who furnish the material or perform the labor, before such material is furnished or such labor is performed, to make and enter into a contract in writing, setting forth the terms thereof, which shall be signed by the owner and his wife, and privily acknowledged by her, as is required in making sale of homestead. And such contract shall be recorded in the office of the county clerk in the county where such homestead is situated, in a well bound book to be kept for that purpose. When such contract has been made and entered into by the husband and wife and the contractor or builder, and the same has been recorded, as heretofore provided, then the same shall inure to the benefit of any and all persons who shall furnish material or labor thereon for such contractor or builder.

It has of course been many times held that in order to create the lien provided for by the Constitution and statute, there must be a contract entered into in writing and acknowledged by the wife before the material is furnished or the labor is performed. Nor can the failure to comply with the requirements of the law be waived, or ratified, by any contract made after the material is furnished or the labor done. *Collier v. Valley Building & Loan Association*, Tex. Com. App., 62 S.W.2d 82, and authorities there cited.

* * *

This manifestly has application to those who furnish labor and material to the contractor or builder, and has nothing to do with creating a lien in favor of the contractor or builder. This is made clear by the succeeding articles. For instance, article 5461 provides how persons, "except the original contractor or builder," shall proceed with the matter of enforcing the lien given by the concluding portion of the statute. There is no contention that plaintiff in this instance attempted to comply with the latter provisions of the law, even if he could have done so.

The judgments of the Court of Civil Appeals and of the district court, in so far as they decree foreclosure of lien against the homestead property of plaintiffs in error, are reversed, and judgment is here rendered denying such lien. The judgments in all other respects are affirmed.

ZELLER
v.
UNIVERSITY SAVINGS ASSOC.

580 S.W.2d 658
(Tex. Civ. App.—Houston [14th Dist] 1979, no writ)

J. CURTISS BROWN, CHIEF JUSTICE.

Summary judgment was rendered against plaintiffs in their suit to set aside the foreclosure sale of their residence.

The property in question was owned by Charles Zeller and wife (appellants) subject to a purchase money mortgage and lien. On July 22, 1976, appellants, to secure a loan for home improvements by University Savings Association (Association), executed three promissory notes and subjected the residence to a second-lien deed of trust. Appellants made payments on the notes for seventeen months during which time the Association accepted numerous payments that were from one week to a month late. In March 1978, when neither the February nor March 1978 payments had been paid, Henry Serafin, II (Serafin), as substitute trustee, was instructed by the Association to accelerate the notes and to institute foreclosure proceedings under the deed of trust. On March 27, 1978, appellants received notice by certified mail of foreclosure sale proceedings to be held on April 4, 1978. Appellants filed for a temporary injunction to halt the sale, but subsequently withdrew that suit and entered into the following agreement in open court:

> With respect to a foreclosure duly posted for sale on property of Mr. Zeller, the plaintiff . . . has agreed to take a non-suit and withdraw . . . the petition for injunction. . . . But in the event the sale is held today and University Savings becomes purchaser, that it will between now and the next date of sale under the statute . . . reconvey its interest . . . subject to the first lien. . . .

The substitute trustee held the sale as scheduled and the property was conveyed by Serafin to David Lawson (Lawson) subject to the first lien. Appellants then filed suit against the Association, Serafin, and Lawson to set aside the sale, alleging as grounds improper notice and posting; conspiracy among the defendants; that the Association had waived prompt payment by acceptance of late payments; and that labor and materials were furnished before the contracts for the improvements were executed. When the defendants' motions for summary judgment were granted, appellants brought this appeal.

The standard to be applied in reviewing summary judgment cases is well established. The controlling question is whether appellees, as the parties moving for summary judgment, established that there were no genuine issues of material fact and that they were entitled to judgment as a matter of law. *Pachter v. Woodman*, 547 S.W.2d 954, 957 (Tex. 1977); *National Founders Corp. v. Central National Bank*, 521 S.W.2d 92, 97 (Tex. Civ. App.—Houston (14th Dist.) 1975, writ ref'd n. r. e.). Further,

> (a)ll conflicts in the evidence are disregarded, and the evidence which tends to support the position of the party opposing the motion is accepted as true. (Citations omitted.) Evidence which favors the movant's position is not considered unless it is uncontradicted. If such uncontradicted evidence is from an interested witness, it cannot be considered as doing more than raising an issue of fact, unless it is clear, direct and positive and there are no circumstances in evidence tending to discredit or impeach such testimony.

E.g., Pachter, supra.

Appellants urge that there is a question of fact with respect to the timeliness of the mailing of the notice of sale. The applicable statute requires that

> the holder of the debt to which the power is related shall at least 21 days preceding the date of sale Serve written notice of the proposed sale by certified mail on each debtor obligated to pay such debt according to the records of such holder. Service of such notice shall be completed upon deposit of the notice, enclosed in a postpaid wrapper, properly addressed to such debtor at the most recent address as shown by the records of the holder of the debt, in a post office or official depository under the care and custody of the United States Postal Service. The affidavit of any person having knowledge of the facts to the effect that such service was completed shall be prima facie evidence of the fact of service.

TEX. REV. CIV. STAT. ANN. art. 3810 (Supp.1978) (emphasis added). In his affidavit, Serafin, the substitute trustee, stated that "(n)otice of the sale was timely and properly sent to plaintiffs as reflected by the notice letter and certified mail receipt. . . ." The notice letter is dated March 13, 1978, which would be "at least twenty-one days preceding the date of sale. . . ." However, the certified mail receipt does not bear the date of deposit of the notice "in a post office or official depository" but does reflect the date of delivery and postmark to be March 27, 1978, only nine days preceding the sale date. Neither the affidavit nor the incorporated notice letter and mail receipt complies with the statutory requirement of "knowledge of the facts to the effect that such service was completed. . . ." Further, the affidavit, notice letter, and certified mail receipt rebut the presumption contained in the trustee's deed "that all prerequisites to said sale required either by law or by said Deeds of Trust have been dutifully and fully complied with. . . ." *Pachter, supra*, 547 S.W.2d at 957. *See also*, *Gulf, Colorado & Sante Fe Railway Co. v. McBride*, 159 Tex. 442, 322 S.W.2d 492 (1958). Therefore, under *Pachter*, there is a question of fact presented on this material issue. However, we agree with the appellees that, by agreeing to allow the sale to proceed at the option of the Association and obtaining the right to repurchase if the interest was acquired by the Association, appellants waived any defects in notice or posting and cannot rely on those grounds for setting aside the foreclosure sale. The appellants' contention that the Association waived prompt payments by a continuous acceptance of late payments is likewise without merit since the notes expressly provided that acceptance of late payments would not give rise to waiver of promptness on subsequent payments.

Appellants also claim that appellees Lawson and the Association acted in collusion to deprive appellants of the right to repurchase as set out in the stipulation. Under the applicable summary judgment rules, it was the appellees' burden to establish that no issues of material fact existed as to conspiracy or collusion. *National Founders, supra*, 521 S.W.2d at 97. In the case at bar the appellees assert by affidavits that there had been no contact between Lawson and the other appellees before the sale other than a telephone inquiry by Lawson concerning the amount owed. The appellees further deny any conspiracy or collusion. The stipulation in open court did not obligate the Association to purchase the property or even bid on it. By agreeing to the stipulation, appellants accepted the risk that someone other than the Association might be that purchaser. Encouraging bidding at such a sale would not be illegal or improper. There is no suggestion that Lawson was acting as straw man for the Association or that he acted in its behalf to avoid the repurchase covenant. Nor is there any intimation that the activities of the Association or Lawson constituted a "combination by two or more persons to accomplish an unlawful purpose or to accomplish a lawful purpose by unlawful means," as required to establish a civil conspiracy. *Schlumberger Well Sur. Corp. v. Nortex Oil & G. Corp.*, 435 S.W.2d 854 (Tex. 1968); *St. Joseph Pro. Bldg. Corp. v. American Nat. Ins. Co.*, 511 S.W.2d 578, 582 (Tex. Civ.

App.—Houston (14th Dist.) 1974, writ ref'd n.r.e.). The affidavits of appellees are sufficient to establish the non-existence of any genuine issues of material fact. MCDONALD, TEXAS CIVIL PRACTICE, § 17.26.8(iv) (rev. 1971). *See, National Founders, supra,* 521 S.W.2d at 97.

Appellants claim that the lien held by the Association was invalid since labor and materials were supplied to the homestead before a written contract covering such was executed. It is true that a mechanics and materialman's lien is unenforceable against the homestead if a contract to cover the labor and materials is not executed before work is begun or materials delivered. TEX. REV. CIV. STAT. ANN. art. 5460 (Supp. 1978). Nevertheless, when appellants recited in the notes that in fact labor and materials had not been furnished before the execution of the contracts, they induced the Association, an innocent third party, to rely on the validity of such liens. It is well settled that in such instances the parties making the recitations are estopped to later argue the invalidity of the liens as a defense to foreclosure. *Ackerson v. Farm & Home Savings & Loan Ass'n.,* 77 S.W.2d 559, 561 (Tex. Civ. App.—San Antonio 1934, writ ref'd); *Farm & Home Savings & Loan Ass'n v. Muhl,* 37 S.W.2d 316 (Tex. Civ. App.—Waco 1931, writ ref'd).

The contention is made on appeal that the interest rates required in the notes were in violation of the usury laws. We do not consider this point since it was not presented to the trial court by "written motion, answer or other response. . . . ." TEX. R. CIV. P. 166-A.

We conclude that appellees met their burden of showing the non-existence of any genuine issue of material fact and their entitlement to judgment as a matter of law. Appellants' points of error are overruled and the summary judgment for the appellees is affirmed.

Questions

1. Why must an agreement to furnish material or perform labor be signed before the labor or material is furnished?

2. Was the principle of "clean hands" a motivating force of the *Zeller* opinion?

---

8. Conveyance of Homestead

As a preface to this section read TEX. FAM. CODE §§ 5.001-.108.

ZABLE
v.
HENRY
649 S.W.2d 136
(Tex. App.—Dallas 1983, no writ)

WHITMAN, JUSTICE.

Appellants, J.I. Zable and his wife, Edith Zable, sought a declaratory judgment that the grant of an option to appellees, Edward J. Henry, Jr. and Edward J. Henry, III, contained in a deed executed by Mr. Zable was void because the property was the Zables' homestead and the deed containing the option had not been signed by Mrs. Zable. Both the Zables and the Henrys filed motions for summary judgment on that issue. The trial court denied the Zables' motion and granted the Henrys' motion and entered judgment dismissing the Zables' action. We affirm.

Mr. Zable conveyed certain real property to the Henrys and in the deed granted the Henrys an option to purchase other real property which the Zables contend was homestead property both at the time the deed was signed and as of the date of hearing on the motions for summary judgment. Mrs. Zable did not join in the execution of the deed containing the grant of the option. For purposes of their motion for summary judgment the Henrys conceded that the option property was the Zables' homestead both at the time the deed was signed and as of the date of hearing on the motion for summary judgment. The option reads:

> As a further consideration herein, Grantor does hereby grant and convey unto Grantees, their heirs and assigns, the right of first refusal to purchase for a cash consideration of $65,000.00, the real property and all improvements at 3939 Travis Street, Dallas, Texas, and legally described as follows:
>
> [property description deleted]
>
> This right of first refusal shall be for a period of ten (10) years from May 1, 1978, until April 30, 1988, and shall be a covenant running with the land and be binding upon the Grantor herein, his heirs and assigns.

Both the Zables and the Henrys interpret the option to consist of a right of first refusal to purchase the property for $65,000.00 until April 30, 1988, and an absolute option to purchase the property for that price on April 30, 1988. While we do not read the option to grant an absolute option to purchase the property for $65,000.00 on April 30, 1988, we are bound by the interpretation made by all parties and dispose of this appeal on the basis of their interpretation.

At the outset we emphasize that the issue in the present case is limited to voidness vel non. This case does not involve the forced sale of homestead or an action for enforcement of the option by specific performance. At no point have the Henrys suggested that the option would be specifically enforceable while Mrs. Zable continues to occupy the property. The only issue presented by this action is whether the option is presently void, and not whether it is enforceable now or at some future time.

A conveyance by a husband, not joined by his wife, of homestead property, is not void but is merely inoperative while the property continues to be homestead, or until such time as the homestead may be abandoned, or the deed ratified in accordance with law. *Grissom v. Anderson*, 125 Tex. 26, 79 S.W.2d 619, 621 (1935). The principal enunciated in *Grissom* is equally applicable to contracts to convey homestead. In *Wright v. Hays*, 34 Tex. 253 (1870), the Supreme Court of Texas stated that while a husband possibly could not have been compelled to execute a conveyance of homestead property without the consent of his wife, the contract as to him "was not unlawful, but good and valid, and he might have been sued for damages during the life of his wife, and at her death he may be compelled to execute the deed, in compliance with his previous contract. . . ." 34 Tex. at 261. In *Brewer v. Wall*, 23 Tex. 585, 589 (1859), the Supreme Court pointed out that while a bond for title to homestead property executed only by the husband could not be enforced by specific performance so long as the wife refused to execute the deed, the bond became enforceable when the property lost its homestead character. *See also*, *Hudgins v. Thompson*, 109 Tex. 433, 211 S.W. 586 (1919) (contract enforceable after abandonment).

Other decisions reflect that the Texas courts have adhered strictly to the principle that one-spouse homestead transactions are not void, but are merely inoperative while the property remains the non-signing spouse's homestead. *See Reserve Petroleum Co. v. Hodge*, 147 Tex. 115, 213 S.W.2d 456, 458 (1948); *Kunkel v. Kunkel*, 515 S.W.2d 941, 948 (Tex. Civ. App.—Amarillo 1974, writ ref'd n.r.e.); *Davis v. Crockett*, 398 S.W.2d 302, 307 (Tex. Civ. App.—Dallas 1965, no writ); *Lewis v. Brown*, 321 S.W.2d 313, 317 (Tex. Civ. App.—Fort Worth 1959, writ ref'd n.r.e.); *Weinert v. Cooper*, 107 S.W.2d 593, 595 (Tex. Civ. App.—Texarkana 1937, writ dism'd). *See also*, *Hill v. McIntyre Drilling Co.*, 59 S.W.2d 193, 195 (Tex. Civ. App.—Texarkana 1933, writ ref'd). In *Lewis v. Brown*, *supra*, (which, like the instant case, involved an option to purchase property) the law regarding single spouse homestead transactions was summarized as follows:

> Deeds of trust and levies of execution or attachment never become liens on property which is homestead at the time of their execution or levy, even after the homestead status ceases to exist. This is so because Article 16, sec. 50, of the Texas Constitution, Vernon's Ann. St., declares them to be void. The subsequent cessation of the homestead exemption does not give them validity. *But a contract to sell a homestead is not void, and "not unlawful but good and valid."* *Wright v. Hays*, 34 Tex. 253. *It is merely unenforceable so long as the homestead status exists.* *Hudgins v. Thompson*, 109 Tex. 433, 211 S.W. 586; *Hill v. McIntyre Drilling Co.*, Tex. Civ. App., 59 S.W.2d 193. Likewise, while a judgment cannot become a lien on property which is homestead, it does become a lien when the homestead exemption ceases. *Marks v. Bell*, 10 Tex. Civ. App. 587, 31 S.W. 699, error refused. *The sale of the homestead by the husband, without the joinder of the wife, becomes operative when the property ceases to be a homestead.* *Marler v. Handy*, 88 Tex. 421, 31 S.W. 636; *Irion v. Mills and Halbert*, 41 Tex. 310; *Grissom v. Anderson*, 125 Tex. 26, 79 S.W.2d 619; *Weinert v. Cooper*, Tex. Civ. App., 107 S.W.2d 593.

321 S.W.2d at 317 (emphasis added). Moreover, the purchaser whose purchase is frustrated by the refusal of the vendor's spouse to ratify the sale has a cause of action for damages against the signing vendor. *See Goff v. Jones*, 70 Tex. 572, 8 S.W. 525, 527 (1888); *Nelson v. Jenkins*, 214 S.W.2d 140 (Tex. Civ. App.—El Paso 1948, writ ref'd). This right to sue for damages at law is necessarily predicated on the premise that such instruments are not void.

In the present case the option is absolutely exercisable in 1988, and exercisable as a right of first refusal until that time. There is absolutely no way of predicting whether the property will continue to be a homestead until 1988. Should the homestead status cease prior to 1988, the option, subject to its terms, will be enforceable by an action for specific performance. If the homestead status exists when the option is exercised, and Mrs. Zable refuses to ratify the deed, the Henrys have a cause of action for damages against Mr. Zable. In either case, the option is currently valid and should not be declared void merely because it is temporarily unenforceable by specific performance.

At oral argument the Zables conceded that under the law as it existed prior to adoption of TEX. FAM. CODE ANN. § 5.81 (Vernon 1975) the option would not be declared void. The Zables contend, however, that Section 5.81 has changed the long standing rule above discussed and requires that the option be judicially voided in the present case. We disagree.

TEX. FAM. CODE ANN. § 5.81, dealing with sale, conveyance, or encumbrance of homestead provides:

> Whether the homestead is the separate property of either spouse or community property, neither spouse may sell, convey, or encumber it without the joinder of the other spouse except as provided in Section 5.82, 5.83, 5.84, or 5.85 of this code or by other rules of law.

TEX. CONST. art. XVI, § 50, dealing with the homestead and how it is to be protected, provides:

> The homestead of a family . . . shall be, and is hereby protected from forced sale . . . nor may the owner or claimant of the property claimed as homestead, if married, sell or abandon the homestead without the consent of the other spouse. . . . No mortgage, trust deed, or other lien on the homestead shall ever be valid, except for the purchase money therefor, or improvements made thereon, as hereinbefore provided, whether such mortgage, or trust deed, or other lien, shall have been created by the owner alone, or together with his or her spouse, in case the owner is married. All pretended sales of the homestead involving any condition of defeasance shall be void. [emphasis added].

We conclude that the Family Code's prohibition that "neither spouse may sell, convey, or encumber it [the homestead] without the joinder of the other spouse . . ." is no more than a statutory enactment of the constitutional prohibition contained in the underscored language of the Constitution. We hold, therefore, that TEX. FAM. CODE ANN. § 5.81 does not change the long-standing rule in Texas as expressed by the Supreme Court in *Grissom v. Anderson, supra*:

> A conveyance by a husband, not joined by his wife, of the homestead property, is merely inoperative while the property continues to be a homestead, or until such time as the homestead may be abandoned, or the deed ratified in accordance with law. *Marler v. Handy*, 88 Tex. 421, 31 S.W. 636; *Irion v. Mills*, 41 Tex. 310; *Brewer v. Wall*, 23 Tex. 585, 76 Am.Dec. 76; *Goff v. Jones*, 70 Tex. 572, 8 S.W. 525, 8 Am. St. Rep. 619.

79 S.W.2d at 621. Thus, we conclude that the trial court did not err in holding that the grant of an option to purchase property at some future time is valid, despite the fact that the property is currently homestead and the grant was executed only by the husband.

Affirmed.

Notes, Comments & Questions

1. Why would Mrs. Zable's continued occupancy bar enforcement of the option?

2. If Mrs. Zable continues occupancy till her death, what is the Henry's remedy?

3. For another case regarding the effect of a spouse's failure to join, *see Nationwide of Bryan, Inc. v. Dyer*, 969 S.W.2d 518 (Tex. App.—Austin 1998, no writ), in which the court held:

> Darrell signed both the sales contract and arbitration addendum; Sherry signed neither. We find the absence of her signature has no legal significance due to her status as a third party beneficiary. Appellees readily concede Sherry's status as a third-party beneficiary from which she derives her standing to sue on the contract and her presence in this appeal. As a third-party beneficiary, Sherry is bound by the terms of the sales contract, including the arbitration agreement. *See Southwest Health Plan, Inc. v. Sparkman*, 921 S.W.2d 355, 358 (Tex. App.—Fort Worth 1996, no writ) (when insurance contract contained arbitration provision, third-party beneficiary to contract was compelled to arbitrate though beneficiary never signed contract); *see also Stonewall Ins. Co. v. Modern Exploration Inc.*, 757 S.W.2d 432, 434-35 (Tex. App.—Dallas 1988, no writ) (third-party beneficiary "steps into shoes" of contracting party and is subject to all provisions of contract). Additionally, because Sherry's claims are so closely connected to and intertwined with her husband's, she is bound to the arbitration as a matter of contract law. *See Fridl*, 908 S.W.2d at 514. While attempting to enforce the terms of the sales contract, Sherry cannot pick and choose which provisions apply; she is bound by all the contract terms. *Id.*
>
> **The Homestead Exemption**
>
> Notwithstanding Sherry's status as a third-party beneficiary, the Dyers claim that because the mobile home is part of their homestead, the arbitration agreement is invalid absent the signatures of both spouses. Even assuming the mobile home is a part of their homestead, their argument fails fundamentally. The Texas Constitution provides special protections for the homestead, separate and distinct from those protections given other types of property. TEX. CONST. art. XVI, § 50. However, the Constitution specifically allows purchase money, tax, and home improvement liens to be placed on the homestead. *Id.* The signatures of both spouses are required only when a home improvement lien is signed on an existing homestead. *Id.* That requirement does not apply here: the arbitration agreement is not part of a home improvement contract. Instead, the contract with Nationwide is a purchase money contract, clearly enforceable without Sherry's signature under the Texas Constitution. Under *Minnehoma Financial Co. v. Ditto*, 566 S.W.2d 354 (Tex. Civ. App.—Fort Worth 1978, writ ref'd n.r.e.), even if Nationwide sought to enforce the purchase money lien, the contract would not require both spouses' signatures. Thus, the Dyers' first claim fails as a matter of law.
>
> Additionally, the Dyers claim that the arbitration agreement is an "encumbrance" upon their homestead. Again, assuming the mobile home is part of the couple's homestead, the argument fails. An encumbrance is a right to, or interest in, property; it diminishes the value of the homestead and constitutes a burden on its transfer. *See* BLACK'S LAW DICTIONARY 527 (6th ed.1990). By enforcing the arbitration agreement, Nationwide has gained no right or interest in the mobile home. The provision does not diminish the value of the mobile home, nor does it burden the transfer of title. The arbitration addendum is not an encumbrance. The

provision merely provides a procedural avenue to resolve disputes. Accordingly, the Dyers' second claim fails as a matter of law.

We hold the arbitration agreement at issue is valid and enforceable; we sustain appellant's first point of error.

---

9. Survivorship Homestead

As a preface to this section read TEX. CONST.art XVI § 52.

PETRUS
v.
CAGE

128 S.W.2d 537
(Tex. Civ. App.—San Antonio 1939, writ ref'd)

SMITH, C.J.

J.F. Petrus and others, children and heirs at law of Ferdinand Petrus, deceased, brought this suit against Cage Brothers, individually and as partners, to recover the value of caliche admittedly taken by mining operations from the 113-acre homestead of the plaintiffs' parents in Bee County, which is still occupied as a homestead by their mother, the survivor in community of their father, who died intestate. In a trial before the court without a jury, judgment was rendered that J.F. Petrus and his co-plaintiffs recover nothing, and they have appealed. There is no statement of facts with the record.

The facts of the case are well stated in appellants' brief, as follows:

> F. Petrus and wife, Laura Petrus, acquired the 113 acres of land in 1906, as community property, immediately moved upon and improved the same as a farm and homestead, and were so using and occupying it when F. Petrus died on the 6th day of August, 1930, intestate. There was no administration on his estate, and none was necessary. Upon the death of F. Petrus, Mrs. Laura Petrus continued her occupancy of the homestead, without interruption, and down to the trial of this case. The appellants are the children, and all of the heirs of Petrus, deceased.
>
> At the time of the acquisition of the title and the establishment of the homestead rights of the husband and wife, in 1906, and before that time, there was no caliche pit or so called mine for caliche existing on said premises. Some eighteen years later, and in 1924, F. Petrus opened and began to operate a caliche pit and continued to operate it through himself, or his agents and lessees or purchasers of caliche, removing caliche therefrom until his death on August 6, 1930, after which his said widow continued to so operate said caliche pit, using and occupying said premises as her homestead, and selling caliche therefrom.

The caliche pit, or mine, is being operated by appellees under lease from appellants' mother, and this suit was to recover of appellees the value of the caliche taken from the mine under said lease.

The whole case, and this appeal, turn on the question of the character of the estate of the widow in that part of the community homestead which descended to the children in fee upon the death of their father, subject to the homestead rights of their mother.

The rights of survivors in like situations have been the subject of much discussion in the cases arising in this State, resulting in the clarification and settlement of the law upon the subject.

The rule arrived at seems clearly to be that the right of survivors, such as Mrs. Petrus, is more than a mere right of possession and occupancy; it is an estate in land, in the nature of a life estate. She is a tenant for life in the homestead, the measure of her right in which is not the mere privilege of possession and enjoyment. The right encompasses "every element of a life estate, and is therefore at least in the nature of a legal life estate, or, in other words, a life estate created by operation of law." *Sargeant v. Sargeant*, 118 Tex. 343, 15 S.W.2d 589, 593 [Other citations omitted].

The authorities cited further hold that a life tenant by virtue of the operation of law (such as Mrs. Petrus) cannot use the property upon which she is such tenant for any purpose which would work an injury to the inheritance, "save those [purposes] only to which it had been devoted at the time the life estate came into existence," for, "having once had the power of committing waste, he shall not be deprived of it by the act of God." *Swayne v. Oil Co., supra.* [98 Tex. 597, 86 S.W. 742].

Applying the rules stated, Mrs. Petrus, upon the death of her spouse, took an estate for life, by operation of the law, in that part of the homestead which descended in fee, upon the death of the father, to their children, appellants herein, and by virtue of her said estate therein thus acquired, she had the right to continue to take caliche from the mine which had been opened prior to and was being operated at, the time her life estate came into existence, to-wit, at the death of her spouse, intestate.

Appellees contend that in order to constitute the mine an old one within the stated rule, it must have been opened before the homestead right ripened. But there is no merit in this contention. The right to continue operations relates to mines opened prior to the coming into existence of the life estate, which was at the death of the spouse. This seems to be obvious.

The right to operate may be exercised by the surviving spouse in person, or through any other agency selected by her, including lessees, such as appellees in this case.

The judgment is affirmed.

Notes, Comments & Questions

1. What if the land in *Petrus v. Cage* had never been used to mine caliche?

2. *See also* the more recent case of *Riley v. Riley*, 972 S.W.2d 153 (Tex. App.—Texarkana 1998, no writ). In *Riley* the court addressed the issue of a homestead holder's right to income:

> Appellants argue that they are entitled to one half of the royalties received by Bobbie Riley since the date of Elbert Riley's death. Bobbie Riley argues that she is entitled to claim a homestead in the oil and gas royalties under the "open mine doctrine."

The open mine doctrine is an exception to the general rule that a life tenant is entitled to nothing but interest on mineral royalties and bonuses.[25] Under the open mine doctrine, a homestead claimant is entitled to receive and expend all oil and gas royalties from the homestead, where the homestead property was producing oil or gas when the right in the property came into existence.[26] Because the 59.7 acres Bobbie Riley has designated as her homestead were producing at the time her homestead rights in the property came into existence, she is entitled to the royalties from that designation.

However, Bobbie Riley's homestead designation did not include the 15-acre River Place tract. Therefore, the open mine doctrine does not apply to this tract. We have held that the probate court's order dated March 14, 1997, properly granted conveyance of all real property, including the 15-acre River Place tract, to Bobbie Riley. Therefore, the only issue left to be decided is whether Appellants are entitled to a portion of the royalties received from the remaining 15 acres, if such acreage was producing, from the date of Elbert Riley's death to the date of the conveyance.

Oil and gas are realty when in place and personalty when severed from the land by production.[27] At the time of Elbert Riley's death, the minerals in place on the 15-acre River Place tract were realty and passed to his heirs, one half to Bobbie Riley and one half to Appellants.[28] Therefore, Appellants are entitled to one half of any royalties attributable to production from the 15-acre tract from the time of Elbert Riley's death to the time the property was conveyed to Bobbie Riley to reimburse the community estate.

At oral argument, Bobbie Riley argued that all of the royalties received since Elbert Riley's death have been used to pay the debts of the estate and, therefore, cannot be distributed to Appellants. There is no evidence in the record of such use of the royalties.

Bobbie Riley also asserted at oral argument that her homestead designation entitles her to all of the royalties from the River Place because her designation includes the bore sites of the producing wells on the River Place property. As support, Bobbie Riley cites the "rule of capture." The rule of capture is a doctrine of nonliability for drainage.[29] Under the rule of capture, the owner of a tract of land acquires title to the oil or gas produced from wells on his land, though part of the oil or gas may have come from adjoining lands.[30] The rule of capture applies when separate tracts are above a common source of supply.[31] However, this rule does not apply to production from land within a pooled unit.[32]

---

[25] Clyde v. Hamilton, 414 S.W.2d 434, 439 (Tex. 1967).

[26] *Id.*; Youngman v. Shular, 155 Tex. 437, 288 S.W.2d 495 (1956).

[27] Phillips Petroleum Co. v. Adams, 513 F.2d 355, 363 (5th Cir. 1975); Humble Oil & Refining Co. v. West, 508 S.W.2d 812, 814 (Tex. 1974).

[28] TEX. PROB. CODE Ann. § 38(b)(2) (Vernon 1980).

[29] Glassell v. Ellis, 956 S.W.2d 676, 687 (Tex.App.—Texarkana 1997, no writ), citing Bender v. Brooks, 103 Tex. 329, 127 S.W. 168, 168-69 (1910).

[30] Elliff v. Texon Drilling Co., 146 Tex. 575, 210 S.W.2d 558, 561- 62 (1948).

[31] Arkla Exploration Co. v. Haywood, Rice & William Venture, 863 S.W.2d 112, 121 (Tex.App.—Texarkana 1993, writ dism'd by agr.), citing Halbouty v. Texas Railroad Commission, 163 Tex. 417, 357 S.W.2d 364 (1962).

[32] Russell v. City of Bryan, 846 S.W.2d 389 (Tex.App.—Houston [14th Dist.] 1992, writ denied).

Where tracts are pooled or a unit operation plan is in force, the rule of capture is, in a way, abrogated in those instances where a landowner or lessee participates in production from a well on another's land, though there be no well on his own, or where, the well being on his land, he must give up part of the production to another.[33]

We have found nothing in the record to indicate the extent to which the River Place tracts are part of a pool or unit or whether royalty was paid attributable to that acreage. Also, nothing in the record indicates whether the 15-acre tract is a part of a producing tract or, if it is, the amount of royalties Bobbie Riley received attributable to that tract. Without this evidence, we are unable to determine whether Bobbie Riley is entitled to keep all of the royalties.

In the interest of justice, we sever and remand for a new trial the portion of the case involving the royalties, if any, paid attributable to the 15-acre tract. The probate court shall determine if the Appellants are entitled to a share of the royalties received by Bobbie Riley from the time of Elbert Riley's death to the time the 15 acres were conveyed to Bobbie Riley and permit a claim against the estate or Bobbie Riley for any funds due to Appellants. The order of the probate court in all other respects is affirmed.

---

[33] Robert E. Hardwicke, *The Rule of Capture and Its Implications as Applied to Oil and Gas*, 13 TEX. L. REV. 391, 418 (1935).

Table of Cases

-A-

-B-

-C-

-D-

-E-

-F-

-G-

-H-

-J-

-K-

-L-

-M-

-N-

-O-

-P-

-R-

-S-

-T-

-V-

-W-

-Z-